1916 REBELLION HANDBOOK

1916 REBELLION HANDBOOK

MOURNE
RIVER
PRESS

THE MOURNE RIVER PRESS

First published 1916 by *Weekly Irish Times*
This edition published 1998 by The Mourne River Press

ISBN 1 902090 05 5

Index compiled by Helen Litton
Print origination by *Deirdre's Desktop*
Printed by ColourBooks Ltd, Dublin

CONTENTS

INTRODUCTION

The 1916 Rising took most people by surprise. When the rebels struck on Easter Monday, the highest-ranking officer on duty was an adjutant and the routine guards at the General Post Office had rifles but no ammunition. *The Irish Times* (then known to derisive nationalists as *The Squireish Mimes* because of its pro-union line) found itself in the eye of the storm. It prided itself on being the Irish paper of record and so its journalists did their best to collect official and eyewitness accounts. The government censorship prevented any statements by supporters of the rebellion: comment was unfree, but the facts were sacred.

So great was governmental confusion that a predictable editorial calling on loyal citizens to hold fast was spiked on April 27; instead there appeared a piece filled with a jesting desperation that seemed to border on flippancy. Perhaps in protest against the censor's restrictions, the writer mentioned official advice that citizens stay clear of all fields of military manoeuvre: "the Censor may permit us to say that such operations have not been uncommon in Dublin since Monday morning, and that the air of the immediate neighbourhood is apt to be unhealthy". With little to report and communications paralysed, the editorialist urged readers to beguile the time with family conversation, home handiwork or a reading of Shakespeare.

By the following week the world-historical implications of the event were more clear and all joking had ceased. Gallant British soldiers were congratulated on saving "the whole Empire from serious danger". On May 5 the Marriages column contained a laconic entry: "Plunkett and Gifford, 3 May 1916 at Dublin. Joseph Plunkett to Grace Gifford". By the time this note appeared, the groom had died by firing squad. Already the event was being dubbed the Sinn Fein Rebellion, although in strict accuracy Sinn Fein had no formal involvement. Nonetheless, the *Irish Times* handbook issued later in the year (and in an augmented new edition in 1917) is a fascinating and generally reliable source of information on the British forces.

Predictably, it is less informative on the rebels, whose leaders were relatively unknown when it went to print and whose foot-soldiers remained anonymous. I searched in vain for mention of my great-uncle, Edward Keegan, shot through the lung at the South Dublin Union on Easter Monday. He spent months in hospital recovering and was sacked for "disloyalty" from his clerking job at *The Irish Times.* He must have been highly amused to think of his former colleagues producing a handbook in memory of the event.

In 1966 *The Irish Times* published a commemorative supplement so large and comprehensive that its contents later appeared in the form of a book. In 1991 a much smaller supplement included comments which were highly critical of the rebellion. A scientific survey of opinion conducted by the *Irish Independent* in 1991 found that sixty-five per cent of respondents looked back on the Easter Rebellion with pride, as opposed to fourteen per cent who regretted that it had happened. Fifty-eight per cent thought that the rebels were right to take up arms, as opposed to twenty-four per cent who would have preferred them to use peaceful political means. Sixty-six per cent thought that the rebels would oppose the violent campaign of the contemporary IRA, as opposed to sixteen per cent who considered that they would endorse it.

All historians attempt to restore to a past moment the openness which it once had, before hindsight. The republication of this valuable document gives us some idea of how Ireland looked from Westmoreland street in the fateful year of 1916. Larkinism was still considered a menace, but the belief was that it was now on the wane. The rebels were regarded as astute and systematic planners: the entry on Tom Clarke marvels, for instance, at his forethought in securing distress funds. A more fanciful note is sounded, perhaps, with the suggestion that "Pearse intended to occupy the post of Provost of Trinity College in the event of the rebellion being a success". Hidden in the paragraphs on more minor *dramatis personae* are some tales of quiet heroism: Dr Ella Webb, one of the first female graduates of Trinity College's medical faculty, is described as organising hospitals and cycling through the firing line repeatedly to assist the wounded. The author of the notes has no compunction in fingering the Chief Secretary, Augustine Birrell, as the official who underestimated "the Sinn Fein movement" and allowed the situation to go beyond control. *The Irish Times* made no secret of its conviction that the Liberals bore a heavy share of responsibility for the outbreak.

DECLAN KIBERD
Dublin 1998

POBLACHT NA H EIREANN.

THE PROVISIONAL GOVERNMENT
OF THE
IRISH REPUBLIC
TO THE PEOPLE OF IRELAND.

IRISHMEN AND IRISHWOMEN In the name of God and of the dead generations from which she receives her old tradition of nationhood, Ireland, through us, summons her children to her flag and strikes for her freedom.

Having organised and trained her manhood through her secret revolutionary organisation, the Irish Republican Brotherhood, and through her open military organisations, the Irish Volunteers and the Irish Citizen Army, having patiently perfected her discipline, having resolutely waited for the right moment to reveal itself, she now seizes that moment, and, supported by her exiled children in America and by gallant allies in Europe, but relying in the first on her own strength, she strikes in full confidence of victory.

We declare the right of the people of Ireland to the ownership of Ireland, and to the unfettered control of Irish destinies, to be sovereign and indefeasible. The long usurpation of that right by a foreign people and government has not extinguished the right, nor can it ever be extinguished except by the destruction of the Irish people. In every generation the Irish people have asserted their right to national freedom and sovereignty; six times during the past three hundred years they have asserted it in arms. Standing on that fundamental right and again asserting it in arms in the face of the world, we hereby proclaim the Irish Republic as a Sovereign Independent State, and we pledge our lives and the lives of our comrades-in-arms to the cause of its freedom, of its welfare, and of its exaltation among the nations.

The Irish Republic is entitled to, and hereby claims, the allegiance of every Irishman and Irishwoman. The Republic guarantees religious and civil liberty, equal rights and equal opportunities to all its citizens, and declares its resolve to pursue the happiness and prosperity of the whole nation and of all its parts, cherishing all the children of the nation equally, and oblivious of the differences carefully fostered by an alien government, which have divided a minority from the majority in the past.

Until our arms have brought the opportune moment for the establishment of a permanent National Government, representative of the whole people of Ireland and elected by the suffrages of all her men and women, the Provisional Government, hereby constituted, will administer the civil and military affairs of the Republic in trust for the people.

We place the cause of the Irish Republic under the protection of the Most High God, Whose blessing we invoke upon our arms, and we pray that no one who serves that cause will dishonour it by cowardice, inhumanity, or rapine. In this supreme hour the Irish nation must, by its valour and discipline and by the readiness of its children to sacrifice themselves for the common good, prove itself worthy of the august destiny to which it is called.

Signed on Behalf of the Provisional Government,

THOMAS J. CLARKE,
SEAN Mac DIARMADA. THOMAS MacDONAGH,
P. H. PEARSE, EAMONN CEANNT,
JAMES CONNOLLY. JOSEPH PLUNKETT.

Above is a reproduction of the poster by which the Irish Republic was declared on Monday, 24th April, 1916. The poster, it will be observed, bears no date.

The declaration of the Irish Republic was made on Easter Monday, 24th April, 1916. The Provisional Government was composed of the seven men whose signatures appeared on the proclamation poster, and whose photographs are reproduced on this and the following page. All the seven were condemned by courts-martial, and executed after the rebellion had been suppressed.

Photo by] [*Keogh Bros.*

THOMAS ˋ CLARKE, executed on 3rd May.

Photo by] [*Keogh Bros.*

JOHN McDERMOTT, executed on 12th May.

Photo by] [*Lafayette.*

THOMAS MacDONAGH, executed on 3rd May.

Photo by] *[Lafayette.*

P. H. PEARSE, "President," executed on 3rd May.

Photo by] *[Keogh Bros.*

EDMUND KENT, executed on 8th May.

Photo by] *[Lafayette.*

JAMES CONNOLLY, executed on 12th May.

JOSEPH PLUNKETT, executed on 4th May.

In order to prevent the further slaughter of Dublin citizens, and in the hope of saving the lives of our followers now surrounded and hopelessly outnumbered, the members of the Provisional Government present at Head-Quarters have agreed to an unconditional surrender, and the Commandants of the various districts in the City and Country will order their commands to lay down arms.

P. H. Pearse
29th April 1916
3.45 p.m.

I agree to these conditions for the men only under my own Command in the Moore Street District and for the men in the Stephen's Green Command.

James Connolly
April 29/16

On consultation with Commandant Ceannt and other officers I have decided to agree to unconditional surrender also

Thomas MacDonagh

Above is a facsimile reproduction of the document signed by the rebel leaders on surrender.

The Provisional Government

... TO THE ...

CITIZENS OF DUBLIN

The Provisional Government of the Irish Republic salutes the CITIZENS OF DUBLIN on the momentous occasion of the proclamation of a

Sovereign Independent Irish State

now in course of being established by Irishmen in Arms.

The Republican forces hold the lines taken up at Twelve noon on Easter Monday, and nowhere, despite fierce and almost continuous attacks of the British troops, have the lines been broken through. The country is rising in answer to Dublin's call, and the final achievement of Ireland's freedom is now, with God's help, only a matter of days. The valour, self sacrifice, and discipline of Irish men and women are about to win for our country a glorious place among the nations.

Ireland's honour has already been redeemed; it remains to vindicate her wisdom and her self-control.

All citizens of Dublin who believe in the right of their Country to be free will give their allegiance and their loyal help to the Irish Republic. There is work for everyone: for the men in the fighting line, and for the women in the provision of food and first aid. Every Irishman and Irishwoman worthy of the name will come forward to help their common country in this her supreme hour.

Able-bodied Citizens can help by building barricades in the streets to oppose the advance of the British troops. The British troops have been firing on our women and on our Red Cross. On the other hand, Irish Regiments in the British Army have refused to act against their fellow countrymen.

The Provisional Government hopes that its supporters—which means the vast bulk of the people of Dublin—will preserve order and self-restraint. Such looting as has already occurred has been done by hangers-on of the British Army. Ireland must keep her new honour unsmirched.

We have lived to see an Irish Republic proclaimed. May we live to establish it firmly, and may our children and our children's children enjoy the happiness and prosperity which freedom will bring.

Signed on behalf of the Provisional Government,

P. H. PEARSE,

Commanding in Chief the Forces of the Irish Republic,
and President of the Provisional Government.

Above is a reproduction of the poster by which the [illegible] [illegible] addressed the citizens of Dublin.

Easter Sunday
1.20 p.m.

Comm^t
Eamon de Valeara

As Comm^t MacDonagh is not accessible, I have to give you this order direct. Comm^t MacDonagh left me last night with the understanding that he would return or send me a message. He has done neither.

As Chief of Staff, I have ordered and hereby order that no movement whatsoever of Irish Volunteers is to be made today. You will carry out this order in your own command and make it known to other commands.

Eoin MacNeill

Above is a facsimile reproduction of a letter sent by John MacNeill from his home at Woodtown Park, Rathfarnham, Co. Dublin at 1.20 p.m. on Easter Sunday, 1916, to Commandant De Valera.

The following is a copy of another letter issued on Easter Sunday, 1916, by John MacNeill:—

Easter Sunday,
Woodtown Park,
Rathfarnham,
Co. Dublin.

The order to Irish Volunteers printed over my name in to-day's *Sunday Independent* is hereby authenticated. Every influence should be used immediately and throughout the day to secure faithful execution of this order, as any failure to obey it may result in a very grave catastrophe.

EOIN MACNEILL.

THE DARKEST WEEK IN THE HISTORY OF DUBLIN

An Orgie of Fire and Slaughter

The story of the Sinn Fein rebellion in Dublin begins a long way behind Easter Monday, 24th April, 1916, but for the purpose of giving a comprehensive narrative of the rising it will suffice to begin with the operations on St Patrick's Day, Friday, 17th March. On that date the Dublin Battalions of the Irish Volunteers held a field day in the city. The different sections paraded in the morning at various city churches, and later the whole force assembled in College Green, where they gave a display of military manoeuvres, concluding with a march past Mr John MacNeill, the President (whose name was printed Eoin MacNeill in most documents issued by the Volunteers), and the members of the Executive, who had previously inspected the men in the ranks. These operations lasted from 11 o'clock till one o'clock, and for two hours the tram and other vehicular traffic was peremptorily suspended by the volunteers, most of whom carried rifles and bayonets, and whose numbers on that occasion were estimated at 2,000. While the inspection was in progress the pipe bands of the 2nd and 3rd Battalions discoursed music, and among the large crowd of spectators leaflets were distributed containing 'Twenty plain facts for Irishmen.'

The following are extracts:

'It is the natural right of the people of every nation to have the free control of their own national affairs, and any body of the people is entitled to assert that right in the name of the people.'

'The Irish people have not the free control of their own national affairs.'

'Some of the Irish people do desire that freedom, and are entitled to assert the right of the nation.'

'The Irish Volunteers (under the presidency of Eoin MacNeill) are pledged to the cause of the freedom of Ireland.'

'In raising, training, arming and equipping the Irish Volunteers as a military body, the men of Ireland are acquiring the power to obtain the freedom of the Irish Nation.'

'It is the duty of every Irishman who desires for his country her natural right of freedom and for himself the natural right of a freeman, to be an Irish Volunteer.'

This demonstration in the centre of Dublin on St Patrick's Day was the first time the Irish Volunteers had taken aggressive action in daylight, but on several occasions previously they had conducted night manoeuvres and practised street fighting in open spaces, generally between Saturday night and Sunday morning, and one night their operations consisted of manoeuvring around the entrances to Dublin Castle. The police on each occasion were eye-witnesses of the operations, but did not interfere with the movement of the Volunteers.

The Affray at Tullamore

While the proceedings in Dublin on St Patrick's Day were still a matter of public comment, a new development occurred at Tullamore on Monday evening, 20th March. Ill-feeling which had been smouldering in the town for some time against the Sinn Fein Volunteers was manifested at a hurling match in aid of the Wolfe Tone memorial on Sunday, 19th March, when a spectator attempted to remove a flag from one of the Sinn Feiners, who, it was alleged, retaliated by drawing a revolver. The feeling was accentuated the following morning, Monday, 20th, at Tullamore Railway Station, where a number of women were taking leave of their husbands, who are serving in the Leinster Regiment. A body of Sinn Fein Volunteers who appeared on the platform were then the object of a hostile demonstration. These incidents culminated in a shooting affray in the Sinn Fein Hall in William street the same evening. A number of children carrying a Union Jack sang songs in front of the hall: the crowd soon swelled, and amid boohing and cheering stone-throwing began, and the windows of the hall were smashed. The volunteers inside retaliated by firing revolvers, and a large force of police proceeded to search the hall for arms. A general melee then took place, revolvers were fired at the police, and several of them injured. Ultimately several men were arrested and charged next morning with having fired at and attacked with intent to murder County Inspector Crane, District Inspector Fitzgerald, Head Constable Stuart and Sergeant Ahern. Subsequently another batch of volunteers were arrested, and remands were granted several times, as Sergeant Ahern was unable to appear, he having been serious injured and conveyed to Steevens' Hospital, Dublin. The case of these prisoners is dealt with in the portion of this book recording the Courts-martial.

The Mansion House Meeting

On Thursday, 30th March, at the Mansion House, Dublin, a largely-attended meeting was held, under the presidency of Alderman Corrigan, for the purpose of protesting against a recent order for the deportation of certain organisers of the Irish Volunteers. The principal speakers were Mr John McNeill, President of the Irish Volunteers, and two Roman Catholic clergymen. The speeches were of a strong character, and during the proceedings a collection was made amongst the audience for the defence of the organisers. The following resolution was adopted unanimously:

'This public meeting of Dublin citizens in the Mansion House, Dublin, asks all Irish people to join in opposing the Government's attempt, unanimously condemned by national opinion last year, and now renewed, to send Irishmen into banishment from Ireland.'

After the meeting, a number of persons who had attended it marched through the streets, and revolver shots were fired in Grafton street and opposite the Provost's house at Trinity College. One of the revolver shots pierced a pocket in the overcoat of Inspector Barrett, DMP. A young man who was arrested and charged with being a member of a disorderly crowd and breaking a lamp in a motor car, was fined 5s and 5s costs, and ordered to find £1 bail, the alternative being seven days in prison. The following night, March 31st, a public meeting at Beresford place, presided over by Alderman T Kelly, endorsed the resolution passed at the Mansion House meeting the previous night. In view of subsequent events, it is worthy of note here that Mr Sheehy Skeffington was one of the speakers at the Beresford place meeting.

Wounded Irish Fusilier Spat Upon

An Irish Fusilier, who had been wounded at Suvla Bay, wrote to the *Irish Times* on 31st March, that while driving in a cab along Grafton street the previous night some of the men from the Mansion House meeting hurled filthy epithets at him, and one man spat at him through the window. Other soldiers, he added, were jostled and insulted by the crowd.

Seizure of Arms

On Sunday, 9th April, the DMP seized a motor car in College Green, and found it contained a quantity of shot guns, revolvers, bayonets, and ammunition, which was being conveyed to Wexford. Two men in the car, who were identified as Sinn Fein Volunteers from Ferns, were afterwards sentenced to three months' imprisonment.

The same day a parade of the Sinn Fein Volunteers took place through the streets of Dublin by way of protest against the deportation to England of two organisers, Ernest Blythe and William Mellowes. About 1,300 took part in the proceedings. When the procession was passing through St Stephen's Green a tram driver attempted to take his vehicle through between two companies, and sounded his gong by way of warning. A cyclist in Volunteer uniform placed his machine in front of the tram, placed his hand upon his revolver, and dared the driver to proceed. The tram man at once stopped until the whole procession had passed.

Mr Justice Kenny's Remarks

On the following Tuesday, April 11th, Mr Justice Kenny, in opening the proceedings of the Commission for the City of Dublin, referred to a propaganda in the city of an openly seditious character which set all authority at defiance, and seemed to be started in order to counteract the recruiting movement. They had, he said, read of the police, in the execution of their duty, being met and repulsed by men armed with rifle and bayonet, and of street disturbance in which firearms appeared to be freely used. What he regarded as the most serious attempt to paralyse recruiting was the display of large posters, such as, 'England's Last Ditch' and 'The Pretence of the Realm Act,' which must necessarily have a most mischievous and deterrent influence on certain classes of the population. He called attention to it because continuance of that state of things must have a tendency to create incalculable mischief.

In the House of Commons the same day, Mr Augustine Birrell, Chief Secretary, replying to Major Newman, said that it would be contrary to public interest to disclose the information in possession of the Irish Government concerning the Irish Volunteers, or the course of action proposed to be followed in dealing with them. The activities of this organisation, however, were receiving the closest attention.

A Bogus Secret Order

A meeting of the Dublin Corporation on Wednesday, 19th April, afforded the next Sinn Fein sensation. During a discussion of the police rate Alderman T Kelly read the following document, which, he said, had been furnished by Mr Little, editor of *New Ireland*:

'The following precautionary measures have been sanctioned by the Irish Office on the recommendation of the General Officer Commanding the Forces in Ireland. All preparations will be made to put these measures in force immediately on receipt of an Order issued from the Chief Secretary's Office, Dublin Castle, and signed by the Under-Secretary and the General Officer Commanding the Forces in Ireland. First, the following persons to be placed under arrest: All members of the Sinn Fein National Council, the Central Executive Irish Sinn Fein Volunteers, General Council Irish Sinn Fein Volunteers, County Board Irish Sinn Fein Volunteers, Executive Committee National Volunteers, Coisde Gnota Committee Gaelic League. See list A3 and 4 and supplementary list A2. Metropolitan Police and Royal Irish Constabulary forces in Dublin City will be confined to barracks under the direction of the Competent Military Authority. An order will be issued to inhabitants of city to remain in their houses until such time as the Competent Military Authority may otherwise direct or permit. Pickets chosen from units of Territorial Forces will be placed at all points marked on Maps 3 and 4. Accompanying mounted patrols will continuously visit all points and report every hour. The following premises will be occupied by adequate forces, and all necessary measures used without need of reference to Headquarters. First, premises known as Liberty Hall, Beresford place: No. 6 Harcourt street, Sinn Fein Building: No. 2 Dawson street, Headquarters Volunteers: No. 12 D'Olier street, 'Nationality' office: No. 25 Rutland square, Gaelic League Office: No. 41 Rutland square, Foresters' Hall: Sinn Fein Volunteer premises in city: all National Volunteer premises in the city: Trades Council Premises, Capel street: Surrey House, Leinster road, Rathmines. **THE FOLLOWING PREMISES WILL BE ISOLATED, AND ALL COMMUNICATION TO OR FROM PREVENTED: PREMISES KNOWN AS ARCHBISHOP'S HOUSE, DRUMCONDRA: MANSION HOUSE, DAWSON STREET**: No. 40 Herbert Park; Larkfield, Kimmage road: Woodtown Park, Ballyboden, Saint Enda's College, Hermitage, Rathfarnham: and in addition premises in list 5D, see Maps 3 and 4.'

Alderman Kelly said he took the responsibility of reading the document in discharge of his public duty. If they wanted this class of thing, of course there was no help for it, but he and those associated with him would do everything they could to see that discretion and moderation would remain.

'An Absolute Fabrication'

The military authorities in Dublin the same night stated that the foregoing document read by Alderman Kelly at the Corporation meeting was 'an absolute fabrication from beginning to end, and does not contain a word of truth.'

German Attempt to land Arms

On Saturday 22nd April, it was reported from Tralee that a collapsible boat with ammunition and three mysterious strangers had come ashore in that district, and that the Sinn Fein Volunteers had been specially mobilised the previous evening. Two arrests, which caused a considerable sensation in the town, were made the same night. News was also received from Tralee of a mysterious motor car which had taken a wrong turning, and dashed over Ballykissane Quay into the River Laune. The chauffeur escaped, but three passengers in the car were drowned. The bodies of two of the passengers were recovered on Saturday evening, 22nd April, and on them was found revolvers and ammunition and Sinn Fein badges. These events were associated in the public mind with the following announcement, which was made by the Press Bureau, but not until Monday evening, 24th April, at 10.25 p.m.:

Capture of Sir Roger Casement

The Secretary of the Admiralty announces—

During the period between p.m. April 20 and p.m. April 21 an attempt to land arms and ammunition in Ireland was made by a vessel under the guise of a neutral merchant ship, but in reality a German auxiliary, in conjunction with a German submarine The auxiliary sank, and a number of prisoners were made, amongst whom was Sir Roger Casement.

Manoeuvres Cancelled

It was known that the Sinn Fein Volunteers were to hold Easter manoeuvres, which were to be taken part in by all the branches of the organisation in Ireland. These were unexpectedly cancelled in the following announcement signed by Mr Eoin MacNeill on Saturday night, 22nd April, and published in the Sunday papers the following morning:

'Owing to the very critical position, all orders given to Irish Volunteers for tomorrow, Easter Sunday, are hereby rescinded, and no parades, marches, or other movements of Irish Volunteers will take place. Each individual Volunteer will obey this order strictly in every particular.'

With this announcement Mr MacNeill ceased to take any public part in the proceedings of the Volunteers.

On Easter Monday, 24th April, 1916, at noon, the storm burst in Dublin, and for the following six days the city and the suburbs were the scene of grave loss of life and destruction of property. The Irish (or Sinn Fein) Volunteers organised the revolution, and with the Citizen Army, Hibernian Rifles, and other bodies carried it out. The object of the movement, as stated in a proclamation (printed in full on page ix), issued on the day of the outbreak, was to 'proclaim an Irish Republic as a Sovereign Independent State.'

Preparations for the insurrection had been active for months previously: large quantities of arms and ammunition were known to have arrived in Dublin, and an unusual activity in the way of 'bluffing' the police had been going on. 'Let sleeping dogs lie,' was the policy of the Executive authority, and no visible effort was made to deal with the situation that was developing in the city. Then came Easter Monday, when the minds of most people were directed to holiday-making. No one took more than a passing interest in the Sinn Fein Volunteers as they passed along the streets in twos and threes to their appointed positions. Twelve o'clock in the day was the hour fixed for the beginning of the operations, and at that time or shortly afterwards bodies of armed Sinn Feiners quietly entered the buildings to which they had been assigned, turned out the occupants, and took possession. Anyone who resisted was promptly shot. In this way the principal buildings in the city were captured, and the rebels at once set about erecting barricades, and taking precautions against attack.

The Central Fortress

The General Post Office in Sackville street proved to be the central fortress of the rebels. It was here that PH Pearse, the 'Commandant-in-Chief of the Army of the Republic and President of the Provisional Government,' made his headquarters and issued his orders. All corner houses commanding the approaches were garrisoned with snipers, who were hidden behind sandbags. Kelly's ammunition shop at the corner of Bachelor's Walk, and Hopkins's jewellery shop at the corner of Eden quay, were held in this way in great strength. Other houses on each side of Lower Sackville street, and particularly those at the four corners of Abbey street, were garrisoned in like manner, and then the work of provisioning the various garrisons having the Post Office as their centre was actively proceeded with, every variety of foodstuffs being commandeered at the point of the bayonet. All the telegraphic wires were cut, thus isolating the city from the rest of the country. The failure of the Volunteers to seize the Telephone Exchange in Crown Alley proved a great advantage to the military in dealing with the insurgents.

The proceedings at St Stephen's Green Park was somewhat similar. At mid-day small groups of Sinn Fein Volunteers were standing about the entrance gates, and at a given signal they quietly walked inside, closed the gates, posted armed guards at them, and then set about clearing all civilians out of the Park. In half an hour the Park was cleared of non-combatants. The next move of the rebels was tot take possession of a number of houses commanding the approaches, and amongst the places occupied were the Royal College of Surgeons at the corner of York street, and Little's public house at the corner of Cuffe street. The houses at other points were not so advantageously situated, but numerous snipers were placed in them.

Attempt on Dublin Castle

Dublin Castle, the headquarters of the Irish Executive, was attacked by a handful of Volunteers, and had any force of Sinn Feiners joined in the attack they would almost certainly have captured the Castle, as there were only a few soldiers on duty. A policeman on duty at the Upper Castle Yard was shot in cold blood, but the few soldiers came to the rescue and the invaders were driven off. Other bodies of rebels succeeded in taking possession of buildings overlooking the approaches to the Upper Castle Yard. In this way the offices of the *Daily Express* and *Evening Mail* were entered, and the staff were turned out at the point of the bayonet. The City Hall, the rear of which commands the office of the Chief Secretary's Department, the Prisons Board, and other Government offices, was also filled with snipers.

Simultaneously with these incidents, attempts were made to occupy the railway termini in the city. Westland row Station and Harcourt street Station were early in the possession of the rebels, and the rails on the Kingstown line were torn up at Lansdowne road. The Harcourt street Station was found unsuitable for defence, and was abandoned at three o'clock in the afternoon. Abortive attempts were made to secure Amiens street Terminus, Kingsbridge Terminus, and Broadstone Terminus. Where they did not succeed in occupying the stations the rebels either attempted to blow up railway bridges or cut the lines, and nearly all the train communication with the city was stopped for a week.

Watching the Military

All the points in the city which were considered of strategical importance having been occupied by the rebels, their plans were further developed by the taking possession of positions controlling the approaches from military barracks. The Four Courts were early in their hands, and men were posted all over the building to attack troops which might approach along the quays from the direction of the Phoenix Park. The Four Courts Hotel, which adjoins the Courts, was garrisoned. On the bridges over the railway on the North Circular road and Cabra road strong barricades were erected. Liberty Hall was strongly held by the rebels, but the Custom House was left unmolested. Across the river, on the south side, Boland's Mill was fortified in every possible manner, and constituted a stronghold of great strategical importance. Round by Northumberland road, Pembroke road, and Lansdowne road, private houses were occupied and garrisoned to resist the approach of reinforcements for the military from the Kingstown direction.

Portobello Bridge, which commands the approach to the city from the military barracks at that place, was the scene of a short, but severe fight, shortly after mid-day on Monday. The rebels had taken possession of Davy's public house, which is close to the bridge and faces the barracks. Their presence was disclosed at an early stage by an attempt to capture an officer who happened to be passing over the bridge. He fortunately escaped and gave the alarm. A small number of soldiers was turned out at once, but was unable to dislodge the rebels. Strong reinforcements were sent out, and after a short and sharp fight the public house was carried, and the military remained in possession afterwards.

A Workhouse as a Fort

At more remote places in the Southern suburbs rebels had taken up positions of defence, but strong cavalry patrols hunted them from point to point, and finally dispersed them, though not until many of the soldiers had been wounded. The South Dublin Union in James's street and a distillery in Marrowbone lane were two other strong points in the Sinn Fein plan. The workhouse was attacked by the military on Monday, and after a stiff fight, during which many casualties occurred on both sides, the remnant of the rebel garrison was driven into one part of the premises, where they maintained their struggle until Sunday.

Jacob's Biscuit Factory in Bishop street, though it does not occupy a strategical position of any importance, was filled with foodstuffs of various descriptions, and probably in this respect it was deemed necessary to instal in it a large garrison, so as to make certain that supplies would be available for the rebels in other places. If this was the idea it never had the slightest chance of succeeding, as the factory was early in the week surrounded by a military cordon.

The foregoing are outlines of the position on the evening of the first day of the rebellion. Several instances of non-combatants being shot by Sinn Feiners took place during the day in various parts of the city. The most shocking was the shooting down of several members of the Veterans Corps on Haddington road. A large muster of this corps had gone out on a route march to Ticknock, and when they were returning in the afternoon to their headquarters at Beggar's Bush Barracks they were ambushed in Haddington road by a body of Sinn Feiners, who poured volleys of rifle shots into the ranks of the defenceless Veterans. Five were fatally, and many others seriously, wounded. The rest of the Veterans got to their barracks, where they had to remain until the following week.

Looting

On learning that several of his men had been shot by the rebels, the Chief Commissioner of the Dublin Metropolitan Police ordered the withdrawal from the streets of the entire uniformed force within an hour or two of the outbreak. The 'underworld' of the city quickly realised their opportunity, and first tackled the shops in Lower Sackville street. The windows were smashed, and hordes of people crowded into the shops, returning with bundles of wearing apparel of all descriptions. Noblett's, at the corner of Earl street, and Lemon's, in Lower Sackville street, were tit-bits for the younger section of the roughs, who made merry with boxes of chocolates, sweets, etc., all the afternoon. The toyshops were also centres of great activity, and then having exhausted Lower Sackville street the crowd swept round into Earl street and Henry street, where they found an abundance and variety that suited every taste. Boys and girls were swaggering about, dressed in the most fantastic apparel, and all had their arms full of mechanical and other toys, hockey and golf sticks, and all kinds of articles used in popular pastimes.

Military Reinforcements

All through Monday night the military were hastily summoning reinforcements from the Curragh, Belfast, and England, and on Tuesday, April 25, these forces began to arrive in the city. Almost in every instance the soldiers could only be conveyed to within five or six miles of Dublin owing to the interruption of the railway communications, and the men had a long and exhausting march, carrying their full equipment, before they arrived at the barracks to which they had been posted. On the way they were sniped at by Sinn Feiners, and had to be continually on the alert to repel attack.

Meanwhile the available forces of the Crown had been engaged all Tuesday morning in conflict with the entrenched rebels, and many fiercely-contested engagements took place. At daybreak troops were posted in houses overlooking St Stephen's Green Park, and a raking fire was sprayed from machine guns all over the Park, while soldiers picked off every rebel who showed himself. They still, however, managed to hold the Park in much reduced numbers. Another body of troops surrounded Cork Hill, and a fierce struggle took place for the possession of the *Daily Express* building. Artillery was brought into play, and prepared the way for a charge. This was carried out in gallant style by a detachment of the 5th Royal Dublin Fusiliers, under Second Lieutenant F O'Neill, a terrible fight taking place on the only staircase leading to the upper rooms. Many casualties took place at this stage. The military ultimately carried the position, and either killed or captured the garrison.

Artillery at Work

Later on Tuesday the positions occupied near Phibsborough were attacked. The barricades erected at the railway bridges on the North Circular and Cabra roads were destroyed by gun fire, about forty casualties being reported and one hundred prisoners secured. These operations resulted in the whole of the North Circular road being in the hands of the military; the Sinn Feiners who escaped it ran for shelter in the direction of Glasnevin Cemetery. The military net was then drawn closer on the city from the North side, but no attempt was made that day to attack the rebels in their central 'fortresses'.

More looting took place in the streets in the vicinity of Nelson's Pillar. Messrs Lawrence's large photographic and toy emporium in Upper Sackville street was one of the principal places cleared. The crowd of looters had matters all their own way for hours, and revelled in the destruction of the property. Some exciting scenes were witnessed when the fireworks were brought out and exploded. Rockets rushed up in the air and burst with a sound like a cannon, and all the smaller sorts of fireworks were thrown whizzing about amongst the crowd. Finally the premises were set on fire and burned to the ground.

Martial Law Proclaimed

Martial Law was proclaimed in Dublin City and County on Tuesday night, 25th April. On Wednesday, 26th, the position of affairs was worse than before. The Sinn Feiners had been driven to the wall, and were fighting with desperation. More troops, with artillery, were continually arriving in the city, and after a short rest they were brought into action, but they had to fight for every foot of ground they gained. For the most part it was an unseen foe with whom they had to contend. At eight o'clock on Wednesday morning the Admiralty steamer Helga came up the Liffey, and bombarded Liberty Hall, the headquarters of the Citizen Army. Owing to the Loop Line Bridge intervening between the ship and Liberty Hall, direct firing could not be brought to bear upon the building. The ship's gunners, however, dropped shells on the hall, the roof and interior of which were destroyed by bursting shells, but the outer shell of the house was not much injured by fire. The garrison escaped before the bombardment commenced. Artillery brought from Trinity College into Tara street also shelled Liberty Hall.

By the afternoon of Wednesday the military were in possession of Brunswick street, and all the district between that thoroughfare and the river and right up to D'Olier street. Sentries were placed at the entrance of a lane leading from D'Olier street to the Theatre Royal. The soldiers had not been long there before one of the snipers in Kelly's shop at the corner of Bachelor's Walk shot one of them dead. The military then brought a nine-pounder gun into position at Trinity College, facing D'Olier street, and bombarded Kelly's corner. The appearance of artillery and the bombardment greatly alarmed the people who reside in the immediate vicinity. Kelly's shop was riddled with shot, and the garrison had to evacuate the position. One peculiar effect of the gunfire was noticed afterwards. A shell struck an electric light standard at the corner, and bored a hole clean through the metal without bringing down the standard. Looting continued in the back streets all Wednesday, and in the evening several houses were set on fire.

The Great Conflagration

Bad as the previous day had been, the crisis reached its climax on Thursday and Friday. Artillery was brought into play at every point, and the air reverberated with nerve-wracking explosives. All day long the bombardment continued unceasingly, and each night the centre of the city was illuminated with great conflagrations. The Hotel Metropole and all that block of buildings for a long distance into Middle Abbey street were burned down, including the *Freeman's Journal* and *Evening Telegraph* offices, Messrs Easons, Messrs Manfields, and Messrs Thom's printing establishment. Then the General Post Office was given to the flames, and was destroyed—only the bare walls of this fine building remain. This particular fire extended down Henry street as far as the large warehouse of Messrs Arnott and Co., which remained intact, but was flooded with water. The Coliseum Theatre was also destroyed.

On the opposite side of Sackville street all the shops were burned down from Hopkins's corner at O'Connell Bridge right up to the Tramway Company's offices at Cathedral street. The fire extended backwards, and enveloped and destroyed almost all the houses between Eden quay and Lower Abbey street, down to Marlborough street. These included the premises of the Royal Hibernian Academy, with its valuable collection of pictures, and the offices of the *Irish Cyclist*, while on the opposite side of Lower Abbey street the branch of the Hibernian Bank, Mooney's public house, 'the Ship' public house, and Union Chapel were consumed in the flames. Round in Sackville street the scarred skeletons of the DBC restaurant and Clery's Warehouse remained like sentinels in the midst of a scene of desolation that beggars description. The only bit of Lower Sackville street left is the block of shops from Elvery's Elephant House to O'Connell Bridge on the right-hand side looking from the Pillar. The two corner houses on this block, however, were seriously damaged, the one by artillery and the other (occupied by the YMCA as a soldiers' supper room), by fire.

The whole of Sackville street, from the Pillar to O'Connell Bridge, was thickly strewn with *débris.*

The world famous O'Connell Statue is but little injured. Several of the figures have been pitted with bullets, and the figure of the Liberator served as a billet for many bullets, one of them drilling a hole just over the right side.

Collapse of the Rebellion

On Saturday, 29th April, PH Pearse, of St Enda's College, Rathfarnham, one of the leaders of the rebels, who had been described as the 'President' of the Irish Republic, surrendered on their behalf to General Lowe at the Headquarters of the Military Command at Parkgate.

Unconditional Surrender

The following is a copy of the document signed by Pearse:

In order to prevent further slaughter of unarmed people and in the hope of saving the lives of our followers, now surrounded and hopelessly outnumbered, members of the Provisional Government at present at headquarters have agreed to unconditional surrender, and the commanders of all units of the republican forces will order their followers to lay down their arms.

(Signed) PH Pearse.
29th day of April, 1916.

I agree to these conditions for the men only under my own command in the Moore street district, and for the men in the Stephen's Green Command.

April 29th, 1916. James Connolly.

On consultation with Commandant Ceannt and other officers, I have decided to agree to unconditional surrender also.

Thomas MacDonagh.

Cease Fire

It was close on 4 o'clock on Saturday, April 29th, when unexpectedly the order was given to the troops in the centre of the city to cease fire, and shortly afterwards it was officially announced that the rebel forces who held the General Post Office had decided to surrender unconditionally. What the 'cease fire' imparted had been interpreted differently by different people and there was a general feeling of uncertainty on the point until the official statement lifted the matter out of the region of conjecture.

Courts-martial were constituted, and the trials of the prisoners were proceeded with daily, until the principals had been sentenced, some to death, others to varying periods of penal servitude or imprisonment, while a large number of persons were arrested and deported to England.

Those who were sentenced to long terms of imprisonment and penal servitude were ultimately set free by the Government granting a general amnesty in June, 1917 (See page 288), in preparation for the assembling of a Convention of Irishmen to devise a new constitution for the country.

A Scene of Desolation

The revolution having ended, the streets in the central parts of the city on Monday became comparatively safe during daylight, the citizens displayed great anxiety to see for themselves some of the damage that had been done. Residents outside the military cordon on the North side of the city were rigorously excluded from passing through, and on the South side a similar restriction, but not quite so strict, was in force. Those who lived within the cordon were in no way hindered from moving about and viewing the wreck of their once fine city. The spectators appeared as if spell-bound when they came into view of Sackville street. Here and there a cloud of smoke rose from a smouldering ruin. Only a few blackened walls remained of the whole range of business houses on one side of the street between Nelson's Pillar and O'Connell Bridge. On the other side of the street only the walls of the General Post Office remained, the Hotel Metropole was gone, and all the other business places from that point down to Elvery's Elephant House were destroyed.

City Again Normal

By Wednesday, 3rd May, there were indications in almost every district that Dublin was returning to its normal condition. Shops and offices were opened in every street, and business seemed to be proceeding in the usual way. Except at a few points where 'snipers' and suspected persons were supposed to be concealed in private houses there were very few soldiers on the streets, which were once more under the control of the Metropolitan Police. There were welcome signs of an improved condition of life in Dublin, and of returning activity in the various departments of business and commerce. Tram and train services were gradually extended, and the authorities urged employers and workers in all occupations to return to work.

The Seizure of the General Post Office

It was just at noon on Easter Monday, when Sackville street presented the normal Bank Holiday appearance, with closed shops and a sprinkling of people walking along the footways, a party of armed men, some in uniform and some in mufti, came along at a brisk pace up Lower Abbey street, and wheeled to the right. When they arrived opposite the front entrance to the Post Office the order to halt was given, and the party, numbering at that time about sixty, rushed into the public office. They shouted wildly, and fired about twenty revolver shots, without hitting anyone. They ordered the clerks in the different departments all round to put up their hands, and leave the place with all possible haste. Among those who had to submit to the 'hands up' order was a fine specimen of the Dublin Metropolitan Police who was on duty. The invaders jumped over the counters, and took possession of the whole place. Some of the clerks were not allowed time even to take their hats and their coats, and as they were pushed about they were told that they ought to be thankful to be allowed to escape with their lives. There were at that time about twenty or thirty members of the general public in the office, engaged in purchasing stamps, writing letters at the centre tables, or transacting some other business such as is of daily occurrence. These people were simply dumbfounded at what they saw and heard, and, in fact, were very much frightened, indeed, by the revolver firing. They naturally left the place as quickly as they could. The public offices on the ground floor having been in this unceremonious way taken possession of by the Volunteers, and an armed sentry placed at the door to exclude the public, a party proceeded throughout the building, and took possession of the sorting rooms, parcels rooms, telegraph and telephones.

Telegraph Wires Cut

The staffs in these departments surrendered at discretion, and gave place to the rebels. They could do nothing else. The telegraph cables to England and Scotland were cut at 12.20, so that Ireland was completely cut off from communication with Great Britain. Everything in the place was turned topsy-turvy. Not a whole pane of glass was left in any of the windows on the ground floor from the Henry street side round to Prince's street. Up against these glassless windows chairs, stools, mail sacks, etc., were piled in the form of a rough and ready barricade. The noise of the glass falling upon the pavement attracted the attention of the people in the street, who at first could not understand the apparently wanton destruction of property. But they were quickly given to understand that serious business was afoot, for a volley of rifle shots fired through the vacant windows sent the hitherto listless pedestrians scampering at full speed in all directions. 'O Lord save us,' cried a few old women as they hurried away from the scene, 'it's the Citizen Army, and they have taken the Post Office.' And so the first act in this latest of Irish rebellions was performed.

Meanwhile other parties of the revolutionists were not idle, for the noise of fusillading was heard from other parts of the city, notably from Dublin Castle. Excitement grew intense, and women and children who were out for the holiday found themselves cut off from the means of getting to their homes. The tramcar service was suspended at one o'clock, and all the cars were sent to their depots. One large car was perforce kept at the entrance to North Earl street as a sort of street barricade. All the public houses within a certain distance of the Post Office were closed, and trembling spectators gathered on O'Connell Bridge and at the corners of Westmoreland street and D'Olier street, expecting every moment to see the military coming from one direction or another.

Lancers Attacked

Shortly after the trouble began a troop of lancers came along from the direction of the North Wall, escorting four or five wagons of munitions which were being conveyed to the magazine in the Phoenix Park. They crossed from the Eden quay side of Sackville street, and passed up Bachelor's Walk, knowing nothing of what was happening in the neighbourhood. A number of them subsequently returned to the city, and came into Sackville street from the north end. As soon as they got in front of the Post Office they were met with a volley from the occupants of that buildings. The shots came from the most part from men who had got on the roof, from which position they had a great advantage over the lancers. Four of the latter were shot, and the horse of one of them fell dead on the street. The dead bodies of these men were taken to Jervis street hospital. The Lancers withdrew to the Parnell Monument, where they remained for a short while before returning to barracks. Early in the proceedings a part of the Volunteers turned into Abbey street, and, having smashed several large shop windows, entered the Ship Hotel, and 'took' that, too. Armed men posted themselves in the upper windows, but they relinquished that position in the course of the afternoon. The police meantime had withdrawn to their several stations.

Shops Looted

Shop windows in North Earl street were smashed, and the shops were looted. Noblett's sweet shop at the corner, and that of Lewers and Co., next to it in Sackville street, were sacked, and youngsters, male and female, might be seen carrying bundles of sweets, or caps and hats, or shirts, of which those shops were despoiled. There was no one to prevent them from helping themselves as they listed. A public house in North Earl street was looted, and when the looters had partaken of the ardent spirits some of them beat each other with the bottles so violently that they were under the necessity of having their wounds dressed in hospital. Another of the shops that suffered was that of Messrs M Kelly and Son, gunsmiths and gunpowder merchants, at the corner of Bachelor's Walk and Sackville street. The looters took away with them such ammunition as they could lay their hands on. A couple of motor cars were stopped as they were passing the Post Office, and the occupants had to leave them in possession of the rebels. One of the victims of this high-handed procedure was Judge Law Smith, County Court Judge of Limerick, who was accompanied by a couple of ladies.

The Second Day

All through Monday night and Tuesday morning the rebels were busily engaged in Sackville street, taking possession of houses occupying commanding positions. The windows and doors of these premises were strongly barricaded with furniture, bedding, etc., and garrisons were installed in them. At O'Connell Bridge, Kelly's shop at the corner of Bachelor's Walk was garrisoned, and Hopkins's jewellery establishment at the opposite corner was similarly occupied. At the corner of Lower Abbey street, the branch premises of the Hibernian Banking Company were likewise seized, and a strong garrison was installed. Every window overlooking the street was filled with armed men, and preparations to withstand a siege were undertaken. Later in the day a change of plans took place, and a Red Cross flag was hung out of one of the upper windows of the bank, as if to indicate that this building was to serve as an hospital for the wounded when the siege of the Post Office was entered upon.

Barbed Wire in Sackville Street

Close by, in Lower Abbey street, a formidable barrier was erected opposite Wynn's Hotel. To obtain material for the barricade the *Irish Times* paper store was looted, and the big reels of paper were rolled out on the street. A bicycle shop was also looted, and bicycles and boxes were piled high, forming the only really effective barricade in the city. The Wireless School, at the corner of Lower Abbey street, was another of the places seized by the rebels, and messages were being despatched from this place until the rebels were shelled out of the building. Further preparations for the siege were made by stretching lines of barbed wire across Sackville street, and portion of the Imperial Hotel, which is directly opposite the Post Office, was also occupied by a number of the rebels.

Amongst the premises in the immediate vicinity of the Post Office which were occupied by the rebels on Monday night was M'Dowell's jewellery shop, which adjoins the Post Office on the Henry street side, and commands the approach from Moore street. On every side, indeed, the approaches were under strict guard, and anyone who ventured too close to the GPO soon realised the danger.

Machine Guns on Trinity

On Wednesday, Thursday, and Friday the fight for the Post Office was carried on by the military with the greatest vigour. Machine-guns were placed on Trinity College, and from this point gusts of fire swept through Westmoreland and Sackville streets whenever any of the rebels attempted to cross the thoroughfare. The military also drew gradually nearer and nearer through the side streets, and formed a circle of steel through which no rebel had a chance of escape. The circle was slowly contracted until a point had been reached when a further forward movement must be a charge. The authorities brought artillery and machine-guns into action, and liberally 'sprayed' all the positions held by the rebels on each side of the street.

Thus the fight went on day and night. On Thursday night a heavy bombardment was directed against Messrs Hopkins' establishment, which was full of Sinn Feiners. When the house was being brought down about them, as many of the rebels as could escape fled in the direction of the Post Office, only to meet their deaths in the streets. Fire then added its terrors to the awful scene, and in a short time the whole block of buildings from Hopkins' corner up to Lower Abbey street was like a furnace. Onward the fire swept, one house after another enveloped. The flames leapt and curled across Lower Abbey street, and soon the Hibernian Bank Branch and the adjoining houses were also burning. The glare of light made the Post Office and the Hotel Metropole on the opposite side of the street, appear as if they had been illuminated in honour of some festive occasion. When Clery's premises and the Imperial Hotel fell victims, great sheets of fire rushed high in the air, and it seemed as if the whole centre of the city was doomed to destruction. All the houses up to Earl street were soon in flames, which again crossed the street and set fire to Tyler's boot warehouse. The great gap which had been created by the previous fire at Messrs Lawrence's stores was an effective check to the further progress of the process of destruction, and the fire finally burnt itself out there.

Burned Out

On Friday, 28th, the battle with the rebels entrenched in the General Post Office continued with unabated violence. All day long they were shelled with artillery and Maxim guns, and in the evening the whole place went on fire. This fire was, if possible, even more destructive than the one of the previous night. The whole building, except the porch, was quickly consumed by the flames, which spread in all directions, enveloping the Hotel Metropole, Messrs Eason's, and the entire block of adjacent buildings. When daylight broke the scene was one of utter desolation. The palatial buildings which formerly adorned the principal streets in Dublin were lying in ruins, nothing but a naked wall being left standing at short intervals.

Officer's Extraordinary Experience inside the GPO

A series of extraordinary experiences and escapes fell to the lot of Second Lieutenant AD Chalmers, 14th Royal Fusiliers, who was kept a prisoner in the General Post Office from Easter Monday to the following Friday, when, according to a statement he made to a Pressman afterwards, he was given the choice of being shot immediately or running the gauntlet of soldiers' fire to draw it off the escaping rebels.

He was going into the Post Office at noon on Easter Monday when he noticed about a party of Sinn Feiners coming up Sackville street, and remarked to a friend: 'Just look at that awful crowd: they must be on a route march.' Three minutes afterwards a voice outside the Post Office shouted 'Charge!' and a crowd of rebels rushed in. One of them presented a bayonet at his breast, and the other prodded him in the back with a pike, a weapon favoured by many of the rebels. Lieutenant Chalmers, who was in Dublin on sick leave, was unarmed. After being searched for arms, the lieutenant was bound with wire obtained from the telephone box and put into the box, which faced Nelson Pillar. By this time the public had scattered, and the officials, including some from other floors, had been marched out of the office with their hands above their heads. Then there was a rush for the windows, which the rebels smashed with the butt-ends of their rifles and pikes. It was when the troop of Lancers charged that Lieutenant Chalmers had his first narrow escape from bullets which went through the telephone box. After being confined in the box for three hours, the lieutenant was taken to the first floor. The O'Rahilly, a captain, said: 'I want this officer to watch the safe to see that nothing is touched. You will see that no harm comes to him.' Shortly afterwards two guards came down and conducted him to the staff diningroom on the top of the building for a meal. At night he was taken to a room overlooking the Metropole Hotel. There was no bedding whatever, and two guards kept the door with fixed bayonets, so that there was no sleep. On Tuesday, Wednesday, and Thursday there was much firing, and the rebels were running about all over the place. On Friday morning the roof of the Post Office caught fire, probably from shells. Downstairs the rebels had everything combustible smashed up ready to start a fire, and the cellars were packed with explosives. Bullets were then coming into the room where Second Lieutenant Chalmers, Second Lieutenant King, RIF: Lieutenant Mahony, IAMS, and other captives, to the number of sixteen, were imprisoned. Prisoners had been taken in as occasion offered.

Tunnel Blasted by Dynamite

They crouched under a table, as the roof was falling in, and part of an inside wall had collapsed. During the week the rebels had made a tunnel from the Post Office to premises in Henry street, and it was through this that many of them escaped temporarily. The tunnel had been blasted by dynamite. Among the rebels were engineers, electricians, and experts of all kinds, including a man who was said to have come from Berlin. He was an expert in regard to explosives, and remarked that he would never return to civil life, knowing as much as he did about the insurrection business. On Friday, 28th April, the prisoners were taken to a basement right below the building. Here were stores of gelignite, cordite, gun cotton, and dynamite—stacks of it. Men came down to the basement calling for bombs.

A Terrible Trap

The cellar was barricaded with boxes, and a light turned on to one of these revealed packages of gelignite. Bombs with fuses set were placed round the cellar by the rebels, who then left the prisoners in it. In this terrible plight the prisoners decided not to die like rats in a trap if they could help it. They were saved from a horrible death by a rebel and a lieutenant. In response to the calls of the prisoners the lieutenant said: 'It's all right boys,' and took them up again into the burning building and out into the yard at the back. Their next move was through a corridor into a room at the back of the Post Office, where they were put under the charge of a woman in male attire, who flourished a big loaded revolver.

Human Bullet Screen

A little later the prisoners were led to Henry place, to be used by the rebels as a screen to facilitate their escape. Lieutenant Chalmers was placed at the head of the line of prisoners, and on his left hand was a private of the Royal Dublin Fusiliers. Pointing a Mauser pistol at the Lieutenant one of the rebels told him to run or he would fire. About 150 yards away were the troops with a machine gun, and they were firing down a lane. Lieutenant Chalmers started to run, but had not got ten yards before he was shot in the thigh, and the Dublin Fusilier through the head. By a rush some of the prisoners passed successfully the end of the lane down which the troops fired the machine gun, and being called upon by more rebels to stop darted down an alley way to their left, only to find themselves charging a British machine gun. Bullets spattered around them, but by a miracle they escaped injury, and jumped a parapet a yard high. Running round yet another passage, they found themselves in a court yard at the back of Lipton's store, where Lieutenant Chalmers collapsed from his nerve-wracking experiences. He was carried on the back of a sergeant of the RIR into the cellar. The whole building had been burned out. Even then the trials of the Lieutenant, the sergeant, and three privates were not passed. They spent the night in the cellar. Next morning fighting was resumed close beside them. Through the cellar grating they saw a sniper on the roof of the building opposite, and inside was a man grinding bayonets, work which he kept up all day. Towards evening the machine-gun-fire became very hot, and the bullets were falling all around. The prisoners crawled out of the cellar into a van standing in the yard. About 6.30 p.m. there was a call for any more rebels who wanted to surrender, and the sergeant jumped out of the van to discover a corporal and two soldiers with fixed bayonets. By that time the captives had been without food or drink for twenty-four hours.

Bomb's Premature Explosion

Many interesting and valuable observations were made by Lieutenant Chalmers during his stay in the Post Office, and he witnessed some strange sights. The first casualty at the Post Office was that which occurred to a Sinn Feiner who was placing a bomb in position. This man was leaning over a counter when the bomb blew his head right off. These bombs were charged with melinite, and fitted with wicks attached to fuses at the outer end. The rebels had arms of the most various patterns—Mauser and Holtz rifles, Army rifles, automatic rifles, sporting guns and revolvers, and automatic pistols of every conceivable type. They also, he said, had a machine gun on the roof of the Post Office. They used expanding bullets of the sort used for killing big game, and Lieutenant Chalmers had one of these bullets which he took from a bandolier. The rebels got a good deal of amusement out of the telegraph instruments before destroying them. Among their number were telegraphists, who chuckled as they translated messages from the outer world, inquiring frantically what had happened in Dublin, and transmitted evasive replies. Food supplies were in abundance, and in the early mornings carts stacked high with provisions would come rattling along under the guard of an armed rebel.

In Lieutenant Mahony the rebels discovered medical and surgical knowledge, which they called upon him to utilise. They had their own force of nurses, but these displayed very slight knowledge, and their methods were very crude, while medical supplies were of an ill-assorted and useless character. Medical students and nurses came into the Post Office, and rendered good service. Connolly's leg wound was dressed by Lieutenant Mahony, who accompanied him along the tunnel blasted by the Sinn Feiners.

Girls in the GPO

In the making of the barricade at the head of Prince's street the most extraordinary articles were utilised, including cauliflowers and milk cans, and a brand new green motor car taken from the Post Office. The girls serving in the diningroom at the Post Office were dressed in the finest clothes, and wore knives and pistols in their belts. They also wore white, green, and orange sashes.

Bank notes, postal orders, and other securities of value were handed over to Thomas Clarke, one of the members of the Provisional Government, in the diningroom on East Monday. Lieut Chalmers is assured on that point, as he heard all the conversation. It was stated that the money was to be distributed among the relatives and dependents of the Sinn Feiners who fell in the fight. One of the rebels offered the Lieutenant a postal order, remarking, 'Here's your pay,' but this was a pleasantry, as at that time Lieutenant Chalmers was bound.

Soldiers Five Days without Food

On Wednesday, 3rd May, more was heard of the soldiers who had been hostages. Mr FR Ridgeway, managing director of Bewley, Sons, and Co., Henry street, discovered that there were two soldiers alive in the ruins of the Coliseum Theatre. It was not long before they were released, when it was found that they were Sergeant Henry, of the School of Musketry, Dollymount Camp, and formerly of the Royal Irish Constabulary, and Private James Doyle, of the Royal Irish Regiment. Both were unwounded, but weak from want of food, having had nothing to eat since Friday. How did they come to be in the Coliseum? Being of the party imprisoned in the Post Office, when sent forth they had sought refuge in the theatre, and there they stayed unaware of the fact that the fighting about the place had ceased.

Attempt to Blow Up Nelson Pillar

One of the many daring schemes of the rebels which failed was an attempt to blow up the Nelson Pillar in Sackville street. An eye-witness of the effort states that he was proceeding to the south side of the city from the north on Tuesday morning, 25th April, at 7 a.m. On reaching the foot of Rutland square he saw an armed rebel driving the spectators up Sackville street and into Great Britain street. At this corner the crowd lingered, and the rebel ordered the people to 'get out of the firing line,' and added with a dramatic whirl of his bayonet: 'The Nelson Pillar is about to be blown up with bombs.'

Taking cover behind the Parnell Monument the eye-witness awaited developments, and precisely at 7.10 a.m. there was a loud explosion, followed by a cloud of smoke, which rose close to the north side of the Pillar. The monument, however, did not show any signs of collapse, and although this explosion was followed by three others within ten minutes, the Pillar did not even quiver. No further efforts were then made at the destruction of the monument, and at 7.30 the spectators were again permitted to pass by the Pillar.

The Attack on Dublin Castle

The attempt to enter Dublin Castle was one of the most exciting incidents of the uprising. About ten minutes past 12 noon on Monday a small party of Volunteers, with two young women in the rear, marched up Cork Hill towards the gates of the Upper Castle Yard. They were fully equipped, as if for a long adventure. They reached the Castle entrance, which was open, and guarded only by a policeman and a sentry. When the policeman saw they were going to enter the Castle Yard, he moved quickly in front of them, and raised his hand as a sign that they could not come in. But the Volunteers were determined, and did not turn back. They remained where they were for a few brief seconds, facing the constable. Then occurred the deed that revealed the daring object of the Volunteers. One of their number, standing out in front of the policeman, levelled his rifle at him, and before the unhappy man could draw his revolver, fired point- blank. The constable stood a second or two, to fall prone and lie motionless on the ground. At the same time other shots were fired by the attackers at the sentry inside the railings, and at the guardroom to the right. Out from the path sprang the soldier with his rifle at the ready and bayonet fixed. He did not come to close quarters with the rebels. The iron gates were quickly closed, and the Volunteers' attempt to 'seize' the Castle failed at the point. That they intended to do as much harm as possible was apparent, for one of them carried a tin cannister, evidently made up as a bomb, and he threw it across the railings at the guardroom. His aim was good, the bomb bad. It broke the window, but did not explode. All this happened in a brief time. The few spectators did not at first realise what the affair meant. It seemed as though a mere act of bravado on the Volunteers' part in endeavouring to march though the Upper Castle Yard, had ended in the shooting down of a policeman—not the first to fall thus around Dublin Castle. The end, however, was not yet.

City Hall and Newspaper Office Seized

Scattering at the Castle entrance, the Volunteers—of whom there were not more than 12 at the outset—ran down Cork Hill. Four or five of them went into the office of the *Daily Express* at the corner of Parliament street and Cork Hill. They ordered the members of the newspaper staff to leave the house, and one presented a bayonet at a man who took them too coolly for their liking. In a few minutes the Volunteers were in possession of the building. Their object in seizing it was to command Dublin Castle, and wage war upon it. For the same purpose a few others of the party ran up the steps of the City Hall, and climbed the iron gates which were shut on account of the holiday. The shop of Messrs Henry and James also was entered by a man who, having broken the window, climbed in and went up through the house to the roof. Another Volunteer ran down Parliament street with his rifle ready to shoot anyone bold enough to detain him. Nobody attempted to do so: the excitement was great, and most persons made for shelter.

Before long the Volunteers, ascended to the roofs of the buildings, began to fire at the Castle and at any soldiers whom they saw in the streets. One shot, fired at a private, grazed the arm of Miss Woods, who was standing at the door of her father's shop in Parliament street. Another, aimed at a Canadian soldier, wounded an old man in the same thoroughfare. A surgeon, who had come up to attend the policeman, brought off the latest victim in his motor car. Not long after another soldier was shot in the head.

Fierce fighting continued here until the following night, when a brilliant charge by a body of soldiers with fixed bayonets, rushing from the Castle, under cover of artillery fire, ended in the capture of the *Express* office. The dead bodies of 26 rebels were then found on the premises.

A Heroic Girl

This district was the scene of series of gallant actions on the part of a young lady, Miss Florence Williams, 8 Bristol Buildings, Castle street, who was afterwards awarded the Military Medal by the War Office for her conspicuous bravery. She was outside the Castle gates when the policeman was shot, and sometime later dragged two soldiers who were severely wounded, from the street, where bullets were rattling, to her mother's house: here they were given all possible assistance. She went through the fire to the Castle in search of a stretcher to carry the wounded men to hospital, and after that rescued more wounded soldiers, and went out and brought a priest to minister to them. Frequently during the week she went out in the firing line, and secured bread and medicine and bandages for the wounded men in her house from the Adelaide Hospital. She was specially thanked and made the recipient of a presentation from the Commander and officers of the Dublin Fusiliers.

In Dublin Castle Red Cross Hospital

Blackwood's Magazine for December, 1916, contained a long article on the 'Experiences of a VAD at Dublin Castle during the Rebellion,' from which we quote:

'It was shortly after noon on Easter Monday, April 24. I was washing bandages in the Supper Room kitchen, when a man came in and said, "The policeman at the front gate has been shot, and they have carried him in!" There was no hope: death had been instantaneous. The men, who were watching from the windows, said an armed body marched up Cork Hill to the gate, and shot the policeman through the head. We heard afterwards that the original plan had been to seize the Castle, as they had done the GPO: and many reasons were advanced why they had not done so. Connolly told us that when they found no resistance, they thought it must be a trap to entice them in and ambush them, and that Ship street Barracks, at the back, would be too strong for them.

'About 5 p.m. troops arrived. The first definite movement I noticed among them was when an officer and a number of men collected near the gate: they were lined up, and he gave orders. At a signal he and two or three of the men ran towards the gate and disappeared from view: three or four followed, and so on. This turned out to be the famous charge on the City Hall. We had been sent a message: all blinds were to be pulled down and all lights turned out, and to be prepared for noise, as machine-guns were going to start. We groped round in pitch darkness, unable to see who was who, so it was hopeless to try and do anything—and then the guns began. The beds had to be moved from the Picture Gallery and Throne Room to St Patrick's Hall, the corridor of the Officers' Quarters, and the landing outside, which were at the back of the house. The back door of the Supper Room kitchen faces the Operating Theatre, and as both doors were open I could see inside. In the middle of the floor a man was lying on mackintoshes in pools of blood: all round were wounded being stitched up, or having haemorrhage stopped.

Meal Time Difficulties

'At 4.30 a.m. we watched the troops march out of the Yard, with bayonets fixed, followed by the stretcher bearers. The hall was turned into a receiving station, fitted up with screens: supplies of bandages and dressings and kettles of boiling water were kept in readiness. The men's dining-room was packed, and the corridor thronged with soldiers waiting for breakfast. Such a jolly cheery crowd they were. From 5 a.m. till mid-day the crowd continued; we fed about seven hundred on Tuesday, though there were only supplies for the seventy men originally in the hospital, so we could not treat the visitors too regally. They were allowed a cup of tea and half a slice of bread for breakfast; the same for tea, and a cup of tea for supper. Practically none were able to turn up for more than two meals in the day. From the first morning till some time after the rebellion was over the gas supply was turned off, and our stove was useless in consequence. The Supper Room and anteroom were heated by hot pipes: there were no fires, and so all the water for tea and cocoa for the fifty men had to be carried through St Patrick's Hall to the fire at the top of the main staircase. Even here troubles did not end, as it was a common occurrence to go back to find your saucepan boiling finely—but with somebody's instruments sterilising in it—and your kettle empty, having been used to fill hot jars for a new arrival!

A Stream of Ambulances

'Numbers of the troops came to the Supper Room kitchen for a wash and brush up, amongst them some we had seen march out, soon after dawn, with fixed bayonets. From the windows we could see a constant stream of ambulances and stretchers going in and out of the Yard—the dead had their faces covered. In the evening we watched the men in the Yard bombing the office of the *Evening Mail*. The noise was terrific, but eventually the building was successfully stormed. From then on, we were considered comparatively safe.

'Wednesday in our quarters was heavy with regular routine, but rather uneventful. In the evening, as I came downstairs a procession of policemen with bared heads passed down the corridor—it was the policeman's funeral.

'The officers' dressing-room was turned into a "dressing station," where slight injuries were attended to: over two hundred and fifty cases were treated here. As the room was fitted with basins, several of us had to spend all spare moments there, washing bandages and mackintoshes, which, needless to say, were never-ending. It had been given out that any nurse who had the chance might sit down, so I used to pull a chair over to the basin and scrub away.

The Funerals

'The windows overlook the Castle garden, where all day about twenty men were digging graves. The nearest were for officers, each made separately: then two large graves for Tommies and civilians, and Sinn Feiners. There were over seventy buried in the garden: most of them were removed when the rebellion was over. Only a very limited number of coffins could be obtained: most of the bodies were buried sewn into sheets. The funerals took place each evening after dark. Towards the end of the week the dead were so many they were brought in covered carts instead of ambulances. I saw a cart open once—about fifteen bodies, one on top of the other. It took time to carry them round to the mortuary, and sometimes as one passed two or three bodies would be lying near the side door, dressed in khaki, but so still, so stiff, the hands so blue, and the faces covered. It is difficult to remember which day armoured motor cars made their first appearance, but by Friday the sight of them rushing in and out was quite familiar. It is also impossible to state chronologically the arrival of Sinn Fein prisoners. They only batch I clearly remember were fifteen or sixteen respectable-looking men brought from the Four Courts the Tuesday morning after the surrender.

'On Saturday there was actually a pause in the afternoon, so I seated myself in front of the fire to make toast for the men's tea. One of the men relieved me before long, and made enough for the whole landing. It was a treat! It seemed years, not days, since we had seen anything so civilised. Teas were being brought, and high good humour prevailed over the toast, when someone hurled herself in with: "The Rebels have surrendered unconditionally!" We could hardly believe our ears: it seemed much too wonderful to be true. The news was followed by a damper: "Thirty new nurses have arrived—what are they to eat? I should rather do twice as much again than have rations cut down any further." We echoed the sentiment. It did not occur to us, that once surrender was official, we should be able to get plenty of food. A new nurse and two VAD's were sent to the Throne Room: other wards received similar reinforcements, and we had the amusing and unexpected experience of tumbling over each other.

James Connolly in the Hospital

'The arrival of James Connolly caused an unusual stir. From the window I could see him lying on the stretcher, his hands crossed, his head hidden from view by the archway. The stretcher was on the ground, and at either side stood three of his officers, dressed in the Volunteer uniform; a guard of about thirty soldiers stood around. The scene did not change for ten minutes or more; they were arranging where he should be brought, and a small ward in the Officers' Quarters, where he could be carefully guarded, was decided upon. The nurses in charge of him acknowledged, without exception, that no one could have been more considerate, or have given less trouble. About a week after his arrival he had an operation on the leg. All through, his behaviour was that of an idealist. He was calm and composed during the court-martial, and he is reported to have said:

"You can shoot me if you like, but I am dying for my country." He showed no sign of weakness till his wife was brought to say goodbye to him, the night he was to be shot. When she had left, he saw the monks, and about 3 a.m. he was carried down on a stretcher to the ambulance that was to bring him to Kilmainham.

'Since the firing had stopped on Saturday the ambulances could drive through the streets in safety, and a great number of wounded were brought in.

About 9 p.m. the day staff retired, and left one staff nurse, one probationer, and me to look after the twenty-seven patients in the Picture Gallery. I never thought I should have seen such suffering as was in that ward that night: the groaning was indescribable.

'Early on Sunday morning orderlies from King George V Hospital appeared on the scene. They were a great help: they used to look after the fires and make themselves generally useful. The convalescent patients, who always worked like blacks, were very critical of them.

Sniping

'The sniping was worse than usual on Monday night, and we heard rumours that the Sinn Feiners had reinforcements, and the surrender was withdrawn. Two men were killed in the Yard just outside our door a few minutes after I had come across. Night duty was not without its excitements. One of the nurses going her rounds had an electric torch, which she switched on when she entered the ward. She was faced by a burly Australian, his fists clenched and a ferocious expression on his face, just going to make a spring for her throat! He had mistaken her muffled footsteps for a Sinn Feiner. After supper, next morning I had to move my belongings to the Night Nurses' Quarters. Everything was quiet, and the Yard was safe to cross. The troops were lying in all directions, and with armloads of pillows, sheets, and similar baggage, I had to pick my way between them.

'We were at dinner in the kitchen, when a stretcher-bearer offered us his newspaper, the now famous paper (*Irish Times*), with three dates. It was the first communication we had held with the outside world for over a week, and we nearly tore it to pieces in our excitement.

Strange Scenes

'The hospital itself presented an unusual appearance. Sentries, with fixed bayonets, sat or stood at the top and bottom of every staircase, and outside every ward in which was a Sinn Feiner: one guarded each of the doors of Connolly's room, and another was in his room. Those who were not on duty sat round the fire at the top of the main staircase, and some turned the "baths" used in peace times for palms and plants, into beds. There are two of these tanks, and about six men fitted into each, three at either end, their feet overlapping in the middle. One man looked too funny: in his well-worn khaki and muddy boots, his face and hands very dirty, he slept peacefully on a lace-edged pillow! I did not know the hospital boasted such a smart one.

'On Tuesday morning we were allowed to go to early Service, held in the Matron's office by one of the chaplains. It was in keeping with "active service." The clergyman robed in a corner of the room: the Bread and Wine were placed on an ordinary table covered with a white cloth.

'The Boiler Room, where we filled our hot jars, was always packed with Tommies—some lying full length on the table, others lolling round. The beloved goat—I forget what regiment it belonged to—made its headquarters there, and the 4th Hussars' dog, which had come up uninvited.

'As the hospital was three-quarters empty when the Rebellion broke out, more than half the staff were on leave and could not return. There were only about thirty altogether for day and night duty, and of these seven had to be spared as waitresses in the buffets. The Matron and the Assistant Matron rarely took more than one hour's rest in the twenty-four and, in addition to the responsibility and strain attached to their posts, they took the place of staff nurses in the wards when it was necessary.

'A Staff Nurse who developed appendicitis refused to give in until the reinforcements arrived. She probably saved several lives by her unselfishness, but it very nearly cost her own.'

In Stephen's Green

One of the boldest acts of the rebels was their seizure of St Stephen's Green Park, and the systematic way in which they set about digging themselves in. There was no parade about the earlier proceedings. The men came up shortly after mid-day in twos and threes, fully armed, and carrying packs on their backs, and quietly took possession of the gates, which they locked against the public. They all seemed to have been previously instructed as to their duties, as they at once set to work. Guards were posted at the various gates, the ammunition boxes were opened, and their contents placed within easy reach of the guards. Squads of men were told off to clear out members of the public who were in the Park at the time, while other squads engaged in trench digging.

Along St Stephen's green, North, the preliminary acts of the rebels were of an equally thorough-going description. If one had the rashness to walk along the pathway outside the railings one could observe men lying in the shrubbery with rifles pointing outwards. One of the armed men, carrying a revolver in one hand and a hatchet in the other, and attended by several men carrying rifles, came out on the roadway, and coolly selected houses in which to post his 'sharpshooters'. Having chosen his house, he smashed in the window, and ordered his men to take post in the house. This was repeated in several instances on the North side of the Green, and then the leader and his men turned their attention to the traffic. An effort was made to stop all wheeled traffic, and if the drivers did not stop they were fired upon.

On Tuesday the military took up positions in the Shelbourne Hotel and other houses overlooking the Park and vigorous sniping of the rebels followed. Gradually they were driven away from the gates and railings. They then fired at the soldiers from trenches in the interior of the Green, and from the shrubberies. Many casualties took place on both sides, the dead bodies of the Sinn Feiners being seen lying at full length on the ground. The military were also sniped from the College of Surgeons, from Little's public house, and from other houses.

Day after day, and night after night, the sniping continued until the rebels had been severely punished. Towards the end of the week the Green was evacuated during the night, but the firing continued from the College of Surgeons, and from other houses where Sinn Feiners were concealed. The Countess Markievicz was in command of the rebels here.

Inside the Royal College of Surgeons

The Royal College of Surgeons in St Stephen's Green was one of the last 'forts' to capitulate. After a week's occupation the surrender took place at two o'clock in the afternoon of Sunday, the 30th ult. Major Wheeler, son of the late Surgeon Wheeler, accompanied by a force of military, attended at that hour, and was received by the rebel leader, the Countess Markievicz. She was still wearing top boots, breeches, service tunic, and a hat with feathers. In the presence of the military she first shook hands with her 'officers,' and then produced her revolver, which was enclosed in a case. After affectionately kissing the weapon, she handed it to Major Wheeler, together with a quantity of ammunition, which on examination was found to include military and also round nosed (expanding) bullets. The prisoners taken at this place numbered about 110 men and young women.

Down in the kitchen large quantities of canned foods and provisions of every description were discovered in disorderly array. Some sort of discipline seems to have been maintained in the commissariat department. A slate was discovered on which was inscribed:

'IRA. Orderly for this kitchen Miss ...

In her absence ...'

Structurally the College suffered little damage, but some of the portraits in the Boardroom have been irretrievably ruined. The life-sized portrait of Queen Victoria, which was painted by the late S Catterson Smith, RHA, and placed in the College in 1887, in commemoration of Her Majesty's Jubilee, was ruthlessly cut out of the frame and torn into fragments. The adjoining Examination Hall was used by the rebels as a sleeping apartment. The carpet which formerly covered the floor was cut into suitable lengths and used as blankets.

The caretaker's rooms were reserved as bedrooms for the female invaders. It was here that Countess Markievicz slept, and she and the others appeared to have had a partiality for chocolates and other similar articles, many broken packages of sweetstuffs being left behind.

A gruesome discovery was made in the Chemical Lecture Theatre. The space beneath the gallery had been converted into a mortuary, slabs for bodies being taken from the Anatomy Room, and benches—originally in the Irish House of Lords—were taken from the Examination Hall for seats. A rude crucifix, composed of black metal coffin breastplates, the central plate bearing the letters 'RIP,' was affixed to the wall. An electric light wire was carried into this mortuary, and other extensions of electric lighting were made in different parts of the house, showing that some skilled workmen were amongst the rebels.

Loot from adjoining shops was found all over the place—new dustcoats, raincoats, and all sorts of male attire, as well as articles of women's apparel. A large number of blood-stained sheets and towels were collected.

The Operations at Trinity College

Trinity College, Dublin, in the crisis, proved true to its traditions. The surprise which was sprung upon the city by the rebels left the College unmoved. The garrison was at the time small, but the spirit of the few collegians who happened to be within the gates was indomitable. When the insurrection occurred the guard numbered eight, but it was sufficient to hold the fort until reinforcements gradually arrived, and by Wednesday the men in College mustered the respectable number of 150. For three days the position was extremely critical. The College, from a strategical standpoint, is of great importance, as it commands the heart of the city. Nassau street, Grafton street, Dame street, Great Brunswick street, Westmoreland street, and the southern end of Sackville street are all commanded from Trinity College, so that is possession by members of the Dublin University Officers' Training Corps was a sore thorn in the side of the rebels. When it was realised that the Sinn Feiners were intent on capturing the principal buildings in the city the front entrance was immediately barricaded, and messengers were hurriedly despatched to various parts to summon every available man to man the fort. The response was immediate. Every graduate who could be rounded up readily answered the call, with the result that the number of the garrison steadily increased. Stray soldiers passing through College Green were apprised of the situation, and they, too, willingly helped to augment the forces.

A Gallant Garrison

At seven o'clock on Monday evening the gallant garrison numbered 44 men. They were supplied with uniforms from the stores in the College, and many others who subsequently came in were fortunate in bringing their uniforms in parcels, thus dodging the snipers, who were very active in various quarters of the city. The problem set to those who were in charge was rather difficult. Would it be better to concentrate the defences on College Green or would it be advisable to watch the rebels who had seized the railway station at Westland row? With only 44 men, and with a wide area to protect, it was not easy to solve the problem. After calm consideration, however, it was decided to place guards on the principal gates, and direct the attention of the main body on the railway station. Headquarters were established at the eastern end of the grounds, with the object of holding the rectangle extending from College Green to Westland row, and from the Library to Great Brunswick street. Windows were fortified with sandbags, and every point of vantage was effectively utilised. The distance from the boundary wall to the railway line, which was being patrolled by the rebels, is only about twenty yards. The operations during the night were confined to keeping the rebels in check, and they proved eminently successful. On Tuesday morning, when the danger of an attack from the eastern end of the grounds had been averted and when the force of the garrison had been increased, it was widely decided to fortify the western end at the main entrance at College Green.

Colonial Sharpshooters

The upper windows were strongly barricaded, and machine guns were placed in positions on the parapet, while snipers took up favourable positions on the roof. Dawn had scarcely appeared when the effect of these precautions was demonstrated. Rebel scouts on bicycles rushed up Dame street in an attempt to get in touch with St Stephen's Green, where the rebels were entrenched. The leaders, however, had scarcely turned the corner of Grafton street when they were laid low by well-directed shots by two Colonial sharpshooters. The others scattered pell-mell up the side streets. Rebel snipers on the roofs of houses in Fleet street and Nassau street were speedily driven into their lairs, and volleys were fired at the General Post Office. Thus the way was kept clear for military operations in the vicinity, and a constant fire was maintained during the day. In the afternoon the small garrison, after heroic operations, was relieved by regular troops. After that the College forces were confined to providing posts and guards at various points.

During the following week many regular troops were quartered in the College grounds, and in this way Trinity has also proved of incalculable advantage to the military authorities. To accommodate a brigade of infantry, a battery of artillery, and a regiment of cavalry is surely something of which the College can be proud. The spacious quadrangles and lawns afforded excellent accommodation for the troops, and it was surely a sign that Trinity had given itself wholly over to the military when one found soldiers playing football on the tennis courts.

How a Larkinite was Caught

Among the troops who had come into the College was one man dressed in battered khaki, without any distinguishing badges. His knowledge of military matters seemed rudimentary, which he excused by saying that he was in the ASC. Nevertheless, a close watch was kept on him, which was not relaxed when he was suddenly taken ill in the middle of the night: nor was he allowed to escape when he asserted that his sister and wife were dangerously ill and he wished to go and see how they were progressing. He was not allowed out, and in the morning was recognised as a man who had been one of Larkin's chief assistants.

Deadly Battles in Pembroke Township

Some of the most desperate fighting of the rebellion took place in Lansdowne road, Pembroke road, Northumberland road, Haddington road, and Mount street. On Easter Monday a body of rebels, who had taken possession of a corner house at Haddington road and Northumberland road, fired upon and killed several members of the Veterans' Corps. The 'GR's' had been on a route march during the day to Ticknock, and were returning to their headquarters at Beggar's Bush Barracks. The first man killed was hit by a shot fired from the railway bridge at the end of Haddington road, and the Veterans were the objects of three volleys fired by the rebels from the house in Northumberland road. Though the Veterans had rifles they were entirely without ammunition. They made no demonstration against the rebels, and were shot down without any warning.

Soldiers Ambushed

On the same day a body of rebels took up positions in the grounds of the Trinity College Botanic Gardens, which command the junction of Lansdowne and Pembroke roads. They occupied these positions with little challenge until Wednesday, when the first regiment of British troops began to arrive from Kingstown. Early that Wednesday a battalion of Sherwood Foresters marched up to Lansdowne road, and fire was instantly opened on them. It was erroneously believed that the rebels occupied Carisbrook House as a fort, but the fact is that while they entered it on Easter Monday they left it immediately they found there was no back lane. The soldiers appear to have been taken by surprise, but although they were almost without cover, and the enemy fire was well directed, these young soldiers, who were taking part in their first action, fought with conspicuous coolness and bravery. The fight continued during the day, and there were several military casualties. The dead and wounded were taken to the Royal City of Dublin Hospital in Baggot street. The hospital resources were sorely tried during the week, but they rose nobly to the occasion. Doctors and nurses were almost in the thick of the fighting, and risked their lives many times a day with magnificent audacity. A tribute must also be paid to the bravery of civilians in Pembroke and Northumberland roads, women as well as men, who brought food and drink to the soldiers when the latter were heavily under fire.

Clanwilliam House Bombed

The attack on Clanwilliam House in Clanwilliam place was one of the fiercest incidents of the whole insurrection in Dublin. At this place the house was strongly held, and the main body of the Sherwood Foresters as they advanced had little or no advantage of cover. Again they came on with fine courage, and again they paid a heavy toll of life. Both here and at 25 Northumberland road the Foresters used hand grenades and small bombs: but the final *coup de guerre* at Clanwilliam House was given by a small party of RNR men, who brought up a Gatling gun and cleared out the place with six shots. The house was in flames at 9 o'clock. From the place some dead and many wounded soldiers were taken to the Royal City of Dublin Hospital.

The whole area bounded by Lansdowne road, Northumberland road, Pembroke road, the Grand Canal, and Upper Baggot street, was throughout the week a centre of the fiercest and most persistent sniping. When the main body of the rebels had surrendered, this district was still being terrorised by a small body of snipers. The bullets hummed up and down the roads, and sentries warned passengers that they were moving about at their own risk. The extinction of these scattered handful of rebels was, of course, only a matter of time.

During Sunday several large bodies of prisoners were brought to the military headquarters in the Royal Dublin Society's premises at Ballsbridge. They were strongly guarded by soldiers, and a white flag was carried in front of the procession. The appearance of these prisoners was dejected and miserable in the extreme, and many of them carried ugly wounds. A sad feature of these parties was the extreme youth of some of the prisoners.

Snipers at Ballsbridge

News of the surrender of the main body of the rebels was received in Sandymount and Ballsbridge, among other suburbs, at about six p.m. on Saturday, 29th April, and produced profound relief. This, however, was short-lived, for barely an hour afterwards a party of rebels made known their presence near the top of Serpentine avenue, and fighting began in that quarter. At about half-past seven, when it was dusk, there was the crackle of a considerable number of shots, apparently from revolvers for the most part, and a heavy reply from military rifles. The interchange of shots did not last very long, and gave the impression that the rebels were retreating across the fields between the main road and the railway. There were also some bomb explosions. The night was disturbed by a good deal of rifle firing, especially after midnight, a favourite time for the rebels to commence their business. A good part of Sunday passed peacefully, but at about five o'clock considerable sniping broke out again in the neighbourhood, and fighting was renewed with vigour for a short time.

Heavy Casualties at Mount Street Bridge

The fighting in the vicinity of Mount street Bridge was exceptionally heavy. On Easter Monday, about mid-day, the rebels occupied Boland's Bakery, and at the same time turned out the resident apothecary of the Grand Canal Dispensary, which is hard by. The next hostile act was the breaking open some large holes in the walls of the bakery directly opposite the entrance to Sir Patrick Dun's Hospital. About three o'clock in the afternoon the rebels shot dead in front of the hospital a Scots Guard named Peter Ennis, who was home on leave. He was out for a walk at the time, and was quite unaware of the presence of the rebels.

On Tuesday morning, 25th April, a man in the hospital, whose head was bound up, as he was suffering from erysipelas, while looking out of one of the front windows of the hospital, was shot at from Boland's Bakery, the bullet passing quite close to his head. On the same morning Mr R Waters, of Monkstown, was shot dead at Mount street Bridge, while being driven to Dublin in a motor car by a captain of the RAMC. Neither Mr Waters nor the captain were armed, and the car was not challenged or asked to stop. Fortunately the RAMC captain escaped.

The total casualties treated during Easter week in Sir Patrick Dun's Hospital was 142—73 military and 69 civilians. Of the military, 10 were either dead on arrival or subsequently succumbed. Eleven of the civilians were either dead on arrival or died afterwards. Nearly all of these casualties occurred in the vicinity of Mount street Bridge, and they were brought into the hospital through the Sir Patrick Dun's Nursing Home in Lower Mount street, from which there is a passage to the hospital.

Girl Wins Military Medal

Sir John Maxwell in his despatch, specially referred to the severity of the fighting at Mount street Bridge, 'where,' he said, 'our heaviest casualties occurred.' He further said he should 'like to mention the gallant assistance given by a number of medical men, ladies, nurses and women servants, who at great risk brought in and tended to the wounded.' Early in 1917, in a list of military honours issued by the War Office there appeared the name of Miss Louisa Nolan, who was awarded the Military Medal. Miss Nolan tended quite a number of wounded officers and men during the fighting at Mount street Bridge, on the Wednesday of Easter week, and brought water and other comforts to the soldiers while bullets were flying thick through the air. Miss Nolan's conduct was highly spoken of at the time of the occurrence, and great satisfaction was expressed when it became known that she had been awarded the Military Medal.

First Blood for the VTC

The Irish Volunteer Training Corps, or the 'GR's' by which they were better known, were the first Volunteers to have the honour of shedding their blood in their country's cause. On Monday, April 24th, the 1st (Dublin) Battalion paraded at Beggar's Bush Barracks. There were four companies composed of the Irish Rugby Union Football Corps, the St Andrew's Corps, the Dublin Veterans Corps, the Glasnevin Corps, as well as City and Railway

Corps, and some motor cyclists. The whole force, in spite of the number of units, was only about a hundred and twenty strong. It marched out of Dublin to Ticknock and took part in some field exercises in which the object was to drive back a force of Kingstown and Greystones Volunteers. We imagine that what followed is the only case on record of a sham fight turning into the real thing. Early in the afternoon the sham fight was over, and the VTC of both sides began to march back to their quarters. Then came to the Dublin Volunteers the amazing news that the Sinn Feiners were in revolt, and that several buildings in Dublin were in their hands. Major Harris, the commander of the 1st Dublin Battalion decided without a moment's hesitation what to do. The battalion marched for an hour and twenty minutes without a halt, and in this time covered the distance from Ticknock to Beggar's Bush Barracks, which they approached about 4 p.m. They found the barracks being besieged, and on approaching them came under a sharp fire from the Sinn Feiners, who occupied the railway bridge which commands Haddington road. They had no ammunition for their rifles: they did not even carry bayonets. Meanwhile their 'GR' brassards made them easy targets. Their commander with an advance party managed to enter the barracks by the front entrance, taking with him Corporal Clery of A Company, who was mortally wounded. The remainder of the column was ordered to retire up Lansdowne lane—a difficult and trying movement which was carried out with complete steadiness. This part of the column made its way to the back of the barracks at the rear of Northumberland road, marching in single file till a place was reached where it seemed possible to climb over the wall. Eighty-one men and nine officers climbed over and joined the besieged garrison. There were only seventeen Lee-Enfield rifles in the barracks, and the Volunteers had only six which would take the .303 cartridge. The Volunteers were instructed to use their old Italian rifles as clubs if the Sinn Feiners attempted to rush them. A member of the battalion who had not taken part in the day's exercises pluckily came to the barracks in plain clothes, bringing a few more rifles. Firing was kept up by the enemy from the houses in Northumberland road, and especially from No. 25, at the corner of Haddington road. It was from this house that fire was opened on the remainder of the Volunteers, numbering about forty of all ranks, commanded by Mr FH Browning, with such fatal results, four being killed and nine wounded. The trees on the road afforded a slight temporary protection to others of this body, but they got shelter in neighbouring houses. The occupiers of Nos. 29, 31, and 33 took in several till they were able to proceed home. All the wounded 'GRs' except two were dressed at No. 31 and here also all the others, with one exception, were supplied with change of clothing. In No. 33 the Sherwood Foresters had a dressing station all day on Wednesday, 26th. Two NCO's of B company managed to get down the lane behind Northumberland road and over the wall into barracks. Mr Edward Webb, Commandant of C Company (Glasnevin), ran for the front gate of the barracks, keeping close to the wall, and got in unhurt.

Continuous Sniping

No attacks were made on the barracks save by rifle fire from these and other distant points, and, so far from the garrison being besieged, motors with rations and stores and other vehicles went in and out, but not without coming now and then under fire. On Monday evening Colonel Sir Frederick Shaw, DSO, Commanding the 2nd (Garrison) Battalion RI Fusiliers, drove in in his trap, and his coachman drove in and out on subsequent days. The intensity of the fire varied from hour to hour: the sniping increased towards evening, and rendered the crossing of the barrack square hazardous at times. The only casualty that occurred out of doors was on Wednesday, the 26 ult, when Mr RA Anderson was wounded by a charge of buckshot while in the 'detention' post, commanding the corner of Northumberland road and Haddington road. He was taken to Portobello Hospital. Happily, the wounds were not serious, and he reappeared with his arm in a sling before the force left barracks on Tuesday, 2nd May.

Later in the week Mr Joseph Hosford, of C Company, was killed in the barrack room. He had gone up to get his overcoat, and stood for a moment opposite a window. A bullet came through the glass and went through his body.

Mr Charles Dickinson, commandant of B Company, and a few others made their way into the barracks on the Tuesday, and on Wednesday afternoon the garrison was strengthened by a part of the Notts and Derby Territorials, who had landed at Kingstown that morning and marched in to Ballsbridge. They knew nothing of the district, much less of the existence of the barracks: but fortunately for them they came down Shelbourne road, and were seen by the sentries on the Shelbourne post. Word was passed down the line of sentries, and they halted. A ladder was let down over the wall, which is very high above the road, and they climbed into barracks, heavily laden as they were. Most of them had been only three months in training at Watford, and some had never fired a service rifle save at a miniature range. They were used to strengthen the guards. Later in the afternoon an attempt was made to dislodge the Sinn Feiners from the railway, but the latter were too strongly entrenched. Sergeant-Major Gamble, from the garrison, accompanied the sortie party, and was killed on the line, while Lieutenant Gerrard, RFA, who was in command of the party, was severely wounded in the right arm.

Short Rations

Food supplies began to run short, and the men were put on half rations. The canteen, where such things as tinned meats, biscuits, minerals, tobacco, and matches were at first to be had, gave out, and it was only in the last couple of days that fresh supplies came in. The Volunteers and the Tommies took their meals together: breakfast at 8, dinner between 12 and 1, and tea at 5. Each guard was on for four hours in the day and four hours at night. Subsequently, as an extra precaution, and to ensure the men being ready for duty at the appointed hour, they slept in the verandah instead of in the barrack rooms. For example, the guards on duty from 1-5 a.m. went to the verandah at 9 p.m., and the 5-9 a.m. guards at 1 a.m. Sunday was not a day of rest. Sniping went on on both sides. Two Services were held in the church. Sergeant Robinson of A Company, acted as chaplain, and preached a stirring sermon in the morning, taking as his text, 'Keep your heads down and your hearts up.' At first the men had to sleep on the floor: afterwards square cushions, popularly known as 'biscuits' from their shape, were provided, and blankets later on. Fortunately, fine weather prevailed all the time, and the nights were not cold, considering the time of year.

Bombardment of Liberty Hall

For many years past Liberty Hall has been a thorn in the side of the Dublin Police and the Irish Government. It was the centre of social anarchy in Ireland, the brain of every riot and disturbance. When it was determined to use artillery to defeat the rebels, Liberty Hall was singled out for the first target, both because of its great notoriety and because it and two neighbouring houses were strongly held by the insurgents.

On Tuesday, 25th April, artillery arrived in Trinity College, and it was decided to start the shelling next morning. But the recoil of modern artillery is so violent that, in spite of the buffer, it is necessary to fix the trail of the gun in the ground. Under ordinary circumstances the recoil drives a spade-shaped plate of iron on the trail into the ground: but the streets of Dublin, being paved, prevented this arrangement from working. Accordingly it was necessary to dig up the cobble stones before the guns could come into action, and the closeness of the range from which it had been determined to fire (some 250 yards) made it fairly certain that any working party of soldiers would be shot down before their task was completed. However, it was thought possible to employ men in civilian clothes, and so in the early hours of Wednesday morning six volunteers from Trinity College—partly civilians and partly members of the OTC—started out to dig holes for the trails near Butt Bridge, at the end of Tara street.

Dublin's Tough Streets

Armed with two picks, two crowbars, and two spades they began to work. But the task proved unexpectedly difficult. Dublin streets are paved with cobble stones some six inches long by four wide, and at last six or seven inches deep. These are set in a cement of tar, and are placed so close to each other that there is no room for a pick to enter between them. After half an hour only one stone had been removed in each position, and one crowbar had been broken. Accordingly a message was sent back for reinforcements and new tools.

Meanwhile the inhabitants of the neighbouring houses were much perplexed as to what was going on, and incredulous of the explanation that the gas supply of Trinity had failed and some attempt was being made to put it right. The arrival of soldiers, who formed up in the cover of the side streets and took possession of the corner house to cover the digging party caused them further alarm and curiosity.

18-pounders from Trinity

Unfortunately, in Trinity College further tools were not procurable, and as delay seemed undesirable it was determined to attack at once, utilising what holes had been made. The guns cantered out by the Brunswick street gate, and came swiftly along Tara street. When they reached the two side streets which intersect it, about thirty yards from the quays, they turned off in these and unlimbered, the ammunition limbers being left there, while the guns were manhandled into the prepared positions. The volunteers from Trinity College left their work, and three of them formed a party to carry ammunition from the side streets to the guns.

The two 18-pounders opened fire almost simultaneously. At the first report every pane of glass in the street was shattered, and even in Trinity College the solid buildings seemed to quake under those who were lining the parapets. Machine guns placed on the tower of the Fire Station, the Custom House, and the Tivoli mixed their noise with that of the rifles, to form an indescribable and hideous medley of sound almost deafening the gunners in the narrow Tara street. Liberty Hall and the adjacent houses were wreathed in dust and smoke, and appeared to be replying vigorously from machine guns and rifles. This was subsequently discovered not to be the case, as the rebels had got wind of the move, and partially evacuated their position on the previous night. Shell after shell was fired, throwing down a portion of Northumberland House, and making the others mere empty shells.

Shelled from the River

On Wednesday, the 26th April, the steamer Helga, which was formerly a police patrol boat belonging to the Fisheries Department, and lately employed by the Admiralty in connection with the war, was brought up the Liffey, and anchored nearly opposite the Custom House, with the intention of bombarding Liberty Hall, the headquarters of the Citizen Army. As most people are aware, the loop line railway bridge intervenes between the Custom House and Liberty Hall, and in addition to this formidable obstruction to the line of fire one of Guinness's steamers was lying close to Butt Bridge. It was impossible under these conditions to bring direct fire to bear upon the objective. The gunners of the Helga were accordingly obliged to adopt a plan of dropping fire. The military in occupation of the Custom House prepared to co-operate, and by removing portions of the wall facing Liberty Hall were able to obtain effective positions for their machine guns.

The bombardment commenced about eight o'clock in the morning, and for over an hour a continuous cannonade was maintained. There was no return fire from the rebels, who were supposed to be in occupation of Liberty Hall, but the bombardment caused intense excitement in the district, where there is a large population of the poorer class of residents. With every shot the houses were shaken, and the people were almost panic stricken. After the expenditure of a great amount of ammunition, the Helga withdrew further down the river. It was then seen that the outer shell of Liberty Hall had been very little damaged. All the windows had been blown in, but the surrounding brickwork was only slightly injured. The interior, however, was a mass of *débris*. The adjoining premises, known as Northumberland House, were badly damaged. It was stated that during the previous night the 'garrison' had been warned of the approach of the Helga, and made good their escape.

Some Discoveries

An examination of the remains of Liberty Hall rewarded the searchers by yielding a number of important documents. A printing press had been installed there, and from this place the literature of the rebellion seems to have been issued. Some of the 'finds' included commissions dated Easter Sunday, and signed by members of the 'Staff', appointing certain named persons to commands in the 'Citizens' Army'. Bundles of the proclamation declaring Ireland a Republic were also discovered.

Another important 'find' in Liberty Hall was a large number of copies of the document which was read at the meeting of Dublin Corporation on the 19th April. At that meeting certain of the members of the Council denounced the Government as the authors of the leaflet, but the discovery made in the printing room of Liberty Hall puts a new complexion on the matter. This document purported to be a statement of certain 'precautionary measures' which were to be put into force by the military on receiving an order from Dublin Castle. The military were to take charge of the city, certain premises were to be seized, and others were to be isolated.

Gunboat in Action at Ringsend

Ringsend was the scene of warm work during the rebellion. On Easter Monday the Volunteers appeared in force at several points in the district. That they had laid their plans well was seen by the commanding positions they took up. Boland's Mill, a high stone building overlooking the Basin of the Grand Canal and affording a wide view over the river mouth, was one of their main strongholds, and, as events proved, one of the hardest to overcome. Having taken possession, the rebels lost no time in fortifying the walls around the mill by placing upon them bags of flour to protect themselves against attackers' bullets. About the same time another party took over the old distillery on the other side of the drawbridge, and prepared for resistance to the forces of the crown. A third body went into a field at the Gas Works. Other strategic positions which the rebels occupied were the bridges on the railway line from Westland row to Lansdowne road. These naturally commanded the approaches to the district, and made it impossible for military to enter Ringsend directly, without having to pass through the line of fire of concealed riflemen.

Firing on Beggar's Bush Barracks

In this, as in other parts of Dublin, the insurgents had evidently in mind the importance of concentrating upon any military barracks from which an attempt might be made to subdue them. Hence, the men who held the positions described fired heavily upon Beggar's Bush Barracks, and caused some loss to the loyalists. Such was the situation in the early days of the rising.

The rebels had prepared themselves so well for their work, were so daring, and in such number, that they suspended the normal life of the district for an entire week. With the best will in the world, it was not always possible to distinguish harmless persons from the foes of public peace and order; and when machine guns came into action the likelihood of being struck by a stray bullet was increased. To defeat the desperate men who fired from strong buildings like Boland's Mill and Ringsend Distillery more than rifle-fire was wanted. This mode of attack they had foreseen, but it is doubtful whether they had calculated upon the use of heavy guns against them. At each point where ordnance was brought up the tide of fortune quickly turned; a Martini-Henry rifle or an automatic pistol is a poor weapon in the face of a nine-pounder handled by good gunners.

The Helga in Action

At Ringsend the heavy guns were used not on land, but from water. On Wednesday the gunboat Helga came up the Liffey and joined battle with the insurgents sheltered in Liberty Hall. To the Helga also fell the duty of coping with the rebel fortresses at Ringsend. The gunboat did that duty well, and has left its mark upon both buildings. What the Volunteers within thought of the bombardment has not yet been disclosed. But it is easily realised that the heavy firing brought great uneasiness to the good folk of Ringsend.

With the surrender of the rebels in the mill and the distillery the rising in this quarter of Dublin was not altogether at an end. There were still stragglers who had not heard or did not accept their leaders' order to desist. The most obdurate were on the railway, and it was not until the following Monday that the military occupied the line. During this week of rebellion there were many narrow escapes and a few sad deaths in Ringsend. While bullets were flying through the streets, only an urgent necessity could force the law-abiding to go their customary ways. Before much of the week had passed the need arose in the form of food. The poor buy their food in small quantities: they had no store upon which to draw. Some went to seek sustenance. Of their number was an old woman who ventured forth alone. She got her bread in a time when bread was scarce—four loaves: but she never reached her home again, for, as she crossed Victoria Bridge, she met with the bullet that brought her life to an end. Another death of the kind occurred on Saturday, when a man was shot at the Ringsend Bottle Works. The work of bearing the wounded was fraught with no little danger: as the Pembroke Ambulance was approaching London Bridge part of the seat was shot away.

The Surrender

Dr Myles Keogh, who, in company with Mr LG Redmond Howard and others, acted so bravely in rescuing the wounded, tells of the actual incident of the surrender of De Valera near Ringsend. Dr Keogh had just returned at half-past twelve from Glasnevin Cemetery, where he conveyed under the Red Cross flag the remains of a civilian who had been fatally wounded at Mount street Bridge. Dr Keogh had dismounted from the hearse and entered the hall of Sir Patrick Dun's Hospital, when two men came out of the Poor Law Dispensary opposite, in which the Sinn Feiners were installed. One was a military cadet who had been captured by the Sinn Feiners, the other was the Sinn Fein leader De Valera. 'Hullo!' cried De Valera. 'Who are you?' replied Dr Myles Keogh. The response was, 'I am De Valera,' from one, and from the other it was: 'I am a prisoner for the past five days. They want to surrender.' De Valera asked permission to use the hospital telephone, in order to communicate with the military authorities. Dr Keogh sent for Sir Arthur Ball, MD, who informed De Valera that the telephone communication had been cut off, and suggested that he should proceed to the nearest military position, at the head of Grattan street, off Lower Mount street. De Valera did so and after some preliminaries the Sinn Feiners were marched out of the dispensary and up Grattan street. At the opening of surrender negotiations De Valera said to the military, 'You may shoot me, but my men must be unmolested when surrendering.' An expression attributed to De Valera at the surrender was, 'If only the people had come out with knives and forks,' but afterwards this statement was said to have been made earlier in the proceedings to an employé of Messrs Boland's, who had been detained by the Sinn Feiners to attend to that firm's horses.

At Portobello Bridge

One of the most exciting of the events of the early part of Easter Monday took place at Portobello Bridge, resulting in the wrecking of Davy's public-house and injury to at least four persons. It was shortly after mid-day when the rebels appeared on the scene. They at once took possession of the public house, which commands the approaches to the bridge, and posted their men at the windows. Some of the rebels were outside on the footpath, and a military officer who was passing was fired at. He returned to the barracks, and a strong armed guard turned out. The soldiers were subjected to some volley firing from the windows of the public house as they approached the bridge, but the men quickly took cover at the bridge wall, from which position they returned the fire of the rebels. The heavy firing doubtless alarmed the authorities in the barracks, as strong reinforcements, with machine guns, were rushed up, to the accompaniment of the hearty cheering of the crowds on the Rathmines road. The people on the roadway were in great danger, and Superintendent Kiernan and Station-Sergeant Crosbie, with a force of police, had a busy time endeavouring to keep them out of rifle shot. The tramway wires had been cut at the bridge, and long lines of cars were drawn up on the roadway. Meanwhile the military had quickly matured their plans. An attack on the public house was decided upon, and, led by a senior officer, the soldiers at once advanced to the 'fortress'. Applying the butt-ends of their rifles, they soon hacked their way through the plate glass windows, and rushed into the house, which they searched from garret to cellar, only to find, as was supposed, that the rebels had made good their escape. In the attack the officer commanding was wounded, but not seriously. A soldier also sustained a bullet wound on the face. He was taken off to the military hospital in the barracks. In the earlier part of the shooting Constable Myles, 99E, was shot in the left wrist. He received first aid at Dr Joyce's surgery close by, and later on was removed to hospital. A civilian, who was too venturesome, and who was being shepherded by Superintendent Kiernan into comparative safety, was also shot by the rebels. The bullet just grazed the officer's body and struck the civilian, happily inflicting only a slight wound. Both men had a narrow escape from being killed. In the afternoon the military took charge of the streets leading to Portobello Bridge, and stopped all traffic.

At Jacob's Factory

At Jacob's bakery establishment in Peter street a considerable body of the rebels entrenched themselves behind bags of flour, which they had placed in windows in the upper flats, and from this place of comparative safety they steadily discharged shots, aimed mainly in the direction of Ship street military barracks, which stands in the hollow between the bakery and the rear of the Castle. It was extremely difficult to come to close quarters with them, for the bakery is surrounded by houses which hamper access to the building. A narrow lane runs close to one of its sides, but to enter it would have proved a death-trap to the soldiers. Gradually, however, the soldiers succeeded in overcoming their difficulties, and by wearing down the defence of the rebels compelled them to give up what they rightly recognised was for them a hopeless struggle. A number of deaths occurred at this place. The surrender took place on Sunday, 30th April. It was a member of the Carmelite Order from Whitefriar street who was instrumental in persuading them to yield. Amid the cheers of the crowd gathered about the building, the clergyman was hoisted by a number of men up to one of the lower windows, from which the bags of flour used instead of sand by the rebels had been pulled. He went inside the factory, and not long after a party of Volunteers walked out. The garrison, leaving their flag flying, came out of the factory one by one on Sunday night, many of them dressed in civilian attire, which had been passed into them by their friends at the rear of the factory. The crowd then indulged in looting on an extensive scale, many bags of flour and boxes of biscuits being carried off.

At the South Dublin Union

After a week's occupation of portion of the South Dublin Union, the rebels surrendered on Sunday night, April 30th. Their number was greatly reduced from its original strength, but those who insisted, despite the utter hopelessness of their plight, in continuing a forlorn fight, caused great uneasiness in the district. They had several opportunities during the week of surrendering, but they refused every time. Their last stand was made in the Boardroom of the institution, which they fortified as best they could, the official ledgers and other formidable books being piled through the windows as part of the defences. Apart from bullet perforation in the windows and some loose tiles on the roof the frontage at James's street was not badly damaged, and it was obvious that the military dealt leniently with it in consideration of the inmates and other innocent persons whose lives were endangered.

Throughout the week the Union was the centre of severe fighting, in the course of which Nurse Keogh was accidentally killed by a shot while discharging her duty. The rebels took up suitable sniping positions at Dolphin's Barn, Marrowbone lane, Watling street, Kingsbridge, Kilmainham, Rialto, and Inchicore, while a party which seized Messrs Roe's malting stores near Mount Brown also gave trouble. On Wednesday the latter were driven out by heavy fire, but in the evening made their way along the banks of the River Camac, with the object apparently of getting towards the open country. Their progress, however, was barred by firing parties judiciously posted, and some of them were killed, while others were rounded up and captured. There were unfortunately some casualties amongst civilians. Two children were shot in the vicinity of Dolphin's Barn. At Watling street, near the river, snipers shot across in the direction of the Royal Barracks, but they were disposed of without causing serious damage. Exhaustive searches were made in houses in the neighbourhood, and some rifles and ammunition were found. Most of the prisoners were taken to Kilmainham Jail under strong escorts.

At the Four Courts

Not far from Charles street are the Four Courts, which formed one of the Volunteers' strongholds. The Courts of Law presented an extraordinary appearance. The gates were closed and barricaded with all kinds of furniture, and inside each was a Volunteer sentry. The buildings within were held by the rebels, whose number could not be ascertained. That many hands had been at work was apparent. Most of the windows were blocked with books and other things taken from the offices, many of which doubtless contained valuable records. Church street Bridge was a centre of interest. It had been barricaded by the Sinn Feiners on Monday. A couple of sentries, marching up and down, did not allow the many inquisitive sightseers to cross into the space at the end of Church street. It was possible to go up the Southern quays, but not up the Northern, owing to the position of the Volunteers. The next bridge was open to pedestrians, but was not free from danger. The rebels took in a number of prisoners, and kept them until they surrendered on Saturday. The Mendicity Institute, not far off, had been one of the rebels' fortresses, but had been successfully enfiladed by the soldiers on Monday.

Easter Sittings should have commenced on Thursday, 27th April, but at the time when the Lord Chancellor would, under ordinary circumstances, have been standing in the Central Hall, wearing his State robes and receiving the judges, the building was in possession of the insurgents, and bloody war had usurped the place of law.

Much anxiety was felt as to what was going on in the Record Office, where thousands of valuable historical documents, wills, deeds, etc., are stored, and great relief was experienced when it was found that the majority of these documents, though much tossed about, had not been seriously damaged. Some bundles containing wills had been thrown out on the adjoining streets, and had been taken away by residents in Church street, not so much, it is believed, as 'loot,' but rather as curious souvenirs of the rebellion. When these people learnt that the authorities were again in possession of the Record Office, it is to their credit that many of them brought these documents back to their custodian.

North King Street

Nowhere was the fighting more intense than in the area of which North King street is the centre. The narrow thoroughfares had been barricaded by the Sinn Feiners, and the task of the military was one of great difficulty and danger, as many of the houses were occupied by snipers. The women and children were urged to leave the district, but declined to do so, and, unfortunately, there is no doubt that people who were not taking part in the operations were killed. Many charges were made against the military, and these were dealt with by the Commander-in-Chief in his despatches, and in a special statement to a Press representative.

SIR JOHN MAXWELL ANSWERS CHARGES OF BRUTALITY

General Sir John Maxwell made the following statement to a correspondent of the *Daily Mail* on Thursday, 18th May:

'The allegations of brutality seem almost exclusively concerned with the fighting in North King street. Our policy during the suppression of the rebellion was to put a military cordon round the chief rebel area in Sackville street, but when we had done so we discovered that there was another centre of importance at the Four Courts, and we determined also to encircle that. One line of this cordon was to pass through North King street. We discovered, however, that instead of being outside the rebel area, this line actually cut through it, and very desperate fighting occurred before we could complete the cordon in this street. With the one exception of the place at Ballsbridge, where the Sherwood Foresters were ambushed, this was by far the worst fighting that occurred in the whole of Dublin. At first the troops, coming from one end of the street, were repulsed, and it was only when we made an attack from both ends that we succeeded after twenty-four hours' fighting in capturing the street.

Moving from House to House

'The casualties were very heavy during this fighting. The troops were continually fired at from the roofs and upper windows of the houses. With modern rifles it is impossible to tell by the sound the exact direction from which a bullet comes. The rebels were moving from house to house. As the troops, for instance, moved along the street the rebels would escape round the back doors and fire again on the troops from behind practically every house there. Five had to be searched and occupied. Always we found that the rebels sought to cloak themselves behind their women. When we began to search a house they threw away their rifles and joined the women herding at the back, pretending that they had been there all the time. These rebels wore no uniform, and the man who was shooting at a soldier one minute might, for all he knew, be walking quietly beside him in the street at another. We tried hard to get the women and children to leave the North King street area; they would not go; their sympathies were with the rebels, and this must be remembered in connection with their allegations now. It was impossible from headquarters to exercise direct control over the sort of fighting that occurred, since the telegraph and telephone wires were out of order. Nearly everything had to be left to the troops on the spot.

Treacherous Assailants

'Possibly unfortunate incidents, which we should regret now, may have occurred. It did not, perhaps, always follow that where shots were fired from a particular house the inmates were always necessarily aware of it or guilty, but how were the soldiers to discriminate? They saw their comrades killed beside them by hidden and treacherous assailants, and it is even possible that under the horrors of this peculiar attack some of them "saw red". That is the inevitable consequence of a rebellion of this kind. It was allowed to come into being among these people, and could not be suppressed by velvet-glove methods where our troops were so desperately opposed and attacked. Some, at any rate, of the allegations are certainly false, and are probably made in order to establish a claim for compensation from the Government. I have ordered a very strict military inquiry into all the allegations that are made. Officers unconnected with the units charged will visit all houses where complaints are made in order to investigate the circumstances impartially on the spot. Battalions concerned will be paraded in order that witnesses who are making allegations of brutality, which they claim to have seen personally, may have an opportunity, if they can, of identifying officers or men responsible, and every such case will be fully inquired into. Any man proved guilty will be properly punished and the full results of the inquiry made public as soon as possible.

'Meanwhile I am happy to note that, in spite of these allegations, the people of Dublin continue on excellent terms with the troops. Even in North King street itself, which I visited yesterday, I saw the soldiers talking in the friendliest way with the women at their doors. Indeed, I think that the popularity of the soldiers in Dublin today is most gratifying and is one of the best possible proofs of the exaggeration, to say the least of it, shown in these allegations.'

Two Bodies Buried in a Cellar

Dr Louis A Byrne, City Coroner, in the Morgue on Tuesday, 16th May, conducted inquests on the bodies of Patrick Bealen, aged 30, who had been employed as foreman at Mrs Mary O'Rourke's licensed house, 177 North King street, Dublin, and James Healy, aged 44, employed as a labourer at Messrs Jameson's Distillery, Bow street, and residing at Little Green street. The bodies, which bore marks of bullet wounds, had both been disinterred on 10th May in the cellar of 177 North King street by the sanitary authorities. At the opening of the inquest the previous Friday evidence was heard, and suggestions were made against the military who had been on duty in North King street. The Coroner then adjourned the further hearing of evidence until Tuesday, and notified the military authorities of the adjourned sitting.

Major Rhodes, Assistant Provost Marshal, 59th Division, and Captain Sheppard were present on Tuesday on behalf of the military authorities.

Mr JCR Lardner, MP (instructed by Mr John J McDonald) appeared for the next-of-kin of the deceased men.

Inspector Travers represented the police authorities.

Mrs O'Rourke's Evidence

Mrs Mary O'Rourke, owner of the licensed premises 177 North King street, said, in reply to Mr Lardner, that the military entered her house about 12 o'clock midnight on 28th April. Her three children, the cook, Patrick Bealen, and herself were then in the cellar for safety. They were there several hours when the military came in. A sergeant and a private came down and searched Bealen and witness's son, who was not 13 years of age. The soldiers subsequently took them all to the kitchen, which was on the second flight of stairs. Two soldiers remained with them, and later on a third came in. An officer came in on Saturday morning, and ordered the soldiers out of the kitchen, saying: 'It is a shame to put them in the kitchen, as it is so small.' To the soldiers he said: 'You have no right to be here: leave the kitchen to the ladies.' Bealen was taken away an hour or two previous to the arrival of the officer.

Dr Meldon gave evidence as to the wounds which caused the death of Bealen. In his opinion the shots which killed the man had been fired from a considerable distance.

Dr Matthew Russell, Assistant Medical Officer of Health for Dublin, gave evidence as to the exhuming of the body of the deceased. It had been buried in the cellar, about 12 inches from the surface. The body was fully dressed. Underneath the body a second body, that of James Healy, was discovered, also fully dressed.

Mr MA Moynihan, Borough Surveyor, stated on searching the cellar he found a portion of the floor softer than the surrounding parts. He made an excavation where it was soft, and the sanitary staff continued the excavation in his presence until they came upon the two bodies. He added that he found the 'spoil' from the grave under the slide by which the barrels were lowered from the street.

Michael Brophy, attendant in the Coroner's Court, said he found tied with a bootlace at the back of Bealen's shirt £7 in notes and gold and one penny in his coat pocket.

Woman's Account of the Shooting

Mrs Roseanna Knowles, 23 Lurgan street, which is close to 177 North King street, stated that during the week of the disturbances a number of soldiers were billeted in her house. She had some conversations with them. She asked the soldiers, 'Was there much killed?' One of them said, 'There was a good deal of our men killed and a good deal of the others.' He further said: 'I only pitied the poor fellow at the corner (O'Rourke's) and the woman who was fainting.'

Did he say why he pitied him? He said, 'I pitied him from my heart, though I had to shoot him. He had made tea for me.'

What else did he say? He said they had brought the prisoner downstairs in O'Rourke's. The soldier said that the man gave him his penknife and his ring. He produced the penknife, but said he had lost the ring.

What happened then? He said that when they brought him downstairs he had not the heart to shoot him straight, and that they told him (the deceased) to go up again, and at the foot of the stairs they shot him—that they 'let bang' at the foot of the stairs.

Military Statement

The Coroner—Major Rhodes, do you wish to say anything?

Major Rhodes—No, but I would ask you to read a statement that had been made by Lieutenant-Colonel H Taylor, Commanding the 2nd/6th South Staffords.

The statement was then read by the Coroner. It was as follows:

'I cannot discover any military witnesses as to the manner in which the two men, Patrick Bealen and James Healy, met with their deaths, but I cannot believe that the allegations made at the inquest can be correct. Patrick Bealen was certainly never brought to the guardroom. To the best of my knowledge and belief, during the military operations in Capel street and King street, which lasted from 6 a.m. on Friday, 28th April, until the truce was declared on the afternoon of Saturday, 29th (and which were, in fact, continued for some hours after that by the rebels in that area), only those houses were entered by the military which the exigencies of the case rendered actually necessary, and no persons were attacked by the troops other than those who were assisting the rebels, and found with arms in their possession.

Firing from Houses

'The premises No. 177 North King street were indicated to me as one of the houses from which the troops had been repeatedly fired upon, and the troops were also continually fired upon both during the night of the 26th April and the whole of the following day from the distillery, at which the deceased man, James Healy, was stated to have been employed. The operations in the portion of King street, between Linenhall street and Church street, were conducted under circumstances of the greatest difficulty and danger for the troops engaged, who were subjected to severe fire, not only from behind several rebel barricades, which had been constructed across King street, and other barricades in Church street and the side streets, but also from practically every house in that portion of King street and other buildings overlooking it.

'Strong evidence of these difficulties and dangers is afforded by the fact that it took the troops from 10 a.m. on the 28th April until 2 p.m. on the 29th to force their way along King street from Linenhall street to Church street, a distance of some 150 yards only; and that the casualties sustained by the regiment (the great majority of which occurred at this spot) numbered five officers (including two captains) wounded, 14 nco's and men killed and 28 wounded.

'I may add (1) that the rebels for some hours after

the truce was declared continued firing on my men, who, although they sustained several further casualties, did not reply; and (2) that during these continued hostilities after the truce the rebels, by firing on the RAMC (one of whom they wounded) prevented the removal of some of our wounded for several hours, and the latter could only be ultimately removed by means of an armoured car.

'I am satisfied that during these operations the troops under my command showed great moderation and restraint under exceptionally difficult and trying circumstances.'

Verdict of the Jury

The Coroner having briefly addressed the jury, the following verdict was returned:

'We find that the said Patrick Bealen died from shock and hemorrhage, resulting from bullet wounds inflicted by a soldier, or soldiers, in whose custody he was, an unarmed and unoffending prisoner. We consider that the explanation given by the military authorities is very unsatisfactory, and we believe that if the military authorities had any inclination they could produce the officer in charge.'

Inquest on James Healy

The adjourned inquest on the body of James Healy, which was also found buried in the cellar of 177 North King street, was then resumed.

The jury returned a verdict in terms similar to that recorded in the case of Bealen.

Mr Asquith and Courts of Inquiry

A large number of questions were put in the House of Commons from time to time regarding alleged shooting of civilians in the North King street area, and various members urged the Government to hold a public inquiry. On Monday, 17th July, Mr Asquith said he undertook that these cases should be carefully investigated, but there had never been any promise of a public inquiry. Accordingly, after all available evidence had been secured, courts of inquiry were held, and the witnesses examined. The conclusion arrived at after a full hearing in all the cases was that the deaths occurred in the course of continuous and desperate street and house-to-house fighting, which lasted for nearly two days, and in which the soldiers were constantly exposed to sniping from the windows and roofs of the houses. There could be little doubt that some men who were not taking an actual part in the fighting were in the course of the struggle killed by both rebels and soldiers, but, after careful inquiry, it was impossible to bring home responsibility to any particular person or body of persons. He had himself read the evidence taken by the courts of inquiry. He was of opinion that further inquiry would not be likely to lead to any different result.

THE ATTACK ON THE MAGAZINE FORT

About noon on Easter Monday eight or nine motor cars dashed into the Phoenix Park through Island Bridge gate. Each of these was crowded with men dressed in their ordinary clothes, and, having regard to the occasion, any passer-by would have taken it for granted that they were out for a holiday, and probably on their way to Fairyhouse Races. Immediately afterwards seven men in uniform, driving on a couple of outside cars, the numbers of which were concealed, arrived on the scene. The Fort was occupied by Mrs Playfair, the wife of the commandant (then at the front in France), and her family of two sons and a daughter. The garrison consisted of only a few soldiers, of whom the sentry was immediately disposed of, and the assailants, rushing into the guardroom, covered the others with revolvers. One of the men in uniform seized Mrs Playfair by the arm, and, presenting a revolver, ordered her to show him the telephone, which he promptly cut. Then he gave them six minutes to get out of the Fort before he blew it up. The elder of Mrs Playfair's boys rushed down to Park place, about a hundred yards from the Fort, to a house in which he thought there was a telephone, and just as the lady of the house had opened the door a Sinn Feiner rode up to the gate on a bicycle, and, rushing to the door, discharged three shots point blank into the unfortunate lad, from the effects of which he died next morning. The assailant escaped down Conyngham road to the city. Fortunately the design of the rebels on the Magazine was only successful to a limited extent. They set the outer portion of it, which contains only small arms, on fire, and evidently being in a great hurry to get away, and unaware that the high explosives were stored in a different compartment, they fled from the scene, after a stay of about twenty minutes. For a time, of course, the danger of an explosion was imminent, but the soldiers who arrived on the scene worked very pluckily and successfully to get the upper hand of the fire, and, aided by the Fire Brigade, they managed to extinguish it before the next morning.

THE FIGHT AT NORTH CIRCULAR ROAD AND CABRA

The northern suburbs perhaps more than any other part of the Dublin Metropolitan area were affected by the general hold up of traffic. From Wednesday, 26th April, they were cut off from all communication with the centre of the city. All traffic along the Phoenix Park road and to Cabra road was stopped, and the military pickets had the most peremptory orders to prevent people from passing through.

All this was following a fight which took place on Tuesday in the Cabra district. The rebels had placed barricades both on the Park road and on Cabra road near the point at which Charleville road links up these thoroughfares. Houses overlooking the barricades had been occupied by the revolutionaries on the Monday, and these positions were held until the arrival of the Dublin Fusiliers from Templemore. The military at once attacked the houses, where, after a sharp fight, some of the rebels surrendered, while others escaped, it was believed, towards Glasnevin and Finglas, going across country.

Following this the closest military precautions were taken. At first the entrance to the Glasnevin road from the North Circular road was barred by a strong picket, and later on the pickets were pushed out as far as the Cross Guns Bridge, commanding the canal and railway line running to the North Wall, the Whitworth road, and the Finglas road.

At Glasnevin

The people in Phibsborough were kept within the cordon, while the people in Glasnevin were rigidly excluded, and only on the most urgent business could permission be obtained to pass. On Thursday it became apparent that something approaching a food famine was imminent. The alarm was instantaneous. Immediately the provision shops in the district were besieged, the flour mills at Cross Guns Bridge, were crowded, and men and women of all classes were seen carrying away parcels of flour, potatoes, bread, and everything that could be procured in the way of foodstuffs. The butchers' shops were soon cleared and the provision stores were sold out by Saturday. Many people went out to the Finglas village where the local butchers did a tremendous trade. While the food crisis was in progress the anxiety of the residents of this district was increased by the alarming rumours which were in constant circulation as to alleged happenings in the city. The rumours, needless to say, became more alarming as they were passed about from one group to another, and all the time there was nothing official, nothing definite. As night fell the anxiety was not eased. The constant sniping, the occasional big gun firing, and then the sky lit up by the reflection from some blazing building all combined to make the night more terrible even than the day. Many pathetic sights were witnessed in connection with funerals going to Glasnevin Cemetery. Owing to the rigid regulations in force only the driver of the hearse and at most one mourner were allowed to accompany the remains. But many were driven through the military cordon accompanied only by the driver of the hearse. These regulations were relaxed with the utmost speed by the military. Up to Wednesday, 3rd May, the residents found it a matter of difficulty to obtain permits from the military station at Cross Guns Bridge, and business people were subjected to long delays before they could resume duty in the city.

At Drumcondra

The district from the Cross Guns Bridge to Glasnevin was entirely free from the presence of active rebels, but they were present in considerable numbers from the Whitworth road to Mountjoy square. Even after the general surrender on Saturday, 29th April, the sniping in that district gave the military and the civil inhabitants a great deal of trouble. Dorset street and the streets off it were in a very disturbed state. The large warehouse of Messrs Baker and Sons in Dorset street had its windows smashed, and some drapery goods were carried off by looters. Sniping was heard on Monday, 1st May, in that district, in spite of the search of houses carried out by the military.

Battle at Fairview

The residents in Fairview had a lively time during the rebellion. On Easter Monday evening the rebels took possession of Ballybough Bridge and the houses around, and began to question those who came along, to search them, and to turn some of them back. They also seized several motor cars. At Annesley Bridge their tactics were the same. On the Wharf road they broke into the Dublin and Wicklow Manure Works, and took possession of houses at Fairview Corner and Philipsburgh avenue. In short, they occupied the whole of Fairview district until Wednesday, when soldiers arrived in the district. Having taken up positions along the railway embankment, they entered into action with the rebels, and ultimately drove them out with machine guns. The engagement lasted until Saturday, by which time all the Volunteers had gone from Fairview, either having been accounted for in one of several ways or having deemed discretion the better part of valour. While the action was in progress several persons were wounded through exposing themselves in the line of fire.

Dublin and South-Eastern

The Dublin and South-Eastern Railway was particularly unfortunate in that both extremes of the system, that is, Dublin and Wexford, were the scenes of active rebellion, and in consequence the traffic along the line was almost entirely suspended, except for military purposes, thus causing a higher proportion of loss to this railway company than to the other railway companies having termini in Dublin. The line between Dublin and Kingstown was under entire military control, and under partial control between Kingstown and Ferns, Co. Wexford, at which latter point the Sinn Feiners had taken possession of the railway. The effect of this was to leave the counties which this company serves without any means of communication for passengers or for transit of goods and supplies, so that the counties of Wicklow and Wexford, and the southern portion of County Dublin, were left to test their ability to support themselves.

About mid-day on Easter Monday the Sinn Feiners took possession of Westland row and Harcourt street stations, and remained in possession of the former station until 3rd May, but they gave up possession of Harcourt street Station on 25th April, having held it for less than 24 hours, after which the military came into occupation. The locomotive, carriage, and wagon works at Grand Canal street were also occupied by the Sinn Feiners on Easter Monday, and held throughout the whole period of the rebellion. The company's property suffered damage to the extent of about £2,000 as the result of the occupation of the Sinn Feiners and military, and the loss of receipts to the company has been estimated at about £14,000. A sum of £731 was granted by the Goulding Commission for structural damages, this being substantially the amount claimed.

Midland Great Western Railway

The material damage to the railway of the Midland Great Western Company was inconsiderable, the cost of repairs not exceeding £600 or £700, but the resulting loss of revenue, whilst the line was controlled by the military authorities, amounted to about £20,000—a serious reduction in war times.

Contrary to statements freely made at the time, the Dublin passenger station of the company at Broadstone did not fall into the hands of the rebels, although under attack for four days. On Easter Monday the bridges carrying the Cabra and North Circular roads over the railway were occupied by the insurgents, who, in the first instance, erected barriers across the roadways, and subsequently made repeated attempts—which were unsuccessful—to blow up the bridges, apparently with the double object of rendering the roads impassable for troops and of blocking the railway. The North Circular road bridge commanded the station yard and platforms, as well as a private pathway constructed by the company for the use of employés passing to and from their work, and during the morning of Easter Tuesday occasional shots were fired at the station premises from this bridge: otherwise the first twenty-four hours after the outbreak passed at Broadstone without incident. At about two o'clock on the same day troops advanced along the Circular road from the direction of the Park, and, having brought field guns into position, proceeded to shell the barricade, and, having destroyed it, cleared the rebels out of the adjoining houses which had been occupied by them. A company of the Royal Dublin Fusiliers then proceeded by the private pathway to Broadstone, with which communication was established about 4 o'clock p.m. Immediately afterwards the station was attacked from the front, no doubt in ignorance of the previous arrival of troops, but on their fire being returned, the rebels quickly took cover, and did not again appear in the open during the four days fighting which ensued. During this time sniping took place almost continuously, the station being fired on from several directions.

Line Torn Up—Cattle Train Wrecked

During Monday night troops had been ordered over the line, and the rebels having become aware of the fact, took steps with the object of wrecking the expected troop train. An abortive effort to destroy a culvert near Liffey Junction was made, and during the early hours of the morning of the Tuesday, 25th April, the permanent way at Blanchardstown was blown up, and a cattle special proceeding in advance of the troop train was derailed and wrecked. On the same morning an engine in steam at Broadstone was seized by rebels, placed on the up line, and started, those in charge jumping clear as soon as the engine began to gather speed. This act would have resulted in disaster if the runaway locomotive had met a passenger or troop train coming in the opposite direction, but fortunately it was thrown off the line at the Liffey Junction points, after running uncontrolled for about a mile. Meantime, in consequence of the Blanchardstown derailment, the troops had been diverted to another station, where they detrained without mishap.

In the provinces little interference with the railway was experienced by this company, save in the section between Athenry and Galway, where the permanent way was torn up for a short distance on three separate occasions, telegraph wires were cut, and the electric instruments in a signal cabin were destroyed.

By order of the military authorities, the running of public trains from and to Dublin was completely suspended from the 24th April until the 3rd May, when a restricted service of 'refugee' trains from Dublin was established. The running of ordinary passenger trains to and from Dublin was resumed on 5th May, but the full service was not brought into operation until the 8th.

Great Northern Railway

On Easter Monday the last ordinary trains to leave Amiens street Station were the 2.0 to Dundalk, and the 2.45 to Howth. Later in the day, by permission of the military authorities, two special trains conveyed excursionists who had arrived in the morning back to Belfast. Trains that were on their way from the North at 3.30 p.m. arrived safely at Amiens street.

The ordinary passenger train service was not resumed until Wednesday, 3rd May, when one train ran each way between Dublin and Howth. The rebels were not in evidence at Amiens street at all. On Tuesday night the military occupied the station, and made it their headquarters for the North side of the city. There was no damage done at Amiens street.

On Easter Monday, about 2.30 p.m., an attempt was made to blow up the down line over the Rogerstown Bridge between Donabate and Rush and Lusk, and the line was damaged to the extent of £250, for which a claim has been made on the county. Traffic was worked over the up line.

There was also an attempt made to blow up the down line between the middle arch at Fairview sloblands and the Wharf road, and the rails were damaged, but traffic was worked over the up line.

Great Southern and Western Railway

At the annual general meeting of the shareholders of the Great Southern and Western Railway Company, at the Kingsbridge terminus, on February 28th, 1917, Sir Wm J Goulding, Bart, DL, Chairman of the Company, referred to the rebellion, which, he said, resulted in practically no trains being run over the Great Southern and Western Railway in and out of Dublin until May 1st, when two trains a day were run until Monday, May 8th, when they gradually increased the service. The loss of revenue to the company was estimated at £21,000, for which a claim had been made to the Government. He was glad to say that the company was able to give great assistance to the authorities by turning out five armoured cars, which saved much life to the soldiers, and the company had put up a very large number of military at Kingsbridge, and provided food for the officers.

The Tramway Service

The extent to which the tramway service of Dublin suffered during the rebellion was made plain by Mr Wm Martin Murphy, the Chairman of the Dublin United Tramways Co., Ltd., at the thirty-seventh ordinary meeting of the company, held on Tuesday, 26th February, 1917. Mr Murphy said that compared with many of their neighbours the company's property escaped very serious damage wonderfully well during that destructive time. Their generating station was in great jeopardy for a time, as it was in the undisputed possession of the rebels, who, however, he was bound to acknowledge, did no damage of any kind there. As it was, the material damage to their property was comparatively small, viz., the loss of two tramcars burned in the streets and some damage to the overhead wire system. None of their buildings was damaged by fire, not even their offices, though the conflagration which consumed nearly the whole of Lower Sackville street did not stop till it reached the narrow street which separates them from Mr Lawrence's premises, that had been burned to the ground. Honourable mention was due to their traffic manager, Mr D Brophy, in connection with the escape of the offices from the fate of the adjoining buildings. He remained in charge until the fire reached the opposite side of the lane, when in the early hours of Friday morning, 28th April, he succeeded in making his way to the Pro-Cathedral, where many people had taken refuge. While there he found the officer in charge of the military operations preparing to bombard the building in the belief that rebels were sniping from the windows, but Mr Brophy was able to satisfy him that the report he received was entirely devoid of truth, as he, Mr Brophy, had just come from there himself. Though their direct loss of property was small, and was compensated for to some extent by the Government, the company suffered a heavy loss of traffic by the entire stoppage of their tramway service for ten days and its dislocation for a long time after, for which they had so far received no compensation. They were told that the loss did not come within the scope of either of the committees set up in this country for considering claims against the Government in connection with the rebellion, but the company intend to press their very equitable claim by every means in their power. It was no exaggeration to say that the company had suffered a loss of at least £15,000 owing to the events of last Easter Week, and he was still in hopes of getting back a substantial part of it.

Grand Canal Company

At the annual general meeting of the shareholders of the Grand Canal Company, held on Thursday, 15th February, 1917, at the offices, James's street Harbour, Dublin, the Right Hon LA Waldron, Chairman, referred to the rebellion, and said the rebels were in possession of what were formerly Messrs William Jameson's premises, now owned by the Dublin Distillers' Company, and the King's troops were in Messrs Guinness's large store; so that over the premises in which they were now sitting and the yard and harbour in front of them bullets were flying for some days. That was not an atmosphere in which the carrying trade could be pursued and for fourteen days traffic was totally interrupted. They had claimed in respect of this from the Government a sum of £2,148, but they were told that for this description of damage it was intended to make no compensation. The reason or equity of this decision was not apparent, and they had pressed, and would press their claim.

STORY OF THE GREAT FIRES
Told by Captain Purcell, Chief of Dublin Fire Brigade

£2,500,000 is put down as an approximate value of all the buildings and stock destroyed by the fires in Dublin during the rebellion. It is the estimate of Captain Purcell, Chief of the Dublin Fire Brigade. The total number of buildings involved in the fires is over 200. With the assistance of a specially coloured map, Captain Purcell, on Monday, 1st May, described to a representative of the *Irish Times* the area of the fires as follows:

The total area burnt on the east side of Sackville street district includes—Portion of the block between Cathedral street and Earl street, the whole block between Earl street and Sackville place, bounded by Nelson lane at the back: portion of the block between Sackville place and Abbey street, the whole block between Abbey street and Eden quay, bounded by Marlborough street on the east. The area of this east side district is 27,000 square yards. Among the principal establishments in the area were the Royal Hibernian Academy, Clery's warehouse, the Imperial Hotel, the DBC, the branches of the Hibernian Bank and the Munster and Leinster Bank, Wynn's Hotel, Hoyte's, the druggist; Messrs Hamilton and Long's, Sir Joseph Downes's new restaurant and bakery, Lawrence's shops and warehouse, Messrs Hopkins and Hopkins' jewellery establishment, and the four public houses—Messrs Nagle's and Sheridan's, in North Earl street: Messrs Mooney's in Lower Abbey street, and Messrs Mooney's on Eden quay, etc.

On the west side of Sackville street the area destroyed by fire is as follows: Portion of the block bounded by Henry street, Henry place and Moore street; portion of the block fronting Henry street, between Moore street and Cole's lane, running back in part to Samson's lane: the whole block from the General Post Office back to Arnott's warehouse, fronting to Henry street back to Prince's street: the greater portion of the block from Sackville street fronting to Lower Abbey street back to Prince's street and towards Liffey street, within a short distance of the *Independent* Printing Office, where the fire was stopped; portion of the block to the south side of Middle Abbey street, with two houses fronting to Sackville street, up to and including No. 62 Middle Abbey street. This area of the fires on the west side of Sackville street is 34,000 square yards in extent. The principal buildings burnt are the General Post Office, the Hotel Metropole, Messrs Eason and Son's, Messrs Manfield's new warehouse, the *Freeman's Journal* Office, Messrs Bewley's, Messrs Alexander Pierie's wholesale paper warehouse, Hampton Leedom's, Messrs Curtis and Son's brass foundry and munition factory, where much work has been going on recently; the Oval Bar, Messrs Thom's Printing Works, Messrs Sealy, Bryers and Walker's, and Messrs Fitzgerald's, etc.

Outside these principal areas there were fires in two houses in Harcourt street of £85 valuation, and at Nos. 1, 2 and 3 Usher's quay, and round the corner into Bridge street, including two tenement houses, and Doherty's Hotel, Nos. 18 to 21 Bridge street, where the fire was stopped before it reached the Brazen Head Hotel. These places have a total valuation of £277.

Another area of fire outside the Sackville street districts is that including the ancient Linen Hall Barracks, one of the landmarks in the history of a great national industry, recently the seat of the Civic Exhibition, and latterly the office of the Army Pay Department. Here 32 clerks were employed. They were surrounded and besieged for four days and unable to get food. Twice this place was fired. The staff dealt with it themselves. The Fire Brigade could not approach it. It is stated that on the fourth day the rebels, by means of the bombs at the rear, ignited the building by setting fire to a wooden structure, erected at the time of the Civic Exhibition. This was a ready prey to flames. This fire involved the portion of the Linen Hall occupied by Messrs Hugh Moore and Alexanders, Ltd., wholesale druggists and drysalters. The premises, which covered about two acres, contained huge stores of oils and chemicals.

Some small conception of the work of the Brigade and the danger to the city of utter ruin may be gathered from the history Captain Purcell gave of the fires that occurred and how the Brigade dealt with them. Captain Purcell's story is as follows: The first call came at 3.58 p.m. on Monday, 24th April. It was from the Ordnance Department at Island Bridge, stating there was a fire at the Magazine in the Phoenix Park. A detachment was sent with a motor engine from the Thomas street section. They made their way round Steevens' lane and Kingsbridge, and managed to get to the Magazine without opposition. They found one section of the Magazine on fire. This contained large quantities of small arms and a large number of boxes of ammunition. That section of the Magazine was more or less destroyed, but the remainder was saved. In the meantime Lieutenant Myers, who attended with another motor engine, was held up at a barricade by Sinn Feiners with loaded revolvers. One of these weapons was placed at the head of the driver, and he was ordered to return.

(The *Irish Times* on Friday, 5th May, published the following: 'Lieutenant Myers, of the Dublin Fire Brigade, requests us to contradict the statement, in a recent issue, that he was held up at a barricade by Sinn Feiners with loaded revolvers while proceeding to the fire at the Magazine in the Phoenix Park.')

The following is the entry in the log book at the Tara street Central Fire Station:

'Monday, 24th April, 1916.

'3.58 p.m.—By 'phone from Ordnance Department, Island Bridge, 'phone no. 3739. Fire in Magazine Fort, Phoenix Park. Sent same to A Station to attend, C and D to stand by, also to police and water control.

'3.59 p.m.—Motor left for same.

'4.6 p.m.—Motor returned, street barricaded at Church street Bridge. Officer in charge of Volunteers refused to let brigade pass.'

At 10.6 p.m. on Monday a box call came from the alarm at Nelson's Pillar that there was a fire in the Cable Shoe Company's shop in Sackville street. The fire looked dangerous, and at 10.24 p.m. the Buckingham street section sent for more help. The Tara street section also arrived. The fire was extinguished at 10.59 p.m. At 11.30 p.m. there was a call of fire in the True Form Shoe shop, also in Sackville street. This place, like the Cable Shoe shop, had been looted, and papers, etc., set alight. The fire was extinguished at 1.30 a.m. on Tuesday morning.

The Second Day

Tuesday, 25th, began with three simultaneous fires in being. At 12.1 a.m. Tuesday, continued Captain Purcell, we were told that No. 4 North Earl street, was burning. The outbreak was extinguished at 12.53 a.m. At 4.11 p.m. on the same day the fire at Lawrence's, in Sackville street, began. A call for more help was made at 4.15 p.m. We fought it until a quarter past eight, when it was practically extinguished, and about half of Lawrence's premises were saved. While working at Lawrence's fire volleying and firing was going on at the General Post Office, and Lawrence's was in the line of fire. While the Brigade was working a man and a woman were shot beside the engine at the Henry street-Sackville street corner. A man, the brother of one of the brigade turncocks, was shot beside the engine driver at Cathedral place. The man leaves a wife and seven children. From the top floor of Lawrence's the Brigade by means of an escape rescued a man and woman from a top window.

The Third Day

At 12.59 p.m. on Wednesday, 26th, Williams's Stores at the back of Henry street caught fire. The stores were being looted at the time. Five men whom the flames prevented from getting out by the way they had entered ran right through to Henry street when the firemen arrived. The fire was extinguished at 2.51 p.m. The Brigade saved the building but the contents had been looted. At 5.14 p.m. further fires took place at Williams's and were extinguished. At 6.59 p.m. there was a fire at the North Wall in a quantity of jute. We did not go to it as the bridges were up and we could not get there. One of the company's men kept it down, and there was no fear of it spreading to anything else. An outbreak in Upper Sackville street was notified at 8.7 p.m. on Wednesday, but it was small.

Thursday, 27th

We attended a fire at Harcourt street at 5.7 a.m. on Thursday, 27th. It was just behind the Russell Hotel. By 7 o'clock we had saved half the house and we soon extinguished the fire. Here we found a rifle, a bag of ammunition, and two revolvers. A dead volunteer lay outside at the corner. The Linen Hall fire was reported at 9.30 a.m., but was suppressed by the private appliances there.

Where the Great Fire Began

We were informed at 12.32 p.m. that there was a fire in the *Irish Times* Reserve Printing Office in Abbey street. As that area was the scene of terrible rifle firing at the time I did not, said Captain Purcell, allow the Brigade to attend. The fire spread very rapidly owing to the barrier of furniture and bales of paper that had been placed across the street. The barrier extended from the *Irish Times* Office to Wynn's Hotel, and carried the fire straight across to that side. That was where the great fire began. As to how it grew I know nothing, except that heavy cannonading was going on. The military were shelling that district.

The Fire Spread Rapidly

At 2.52 p.m. we were informed that it had reached Sackville place, in the rear of the *Irish Times* building. All I could do was to observe through a glass from our tower the progress of the flames. I saw the fire creeping along Abbey street in both directions on both sides, on the one hand up towards the Hibernian Bank at the corner of Sackville street, and eastwards towards the Methodist church in Lower Abbey street, and then again on the south side Wynn's Hotel made a terrible blaze. I saw the fire gradually work up to Hoyte's corner, and through the shops in Sackville street down to the DBC restaurant. That being a very high building I knew that it would stop the fire for a time, and as I saw the Grand Restaurant with its annex behind in Harbour Court at the rear I had a faint hope that the DBC might survive. It made a brave stand for hours. Then I noticed an ominous light in the upper lantern windows. It was at once an indication that the place was doomed. Little by little the smoke and flames gathered strength, and then burst through the ventillators and windows. After another half hour the roof showed up alight and the lantern on top was wrapped in flames, and the whole made a weird sight. It was then getting dark: it was about half past seven. Once that fire was fully under way nothing could have saved the block. It burnt away all night. I traced the fire's path from the station tower through the various shops down to Hamilton and Long's, and out to the rear of the offices of the London and North-Western Railway Company, leaving a little oasis about the corner in which were Scott's, the tailors, Hopkins's, and Lanigan's, with Lipton's illuminated advertisement on the front on Eden quay. It was only after long hours that this corner succumbed.

Hoping against Hope

As to how the fire was going northwards I could form no accurate opinion owing to the huge volumes of fire between us and Clery's. At intervals, when the wind wafted away great volumes of flame and smoke we got glimpses of Clery's still standing intact. I was hoping against hope that it might stop the fire. But before morning Clery's had gone the way of the rest. For the time being the northern wall and gable of Clery's withstood the fire and prevented it from going farther in a northerly direction. But the flames made their way behind Allen's, and took in Sir Joseph Downes's new bakery and restaurant. At this period I got into telephonic communication with Hickey's on the north of North Earl street, and was able to learn of the situation on that side. This was at 5 a.m. on Friday, 28th.

Friday's Fires

It is needless to say, observed Captain Purcell, that it was with awful pain, amounting to anguish of mind, that I witnessed this terrible destruction, that I felt I could have stopped easily if I could only have been allowed with any reasonable degree of safety to approach these premises earlier. However, added the captain, we took our courage in our hands. I decided that I would make an effort, even at the eleventh hour, to stop the ruin. We proceeded with the Tara street section to Cathedral place, and under cover of Hickey's shop and through the rooms above the warehouse we threw volumes of water into Sir Joseph Downes's restaurant, and extinguished the fire, which was right in front and likely to ignite Hickey's warehouse. For the time being we saved the situation. Unfortunately, owing to the sniping that was going on in front from the Marlborough street direction, I could not risk the men's lives in the open, and was prevented from doing what I should have wished to do—to get at the rear of Downes's premises and examine the backs of Winstanley's and Meagher's, which were then intact. We worked there in the open, and some of my men's lives were threatened by men, who told them that if they did not clear off they would be shot. We had to retire. That was at 9 a.m. on Saturday.

Saturday's Outbreaks

While we were thus watching or working on Friday at the great fire we had fires in other parts of the city at the same time. At 3.5 p.m. on Friday there came a call of fire in Lower Bridge street. That was attended by the Thomas street section, and after several hours' work it was prevented from extending. Again at 6.40 a.m., while we were fighting at North Earl street, another call came from Harcourt street. This was a dwellinghouse, in which the fire was extinguished at 8.59 a.m. by the Buckingham street section. On Saturday we knew that the GPO was burning, but we could not go near it. As I had anticipated in regard to North Earl street, the fire worked into Winstanley's and Meagher's public house, and other shops at the corner of Sackville street. Then it crossed Earl street by another barrier of furniture into Tyler's boot shop at the north corner of Earl street and Sackville street. It crept eastward through Rowe's drapery house adjoining Sheridan's public bar. I had information of all this, but could do nothing to stop it.

Message from the Military

At 3.40 p.m. on Saturday the Commanding Officer of the troops in Dublin sent me, said Captain Purcell, a special despatch to say that they had the leaders of the rebels in their custody, and that they would now cease military operations; that matters in the city were getting normal, and that I might now make an effort to stop the fires in Sackville street and Abbey street. I immediately turned out the whole force of the Brigade. We proceeded to the great fire area and got to work. We had our two motor engines, and started on the north-west side of O'Connell Bridge, lifting water from the Liffey with four lines of delivery hose. We had out six other lines of hose from hydrants in the vicinity of the fires all at work. At that time the Post Office was gone, the Hotel Metropole and Eason's were going badly, and Manfield's at the corner, and five other houses from the corner of Sackville street, and extending to the south side of Abbey street, were burning.

Firemen Deliberately Fired At

We were making excellent progress towards stopping the fire on both sides of Abbey street when the bullets began to fly amongst us. We were being deliberately fired at. I had two men up on fire escapes, and bullets struck their ladders. Our engines were shot at from the directions of Westmoreland street and Aston's quay. Bullets hit the engines, going through the mudguards and through the tires. I instantly called the men off to take cover. I abandoned the engines and hose on the streets, and rushed the men in batches in motor ambulances home to their stations. Then we saw the fires ripping away in every direction from the west along Abbey street and along Henry street. At 4.40 and 4.50 p.m. I had transferred the men back to their stations. They had been allowed to work only little more than half an hour. At 5.30 p.m. I received a telephone message from the Pro-Cathedral in Marlborough street to say that Nagle's was burning furiously, and that Hickey's, the adjoining warehouse, was taking fire. This was the place I had taken so much trouble to save. Of course I knew that when it got to Hickey's, Boyer's new and extensive warehouse would be taken in, and that the fire would extend along the north side of Earl street and probably involve the cathedral in the rear.

Volunteers

After our previous painful experience I felt that I was not justified in ordering any members of the Brigade to attend this new outbreak. But being fully impressed with the gravity of the situation I appealed for four volunteers from amongst the Brigade in my station to go and stop this fire. Four men instantly came forward and proceeded in charge of Lieut Myers to the place and succeeded in stopping the fire at Nagle's before it had done much harm. They also insured the safety of the remainder of the north side of Earl street, including the cathedral at the back.

The Culminating Call

While the men were working there I received what I call the culminating call of the many from the doctors and clergymen in Jervis street Hospital. This was at 8 p.m. on Saturday. I was informed that the fires were spreading closely in the direction of the hospital, that sparks were raining on the glass roof of their verandah, and they said that if I could not do something to stop the fire's course then I must make immediate arrangements for the removal of the patients. To the firemen's credit, they one and all declared that they would save the hospital, even under the bullets. We immediately hurried our available force out, recovered our engines and other apparatus from O'Connell Bridge, and started on for the big fight. I also called for the assistance of any available men and apparatus from Messrs Powers' Distillery and Guinness's Brewery. Both sections kindly responded to the appeal, and sent men and means which I ordered to work at various points. We fought during all Saturday night, stopping the fire where it was possible to stop it, and saved the hospital. In other directions since we had been prevented by shooting in the afternoon of Saturday from working, fires had multiplied and increased in volume a hundred fold. So our work now consisted of not attempting to extinguish what were already hopeless cases, but cutting off in sections and preventing the fires from spreading further. In this we succeeded. During the operations the popping of rifle ammunition and the explosion of bombs left behind in buildings occurred, and gave us peculiar sensations, but they were not to be compared with the sensations caused by the sniping.

By 7 o'clock on Sunday morning we had the conflagration, as we may call it, completely under control. But since then we have had to deal by detachments with other outbreaks or dangerous re-kindlings over the whole area.

Well-known Houses Destroyed and Damaged

A representative of the *Weekly Irish Times* compiled a list of houses which had been destroyed by fire in the central streets of Dublin. In the case of many houses only the name of the chief firm doing business there is given; and other persons have offices or rooms in the building as well. In some instances the premises are only partially destroyed.

The rateable annual value of the various properties set out in this list, based upon the new valuations given in *Thom's Directory* for 1916, exclusive of any estimate for stocks of goods in the different premises, and also excluding any figure for the General Post Office, the Royal Hibernian Academy, the Presbyterian Union Chapel, or the Methodist Church in Abbey street, amounts to £241,870.

Lower Sackville Street

1—Hopkins and Hopkins, jewellers.
2—William Scott and Co., tailors.
3—Hamilton, Long and Co., apothecaries.
4—Francis Smyth and Son, umbrella manufacturers.
The Waverley Hotel and Restaurant.
6—Great Western Railway of England.
6 and 7—Dublin Bread Company Restaurant, popularly known as the DBC.
Frank R Gallagher, cigar merchant.
8—Grand Hotel and Restaurant.
9—ER Moore, jeweller.
10 and 11—Charles L Reis and Co., fancy goods warehouse.
The Irish School of Wireless Telegraphy.
12 and 13—The Hibernian Bank.
14—Robert Buckham, gentlemen's outfitter.
15—City and County Permanent Building Society.
16—F Sharpley, ladies' and children's outfitters.
17—Hoyte and Son, druggists.
GP Beater, architect and civil engineer.
18—The True-Form Boot Company.
19—JP Callaghan, tailor and hosier.
20—George Mitchell (Ltd.), cigar and wine merchants.
21 to 27—The Imperial Hotel.
Clery and Co. (Ltd.), drapers.
28—Richard Allen, tailor.
29—Frs O'Farrell (Ltd.), tobacco importer.
30—The Munster and Leinster Bank (branch).
31—The Cable Boot Company (Ltd.).
32—Dunn and Co., hatters.
33—Lewers and Co., boys' clothiers and outfitters.
34—Noblett's Ltd.
35—Kapp and Peterson, Ltd., tobacconists.
35 to 39—Hotel Metropole.
39—Henry Grandy, tailor.

40—Eason and Sons, general newspaper and advertising office and subscription library.
41—David Drimmie and Sons, insurance agents.
42—The Misses Carolan, milliners.
43 and 44—Manfield and Sons, boot and shoe manufacturers.
46 and 47—John W Elvery and Co., waterproof and gutta percha manufacturers.

Upper Sackville Street

1—John Tyler and Sons, boot merchants.
2—Dublin Laundry Co. and Dartry Dye Works.
3—John McDowell, jeweller.
4—E Nestor, milliner.
5, 6 and 7—William Lawrence, photographer and stationer.
8—Henry Taaffe, gentlemen's outfitter.

Sackville Place

11—Vacant.
13—Corrigan and Wilson, printers.
14—John Davin.
16—Denis J Egan, wine and spirit merchants.

Henry Street

6—Samuel Samuels, jewellers.
16—James O'Dwyer and Co., tailors.
17—Harrison and Co., cooks and confectioners.
18, 19 and 20—Bewley, Sons, and Co. (Ltd.), provision and general merchant.
21—Irish Farm Produce Co.
22 and 23—E Morris, merchant tailor.
24—The Coliseum Theatre.
25—HE Randall, boot and shoe manufacturers.
26 and 28—MacInerney and Co., drapers.
27—McDowell Brothers, jewellers.
29—Adelaide Repelto, fancy warehouse.
30—The World's Fair 6½d Stores.
34—Dundon and Co., tailors and outfitters.
35—A Clarke and Co., millinery and general fancy warehouse.
36—Madame Drago, hairdresser.
37—E Marks and Co. (Ltd.), Penny Bazaar.
38—R and J Wilson and Co., confectioners and fancy bakers.
39—McCarthy and Co., costume and mantle warehouse.
40—Bailey Brothers, tailors.
40a—Mrs Charlotte Gahagan, ladies' outfitter.
41a—Joseph Calvert, provision merchant.
41—Patrick M'Givney, cutler and optician.
42—John Murphy, spirit merchant.
43—R and J Dick, boot and shoe manufacturers.
44—Caroline E Fegan and Co., underclothing factory.
49—Menzies and Co., milliners.
50—Hampton, Leedom and Co., hardware merchants.
51—Hayes, Conyngham, and Robinson, chemists.
52—Miss White, milliner.
53—Maples and Co., tailors.

Lower Abbey Street

1—Young and Co., Ltd., wine and spirit merchants.
2—JJ Kelly and Co., cycle agents.
3—JJ Keating, cycle and motor dealers.
4—*Irish Times*, Ltd., reserve printing offices.
5—Ship Hotel and Tavern.
6—The Abbey Toilet Saloon, Ltd.
7—John Hyland and Co., wholesale wine merchants.
8—CG Henry, wholesale tobacconist.
Presbyterian Church—Rev John O Johnston, MA, minister.
23—Patrick Foley, wine and spirit merchant.
29—Denis Nolan, private hotel.
30—Francis Marnane, furrier.
31—William Collins, oil importer and hardware merchant.
32—Humber, Ltd., cycle and motor manufacturers, wholesale depot.
32—The *Leader* Newspaper.
32 and 33—Keating's Motor Works.
32 and 33—The Irish Commercial Travellers' Association.
33 and 34—Percy, Mecredy and Co., Ltd., publishers; Irish Homestead Publishing Co.; James M'Cullagh, Son, and Co., wholesale wine merchants: the Royal Hibernian Academy.
35, 36 and 37—Wynn's Hotel.
37—Smyth and Co., Ltd., hosiery manufacturers.
38—J Ferguson and Co., hair dressers.
39—Peter Callaghan, gentlemen's outfitter.

Middle Abbey Street

62—Patrick Gordon, wine agent.
66—WJ Haddock, ladies' and gentlemen's tailor.
67—Collins and Co., tailors.
68—George Young, builders and general ironmongers.
69 and 70—Sharman Crawford, wine merchant.
71—Dermot Dignam, advertising agent.
73—James Allen and Son, auctioneers and valuers.
74 and 75—Gaynor and Son, cork merchants.
76—YMCA Supper Room for Soldiers and Sailors.
78—John J Egan, wine and spirit merchant, The Oval.
79 and 80—Eason and Son, Ltd., wholesale newsagents.
81 and 82—Do.
83—*Evening Telegraph* Office.
84—*Weekly Freeman* and *Sport* Office.
85—Sullivan Brothers, educational publishers.
86—Sealy, Bryers, and Walker, printers and publishers.
87 to 90—Alexander Thom and Co., Ltd., Government printers and publishers.
91, 92 and 93—Fitzgerald and Co., wholesale tea, wine and spirit merchants.
94—The Wall Paper Manufacturing Co.
96—Maunsel and Co., publishers.
96—Francis Tucker and Co., Ltd., church candle and altar requisites manufacturers.
97—W Dawson and Sons, Ltd., wholesale agents.
98 and 99—W Curtis and Sons, brass and bell founders, plumbers, electrical and sanitary engineers.
100—J Whitby and Co., cork merchants.
101—John Kane, art metal worker.
102 to 104—National Reserve Headquarters.
105—Perfect Dairy Machine Co.

Earl Street

1a—James Tallon, newsagent.

1—T Carson, tobacconist.
2—A Sullivan, confectioner.
3—JJ Lalor, Catholic art repository.
4—Philip Meagher, vintner.
5—James Winstanley, boot warehouse.
6—Noveau et Cie, costumiers
7—Sir Joseph Downes, confectioner.
25—J Nagle and Co., wine and spirit merchant.
26—Mrs E Sheridan, wine and spirit merchant.
27—Delany and Co., tobacco and cigar merchants.
27a—J Alexander, merchant tailor.
28—M Rowe and Co., general drapers.
29, 30 and 31—John Tyler and Sons (Ltd.), boot manufacturers.

Eden Quay

1 and 2—Barry, O'Moore, and Co., accountants and auditors.
3—Gerald Mooney, wine and spirit merchant.
4—The London and North-Western Railway Co., General Inquiry Office.
5—GR Mesias, military and merchant tailor.
6—The Midland Railway of England, receiving, booking and inquiry office.
6—Wells and Holohan, railway and shipping agents.
7—J Hubbard Clark, painter and decorator.
8—The Globe Parcel Express.
9—Henry Smith, Ltd., ironmonger.
10—Joseph M'Greevy, wine and spirit merchant.
11—The Douglas Hotel and Restaurant.
12—Mr John Dalby.
13—The Mission to Seamen Institute.
14—E Moore, publican.

Prince's Street

3—Princes Stores.
4 to 8—*Freeman's Journal* (Ltd.).
13—Stores.
14—Vacant.
15—Pirie and Sons, stores.

Moore Street

1 and 2—J Humphrys, wine and spirit merchant.
3—O Savino, fried fish shop.
4—Miss B Morris, dairy.
5—MJ Dunne, pork butcher.
6—R Dillon, fruiterer.
59—Francis Fee, wine and spirit merchant.
60—Miss M'Nally, greengrocer.
61—C O'Donnell, victualler.
62—Miss Ward, victualler.

Lower Bridge Street

18—Tenements.
19 and 21—Doherty's Hotel.
20—Brazen Head Hotel.

Usher's Quay

1—H Kavanagh, wine and spirit merchant.
2 and 3—Dublin Clothing Co.
4—Tenements.

Bolton Street

57—George Freyne, hardware merchant.
58—D Dolan, chemist.
59—W Leckie and Co., printers and bookbinders.
60—Tenements.

Marlborough Street

112 —J Farrell, wine and spirit merchant.
113—Marlborough Hotel.

Clanwilliam Place

1 and 2—Private Houses.

Yarnhall Street

1—Hugh, Moore and Alexanders, Ltd., wholesale druggists.
Linenhall Barracks.
4, 5, 6 and 7—W Leckie and Co.'s workshops.

Beresford Place

16 and 17—Offices.
Liberty Hall, headquarters of Irish Transport and General Workers' Union.

Harcourt Street

96—Norma Reeves, tailor.
97a—Mrs Elizabeth Bryan, fruiterer.

Many Constabulary Killed in Co. Meath

On Friday, 28th April, the police authorities received information that Ashbourne police station had been attacked. County Inspector Gray, District Inspector Harry Smyth, of Navan, and fifty Constabulary left in motor cars for the district, passing through Slane and Balrath towards Kilmoon, where there is another small barracks a short distance from Ashbourne. The motor cars had proceeded a short distance from Kilmoon, which is on an eminence, and at the foot of which a small road branches off. The police did not know the rebels were at hand, the intention being to get out of the motor cars and march to Ashbourne. The Sinn Feiners had, however, secreted themselves in a small grove by the roadside at a place near Rathgate. They had entrenched themselves in the field, and at each end of the road they had taken up a position for attack. Hardly had the police got out of the motor cars at the ascent of the hill than a fusillade of bullets was sent into their midst. Sergeant J Shanagher, of Navan, was shot through the heart almost as he was leaving his car. The small police party at once took what cover they could obtain beside the motor cars and in the ditches. The rebels, however, closed in from all directions, and sent a messenger to the county inspector demanding the surrender of all his men.

How District Inspector Smyth met his Death

County Inspector Gray declined, and gave directions to his men to return the fire. Handicapped by their cramped position, the police nevertheless held their ground, and the county inspector fell wounded, shot through both hands and part of the body. Several other casualties occurred among the police, and sniping proceeded for over four-and-a-half hours. District Inspector Smyth, of Navan, was twice wounded, but, followed by a sergeant and some constables, he pluckily crept along the roadside ditch towards the rebels, who were gradually closing in. Sergeant Young, of Kilmoon, was next shot dead. Other constables were being hit, but one wounded policeman from beneath a motor car continued to fire to the last. Suddenly the rebels appeared on the ridge overhead, and the district inspector fell dead with a bullet through his forehead. An unarmed chauffeur named Kepp, in the employ of the Marquis Conyngham, of Slane Castle, was shot in the leg by an explosive bullet, and had to have his leg amputated, but he died. The police fought until they had expended their last cartridge, and when they saw that further resistance was useless they surrendered. The rebels took possession of the policemen's rifles and seized some of their equipment, but the men were afterwards released.

Two men—JJ Carroll, of Kingstown, and J Hogan—said to be commercial travellers, who were passing at the time, were shot dead.

The names of the men of the Royal Irish Constabulary killed and wounded in the engagement will be found in the official casualty lists on page 54.

Shells from a Destroyer in Galway Bay

On Easter Tuesday morning it was definitely announced by the authorities that about four hundred of the Sinn Fein party were marching on Galway and had reached Merlin Park, the residence of Captain and Lady Philippa Waithmore. Great alarm was naturally felt, and the loyal citizens got together every available firearm. The police acted splendidly. Although many of the men had been out on duty for eighteen hours, they responded to the call, and, in spite of the fact that a comparatively small number only could be spared to go in the direction of Merlin Park, they obeyed the order to go there. Another body went out on the Tuam road, as it was expected that the rebels would cut across from the Oranmore road and storm the town from the Bohermure side. In the meantime a number of the citizens and county gentlemen residing in the danger zone had armed themselves. However, in the midst of all the excitement and bustle, the booming of big guns rang out in the bay, and Galway was saved. Shells had burst close to the insurgents, and they fled for their lives back to Oranmore. One shell, which fell close to the village, showed them that they were not out of danger, and they started for the old uninhabited Castle of Moyode, which is about three miles from Craughwell. A body of the rebels had taken possession of the Model Farm at Athenry, but, fearing the shell-fire from the warship, they were ordered to proceed to Moyode.

Constable Killed at Carnmore

Affairs at Carnmore on the previous evening were exciting, and resulted in the death of Constable Patrick Whelan. District Inspector Heard motored out late at night with a body of fully armed police to Carnmore, about three miles from Galway. On arriving there a number of shots were fired, and as Mr Heard and Constable Whelan were stepping from the motor, the constable got a full charge of No. 3 shot in the head, blowing off the side of his face and killing him instantly. Mr Heard at once started firing at the gang. The man who fired the fatal shot was seen to be carrying a gun of antique pattern, and it is believed that he was shot in the back while getting over a stone wall.

The Oranmore District

In Oranmore some exciting scenes took place. The

police barracks were rushed and the police captured. Sergeant Healy got away and barricaded himself in a house on the opposite side of the street. A man came to the door and demanded the sergeant's surrender. No reply was given, and the rebels endeavoured to force the door. Sergeant Healy fired a revolver shot through the door, and the crowd dispersed. Ten minutes later County Inspector Ruttledge, from Galway, accompanied by a body of police, charged up the street in a gallant manner. The rebels fled.

The arrests of several well-known men in Galway caused some excitement. The police returned to their quarters at Oranmore Barracks, but a large number of extra men remained in Galway. Three large motor cars, capable of carrying forty persons, for several days made two daily trips to country districts, and on each occasion returned with about sixty prisoners.

The Enniscorthy Rising

The first armoured train used in Ireland was employed in connection with the Enniscorthy revolt. 'It was a home made fighting machine, slung together hurriedly, but very effectively, of materials to hand. It consisted of an ancient, but still serviceable engine, in the proud charge of a richly humorous Hibernian. There were two or three shell trucks sheckled to the engine, armoured with hastily-pierced sheets of iron, and the whole amazing contraption was painted slate colour.'

The Enniscorthy rebels waited for information from their leaders that the City of Dublin had been captured, and when this information came to hand the local rebels immediately gave orders to their forces to begin action. They first seized the business houses of the town and also the railway station, and held up a train which was on its way from Wexford with 300 workmen for Kynoch's factory. The engine was detached from the train, and the men were permitted to walk back to Wexford by the railway line. The rebels then debated amongst themselves the advisability of blowing up the fine bridge at Enniscorthy, but fortunately abandoned the idea. They then attempted to blow up the bridge of Scarawalsh, which crosses the River Slaney on the main road between Wexford and Enniscorthy. Before doing so they warned the old and respected blacksmith, named Carton, who, with his family, lived in a house close to the bridge. The signalling wires on the railway were cut, and the instruments in the cabin were destroyed. Between Enniscorthy and Ferns an extensive trench was dug, and the rebel forces advanced and captured the town of Ferns, making the ancient mansion of St Aidan's their headquarters. They, when they thought they were firmly entrenched, they advanced a little in the Gorey direction, but just then a train which contained a few military arrived at Camolin Station. On seeing the soldiers, who were there for ordinary guard duty, and had no knowledge of the 'rising', the rebels hastily retreated to their stronghold at Enniscorthy. Here, however, they learned to their dismay that a military armoured train, including the now famous 'Enniscorthy Emily', a 15-pounder gun, was on the south side of the town, and only about six miles distant.

Some of the rebels had taken up positions on Vinegar Hill, which overlooks the town of Enniscorthy. A council of war was held, but the deliberations were brought to an abrupt conclusion by a well planted shell which the gunner of 'Enniscorthy Emily' discharged at the hill. The shell, which, it is stated, was a blank one, landed plump amongst the rebels, who hoised white flags on the hill, while two hundred of the insurgents bolted for the hills. Many of the escaping rebels were captured. The others laid down their arms unconditionally.

Affray at Fermoy

Although there was considerable movement in Cork City and County, no disturbance took place, apart from that near Fermoy, where Head Constable Rowe, of the Royal Irish Constabulary, met his death. Early on Easter Tuesday a body of police proceeded to make an arrest at Bawnard House, Castlelyons, near Fermoy, occupied by Mrs Kent, a farmer's widow, and her four sons. Resistance was offered to the police by the Kents, and in the fighting Head Constable Rowe was shot dead. Military assistance was procured, and the Kents surrendered. Richard Kent attempted to make his escape, and was shot, with fatal results. Thomas Kent was tried at Cork by court-martial for the murder of the Head Constable, found guilty, and executed. William Kent was tried on the same charge and acquitted. David Kent was tried later in Dublin on the same charge, found guilty, and sentenced to death, with a recommendation to mercy on account of his previous good character, and his sentence was commuted to five years' penal servitude.

Destroyers Land Troops at Skerries

Of the outlying portions of County Dublin affected by the rising, Skerries had not the least exciting experience.

On Easter Monday a war demonstration had been advertised, with Mr John J Clancy, KC, member for North Dublin, in the chair, and speakers from the Recruiting Department. When the occupants of the platform had taken their places word reached the local committee that the bridge at Donabate had been just blown up, that the train bringing the Chairman and speakers was held up, and that the Sinn Feiners were out.

Notwithstanding this grave news, it was decided not to alarm the audience, but to hold the meeting. Mr Battersby, KC, was accordingly moved to the chair. Local speakers—Captain Taylor, Mr Fitzpatrick, and Mr Malone, with Lieutenant Clancy—took the place of the absentees, and certificates were given to the relatives of Skerries soldiers—one hundred in all—and the meeting passed off successfully.

On Tuesday, 25th April, the police got word that the Marconi station recently erected by the Admiralty was to be attacked and some of the principal houses raided. There was consternation at this report, as the wireless operators were unarmed, and there were only seven soldiers to guard the station, while the police force, under Sergeant Burke, to whose energy and ability throughout the week a warm tribute must be paid, was wholly inadequate to protect the town. So great was the alarm that some of the townsfolk left their houses, and paced the shore as the safest place in case of a raid. The attack, however, did not come off; but on Wednesday morning information was received of the capture in succession of Swords, Donabate, where a second attempt was made to blow up the railway, and Lusk, which had the reputation of being a hot-bed of Sinn Feiners, and it was definitely stated that the rebels were on their way to Skerries. Preparations were at once made to receive them.

Captain Battersby, on sick leave, wounded, took command of the small force in charge of the wireless station. Miss Battersby, with the assistance of Miss McGusty and the Misses Clifford and Dr Healy, organised a Red Cross hospital in the Carnegie Library.

Boatloads of Soldiers

People form the village gathered on the hill above the Marconi station in order to see the coming fight, when a destroyer was seen steaming at a great pace from Lambay Island. As she drew nearer, it was seen that she was crowded with soldiers. A rush was made by the townsfolk to the harbour, and in a very few minutes boatloads of military were quickly rowed to the pier, and two hundred men of the North Staffordshires, under the command of Captain Clay, were landed and marched to the wireless station, where they entrenched in the ditches surrounding the station. The town was saved, and in the offing two gunboats patrolled, their guns being within reach of the coast roads, by which the rebels were expected to arrive.

On Thursday, 27th April, the Staffords dug themselves in, put up barricades of carts and sandbags on all the roads leading into Skerries, and made every preparation for a siege.

The Harristown and Ashbourne rebels were stated to have joined the Lusk contingent, but if this were so they must have received news of the military force which had landed, and of the guns of the warships trained on the town and roads, and come to the conclusion that discretion was the better part of valour, as the next news was that they had returned to Dublin. The scare was consequently at an end.

The North Staffords remained some time in Skerries, and nearly twenty persons were arrested and sent to Dublin.

Further details of Sinn Fein proceedings in various parts of the country will be found in the evidence submitted by police officials to the Commission of Inquiry presided over by Lord Hardinge.

OFFICIAL REPORTS AND STATEMENTS

German Attempt to Land Arms

Capture of Sir Roger Casement

The Secretary of the Admiralty made the following announcement on Easter Monday night, April 24:

During the period between April 20 and April 21 an attempt to land arms and ammunition in Ireland was made by a vessel under the guise of a neutral merchant ship, but in reality a German auxiliary in conjunction with a German submarine. The auxiliary was sunk, and a number of prisoners were made, amongst whom was Sir Roger Casement.

Mr Birrell's Bulletin

On Tuesday evening, 25th April, Mr Birrell supplied the London Press with the following:

'At noon yesterday serious disturbances broke out in Dublin.

'A large body of men, identified with the Sinn Feiners, mostly armed, occupied Stephen's Green, and took possession forcibly of the Post Office, where they cut the telegraph and telephone wires. Houses were occupied in Stephen's Green, Sackville street, Abbey street, and along the quays.

'In the course of the day soldiers arrived from the Curragh, and the situation is now well in hand. So far as is known here three military officers, two loyal volunteers, four or five soldiers, and two policemen have been killed, and four or five military officers, seven or eight soldiers, and six loyal volunteers wounded.

'No exact information has been received of casualties on the side of the Sinn Feiners. Reports received from Cork, Limerick, Ennis, Tralee, and both Ridings of Tipperary show that no disturbances of any kind have occurred in these localities.'

Rebels Surrounded by Troops

The following was issued by the General Officer Commanding-in-Chief in Dublin on Wednesday, 26th April:

There is now a complete cordon of troops around the centre of the town on the north side of the river. Two more battalions are arriving this afternoon (Wednesday) from England. There has been a small rising at Ardee, Louth, and a rather more serious one at Swords and Lusk, close to Dublin. The last report I have shows the total of fifteen killed and twenty-one wounded, besides two loyal Volunteers and two policemen killed and six loyal Volunteers wounded.

Mr Asquith's Statement in The Commons

In the House of Commons on Wednesday, 26th April, in reply to questions about the rebellion, Mr Asquith said—Troops have arrived from Belfast and from England. A building called Liberty Hall is already occupied by soldiers. So, also, is Stephen's Green. Martial law has been proclaimed in Dublin City and County. Drastic action both to suppress the movement and to secure the arrest of all concerned is at this moment being taken. Outside Dublin the country is tranquil, and only three minor cases of disturbance are reported. Steps have been taken to give full and accurate information to our friends abroad as to the real significance of this most recent German campaign.

The Prime Minister afterwards read the following telegram from the Viceroy:

Drogheda National Volunteers Assist the Military

'Situation satisfactory. St Stephen's Green captured. Eleven insurgents killed. Provincial news reassuring. Inspector-General, Royal Irish Constabulary, reports that at Drogheda the National Volunteers turned out to assist the military. (Cheers.) Many private persons have offered assistance.'

Mr Asquith added it was not the case that the rebels had machine guns.

Mr Birrell Anxious about Neutrals

Mr Birrell said—We were very anxious, indeed, during these last few days that news should not reach the neutral countries, and particularly our friends in America, which would be calculated to give them an entirely false impression as to the importance of what has taken place, important as that is. Therefore, during the short period there has been a censorship—that is to say, people were told they were not to communicate to the Press except what had passed through the Press Bureau, and that, I hope, will be taken off almost at once.

Lord Lansdowne's Statement

Lord Lansdowne, in the House of Lords on Wednesday, 26th April, said the Dublin garrison had had reinforcements from Belfast and England, and the Sinn Feiners had been driven out of Stephen's Green with a certain number of casualties. On Tuesday evening the military had succeeded in protecting the line from Kingsbridge Station, *via* Trinity College, to the Customs House and the North Wall. By mid-day on Wednesday it was learned that Liberty Hall, the headquarters of the Citizen Army and formerly of Mr Larkin, had been wholly or partially destroyed and occupied by the military. Lord Lansdowne added that the latest details showed that there was a cordon of troops round the centre of the town on the north bank of the river, that two more battalions were to arrive in Dublin that afternoon from England, and that there had been a small rising at Ardee, in County Louth, and a rather more serious one at Swords and Lusk, near Dublin. The casualties he put at 19 killed and 27 wounded.

Lord Lansdowne gave an interesting addition to the official account of the attempted German landing on the west coast of Ireland. A German vessel disguised as a Dutch trading vessel, and a German submarine, brought the invaders. From the submarine there landed in a collapsible boat three individuals, of whom two (one Sir Roger Casement) were made prisoners. The disguised German ship was stopped by one of His Majesty's ships, and while she was being taken into Queenstown Harbour, no prize crew having been put on board, she exhibited the German flag and sank herself.

Sir John Maxwell's Appointment

In the House of Commons on Thursday, 27th April:

Mr Asquith said—The Cabinet have decided to-day that the Irish Executive must at once proclaim martial law over the whole of Ireland. General Sir John Maxwell left this afternoon for Ireland, and has been given plenary power to proclaim martial law over the whole of the country, and the Irish Executive have placed themselves at his disposal to carry out his instructions. He added that there were indications of the movement spreading, especially in the West, and that the rebels continued to hold important public buildings in Dublin.

Large Reinforcements from England

The Lord Lieutenant issued the following from the Viceregal Lodge on Thursday, 27th April:

In the last forty-eight hours satisfactory progress has been made. Enemy activity is confined to sniping from houses in certain restricted areas. Large additional reinforcements have arrived from England, and are in hand for disposal as required.

Reports from Viscount French

Hemming in the Rebels

The following communication was issued by Field-Marshal Viscount French, Commanding-in-Chief the Home Forces, early on Saturday morning, 29th April:

The military operations for the suppression of the rebellion in Dublin are proceeding satisfactorily. What may be described as the organised forces of the rebels are confined to a few localities, the principal one being the Sackville street district, in which the rebels' headquarters appear to be the General Post Office. The cordon of troops round this district has been drawn closer, and the rebels in this locality appear now to be confined behind the line of their barricades.

Sniping from houses in which small parties of the rebels have established themselves in various parts of the city still continues. The district where this is most prevalent is that to the north-west of the Four Courts, which is still in possession of the rebels. The clearance of the snipers is a matter of time.

Considerable damage was caused by fires on Thursday, and a large fire is still burning in Sackville street.

In other parts of Ireland the principal centres of disturbance are County Galway and Enniscorthy. Disturbances have also been reported at Killarney, Clonmel, and Gorey.

Other parts of Ireland appear to be normal.

The general trend of the reports received indicates that the disturbances are local in character.

On the Verge of Collapse

The following was issued by Field-Marshal Viscount French, Commanding-in-Chief Home Forces, on Saturday night, 29th April:

Dublin—The situation this morning had improved considerably, but the rebels were still offering serious resistance in the neighbourhood of Sackville street.

The cordon of troops encircling this quarter was, however, steadily closing in, but the house to house fighting necessarily rendered this progress slow. The Post Office and a block of buildings east of Sackville street have been destroyed by fire. A party of rebels have been driven out of Boland's mills, Ringsend, by guns mounted on motor lorries.

One of the rebel leaders, a man named Pearse, was said to be in this area, and was wounded in the leg. A report received this evening states that Pearse has surrendered unconditionally, and that he asserts he has authority to accept the same terms of surrender for his followers in Dublin.

Another leader, James Connolly, is reported killed.

The Fourt Courts district, which is still held by the rebels, is also surrounded by a cordon of troops, which is gradually closing in.

All the information to hand points to the conclusion that the rebellion, so far as Dublin is concerned, is on the verge of collapse. A considerable number of rebels are prisoners in military custody.

Reports received this evening from the rest of Ireland are generally satisfactory. The conditions in Belfast and the Ulster Province are normal, and the situation in Londonderry is stated to be quite satisfactory.

The district within fifteen miles of Galway is also reported to be normal, but a band of rebels has been located between Athenry and Graughwell.

Nineteen rebel prisoners have been captured and are on their way to Queenstown.

Another band of rebels are reported to have entrenched themselves at Enniscorthy, but the police are still holding out, and the roads and railways are clear to within four miles of the town.

The damage to the Barrow Bridge on the Dublin and South-Eastern Railway, is now reported not to be serious.

Division of Troops in Dublin

An official intimation was circulated among the Royal Irish Constabulary in County Dublin on Saturday, 29th April, as follows:

The Sinn Fein rebels in the area of Capel street, Great Britain street, and Lower Gardiner street are completely surrounded by a cordon of troops, which is gradually closing on the centre. The troops in the district are gradually overcoming resistance. One of the principal rebel leaders, PH Pearse, is known to

Photo by] [*Lafayette.*
GENERAL SIR JOHN G. MAXWELL, Commander-in-Chief of the Forces in Ireland.

Photo by] [*Lafayette.*
MAJOR-GENERAL A. E. SANDBACH. Commander of the troops in the Dublin Area.

Photo by] [*Lafayette.*
MAJOR-GENERAL L. B. FRIEND, who Commanded the Forces in Ireland before Easter.

Photo by] [*Lafayette.*
BRIGADIER-GENERAL W. H. M. LOWE, to whom P. H. Pearse surrendered.

be inside the cordon with a fractured thigh. The woman generally known as Countess Markievicz has also been seen inside. Another leader, James Connolly, is reported killed. The additional area containing the Four Courts is also surrounded by a cordon, which is closing in on the centre. It contains within it most of the rebels.

A division complete with artillery is now operating in the Dublin area, and more troops are constantly arriving. Arrangements are being made to intern in England all the Sinn Feiners captured or wounded who are not dealt with here.

Sir Roger Casement has declared that Germany has sent all the assistance she is going to send, and that is now at the bottom of the sea.

The Unconditional Surrender

On Saturday evening, 29th April, it was officially announced in Dublin that the leaders of the rebels had surrendered. The following is an exact copy of the document:

In order to prevent the further slaughter of unarmed people, and in the hope of saving the lives of our followers, now surrounded and hopelessly outnumbered, Members of the Provisional Government present at Headquarters have agreed to an unconditional surrender, and the Commanders of all Units of the Republican Forces will order their followers to lay down their arms.

(Signed),
PH Pearse,
29th April, 1916, 3.45 p.m.

I agree to these conditions for the men only under my own command in the Moore street District and for the men in the Stephen's Green Command.

James Connolly,
April 29/16.

On consultation with Commandant Ceannt and other officers I have decided to agree to unconditional surrender also.

Thomas MacDonagh.

Dealing with the Remnant

The following communication was issued by the Lord Lieutenant from the Viceregal Lodge, Dublin, on Sunday, April 30th:

'Yesterday Pearse, the rebel leader, surrendered, and the great bulk of his supporters in the city and throughout the country have done likewise.

'Only a few detached bodies have not yet made their submission, and they are being effectively dealt with.'

A Truce at Enniscorthy

The following was issued by Field-Marshal Viscount French, Commanding-in-Chief Home Forces, on Sunday, 30th April, 6.45 p.m.:

The General Officer Commanding-in-Chief Irish Command has reported that the situation in Dublin is much more satisfactory.

Throughout the country there was still much more to be done, which would take time, but he hopes that the back of the rebellion has been broken.

Last night messengers were sent out from the leaders of the rebels in Dublin to rebel forces in Galway, Clare, Wexford, and Dublin counties ordering surrender, and the priests and the Royal Irish Constabulary are doing their utmost to disseminate this information.

As regards the situation in Dublin rebels from the areas of Sackville street, Post Office, and Four Courts are surrendering freely.

More incendiary fires took place in Sackville street last night, but the fire brigade have now been able to resume work.

It is further reported that up to the present 707 prisoners have been taken. Included among these is the Countess Markievicz.

The rebels at Enniscorthy were reported to be still in possession of this place, and a mixed column of cavalry, infantry, and artillery, including 4.7in guns, has been sent from Wexford with a view to engaging the rebels.

The latest information from Enniscorthy shows that the rebel leader at this place does not believe in the rebel leader's message from Dublin, and has proceeded to that city in a motor car under escort to verify the information. In the meantime a truce exists.

A deputation for a similar purpose from the rebels at Ashbourne has also been sent to Dublin.

In Galway the rebels are believed to be disbanding, and a few arrests have been made.

The situation at New Ross, Gorey, Wicklow, Bagenalstown, and Arklow is reported to be normal. Carlow and Dunlavin are believed to be quiet.

Flying Column to Stimulate Surrenders

The following was issued on Sunday, 30th April:

Yesterday (Saturday) the Sinn Fein leaders, including James Connolly, unconditionally surrendered to the General Officer Commanding-in-Chief in Ireland. These leaders, anxious to avoid further bloodshed, have signed a notice to other leaders of their party, both in Dublin and in the country, calling on them to surrender, as their cause is hopeless. These notices are being circulated by the RIC to all stations. A large number of men surrendered last night and this morning, and it is expected that others will follow during the course of the day. A flying column will at once proceed to various points to stimulate the surrender of parties in the country. Emissaries have come in from the Sinn Fein party at about Ashbourne, Swords, and from Wexford to verify the fact of the above surrender with a view to their immediate surrender.

1,000 Rebels Surrender in Dublin

The following was issued by Field-Marshal Viscount French, Commanding-in-Chief the Home Forces, on Monday, 1st May, 7.5 p.m.:

All the rebels in Dublin have surrendered, and the city is reported to be quiet. The rebels in the country are surrendering to mobile columns. There were 1,000 prisoners in Dublin yesterday, of whom 489 were sent to England last night.

It is reported from Queenstown that hopes were entertained that arms would be handed in to-day in the City of Cork.

Enniscorthy: During the night of April 30-May 1, Sunday, the rebels at Enniscorthy made an effort to surrender their leaders and arms, on condition that the rank and file were allowed to return to their homes. They were informed that the only terms we would accept were unconditional surrender. It has been reported at a later date that the rebels are now surrendering today on these terms.

Ferns: A column, composed of soldiers and Royal Irish Constabulary, captured seven prisoners in the neighbourhood of Ferns, Co. Wexford, today.

Wicklow, Arklow, Dunlavin, Bagenalstown, Wexford, New Ross, Counties of Cork, Clare, Limerick and Kerry are generally quiet.

The whole of Ulster is reported quiet.

Affray at Fermoy. No Rising in Cork

The following was issued by Field-Marshal Viscount French, Commanding the Home Forces, on Tuesday, 2nd May:

Dublin is gradually reverting to its normal condition. The work of clearing some small districts around Irishtown is being carried out by an ever-contracting cordon.

Cork: All is quiet in this county with the exception of an affray in the Fermoy district, where the police on attempting to arrest two men in their house met with armed resistance, the head constable being shot dead. On arrival of military reinforcements the occupants of the house, all of whom were wounded, surrendered.

The Sinn Feiners in Cork City, where there has been no rising, have handed in their arms.

Wexford: The column which went to Enniscorthy is carrying out the arrest of rebels in Co. Wexford.

The rest of the South of Ireland is reported quiet.

Trials of Rebels

The following communication was issued on Tuesday, 2nd May, from the Irish Command Headquarters:

Rebels considered suitable for trial are being tried by Field General Courts-martial under the Defence of the Realm Act in Dublin. As soon as the sentences have been confirmed the public will be informed as to the results of the trial.

Those prisoners whose cases could not be immediately dealt with are being sent to places of confinement in England. Their cases will receive consideration later.

The cases of the women taken prisoners are under consideration.

The work of dealing with these trials is one of great magnitude, and is being proceeded with with despatch.

The Provinces

Normal: Great Southern and Western Railway, Dublin, Cork, Tralee, Limerick.

Quiet: Waterford, King's County, Queen's County, Wicklow, Carlow, Cork, WR: Galway, ER, Mayo, Belfast, and Ulster Counties.

No Shooting without Trial

The Irish Command Headquarters on Tuesday, 2nd May, issued the following:

i Reports as to the shooting without trial of any rebels after their surrender may be denied in the Press. Trials are not yet completed.

ii Passes: (a) Communication is open and free inside Dublin City within the cordon of North and South Circular roads. (b) Passes will be required for some few days by people proceeding through that cordon, but examination posts have been established at convenient points along the North and South Circular roads, at which inhabitants of Dublin and environs may be passed through by the police. (c) Women, children, and coal and food carts have free passage in and out of Dublin.

iii A restricted railway service will begin from tomorrow, May 3rd, to and from Dublin, but passengers must be scrutinised by the police both on entering and quitting railway stations.

iv A Proclamation has been issued that only the ports of Dublin, Kingstown, Belfast, and Greenore are available for embarkation of passengers, subject to the scrutiny of the police. Intending passengers must show due cause for their proposed journey.

Rebels Dispersed in Galway

The following report from Field-Marshal Viscount French, Commander-in-Chief of the Home Forces, was issued at Dublin on Wednesday, 3rd May, at 7.20 p.m.:

The situation in Ireland is reported as quiet. The collection of arms and the arrests of fugitive rebels progresses satisfactorily. A strict cordon is still maintained.

Galway—The police barracks at Oranmore, about seven miles from Galway, were attacked by parties of rebels, but held out until relieved. In the West Riding of Galway the police reported that the situation is well in hand, and that the rebels have been dispersed.

The South of Ireland is quiet. Steady progress is being made towards the restoration of normal conditions.

The situation in Ulster is normal.

Irishtown the Last Spot

The following notice was issued on Thursday, 4th May:

Passes

From tomorrow, May 5th, 1916, passes are not required for any persons moving in and out of Dublin. But the cordon of troops all round Dublin will be maintained, and people will be required to pass through this cordon at fixed examination posts, when they will be subject to scrutiny by the civil police. This order does not apply to the Irishtown Area, round which the Commander, 177th Infantry Brigade, has established a close cordon. Only women and children are allowed to pass through this close cordon.

AE SANDBACH
Major-General
Commanding Troops in Dublin Area
Dublin, 4th May, 1916

300 Arrests by Belfast Police

The following official notification was issued at Belfast on Monday, 8th May:

The police, acting under instructions, made on Friday last a large number of domiciliary visits in the city and suburbs of Belfast, and arrested some twenty-six persons who were suspected of being connected with the Sinn Fein movement. These prisoners, together with eight others who had been arrested in County Louth, were sent on to Dublin on Saturday last.

On Easter Tuesday, 25th April, a party of Belfast police, numbering 200, left the city by motor transport, and until Saturday morning they had been actively engaged in rounding up about 1,500 rebels in various parts of the country. They have effected some 300 arrests, and of these prisoners 136 have been sent to Dublin, while 130 are confined elsewhere.

Instruction to Sir John Maxwell

The instructions to Sir John Maxwell by the Army Council with regard to the steps to be taken by him as to the outbreak in Dublin were issued on Wednesday, 10th May, in a letter to the Field-Marshal Commanding-in-Chief Home Forces:

'His Majesty's Government desire that Sir John Maxwell will take all such measures as may in his opinion be necessary for the prompt suppression of insurrection in Ireland, and be granted a free hand in regard to all troops now in Ireland, or which may be placed under his command hereafter, and also in regard to such measures as may seem to him advisable under the Proclamation dated April 26, issued under the Defence of the Realm Act, 1915.

'In regard to the question of administration, as also military and martial law, Sir John Maxwell will correspond direct with the War Office under the same system that obtained in peace time.

'In the event of Sir John Maxwell applying to you for further reinforcements, I am to request that you will be good enough to inform the Army Council of the nature of the demand, and your proposed action in the matter.'

Removal of the Dead

The following announcements were made by the civic authorities on Wednesday, 3rd May:

'The removal of bodies in Dublin is being carried out by the military authorities and the sanitary authorities, and citizens are required to give information of discoveries of bodies to the police, or to the Medical Officer of Health, Castle street. Bodies may yet be lying on roofs or concealed in chimneys, from which snipers fired.'

Prevention of Epidemic

'Persons discovering dead bodies should inform the police or the Chief Medical Officer of Health, Municipal Buildings, Castle street, immediately.'

PROCLAMATIONS

Restrictions upon Citizens

On the day the rebellion broke out the following Proclamation was issued by the Viceroy:

Whereas, an attempt, instigated and designed by the foreign enemies of our King and Country to incite rebellion in Ireland, and thus endanger the safety of the United Kingdom, has been made by a reckless, though small, body of men, who have been guilty of insurrectionary acts in the City of Dublin:

Now, we, Ivor Churchill, Baron Wimborne, Lord Lieutenant-General and Governor-General of Ireland, do hereby warn all His Majesty's subjects that the sternest measures are being, and will be taken for the prompt suppression of the existing disturbances, and the restoration of order;

And we do hereby enjoin all loyal and law-abiding citizens to abstain from any acts or conduct which might interfere with the action of the Executive Government, and, in particular, we warn all citizens of the danger of unnecessarily frequenting the streets or public places, or of assembling in crowds:

Given under our Seal, on the 24th day of April, 1916.

WIMBORNE.

Martial Law Proclaimed in Dublin

The following day, Tuesday, 25th April, the Viceroy issued a second proclamation, in which Martial Law was applied to the City and County of Dublin for a period of one month. The people were warned of the danger of frequenting places where the military were operating, and ordered to remain indoors between 7.30 p.m. and 5.30 a.m. In the Dublin area all licensed premises were ordered to be closed, except between the hours of 2 and 5 p.m.

On Wednesday, 26th April, a Proclamation was issued commanding all persons in Dublin City and County to keep within their homes between the hours of 7.30 p.m. and 5.30 a.m., unless provided with the written permission of the military authorities. This notice was signed by Major-General LB Friend, CB, the then Commander-in-Chief of the Forces in Ireland.

On Wednesday, 26th April, a Proclamation was issued suspending in Ireland Section I. of the Defence of the Realm Act, which gives the right to a British subject charged with offence to be tried by Civil Court.

All Ireland under Martial Law

On Wednesday, 26th April, a Proclamation was issued placing the whole of Ireland under martial law for the period of one month, and on Saturday, 29th, this Order was extended for one month.

Sir John Maxwell Adopts Rigorous Measures

The first proclamation to be issued by General Sir John Maxwell on taking over command of His Majesty's troops in Ireland on Friday, 28th April, was as follows:

'Most rigorous measures will be taken by me to stop the loss of life and damage to property which certain misguided persons are causing by their armed resistance to the law. If necessary, I shall not hesitate to destroy all buildings within any area occupied by rebels, and I warn all persons within the area now surrounded by His Majesty's troops, forthwith to leave such areas under the following conditions: (a) Women and children may leave the area from any of the examining posts set up for the purpose, and will be allowed to go away free: (b) men may leave by the same examining posts, and will be allowed to go away free, provided the examining officer is satisfied they have taken no part whatever in the present disturbance: (c) all other men who present themselves at the said examining posts must surrender unconditionally, together with any arms and ammunition in their possession.'

Surrender of Arms

On Tuesday, 2nd May, the following was issued:

I, General Sir John Grenfell Maxwell, KCB, KCMG, CVO, DSO, Commanding-in-Chief His Majesty's Forces in Ireland, hereby Order that all members of the Irish Volunteer Sinn Fein Organisation or of the Citizen Army, shall forthwith surrender all arms, ammunition, and explosives in their possession to the nearest Military Authority or to the nearest Police Barracks. Any member of either of these organisations found in possession of any arms, ammunition, or explosives, after 6th May, 1916, will be severely dealt with.

On Saturday, 6th May, an Order was issued by Major-General AE Sandbach, commanding the troops in the Dublin area, requiring all licensed premises within the A, B, C, D and E Divisions of the Dublin Metropolitan Police district to be kept closed throughout Saturday, May 6th, and thereafter to be kept closed except between the hours of 2 p.m. and 5 p.m.

On Friday, 12th May, an order was issued fixing the hours at which citizens must remain indoors—from twelve midnight until four a.m. This came into operation on Sunday, 13th May, when a full tram service was run for the first time after the outbreak of the rebellion.

Political Meetings Banned

The following Order was issued on Saturday, 13th May, by Sir John Maxwell, General Commanding-in-Chief the Forces in Ireland:

Political Meetings, Parades, or Processions.

I, General Sir John Grenfell Maxwell, KCB, KCMG, CVO, DSO, Commanding-in-Chief His Majesty's Forces in Ireland, hereby order that no parade, procession or political meeting or organised football, athletic or hurling meeting, shall take place anywhere in Ireland without the written authority, previously obtained, of the local County Inspector of Royal Irish Constabulary, or, in Dublin City, of the Chief Commissioner of the Dublin Metropolitan Police.

This Order was modified at the end of June by a new Order, deleting the words 'organised football, athletic, or hurling meeting' from the original.

The remainder of the Order remains in force. This means that, while processions, parades, and political meetings shall not take place without written authority, no such authority is needed for football, athletic, or hurling meetings.

Carrying of Arms Prohibited

Under the Defence of the Realm (Consolidation) Regulations, General Sir John Maxwell on 17th July issued an Order which prohibits the carrying of firearms or military arms in Ireland except by members of His Majesty's naval or military forces, or of the Dublin Metropolitan Police or the Royal Irish Constabulary. It does not apply to duly licensed persons carrying shot guns for sporting purposes, to occupiers of land who desire to scare birds or kill vermin on their land, or to persons specially authorised, in writing, by the competent military authority to carry firearms.

Martial Law until Further Orders

A proclamation was issued on Saturday, 27th May, by the Lords Justices General and General Governors of Ireland, stating that, as 'disaffection and unrest still prevail in certain parts of Ireland... martial law shall continue to exist throughout Ireland until further order.'

This order remained in force in April, 1917, when this edition was prepared for the Press.

Drilling in Ireland Prohibited

On 28th November an order was issued by the Chief Secretary making it an offence against the Defence of the Realm Act for any body in Ireland to take part in any drill of a military nature without a permit from a competent naval or military authority.

Carriage of Letters

An order was also issued by General Sir John Maxwell, by which it became an offence under the Defence of the Realm Act for any person to sent letters (shippers' advices excepted) to the United Kingdom or elsewhere by any means except that of the Post Office.

Licensed Houses in Dublin

When the rebellion occurred publicans were only allowed to open their licensed premises daily between the hours of 2 and 5 p.m. On May 12th a new Order extended the hours from 10 a.m. to 5 p.m., and on the 15th May another Order permitted the public houses to remain open between 7 a.m. and 10 p.m. on four days of the week, between 7 a.m. and 9.30 p.m. on two days, and from 2 p.m. to 5 p.m. on Sundays. This was curtailed by an Order operating from 24th May, and which restricted the hours for the sale of liquor from 10 a.m. to 8 p.m. On Monday, 26th June, the hours were again extended to 9 a.m. to 9.30 p.m.

THE PROCLAMATIONS OF THE REBELS
Some Historic Documents

The first thing the rebels did when they secured possession of the Post Office was to post up on that building and others around it a Proclamation by which they declared an Irish Republic. A facsimile reproduction of the poster appears on page ix. The following are copies of other orders and manifestoes issued by the rebels:

Easter Manoeuvres Cancelled

Dublin Brigade Order
23rd April, 1916
HQ

1. As publicly announced, the inspection and manoeuvres ordered for this day are cancelled.

2. All Volunteers are to stay in Dublin until further orders.

Thomas MacDonagh,
Commandant.
Ed de Valera

The Fatal Parade

Dublin Brigade Order
HQ
24th April, 1916

1. The four city battalions will parade for inspection and route march at 10 a.m. today. Commandants will arrange centres.

2. Full arms and equipment and one day's rations.

Thomas MacDonagh,
Commandant.
Coy. E3 will parade at Beresford place at 10 a.m.
PH Pearse,
Commandant.

Address to the Citizens of Dublin

The following is a copy of a manifesto issued by PH Pearse to the citizens of Dublin during Easter week:

The Provisional Government to the Citizens of Dublin

The Provisional Government of the Irish Republic salutes the Citizens of Dublin on the momentous occasion of the proclamation of a

Sovereign Independent Irish State,

now in course of being established by Irishmen in arms.

The Republican forces hold the lines taken up at twelve noon on Easter Monday, and nowhere, despite fierce and almost continuous attacks of the British troops, have the lines been broken through. The country is rising in answer to Dublin's call, and the final achievement of Ireland's freedom is now, with God's help, only a matter of days. The valour, self-sacrifice and discipline of Irish men and women are about to win for our country a glorious place among the nations.

Ireland's honour has already been redeemed: it remains to vindicate her wisdom and her self-control.

All citizens of Dublin who believe in the right of their country to be free will give their allegiance and their loyal help to the Irish Republic. There is work for everyone: for the men in the fighting line, and for the women in the provision of food and first aid. Every Irishman and Irishwoman worthy of the name will come forward to help their common country in this her supreme hour.

Able-bodied citizens can help by building barricades in the streets to oppose the advance of the British troops. The British troops have been firing on our women and on our Red Cross. On the other hand, Irish regiments in the British Army have refused to act against their fellow-countrymen.

The Provisional Government hopes that its supporters—which means the vast bulk of the people of Dublin—will preserve order and self-restraint. Such looting as has already occurred has been done by hangers-on of the British Army. Ireland must keep her new honour unsmirched.

We have lived to see an Irish Republic proclaimed. May we live to establish it firmly, and may our children and our children's children enjoy the happiness and prosperity which freedom will bring.

Signed on behalf of the Provisional Government,
PH Pearse,
Commanding-in-Chief of the Forces of the Irish Republic, and President of the Provisional Government.

The War Stop Press Edition

The rebels on the second day of the rising issued a small newspaper of four pages, measuring ten inches by seven and a half inches. The title on the front page read:

Irish War News.
The Irish Republic
Vol. 1. No. 1. Dublin, Tuesday, April 25, 1916.
Price One Penny

The leading article, which was entitled 'If the Germans Came to England,' occupied the whole of the front page, but the principal item of news was printed on the fourth page, and was as follows:

Stop Press!
The Irish Republic

'(Irish) War News is published today because a momentous thing has happened. The Irish Republic has been declared in Dublin and a Provisional Government has been appointed to administer its affairs.

'The following have been named as the Provisional Government:

Thomas J Clarke
Sean Mac Diarmada
PH Pearse
James Connolly
Thomas MacDonagh

Eamonn Ceannt
Joseph Plunkett

'The Irish Republic was proclaimed by poster which was prominently displayed in Dublin.

'At 9.30 a.m. this morning the following statement was made by Commandant-General PH Pearse:

'The Irish Republic was proclaimed in Dublin on Easter Monday, April 24, at 12 noon. Simultaneously with the issue of the proclamation of the Provisional Government the Dublin division of the Army of the Republic, including the Irish Volunteers, Citizen Army, Hibernian Rifles, and other bodies occupied dominating positions in the city. The GPO was seized at 12 noon, the Castle attacked at the same moment, and shortly afterwards the Four Courts were occupied. The Irish troops hold the City Hall and dominate the Castle. Attacks were immediately commenced by the British forces, and were everywhere repulsed. At the moment of writing this report (9.30 a.m. Tuesday) the Republican forces hold their positions and the British forces have nowhere broken through. There has been heavy and continuous fighting for nearly 24 hours, the casualties of the enemy being much more numerous than those on the Republican side. The Republican forces everywhere are fighting with splendid gallantry. The populace of Dublin are plainly with the Republic, and the officers and men are everywhere cheered as they march through the streets. The whole centre of the city is in the hands of the Republic, whose flag flies from the GPO.

Commandant-General PH Pearse is Commandant-in-Chief of the Army of the Republic and is President of the Provisional Government. Commandant-General James Connolly is commanding the Dublin districts.

'Communication with the country is largely cut, but reports to hand show that the country is rising. Bodies of men from Kildare and Fingal have already reported in Dublin.'

'To the Officer in the DBC'

The following is a copy of orders issued by James Connolly, the 'Commandant' of the Dublin Division of the 'Republican Army.' Connolly, who was in charge of the rebels in the General Post Office, was executed in Dublin on Friday, 12th May:

'Army of the Irish Republic,
'(Dublin Command).
'Headquarters, Date, 25th April, 1916.

'To the Officer in Charge, Reis and DBC

'The main purpose of your post is to protect our wireless station. Its secondary purpose is to observe Lower Abbey street and Lower O'Connell street. Commandeer in the DBC whatever food and utensils you require. Make sure of a plentiful supply of water wherever your men are. Break all glass in the windows of the rooms occupied by you for fighting purposes. Establish a connection between your forces in the DBC and in Reis's building. Be sure that the stairways leading immediately to your rooms are well barricaded. We have a post in the house at the corner of Bachelor's Walk, in the Hotel Metropole, in the Imperial Hotel, in the General Post Office. The directions from which you are likely to be attacked are from the Custom House, or from the far side of the river, D'Olier street, or Westmoreland street. We believe there is a sniper in McBirney's on the far side of the river.

'JAMES CONNOLLY,
'Commandant-General.'

'The Hour of Victory'

The following is a copy of an order which was found on the body of the O'Rahilly, one of the rebel commandants, who was shot dead while fighting in Henry place, opposite the General Post Office, Dublin. It was presumably written in the Post Office, which the rebels had made their headquarters, and is dated April 28, the day before the Sinn Fein garrison surrendered:

Army of the Irish Republic
(Dublin Command),
Headquarters, April 28, 1916.

To Soldiers,

This is the fifth day of the establishment of the Irish Republic, and the flag of our country still floats from the most important buildings in Dublin, and is gallantly protected by the officers and Irish soldiers in arms throughout the country. Not a day passes without seeing fresh postings of Irish soldiers eager to do battle for the old cause. Despite the utmost vigilance of the enemy we have been able to get in information telling us how the manhood of Ireland, inspired by our splendid action, are gathering to offer up their lives if necessary in the same holy cause. We are here hemmed in because the enemy feels that in this building is to be found the heart and inspiration of our great movement.

Let us remind you what you have done. For the first time in 700 years the flag of a free Ireland floats triumphantly in Dublin City.

The British Army, whose exploits we are for ever having dinned into our ears, which boasts of having stormed the Dardanelles and the German lines on the Marne, behind their artillery and machine guns are afraid to advance to the attack or storm any positions held by our forces. The slaughter they suffered in the first few days has totally unnerved them, and they dare not attempt again an infantry attack on our positions.

Our Commandants around us are holding their own.

Commandant Daly's splendid exploit in capturing Linen Hall Barracks we all know. You must know also that the whole population, both clergy and laity, of this district are united in his praises. Commandant MacDonagh is established in an impregnable position reaching from the walls of

Dublin Castle to Redmond's Hill, and from Bishop street to Stephen's Green.

(In Stephen's Green, Commandant — holds the College of Surgeons, one side of the square, a portion of the other side, and dominates the whole Green and all its entrances and exits.)

Commandant De Valera stretches in a position from the Gas Works to Westland row, holding Boland's Bakery, Boland's Mills, Dublin South-Eastern Railway Works, and dominating Merrion square.

Commandant Kent holds the South Dublin Union and Guinness's Buildings to Marrowbone lane, and controls James's street and district.

On two occasions the enemy effected a lodgement and were driven out with great loss.

The men of North County Dublin are in the field, have occupied all the Police Barracks in the district, destroyed all the telegram system on the Great Northern Railway up to Dundalk, and are operating against the trains of the Midland and Great Western.

Dundalk has sent 200 men to march upon Dublin, and in the other parts of the North our forces are active and growing.

In Galway Captain — , fresh after his escape from an Irish prison, is in the field with his men. Wexford and Wicklow are strong, and Cork and Kerry are equally acquitting themselves creditably. (We have every confidence that our Allies in Germany and kinsmen in America are straining every nerve to hasten matters on our behalf.)

As you know, I was wounded twice yesterday and am unable to move about, but have got my bed moved into the firing line, and, with the assistance of your officers, will be just as useful to you as ever.

Courage, boys, we are winning, and in the hour of our victory let us not forget the splendid women who have everywhere stood by us and cheered us on. Never had man or woman a grander cause, never was a cause more grandly served.

(Signed) JAMES CONNOLLY,
Commandant-General,
Dublin Division.

MANIFESTO BY PH PEARSE ON THE EVE OF SURRENDER

The following is a copy of a manifesto issued from the Headquarters of the Insurgents, General Post Office, Dublin. It was written on Government paper bearing the Royal Arms embossed in left top corner:

'Headquarters, Army of the Irish Republic,
'General Post Office, Dublin,
'28th April, 1916, 9.30 a.m.

'The Forces of the Irish Republic, which was proclaimed in Dublin, on Easter Monday, 24th April, have been in possession of the central part of the capital, since 12 noon on that day. Up to yesterday afternoon Headquarters was in touch with all the main outlying positions, and despite furious, and almost continuous assaults by the British Forces all those positions were then still being held, and the Commandants in charge, were confident of their ability to hold them for a long time.

'During the course of yesterday afternoon, and evening, the enemy succeeded in cutting our communications with our other positions in the city, and Headquarters is today isolated.

'The enemy has burnt down whole blocks of houses, apparently with the object of giving themselves a clear field for the play of artillery and field guns against us. We have been bombarded during the evening and night by shrapnel and machine gun fire, but without material damage to our position, which is of great strength.

'We are busy completing arrangements for the final defence of Headquarters, and are determined to hold it while the buildings last.

'I desire now, lest I may not have an opportunity later, to pay homage to the gallantry of the soldiers of Irish Freedom who have during the past four days been writing with fire and steel the most glorious chapter in the later history of Ireland. Justice can never be done to their heroism, to their discipline, to their gay and unconquerable spirit in the midst of peril and death.

'Let me, who have led them into this, speak in my own, and in my fellow-commanders' names, and in the name of Ireland present and to come, their praise, and ask those who come after them to remember them.

'For four days they have fought and toiled, almost without cessation, almost without sleep, and in the intervals of fighting they have sung songs of the freedom of Ireland. No man has complained, no man has asked 'why?' Each individual has spent himself, happy to pour out his strength for Ireland and for freedom. If they do not win this fight, they will at least have deserved to win it. But win it they will, although they may win it in death. Already they have won a great thing. They have redeemed Dublin from many shames, and made her name splendid among the names of cities.

'If I were to mention names of individuals, my list would be a long one.

'I will name only that of Commandant-General James Connolly, Commanding the Dublin Division. He lies wounded, but is still the guiding brain of our resistance.

'If we accomplish no more than we have accomplished, I am satisfied. I am satisfied that we have saved Ireland's honour. I am satisfied that we should have accomplished more, that we should have accomplished the task of enthroning, as well as proclaiming, the Irish Republic as a Sovereign State, had our arrangements for a simultaneous rising of the whole country, with a combined plan as sound as the Dublin plan has been proved to be, been allowed to go through on Easter Sunday. Of the fatal countermanding order which prevented those plans from being carried out, I shall not speak further. Both Eoin MacNeill and we have acted in the best interests of Ireland.

'For my part, as to anything I have done in this, I

am not afraid to face either the judgment of God, or the judgment of posterity.

'(Signed) PH PEARSE
'Commandant-General,
'Commanding-in-Chief, the Army of the Irish Republic and President of the Provisional Government.'

An Order of the IR Government

The following is a copy of a credit left on the premises of Messrs Alex Findlater and Co. for goods taken by the rebels:

No .... Date, 24/4/16. Time ....
Place ....
To Alex Findlater ....
Place ....

Commandeered by the Irish Republic, to be paid for goods to the value of about £25.

By Order of the IR Government.

A Commission in the Citizen Army

The most interesting 'find' at the Royal College of Surgeons after the surrender of the rebels was the following partly printed, partly written, commission:

'Irish Citizen Army'
'Headquarters, Liberty Hall, Dublin.
'Commandant James Connolly.
'Date, 24th April, 1916.

'By warrant of the Army Council, I hereby appoint Michael Kelly to take the rank of Lieutenant, with full power to exercise all the rights and perform all the duties belonging to that rank.

(Signed) 'JAMES CONNOLLY,
'Commandant.'

The Outfit of the Fighting Men

The following is a copy of the leaflet issued from the headquarters of the Irish Volunteers giving instructions to the men regarding their equipment:

FIANNA FAIL
The Irish Volunteers
Service Kit

The following are the articles prescribed by Headquarters for the personal equipment of Volunteers on field service. Items printed in heavy type are to be regarded as important:

For All Volunteers

(a) as to clothes: uniform or other clothes as preferred; if uniform not worn clothes to be of neutral colour; nothing white or shiny (white collar not to be worn); **Soft Brimmed hat** (to be worn in lieu of cap on field service): strong comfortable boots; overcoat.

(b) As to arms: **Rifle**, with sling and **cleaning outfit**; 100 rounds of **ammunition** with **bandolier** or **ammunition pouches** to hold same; **bayonet**, with scabbard, frog and belt; strong knife or slasher.

(c) As to provision for rations: **Haversack, water-bottle**, mess tin (or billy can), with knife, fork, spoon, tin cup; one dry stick (towards making fire); emergency ration.

(d) **Knapsack** containing: spare shirt, pair of socks, towel, soap, comb, scissors, needle, thread, safety-pins.

(e) In the pocket: clasp knife, note book and pencil, matches in tin box, boot laces, strong cord, a candle, **coloured** handkerchiefs.

(f) Sewn inside coat: **First field dressing.**

For Officers

(a) As to clothes: uniform is very desirable for officers; if not worn a sufficient, but not unduly conspicuous, distinguishing mark of rank to be worn.

(b) As to arms: **automatic pistol** or **revolver**, with **ammunition for same**, in lieu of rifle: sword, sword bayonet, or short lance.

The rest of the equipment as for ordinary Volunteers, with the following:

(c) Additions: **Whistle on cord**; **watch**; **Field despatch book**; fountain pen or **copying ink pencil**; field-glasses, pocket compass, range finder, map of district, electric torch, hooded.

Sub-officers and **scouts** should, as far as possible, be provided with the additional articles prescribed for Officers.

By Order.

OFFICIAL LISTS OF CASUALTIES

On Thursday, 11th May, it was officially intimated that the total casualties caused by the revolt were as follows:

	Killed	Wounded	Missing	Total
Military officers	17	46	—	63
Military, other ranks	86	311	9	406
Royal Irish Constabulary officers	2	—	—	2
Royal Irish Constabulary, other ranks	12	23	—	35
Dublin Metropolitan Police	3	3	—	6
Civilians and insurgents	180	614	—	794
	300	997	9	1,306

It was stated that according to reports received from the police and medical authorities, 80 persons were killed and 614 passed through the hospitals. Beyond this the casualties of the rebels were not ascertainable. Many of the rebels were not in uniform, and it was not possible to distinguish between them and civilians, hence they are all included in the last figures given. Since these figures were issued the deaths of wounded persons have increased the total death roll considerably, but no complete official list is available.

The following lists of casualties were complied from those issued on different dates by the War Office:

OFFICERS

Killed or Died of Wounds

Acheson, Maj PH, Army Service Corps.
Allatt, Colonel HTW.
Browne, Sec-Lt MB, Sherwood Foresters.
Calvert, Sec-Lt JH, Royal Irish Rifles.
Crockett, Sec-Lt CLR, Innis Fus.
Daffen, Lt HC, Sherwood Foresters.
Dietrichsen, Capt FC, Sherwood Foresters.
Gray, Sec-Lt GR, RDF.
Hawken, Lt WV, Sherwood Foresters.
Hunter, Sec-Lt GJ, Lancers.
Lucas, Sec-Lt A, King Edward's Horse.
Neilan, Lt GA, RDF.
Perry, Lt PC, Sherwood Foresters.
Pinfield, Sec-Lt GV, 8th Hussars.
Purser, Lt PA, Army Service Corps.
Ramsay, Lt AL, Royal Irish Regiment.
Warmington, Capt AE, Royal Irish Regiment.
Worswick, Sec-Lt B, King Edward's Horse.

Wounded

Addis, Sec-Lt THL, RDF.
Bagley, Capt AB, RDF.
Black, Maj CAJA, RAMC.
Battersby, Sec-Lt JA, Royal Irish Rifles.
Bayliss, Capt PS, South Staffordshire Regiment.
Blake, Sec-Lt RDC, Hussars.
Broad, Sec-Lt JE, Sherwood Foresters.
Burrowes, Lt TJ, Rifle Brigade.
Chalmers, Sec-Lt AD, Royal Fusiliers.
Charlion, Capt RA, Sherwood Foresters.
Church, Capt H, Royal Scots.
Cursham, Capt FG, Sherwood Foresters.
Curtis, Sec-Lt WH, Sherwood Foresters.
Delany, Capt AS, RDF.
Denning, Capt GF, RAMC.
Dunn, Sec-Lt JA, RDF.
Dunsany, Capt EJMD, Lord, Royal Inniskilling Fusiliers.
Dunville, Sec-Lt RL, Grenadier Guard.
Elliott, Lt CP, Sherwood Foresters.
Fane, Lt-Col C, DSO, Sherwood Foresters.
Fisher, Sec-Lt WF, Sherwood Foresters.
Gerrard, Sec-Lt E, RFA.
Hanson, Maj H, Sherwood Foresters.
Hartshorn, Sec-Lt JE, Sherwood Foresters.
Hawe, Sec-Lt JA, RDF.
Helliwell, Sec-Lt GD, South Staffordshire Regiment.
Hickling, Capt FG, Sherwood Foresters.
Jollands, Sec-Lt BE, Yeomanry.
Lamb, Sec-Lt FM, Sherwood Foresters.
Leatham, Maj WSB, Royal Irish Rifles.
Leslie-Melville, Capt and Adjt AB, Sherwood Foresters.
Malone, Lt G, Royal Irish Regiment.
McCammond, Sec-Lt CRW, Royal Irish Rifles.
McClughan, Capt JC, Royal Irish Rifles.
McCullagh, Capt JT, RAMC.
Mooney, Lt HL, RAMC.
Norman, Sec-Lt HW, Leinster Regiment.
North, Sec-Lt FW, Royal Irish Regiment.
O'Neill, Sec-Lt J, Royal Dublin Fusiliers.
Pragnell, Capt F, Sherwood Foresters.
Quibell, Capt AH, Sherwood Foresters.
Rigg, Maj WT, Royal Irish Rifles.
Sheppard, Capt J, South Staffordshire Regiment.
Thompson, Lt HH, Duke of Lancaster's Own Yeomanry
Tissington, Sec-Lt HG, RE.

RANK AND FILE

All are privates unless otherwise stated. The towns following the names are those in which the next-of-kin of the soldier reside.

Sherwood Foresters

Killed or Died of Wounds

Barks L-Cpl G (Newark).
Barratt G (Loughborough).
Blissett J (Nottingham).
Bradford 5617, JH.
Chapman L-Cl H (Southwell).
Davenport E (Mansfield).
Dixey Co. S-MH (Newark).
Dixon CT (Nottingham).
Elliott AG (Notthingham).
Farnworth E (Nottingham).
Forth JR (Worksop).
Goss J (Radford).
Holbrook A (Nottingham).
Holland L (Sutton in A'field).
Hoyle Capl C.
Jeffs P (Bulwell, Notts).
Kitchen AJ (Newark).
Millar TH (Canterbury).
Rodgers H (Whitewell).
Sibley A (Beeston, Notts).
Tunnicliffe WA (Long Eaton).
Tyler 4905, A.
Warner A (Mansfield).
Woard AE (Newark).

Wounded

Allen H (Carrington, Notts).
Ankers L (Riddings, Alfreton).
Applegate A (Nottingham).
Baguley T (Mansfield).
Ball Bglr TW (Nottingham).
Beastall C (Snelton Dale).
Beazley F (Mansfield).
Becke Sgt C (Maidenhead).
Belton JP (Newark).
Bettney H (Calver).
Blore L-Cpl H (Nottingham).
Boissitt J (Nottingham).
Bowley WC (Stapleford).
Bradford S (Nottingham).
Bradley JR (Huthwaite).
Bird E (Newark).
Brindley R (E Kirby).
Buckman AS (Matlock).
Carlin Cpl M (Chesterfield).
Chambers C (Nottingham).
Champelovier JN (Nottingham).
Clarke 2481 CF.
Clayton L-Cpl H (Nottingham).
Collin G (Nottingham).
Conneley J (Mansfield).
Cooper S-Drm R (Mansfield).
Cox A (Mansfield).
Cox A (Nottingham).
Cupitt 5676, F.
Davey A (Nottingham).
Denham JH (Daybrook).
Dickinson A (Nottingham).
Dillon C (Mansfield).
Ditchfield R (Mansfield).
Dixie J (Nottingham).
Dixon J (Worksop).
Dixon OB (Elkington).
Dolphin JJ (Mansfield).
Dove L-Cpl F (Sutton-in-A'field).
Doyle W (Nottingham).
Duncombe G (Mansfield).
Eden J (Nottingham).
Edney T (Mansfield).
Elliott HC (Nottingham).
Ellis F (Radford).
Fish AL (Nottingham).
Foster R (Arnold, Notts).
Freestone W (Newark).
Godbor JA (Radford).
Goddard J (Nottingham).
Graveney L-Sgt A (Newark).
Hadden J (Carlton).
Hawley Cpl E (Netherfield).
Hazledene A (Long Eaton).
Higgins JT.
Hill L Cpl W (Basford).
Hocking J (Stanton Hill).
Hogg L-Sgt J (Alfreton).
Hopcroft R (Nottingham).
Iles F (West Bridgeford).
Illingworth E (Retford).
Jackson Sgt W (Newark).
Kerry L (Alfreton).
Lane JH (Newark).
Lawrence Co. S-MH (Newark).
Laxton E (Snilton, Notts).
Limb BM (Draycott).
Lindley H (Mansfield).
Lock A (Basford, Notts).
Lowde 3353 SH.
Mapletoft J (Warsop, Notts).
Marriott 550, Co. Sergt-Maj EC.
McMahon N (Chesterfield).
Middleton S (Long Eaton).
Midgeley N (Fisherton).
Millership G (Sutton-in-A'field).
Moorby GN (Broadbottom).
Mottley W (Annesley, Woodhouse).
Newcombe Cpl A (Notts).
Nicholson Cl A (Old Basford).
Norman CH (Nottingham).
Northbridge H (Mansfield).
Nunn Sgt G (Worksop).
O'Mara J (Mansfield).
Oldham TH (Beeston).
Olley BD (Nottingham).
Padmore E (Nottingham).
Parsons Sgt WG (Notts).
Pattinson A (Carlisle).
Pearce 5416, H.
Pickering Cpl A (Watford).
Plowman W (Stapleford).
Plowright H (Nottingham).
Poppitt L-Cpl J (Worksop).
Presswood E (Worksop).
Proctor AF (Bontham).
Reynolds FN (Nottingham).

Ridge H (Southwell).
Roberts H (Bootle).
Robson AN (Nottingham).
Rooks CE (Elmham).
Rowe G (Carrington).
Saltinstall A (Nottingham).
Savage F (Mansfield).
Scothon G (Sherwood).
Scrutton DG (Farndon).
Sharpe 5553, S.
Shaw W (Ilkeston).
Sheldon H (Lenton).
Simmonds J (Nottingham).
Skerritt W (Arnold).
Smedley H (Nottingham).
Smith A (Nottingham).
Smith H (West Bridgeford).
Smith W (Mansfield).
Snowden F (Retford).
Strickson 5383, G.
Stroud W (Reading).
Taylor WH (Worksop).
Thorpe C (South Scarle).
Vestey 5521, B.
Waplington W (Tuxford).
Ward J (Radford).
Webster C (New Basford).
Whitby B (Radford).
Wiles 5619, W.
Williamson J (Buxton).
Wyer C (Southwell).

South Staffordshire Regiment
Killed or Died of Wounds

Banks A (Wednesfield).
Banting FC (Wolverhampton).
Barrett Cpl J (Wolverhampton).
Bourne H (Sedgeley).
Bowcott J (Wolverhampton).
Chick J (Wombourne).
Collins 3151, TA.
Fox E (Willenhall).
Humphries WH (Mansfield).
Jobbert T (Willenhall).
Saunders O (Brierley).
Sherwood JH (Bolton)—accidentally.
Speed B (Wolverhampton).
Tempest Co. QMS DP (Wolverhampton).
Wright P (Nuneaton).

Wounded

Banks Sgt A (Willenhall).
Bayliss 5051, R.
Benfield F (Smethwick).
Buckerfield GA (Wolverhampton).
Buckoke HL (Balham).
Bulloch H (Bilston).
Davies F (Wolverhampton).
Davies W (Wolverhampton).
Foley J (West Bromwich).
Goody Sgt A (Clapham).
Hancox W (Old Hill).
Harris WE (Walsall).
Harvey Sgt J (Walsall).
Hope TS (Wolverhampton).
Jones Sgt H (Heath Town).
Millington T (Kirk Ireton).
Roberts C (Wolverhampton).
Rowbotham 4271, A.
Slaney L.(Wolverhampton).
Stringer F (Dudley).
Tudor L-Cpl SF (Wolverhampton).
Venables M (Wolverhampton).
Waterhouse G (Stockport).
Webb S (Walsall).
Worton Sgt F (Brierley Hill).

North Staffordshire Regiment
Killed or Died of Wounds

Brindley H (Burslem).
Cornwall L-Sgt C (Burton-on-Trent).

Wounded

Cornwall Sgt J (Burton).
Cook CE (Stafford).
Johnson W (Stoke-on-Trent).
King L-Cpl C (Burton-on-Trent).
Merrick G (Uttoxeter).
Talbot HG (Newport, Salop).
Warburton L-Sgt H (Burton-on-Trent).

Royal Irish Rifles
Killed or Died of Wounds

Coyle Co. QMS J (Middlesborough).
Duggan C (Belfast Enlt).
Hanna J (Belfast).
Mulhern J (Dublin).
Morton L-C N (Belfast).
McCullough J (Belfast).
McClelland A (Down).
Nolan J (Dublin).
Wilson D (Glasgow).

Wounded

Atkins M (Kilkenny).
Brady D (Dublin).
Cleyland WD (Belfast).
Collard Sergt G (Poplar).
Cunningham J (Youghal).
Doyle L (Dublin).
Duffy JT (Kilteel, Co. Kildare).
Gilmore J (Toomebridge, Co. Antrim).
Gould S (Manchester).
Graham A (Manchester).
Henderson JA (Belfast).
Holohan T (Waterford).
Hutchinson S (Belfast).
Irvine G (Newry).
Johnston D (Belfast).
Maher Cpl H (Dublin).
Mangan Cpl J (Dublin).
McCord L-Cpl R (Belfast).
McMaster Sgt A (Belfast).
Mitchell R (Belfast).
Mulholland Sgt H (Belfast).
Mulholland Sgt J (Belfast).
Murray P (Dublin).
O'Reilly E (Stillorgan).
Patton S (Ballymoney).
Smyth W (Carrick-on-Shannon).
Southam Co. Sgt-Maj R (West Bromwich).
Swan Cpl D (Belfast).

Taylor A (Dublin).
Taylor Co. Sergt-Maj W.
Wilson B (Mossley, Antrim).
Wilson C (Waterford).

Royal Irish Fusiliers
Killed or Died of Wounds

Burke L-Sergt WR (Gravesend).
Byrne J (Dublin).
Coxon R (Durham).
Ellis A (Leeds).
Hare Sgt H (Dublin).
Humphreys CH (Dublin).
Lucas F (Halton, Leeds).
Thompson JA (Enniskillen).
Watchorn A (Williamstown, Co. Carlow).

Wounded

Baird W (Dublin).
Barnes JW (Dublin).
Brennan FA (Dublin).
Byrne D (Dublin).
Byrne H (Lucan, Co. Dublin).
Campbell J (Dublin).
Carolan QMS T (Sittingbourne).
Conway P (Donnybrook).
Cope L-Cpl E (Dublin).
Coroner J (Dublin).
Cox L-Cpl T (London).
Craddock C (Clonmel).
Dolan Cpl M (Dublin).
Ellis A (Leeds).
Healy JE (Clare).
Healy P (Cork).
Herbert L-Cpl P (Dublin).
Kerrigan L-C M (Dublin).
Lawlor J (Dublin).
M'Alister B (Longford).
M'Nally M (Dublin).
Merry L-Cpl M (Dublin).
Nolan H (Manchester).
Nolan L-C M (Monasterevan).
O'Riordan W (Cork).
Smith RA (Dromore).
Smuller L-C M (Dublin).
Walsh RH (Dublin).
Wheatman R (Dublin).

Royal Irish Regiment
Killed or Died of Wounds

Brennan Cpl J (Gowran).
Carr M (Mulhuddart).
Cavanagh J (Glasgow).
Duffy J (St John's, NB).
Flynn W (Carrick-on-Suir).
Gamble Co. QM Sgt (Golder's Green, NW).
Treacy T (Killenaule).

Wounded

Crotty J (Newcastle, Tipperary).
Cullen E (Cashel).
Doyle P (Dublin).
Goodchild E (Waterford).
Grayson M (Thurles).
Humphries A (Taunton).
Keating J (Mulhuddart).
McGrath A-C M (Waterford).
Moulton J (Liverpool).
Murphy L-Sgt F (W'ford).
Norman J (Bedford).
Traynor MT (Dublin).
Walsh P (Mooncoin).
Walsh W (Kilkenny).

Royal Inniskilling Fusiliers
Killed or Died of Wounds

Knox FW (Wicklow).

Wounded

Ferguson H (Belfast).
Foley J (Cork).
Gerrard F (Navan).
Hawkins Sergt F (Derry).
Maguire L-C P (C Ins).
M'Alonen Sgt J (Belfast).

Royal Irish Fusiliers
Killed or Died of Wounds

Brosnan Sgt-Maj P (Dublin).
Cullen J (Belfast).

Wounded

Beatty R (Killigar, Co. Leitrim).
Burnison J (Lurgan).
Carroll E (Manchester).
Clarke J (Newbliss).
Padmore L-Cpl B (Saltley).
Somerville G (Lurgan).

Leinster Regiment
Killed

Moore C (Dublin).

Wounded

Callaghan J (Trim).
Dardas H (Navan).
Fitzgerald Cpl R (Glossop).

Royal Field Artillery
Killed

Cartlidge Gnr R (Hanley).

Wounded

Barnes Dvr C (Choulton).
Pepper Bdr E (Ashton-under-Lyne).
Toole Gnr T (Dublin).

Leicestershire Regiment
Wounded

Bannister T (Leicester).
Scothey 2896 W.

Royal Engineers
Wounded

Cripps Spr RF (Ballincollig, Co. Cork).
Moore Spr L (Long Eaton).
Westwood Spr T (Walsall).
Wooley Spr F (Brownhills).

Connaught Rangers

Wounded

Meenehan Cpl A (Ballinrobe).

Army Service Corps

Killed or Died of Wounds

Cobbold AE (Bedford).
Harrison T (Salford).
Mulvey JA (Wildstone).

Wounded

Davies CF (Manchester).

Royal Army Medical Corps

Wounded

Devey AA (Wolverhampton).
Fewkes Sgt HC (Nottingham).
Mills Cpl C (Dublin Enlt).

Lancers

Killed or Died of Wounds

Blundell J (Appley B'ge).
Headland Sergt JDA (Finsbury).
Hughes F (Kingston).
Leen P (Limerick).
Newland A (Millwall E).
Osborne L-C C (Brighton).
Scarlett A (Battersea).
Shepherd Sgt (Bristol).
Walker W (Glasgow).

Wounded

Addis W (Pengam).
Austin F (Burton-on-Trent).
Bonser TB (London, SW).
Chapman WE (Leeds).
Coote Sgt C (Colchester).
De Bank A (Faringdon).
Fitch H (Rotherhithe, SE).
Gibbs I (Stantonbury).
Gibson Sh-Smith WJ (Exeter).
Goodliffe Sgt F (York).
Hawdon PCW (Loughton).
Huxley Cpl H (Woking).
King R (New Barnet).
Knight L-Cpl S (New Barnet).
Liddon GW (Dublin).
Murphy L-Cpl PS (Dublin).
Peers A (Wigan).

Hussars

Killed or Died of Wounds

Cordwell 24522 HJ.
Mulraney W (Dublin).
O'Gorman SH.
Smith C (Kilburn, NW).
Smith AC (Hexbridge).
Walton L-Cpl AJ (Reading).

Wounded

Hall L-C CJ (Windsor).
Jolliffe Sgt R (Londonderry).
M'Donnell S (Dublin).
Mullally J (Claremorris).
Pinner Act L-Cpl T (Northwood, Hanley).
Tait Act Cpl PB (Edinburgh).
Tudbury T (Heb-on-Tyne).

Yeomanry

Killed or Died of Wounds

James—(Pembroke).
James M (Caeran).
Llewellyn G (Neyland).

Wounded

Asbury H (Hope, Flint).
Blenkinship A (Carlisle).
Charlton JG (Carlisle).
Jones I (Swansea).
Lees E (Stockport).
Partington JR (Carlisle).
Richards RD (Oswestry).
Regan J (Bootle).
Williamson L-Clp PW (Cockermouth).

2nd King Edward's Horse

Killed

Hewitt Cpl H (Stoke-Devonport).

Wounded

Browne EFL (Maidenhead).
D'Alroy, L-Cpl F.
Milton Sgt AC (Kensington, W).
Presnall FJ (S Norwood).
Wood Cpl R (London).

Naval List

Killed

Glaister Robt FRA, RNR, 1907, EA.

Wounded

Bowle Neil, Stoker, RNR, 8659, S.
Herbert Pickering, Fireman, Mercantile Marine.
Miller George Thomas, Pte, RMLI, Ply S 1125.

Severely Wounded

Sugden Joshua, Pte, RMLI, Ply S 1295.

Royal Irish Constabulary

Killed

County	*Locality of casualty*	*Name*	*Rank*	*Age. Years*	*Period of Service Y*	*M*
Meath	Ashbourne	Gray, Alexander	County Inspector	57	33	5
Meath	Ashbourne	Smyth, Harry	District Inspector	41	16	9
Meath	Ashbourne	Shanagher, John	Sergeant	48	25	3
Meath	Ashbourne	Young, John	Sergeant	42	19	5
Meath	Ashbourne	Hickey, James	Constable	49	25	7
Meath	Ashbourne	Gormley, James	Constable	25	3	7
Meath	Ashbourne	McHale, Richard	Constable	22	3	2
Meath	Ashbourne	Cleary, James	Constable	28	6	9
Galway (WR)	Carnmore	Whelan, Patrick	Constable	34	8	6
Tipperary (SR)	Lisvernane	Rourke, Thomas F	Sergeant	42	22	3
Tipperary (SR)	Lisvernane	Hurley, John	Constable	23	3	1
Louth	Castlebellingham	McGee, Charles	Constable	23	3	5
Cork (ER)	Coole, Lower	Rowe, William N	Head Constable	49	28	7
Belfast	Dublin City	*Millar, Christopher	Constable	29	8	3

*Constable Millar was in Dublin at the School of Instruction for non-commissioned officers at Portobello Barracks. He took part with the military in the attack on the South Dublin Union.

Wounded

County	*Locality of casualty*	*Name*	*Rank*	*Age. Years*	*Period of Service Y*	*M*
Meath	Ashbourne	Scully, Patrick J	Sergeant	48	30	6
Meath	Ashbourne	Glennon, Francis P	Constable	37	15	7
Meath	Ashbourne	Murtagh, Peter	Constable	41	20	10
Meath	Ashbourne	Leckey, Henry	Constable	36	13	4
Meath	Ashbourne	Johns, William E	Constable	20	1	7
Meath	Ashbourne	Cunningham, Patrick	Constable	30	8	7
Meath	Ashbourne	Duggan, Michael J	Constable	19	1	3
Meath	Ashbourne	Finan, Tim	Constable	28	1	11
Meath	Ashbourne	Drinan, Patrick	Constable	26	3	5
Meath	Ashbourne	McGann, Henry	Constable	23	1	0
Meath	Ashbourne	Murphy, John	Constable	26	2	7
Meath	Ashbourne	Kenny, Francis	Constable	23	5	4
Meath	Ashbourne	McKeon, Patrick	Constable	24	4	6
Meath	Ashbourne	Mulvihill, Martin	Constable	31	9	4
Meath	Ashbourne	Conneely, Patrick	Constable	30	6	0
Dublin	Donabate	Thorpe, Joseph G	Constable	40	20	3
Galway (ER)	Oranmore	Ginty, Joseph	Constable	44	21	4
Galway (WR)	Carnmore	Hamilton, Hugh	Constable	31	9	10
Galway (WR)	Clarenbridge	Manning, David	Constable	32	10	0
Galway (WR)	Dublin City	*Meany, Martin	Constable	26	4	2
Kerry	Firies	Cleary, Michael	Constable	23	2	7
Kerry	Firies	McLoughlin, Thomas	Constable	23	3	8
Wexford	Enniscorthy	Grace, Patrick	Constable	26	6	9

*Constable Meany was in Dublin at the School of Instruction for NCO's at Portobello Barracks. He took part with the military in the attack on the South Dublin Union.

Dublin Metropolitan Police Force

Killed

Constable James O'Brien, 168 B, who was on duty at the Cork Hill entrance to Upper Castle Yard, was shot through the head between 11 a.m. and 12 a.m. by a volunteer who rode up to the gate on a bicycle. The body was removed to Castle Hospital. He was about 45 years of age, and had over 21 years' service.

Constable Michael Lahiff, 125 B, who was on duty at Stephen's Green, West, was shot by the rebels at about 12 noon on 24th April. He was hit three times before he collapsed. He was brought to the Meath Hospital, where he died shortly after admission. He was 28 years of age, and had five years' service.

Constable William Frith, 174 C, was shot dead by a bullet through the head in a bedroom of Store street Police Station on 27th April. He was 37 years of age, and had over 17 years' service.

Wounded

Constable Edward Dunphy, 35 C, was taken prisoner by the Sinn Fein Volunteers in the vicinity of Sackville street on the 24th April, and brought into the GP Office. He was put out of the place on the 28th April, and whilst making his escape received a bullet in the back of the left hand, and pellets on the left cheek and forehead. The bullet was extracted in Jervis street Hospital. He was on sick report from the injuries for 45 days. He is 44 years of age, and has over 23 years' service.

Constable Thomas Donohoe, 30 D, while passing on duty through Christchurch place between 12 noon and 1 p.m., 24th April, received a gunshot wound on the left forearm. He was medically treated at Bridewell Station, and was on sick report from his injuries for 27 days. He is 47 years of age, and has over 25 years' service.

Constable Charles Hales, 119 D, while passing on duty along Church street between 2 p.m. and 3 p.m., 24th April, was stopped by rebels, one of whom fired at him with a revolver and wounded him slightly on the back of the left hand. He was then arrested by rebels and brought into the Four Courts, where one of them dressed his hand. He was released shortly after, and was nothing the worse for his slight injury. He is 54 years of age, and has 36 years' service.

Constable Patrick J Myles, 99 E, while on duty at Portobello Bridge on 24th April had his left forearm shattered by a bullet. He was brought to City of Dublin Hospital, where he remained till 31st May. He was unable to resume duty till 20th September. He is 35 years of age, and has over 12 years' service.

Station Sergeant John Hughes, 6 D, while off duty in plain clothes returning to Green street Barracks, was stopped, searched, and arrested by rebels at Stephen's Green, West, between 12 midnight and 1 a.m., 25th April, and was kept in Stephen's Green Park till about 9 a.m. same date, when he was released by Countess Markievicz. When endeavouring to leave the park his right forearm was shattered by a gunshot fired by one of the rebels entrenched there. He remained lying in the park for about five hours, when he was discovered by Mr Carney, Superintendent of Board of Works, who had him removed in the Corporation Ambulance to Mercer's Hospital. He had to undergo two operations for the wound, and remained a patient until 22nd July, but was unable to resume duty until 6th January, 1917. He is 48 years of age, and has over 27 years' service.

Constable John McGrath, 188 B, while on duty keeping watch from a window in College Barrack between 1 p.m. and 2 p.m., 26th April, in company with Corporal Henry Bushe, Military Provost Staff, was shot through the lower part of the body by a rifle bullet, fired from the D'Olier street direction. He was under treatment in St Vincent's Hospital till 22nd July, and in Stillorgan Convalescent Home till 4th November. On 14th January, 1917, he was discharged from the force on pension as unfit for further duty owing to the injuries he had received. He is 32 years of age, and had over 12 years' service.

Constable Cuthbert O'Connell, 45 E, while on duty in uniform with a military search party at Tritonville road, received a bullet wound in the calf of the left leg on 2nd May. He was brought to the City of Dublin Hospital, where he remained till 29th May. He resumed duty on 1st July, and is now quite well. He is 34 years of age, and has over 13 years' service.

'The GR's'

In the 1st (Dublin) Battalion Associated Volunteer Training Corps the following casualties occurred between 24th and 26th April, 1916:

Killed, or Died of Wounds

Name	*Rank*	*Dependents*
FH Browning	Sub Commandant	Widow and one son
Thos Harborne	Pte (Motor Cyclist)	Widow and four children
John H Gibbs	Private	Widow
Reginald F Clery	Lance Corporal	Unmarried
Joseph Hosford	Private	Widow and one child

Wounded

Name	*Rank*	*Dependents*
LH Ford	Sergt (severely)	Wife and children
WJ Horne	Pl Com (severely)	Wife and two children
H Green	Pte (severely)	Wife
J Redding	Co. Sgt Maj	Wife and six children
W Scott	Private	Wife
George May	Corporal	Wife and four children
RA Anderson	Pl Com (slightly)	No dependents

250 Bodies Interred at Glasnevin Cemetery

The following list gives the names of identified persons interred at Glasnevin Cemetery, and whose deaths occurred as a result of bullet or gunshot wounds arising out of the rebellion. The list includes several persons who were trampled to death by crowds in the streets. Two hundred and fifty bodies buried in this cemetery between Easter and 11th July were those of persons whose deaths were directly attributable to the rising:

Adams, J, (38), 109 Cork street.
Allen, Bridget, (16), 27 Arran quay.
Allen, T, (30), 19½ Monck place.
Andrews, J, (14), 8 Stephen's place, Mount street.
Armstrong, JH, (43), 2 Great Longford street.
Barnbrick, Alice, (44), 8 Willet place.
Barry, Bridget, (36), 44 Lower Dominick street.
Barter, W, (23), 14 Elliott place.
Blayney, J, (65), 18 First avenue, Seville place.
Brennan, J, (45), 6 Great Longford street.
Brennan, M, (45), 85 Capel street.
Brunell, Julia, (20), 2 Grattan street.
Brunswick, Mary, (15), 57 Lower Wellington street.
Butler, R, (45), 10 Woodgate street, London.
Byrne, E, 30 Corporation Buildings, Foley street.
Byrne, J, (60), 68 Shelbourne road.
Byrne, J, 31 Lower Stephen street.
Byrne, P, (42), 1 O'Brien's place, Co. Dublin.
Caffrey, Christina, (20), 27 Corporation Buildings.
Caldwell, Anne Jane, (24), 43 Corporation Buildings.
Casey, J, (33), 55a Townsend street.
Cashman, J, Rosemount, Dundrum.
Cathcart, C, (9), 28 Charlemont street.
Clarke, P, (40), 65 Cork street.
Clarke, R, (73), 61 Mespil road.
Coade, JJ, (19), 28 Upper Mount Pleasant avenue.
Coghlan, Thos, 155 North strand.
Cole, Mary Anne, (37), 14 Upper Gloucester street.
Condon, Julia, (44), 56 Summerhill.
Connolly, J, (33), 108 Philipsburgh avenue.
Connolly, Mary, (23), 4 North Richmond street.
Connolly, W, (37), 27 Usher's quay.
Connor, C, (21), 31 Strandville avenue.
Corbin, Mr, Jervis street Hospital.
Corrigan, C, North Frederick street.
Corrigan, Mary Anne, (38), 8 Engine Alley, Moore lane.
Cosgrave, E, (43), 65 Lower Dominick street.
Costello, J, (32), 9 Wall square.
Costello, Jane, (24), 113 Seville place.
Costello, Mr, Kingstown.
Courtney, C, 24 York street.
Coyle, H, (29), 32 Leinster avenue.
Crawford, Julia, (20), 7 Irvine Crescent.
Creevan, J, St Aloysius road.
Cromien, J, (23), 13 Fingal place.
Cunningham, Mary, (62), 7 Chancery street.
Curley, F, (51), 16 Green street.
Daly, Margaret, (60), 57 Queen street.
Dargan, D, (58), 12 Henrietta street.
Davis, Catherine, (59), 6 Stratford row, Summerhill.
Derrick, P, (24), 22 Eustace street.
Dickson, T, (31), 12 Harrington street, newspaper editor, shot by military in Portobello Barracks.
Dignan, P, (51), 22 Lower Ormond quay.
Dillon, R, (65), 8 Moore street.
Donnelly, J, (44), 6 Newfoundland street.
Donnelly, T, (52), 35 North Cumberland street.
Donoghue, J, (19), 97 Marlborough street.
Donohue, TD, (22), 4 North Brunswick street.
Doyle, D, (46), 27 Upper Liffey street.
Doyle, J, (18), 25 Summerhill.
Doyle, J, (36), 16 Moore street.

Doyle, M, (16), 7 Whitefriar street.
Doyle, SP, (50), 27 Wellington quay.
Doyle, T, (50), 12 Upper Mercer street.
Dunlea, R, (35), 83 Marlborough street.
Dunne, E, (39), 91 North King street.
Dunne, M, (28), 36 Wexford street.
Dunphy, J, Adelaide Hospital.
Dwan, J, (24), 1 Lower Gardiner street.
Ennis, E, (31), 5 Dromard avenue, Sandymount.
Ennis, G, (50), 174 North King street.
Fahey, P, (23), 18 Usher's Island.
Farrell, J, (48), 20 City Quay.
Farrelly, J, (35), 3 Monks' Cottages, Lower Sheriff street.
Fennell, P, (33), 13 Portobello road.
Ferris, Arthur, (35), 22 Lower Kevin street.
Fetherstone, P, (12), 1 Long lane, Dorset street.
Finegan, W, 48 Marlborough street.
Finnegan, J, (40), 27 North King street.
Foran, T, (28), 22 Patrick street.
Foster, JF, (2 years 10 months), 18 Manor place, Dublin.
Fox, Wm, 6 Holycross road.
Fraser, J, 68 Caledon road.
Friel, P, (59), 17 St Joseph Villas, Strand street.
Geraghty, J, (21), 16 Middle Gardiner street.
Geraghty, P, (39), 64 Lower Dominick street.
Gibney, J, (5½), 16 Henrietta place.
Glaister, R, (55), Ryicote, Silloth, Cumberland (naval petty officer).
Glennon, D, (65), 99 Upper Church street.
Glynn, M, (57), 24 C Corporation Buildings.
Goulding, A, (45), 18 Upper Buckingham street.
Hanratty, Elizabeth, (30), 39 Moore street.
Harris, P, (35), 23 Marlborough place.
Hayes, M, (45), 8 Christchurch place.
Healy, J, (14½), 188 Phibsborough road.
Healy, JP, (33), 143 Church street.
Heavey, W, (32), 57 Moore street.
Heeney, RP, (40), 14 North Great George's street.
Higgins, Christopher, (26), 40 Jervis street.
Hoey—Ryder's row.
Hoey, P, (25), 27 North King street.
Hogan, J, (28), 31 Upper Rutland street.
Howard, JB, (17), 26 Temple Cottages, Broadstone.
Hughes, M, (34), 172 North King street.
Hyland, CH, (29), 3 Percy place.
Ivors, P, 15 Cumberland street.
Jessop, James, (12), 3 Upper Gloucester street.
Johnston—18 Denzille street.
Jordan—Holles street Hospital.
Kavanagh, E, (32), 30 Oxford road, Ranelagh.
Kane, Jane, (40), 109 Amiens street.
Kavanagh—(15), 4 North King street.
Keegan, F, (60), 29 Upper Ormond quay.
Kelly, D, Jervis street Hospital.
Kelly, James, (18) 205 Phibsborough road.
Kelly, L, (50), 1 Lower Clanbrassil street.
Keogh, M, Holles street Hospital.
Knowles, H, (40), 6 East Essex street.
Lahiff, M, (28), Dublin Metropolitan Police Barracks, Great Brunswick street.
Lawless, PJ, (21), 27 North King street.
Lawlor, C, (46), 6 Halston street.
Leahy, M, (62), 3 Inns quay.
Lennon, Kate, (55), 5 Upper Gloucester place.
Lennon, Mary, (64), 43 Corporation Buildings.
Long, Samuel, (44), 25 Great Clarence street.
Macken, P, (37), 13 Nassau place.
Maguire, W, (40), 92 Marlborough street.
Mallon, J, (29), 96 Upper Dorset street.
Manning, PP, (25), 4 Broadstone Avenue.
Martin, P, (42), 22 Lower Gardiner street.
M'Cabe, Henrietta, (48), 34 Marlborough street.
M'Cartney, J, (36), 16 Exchange street.
M'Cormack, J, Baldoyle.
McCormick, J, (40), 44B Corporation Buildings.
McDowell, W, (49), 10 Merchant's quay.
McElvery, J, (56), 15 Verschoyle place.
M'Galey, E, (57), 4 Lower Bridge street.
M'Kane, Bridget, (16), 10 Henry place.
M'Killop, M, (33), 22 Lower Gardiner street.
McLoughlin, R, (62), 28 John street, Blackpitts.
M'Manus, P, (61), 12 Moore street.
Meagher, J, (49), 12 Langrishe place.
Meegan, J, (53), 90 Lower Gardiner street.
Meron or Merna, Julia, (60), 32 Great Charles street.
Molcady, T, Irvine place, Fairview.
Moore, J, (29), 15 Little Britain street.
Morris, Mary, (27), 31 Upper Mount street.
Moy, WE, Richmond Hospital.
Mullen, W, (9), 8 Moore place.
Murphy, Catherine, (68), 63 Railway street.
Murphy, E, (32), 9 Upper Pembroke street.
Murphy, J, (60), 42 Henry street.
Murray, DJ, (28), 35 Lower Mount Pleasant avenue.
Murray, J, (40), 28 Empress terrace.
Neal, John, The Castle Yard.
Nealon, P, (62), 88 Bridge street.
Neill, Wm, (16), 93 Church street.
Nolan, Margaret, (26), 6 Lower Wellington street.
Nunan, M, (34), 174 North King street.
O'Callaghan, J, Iveagh House.
O'Carroll, R, (40), 49 Cuffe street.
O'Connor, Ellen, (50), South Union Workhouse.
O'Donoghue, J, (42), 31 Cabra park.
O'Duffy, J, (82), 54 Rutland square.
O'Grady, E, (25), 2 Lower Sheriff street.
O'Grady, P, (45), Daisy Market.
O'Neill, W, (16), 93 Church street.
O'Rahilly, MJ, (The) (40), 14 Herbert park.
O'Reilly, J, (28), 12 Lower Gardiner street.
O'Reilly, TJ, (21), 43 Geraldine street.
Pentony, T, (48), 34 North Cumberland street.
Pierce, G, (20), 12 South Earl street.
Power, J, (60), 9 Buckingham place.
Purcell, Christina, (30), 37 Wentworth place.
Quinn, J, (42), South Union Workhouse.
Quirke, Elizabeth, (22), 11 Liffey street.
Redmond, C, (21), 32 Hanover street East.
Redmond, Mary, (16), 8 Mary's Abbey.
Reilly, J, (51), 75 Capel street.
Ryan, F, (18), 3 High street.
Ryan, P, (13½), 2 Sitric place.
Scott, WE, (8), 16 Irvine crescent.
Sheehy-Skeffington, FCJ, (37), journalist, 11 Grosvenor place, shot by military in Portobello Barracks.
Shiels, F, (27), 45 Jervis street.
Simpson, VP, (23), 6 Enniskerry road.
Smyth, Elizabeth, (19), 5 Sandwith place.
Spellman, T, (68), 62 Arbour Hill.
Stephenson, P, (50), 76 Lower Gloucester street.
Stillman, J, (35), 8 Leitrim place.
Taaffe, Rosanna, (41), 26 Corporation street.

Tierney, P, 123 Dorset street.
Timmons, May, 4 Harmony row.
Traynor, JJ, (18), 3 Shannon terrace, Kilmainham.
Trevor, P, Ryder's row.
Veale, Margaret, M, (13), 103 Haddington road.
Walsh, E, (43), 8 Lower Dominick street.
Walsh, J, (34), 172 North King street.
Walsh, JJ, (19), 14 Upper Kevin street.
Walsh, P, (12), 10 Hackett's court.
Walsh, P, (27), 43 Manor place.
Watson, W, Swift's row.
Watters, Very Rev FJ, DD, SM, (66), 96 Lower Leeson street.
Wenny, Mrs, (63), 18 Upper Buckingham street.
West, W, (52), 16 Belvedere place.
Whelan, C, (15), 30 North Great George's street.
Whelan, D, 122 Parnell street.
Whelan, P, (23) 25 Pembroke Cottages, Ringsend.
Whelan, Sarah, (28), 16 Great Clarence street.

The bodies of about twenty persons whose identity was not clearly established were also interred at Glasnevin. These were brought from Holles street, Richmond, Jervis street, Mater and Mercer's Hospitals, Trinity College, the Castle Yard, South Dublin Union, and Daisy Market.

---

24 in Mount Jerome Cemetery

The following is the list of remains brought to Mount Jerome Cemetery for interment as a result of the rebellion:

Ballantyne, John, (79), 40 Merrion square.
Bond, Henry, (33), 38 South Frederick street.
Cowley, Thos, K, (65), 93 Haddington road and Christian Union Buildings.
Dockeray, Cecil, E, (44), 4 Warwick terrace, Leeson park.
Frith, Wm, (174C, DMP), (32), Store street Police Station.
Fryday, Private Neville, N, (75th Batt Canadian Regiment), (16½), Mercer's Hospital.
Gibbs, John, H, Vet Corps, (55), 58 Belgrave square, Rathmines.
Hall, Robert, C, (29½), 3 Serpentine avenue.
Halliday, Wm, Jas, (23), near Herberton Bridge.
Hayter, Charles, (77), Grand Canal street Bridge.
Jozé, Thos, M, (60), Arran quay.
Macnamara, John, H, (12½), York street.
McLoughlin, James, (52).
Myers, Miss Annie, (54), 13 North Earl street.
Neil, James, C, (29), 16 Fitzroy avenue.
Neil, Mary, (40), Aungier street.
Ramsay, Lieutenant Alan, L, (25), Royal Irish Regiment.
Rice, Wm, John, (35), Glenholme, Sandford terrace.
Sainsbury, George, P, (9½), 54 South Circular road.
Stodart, Holden, (33), Winona, Victoria Villas, Blackrock.
Vantreen, Mrs Prudence, (70), 22 Werburgh street.
Warbrook, Miss Eleanor, (15), 7 Fumbally's lane.
Wilkinson, Miss Elizabeth, (60), 4 Woodstock Gardens, Ranelagh.
Wilson, David, 5852, 3rd RIR, Adelaide Hospital.

---

49 in Dean's Grange Cemetery

The following is the list of known persons whose deaths resulted from bullet or gunshot wounds, and whose remains were interred in Dean's Grange Cemetery:

Blissett, Private JH, Sherwood Foresters.
Brown, Sec-Lt, MB, Sherwood Foresters.
Browning, Francis, Henry, (47), 17 Herbert park, Donnybrook.
Byrne, Private Edward, Sherwood Foresters.
Carroll, James, Joseph, (24), the Municipal Buildings, Kingstown.
Cunningham, Andrew, (24), 77 Park View, Pigeon House road, Dublin.
Dietrichsen, Capt Frederick, Christian, Sherwood Foresters, 5 Weston terrace, Nottingham.
Doyle, John, (20), 104 Ringsend road.
Elles, Private J, Scots Guards.
Ellis, Private A, Royal Dublin Fusiliers.
Farmsworth, Private A, Sherwood Foresters.
Flynn, John, (63), Dodder View.
Gregg, Wm, (64), 2 Simpson's lane, Irishtown.
Hickey, Christopher, (16), 168 North King street.
Hickey, Thomas, (38), 168 North King street.
Hogan, Jeremiah, (26), 9 Summerhill.
Keely, John, (30), Ballyboden, shot in the Post Office.
Kelly, Mary, (12), 128 Townsend street.
McCarthy John (54) Island Bridge Barracks
McGuinness, Margaret, (50), Pembroke Cottages, Ballsbridge.
McIntyre, Patrick, (38), newspaper editor, 21 Fownes street, Dublin, shot by military in Portobello Barracks.
O'Flaherty, Joseph, Northumberland road.
Saunders, Private Charles, South Staffordshire Regiment.
Stewart, Bridget, (11), 3 Pembroke place, Ballsbridge.
Synnot, George, (58), 98 Haddington road.
Waters, Richard, (49), 'The Recess', Monkstown.

The bodies of the following, whose addresses are not recorded, were brought from Sir Patrick Dun's Hospital for interment:

Joseph Byrne
Joseph Clarke
John Costello
Wm Carrick
John Loughlin
Joseph Maguire
Annie Walsh
David Swords
Christopher Woodcock

From St Vincent's Hospital
John Keynon, Joseph Shergoing

Twelve unknown persons were also buried. These bodies came from St Vincent's, Sir Patrick Dun's, Royal City of Dublin and the Mater Hospitals.

Rebels Killed while Fighting

A card issued by the Irish National Aid and Volunteers' Dependents' Fund, bearing the imprint of the Gaelic Press, Dublin, gave, in addition to a list of those executed, the names of the following, as 'men who were killed whilst fighting for Ireland during Easter Week, 1916':

Adams John
Allen Thomas
Burke Frank
Byrne Andrew
Byrne James
Byrne Joseph
Carrigan Charles
Clarke Philip
Connolly Sean
Corcoran James
Costello John
Coyle Harry
Crinigan John
Cromean John
Darcy Charles
Darcy Peter
Donelan Brendan
Doyle Patrick
Dwan John
Ennis Edward

Farrell Patrick
Fox James
Geoghegan George
Healy John
Howard Sean
Hurley John
Kealy John
Keating Con
Keily John
Kent Richard
Keogh Gerald
Macken Francis
Macken Peter
Malone Michael
Manning Peter
McCormack J
M'Dowell William
Murphy D
Murphy Richard
Murray D

O'Carroll Richard
O'Flanagan Patrick
O'Grady John
O'Rahilly The
O'Reilly J
O'Reilly Richard
O'Reilly Thomas
Owens J
Quinn James
Rafferty Thomas
Reynolds George
Ryan Frederick
Sheehan Domhnall
Sheehy Patrick
Traynor John
Walsh Edward
Walsh Philip
Weafer Thomas
Whelan Patrick
Wilson Peter

PUNISHMENT OF THE REBELS
Fifteen Men Executed

Sir John Maxwell's Statement

The following announcement was issued at the Irish Headquarters Command on Thursday, 11th May:

In view of the gravity of the rebellion and its connection with German intrigue and propaganda, and in view of the great loss of life and destruction of property resulting therefrom, the General Officer Commanding-in-Chief has found it imperative to inflict the most severe sentences on the known organisers of this detestable rising and on those Commanders who took an active part in the actual fighting which occurred. It is hoped that these examples will be sufficient to act as a deterrent to intriguers, and to bring home to them that the murder of His Majesty's liege subjects, or other acts calculated to imperil the safety of the Realm will not be tolerated.

The Prime Minister's Statement

With the execution on Friday, 12th May, of James Connolly and John McDermott, the last of the seven men who signed the declaration of the Irish Republic on Easter Monday paid the death penalty. In the House of Commons the previous night Mr Dillon made a remarkable speech, in which he demanded the cessation of the executions, but the Prime Minister, while expressing the hope that it would not be necessary to carry out the full punishment in many other cases, said there were two men who would have to endure the extreme penalty. The following morning it was announced that Connolly and McDermott had been executed.

The total number of rebels executed was fifteen. They were:

PH Pearse
Thomas MacDonagh
Joseph Plunkett
Edmund Kent
Thos J Clarke
Jas Connolly
John McDermott

The above were the seven men who signed the declaration. The others who were executed for taking a prominent part in the rebellion were:

Edward Daly
Wm Pearse
Cornelius Colbert
JJ Heuston
Michael O'Hanrahan
John McBride
Michael Mallin

For the murder of Head Constable Rowe at Fermoy on 2nd May

Thomas Kent

was executed on 9th May at Cork.

Three Shot on Wednesday, 3rd May

The following was officially communicated from the Command Headquarters, Parkgate, Dublin on Wednesday morning, 3rd May:

Three signatories of the notice proclaiming the Irish Republic,

PH Pearse, T MacDonagh and TJ Clarke

have been tried by Field General Courts-martial and sentenced to death. The sentence having been duly confirmed, the three above-mentioned men were shot this morning.

Four Shot on Thursday, 4th May

It was officially announced on Thursday, 4th May, that four more rebel leaders had been convicted by court-martial and sentenced to death. They were:

Joseph Plunkett
Edward Daly
Michael O'Hanrahan
William Pearse

The above were shot that morning, after confirmation of the sentences by the General Officer Commanding-in-Chief:

The following were convicted and sentenced to death, but the sentences commuted by the General Officer Commanding-in-Chief to 10 years' penal servitude:

Thomas Bevan
Thomas Walsh
Finian Lynch
Michael Mervyn
Dennis O'Callaghan
PE Sweeney
Patrick McNestry
Peter Clancy
William Tobin
George Irvine
John Doherty
JJ Walsh
James Melinn
JJ Reid
John Williams

Convicted and sentenced to death, but commuted to eight years' penal servitude by the General Officer Commanding-in-Chief:

John M'Garry

Convicted and sentenced to ten years' penal servitude, and sentence confirmed by the General Officer Commanding-in-Chief:

Francis Fahy, Richard Davys

One Shot on Friday, 5th May

The following was officially communicated from the Irish Headquarters on Friday, 5th May:

Trials by court-martial of rebels proceeded yesterday, and 36 men were tried. Confirmation has only taken place in three cases—namely, those of Thomas Hunter, John McBride, and William Cosgrave.

All three of these men were sentenced to death, but the General Officer Commanding-in-Chief commuted the death sentence to penal servitude for life in the case of Hunter and Cosgrave.

The death sentence on John McBride was carried out this morning.

Photo by] [*Keogh Bros.*
WILLIAM PEARSE, executed on 4th May.

Photo by] [*Keogh Bros,*
M. O'HANRAHAN, executed on 4th May.

Photo by] [*Keogh Bros.*
EDWARD DALY, executed on 4th May.

Photo by] [*Keogh Bros,*
JOHN MacBRIDE, executed on 5th May.

The following men were tried on the 2nd May:
Edward Duggan, Pierce Beasley, and
Joseph Maguinness.

These men were each sentenced to three years' penal servitude, and the sentence was confirmed by the General Officer Commanding-in-Chief.

Countess Markievicz Gets Life Sentence on Saturday, 6th May

The following results of trial by Field General Court-martial were officially announced on Saturday, 6th May:

Sentenced to death, but commuted to penal servitude for life by the General Officer Commanding-in-Chief:

Constance Georgina Markievicz,
Henry O'Hanrahan

Sentenced to death—commuted to ten years' penal servitude:

George Plunkett, John Plunkett

Sentenced to death—commuted to five years' penal servitude:

Philip B Cosgrave

Sentenced to death—commuted to three years' penal servitude:

W Meehan, R Kelly, W Wilson, J Clarke, J Marks,
J Brennan, P Wilson, F Brooks, R Coleman,
T Peppard, J Norton, J Byrne, T O'Kelly

Sentenced to penal servitude for twenty years—ten years remitted:

James T Hughes

Sentenced to penal servitude for ten years—duly confirmed:

Peter Doyle

Sentenced to two years' imprisonment with hard labour—duly confirmed:

J Wilson

Sentenced to two years' imprisonment with hard labour—one year remitted:

E Roach

Four Shot on Monday, 8th May

The following official communication was issued on Monday, 8th May, at the Headquarters of the Irish Command:

The following are further results of trials by Field General Court-martial:

Sentenced to death, and sentence carried out this morning:

Cornelius Colbert, Edmund Kent
Michael Mallin, JJ Heuston

All these four men took a very prominent part in the rebellion.

Sentenced to death, commuted to eight years' penal servitude:

James O'Sullivan

Sentenced to death, commuted to five years' penal servitude:

Vincent Poole, William P Corrigan.

Sentenced to death, commuted to three years' penal servitude:

John Downey	John Faulkner
James Burke	Michael Brady
James Morrissy	George Levins
Maurice Brennan	John F Cullen
Gerald Doyle	J Dorrington
Charles Bevan	W O'Dea
John O'Brien	P Kelly
Patrick Fogarty	James Dempsey

Sentenced to ten years' penal servitude, seven years remitted:

Michael Scully

Sentenced to two years: imprisonment, with hard labour, one year remitted:

J Crenigan, William Derrington

Acquitted and released:

John R Reynolds, Joseph Callaghan

Execution for Murder on 9th May

The following official communication was published on Tuesday, 9th May, at the headquarters, Queenstown:

The following results of Field General Court-martial are announced:

Thomas Kent, of Coole, near Fermoy, was sentenced to death, and the sentence duly confirmed by the General Officer Commanding-in-Chief in Ireland. The sentence was carried out this morning.

William Kent, of Coole, near Fermoy, was acquitted.

Two Life Sentences on 11th May

The following results of trials by Field General Court-martial were announced at the Headquarters, Irish Command, Dublin, on Thursday, 11th May:

Sentenced to death, and sentence commuted to penal servitude by the General Officer Commanding-in-Chief:

Edward de Valera, penal servitude for life.

John McArdle, three years
C O'Donovan, five years
John Shouldice, five years
Thomas Ashe, penal servitude for life
Frank Lawless, ten years
James Lawless, ten years.

Sentenced to penal servitude and confirmed by the General Officer Commanding-in-Chief:

Richard Hayes, twenty years
Henry James Boland, ten years (five years remitted)
Gerald Crofts, ten years (five years remitted)
Frank Drennan, twenty years (ten years remitted)

Sentenced to imprisonment with hard labour:
Charles O'Neill, one year.

The trials for the murder of Head Constable Rowe

Photo by] [*Keogh Bros.*
CORNELIUS COLBERT, executed on 8th May.

Photo by] [*Keogh Bros.*
J. J. HEUSTON, executed on 8th May.

Photo by] [*Lafayette.*
COUNTESS MARKIEVICZ, sentenced to penal servitude for life.

Photo by] [*Keogh Bros.*
HENRY O'HANRAHAN, brother of M. O'Hanrahan, sentenced to penal servitude for life.

took place at Cork on the 4th May with the following results:

Wm Kent, acquitted
Thomas Kent, found guilty and sentenced to death.

The finding and sentence were confirmed by the GOC in Chief, and the execution took place on the 9th inst.

Two Shot on Friday, 12th May

The following communiqué was issued on Friday, 12th May, from the Headquarters, Irish Command, Parkgate, Dublin:

The trial of two prominent leaders in the rebellion, whose names appeared in the proclamation issued by the so-called 'Provisional Government'—namely:

James Connolly and John McDermott,
took place on the 9th May.

Sentence of death was awarded in each case. These sentences were confirmed by the General Officer Commanding-in-Chief on the 9th May, and they were carried out this morning (May 12th).

Countrymen Sentenced on Monday, 15th

The following results of the trials by Field General Courts-martial were announced on Monday, 15th May:

Sentenced to death, and sentence commuted to penal servitude, by the General Officer Commanding-in-Chief, as shown:

Bryan Molloy, Galway—ten years.
Michael de Lacy, Enniscorthy—five years.
John R Etchingham, Enniscorthy—five years.
Robert Brennan, Enniscorthy—five years.
James Rafter, Enniscorthy—five years.
Richard F King, Enniscorthy—five years.
James Doyle, Enniscorthy—five years.

Sentenced to penal servitude, and sentence confirmed, by the General Officer Commanding-in-Chief:

James Joyce, Dublin—penal servitude for life, commuted to five years' penal servitude.
Fergus O'Connor, Dublin—ten years (seven years remitted).
Philip Joseph MacMahon, Dundalk—five years (two years remitted).
Michael Reynolds, Dundalk—five years (two years remitted).
John Quinn, Dundalk—three years.

Sentenced to imprisonment with hard labour, and confirmed by the General Officer Commanding-in-Chief:

Michael Grady, Athenry—one year.
Charles White, Athenry—one year.
John Haniffy, Athenry—one year.
Martin Bansberry, Athenry—one year.
Michael Higgins, Athenry—one year.
John Grady, Athenry—one year.
James Murray, Athenry—one year.
Thomas Barrett, Athenry—one year.
Patrick Kennedy, Athenry—one year.
Thomas Kennedy, Athenry—one year.
Murtagh Fahy, Athenry—one year.
Michael Donohue, Athenry—one year.
Patrick Weafer, Maynooth—two years (eighteen months remitted).
John Greaves, Maynooth—two years (eighteen months remitted).
Joseph Ledwich, Maynooth—two years (eighteen months remitted).

Acquitted:
John Kennedy, Athenry

Friday, May 19th

The following results of trials by Field General Court-martial were issued on Friday, 19th May, at Richmond Barracks, Dublin:

Conor McGinley, Dublin—ten years' penal servitude (seven years remitted).
John Carrick, Oranmore—five years' penal servitude (two years remitted).
Michael Hehir, Oranmore—five years' penal servitude (two years remitted).
Christopher Carrick, Oranmore—five years' penal servitude (two years remitted).
William Corcoran, Oranmore—five years' penal servitude (two years remitted).
Patrick Fury, Oranmore—five years' penal servitude (two years remitted).
Eddy Corcoran, Oranmore—five years' penal servitude (two years remitted).
Thomas Fury, Oranmore—five years' penal servitude (two years remitted).
Patrick Flanagan, Oranmore—five years' penal servitude (two years remitted).
James Loughlin, Oranmore—five years' penal servitude (two years remitted).
Michael Toole, Oranmore—five years' penal servitude (two years remitted).
Joseph Burke, Oranmore—five years' penal servitude (two years remitted).
Joseph Howley, Oranmore—five years' penal servitude (two years remitted).
Another Thomas Fury, known as Fred, Oranmore—five years' penal servitude (two years remitted).
Timothy Brosnan, Kerry—twenty years' penal servitude (fifteen years remitted).
James Kennedy, Kerry—acquitted.
Michael Duhig, Kerry—acquitted.
John Brosnan, Kerry—acquitted.
Abel Mahony, Kerry—acquitted.
Michael McKenna, Kerry—acquitted.
Daniel O'Shea, Kerry—acquitted.
Colan O'Geary, Mayo—fifteen years' penal servitude (five years remitted).
John Tomkins, Wexford—twenty years' penal servitude (ten years remitted).

Photo by] *[Keogh Bros.*

THOMAS ASHE, sentenced to penal servitude for life.

Photo by] *[Keogh Bros.*

EDWARD DE VALERA, sentenced to penal servitude for life.

Photo by] *[Lafayette.*

THE O'RAHILLY shot dead while fighting in Henry place, opposite G.P.O.

JOHN MacNEILL, sentenced to penal servitude for life.

Monday, 22nd May

The following further results of trials by Field General Court-martial were announced on Monday 22nd May:

Sentenced to death, sentence confirmed by the General Officer Commanding-in-Chief, but commuted to penal servitude as stated:

Jeremiah C Lynch (Dublin), 10 years' penal servitude

Peter Gallighan (Wexford), 5 years' penal servitude

Sentenced to penal servitude and confirmed by the General Officer Commanding-in-Chief:

Patrick Fahy (Galway), penal servitude for life. Commuted to 10 years' penal servitude.

Thomas Desmond Fitzgerald (Dublin), 20 years' penal servitude (10 years remitted)

William Partridge (Dublin), 15 years' penal servitude (5 years remitted)

Michael Fleming, senior (Galway), 5 years' penal servitude (2 years remitted)

John Corcoran (Galway), 5 years' penal servitude (2 years remitted)

William Hussey (Galway), 5 years' penal servitude (2 years remitted).

Sentenced to imprisonment with hard labour and sentence confirmed by the General Officer Commanding-in-Chief:

Michael Fleming, junior (Galway), one year.

John MacNeill Gets Life Sentence

The trial of Mr John MacNeill, the former President of the Irish Volunteers, by court-martial commenced on Monday, 22nd May, 1916, at Richmond Barracks, Dublin. The Court consisted of thirteen officers, of whom the president was Colonel (temporary Brigadier-General) CG Blackader, DSO, ADC, Commanding the 177th Brigade. The case for the prosecution was presented by Lieutenant WC Wylie, KC, of the Officers' Training Corps, Territorial Force. Mr James Chambers, KC, and Mr Arthur Clery (instructed by Messrs Gerald Byrne and Co.) appeared for the defence of Mr MacNeill. No newspaper reporters were admitted to the Court, but a full note of the evidence was taken by a staff of police shorthand writers. The proceedings occupied three days.

The official report supplied from the Military Headquarters in Dublin on Tuesday, 30th May, was as follows:

The following result of the trial by General Court-martial is announced:

'John MacNeill convicted and sentenced to penal servitude for life. Sentence confirmed by the General Officer Commanding-in-Chief.'

Subsequently MacNeill was removed with other prisoners to Dartmoor Convict Prison.

Mr Asquith, in the House of Commons at a later date, informed Mr Ginnell that twelve charges were made against Professor MacNeill, and he was found guilty of all of them. Eight were charges of attempting to cause disaffection among the civil population in Ireland, and four were of acting in a way likely to prejudice recruiting.

Condemned Rebel's Marriage in Prison

Among the men who signed the proclamation of an Irish Republic was Joseph Plunkett. He was tried by court-martial, sentenced to death, and shot on Thursday, 4th May. The previous evening about five o'clock a young lady drove up to a jeweller's shop in Grafton street. The jeweller had put his stock away for the night, and was about to shut the shop. The lady asked for a wedding ring of any kind. She was to be married to Joseph Plunkett, who was to be shot next morning. Permission had been granted for the marriage. The jeweller went over his stock, and gave the lady a ring, and she went away. In the *Irish Times* of Friday, 5th May, there appeared the following marriage notice:

Plunkett and Gifford—May 3, 1916, at Dublin, Joseph Plunkett to Grace Gifford

It is understood that the marriage ceremony took place a short time before the execution. A sister of the lady who was married under such tragic circumstances, was the wife of Thomas Macdonagh, who was also executed.

The Telephone Exchange

One of the most remarkable and providential facts in the rebellion was the way in which the Dublin Telephone Exchange kept at work meeting military needs. The story is concerned largely with the devotion of women to their duty, continued in spite of nerve-wracking conditions, which reduced them at times to tears. Only just before the rebels entered the General Post Office the military in Dublin got a telephone call through to the Curragh, and the girl operator at the Post Office left the connection intact when she was ordered out of the building, realising fully the gravity of the occasion. Later on communication was established with the Curragh, Maryborough, and Belfast by linesmen, who connected the trunk wires, at points such as Lucan, with the Exchange by minor circuits, the regular trunk lines to the General Post Office having been cut. For the first two days groups of girl operators relieved each other, returning to their work in trepidation, but impelled to make their perilous journeys by a sense of duties devolving upon them. By Wednesday morning conditions had become too bad for them to return home, and they had to settle down in their fortress for the rest of the week, their only communication with the outside world being the slender wires.

PRISONERS DEPORTED AND RELEASED
Official Lists

Over three thousand persons were arrested in connection with the outbreak and detained for various periods at various places. The majority were transported to prisons across the Channel, and considerable numbers were released and allowed to return to Ireland after a short period of detention. An Advisory Committee was appointed by the Government, and began its sittings late in June. The Committee, which consisted of Mr Justice Sankey, Mr Justice Pim, Mr Justice Younger, Colonel Lockwood, MP, Mr J Mooney, MP, Mr McLean, MP, and Mr Baldwin, held numerous sittings, at which prisoners were allowed to state their case, and on Wednesday, 12th July, Mr Herbert Samuel (Home Secretary) announced in the House of Commons that the Committee had arrived at the opinion that a large number of men who took part in the rebellion were successfully kept in ignorance by their leaders, and thought they were being called up for a route march on Easter Monday. On Thursday, 27th July, Mr Samuel intimated that the cases of 1,200 or 1,300 prisoners had been considered, and 860 men and two women recommended for release.

Release of Interned Men

From then onwards a constant agitation was maintained by the leaders of the Irish Nationalist Party in Parliament and elsewhere for the release of the interned men. When Mr Lloyd George made his first appearance as Prime Minister in the House of Commons on Tuesday, 19th December, Mr John Redmond appealed to him 'as a Christmas gift to the Irish people' to release the 500 or 600 prisoners then in confinement. On Thursday, 21st, Mr Duke, the Chief Secretary, intimated that the Government had agreed to the release of the men.

The prisoners at Frongoch Camp were released at 6 p.m. on Friday, 22nd December. One hundred and thirty of them landed at Kingstown by the mail packet from Holyhead on Saturday morning. Sixty-three of these travelled by the mail train which enabled them to proceed by the Great Southern and Western Railway to the South, and by the Midland Great Western to the West of Ireland. A tram arriving in Westland row at 7.40 landed sixty-seven of the liberated men in the city. They carried their personal belongings in small bags on their shoulders. The men formed into line and marched along Great Brunswick street into Sackville street. Many of them proceeded to the Broadstone station, and took train for the West. There was nothing in the shape of a demonstration of welcome, and everything passed off quietly.

Forty of the released prisoners arrived at the North Wall on Saturday morning at 6.30 by one of the London and North Western Co.'s cargo boats. There were also aboard a large number of soldiers and munitions workers coming home for the holidays. As they were recognised by their friends they were cordially greeted, but nothing in the nature of a demonstration occurred, and there was a small force of police present. The prisoners, most of them wearing 'Sinn Fein' badges, marched along the quays in military formation, accompanied by their friends. Their progress went almost unnoticed as only a few persons were about in the vicinity of O'Connell Bridge. They quietly dispersed into groups, and made their way homewards. When questioned as to their treatment at Frongoch they stated that they had no complaints to make, and were thoroughly satisfied in that regard.

On Sunday (Christmas Eve) some 130 released prisoners arrived at Westland row by the 7.40 a.m. train from Kingstown, having come across by the mail steamer from Holyhead. Upwards of 300 men from Frongoch Camp came by steamer to the North Wall. On Christmas morning twenty-eight of the released men arrived at Carlisle Pier from Holyhead, of whom eight proceeded to their destinations in Belfast and the North by through trains, and twenty travelled to Westland row.

The latest official figures regarding the number of men arrested were those issued from the Military Headquarters, Dublin, on 11th July, 1916, as follows:

Total number of prisoners who passed through Richmond Barracks:

Men 3,149 Women 77	3,226
Men released	1,104
Convicted by court-martial	160
Acquitted by court-martial	23
Men interned	1,852
Women released 72, interned 5	77
	3,226

Names of Deported Prisoners

The following are the names of the persons who were deported, so far as they have been published by the military. These lists were all officially issued to the Press for publication by the military authorities on the dates mentioned:

200 to Knutsford on 1st May

The following list of two hundred prisoners who were removed from Richmond Barracks, Dublin, on April 30th, and lodged in Knutsford Detention Barracks, England, on May 1st, was issued on Wednesday, 10th May:

Alexander, N, 34 Newbridge street—Weaver.
Begley, D, 16 Whitworth road—Carman.
Begley, J, 387 NCR—Shorthand-typist.
Bermingham, J, St Ignatius road—Body maker.
Berry, W, 51 Sheriff street—Shop assistant.
Billings, J, Baymount avenue—Upholsterer.
Blanchfield, M, Carnew street—Boot cutter.
Bradley, P, 15 St Mary's terrace, Kells—Labourer.
Brophy, D, Lusk, Co. Dublin—Labourer.
Buckingham, J, 24 St Ignatius road—Tailor.
Burke, B, New Brook, Rathfarnham—Labourer.

Burns, J, 47 St Paul's street—Goods checker.
Byrne, C, 24 Manor place—Chauffeur.
Byrne, J, 44 Lr Mayor street, North Wall—Library assistant.
Byrne, J, 190 North Portland road—Electrician.
Byrne, P, St Mary's Abbey—Shop assistant.
Byrne, T, 94 Capel street—Baker.
Byrne, T, 30 Summerhill—Porter.
Caffrey, M, Lr Rathfarnham, Co. Dublin—Van driver.
Callan, J, 15 Clonliffe avenue—Motor driver.
Campbell, G, 18 Hardwicke street—Law clerk.
Canny., 70 North Strand road—Grocer.
Carmichael, B, Larkfield, Kimmage—Carpenter.
Carpenter, P, 110 Foley street—Labourer.
Carraty, T, 2 George's hill—Carpenter.
Carroll, P, Collinstown, Lusk—Farmer.
Cassells, J, Lr Mayor street, North Wall—Clerk.
Cathan, J, 39 North Cumberland street—Labourer.
Charlton, M, 27 Portland place—Compositor.
Clarke, J, 31 Bachelor's Walk—Shop assistant.
Coleman, P, Larigan, Cariskaboy, Co. Cavan—Labourer.
Condron, L, 4 Blackhall parade—Farrier.
Conroy, H, 4 Marino avenue, Clontarf—Vanman.
Conway, J, 8 Moore Cottages, Rutland street—Office boy.
Courtney, D, 43 Bessborough avenue, North Strand—Labourer.
Cox, R, 22 Wiley road, Wallowfield, Manchester—Grocer's assistant.
Craven, T, 20 North Frederick street—Wax bleacher.
Croke, T, 4 College view, Drumcondra—Porter.
Daniel, H, 6 Lower Daniel street—Vice-maker.
Decceur, E, 29 Charlotte street West—Labourer.
Delaney, H, 26 Harold's Cross—Labourer.
Doherty, J, 7 Ballybough road—Labourer.
Donnelly, C, 10 Willbrook terrace, Rathfarnham—Grocer's assistant.
Donnelly, M, 113 Stephen's Green West—Labourer.
Donohue, W, Killalong, Clonmore, Hackettstown—Grocer.
Doyle, E, 13 Broadstone avenue.
Doyle, J, 13 Granville street—Actor.
Doyle, T, Ashleaf House, Crumlin, Co. Dublin—Farmer.
Dreeland, W, 53 Bridgefoot street—Boilermaker.
Duffy, P, 34 Commons street, North Wall—Bookbinder.
Dunn, A, 179 Great Brunswick street—Labourer.
Ellis, J, 19 Blessington street—Cabinet maker.
Ellis, S, 19 Blessington street—Wood worker.
Farren, S, 2 Close Bank, Henry street—Paper ruler.
Flanagan, J, 40 Belvedere road—Insurance agent.
Fogarty, T, 79 Fitzroy avenue, Drumcondra—Tailor.
Foley, N, 26 Talbot street, Dublin—Grocer's assistant.
Foran, J, 68 Foley street—Carter.
Foy, M, 21 Little Denmark street—Labourer.
Frawley, D, 155 Lower King street—Plumber.
Friel, B, Larkfield, Kimmage—Plumber.
Gannon, H, Main street, Rathfarnham—Painter.
Gaynor, A, 9 Aughrim Villas—Student.
Gleeson, W, 50 Lr Dominick street—Labourer.
Good, J, 44 Eccles street—Electrician.
Halpin, P, 24 Lower Summerhill—Attendant.
Harnett, J, 37 Mulrow Cottages—Fireman.
Healy, R, 93 Parnell street—Grocer's asst.
Hegarty, J, 31 St Peter's road—Clerk.
Hickey, R, Harold's Cross—Cabinet maker.
Holohan, H, 77 Amiens street—Clerk.
Houghton, G, 33 Sitric road—Plumber.
Howlett, M, 8 Granville street—Labourer.
Hughes, P, 30 Little Denmark street—Caretaker.
Hunter, J, 32 Sackville avenue—Joiner.
Humphreys, R, 108 Seville place, North Strand—Clerk.
Hyland, T, 11 Lr Bridge street—Range fitter.
Hynes, J, 4 Queen street—Brushmaker.
Jackman, N, Kinmorgam, Co. Wexford—Gardener.
Kelly, J, Commons West—Labourer.
Kenny, J, Mountain View, Terenure—Grocer's asst.
Kavanagh, J, Lower Gardiner street—Cabinet maker.
Kavanagh, P, 28 Upper Gloucester street—Painter.
Kelly, F, 152 Parnell street—Chemist's assistant.
Kelly, M, 3 Back lane—Labourer.
Kelly, W, 8 Bishop street—Labourer.
Kennealy, J, 7 Lr Jervis street—Locksmith.
Kennedy, J, 118 Upper Church street—Fitter.
Kenny, A, 85 Blessington street—Grocer's assistant.
Kenny, H, 110 Marlborough street—Painter.
Keogh, C, 25 Elmgrove, Ranelagh—Actor.
Keogh, E, 2 Richmond parade—Hole borer.
Keogh, J, 24 Park street, Inchicore—Labourer.
Lafferty, J, Burghs, Magilligan, Derry—Labourer.
Lawler, L, Ardrigh road—Carpenter.
Lawless, E, Swords—Farmer.
Lee, J, Rathfarnham—Labourer.
Lee, T, 14 Lr Buckingham street—Riveter.
MacGuire, T, 3 Nugent's lane, Broadstone—Loco fireman.
McAulliffe, G, 77 Parnell street (Co. Limerick)—Clerk.
McCormack, B, 1 Elm Grove—Prov Acct.
M'Cormack, R, 62 North King street—Labourer.
M'Dermott, R, 28 Harcourt street—Canvasser.
M'Donald, W, 13 Upper Oriel street—Coach-builder.
M'Gill, J, 34 Killeen road, Rathmines—Draper.
M'Ginley, W, 2 Fitzgibbon street—Labourer.
M'Grath, PB, 55 Belgrave square—Shop assistant.
M'Grath, T, 13 Granville street, Mountjoy—Vanman.
M'Laughlin, J, 4 North street—Mattress maker.
M'Manus, P, 28 North Frederick street—Farmer.
McNally, F, 10 Sullivan avenue, Ballybough road—Labourer.
M'Nally, J, Lusk, Co. Dublin—Labourer.
M'Namara, J, 74 Parnell street—Grocer.
M'Namara, P, 12 South Richmond street—Shop assistant.
M'Neive, W, 58 Parnell street—Shop assistant.
M'Quade, T, Mount Temple road—Plumber.
Mahon, P, 23 Great Nicholas street, Wexford—Labourer.
Maloney, J, Norseman place—Fireman.
Monahan, J, 5 Henrietta street—Fireman.
Mooney, J, 130 Cloth street—Draper.
Mooney, P, 15 Fleet street—Shunter.
Moran, P, 5 Wentworth place—Slater.
Morkan, M, 1 Ellis quay—Clerk.
Mulkearns, J, 21 Royal Canal Bank—Loco fireman.
Mulligan, A, 7 Wilfred place, off Summer Hill—Labourer.
Mulvey, D, Fountain avenue, Rathfarnham—Singer's agent.
Mulvey, W, Fountain avenue, Rathfarnham—Cash desk.
Murphy, E, 33 Sullivan street, Wexford—Porter.
Murphy, F, Brimbane, Curry, Co. Sligo—School teacher.
Murphy, M, 46 Manor street, Shop assistant.
Murphy, Wm, 18 Botanic avenue—Groom.
Neary, D, 30 Little Mary street—Clerk.
Neilan, A, 4 Mt Herald terrace, Harold's Cross—Clerk.
Nelson, P, 40 Gardiner's lane, Mountjoy Square—Labourer.
Neville, P, 15 Lower Marlborough street—Printer.
Nicholls, H, 1 Church avenue, Rathmines—Engineer.

Nolan, P, 8 Rutland Cottages—Electrical Fitter.
Norton, J, 41 Parnell square, Shop assistant.
Nugent, P, 8 Charleville avenue, North Strand—Labourer.
O'Brien, J, 487 NCR, Dublin—Apprentice.
O'Brien, Ml, 29 Guild street, North Wall—Artist.
O'Brien, W, 1 Becham terrace—Compositor.
O'Brien—385 North Circular road—Clerk.
O'Brien, 2 Tivoli avenue—Checker.
O'Cahill J, 22 Merchant's quay—Cooper.
O'Callaghan, D, 3 Upper Fownes street—Apprentice.
O'Carroll, J, 24 Mount Temple road—Clerk.
O'Carroll, P, 92 Manor street—Poulterer.
O'Carroll, W, 92 Manor street—Clerk.
O'Connor, P, 3 Tivoli terrace, Harold's Cross—Librarian.
O'Donohue, T, 4 Middle Mountjoy street—Electrician.
O'Neill, J, 102 Lindsay road—Upholsterer.
O'Neill, P, 183 Townsend street—compositor.
O'Neill, W, 12 Upper Mayor street—Carter.
O'Reilly, L, 1 Aughrim street—Grocer.
O'Reilly, H, 3 O'Connell Villa, Foster terrace—Insurance inspector.
O'Reilly, SP, 181 North Circular road—Engineer.
O'Ryan, O, Maynooth College—Waiter.
O'Shea, J, 28 Coombe—Labourer.
O'Shea, M, Kinmay road—Labourer.
O'Shea, R, 37 Upper Gardiner street—School Attendant.
Power, W, 28 North Frederick street—Plumber.
Prendergast, J, 11 Stafford street—Packer.
Purcell, C, 35 St James' avenue, off Clonliffe road—Baker.
Redmond, J, 16 Lower Oriel street—Clerk.
Regan, M, Ring, Dungarvan—Grocer's assistant.
Reid, J, 41 St Mary's terrace, Ballybough road—Porter.
Reilly, M, 22 Ailesbury road—Chauffeur.
Reilly, P, 5 Charleville road, North Strand—Porter.
Ridgway, A, 163 Parnell street—Hairdresser.
Robbins, F, 39 North William street—Driller.
Rocarter, O, 2 Sallypark Cottage, Fairview—Painter.
Roche, M, 31 Bachelor's Walk—Shop assistant.
Rooney, J, 36 Fairview Strand, Clontarf—Coach-builder.
Russell, J, 68 North Strand road—Grocer.
Saurin, C, The Cottage, Vernon avenue, Clontarf—Clerk.
Savage, M, 21 Bachelor's Walk and Streamstown, Ballysodare, Sligo—Barman.
Sexton, J, 11 Upper Gloucester place—Labourer.
Shannon, M, 12 Coombe—Labourer.
Sheilds, A, 3 Seafield road—Actor.
Sheppard, M, 19 St Michael's road, Glasnevin—Clerk.
Sheridan, J, 16 Mountain View avenue, Harold's Cross road—Painter.
Simpson, T, Upton Cottage, Goose Green, Drumcondra—Painter.
Stephenson, P, Lower Gloucester street—Labourer.
Stynes, J, 25 Mary's avenue—Grocer's assistant.
Sweeney, J, 12 Lr Dominick street—Cabinet maker.
Tallon, C, 2 Granville, North Richmond street—Night watchman.
Toomey, J, 10 Clonmore terrace—Electrician.
Toomey, T, 30 Clonliffe avenue—Fitter.
Traynor, C, 55 Jones' road—Printer.
Trell, P, 178 North King street—Draper's assistant.
Tuke, E, 83 Queen street—Labourer.
Tully, 2 Nugent Cottages, Monck place—Cabinet maker.
Ward, G, 44 Home Farm road—Belt-maker.
Warham, T, 154 Thomas street—Shirt cutter.
Whelan, M, 31 Ballybough road—Carpenter.
Whitley, T, 251 Richmond road, Drumcondra—Law clerk.
Williams, P, 6 Coombe—Labourer.

289 to Stafford on 1st May

The following list of 289 prisoners who were removed from Richmond Barracks, Dublin, on the 30th of April, and lodged in Stafford Detention Barracks on the 1st May, was issued on Thursday, 11th May:

Agnew, A, 11 Emerald street, Dublin: home address 33 Clare st, Liverpool.
Bagley, T, 16 Whitworth row, Seville place.
Bird, J, 4 Rutland Cottages, Dublin.
Boland, 8 Viking rd, Arbour hill, Dublin.
Bolger, J, Blackwater, Co. Wexford.
Brennan, E, 19 Ardrigh road, Arbour Hill, Dublin
Breslin, J, 50 New street, Dublin.
Breslin, T, 49 New street, Dublin.
Breslin, P, 50 New street, Dublin.
Bridgeman, E, 19 Richmond hill, Rathmines, Dublin.
Broughman, J, (?) 10 St Lawrence street, Dublin.
Bryan, T, 31 Guild street, Dublin.
Byrne, A, 42 Arran quay, Dublin.
Byrne, C, 3 Camden place, Dublin.
Byrne, C, 45 St Mary's rd, Church rd, Dublin.
Burke, E, 63 Meath street, Dublin.
Burke, F, Hermitage, Rathfarnham, Dublin.
Byrne, J, 28 Malachi rd, NCR, Dublin
Byrne, J, 6 Whitworth place, Dublin.
Byrne, J, Erin place Lower, Dublin.
Byrne, J, 45 St Mary's road, Dublin. (Church rd)
Byrne, L, 42 Arran quay, Dublin.
Cassidy, T, 22 Bolton st, Dublin.
Chaney, W, 5 Northcourt Ave, Church rd, Dublin.
Coates, P, 12 Upper Oriel street, Dublin.
Cody, J, 12 Bessboro ave, N Strand, Dublin.
Cole, P, 1 Aughrim street, Dublin.
Coughlan, J, Larkfield, Kimmage, Dublin.
Connaughton P, 23 Nicholas street Dublin. (home address: Market Square, Longford.)
Cowling, J, 6 Sussex terrace, Mespil rd, Dublin.
Craven, B, 21 Poole street, Dublin.
Croke, M, 4 Milbourne Ave, Drumcondra, Dublin.
Cullen, J, 6 Whitworth place, Dublin.
Callaghan, J, 18 Moss street, Dublin.
Carroll, M, 24 George's quay, Dublin.
Carroll, R, 38 Susanville rd, Drumcondra, Dublin.
Carton, O, 21 Temple street, Dublin.
Casey, H, 11 St George's ave, Drumcondra, Dublin.
Cassidy, J, 508 NCR, Dublin. (home address: Aughanagh, Letterbreen, Enniskillen.)
Chaney, P, 5 North Court Ave, Church rd, Dublin.
Clifford, D, 4 Upper Gardiner street, Dublin.
Clinch, P, 28 North Frederick street, Dublin.
Coffey, J, 34 Botanic road, Glasnevin, Dublin.
Collin, P, 12 Parnell st, Dublin.
Collins, M, 16 Rathdown rd, NCR, Dublin.
Conroy, J, 40 Railway street, N Strand, Dublin.
Corbally, R, 7 Moor row, off Gardiner st, Dublin.
Corbally, T, 38 St Patrick's Cottages, Willbrook, Rathfarnham, Co. Dublin.
Cosgrove, M, Abbotstown, Castleknock. (home address: Coolridge, Kilcock.)
Coughlan, F, 35 Dargle road, Dublin.
Cowley, M, Orchardstown, Rathfarnham, Co. Dublin.

Coyle, W, 21 Temple street, Dublin.
Cremen, M, Rockbrook, Rathfarnham, Co. Dublin.
Dalamere, E, 34 Patrick street, Dublin.
Daly, D, Main street, Caherciveen, Co. Kerry.
Darcy, W, 51 Lower Camden street, Dublin.
Darritt, D, 4 Russell st, NCR, Dublin.
Dennany, P, 9a Block Buckingham Building, Dublin.
Dervin, P, 14 Summer place, Dublin,
Doggett, C, 8 Charlemont street, Dublin.
Donegan, J, 17 Grantham street, Dublin. (parents' address: 6 Wye street, Birkenhead.)
Donnelly, P, Hermitage, Rathfarnham, Co. Dublin.
Donohoe, R, 2 Eccles street, Dublin.
Donohoe, S, 14 Montpelier street, Dublin.
Dore, E, Main st, Glin, Co. Limerick.
Dowling, A, Main road, Castleknock, Co. Dublin.
Dowling, J, Main road, Castleknock, Co. Dublin.
Doyle, J, 8 Church lane, Lr Kevin st, Dublin.
Doyle, J, 8 Harbour rd, Bullock, Dalkey.
Doyle, J, 117 Capel st, Dublin.
Duffy, C, 3 River road Cottage, Castleknock, Co. Dublin.
Duffy, J, 11 Emerald street, Dublin.
Duffy, J, 7 Rueben ave, Dublin.
Dunne, J, 13 Upper Liffey street, Dublin.
Dunne, P, 23 North Great George's street, Dublin.
Dunne, T, 14 Upper Liffey street, Dublin.
Dwyer, J, 7 Inns quay, Dublin.
Early, J, 607 Richmond place, Dublin.
Edwards, M, 25 St Michael's tce, Bellerville, SCR, Dublin.
English, P, Dunsink Cottage, Castleknock, Co. Dublin.
Ennis, T, 3 Richmond crescent, Dublin.
Farrell, M, 20 Lower Dorset street, Dublin.
Farrelly, J, 5 Temple Cottages, Broadstone, Dublin.
Feeney, G, 20 Henry street, Dublin.
Fitsimonds, M, 8 Blessington place, Dublin.
Fitzharris, J, 2 Oriel place, Dublin.
Fitzmaurice, G, 2 Orchard tce, Dublin.
Flanagan, M, 40 Moore street, Dublin.
Flanagan, F, 30 ½ Moore street, Dublin.
Flanagan, G, 30 ½ Moore street, Dublin.
Flanagan, M, 14 St Clement's, road, Drumcondra, Dublin.
Flood, J, 19 Summerhill parade, NCR, Dublin.
Ford, J, 30, Upper George street, Kingstown.
Fox, J, 9 Hawtorne terrace, Church rd, Dublin.
Fox, M, Brasscastle, Knockmaroon, Chapelizod, Dublin.
Foy, F, Lower Palmerstown, Chapelizod, Co. Dublin.
Fullam, T, 15 Synnott place, Dublin.
Gahan, M, 9 Nicholas street, Dublin.
Gallagher, P, Edmondstown, Rathfarnham, Dublin.
Garland, P, 27 Lower Kevin street, Dublin.
Garvey, M, 51 Lower Camden street, Dublin.
Gavan, J, 283 Richmond rd, Fairview, Dublin.
Geoghan, JJ, 134 North Strand road (parents, Ballingrone Junction, Co. Limerick).
Geraghty, C, 3 Fingal place, Dublin.
Gleeson, T, 50 Lower Dominick street, Dublin.
Gough, J, 1 North Richmond st, home address, Newroad, Baldoyle, Co. Dublin.
Halpin, P, 35 Oxmanstown rd, Dublin.
Hammill, T, 17 St James' terrace, SCR, Dublin.
Hands, N, 12 Great Longford street, Dublin.
Harper, J, 70 Benburb street, Dubin.
Hayden, J, 126 James's street, Dublin.
Hayes, J, 77 Heytesbury street, Dublin.
Hayes, J, 5 Marino ave, Malahide rd, Dublin.
Healy, J, 12 Upper Gardiner street, Dublin.
Healy, P, 86 Phibsborough road, Dublin.
Heery, J, (?46), 40 Fitzroy ave, Drumcondra, Dublin.
Henderick, E, 12 Up Dominick st, Dublin.
Henderson, F, 5 Windsor Villas, Fairview, Dublin.
Henderson, M, 14 St Kearin's rd, SCR, Dublin.
Henderson, T, 14 St Kearin's rd, SCR, Dublin.
Henry, F, 25 Charlemont street, Dublin.
Henry, F, 6 Fennell's Cottages, Charlemont street, Dublin.
Foran, J, 4 Francis street, Tralee.
Hughes, T, 8 Summer hill, Dublin.
Jackson, P, 40 St Augustine street, Dublin.
Joyce, B, Hermitage, Rathfarnham, Dublin.
Joyce, E, 29 Charles street, Dublin.
Karns, P, 10 Daniel street South, Dublin.
Kavanagh, J, 45 Sth Gt George's st, Dublin.
Kavanagh, P, 24 St Mary's rd, N Strand, Dublin.
Kearney, T, Ballyboden, Rathfarnham, Co. Dublin.
Keating, C, 14 Portland place, Dublin.
Kelly, P, Coolgariff, Stillorgan, Co. Dublin.
Kelly, J, 93 Lower Dorset street, Dublin.
Kelly, FM, 53 Gordon st, Ringsend, Dublin.
Kelly, P, 14 Watkin's Cottages, off Ardee st, Dublin.
Kenny, J, 25 North Brunswick st, Dublin.
Keogh, J, 11 Brabazon st, off Coombe, Dublin.
Kerr, J, 31 Upper Sackville st, Dublin.
Kerwin, P, Maynooth, Co. Kildare.
Kilgallon, J, The Hermitage, Rathfarnham, Co. Dublin.
King, G, 25 St Ignatius road, Dublin.
King, G, Larkfield, Kimmage, Dublin.
King, M, 25 St Ignatius road, Dublin.
King, P, Larkfield, Kimmage, Dublin.
Lawlor, L, 29 Ardrigh road, Dublin.
Ledwith, P, 65 Blessington street, Dublin.
Little, J, 31 rear Up Clanbrassil st, Dublin.
Lowe, A, 3 Deane street, Dublin.
Lundy, J, Larkfield, Kimmage, Dublin.
Lynch, M, 7 St Bridget's ave, N Strand, Dublin.
Lynch, P, 14 Nelson st, Dublin: home address, John's Brook, Kells, Co. Meath.
Lyons, J, 39 Finglas rd, Glasnevin, Dublin.
McArdle, J, 10 North Portland row, Dublin.
McArdle, P, 4 North Portland row, Dublin.
McCormack, J, 220 Parnell st, Dublin.
McDonough, J, 18 Cottages, Station road, Baldoyle.
M'Elligott, M, 11 Lr St Columba's rd, Dublin.
M'Entee, JF, 42 Mill street, Belfast.
M'Erratt, L, 31 Usher's quay, Dublin.
M'Grath, M, Kimmage, Larkfield, Dublin. (Brother's address, 1 Herbert st, Kentish Town, London.)
M'Guire, FJ, c/o T M'Guire, Derrygonnelly, Co. Fermanagh.
M'Guire, R, 65a Rathmines road, Dublin.
McGuirk, P, 54 Donore avenue, Dublin.
McKeon, O, Unversity Coll, Earlsfort tce, Dublin.
McMahon, D, 11 Newmarket, Dublin.
McNulty, M, The Mill Blanchardstown, Co. Dublin.
McNulty, P, The Mill Blanchardstown, Co. Dublin.
McPartlin, P, 32 St Joseph's place, Dorset st, Dublin.
MacGinley, E, 108 Drumcondra road, Dublin.
Madden, J, 27 Clonliffe avenue, Dublin.
Magee, (R) M, 20 Ostman place, Dublin.
Maghar, J, 1a Montague street, Dublin.
Mahon, J, 4 Nixon street, Dublin.
Marie, L, 17 Grantham street, Dublin.
Mason, (?Frank), 4 Lr Dominick st, Dublin.
Mason, F, 4 Lower Dominick street, Dublin.
Meade, H, 68 Cabra park, Phibsborough, Dublin.

Meade, W, 68 Cabra park, Phibsboro', Dublin.
Meagher, P, 138 Upper Dorest street, Dublin.
Meekin, G, 38 East Essex street, Dublin.
Monks, A, 1 Malpas terrace, off New st, Dublin.
Mooney, J, River road Cottage, Castleknock, Co. Dublin.
Mooney, P, Riverview, Castleknock, Co. Dublin.
Moore, J, 16 St Joseph sq, Vernon ave, Clontarf, Dublin.
Munroe, T, 7 Little Denmark street, Dublin.
Murnane, W, 14 Blackhall place, Dublin.
Murphy, F, 9 North Wall, Dublin.
Murphy, F, The Hermitage, Rathfarnham.
Murphy, H, 31 Usher's quay, Dublin.
Murphy, J, 31 Kilmore Cottages, Artane, Co. Dublin.
Murphy, P, 45 Broughton street, Dundalk.
Murtagh, FD, 196 Parnell street, Dublin.
Murtagh, L, Lower Palmerstown, Chapelizod, Dublin.
Murray, T, 102 Lower Gardiner street, Dublin.
Murphy, C, 9 Upper St Brigid's rd, Drumcondra.
Musgrave, L, 4 St Patrick's rd, Drumcondra, Dublin.
Nolan, M, Burrowfield, Co. Dublin.
Nolan, T, 8 Norseman place, Dublin.
Noonan, C, 28 Blackhall place, Dublin.
Noonan, E, Larkfield, Kimmage, Dublin.
Noonan, J, Larkfield, Kimmage, Dublin.
O'Brien, J, 8 Dolphin's Barn, Dublin.
O'Brien, M, 2 Walker's Cotatges, Rathmines.
O'Brien, O, 7 Bessborough pde, Rathmines, Dublin.
O'Brien, P, 26 St Michael's terrace, SCR, Dublin.
O'Brien, W, 75 Fairview Strand, Clontarf, Dublin.
O'Brien, T, 6 Parkgate street, Dublin.
O'Byrne, J, 32 Connaught street, Dublin.
O'Byrne, J, 2 Camden place, Dublin.
O'Connell, M, 44 Mountjoy street, Dublin.
O'Connor, J, 18 Francis street, Dublin.
O'Connor, J, 77 Parnell St (home address, White Lion street, London).
O'Connor, J, 10 Beresford place, Dublin.
O'Connor, J, 4 Lower Sherrard street, Dublin.
O'Connor, T, 58 1/2 Harold's Cross, Dublin.
O'Doherty, W, 15 Shamrock tce, Blarney, Co. Cork.
O'Gorman, W, 16 Drumcondra park, Dublin.
O'Hanlon, P, 31 Up Wellington st, Dublin.
O'Higgins, B, Finglas, Co. Dublin.
O'Kelly, M, 27 Upper Rutland street, Dublin.
O'Neal, M, 69 North King street, Dublin.
O'Neill, J, 4 Russell terrace, Church road, Dublin.
O'Neill, J, 18 Manor place, Dublin.
O'Neill, T, 8 St Mary's rd, off Church rd, Dublin.
O'Neill, W, 7 North Gt George's st, Dublin.
O'Reilly, D, 181 North Circular road, Dublin.
O'Reilly, J, 32 Commons street, Dublin.
O'Reilly, J, 3 Ballybough lane, Dublin.
O'Reilly, 35 Drumcondra road, Dublin.
O'Reilly, J, Chapel st, Bantry, Co. Cork.
O'Reilly, P, 43 Geraldine street, Dublin.
O'Reilly, T, 10 St Michael's Hill, Dublin.
O'Reilly, W, 14 Arbutus place, SCR, Dublin.
O'Borke, J, 14 Carlingford tce, Drumcondra, Dublin.
Oman, R, 8 Daniels street, Dublin.
Pollard, F, 31 Lower Dominick st, Dublin.
Perry, W, 19 Usher's Island, Dublin.
Poole, C, 2 Lower Rutland street, Dublin.
Poole, P, 50 Marlborough street, Dublin.
Price, J, 15 Killarney parade, NCR, Dublin.
Rankin, P, 24 Queen street, Newry.
Rat, T, 12 Grand Canal Harbour, Dublin.
Redmond, A, 15 Curzon street, Dublin.
Richmond, J, 275 North Circular road, Dublin.
Ring, C, 5 Sackville Gardens, Dublin.
Ring, J, 17 Clonmore terrace, Dublin.
Ring, W, 4 Sackville gardens, Dublin.
Ross, W, 11 Lr Sherrard street, Dublin.
Ryan, D, St Enda's College, Rathfarnham.
Ryan, J, 19 Ranelagh road, Dublin.
Ryan, L, 4 Portobello Harbour, Dublin.
Seery, J, 10 Beresford place, Dublin.
Shelly, C, 78 St Augustine street, Dublin.
Sheridan, J, 10 Carters' lane, off Smithfield, Dublin.
Shortall, W, 3 St Joseph's terrace, Upper Wellington street, Dublin.
Shouldice, F, 3 Marino Crescent, Clontarf, Dublin.
Skeils, T, 36 Moyelta road, West road, Dublin.
Smith, J, 3 Pile's Buildings, Wood st, Dublin.
Steinmayer, C, 70 Lombard street, SCR, Dublin.
Sullivan, J, 4 Camden place, Dublin.
Sullivan, J, 550 NCR, Dublin.
Summers, J, 7 Henrietta street, Dublin.
Swan, P, 15 Belvedere ave, NCR, Dublin.
Sweeney, J, The Hermitage, Rathfarnham, Co. Dublin.
Sweeney, J, Butterfield avenue, Rathfarnham.
Sweeney, P, Butterfiel ave, Rathfarnham.
Thornton, H, Larkfield, Kimmage road, Dublin.
Toban, M, 33 Sullivan street, Dublin.
Tobin, M, 28 Castlewood ave, Rathmines, Dublin.
Tuohy, S, 73 Bride street, Dublin.
Turmley, J, 17 Garden lane, Dublin.
Turner, H, 10 Summerhill, Dublin.
Tyrrall, T, Maynooth, Co. Kildare.
Vize, J, 70 Seville place, Dublin.
Water, P, Shannon Hill, Enniscorthy, Co. Wexford.
Walpole, H, 3 Ranelagh rd, Dublin.
Walsh, J, 74 Parnell street, Dublin.
Walsh, J, 3 Sherrard avenue, NCR, Dublin.
Ward, G, 44 Home Farm road, Drumcondra, Dublin.
Ward, T, 74 Paarnell street, Dublin.
Whelan, G, 19 Russell street, Dublin.
Whelan, J, 50 Marlborough street, Dublin.
Whelan, J, 14 Marlborough street, Dublin.
Whelan, W, 31 Ballybough road, Dublin.
White, J, 10 Summer street, Dublin.

308 to Knutsford on 3rd May

The following is a list of 308 prisoners who were removed from Richmond Barracks, Dublin, on May 2nd, and lodged in Knutsford Detention Barracks on May 3rd, was issued on Friday, 12th May:

Archibold, Wm, 6 Synnott street, North Strand, Dublin—Commission agent's clerk.
Blanchfield, Peter, 44 Ccarnew street, NCR—Cabinet-maker.
Boland, Gerald, 9 Vincent street, SCR—Fitter.
Bowman, Joseph, 21 Sth terr, Inchicore—Fitter.
Boylan, Thos, 6 Ashbrook terr, SCR—Teacher.
Bracken, Thos, 7 Lower Gloucester st—Labourer.
Brady, Jas, 71 Bride street, Dublin—Lamplighter.
Breslin, Patrick, 111 Foley st—Labourer.
Brian, Ptk, 42 Upper Gloucester st—Machinist.
Brogan, (Drogan), Ptk, Collinstown, Lusk—Labourer.
Buckley, Daniel, Maynooth, Kildare—General merchant.
Buckley, Wm J, 43 Gt Charles street, NCR—Cotton merchant.
Burke, M, 9 Brabazon street, Dublin—Labourer.
Burne, James, 2 Alexander tce, Terenure—Carpenter.
Betler, Chris, 61 Emmet rd, Inchicore—Cooper.
Byrne, Joseph, 99 Marlborough street—Corporation labourer.

Byrne, Michael, 1 Maxwell st—Labourer.
Byrne, Wm, Fingall street, Cork street, Dublin—Despatch clerk.
Byrne, Jos, 5 Armstrong street, Harold's Cross—Carpenter.
Byrne,Thomas, 37 Blackpitts, Dublin—Carpenter.
Byrne, Patrick, 9 Ring terrace, Inchicore, Dublin—Brass polisher.
Byrne, M, Salem place, Donore, Terenure ave, Dublin—Carpenter.
Byrne, Lawrence, 15 Havelock square, Dublin—Engineer's Fitter.
Byrne, Hugh, Harold's Cross rd, Dublin—Labourer.
Byrne, Frank, 2 Aberdeen terrace, Dublin—Inspector GPO telephones.
Byrne, Christopher, 16a (169) Up Basin street—Corporation labourer.
Byrne, Wm, 4 Smithfield ave—Labourer.
Byrne, Patrick, 2 Alexander terrace, Terenure—Compositor.
Byrne, Patrick, 20 Dunore avenue—Machinist.
Byrne, John, 31 Nth Cumberland st—Labourer.
Byrne, Charles, 35 Mount Pleasant sq—Clerk.
Byrne, Joseph, 56 Summerhill—Labourer.
Caffrey, F, 116 Lr Gardiner street, Dublin—Baker.
Caffrey, Leo, 116 Lr Gardiner st, Dublin—Baker.
Callan, P, 59 Millmount avenue, Dublin—Carpenter.
Carlton, TG, Kimmage road, Dublin—Warehouse clerk.
Carroll, Bartholomew, 5 Mallon tce, Grove road, Harold's Cross—Plumber.
Carroll, James, 4 Almeida ave—Engine driver.
Carroll, Peter, 8 Lr Rutland st—Labourer.
Carty, Thos, Castleknock, Co. Dublin—Clerk.
Casey, Jas, Iveagh House, Dublin—Boot salesman.
Cassidy, H, 36 Coombe street, Dublin—Labourer.
Caulfield, John, 1 (4?) Marlborough place—Wine porter.
Cavanagh, Martin, 20 Phoenix st—Brass moulder.
Cavanagh, Thos, 20 Phoenix st—Machine minder.
Christie, Peter, Artane Village, Co. Dublin—Labourer.
Clarke, Jos, 7 Clifton terr, Ranelagh rd—Plumber.
Collins, John, 98 Marlborough st—Tailor.
Commerford, Andrew, 4 Up Kevin st—Range setter.
Corcoran, Jos, 19 Kennedy's Villas, James's st—Bootmaker.
Cordy (Coady), Wm, 8 Nicholas pl—Silk-weaver.
Corrigan, James, 11 Lr Baggot st, Dublin—Shop assistant.
Cotter, Joseph, 2 St Anne's rd, Drumcondra—Clerk, Civil Service.
Coughlan, Jas, 21 Up Bridge st, Dublin—Mechanic.
Cullen, John, 37 Wexford st—Chauffeur.
Curran, W, 3 Vauxhall ave, Dublin—Brass polisher.
Cahill, Arthur, 444 NCR, Dublin—Chemist.
Corrigan, Wm, 84 Lr George's street, Kingstown—Shopman (grocer ?).
Cotter, Joseph, 32 St Anne's rd, Drumcondra—Clerk.
Cotter, Richard, 2 St Anne's rd, Drumcondra—Clerk, Civil Service.
Cunningham, James, 3 Upper Oriel st—Tailor.
Daly, Philip, 12 Pim st, Dublin—Draper's assistant.
Delany, M, 31 Patrick street, Dublin—Labourer.
Dempsey, Wm, 32 Reginald st, Dublin—Labourer.
Devine, John, Lusk—Labourer.
Doherty, John, St James' terrace, Dolphin's Barn, Dublin—Cooper.
Donoghue, Thos D, Lr Abbey st—Labourer.
Doolan, Joseph, 6 Brighton Gardens (Bright's Yard?), Terenure—Insurance agent.
Doyle, Peter, 74 Summerhill—Bricklayer.
Dowling Edward, 99 Marlborough street—Carter.
Doyle, Patrick, Coombe Hospital—Medical student.
Doyle, Thos, 19 Harman street, Donore ave, Dublin—Carpenter.
Doyle, Joseph, 22 Chamber st—Porter.
Doyle, Thomas, 18 Lr Mayor st—Porter.
Doyle, Christopher, 3 Dolphin's Barn st—Labourer.
Doyle, Wm, Leisson hall, Swords—Farm labourer.
Dunne, Denis, 22 Brighton Gardens, Terenure—Insurance agent.
Dunne, P, 31 Darley's terr, Donore ave—Labourer.
Dunne, John Joseph, 28 SCR—Clerk.
Drumm (Drohan?), Thos, 3 Byrne's Cottages, Dollymount—Gardener.
Durham, Matthias, Skerries—Carpenter.
Edwards, John, 25 St Michael's terr, Dublin—Cooper.
Egan, Patrick, 31 Gardiner st—Van driver.
Ennis, Michael (Christopher?), 4 Bessboro ave, N Strand—Gas fitter.
Farrell, Wm, 25 Grenville st, Dublin—Plumber's assistant.
Farrell, M, 84½ Cork street, Dublin—Wine porter.
Farrell, Jas, 18 Lower Drumcondra rd—grocer
Fitzpatrick, Andrew, 1 Chawoit (Talbot ?) terrace—Electric worker
Fitzpatrick, John, 118 Parnell st, Dublin Grocer' sassistant.
Fitzpatrick Jas, 7 Carrickfoyle terr, Kilmainham—Coachmaker.
Fitzsimmons, John, 118 Lr Gardiner st, Dublin—Vanman.
Fleming M, Shillelagh, Co. Wicklow—Fireman.
Fogarty, James, 7 Parnell place, Harold's Cross—Saddler.
Foran, James, Camac House, Dolphin's Barn—House painter.
Fullerton, Geo, 22 Bow lane, Dublin—Machinist.
Furlong, Matthew, 70 Seville place—Tool maker.
Furlong, Joseph, 70 Seville place—Turner.
Gahan, (Galvin?) Timothy, Wood quay—Student or Steward.
Goulding, Charles, 5 Cottage place, NCR, Dublin—Painter.
Goulding, James, 5 Cottage place, Dublin—House painter.
Graham, Jas, 27 Emerald sq, Dolphin's Barn—Labourer.
Graham, Thos, 44 Reginald st—Labourer.
Grant, Patrick, GNR Cottage, Baldoyle—Motor mechanic.
Gregory, John, 28 Cadogan rd—labourer.
Griffen, John, 3 Grenville lane, off Gardiner place—Tailor.
Gunning, J, 79 Lr Gardiner st—Plate polisher.
Hagan, James, 30 Gray st, Dublin—Labourer.
Hannon, Jas, 12 Lawrence st, Dublin—Checker.
Harney, John, 79 Lr Gardiner street—Old age pensioner and painter.
Hanney, Fras (John?), 79 Lr Gardiner st—Printer.
Harvey, Robert, 79 Lr Gardiner st—Cycle mechanic.
Harvey, Thos, 5 D'olier st—Waiter.
Heron, Jas, 23a Bessboro's ave, North Strand—Butcher.
Holland, (Haloran) Dl, 157, Silverdale terr, Inchicore—Carpenter.
Holland (Hailington), Robt., 157 Silverdale terr, Inchicore—Butcher.
Hutchinson, Jos, 12 Summerhill parade, Summerhill, Dublin—Printer's assistant.
Jordan, Michael, 53 Mountjoy street—Porter.
Joyce, J, Ashdall road, Terenure—Student.
Judge, J, 2 Cassimir road, Dublin—Butcher.
Kavanagh, Jas, 78 Marrowbone lane, Dublin—Messenger.
Kavanagh, P, 13 Up Dorset street—Grocer's assistant.
Kearns, Jos, 13 St Clement's rd—Clerk.

Kearns, Frank, 13 St Clement's rd—Clerk.
Kearns, John, 13 St Clement's rd—Student.
Kearns, Thos, 13 St Clement's rd—Clerk.
Keating, Jas, 42 Up Gloucester st—Labourer.
Kelley, Thos, Corduff, Lusk—Labourer.
Kelly, Thomas, 71b Corporation Buildings, Dublin—Flour packer.
Kelly, Henry, 31 Bachelor's Walk—Grocer's assistant.
Kelly, Joseph, 12 Killarney parade, NCR—Private means.
Kelly, J, Skerries, Co. Dublin—Grocer's assistant.
Kelly, Wm, 11 Donohue st, Inchicore—Labourer.
Kelly, P, 100 Lr Drumcondon (Drumcondra ?) rd—Clerk.
Kelly, Joseph, Corduff, Lusk—Workhouse wardmaster.
Kelly, Isaac, 23 Longwood ave, SCR, Dublin—Bank clerk.
Kelly, Matthew, 42 Up Gloucester st—Van driver.
Kennedy, Joseph, 2nd Lock, Grand Canal—Clerk.
Kenny, James, Priestfield terr, Dolphin's Barn, Dublin—Harness maker.
Kenny, K, 42 Reuben st, SCR, Dublin—Draper.
Kenny, J, 92 North Strand rd—Plaster.
Keogh, James, 8 High street—Hairdresser.
Kerr (Carr), Neill, 6 Florinda street, Larkhill, Liverpool—Seaman.
Kerr, Michael, Terenure—Labourer.
Kerr, Thos, Kimmage (11 Emerald street)—Labourer.
Kerrigan, Owen, 82 Up Rathmines—Upholsterer.
Killeen, Robert, 14 St Joseph's parade, off Dorset st, Dublin—Labourer.
King, John, 45 St Patrick's road, Drumcondra—Bookseller's clerk.
Laughlin, Ptk, 172 James' st, Dublin—Silk-weaver.
Lawless, Jas, 20 (21?) First ave, Seville place—Clerk.
Lawless, Jas, Swords, Co. Dublin—Fireman.
Liston, M, 27 South square, Inchicore—Fitter's apprentice.
Losty, Thos, 5 Nxon st, North Wall—Checker.
Lynch, Ml, 2 Grantham st—Clerk (Corporation).
Lynch, Wm, 1 Nixon st—Clerk.
Lynch, John, 1 Nixon st, Dublin—Clerk.
Lyons, E, 15 Factory terr, Ballybough rd, Dublin—Brass finisher.
MacKay, Lawrence, 23 (? 33) Nth William st—Blacksmith.
McCabe, P, Roymount House, Harold's Cross—Painter.
McCabe, Edward, Roymount House, Kimmage, Harold's Cross—Painter.
McCabe, Wm, Roymount House, Kimmage rd—Painter.
McCormack, John, 70 Corporation st, Dublin—Grocer's assistant.
M'Donnell, Jn, Victoria Cottage, Stillorgan rd, Doonybrook—Labourer.
M'Glynn, John, 4 Portobello Harbour—Plasterer.
M'Gloughlin, M, 9 Northumberland square, Dublin—Printer.
M'Grath, John, 49 Belleview Buildings, Thomas street, Dublin—Clerk at Guinness's Brewery.
M'Grath, Patrick, 49 Bellevue Buildings, Dublin—Labourer.
M'Guire, Jas, 32 St Michael's terrace—Labourer.
Malone, Wm, 57 Corporation street, Dublin—Grocer's porter.
Malony, J, 21 Longwood avenue, SCR, Dublin—Traveller.
Martin, Peter, 32 Commons street, North Wall—Checker.
Meade, Dnl, 11 Emerald sq—Atttendant (labourer).
Molloy, Chas, 118 Parnell st, Dublin.
Molloy, Ml Jos, 45 Bayviw ave—Compositor.
Molloy, Richard, 50 Sitric rd, Dublin—Painter.
Morgan, John, 10 Gray st, Dublin—Labourer (messenger).
Mullen, Martin, 10 Launderdale terrace, New row, Dublin—Bricklayer.
Murphy, M, 9 Synnott place, Dublin—Bricklayer.
Murphy, John, 1 Lower Clanbrassil street, Dublin—Van driver.
Murphy, Jn, 5 Behan's Cott, James's st—Labourer.
Murphy, James, 17 St Mary's terrace, Rathfarnham—Traveller.
Murray, Ger, 31 Effra rd Rathmines—Clerk.
Murray, G, Tintern, Effra rd, Rathmines—Clerk.
M'Allister, Bernard, Donabate, Co. Dublin.
M'Cabe, Kevin, 539 NCR, Dublin—Watchmaker.
M'Cann, John, Back lane, Lusk—Labourer.
M'Donagh, John, 34 Bloomield ave—Theatre manager.
M'Donald, Ml, 84 North Strand rd,—Labourer.
M'Donald, J, 17 Lr Driel st—Clerk.
M'Donald, John, 6 St Brigid's ave, Nth Strand—Linotype operator.
M'Donnell, Matthew, 11 North Portland place, NCR, Dublin—Painter.
M'Donnell (M'Donald), Patrick, 4 Up Gardiner street—Draper's assistant.
M'Donnell, Seamus (James), Little Strand street, Skerries—Druggist.
M'Evoy, James, 8 Redmond's Hill—Cinematograph operator.
M'Ginley, Patrick, 2 Fitzgibbon st, Dublin—Tailor.
M'Keag (M'Kerg), David, 25 Lr Abbey st—Glazier.
M'Kee, Richard, Finglas Bridge—Compositor.
M'Kenna, Bernard, 1 Maxwell st—Van driver.
M'Loughlin, Peter, 6 King street South—Tailor.
M'Mahon, Peter, Up Gardiner street—Clerk to ship-broker.
M'Quaid, John, 1a Rose terrace, Wharf road, Fairview—Tramway clerk.
M'Veigh, James, Emerald square, Dolphin's Barn—Labourer.
Mackey, Ml, 23 Nth William st—Blacksmith's improver.
Makanaltis, Antli, (Russian), Belfast—Seaman.
Malony, Hy, Lr Gloucester st—Foreman.
Masterson, James, Lusk—Labourer.
Maxwell, Thomas, Sutton, Co. Dublin—Gardener.
Meldon, Thos, 45 Gardiner st—Tailor and.
Meldon, John, same address—Clerk, brothers.
Moore, John, 29 Guild st, Dublin—Labourer.
Moore, Wm, 21 Cardigan rd, (? Cadogan rd)—Clerk.
Moran, Ptk, 160 Phibsboro' rd, Dublin—Grocer's assistant.
Mulen, Martin, 9 Emerald tce, Cork st—Labourer.
Mullen, Patrick, 9 Emerald tce,—Fitter's apprentice.
Mulcahy, Richard, Bayview, Sutton—Clerk.
Murphy, Patrick, 9 Church st, Nth Wall—Labourer.
Murphy, F, 42 Chamber St—Labourer (Boot-maker).
Murphy, Jos, 30 Corporation st, Dublin—Labourer.
Murray, Nicholas, 107 North Strand—Decorative artist.
Murray, Henry, 31 Effra rd, Rathmines—Clerk.
Murtagh (? Morton), Bernard, 63 Lombard street W—Labourer.
Neary, Jos, Marlborough House, Glasnevin—Waiter.
Nolan, Thomas, 106 Cork street—Labourer.
O'Brien, Wm, 43 Lombard street, West, SCR, Dublin—Clerk.

O'Brien, Lorcan, 8 Pim st—Clerk.
O'Brien, Denis, 1 Greenville terrace—Slater.
O'Brien, Peter, 7 Bessboro' Parade, Rathmines—Law clerk.
O'Byrne, John, 5 Shamrock Villas, Harold's Cross—Painter.
O'Byrne, Joseph, Crehelp, Dunlavin, Co. Wicklow—Grocer.
O'Callaghan, Michael, 6 Shannon terrace, Old Kilmainham—Coachbuilder.
O'Callaghan, J, 20 Leinster st—Commercial clerk.
O'Connell, J, 9 Parnell Cott, Malahide—Labourer.
O'Connor, Thos, 4 Lower Sherrard street, Dublin—Seaman.
O'Donnell, Jas, 28 Francis st—Hairdresser.
O'Dwyer, Michael, 49 Cork st, Dublin—Cooper.
O'Flaherty, Martin, 22 Rialto st—Clerk.
O'Flaherty, Liam, 22 Rialto st—Clerk.
O'Gorman, John, 1 Coulson ave, Rathgar—Railway clerk.
O'Neill Frank, 14 Lower Gardiner street, Dublin—Tea packer.
O'Neill, E, 14 Ring street, Inchicore—Fitter.
O'Neill, Joseph, 14 Lower Gardiner street, Dublin—Tea packer.
O'Neill, Michael, 49 Phoenix st—Blacksmith.
O'Halloran, C, Auburn Villas, Kingstown.
O'Rafferty, John, Main st, Lusk—Groom.
O'Rourke, Ml, 2 Seville place—Clerk.
O'Rourke, P, 78 Marrowbone lane, Dublin—Coal agent (labourer).
O'Reilly, Ptk, 44 Reuben st, Dublin—Silk-weaver.
O'Shea, Dermott, 10 Temple street, Dublin—Warehouse clerk.
Perry, Jas, 42 Up Gloucester st—Labourer.
Perry, Greo, 42 Up Gloucester st—Foreman.
Phelan, Michael, 4 Portobello place, SCR—Carpenter.
Phillips, John, 9 Sth Brown st—Carrier.
Power, Thomas, 14 Lr Gardiner street—Tailor.
Power, Joseph, Bluebell, Inchicore—Machinist.
Power, Arthur, Bluebell, Inchicore—Labourer.
Power, Wm, Bluebell, Inchicore—Drilling machinist.
Price, Edward, 15 Killarney Parade, NCR—Clerk, Civil Service.
Pugh, Thos, 9 Charville Mall, Nth, Strand—Clerk.
Quigley, John, Police Barracks, Store street, Dublin—Ex Policeman.
Reardon, Michael (? Reardon), 22 Ring terrace, Inchicore—Apprentice coachbuilder.
Redmond, Patrick, 24 Phillipsburgh avenue, Dublin—Labourer.
Reynolds, Charles, 70 Gardiner st,—Ship's fireman.
Roche, Thomas Q, 4 Sidney tce, SCR—Book-keeper.
Roche, Wm, 4 Sydney tce, SCR—Clerk.
Rooney, James, Lusk, Co. Dublin—Farmer.
Rooney, Edward, Luck, Co. Dublin—Farmer.
Rungien, (Runaungie) Richard, Lusk—Carpenter.
Russell, J, Chalgrove ter, SCR, Dublin—Butcher.
Saul, John, 37 Parkview terrace, Kilmainham—Labourer.
Schweppe, Fred, 3 Mountain place, Dublin—Pattern case maker.
Server, Thomas, Lusk—Farmer.
Shanahan, Philip, 134 Foley street—Grocer.
Sheils (? Sheeln) Jas, 33 Bessboro' ave—Clerk.
Shorthall, P, 10 Castlewood pl, Rahtmines—fireman.
Shelley, Denis, 4 Seville pl—Cabinetmaker.
Shelley, Thos, 4 Seville pl—Cabinetmaker.
Sieman, Charles, 143 James's st—Clerk.
Smith, Ml, 2 Bayview ave, Nth Strand—Painter.
Smith, Thomas, 61 Lr Dominick st—Postman.
Slattery, Jas, 9 Woodville, Botanic ave, Dublin—Cabinet makers apprentice.
Stafford, Edward, Swords, Co. Dublin—Butcher's assistant.
Stapleton, Wm, 30 (13) Gt George's st—Painter.
Stokes, Richaard, 30 Hollybank road, Dublin—Draper's assistant.
Swanzy, Patrick, 108 Phillipsburgh ave, Fairview, Dublin—Baker.
Tobin, Michael, 118 Parnell st, Dublin—Grocer's assistant.
Toole, John, 13 Gray st—Labourer.
Tracy, John, 7 Rathmines terr—Grocer's assistant.
Troy, Patk, 179 Emmet rd, Inchicore—Skilled labourer.
Troy, Daniel, 179 Emmet rd, Inchicore—Body-maker.
Venables, Thos, 7 Chamber st—Silk-weaver.
Walsh, Patrick J, 17 Glenarm ave—Furniture salesman.
Walsh, Ptk, 47 Grove park, Rathmines—Motor mechanic.
Ward, Patrick W, 100 Lr Gloucester street, Dublin—Grocer's porter.
Weston, Bartle, Turvey, Donabate—Bricklayer.
Weston, Charles, Donabate, Co. Dublin—Bricklayer.
Whelan, Richard, Herberton Buildings, Rialto—Railway clerk.
Whelan, M, 7 Emerald square, Dolphin's Barn—Basket maker.
Whitmore, William, Clonee, Camolin, Co. Wexford—Farmer.
Whiteham, Chris, Patrick street, Mullingar—Labourer.
Williams, W, 19 Sydney terr, West rd—Bookbinder.
Young, Robert, 17 Sandford ave—Shop Asst.
Young, Thomas, 17 Sandford ave—Apprentice to brass moulder.

376 to Wakefield on 6th May

The following list of 376 prisoners arrested by the military authorities, and received at Wakefield Detention Barracks on May 6th, was issued on Saturday, 13th May:

Ballsbridge Party

Allwell, Jos, 144 Townsend street—Dairyman.
Boland, Michael, Lower Rathfarnham—Carter.
Bracken, John (jun), 14 Charlemont Mall, Portobello—Painter's app.
Bradley, Richard, 82 Lr Gardiner st—Printer.
Byrne, Chris, 37 Blackpitts—Plasterer.
Byrne, Lawrence, 16 Gloucester place—Carter.
Banks, Henry, 53 Shelbourne road—Cabman.
Banks, Henry, 7 Upper Camden st—Storekeeper.
Birmingham, Patk, 119 Haddington rd—Labourer.
Bracken, John (sen), 14 Charlemont Mall, Portobello—House painter.
Breen, John, 20 Charlotte street, SCR—Grocer's assistant.
Brennan, Patk, The Gardens, Milltown Park—Market gardener.
Brennin, 33 Summerhill—Confectioner.
Breslin, TF, 2 Fairview Corner—Book-keeper.
Burton, Fredk, 18 Herbert lane—Carter.
Byrne, Patk, 3 Camden place—Tailor.
Byrne, Henry, 3 Camden place—Porter.
Byrne, Michael, 135 Townsend street—Labourer.
Byrne, J, 7 Barrow street—Law clerk.

Byrne, John, 31 Clarendon street—Mess man.
Byrne, Ed, no residence—Labourer.
Byrne, Peter, 7 Barrow street—Law clerk.
Cahill, Patrick, 74 Church street—Labourer.
Campbell, Mich J, 81 Lr Gardiner st—Electrician.
Carberry, Chris, 3 Myrtle terrace, Church road—Stock book-keeper.
Carroll, Thos, 10 Repeal place—Labourer.
Carroll, Nick, 10 Repeal place—Labourer.
Carroll, Dudley, 17 Clarendon street—Hairdresser.
Carter, Richard, Booterstown avenue, Willow park—Gardener.
Casey, Leo, 60 Shelbourne rd—Dentist's apprentice.
Cassidy, Thos, 13 Denzille street—Coach builder.
Christian, Wm, 94 Bride street—Porter.
Clarke, Joseph, 6 Harcourt street—Vanman.
Coffey, Wm, 7 Main street, Blackrock—Grocer's assistant.
Colgan, Daniel, 65 Gt Brunswick street—Clerk.
Cooper, Robert, 27 Clarendon street—Case maker.
Cosgrove, John, 1 Grattan Court—Motor driver.
Cranwell, Ed, 5 Margaret's Cottages—Nagsman.
Cregg, Laughlin, 74 Parnell street—Barman.
Cuff, James, 4 Greenfield place—Book-keeper.
Cuffe, Patk, 4 Greenfield place—Railway porter.
Cullen, Michael, 67 Percy place—Clerk.
Cullen, John, 67 Percy place—Clerk.
Delaney, Joseph, 3 Waterford street—Blacksmith.
Dempsey, Charles, 5 Emerald street—Winchman.
Donnelly, Simon, 34 Wexford street—Plumber.
Dowling, Thos F, 96 Donore terr, SCR—Dentist.
Dowling, Chas, 96 Donore terr, SCR—Dentist.
Dowling, Lewis, 96 Donore terr, SCR—Dentist.
Dowling, Stephen, 46 Marborough street—Carter.
Doyle, Jas, Edenville, Haddington rd—Clerk, Gas Company.
Doyle, James, 39 Lr Kevin street—Labourer.
Doyle, Patk, 96 SCR—Ship plater.
Ducia, Pat, Upper Mount Town, Kingstown—Driver.
Dunne, James, Allanwood, Robertstown, Co. Kildare—Boatman.
Duffy Thomas, 15 Thomas street—Labourer.
Duff Henry, 21 Lullymore terrace, SCR—Retired railway official.
Dunne,John, 6 South Dock place—Dray man.
Dunne, Joseph, 46 Malborough street—Blacksmith.
Dunne, Timothy, 2 Haddington road—Turf dealer.
Dunne, James, 28 Great Clarence street—Labourer.
Dunne, Andrew, Allanwood, Robertstown, Co. Kildare—Boatman.
Dunphy, John, 15 Pleasants street—Cycle salesman.
Fay, James, 46 Marlborough street—Carter.
Finn, Timothy, 9 Brosna cottages, Blackrock—Tailor.
Finn, Luke, 12 Grenville street—Coal labourer.
Flannigan, Patrick, New street, Portumna (11 Reginald street)—Joiner.
Fleming, Michael, 9 Hamilton row—Motor fitter.
Fulham, Thos, 54 Denzille street—Labourer.
Gaffikin, Ed Digby, 67 Lr Gardiner street—Mechanic.
Gaskin, Frank, 55 Reuben avenue, SCR—Moulder.
Gibbons, Patrick, 46 Marborough street—Rivetter.
Gill, James, 3 Lauderdale terrace—Wine porter.
Gillies, Thos, 31 Leinster road—Electrician.
Goulding, John, 6 Vincent street, SCR—Shop asst.
Grace, James, 29 Longwood avenue, 3 Stanley Cottages, Mespil road—Clerk.
Griffen, M, 17 Vavasour square, Sandymount—Tailor.
Guilfoyle, John, 47 Pleasants street—Electrician.
Guilfoyle, Jos, 47 Pleasants street—Stationer.
Hannon, James, 1 Bayview avenue, Fairview—Railway porter.
Hardy, Octavus, 17 Belgrave road—Insurance clerk.
Hardy, Joseph, Mount Prospect, Ballinasloe—farmer.
Harvey, Patk, 8 Lr Mt Pleasant ave—Hairdresser.
Harvey, Jos C, 8 Lr Mt Pleasant ave—Electrician.
Hayes, Augustine, 16 Hume street—Tailor.
Henry, Jas, 4 Lr Orme place—Cabinet-maker.
Hickey, Michael, 30 Lennox street—Clerk.
Hill, Sam H, 18 Lr Ormond quay—Legal searcher.
Hynes, John, No Commons, Lusk—Labourer.
Irwin, Samuel, 22b Nicholas street—Laboratory assistant
Jackson, Francis, 26 South King street—Baker's assistant.
Jackson, Joseph, 26 South King street—Chauffeur.
Jennings, MO'S, 49 Londonbridge road—Independent.
Johnson, Ed, 2 Hamilton row—Waiter.
Jones, Peter, 81 Marlborough street—Pig minder.
Joyce, John, 1 Healy street—Case maker.
Joyce, John, Kilmore road, Artane—Gardener.
Judge, Richard, 26 Cumberland street—Billposter.
Kavanagh, Patrick, 25 Rathmines terrace—Labourer.
Kavanagh, Peter, 4 Ross road—Plumber's assistant.
Kavanagh, Patrick, 4 Ross road—Fitter's assistant.
Kavanagh, Jas, 8 Bishop street—Factory hand.
Kavanagh, Michael, 5 Pleasants street—Clerk.
Kavanagh, Wm, 5 Pleasants street—Clerk.
Kelly, Michael, 4 Poole's Arch, Dublin—Labourer.
Kelly, Thos, 1 Lambert cottages, off Linn street—Labourer.
Kelly, Richard, 3 Sth Gloucester st—Labourer.
Kelly, Patk, 5 St Nicholas road—Stationery.
Kenny, Charles, 7 Richmond place, Portobello—Wood cutter.
Kenny, James, 31 Leinster road—House agent.
Kerford, Patk, 59 Marlborough street—Newsman.
Kiernan, Ed, 13 Camden row—Storekeeper.
Kinsella, John, 23 Annaville avenue, Ranelagh—Bookbinder, edge gilder.
Knightly, Michael, 16 Gardiner's place—Reporter.
Lamgare, Patk, Kilmore road, Artane—Labourer.
Lang, Francis, 9 Shandon road—Civ Ser GPO.
Largan, Michael, 12 Waterford street—Munitions.
Lawlor, Ed, 11 New Grove avenue—Commercial traveller.
Layden, Mathew, 105 Parnell street—Messenger.
Leonard, Michael, 2 Grattan Cottages, off Grattan street—Gas stoker.
Leonard, Jos, 29 Nottingham st—Electrician.
Lindsay, John, 18 Primrose ave—Railway guard.
Lyng, Thos, 53 Lr Clanbrassil street—Pawnbroker's assistant.
Lynch, Daniel, 46 Marlborough st—Labourer Gen.
Lynch, John, 25 Annesley avenue—Car owner.
Lyons, Geo, 14 Duke street—Printer's clerk.
Mahon, John, 6 Duker's lane—Engine driver.
Mahon, James, 6 Duker's lane—Labourer.
Malone, Robert, 17 Pigeon House road—Labourer.
Mallen, James, 19 George's quay—Hair dresser.
Mannering, Ed, 15 Charlemont st—Labourer.
McCabe, Patrick, 13 Townsend st—Coach painter.
McCarthy, Bernard, 32 Penrose street, Ringsend—Jeweller.
McCline, Hubert, 82 Lr Gardiner st—Book-keeper.
M'Dermott, Joseph, 12b Mark street—Bootmaker.
M'Ginn, Michael C, Stranville, Strand road—Clerk.

M'Grath, John, 20 East Essex st—Warehouseman.
M'Kenna, Joseph, c/o M Redmond, Forge, Milltown—Horse shoer.
M'Loughlin, Patrick, Sandymount Castle—Handyman.
McMahon, John J, 113 middle Abbey st—Property master.
McNamara, John, 114 Main street, Bray—Draper's assistant.
Meagher, Michael, 27 Sandwith place—Carpenter.
Meagher, Patk, 27 Sandwith terrace—Joiner.
Miller, Geo, Booterstown avenue, Willow Park—Groundsman.
Moriarty, Denis, 11 Heytesbury street—Baker.
Mullaly, Joseph, 38½ Talbot street—Grocer's asst.
Murphy, Peter, 32 Prospect avenue, Glasnevin—Labourer.
Murphy, John, 4 Lr Leeson street—Baker and confectioner.
Murphy, Jas, 248 Mountpleasant Buildings—Labourer.
Murray, Joseph, 3 Hamilton row—Labourer.
Murray, Frank, Verbina House, Drumcondra—Student.
Murray, Chris, 13 Waterford street—Porter.
Martin, Joseph, 49 Heytesbury street—Brass fitter.
M'Bride, Patk, 12 Boyne street—Messenger.
M'Cabe, Wm, 57 Lr Dominick street—Smith's helper.
M'Carthy, Michael, 16 Annaville avenue, Ranelagh—Painter.
McDermott, Owen, Artane village—Carpenter.
M'Dowell, Cecil, 1 Prospect place—Architect.
M'Mahon, John, 5 Sandwith street—Clerk.
Molloy, Joseph, 2 Palace street—Dockyard labourer.
Murphy, Wm, 35 Sth William street—Coat maker.
Murphy, Charles, 7 Albert place. E—Clerk.
Murray, Jas, 24 Michael's lane—Carter.
Navin, Michael R, 13 Seaforth avenue, Sandymount—Porter.
Nolan, Patrick, 171 Townsend street—Wheelwright.
Nolan, Peter, 2 Turner's Cottages, Ballsbridge—Tram Coy.
O'Brien, Tim, 3 Charleville road—Teacher.
O'Brien, Patk V, 43 Lombard street, W—Corporation employé.
O'Brien, Peter, 8 Duke's lane—Cabinet-maker.
O'Byrne, Wm, 6 Seaforth avenue—Van driver.
O'Byrne, Thos, 6 Seaforth avenue—Motor driver.
O'Connor, Joseph, 11 Harty place—Clerk.
O'Connor, Joseph, 7 Rathmines terrace—Provision assistant.
O'Connor, Thos, 14 Adelaide road, Sandycove—Plumber.
O'Connor, Alf, 82 Lr Gardiner st—Junior clerk.
O'Donaghue, Thos, 19 Up Sheriff street—Clerk.
O'Duffy, James P, 162 Rathmines road—Clerk.
O'Grady, Anthony, 33b Nicholas street—Draper's porter.
O'Hanlon, John, 12 Queen's square—Caretaker.
O'Leary, Arthur, Homestead, Cabra—Caretaker.
O'Malley, Chris, 1 Lr Buckingham st—Clerk.
O'Mara, Peter, 46 John Dillon street—Book maker and window dresser.
O'Moore, Patk, 6 Lr St Columba's rd—SS clerk.
O'Neill, Andrew, 197 Railway street—Porter.
O'Reilly, Chris, 12 Sandwith place—Lawyer.
O'Reilly, Patk, 95 Townsend street—Grocer's asst.
Parle, Richard, 13 Cardiff lane, South Wall—Messenger.
Peate, Thos, 169 Parnell street—Labourer.
Pender, James, 44 John Dillon street—Tailor.
Pender, Wm, 51-6 Corporation Buildings—Labourer.
Phelan, Patk, 81 Marlborough street—Yardman.
Porter, Owen, 21 Warrenmount place—Upholsterer.
Power, Patk, 62 Gt Brunswick street—Workman.
Purcell, Phillip, 82 Lr Gardiner st—Canvasser.
Quinn, Thos, 2 Adelaide place—Labourer.
Quinn, John, 26 Hanover street E—Assistant.
Rafferty, Thos, 59 Dufferin ave, SCR—Carpenter.
Reilly, James, 33 Summerhill—Carter.
Reilly, Robt, 24 Upper Gloucester place—Carrier.
Ribton, Thos, 21 Delahunty's Buildings—Porter.
Robinson, Thos, 2 Park View, Ashtown—Clerk.
Rowley, Wm, 24 Bath avenue, Ringsend road—Painter.
Ryan, Cornelius, 42 Castle st—General worker.
Ryan, John, 43 Patrick st, Kingstown—Van driver.
Ryan, John, 74 Parnell st—Barman.
Scully, Thos, 7 Pitt street—Seaman.
Shelly, John, 3 Waterford street—Bullockman.
Slack, Patk, 4 Young's Cottages—Labourer.
Smith, Albert, 3 Charlemont Mall, Portobello—Porter.
Tannan, Michael A, rear 3 Wilton terr, Dublin—Clerk.
Tevercuse, Patk, 17 Lower Gardiner street—Blacksmith.
Thackaberry, Wm, 1 Charlgrove terr, SCR—Baker.
Timbrenan, Tobias, Ballagh, Monasterevan.
Tobin, Patk, 4 Cottage place—Labourer.
Tobin, Martin, 7 Main street, Blackrock—Grocer's assistant.
Trayner, Thos, 20 Synnott place—Boot maker.
Treacy, Jas, 10 Tramway terrace, Sandymount—Tram conductor.
Tully, William, 18 Upper Gloucester place—Labourer.
Tully, Geo, 18 Upper Gloucester place—Filer.
Turner, Frank, 10 Summerhill—Machinist.
Turner, Joseph, 10 Summerhill—Concreter.
Tyrell, Jas, 77 Upper George's st, Kingstown—Electrician.
Walker, John, 6 Pigeon House road—Labourer.
Wall, Michael F, 3 Eldon terr—Stone-cutter.
Wall, Wm, 3 Eldon terr—Marble polisher.
Walpole, Leo, 3 Ranelagh road—Tailor.
Walsh, Richard, 22 Lr Kevin st—Baker.
Walsh, Colman, 95 Talbot st—Tailor.
Ward, Patk, 81 Bath avenue—Van driver.
Walters, Jas SE, James st—Labourer.
Welch, Jas, 12 Turner's Cottages, Ballsbridge—Coal merchant.
Williams, Patk, 25 Stafford street—Labourer, Corporation.
Woodcock, Wm, 16 Lr Grand Canal st—Case maker.

List from Kilmainham

Allen, George, Boys' Home, Abbey street.
Arnold, James, 47 Dolphin's Barn St, Dublin.
Barry, Joseph, 32 Parliament street.
Breen, Patrick, 16, Fitzwilliam lane.
Buckle, J, High street, Cork—Draper's assistant.
Burke, Michael, 8 Basin lane.
Byrne, James, 49 Albion terrace.
Byrne, Joseph, 10 Braithwaite street.
Carter, John, 13 Denzille street, Merrion square.
Clarke, James, 72 Middle Abbey street.
Condron, William, 3 Mullins terr, Grove road.
Coney, Patk, 1 Springfield terr, Dolphin's barn.
Cooney, William, 17 Prebend street.
Cooper, John, 43 Lanark street.
Cullen, Thomas, 26 Landerdale terr, New row.
Cullen, William, 3. St Joseph's terr, Philipsburg Av.
Cullen, Michael, 37 High street.

Cunningham, Patk 3 High street.
Cunningham, John, 3 High street.
Darby, Charles, 8 West Essex street.
Darcy, John, 15 Tyrconnell street, Inchicore.
Darney, John E, 9 Clonliffe avenue.
Dowling, Michael, Buckingham place.
Doyle, Thomas, 1 Queen's lane.
Doyle, William, 28 N Frederick street.
Duffy, James, 202 Phibsborough road.
Duggan, Edward, Ballyheada, Ballinhassig, Cork.
Dunne, Frank, 1 Clonmore road.
Farrell, Joseph, 11 Prebend street.
Farrelly, James, 26 Parnell street.
Farrington, Leo, Boys' Home, Abbey street.
Filey, Matthew, 70 Rialto Buildings,
Fitzpatrick, Thos, 2a Bride street.
Fitzpatrick, Martin, 92 Emmet road.
Gibson, Edward, 31 St Michael's terr, Blackpitts.
Giffney, Michael, 10 Seville place Cottages.
Goga, John, 194 Rathgar road.
Halpin, Joseph, 7 St Joseph's parade.
Halpin, James Francis, 3 Goldsmith street.
Humphries, Richard, 54 Northumberland road.
Kelly, Daniel, 2a Bride street.
Kelly, Michael Joseph, 1 Bailey's row, Summerhill.
Kelly, Thomas 13 St Augustine street.
Kelly, Patk Bealan. 29 Cabra Park, Dublin.
Kenny, Joseph, 160 Phibsborough road.
King, Leo, 4 Sackville Gardens.
Lambert, Thomas, Old Bridge House, Milltown.
Larkin, John, 160 Phibsborough road.
Leeson, John, Hackett's Court, Capel street.
Lennon, Michael John, 6 Longwood avenue.
Lyndon, Patrick, 15 Railway street.
Lynch, James, 2 Curzon street, SCR.
Macken, Aloysius, 44 Mountjoy square.
Magee, George, 40 Corn Market.
Maguire, John, 86 Capel street.
Manning, Michael, 5 Thomas Davis street, Golden Bridge.
McGill, Edmund, 5 Phibsborough place.
McMahon, Dan Joseph, 2 Richmond row, Portobello.
Moore, Patk, 16 St Joseph's sq Vernon ave, Clontarf.
Moore, Peter, 5 Lower Gloucester street.
Morgan, Henry, 14 Henrietta street.
Moroney, Thomas, 18 Werburgh street.
Murphy, Joseph, Donoghue street.
Murphy, Thomas, 26 Ring's terrace.
Newman, John, Marine Lodge, Fairview.
Nolan, John, 13 Upper Mayor street.
Norries, David Henry, Memorial Hall, Londonderry.
Nugent, Michael, 77 Angel street.
O'Brien, Stephen, 3 Tivoli avenue.
O'Connell, Edward, 8 Corn Market.
O'Connor, Patk, Main street, Rathfarnham—Draper.
O'Kelly, John, 32 Connaught street.
O'Kelly, Frank, 10 Castlewood place, Rathmines.
O'Neill, George, 9 York Villas.
O'Reilly, John, 43 Geraldine street.
O'Toole, William, 31 Lower Erne street.
Parker, George, 10 Rutland square.
Phelan, Thomas, 160 Phibsborough road.
Quinn, Hugh, 41 Blessington street.
Rowman, William, 77 Angel street.
Saul, James, 37 Park view terr, Brookfield road.
Staines, Michael, 63 Murtagh road.
Stritch, James, 51 Mountview street.
Sweeney, Michael, 5 Harold's Cross.
Tallon, Joseph, 2 Brana Villas, N Richmond st.
Wall, Thomas, 31 Liffey street.
Whelan, Patk, 1 Lr Sherrard street.
Whelan, John, James's street Warehouse.

List from Arbour Hill

Beggs, Joseph, The Square, Skerries—Fishmonger.
Bent, John, 4 Swift's row—Sheet metal worker.
Cadden, Matthew J, 22 Gt Ship street, Dublin—Tailor.
Corcoran, Patk, 42 Waterford st—Asst dentist.
Cusack, John, 32 Dargle road, Drumcondra—Carpenter.
Daly, James, Cluny, Clontarf—Fitter and turner.
Derham, Rbt, Hoar Rock, Skerries—Motor mechanic.
Dunne, Patk, 35 Vicar street, Dublin—Driver.
Du Bourdien, Arthur, 50 Park ave Sandymount—Asst Supt Tel, GPO.
Farrell, John, 60 Up Dominick st, Dublin—Chauffeur.
Fitzgerald, Leo, 173 Gt Brunswick st—Painter.
Fitzgerald, Thomas, 173 Gt Brunswick street—Painter.
Fitzgeral, James, 173 Gt Brunswick st—Painter.
Ganley, William, Ballingham, Skerries—Farmer.
Gibbons, Pete, Ballingham, Skerries—Farmer.
Gibson, James, 115 James's street—Labourer.
Gibson, Denis, 115 James's street—Porter.
Griffiths, Nicholas, 32 Benburb st—Shop assistant.
Griffiths, Patrick, 32 Benburb st—Shop assistant.
Griffiths, William, 32 Benburb st, Dublin—Motor mechanic.
Hand, Thomas, Milverton, Skerries—Traveller.
Jenkinson, Wm, 37 Up Gardiner street—Labourer.
Jordan, Patk, 34 Usher's quay—Labourer.
Keane, Peter, Strand street, Skerries—Teacher.
Keogh, Patk, 115 James's street—Baker.
Kilmartin, Patk 24 Stoneybatter, Dublin—Shopkeeper.
Lacey, Michael, Strifeland, Balbriggan—Blacksmith.
Leggett, Rbt, 3 Hardwicke pl, Dublin—Painter.
Lynch, James, 4 Prussia lane—Labourer.
Maguire, Denis, Strifeland, Balbriggan—Farmer.
Maguire, Philip, 36 Thomas street—Labourer.
McCarthy, D, Blessington st—Coach builder.
McCormack, Peter, 92 Lr Dorset st, Dublin—Vanman.
McDermott, Patk, Drumcliff, Co. Sligo—Labourer.
McDonald, Joseph, 155 James's street—Labourer.
McGuinness, Joseph, Cross st Skerries—Bootmaker.
McHugh, William, 115 James's street—Labourer.
McHugh, Miles, 115 James's street—Labourer.
McHugh, Edward, 115 James's street—Messenger.
McHugh, Patk, 115 James's street—Messenger.
Moore, J Wm, 26 Stoneybatter, Dublin—Traveller.
Moran, John, Phoenix Hill—Clerk.
Munster, Thomas, 121 Chord road, Drogheda—Chauffeur.
Oglesby, Joseph, 12 St George's place—Labourer.
O'Toole, John, 115 James's street—Labourer.
O'Reilly, Thomas, North Bank, Skerries—Baker.
O'Reilly, John, 80 Delahunty's Buildings, Dublin—Plumber's assistant.
Reynolds, Henry, Balbriggan st, Skerries—Warehouseman.
Ryan, Michael, 115 James's street—Labourer.
Shanley, Michael, Hoar Rock, Skerries—Vanman.
Sheridan, John, 91 St Ignatius road, Dublin—Grocer's assistant.
Sherlock, John, Town Park, Skerries—Labourer.
Shiels, Joseph, Cross street, Skerries—Clerk.

Tallon, James, 2 Brana Villas, N Richmond st—Clerk.
Tarpey, Patk 7 Inns quay—Clerk.
Whelan, Daniel, 20 Middle Gardiner st—Carpenter.

203 to Stafford on 8th May.

The following list of 203 prisoners who were removed from Richmond Barracks, Dublin, on the 8th May, 1916 and lodged in Stafford Detention Barracks on 9th May, 1916, was issued on Sunday, 14th May :

Allen, A, 3 Castle street, Enniscorthy.
Alexander, W, 4 Brookfield avenue, Blackrock.
Barnes, J, St James's Park, Falls road, Belfast.
Barrett, J, 13 Dublin street, Dundalk.
Black, E, 1 Hospital lane, Enniscorthy.
Boland, C, Upper Abbey street.
Boyne, W, 50 Irish street, Enniscorthy.
Brandon, J, 45 Temple street, Blackrock, Co. Dublin.
Byrne, J, 19 Island road, Enniscorthy.
Byrne, P, Island road, Enniscorthy.
Byrne, J, 117 Lr George's street, Kingstown.
Bulfin, E, Derrinlough House, Birr.
Cahill, M, Shannon Hill, Enniscorthy.
Carney, FJ, 24 Cadogan road, Fairview.
Carolan, M, 80 Chief street, Belfast.
Carroll, J, 27 Irish street, Enniscorthy.
Carty, M, 1 Slaney street, Enniscorthy.
Casey, P, Castletown road, Dundalk.
Chapman, T, Busherstown, Ballynetty, Co.Wexford.
Chapman, P, Busherstown, Ballynetty, Co.Wexford.
Colgan, P, 28 Leinster Cottage, do.
Clear, T, 57 Agincourt avenue, Belfast.
Coady, J Irish street, Enniscorthy.
Coady, P, Irish street, Enniscorthy.
Coady, J, 24 Irish street, Enniscorthy.
Conlon, J, River road Cottages, Castleknock.
Connor, M, John street, Enniscorthy.
Connors, P, Hospital lane, Enniscorthy.
Connolly, M, 58 Lower Gloucester street, Dublin.
Conway, J, do.
Corish, R, 35 William street, Wexford.
Courtney, C, 5 New Enniscorthy, Co. Wexford.
Courtney, J, Ross road, Enniscorthy.
Courtney, W, Ross road, Enniscorthy.
Cullen, T, Gibberpatrick, Co. Wexford.
Cullen, M, Ross road, Enniscorthy.
Cullen, J, 6 Court street, Enniscorthy.
Cummins, M, 49 South Gt George's street.
Darcy, P, 27 Upper Abbey street.
Darcy, P, Woodside, Dalkey.
Davis, M, Lower Church street, Enniscorthy.
Derham, M, 2 St Joseph street, Synnot place.
Devereux, Deancastle, Bannow, Co. Wexford.
Devitt, E, 47 St Mary's road, North Wall.
Doherty, J Tramway Cottages, Sandymount.
Donoghue, J, Ross road, Enniscorthy.
Donnelly, N, 31 Templeshannon, Enniscorthy.
Dorin, D, 5 Hill View terrace, Enniscorthy.
Doody, P 66 Jervis street.
Doolan, J, 38 John street, Enniscorthy.
Doyle, T, Lower Church street, Enniscorthy.
Doyle, PJ, Temple Shannon, Enniscorthy.
Doyle, A, (jun) Shannon Hill, Enniscorthy.
Doyle, R, 66 Irish street, Enniscorthy.
Doyle, T, Shannon Hill, Enniscorthy.
Doyle, A, Shannon Hill, Enniscorthy.
Du Bourdiun, J, 50 Park avenue, Sandymount.
Dwyer, J, Hospital lane, Enniscorthy.
Ellett, E, 2 Eitlon terrace, Phibsborough.
Ennis, M, Tomalassat, Enniscorthy.
Ernis, M, Ballinkeel, Co. Wexford.
Farnon, L, 10 Hollybrook road, Clontarf.
Farrell, H, Somerset street, Ballsbridge, HM ex-Launch 125, c/o Coastguard Office, Queenstown.
Fielding, T, Seaview, Barntown, Co. Wexford.
Finn, E, 27 Brookfield, Blackrock.
Fitzharris, J, Clonafton, Enniscorthy.
Fitzpatrick, P, 15 Court street, Enniscorthy.
Fitzpatrick, M, 66 Bride street.
Fortune, R, 55 Marlborough street.
Fortune, W, 5 Slaney place, Enniscorthy.
Fox, B, Brookfield avenue, Blackrock.
Fox, T, Main street, Maryborough.
Franklin, J, 60 St John street, Enniscorthy.
Franklin, M, St John street, Enniscorthy.
Furlong, J, Bargy Common, Clearistown, Co.Wexford.
Gahin, W, Duffrey street, Enniscorthy.
Garrett, J, Temple Shannon, Enniscorthy.
Gascoigne, J, 74 Brookfield Buildings, Blackrock, Co. Dublin.
Goodall, J, Mandling Folly, Enniscorthy.
Gorman, W, 3 Urban Council terrace, Enniscorthy. (Home address, 12 Vergemount, Clonskeagh, Co. Dublin).
Hayes, TJ, 6 Court street, Enniscorthy.
Hayes, T, 7 Court street, Enniscorthy.
Heffernan, M, Myra Lodge, Inchicore.
Hegarty, J, 11 Eden terrace, Kingstown.
Hendrick, W, 2 New street, Enniscorthy.
Hickey, B, Grove View, Stillorgan.
Holbroke, M, Templeshannon, Enniscorthy.
Holmes, D, 17 Railway street, Dublin.
Hutchin, W, 117 Upper Abbey street.
Hyland, J, 11 Lower Bridge street.
Halpin, P, Burn's row, Dundalk.
Hayes, J, Bridgeton, Co. Wexford.
Horan, M, 2 Anglesey avenue, Blackrock.
Irwin, CJ, Kilcannon House, Enniscorthy.
Jordan, J, 11 New street, Enniscorthy.
Kane, C, 145 Townsend street.
Kavanagh, P, 35 John street, Enniscorthy.
Kavanagh, M, Castleconnor, Ballina.
Kavanagh, J, Gibberwell, Duncormick, Co.Wexford.
Keegan, P, 10 Irish street, Enniscorthy.
Keeffe, P, Hospital lane, Enniscorthy.
Kehoe, P, Ballybough, Bridgetown, Wexford.
Kehoe, P, Riversdale, Enniscorthy.
Kehoe, J, Ballinapierce, Enniscorthy.
Kehoe, P, Skeeter Park, Cleriestown, Co.Wexford.
Kelly, M, Corduff, do.
Kelly, P, Slaney street, Enniscorthy.
Keogh, P, 15 Dolphin's Barn street.
Kingarroff, T, Claremorris, Co. Mayo, (Dunmore, Co. Galway).
Lacey, J, Shannon Hill, Enniscorthy.
Lacey, J, Temple Shannon, Enniscorthy.
Maguire, J, Crew Hill, Maynooth.
Maguire, M, Crew Hill, Maynooth, Co. Kildare.
Maher, J, 19 Cross Avenue, Kingstown.
Maher, D, 29 Longford avenue, SCR.
Maher, T, 33 Island road, Enniscorthy.
Mahon, P, 71 Summerhill, Dublin.
Mangan, T, Maynooth, Co. Kildare.
Mardley, F, 21 Summerhill.

Mardock, W, Gibberpatrick, Co.Wexford.
M'Carthy, T, 17 George street, Enniscorthy.
M'Gowan, J, 3 Victoria lane, Botanic avenue, Drumcondra.
McMacken, B, 80 Chief street, Belfast.
Moran, J, Fiory place, Co.Wexford.
Moran, P, Little Forest, Cloughran.
Moran, T, Johnstown, Duncormick, Co. Wexford.
Moran, M, Fiory place, Co. Wexford.
Moran, J, Church street, Enniscorthy.
Murphy, P, Lower Church street, Enniscorthy.
Murphy, J, 4 Main street, Enniscorthy.
Murphy, P, 14 New street, Enniscorthy.
Murphy, J, Old Hall Bridge Town, Co.Wexford.
Murphy, W, 2 New Range, Enniscorthy.
Murphy, J, 15 Ross road, Enniscorthy.
Murphy, P, 31 Templeshannon, Enniscorthy.
Murray, B, 28 Ross road, Enniscorthy.
Nash, P, 52 Gibson street, Belfast.
Neill, J, Hospital lane, Enniscorthy.
Nolan, M, 3 Hospital lane. Enniscorthy.
O'Brien, J, 48 Irish street, Enniscorthy.
O'Brien, D, 48 Irish street, Enniscorthy.
O'Brien, M, Hospital lane, Enniscorthy.
O'Connell, R, 9 Main street, Blackrock.
O'Connor, D, 11 Main street, Enniscorthy.
O'Donoghue, H, 12 Leeson Park.
O'Driscoll, R, Ashtown.
O'Hara, P, Swift row.
O'Kane, J, 4 Divis Drive, Falls road, Belfast.
O'Keegan, T, Irish street, Enniscorthy.
O'Leary, P, 36 East Essex street.
O'Neill, J, Fiory Hill, Enniscorthy.
O'Neill, M, 8 Irish street, Enniscorthy.
O'Reilly, J, Temple Shannon, Enniscorthy.
O'Reilly, J, Bruce, Clonevin, Gorey.
O'Shea, J, Knocktopher, Tonistown, Co. Kilkenny.
Osborne, H, 69 Smithfield, Belfast.
Parker, T, 12 Hollaf row, Dublin (Pte 2nd Leinster Regiment).
Reddin, GM, Rockfield, Artane.
Reddin, K., Rockfield, Artane.
Reddin, T, Rockfield, Artane.
Redmond, E, 15 Court street, Enniscorthy.
Reinhardt, WJ, 12 Bolton street.
Reynolds, P, 16 Clonmore road, Ballybough.
Rigley, P, 10 Court street, Enniscorthy.
Ring, P, 6 Sackville Gardens, Ballybough road.
Robinson, J, 10 Robson street, Glasgow.
Rogers, M, Hermitage Lodge, Rathfarnham.
Rossiter, J, 62 St John street, Enniscorthy.
Royce, W, 6 Slaney street, Enniscorthy.
Ruth, W, 72 John street, Enniscorthy.
Ryan, P, Collinstown, Cloghran.
Sharkey, T, 7 Dublin street, Dundalk.
Sheehan, P, 28 Irish street, Enniscorthy.
Sherwin, P, New Haggard, Lusk.
Shiel, M, 30 Slaney street, Enniscorthy.
Sinnott, J, 8 Main street, Enniscorthy.
Sinnott, TD, 21 Slaney place, Enniscorthy.
Smyth, P, 3 Castle street, Enniscorthy.
Stafford, W, Cools Barnton, Co.Wexford.
Stafford, T, Cools Barnton, Co.Wexford.
Stafford, J, Scarmill, Duncormick, Co. Wexford.
Stokes, T, 11 Duffy street, Enniscorthy.
Synnott, J, 7 Grattan terrace, Wexford.
Thorpe, W, Shannon Hill, Enniscorthy.
Thorpe, W, Shannon Hill, Enniscorthy.
Treanor, T, Island View Cottage, Enniscorthy.
Tumbleton, P, Mary street, Enniscorthy.
Tyrell, P, 10 Duffrey Hill, Enniscorthy.
Walker, J, 37 Addison road, Fairview.
Walker, M, 37 Addison road, Fairview.
Walsh, J, 29 Coombe street, Dublin.
Walter, JJ, Maxwell terrace, Dundalk.
Welsh, P, Old Church, Enniscorthy, Co. Wexford.
Whelan, J, 10 New street, Enniscorthy.
Whelan, J, John street, Enniscorthy.
White, M, Castle street, Enniscorthy.
Williams, H, 72 Cadogan road, Fairview.
Wilson, M, 48 N Gt George's st, (2 Nth King st, Dublin).
Wilson, J, 2 Hospital lane, Enniscorthy.
Wilson, R, Hospital lane, Enniscorthy.

197 to Wandsworth on 9th May.

The following lists of 197 prisoners who were removed from Richmond Barracks, Dublin on May 8th, and lodged in Wandsworth Detention Barracks, London, on May 9th, was issued on Monday, 15th May :

Amos, George, 21 Chapel street, Athlone.
Armstrong, James, Galbally.
Barnes, Michael, Ferns, Co. Wexford.
Barnes, Thomas, Ferns, Co. Wexford.
Bevan, Joseph, 58 Lower Dominick street.
Boland, William, 8 Sackville place.
Boylan, Edward, Dunboyne, Co. Meath.
Boylan, Peter, John and Joseph, same address.
Bracken, Joseph, 106 St Lawrence road, Dublin.
Brady, Christopher, 32 Foley street.
Breen, Miles, Finnish Rule, Co. Wexford.
Breen, Joseph, Finnish Rule, Co.Wexford.
Brennan, Mathew, Camolin, Co.Wexford.
Breslin, James Francis, Ferns.
Brown, Arthur, 9 Chapel ave, Irishtown, Dublin.
Burke, Thomas, 92 Duleek street, Drogheda.
Burke, Wm, 118 Parnell street, Dublin.
Burke, John, 33 Richmond street, Dublin.
Burke, Wm, Skehana, Peter's Wall, Galway.
Burke, John, Catherine, Kenvare, Dublin. (?)
Byrne, Wm, 437, NC road, Dublin.
Byrne, John, 62 Meath street, Dublin.
Byrne, John, Gorey avenue, Gorey.
Carberry, Charles, 61 Donaghmore, Co. Tyrone.
Car, Joseph, Blackbull, Drogheda.
Casidy, Patrick, Mullingar.
Carter, James, Charleville Gardens, Shanballa. Galway.
Coghlan, Wm, 81 Charlemont street, Dublin.
Collins, Maurice, 230 Clonliffe road, Dublin.
Collins, Michael, 23 Leigh st, Attcliffe Common, Sheffield.
Cooley, Patrick, Tonroe, Oranmore, Galway.
Condon, Thomas, Cloonana, Ashbourne, Co. Meath.
Connelly, Joseph, Fire Station, Tara st, Dublin.
Connors, John, Kilthomas, Ferns, Co.Wexford.
Conroy, Edward, Brenloughlane, Galway.
Cornese, PJ, De Courcy square, Glasnevin.
Cullen, Alexander, Fernback, Dundrum, Co. Dublin.
Cummins, Joseph, Coldwood, Athenry.
Cunningham, John, Campfield, Dundrum, Co. Dublin.
Daly, James, 9 Vance's Buildings, Bishop st Dublin.
Derham, Joseph, 26 North Frederick st, Dublin.

Donoghue, Daniel, 15 Donore avenue, Dublin.
Doyle, Patrick, 41 Lr Camden street, Dublin.
Doyle,Henry, 104 South Lotts road, Ringsend.
Doyle, Michael, Crawnford, Gorey.
Doyle, James, Ferns.
Duff, Thomas, Swords, Co. Dublin.
Duke, Thomas, St Margaret's, Co. Dublin.
Duke, Richard, same address.
Dunbar, Martin, Castle place, Ferns.
Dunleary, Christopher, 21 Gray street, Dublin.
Evans, Robert, 22 Harold's Cross, Dublin.
Fahy, Patrick J, Kinvara, Galway.
Earley, PJ, Swords, Dublin.
Farrell, Denis, 7 Miller place, Rutland st Dublin.
Farrelly, James, Railway terrace, Ardee.
Finnigan, Joseph, 1 Peter street, Drogheda.
Fox, Peter, Carrickmore, Tyrone.
Flannigan, Thomas, Merchants road, Galway.
Flynn, Frank, 181 NC road, Dublin.
Flynn, John, 103 Gt Brunswick st, Dublin.
Fuge, Joseph, Kilbride, Courtown, Harbour, Wexford.
Fuller, John, Williamara, Galway.
Gahan, Joseph, 19 Nicholas street, Dublin.
Galvin, James, 18 Blare's lane, Waterford.
Gaskin, Thos, 55 Reuben ave, SCR, Dublin.
Gaynor, Patrick, 4 Portobello square, Dublin.
Geoghegan, E, 29 Longwood ave, SC road, Dublin.
Gleeson, Martin, 22 Harold's Cross, Dublin.
Glynn, John, Duras, Kinvara, Galway.
Golding, Francis, 6 Vincent street, Dublin.
Golding, Thomas, 6 Vincent street, Dublin.
Golding, James, 6 Vincent street, Dublin.
Grogan, James, Tromague, Carrickmore, Tyrone.
Halpin, Thomas, 2 Stockwell lane, Drogheda.
Hampton, James, 18 Mary's Abbey, Dublin.
Hanbury, P, Dongora, Kinvara, Co. Galway.
Hanlon, Michael, Crushor, Kinvara, Co. Galway.
Hannigan, Thos, 19 Great Western sq, NCD.
Hardiman, Francis, Town Hall, Galway.
Hart, Henry, Dungannon, Tyrone.
Haskin, Michael, 'Drogheda Advertiser' office.
Hastings, John, 28 Magdalen street, Drogheda.
Hogan, Patrick, Main street, Gorey, Co. Wexford.
Hogan, Patrick, 53 Clonliffe road, Dublin.
Hogan, William, 111 Up Leeson street, Dublin.
Howley, Peter, Lime Park, Peterswell, Galway.
Hughes, William, Donaghmore, Tyrone.
Humphreys, James, Moore st, Dublin (49 Praed st).
Hynch, John, Ferns, Co. Wexford.
Hynes, Thomas, Cranmore Court, Galway.
Kain, Thos, 11 Arran quay, Dublin.
Kavanagh, John (or Michael) Ferns, Co. Wexford.
Kavanagh, JJ, 3 Sth Prince's street, Dublin.
Kavanagh, Wm, Ferns, Co. Wexford.
Keenan, Ml, 63 Beamore road, Drogheda.
Kelly, Joseph, 11 Upper Dominick street, Dublin.
Kelly, Thos, Charlemount, Dungannon, Co. Tyrone.
Kelly, Peter, Swords, Co. Dublin.
Kelly, Alderman, JJ (since released).
Kenny, Moses, 65 Main street, Gorey.
Kent, Matthew, Ballycarey, Ferns, Co. Wexford.
Keogh, Michael, 18 Synge street, Dublin.
Kilkelly, Michael, Towna, Kinnaird, Co. Galway.
Kilkelly, Patrick, Towna, Kinnaird, Co. Galway.
Kinsella, Robert, Ferns, Co. Wexford.
Kirwan, Patrick, 10 Gt Ship street, Dublin.
Leech, Stephen, Loughcurra, Kinvara, Co. Galway.
Logue, Edward, 21 Usher's quay, Dublin.
Lyons, Chas, 14 Portland place, Drumcondra.
Lynch, John, 5 St Joseph's terr, NCR, Dublin.
Lysham, Chris, Dunboyne, Co. Meath.
Mannion, John, 60 Gantry, Curraghwell, Co. Galway.
Mathews, Thos, Moorhall, Ardee, Louth.
Mathews, John, 22 Eugene street, Dublin.
McAlduff, Jas, Aughrogan, Carrickmore, Tyrone.
McCann, Andrew, Caskinera, Gorey.
McDonagh, (?), George street, Gorey.
McDonald, Edward, Kilborea, Camolin, Co. Wexford.
McElvogue, Jas, Donoghmore, Co. Tyrone.
McElvogue, John, Dungannon, Co. Tyrone.
McGill, William, Barrack st, Dunmore, Co. Galway.
McGrane, Thos, Seatown, Dundalk.
McGuire, James, 26 Prieston road, Dublin.
McGuirk, Patrick, Crevagh, Lr Garland, Dungannon.
McManus,Wm, 55 Marlborough street, Dublin.
McTaggart, Thos, 13 Church street, Dundalk.
Molloy, John, 111 Upper Leeson street, Dublin.
Moran, Chris, Swords.
Moroney, John, 33 Sth. Richmond street, Dublin.
Mullally, Michael, Cottage pl, Belvedere, Dublin.
Murphy, Patrick, 7 Mark's alley, Dublin.
Murphy, James, Ferns, Co. Wexford.
Murphy, Matthew, Ferns, Co. Wexford.
Murphy, Patrick, Ferns, Co. Wexford.
Murray, Patrick, Chapel lane, Dublin.
Nelson, Thomas, 40 Gardiner's lane, Dublin.
Nicholls, Geo, 2 University road, Galway.
Norgrove, Alfred, 15 Strandville avenue, Dublin.
Nugent, Chris, Swords.
O'Brien, Wm, 11 Leinster avenue, Dublin.
O'Brien, Jas, Morris Castle, Kilmuckridge, Gorey.
O'Brien, William, 10 Anna Villa, Ranelagh, Dublin.
O'Byrne, John, Cooleshall House, Gorey.
O'Connor, Thos Jos, Saggart, Co. Dublin.
O'Dwyer, Jas, 20 Rutland Cottages, Dublin.
O'Grady, Standish, 5 Wilton place, Dublin.
O'Hehir, Michael, 31 Little Strand street, Dublin.
O'Leary, Philip, 4 Middle Gardiner street, Dublin.
O'Leary, Cornelius, Costello, Co. Galway.
O'Maille, Patrick, Maam, Co. Galway.
O'Reilly, John, N, 181 North Circular road.
O'Neill, John, 111 Upper Leeson street.
O'Neill, Peter, St Michael's place, Gorey.
O'Reilly, Kevin, 181 North Circular road.
O'Rourke, Michael, Moree, Oranmore, Co. Galway.
Parnell, Matthew, 38 Susanville road, Dublin.
Pedlar, Wm, 27 Brookfield terrace, Dublin.
Poole, John, 50 Marlborough street, Dublin.
Quigley, James, County Surveyor, Navan.
Quinn, Wm, Caheravon, Kinvara, Co. Galway.
Quinn, James, Camolin Park, Wexford.
Redmond, Joseph, 28 Nth Frederick street.
Redmond, Owen, Ferns, Co. Wexford.
Riley, Thos, Ivy Cottage, The Ward, Dublin.
Ronayne, Michael, Dunmore, Co. Galway.
Roche, Thos, Ferns.
Ronan, Patrick, Ferns.
Ryan, James, Claremorris, Co. Mayo.
Scallon, Thos, Gorey.
Sears, Wm, 24 Leinster road, Rathmines.
Sexton, Michael, 28 Broadstone avenue, Dublin.
Sheehan, Patrick, 16 Hollybrook, road, Clontarf.

Sherrin, Thos, 50 Seville place, Dublin.
Smith, John, St Nevin's road, Valstreet, Scotland.
Smullen, Patrick, Ferran's lane, Broadstone.
Steinberger, Val, Belmore, Co. Galway.
Sweetman, John, Drumbaragh, Kells.
Taylor, Joseph, Swords.
Taylor, Thos, Swords.
Taylor, Chri, Swords.
Thornton, Michael, Spiddal, Co. Galway.
Waldron, Richard, London Bridge rd, Sandymount.
Ward, Bernard, Glenmalure House, Rialto Bridge, Dublin.
Ward, Patrick, Glenmalure House, Rialto Bridge, Dublin.
Welsh, Thomas, Merville, Taylor's Hill, Galway.
Whelan, Jas, Duris, Kinvara, Co. Galway.
Whelan, John, Duris, Kinvara, Co. Galway.
Whelan, Patrick, Woodlands, Ferns.
Whelan, Thos, Ferns.
White, Patrick, 27 Upper Abbey street.

54 to Wandsworth on 13th May

The following list of 54 prisoners who were removed from Richmond Barracks, Dublin, on 12th May, and lodged in Wandsworth Detention Barracks, London, on 13th May, was issued on 16th May:

Bermingham, Thomas, 91 Upper Rathmines.
Burke, Patrick, Benduff, Castlegar, Co. Sligo.
Cole, DL, 3 Mountjoy square, Dublin.
Conway, Andrew, Edenreva, Cliffoney.
Corcoran, John, Kiltimagh, Co. Mayo.
Cryan, Barty, Bridge street, Westport.
Cryan, Thos, Seefin, Cloonloo, Boyle.
Crystal, Hugh, Creevykeel, Cliffoney.
Curtis, W O'Leary, 34 N Gt George's st, Dublin.
Daly, Patrick Thomas, 22 Fitzroy avenue, Dublin.
Derry,Thomas, High street, Westport.
Derry, Michael, Octagon, Westport.
Duffy, Michael, Bridge street, Westport.
Fagan, John, 10 Havelock square, Dublin.
Fagan, James, 10 Havelock square, Dublin.
Foley, Hugh, Benduff, Castlegar, Co. Sligo.
Gammon, Edward, High street, Westport.
Gardiner, George, Edenreva, Cliffoney.
Gavin, Charles, High street, Westport.
Gavin, John, Murrisk.
Geraghty, Martin, James street, Westport.
Gilmartin, Charles, Carnduff, Cliffoney.
Gilmartin, John, Creevykeel, Cliffoney.
Gilmartin, John, Creevykeel, Cliffoney.
Gilmartin, Wm, Creevykeel, Cliffoney.
Griffith, Arthur, 122 St, Lawrence road, Clontarf.
Gunnigle, Lawrence, Carnduff, Cliffoney.
Gunnigle, Robert, Carnduff, Cliffoney, Co. Sligo.
Hannon, John, Creevykeel, Cliffoney.
Hannon, Edward, Cliffoney.
Harrin, Edward, James street, Westport.
Heraty, Hubert, Altamount street, Westport.
Hickey, Charles, James street, Westport.
Hughes, Owen, Larkhill, Westport.
Keane, Manus, Clonskill, Loughagower.
Kenny, Patrick, S Shop street, Westport.
Logan, John, Bridge street, Westport.
McDonnell, Francis, 91 Upper Rathmines.
McDonough, John, High street, Westport.
Malone, James, Quay road, Westport.
McDonnell, Paul, 91 Upper Rathmines.
McGarrigle, Charles, Creevykeel, Cliffoney.
Meehan, Bernard, Creevykeel, Cliffoney.
O'Brien, Thomas, Moyhasten, Westport.
O'Rourke, Peter, Abbeytown, Boyle.
O'Shea, John P, 29 Arran rd, Drumcondra, Dublin.
Ralph, Thomas, Mill street, Westport.
Redmond, Myles, 6 Parnell street, Wexford.
Reilly, Michael, Fair Green, Westport.
Ring, MJ, Drimmindoo, Westport.
Rooney, Patrick, Carnduff, Cliffoney, Co. Sligo.
Ruddy, Joseph, Church street, Westport.
Sammol, Edward, Peter street, Westport.
Tunny, Patrick, Derrykillew, Westport.
Walsh, Thaddeus, Mill street, Westport.

58 to Stafford on 13th May

The following list of 58 prisoners who were removed from Richmond Barracks, Dublin, on May 12th, and lodged in Stafford Detention Barracks on the 13th May, was issued on 17th May:

Barrett, Christopher, Court lane, Athenry—Painter.
Burke, Ptk, Caheroyn, Athenry—Labourer.
Cahill, Ml, Boyhill, Athenry—Labourer.
Callinan, Thos, Rockfield, Athenry—Groom.
Caulfield, Chas, Bozhill, Athenry—Postman.
Cleary, Thos B, Athenry—Farmer and builder.
Cleary, Joseph, Abbeygrove, Athenry—Apprentice.
Coady, Wm, Claregalway—Farmer.
Commins, Michael, Coldwood, Athenry—Farmer.
Commins, Edward, Tarmind, Clarenbridge—Farmer.
Commins, Wm, Coldwood, Athenry—Farmer.
Conniffe, Michael, Court lane, Athenry—Labourer.
Costello, Martin, Gortral, Athenry—Farmer.
Costello, Ml, Gortrall, Athenry—Farmer.
Costello, Patrick, Glenascaul, Oranmore, Co. Galway.
Coyle, Martin, Kittrogue, Claregalway.
Cullinane, John J, Mount Brown, Athenry—Farmer.
Dunleary, Ml, Ballygurrane, Athenry—Farmer.
Fahy, Lawrence, Tullyho, Athenry—Farmer.
Fallon, Ml, Two-Mile-Ditch, Co. Galway—Farmer.
Favrell, Ml, Parkmore, Athenry—Labourer.
Freany, Wm, Ballydonnell, Athenry—Farmer.
Freany, Ml, Ballydonnell, Athenry—Farmer.
Feeny, Jas, Two-Mile-Ditch, Co. Galway—Farmer.
Galvin, Jeremiah, Slieverne, Athenry—Farmer.
Gardiner, Jas, Knockbrack, Movivea, Athenry—Carpenter.
Glynn, Ml, Lidecan, Claregalway—Farmer.
Grealish, Ptk, Carnmore, Galway—Farmer.
Henegan, Peter, Derrydonnell, Athenry—Milesman, GS and W Railway.
Henegan, Patk, Ballydonnell, Athenry—Farmer.
Higgins, Wm, Coshla, Athenry,—Farmer.
Howley, Wm, Limepark, Peterswell, Co. Galway—Farmer.
Howley, Ml, Limepark, Peterswell, Co. Galway—Farmer.
Hughes, Ptk, Caheroyn—Farmer.
Hynes, Martin, Cross st, Athenry—Stonemason.
Kane, Ptk, Church st, Athenry—Labourer.
Kane, Ml, Derrydonnell, Athenry—Farmer.
Kennedy, Martin, Lackroo, Athenry—Farmer.
Kennedy, Ptk, Caheroyn, Athenry—Farmer.
Kenny, Ptk, Caheroyn, Athenry—Labourer.

King, Peter, Kiltullagh, Oranmore, Galway—Farmer.
King, John, Kiltullagh, Oranmore—Farmer.
Lynskey, Ptk, Kingsland, Athenry—Farmer.
M'Evoy, Martin, Rool, Craughwell—Farmer.
M'Keon, Peter, Cross st, Athenry—carpenter.
Monaghan, John, Oranmore—Labourer.
Mulryan, Wm, Kiltullagh, Oranmore—Farmer.
Murphy, John, Church st, Athenry—Labourer.
Murphy, Philip, Liecan, Clare, Galway—Farmer.
Newell, Thomas, Castlegar, Clare, Galway—Farmer.
O'Flaherty, Joseph, Loughrea—Draper.
O'Leary, Ml, Tarmind, Clarenbridge—Farmer.
Ryan, John, Ballydavid, Athenry—Farmer.
Silk, Thomas, Briarhill, Castlegar, Galway—Farmer.
Sweeny, Peter, Loughrea—Builder.
Waldron, John, Mulpit, Athenry—Farmer.
Walsh, Martin, Church st, Athenry—Carpenter.
Wilson, Richard AL, Loughrea—Ph Chemist.

273 to Wakefield on 13th May

The following list of 273 prisoners, who were removed from Richmond Barracks on May 12th, and lodged in Wakefield Detention Barracks on the 13th May, was issued on Thursday, 13th May:

Atkinson, Wm, New st, Dundalk—'Bus Driver.
Barry, Denis, Monster House, Kilkenny—Draper's assistant.
Begley, Jos, Castle road, Bandon—Apprentice.
Behan, Thomas, Rathangan—Labourer.
Birrell, Lawrence, Moss st, Dublin—Coal porter.
Blaney, John, Coosane, Athlone—Farmer.
Bowen, Barth, Melrose, Howth—Science teacher.
Boyce, Lawrence, Viking place, Arbour Hill—Motor driver.
Brady, Jas, Booterstown ave, Dublin—Clerk.
Brett, P, Blackmill st, Kilkenny—Motor mechanic.
Brown, Charles, do—Labourer.
Buckley, James, Millstreet—Carpenter.
Buckley, Wm, Kilcorney, Banteer—Shopkeeper.
Burke, Patk, Wolfe Tone st, Kilkenny—Labourer.
Burke, Finton, George st, Enniscorthy—Carpenter.
Byrne, Nich, Ballsbridge—Teacher.
Byrne, John, Donore, Naas—Blacksmith.
Byrne, Martin, Marrowbone lane, Dublin—Labourer.
Buren, Chris, Kilcullen road, Naas—Monotype operator.
Callaghan, John, Cork road, Bandon—Labourer.
Carmody, Patrick, Millstreet, Co. Cork—Baker and grocer.
Casey, William, King street, Mitchelstown—Trader.
Clegg, Jas, South st, New Ross—Draper's assistant.
Cogan, Robert, Allen Villas, Mardyke, Cork—Draper's assistant.
Collins, Ed, Cotballis, Donabate—Farmer.
Comerford, E, Wellington sq, Kilkenny—Electrician.
Connors, Ml, Ross road, Enniscorthy—Labourer.
Corkerry, Daniel, Cork st, Macroom—Shopkeeper.
Cox, JE, Oaklands Park, Ballsbridge—Surveyor.
Cox, Ed J, Oaklands Park, Ballsbridge—Clerk CDB.
Coyne, James, Bishop's Hill, Kilkenny—Baker.
Crowe, Martin, Ballyteigue, Corofin, Clare—Farmer.
Crowley, Wm, Gurteen, Bandon—Farmer.
Crowley, Patk, Gurteen, Co. Tipperary—Labourer.
Crowley, Ml, Rosbercon, New Ross—Shop assistant.
Crowley, John, Clonakilty—Farmer.
Crowley, Tim, Clonakilty—Farmer.
Daly, Francis, Cluny, Clontarf—Engine fitter.
Davies, Jas J, Harold's road, Kilkenny—Banker.
Deban, Patk, Cork road, Fermoy—Gaelic teacher.
Deene, Conor, Goold's Cross—Grocer.
Degan, M, South st, New Ross—Draper's assistant.
de Loughrey, Lawrence, Kilkenny—Ironmonger.
Dempsey, Patk, Locan st, Belfast—Shop assistant.
Dempsey, James, Locan st, Belfast—Shop assistant.
Denn, W, Tabbot's Inch, Kilkenny—Cab maker.
Desmond, Denis, Kinsale—Farmer's son.
Dobbyn, Henry, 21 Clonard Gardens, Belfast—Brick layer.
Dobbyn, Jas, 21 Clonard Gardens, Belfast—National school teacher.
Donnelly, Ml, Cornally, Silverbridge, Co. Armagh—Barman.
Donovan, Peter, Clonakilty—Farmer.
Donovan, John, Clonakilty—Student.
Doorley, Ed, Castle st, Roscommon—Butcher.
Doorley, JJ, Castle st, Roscommon—Garage owner.
Doyle, Michl, 32 Lr Gardiner st, Dublin—Labourer.
Doyle, John, South st, New Ross—Draper's assistant.
Doyle, Wm, Robert st, New Ross—Porter.
Doyle, Chas, Ballycarney, Ferns—Labourer.
Driscoll, Thomas, Bandon—Van driver.
Duffy, Ed J, Foyle st, Derry—Book-keeper.
Duncan, Patk, Meeting House st, Strabane—Van driver.
Dwyer, Stephen, Up Patrick st, Kilkenny—Reporter.
Evoy, Daniel, Prior lane, New Ross—Carpenter.
Fanning, John, William st, New Ross—Commission agent.
Finegan, John, St Patrick's terr, Dundalk—Porter.
Fitzgerald, John, Newbridge—Bootmaker.
Fitzgerald, James, Fast Hill, Queenstown—Engineer fitter's apprentice.
Fitzgerald, Thos, Dingle, Co. Kerry—Engine driver.
Foley, Ml, New Ross—Porter.
Fortune, Daniel, Ballycarnew, Gorey—Labourer.
Franklin, James, Barrackton, Cork—Shoemaker.
Furlong, Thos, Michael st, Kilkenny—Painter.
Furlong, Richard, Killashee, Naas—Labourer.
Gribban, Hugh, Castledawson, Co. Derry—Farmer.
Gallagher, John, Shannon Hill, Enniscorthy—Ledger clerk.
Gallon, Patk, Six-Mile Cross, Tyrone—Shop assistant.
Gibbons, John, Ballylarkin, Freshford—Farmer.
Grehan, Patk, Main street, Naas—Merchant.
Grieve, James, Glenmoran Mills, Strahane—Farmer.
Haden, Ptk, South st, New Ross—Draper's assistant.
Hales, Wm, Knockacurra, Bandon—Farmer.
Hales, Robert, Knockacurra, Bandon—Farmer.
Hall, Saml, Jocelyn st, Dundalk—Tailor.
Hamill, Thos, Broughton st, Dundalk—Van driver.
Hamilton, Chris, Kyle street, Cork—Carpenter.
Hanley, Danl, New Ross—Harness-maker.
Hannigan, James, The Square, Mitchelstown—Company agent.
Hanratty, Jas, Mill st, Dundalk—Printer.
Hartley, J, South st, New Ross—Grocer's assistant.
Harrington, Daniel, Macroom—Farmer.
Hart, Bernard, Dalkey—Railway clerk.
Hart, John, Claddagh, Clifden, Kilkenny—Farmer.
Kealy, Matt, Roughgrove, Bandon—Clerk.
Healy, Denis, Bodyke, Co. Clare—Farmer.
Heber, John, Lord Edward st, Limerick—Teacher.
Hedley, Jas, Irish st, Enniscorthy—Labourer.

Heduvan, Lawrence, Main st, Charleville—Teacher.
Hegarty, Patrick, Westland avenue, Derry—Tobacconist's assistant.
Hegarty, Daniel, Fair street, Mallow—Builder's foreman.
Hehoe, Tim, John st, New Ross—Grocer's assistant.
Henderson, Leo, Windsor Villas, Fairview, Dublin.
Higgins, Maurice, Up John st, Kilkenny—Law clerk.
Hughes, Gilbert, Coosane, Athlone—Farmer.
Hunt, Hubert, Corofin, Co. Clare—Farmer.
Hunt, Wm, Corofin, Co. Clare—Farmer.
Hyde, Patk, Ballinhassig, Cork—Farmer.
Hyde, Michael, Ballinhassig—Labourer.
Hyde, Jos, Gurteen, Bandon—Farmer.
Hyde, John, St Finn Barr's College, Cork—Student.
Jordan, Daniel, Farnalough, Newcester, Cork—Farmer's son.
Kavanagh, John, Miltown, Ferns—Labourer.
Kealey, Martin, Park Clifeden, Kilkenny—Farmer.
Kearns, John, Loughrea—Labourer.
Keegan, Michael, Queen st, Dublin—Labourer.
Keirse, Thos, Kileen, Co. Clare—Farmer.
Kelly, Daniel, Cashernageran, Gortahork, Donegal—Stationmaster.
Kelly, John, Clonee, Camolin, Wexford—Labourer.
Kelly, John E, Brown st, Dolphin's Barn, Dublin—Clerk.
Kelly, Robert, Mary st, Newry—Stone-cutter.
Kelly, John, Irish st, Belfast—Clerk.
Kelly, James, Clonee, Wexford—Farmer's son.
Kenny, Chris, Rathangan, Kildare—Postman.
Kenny, Ptk, Woodlands, Ferns—Labourer.
Kenny, Michael, Rathangan—Labourer.
Kenny, Patk, Kildare—Postman.
Kenny, Jos, Rathangan—Postman.
Kent, John, South st, New Ross—Grocer's assistant.
Kerr, P, Castletown rd, Dundalk.
Kiniry, Martin, Patrick st, Fermoy—Shopkeeper.
Kiniry, Martin, do—Cardriver.
Lalor, Jas, Eriary st, Kilkenny —Builder.
Lennon, Wm, Mylers Park, New Ross—Farmer.
Lynch, John, Bridge, Macroom—Draper's assistant.
Lynch, Patrick, New Ross—Contractor.
Lynch, Tim, Ballyfeard, Co. Cork—Farmer.
Lynch, Lawrence, Court st, Enniscorthy—Maize oil extractor.
Lyng, James, Balnabanough, Wexford—Labourer.
Madigan, Jas, Abbey street, Kilkenny—Mason.
Mannion, Tim, Craughwell, Galway—Farmer.
Martin, Ed, St Mary's terr, Athlone—Clerk.
May, Patk, North st, New Ross—Grocer's assistant.
McAllister, Dan, Staffordstown, Donabate—Farm manager.
McCarthy, John, Donoughmore, Timoleague—Do.
McCarthy, Joseph, South st, New Ross—Grocer's assistant.
McCormack, Ml, Drumrany, Athlone—Farmer.
McCrann, Alfred, Roscommon—Draper.
McDonnell, Wm K, Bandon—Merchant.
McDermott, Ed, Westland avenue, Derry—Clerk.
MacGough, O, Clanbrassil st, Dundalk—Accountant.
McGrath, T, John st, New Ross,—Grocer's assistant.
McGrath, M, Ballywilliam, Co. Wexford—Labourer.
McGuinness, Francis, Longford—Merchant.
McGuirk, Anthony, Collarduff, Knocklounghran, Co. Derry—Farmer.
M'Inerney, Thos, Lock quay, Limerick—Motor engineer.
McLoughlin, Fred, Glenmore, Wexford—Boot dealer.
M'Mahon, Ed, 26 Talbot st, Dublin—Grocer's assistant.
McQuill, Joseph, Bridge st, Dundalk—Undertaker.
McQuillan, Phil, Maxwell row, Dundalk—Gas inspector.
Mooney, Patk, Millbrook Villas, Naas—Chauffeur mechanic.
Mooney, Thomas, Rathangan—Labourer.
Moran, Louis, Ballysax, Curragh—Butcher.
Moran, Ed, Ballysax, Curragh—Farmer.
Mullally, Antony, Parnell st, Kilkenny—Painter.
Mullally, John J, Barnard st, Athlone—Compositor.
Murphy, Ed J, Quay st, New Ross—Rate Collector.
Murphy, Francis, Lusk, Co. Dublin—Apprentice fitter.
Murphy, Jer, The Harrow, Ferns—Grocer's assistant.
Murphy, D, The Harrow, Ferns—Grocer's assistant.
Murphy, Jas, Market sq, Newtownbarry—shop assistant.
Murphy, Wm, Bridge st, New Ross—Merchant.
Murphy, John, Quay st, New Ross—Merchant.
Murphy, John, New Ross—Merchant.
Murray, James, Portland st, Nth, Dublin—Labourer.
Murray, Peter, Upper Irishtown, Athlone—Weaver.
Murtagh, Peter, Cecil ave, Clontarf—Electrician.
Neary, Thos, Coulgour, Kilkenny—Van driver.
Neill, John, Irish st, Enniscorthy—Labourer.
Noctor, John, Dean's Grange, Blackrock—Gardener.
Noonan, John, Ballyfeard, Cork.
Noonan, William, Ballyfeard, Cork.
Nowlan, Jas, Bishop's Hill, Kilkenny—Cooper.
O'Breslin, Chas, William st, Derry—Teacher.
O'Brien, Wm, Tracton, Co. Cork—Farmer.
O'Brien, Jas, Carnamaddy, Athlone—Tailor.
O'Brien, John, Upper Irishtown, Athlone—Clerk.
O'Brien, John, Tracton, Co. Cork—Farmer.
O'Brien, Wm, Queenstown—Chemist's assistant.
O'Brien, John, Clancy st, Fermoy—Gardener.
O'Connell, Chris, Beecher street, Mallow—Railway employé.
O'Connell, John, 22 Upper Cecil street, Limerick.
O'Connor, Patrick, Bridge st, Killaloe—teacher.
O'Connor, James, Rickardstown, Cloghran, County Dublin—Apprentice.
O'Connor, Stephen, New st, Macroom—Blacksmith.
O'Connor, Patrick, New st, Macroom—Blacksmith.
O'Doherty, Joseph, Creggan st, Derry—Clerk.
O'Doherty, Andrew V, do—Butcher.
O'Dwyer, Ml, John st, Kilkenny—Sculptor.
O'Dwyer, Patrick, Hill terrace, Bandon—Egg packer.
O'Halloran, John, Ballingeary, Co. Cork—Farmer.
O'Halloran, Tim, Ballingeary, Co. Cork—Farmer.
O'Keeffe, Ml, William st, New Ross—Porter.
O'Kelly, Michael, Naas—Journalist.
O'Kennedy, John, Quay st, New Ross—Brewer's secretary.
O'Kennedy, Philip A, do—Mercantile clerk.
O'Kennedy, Michael J, do—Mercantile clerk.
O'Leary, John, Ballinhassig—Tailor.
O'Leary, S, Quay st, New Ross—Grocer's assistant.
O'Leary, Jas, Rossmore, Ballineen—Farmer.
O'Neill, J, John st, New Ross—Grocer's assistant.
O'Neill, Michael, Ferns—PO Clerk.
O'Neill, Arthur, Hill st, Dundalk—Machinist.
O'Shea, Patrick, King st, Fermoy—Engineer.
O'Sullivan, Patrick, Bank place, Mitchelstown—Carpenter.
O'Toole, W, Lr Church st, Enniscorthy—carpenter.
Parsons, Patk, Wolfe Tone st, Kilkenny—Tailor.
Prendergast, Jas, Quay st, New Ross—Grocer's assistant.
Purcell, Ml, High st, Kilkenny—Baker.

Quigley, Jas, Garryowen, limerick—Mill foreman.
Quinn, Thos, Cork st, Dublin—Poplin weaver.
Quinn, George, Cork st, Dublin—Poplin weaver.
Rearden, Tim, Ballinhassig, Cork—Farmer.
Reardon, John, Macroom—Labourer.
Richardson, Jos, Ashcroft, Togher—Farmer.
Riordan, Michael, Millstreet, Cork—Shop assistant.
Riordan, Jeremiah, Millstreet, Cork—Baker.
Roche, John, Church st, Ferns—Labourer.
Rodgers, Hugh, Six-Mile Cross, Tyrone—Chauffeur.
Ruttle, SM, Kilcurley, Adare, Co. Limerick—Accountant.
Ryan, M, Bishop's Hill, Kilkenny—Grocer's assistant.
Rynne, Wm, Cloyne South, Ennistymon, Co. Clare—Shop assistant.
Roche, John, Knockacurra, Bandon—Farmer.
Savage, Michael, Kilshannig, Fermoy—Labourer.
Selby, Joseph, Quay corner, New Ross—Jeweller.
Shane, Robert, Six-Mile Cross, Tyrone—Carrier.
Shannon, MJ, Quinn Co. Clare—Labourer.
Sheehan, Michael, Dundrum, Co. Tipperary—Forester.
Sheehan, Ml, North st, New Ross—Merchant.
Shiels, Patrick, Bogside, Derry—Clerk.
Southwell, John, Queen st, Newry—Van man.
Smith, Louis, Magherafelt, Co. Derry—Merchant.
Smith, Patrick, Ballybehan, Roscommon—Farmer.
Smith, Chas, Kilkenny—Carpenter.
Spillane, John, Lohort, Fermoy—Carpenter.
Stephens, W, High st, Kilkenny—Draper's assistant.
Stokes, John, Rath st, Irishtown, Dublin—Labourer.
Sullivan, Ed, Clonakilty—Farmer.
Sunderland, John, Ferns—Labourer.
Sweeney, Owen, Clonbruske, Athlone—Farmer.
Synott, Pierce, St Michael's place, Gorey—Brick-layer.
Synnott, Ml, Ballinakill, Ferns—Farmer.
Toomey, Richard, Ballymountain, Bandon—Labourer.
Toomey, James, Millstreet, Co. Cork—Baker.
Thornton, Jos, Skerries, Co. Dublin—Seed merchant.
Travers, John, Ballymurthy, Enniscorthy—Engine driver.
Travers, Martin, New Ross—Boot dealer.
Tuite, Daniel, Castletown rd, Dundalk—Painter.
Waldron, Ed, Hotel, Ennistymon—Gaelic teacher.
Wallace, John W, Eyre st, Newbridge—ASC.
Wall, James, Kerry—Motor mechanic.
Walsh, Jas, South st, New Ross—School teacher.
Walsh, Lawrence, Dunmore, Kilkenny—Gardener.
Walsh, Lawrence J, Duleek st, Drogheda—Carrier employé.
Walshe, Daniel, P, Main st, Fethard—Farmer.
Walsh, Redmond, Bandon—Farmer.
Walsh, James, Knockey, Co. Cork—Labourer.
Warner, Peter, Quay st, New Ross—Hairdresser.
Wickham, Mark, Merchant's quay, Cork—Tinsmith.
Wilson, HJC, Longford—Merchant.
Windram, SW Dominick st, Limerick—Engineer.

197 to Glasgow and Perth on 20th May

On Wednesday, 24th May, two lists were issued containing the names of 197 prisoners, who were removed from Dublin on the 19th May to Barlinnie Detention Barracks, Glasgow, and to Perth Detention Barracks:

To Perth

The following are the names of the prisoners lodged at Perth:

Boland, Patrick, Ferns, Co. Wexford.
Browne, John, Hollypark, Craughwell, Co. Galway.
Burke, Thomas, Lurgin, Gort.
Burke, Ed, Raford Mills, Kilturra, Co. Galway.
Burns, Michael, Colmanstown, Co. Galway.
Carroll, James, Ferns, Co. Wexford.
Coen, James, Ballycholin, Gort.
Coen, Martin, Ballycholin, Gort.
Collohan, Thomas, Craughwell, Co. Galway.
Collohan, Patrick, Castleall, Athenry.
Conner, Bryan, Ballycholin, Gort.
Connolly, Thomas, Derryhole, Co. Galway.
Corbett, Thomas, Craughwell, Co. Galway.
Corbett, Peter, Craughwell, Co. Galway.
Corbett, Patrick, Craughwell, Co. Galway.
Coughlan, Charles, Castle street, Loughrea.
Coy, James, Derryhole, Co. Galway.
Coy, Patrick, Derryhole, Co. Galway.
Co, Michael, Derryhole, Co. Galway.
Coy, Patrick, Galway road, Loughrea.
Craven, John, Clonoshecahill, New Inn, Co. Galway.
Cunniffe, Thomas, Ballycholin, Gort.
Cunniffe, Michael, Ballycholin, Gort.
Cunniffe, Patrick, Bride street, Loughrea.
Currin, James, Newtownbarry, Co. Wexford.
Delahunty, Michael, Loughrea.
Dempsey, Patrick, Lissilondon, Craughwell.
Donnellan, Patrick, Newcastle, Athenry.
Doyle, Thomas, Kiltulla, Athenry.
Duffy, William, Attymon, Athenry.
Earl, Joseph, Lisduff, Athenry.
Egan, Michael, Ballycholin, Gort.
Egan, Martin, Armagh, Gort.
Fahey, John, Lurgan, Gort.
Fahey, Michael, Lurgin, Gort.
Fahey, Patrick, Bride street, Loughrea.
Flynn, James, Main street, Loughrea.
Forde, Patrick, Kiltulla, Athenry.
Forde, Michael, Craughwell, Co. Galway.
Forde, John, Craughwell, Co. Galway.
Frowley, John, Wolfhill, Queen's County.
Gardiner, James, Coolraugh, Cringhwell.
Gegan, Michael, Craughwell, Co. Galway.
Gillighan, Patrick, Kiltulla, Athenry.
Grealish, Thomas, Pollacoppal, Athenry.
Greene, Martin J, Main street, Loughrea.
Haniffy, Michael, Tallybo, Athenry.
Haniffy, James, Glebe, Cringhwell.
Haverty, Richard, Clonoshecahill.
Healy, Michael, Athenry.
Hession, Michael, Athenry.
Higgins, Patrick, Lisheenkyle.
Hynes, Denis, Gregatorla, Co. Galway.
Hynes, John, Gregatorla, Co. Galway.
Hynes, Michael, Craughwell, Co. Galway.
Keane, James, Rockmore, Athenry.
Kearns, Daniel, Oldcastle, Athenry.
Keating, Michael, Atymon, Athenry.
Keating, Joseph, Attymon, Athenry.
Kellahen, James, Ballycholin, Gort.
Kelleper, Daniel, Gort.
Kellerker, Martin, Gort.
Kelly, Michael, Kiltulla Post Office. Athenry.
Kelly, William, Clondaw, Co. Wexford.
Kelly, Michael, Athenry.
Kennedy, Martin, Cringhwell.

Lawless, John, Attymon, Athenry.
Lawless, Patrick, Attymon, Athenry.
Loughery, John, Ballycohalin, Gort.
Lyons, William, Ferns, Co. Wexford.
McGigne, Patrick, Athenry road, Loughrea.
McGlynn, Martin, Gregatorla, Co. Galway.
McGlynn, Michael, Gregatorla, Co. Galway.
McNamara, Thomas, Gantry, Co. Galway.
Maloney, John, Cringhwell.
Martin, Patrick, Galway road, Loughrea.
Melody, Michael, New Inn, Co. Galway.
Molloy, Michael, Monivea, Co. Galway.
Moloney, John, Monivea, Co. Galway.
Moran, Martin, Cringhwell.
Mullins, Thomas, Kiltulla, Athenry.
Naughton, Patrick, Donsindle, Athenry.
Nestor, Michael, Rockfield, Athenry.
O'Brien, Augustus, Turlooughmore, Co. Galway.
Roche, Ed, Kelly street, Loughrea.
Roughan, Peter, Ballycohalin, Gort.
Rudy, HC, 14 Seaforth parade, Blackrock.
Stafford, Mat, Derryhole, Cringhwell.
Sweeney, Patrick, Moore street, Loughrea.
Walsh, Patrick, Old Church street, Athenry.
Walsh, Walter, Athenry.
Ward, James, Athenry.
White, Patrick, Attymon, Athenry.
White, Joseph, Attymon, Athenry.

To Glasgow

The following were lodged in Glasgow:

Benn, W, Church street, Tipperary.
Berry, John, Lanmore, Westport.
Blake, Michael, Coonaserunin, Athenry.
Brennan, M, Carrowkeel, Roscommon.
Burke, William, Tiaquin, Athenry.
Burke, S, Gurrane, Athenry.
Burns, Ml, Oranmore, Co. Galway.
Burns, James, Bellamona, Oranmore.
Burns, Patrick, Cave, Oranmore.
Casserly, Martin, Kinska, Claregalway.
Clifford, Peter, Casey place, Dundalk.
Connolly, Robert, Monivea, Athenry.
Connolly, John, Kiltulla, Oranmore.
Connolly, John, Coshla, Athenry.
Connor, Jas, Coldmanstown, Ballinasloe.
Cooney, Dominick, Lissaloudoon, Craughwell.
Corteen, Joseph, Boyhill, Athenry.
Cullinan, John, Loughcurra, Galway.
Cunniff, Thomas, Oranmore, Co. Galway.
Cunningham, P, Main Guard, Clonmel.
Dalton, LJ, Galtee view, Tipperary.
Daly, Patrick, Cross street, Athenry.
Deely, Jermiah, Templemartin, Craughwell.
Drohan, F Irishtown, Clonmel.
Egan, J, Clarenbridge, Oranmore, Co. Galway.
Fahy, Ml, Tawin, Oranmore, Co. Galway.
Fahy, John, Templemartin, Craughwell.
Fallon, Bernard, Moore street, Loughrea.
Flanagan, Patrick, Cave, Oranmore.
Foley, Edward, 14 Lr Main street, Wexford.
Forde, P, Rian, Kilcolgan Co. Galway.
Forde, Wm, 1 Richmond terrace, Bray.
Garvey, Law, Mulligh, Loughrea, Co. Galway.
Glynn, Jas, Curreentarmid, Monivea.
Golding, Patrick, Ballywinna, Craughwell.
Greany, Hugh, Stoneleigh, Craughwell.
Halpin, Thomas, 39 Kickham street, Clonmel.
Hassett, Daniel, Newcastle, Athenry.
Haverty, Jas, Spring Lawn, Moylough.
Hawkins, Thomas, Monymore, Oranmore.
Healy, Patrick, Newcastle, Athenry.
Heffernan, J, Gurteen, Colbrooke, Co. Tipperary.
Hilton, Thomas, 92 Marlborough st, Dublin.
Hughes, Patrick, Lankill, Westport.
Hynes, Wm, Drinbeg, Oranmore, Co. Galway.
Ivers, Thos, Ivy Ctge, Mount Pleasant pl, Ranelagh.
Joyce, Michael, Carrlne, Athenry.
Joyce, P, Monroe, Kilcolgan, Co. Galway.
Keane, Martin, Derrydonnell, Athenry.
Keane, D, Clarenbridge, Oranmore, Co. Galway.
Kearney, Fras, Ballinadurty, Oranmore, Co. Galway.
Kelly, Jas, Coldwood, Athenry.
Kelly, Thomas, 6 North street, New Ross.
Kelly, William, Coldwood, Athenry.
Kelly, Patrick, Hilleeaan, Craughwell.
Kelly, James, Kiltulla, Athenry.
Kennedy, John, Cackarrow, Athenry.
Kennedy, Patrick, Carrine, Athenry.
Kilkelly, P, Kilcolgan, Co. Galway.
M'Guire, John, Fennishrule, Wexford.
M'Kenna, John, 117 Cork street, Dublin.
Mackey, D, Upper Gladstone street, Clonmel.
Maloney, PJ, Church street, Tipperary.
Mitchell, John, Knockroe, Attymon.
Moloney, Martin, Belle Villa, Monivea.
Moore, Jas, 4 King's street, Fermoy, Co. Cork.
Moran, B, 54 St Mary's lane, Dublin.
Morin, John, Cloon, Claregalway.
Morrissey, Gilbert, Cahercrin, Athenry.
Morrissey, Richard, Cahercrin, Athenry.
Morrissey, J, 8 William street, Clonmel.
Morrissey, Patrick, Cahercrin, Athenry.
Morris, M, Mellison, New B'ham, Co. Tipperary.
Mullen, Moyvilla, Athenry.
Murphy, Thomas, Borelia, Kilcotty, Enniscorthy.
Murphy, Martin, Curreentarmid, Monivea.
Murphy, John, Tiaquin, Athenry.
Nelly, JJ, Gort, Co. Galway.
Newell, Martin, Caheradain, Craughwell.
Noone, Patrick, Brickmoon, Kiltulla.
Noone, James, 12 Geraldine Square, Dublin.
O'Connor, Matthew, 4 Nt Main st, Wexford.
O'Hanlon, P Kingstown.
O'Kennedy, TJ, Priory street, New Ross.
O'Reilly—30 Cork street, Dublin.
Piggett, P, Gort, Co. Galway.
Quinn, John, Caherfurvause, Craughwell.
Rogers, TF, James street, Tipperary.
Rooney, Martin, Cahercrin, Athenry.
Rooney, John, Cahercrin, Athenry.
Ryan, J, 12 Parnell street, Clonmel.
Ryan, WE, St Michael street, Tipperary.
Stephenson, T, Gort, Co. Galway.
Tally, Thos, Kilbeg, Monivea.
Toole, Martin, Oranmore.
Trayers, M, Gort, Co. Galway.
Walsh, Patrick, Killeenan, Craughwell.
Walsh, D, Gaggan, Bandon, Co. Cork.

40 to Woking on 20th May

It was announced on Thursday, 25th May, that the 40

prisoners named below were moved from Richmond Barracks, Dublin, on May 19th, and lodged in Woking Detention Barracks the following day:

Barrett, Pat, farmer, Ballinageane, Craughwell, Galway.
Burke, Patrick, farmer, Chermore, Kinvara.
Burke, Peter, farmer, Chermore, Kinvara.
Cleary, James, horse-shoer, Irish st, Enniscorthy.
Cleary, Thos, plasterer, Abbeyrow, Athenry.
Connolly, Patrick, farmer, Tysaxon, Athenry.
Cullen, Jas Jos, 8 Harney street, Enniscorthy.
Cullen, James, lino operator, Belfield, Enniscorthy.
Daley, John, agric overseer, Lakeview, Manorhamilton.
Devereux, Eugene, cycle agent, 18 George st, Enniscorthy.
Doherty, John, farmer, Northgate street, Athenry.
Dolan, James, N, shopkeeper, Ballyboy, Manorhamilton.
Dooley, John, farmer, Esker, Athenry, Co. Galway.
Dooley, Ml, farmer, Esker, Athenry, Co. Galway.
Doyle, Patrick, farmer, Kiltulla, Athenry.
Dwyer, Peter, engine driver, Tomalossett, Enniscorthy.
Egan, Thos, labourer, Abbeyrow, Athenry.
Fahy, Thos, farmer, Lavally, Craughwell, Galway.
Fenlon, Wm, labourer, Hospital lane, Enniscorthy.
Flanagan, Jas, farmer, Frenchfort House, Oranmore.
Gardiner, John, carpenter, Knockbrock, Athenry.
Gilgan, Bryan, electrician, Ballyboy, Manorhamilton.
Gilgan, Thos, farmer, Ballyboy, Manorhamilton.
Henehan, Pat J, grocer asst, Fethard, Tipperary.
Hynes, Martin, farmer, Durns. Kinvara, Co. Galway.
Hynes, Pat, farmer, Creggan, Craughwell, Galway.
Kenny, John, valet, Maynooth Col, Main street, Maynooth.
Larden, Jas, clerk, Shannon (Temple), Enniscorthy.
Lawless, Peter, farmer, Corrin Ramid, Athenry.
Mahon, Peter, farmer, Newcastle, Athenry.
Murphy, Ml, labourer, Church street, Athenry.
Murphy, Jas, spinner, Carley's Bdge, Enniscorthy.
O'Connor, R, clerk, 38 Serpentine ave, Ballsbridge.
O'Loughlin, Jas, coachbuilder, Ballyboy, Manorhamilton.
O'Loughlin, Thos, coachbuilder, Ballyboy, Manorhamilton.
Rooney, Jos, labourer, Caheroryan, Athenry.
Rossiter, Ed, clerk, Templeshannon quay, Enniscorthy.
Wafer, John, clerk, Shannon, Enniscorthy.
Walsh, Ml, carpenter, Athenry, Co. Galway.
Young, Joe, labourer, High street, Dublin.

59 to Lewes on 20th May

The following fifty-nine prisoners were removed from Richmond Barracks on May 19, and lodged in Lewes Detention Barracks on the following day:

Abernatty (? Mahernatty), Henry, lab, Shannon Hill, Enniscorthy.
Burke, Martin, lab, Glauscauly, Galway.
Byrne, Alphonsus, clerk, 36 Mt Pleasant place, Dublin.
Cassidy, John, sewing machine agent, Ballybofey, Strabane.
Coleman, JJ, publican, Ballaghadereen, Mayo.
Concannon, Pat, farmer, Claregalway, Galway.
Connolly, Thos, lab, Drumgoold, Enniscorthy.
Culligan, Ber, lab, 95 Pembroke cot, Donnybrook.
Cummins, Pat, farmer, Claregalway, Galway.
Cunniffe, Jas, butcher, Ballaghadereen, Mayo.
Daly, Pat, surveyor, Carrickmacross.
Daly, Thos, lab, 13 Lr Gloucester pl, Dublin.
Darcy, Jas, lab, Milltown, Co. Dublin.
Darcy, John, postman, 17 Ballsbridge terr, Dublin.
Davis, John, carpenter, Shannon, Enniscorthy.
Doherty, Daniel, clerk, Butcher st, Strabane.
Doyle, Michael, labourer, Shannon Hill, Enniscorthy.
Flannery, BJ, clerk, Ballaghadereen, Co. Mayo.
Fox, John, dock labourer, 112 st, Columba's Wells, Derry City.
Goen John, farmer, Ballymaguire, Ardaahane, Galway.
Grealy, Peter, farmer, Glanscauly, Galway.
Hyland, Matthew, labourer, Drumgoold, Enniscorthy.
Jennings, James, plumber, Bachelor's Walk, Dundalk.
Kavanagh, James, foundry labourer, 17 Alexandra place, Derry City.
Kelly, Joe, no occupation, Ballaghadereen, Co. Mayo.
Kelly, WJ, poultry merchant, Charlemont street, Dungannon.
Kyne, Michael, farmer, Branloughane, Galway.
Lennon, Philip, shop asst, John st, New Ross.
Loughran, WJ, waiter, O'Neills Hotel, Carrickmacross.
Martin, Thos, farmer, Maghercloone, Carrickmacross.
M'Cormick, Thos, merchant, Ballaghadereen, Mayo.
M'Grath, Patrick, machine man, Duffry Hill, Enniscorthy.
M'Kenna, B, carpenter, Railway st, Strabane.
Molloy, John, farmer, Cullough, Co. Galway.
Morley, JF, clerk, Ballaghadereen, Co. Mayo.
Murphy, Arthur, labourer, 50 John st, Enniscorthy.
Murphy, F, labourer, Spring Valley, Enniscorthy.
Murphy, Michael, clerk, 19 Up Sherrard st, Dublin.
Neeson, John, teacher, 310 Cupan st, Belfast.
Nolan, Thos, clerk, WC, Carrickmacross.
O'Brien, James, carpenter, Carrickmacross.
O'Brien, John, clerk, 4 Old Church, Enniscorthy.
O'Byrne, Thos, shop asst, Clanbrassil st, Dundalk.
O'Connor, Denis, clerk, 26 Main st, Enniscorthy.
O'Donnell, A, teacher, Tullycrine, Co. Clare.
O'Gara, Bartley, draper's asst, Ballaghadereen, Co. Mayo.
O'Hara, TF, shop asst, Ballaghadereen, Co. Mayo.
O'Neill, James, teacher, Rockwell College, Cashel, Co. Tipperary.
O'Reilly, Pat, bootmaker, Bath st, Carrickmacross.
Quill, Michael, labourer, 58 Douglas st, Cork.
Raul, Laurence, 10 Foxtall tce, Mornington road.
Ryan, Patk J, merchant, Ballaghadereen, Mayo.
Sargeant, Phillip, trimmer, 59 Hollybank road, Drumcondra.
Sinnott, Patk, asst agent, Belfield, Enniscorthy.
Trimble, Joe, no occupation, Ballaghadereen, Mayo.
Tobin, Patk, labourer, Bohreen Hill, Enniscorthy.
Wade, Michl, labourer, 24 N Gt George's st, Dublin.
Ward, Thos, farmer, Coolfore, Carrickmacross.
Watkins, Thos, clerk, Temple Shannon, Enniscorthy.

100 to Wakefield on 2nd June

On Saturday, 3rd June, it was announced that the following 100 prisoners had been removed from Richmond Barracks, Dublin, on the 1st June, and lodged in Wakefield Detention Barracks on the following day:

Ahern, M, Dungourney, Midleton.
Ahern, Con, Dunmanway.
Barrett, Ed, Kilbrittain.
Brennan, John, Carrowkeel, Roscommon.
Burke, Thos, James's street, Dublin.
Burns, Peter, 7 Lindon street, Belfast.
Butterly, John, Dunleer.
Collins, David, Ballard's lane, Cork.
Conway, Michael, Grinnage, Craughwell.
Cornan, John, Macroom.

Cotton, AW, Rosemount Gardens, Belfast.
Curtin, Thos, Thomas Davis street, Cork.
De Loughrey, Peter, Kilkenny.
Duggan, William, Dunmanway.
Fahey, John, Carnakelly, Kiltulla, Athenry.
Fahy, John, Caheravoneen, Co. Galway.
Fahey, John J, Bride street, Loughrea.
Fahey, Peter, Carnakelly, Kiltulla, Athenry.
Fahey, Patk, Templemarhin, Craughwell.
Fergus, Tim, Knocktor, Kiltulla, Athenry.
Flaherty, M, Binckey, Castlegar, Galway.
Fleming, Patk, Clarenbridge, Oranmore.
Fleming, George, Kinvara, Co. Galway.
Flannery, Ml, Castlegar, Coolough, Galway.
Fury, Stephen, Lecarrow, Craughwell.
Fury, Ml, Lecarrow, Craughwell.
Gantley, Patrick, Roscrea.
Geraghty, George, Roscommon.
Gill, Joseph, Westport.
Glynn, James, Fairbrothers' Fields, Dublin.
Grealish, John, Kingsland, Athenry.
Grealish, Pat, Curraghgreen, Galway.
Gregan, James, Lower George's street, Kingstown.
Gregan, Ed, Seville place, Nth Strand rd, Dublin.
Griffing, M, Ballinadell.
Halloran, Denis, Kiltulla, Athenry.
Hanley, John, Bruchy, Castlegar, Galway.
Hanniffy, Martin, Clarenbridge, Galway.
Hanrahan, Ed, North Strand road, Dublin.
Harris, TF, Tower street, Cork.
Harris, MJ, Tower street, Cork.
Harte, Pat, Oranmore, Galway.
Haskins, Robert, no fixed address.
Henlon, David, Loughcurra, Kinvara, Galway.
Heron, Sam, Doris street, Belfast.
Higgins, James, Ellesmere avenue, NCR, Dublin.
Howley, Patk, Granna, Ardrahan, Galway.
Hourihane, John, Lick, Skibbereen.
Hurley, John, Excise street, Athlone.
Hynes, Thos, Lisduff, Craughwell, Galway.
Jordan, Pat, Newcastle, Monivea, Co. Galway.
Keane, Pat, Currane, Co. Galway.
Kelly, Thos, Grange, Dunleer.
Kelly, Thos, Skehana, Peterswell, Co. Galway.
Kelly, James, Grange, Dunleer.
Kelly, T, Feakle, Co. Clare.
King, Pat, Kiltulla, Oranmore.
Langley, WT, Tuam.
Layng, Jos, Dunleer, Co. Louth.
Leahy, M, Ballywilliam, Queenstown.
Lynch, M, Grannig, Kinsale.
Mahon, Pat, Kiltulla, Oranmore.
Mahon, Thomas, Kiltulla.
Malinn, Peter, Mardyke, Athlone.
Malone, James, Crescent College, Limerick.
Manning, Daniel, Kilbrittain, Co. Cork.
Manning, Denis, Kilbrittain, Co. Cork.
McBride, Joseph, Westport.
McKeever, Andrew, Court street, Enniscorthy.
McSerrny, TJ, Gardiner's terr, Victoria rd, Cork.
Meade, WJ, Kilgarriff, Clonakilty.
Meade, JW, Kilgarriff, Clonakilty.
Mulrenan, Wm, Kilkilla, Co. Galway.
Mulroyan, Bart, Kiltulla.
Mulroyan, John, Kiltulla.
Murphy, Ml, Aldborough Parade, Dublin.
Murphy, J, Crossmahon, Bandon.
Murray, James, Gardiner's place, Dublin.
Newell, Wm, Castlegar, Co. Galway.
Newell, James, Castlegar, Co. Galway.
O'Dea, Jn, Charleville, Co. Cork.
O'Driscoll, J, Castletownshend, Co. Cork.
O'Dwyer, Ed, Ballagh, Goold's Cross, Tipperary.
O'Hourihane, Peter, Skibbereen.
O'Leary, Jos, 11 Tremaddock road, Clapham.
O'Loughlin, T, Carron, Co. Clare.
O'Madden, PL, St Ignatius coll, Galway.
O'Mahony, John, Gardiner's place, Dublin.
O'Mahony, C, Ahiohill, Enniskeen, Co. Cork.
O'Shea, P, New lane, Killarney.
O'Shea, T, Dunmanway.
O'Sullivan, M, Fairhill, Killarney.
Rickard, James, Balbriggan.
Ruane, Michael, Glanscaul, Oranmore.
Scullen, Patk, North Circular road, Dublin.
Tomkins, Patk Tonbrick Ballycarney, Ferns.
Tracey, T, Dean street, Kilkenny.
Tracey, M, Athenry.

49 to Wandsworth on 2nd June

On Saturday, 3rd June, it was announced that the following 49 prisoners had been removed from Richmond Barracks, Dublin, on 1st June, and lodged in Wandsworth Detention Barracks on the following day:

Bindon, John, Stradbally.
Byrne, Jos, no fixed address.
Casserly, Peter, Claregalway.
Collins, J, Waterdale, Claregalway.
Cuffee, Thomas, 4 Pleasants street, SCR.
Cullaghan—Millstreet, Co. Cork.
De Bourca, P, Carrickmacross.
Donoghue, D, Ballinadee.
Donnelly, Pat, Mountbagna, Carlingford.
Feeney, Pat, Claregalway.
Ferguson, Michael, Castletown, Co. Louth.
Fitzgerald, R, College street, Killarney.
Foley, J, Ardcluggan, Castletownbere.
Hanlon, James, Castletown, Co. Louth.
Hennessy, W, Pope's quay, Cork.
Horgan, Wm, Lower New street, Killarney.
Larkin, John, 99 Lr Dorset street, Dublin.
Lyons, John, Portland place.
Maguire, Bernard, 4 Glenfarm, Co. Leitrim.
Malone, Thos, Tyrrell's Pass, Westmeath.
Martin, Ambrose, Ballycash, Co. Wexford.
McArten, B, Askabuoy, Carrickmore, Tyrone.
McCrory, Hugh, Dunmoyle, Co. Tyrone.
Minahan, Jas, Tivoli Theatre.
Mullen, D, 66 Moyne road.
Murphy, M, Florence Villas, Drumcondra.
Newell, Michael, Castlegar, Galway.
Newell, Edward, Cungwell, Galway.
Neyland, Thos, Stradbally, Galway.
Nogan, J, Baltimore.
Nolan, Bart, Banmore, Galway.
O'Brien, Pat, Waterdale, Claregalway.
O'Connor, B, 1 Brendon road, Donnybrook.
O'Donovan, Thos, New Birmingham, Thurles.
O'Hehir, Hugh.
O'Kelly, John, T, 27 Upr Rutland street, Dublin.
O'Leary, J, Clonakilty.
O'Neill, John, Ballybough road, Dublin.
O'Neill, John, Grenville street, Dublin.
O'Connell, J, Lower Leeson street, Dublin.

O'Dea, Michael, Stradbally, Kilcugan.
O'Keeffe, Pat, Lower Camden street.
O'Sullivan, S, Mountjoy street, Dublin.
Raffley, Michael, Ballybritt, Co. Galway.
Scullen, JJ, St Joseph's avenue, Drumcondra.
Shannon, Chas, 27 Canning street, Belfast.
Smyth, Michael, no address.
Ward, P, 24 Hamilton street, SCR.

50 to Knutsford on 2nd June

On Saturday, 3rd June, it was announced that the following 50 prisoners had been removed from Richmond Barracks, Dublin, on the 1st June, and lodged in Knutsford Detention Barracks on the following day:

Booth, Frank, Alexander street, W, Belfast.
Bindon, Thos, Stradbally, Kilcolga.
Birrell, PT, Williamson's place, Dundalk.
Carr, Martin, Cloonacorneen, Castlegar.
Connell, John, Clarenbridge, Oranmore.
Fallon, Bernard, Two-Mile-Ditch, Castlegar.
Foran, T, Clonliffe road, Drumcondra.
Hessin, Michael, Templemartin, Craughwell.
Johnson, James, Limaveane, Sandown rd, Belfast.
Keane, John, Derrydonnell, Athenry.
Keigheny, M, Ballyboy, Ardrahan.
Kelly, Wm, Attymon, Athenry.
Kilkelly, John, Canshow, Kinvara.
Lally, Frank, Tallyho, Athenry.
Larkin, Jos, Lower Dorset street.
Lynch, Michael, St Clement's road, Drumcondra.
Mannion, Michael, Athenry.
Mason, Thos, St Jones's ave, Clonliffe rd, Dublin.
McCann, Pierce, Ballyowen, Cashel.
McCullough, Denis, Grosvenor road, Belfast.
McDowell, Chas, Logan street, Belfast.
McInery, Thos, Cashenmoore, Kinvara.
McNally, Peter, Belvedere place, Dublin.
Mitchell, Pat, Anne street, Dublin.
Monaghan, Pat, Kiltulla, Athenry.
Merriman, Thos, Emmet road, Inchicore.
Neasly, Frank, Chapel lane, Dundalk.
Nolan, Jas, Athenry.
O'Dea, John, Stradberry, Kilcolgan, Galway.
O'Neill, Felix, Barrack street, Dundalk.
Quirke, Martin, Ballnagran, Craughwell.
Rourke, Jas, Coxtown, Ardrahan.
Ronan, Pat, Castlegar, Co. Galway.
Ryder, Michael, Ballinamanna, Oranmore.
Shaughnessy, Michael, Ballylin, Craughwell.
Silver, Patrick, Ardrahan.
Smith, Jas, Belfast.
Stanley, JM, Upper Liffey street.
Stanton, Michael, Cloonarke, Kinvara.
Tanner, Wm, 3 Wilton terrace, Dublin.
Thomson, Martin, Granna, Ardrahan.
Thompson, Martin, Ballyhene, Ardrahan.
Thompson, Wm, Ballyboy, Ardrahan.
Walsh, Michael, Knockatoher, Kiltulla.
Walsh, Thos, no fixed address.
Walsh, Michael, Glenscaul, Oranmore.
Wall, Martin, Brockey, Castlegar.
Ward, Joseph, Kiltulla, Athenry.
Wilson, Thos, Albert Bridge road, Belfast.

41 to Knutsford on 7th June

On Thursday, 15 June, it was announced that the following prisoners were removed from Richmond Barracks, Dublin, on the 6th June, and lodged in Knutsford Detention Barracks on the following day:

Barrett, James, house painter, Athenry, Co. Galway.
Brennan, James, organ builder, 59 Bride street, Dublin.
Byrne, Joseph, gardener, St Mary's College, Rathmines, Dublin.
Clery, John, plasterer, Athenry, Co. Galway.
Connell, Thomas, farmer, Barretspark, Athenry.
Conolly, Alex, Labour Exchange clerk, 2 Alamada terrace, Falls road, Belfast.
Conolly, Joseph, house furnisher, 38 Divis Drive, Glen rd, Belfast.
Connors, Joseph, farmer, Derrogh, Co. Galway.
Daly, Thomas, clerk, Mountain View, Tipperary.
Duggan, Thomas, farmer, Ross Hill, Galway.
Dundon, Edward, medical practitioner, Borris, Co. Carlow.
Gunne, Arthur, grocer's assistant, 3 Irish street, Enniscorthy.
Fury, Thomas, farmer, Rhen, Oranmore, Galway.
Healy, FF, barrister, Wilmount House, Queenstown.
Howlett, John, messenger, 21 Great Ship street.
Kennedy, Luke, whitesmith, 58 Great Charles street, Dublin.
Lalor, Patrick, artist, 16 Valentia Parade, Dublin, NCR.
M'Carthy, Daniel cooper, East Green, Dunmanway, Co. Cork.
M'Linn, Joseph, insurance agent, Tralee.
Milroy, John, confectioner, 82 Talbot street, Dublin.
Monaghan, Philip, school teacher, 7 Carlingford terrace, Drumcondra, Dublin.
Morris, William, butler, St Mary's College, Rathmines, Dublin.
Morrisey, Martin, shop assistant, Athenry, Co. Galway.
Murphy, Eugene, labourer, Barna Upton, Co. Cork.
Murphy, Con, farmer, Ballydary, Millstreet, Co. Cork.
Murphy, NJ, commercial traveller, 11 Monck street, Wexford.
O'Brien, William, master tailor, 43 Belvedere place, Dublin.
O'Connor, MJ, Trade Union Secretary, clerk, Upper Rock street, Tralee.
O'Keefe, Eugene, farmer, Courlea, Clonakilty.
O'Reilly, Paul, machinist, 39 Daniel street, Dublin.
Redmond, Lawrence, labourer, 2 Caroline row, Ringsend.
Roughan, Bryan, farmer, Derrouah, Co. Galway.
Ryan, John, farmer's son, Castlegare, Co. Galway.
Sexton, Timothy, farmer, Skaif, Timoleague, Co. Cork.
Silver, Michael, farmer, Rathbairn, Ardrahan.
Spillane, Michael, boot and shoe maker, Killarney, Kerry.
Sullivan, Con, priest's boy, The Presbytery, Dunmanway.
Supple, Patrick, clerk, no fixed address (Dublin).
Wall, John, farmer's son, Kiltulla, Oranmore, Co. Galway.
Walsh, John, carpenter, Athenry, Co. Galway.
Walsh, Michael, farmer, Rathroon, Bandon, Cork.

25 to Knutsford on June 16th

On Wednesday, 21st June, it was announced that the following 25 prisoners, who were removed from Richmond Barracks, Dublin, on 15th June, 1916, were lodged in Knutsford Detention Barracks on the following day:

Costello, Martin, blacksmith, Oranmore.
Donoghue, Con, Ratrout, Ballinadee, Bandon.
Donoghue, Patk, Ratrout, Ballinadee, Bandon.
Fahy, Patk, farmer, Lavally, Craughwell.
Finlay, John, 40 Nth Camming st, Dublin.
Freaney, Ml, Mountain West, Oranmore.
Hales, John, farmer, Knocknacurra, Bandon, Cork.
Halpin, Wm Robt, shipbuilder, 6 St Valentine's terrace, West road, Dublin.
Halpin, Wm Thos, 53 Lr Dominick st, Dublin.
Hanratty, Jas, compositor, Mill street, Dundalk.
Hearne, Edward, Spring Valley, Enniscorthy.
Herty, Thomas, cardriver, 17 Bridge st, Dundalk.
Jourdan, Stephen Jos, bootmaker, Davis st, Athenry.
Kelly, John, foreman, 5 Swift's row, Dublin.
Kelly, Ml, farmer's son, Caherleriscaun, Athenry.
Larkin, Stephen, Danish Island, Latter Mullen.
McCrave, Thomas, carter, Seatown, Dundalk.
Murphy, Richd, farmer, Cross street, Athenry.
Nielan, Martin, farmer, The Weir, Kilcolgan.
Nolan, Patk Jos, 6 Newfoundland st, Dublin.
O'Dea, Thomas, farmer, Stradbally, Kilcolgan.
O'Dea, Patk Jos, Stradbally, Kilcolgan.
Reilly, Francis, Blacksmith, Cross street, Athenry.
Stokes, Thos Jos, 11 Duffrey st, Enniscorthy.
Thornton, Jos, shopkeeper, Skerries, Co. Dublin.

---

211 PERSONS DETAINED AT RICHMOND BARRACKS

The following official list of the persons confined at Richmond Barracks was issued on Saturday, 20th May:

Allen, James; Allen, Wm; Allen, Thos.
Burke, TF; Birrell, PJ; Booth, Frank; Byrne, Peter; Burke, James; Burke, Michael; Brennan, Thos; Burke Thos; Bindon, Thos; Bracken, Peter; Brennan, JM; Butterly, John; Butterly, Nich; Byrne, Jos; Balfe, Robt; Brennan, John; Biggs, Patk; Broderick J; Brennan, MJ; Brennan, Patk; Brennan F; Byrne, Thos.
Cullen, James; Cullen, C; Campbell, J; Connor, Thos; Collins, John; Corbett, Dominick; Costello Mich; Carr, Martin; Cuffe, Thos; Connolly, Jos; Connolly, Alex; Cotton, AW; Cleary, TV; Casserly, Pat; Cowley, John; Cooney, John; Chardyce, Bertie; Cusack, Paul; Cassidy, Michael; Coen, Michael; Corbett, John; Clarke, James.
Donoghue, Peter; Dunlevy, Patk; Daffy, Pat; Daly, Matt; Dixon, Henry; Dorris, Pat Jos; Duggan, Thos; De Bourca, P; Dundon, Ed; De Loughrey, Peter; Dillon, Hubert; Delaney, John; Duggan, Thos.
Elliott, JJ.
Fitzgerald, T; Fogan, Michael; Fogan, Thos; Fahey, Michael; Fahey, James; Fahey, Martin; Fallow, Bern; Faran, T; Figgis, Darrell; Feeney, Patk; Fallon, Michael.
Gregan, James; Gaffney, Jos; Grealish, John; Grealish, Bern; Garland, P; Gerathy, George; Grealish, Patk; Gill, Jos; Graham, Jos.
Hurley, John; Hynes, Thos; Haskin, Robt; Heron, Sam; Herty, Thos; Harte, Wm; Heely, FJ; Harris, FF; Harris, MJ; Harte Patk; Holland, Patk; Hanley, Ed; Higgins, James; Hogan, Thos; Hughes, Chas.
Inskipp, Peter.
Johnson, J; Jordan, Patk.
King, Patk; Kavanagh, John; Kirwin, W; Kennedy, Luke; Kelly, James; Kelly, Thos; Kelly, T; Keene, Patk.
Lehey, Denis; Lally, Michael; Larkin, J; Larkin, J; Layng, Jas; Lyon, John; Loughley, W; Lehey, Michael; Lynch, M.
McCarthy, JJ; Melinn, Peter; Murray, Frank; Mulroyan, Wm; McLoughlin, Patk; McCullough, Denis; McDowell, Chas; Morrissey, Patk; Mahon, Patk; Mullen, Ffrench; Murray, Jos; Murphy, M; Monaghan, Phil; Milroy, John; McCarten, B; McCrory, Hugh; McGuire, Bern; Mellowes, H; Minahan, Jos; Molone, Thos; Mooney, Jos; Mahon, Patk; Molone, Thos; Manning, Patk; Mulroy, Bart; Mulroy, John; Maron, John; Malone, Jas; Malin, Jos; McBride, Jos; McNally, Henry; Morris, Joe; Mahoney, Abel.
Newell, Wm; Newell, Jas; Neasey, Frank; Newell, Ed; Newell, Michael; Nolan, Bart.
O'Leary, Patk; O'Neill, John; O'Neill, Felix; O'Reilly, John; O'Brien, W; O'Brien, Patk; O'Connor, B; O'Connor, John; O'Hehir, Hugh; O'Mahoney, John; O'Kelly, TG; O'Neill, John; O'Keefe, Patk; O'Reilly, Paul; O'Donovan, Thos; O'Neill, John; O'Neill, JJ; O'Sullivan, G; O'Connell, J; O'Madden, PL; O'Donnell, Philip; O'Conor, NJ; O'Dea, J; O'Dwyer, Ed; O'Hourihane, Peter; O'Loughlin, T; O'Rourke, B.
Purcell, Jer; Parker, Thos.
Quinn, Chas; Quigley, Jas.
Raffly, Michael; Ryan, Michael; Ruane, Michael; Ruane, Martin; Ryan, Thomas.
Sheridan, F; Stack, Austin; Sweeney, Terence; Sally, Jas; Smith, Jas; Stanley, Jos M; Somerly, Thos; Scullen, JJ; Smythe, Michael; Scullen, Patk; Shannon, Chas.
Tracey, I; Treacy, Michael.
Wall, John; Wilson, Thos; Walsh, Thos; Ward, P; Warwick, Jas; Whelan, Jas; Weston, Thos.

Among the names of deported persons officially supplied was that of 'Andrew Comerford, 4 Upper Kevin street.' E Murray of that address wrote to say that no one of the name of Commerford lived there.

In the official list of deported prisoners issued on 16th May there appeared the name of Myles Redmond, 6 Parnell street, Wexford. Subsequently the *Irish Times* was requested to state that Myles Redmond did not reside at that address.

Mr Octavus Hardy, of 17 Belgrave road, Rathmines, was arrested at the address in connection with the Easter rising in Dublin. He was released soon afterwards, and received a communication from the War Office enclosing an extract from a statement from General Headquarters at Dublin. This statement says: 'It was made clear that Mr Hardy was a thoroughly loyal subject, and that his arrest was merely one of the unfortunate incidents which are bound to arise in the course of such military operations as those which took place in the Dublin area.'

Mrs Mary McQuade, of 82 Upper Rathmines, pointed out that in the list of deported prisoners officially issued on Friday, 12th May, the name Owen Kerrigan, 82 Upper Rathmines, appears. She wished to state that no such person ever resided at 82 Upper Rathmines.

Names of Prisoners released

206 up to 12th May

The military authorities on Wednesday, 24th May, announced that after fully investigating the cases of the following men they were released. This list was m ade up to the 12th May:

A
Adams, John, Dublin
B
Bannon, Thos, Dublin
Bateson, Frank, Louth
Begley, F, Bandon, Cork
Behan, Jas, Fairview
Bennett, T, Castleknock
Boyne, John, Dublin
Brady, Thos, Dublin
Breenty, Wm, Dublin
Brennan, Thos, Finglas
Brennan, L, Dublin
Brophy, Thos, Dublin
Brown, Jas, Dublin
Buryne, Peter, Dublin
Butler, Geo, Dublin
Butler, Jas, Dublin
Byrne, John, Dublin
Byrne, PJ, Enniscorthy
Byrne, V, Dublin
Byrne, Ed, Dublin
C
Cardigan, Jas, Dublin
Carney, Alfred, Dublin
Carroll, Bernard, Dublin
Carroll, Pat, Dublin
Chavasse, Claud, Dublin
Clarke, Pat, Dublin
Coade, John, Dublin
Codlin, J, Enniscorthy
Condron, J, Irishtown
Coughlan, Ml, Dublin
Conly, M, Dublin
Conmore, P, Enniscorthy
Conroy, Jas, sen, Dundalk
Conroy, Jas, jun, Dundalk
Corcoran, Pat, Dublin
Corrigan, Jas, Kilkenny
Cosgrove, Ed, Newbridge
Crushue, Thos, Galway
Curtis, Jas, Dublin
D
Dalton, Pat, Dublin
Darcey, M, Dublin
Delaney, Thos, Dublin
Devine, Jas, Strabane
Devine, Ed, Strabane
Dillon, Jas, Dundrum
Divine, Thos, Dublin
Donnelly, Jas, Dublin
Donovan, M, Dublin
Doyle, Sylvester, Dublin
Doyle, Thos, Dublin
Dowling, Thos, Dublin
Dunne, Thos, Dublin
Dune, Thos, Dublin
Dunbar, Jas, Ferns
Dyass, Albert, Dublin
E
Egan, Wm, Dublin
Enright, John, Dublin
F
Flanagan, Rev Patrick, Ringsend
Flannagan, T
Feehan, Jas, Dublin
Fitzgibbon, M, Fermoy
Flynn, P, Phibsborough
Fitzpatrick, Thos, Dublin
Fitzsimmons, John, do
G
Gavin, Thos, Co. Louth
Geoghan, Stephen
Gerathy, Pat, Dublin
Gogan, Richard, Dublin
Gordon, Ed, Dublin
Green, Arthur, Dundalk
Green, Pat, Dublin
H
Hannon, Arthur, Dublin
Harper, Thos, Dublin
Harrison, Pte, Robt
Heffernan, Wm, Dublin
Hennessy, Pat
Hevry, Thos, Enniscorthy
Hogan, Ml, Co. Wexford
Holmes, Thos, Dublin
Holton, John
Howard, Ed, Dublin
Howard, Cornelius, do
Hunter, John, Dublin
Hussey, G, Dublin
Hynes, M, Co. Galway
J
Jennings, Thos, Dublin
Jordan, Ml, Enniscorthy
K
Kane, Jos, Dublin
Kavanagh, Art.
Kavanagh, Ed, Dublin
Kavanagh, John, Dublin
Kavanagh, M, Dublin
Kelly, Ald JJ, Dublin
Kelly, Jos, Dublin
Kelly, JM, Dublin
Kelly, Matt, Dublin
Kelly, Ml, Dublin
Keenin, Thos, Dublin
Kennedy, J, Athenry
Kenny, Ml, Dublin
Keogh, Thos, Dublin
Kinsella, Ml, Dublin
Kirwan, Thos, Dublin
L
Lalor, Fenton, Co. Louth
Lallor, Pat, Dublin
Lambe, Pat, Dublin
Lawlor, Pat, Clontarf
Leech, Thos, Dublin
Lee, Hugh, Dublin
Lemas, John, Dublin
Lynch, Pat
M
Mackey, Robt
Mahoney, J, Bandon
Mangin, M, Dublin
Mapother, Pat F, Dublin
Mapother, Ml J, Dublin
Markham, TJ, Fairview
Mason, Pat, Dublin
M'Cabe, Ml, Dublin
M'Carthy, Barry, Dublin
M'Carthy, M, Co. Cork
M'Clean, Wm, Dublin
M'Cormack, Chris, Dublin
M'Dermott, Louis, Dublin
MacDonald, Jas, Dublin
M'Donell, Andrew, Dublin
M'Grane, Ml, Dublin
M'Guire, J, Enniscorthy
M'Kenna, John, Dublin
M'Namara, GF, Dublin
M'Namara, T, Limerick
M'Quillan, Wm, Louth
Meade, Ml, Dublin
Moloney, J, Finglas
Moore, Andrew, Dublin
Moore, Peter, Dublin
Monks, Christopher, do
Morriman, Ed, Dublin
Murragh, Jos, Dublin
Murphy, Robt, Dublin
Murphy, A, Dublin
Murphy, R, Co. Cork
Murray, J, Enniscorthy
Murray, Pte Jas
N
Naughter, Jas, Dublin
Newsome, F, Enniscorthy
O
O'Brien, Pat, Dublin
O'Brien, Denis, Dublin
O'Connor, Peter, Dublin
O'Donnell, Chris, Dublin
O'Donnell, Wm, Dublin
O'Dwyer, Ml, Dublin
O'Kiely, John, Drogheda
O'Mahoney, Ed, Dublin
O'Moore, Donough, do
O'Morray, Ed, Dublin
O'Neill, John, Clare
O'Neill, Clarence
O'Neill, Ald L, Dublin
O'Neill, Pat, Dublin
O'Norton, Owen
O'Reardon, N, Dublin
O'Reilly, Pat, Dublin
O'Reilly, John, Dublin
O'Rourke, Fred, Dublin
O'Shea, John, Dublin
O'Toole, Fras, Dublin
Oman, Wm, Dublin
P
Parker, George, Dublin
Peelo, Denis, Dublin
Phillips, Matthew, Dublin
Picker, J, Galway
Ponder, Henry, Dublin
Pringle, Robt, Dublin
Q
Quinn, John, Dublin
Quinn, Patrick, Dublin
R
Rafter, William
Radbonrae, Avid, Dublin
Regan, Lawrence, Dublin
Ridgeway, Robt, Dublin
Rowan, Laur, Kildare
Russell, T, Bandon, Cork
Ryan, J, Dublin
S
Sanders, W, Dublin
Scott, William
Sears, David, Dublin
Seavers—Athlone
Sheppard, William
Sheridan, John, Cork
Stafford, Geo, Dublin
Stamford, Ml, Dublin
Stoke, P, Enniscorthy
Sutton, Ml, Enniscorthy
Swann, Ant, Dublin
Sweeney, A, Kildare
Synnott, James, Ferns
T
Tahan, Richard, Dublin
Tanning, M, Finglas
Thornton, Pat, Dublin
Treling, M, Dublin
W
Wall, Joseph E, Dublin
Walsh, Wm, Dublin
Wills, Henry, Dublin
Wills, Robert
White, Ml, Dublin
Y
Young, Ed, Dublin

64 Women up to 22nd May

On Monday, 29th May, the military authorities announced that having fully investigated the cases of the following men and women, they had been released. This list was made up to the 22nd May:

Names of sixty-four women prisoners who were released:

B
Barrett, Kitty
Brady, Bridget
Brown, Kate
Brown, Martha
Byrne, Mary
Byrne, Katie
Byrne, Eileen
C
Carron, May
Cooney, Lily
Cooney, Annie
Cooney, Eileen
Cosgrave, Marcella
D
Davis, Bridget
E
Ennis, Ellen
F
Fleming, Kathleen
G
Gahan, May
Goff, Bridget
Grenan, Julia
H
Hackett, Rosanna
Hegarty, Bridget
Humphreys, Ellen
J
Joyce, Maggie
K
Kelly, Kitty
Kelly, Martha
Kelly, Josephine
Kenny, Bridy
Kennedy, Margaret
L
Liston, Catherine
Liston, Mary
Lynch, Bessie
Lyons, Bridget
M
Maher, Kathleen
Markhan, Pauline
Martin, Kate
McCauley, Julia
McGowan, Josephine
McLaughlin, Maggie
McNamara, Rose
McNamee, Agnes
Mead, Florence
Mitchell, Caroline
Mullally, Rose
Mulhall, Lizzie
Murphy, Kathleen
Murtagh, Bridget
N
Norgrove, Annie
Norgrove, Emily
O
O'Brennan, Lilly
O'Daly, Nora
O'Flaherty, Margaret
O'Hanlon, Sheila
O'Keeffe, Josephine
O'Keeffe, Emily
O'Moore, May
O'Sullivan, Louisa
P
Partridge, Mary
Q
Quigley, Priscilla
Quigley, Maria
R
Retz, Barbara
S
Seery, Kathleen
Shanaharan, Jane
Spicer, Josephine
Sullivan, Mary
T
Treston, Catherine

139 Men up to 22nd May

Names of male prisoners released from 13th May to 22nd May, inclusive:

A
Allen, Geo, Dublin
B
Boylan, Edward
Boylan, Joseph
Boylan, Peter
Breen, Pat
Brosnan, John, Tralee
Butler, D, Courtown
Byrne, John, Dublin
Byrne, Lce, Dublin
Byrne, Joseph
C
Caffrey, Frs, Dublin
Carney, T, Oranmore
Carr, Jos, Drogheda
Casey, James
Cassidy, P, Mullingar
Clarke, Jas, Dublin
Collins, Ed, Donabate
Corless, Patk, Clarenbridge
Corcoran, Thos, Clarebridge
Courtney, Wm, Enniscorthy
Crowe, Martin, Ruane, Co. Clare
Cudden, Matt, Dublin
D
Duggan, E
Dempsey, Chas, Dublin
Duffy, Thos, Dublin
Donohue, Jas, Enniscorthy
Doyle, Richard, Enniscorthy
Dougherty, John, Sandymount
Dowling, Ml, Dublin
Donoghue, Dan, Dublin
Dunne, John, Dublin
Duke, Rich, St, Margaret's
Duff, Anthony, Skerries
Dulig, Ml, Tralee
Doyle, John, A
Doyle, Thos, Dublin
Devitt, E, Dublin
E
Edelstein, J
Elliott, John J, Athlone
F
Fay, James, Dublin
Flannagan, T, Oranmore
Fitzgerald, John, Glasnevin
Fulham, Thos, Dublin
G
Graffigan, Ed, Digby, Dublin
H
Halpin, JF, Dublin
Halpin, J, Dublin
Hughes, Gbt, Athlone
Hardy, O, Dublin
Hardy, J, Dublin
Humphreys, J, Dublin
Harnett, Richard, Dublin
Hastings, John, Dublin
Halloran, J, Oranmore
Hanvey, John, Dublin
Hanvey, Robert, Dublin
Hanvey, Francis, Dublin
Hynes, Wm, Oranbeg
Hogan, Wm, Dublin
J
Jennings, MOF, Dublin
Jones, Peter, Dublin
K
Kavanagh, Pat, Enniscorthy
Kavanagh, John, Milltown, Ferns
Kelly, PB, Cabra Pk
Keogh, Ml, North Strd
Kennedy, John, Dublin
Kilcoyne, Arthur, Dublin
Kennedy, Jas, Tralee
L
Lyndon, P
Laden, Matt, Dublin
Larkin, John, Dublin
Lacey, Ml, Skerries
Lang, Francis, Dublin
Lawler, Chas, Glasnevin
M
McGill, Edmund
McGloughlin, Ml, Dublin
Murray, Ben, Enniscorthy
Murphy, Rbt, Enniscorthy
Moran, Ml, Enniscorthy
McManus, Wm, Dublin
McAllister, Dl, Donabate
Murray, Peter, Athlone
Maloney, HJ, Dublin
Murray, Jos, Westland row
Matthews, John, Dublin
Munster, Thos, Drogheda
McHugh, Phil, Inniskeen
Mahoney, Abel, Tralee
McKenna, Ml, Tralee
MacMahon, Fred W, Dublin
McGrath, Pat, Dublin
Moore, John, Dublin
Martin, JP, Galway
Molloy, John, Dublin
Moroney, John, Dublin
N
Nolan, Ml, Enniscorthy
Norrie, David H, Londonderry
O
O'Brien, John, Athlone
O'Neill, Geo, Dublin
O'Brien, Pat Vin, Dublin
O'Shea, Dl, Tralee
O'Reilly, John, Dublin
O'Donoghue, Dr, Harry, Dublin
O'Neill, John, Dublin
O'Donnell, Phil, Clonmel
P
Phelan, Thos, Dublin
Power, Jos, Inchicore
Power, Wm, Inchicore
Power, Arthur, Inchicore
Phillips, BJ, Dublin
Parnell, Mat, Dublin
Perry, Geo, Dublin
Q
Quinn, Hugh, Dublin
Quigley, J, Dublin
R
Rigley, Pat, Enniscorthy
Reddin, Kerry, Howth
Reddin, Gerard, Howth
Reddin, Kenneth, Howth
Redmond, Mat, Dublin
Reilly, Martin
Farrell, Wm, Dublin
Reilly, Matthew, Dublin
S
Scully, Thos, Dublin
Sweeney, Owen, Athlone
Sherlock, John, Skerries
Shanley, Ml, Skerries
Smith, John, Dumfries
Sweetman, John, Kells
Sweeney, Ml, Harold's Cross
Shelly, John, Dublin
Steinberger, Prof, Galway
Southwell, John, Newry
Scott, Wm
T
Thackaberry, Wm, Dublin
W
Walsh, Coleman, Dublin
Wilson, Rbt, Enniscorthy
Whelan, Pat, Ferns
Walker, Ml, Dublin
Walker, John, Dublin
Williams, H, Fairview
Waldron, Rich R, Sandymount

238 Men up to 29th May

It was announced on Friday, 2nd June, that the military authorities, having fully investigated the cases of the following men, had ordered their release. This list was made up to the 29th May:

Allen, Thos, Summerhill, Co. Meath
Allen, W, Summerhill, Co. Meath
Allen, Jas, Summerhill, Co. Meath
Ahearne, Jas, Garranfeen, Kilbrittain
Alexander, William E, Brookfield, Blackrock
B
Brien, Jas, Dublin
Brien, Patrick, Dublin
Bracken, Thos, Dublin
Brown, Arthur, Irishtown
Boland, Wm, Sackville st
Byrne, John, Dublin
Burke, Wm, Dublin
Boland, Chas, Dublin
Birmingham, T, 91 Up Rathmines
Boylan, L, Booterstown
Broderick, Ml, Clarenbridge
Behan, Thos, Rathangan
Burke, Wm, Peterswell
Burke, John, Dublin
Biggs, Pat, Galway
Brennan, J, Ballinadee
Broderick, J, Galway
Barrett, John, Kilbrittain
Byrne, L, 16 Havelock sq
Berry, John, Bandon
Byrne, Jos, 19 Marlborough st
Byrne, John, J, Kingst'n
Blake, Thos, Dublin
C
Corcoran, Pat, Dublin
Condon, T, Ashbourne, Meath
Casserly, John
Campbell, G, Dublin
Carroll, Jas, Ferns
Collins, John, Dublin
Collins, Ml, Sheffield
Cuffe, Jas, Harold's Cross
Cuffe, Pat, Harold's Cross
Cahill, Wm, Craughwell
Cogan, R, Mardyke
Connor, J, Tiaquin, Co. Galway
Conway, John, Dublin
Cooney, Dom, Craughwell
Collins, Tim, Ballinadee
Campbell, Jas, Fintona
Chapman, Thos, Duncormick
Conway, John, Hollymount
Conroy, Ed, Ballintemple, Co. Galway
Crowley, Tim, Ballinadee
Cullen, James, Dublin
Cullen, Thos, Duncormick
D
Donoghue, Thos, Dublin
Doyle, Jas, Ferns
Doyle, Ml, Gorey
Daly, PE, Dublin
Delaney, Ml, Dublin
Dowling, Ed, Dublin
Doyle, Thos, Crumlin, Co. Dublin
Dunbar, Martin, Ferns,
Daly, Pat J, Athenry
Dalton, LJ, Tipperary
Dempsey, Wm, Dublin
Dunleary, Chris, Dublin
Duffy, Pat, Clandoogan, Co. Mayo
Donaghy, P, Fintona
Dwyer, Stephen, Kilkenny
Dempsey, Jas, Belfast
Dorney, JC, Dublin
Doyle, Ml, Dublin
Dunne, James, Dublin
Delaney, Henry, Dublin
Doyle, Pat, Dublin
Darcy, John, Dublin
Doyle, John, Killarney
Daly, John, Rathballymore, Co. Cork
Doyle, Pat, Athenry
Darcy, Pat, Dalkey
Doherty, John, Athenry
E
Egin, Pat, Dublin
Evans, Robert, Dublin
Ennis, Matt, Enniscorthy
F
Funge, Joseph, Gorey
Flynn, JA, Dublin
Flynn, Frank, Dublin
Fegan, Thos, Clandoogan, Co. Meath
Fegan, Ml, Clandoogan, Co. Meath
Fagan, James, Dublin
Fagan, John, Dublin
Fanning, J, New Ross
Fitzgerald, Theo, Dublin
Fox, Bernard, Blackrock
Fitzgerald, W, Inchicore
Fallow, Pat, Balla, Co. Mayo
Fielding, Thos, Barntown, Co. Wexford
G
Gunnigle, L, Cliffoney, Co. Sligo
Griffin, Maurice, Tralee
Goulding, Jas, Dublin
Creany, Hugh, Craughwell
Goodwin, John
Gillgwm, Bryan, Manorhamilton
Gilmartin, J, Cliffoney, Co. Sligo
Geraghty, Martin
Gilmartin, Chas, Cliffoney, Co. Sligo
Gaynor, Pat, Dublin
Goulding, Thos, Dublin
Geoghegan, Ed, Dublin
Gavin, J, Westport
Gardiner, Jas, Monivea
Goulding, Ml, Balla, Co. Mayo
Grealish, J, Craughwell
H
Harkin, Ml, Drogheda
Hanley, Ed, Galway
Heraty, Hubert, Westport, Co. Mayo
Hyde, John, Cork
Hannon, Ed, Cliffoney, Co. Sligo
Hannon, John, Cliffoney
Hill, SH, Dublin
Hayes, Thos, (sen) Enniscorthy
Hughes, Pat, Westport
Hogan, Pat, Gorey
Halpin, Patrick, Dublin
Houghton, Chris, Dublin
Hyde, Joseph, Bandon
Harvey, Thos, Dublin
Hoban, John, Castlebar
I
Inskipp, Jos, Dublin
J
Jordan, Ml, Killeshandra
Jordan, Pat, Dublin
K
Kelly, MJ, Summerhill
Kelly, Patrick, Dublin
Kelly, Matt, Dublin
Kelly, Isaac, Dublin
Keating, Jas, Dublin
Kehoe, J, Enniscorthy
Kavanagh, Jas, Dublin
Kelly, James, Athenry
Kenny, SJ, Westport
Kenny, Moses, Gorey
Keane, Martin, Athenry
Kavanagh, Ml, Enniscorthy
Kelly, Pat, Craughwell
Kelly, Thos, New Ross
Kilmartin, Pat, Dublin
Keegan, Thos, Enniscorthy
Kenny, Chris, Rathangan
Kennedy, Martin, Athenry
Kearney, Pat, Dublin
Keane, John, Clarenbridge
Keville, Pat, Balla, Co. Mayo
Kavanagh, J, Duncormick
L
Lohan, John, Westport
M
M'Loughlin, Pat, Sandymount
Murphy, Jos, Dublin
McQuaid, Thos, Dublin
Murray, F, Drumcondra
Moran, John, Galway
McDonald, Ed, Camolin
M'Evoy, Jas, 8 Redmond's Hill
Murphy, Matt, Ferns
M'Donnell, Fras, Dublin
McDonnell, Paul, Dublin
McGarrigle, C, Cliffoney
Mahon, J (sen) Dublin
McTeggart, Thos, Dundalk
Mitchell, John, Athenry
McGuinness, F, Longford
Moore, JW, Dublin
Murphy Ml, Athenry
McLoughlin, Pat, Summerhill, Co. Meath
McElligott, J, Drumcondra
Maloney, M, Athenry
Makipaltis, Antle Zecks, Finland
Manning, Pat, Kilsallaghan
McCrann, A, Roscommon
Mooney, Thos, Rathangan
Marie, Louis, Dublin
Murray, Francis, Dublin
Murphy, Tim, Ballydaly
Mannion, John, Craughwell
Mullane, Jer, Cork
McCann, Rob, Dublin
Maddock, Wm, Duncormick
Mulvey, Dominick, Rathfarnham
Murphy, Thos, Castlebar
McHugh, M, Castlebar
N
Nestor, Thos, Galway
Noone, James, Dublin
Nolan, John, Dublin
O
O'Donnell, JP, Tralee
O'Neill, Ml, Inchicore

O'Shea, JP, Dublin
O'Neill, Peter, Gorey
O'Connor, John M, Dublin
O'Leary, Pat J, Cavan
O'Connell, John Vin, Limerick
O'Loughlin, J, Manorhamilton
O'Connor, TJ, Taggart
O'Hehir, Ml, Dublin
O'Brien, J, Ballybeard
O'Brien, W, Ballybeard
O'Neill, MJ, Ferns
O'Leary, Jas, Ballineen
O'Grady, Standish, Dublin
O'Rourke, Pat, Dublin
O'Brien, Thos, Westport
O'Neill, John, Fintona
O'Rourke, B, Inniskeen
P
Phelan, Pat, Dublin
Power, TP, Dublin
Perry, Jas, Dublin
Q
Quinn, John, Craughwell
R
Reynolds, Chas, Dublin
Ryan, T, Kilsallaghan
Ryan, Jas, Claremorris
Reilly, Jas, Balla
S
Smyth, Fras, Dublin
Smullen, Pat, 7 Farrell's lane
Spicer, Geo, Killarney
Sreehan, Ml, New Ross
St Clair, Martin, Cork
Sheehan, Pat, Dublin
Stafford, John, Duncormick
T
Treacy, Jas, Sandymount
Timmins, Rose
Turner, Pat, Dublin
Tobin, Maurice, Rathmines
W
Whelan, Ed R, Dublin
Ward, BM, Dublin
Ward, PJ, Dublin
Walsh, R, Dublin
White, Pat, Dublin
Windrum, SW, Limerick
Ward, Pat, Dublin
Wiseman, Wm, Cork
Wallace, JE, Newbridge
Watkins, T, Enniscorthy
Y
Young, John, Dublin

191 up to 2nd June

The military authorities on 8th June announced that, having fully investigated the cases of the following 191 prisoners, they had ordered their release. This list was made up to 2nd June, inclusive:

B
Burke, Ed, Athenry
Blayney, John, Athlone
Barry, Jos, Dublin
Byrne, Chris, Naas
Byrne, Nicholas, Naas
Brown, John, Sligo
C
Corcoran, Pat, 42 Waterford st
Callanan, T, Craughwell
Corbett, Pat, Craughwell
Corbett, T, Craughwell
Cunniffe, Pat, Loughrea
Coyne, JF, Kilkenny
Clegg, Jas, New Ross
Crowley, Pat, Bandon
Crowley, Wm, Bandon
Crowley, MJ, New Ross
Cooney, PJJ, Dublin
Crowley, Ml, New Ross
Coyne, Michael, Sligo
Connolly, Ml, Dublin
Comerford, E, Kilkenny
Cunniffe, T, Oranmore
Clery, Thos, V, Dublin
Carney, Fran J, Dublin
Corish, R, Wexford
Carroll, J, Enniscorthy
D
Derham, Rbt, Skerries
Doyle, Wm, New Ross
Delahunty, M, Loughrea
Doyle, John, New Ross,
Deegan, Martin, do
Dunne, Tim, Dublin
Dunne, Andrew, Naas
Dunne, Jas, Naas
Dowling, TF, Dublin
Dowling, Louis, Dublin
Dowling, C, M, Dublin
Duff, Henry, Dublin
Darcy, JF, Inchicore
Duffy, EJ, Londonderry
De Loughrey, Lawrence, Kilkenny
Dooley, Ml, Athenry
Dooley, JJ, Athenry
Du Bourdieu, J, Dublin
Darcy, Pat, Dublin
Doody, Pat, Dublin
Dunleavy, Pat, Tuam
Dunne, John J, Dublin
E
Egan, Martin, Gort
F
Fahey, Pat, Loughrea
Fitzgerald, Thos, Kerry
Farrell, John, Dublin
Fortune, Daniel, Gorey
Fitzgerald, J, Newbridge
Forde, J, Craughwell
Furlong, T, Kilkenny
Fahey, Mat J, Dublin
Furlong, R, Kilashee
Fahey, T, Craughwell
Fortune, Francis, Dublin
Farrell, Jos, Broadstone
Finn, Eugene, Blackrock
Fortune, E, Enniscorthy
Fallon, Ml, Craughwell
Farrell, Ml, Athenry
Fahy, Pat J, Kinvara
G
Green, MJ, Loughrea
Gegan, Ml, Craughwell
Gallon, Pat, Co. Tyrone
Grehan, Pat F, Naas
Gorman, W, Enniscorthy
Grady, Thos, Feakle
H
Humphreys, R, Dublin
Haverty, R, New Inn
Hynes, Ml, Craughwell
Hunt, Hubert, Corofin
Hunt, Wm, Corofin
Hanniffy, Ml, Athenry
Higgins, MF, Kilkenny
Hart, B Vin, Dalkey
Harte, John, Kilkenny
Hartley, John, New Ross
Hayden, Pat, New Ross
Hayes, Jas, Bridgetown
Hession, Ml, Craughwell
Holmes, Denis, Dublin
J
Jordon, Daniel, Bandon
Judge, Richard, Dublin
K
Kennedy, M, Craughwell
Kenny, Ml, Rathangan
Kenny, Jos, Rathangan
Kenny, Pat, Rathangan
Kavanagh, P, Dublin
Kearns, John, Loughrea
Kelly, Thos, Dublin
Kent, John, New Ross
Kealy, Martin, Kilkenny
Kavanagh, J, Dublin
Kelly, Thos, Dublin
Kehoe, Tim A, New Ross
Keane, Peter, Skerries
Keogh, Jos, Dublin
Kelly, J, Ballaghadereen
Kelly, Henry, Dublin
Kirwan, Wm, Dublin
L
Lyons, Wm, Ferns
Loughrey, Ml, Gort
Lindsay, John, Dublin
Lehane, Pat, Cork
Lygg,(?) Thos, Dublin
Lynch, Pat, New Ross
M
McTigue, Pat, Loughrea
Martin, Pat, Loughrea
Murphy, Ed J, New Ross
Murphy, John, New Ross
McGrath, T, New Ross
Maguire, D, Balbriggan
McDonnell, WK, Bandon
McCarthy, J, Timoleague
Murphy, Jas, Barry
Morgan, M, Craughwell
May, PC, Goresbridge
Mullally, A, Kilkenny
Madigan, Jas, Balbriggan
Moore, Peter, Dublin
McHugh, Wm, Dublin
Miller, G, Booterstown
Murphy, Wm, New Ross
McHugh, Myles, Dublin
McHugh, Pat, Dublin
Mullany, JJ, Athlone
Murphy, Pat, Dublin
Moroney, Thos, Dublin
Martin, Jas, Dublin
Moran, Lewis J, Curragh
McDonald, John, Dublin
Meehan, J, Dublin
McLaughlin, J, Kilmainham
Murray, Pat, Dublin
N
Neary, Thos, Kilkenny
Noone, Pat, Athenry
Nolan, P, Ballsbridge
O
O'Connor, Alf G, Dublin
O'Kelly, Ml, Naas
O'Neill, John, New Ross
O'Leary, Simon, do
O'Connor, R, Blackrock
O'Kennedy, MJ, New Ross
O'Kennedy, PA, New Ross
O'Kennedy, J, New Ross
O'Doherty, Wm D, Drumcondra
O'Dwyer, Ml, Kilkenny
O'Halloran, T, Kinsale
O'Halloran, J, Kinsale
O'Byrne, John, Dublin
O'Hara, Peter, Dublin
O'Brien, Dan, Tipperary
O'Flanagan, Ml, Dublin
O'Keeffe, John, Cork
P
Purcell, Ml, Kilkenny
Parsons, Pat, Kilkenny
Prendergast, J, New Ross
Purcell, Phil P, Dublin

R
Ronghan, Peter, Fort
Ryan, Ml, Kilkenny
Rynne, Wm, Ardee
Roche, John, Bandon
Rudy, Hans C, Blackrock
Rodgers, H, Sixmilecross
Rooney, P, Craughwell
Ralph, Thos, Westport
S
Shannon, Ml J, Clare
Saul, James, Dublin
Sweeney, Pat, Loughrea
Smyth, Chas, Kilkenny
Schelly, Jos, New Ross
Stafford, Thos, Taghmon
Slane, R, Sixmilecross
Smyth, L, Magherafelt
Shaughnessy, J, Craughwell
Stokes, T, Enniscorthy
T
Travers, M, New Ross
Tuohy, Jos, Feakle
W
Walsh, Thos, Athenry
Warner, Peter, New Ross
Walsh, L, Kilkenny
Waldron, John, Athenry
Walsh, Pat, Athenry
Walsh, LJ, Drogheda
White, Ml, Enniscorthy
Ward, Pat J, Dublin

212 up to 7th June

The military authorities announced on 13th June that, after fully investigating the cases of the following 212 men, they had ordered their release. This list is made up from the 4th to the 7th June, inclusive:

A
Ashe, Ml J, Dublin
Allen, A, Enniscorthy
Archbold, Wm, Dublin
B
Brown, J, Craughwell
Byrne, Martin, Dublin
Brennan, J, Dublin
Banks, Henry, Dublin
Birrell, L, Dublin
Byrne, James, Dublin
Burke, Michael, Dublin
Bradley, R, Dublin
Buckley, Jerh, Dublin
Byrne, Jos, Dunlavin
Byrne, Joseph, Dublin
Birmingham, P, Dublin
Brett, Pierce, Kilkenny
Broderick, Ml, Athenry
Burke, Patk, Athenry
Boyne, Wm, Enniscorthy
C
Coyne, M, Loughgeorge
Coy, Jas, Craughwell
Coy, Ml, Craughwell
Cooney, Wm, Dublin
Carter, R, Booterstown
Cunningham, J, Dublin
Cunningham, P, Dublin
Cusack, J, Drumcondra
Colgan, Danl, Dublin
Cahill, Patk, Dublin
Cooney, Ml, Dublin
Campbell, John, Dublin
Cremen, M, Rathfarnham
Connolly, T, Derryhoyle
Carter, John, Dublin
Chaney, WJ, Dublin
Chaney, Patk, Dublin
Caffrey, Leo, Dublin
Cullen, Ml, Dublin
Cregg, Laughlin, Dublin
Creswell, Ed, Dublin
Carroll, Thos, Dublin
Carroll, Nicholas, Dublin
Carty, M, Enniscorthy
Curtis, O'Leary
Chapman, P, Ballyneety
D
Duffy, Wm, Athenry
Dempsey, P, Craughwell
Du Bourdieu, A, Sandymount
Darby, Chas, Dublin
Delaney, Jos, Dublin
Devereux, Patk, Dublin
Duffy, Jas, Dublin
Dowling, S, Dublin
Dillon, Hubert, Attymon
Doyle, Ml, Athenry
Drinnan, Wm, Dublin
Dunne, Jos, Dublin
Donohoe, S, Dublin
Devane, Patk, Fermoy
Doyle, JL, Wexford
Doyle, PJ, Enniscorthy
E
Earls, Joseph, New Inn
F
Fitzpatrick, M, Dublin
Fitzsimons, J, Dublin
Fitzpatrick, J, Dublin
Farrell, James, Dublin
Fitzpatrick, P, Enniscorthy
Farrell, H, Dublin
Farrington, Leo, Dublin
Frawley, Denis, Dublin
Fox, T, Maryborough
Fitzpatrick, M, Dublin
Farnon, L, Clontarf
Fitzharris, J, Enniscorthy
G
Gardiner, J, Craughwell
Gilligan, P, Athenry
Gibson, Jas, Dublin
Gibbons, P, Dublin
Gunning, J, Dublin
H
Hynes, D, Craughwell
Hynes, John, Craughwell
Hanniffy, J, Craughwell
Hamilton, Chris, Cork
Harvey, P, Ranelagh
Hannon, Jas, Dublin
Hanley, DJ, New Ross
Hogan, Patk, Dublin
Howley, Ml, Galway
Hutchin, Wm, Dublin
Hickey, B, Stillorgan
Hynch, John, Ferns
J
Joyce, John, Dublin
Jackson, F, Dublin
Jenkinson, W, Dublin
K
Keating, Ml, Athenry
Keane, Jas, Athenry
Kearns, Danl, Athenry
Kerford, Patk, Dublin
Kirwan, Ed, Dublin
Kelly, Wm, Athenry
Kenny, John, Dublin
Keogh, Patk, Dublin
Keirwin, P, Dublin
Kennedy, J, Athenry
Keeffe, P, Enniscorthy
Kehoe, P, Enniscorthy
Kelly, P, Enniscorthy
Kelly, Alderman Thos, Dublin
L
Largan, Ml, Dublin
Lyng, J, Ballywilliam
Leeson, John, Dublin
Lennon, W, New Ross
Lynch, Jas, Dublin
Lynch, Danl, Dublin
Leonard, M, Dublin
Lawless, S, Attymon
Lynch, J, Dublin
M
Mullin, T, Athenry
Magee, Geo, Dublin
Mooney, Patk, Naas
Moran, JJ, Dublin
Mullally, M, Dublin
Maguire, Louis, Dublin
M'Loughlin, C, Glenmore
Molloy, C, Dublin
Maguire, P, Dublin
Moore, J, Fermoy
M'Cormack, J, Dublin
M'Donangh, E, Gorey
Murtagh, Peter, Dublin
M'Keog, David, Dublin
M'Namara, J, Bray
M'Hugh, Ed, Dublin
M'Mahon, Ed, Dublin
Murtagh, B, Dublin
M'Donnell, JJ, Donnybrook
Malone, Wm, Dublin
Manning, Ml, Inchicore
M'Cormack, M, Moate
Merriman, T, Inchicore
Mehan, Geo, Dublin
M'Ginley, W, Dublin
M'Donnell, Jos, Dublin
Moriarty, D, Dublin
M'Evoy, Danl, New Ross
M'Glynn, M, Craughwell
M'Glynn, Martin, Craughwell
Murray, C, Dublin
Madhey, R, Dublin
Macken, AF, Dublin
M'Clane, H, Dublin
M'Guire, J, Dublin
Murphy, P, Glasnevin
Murphy, J, Inchicore
Moran, B, Dublin
Murphy, John, Wexford

M'Dermott, P, Drumcliffe
Moran, T, Duncormick
N
Naughton, Pat, Athenry
Noonan, J, Ballyfeard
Noonan, Wm F, do
Nyhan, John, Dublin
Nowlan, Jas, Kilkenny
O
O'Callaghan, J, Bandon
O'Neill, Andrew, Dublin
O'Brien, Ml J, Dublin
O'Kennedy, TJ, New Ross
O'Brien, Peter, Dublin
O'Rourke, P, Roscommon
O'Keeffe, Ml, New Ross
O'Connor, R, Dublin
Oglesby, Jos, Dublin
O'Malley, Chris, Dublin
O'Duffy, Jas P, Dublin
O'Neill, M, Enniscorthy
O'Brien, T, Rathmines
O'Neill, J, Enniscorthy
P
Pender, Wm, Dublin
R
Ripton, Thos, Dublin
Reilly, Jas, Dublin
Ryan, Ml, Dublin
Reynolds, JH, Skerries
Rafferty, Thos, Dublin
Reilly, Robt, Dublin
Reardon, M, Millstreet, Cork
Ruth, Wm, Enniscorthy
S
Stratford,(?) M, Craughwell
Savage, Ml, Castleyour
Shiels, Jos, Skerries
Shiels, ML, Enniscorthy
Sheridan, Jas, Dublin
Summers, Jos, Dublin
Smyth, P, Enniscorthy
Sheehan, Pat, do
Sheridan, Fran, Dublin
T
Tobin, Pat, Dublin
Tarpey, Pat, Dublin
Turner, Jos, Dublin
Turner, Frank, Dublin
Tully, Wm, Dublin
Tully, Geo, Dublin
Tobin, Ml, Dublin
Tobin, Ml, Dublin
W
Whyte, Jos, Attymon
Whyte, Pat, Attymon
Walsh, R, Dublin
Ward, Jos, Athenry
Ward, Tim, Dublin
Whelan, J, Enniscorthy
Walsh, Jas, Dublin
Whelan, J, Enniscorthy
Whelan, Jos, Dublin

War Office, 21st July 1916

The following despatches have been received by the Secretary of State for War from the Field-Marshal Commanding-in-Chief, Home Forces:

General Headquarters, Home Forces,
Horse Guards, London, WW,
29th May, 1916

My Lord,

I have the honour to forward herewith a Report which I have received from the General Officer Commanding-in-Chief, Irish Command, relating to the recent outbreak in Dublin and the measures taken for its suppression.

1. It will be observed that the rebellion broke out in Dublin at 12.15 a.m on April 24th, and that by 5.20 p.m. on the same afternoon a considerable force from the Curragh had arrived in Dublin to reinforce the garrison and other troops were on their way from Athlone, Belfast, and Templemore. The celerity with which these reinforcements became available says much for the arrangements which had been made to meet such a contingency.

2. I was informed of the outbreak by wire on the afternoon of the 24th ult., and the 59th Division at St Albans was at once put under orders to proceed to Ireland, and arrangements were put in train for their transport. After seeing General Friend I gave orders for the movement of two brigades to commence as soon as their transport could be arranged. I am aware that in doing so I was acting beyond the powers which were delegated to me, but I considered the situation to be so critical that it was necessary to act at once without reference to the Army Council.

3. On the morning of the 28th April General Sir John Maxwell, KCB, KCMG, CVO, DSO, arrived in Ireland to assume command.

4. I beg to bring to your notice the assistance afforded to me by the Lords Commissioners of the Admiralty, who met every request made to them for men, guns, and transport with the greatest promptitude, and whose action enabled me to reinforce and maintain the garrison in the South and West of Ireland without unduly drawing upon the troops which it was desirable to retain in England.

I have the honour to be,
Your Lordship's most obedient servant,
FRENCH, Field-Marshal,
Commanding-in-Chief, Home Forces.

Sir John Maxwell's First Despatch

From the general Officer,
Commanding-in-Chief,
The Forces in Ireland.
To the Field-Marshal,
Commanding-in-Chief,
The Home Forces.

Headquarters,
Irish Command, Dublin,
25th May, 1916.

My Lord,

I have the honour to report the operations of the Forces now under my command from Monday, 24th April, when the rising in Dublin began.

1. On Easter Monday, 24th April, at 12.15 p.m., a telephone message was received from the Dublin Metropolitan Police saying Dublin Castle was being attacked by armed Sinn Feiners. This was immediately confirmed by the Dublin Garrison Adjutant, who reported that, in the absence of Colonel Kennard, the Garrison Commander, who had left his office shortly before, and was prevented by the rebels from returning, he had ordered all available troops from Portobello, Richmond, and Royal Barracks to proceed to the Castle, and the 6th Reserve Cavalry Regiment towards Sackville street.

The fighting strength of the troops available in Dublin at this moment were:

6th Reserve Cavalry Regiment, 35 officers, 851 other ranks.

3rd Royal Irish Regiment, 18 officers, 385 other ranks.

10th Royal Dublin Fusiliers, 37 officers, 430 other ranks.

3rd Royal Irish Rifles, 21 officers, 650 other ranks.

Of these troops an inlying picquet of 400 men, which for some days past had been held in readiness, proceeded at once, and the remainder followed shortly afterwards.

At 12.30 p.m. a telephone message was sent to General Officer Commanding, Curragh, to mobilise the mobile column, which had been arranged for to meet any emergency, and to despatch it dismounted to Dublin by trains which were being sent from Kingsbridge.

This column, under the command of Colonel Portal, consisted of 1,600 officers and other ranks from the 3rd Reserve Cavalry Brigade.

Almost immediately after the despatch of this message telephonic communication in Dublin became very interrupted, and from various sources it was reported that the Sinn Feiners had seized the General Post Office in Sackville street, the Magazine in Phoenix Park, the Four Courts, Jacobs' Biscuit Factory, and had occupied many buildings in various parts of the city.

As the occupation of the General Post Office by the Sinn Feiners denied the use of the telegraph, a message reporting the situation in Dublin was sent at 1.10 p.m. to the naval centre at Kingstown, asking that the information of the rising might be transmitted by wireless through the Admiralty to you. This was done.

First Actions of the Troops

2. The first objectives undertaken by the troops were to recover possession of the Magazine in Phoenix Park, where the rebels had set fire to a quantity of ammunition, to relieve the Castle, and to strengthen the guards on Viceregal Lodge and other points of importance.

The Magazine was quickly re-occupied, but the troops moving on the Castle were held up by the rebels, who had occupied surrounding houses, and had barricaded the streets with carts and other material.

Between 1.40 p.m. and 2 p.m., 50 men of 3rd Royal Irish Rifles and 130 men of the 10th Royal Dublin Fusiliers reached the Castle by the Ship street entrance.

At 4.45 p.m. the first train from the Curragh arrived at Kingsbridge Station, and by 5.20 p.m. the whole Cavalry Column, 1,600 strong, under the command of Colonel Portal, had arrived, one train being sent on from Kingsbridge to North Wall by the loop line to reinforce the guard over the docks.

3. During the day the following troops were ordered to Dublin:

(a) A battery of four 18-pounders RFA, from the Reserve Artillery Brigade at Athlone.

(b) The 4th Dublin Fusiliers from Templemore.

(c A composite battalion from Belfast.

(d) An additional 1,000 men from the Curragh. This message being sent by one of the troop trains returning to the Curragh.

During the afternoon and evening small parties of troops were engaged with the rebels.

Gallant Stand by Cavalry

The 3rd Royal Irish Regiment on their way to the Castle were held up by the rebels in the South Dublin Union, which they attacked and partially occupied; a detachment of two officers and 50 men from the 6th Reserve Cavalry Regiment, which was convoying some ammunition from the North Wall, was surrounded in Charles street, but succeeded in parking their convoy and defended this with great gallantry for 3½ days, when they were relieved: during this defence the officer in command was killed and the remaining officer wounded.

The rebels in St Stephen's Green were attacked, and picquets with machine guns were established in the United Service Club and the Shelbourne Hotel with a view to dominating the square and its exits.

At 9.35 p.m. Colonel Kennard, Officer Commanding Troops, Dublin, reached the Castle with another party of 86 men of the 3rd Royal Irish Regiment.

The defence of the docks at North Wall was undertaken by Major HF Somerville, commanding a detachment from the School of Musketry, Dollymount, reinforced by 330 officers and men of the 9th Reserve Cavalry Regiment.

The occupation of the Customs House, which dominated Liberty Hall, was carried out at night, and was of great assistance in later operations against Liberty Hall.

4. The situation at midnight was that we held the Magazine, Phoenix Park, the Castle, and the Ship street entrance to it, the Royal Hospital, all barracks, the Kingsbridge, Amiens street, and North Wall railway stations, the Dublin telephone exchange in Crown alley, the Electric Power Station at Pigeon House Fort, Trinity College, Mountjoy Prison, and Kingstown Harbour. The Sinn Feiners held Sackville street and blocks of buildings on each side of this, including Liberty Hall, with their headquarters at the General Post Office, the Four Courts, Jacobs' biscuit factory, South Dublin Union, St Stephen's Green, all the approaches to the Castle except the Ship street entrance, and many houses all over the city, especially about Ballsbridge and Beggar's Bush.

5. The facility with which the Sinn Feiners were able to seize so many important points throughout the city was, in my opinion, due to the fact that armed bodies of civilians have been continually allowed to parade in and march through the streets of Dublin and throughout the country without interference.

The result was that the movement of large forces of armed civilians, particularly on a holiday such as Easter Monday, passed, if not unnoticed, unchecked, and no opposition could be offered to them at the moment when they decided to act.

Dublin Police Powerless

Further, the Dublin police, being unarmed and powerless to deal with these armed rebels, were withdrawn from the areas occupied by them.

6. At the time of the rising Major-General Friend, then commanding the troops in Ireland, was on short leave in England, and when visiting your headquarters at the Horse Guards on that day heard the serious news from Dublin. He returned that night, and arrived in Dublin early on the morning of the 25th April.

He has informed me that at a conference with you it was decided to despatch at once two infantry brigades of the 59th Division from England to Ireland, and that the remaining infantry brigade and artillery of this Division were to be held in readiness to follow if required.

7. On April 25th, Brigadier-General WHM Lowe, Commanding the Reserve Cavalry Brigade at the Curragh, arrived at Kingsbridge Station at 3.45 a.m. with the leading troops from the 25th (Irish) Reserve Infantry Brigade, and assumed command of the forces in the Dublin area, which were roughly 2,300 men of the Dublin garrison, the Curragh Mobile Column of 1,500 dismounted cavalry men, and 840 men of the 25th Irish Reserve Infantry Brigade.

Rebel Forces Cut in Two

8. In order to relieve and get communication with the Castle, Colonel Portal, Commanding the Curragh Mobile Column, was ordered to establish a line of posts from Kingsbridge Station to Trinity

College via the Castle. This was completed by 12 noon, 25th April, and with very little loss. It divided the rebel forces into two, gave a safe line of advance for troops extending operations to the north or south, and permitted communication by despatch rider with some of the Commands.

The only means of communication previous to this had been by telephone, which was unquestionably being tapped.

The Dublin University OTC, under Captain EH Alton, and subsequently Major GA Harris, held the College buildings until the troops arrived. The holding of these buildings separated the rebel centre round the General Post Office from that round St Stephen's Green: it established a valuable base for the collection of reinforcements as they arrived, and prevented the rebels from entering the Bank of Ireland, which is directly opposite to and commanded by the College buildings.

(9) During the day the 4th Royal Dublin Fusiliers from Templemore, a composite Ulster battalion from Belfast and a battery of four 18 pounder guns from the Reserve Artillery Brigade at Athlone arrived, and this allowed a cordon to be established round the northern part of the city from Parkgate, along the North Circular road to North Wall. Broadstone Railway Station was cleared of rebels, and a barricade near Phibsborough was destroyed by artillery fire.

Heavy Fire on the Castle

As a heavy fire was being kept up on the Castle from the rebels located in the Corporation buildings, *Daily Express* offices, and several houses opposite the City Hall, it was decided to attack these buildings.

The assault on the *Daily Express* office was successfully carried out under very heavy fire by a detachment of the 5th Royal Dublin Fusiliers under 2nd Lieutenant F O'Neill.

The main forces of the rebels now having been located in and around Sackville street, the Four Courts, and adjoining buildings, it was decided to try to enclose that area north of the Liffey by a cordon of troops so as to localise as far as possible the efforts of the rebels.

(10) Towards evening the 178th Infantry Brigade began to arrive at Kingstown, and in accordance with orders received, the brigade left Kingstown by road in two columns.

The left column, consisting of the 5th and 6th Battalions Sherwood Foresters, by the Stillorgan-Donnybrook road and South Circular road to the Royal Hospital, where it arrived without opposition.

The right column, consisting of the 7th and 8th Battalions Sherwood Foresters, by the main tram route through Ballsbridge, and directed on Merrion square and Trinity College.

Severe Casualties at Northumberland Road

This column, with 7th Battalion leading, was held up at the northern corner of Haddington road and Northumberland road, which was strongly held by rebels, but with the assistance of bombing parties organised and led by Captain Jeffares, of the Bombing School at Elm Park, the rebels were driven back.

At 3.25 p.m. the 7th Battalion Sherwood Foresters met great opposition from the rebels holding the schools and other houses on the north side of the road close to the bridge at Lower Mount street, and two officers, one of whom was the Adjutant, Captain Dietrichsen, were killed, and seven wounded, including Lieutenant-Colonel Fane, who, though wounded, remained in action.

At about 5.30 p.m. orders were received that the advance to Trinity College was to be pushed forward at all costs, and therefore at about 8 p.m., after careful arrangements, the whole column, accompanied by bombing parties, attacked the schools and houses where the chief opposition lay, the battalions charging in successive waves, carried all before them, but, I regret to say, suffered severe casualties in doing so.

Four officers were killed, 14 wounded, and of other ranks 216 were killed and wounded.

The steadiness shown by these two battalions is deserving of special mention, as I understand the majority of the men have less than three months' service.

In view of the opposition met with, it was not considered advisable to push on to Trinity College that night, so at 11 p.m. the 5th South Staffordshire Regiment from the 176th Infantry Brigade, reinforced this column, and by occupying the position gained allowed the two battalions Sherwood Foresters to be concentrated at Ballsbridge.

Heroic Civilians

In connection with this fighting at Mount street Bridge, where our heaviest casualties occurred, I should like to mention the gallant assistance given by a number of medical men, ladies, nurses and women servants, who at great risk brought in and tended to the wounded, continuing their efforts even when deliberately fired at by the rebels.

(11) Meanwhile severe fighting had taken place in the Sackville street quarter. At 8 a.m. Liberty Hall, the former headquarters of the Sinn Feiners, was attacked by field guns from the south bank of the River Liffey, and by a gun from the patrol ship Helga, with the result that considerable progress was made.

During the night of 26th-27th April several fires broke out in this quarter and threatened to become dangerous, as the fire brigade could not get to work owing to their being fired upon by the rebels.

Throughout the day further troops of the 176th Brigade arrived in the Dublin area.

(12) On 27th April, the

5th Leinsters,
2/6th Sherwood Foresters,
3rd Royal Irish Regiment,
The Ulster composite battalion,

under the command of Colonel Portal, began and

completed by 5 p.m. the forming of a cordon round the rebels in the Sackville street area, which operation was carried out with small loss.

About 12.45 p.m. Linen Hall Barracks, which were occupied by the Army Pay Office, were reported to have been set on fire by the rebels and were destroyed.

By night-fall the 177th Infantry Brigade had arrived at Kingstown, where it remained for the night.

Sir John Maxwell's Arrival

13. At 2 a.m. on the 28th April I arrived at North Wall and found many buildings in Sackville street burning fiercely, illuminating the whole city, and a fusilade of rifle fire going on in several quarters of the city.

Accompanied by several Staff Officers who had come with me, I proceeded to the Royal Hospital.

After a conference with Major-General Friend and Brigadier-General Lowe, I instructed the latter to close in on Sackville street from East and West, and to carry out a house-to-house search in areas gained.

I was able to place the 2/4 Lincolns at his disposal for the purpose of forming a cordon along the Grand Canal, so enclosing the southern part of the city and forming a complete cordon round Dublin.

During the afternoon the 2/5th and 2/6th South Staffords arrived at Trinity College, and this additional force allowed me to begin the task of placing a cordon round the Four Courts area in the same way as the Sackville street area, which had already been successfully isolated.

During the afternoon, the 2/5th and 2/6th Reserve Cavalry Regiment, which had been escorting ammunition and rifles from North Wall, and had been held up in Charles street, was relieved by armoured motor lorries, which had been roughly armoured with boiler plates by the Inchicore Railway Works and placed at my disposal by Messrs Guinness.

Field Artillery Hastens the Surrender

Throughout the night the process of driving out the rebels in and around Sackville street continued, though these operations were greatly hampered by the fires in this area and by the fact that some of the burning houses contained rebel stores of explosives which every now and again blew up.

In other quarters of the city the troops had a trying time dealing with the numerous snipers, who became very troublesome during the hours of darkness.

14. Owing to the considerable opposition at barricades, especially in North King street, it was not until 9 a.m. on the 29th April that the Four Courts area was completely surrounded.

Throughout the morning the squeezing out of the surrounded areas was vigorously proceeded with, the infantry being greatly assisted by a battery of Field Artillery commanded by Major Hill, who used his guns against the buildings held by the rebels with such good effect that a Red Cross Nurse brought in a message from the rebel leader, PH Pearse, asking for terms. A reply was sent that only unconditional surrender would be accepted. At 2 p.m. Pearse surrendered himself unconditionally, and was brought before me, when he wrote and signed notices ordering the various 'Commandoes' to surrender unconditionally.

During the evening the greater part of the rebels in the Sackville street and Four Courts area surrendered.

15. Early on the 30th April two Franciscan monks informed me that the rebel leader, Macdonagh, declining to accept Pearse's orders, wished to negotiate.

He was informed that only unconditional surrender would be accepted, and at 3 p.m., when all preparation for an attack on Jacobs' Biscuit Factory, which he held, had been made, Macdonagh and his band of rebels surrendered unconditionally.

In the St Stephen's Green area, Countess Markievicz and her band surrendered and were taken to the Castle.

These surrenders practically ended the rebellion in the City of Dublin.

16. Through out the night of the 30th April/1st May isolated rebels continued to snipe the troops, but during the 1st May these were gradually cleared out, and in conjunction with the police a systematic house-to-house search for rebels and arms was continued.

Anxiety about the Country

17. During the severe fighting which took place in Dublin the greatest anxiety was caused by the disquieting reports received from many parts of Ireland, and chiefly from:

(a) County Dublin
(b) County Meath
(c) County Louth
(d) County Galway
(e) County Wexford
(f) County Clare
(g) County Kerry

18. On the 27th April, as soon as the troops became available, a detachment was sent by sea from Kingstown to Arklow to reinforce the garrison at Kynoch's Explosive Works, and a small party was sent to assist the RIC post over the wireless station at Skerries.

On the 28th April a battalion of the Sherwood Foresters was despatched by rail to Athlone to protect the artillery and military stores there and to hold the communication over the River Shannon.

19. Brigadier-General Stafford, the Garrison Commander at Queenstown, was directed to use his discretion in the employment of troops under his command, and on 30th April he was reinforced from England by one battalion of the 179th Brigade, 60th Division, a battalion of the Royal Marines, and later by the remainder of the 179th Brigade.

20. Brigadier-General Hackett-Pain, who assumed command of the troops in Ulster, made effective use of the troops under his command, and it was largely due to the dispositions made by these two Commanders that the Sinn Feiners in the South and North of Ireland were restrained from taking a more active part in the rebellion.

Assistance from the RIC

I received the greatest assistance from the Inspector-General Royal Irish Constabulary, and from all his inspectors and men, and throughout the rebellion I worked in the closest co-operation with them. In many districts small posts of these gallant men were isolated and had to defend themselves against overwhelming numbers, which they successfully did except in very few cases.

It was with great regret I received the report of 28th April that a body of Royal Irish Constabulary, under Inspector Gray, had been ambushed by the rebels at Ashbourne, which resulted in Inspectors Gray and Smith and eight constables being killed and 14 wounded.

It was not until 30th April that I was able to spare a mobile column to deal with this body of rebels, the leaders of which were secured.

Despatch of Mobile Columns

In other parts of Ireland similar attacks on police posts had been made by armed bands of Sinn Feiners. In order to deal with these, as soon as the Dublin rebels had been crushed, I organised various mobile columns, each consisting of from one to two companies of infantry, a squadron of cavalry, one 18-pounder gun and an armoured car.

Each column was allotted a definite area, which, in close co-operation with the local police, was gone through, and dangerous Sinn Feiners and men who were known to have taken an active part in the rising were arrested; in addition many arms belonging to Sinn Feiners were surrendered or seized.

I am glad to be able to report that the presence of these columns had the best possible effect on the people in country districts, in many of which troops had not been seen for years.

22. That splendid body of men, the Dublin Metropolitan Police, could give me little or no assistance, because they were unarmed. Had they been armed I doubt if the rising in Dublin would have had the success it did.

23. I am glad to report that the conduct of the troops was admirable: their cheerfulness, courage, and good discipline, under the most trying conditions, was excellent.

Although doors and windows of shops and houses had to be broken open, no genuine case of looting has been reported to me, which I consider reflects the greatest credit on all ranks.

Acknowledgments

24. I wish to acknowledge the great assistance I received from the Provost of Trinity College; the clergy of all denominations; civilian medical men; Red Cross nurses, who were untiring in their attention to the wounded, often rendered under heavy fire; ambulances provided by Royal Ambulance Corps; the Irish Volunteer Training Corps and members of St John's Ambulance Corps; the Civilian and Officers' Training Corps motor cyclists, who fearlessly carried despatches through streets infested with snipers; telegraph operators and engineers; and from the lady operators of the Telephone Exchange, to whose efforts the only means of rapid communication remained available.

I am glad to be able to record my opinion that the feelings of the bulk of the citizens of Dublin being against the Sinn Feiners materially influenced the collapse of the rebellion.

25. I deplore the serious losses which the troops and the civilian volunteers have suffered during these very disagreeable operations.

I have the honour to be,
Your most obedient servant,
JG MAXWELL,
General.

Difficulties of the Troops

From the General Officer Commanding in Chief, the Forces in Ireland, to the Secretary of State for War.

Headquarters, Irish Command.
Dublin, 26th May, 1916.
My Lord,

In amplification of the report of the operations undertaken by the troops in Dublin, which I forwarded to Field-Marshal Lord French on 25th May, I think it desirable to bring to your notice the difficult conditions under which the troops had to act.

Confused and Trying Conditions

1. The rebellion began by Sinn Feiners, presumably acting under orders, shooting in cold blood certain soldiers and policemen, simultaneously they took possession of various important buildings and occupied houses along the routes into the City of Dublin which were likely to be used by troops taking up posts.

2. Most of the rebels were not in any uniform, and by mixing with peaceful citizens made it almost impossible for the troops to distinguish between friend and foe until fire was opened.

3. In many cases troops having passed along a street seemingly occupied by harmless people were suddenly fired upon from behind from windows and roof-tops. Such were the conditions when reinforcements commenced to arrive in Dublin.

Shooting of Civilians

4. Whilst fighting continued under conditions at once so confused and so trying, it is possible that

some innocent citizens were shot. It must be remembered that the struggle was in many cases of a house-to-house character, that sniping was continuous and very persistent, and that it was often extremely difficult to distinguish between those who were or had been firing upon the troops and those who had for various reasons chosen to remain on the scene of the fighting, instead of leaving the houses and passing through the cordons.

5. The number of such incidents that has been brought to notice is very insignificant.

6. Once the rebellion started the members of the Dublin Metropolitan Police—an unarmed uniformed force—had to be withdrawn, or they would have been mercilessly shot down, as, indeed, were all who had the bad luck to meet the rebels. In their absence a number of the worst elements of the city joined the rebels and were armed by them. The daily record of the Dublin Magistrates' Court proves that such looting as there was was done by such elements.

Deliberate Firing on Ambulances and Firemen

7. There have been numerous incidents of deliberate shooting on ambulances, and those courageous people who voluntarily came out to tend to the wounded. The City Fire Brigade, when turned out in consequence of incendiary fires, were fired on and had to retire.

8. As soon as it was ascertained that the rebels had established themselves in various centres, the first phase of operations was conducted with a view to isolate them by forming a cordon of troops around each.

9. To carry out this streets were selected, along which the cordon could be drawn. Some of these streets, for instance, North King street, were found to be strongly held rebels occupying the roofs of houses, upper windows, and strongly-constructed barricades.

10. Artillery fire was only used to reduce the barricades, or against a particular house known to be strongly held.

11. The troops suffered severe losses in establishing these cordons, and, once established, the troops were subjected to a continuous fire from all directions, especially at night time, and invariably from persons concealed in houses.

The Military Losses

12. To give an idea of the opposition offered to His Majesty's troops in the execution of their duty, the following losses occurred:

	Killed	Wounded
Officers	17	46
Other ranks	89	288

13. I wish to draw attention to the fact that, when it became known that the leaders of the rebellion wished to surrender, the officers used every endeavour to prevent further bloodshed; emissaries were sent in to the various isolated bands, and time was given them to consider their position.

14. I cannot imagine a more difficult situation than that in which the troops were placed; most of those employed were draft-filling battalions or young Territorials from England, who had no knowledge of Dublin.

15. The surrenders, which began on April 30th, were continued until late on May 1st, during which time there was a considerable amount of isolated sniping.

16. Under the circumstances related above, I consider the troops as a whole behaved with the greatest restraint, and carried out their disagreeable and distasteful duties in a manner which reflects the greatest credit on their discipline.

Allegations against Troops

17. Allegations on the behaviour of the troops brought to my notice are being most carefully inquired into. I am glad to say they are few in number, and these are not all borne out by direct evidence.

18. Numerous cases of unarmed persons killed by rebels during the outbreak have been reported to me. As instances, I may select the following for your information:

J O'Brien, a constable of the Dublin Metropolitan Police, was shot while on duty at Castle Gate on April 24th. On the same day another constable of the same force, named M Lahiff, was shot while on duty at St Stephen's Green. On April 25th R Waters, of Recess, Monkstown, Co. Dublin, was shot at Mount street Bridge, while being driven into Dublin by Captain Scovell, RAMC.

All these were unarmed, as was Captain Scovell. In the last case, the car was not challenged or asked to stop.

19. I wish to emphasise that the responsibility for the loss of life, however it occurred, the destruction of property, and other losses, rests entirely with those who engineered this revolt, and who, at a time when the Empire is engaged in a gigantic struggle, invited the assistance and co-operation of the Germans.

I have the honour to be, my Lord,
Your obedient Servant,
(Sgd.) JG Maxwell, General.

VISCOUNT FRENCH'S DESPATCH
German Attack on Yarmouth to Assist the Irish Rising

The Secretary of State for War, on Tuesday, 23rd January, 1917, issued the following despatch from Field-Marshal Viscount French, GCB, Commanding-in-Chief, Home Forces, dated from:

General Headquarters, Home Forces,
Horse Guards, London, SW,
31st December, 1916.

On the 24th April the rebellion broke out in Dublin. I have already referred to this in my despatch of the 29th May covering a report from the

General Officer Commanding-in-Chief in Ireland, which dealt fully with the occurrence. I will only add that both in England and in Ireland the military arrangements for its suppression proved everywhere adequate, and reflect great credit on all concerned.

On April 25th, the morning after the outbreak in Dublin, a hostile squadron, accompanied by submarines, appeared off Lowestoft. No doubt, the object of this demonstration was to assist the Irish rebellion and to distract attention from Ireland. It failed entirely to accomplish its object.

The enemy opened fire at long range on the towns of Yarmouth and Lowestoft, and continued the bombardment for about twenty minutes, after which they were engaged by our cruisers and torpedo boat destroyers, and they steamed away to the north-east.

In addition to the heavier ships and submarines, the squadron was accompanied by a number of destroyers, but the results of the bombardment were comparatively small, and no damage whatever of military importance was done.

HONOURS AND AWARDS FOR SERVICES

Promotions and Decorations

No special list of honours was issued in connection with the services rendered by the military during the rebellion, but in two supplements to the 'London Gazette', issued by the War Office on 24th and 25th January, 1917, there appeared the names of the following officers and men who were known to have been engaged in Dublin and other parts of Ireland at the time of the rising.

CB

Maj. and Bt. Lt-Col. (Hon. Brig.-Gen.) Joseph Aloysius Byrne, ret. pay, late R Innis. Fus.

Order of St Michael and St George, CMG

Maj. and Bt. Lt-Col. (temp. Lt.-Col.) Cecil Fane, DSO, Lrs, attd. Notts. and Derby R.

To be Honorary Major-General

Col. (temp. Brig.-Gen.) WHM Lowe, CB, ret. pay.

To be Brevet Colonel

Lt.-Col. Sir AA Weldon, Bt., CVO, DSO, Leins R., Spec. Res.

To be Companions of the Distinguished Service Order

Maj. GA Harris, Unattd. List, TF.
Temp. Maj. Ivor H Price, Spec. List.
Capt. AH Quibell, Notts. and Derby R.
Capt. (temp. Lt.-Col.) F Rayner, Notts. and Derby R.
Maj. HF Somerville, Rif. Brig.

Awarded the Military Cross

Lt. (temp. Capt.) EH Alton, TF and OTC.
2nd Lt. (temp. Capt.) HA Hewitt, Notts and Derby R.
Capt. (now Maj.) MC Martyn, Notts and Derby R.

Awarded the Distinguished Conduct Medal

1126 Pte. E Carroll, R Ir. Fus.
2543 Sgt. Dmr RM Cooper, Notts. and Derby R.
9188 ASM T Cumming, PS, attd. Notts. and Derby R.
76050 Pte. AA Devey, RAMC.
3886 Pte. J Hill, Notts. and Derby R, now Cpl., R. War. R.
4045 Pte. F Snowdin, Notts. and Derby R, now 40861, Manch. R.

Awarded the Military Medal

Miss Louisa Nolan.
Miss Florence Williams.

Mentioned in Despatches for Distinguished Services in Connection with the War

Allatt, Col. HTW, R Ir. Rif. (deceased).
Baker, Lt. AWW, Dublin University OTC.
Battenberg, Capt. His Highness Prince Alexander of, GCVO, G Gds.
Byrne, Maj. and Bt. Lt.-Col. (temp. Brig.-Gen.) JA, R Innis. Fus.
Cheylesmore, Maj.-Gen. HF, Lord, KCVO, ret. pay.
Cowan, Col. HV, CB, CVO, ret pay.
de Courcy Wheeler, Maj. WI, RAMC.
Dietrichsen, Capt. and Adjt. FC, Notts. and Derby R (killed).
Downie, Capt. F, Lond R.
Fanshawe, Lt.-Col. (temp. Col.) RW, APD.
Friend, Maj..-Gen. Right Hon LB, CB.
Harris, Maj. GA, Unattd List.
Hill, Maj. GN, RFA.
Kennedy, Sec. Lt. TJ, R Innis. Fus.
McCammond, Lt.-Col. TVP, R Ir. Rif.
North, Sec. Lt. FW, R Ir. Regt.
Oates, Lt. (temp. Capt.) JSC, MC, Notts. and Derby R.
Oates, Lt.-Col. WC, Notts. and Derby R.
O'Neill, Sec. Lt. F, R Dub. Fus. (killed).
Owen-Lewis, Maj. AF, DSO, Capt, ret. pay, Res. of Off.
Pain, Col. (temp. Brig.-Gen.) GWH, CB, ret. pay.
Portal, Lt. Col. and Bt. Col. BP, DSO, Res. of Off., late Hrs.
Price, Maj. IH, Spec. List.
Quibell, Capt. AH, Notts. and Derby R.
Sheppard, Capt. J, S Staffs. R.
Somerville, Maj. HF, Rif. Brig.
Stafford, Col. (temp. Brig. Gen.) WFH, CB, ret. pay, late R E.
Weldon, Lt.-Col. Sir AA, Bt., CVO, DSO, Leins. R.
Wylie, Sec. Lt. (temp. Lt) WE, Unattd. List, Dublin University OTC.
Barrett 4276 Actg Cpl. JS, Staffs R. (killed).
Burke, 25692 L.-Sgt. FWR, R Dub. Fus. (killed).
Dixey, 2454 Co. Sgt-Maj. HC, Notts and Derby R (killed).
Hewett 1474 L. Cpl. H, King Edward's Horse.
King, 3057 Actg. Cpl. C, N. Staffs R.

King's Medal Awarded to Police Officers

On Monday, 13th February, 1917, it was announced that His Majesty the King had been pleased to award the King's Police Medal to the following officers of the Royal Irish Constabulary and the Dublin Metropolitan Police in recognition of conspicuous gallantry during the Irish rebellion.

County Inspector George Bedell Ruttledge, Royal Irish Constabulary, in charge of the County Galway. He showed conspicuous courage and ability during the rebellion, when, as practically no troops were available, he was entirely responsible for the security of the county. The measures taken by him were prompt and energetic, and the operations of the police in attacking and dispersing bodies of armed rebels, greatly superior in numbers, were conducted under his personal leadership.

Sergeant William O'Connell, RIC, Drumconrath, Co. Meath.—Conspicuous gallantry during an attack by a large body of rebels on a party of police, who lost eight killed and fifteen wounded. By his personal example he encouraged the men under his command to offer a prolonged resistance.

Sergeant Thomas Reilly, RIC, Portadown, Co. Armagh—Conspicuous gallantry in arresting and disarming a leading rebel, whose capture during the early part of the rebellion was of the greatest importance.

Constable Eugene Bratton, RIC, Navan, Co. Meath—Conspicuous gallantry during the rebellion. As a motor cycle despatch carrier he risked his life on several occasions. He volunteered to act as chauffeur in the place of a man who had run away, and, after driving the police to a spot where fighting was taking place, joined in the fighting. He was captured by the rebels, but escaped, and cycled to the Post Office to telephone for help, afterwards returning to the scene of the fight.

Sergeant Patrick Haugh, Dublin Metropolitan Police—Conspicuous gallantry under fire in rescuing from a position of great danger a police officer who had been seriously wounded.

Constable Thomas Barrett, 67 B, DMP—Conspicuous gallantry in arresting and disarming a man who was threatening to shoot two soldiers.

Constable John Barton, 37 B, DMP—Conspicuous gallantry and exceptional ability and devotion to duty during the past year. He has been instrumental in the detection and apprehension of a very large number of criminals. During the first night of the rebellion he arrested at great personal risk twenty-seven persons who were looting in the vicinity of O'Connell Bridge, which was dominated by rebel fire, and on the same night, with the assistance of another officer, he arrested two armed men who were carrying a large quantity of ammunition.

Constable James H Coulter, 187 A, DMP—Conspicuous gallantry in conveying ammunition under fire to Dublin Castle, and subsequently in disarming, after a severe struggle, a rebel who was attacking passers-by with rifle and bayonet.

THANKS TO THE FORCES OF THE CROWN

King's Message to Soldiers and Police

The following message was received from His Majesty the King:

'Windsor Castle, 4th May, 1916.
To General Sir John Maxwell, GOC in C,
Irish Command, Dublin.

Now that the recent lamentable outbreak has finally been quelled I wish to express to my gallant troops in Ireland, to the Royal Irish Constabulary, and the Dublin Metropolitan Police my deep sense of the whole-hearted devotion to duty and spirit of self-sacrifice with which throughout they have acted.

GEORGE RI.'

Sir John Maxwell's Thanks to his Men

The following General Order was issued to the troops by Sir John Maxwell, General Commanding-in-Chief the Forces in Ireland:

I desire to thank the troops who have been engaged in the City of Dublin for their splendid behaviour under the trying conditions of street fighting which I found it necessary to order them to undertake. Owing to the excellent direction of the officers and the tireless effort of the troops all the surviving rebels in Dublin have now surrendered unconditionally.

I especially wish to express my gratitude to those Irish regiments which have so largely helped to crush this rising.

Many incidents of very gallant behaviour have been brought to my notice, which I am unable to refer to in this Order, but I must express my admiration of the conduct of a small detachment from the 6th Reserve Cavalry Regiment, which, when convoying ammunition, was attacked in Charles street, and, after a splendid defence for three and a half days, during which their leaders were struck down, safely delivered the ammunition.

JG MAXWELL
General Commanding-in-Chief the Forces in Ireland,
Headquarters, Irish Command, May 1, 1916.

Tribute to Doctors and Nurses

Sir John Maxwell issued the following: 'Headquarters, Irish Command, Parkgate, Dublin, 7th May 1916. I desire to express my sincere appreciation of the services rendered during the recent disturbances in Dublin by the medical, surgical, and nursing staff of many of the city hospitals, and in particular of the gallantry shown by those nurses who exposed themselves to a heavy fire in attending to and removing the wounded. Also to the members of the Red Cross and St John Ambulance Societies, and the many medical men and private individuals who gave assistance in attending to the wounded or placed their houses at the disposal of the military for use as dressing stations. In numerous instances these services were rendered at considerable personal risk and under circumstances reflecting the greatest credit on those engaged in them. (Signed) JG Maxwell, General, Commanding-in-Chief the Forces in Ireland.'

Lord Lieutenant's Tribute to DMP

The Lord Lieutenant addressed the following letter to the Chief Commissioner of the Dublin Metropolitan Police:

Viceregal Lodge,
Dublin, 8th May, 1916

Dear Colonel Johnstone

I wish to convey to you my very warm appreciation of the conduct of the officers and men under your command during the recent disturbances in Dublin. Although they were without arms, your men carried out their duties in very difficult and trying circumstances with resolution and courage, and I congratulate you warmly on their conduct. I deeply regret the casualties that have occurred in the ranks of the force.

Yours sincerely,
WIMBORNE.

Lord Wimborne thanks the RIC

The Inspector General of the Royal Irish Constabulary directed that the following copy of a letter received by him from His Excellency the Lord Lieutenant should be communicated to all ranks of the Reserve and Depot forces:

Dear Sir Neville Chamberlain,—Now that the disturbances due to the Sinn Fein rising have been suppressed, I have to express to you my deep appreciation of the gallantry and devotion to duty displayed by the officers andmen under your command during the crisis. In a number of instances small parties of constabulary have found themselves in circumstances of great danger, but on every occasion they have shown courage and resolution in every respect worthy of the great traditions of the force to which they belong. I deeply regret that some members of the constabulary should have lost their lives while gallantly doing their duty, and I shall use every endeavour to see that the claims of their families meet with every consideration—Yours, sincerely,

(Signed) "WIMBORNE"

Viceregal Lodge, 8the May, 1916

Sir John Maxwell's Review at Trinity College

Something like a thousand men must have been on parade in the park of Trinity College on Saturday, 6th May, when General Sir John Maxwell, KCB, DSO, inspected the Officers' Training Corps of Dublin University and of the Royal College of Surgeons, several corps affiliated to the Irish Association of Volunteer Training Corps, and St John and Red Cross Ambulance units.

Mr Asquith was among the distinguished visitors. Lady Wimborne, attended by Miss Grosvenor, watched the proceedings with keen interest from the platform, over which waved the Union Jack, and the Provost of Trinity College (Rev. Dr Mahaffy) was in the company. General Maxwell carried out the inspection, accompanied by Major GA Harris, Dublin University OTC, who was in command. Sir John said that he was glad to have the opportunity of thanking the Provost and the officers and men of the University Officers' Training Corps for all they had done during recent events. It was thanks to their prompt assistance that that part of the city was kept from being ruined.

A march past concluded the proceedings, and General Maxwell, standing by the Union Jack, gracefully acknowledged the salutes of the officers of the various corps. Only the members of the University Corps carried arms. The officers on parade were:

Dublin University OTC and Royal College of Surgeon OTC—Major Harris, Major Tate, Captain Alton, Lieutenants Baker, Smith, Mitchell: Second Lieutenants Crawford, Henry Baxter, Wylie, Col. Smith, and Millar.

Mr CH Dickinson was battalion commander of the Volunteer Training Corps, and Mr GB Butler, Staff officer, attended.

Rugby Union Corps—Company Commander, HJ Miller: second in command, R McC. Dillon: platoon commanders, EA MacNair, WGF Allen, ASM Imrie, and JW Frith.

Veterans' Corps—Lord Justice Molony and Mr Justice Barton (hon. officers): company commander, J Wilson, Captain Knox Foote: platoon commanders, CA Munro and RA Anderson: quartermaster, CH Gick.

Glasnevin Corps—Company commander, E Webb: platoon commanders, RW Todd and CM Harris.

D Company (GNR, GS and WR, North City, and South City)—Company commander, J Walsh: platoon commanders, A Agnew, P Wharton, CE Riley, W Cunningham, HJ Matthews, HB Turner, Captain Alan Smythe, and D Bole: sergeant-major, TV Shellard: quartermaster-sergeant, W Bullick.

Greystones Corps—Company commander, Captain AW Blake (Indian Army Reserve), second in command, Lieutenant Colonel JC Beare: Sergeant-Major Scuffle: Sergeants Fry and Barry.

Bray Corps—Company commander, H Malley: platoon commander, RD Bolton: adjutant T Lang.

St John Ambulance and British Red Cross VAD's—Dr J Lumsden, vice-chairman of the Joint VAD Committee for Ireland: assistant director, Dr R Peacocke: commandant, O'C. FitzSimon: district superintendent, WG Smith: district officer, A Moore: district surgeon, Captain Stevenson: district treasurer, Dr Cope: corps superintendent, JH Webb and R Keating. The VAD's represented were: Four Courts, Land Commission, Royal College of Science, RIC, Rathmines, City of Dublin, Howth, Pembroke, Kingstown, Carrickmines, Glenageary, Dublin Building Trades, Guinness, Jacob's and Powers.

Indian students from the King's Inns, who performed ambulance work, paraded with the Rathmines unit.

The Brave Carters

The fifteen carters of the London and North-Western Railway Co., who bravely looked after five lorry loads of ammunition and horses, escorted by Lancers, which were ambushed by the rebels on Ormond quay, also paraded. The five men who set out with the lorries were relieved by another five bringing provender for the horses, and a second relief of five men did the same. All were under fire during the three days, when the lorries were defended in Charles street by their escort. The men were: D O'Keefe, M Byrne, T Taafe, T Noone, and C Kelly: W Milling, M Foy, M Greene, R McKenna and R Breen: R Lane, M McEvoy, T Painter, T Kelly and J Lacey.

Mr HG Burgess, manager in Ireland for the company, was presented to General Maxwell when he inspected the carters.

Sir John Maxwell Inspects Ambulances

General Sir John Maxwell inspected some units of the Irish Automobile Club Ambulance Service at the Royal Barracks, Dublin, on Saturday, 27th May. The vehicles were those which played a useful part in removing to hospital soldiers and citizens wounded during the rebellion, with the Dublin Corporation ambulance and the two motor ambulances of the Pembroke Urban Council. Several of the machines bore bullet marks on their sides or holes through their canopies, showing at what risk the drivers and orderlies had carried out their splendid work. Accompanied by Major-General Friend, Mr Edward White (Chairman of the Irish Automobile Club), Mr W Sexton (Hon. Secretary and Treasurer), and Mr HS Chaytor (Secretary), General Maxwell made a leisurely inspection of the ambulances, and had a few kindly words for each of the drivers and orderlies, making keen inquiry about their experiences during Easter week. He was particularly interested to meet Martin Redmond, who was wounded while driving an ambulance, which he nevertheless brought safely back. Redmond came from hospital that Saturday to take part in the function. The drivers on parade were:

Mr ST Robinson, Mr W Peck, Mr W Chevers Roche, Mr J Gibson, Mr M Robinson, Mr K King, Mr A Camp, J McClaren, E O'Brien, J White, P Boyle, C Crampton Stokes, M Gleeson, and N McCoy. Capt. JJ Hutson, Chief of the Pembroke Brigade, brought his drivers, Assistant M Broughton and Firemen C Moynihan, A McManus and James Gorman: and from the Dublin Brigade, John O'Connor (driver), J Williams, and Joseph Lynch attended.

The orderlies present were:

G Kiverson, WJ Douglas, L Bennett, A Dowie, J Lee, I Bodkin, RH Scott, James Giltrap, J Gahan, Andrew Know, R Brown, GC May, NS Norway, W Emery, HJ Scott.

Sir John Maxwell, in a brief address, said the military in Dublin were deeply thankful for the work done by the ambulances.

Kingstown Volunteer Corps

The Kingstown Volunteer (GR) Corps were paid a high compliment by General Sir John Maxwell, the General Officer Commanding the Troops in Ireland, who, on Tuesday, 9th May, accorded the Corps the official recognition of an inspection by Major-General Sandbach, the General Officer Commanding the Dublin Area. The inspection took place in front of the Royal Marine Hotel, where the members of the Kingstown and District Volunteer (GR) Corps paraded in the green, along with the local corps of Boy Scouts, Girl Guides, nurses of the St John Ambulance Association, and a number of special constables. During the previous fortnight all these bodies had lent active assistance to the military.

The Kingstown and District Volunteer Corps, which is affiliated to the Irish Association Volunteer Training Corps, whose headquarters are at Beggar's Bush Barracks, in the very beginning of the rebellious outbreak in Dublin offered its services to the military authorities. These were accepted, and the Volunteers were afterwards the very guides and lights of the military in what to them was a strange terrain. In the early stages of the insurrection the Volunteers undertook the protection of the local gas works. Night and day they assisted in the work at the town barriers, to which they were deputed under general orders. The chief officer, Mr T Morgan Good, was appointed Town Commandant, and to him the Provost Marshal expressed his appreciation of the Corps' services, and declared that they had been indispensable. Amongst the many efficient services rendered by the Corps was that of organising a supply of motor cars, motor cycles, and bicycles for the use of the military. The Corps also policed the Carlisle Pier and the railway stations with the military. The Boy Scouts were most useful, acting as messengers and assistant at the Soldiers' Buffet, while the Girl Guides afforded a great deal of very acceptable service in a variety of offices. Especially helpful were they in the Provost Marshal's and the Town Commandant's offices. They assisted in the heavy work of the issuing of permits. Miss Nancy Gosling gave her services voluntarily as typist to the APM, and Miss Baird and Miss Lucy Gosling acted in the same office as telephone clerks.

The Parade

The Volunteers paraded in front of the Marine Hotel to the number of 75, including all ranks, and were under the command of their officers—Mr T Morgan Good, Town Commandant: Mr SA Quan Smith, Mr R Norman Potterton, Mr EF Scanlan, and Dr Matthew Good. Fifty of the Volunteers wore uniform and about 24 or 26, with some special constables, were in mufti. There were some 40 Boy Scouts on the ground, under the command of Mr SA Quan Smith, senior Vice-President for the county, and Mr Evelyn Wilkinson, Acting Scoutmaster. Sixteen Girl Guides, in their neat navy blue uniform, also under the command of Mr Quan Smith, were present, and three nurses, representing the St John Ambulance Association—viz., Mrs Robinson, Lady Corps Superintendent, Co. Dublin; Mrs Middleton Curtis, Lady Corps Treasurer, City of Dublin; and Miss Mowbray, Lady Divisional Superintendent. About 250 men, new drafts for the North Midland Divisional Artillery, were also paraded.

Major General Sandbach made a close and interested inspection of the Volunteers, who were drawn up in two lines. He questioned many, and spoke in flattering terms of the parade to Mr Good. He inspected the boys and girls very carefully, and especially noted those wearing war service badges, granted for aid to the military since the war began in 1914.

Having inspected the Girl Guides and nurses, Major-General Sandbach said Sir John Maxwell had asked him to convey his thanks for the work they had done during the crisis.

COURTS-MARTIAL AT RICHMOND BARRACKS

The Shooting of Francis Sheehy Skeffington

The courtmartial on Captain JC Bowen-Colthurst, Royal Irish Rifles, in connection with the shooting of three men named F Sheehy Skeffington, Thomas Dickson, and Patrick MacIntyre at Portobello Barracks, Dublin, on the 26th April last, opened at the Richmond Barracks, Dublin, at 10 o'clock on Tuesday, 6th June.

Admission to the court was by ticket, and at the opening of the proceedings there were about 100 civilians present, including a number of ladies. Dr Skeffington, MA, LLD, JP, father of Mr Sheehy Skeffington, and Mrs Sheehy Skeffington (widow) were present during the proceedings. The Court was constituted as follows: Major-General Lord Cheylesmore (presiding), Colonel HM Thoyts, Lieutenant-Colonel Murray, Temporary Lieutenant-Colonel H Taylor, Temporary Lieutenant-Colonel LG Redding, Temporary Lieutenant-Colonel Simmons, Temporary Lieutenant-Colonel WJ Kent, Major WER Collis, Major DS Matthews, Temporary Major EC Hamilton, Temporary Major H Montgomery, Temporary Major MA Tighe, and Temporary Major H Johnson.

Waiting Members—Major ABL Wood, DSO: Temporary Major Davenport, Temporary Major Hon JRN Ridley.

Prosecutor—Major Kimber, Judge Advocate—Mr Marshall.

Mr James Chambers, KC, MP and Mr Andrews (instructed by Mr CH Denroche) appeared for the prisoner. Mr TM Healy, KC MP and Mr P O'C White (instructed by Mr Lemass), appeared on behalf of Mrs Sheehy Skeffington, but they did not intervene in the proceedings.

The Indictment

The Judge Advocate read the charges against Captain Bowen-Colthurst, which were:

1. That on the 26th April, 1916, at Portobello Barracks, he murdered Francis Sheehy-Skeffington.
2. That he was guilty of the manslaughter of Francis Sheehy-Skeffington.
3. That on the 26th April, at Portobello Barracks, he murdered Thomas Dickson.
4. That he was guilty of the manslaughter of Dickson.
5. That on the 26th April, at Portobello Barracks, he murdered Patrick MacIntyre.
6. That he was guilty of the manslaughter of MacIntyre.

The prisoner, in a loud clear voice, pleaded 'not guilty' to the several charges.

The Story of the Tragedy

Major Kimber, the prosecutor, stating the case, said the accused was charged with the murder of three persons—Mr F Sheehy Skeffington, Mr Thos Dickson, and Mr P MacIntyre—and in the alternative he was charged with the manslaughter of these men. About six o'clock on the evening of Tuesday, April 25, the accused was with part of his regiment (the Royal Irish Rifles) at Portobello Barracks, Dublin. At Portobello Bridge there was stationed a picket of about thirty men under command of Lieutenant Morris, guarding the bridge. Near the bridge was a publichouse called Davy's, and a short distance from the publichouse was Jacob's factory, which was held by the rebels. Firing was going on from the factory towards Portobello Bridge, and information had reached Lieutenant Morris that there was a possibility—nay, more—that there were thoughts of an attack on Portobello Barracks. There were about 300 men stationed in the barracks, but, of course, a considerable part of that number was on duty in the streets about that time. In the other direction from the bridge lay Portobello Barracks—the opposite side from Jacob's. The rebels were advancing from that direction. Between 6 and 7 o'clock on Tuesday night firing was going on from Jacob's direction, and also from the rebels who were coming up in the direction of Portobello Barracks. One of the deceased men—Mr Sheehy Skeffington—advanced, followed by a crowd, from the direction of the factory towards the Portobello Barracks. It was only fair to say that he was going in the direction of his home. Lieutenant Morris allowed him to pass, but two soldiers followed him and took him to the guardroom.

Mr Skeffington before the Adjutant

About half-past 8 o'clock that evening Mr Skeffington was brought before the Adjutant. The Adjutant asked him if he was a 'Sinn Feiner', and he replied that he was in sympathy with the movement, but not in favour of militarism. He was taken back to the guardroom. Meanwhile two other men, Dickson and MacIntyre, were brought in, and they were, with six or eight others, placed in the guardroom. Dickson was the editor of a paper called *The Eye Opener*. MacIntyre was the editor of a paper called the *Searchlight*, and Skeffington was a well-known journalist in Dublin. The men were left in the guardroom during the night. The rebellion continued, and firing went on throughout the night around the barracks, and the rebels were in possession of the points he had mentioned. The accused officer went to the guardroom about 10.20 on Wednesday morning. There were other officers there and the sergeant of the guard. He said to one of the officers: 'I am taking these prisoners out of the guardroom, and I am going to shoot them, as I think it is the right thing to do.' One of the officers proceeded to the orderly room, and reported to the Adjutant what he had heard, and the Adjutant sent a message to the accused. He (prosecutor) did not know if that message reached the accused. He rather thought it did not: but the fact was that the accused returned to the guardroom and ordered the three men out into the yard. He took seven men, armed with rifles and ammunition, with him. The yard at the back of the guardroom was enclosed by a wall twelve feet high. The accused had the men placed against the wall, and he ordered the soldiers to load and fire. The three men were shot by his orders. Having done that, he went to the orderly room and reported that he had ordered the three men to be shot, giving as his reasons first, to prevent any possibility of escape: second, to prevent their being rescued by armed force. Apparently he then began to think that he had probably done what he ought not to have done, and he went in search of the commanding officer of the battalion (Major Roxburgh), who was at the time in barracks, and who instructed him to make a report of the matter. This the accused did, and the whole affair was submitted to the Commander-in-Chief.

Photo by] [Elliott and Fry.
MAJOR-GENERAL H. F. LORD CHEYLESMORE, who presided over the Courts-martial at Richmond Barracks.

Lieutenant Morris

Lieut. MC Morris, 11th East Surrey Regiment, gave evidence that he was attached to the 3rd Royal Irish Rifles at Portobello Barracks, and was in command of a picket of 30 men of that regiment on Tuesday, 25th April. He bore out the prosecutor's statement of the approach and arrest of Mr Sheehy-Skeffington, who was not armed. In reply to questions by Mr Chambers, witness said his men reported that a machine gun was seen on the top of a house near Jacob's factory, and he saw men in civilian clothes moving something across a roof in the direction where the firing was going on. A machine gun was fired in that direction.

Sergeant Maxwell

Sergeant John Arthur Maxwell, 7149 3rd Royal Irish Rifles, stated he was at Portobello Barracks on the 25th April last, and acting on instructions he took Mr Sheehy Skeffington to the orderly room to be examined by the Adjutant. He heard Mr Morgan ask Mr Sheehy Skeffington was he in sympathy with the Sinn Feiners, and he made answer to the effect that he was, but that he did not believe in passive resistance. He said something about militarism, which witness could not understand.

Lieutenant Morgan

Lieut. Samuel Valentine Morgan, adjutant, 3rd Royal Irish Rifles, said at about 8.15 o'clock that evening he asked Mr Sheehy Skeffington if he was a Sinn Feiner. He said he was not. Witness also asked him was he in favour of the Sinn Fein movement. He said he was in sympathy with the Sinn Feiners, but he was not in favour of militarism.

Next morning the accused came to the orderly room about 10.20 o'clock, and reported that he had shot three prisoners—Sheehy Skeffington, and the editors of the *Spark* and the *Eye Opener*. He said he feared they might be rescued by armed force. He also said that he had lost a brother in this war, and that he was as good an Irishman as the men he had shot. Witness reported to Major Smith of the Headquarters of the Irish Command, and to Major Rosborough, who was in command of the battalion.

Cross-examined by Mr Andrews, witness said that sniping went on in the immediate vicinity of the barracks, and actually at the barracks. Among the casualties sustained by those stationed at the barracks were a second lieutenant killed, four officers wounded, while there were sixteen casualties in the rank and file. They all belonged to the same battalion as the prisoner.

Second Lieutenant Wm Price Dobbin, of the 3th Royal Irish Fusiliers, stated that he was at Portobello Barracks on the 26th April, in command of the main guard. There were, he thought, eight civilian prisoners in the guardroom. He did not know either Skeffington, Dickson, or MacIntyre. He saw the accused going into the guardroom that morning. He came out again, and then said to witness, to the best of his belief, 'I am taking these men out of the guardroom, and I am going to shoot them, as I think it is the right thing to do,' or words to that effect. Witness, continuing, said that at the back of the guardroom was a yard enclosed by a wall ten or twelve feet high. The three men were taken out into the yard, and he heard shots fired as from the yard. He went into the yard and saw three men lying dead there. He knew Sheehy-Skeffington from his appearance the night before, when he heard his name mentioned. Witness knew the body. He did not examine the bodies that he saw on the ground, but he saw blood on the ground. He did not examine Sheehy Skeffington's body to see whether he was dead or alive. He was some distance from the bodies.

Cross-examined by Mr Chambers, the witness said he and other men were constantly on duty for three days. There was shooting going on in the neighbourhood of the barracks. Some of his men were wounded on Portobello Bridge. He had heard that a machine gun had been trained on the roof of some house by the rebels, but he did not see it.

Replying to questions put by the President witness said that when Capt. Colthurst came out of the guardroom he appeared in an excited state, which was not his usual manner.

'To Shoot Again'

In your previous evidence you made a statement which you have not corroborated to-day. You were asked by by the prosecutor if you noticed anything regarding one of the bodies, and you said "Nothing in particular." That is your answer to the prosecutor to-day. Did you notice anything particular about one of these bodies? I did.

What was it? I noticed a movement of one of the legs of Sheehy Skeffington.

What did you do then? I sent for an officer to the orderly room. That officer was Lieut. Tooley, and what I wanted to know was what steps I was to take.

Did you send the officer specially to the accused? No, but simply to the Orderly.

What was the answer received by you? The order was that I was to shoot again.

Who sent that order? Capt. Colthurst.

How do you know it was he? Lieutenant Tooley told me.

What did you do then? I stood by four men of my guard, and I complied with the order.

The President: Perhaps after this evidence counsel for the defence would like to cross-examine the witness.

Mr Chambers (to witness): What sort of a movement was it that you saw—was it a twinge of a muscle? I don't know.

Did you believe Skeffington to be then dead, or that he was living? I believe he was dying.

That he was dead? I cannot say. In my opinion he was done for.

The President: By 'done for' you mean dead? Yes.

Sergeant Aldridge, 10th RDF

Sergeant John William Aldridge, 10th Batt. Royal Dublin Fusiliers, said he was at Portobello Barracks on the 26th April last attached to the Royal Irish Rifles. At about 9 a.m. on that date he relieved a sergeant of the Royal Irish Rifles, who is now at the front. At about 10.20 Capt. Bowen-Colthurst told him he wanted men named MacIntyre, Dickson, and Sheehy Skeffington in the yard—that he wanted to shoot them. Witness identified prisoner as the officer who made that statement. The accused ordered portion of the guard to go out with them. There were seven of them, and they were all armed. Each magazine of each man's rifle was charged. Witness followed them into the yard.

The Shooting

The Prosecutor: When you got the yard what happened? Capt. Bowen-Colthurst told the three prisoners to go to the farther end of the yard, which they did. He then told all the men to load—to pull off the catch and pull out the bolt of their rifles. Then he told them to 'present' and to 'fire'. The three prisoners, to my belief, were shot dead, sir.

One volley? One volley, sir.

Did you examine the three bodies? I went up to them, and so far as I could see, and so far as my judgment went, I took them all three to be dead.

Did you see wounds on them? No, sir, but I saw at the back of the coat where the bullets penetrated through.

Now what did Mr Dobbin do? He stood in the yard, and at the time he thought there was a movement in Sheehy Skeffington. He went away and came back in about two minutes, and another volley was fired by four men at that one particular man.

What was your own impression? My own impression was that the man was dead before that volley was fired.

Cross-examined by Mr Andrews: Witness said his impression was that the three men were killed the first time. It was the general belief that there were not sufficient forces to protect the barracks if an attack was made on it.

By the President: No special orders were given with regard to Mr Sheehy-Skeffington or any of the prisoners. Mr Skeffington was kept in the guardroom, and Messrs Dickson and MacIntyre in the detention room. Witness was present when the accused gave the order to the seven men to load and shoot the three prisoners.

Second Lieutenant Wilson

Second Lieut. L Wilson, 5th RIF, attached RIR, said that on the Tuesday night he was with a party of men, about forty, under Capt. Bowen Colthurst. They had charge of Mr Sheehy Skeffington, who was taken as a hostage, and went to 'Kelly's Corner'. Capt. Colthurst left witness, twenty men, and Mr Skeffington on Portobello Bridge.

The Prosecutor: What orders did he give you before he went? He said that if any of his men were fired upon I was to shoot Skeffington immediately, and if he (accused) were knocked out of action witness was to take command. Witness understood the accused was going to raid Kelly's shop. Captain Colthurst came back with five prisoners, including Messrs Dickson and MacIntyre. Two prisoners were allowed to go away, and two were taken into the guardroom.

THE LATE MR. FRANCIS SHEEHY-SKEFFINGTON was a well-known figure in Dublin.

Major Rosborough

Major James Rosborough, 3rd RIR, stated that he was temporarily in command at Portobello Barracks during the rebellion. About three hundred men were in barracks. Witness saw the accused on the Wednesday morning. Captain Colthurst came to witness as he was crossing the barrack square, and said that he had just shot three prisoners, and that he expected he would get into trouble. Accused did not say whether the prisoners were military or civilian prisoners, but witness presumed that they were civilians.

Cross-examined by Mr Andrews, witness said that they received a telephone communication from the garrison adjutant that an attack might be made on the barracks. He considered that they should be prepared for an attack.

Where you aware that Skeffington had been taken out by Capt. Colthurst? I did not know.

May I take it that to the best of your knowledge the taking of hostages in warfare or rebellion is quite an obsolete practice? I certainly would not do it.

The President: No reports were made to you, as commanding officer, that there were prisoners in the guardroom? No reports were made to me.

You understand, I presume, that as commanding officer you are responsible for those prisoners? Yes.

When did it come to your knowledge that the accused took one of the prisoners out of the guardroom? I heard that next day.

Did you take any action on that? I took no particular action.

You, as commanding officer, being responsible for the safe custody of prisoners, took no notice whatever on hearing that one of your prisoners had been removed without your authority from the guardroom? What I understand was that he was taken as a guide.

Witness said that the accused met him on the barrack square at about 11 a.m. on April 26th.

Was the accused in an excited state at the time? He was not in an abnormally excited state.

Lieutenant Morgan, re-called, was asked by the President: Did it come to your knowledge that the accused had taken out Skeffington with a body of men to the bridge? Yes.

When did you come to know that? That night, about 10.40.

Did you make any report of that to your commanding officer? Yes.

When? I reported it immediately when I heard of it.

Can you tell us when Skeffington was brought back to the guardroom that night? I should say about 20 minutes past 11 o'clock.

Was any other prisoner taken out, to your knowledge? No.

Chaplain's Evidence

Rev. FE O'Loughlin, RC Chaplain to the military at Portobello Barracks, was the next witness. He said he was at the barracks on the 25th and 26th April. He knew Skeffington, Dickson, and MacIntyre by appearance. In consequence of a report which he had received from the adjutant he went to the mortuary, and there he saw the dead bodies of the three men named. They were buried at 11.15 on Wednesday night, and he was present at their interment and subsequent exhumation.

Peculiar Incident

Lieutenant Wilson was re-called for cross-examination by Mr Chambers.

You spoke of the night when Mr Sheehy-Skeffington was taken out as a hostage? Yes.

What was the condition of the accused on that occasion? I considered that he was in a highly excited condition.

Do you remember any incident of a peculiar nature occurring? Well, he ordered Mr Skeffington to say his prayers, and he made the men take off their hats.

Did he say any prayer himself? He did.

What was it? As far as I can remember it was as follows—'O Lord God, if it should please Thee to take away the life of this man forgive him for Our Lord Jesus Christ's sake'.

The President: When was it that he ordered him to say his prayers? Just outside the guardroom, previous to his being taken out as a hostage.

Sergeant James Geoghegan, RAMC, said he went from the guardroom into the yard at back, and found there three dead bodies which he did not identify because he had not seen them before. The medical officer was not called. He took the three bodies on a stretcher and had them conveyed to the mortuary.

Was there any blood there? Yes, there was blood on their clothes.

Can you say from what you saw if the men had been hit at all? Yes.

How? With bullets.

Whereabouts? In the body. I did not see whether or not the bullets passed through the bodies.

Did you form any opinion of how they died? They died from the effects of bullet wounds.

Lieutenant Wilson was recalled.

Mr Chambers: I forgot to ask you whether on the way down from Portobello Barracks to Kelly's tobacco shop, Capt. Colthurst did anything with his rifle? Yes, he was firing it off.

In the air? Yes.

How often did he fire it off between the barracks and Kelly's? Several times, sir.

The President: You mean that he was firing indiscriminately, without taking aim? In the air, sir.

Lieutenant Morris Recalled

Lieut. Morris was then recalled and examined by Mr Andrews: Do you remember on the Tuesday evening when you were proceeding with the prisoner Skeffington and Capt. Colthurst in the direction of Portobello Bridge? I had nothing to do with Capt. Colthurst that evening in connection with the prisoner. I saw Capt. Colthurst about midnight, when he was going from the barracks with Mr Skeffington, and he was then proceeding to raid Kelly's tobacco shop. He had Mr Sheehy Skeffington with him, and was in a very excited condition indeed, and it struck me as very stupid of him to warn Sheehy Skeffington that if he was fired on Sheehy Skeffington would be shot at once. I did not see how Sheehy Skeffington could, or anyone could, stop anyone from firing on the troops.

Did you consider Captain Colthurst to be in an abnormal condition at the time? He did not seem quite right in his head at the moment—he seemed to be labouring under tremendous excitement.

When did you see him the nearest time after the shooting took place? I saw him when he announced to the Adjutant that he had shot the prisoners. I was there when he made the announcement. He seemed then rather worse than the night before—he was perfectly stupid.

Perfectly stupid? He was extremely agitated and excited. I do not know Captain Colthurst very well—indeed he did not strike me at the time as a man who should be at any time in command of troops.

Did he appear to you on these two occasions to be in an entirely different frame of mind from previous occasions? I had not seen him previously, but I have seen him since, and he was then totally different. Then there was a third occasion when I saw him—that was in the officers' mess at tea time on the same day—the Wednesday about 4.30 or 5 o'clock—I am not quite certain. There were several junior officers present. Most of us were strangers to the barracks, and Captain Colthurst made a very ridiculous set speech, indeed, as to Sir Francis Vane doing all sorts of wicked things and being a Sinn Feiner and a pro-Boer. On that occasion he did not seem to be right in his head.

Did he say anything else about Sir Francis Vane? He said he should not be allowed in the barracks, and that he should be shot. I took it upon myself to tell the other officers not to pay any attention to what Captain Colthurst had said, and that I thought he was not quite himself at the time.

Did you consider he was in any way capable of discriminating between legal right and legal wrong? No, sir, I do not.

The Defence

Mr Chambers proceeded to call his witnesses. In reply to the President, he said that he would not call the accused, nor had the accused any written statement to hand in.

Major-General Bird

Major-General Bird was questioned as to the general character of the accused, and his demeanour in 1914. Witness said that he found him eccentric. Accused seemed to be unable to concentrate his mind on a subject, and was certainly at times eccentric. Apart from that, he was a man of high character, and set a very good example to everybody. The accused took part in the battle of Mons, and the morning after the battle he was in charge of the leading company of a battalion. Witnesses found that whenever he rode away from the head of the battalion it moved off. When witness went back and asked why that occurred nobody could tell him, but when he turned his back he heard Captain Colthurst giving an order in rather a weak voice for the company to advance. Captain Colthurst's reply and his demeanour convinced witness that he was quite incapable of leading men, and witness suspended him from duty for a time. Accused was quite broken down, and was not fit to exercise judgment. He was wounded about a fortnight later at the Aisne. Witness's opinion was that when unusually fatigued and in a state of excitement Captain Colthurst was not quite responsible for his actions.

Cross-examined, witness said that in April, 1914, he made a report about Captain Colthurst. The report was over-ruled, and witness had to tell him on one occasion that he would have to report unfavourably upon him. On another occasion the accused bellowed at him: 'Do you mean to say anything against my company?' That was extraordinary, and witness reprimanded him there and then.

To the President: Witness reinstated Captain Colthurst in his old position of company commander three or four days after he had been removed from it. He attributed the movement of the battalion after Mons to the orders of Captain Colthurst.

Major Goodman

Major Goodman, stationed at the Curragh Camp, examined by Mr Andrews, said he had known Captain Colthurst since November, 1904. Taking him generally, he was a kindly and considerate man towards his fellow-officers and the men under him. He had known him occasionally to have done acts of an eccentric character.

The President: Can you give us one instance of the eccentric acts he did? Yes.

What is it? I had been on a shooting expedition with him in India, and we put up for a night at a bungalow. There were dogs barking all night, and we did not sleep. At breakfast next morning I said I wished that dog was shot that kept us awake. He got up from the breakfast table without saying a word to anyone, and went out. I heard a rifle shot fired, and it was followed by the piteous howling of a dog. Captain Colthurst came back and said he had shot the dog. I asked if he had killed the dog, and he said, 'No'; and he added that the dog was sufficiently wounded to die. I mention that as an eccentric act, because it was entirely against the nature of Captain Colthurst to do that.

Captain EP Kelly

Captain Edward Phillip Kelly, examined by Mr Chambers, KC, MP, stated that he met Captain Bowen Colthurst for the first time on Easter Monday at Portobello Barracks. Witness thought his manner was rather peculiar on the Monday and Tuesday. On the Wednesday, his manner seemed strange. He was half lying across the table with his head resting on his arm, and he looked up occasionally and stared about the room, and then fell forward again with his head on his arm. Witness came to the conclusion then that he was off his head, and he saw Capt. McTurk and said something to the effect, 'For Goodness sake, keep an eye on Captain Colthurst: I think he is off his head.'

Captain M'Turk, RAMC

Captain James McTurk, RAMC, stated, in reply to Mr Andrews, that he had known Captain Bowen-Colthurst for about eight months. Both as a medical man and one who had known him for nine months, witness thought he was not responsible for his actions, and was not capable of exercising any sound judgment or discriminating between right and wrong.

Cross-examined by the Prosecutor: Witness had no special training in mental diseases.

By the President: I have been in Portobello Barracks for nine months.

On the Wednesday, at lunch time, did you think the accused was responsible for his actions? I do not think so.

Can you give us any particular reasons for stating that? His general demeanour at lunch.

Did you report that to anyone? Well, Captain Kelly reported it to me.

That is not the question I asked—you were there as Medical Officer—the question is, did you report this to anybody there? I reported it to Captain Kelly. I told Captain Kelly that I had prescribed ten grains of potassium bromide for the accused.

Did you realise that it was your duty to report an officer unfit for duty? I reported the matter to Captain Kelly.

At this time did he tell you that he had been responsible for the shooting of three men? He did not; he never said that.

Would you say his condition was due to anxiety for what he had done? He said it was a terrible thing to shoot one's own countrymen.

Dr Parsons

Dr Parsons, FRCP, physician to the Royal City of Dublin Hospital, gave evidence that he met Captain Colthurst several years ago, when he paid a professional visit. Witness saw the accused on November 21st, 1914, when he had returned from the front, and reported on his condition. There was loss of power, owing to wounds, in accused's left arm, and, in addition, Captain Colthurst was in a condition of marked nervous exhaustion. Witness reported that he was unfit for duty: should have two months' leave of absence, and, after that, a period of light duty. He was quite unequal to any strain, which would probably have brought about a nervous breakdown, probably affecting him mentally. In February the accused had improved physically, and the rest had done his mind good, but he was not fit for duty.

Witness last saw accused professionally the previous Friday. He found him labouring under considerable excitement and restless. He did not seem to realise his position in regard to the present charge. In the course of a long conversation accused talked about the fighting at Mons and the retreat.

Did he make any reference to the shooting incident? Yes, he told me that on Wednesday morning he went to bed at three and read his Bible, and that he came across a passage in it which seemed to have exercised a very powerful influence on his mind. The passage was to the effect: 'And these my enemies which will not have me to rule over them, bring them forth and slay them.' So far as I could gather from him the way that affected his mind was that it was his duty to slay men who would not have His Majesty to rule over them.

Having regard to that and other parts of the conversation, did you form any opinion as to the state of his mind? I came to the conclusion that his condition was far from normal, and that he was unbalanced. I felt that a very trivial incident at the time would absolutely upset his balance.

Witness would not say that accused was responsible for his actions in March, 1915. The bearing of Captain Colthurst on the Wednesday might be consonant with manifestations of remorse and regret on the part of a sane man. Witness said that the accused made it quite clear to him that he (accused) had done right and carried out his duty. His words were to the effect that in any other country except Ireland it would be recognised as right to kill rebels.

Dr Leeper

Dr Leeper, FRCSI, examined by Mr Andrews, said he held a certificate for knowledge of mental diseases, that he was medical superintendent of St Patrick's Hospital, Dublin, and late examiner in mental diseases in the University of Dublin. He first saw the accused on Friday last, in company with Dr Parsons, and listened to the conversation which he had with Captain Colthurst. The accused seemed to be in a very restless, agitated state, pacing up and down the room, and not able to control himself. He did not appear to realise the seriousness of the charge against him, or to have the ordinary self-protective feeling of a man against whom there was a serious charge pending. He (witness) had come to the conclusion that the man was exceedingly nervously shaken, and that if his condition remained as it was, he was on the eve of a complete breakdown.

Evidence as to Character

Captain Wade Thompson, DL, Clonskeagh Castle, was called, and stated that he had known the accused for ten years. During that time he was one of his staunchest friends, and he had found him an honourable, straightforward gentleman. He considered him a little erratic in his manner at times, and a little inconsequent in his conversation occasionally. He was a straightforward, kindly gentleman in every way, incapable of anything dishonourable, under natural circumstances.

Colonel Sir Frederick W Shaw described the accused's character as of the very best. He was not cruel or given to harsh acts. Since Captain Colthurst's return from France his mind was more unbalanced than before.

Lieutenant-Colonel Hamilton Bell and Colonel JS Brown gave accused a high character.

Major Eckford said that he knew accused best in India. He thought he was rather gullible as far as the men were concerned.

Medical Testimony

Capt. George Lawless, Medical Superintendent of the Armagh District Lunatic Asylum, said, in reply to Mr Chambers, that he had examined the accused. His opinion was that Capt. Colthurst was in a state of mental instability, and that he was restless and unstrung. His history for over a year was one of mental weakness. Witness was a member of a medical board before which Capt. Colthurst presented himself in March, 1915. A report was then made as to his mental and bodily condition. Witness saw him again the previous Saturday, when he was with him for about two hours. The result of his examination was that he considered Captain Colthurst was at present mentally in an unsound state, and that he was not responsible.

Major Francis Purser, who had also examined the accused, agreed with the evidence given by Capt. Lawless.

Telegram from Sir Francis Vane

The President said that before the Court retired he should like to read the following telegram which he had received from Major Sir Francis Vane:

As Captain Colthurst's alleged speech about myself, as reported in papers, give false impression, I consider public announcement should be made from Bench. Please note I was recommended by Brigadier 178th Brigade for mention in despatches for work done in the rebellion, and for re-organising defences Portobello Barracks, but did not sanction unnecessary harsh actions.

The Court then retired.

Findings of the Courtmartial

The finding of the General Courtmartial on Captain Bowen-Colthurst, held at Richmond Barracks on June 6th and 7th, 1916 was promulgated on Saturday, 10th June.

The Court found Captain Bowen-Colthurst guilty of the first third and fifth charges of murder, and also found this officer was insane at the time that he committed these acts. The finding was confirmed by the General Officer Commanding-in-Chief.

To be Detained in an Asylum

The following *communiqué* with reference to the courtmartial on Captain Bowen Colthurst was issued from the Military Headquarters in Dublin on Thursday, 29th June:

The Army Council has notified that the case of Captain JC Bowen Colthurst, who was found guilty by courtmartial of the murder of Sheehy-Skeffington, Thomas Dickson, and Patrick MacIntyre during the recent rebellion, has been submitted to the King, in accordance with Section 130 of the Army Act, and His Majesty has been pleased to direct that Captain Bowen Colthurst be detained in a criminal lunatic asylum during His Majesty's pleasure.

THE RISING IN COUNTY LOUTH

Murder of Constable McGee

A Courtmartial assembled on Friday, 9th June, at Richmond Barracks, Dublin, for the purpose of trying four young men on a charge of killing a police constable of the RIC at Castlebellingham on Easter Monday, and attempting to kill a military officer. Major-General Lord Cheylesmore, KCVO, presided, and the Court consisted of twelve other officers. Mr Kenneth Marshall acted as Judge Advocate.

The accused were:

John McEntee, electrical engineer, Belfast
Frank Martin, house painter, Dublin
Denis Leahy, labourer, Dundalk,
James Sally, coach painter, Dundalk.

The first charge against them was: 'Doing an act of such a nature as to be calculated to be prejudicial to the public safety and the Defence of the Realm, with the intention of, and for the purpose of, assisting the enemy, in that they, near Castlebellingham, Co. Louth, on the 24th April, 1916, whilst engaged in armed rebellion and the waging of war against His Majesty the King, feloniously and of their malice aforethought, did kill and murder Constable McGee of the Royal Irish Constabulary.' The second charge against them was: 'Doing an act of such a nature as to be calculated to be prejudicial to the public safety and the Defence of the Realm, with the intention and for the purpose of assisting the enemy, in that they, on the 24th April, near Castlebellingham, whilst engaged in armed rebellion, and waging war against the King, did attempt to kill and murder Lieutenant Robert Dunville, Grenadier Guards': and the third charge was 'the doing of an act prejudicial to the public safety and Defence of the Realm, with the intention and for the purpose of assisting the enemy, in that they took part in an armed rebellion in Ireland and the waging of war against the King.'

Major Kimber, DSO, conducted the case for the prosecution. Mr TM Healy, KC, MP, and Mr Cecil Lavery (instructed by Mr Hamill, Dundalk) appeared for the accused, with the exception of McEntee, who was defended by Mr Hanna, KC, and Mr McGrath (instructed by Mr John Gore).

The Facts of the Case

The Prosecutor (Major Kimber) briefly stated the facts of the case. He said on Sunday morning, April 23rd, a party of 73 men set out from Dundalk at ten o'clock in the morning. Nineteen of them were armed, and they went to Ardee. On the way they were met by a man in a motor car, in which there were rifles. These rifles were distributed to the men, who adopted military formations. McEntee was in charge of the party. They stayed at Ardee that night, and early on the morning of the 24th they started back towards Castlebellingham. At six in the evening they were at Lurgan Green, the party having been reduced to about 50. A man named Patrick McCormack, a farmer, came towards Sergeant Wymes, who had been following the party throughout, and accused McEntee of having wounded him in the hand with a revolver, and asked him to arrest him. McEntee replied: 'I did it as a matter of duty. Ireland is proclaimed a Republic, and you must stand or fall by that fact.' Sergeant Wymes, whom they knew well, and two other constables, were made prisoners, and placed under an armed guard. Several motor cars passed on the road, and every vehicle passing was stopped and searched. That continued until 6.30, when the rebels went to Castlebellingham. About seven o'clock a party arrived at Castlebellingham and pulled up on the middle of the road, near the police barrack. McEntee and Martin came up and covered three policemen with revolvers. They were taken and placed with their backs against a railings. Martin was put in charge of them, and he said to them that if they stirred they would be shot. Whilst this was going on Constable McGee came up, riding a bicycle. McEntee ordered him to dismount and to deliver what despatches he had to him. The constable was searched, and his despatches taken from him. McGee was placed against the rail, and about twenty armed Volunteers were addressed by McEntee, who said: 'See that your revolvers are properly loaded, and be ready to obey me.' Then Lieutenant Dunville in his motor car came on the scene. He was stopped and ordered out of his car, and he and his chauffeur were put with the three men with their backs to the railings. The prisoner Leahy pointed his rifle at Lieutenant Dunville and then McEntee gave an order. The rebels got back to their cars, and shots were heard. Lieutenant Dunville was hit, and the charge went through his lung. Almost immediately Constable McGee was hit. He fell, and died in a couple of hours.

The Rebels' Password

Sergeant M Wymes, RIC, Dundalk, said that on Sunday, April 23rd, at 10 o'clock in the morning, he saw a body of twenty men, leaving a hall in the town. Nineteen of them were armed with rifles, double and single barrels, and they went on towards Ardee, accompanied by five cars. At Ardee he saw the prisoners, and he saw ammunition being handed out. They arrived at Slane about 8 o'clock, and stayed on the road till 12 o'clock at night, where they encamped. At a quarter to three in the morning they proceeded towards Collon. He traced their movements during the day to Castlebellingham. The party numbered fifty at Lurgan Green, mostly armed. That was at 6 p.m. Patrick McCormack, a farmer, came along with McEntee, and McCormack said that McEntee had shot him in the hand, and the latter said he did it as a matter of duty: that Ireland was proclaimed a Republic, and that he was prepared to stand or fall by his acts. He made witness a prisoner. Two Constables then came up, and they and he were searched and placed under an armed guard. The cars that passed were all commandeered and taken possession of by the Sinn

Feiners. Witness was there for an hour and a half altogether under an armed guard. The main party of Sinn Feiners went away. He was allowed eventually to go away, and was given the password 'Limerick,' by which he was enabled to pass the rest of the rebels. He saw three of the accused, Martin, McEntee and Sally bearing arms. He did not see Leahy there at all.

Police Held Up

Acting Sergeant Patrick Kiernan, Castlebellingham, stated that on Easter Monday he saw a party of armed men passing through the village between 4.30 and 5 p.m., going towards Dundalk. They were on foot. There were a couple of vehicles behind them. Some of them came back about 6.45—three cars and eleven armed men came back. They had shot guns and rifles. Witness did not recognise them as being in the first party. About fifteen minutes later about fifty men came from the Dundalk direction, armed with rifles, shot guns, and revolvers. The cars stopped near the end of the village, the last car being about 120 yards from the barracks. Witness took a constable with him down after the cars. As he approached McEntee, Martin, and two others presented revolvers at them, and ordered them to stand by the railing. McEntee said if they stirred one way or the other they would be shot dead. While standing there, Constable McGee came up on his bicycle, and McEntee and several others went towards him and ordered him to dismount. He got off, and they told him to stand with his back to the railings. McEntee asked him had he arms, and he said not, and McEntee ordered him to deliver up all papers on him, otherwise he would be shot. Constable McGee then handed what witness believed to be two despatches to McEntee. The constable was then searched for arms. After the search McEntee came down, and stood about a yard in front of witness, facing him. There would be about twenty others present, just behind the last motor car, all armed. McEntee said: 'Now, men, keep your rifles at proper load, and be able to obey me when I give the order.' Martin was then present. Lieutenant Dunville then came up in a motor car, and was stopped by McEntee and several others with revolvers and rifles. They pointed their weapons towards Lieutenant Dunville, who was taken out of the car and put standing by the railings. Witness saw the accused, Denis Leahy, standing about three yards away. Witness also saw James Sally present. The chauffeur was also ordered to leave the motor car. There were about twenty men at least covering witness and the other four men with rifles and revolvers. He then heard a shot from the direction of the first motor car. Lieutenant Dunville said, 'I am shot,' and commenced to fall back against the railings. Witness did not then see where he was shot, but afterwards found he was shot through the body. Another shot followed, and witness and Constable Donovan ran into a house. Two shots were fired as they crossed the road. Witness and the other policeman went out backwards and got to the barracks. He returned to the scene immediately, and found Constable McGee shot. The constable died within a few hours. All the cars went away, except one which broke down. That car contained a large amount of ammunition for rifles, revolvers, and shot guns.

American Ammunition

The President said the rifle cartridges were American ammunition. The shotgun ammunition was a mixture of buckshot and ordinary shot.

Constable Patrick Donovan, RIC, stationed at Castlebellingham, answering Major Kimber, said he remembered going before the rebels' cars to stop them on Easter Monday about 7 p.m. As he got in front of the cars he was 'halted' by four men, of whom two were the accused, McEntee and Martin, both being armed with revolvers. McEntee placed him beside the railing, and put Martin in charge of him, with directions that if he did anything he should be shot. The police were in uniform, but they had no arms. He saw McEntee stop Constable McGee with a revolver pointed at him. McEntee told him that if he resisted he would be shot. There were a lot of rebels round about, and they were all armed. He saw Lieutenant Dunville and his chauffeur ordered out of their car by McEntee, who covered them with his revolver. Witness asked the men who placed them against the railing not to shoot them.

Lieutenant Dunville's Narrow Escape

Second Lieutenant Robert Dunville, of the Grenadier Guards, said he was travelling by motor car from Belfast to Kingstown on Easter Monday, accompanied by his chauffeur. They arrived at Castlebellingham about ten minutes to seven. When he entered the village he saw three policemen on the left hand side of the road near the railings. He also saw a considerable number of men in motor cars, and some on the road—all armed, some with revolvers, some had automatic pistols, others carbines and ordinary rifles. As he could not get through he pulled his car up, and a man whom he identified as the accused, Leahy, came up and pointed a rifle at him. Then McEntee came up and presented a pistol at him. Witness asked them what it was all about, told him that he wanted to catch the boat from Kingstown, and to let him pass. His chauffeur and himself were placed with the police at the railings. Then a man got out of one of the cars, and aimed a long rifle at him. He heard a report, and somebody at his right hand side shouted, and he found that he himself had been shot: that the bullet passed through his breast from left to right. He saw a rifle still pointed at him after he was hit. After that he fell, and he was removed to his car. Besides McEntee, who seemed to be in command, he saw Leahy and Martin. He could recognise the man who pointed the long rifle, but he was not one of the accused.

Dr Patrick J O'Hagan, Castlebellingham, described the nature of Constable McGee's injuries. He was suffering from four bullet wounds, two in the left arm, and two in the body. Witness was present at the *post-mortem* and attributed death to shock and hemorrhage, resulting from bullet wounds. Witness also attended Lieutenant Dunville, and found two wounds on the chest, one on the left, being apparently the wound of entry.

Aid of a Foreign Power

Sergt. Chr. Sheridan, RIC, stationed at Dundalk, said he searched McEntee's lodgings in Anne street, Dundalk, on May 17th, and found a number of papers and documents, and a book in which the following was written:

Proposed and seconded, that a meeting be held in the Town Hall on Easter Sunday. First, Ireland to reach independence in two ways—1. by the development of limited autonomy: 2. at one stroke by her own unaided exertion, or by the aid of a foreign power—the latter the more feasible. Should she gain it by the first ipso she would be strong enough to hold it, and by the second we will consider.

The other documents composed copies of Sinn Fein newspapers, such as the *Spark* and the *Volunteer*, and a manuscript in which was entered some dates in history, as far back as the fifteenth century, at which rebellions took place, not only in Ireland, but on the Continent. Then there were books of military instruction, and a pamphlet on Sinn Fein policy. One of the letters found was a reply from the War Office authorities to an application of McEntee's for a commission in His Majesty's Army.

Mr Healy and the Government

Cross-examined by Mr Healy: Was there a Government in Ireland while all this was going on? Were the police in Dundalk? Yes.

Did you allow all these young men to be brigaded, drilled, organised, armed, and pro-Germanised without taking any steps to stop it? We did not interfere.

Did you ever caution them? No.

Head Constable Donnelly, Dundalk, told the Court that on the 28th April last he opened the desk which McEntee had at the power house, Dundalk, and found a quantity of papers and letters, among the latter being a letter from the late PH Pearse, who was the Commander-in-Chief of the rebels, recommending McEntee to push on the work and complete their equipment and training. He also produced a book containing what he took to be a list of names of the Volunteers in Dundalk, and a circular from Cumann na Bhan relating to a drawing for the distribution of arms to be held on the 8th April.

Leahy's Statement

Head Constable Kinahan proved a statement made by Leahy on April 27 to District Inspector Smith before that officer was killed, in which he stated that on the previous Sunday they walked into Ardee, where they got rifles there from a strange car. They then went to Collon, and from that to Slane, where they stopped till 3 o'clock next morning. They walked through Dunleer into Castlebellingham, and on to Lurgangreen, where they met a strange man in a car, who said he came from Dublin, and that fighting was going on there. 'So,' continues the statement, 'we were all taken together to get our guns ready. We were told that if we moved we would be shot. All the motor cars that were coming in from the races were held up with revolvers, and the cars were taken possession of. We went on to Dunshaughlin, and as the motor cars ran short of petrol we had all to get out and walk. A few of us got together, and said we would not go. So we had to hand up our rifles and ammunition. We had to leave them, and walk where we were arrested.'

Percy Alfred Spalding, Engineer, and Manager of the Electricity Works, Dundalk, under whom the accused, McEntee, had been employed, gave him an excellent character from the personal point of view, as well as from the professional. Testimonials from officials in Belfast were also read. The witness said that McEntee had left on the Thursday before Easter for his holiday, promising to be back at his work on Monday morning.

This closed the evidence for the prosecution.

Mr Healy opened the case for the defence of his clients.

Thomas Harty, car driver, Dundalk, examined by Mr Lavery, deposed to having driven a party of Volunteers on the Sunday and Easter Monday through the country, and that he was with Sally at Lurgangreen when the constable was shot at Castlebellingham.

McEntee's Statement

John McEntee, one of the accused, here read to the Court a statement which he had prepared since the trial began. At the outset he positively denied the charge of murder. In obedience to the order of his commander, he stopped the constable and searched him. He took from him one envelope, which he brought to his commander. The constable received no abuse from him, and he lamented his death; the constable was his fellow-countryman, discharging his duty. He saw Dunville sink to the ground, and would have gone to assist him but that their commander thought it imperative, from information which he had received, that they should no longer remain there. He was charged with having given assistance to the King's enemies. He absolutely denied that he had given, directly or indirectly, assistance to the King's enemies. Anything he did was done out of love for Ireland, and not to assist the King's enemies in any way. Such an idea never occurred to him. He admitted that for some months up to April 24 he was an active and enthusiastic Volunteer: and he was a Volunteer, first of all, because, being an Irishman, he thought that the economic and industrial future of his country could only be assured by such government as was enjoyed by the Empire's free Dominions. He recognised that the Home Rule Act was such a measure, and he thought he saw in the promise of an Amending Bill a proposal whereby Ulster should be cut off and separated from the Ireland which he loved. He saw his hopes falsified by the promise of an Amending Bill, and he saw no protection against it but some such organisation as the Ulster Volunteer Force. He admitted that he took part in events which he afterwards discovered were a rebellion; but his sole aim and object was to resist the suppression of the organisation whose maintenance he regarded as a great safeguard against the repeal of Home Rule. Throughout the whole proceedings he had no idea or desire to assist the enemy. When General Parsons was raising the 16th Division he applied to him for a Commission, but owing to the difficulty of getting to Mallow the application fell through, and he then decided to devote himself to his profession. In conclusion, he said he was not aware of any of the plans for the late unfortunate insurrection.

Highway Robbery in Broad Daylight

Mr T Erskine Alexander, solicitor, Belfast, said he was motoring from Fairyhouse Races to Belfast, when he was stopped at Dromiskey by about thirty armed men. McEntee was there, and but for McEntee the other men would have behaved badly to him (witness) and the other persons whom they had stopped. His car had been taken from him, but it was returned later on.

The Prosecutor: Do you agree with me that this was highway robbery of your car in broad daylight? Yes.

McEntee was apparently in authority? He was the only one that I identify. I don't remember having seen any of the others. The whole crowd surrounded us and pointed their revolvers at us.

Alderman John McGrath, Belfast, who travelled with Mr Alexander, corroborated his evidence.

A chauffeur named Dickson, who drove another motor car going to Belfast, gave evidence of having been stopped by the rebels, who took possession of his car, after having turned out the owner. McEntee sat beside him as he drove back to Castlebellingham from Lurgangreen. There were five other rebels in the car sitting behind him, and one of them put his rifle to his left shoulder and fired at the police who were lined up against the railings at Castlebellingham. He heard the man say that he had got first blood. McEntee had only a little automatic pistol. McEntee gave him money to buy food.

Wm Donnelly, another chauffeur, said that he heard McEntee refuse to give ammunition to those who demanded it.

Patrick Byrne, publican, Castlebellingham, said that he saw the five persons, including the three policemen, lined up against the railings, and he saw Constable Magee shot, but it was not done by McEntee.

Mr Joseph Devlin, MP: Mr Joseph Donnelly, Treasury Solicitor for Ireland, and Mr T Callan Macardle, Dundalk, gave evidence testifying to the respectability of McEntee.

Sentences

The following result of the trial was subsequently issued:

John McEntee, Francis Martin, and Denis Leahy were sentenced to death: these sentences were confirmed by the General Officer Commanding-in-Chief, but commuted to penal servitude as under:

John McEntee—Penal servitude for life.

Francis Martin—Ten years' penal servitude.

Denis Leahy—Ten years' penal servitude.

James Sally was sentenced to penal servitude for ten years, which was confirmed by the General Officer Commanding-in-Chief, with a remission of five years of the sentence awarded.

THE BATTLE OF ASHBOURNE

Meath County Surveyor Acquitted

The trial by courtmartial of James Quigley, County Surveyor of County Meath, began on Wednesday, 7th, and concluded on Friday, 9th June, at Richmond Barracks, Dublin. The charge against Mr Quigley was that, during the rising of Sinn Fein rebels in the County Meath on April 28th, when the police were ambushed near Ashbourne and several officers and men were killed and a number wounded, he conveyed information by signal to them as to the whereabouts of the police, which might be helpful to them, and prejudicial to the peace and welfare of the King's subjects. The accused denied the charge, and, further, stated that he had neither hand, act nor part in the rebellion, and that he had no knowledge of the acts of the rebels, and that he had no sympathy with them.

The accused pleaded not guilty, and was defended by Mr Henry Hanna, KC, and Mr Lardner, MP (instructed by Mr JJ McDonald).

Case for Prosecution

Major Kimber, the Prosecutor, said the facts of the case were that during the week of the rebellion a man named Ashe set out with a doctor named Hayes and a number of armed rebels, and they deliberately took possession of various police barracks, took the policemen prisoners, and ultimately came to a pitched battle with the police at a place called Ashbourne, where the County Inspector was mortally wounded, the District Inspector killed, and 16 policemen were wounded, and four or five others killed. The expedition of the police started from Navan on the 28th April at about 11.15 a.m. They were in motor cars, in command of County Inspector Gray and District Inspector Smith. They started to relieve the policemen besieged at Ashbourne, a distance of about 20 miles from Navan. At a spot on the road between Balrothery and Kilmoon the police met the accused, James Quigley, with his motor cycle. The accused was a man of importance in the County Meath, occupying an official position as County Surveyor. He was standing at the cross roads when the police passed, and when they got close to Kilmoon they again passed the prisoner on the road. Near Ashbourne the police were fired upon by the rebels. The accused came up on his cycle behind them, left the cycle on the side of the road and ran across in a stooping position to a wood. It was important to recollect that because during the fight which followed the police were fired upon from the wood, and the police force was cut off from the rear and surrounded. The police finally surrendered, and when they surrendered they saw the accused talking with rebels and shaking hands with Ashe. When the premises of the accused were searched, a rifle, a shot gun, ammunition, and seditious literature were found there.

Acting Sergeant Joseph Stephenson, RIC, deposed that he was on duty at Slane on the 26th April. On that day he saw Mr Quigley come into the village on his motor bicycle and take observation of the police, who numbered 20 or 30, standing about the local police station. He thought the accused was spying on the police.

Rifles and Ammunition Produced

District Inspector HB Molony, RIC, who had been in charge of the Navan district from the 2nd till the 31st May, produced three rifles, 54 rounds of ammunition, a button badge of the Volunteers, a copy of *Nationality*, some copies of a 'Cumann-na-Bhan' leaflet, and some books and manuscript, which were found at the house of the accused.

Sergeant John Griffith, RIC, stated that he was in charge of Bohermeen Barracks, five miles from Navan. On the 28th April last he was at Slane and left with a party of police, under County Inspector Gray and District Inspector Smith. It was about 11 o'clock. They went towards Ashbourne. Witness had known the accused about three years, and saw him first that day standing with a motor cycle on the road next Kilmoon. The accused passed the motor cars in which the police were, and went on towards Kilmoon and Ashbourne. Witness afterwards saw accused talking to two men on the side of the road, and saw him a third time nearer Ashbourne, where he left his cycle and went across the fields. The accused waved his hands. Shortly afterwards there was a fusilade of bullets against the police. The police were practically in a trap, being fired upon from every direction. The fighting continued from noon till about 5 p.m., when the police surrendered, having no more ammunition. The County Inspector, the District Inspector, two sergeants and four constables were killed, and about 16 men wounded. After the fighting witness saw the accused talking to a number of men in the Irish Volunteer uniform.

Constable William Gray, RIC, Kells, gave corroborative evidence, identifying the accused as being present at the spots already alluded to. The police were not fired on from the rear until a quarter of an hour before the end of the fight. All the firing before that came from the direction of Kilmoon and from the right and left front.

The Battle between Police and Rebels

Constable Oliver Watson, RIC, Kells, said that he was one of the police party that left Slane on the morning of the 28th April on motor cars for Ashbourne. He saw the accused at twelve o'clock that day where the battle took place. The accused was standing on the side of the road where he saw him that evening after the battle at Rath Cross. The battle between the police and the rebels was a hot one. It went on for five hours. He estimated that there were forty rebels between himself and the police barracks at Kilmoon. Witness kept firing as long as his ammunition lasted, after which he surrendered with the other police. When he surrendered he was taken to Rath Cross, and there he saw a lot of wounded men and Mr Quigley. He saw Mr Quigley halted by a man whom he afterwards learned was named Ashe. Ashe, apparently, was a commander, and was in uniform. Quigley said to Ashe: 'Don't mind me: I am an independent man. I am a country road surveyor.' Quigley gave Ashe a red card. The prisoner did not shake hands with Ashe in witness's presence.

Constable Eugene Bratton, RIC, Navan, gave evidence as to having seen the accused on the road near Ashbourne with his motor cycle. Witness was taken prisoner by the rebels about an hour after the fight started. He was detained about half an hour, and the rebels then told him to go and sit in a field at the back of a ditch. (Laughter). He did so, and escaped some time later, borrowing a bicycle, on which he rode to Balrath Post Office and 'phoned for assistance. When he returned to the scene of the fighting at about 6 p.m. it was all over. Witness, who had been in plain clothes driving a motor car, found that the car had gone away, and got another car, and was in the act of turning it when he saw Mr Quigley come to the back of the car and look at the number. Accused had a pencil and paper in his hand, and took some notes.

Sergeant Terence MacDermott, RIC, stationed at Ballivor, Co. Meath, stated that he was one of the police party, and that he saw the accused not far from Ashbourne. Witness was one of those who surrendered to the rebels near Ashbourne. A quarter of an hour after the conclusion of the battle he saw the accused come along the road through the Sinn Feiners, of whom there were about one hundred. The accused was not molested by them. He spoke to the commander, Thomas Ashe, with whom he seemed to be on friendly terms, because he shook hands with him and spoke to him for a couple of minutes. Witness was standing among the wounded policemen, trying to assist them.

Statement by Accused

At the sitting of the Court on Thursday, 8th June, two witnesses for the prosecution were examined before the public were admitted.

This closed the case for the prosecution.

Mr Hanna said the accused could not be examined on oath, but he could make a statement.

The accused then read a statement, in the course of which he said that some time early in 1913 a corps of Volunteers was formed at Navan as a counterblast to the Ulster Volunteers. He joined the corps, and was appointed secretary. A meeting of delegates from similar corps in the County Meath assembled in Navan to discuss the question whether or not they should join the Dublin corps of Volunteers. They had about one hundred men, and they had no fixed policy. The majority of them were incapable of military service. At their first meeting he proposed a resolution of loyalty to the King and the Constitution of the Realm. That was defeated by an amendment that the matter be left to an All-Ireland meeting, and he took no further part in their deliberations. They continued route marching until their instructor left to join the Army when the war broke out. He was anxious that Lord Fingall should take command of the Volunteers. He did not succeed in getting Lord Fingall, and he waited on Colonel Hammond and asked him to take command. He also refused, and they tried to get Lord Gormanston, but there was an objection to such a prominent Unionist taking command. Subscriptions were raised, and sixteen rifles and some ammunition were purchased. One of the rifles was given to him, but it was out of order, and the twenty cartridges remained in his house. The rifles and ammunition were purchased openly at James Sheridan's, of Navan. He had been advised to resign his connection with the Volunteers lest the men employed by the County Council might not be pleased with him. He did not resign, but he took no part in the proceedings of the Volunteers. He never had any connection with the Irish Volunteers, and he had never met or spoken to any of them as far as he knew, with the exception of John McNeill, who came to Navan. Not a single man of those who had taken part in the recent rebellion was known to him. He had not hand, act, or part in the rebellion or the disturbances that took place. He was at Fairyhouse Races when he heard of the outbreak in Dublin. He refused to believe at first that it was more than a riot. He knew of no Irish Volunteers in the County Meath. His diary would account for his movements every day in the year. He was engaged on the 28th April on his official duties, and in attending a meeting at Ardee. It was in returning from that meeting on his motor bicycle he met the police near Ashbourne. He found himself in danger from the firing, and had to take shelter in a cottage. He denied that he had waved his hands to the rebels, as stated by the police witnesses. He had never said that the police should not have been driven in cars that day. His speaking to the 'rebel leader', alluded to, was merely to ask him to allow him to pass in order to fetch a doctor to the wounded police and civilians. He did not shake hands with the rebel leader. He had never belonged to any Sinn Fein organisation, nor did he subscribe to any such society. No man in Ireland knew less about the late disturbance than he did, and he was absolutely innocent of any connection with the outbreak. As to the empty gelignite box found at his house that was brought from a quarry two years ago, and the Volunteer button badge had been given to him at a tobacco shop. The 'Cumann na Bhan' circular had been sent to his house by post. He had never written or spoken a word indicating that he was dissatisfied with the British Empire. He had spent the greater part of his life in England, and had as many English as Irish friends. He had tried to join the Army when he was a young man. If he had been accepted then his career might have been different from what it was.

John Conroy, Assistant Surveyor, County Meath, examined by Mr Hanna, said that some roads in the county were regularly inspected by Mr Quigley once or twice a month. Mr Quigley was out on inspection duty on the 28th of April.

Accused not Active

John J Gallen, Secretary to the County Committee of Meath, said he was Treasurer of the Volunteer Corps at Navan. Mr Quigley had been president of the branch all the time, but it was almost a year since he took any active part. He knew that Mr Quigley proposed an address to the King declaring their loyalty when the branch was formed in 1914.

Witness said that since the war began the National Volunteers had not been active, and they had no meetings since the middle of last year. The subscriptions which they had received came from people of all denominations in the county. The rifles they bought were still in the hands of the Volunteers. None except those that were lifted by the police were given in.

Purchase of Rifles

PJ McQuillan, publican and farmer, Navan, in his evidence stated that he was a member of the Committee of the Navan Volunteers, and that none of their members had anything to do with the Sinn Fein outbreak at Ashbourne. They were all absolutely opposed to the principle of Sinn Fein. He knew some persons who were reputed to be Sinn Feiners, but none of them were members of the Volunteers to which he belonged. None of his Volunteers, with the exception of Mr Quigley, had been arrested. He remembered the purchase of sixteen rifles from Mr James Sheridan, of Navan. Fourteen were kept for drilling purposes, and two were sent to men at Kilbarry. They had paid £4 for each rifle. Mr Quigley was a trustee of the funds, and there was about £40 in bank. Mr Quigley had the confidence of the people who supported the Irish Parliamentary Party.

In reply to the Prosecutor, the witness said that not many of his members left him at the 'split', and there was no body of the Irish Volunteers near.

A shop assistant in the employment of Mr Sheridan, Navan, produced an account book showing a sale of rifles on the 12th August, 1914, to the Committee of the Navan Volunteers.

Mr P Boyle, of Slane, and Mr John P O'Brien, Assistant County Surveyor, proved that the accused attended a meeting of the Ardee No. 2 Rural District Council in his capacity as County Surveyor on April 28th.

County Surveyor's Evidence

Mr Francis Bergin, CE, Acting County Surveyor for Kildare, produced a map showing elevations and measurements of portions of the road where the accused was seen by the police on the day of the fight. The portion of the road to Ashbourne known as the Causeway was visible from the country all round.

Joseph Conroy, a road ganger in the employment of the Meath County Council, gave evidence that on the 28th April, while he was at his duties on the road between Balrath and Duleek, the accused came to him about 11.05 a.m. and remained with him giving instructions for three-quarters of an hour. He left, going towards Navan, about 12 o'clock.

Mr P White, MP

Mr Patrick White, MP for North Meath, said he had known the accused since he was appointed County Surveyor, eight or nine years ago. From that time Mr Quigley was always a supporter of the Irish Parliamentary Party and a subscriber to their funds. When the Volunteers were started at Navan, the accused took a prominent part in carrying them on. Witness said he was present at a review of National Volunteers at Slane about two years ago. Mr Quigley was there, and so were many noble lords, including Lord Fingall, Lord Dunsany, the Marquis of Headfort, the Marquis Conyngham, and several minor lords. There was nothing Sinn Fein in that demonstration.

Miss Quigley, a sister of the accused, said she was a qualified nurse, and that she volunteered for war service at the outbreak of the war. She was called up in January, 1915, and after serving three months in England she went to Egypt. She had several letters from her brother while she was abroad. She knew his views on the war, and he said to her when she volunteered for service that it was the best thing that she could do. He said to her that if she wanted anything she was to write to him for it, and that he would be glad to welcome her home as his Inniskilling dragoon. (Laughter.)

Mr John Rogers, Piercetown, County Meath, stated that he saw the accused coming along the road from Kilmoon police barrack. He told witness that he had better not go up, or he might be shot. Both went for shelter behind a labourer's cottage, and listened to the firing. When there was a lull they went down the road about 400 yards, and both sat on the back of the ditch. When the firing ceased Quigley said he would go up for his bicycle, and witness mounted his own bicycle and rode off in the opposite direction.

Nicholas Kinsella gave evidence, in which he stated that, having seen a man with a motor bicycle coming across a field which was sown with corn, he waved his arms to him to keep off. He found it was the accused, who came into his house, and stayed for ten minutes.

Dr E Byrne

Dr Eugene Byrne, of Slane, said that he, having heard of the fight at Ashbourne, was proceeding in that direction between 2 and 3 o'clock in his motor car, when he was arrested by the 'Sinn Feiners', and detained for two-and-a-half or three hours. A 'Sinn Feiner' sat in his motor car, and as they were driving along to the place where the wounded were they passed Mr Quigley and another man. The 'Sinn Feiner,' who was guiding him to the place, said that the men they had passed wanted a 'lift', and he stopped and took him into the motor car. Mr Quigley said he would come and help him to dress the wounded. He also said that he had come there that morning to survey the road, and he added: 'Isn't it a terrible thing that Irishmen should be killing one another like this?'

Thomas McGrane, servant to Dr O'Reilly, said that on the day of the 'battle of Ashbourne' the accused rode up on a motor bicycle to Dr O'Reilly's house at Ratoath. The doctor was not a home, and Mr Quigley left a message for him that he should, when he came home, go to Ashbourne as quickly as possible, where he was wanted to attend to wounded police, and to bring medical appliances with him. That was between 5 and 5.30 o'clock in the evening. The doctor did not reach home till 6.30, and then he went off to Ashbourne, taking two clergymen with him.

Patrick Boyle was recalled, and he proved that the Meath County Council, at a meeting since Mr Quigley was arrested, passed a resolution bearing testimony to his good character and to his efficiency as an officer; and also expressing the hope that he would be soon released, as the Council believed there were no grounds for his arrest.

Rev. Mr Kinahan and Cornelius Corcoran having been examined, the evidence for the defence closed.

Acquitted

The Court, having retired to consider their verdict, returned after an absence of about half an hour.

The President: Having considered all the evidence, the Court find that the accused, James Quigley, is not guilty of the charge. The finding is read in open court, and the accused is released.

The announcement was received with slight applause, and the accused, having bowed to the Court, left in company with a number of relatives and friends.

OFFICERS AND CIVILIANS SHOT AT GUINNESS'S

Quartermaster-Sergeant Acquitted

A General Court-martial assembled on Monday, 12th June, at Richmond Barracks for the purpose of trying Company Quarter-master Sergeant Robert Flood, of the 5th Battalion Royal Dublin Fusiliers, on a charge of having, on April 28th, at Dublin, murdered Lieutenant A Lucas, of the 2nd King Edward's Horse. He was also charged with having murdered William John Rice, an employé of Guinness's Brewery, on the same date. The accused pleaded not guilty, and was defended by Mr Henry Hanna, KC (instructed by Mr Joseph Gleeson).

The prosecution was conducted by Major EG Kimber, DSO (instructed by Mr Robertson, of the Chief Crown Solicitor's Office).

Major-General Lord Cheylesmore, KCVO, presided over the Court, and Mr Kenneth Marshall was Judge Advocate.

Prosecutor's Statement

Major Kimber stated the facts of the case for the prosecution. On the evening of April 28th, Colonel Williams, who was in charge of the military in the area in which Guinness's Brewery is situate, ordered Captain McNamara, of the Dublin Fusiliers, to place a guard in the malthouse, which is at the south-western corner of the premises. Captain McNamara went there, with Quartermaster-Sergeant Flood (the accused) and nine men. It was a pitch dark night and that was a matter to be recollected. The orders which Colonel Williams gave to Captain McNamara were that he was not to return the snipers' shots, and not to fire at all unless there were attempts made to enter the brewery. At 11 o'clock that night Captain Rotheram was ordered by Colonel Williams to take down Second Lieutenant Lucas (who was subsequently killed) to the brewery, in order to relieve Captain McNamara. Mr Lucas belonged to King Edward's Horse, and at that time officers had been reporting all over Dublin, and had been sent to different jobs. The guard in the malthouse belonged to the Royal Dublin Fusiliers, and, of course, Mr Lucas was unknown to the company quartermaster-sergeant or any of the guard. Captain Rotheram took with him extra men, and when he left Mr Lucas the guard numbered fifteen men. They were put out at different sentry posts in the building, and the orders which Colonel Williams had given to Captain McNamara were repeated to Mr Lucas in the presence of the accused, and, in addition to that, Captain McNamara said it was inadvisable to open any of the windows, but if it was necessary to fire it would be better to fire through the windows rather than open them and attract the attention of the rebels. He also told the accused that Mr Lucas was relieving him. The official who acted as guide told the guard that there was no one in the building except three watchmen, who, when they went their rounds, carried lights. It seemed that lights were seen by several of the guard during the evening from the houses round, and from the direction of the adjacent distillery. It was feared that the rebels might make an attack on the brewery from two directions, so that lights would cause considerable suspicion, as they might be regarded as signals. At any rate, whatever it was, the guard got into a state of jumpiness, and the consequence was that when Lieutenant Lucas went round with Mr Rice, one of the brewery officials, the sentries on several occasions got the idea that he was a stranger who had no business there. The conversations he had with them were misinterpreted, and they came to a conclusion which was utterly false, and, unfortunately, it was shared by the accused. Lieutenant Lucas opened a window. The men knew that orders had been given that the windows were not to be opened. It looked very suspicious. The state of mind into which accused had got at that time led him to arrest Lieutenant Lucas and Mr Rice, who were subsequently shot. The officer, before being shot, asked permission to say his prayers, and, having done so, he said he was sorry, but 'the boys led him into it.' Soon afterwards another officer was coming down the staircase. He was challenged and searched, and rushed at the sergeant, knocking him down. The men of the guard fired, and the second officer, Lieutenant Worswick, was killed, and also a civilian who was with him, Mr Dockeray, an employé of the brewery.

Captain McNamara

Captain Charles McNamara, 5th RDF, examined, said that on the 28th April last he was in Dublin; he had been ordered by Colonel Kennard to take fifteen men to Guinness's Brewery. He did so, and he put nine men with the accused to guard the malthouse in Robert street. His orders were to occupy the building, and not to answer any snipers by firing, unless actually attacked by the rebels; not to open the windows, and to hold the place during the night. The rebels occupied some of the houses all round and in front. He was told that the only officials of the brewery that would be on the premises were three watchmen, and that they would have lamps. That was known to the accused, who heard the instruction and the orders. He encountered no firing and saw no lights while he was there. At 11 o'clock Captain Rotheram came to him, bringing with him Lieut. Lucas and seven men. They were conducted by a guide. He handed over command to Lieut. Lucas, and told him what his orders were. He told him that he was not to open the windows lest the Sinn Feiners might hear, and thereby might become aware that the brewery was occupied. He also told Lieut. Lucas that in view of the difficulty of getting away in daylight he had better get out of the building about dawn. All the orders that were transmitted to Lieut. Lucas were heard by Quartermaster-Sergeant Flood. It was a pitch-dark night, and it was possible that Flood may not have seen what Lucas's rank was.

Cross-examined by Mr Hanna, witness agreed that, from the military point of view, this was a difficult place to guard. It was a dark night and a very uncanny place.

In reply to the President, the witness said that he had not known Lieut. Lucas before he met him that night. He wore a great coat, and his rank could not have been distinguished in the dark by Sergeant Flood.

Finding the Dead Men

Captain AR Rotheram, of the 10th Reserve Cavalry, stated that he was on duty in the vicinity of Guinness's Brewery on the night of the 28th April. About 2 in the morning Lieutenant Worswick and Mr Dockeray (of Guinness's Brewery) came to him in James's street. They said a telephone message had been received from the malthouse saying that Mr Rice was a prisoner. He gave Lieut. Worswick instructions to do nothing till daylight. He received no other communication till 3.30 in the morning, when he was told that there was a sergeant outside who wanted to see him. He went out and saw the accused and about fourteen men. They seemed very excited. The accused reported to him that he had shot two men, and that he thought the malthouse was full of rebels.

The Prosecutor: Did you ask him where Mr Lucas was? Yes, and he said he thought he had shot him. He left accused with his picket, and brought some of his men back to the malthouse, where he found the dead bodies of Lieut. Worswick and Mr Dockeray on the third storey. On the next floor below witness said he found the bodies of Lieut. Lucas and Mr Rice, also dead. Witness put some men in charge of the bodies, and he reported the matter to Colonel Williams.

Cross-examined by Mr Hanna: Lieut. Worswick was in command of one of his (witness's) pickets in Watling street. He had no duty to do in the brewery.

Captain McNamara, re-called, in answer to Mr Hanna, said that he had been at the brewery on the day previous (Thursday), and that he saw in one of the offices a box of German ammunition. They were dum-dum bullets.

How the First Officer was Shot

Private Maurice McCarthy, of the 5th RDF, said he was on duty on the night of April 28th under Sergeant Flood at the brewery. He was called upstairs by Flood, and there he saw a civilian and an officer. He was ordered by Flood to search a civilian, and he did so, and found on him a bunch of keys. Sergeant Flood turned an electric torch on the officer and said, 'I know you.' He took it from the look of the civilian and the officer at each other that they knew each other. The sergeant placed the two men together at some distance from the window and he (witness) was ordered to cover them with his rifle. He kept them so covered for an hour. There were lights flashing outside the building, and one of the soldiers said he saw men's forms moving in the darkness on the road outside. Flood sent Private Short to go out and report as to the lights. Short returned saying that he could not get out.

The Prosecutor: While you kept the officer and the civilian covered what did the accused do? He ordered the officer to take off his coat and not to disgrace it.

Did you see any badge on the coat? There was a badge of some kind.

Did Flood say anything about firing? He said he would have to fire, as things were looking as if an attack was going to be made.

What happened then? The officer said he was a poor farmer's son and that he was sorry that he had been let into it by others.

Prayers

Did he say anything else? He asked to be allowed to say his prayers. The sergeant gave him permission to say his prayers, and he knelt down. He was crying when he got up. The sergeant had his torch in his hand, and it was shining on the officer all the time.

Did Flood give any orders? He gave the order to present and fire, and we obeyed the order.

How many of you did that? Five.

What was the result? We fired, and the officer fell down, and the civilian was standing. We got the second order to fire at the civilian, Mr Rice, and he fell.

Did you examine him? He did not appear to be quite dead, and the sergeant (the accused) gave me the order to shoot at him again, which I did.

Did you examine the bodies? No; apparently to me they were both dead.

What happened then? I was moved downstairs to another floor, and was nearly half an hour there at the window. We heard footsteps in the room, as from behind. The accused was with us there.

Did he do anything? He turned round and shone his torch towards where the footsteps were heard. I saw by the light of the torch a civilian and an officer. I could not say what the officer's rank was. This would be about 1 o'clock in the morning. I had not seen the civilian before.

The Second Shooting

What happened then? Sergeant Flood said to the officer: 'Who are you?' The officer replied, 'I refuse to say who I am.' He refused to give any account of himself. By order of Sergeant Flood I searched him, and then covered him with my rifle. Other men covered the civilian.

Did the officer say anything? He said 'I don't know who you are. You may be Sinn Feiners for all I know.' Then he made a plunge at the sergeant and knocked him down.

What happened then? The sergeant said, 'Men, fire.' We did, and both fell.

This was on the floor below that on which you had shot the other two men? Yes. The dawn was breaking, and the sergeant said: 'We had better get out and report the matter.' I tried to get out, but could not, as the doors were locked. I found that one of the keys on the bunch found on the civilian unlocked the door. Against one of the doors was a metal drum, and Sergeant Flood said it looked as if it contained an explosive.

In reply to further questions, the witness said that some officer in the brewery, addressing Private Short, asked him if he was Irish. On being told that he was the man said: 'Then fire high; sure you won't shoot your own countrymen.' Then the officer stopped, and said: 'I am sorry I have been led into it by others.'

Had no Doubt he was an Officer

Lance-Corporal William Thompson, 5th Royal Dublin Fusiliers, corroborated the evidence of the previous witness in all particulars, except that he said the officer, when he was crying, said he was crying not for himself, but for his wife. He had no doubt that the gentleman was an officer, judging from his uniform. When both the civilian and the officer dropped dead, the soldiers left their bodies where they fell. There was only half an hour between the two shootings.

Private Michael O'Reilly, 5th RDF, in his evidence, generally corroborated the foregoing.

Contrary Orders

Private Murphy said that he was with the party in the malthouse when a strange officer came to relieve Captain McNamara. When this strange officer (Lieutenant Lucas) took charge he gave orders contrary to those that Captain McNamara had given. He told them not to fire upon anyone without orders from him.

Were these two persons, in your opinion, rebels? We understood they were.

Why did you understand that? Because when the officer came he turned all the previous orders upside down.

Did you fire on him? I was covering him, and so when I got orders I fired at him.

Captain McNamara, again recalled, said that when he was leaving Lieutenant Lucas in charge he told Flood his name. He had selected Flood for that duty because he considered him a reliable man.

Guarding the Bridge

Privates Wm Hunter and Wm Fox also corroborated. The latter said that while they were at the brewery a civilian came to him and said to him that he ought to be very careful, because the building was a nest of Sinn Feiners. When the strange officer took charge he placed him (Fox) and two other men to guard the bridge that crosses the canal near the brewery. While they were there Rice made a dash to get over the bridge, as if trying to escape. Witness stopped him.

Private Patrick Short said that a man in the brewery spoke to him about four o'clock on the 28th April, and said that as Irishmen they should fire high. He told him, in reply, that they would not. That night in the malthouse Mr Rice asked him and the men with him if they were Irish. Sergeant Flood replied that they were, but that they were not Sinn Feiners. He was suspicious that the presence of the two men was a trap.

Lieutenant Lucas's Career

Captain RE Campbell, 2nd King Edward's Horse, was called, but did not appear. A signed statement of his was read. It gave an account of Lieutenant Lucas's career. Mr Lucas, it stated, joined the reserve squadron, after having been in the Officers' Training Corps, in April, 1915, and was attached to the British Expeditionary Force. He was signalling officer to the regiment. He was wounded in France, and was invalided home. He joined the reserve in December last, and since then Captain Campbell knew Lieutenant Lucas and his wife very well. He was educated at a public school, and went to the University. He then went out to Canada as schoolmaster. He left that, and went to Montreal Stock Exchange, and made a lot of money there. He married a Canadian lady, and they lived in Montreal. Regarding Lieutenant Worswick, he joined at the Curragh in October, 1915, and he was a steady, hard-working man. He had travelled a good deal, and had some property in Canada. Both officers bore an excellent character.

This concluded the case for the prosecution, and the Court adjourned.

At the hearing of the case on Tuesday, 13th June, Lieut. Evelyn Toler, of the Inniskilling Fusiliers, said he had met Lieut. Lucas at dinner on the evening of the 28th April. He was dressed in the uniform of his regiment, and his shirt was the ordinary flannel. He wore the uniform collar and tie. He had been in mufti before that.

Evidence of the Accused

Sergeant Robert Flood, the accused, was sworn, and was examined by Mr Hanna. He said he joined his battalion in January, 1899, in London, when he was fourteen years and nine months old. He had served in South Africa, Malta, Khartoum, and India. He arrived in Dublin from the Curragh on the day following the outbreak of the rebellion in Dublin. He was taken to the Castle, and subsequently had charge of the arrangements for the defence of St Catherine's Church, James's street. He received orders from Capt. McNamara on Thursday to go to Guinness's Brewery with fifteen men, and the Captain told them that they were to take no notice of snipers, unless an attempt was made by the reels to enter. When he first got into the brewery, in the clerks' room he observed a box of foreign ammunition on a table, and a civilian standing against the table. He asked the civilian what he was doing with the ammunition, and he made no reply. Witness took the box and gave it to Capt. McNamara. All the men under him, he believed, saw the box. Nothing happened on Thursday night except that one shot hit the wall of the house the men were posted in. On Friday the party were led up into the malthouse. He remembered Capt. McNamara and a civilian coming to him. The civilian was pointing out to Capt. McNamara the different places, and he pointed out to him a small footbridge on the left over the canal, and he said that they expected an attack on the brewery at that particular spot, and that it ought to be well watched. The civilian and Capt. McNamara went upstairs to the second floor of the malthouse, and witness and his men were shown the positions they were to occupy. They went up to the third floor, and the Captain left it to him to choose which floor he thought best for observation. He chose the third. He did not know the name of the civilian who went round the place with Captain McNamara. He was not the man he subsequently heard called Mr Rice. They went back then to the clerk's room, and he was ordered to fall in eight men, and they marched across to the malthouse accompanied by Captain McNamara and a gentleman who he took to be a guide, was like a clerk.

The Instructions

The witness, continuing, said he posted his men in pairs at the windows on the third floor of the malthouse. The guide had already said that there would be three night watchmen on the premises, and that they usually carried lamps. Capt. McNamara said that no other people were to be allowed into the building but the night watchmen. Capt. McNamara gave him instructions that the windows were not to be opened, and that the men should not expose themselves, but to fire from cover of the side walls at the windows. They were also not to reply to snipers or let it be known that there was a part of soldiers in the brewery, but if an attempt were made to rush the brewery they were to fire. He said that if the Sinn Feiners were seen crossing the road to get into the brewery he (witness) was to open fire by pushing the rifles through the glass. Capt. McNamara later said that seven men would be brought up by another officer. Witness said he acted under his orders, and Capt. McNamara left, along with the civilian, about 8 o'clock. About 11 he heard footsteps coming up, and he ascertained that it was Captain McNamara and the remainder of the party of fifteen men. He had an officer and a guide with him. Captain McNamara said: 'This is the officer who is to relieve me for the night.' He did not remember if the officer's name was mentioned. At that time it was pitch dark.

Were you able to see whether or not the man referred to was an officer? I took it when Capt. McNamara said he was an officer that he was an officer, and afterwards I saw that he was in the uniform of an officer.

When Captain McNamara left had you any suspicion of this officer? None whatever.

The witness here related how he posted his men, some at the footbridge, and others at the windows on the third floor. The officer then in charge gave them instructions that they were not to fire until some person was seen coming towards the bridge. This officer moved out towards the centre of the bridge, where he might have been seen by the rebels. It struck witness at the time that that was a strange thing for the officer to do, after the instructions he had received from Captain McNamara. Witness and the officer returned to the third floor, and witness took up his position at the window. The officer seemed to be familiar with the catch on the window, and went as if to open it. Witness said to him that his instructions from Captain McNamara were not to open the windows.

What did he say in answer to that? As far as I remember he opened the window, and said: 'I am in charge here, and you are to do as I tell you.'

Taken for a Sinn Feiner

Did you notice anything about his manner that struck you as rather unusual in an officer? Yes. When he opened the window he said that he had been in America, and that he had twice been taken for a Sinn Feiner. Then he moved away to the other end of the room, and soon afterwards witness heard a conversation going on, and a noise as if a window was being opened.

And this was contrary to the orders you had got? Exactly the opposite. Soon afterwards I heard footsteps on the stairs, and I shouted 'Halt' twice, and got no reply. I went over to see who it was. I turned my torch on him, and I saw a tall civilian whom I had never seen before.

What did you do next? I called the officer. I could not see him, and said: 'There is a civilian here. He won't reply, and I don't know who he is.' The officer then came over and stood close to the civilian. I had my torch still shining on the civilian. When the officer came the light of the torch fell on his face, and I recognised him.

Was that the first time you had seen his face from the time Captain McNamara had brought him? Yes.

Did you believe you had seen him before? I was sure I did.

Where? On the previous day we were taken to Guinness's luncheon room about 7 o'clock, and I recognised this officer as the civilian who had taken us to the luncheon room.

Was he in civilian clothes at that time? Yes.

Was that the only time at which you had seen him in civilian clothes? On the Wednesday before I thought I had seen him at St Catherine's Church.

When you shone the torch on the two of them, did you see any look pass between them? I did. I saw a look of recognition pass between the officer and the civilian, and a sort of smile.

Did you then mention to the officer that your instructions were that only the night watchman was to be allowed into the building? I did.

What did he say to that? He made no remark. I said, 'Civilians have no right here. You will have to place him under arrest, as he will not give any account of himself.'

Did the civilian say anything? I don't remember that he made any reply.

Lights Outside

Did the officer say anything to the civilian? He made a remark which I did not catch, and then the two of them moved over towards my position at the window, and he ordered the civilian to sit down close just behind him. About that time one of my men shouted that there were lights outside, right, left and front, and I myself saw lights like signals, but not military signals. I thought it peculiar that the officer who was close to me did not take any notice of the lights. I turned round to call his attention to them, and then I saw him bending down as if in conversation with the civilian, who had been placed under arrest.

What did you do? Then my suspicion was aroused. I was sure there was treachery.

What did you do? I covered the officer, and said: 'There is treachery here: I'll have to place you under arrest,' thinking at the time that he was not an officer. My opinion was that he was a civilian and not an officer.

Tell us the facts that operated upon your mind creating the belief that there was treachery going on? The first thing was the finding of the box of foreign ammunition in the clerks' room the previous evening; the second was that a civilian should be in the place against the orders given, and the third was that the officer recognised the civilian, and that I saw him bending down and in conversation with him, and also that the officer took no notice of the lights, and that he had reversed the orders given by Capt. McNamara.

When you put him under arrest you were not aware of what he said to Privates Murphy or O'Reilly as to their being Irishmen? I was not. I only heard of it in their statements.

From the moment you put him under arrest did he protest or remonstrate with you in any way? He collapsed: he made no reply of any kind.

The witness then told how he ordered the two men to be searched, and how Private McCarthy took his revolver, money, and some papers from the officer, and a bunch of keys from the civilian. He ordered the officer to take off his 'British warm' (or overcoat), and in the search he noticed that he wore a kind of shirt that he believed officers did not wear. That added to his suspicions. Having searched the men he sent Private Short to the telephone to communicate with Captain McNamara, who had asked him to do so if anything happened during the night. He told Short to tell Captain McNamara that they had an officer, or rather a civilian in officer's clothing, and another civilian under arrest.

Had Rice at that time told you his name? He asked me to inquire by telephone about his identity, and said he was Mr Rice. Short came back and said he could not find Captain McNamara, that he was not in the luncheon room, but that the person who answered had a shrewd suspicion where he was.

When you could not get into touch with Captain McNamara what did you determine to do? I determined to get them out of the brewery somehow, and hand them over. I knew there was a picket in James's street. In the attempt to get out of the building the civilian darted off as if to make his escape by the footbridge, and witness covered him with his rifle. He was determined that the man should not get away, and added the witness: 'It was only restraint that I did not fire.' He said to the civilian: 'You intend to escape :if you can. We will go back up the steps and I will keep you there till dawn.' They got back into the room.

Attempt to Report to the Castle

What did you do then? I ordered two men to cover them, and I detailed two men to try and find a way to get out of the building, and report the whole occurrence at the Castle. Private Short returned and said he could not get out, as all the doors were locked. I saw lights flashing from different directions, and I thought there were lights on the floor below that on which we were. Private Byrne reported to me that he saw a man at the stable door opposite, and getting ready as if to rush into the place.

You had the officer and the civilian still covered? Yes. I said to them that I was sure that from the time I came into the place there was treachery, and that they were not going to come into the brewery and endanger the lives of my men.

Did you believe at that time that an attempt was about to be made by the Sinn Feiners to enter the brewery? I was sure they were on the point of rushing the place.

And, of course, having these two men under cover of five of your men, weakened your force considerably? It did, by one-third.

Did you inform the two men that you were going to fire on them? Yes, I remember I said, 'I am sorry that there is treachery going on. My men's lives are at stake, and I will have to give an order to fire.' I thought then, and I do still, that had I not done so the brewery would have been taken.

When you said you were going to fire did they say anything? The officer said, 'Don't fire, sergeant: I am only a poor farmer's son.' There was something else said which I cannot remember.

Asked Leave to Say his Prayers

Did he say anything about being allowed to say his prayers? I was on the point of giving the order. I had said 'ready.' He knew then I was determined, and he asked if he could say a few prayers. I said he could.

Did the civilian say anything? Nothing.

After the officer had prayed and stood up again, you gave the order? I did. When he prayed he got up and stood at the window, and he was crying. I asked him why he was crying, and he said he was thinking of his wife and child.

The men subsequently fired at your orders? I gave the order to fire.

And a second volley was fired at Mr Rice? I remember giving the order to fire. The two men were standing close together. I thought the men nearest to Mr Rice would cover him. When I gave the order to fire the officer fell, and the civilian was still standing: but when the order to fire was given I thought the full number of shots had not gone off, and that was why the civilian was still standing. I gave a second order to fire, and the civilian fell.

While these men were covered by the rifles did any man call your attention to the civilian moving? Yes, Private Murphy said: 'You will have to fire: that civilian will get away.' I saw the civilian moving as if to make a rush at me.

The Second Shooting

The accused next referred to the incidents on the second floor. They went down to the second floor, and were there in positions similar to those which the guard occupied above. They were there about twenty minutes when he heard footsteps, and he shouted 'Halt' twice, and got no reply. He turned his torch, and saw an officer and a civilian standing in the room. He said to them that his orders were not to allow any civilian into the building but a night watchman. He asked them what they were doing. They made no reply. He called two of his men to cover and search them.

Did the officer submit to being searched? I remember he handed his property over himself. He had six Treasury notes and some silver. He had no arms, and he had not even an officer's belt on. The civilian had keys on him. The only remark I heard from them was 'Sinn Feiners,' and I got a staggering blow, and was felled to the ground.

What happened then? The men fired.

You had given no order to fire on this occasion? None whatever.

When you got up you had an opportunity of seeing what had happened, and you found that the officer and the civilian had been shot? I did.

At the time you ordered the first two to be shot did you honestly believe it was necessary for the safety of yourself and your men? I did.

Did you think it necessary for the purpose of carrying out your military duty? I did.

This closed the evidence.

The Verdict

The President shortly afterwards announced that the accused had been found not guilty. The result was received with applause in court, and the accused was released.

Mr Sydney Matthews (Messrs Hoey and Denning), for Mrs Rice, said that an impression would be conveyed from the reports in the papers that Mr Rice and Mr Dockeray were in some way connected with the Sinn Fein movement. In fairness to the relatives of both the deceased, it was thought necessary to refute any such suggestion. To those who knew them it was unnecessary to say that they had no sympathy with the Sinn Fein movement.

Mr CJ Law (Messrs Malcomson and Law) made a similar statement on behalf of Mrs Dockeray.

Mr Alan McMullen, from the brewery, said that Mr Dockeray had been twenty-four years, and Mr Rice sixteen years, in the service of Messrs Guinness. They were both night clerks, and the management had the highest opinion of them. They had been specially selected for duty in the brewery during the rebellion as having been most trustworthy in every way.

This concluded the proceedings.

Lieutenant Lucas's Position

During the hearing of a subsequent trial on Saturday, the 17th June, the President said he had received some messages with regard to the case of Lieut. Lucas, who had been shot at Guinness's Brewery. The impression which his friends seemed to have received from the reports of the evidence was that he was in some way or other connected with the Sinn Fein movement, which he was not. He wished to state, and it was the opinion of the other members of the Court as well as his own, that there was no evidence produced to the courtmartial to give rise to such a suggestion. There was nothing whatever against the personal character of the late Lieutenant Lucas.

Messrs Rice and Dockeray

The following statement was published on 16th June:

Messrs Arthur Guinness, Son, and Co., Limited, are authorised by Lord Cheylesmore to state that there was nothing in the evidence at the recent court-martial to justify any suggestion that either Mr Dockeray or Mr Rice was in any way connected with, or in sympathy with, the Sinn Fein rebellion. He regrets that any such idea should have arisen.

(Signed) HW Renny Tailyour,
Managing Director
16th June, 1916.

NAVAL ARTIFICER SHOT AT AMIENS STREET

Soldier Charged with Murder

A General Courtmartial assembled at Richmond Barracks, on Wednesday, 14th June, for the trial of Henry Joseph Wyatt, a private in the 6th Royal Irish Lancers, attached to the 6th Reserve Regiment of Cavalry, on a charge of having murdered Robert Glaister, an engine-room artificer, in Dublin, on the 28th April. He was also charged with having attempted to murder Wm Francis Gray, hotel proprietor, at the same time and place, and in a second count with having caused him grievous bodily harm. The accused pleaded not guilty, and was defended by Second Lieut. JP Coghlan, Barrister-at-Law.

Major EG Kimber, DSO, conducted the case for the prosecution.

Major-General Lord Cheylesmore, KCVO, presided over a Court of twelve officers.

Lieut. Norris Goddard, RNR, attended on behalf of the Naval authorities.

Wm Francis Gray, proprietor of the Northern Hotel, Amiens street, stated that about 6.30 pm on Friday, April 28th, he was seated along with some guests at his hotel on a seat outside the door. The accused was on sentry in the immediate vicinity. Mr Glaister proposed to him (witness) that they should stroll down the street, everything being at the time very quiet. They had not proceeded many paces when the accused challenged them to halt, which they did. He put his rifle against Glaister's chest and fired. Witness thought the man was joking, and Glaister pushed the weapon aside, with the result that the charge went through Glaister's arm. He fell on his knee, but soon recovered himself, and witness and the wounded man walked back to the hotel. They were going up the steps when the sentry fired again, but did not hit either of them. They were closing the door when the accused again put his rifle up to Glaister's chest and shot him dead. He also pointed the weapon at him (witness), and probably would have shot him too, were it not that a waitress turned the weapon off. The accused entered the hotel, and ordered everyone in the house to go upstairs. Mrs Gray took her children, and as she was proceeding up the stairs the accused fired at her. When he had done this the accused said: 'These officers are great fellows: but I can show you what a private can do. I would do the same to General Friend.' The accused was excited, and appeared to have had some drink. The accused fired five shots altogether—two in the street, one that killed Glaister, one at witness and one at Mrs Gray.

Private Smith, 12th Lancers, stated that he was on duty about sixty yards from the Northern Hotel, and saw the accused fire a shot at a naval officer who was standing on the steps of the hotel door. He asked the accused what the matter was, and he replied that he had challenged the man, and that he had refused to answer; that he (accused) had first fired over the man's head, and then fired at him. He went into the hotel and saw the naval officer lying on the floor.

In reply to Lieut. Coghlan, the witness said the orders he had received when going on duty was that all doors and windows were to be kept closed, and that nobody was to be allowed on the streets except those who had passes from the Castle. He entered the hotel with the accused, but he saw nobody in the hotel but the naval officer. The accused did not fire in the hotel.

The President: In your previous statement, which you signed, you said you saw the accused fire one round at a woman on the way upstairs in the hotel? No, sir, I did not say that. I was told that he fired at a woman.

Excited but Sober

The President: Your previous statement is: 'The accused appeared very excited, but he did not appear to be drunk. He fired one round at a woman running upstairs. She had two children with her at the time.' Now you say that is all incorrect? Yes, sir.

Lance-Corporal Smedley said he was one of the picket in Amiens street. The accused was in a very excited condition, but quite sober. He said that the naval officer defied him. He did not say that in his original statement, because he was confused.

Mrs Elizabeth Lynch, whose residence is next to the hotel, said she saw an altercation going on between the sentry and the naval officer, and she saw the sentry fire at the man.

What happened then? The sentry stood behind the naval officer and struck him on the wrist, and said, 'One, two, three,' and a second shot was fired.

Did the accused fire into the hotel? Yes.

Captain Clarke, RAMC, said he had seen the naval officer, and heard him challenged by the sentry. Almost immediately he heard a shot, and again a second shot. When witness looked back he saw the sentry on the steps of the hotel.

Was the man defying the sentry? Yes. He was disobeying orders. I saw no one else in the street.

In reply to the President, the witness said he had come out of the railway station; he made no inquiry as to what happened, and walked on not knowing whether the man had been shot or not.

Captain Gaffikin, RAMC, stated that he saw the dead body of Glaister at the hotel. Death was caused by a gun shot wound. The accused was at the hotel.

What condition was he in? He was very excited, and apparently labouring under emotion. He was sober. He did not think the shot was fired at close range as there was no mark on deceased's clothes. There had been three or four cases in the same area where the men had been drunk.

Capt. E Bryce Wilson, 5th Royal Irish Rifles, who was in command at Amiens street Station, said the accused was in his detachment. The accused was brought before him by Lance-Corporal Smedley, who charged him with having shot a naval man. Witness placed the man under arrest and had him brought before the senior officer.

The President: Were any orders given with regard to shooting? Yes. I am very particular about that. I sent word that there was to be no shooting, except at snipers in the day time, unless in very grave circumstances: and especially that there should be no shooting against unarmed citizens. The accused stated that he took the deceased for a postman.

Accused's Version

The accused was examined on oath. He stated that it was about 6.30 pm when he was standing about fifteen yards from the Northern Hotel. He saw seven or eight persons come out of the hotel, some ladies being among them He ordered them to get back, and all obeyed the order except the man in blue, whom he took at the time to be a railway official. He told the man several times to 'get back', and he refused, saying that he was a naval man. Witness told him that he had his orders. 'Damn your b— orders, you don't stop me,' replied the naval officer. Witness again challenged him and told him to 'get back,' and he still refused. He edged back a pace or two, but still defied witness. Witness fired over him, and the man went back slowly to the steps of the hotel. 'He then called me a dog,' said witness, and added, 'You don't frighten me. Fire away.' And he also said, 'If that is all you can do try another shot.' I then fired again, on the doorstep, continued witness, and I saw him disappear into the hall. He denied making the statement with regard to General Friend that Mr Gray said he made. In reply to questions, the witness said that he got a cup of tea from a house in Talbot street about four o'clock that day, and that some time after having taken it he felt a 'little strange.' Shots were fired by snipers on the roofs during the day.

The President: What were your orders about shooting? To let nobody past the post.

And about shooting? If people refused to obey orders? If they refused to obey orders, to fire on them.

Contradictory Statements

That is a distinct contradiction of what your officer and other witnesses have said. You admit firing three shots indiscriminately without aiming at anybody? Yes. I fired to frighten him. Did you consider it your duty to fire after having received the orders you had received? Yes; to fire if they refused to obey orders.

Who gave you those orders about firing? Lance-Corporal Smedley.

You never fired in the hotel? No.

After you fired the third shot did you hear any other shot fired? I cannot say that I did.

Private Mines, who was on duty in Talbot street at the time of this occurrence, stated that he saw nobody sitting outside the hotel.

In answer to Major Kimber, the witness said that he was with the accused all that day. The accused did not fire upon any sniper that day. Witness himself fired three times at snipers, but the accused did not fire at all.

Private McLeesh said the accused told him that he had challenged the naval man, and that he fired one or two shots, but that the fatal shot was fired afterwards.

Major Kimber: Are you sure he said that he fired at the naval officer? He simply stated that he fired at the naval officer.

Two other private soldiers and two constables having been examined, the evidence for the defence closed.

Sentence of Five Years' Penal Servitude

On Thursday, 22nd June, the result of the trial was announced in an official report issued from the Military Headquarters, as follows:

Private Henry Joseph Wyatt, 5th Royal Irish Lancers, was tried on the 13th and 14th instant. He was found guilty of the manslaughter of Robert Glaister, an engine room artificer, Royal Navy, and sentenced to penal servitude for five years, which was confirmed by the General Officer Commanding-in-Chief.

ATTEMPTED GUN RUNNING IN CO. KERRY

The Landing of Casement

A General Courtmartial at Richmond Barracks on Friday, 16th June, began the trial of Austin Stack, solicitor's clerk, residing at Tralee, and Cornelius Collins, clerk in the General Post Office, Dublin, residing at 500 North Circular road, Dublin. The charges against the accused were: 1. That, in or about the month of April, 1916, they conspired and agreed with certain other disloyal and disaffected persons to bring about a rebellion in Ireland, and to spread disaffection amongst the civil population of the country, such act being of such a nature as to be calculated to be prejudicial to the public safety and the defence of the realm, and being committed with the intention and for the purpose of assisting the enemy. 2. That, in or about the month of April, knowing, or having reasonable grounds for supposing, that certain persons, by name Monteith and Bailey, were then engaged, contrary to the regulations for the defence of the realm, in the importation of arms and ammunition into Ireland, without previous permit of the competent military or naval authority—which said arms and ammunition, as they (the accused) then well knew, or had reasonable grounds for supposing, were intended to be used in aid and in furtherance of the rebellion in Ireland—they did harbour the said persons, Monteith and Bailey, such act being calculated to be prejudicial to the public safety and the defence of the realm, and being committed with the intention and for the purpose of assisting the enemy.

Major-General Lord Cheylesmore, KCVO, presided, and Mr Kenneth Marshall was Judge Advocate.

Major EG Kimber, DSO, conducted the prosecution.

Mr EJ McElligott, KC, and Mr Arthur Clery (instructed by Mr John O'Connell, LLD, Tralee) appeared for the accused.

Case for the Prosecution

Major Kimber stated the case for the prosecution. Stack, he said, was a well known commander of the Irish Volunteers, and Collins was a clerk in the employment of His Majesty in the Dublin Post Office. The events which brought about the charge occurred immediately before the rebellion. They were charged with doing acts that were calculated to assist the enemy. They were in touch with people who came to this country, accompanied by German officers and German bluejackets, who were taken prisoners at Cork and interned. Counsel described the movements and sinking of the arms ship, and the landing and capture of Casement, and, continuing, said the next part of the story was picked up at Tralee, where early that morning two strangers entered a newspaper shop and asked to be directed to the local commander of the Irish Volunteers. One of them gave the name of Murray, but it afterwards turned out that his real name was Monteith. The other gave the name of Mulcahy, and he turned out to be Bailey, who was afterwards charged in London. Messages were sent out, and the result was that the two accused men arrived at the shop. Stack, Collins, and Monteith shut themselves up in the parlour, and Bailey remained in the kitchen, where all four had been first. The first man to leave was Stack, who went to engage a motor car. Then Bailey and Collins left, and Monteith remained in the house and had refreshments. Meanwhile, the Irish Volunteers had assembled, and he was taken to the hall of the Hibernians. At 11 o'clock that morning Stack, Bailey and Collins set out in a motor car for Ballyheigue.

Hue and Cry Raised

Returning to the events on the shore, the Prosecutor said that when the boat was found a hue and cry was raised. The police were sent out, and a sergeant and a constable found Casement in an old fort between Currahane and Ardfert. He had with him some sandwiches made of German sausage and black bread. Prosecutor's theory was that Stack and Collins had set out to search for Casement, and twisted and turned through the country, but they were met by the police everywhere and searched. They were driven to return to Tralee without finding Casement. At six o'clock that evening Head Constable Kearney arrested Collins in a publichouse in Tralee. Collins said that he had come to Tralee the night before on a holiday, and that he had been out for a motor drive with Stack and Mulcahy, who, he said, lived in Mountjoy street, Dublin. Collins, when searched, had a Browning revolver, 55 rounds of ammunition, £35, and an English-German dictionary in his possession. Stack came to the police station to see Collins, and he was there and then arrested. A number of documents were found at Stack's lodgings in Tralee. Among them was a letter from Liberty Hall, signed James Connolly, in which it was stated: 'It is not our purpose to disrupt, but rather to enforce and strengthen the true National movement, and in a town the size of Tralee there is no necessity for any other military body than the Volunteer Corps which has stood out so splendidly by the true Irish ideal—the corps that you command.' Attached to that letter was a piece of printed matter in these words: 'The humanising of war—you might as well talk of humanising hell! When a silly ass at The Hague got up and talked about the amenities of civilised warfare, and putting your prisoners' feet in hot water, and giving them gruel, my reply, I regret to say, was considered totally unfit for publication. As if war could be civilised! If I am in command when war breaks out, I shall issue as my orders: The essence of war is violence: moderation in war is imbecility: hit first, hit hard, and hit everywhere … if you rub it in both at home and abroad that you are ready for instant war with every unit of your strength in the first line, and intend to be first in, hit your enemy in the belly, and kick him when he is down, and boil your prisoners in oil (if you take any), and torture his women and children; then people will keep clear of you.'

Other documents consisted of maps showing parts of Tralee, telegraph and telephone wires—in order, no doubt, that they might be readily cut. He submitted to the Court that the plan found was one to assist the landing. Further, there was a code arrangement, and information as to food supplies and other matters.

The Evidence

Frank Goodwin, a pilot, residing at Scraggen Point, Tralee Bay, answering Major Kimber, told how he watched the strange boat in Tralee Bay. She was painted black, with a black funnel which had a white band on top of it. Two flags were painted on her sides—the Norwegian flag.

John McCarthy, farmer, Currahane; Mary Gorman, servant, Ardfert; and Sergeant Thos Hearn, RIC, stationed at Ardfert, repeated the evidence given by them at the trial of Casement.

Constable Wm Larke, RIC, stationed at Ardfert, corroborated the evidence of Sergeant Hearn as to the finding of articles on the Currahane Strand, and the taking of them to the police station.

Constable Bernard Reilly, stationed at Ardfert, also corroborated the sergeant's evidence as to the finding of Sir Roger Casement in McKenna's fort.

Maurice Moriarty, a chauffeur, in the employment of Mr Nolan, Tralee, stated that on the 21st April he drove Stack out along the road from Tralee. They met two men on the road, and Stack said he was to pick them up. The men, one of whom was Collins, got into the car: the other was Bailey.

Sergeant Daniel Crowley, RIC, deposed to having met the motor car at Banna Strand. He saw two men in the car, one of whom he had seen since at Bow street, London, where his name was given as Bailey.

Constable Neazer, Tralee, said Collins gave his correct name and address when asked. He said that he had been stopped by the police at several places, and that he intended to spend his Easter holidays in Tralee, but that he had changed his mind.

Signalman Waghorne, of HMS Bluebell, repeated the evidence that he gave in London as to the overhauling of the steamer Aud, which was sunk by her crew.

The Arrests

Head Constable John Kearney, Tralee, stated that he had known Stack for three years, and that he was the commandant of the Volunteers in Tralee. The witness said that he met Collins in Tralee on the night of April 21st. He said he had been for a motor drive to Ardfert, Ballyheigue, and Causeway with a man named Mulcahy, of Mountjoy street, Dublin, and Mr Stack. He said that he had met Mulcahy once or twice before. He also said that he had been stopped and searched several times during the day. Witness arrested him on a charge of conspiracy to land arms. He made no further statement. Witness searched him, and Collins handed him a revolver and sixty-one rounds of ammunition. He said he usually carried the weapon in Dublin because he was out late at night and early in the morning. The prisoner also had £35 in his possession. Among other things found on him was a soldier's English-German dictionary. At the police station Collins said that he wanted to see Stack, and Stack was sent for. When he came to the station witness arrested him. He asked witness if he was serious in arresting him. He searched him and found documents on him, and others at his lodgings. Among these was a map of Tralee, showing the post office, the railway station, the GPO store at the station, and other leading places.

A Form of Oath

Witness also found a paper on which was written a form of oath as follows: 'I swear in the presence of God that, if I become a member of the Irish Volunteers, I will do all in my power to assert the independence of Ireland, keep the secrets of the organisation, and obey the commands of my superior officers.' He also found a letter addressed to Stack from the Irish Volunteers in America, which contained the phrase: 'The news from Ireland that recruiting is a failure is very gratifying, and has given us renewed hope.' The letter was signed Patrick Griffin. There was also a letter from a person in British South Africa, in which occurred the statement: 'Now is the moment for Young Ireland to assert itself.' There was a bundle of letters, all directed to Stack, on matters relating to the Volunteers, from members of that body in Dublin, such as Bulmer Hobson and the late PH Pearse.

Cross-examined: You will agree that the newspaper cutting which Major Kimber read in his opening statement is a very brutal document? I should say so.

Did the prisoner tell you that it was an extract from 'The Review of Reviews' of February, 1910? No.

Or that the article in the 'Review' professed to give the very words as the sentiments of Admiral Lord Fisher? Yes; he said they were the words of Lord Fisher.

Did you confirm that as being cut out of the 'Review of Reviews' of February, 1910? No.

A copy of the magazine was handed to witness, and, at counsel's request, he read from an article giving a character sketch of Lord Fisher, the part quoted by Major Kimber in his opening statement.

John Dempsey, a diver in the employment of the Admiralty at Queenstown, repeated the evidence given by him at the Casement trial.

Mr SJ Harrison, first class clerk in the GPO, Dublin, said that Collins had been on the Post Office staff at a weekly salary of 47s. 6d., and that he was entitled to twenty-one days' leave in the year. He had his choice of two periods—from the 21st March to the 13th of April or from the 14th of April to the 11th of May. Collins chose the latter period, and he went away on his holiday.

Constable Daniel Coffey, of the Dublin Metropolitan Police, stated that he knew Collins for the past three years, and that he had seen him several times entering the house in Rutland square which was the head-quarters of the Gaelic League, and which was also used as the drill hall of the Irish Volunteers. He also saw him in company with several leaders of the Volunteers. He also saw him at a concert which was given for the benefit of the Irish Volunteers, when John MacNeill and other Sinn Fein leaders were present. He also knew Monteith, who was an instructor of the Irish Volunteers and marched through the streets with them. Monteith had been served with notice to leave Dublin, and he did leave, but he returned in August last, and remained for a few days. He had not seen him since.

Constable McKeown, DMP, said he had seen Collins at the shop of the man Clarke, a leader of the Sinn Feiners, who had recently been executed.

Statements by Stack and Collins

Stack handed in a written statement which was read by the President. In it he said that he had always been a believer in the right of Ireland to self-government. When the Irish Volunteers were formed with the object which their constitution states—namely to defend and maintain the rights and liberties of the threatened by a rising of the armed Volunteers of Ulster—he became an active Irish Volunteer. When compulsory service was proposed he was preparing to resist it by means similar to those which the Ulster Volunteers used against Home Rule. He continued an ardent worker in the Irish Volunteers up to the date of his arrest. As to Monteith and Bailey, these men may have come to Tralee from some part of Ireland, or from Timbuctoo, or from somewhere else, as far as he could see.

Collins's statement (also read by the President) was that he had been in the service of the Post Office since May, 1902. In April of this year he was spending his annual leave in Limerick and Kerry, Limerick being his native county. On April 20th he went to Tralee where had had been accustomed to go for a number of years to spend portion of his holidays and in visiting friends. He had no knowledge of any contemplated landing of arms on the Kerry coast then or at any other time. He had not been a member of any Volunteer force for upwards of eighteen months. As to his alleged connection with Monteith or Bailey he knew nothing of them, and they might have come to Tralee from Dublin or Cork, or any other part of Ireland for anything he knew to the contrary.

Accused's Good Character

Mr M Flavin, MP: Mr Thos O'Donnell, MP: Mr DJ Liston, solicitor, and the Rev. Father O'Quigly, OP, each gave Stack a very high character.

Mr Thomas Hurley, a member of the Limerick County Council, and Chairman of the District Council of Newcastle West, Co. Limerick, gave Collins a good character.

Mr Browne, who is in charge of the Accountant's Department at the GPO, said the accused Collins was a member of the staff, and was a steady man who did his business satisfactorily. Until March, 1915, there was no record against him. At that time it came to the notice of the Secretary that he was connect with the Irish Volunteers, and he was warned under threat of instant dismissal to sever his connection with that or any other political movement with which he might be connected. He was, witness thought, reminded of that warning once since March, 1915. Since then the Department had no information that he had not kept his promise to leave the Volunteers.

Sentence of Penal Servitude for Life

The result of the trial was announced in a report issued from the Military Headquarters on Thursday, 22nd June, as follows:

Austin Stack and Cornelius Collins were tried on the 15th and 16th instant. They were found guilty of complicity in the attempt to land arms and ammunition in Kerry, and of conspiring to bring about rebellion in Ireland. They were sentenced to penal servitude for life, which was confirmed by the General Officer Commanding-in-Chief.

THE REBELLION IN COUNTY CORK

SHOOTING OF HEAD CONSTABLE ROWE

A general courtmartial assembled on Wednesday, 14th June, at Richmond Barracks, and began the trial of David Kent on a charge of having, on the morning of May 2nd, at Coole Lower, near Fermoy, Co. Cork, wilfully murdered Head Constable Rowe, of the Royal Irish Constabulary, while that officer was engaged in effecting the arrest of Kent on a charge of treason. There was a second charge against the accused—namely, that he was aiding and abetting an armed rebellion against the King. Both charges were brought under the Defence of the Realm Act, 1914. The accused pleaded not guilty.

Major-General Lord Cheylesmore, KCVO, presided.

Mr Kenneth Marshall acted as Judge Advocate.

Major Kimber, DSO, (instructed by Mr Robertson, of the Chief Crown Solicitor's Office), conducted the case for the prosecution.

Mr Patrick Lynch, KC, and Mr JF Moriarty (instructed by Mr James J McCabe, Cork) appeared for the accused.

Major Kimber stated the facts of the case. Early in the morning of May 2nd, Head Constable Rowe and a party of police went to the house of the accused, and knocked at the door. A voice from an upper window asked, 'Who is there?' and the head constable replied, 'Police. Come down and open the door.' The voice inside the house said, 'We will never surrender. We will leave some of you dead.' One of the sergeants with the head constable advised him to take cover, for they would surely fire from the house. The head constable went to one side of the yard, where there was a gap in the wall, and the sergeant went in another direction. Almost immediately a shot was fired from the window in the direction where the head constable was standing. A shot was fired in reply by the police, and another shot came from the house, and in the direction of Sergeant Caldbeck. He moved aside, and the shot killed the head constable.

Police Sergeant Samuel Caldbeck gave evidence as to the occurrence. He said that he was one of the police party—four constables and two sergeants—who were with the head constable at the house of the Kents. Four sons—Thomas, William, Richard, and David—lived there with their mother. When the head constable knocked at the door about a quarter to four o'clock, and said the police were there, a voice from inside said, 'We will never surrender. We will leave some of you dead.' Then a shot was fired from the lobby window, which was open, and witness replied with another shot. He did not know what effect that shot had. Another shot was fired from the eastern side of the house, and witness was re-loading when he saw a gun thrust again through the open window, covering himself. A shot was fired, and in a moment a man at his side said that the head constable was killed. Witness fired again, and the firing was continued until about 4:50 when a cry came from the house. 'There is a man dying; send for a priest.' Witness said in reply that he would send for a priest if those inside threw out their arms and ammunition. About ten minutes afterwards they flung out two shot guns, but no ammunition. The military arrived about 6.40, and one of the brothers said from a window that he would surrender to the officer. They surrendered, and the four brothers and their mother came out of the house. He saw that David (the accused) was wounded. Thomas had since been tried, and was executed. Richard was preparing to run away. Witness called upon him to stand, but he did not do so. The military fired and wounded him, and he died. William had been tried, and was acquitted. The military searched the house, and found two rifles and 49 rounds of service ammunition, and seven rounds of cartridges for a shot gun. There were five rounds in the magazine of one rifle.

Police Constables King and Norris, RIC, gave evidence in corroboration of that given by the sergeant. The latter said that he found on the 13th January a revolver and 27 rounds of ammunition, 54 rounds of ball cartridges, and 409 sporting cartridges at the house of the Kents. There was a shot gun there which the police did not take. The accused belonged to the Irish Volunteers. He had never seen him in the Volunteer Uniform, but he had seen his brother Thomas so dressed.

Second Lieutenant Page Green, of the 14th Royal Fusiliers, and Second Lieutenant Chesney, of the 15th Royal Fusiliers, who were in charge of the party of military who arrived at the house of the Kents, gave evidence as to the surrender of the accused and his brothers.

Dr GH Purcell, RAMC, who accompanied the military, said the top of the head of the head constable had been blown off.

At the hearing of the case on Thursday, the accused handed in a written statement in which he said that he had not hand, act or part in the attack on the police. When he heard the noise in the house that morning he got out of bed and went downstairs and was shot from outside.

Brother's Evidence

William Kent, brother of the accused, said that he had been tried and acquitted. His mother, who was the owner of a farm of 200 acres, was close on ninety years of age. His brother Richard, as a result of an accident, had been for a while in a lunatic asylum. When he was awakened that morning by the peculiar noise he went out on the landing and met his brother Richard there with a shot gun in his hand. He asked him what he was doing with it, and the reply was that the police were outside. Any shooting that was done from the house was done by Richard. There were shots from the police all around the house. He heard his brother (accused) say that he was shot, and it was then that he shouted out for the police that his brother David was shot, that he believed he was dying, and asked him if he would send for a priest. It was then that he threw out the two guns—a rifle and a shot gun—that he found on the lobby. If he had known that there were any other arms in the house he would have surrendered them. The accused had no gun.

Cross-examined by Major Kimber: It is all the fault of your brother Richard? That is my belief.

Do you suggest that it was your brother Richard who fired all the guns? I have no doubt that he did.

You will agree with me that it was strange that there were four men in the house, and four weapons, and that all four had been used? It is rather strange.

District Inspector Lewis was called. He said that apart from this case the accused was a man of exceptionally good character.

The President said this concluded the proceedings in open Court.

Sentence of Five years' Penal Servitude

The result of the trial was communicated in a report issued from the Military Headquarters, on Thursday, 22nd June, as follows:

David Kent was tried on the 14th and 15th instant. He was found guilty of the murder of Head Constable Rowe, Fermoy, and of aiding and abetting in the recent rebellion, and was sentenced to death, with a strong recommendation to mercy on account of his previous good character. The General Officer Commanding-in-Chief confirmed this courtmartial, but commuted the sentence to one of five years' penal servitude.

Tullamore Prisoners Discharged

An official report issued on Thursday, 22nd June, from Military Headquarters in Dublin, stated:

The following prisoners from Tullamore, viz.: James O'Brennan, Frank Brennan, John Delaney, Joseph Morris, Thomas Duggan, Joseph Graham, Peter Bracken, Thomas Byrne, James Clarke, Henry McNally, Thomas Hogan, Joseph Rafter were tried by General Courtmartial on the 26th May. They were charged with the attempted murder of County Inspector Crane, District Inspector Fitzgerald, and Sergeant Ahearn while an attempt was being made by the police to enter the Sinn Fein Hall at Tullamore on 20th March, and disarm a number of men who were in possession of the hall, from which shots were being fired, and Sergeant Ahearn received a bullet wound which placed his life for several weeks in danger. The prisoners, after being brought before the local magistrates, were handed over to the military, and at their courtmartial which followed, Mr Healy, KC, who appeared for them, contended that they had been illegally transferred from the civil to the military authorities. The General Officer Commanding-in-Chief has not confirmed the proceedings, and has ordered their release from military custody.

SIR ROGER CASEMENT'S TRIAL AND EXECUTION
A Historic Case

Sir Roger Casement appeared on Monday, 15th May, at Bow street Police Court, London, to answer the charge of high treason preferred against him as a consequence of his conduct in Germany during the war, and his landing in Ireland a few days before the rebellion broke out. Seldom has a case attracted so much public attention as this, in which a British ex-Consul, after an amazing career in an enemy country, was called upon to stand his trial on one of the gravest charges to be heard in British courts. Casement was brought from the Tower of London in a taxi-cab, and to the surprise of almost everybody in court, on entering the dock, he was accompanied by a second prisoner, who proved to be an ex-soldier named Daniel Julian Bailey. Unkempt and unshaved, Bailey, a fair-haired, fresh-complexioned man, about thirty-five years of age, to judge by appearances, presented a marked contrast to his fellow-prisoner. Casement, swarthy, and with sunken eyes, his face wearing a set expression of brooding, was well groomed and distinguished-looking. Both men bowed to Sir John Dickinson on entering the court, and were allowed to be seated. Casement, thereafter, bent his tall figure, and supporting his head with his hand, and his elbow on his knee, followed the speech of the Attorney-General, in opening the prosecution, with a searching interest. Bailey, on the other hand, sat staring fixedly ahead of him throughout the hearing. Once only he smiled, when he recognised a witness who had met him when they were both prisoners of war in Germany.

The Charge

Both prisoners were called on to answer the following charge:

For that they did, between the 1st day of November, 1914, and on divers other occasions between that day and the 21st day of April, 1916, unlawfully, maliciously, and traitorously commit high treason without the Realm of England, in contempt of our Sovereign Lord the King and his laws, to the evil example of others in like case, contrary to the duty and allegiance of the said defendants.

The case for the Crown was in the hands of the Attorney-General (Sir FE Smith), Mr AH Bodkin, and Mr Travers Humphreys.

Defending the accused men were Mr Artemus Jones and Mr JH Morgan, instructed by Mr George Gavan Duffy.

Sir FE Smith's Statement

Sir Frederick E Smith began by outlining the career of Sir Robert Casement. Born on September 1st, 1864, Casement was in the service of the Niger Coast Protectorate in 1892, and became HM Consul in the Portuguese Province of Lorenzo Marques in June, 1895. In 1898 he was appointed Consul to the Portuguese possessions in West Africa, and during the South African War he was employed on special service in Cape Town, receiving at the conclusion of hostilities a British South African medal. Subsequently he served in the French Congo, and in June, 1905, he was made a CMG, and appointed Consul to the State of San Paulo. He was promoted Consul-General, and transferred to Rio Janeiro in 1908, and in 1911 he was knighted, receiving in the same year the Coronation medal. Alluding to Casement's investigation into the conditions of the rubber industry in South America between 1909 and 1912, Sir Frederick remarked that Casement's record showed a career of considerable public usefulness, and he had retired with a pension. Acknowledging the intimation that he was to be knighted, Casement, in June, 1911, wrote:

Thanks for Knighthood

Dear Sir Edward Grey, I find it very hard to choose words with which to make acknowledgment of the honour done me by the King. I am much moved at this proof of confidence and appreciation of my services on the Putumayo, conveyed to me by your letter, wherein you tell me the King has been graciously pleased, on your recommendation, to confer upon me the honour of Knighthood. I am, indeed, grateful to you for this signal assurance of your personal esteem and support. I am very deeply sensible of the honour done me by His Majesty, and would beg that my humble duty might be presented to His Majesty, and that you do me the honour to convey to him my deep appreciation of the honour he has been so graciously pleased to confer upon me.

Sir Frederick remarked that that letter showed what Casement's feelings then were towards the country he had served so long. He was then a man of mature years, being 47 years old, and he had had 19 years experience of Government work. A man of cultivated understanding, he had also a considerable knowledge of history. Casement drew his pension till September 30, 1914.

Turning to the case of Bailey, Sir Frederick said that this defendant had made a statement in which he said he was born in Dublin. He had joined the Royal Irish Rifles in 1904, and had served with his regiment in India. When the war broke out he was employed as a goods porter at Paddington, and was called up as a reservist. He sailed with the original Expeditionary Force to France. He shared the fortunes of the force during the early days of the campaign, and was taken prisoner by the Germans on September 4, 1914. Among the British soldiers taken prisoners were a considerable number of Irish soldiers. Between the Irish and other prisoners there was at first apparently no differentiation, but about December, 1914, Irish prisoners were removed from the different camps and collected together into a large camp at Limberg. At that time Casement was in Germany.

Terms for the Irish Brigade In Berlin

The part Casement was destined to play was that of a man who hoped to seduce from their allegiance to the King the Irish prisoners of war, who were collected for the purpose of listening to addresses and lectures from Casement. They were addressed collectively, and in some cases individually by Casement, who moved about the camp freely, with full approval of the Germans. This went on between 3rd January and 19th February, 1915. Casement introduced himself as Sir Roger Casement, the organiser of the Irish Volunteers. He stated that he was forming an Irish Brigade, and he invited all the Irish prisoners in the country to join him. He pointed out repeatedly, and with emphasis, that in his opinion everything was to be gained for Ireland Germany winning the war, and that now was the day for striking a blow for Ireland. He stated that those who joined the Irish Brigade would be sent to Berlin; they would become guests of the German Government, and in the event of Germany winning a sea battle he would land a brigade in Ireland and defend the country against the enemy, England. In the event of Germany losing the war either he or the Imperial German Government would give each man of the brigade a bonus of from £10 to £20 and a free passage to America.

ROGER DAVID CASEMENT.—Executed on 3rd August.

Hissed by Prisoners of War

The vast majority of the Irish prisoners treated the rhetoric and persuasions of Casement with contempt. He was received with hisses, and at least on one occasion booed out of camp. The Munster Fusiliers were particularly prominent in their loyalty and in their resentment to the treacherous proposals made to them. One man actually struck Casement, who was saved from further violence by the intervention of an escort of the Prussian Guard assigned to give him their protection. The Irish prisoners who refused to receive the proposals were punished by a reduction of their rations, which before this had not been in any way excessive. A man named Robinson who refused to join the Irish Brigade was transferred to another camp for punishment. The few men who were seduced from their allegiance were rewarded by being given a green uniform with a harp worked upon it, by being left at liberty, and by exceptionally liberal rations, both in quality and in quantity. Amongst the Irish prisoners at Limberg was the prisoner Bailey, who was wearing the green uniform and also side arms in the German fashion. Evidence would be given that Bailey joined the so-called Irish Brigade, and was promoted at once to the rank of sergeant by the Germans, who encouraged the formation of the brigade. The witnesses to these acts of high treason and treachery included a Royal Munster Fusilier, a lance-corporal of the Royal Irish Rifles, and several other soldiers. All of these men had been wounded, and had since been exchanged, and were at the disposal of the Crown as witnesses.

Photo by] [L. N. A.
DANIEL JULIAN BAILEY, who came over in the German submarine with Casement.

Bailey's Statement

Counsel then read the statement made by Bailey after his arrest of April 21st. He stated that he was born in Dublin. In 1904 he joined the Royal Irish

Rifles. He was a reservist at the outbreak of war, and, being called to his depot at Belfast, was immediately sent out with the Expeditionary Force. He was taken prisoner in September, 1914, and taken, with other Irishmen, to the camp at Limberg, where he was well treated for a time: 'I saw Sir Roger Casement about April, 1915 (the statement proceeded). He spoke to me about joining the Irish Brigade solely for the purpose of fighting for Irish freedom, and I joined so that I could get out of the country, and was made sergeant straight away.' Bailey went on to say that he was sent to Berlin at the end of March, 1916, and, with a Mr Monteith, went to a school to get instruction in the use of explosives. After three hours he went to another place in Berlin for further instruction.

To Ireland in a Submarine

On the 11th he and Mr Monteith and Sir Roger Casement were driven to the War Office. There he was given a railway ticket, and the three of them went to Wilhelmshaven. There they were put on a submarine. Owing to a slight accident they had to put in at Heligoland. They left there on the 13th of April and came round by the Shetlands. 'I then knew (the statement continued) where I was going, but I had no instructions. I knew when I got near to Tralee that it was in connection with the Volunteer movement. The submarine steered in as close as it could, and then lowered a collapsible boat and put us off. We took revolvers, ammunition, etc., and I was ordered to bury them. The boat put off at 1 a.m. in the surf. It was overturned, and we had to wade ashore. I went back two or three times to fetch the stuff. We buried the arms, etc., not far from where we landed. We left our coats there, and I was taken by Monteith to Tralee. People were going to Mass when we got there.' At Tralee (Bailey's statement continued) they got something to eat, and then went to a shop. Four men came in separately, and Monteith conversed with them. Afterwards they got into a motor car, and one of the men asked where the arms were. They travelled about looking for the place, and a tyre was punctured. Before they could get out of the car the police came up, and afterwards they drove off in an opposite direction. He was afterwards directed to a castle, and remained there until he was arrested.

Arms Ship Disguised

When on the submarine (the statement went on) I overheard conversation from time to time about a small Wilson liner which was being piloted into Tralee. It had on board 20,000 rifles and a million rounds of ammunition. It was disguised as a timber ship, and there were also ten machine guns and bombs and fire bombs, and it was said that Dublin Castle was to be raided. From that statement, counsel resumed, it appeared that the three passsengers, Casement, Monteith, and Bailey, were put into a small boat and landed on the sands near Ardfert, probably about 2 o'clock on the morning of Good Friday, April 21. On the Thursday night at 9.50 a labourer saw a light flashing about half a mile out at sea, and it was, probably, not unconnected with what happened afterwards—probably those on board were taking part in a common adventure with the prisoners.

The Raider Challenged

The next phase of the case dealt with by counsel was the challenging of the accompanying ship by the sloop Bluebell, which on April 21 was patrolling in the neighbourhood of Tralee. Sighting a suspicious ship, flying the Norwegian ensign, and with four Norwegian ensigns painted fore and aft on the vessel, the captain of the Bluebell hoisted a signal demanding the vessel's name and destination. The vessel replied that she was the Aud, of Bergen. The captain of the Bluebell ordered her to follow him into harbour. The Aud replied in broken English: 'Where are you taking me to?' The Bluebell went ahead, but the Aud remained without moving. A round was accordingly fired across her bows, and she then signalled: ''What am I to do?' She was told to follow, and did so without further trouble until the next morning, when the Aud hoisted a signal: 'Where am I to enter?' On arriving in the harbour she was told to await orders, and continue to follow the Bluebell. Near the Daunt Rock lightship the Bluebell headed for harbour, but the Aud stopped. The Bluebell then went back about a cable's length, and saw a small cloud of white smoke issuing from the after-hold. At the same time two German naval Ensigns were flown from the mast, and two boats were launched, one from either side. The Bluebell went round across the bows, and the occupants of the two boats, coming towards her, hoisted a flag of truce, and put up their hands. They were taken prisoners on the Bluebell. The Aud sank almost imediately afterwards. If, said counsel, one might connect all these matters, it was established that Casmeent was attempting to seduce Irish soldiers from their allegiance, with the object of forming a brigade to take part in an insurrection in Ireland. The association of the events described appeared to be obvious. About 4 o'clock in the morning there were found buried three Mauser pistols, a flash lamp, a large flag, two lifebelts, maps and other articles. Counsel here 'produced' a large green Irish flag, and the prisoners joined in the interested scrutiny of the exhibit.

The Arrest of Sir Roger Casement

Describing Sir Roger Casement's arrest, Sir Frederick said he was found in hiding at McKenna's Fort. 'It is called a fort, but I am informed it is not so much an edifice as an excavation.' Asked by the police who he was, Casement replied: 'Richard Morton, of Denham, Bucks.,' and described himself as an author. He said he arrived from Dublin on 19th April, and slept at a farmhouse close by, and that he intended to go to Tralee. While being taken to Ardfert Barracks he was seen by a farmer named

Collins to drop a paper from his coat. This was found to be a code.

This code consisted of such contemplated messages as the following: 'Wait further instructions,' 'Wait further opportunity,' 'Send agent at once,' 'Proposal accepted,' 'Proposal received,' 'Please answer by cablegram,' 'Have decided to stay,' 'Communication again possible,' 'Railway communications have been stopped,' 'Further ammunition is needed,' 'How many rifles will you send us?' 'Will send plans about landing,' 'Preparations are made about —' 'Send another ship to —' 'Cannons with plenty of ammunition are needed,' 'Send more explosives,' 'Send a vessel, if possible.' Such, commented counsel, were the contemplated communications required to develop the situation in Ireland. Casement was charged at Ardfert Barracks with landing arms and ammunition. He asked for legal assistance. On April 22nd he was brought to England, and to an inspector of the Metropolitan Police he said he was Sir Roger Casement.

The Aud's Cargo

Divers sent down to the Aud had discovered on board Russian rifles of a pattern of the year 1905. Concluding his speech, the Attorney-General described the arrest of Bailey, who, he said, was stopped by the police near where the arms were found. He was in a motor car with some other men and stated that he came from Mountjoy street, Dublin. They were arrested between Causeway and Tralee, on the evening of April 22nd.

Police Inspector Parker's Evidence

The first witness was Inspector Parker, of Scotland Yard, who stated that he went to the Tower at 7 o'clock that morning, and read the warrant over to Casement, who was conveyed to Bow street. Bailey was also brought that morning from Wandsworth Prison. When the two prisoners were charged together at Bow street, Casement, pointing to Bailey, said: 'Well, that man is innocent. I think the indictment is wrongly drawn against him. Is it within my power to pay for the defence of this man? I wish him to be in every way as well defended as myself, and if he has no means to undertake his defence I am prepared to pay for him.'

Ex-War Prisoner's Stories

John Robinson, Ross street, Belfast, formerly a corporal in the RAMC, said that on August 24th, 1914, he was taken prisoner in France, and interned at a prisoners' war camp at Sanneelageer, and after a few months there the Irish soldiers there received an order that they were to be put together, and they were treated a little, but not much, better. They were given lighter work than the English prisoners, and were put in huts by themselves. In December, 1914, some three Irish soldiers were moved to Limberg, where the accommodation was good, but the food bad. Casement visited the Irish soldiers, and 'spouted' to them. He said that now was the time to fight for Ireland. He wanted the Irish prisoners there to form an Irish Brigade, and said that Germany was going to free Ireland. Sometimes he got a very poor reception. The men tried to hiss him out of the camp, and one fellow shoved him. When the man pushed Casement, witness added, the German guard got him away. Casement visited the camp four times, about a week between each visit. Casement promised them £10 each if they joined, and if Germany lost the war they would be sent to America. Witness added that copies of a paper, the *Gaelic American*, and a book, 'The Crime Against Ireland,' were circulated in the camp. Forms were handed to them.

The Mode of Temptation

One of the questions asked was: 'Are you willing to fight for your own country, with a view of securing the national freedom of Ireland? With the moral and material assistance of the German Government an Irish Brigade is being formed.'

Counsel produced a copy of this form, also a pamphlet circulated among the Irish prisoners. Quoting from it, he read:

'Irishmen, here is a chance for you to fight for Ireland. You have fought for England, your country's hereditary enemy. You have fought for Belgium, though it was no more to you than the Fiji Islands. Are you willing to fight for your own country, with a view of securing the national freedom of Ireland? The object of the Irish Brigade shall be to fight solely the cause of Ireland and in no circumstances shall it be directed to the interests of Germany.'

The pamphlet went on to declare that the Brigade would fight under the Irish flag alone, with a distinctive Irish uniform, and Irish officers. At the end of the war the German Government undertook to send those who desired it to America, with the necessary means of landing. It was further stated that the Irish in America were raising money for the Brigade. If interested, men were to see their company commanders. It concluded:

'Remember Bachelor's Walk. God Save Ireland.'

Signing the Form

Witness, proceeding, said that out of over a thousand men he thought between fifty and sixty signed the form. He never joined the Brigade. Witness said he recognised the prisoner Bailey, and also remembered a Corporal Quinless at Limberg. Both joined the Irish Brigade. Witness added, in conclusion, that he was exchanged from the 8th of October last year, and returned to this country.

Private John Crone

Private John Crone, of 2 Camel's place, John street, Cork, formerly in the 2nd Battalion Royal Munster Fusiliers, gave somewhat similar evidence. He was wounded on August 22, he said, taken prisoner, and on December 22nd was conveyed with 21 other

Irish prisoners to Limberg, where he saw Bailey. Casement occasionally visited the camp. Once he heard him say—'Why do you stay here in hunger and misery, when you might be enjoying yourselves by joining the Irish Brigade, and becoming guests of the German Government?'

William Egan

William Egan, 14 Barrow street, Dublin, another ex-prisoner, said he knew Bailey at St Vincent de Paul School, Glasnevin, Dublin, and later he was in Bailey's regiment. He was wounded and captured at Neuve Chapelle in October, and he again met Bailey at Limberg. On one of the forms given to the Irish prisoners was the question—'In what state were the people of Ireland when the war broke out?' Witness identified Bailey and Quinless as two prisoners who joined the Irish Brigade. Bailey joined with soldiers named Greer and Scanlan. There were 2,500 Irishmen in the camp, and only 52 joined the Brigade.

Daniel O'Brien

Daniel O'Brien, formerly in the Leinster Regiment, said he was taken from Doeberitz Camp with a hundred other Irish prisoners to Limberg. Witness corroborated the evidence as to Casement's remarks to the Irish prisoners. Witness said that Bailey drew a map of Ireland, which was shown round the camp. Recruiting for the Irish Brigade continued till February, and was carried on by a man called Father Nicholson, a supposed American.

Corporal Michael O'Connor

Corporal Michael O'Connor, a one-armed man, who appeared in khaki, and wore South African medals, said that his home was in Wexford. At Limberg, he said Casement told them that England was nearly beaten. On January 3rd Casement said to the men booing him—'You are followers of the recruiting officer for the British Army, Johnnie Redmond.' On that occasion a Coldstream Guard Colour-Sergeant called Casement a traitor, and was sent to a punishment camp. While in hospital witness was given a book entitled 'The King, the Kaiser, and Ireland.'

James Wilson

James Wilson, formerly a private in the Royal Dublin Fusiliers, living at 560 North Circular road, Dublin, another prisoner from Limberg, spoke to a man whom, owing to his impaired eyesight he could not identify, urging the Irishmen in the camp not to prolong their misery, but to better themselves by joining the Irish Brigade. He spoke of the blood of their forefathers flowing in their veins, and urged them not to take any notice of 'the uncrowned king, John Redmond.' Some of the men called the man a renegade, and one told him he was 'up the pole.' (Laughter.)

John McCarthy

When the case was resumed on Tuesday, 16th May, John McCarthy, a farmer living near the Banna Strand, examined by Mr Bodkin, said that on the morning of Good Friday, about 4 o'clock, he noticed a boat being washed in by the tide, with four oars floating around. He waded in and took hold of the boat, and found a dagger (produced). In the sands, covered up, he also found a tin box (box produced) about 15 inches square and a foot deep. On the sands he also saw footmarks, apparently of three or four persons. The footprints led to his farm. He and his man, Pat Driscoll, pulled the boat out of the water. As they were coming back they saw McCarthy's daughter, aged seven, playing with three revolvers. The revolvers, formidable weapons of the Mauser pattern, were produced. Witness said he also found a small bag (produced along with a brown and a black bag found by the police).

A Light At Sea

Michael Hussey, a typical Irish labourer, whose brogue was so pronounced that it was only with difficulty he was understood, answering Mr Travers Humphreys, said that the night before Good Friday he was 'out visiting for a bit of the night,' and about half past nine he saw a dark red light at sea. He saw it for about two seconds, or perhaps a little longer. He went down to the edge of the sea, but saw no one there. The light had been seen about half a mile out from low water mark. Next morning he saw the boat on the beach opposite where the light had been at sea.

Mary Gorman

Next there stepped into the witness box a young Irish servant named Mary Gorman, and her accent completely puzzled counsel. Mr Bodkin had to get her address 'Rathoneen.' She described how at half-past four on Good Friday morning, three men passed close to her, going in the direction of Ardfert. One was a tall man, another nearly as tall and the third smaller. The tall man carried a coat, a green knapsack across his shoulders, and a walking stick. The two others had overcoats. They were all walking quickly. She was able to see the tall man's face, and she identified him as Sir Roger Casement. She did not recognise Bailey.

Sergeant Hearn. Royal Irish Constabulary

Sergeant Thomas J Hearn, of the RIC, told how he received the various articles found in the sand by M'Carthy, in whose house the bags were opened. In one of the bags witness found five hundred rounds of ammunition. The pistols found were loaded. Subsequently the witness with another officer found a man in the old rath or fort. It was the prisoner. Witness said he asked Casement what he was doing there, and he replied, 'By what authority do you ask me the question?' Witness replied that he could ask any question he chose, and added that he should arrest him under the Defence of the Realm regulations. He then asked Sir Roger Casement his name, and the prisoner replied Richard Norton, of Denham, Bucks. Sir Roger Casement added that he had written a book and told the witness the name of it. Further answering the witness, Sir Roger Casement said he was going to Dublin, but had no passport papers. He got to the fort at eight o'clock that morning; his clothes were wet; he intended going on to Tralee. At Ardfert Barracks Sir Roger Casement, when charged with landing arms, said, 'Can I see your order?' Among the articles found on him was some kind of sausage wrapped in paper, also two documents, one in a foreign language, and evidently an itinerary of Sir Roger Casement's movements in Germany.

Constable Reilly

Constable Reilly, of the Royal Irish Constabulary, deposed that on Good Friday morning he saw a man at M'Kenna's fort. His head and shoulders appeared over the side of the fort. Witness went towards the man, who was Sir Roger Casement, 'covered' him, and called on him not to move. Sir Roger Casement replied, 'This is a nice way to greet an English traveller.' He also said, 'I am not armed. I will do you no harm.' The Sergeant then came up. In the inside pocket of Sir Roger Casement's waistcoat, witness added, was a slip of white paper. 'I read something on it,' said witness, 'and said, "that isn't Irish".' (Laughter) Casement replied, 'I don't know, I have never seen that before.' Witness made a further search at the fort and found three overcoats. He noticed Casement was wearing a green woollen muffler, the ends of which were wet and sandy. There was also sand in his boots.

A Twelve-Year-Old Witness

Martin Collins, the twelve-year-old son of an Ardfert farmer, was the next witness. A bright faced, intelligent boy, he gave his evidence with great self possession. He told how he was driving a pony and cart past McKenna's fort on the way to a neighbouring farmer's, when he saw Sergeant Hearn and Constable Reilly with a stranger, whom he recognised now as Sir Roger Casement. The stranger put his hands behind his back, rolled up a piece of paper behind him, and dropped it. Witness said he drove the man as far as the farm, where Mary Gorman identified him as one of the men she had seen in the morning. On his way home after dinner witness said he stopped at the fort, and asked a boy to pick up the paper Sir Roger Casement had dropped. Witness opened it and found it was torn in two. He read some of it, and when he got back to Ardfert handed it over to Constable Reilly.

Constable Larke

Constable Robert William Larke, RIC, answering Mr Bodkin, said that on Good Friday morning he went to the sands at Curraghane, where he discovered buried in the sands near where the revolvers were picked up a black bag about two hundred yards from McCarthy's house.

Casement's Journey through Dublin

Sergeant Bracken, of the Military Foot Police, stationed at the Ship street Barracks, Dublin, deposed that on 22nd April he went to Arbour Hill Military Detention Barracks with an escort, and there received from the sergeant-major in charge the prisoner Casement. He brought him via Holyhead to Bow street Police Station, where he handed over Casement to the Metropolitan Police.

Sergeant James Butler, of the RIC, who took Casement from Tralee to Dublin, said that the train stopped at Killarney Station, and while there the prisoner asked permission to get a paper. Witness granted the request. At the station a head constable came to the carriage door and said to witness, 'Did you hear what happened to the two lads at Puck?' Witness answered, 'No,' and the head constable went on, 'They ran into the tide, and were drowned.' After leaving the station the prisoner started to cry, and remained crying for some time. He then turned round to the witness and said, 'Where is Puck; is it near Castlemaine Bay?' Witness answered 'Yes.' Sir Roger Casement then said, 'I am very sorry for these two men. It was on my account they were there. They were two good Irishmen.' On arrival at Mallow witness asked if he had been there before, and he answered, 'Yes, I know Blackwater well.'

Sergeant-Major Whittaker, Military Provost's Staff Corps, stationed at Arbour Hill Barracks, Dublin, spoke to receiving three bags and a parcel from Sergeant Butler, who also handed over the prisoner Casement. The parcel contained three great coats.

Inspector Sandycock

Inspector Joseph Sandycock, CID, Scotland Yard, stated that at Euston Station on the morning of April 25 he received into custody Sir Roger Casement from Sergeant Bracken. He conveyed him to New Scotland Yard, where prisoner said, 'I am Sir Roger Casement, and the only person to whom I have disclosed my identity is a priest at Tralee, in Ireland.' I then cautioned him, and later in the day he was conveyed to Brixton Prison, and afterwards to the Tower of London.

Motor Car's Movements

Maurice Moriarty, motor car driver, stated that shortly before 11 o'clock on Good Friday morning he got his car ready for a Mr Stack, a solicitor's clerk in Tralee. They started off, and a little way out stopped to pick up two men named Collins and Mulcahy. He identified the latter as the prisoner Bailey. They drove on through Ardfert to the Banna Strand, where a tyre burst. Sergeant Crowley came up and questioned them, and they then went on to Ballyheigue. On the way Mr Stack stopped to speak to someone at a house, and Sergeant Crowley again rode up on a bicycle from Ballyheigue. They went on to the Causeway, where they were searched by the police. They returned by another route to Tralee. Witness did not notice whether Bailey was in the car or not when they got back. He had to stop on the road to fix the footboard of the car, and Bailey got out then. In Tralee they stopped at the house of a Miss Slattery, in Rock street, and Stack and Collins went inside.

Sergeant Crowley

Sergeant Daniel Crowley, of the RIC, said he saw the car driven by Moriarty, and questioned the occupants. One of them, whom he recognised as Bailey, gave his name as David Mulcahy, of 44 Mountjoy street, Dublin. Another man gave the name of Stack, of Rock street, Tralee, and the third man described himself as Collins, accountant, General Post Office, Dublin.

Constable Cotter

Constable George Cotter, RIC, said that on the 22nd of April he obtained some information about a man, and in consequence searched for him in the neighbourhood of Killahan, with another constable. He saw a man who was a stranger to him, and, continued witness, I asked him: 'What are you doing about here?' He answered: 'Nothing: I am just knocking around.' I asked him where he slept the previous night, and he refused to tell me. Then I asked him where he intended to sleep that night, and he refused to tell me. I asked him: 'Where are your chums?' and he replied that he did not know. I asked him where he came from, and he said: 'From Dublin, on Thursday, on by motor car.' I asked him the number the car bore, and he said he did not know. I asked him upon other points, and he refused to answer my questions. I then arrested him under the Defence of the Realm Regulations. At the police barracks he searched the prisoner, and found ten sovereigns tied up in a handkerchief, 31s in silver, and some copper, as well as a notebook, and a piece of paper on which was written, 'The Castle, near Tralee, is quite a quaint old structure of stone.' The man arrested was the prisoner, Bailey? Yes, sir.

Detective Inspector O'Connell

Detective Inspector Daniel O'Connell, New Scotland Yard, deposed that on April 28th he went over to Dublin and received the prisoner Bailey into custody at the Depot of the RIC in Phoenix park.

Detective Inspector Parker

Detective Inspector Parker, recalled, gave further detailed evidence as to several of the exhibits. A leather satchel bag contained some pistol ammunition, a flash lamp, and other articles enumerated in a list attached to the bag. In a black bag were certain maps and portions of maps, a green flag with a Latin motto, forty rounds of ammunition, a flash lamp, notebook, etc., explaining some of the maps. Witness said that there were two maps of Ireland, made up into fourteen sections, each section being numbered and bearing the name of a district. On number 14 was a list of the different sections.

The Arms Ship

Sidney Ray Waghorn, leading signalman on HMS Bluebell, stated that on Good Friday he was on board that ship on the south-east coast of Ireland. The ship was on patrol duty. About six o'clock in the evening another ship was sighted flying the Norwegian colours, and having the Norwegian colours painted on her sides.

Witness said he was ordered to signal and ask the name and destination of the ship. She signalled back that her name was Aud, and she was bound from Bergen to Genoa. She was told to follow the Bluebell, which was then, roughly speaking, over 130 miles from Queenstown. They were about 90 miles from land. The ship did not follow as she was ordered until a shot was fired. Near the entrance to Queenstown Harbour the Aud stopped her engines, when the Bluebell was about a cable's length away. When witness looked back he saw smoke issuing from the after-hold of the Aud on the starboard side. At the same time two German ensigns were flown at the masthead. Two boats were lowered, and rowed towards the Bluebell. The latter fired a round, and the boats showed two flags of truce, and the occupants put their hands up. They were taken on board as prisoners. They wore German bluejackets, and wore German uniforms. There were twenty-three of them, and they were placed under an armed guard on board the Bluebell. The Aud sank in ten minutes, one and a quarter miles south-east of the Daunt Lightship.

Admiralty Diver's Account

John Dempsey, of Ringaskiddy, Co. Cork, an Admiralty diver, stated that on May 10th he received instructions to go from Queenstown to the wreck of the ship, whose position was marked by a buoy. The ship had sunk in from 17½ to 20 fathoms of water. He inspected the wreck, and found that the vessel had the Norwegian flag painted on her side. There was a hole in the side of the ship 12 to 14 feet in diameter, and abreast of the hole, on the bed of the sea, were rifles and ammunition. He brought up on of the rifles.

The rifle, with a rusty barrel, was produced in court, together with a number of broken, sea-stained rifle butts, a bayonet case, and a cartridge, which witness had also found on the wreck.

How Bailey Behaved

At the sitting of the Court on Wednesday, 17th May, Constable George Carter, RIC, was recalled, and in cross-examination by Mr Artemus Jones, said that when he asked Bailey for his name at Abbeyderney Police Station he at first refused to give it. He was taken to the police station about 6 p.m. on the Saturday, and remained there all day on Sunday. Constables were walking about the room in which he was kept, and he saw Bailey talking to them and heard him say: 'I have some important information to give which will give you fellows something to do.'

Russian Officer's Evidence

Colonel N Belaeiw, an officer in the Russian Army, was then called by Mr Humphreys to describe the make of some of the munition exhibits. He was in mufti, and said he was a member of the Russian Supply Committee. Shown a rifle, much the worse for wear and asked if it was a Russian weapon, the witness, after examining it carefully, said 'Yes.' It had been manufactured at the Russian Imperial Toula Rifle Works in 1905. Each rifle manufactured by the Russian Imperial Works, he explained, bore a certain number, and the number of this special rifle was 80908.

Lieutenant-Colonel Gordon

Lieutenant-Colonel Philip James Gordon, attached to the Directorate of Military Intelligence at the War Office, was called to speak to certain portions of maps which he was given to examine. In his opinion, these were not printed in the United Kingdom. There were some roads on one map which are not used on the ordnance survey map. There were special patches of colour shown on one map in the neighbourhood of garrisons in Ireland, which are not shown on the English map.

Bailey's Military Record

Second Lieutenant James Leslie Brierley, Wilts Regiment, attached to the Adjutant-General's Staff at the War Office, said Daniel Bailey enlisted on April 7, 1904, at Dublin. He served eight years and 357 days, of which five years and 328 days were served abroad. He was transferred to the Army Reserve at Gosport on March 29th, 1913, and was mobilised at Belfast on August 5th, 1914, being posted to the 2nd Battalion of his own regiment. He is shown on the official papers as a prisoner of war in Belgium, and they also showed a good record.

Bailey's Statement To Sergeant Bestick

Sergeant Bestick, of the Royal Irish Constabulary, said that a man whom he knew as David Mulcahy (who turned out to be Bailey) was detained at Abbeyderney Barracks on April 23rd, and witness made inquiries of him. After he had done so, witness went into his own private room, and the man asked to see him privately. He said: 'I will tell you some of the truth. I came over from America under false colours. I joined a society there. I do not want any person to know who I am.' Witness told the man he would be detained, and his photograph would be taken, and inquiries made. After an interval of about a quarter of an hour the man again asked to see witness, and added: 'Can I get free if I tell the truth?' Witness said he could not guarantee that he would get free, but he guaranteed he would get protection. The man said he was afraid to make a statement, but he did not say of whom he was afraid. Witness told him the superior officer would be there soon, and the man said, 'Send for him quickly. Tomorrow may be too late, as I have important information.' Inspector Brittain arrived about two hours later, and saw the prisoner Bailey. In reply to his question the inspector said he would guarantee protection, but not that the man would go free. The man then gave the inspector the name of a boat which was to reach Ireland the following morning.

Cross-examined by Mr Artemus Jones, witness said that he had treated the man as Mulcahy, and did not press him for his real name.

Mr Jones: Did you say to him: 'If you don't say who you are we will publish your photograph and find out?' No.

Witness said he did not know until about a week later that the man who was captured was Sir Roger Casement.

Mr Jones: Did you in talking to this man, use these words: 'We have got the other fellow. We know he is Sir Roger Casement, and we know all about it?' No.

'You had best make a statement to save yourself?' No.

I suggest that he asked to be allowed to see the military authorities? No.

Mr Jones: I put it to you, sergeant, that at that time you were pressing him to make a statement but he refused? No.

There is no doubt he was in a very anxious frame of mind at that time? Yes.

In great trouble? He seemed to be.

And you agree with me he was very anxious to save his own skin? Well; I can't say that. He asked me if I could get him free. I told him I could not give him a guarantee I could get him free.

Counsel: Let me give his version. You said to him: 'I can't guarantee you will get no punishment, but I can assure you it will be all right?' No; I did not say that.

Bailey here wrote a note and passed it to his counsel, who continued: 'Before you telephoned to the inspector, did he tell you he would make a statement if you would give him a guarantee?'

Witness: No.

Counsel: The first thing he asked the Inspector when he arrived was about the guarantee? Yes: all the Inspector said was that he would guarantee him protection.

District Inspector Brittain

District Inspector Brittain, RIC, said that at half-past one on April 23rd, he received a message from Sergeant Bestick, and arrived at Abbeydorney about four o'clock. In company with Sergeant Bestick he saw Bailey. I told him who I was, witness continued, and said, 'I understand you sent for me, and wish to give me some information. You understand that what you tell me is quite voluntary.' I believed him at the time to be David Mulcahy. He asked me if I would guarantee him protection. I told him that of course I would. He asked me then if I would guarantee him against punishment. I told him it was not in my power to do that. He told me that his information was of the utmost importance, would not wait a minute. 'In fact,' he said, 'it may be too late already.' He again asked me to guarantee him

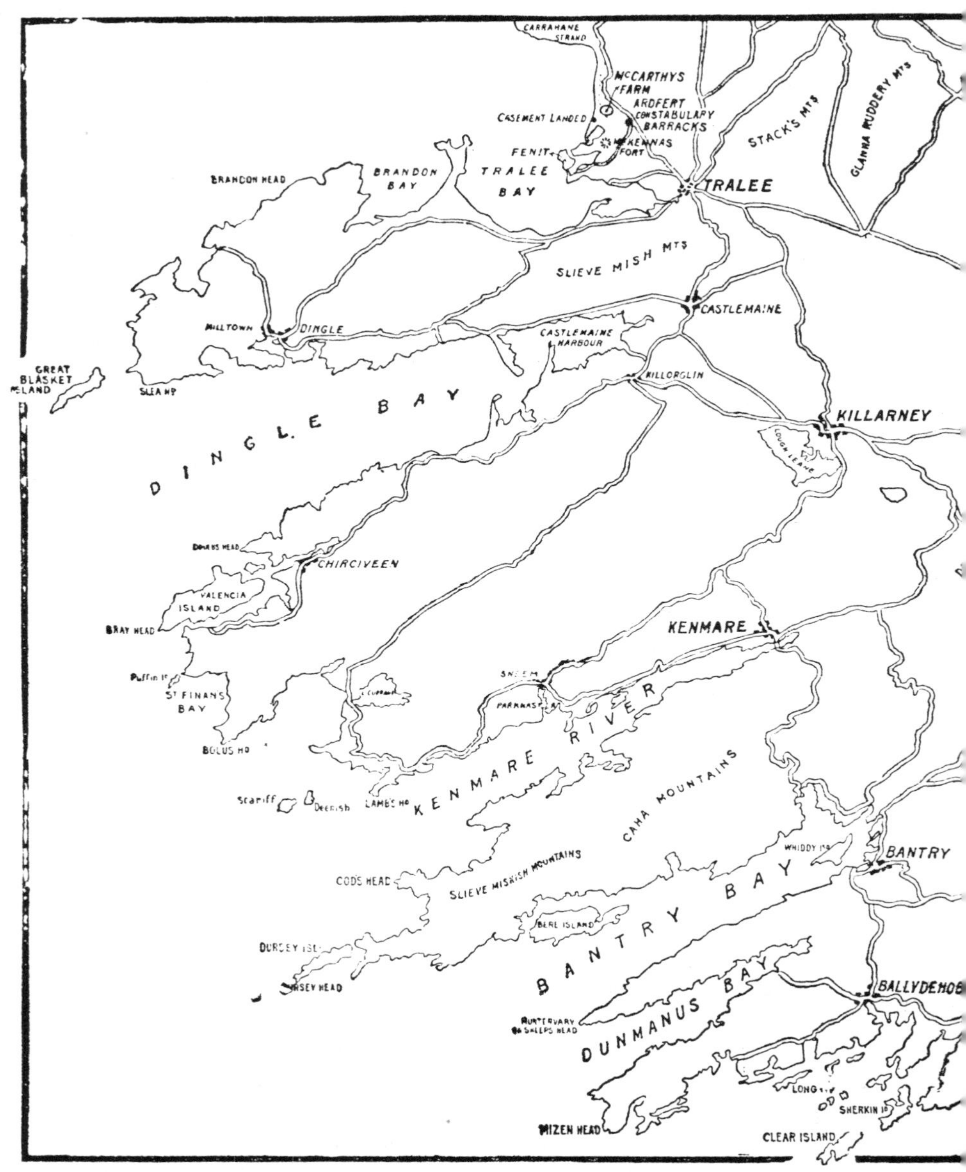

This map shows the place where Casement landed from the German submarine, and the fort at which he was arrested.

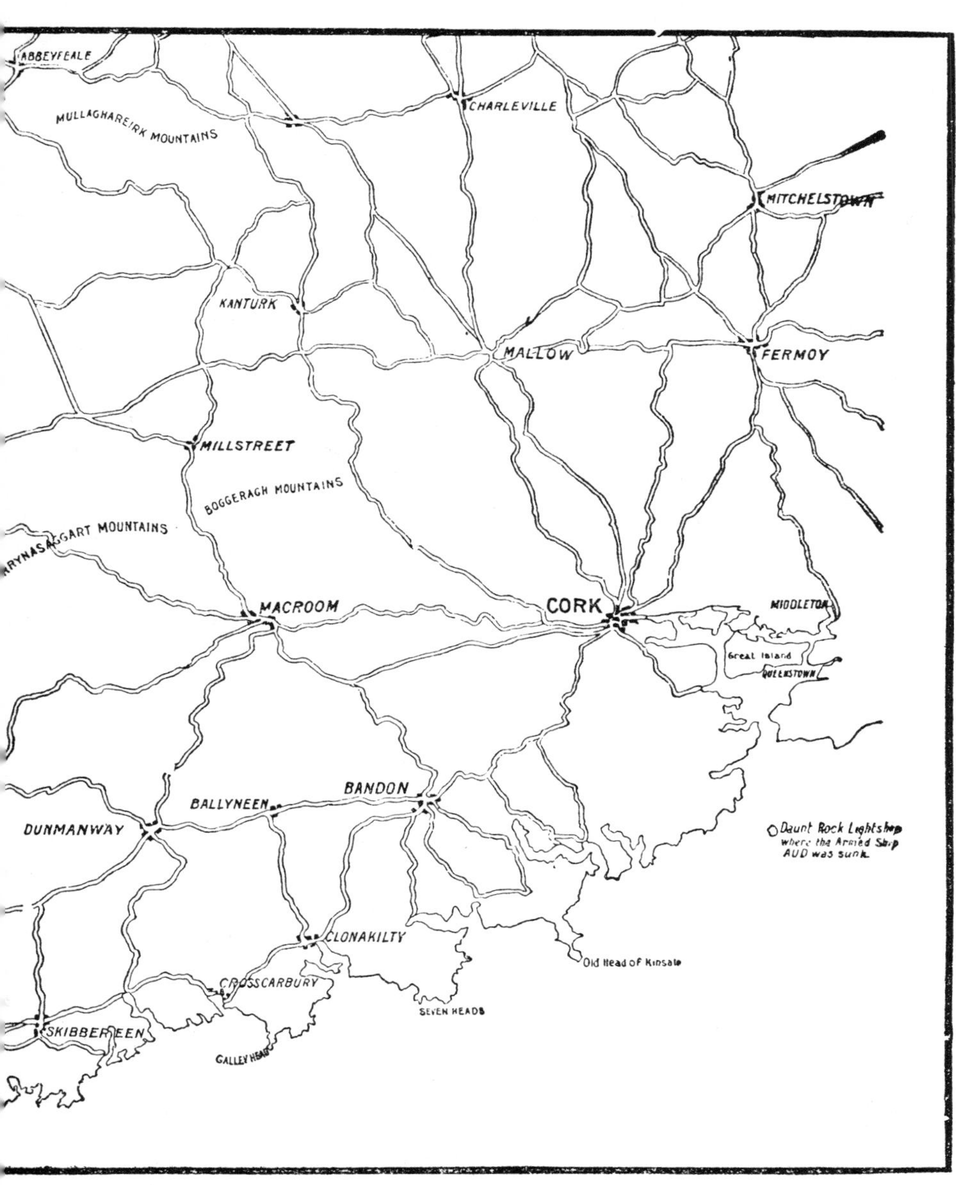

This map shows the spot where the vessel with the arms from Germany was sunk.

against punishment. I told him again it was not in my power to do so, but that I could bring his request under notice, and no doubt it would be considered. He then told me that a Wilson liner which was captured by the Germans at the beginning of the War —

The Attorney-General interrupted at this point. 'I may say,' he said, 'that I have had a letter from a member of the Wilson firm, who are reasonably anxious that it should be made clear that this was a vessel that had been captured by the Germans.'

Witness continued: Bailey told me this vessel was to be piloted into Fenit the following Monday morning, or perhaps sooner—if possible that night—with 20.000 rifles, over a million rounds of ammunition, ten machine guns (two ready for action), bombs, and fire bombs. He then said there was to be a general rising in Ireland simultaneously, and that Dublin Castle was to be attacked or raided. He described to me the lights which the pilot would carry—two green lights—and said the boat was to lie outside. I knew by this time that a vessel supposed to contain arms and ammunition had been sunk. He said 'No, that could not be. The boat was not to come in until Monday or tonight.' I then questioned him as to how he knew, and he then told me his name, and said he was one of three, the others being Casement and Monteith. He also told me that he landed from a German submarine on Friday morning. I told him I would take a statement from him in writing later on, and I left him to take some telegrams. On return I told him I would take a statement from him if he was still willing to give it to me. He asked me if I would promise on my honour not to publish it while he was in the neighbourhood. I told him I would not. He also asked me if I would move him away from there as soon as possible, and I told him I would. The statement he gave to me himself. I questioned him myself, but only to keep his narrative in some sort of order.

Mr Jones Raises An Objection

At this point Mr Jones roses and objected to the admissibility of the statement on the grounds that there existed in the case certain conditions which vitiated anything in the nature of a confession.

Sir Frederick Smith submitted that the statement was evidence.

Sir John Dickinson said it was clear that a confession to be admissible must be free and voluntary, and there must be no promise of any kind of favour or assistance or threat. It seemed to him, upon the evidence, that the man was wishful to make a statement which might or might not be a protection to him in the future. But he was anxious to make it, and also to be protected from the result of the statement. As he was told that any statement must be an entirely voluntary one, he (Sir John Dickinson) could not hold that there was any inducement to him to make a statement.

The District Inspector, resuming his evidence, said that when he had taken the statement Bailey had said—'if you bring it in evidence I will go back on it'. Witness said— 'what else do you suppose I wrote it down for?' After taking the statement, witness sent an escort for Bailey, and he was brought to Tralee. In the sleeve pocket of one of the three overcoats picked up on the sand he found a sleeping car ticket from Berlin to Wilhelmshaven. It was dated April 11-12, 1916.

Cross-examined by Mr Jones, witness said that after Bestick left the room he remained with Bailey about an hour and a half. He was at Ardfert on the Good Friday, and there saw Sir Roger Casement, though he did not then know his identity. He had a very good idea, but he didn't know for certain. He meant when he said he would give him protection that it would be from any violence in the neighbourhood.

Sir Roger Casement's Pension

John Anthony Cecil Tilley, Chief Clerk at the Foreign Office, produced a letter dated June 19th, 1911, written by Sir Roger Casement to Sir Edward Grey in acknowledgement of his knighthood. It was addressed from 'The Savoy', Denham, Bucks. The letter was not read, Mr Travers Humphreys remarking that it had already been given in the Attorney-General's opening statement. Witness also produced from the Foreign Office records the official history of Sir Roger Casement, and said that after September 30th, 1914, the pension of Sir Roger Casement was stopped by direction of the Treasury.

Replying to Mr Jones, the witness said he did not know that the order suspending Sir Roger Casement's pension was not made until February, 1915, nor that the quarterly pension from June to September, 1914, is still lying in Sir Roger Casement's bank. The amount of Sir Roger Casement's pension was £421 13s. 4d. a year.

Joseph Brennan, of Sallins, Co. Clare, formerly a private in the Irish Guards, was the last witness called. He said that he went to France about the end of August, 1914, and was taken prisoner by the Germans after being wounded on September 6th of that year. He was conveyed back to the field hospital, and then to Cologne, afterwards being transferred to Metzberg, and then to Limberg. He reached the camp at the latter place in February, 1913, and found there a large number of Irish prisoners. While there he was not individually addressed by anyone, but he heard a man make a speech to a number of the prisoners. He recognised him as Sir Roger Casement in the dock.

Witness added that he did not hear what Sir Roger Casement said to the men, and did not hear him addressing any of the Irish prisoners.

Sir John Dickinson then formally charged the accused with high treason, and committed them for trial at a place and time to be fixed thereafter.

The Trial

Sir Roger Casement was placed on his trial at the Royal Courts of Justice in London on Monday, 26th June, on a charge of high treason. His judges were the Lord Chief Justice (Lord Reading), Mr Justice Avory, and Mr Justice Horridge. He had an imposing array of legal representatives who were led by Serjeant Sullivan, an Irish KC, and a member of the English Junior Bar. With him were Mr Artemus Jones, and Professor JH Morgan, who watched the interests of accused before the magistrate at Bow street, and a distinguished American lawyer, Mr Francis Doyle, was present in an advisory capacity. For the Crown there appeared the Attorney-General (Sir Frederick Smith), the Solicitor-General (Sir George Cave), and Mr Bodkin and Mr Travers Humphreys, well known representatives of the Director of Public Prosecutions, in cases of lesser importance. The trial was heard in the Lord Chief Justice's Court, the largest court in the building, but not nearly adequate to accommodate all those members of the general public who would have flocked to the proceedings as to a public spectacle.

Casement, deprived then of the fellowship in the dock of Bailey, the ex-soldier, was a new Casement—debonnair and confident, fashionably dressed in a braided morning coat, with vest slip, dark tie, his hair carefully tended and his beard trimmed—once more the cultured civil servant. His sensitive face had lost its wonted air of brooding, and his entry to the court between the parted green curtains was an object lesson in careless grace of movement.

The master of the Crown Office, in the place usually occupied by the Clerk, read the long indictment, and Casement listened, one hand in the trouser's pocket, the other holding his chin, apparently but faintly interested.

The Charge

The indictment against him was in the following terms:

'Sir Roger David Casement, otherwise known as Sir Roger Casement, Knight, on the 1st December, 1914, and on divers other days thereafter, and between that day and the 21st April, 1916, being then to wit, on the said several days a British subject, and whilst, on the said several days an open and public war was being prosecuted and carried on by the German Emperor and his subjects against our lord the King and his subjects, then and on the said several days traitorously contriving and intending to aid and assist the said enemies of our lord the King and his subjects, did traitorously adhere to and did comfort the said enemies in parts beyond the seas, without this realm of England, to wit, in the Empire of Germany.'

Attorney-General's Statement

The Attorney-General then rose to open the case for the Crown. He said that the charge against the prisoner was the gravest known to the law. The law of treason was principally founded upon a statute as old as the reign of King Edward III. In this case the Crown alleged that the prisoner had been guilty of the most heinous crime—that he had adhered to the King's enemies, and had attempted to seduce His Majesty's soldiers from their allegiance. It will be for you to say, continued the Attorney-General, if the case is proved, whether there are any extenuating circumstances, or whether it is aggravated by the relationship in which he formerly stood to the Sovereign, whom he has betrayed and the country which he has struck. The Attorney-General described Casement as an able and cultivated man, versed in affairs, and experienced in political matters. He was not a lifelong rebel against England, and all that England stood for, as others well known in history had been. His career had not been without public distinction, and the earlier stages of it, it might even now be remembered to his credit, were directed, not to the destruction of the power of this great Empire, but to its consolidation and development. The Attorney-General next proceeded to outline the career of Casement, mainly dealing with the Consular posts which he had filled, and to his inquiries relative to the rubber industry while he was Consul-General at Rio de Janeiro. In 1905 he was made a CMG in recognition of his public services, and in 1911 he was made a Knight and received the Coronation medal. After a career of public usefulness he was retired on a pension.

A Well-Earned Pension

This pension, said the Attorney-General, had been honourably earned, and it would, therefore, be neither necessary or proper to refer to it, were it not for the sinister and wicked activities of the period which I am approaching. The pension was drawn between October 2nd, 1913, and October 7th, 1914. Casement did not send in the necessary claim for it after the latter date, and at the same time the Treasury directed that it should cease to be paid. The Attorney-General then repeated the substance of his statement at the opening of the proceedings at Bow street, and concluded by saying that the prisoner, blinded by hatred to this country, as malignant in quality as sudden in origin, had played a desperate hazard: 'He has played it, and he has lost it, and the forfeit is claimed.'

Evidence was then given by John Crone, of Cork, formerly a private in the Royal Munster Fusiliers; Daniel O'Brien, formerly of the Leinster Regiment and the 19th Hussars; Corporal John Robinson, Belfast, RAMC; Michael O'Connor, a one-armed corporal of the Royal Irish Regiment; Private Michael Moore, RAMC, who were prisoners of war in Germany, and heard Casement lecture the Irishmen in the camps. Their evidence was in substance the same as that given at Bow street.

Private John Neill

John Neill, of the 18th Royal Irish, said that at Hanover a German General made a speech.

Serjeant Sullivan objected to the speech as evidence, and this was upheld.

Witness added that it was a very small speech. (Laughter) On one Sunday they were supposed to go to Church Service, but on reaching the barrack room they found Casement on a table getting ready for a speech. He had an Irish Brigade book in his hand. He said he was going away for a fortnight, and when he came back he wished to see fifty names in the book.

The Solicitor-General: Did he say who would take the Irish Brigade?

Witness: The German Government. Witness then gave his recollection of Casement's speech. He said that Irishmen were all to join one brigade, and if Germany gained a naval victory it would land in Ireland, and strike a blow for old Ireland once again to gain Home Rule. He also said that the Germans very much liked the Irish, and the Irish very much liked the Germans. He also said that Ireland now had the strongest Power in the world at her back. No one signed the book, and when Casement returned from Berlin he said he was very disappointed. 'what are you Irishmen thinking of,' he asked, 'that you won't go and fight for your country at this time?' Casement told them that the Irish Brigade was first to help the Turks against the Russians: secondly, the Germans against the British, and then they were to go and shed their blood for their own native country.

John McCarthy

At the sitting of the Court on Tuesday, 27th June, John McCarthy, a farmer, of Currahane, said that at 2 o'clock on the morning of 21st April (Good Friday) he went about a mile from his home. The night was dark. He saw a collapsible boat about twenty yards from the shore. In the boat he found a dagger, and on the bank a tin box. He saw a little girl playing with three revolvers. He gave the things he found to the police, who took them to the barracks.

Cross-examined by Serjeant Sullivan, witness said he went out at that early hour to go to the holy well to say a few prayers. He was never saying prayers at that well before.

Mary Gorman, a servant, repeated her previous evidence, and in answer to Serjeant Sullivan said her usual hour for being up was 4 o'clock in the morning.

Sergeant Thomas Hearn, RIC

Sergeant Thomas John Hearn, RIC, stationed at Ardfert, after re-stating the evidence he gave at Bow street, was cross-examined by Serjeant Sullivan, in answer to whose questions he said that in 1914, before the war, there had been a considerable importation of arms. In consequence of what happened in the North of Ireland people were arming in the South, and bearing arms openly, without interference by the public authorities. Witness agreed that the suspension of the Home Rule Bill aggravated the unrest in the country.

Constable Reilly, RIC, spoke of arresting Casement in the fort, and Martin Collins spoke of finding papers where he had seen the prisoner.

District Inspector Brittain

District Inspector Brittain, RIC, Tralee, produced a first class sleeping ticket from Berlin to Williamshaven, dated 11th-12th April. It was in the prisoner's pocket.

Cross-examined, witness was taken through many speeches and articles published in the Irish newspapers. One speech from the *Irish Times* of July 14th, 1913, pointed out that there was a majority of over thirty against the Home Rule Bill, and added: 'We can rely upon tens of thousands of people in England who are prepared to assist us.' The witness, failing to find the speech in the newspaper, asked whose speech it was.

Serjeant Sullivan: Oh, well, I could give you the name, but I am a little diffident. (Laughter)

Counsel (reading): 'In their determination to resist they would have the support of thousands of people in England, amongst whom I should have the pleasure of reckoning myself.' Serjeant Sullivan added: The author of that is not here to earn his meed of praise at this moment. (Laughter)

Then, under the heading, 'Sir Edward Carson,' Serjeant Sullivan read: 'He could add this, as a word of partial assurance, that they had many powerful friends in England who thought as he did. That it was all very well to talk of the great force which might be marshalled behind the Government, which could be used in the event of extreme necessity in Ulster. The reply to that was that the forces of the Crown were the servants of the nation, and the employment of these forces would be a monstrous crime.'

Serjeant Sullivan was proceeding to read other extracts, but the Lord Chief Justice said that counsel had gone far enough.

Leading Signalman Waghorn, of HMS Bluebell; John Dempsey, diver; Colonel Belaeiw, of the Russian Army, and Lieutenant-Colonel Gordon, Intelligence Department, War Office, having repeated their previous evidence, the latter proved that the maps said to have been dropped by Casement were process copies of the Ordnance Survey maps of Ireland. The maps closely resembled the maps of Middle Europe prepared by the German Government.

Application to Quash the Indictment

Serjeant Sullivan rose to argue his case for quashing the indictment, the matter having been raised by him at the opening of the case, but postponed at the suggestion of the Court. His point was that the indictment disclosed no offence known to the law and tryable before the Court. He would, he said, have to occupy a considerable time, and he was surrounded by piles of law books, from which, when he began, he quoted precedents going back to the earliest time.

The Lord Chief Justice said that whatever time Serjeant Sullivan required was at his disposal, as it was essential that he should have all the time he wished.

Serjeant Sullivan had not concluded his argument when the Court adjourned.

At the sitting of the Court on Wednesday, 28th June,

Serjeant Sullivan asked that the argument for the defence might be resumed by Mr Morgan, as he himself felt a little taxed after his efforts on the previous day.

The Lord Chief Justice said that there was a difficulty in the way. The law provided for only two counsel when counsel were assigned for the defence. The Court would, however, reserve the point, and allow Mr Morgan to appear.

Mr Morgan contended that as far back as Philip and Mary, no offence committed outside the Realm was triable here by the Courts of common law. The evidence was overwhelming.

The Attorney-General submitted that the objection of the defence was ill-founded, and could not be supported.

The Lord Chief Justice

The Lord Chief Justice said that a submission had been made by the counsel for the defence—that the indictment should be quashed on the ground that it disclosed no offence known to the English law. Another way to put the same proposition was that the Court should rule, according to the contention of the defence, that the Crown had failed to prove any offence in law. The case advanced and supported by careful, well reasoned, and able argument by Mr Sullivan and those with him, was in effect that adherence to the King's enemies without the realm was not an offence against the Statute of Edward III, 1351. The argument was that the Court must construe the Statute of 1351, and must pay no regard to any commentary that may have been made by learned authors in the past, however distinguished, in arriving at the meaning of the words—that the Court must interpret the words of the Statute was beyond question. That they were not entitled to do violence to the words of the Statute might be assumed. But if the words of the Statute were not clear, and if it were possible to construe the Statute in two different ways, then the comments of great lawyers, masters of the common law, during the last three or four centuries, could not be allowed to pass without the greatest regard and consideration. He had no hesitation himself in stating that if a man adhered to the King's enemies without the realm he committed the offence of treason at common law, notwithstanding that the offence was committed without the realm. The State assumed that the offence of treason could be committed without the realm, and the Statute of Henry VIII provided for it. The doubts that had arisen from beginning to end, so far as they had been able to trace them, were never as to the offence, but only as to the venue. He had come to the conclusion that the offence, if proved in fact, had been committed in law. Notwithstanding the learned and able arguments that had been put forward, the motion must be refused.

Justices Avory and Horridge concurred.

Sir Roger Casement's Personal Statement

After luncheon the Lord Chief Justice told the jury that the statement the prisoner wished to make was not upon oath, and he could not be cross-examined.

Sir Roger Casement then rose in the dock, and sought, and obtained, the consent of the Court to his reading the statement:

My lords and gentlemen of the jury, he commenced, softly, I desire to say a few words only with reference to some allusions made by the prosecution. As to my pension and the honour of knighthood conferred upon me, I shall say one word only. The pension I had earned by services rendered and it was assigned by law. The knighthood it was not in my power to refuse. But there are mis-statements given in the evidence against me, which I shall refute. First—I never at any time advised Irishmen to fight with Turks against Russians, nor to fight with the Germans on the Western Front. Second—I never asked an Irishman to fight for Germany. I have always claimed that he has no right to fight for any land but Ireland. Third—the horrible insinuation that I got my own people's rations reduced to starvation point because they did not join the Irish Brigade is an abominable falsehood. Rations were necessarily reduced throughout Germany owing to the blockade, and they were reduced to Irish prisoners at exactly the same time and to the same extent as for the German soldiers and the entire population of Germany. The other suggestion that men were sent to punishment camps at my instance for not joining the Irish Brigade is one I need hardly pause to refute. It is devoid of all foundation. Fourth—there is a widespread imputation of German gold. I owe it to those in Ireland who are assailed with me on this very ground to nail this lie once for all. It was published in the newspapers in America, and originated in this country, and I cabled to American and instructed my American lawyer to proceed against those papers for libel. Those who know me know the incredibility of this malicious invention. They know from my past record that I have never sold myself to any man or any Government. From the first moment I landed on the Continent until I came home again to Ireland I neither asked nor accepted a single penny of foreign money, either for myself or for any Irish cause, nor for any purpose whatever, but only the money of Irishmen. I refute so obvious a slander, because it was so often made until I came back.

Money offered in Germany

Money was offered to me in Germany more than once, and offered liberally and unconditionally, but

I rejected every suggestion of that kind, and I left Germany a poorer man than I entered it. Money I could always obtain from my own countrymen, and I am not ashamed here to acknowledge the debt of gratitude I owe to many Irish friends and sympathisers who did freely and gladly help me when I was on the Continent. I take the opportunity here of stating how deeply I have bee touched by the generosity and loyalty of those English friends of mine, who have given me proof of their abiding friendship during these last dark weeks of strain and trial. I trust, gentlemen of the jury, that I have made that statement clearly and emphatically enough for all men, even for my most bitter enemies, to comprehend that a man who in the newspapers is just another Irish traitor may be a gentleman. There is another matter I wish to touch on. The Attorney-General for England thought it consistent with the tradition of which he is the public representative to make a veiled allusion, in his opening address, to the rising in Ireland, of which he has brought forward no evidence in this case, from first to last, and to which, therefore, you and I, as laymen, would have supposed that he would have scrupulously refrained from referring. Since the rising has been mentioned, however, I must state categorically that the rebellion was not made in Germany, that it was not directed from Germany, that it was not inspired from Germany, and that not one penny of German gold went to finance it. Gentlemen, I have touched on these personal matters alone because they were intended to reflect on my honour, and calculated to tarnish the cause that I hold dear.

When he had finished reading, Sir Roger Casement quietly thanked the Court, and resumed his seat, his demeanour having obviously made an impression on the crowded court.

Mr Serjeant Sullivan

Mr Serjeant Sullivan then addressed the Court. He told the jury to put aside all preconceived notions arising from outside the court, and to remember that it was a trial for the life of a man, but more than that—Sir Roger Casement was not a countryman of theirs. He thought differently and acted differently, and that made the task of the jury by no means an easy one. They had to consider the motives and the intentions of a man who was not of their race. It was true that Sir Roger Casement went to Germany. But did he ever ask any Irishman to fight for Germany? No; he asked them to join the Irish Brigade, to fight for their own land, and not one of the men to whom he spoke at Limburg had fired a shot for Germany. Counsel stated that there was no connection whatever between Sir Roger Casement and the ship which sank off Ireland. He objected to the statement of the Attorney-General that Sir Roger Casement was in the employment of England. He was, said counsel, in the service of the British Empire. Then counsel went on to speak of the arming of Ulster and the landing of German rifles there, which at the end of the war would break up Ireland in two halves. It was to fight against this denial of Irish rights that the Irish Brigade was to be formed, especially as Ulster was using these things while the authorities were helpless.

At this point the Attorney-General objected to the statements. There was no evidence that German rifles were landed in the North of Ireland.

The Lord Chief Justice said that the Court had allowed Mr Sullivan great latitude, as he had constantly referred to matters which were not in evidence.

Mr Serjeant Sullivan, who had been speaking with great fervour, apologised and resumed his address. He had not gone far before it was obvious that his strength was failing, and at last he told the Court that he was exhausted, and could go no farther.

The Lord Chief Justice at once adjourned till the morning.

Mr Serjeant Sullivan sat quietly for a short time, and, with the aid of restoratives, recovered sufficiently to be able to leave the court with his friends.

Mr Serjeant Sullivan Absent

When the case opened on Thursday, 18th June Serjeant Sullivan was not present, and sympathetic inquiries were made by the Attorney-General and others.

On the judges taking their seats, Mr Artemus Jones rose, and said that his learned leader, on the advice of his doctor, could not be present, and he asked to be allowed to continue the speech of his leader.

The Lord Chief Justice said he was sorry that Mr Sullivan was not able to be present, but it was obvious that he was labouring under the strain of the previous day's proceedings.

The Court consented to Mr Jones's application.

Mr Artemus Jones, addressing the jury, said Sir Roger Casement had played a part in consolidating the Empire. The Attorney-General had asked what had happened to convert this loyal and dutiful of the Empire to the man he was now said by the Crown to be. That was the question asked by the Attorney-General, and the answer was in the evidence and in the speeches which had been circulated in the Irish newspapers. He then proceeded to read certain passages to emphasise, as he said, that the state of things which prevailed in Ireland prior to the war must have gone on subsequently in Ireland. There was a community full of deep and bitter memories of what they considered to be wrongs, and it was important for the jury to bear that fact in mind, because it was only when there were armed movements in the north that this loyal servant of the Empire became connected with anything in the nature of arms. If the Attorney-General wanted a complete answer to the question he put, he (Mr Jones) suggested that that answer might be found in the newspaper extracts which caused Sir Roger Casement to start the Irish National Volunteer movement.

The Attorney-General

The Attorney-General paid a striking testimony to the ability of Serjeant Sullivan, and went on to ask—Why, at the very moment that Germany made her tiger spring at Europe, did the prisoner go to Germany at all? How did he get there? What was the arrangement by which he went to Germany? How was it, when this country was at war with Germany, when Irish soldiers on the field of battle had been made prisoners by German arms—how was it that they found the prisoner for months a free man in Germany, moving without restriction in whatever part of Germany Irish soldiers were confined, without control, or interference, going among them and attempting to seduce them from their allegiance? No answer had been given to that question, and no answer could be given consistent with the integrity and innocence of the prisoner.

The Lord Chief Justice

The Lord Chief Justice, in summing up, said: 'This is a trial of supreme importance. The charge against the prisoner is the gravest known in law.' Then, after a pause, he joined in the tribute to the way in which the case for the defence had been conducted, and made general recognition of the way in which all counsel had assisted the Court. His Lordship then got back to the enormity of the crime of treason. At all times, he said, to betray the King—that is the State, that means the country, and that means those of us who are subject to the King, who live in a common society—is, and must ever be, the most odious charge. But treason in time of war, by adhering to the King's enemies, by aiding and comforting the King's enemies when all persons in this country are making sacrifices to resist the enemy, when we are all combined, whatever our views may be, to defeat the common enemy—treason in these times is almost too grave for expression. It is because one must feel that, that I desire to caution you in this case to judge of it, as all criminal cases must be considered and judged, calmly and dispassionately; and let me remind you that it is very necessary in a case of this description, where the defence have thought it right and necessary for the purposes of their case to introduce political considerations, to concentrate your attention closely and exclusively upon the evidence before you. Here let me tell you what has been said by the Attorney-General, endorsing the view presented to you by Mr Sullivan, that it is for the Crown to satisfy you beyond reasonable doubt that the prisoner is guilty of the charge against him. It is not for the defence to disprove it.

Politics in Ireland

Proceeding, the Lord Chief Justice said they had heard much about politics in Ireland. For himself, he always felt anxiety in a court of justice when there was any possibility of the introduction of political passion. Justice was ever in jeopardy when passion was aroused. They must pay no more attention to what had been said with regard to the condition of Ireland before the war and after the war than was necessary in order to understand the circumstances in this case, but more particularly to do justice to the defence which had been set up. He urged them not to allow themselves to be influenced by any political opinion. I cannot, said his lordship, but think that counsel for the defence paid the highest compliment to the English Bar that could be imagined, when he had the courage to address you as he did yesterday upon Ireland. It is all to the good that it was done. He did it in the interests of his client, to present to you his client's point of view, so that you might be able to gauge his client's mind. Coming to the charge itself, his Lordship asked how, and under what circumstances, did the prisoner go to Germany. They had no evidence that he went there other than his overt acts. His Lordship explained the meaning of overt acts, and said that, although half-a-dozen might be charged, one overt act proved would call for a verdict of guilty. But before convicting the prisoner they must be satisfied of his intention and purpose. Counsel for the defence had told them it was difficult to define the mind of an Irishman. You never really, said his Lordship, can get at the actual thought passing through a man's mind except by considering his actions. A man's intentions are to be gathered from his acts, and he must be held to have intended the natural and reasonable consequences of his act. It was open to the prisoner to go into the witness box and be cross-examined, but he did not do so. Why did the prisoner arrive in this way in Ireland? Why did he hide in a fort and give a false name? Why did he carry a 'code,' and more important, why did he drop that when arrested? How was it that Germany allowed him to leave Germany, and how was it that the ship was painted with the Norwegian colours, and that before she went down she flew the German flag? If arms had been landed in Ireland to help those who wished to create discontent at that time, it would have been very useful in assisting the enemy, and consequently would be weakening the forces of the King.

THE VERDICT.

It was nearly three o'clock when the jury retired. In a few moments they sent for the original 'code' and for a copy of the indictment. These were supplied to them, but the Lord Chief Justice refused to send them a copy of the evidence, which they also asked for. At ten minutes to four the judges returned. The jury soon followed, and Sir Roger Casement again entered the dock.

The names of the jury having been called over, they were asked if they were agreed upon their verdict. The foreman said that they found the prisoner guilty.

Sir Roger Casement was asked by the Clerk if he had anything to say why sentence of death should not be passed upon him according to law.

The Prisoner's Statement

Sir Roger Casement then read a long statement. At first he appeared to be extremely nervous, but he grew more confident as he proceeded. He said:

My Lord Chief Justice, as I wish my words to reach a much wider audience than I see before me here, I intend to read all that I propose to say. What I shall read now is something I wrote more than 20 days ago. There is an objection, possibly not good in law, but surely good on moral grounds, against the application to me here of this old English Statute, 565 years old, that seeks to deprive an Irishman to-day of life and honour, not for 'adhering to the King's enemies,' but for adhering to his own people.

When this statute was passed in 1351, what was the state of men's minds on the question of a far higher allegiance—that of man to God and His Kingdom? The law of that day did not permit a man to forsake his Church or deny his God save with his life. The 'heretic' then had the same doom as the 'traitor'. To-day a man may forswear God and His heavenly realm without fear or penalty, all earlier statutes having gone the way of Nero's edicts against the Christians, but that Constitutional phantom, 'The King', can still dig up from the dungeons and torture-chambers of the Dark Ages a law that takes a man's life and limb for an exercise of conscience.

If true religion rests on love, it is equally true that loyalty rests on love. The law I am charged under has no parentage in love and claims the allegiance of to-day on the ignorance and blindness of the past. I am being tried in truth not by my peers of the live present, but by the fears of the dead past; not by the civilisation of the 20th century, but by the brutality of the 14th: not even by a statute framed in the language of the land that tries me, but emitted in the language of an enemy land—so antiquated is the law that must be sought to-day to slay an Irishman whose offence is that he puts Ireland first!

Loyalty is a sentiment, not a law. It rests on love, not on restraint. The government of Ireland by England rests on restraint and not on law: and since it demands no love it can evoke no loyalty.

The Dead Hand

But this statute is more absurd even than it is antiquated: and if it be potent to hang one Irishman, it is still more potent to gibbet all Englishmen. Edward II was King not only of the Realm of England, but also of the Realm of France, and he was not King of Ireland. Yet his dead hand to-day may pull the noose around the Irishman's neck whose Sovereign he was not, but it can strain no strand around the Frenchman's throat whose Sovereign he was. For centuries the successors of Edward III claimed to be Kings of France, and quartered the arms of France on their Royal shield down to the Union with Ireland on January 1, 1801. Throughout these hundreds of years these 'Kings of France' were constantly at war with their Realm of France and their French subjects, who should have gone from birth to death with an obvious fear of treason before their eyes. But did they? Did the 'Kings of France' resident here at Windsor, or in the Tower of London, hang, draw, and quarter as a traitor every Frenchman for 400 years who fell into their hands with arms in his hands? On the contrary, they received Embassies of these traitors, presents from these traitors, even knighthood itself at the hands of these traitors, feasted with them, tilted with them, fought with them—but did not assassinate them by law.

Judicial assassination to-day is reserved only for one race of the King's subjects: for Irishmen; for those who cannot forget their allegiance to the Realm of Ireland. The Kings of England, as such, had no rights in Ireland up to the time of Henry VIII, save such as rested on compact and mutual obligation entered into between them and certain princes, chiefs and lords of Ireland. This form of legal right, such as it was, gave no King of England lawful power to impeach an Irishman for high treason under this statute of King Edward III of England until an Irish Act, known as Poyning's Law, the 10th of Henry VII, was passed in 1494, at Drogheda, by the Parliament of the Pale in Ireland and enacted as law in that part of Ireland. But if by Poyning's Law an Irishman of the Pale could be indicted for high treason under this Act, he could be indicted only in one way and before one tribunal—by the laws of the Realm of Ireland and in Ireland. The very law of Poyning, which, I believe, applies this statute of Edward III to Ireland, enacted also for the Irishman's defence, 'all those laws by which England claims her liberty.'

'A Foreign Court'

And what is the fundamental charter of an Englishman's liberty? That he shall be tried by his peers. With all respect I assert this Court is to me, an Irishman, charged with this offence, a foreign Court—this jury is for me, an Irishman, not a jury of my peers to try me in this vital issue, for it is patent to every man of conscience that I have a right, an indefeasible right, if tried at all under this statute of high treason, to be tried in Ireland, before an Irish Court and by an Irish jury. This Court, this jury, the public opinion of this country, England, cannot but be prejudiced in varying degrees against me, most of all in time of war. I did not land in England. I landed in Ireland. It was to Ireland I came; to Ireland I wanted to come, and the last place I desired to land in was England.

But for the Attorney-General of England there is only 'England'—there is no Ireland, there is only the law of England—no right of Ireland; the liberty of Ireland and of Irishmen is to be judged by the power of England. Yet for me, the Irish outlaw, there is a land of Ireland, a right of Ireland, and a charter for all Irishmen to appeal to, in the last resort, a charter that even the very statutes of England itself cannot deprive us of, nay more, a charter that Englishmen themselves assert as the fundamental bond of law that connects the two kingdoms. This charge of high treason involves a moral responsibility, as the very terms of the indictment against myself recite, inasmuch as I committed the acts I am charged with to the 'evil example of others in the like case.' What was this 'evil example' I set to others in 'the like case,' and who were these others? The 'evil example' charge is that I asserted the rights of my own country, and the 'others' I appealed to, to aid my endeavour, were my own countrymen. The example was given not to Englishmen, but to Irishmen, and the 'like case' can never arise in England, but only in Ireland. To Englishmen I set no evil example, for I made no appeal to them, I asked no Englishman to help me. I asked Irishmen to fight for their rights. The 'evil example' was only to other Irishmen who might come after me and in 'like case' seek to do as I did. How, then, since neither my example nor my appeal was addressed to Englishmen, can I be rightfully tried by them?

Appeal for an Irish Trial

If I did wrong in making that appeal to Irishmen to join with me in an effort to fight for Ireland, it is by Irishmen and by them alone I can be rightfully judged. From this Court and its jurisdiction I appeal to those I am alleged to have wronged, and to those I am alleged to have injured by my 'evil example', and claim that they alone are competent to decide my guilt or my innocence. If they find me guilty the statute may affix the penalty, but the statute does not override or annul my right to seek judgement at their hands. This is so fundamental a right, so natural a right, so obvious a right, that it is clear the Crown were aware of it when they brought me by force and by stealth from Ireland to this country. It was not I who landed in England, but the Crown who dragged me here, away from my own country to which I had returned with a price upon my head, away from my own countrymen whose loyalty is not in doubt, and safe from the judgment of my peers whose judgment I do not shrink from. I admit no other judgment but theirs. I accept no verdict save at their hands.

I assert from this dock that I am being tried here not because it is just, but because it is unjust. Place me before a jury of my own countrymen, be it Protestant or Catholic, Unionist or Nationalist, Sinn Feineach or Orangeman, and I shall accept the verdict and bow to the statute and all its penalties. But I shall accept no meaner finding against me than that of those whose loyalty I endangered by my example and to whom alone I made appeal. If they adjudge me guilty, then guilty I am. It is not I who am afraid of their verdict—it is the Crown. If this be not so, why fear the test? I fear it not. I demand it as my right.

That is the condemnation of English rule, of English-made law, of English government in Ireland, that it dare not rest on the will of the Irish people, but exists in defiance of their will—that it is a rule derived not from right but from conquest.

Conquest, my lord, gives no title—and if it exists over the body it fails over the mind. It can exert no empire over men's reason and judgement and affections; and it is from this law of conquest without title, to the reason, judgment, and affection of my own countrymen, that I appeal.

Sympathy from America

I would add, the generous expressions of sympathy extended to me from so many quarters, particularly from America, have touched me very much. In that country, as in my own, I am sure my motives are understood, for the achievement of their liberties has been an abiding inspiration to Irishmen and to all elsewhere rightly struggling to be free.

My Lord Chief Justice, I am not called upon, I conceive, to say anything in answer to the inquiry your lordship has addressed to me why sentence should not be passed upon me. Since I do not admit any verdict in this Court I cannot, my lord, admit the fitness of the sentence that of necessity must follow it from this Court. I hope I shall be acquitted of presumption if I say that the Court I see before me now is not this High Court, of Justice of England, but a far greater, a far higher, a far older assemblage of justices—that of the people of Ireland. Since in the acts which have led to this trial it was the people of Ireland I sought to serve and them alone—I leave my judgment and my sentence in their hands.

Let me pass from myself and my own fate to a far more pressing as it is a far more urgent theme—not the fate of the individual Irishman who may have tried and failed, but the claims and the fate of the country that has not failed. Ireland has out-lived the failure of all her hopes—and yet she still hopes. Ireland has seen her sons—aye, and her daughters, too—suffer from generation to generation always for the same cause, meeting always the same fate, and always at the hands of the same power; and always a fresh generation has passed on to withstand the same oppression. For if English authority be omnipotent—a power, as Mr Gladstone phrased it, that reaches to the very ends of the earth—Irish hope exceeds the dimensions of that power, excels its authority, and renews with each generation the claims of the last. The cause that begets this indomitable persistency, the faculty of preserving through centuries of misery the remembrance of lost liberty, this, surely, is the noblest cause men ever strove for, ever lived for, ever died for. If this be the case I stand here to-day indicted for and convicted of sustaining, then I stand in a goodly company and a right noble succession.

The Ulster Volunteers

My counsel has referred to the Ulster Volunteer movement, and I will not touch at length upon that ground, save only to say this, that neither I nor any of the leaders of the Irish Volunteers, who were founded in Dublin in November, 1913, had any quarrel with the Ulster Volunteers as such, who were born a year earlier. Our movement was not directed against them, but against the men who misused and misdirected the courage, the sincerity, and the local patriotism of the men of the North of Ireland. The manifesto of the Irish Volunteers, promulgated at a public meeting in Dublin on November 25, 1913, stated with sincerity the aims of the organisation as I have outlined them.

Since arms were so necessary to make our organisation a reality and to give to the minds of Irishmen menaced with the most outrageous threats a sense of security, it was our bounden duty to get arms before all else. I decided, with this end in view, to go to America, with surely a better right to appeal to Irishmen there for help in an hour of great national trial than those envoys of 'Empire' could assert for their week-end descents upon Ireland, or their appeals to Germany.

If, as the right hon. gentleman, the present Attorney-General, asserted in a speech at Manchester, Nationalists would neither fight for Home Rule nor pay for it, it was our duty to show him that we know how to do both. Within a few weeks of my arrival in the States the fund that had been opened to secure arms for the Volunteers of Ireland amounted to many thousands of pounds. In every case the money subscribed, whether it came from the purse of the wealthy man or the still readier pocket of the poor man, was Irish gold.

Then came the war. As Mr Birrell said in his evidence recently laid before the Commission of Inquiry into the causes of the late rebellion in Ireland, 'the war upset all our calculations.' It upset mine no less than Mr Birrell's, and put an end to my mission of peaceful effort in America. War between Great Britain and Germany meant, as I believed, ruin for all the hopes we had founded on the enrolment of the Irish Volunteers. A constitutional movement in Ireland is never very far from a breach of the Constitution, as the loyalists of Ulster had been so eager to show us.

The Road to the Dock

The difference between us was that the Unionist champions chose a path they felt would lead to the Woolsack, while I went a road I knew must lead to the dock. And the event proves we were both right. The difference between us was that my 'treason' was based on a ruthless sincerity that forced me to attempt in time and season to carry out in action what I said in words—whereas their treason lay in verbal incitements that they knew need never be made good in their bodies. And so, I am prouder to stand here today in the traitor's dock to answer this impeachment than to fill the place of my right honourable accusers.

We have been told, we have been asked to hope that after this war Ireland will get Home Rule as a reward for the life-blood shed in a cause whoever else its success may benefit, can surely not benefit Ireland. And what will Home Rule be in return for what its vague promise has taken, and still hopes to take, away from Ireland? Home Rule when it comes, if come it does, will find an Ireland drained of all that is vital to its very existence—unless it be that unquenchable hope we build on the graves of the dead. We are told that if Irishmen go by the thousand to die not for Ireland, but for Flanders, for Belgium, for a patch of sand on the deserts of Mesopotamia, or a rocky trench on the heights of Gallipoli, they are winning self-government for Ireland. But if they dare to lay down their lives on their native soil, if they dare to dream even that freedom can be won only at home by men resolved to fight for it there, then they are traitors to their country, and their dream and their deaths alike are phases of a dishonourable fantasy.

But history is not so recorded in other lands. In Ireland alone in this 20th century is loyalty held to be a crime. If loyalty be something less than love and more than law, then we have had enough of such loyalty for Ireland or Irishmen. Where all your rights become only an accumulated wrong: where men must beg with bated breath for leave to subsist in their own land, to think their own thoughts, to sing their own songs, to garner the fruit of their own labours—and even while they beg to see these things inexorably withdrawn from them—then surely it is a braver, a saner, and a truer thing to be a rebel in act and deed against such circumstances as this than tamely to accept it as the natural lot of men.

The prisoner, at the conclusion of his statement, addressing the jury, said that he wished to thank them for their verdict, and that his observations did not in any way reflect on their integrity. He maintained that he had a right to be tried in Ireland, and he asked them how any one of them would feel in a converse case if he had landed in England and been carried over to Ireland by stealth and under a false name to be tried in a country inflamed against him and believing him to be a criminal

Sentenced to Death

The Lord Chief Justice then assumed the black cap and passed sentence of death by hanging in the usual form. Casement paused a moment to smile to friends in Court, and then disappeared below.

DANIEL JULIAN BAILEY DISCHARGED.

When Sir Roger Casement had left the dock, the soldier, Daniel Julian Bailey, was placed there on the same charge.

He pleaded not guilty.

As he had throughout been but a subordinate, and had a good character in the Army, and having always denied any intention of helping the enemy, but, in the words of the Attorney-General, took the course he did to get away from captivity in Germany, the Crown entered a *nolle prosequi*, and he was at once released.

The Lord Chief Justice said that their lordships quite concurred in the verdict of the jury. There was no other course open to them.

Sir Roger Casement Degraded

The following official statements were issued on Friday, 19th June:

The King has been pleased to direct the issue of Letters Patent under the Great Seal of the United Kingdom degrading Sir Roger Casement, CMG, from the degree of Knight Bachelor.

The King has been please to direct that Sir Roger Casement, Knight, shall cease to be a member of the Most Distinguished Order of Saint Michael and Saint George, of which Order he was appointed a Companion in 1906, and that his name shall be erased from the register of the Order.

Appeal Dismissed

Roger David Casement appealed on Monday, 17th July, to five judges against his conviction. He sat in the dock of the Court of Criminal Appeal, London, and listened with much interest to the proceedings. He was dressed in a grey suit, but did not look quite so smart as during his trial a few weeks ago. To the lay mind the day was one of intense weariness, as nothing but ancient rolls and Statutes in Norman French and Latin, was read, and there was virtually nothing to relieve the monotony.

Mr Justice Darling presided, the other Judges being Justices Bray, AT Lawrence, Scrutton, and Atkin.

The Crown was represented by the Attorney-General (Sir Frederick Smith), the Solicitor-General (Sir George Cave), Mr Bodkin, Mr Travers Humphreys, and Mr Branson.

Counsel for the prisoner were Mr Serjeant Sullivan, Professor Morgan, and Mr Artemus Jones.

Serjeant Sullivan's Statement

Mr Serjeant Sullivan said that the prisoner was indicted under the Statute of Edward III, the offence being stated in the following terms:

'Charged with high treason by adhering to the King's enemies elsewhere than in the King's realm—to wit, in the Empire of Germany—contrary to the Treason Act, 1351, 25th Edward III.

The matter of the appeal, he said, would involve two questions—the first, whether the matter described in the charge was a triable offence within the Statute cited, and the second point that would arise was as to whether the definition of the offence as given by the Lord Chief Justice was accurate or defective as an instruction to the jury. Counsel argued his case at great length till the adjournment of the Court.

On Tuesday, 18th, the five judges, headed by Mr Justice Darling, took their seats on the bench, and Casement was brought into the dock by warders. This time he was looking very weary from the long strain, but throughout the day he smiled to a lady who sat near him, and who evidently did all she could by responsive smiles to cheer him.

Serjeant Sullivan fought with wonderful spirit for his client. He did not fear or attack the great lawyers of the past, whose tomes were piled up before the judges for reference and guidance. His arguments rivetted the attention of their lordships, and although he did not succeed in winning his case the judge paid him a high compliment for the way in which he had sustained the greatest traditions of the King's Courts.

Their lordships, when they returned after a brief retirement, told Sir Frederick Smith, the Attorney-General, that they need not trouble him to reply on behalf of the Crown: and after Mr Justice Darling had delivered judgement dismissing the appeal, Casement was taken back to prison. He smiled at friends in court, and waved them a goodbye.

Mr Justice Darling on Treason

Mr Justice Darling intimated that the Court did not want to trouble the Attorney-General, and then, having arranged a mass of law books, from which he quoted, he proceeded to give judgement. He read to the Court the clause of the Act of Edward III in the Norman French, and then its translation, pointing out that the words 'or elsewhere', which in the indictment by the Crown meant 'in the Empire of England,' had caused all the trouble. But before going on his Lordship paid a high tribute to he way in which Mr Serjeant Sullivan had conducted his case. The Court considered that Mr Serjeant Sullivan's arguments were exceedingly well considered and well delivered, and were in every way worthy of the greatest traditions of the King's Courts. It was from no want of respect to his argument that the Court did not call upon the Attorney-General. But the Court, having considered fully and carefully every argument used by Mr Serjeant Sullivan and the authorities advanced, had come to the conclusion that there was no need to call for any refutation from the Crown. The main point raised in the argument of Mr Serjeant Sullivan, his Lordship said, was that this Statute had neither created nor declared that it was an offence to be adherent to the King's enemies beyond the realm of the King, and that the words 'giving aid and comfort outside the realm' did not constitute a treason which could he tried in this country unless the person who gave the aid and comfort outside the realm—in this case the Empire of Germany—was himself within the realm at the time when he gave that aid and comfort, and, therefore, the person could not be tried in any Courts at all for what he had done in Germany unless he was himself actually resident within the realm of the King. That argument was founded on difficulties which must arise owing to the doctrine of venue, under which people were only triable within certain districts. The dearth of cases had been dwelt upon, but a guilty man would in all probability absent himself altogether from the country where he might be punished. Therefore, the Court was not very much impressed with the fact that here was very little precedent for such a prosecution as this. But there was a large amount of authority for the proposition that what the jury had found, and what it was not contested was done by this appellant, was an offence triable in the King's Bench. Mr Serjeant Sullivan had said that the construction was not a true one, but the Court agreed that a person, who, being within this country, gave aid and comfort to the King's enemies in this country, was adherent to the King's enemies, and if he was in this country and gave aid and comfort to the King's enemies outside, the Court agreed that he was then adherent to the King's enemies. But the Court thought that there was another offence, and that the words of the Statute meant something more.

Meaning of the Statute

The court thought the meeting was this—that if a man gave aid and comfort to the King's enemies—and there were words in apposition to explain what was meant by 'adhering to'—by adhering to the King's enemies in his realm, by giving them aid and comfort in this realm, or by adhering to the King's enemies elsewhere—that was, by giving aid and comfort elsewhere—he was equally adherent to the King's enemies, and if he was adherent to the King's enemies then he committed treason which the Statute of Edward III defined. The reason for that might be given as follows: The subject of a King owed him allegiance, and the allegiance followed the person of the subject. He was the King's liege wherever he lived, and he might violate his allegiance in any foreign country. It was known to the Court that there was a great deal of authority for the proposition that adherence outside the King's dominions by a person himself outside constituted exemption. Many persons may have debated that such a person could have been tried, but there was ancient opinion for the proposition that it was treason to do what the appellant had been convicted of doing in this case. Mr Serjeant Sullivan had asked the Court to simply take the Statute and read it as though they had seen it for the first time, and had said that this was the best way to construe any Statute. It was a little difficult for any judge of the King's Bench to say that he read for the first time the Statute of Edward III. They must have read it before that. He did not know that the rule that Mr Serjeant Sullivan laid down was an altogether acceptable one. The learned judge quoted a commentator to the effect that 'long usage is presumed to be the true construction, and the long acquiescence of the Legislature in its interpretation put upon this enactment might perhaps be regarded as some sanction and approval of it.' This Statute, his lordship went on to say, had been understood long before that day by lawyers of great learning, by lawyers of very exceptional erudition, in the sense that the Court understood it. Their authority had been attacked by Mr Serjeant Sullivan, who had also attacked Lord Coke. But if the Court were to accede to Mr Serjeant Sullivan's argument they would have to absolutely disregard the opinion of Lord Coke and other legal authorities, great men, whose opinion had been followed in many questions of extreme difficulty, which had puzzled lawyers for many years past. The Court did not think it necessary to give further reasons for the conclusion at which they had arrived. The Court certainly did not rely on the recent case quoted by Mr Serjeant Sullivan, simply for the reason that they were of opinion that ample authority for the conclusion to which the Courts came in that case was to be found in the decisions and opinions of the great lawyers to whom he had already referred. It remains, remarked his lordship, in conclusion, to say that the appeal is dismissed.

This ended the proceedings.

Special Sitting of Appeal Court

The Court of Criminal Appeal, London, convened in case it was desired to make an appeal on behalf of the convict Roger Casement, sat on Friday, 29th July, at the Royal Courts of Justice. It consisted of the five judges who disposed of Casement's appeal—Mr Justice Darling (who presided), Mr Justice Bray, Mr Justice AT Lawrence, Mr Justice Scrutton, and Mr Justice Atkin.

The Attorney-General, Sir Frederick Smith, KC, and the Solicitor-General, Sir George Cave, KC, were early in the seats they usually occupy, but a long time after the Court was timed to sit no one had put in an appearance on behalf of Casement. The five judges took their seats just before half-past ten, and still the convicted man was apparently unrepresented. A few minutes were spent by Mr Justice Darling in consulting his brother judges, and during the conversation he pulled out a sheaf of letters, and handed one or two sheets around the Bench for perusal.

Mr Justice Darling, addressing the Court, said that the Court had assembled because they were informed some time ago by the King's Coroner that the solicitor representing the convict Casement had been to him, and proposed to make some application for the consideration of some points which were mentioned in the notice of appeal, and which points Serjeant Sullivan stated in court publicly he abandoned, because having considered them carefully, he had come to the conclusion that he could not ask the Court to quash the conviction upon the grounds contained under those heads. The Court had been in considerable doubt from day to day. They could not obtain definite information whether it was intended to make application to the Court or whether it was not. If it was to be made, now was the opportunity to make it. They had that day received a letter from the solicitor, saying that the King's Coroner had been informed quite definitely that the solicitor for the convict would not proceed with the application, which he had mentioned as a possible application. As the matter had become so public, and as people might not understand exactly what were the rights of the question, he desired to say that what he said now he was saying for the whole Court. They were in no way surprised when Serjeant Sullivan rose, and said he abandoned those points which were taken in the notice of appeal, and which points he did not go into. It was conveyed to the King's Coroner—that was why the judges treated the matter so seriously—that Serjeant Sullivan had no authority from those who instructed him to abandon those points. Referring to the reason why the Attorney-General was not called upon by the Court to reply to Serjeant Sullivan's argument, Mr Justice Darling said he wanted to let the public know what the procedure was. The judges before they met to hear any appeal read all the evidence, the notice of appeal, and considered all the points which had been taken, and as far as they could make up their minds without hearing the argument, they decided whether the points were good or bad. The Court had come to the same conclusion as Serjeant Sullivan, that there was nothing in these points. Had they thought otherwise they would have called on the Attorney-General to argue them. It could hardly be alleged with anything approaching plausibility that Serjeant Sullivan had not authority to withdraw those points. There were present in court at the time the solicitor instructing Serjeant Sullivan and his two juniors, and it was inconceivable that during all the time that the Court was out discussing the matters—twenty minutes—if Serjeant Sullivan had not had authority to withdraw the points the solicitor and junior should not have told him so, and the Court should have been allowed to go away with the slightest intimation that these points were not withdrawn with the whole cognisance of everybody concerned for Casement. The Court felt that there should be no sort of misapprehension as to what had occurred in the case.

Mr Powell, KC, having received permission to make a personal explanation, said he had been retained to argue in the House of Lords the points of law arising on the Edward III statute of treason, if the Attorney-General's certificate could be obtained. He was retained for nothing at that court, but was present at the request of their lordships. Mr Artemus Jones, junior counsel for Casement, never for one moment contemplated making the application referred to. He had learned that the proper officer of the Court was informed definitely by the prisoner's solicitor two days ago that the points were abandoned.

Mr Justice Darling: This is really attacking the King's Coroner.

Mr Powell said he wished to attack neither the King's Coroner, who had done everything he could, not any officer of his department.

Mr Justice Darling added that he, Mr Justice Bray, and Mr Justice Scrutton were acquainted step by step with every communication that had been made to the King's Coroner.

The Court then rose.

Casement Executed in London

On Thursday, 3rd August

Roger David Casement was executed in London on Thursday morning, 3rd August.

A large crowd of people assembled outside Pentonville Prison, and when at eight minutes past nine the prison bell tolled, members of the crowd exclaimed—'He has gone!' A second or two later the bell pealed again, and a cheer went up, mostly from children. Ellis was the executioner.

A Roman Catholic priest who attended the condemned man at the execution afterwards informed a Press representative that Casement went to his death 'strong and erect, like the man he was.' The priest said a prayer, and Casement replied, 'Into Thy hands, O Lord, I commend my spirit.' Later the condemned man said, 'Lord Jesus, receive my soul.' Three official notices were afterwards posted on the prison doors. The first was a declaration that judgment had been carried out in the presence of the Under-Sheriff for London, the Governor of the Prison, the Roman Catholic Chaplain of the prison, and others. Another notice stated:

'I, PR Mander, Surgeon of His Majesty's Prison of Pentonville, hereby certify that I, this day, have examined the body of Roger David Casement, on whom judgment of death was this day executed in the said prison, and that on that examination I found the said Roger David Casement was dead.'

'Dated this 3rd Day of August, 1916.

'PR Mander.'

Another notice bore the signature, 'AR Preston, Under-Sheriff of Middlesex.'

The Inquest

The inquest on the body of Casement was held in Pentonville Prison. Mr Gavan Duffy, Casement's solicitor, formally identified the body, and said that the deceased was between 50 and 60. In reply to Mr Duffy, the Coroner said the order for burial was issued by him and handed to the Governor of the prison. As to any matter beyond that, an application must be made to the authorities. Mr Duffy said he had applied to the Home Office for permission to have the body. He considered it a monstrous act of indecency to refuse it. The Governor of the prison said Casement's death was instantaneous. The Catholic priests present performed the rites according to the Catholic faith. Mr Mander, senior medical officer, was asked by Mr Duffy the result of his observation of Casement, and if there was any truth in the suggestion made in the Press. Witness replied that he saw no evidence of insanity. A verdict of death due to execution was returned.

Casement as Agent of Germany

The Statement by Government

The Press Bureau the same night announced that it was instructed to place the following statement at the disposal of the Press:

All the circumstances in the case of Roger Casement

were carefully and repeatedly considered by the Government before the decision was reached not to interfere with the sentence of the law. He was convicted and punished for treachery of the worst kind to the Empire he had served, and as a willing agent of Germany.

The Irish rebellion resulted in much loss of life, both among soldiers and civilians. Casement invoked and organised German assistance to the insurrection. In addition, though himself for many years a British official, he undertook the task of trying to induce soldiers of the British Army, prisoners in the hands of Germany to foreswear their oaths of allegiance and join their country's enemies.

Conclusive evidence has since into the hands of the Government since the trial that he had entered into an agreement with the German Government, which explicitly provided that the brigade which he was trying to raise from among the Irish soldier prisoners might be employed in Egypt against the British Crown.

Cruelty to Irish Prisoners of War

Those among the Irish soldiers, prisoners in Germany, who resisted Casement's solicitations of disloyalty were subjected to treatment of exceptional cruelty by the Germans. Some of them have since been exchanged as invalids, and have died in this country, regarding Casement as their murder.

The suggestion that Casement left Germany for the purpose of trying to stop the Irish rising was not raised at the trial, and is conclusively disproved, not only by the facts there disclosed, but by further evidence which has since become available.

Another suggestion that Casement was out of his mind is equally without foundation. Materials bearing on his mental condition were placed at the disposal of his counsel, who did not raise the plea of insanity. Casement's demeanour since his arrest, and throughout and since his trial, gave no ground for any such defence, and, indeed, was sufficient to disprove it.

WILL OF ROGER CASEMENT

The will, made on a sheet of foolscap, and dated August 1st, 1916, of Roger David Casement, of Malahide, Dublin, Ireland, who died at Pentonville Prison on August 31st, was proved by Mrs Gertrude Parry, of Oxmead, Ewhurst, Surrey (cousin), and George Gavan Duffy, of 45 Connaught street, London, W., solicitor, the value of the estate being sworn at £135 0s. 10d. The testator gave everything he possessed or could dispose of to his cousin, Gertrude Parry. The witnesses were J Middleton, PW, and W Turner, warder.

PERILOUS WORK OF THE AMBULANCE STAFF

Captain Purcell stated on Monday, 1st May, that in addition to the Fire Brigade's duties at the fires, they carried out an incredible amount of work with their ambulance service. During the eight days their three ambulances made on an average 50 journeys daily, picking up the wounded and dead. Sometimes, said Captain Purcell, in fact many times, the recovery and removal of wounded took place under actual fire. Bullets hit the ambulance on many occasions, and in one instance a horse was shot clean through the foreleg; while in another case a civilian who was assisting the firemen to place a stretcher in the ambulance with a woman, who had been shot by snipers, was himself struck by a bullet. In addition to this work, we had to remove people from dangerous areas, and to aid paralytics and invalids. There were hundreds of cases that we could not attend to.

KINGSTOWN

From Wednesday until Friday there was merely a procession of all sorts of troops and trains of supply day and night. Communication was cut off from the outside. Barricades were erected everywhere on all routes from Kingstown: none save soldiers could pass to or from Kingstown without military permits. People were confined in their homes between the hours of 7.30 at night and 5.30 a.m.; the streets were policed with armed men. It was an extraordinary and trying experience, in which the continuing scarcity of food was really alarming. On Saturday night food came in by special boats, and on Sunday morning a number of shops opened to sell it. Bread made in London was eaten that day by people in Kingstown. So rebellion week mainly affected Kingstown. Never a shot was fired in anger within its precincts.

ILLUSTRATED RECORDS

Pictorial records of the rising were issued as follows:

The Record of the Irish Rebellion, published by 'Irish Life'.

Dublin and the Sinn Fein Rising, published by Wilson, Hartnell and Co.

The Sinn Fein Revolt, Illustrated, published by Hely's, Ltd.

Dublin after the Six Days' Insurrection, published by Mecredy, Percy and Co., Ltd.

ROYAL COMMISSION OF INQUIRY
GOVERNMENT NEGLECT REVEALED

The Royal Commission appointed to investigate the facts surrounding the rebellion in Ireland opened its inquiry at the Royal Commission's House, Westminster, on Thursday, 18th May.

The members of the Commission were:

Lord Hardinge (Chairman), Mr Justice Shearman, and Sir Mackenzie Chalmers.

The Chairman said they had to inquire:

1. What system there was in force in Ireland to enable the officials to obtain information as to the movement which led to the present outbreak.
2. What information was obtained as to it.
3. To whom was that information communicated and,
4. What steps were taken upon the information received

They would also deal with the question of the responsibility of persons or associations for this particular outbreak

Sir Matthew Nathan

Sir Matthew Nathan, late Under-Secretary to the Lord Lieutenant of Ireland, was the first witness. He read a statement in which he recounted the history of the Volunteer movement up to the point in September, 1914, when they split, and Mr Redmond's followers were known as the National Volunteers, the name by which the loyal section was subsequently distinguished from the disloyal section or 'Irish Volunteers.' Of the members enrolled previous to this—about 180,000—witness continued, not more than 11,000 adhered to the disloyal section of the original Provisional Committee. By October, 1914, the Volunteers following Mr Redmond had fallen in numbers to 165,000, whilst those following Mr McNeill had gone up to 13,500, including over 2,000 in Dublin, of whom a few belonged to the Citizen Army. From that time the shrinkage in the National Volunteers had steadily continued. From the middle of October to the middle of December the Irish Volunteers were estimated to be about 14,000 strong, and they were increased by about 2,000 men in the provinces. This increase synchronised with several efforts being made by the Department for Recruiting in Ireland to get men for the Colours. Impetus was given to the Irish Volunteer movement by the fear of the Military Service Bill being applied to Ireland. The number of Sínn Fein Volunteers at the time of the outbreak was estimated by the police authorities to be about 15,200, including some 2,850 in the provinces, of whom the majority were actually enrolled as Irish Volunteers, and remained, although still calling themselves National Volunteers, and looked upon John McNeill as their head. There was no difficulty in the country for the Royal Irish Constabulary to know what leader the men acknowledged. The figure of 3,225, including 100 of the Citizen Army, given by the Metropolitan Police of Dublin, was likely to be under-estimated. The Citizen Army were militant members of the Irish Transport Workers' Union, which, under James Larkin, had conducted the strike of 1913, and, when Larkin, at the end of 1914, left Ireland for America, obeyed the orders of James Thomas Connolly. It was believed that the close association between the Citizen Army and the Irish Volunteers only dated from the latter part of 1915. But there was no doubt that in recent months they had worked together, worked under one direction, the Citizen Army leaders urging violent action. In this they were supported by the Irish Republican leaders, which consisted of a small knot of men, of whom some members had, in connection with the dynamite outrages in 1883, been sentenced to penal servitude.

Funds from America

The Irish Volunteers had from the outset funds at their disposal. Before the split between the National and the Irish Volunteers considerable sums were coming from America, and being paid into various banks in Dublin in the name of Mr John MacNeill, President of the General Council and Executive Committee, and another gentleman. Sums roughly amounting to £16,000 continued to be sent into the account up to September, 1914. After that it was not possible to trace the method of receipt in Ireland of funds from America. It was believed that a large part of the funds available for anti-British organisation were expended in the maintenance of seditious newspapers, and the circulation of seditious leaflets, and the employment of organisers to travel the country to win people to join the Irish Volunteers, and become in their turn organisers in this direction. A summary attached to the statement showed that shortly before the outbreak of the insurrection there were supposed to be 1,886 rifles, and a number of shot guns, pistols, and revolvers in the provinces, and 825 rifles and a number of other firearms in Dublin

How arms and ammunition were obtained

The number of rifles was probably under-estimated. Thefts of rifles from the National Volunteers were not taken into account. It was known that a hundred were stolen from the warehouses of the London and North-Western Railway Company. There were thefts of rifles from the military, and they must have been considerable. No doubt further rifles were purchased from soldiers on leave. There was evidence of heavy importation from England before it was stopped on December 8th, 1915. It was also known that revolvers and pistols, much in excess of the number on record, were being brought into Ireland in passengers' baggage and otherwise. For some time it was believed that there was no great supply of ammunition in the hands of the

Volunteers. It was known there had been at least one considerable theft of military ammunition, and also that the rounds carried by soldiers were being purchased. It was also believed that man-killing ammunition was being made for miniature rifles and shot guns. Searches made from time to time in Dublin and the provinces, had revealed no considerable store either of arms or ammunition.

Explosives

On the other hand, evidence was available of considerable thefts of explosives, and the manufacture of bombs. Offences connected with explosives occurred at Enniscorthy, in February, 1913: at Sligo in November, 1915: at Cork in December, 1915: at Castlebellingham and at Lanarkshire, in Scotland, in January, 1915, and at a place in County Kildare in February. Those cases were considered to indicate the intention to commit outrages on persons or buildings.

Describing the steps taken to deal with the movement which led up to the insurrection, Sir Matthew Nathan said that the Irish Volunteers were originally part of the Volunteer force which came into existence at the time of the organisation of the Ulster Volunteers, and the attempt made to deprive them of arms, surreptitiously landed for their use, was declared by a Judicial Commission, which sat shortly after the outbreak of the Continental war, to be illegal. It was accordingly impossible for the Government to take any proceedings against them at that time. The Judicial Commission was a Royal Commission into the circumstances of the landing of arms at Howth. At the end of 1914 it was recognised that in the *personnel* of the Committee, its declaration of policy, the utterances of its leading representatives in the Press and at public meetings, its opposition to the efforts of Mr Redmond and the Irish Parliamentary Party to bring Ireland into line during the national crisis, and its crusade against enlistment into the army, the Irish Volunteer organisation had shown itself to be disloyal and seditious.

Measures against Civil Servant

Henceforth, the proceedings of the organisation were carefully watched, and steps were taken to prevent Civil Servants belonging to the Irish Volunteers. Warnings were given to the seditious Press, and steps were taken to restrict the activity of the organisation. The importation and sale of arms were brought under strict regulation. The policy of not allowing Government servants to belong the organisation was consistently followed, and where membership was proved to continue after warning had been given dismissal followed. Persons were dismissed from the Ordnance Stores, the Post Office, the Inland Revenue, the Ordnance Survey and some other Government or quasi Government Departments. Some of the people who were dismissed proved to be amongst the most violent of those who were against the Government. In the cases of priests assisting the Volunteers in any public way, representations were made to the higher ecclesiastical authority. After explaining the actions taken in dealing with seditious newspapers, witness went on to say that the necessity of placing some check on the activities of the organising instructors was considered by the military and civil authorities in July, 1915. Four men were sentenced, one to four and the others to three months' imprisonment, and ordered to leave Ireland, but they were told that at the expiration of their sentences the order would not be enforced unless their conduct was unsatisfactory. Two of them were deported, and their deportation was followed by somewhat violent demonstrations in Dublin. One of the men, Mellows, returned and led the insurrection in Galway. Of the 496 cases under the Regulation, 153 had been for making use of anti-recruiting expressions and illegal and seditious language, and 34 were for offences in regard to arms and ammunition.

Verdicts against Weight of Evidence

In two bad cases of having explosives in possession, brought before juries in Dublin, verdicts of not guilty were returned against the weight of evidence. Similar miscarriages of justice occurred in Cork in connection with speeches. As the Defence of the Realm Act had done away with trial by courtmartial, and as juries could not be trusted, it was necessary to bring such cases before the magistrates in Dublin and elsewhere, and this meant that the punishment for serious offences could not exceed six months' hard labour.

Proceeding, Sir Matthew said that the Irish Government had considered it of primary importance to prevent the Irish Volunteers becoming a military danger, and that every obstacle should be placed in the way of arms and ammunition getting into their hands. It was difficult to make this policy effective. English manufacturers had been importing freely into Ireland for some time after the commencement of the war, and even after the importation was forbidden, owing to he action of the Customs examiners, it was impossible to prevent forbidden goods from getting through. As late as April 16th a case of 500 bayonets was detected by the police on the way from a Sheffield cutler to a Sínn Fein manager of what was believed to be a reputable firm.

Anxious to start 'Business'

A report was received in March, said witness, to the effect that the young men of the Volunteers were very anxious to start business at once, and were being backed up strongly by Connolly, of the Citizen Army, but the heads of the Volunteers were against the rising at present. One of their leaders said it would be sheer madness unless the help promised by Monteith was forthcoming. It was stated that Monteith had been an Irish Volunteer instructor, and was in Germany. It was reported that there was to be a general mobilisation on April 2nd.

Photo by [*Photo Press.*

LORD HARDINGE. **MR. JUSTICE SHEARMAN.** **SIR MACKENZIE CHALMERS**

These gentlemen constituted the Royal Commission which inquired into the causes of the rebellion.

Photo by [*Photo Press.*

SIR MATTHEW NATHAN, the late Under Secretary for Ireland. **MR. AUGUSTINE BIRRELL**, the late Chief Secretary for Ireland.

After giving evidence before the Royal Commission at Westminster.

Another report of March 22nd stated that there was no fear of any rising by Volunteers standing alone. They were not prepared for any prolonged action, and the majority were practically untrained.

On 17th April there was information contained in a letter which told of the contemplated landing from a German ship made up as a neutral and accompanied by two submarines of arms and ammunition on the South-West coast. The letter was shown to the Inspector-General of the Royal Irish Constabulary, and the Inspectors of the South and South-West counties were put on their guard. On the 19th a report was received by the police from a woman having two brothers in the Irish Volunteers that the Castle would be attacked that night, but nothing unusual occurred. Witness then went on to speak of the events connected with the attempted landing from German vessels and the arrest of Sir Roger Casement.

Easter Sunday Order Rescinded

About that time a notice was published in an Irish newspaper, signed by John MacNeill, 'Chief of Staff, Irish Volunteers,' rescinding the orders for Easter Sunday, and stating that no movement of the Volunteers would take place. In another portion of the paper the discovery of the collapsible boat and the arrest of a man of unknown nationality and of Stack and Collins was announced.

There was no movement of the Irish Volunteers on Easter Sunday, but a report was received of a robbery under arms, and the stealing of five 50lb cases of gelignite, which was believed to have been brought into Dublin by motor car.

Decision to arrest leaders

A consultation took place at the Viceregal Lodge, and it was considered that the position justified the arrest and internment in England of some of the leaders of the movement. This course was, therefore, decided on. Further evidence of their association with the enemy was received from the District Inspector of Tralee, who reported the arrest of one of the men landing in the collapsible boat, and implicating Stack and Collins. He also stated that a vessel containing arms was to be piloted into Fenit that night, and that there was to be a rising and an attack on Dublin Castle. The Chief Secretary agreed to the arrest of the leaders, in view of their definite association with the enemy having been established. Later telegrams were received telling of malicious damage to the railway and telegraphic communications.

The first shot

The first shot was fired a little after noon on April 24th. When matters connected with the general situation were being discussed at the Castle, shots rang out at the gate, and the body of a dying policeman was carried into the yard. The statement proceeded to enumerate the places in Dublin which were taken by the rebels.

The existence of organised bodies of trained and armed men, not under the control of the Government, which in August, 1914, was the recognised state of affairs in Ireland, necessarily involved grave risks to the State. The idea in the early days of the war that these Volunteers should come under control as part of the armed forces of the Crown, for the defence of Ireland against a foreign enemy, did not find favour with the military authorities, and, while those Volunteers who would have accepted such control either enlisted in the Army or became inactive, others turned to national hostility, which enhanced the danger they constituted to the Empire. Suppression of the Volunteers would have meant complete disarmament, and at any rate, strong coercive measures, which to be effective would have had to go outside the Irish Volunteers, and extend to the body from which they had sprung, and were subsequently to some extent recruited.

The difficulty

In the circumstances, especially if the Volunteers to resist Home Rule had been allowed to continue, the Nationalist union would have been completely alienated, and with it that large body of Irish feeling which had been favourable to Great Britain in the war, and had sent some 55,000 Irish Catholics to fight for the Empire. It was rather noteworthy that in the month ending April 15th 1,827 men joined the Army, including 448 in Dublin itself. Since the beginning of the war 18,698 men had joined in Dublin. Even such measures as the suppression of seditious newspapers and the prosecution of persons for inflammatory speeches were taken against the advice of the Irish Parliamentary Party, whose loyalty was undoubted. It was for these reasons that the policy of the Government was not to attempt the suppression of the Volunteers. At the same time, war conditions required that the measures taken should prevent them getting supplies of arms and ammunition, and organising, especially in those parts of Ireland where they might render assistance to a foreign enemy. The possibility of this was always kept in view, and the Royal Irish Constabulary watched their movements.

The Constabulary's part

In spite of the demands of recruiting, it was looked upon as important not to allow any great diminution in the numbers of the Constabulary, but considerably to increase the strength of the garrison (military). It was known that this could supply at short notice a movable force of 2,500, and that 1,000 men could turn out in Dublin and Cork if required. When the insurrection broke out the men quickly turned out from the Dublin barracks, and some hundreds concentrated at the Castle, and other posts were occupied. 2,500 men arrived that evening, and 1,000 men came from Belfast the following day. Further reinforcements arrived from England on the 26th.

Meeting of the leaders

There seemed to have been a meeting of the Volunteer leaders in Dublin on Saturday or Sunday, when it was decided by a majority of one, it was stated, to start an insurrection the following Easter Monday. Had information been obtained of this movement troops would have been concentrated sooner in the Castle. Generally, the tactics which their numbers and armament forced them to adopt, while they made ultimate success hopeless, gave them the mastery of the situation for some time, and would have done so had more troops been available.

The only practical purpose such an insurrection could achieve was to detain a large number of troops in the city for a time, which would be valuable to a hostile force operating elsewhere. Apart from its general ultimate futility, the conduct of the insurrection showed greater organising power and more military skill than had been attributed to the Volunteers, and they also appeared, from reports, to have acted with greater courage.

This concluded the statement, and Sir Matthew Nathan then answered questions put to him.

Witness examined

The President: What is the strength of the Constabulary? The actual strength on the 31st March last was 9,302.

Has there been any increase or decrease of late? There has been a considerable decrease since the beginning of the war.

But with all the activity on the part of Volunteers and other associations, did you not consider it necessary to keep the Constabulary up to establishment? I felt strongly that any big decrease would be quite out of the question.

But the decrease was about 2,000, was it not? It was not as much as that. There were 1,231 wanting to complete establishment, but I think that includes a considerable number that had been wanting for some time.

Abolition of the arms restriction

Replying to Mr Justice Shearman, witness said that on August 5th, 1914, the restriction on the importation of arms into Ireland, which had existed until then, was removed, but he did not know why. He added that the importation of arms was prohibited in 1913. After the removal of the restrictions efforts were made to prohibit importation under the Defence of the Realm Act. There was licence duty to be paid, but it was not enforced.

The Chairman: Why not? It is enforced in England.

Witness was understood to reply that, as the arms were obviously carried for illegal purposes, it was looked upon as trifling to ask for licence duty.

A Statute that was not enforced.

Mr Justice Shearman: is there any statute to prevent armed drilling for illegal purposes? There is a statute against illegal assembly. There is a statute of 1819 which prevents armed persons drilling together, whatever their object, without the permission of the authorities.

You have no experience of that statute being enforced? No.

So there was nothing to enable you to arrest people drilling with armed weapons, unless you could prove they were there for a seditious purpose? There was nothing to prevent loyal or disloyal citizens assembling to any number. We were deterred for political reasons.

Mr Justice Shearman asked if the drilling of young men and the training of young women to give first aid, which witness had described in his report, did not obviously point to a war in Ireland.

Sir Matthew Nathan did not reply.

Mr Justice Shearman asked when the sham attack on Dublin Castle took place.

Witness: On the 6th October, 1915.

The Chairman: Did not it seem 'extraordinary' that these people should be permitted to make an attack on Dublin Castle, and that nothing was done to prevent it? Of course, we were accustomed to all sorts of operations in Ireland.

Leaving it alone

Was the fact that no notice was taken of this in accordance with the general line of policy laid down by those responsible? Generally.

And that a free hand was to be given to any of the Irish Volunteers to behave as they liked, provided they did not go actually to extremities such as taking life?

Witness hesitated a little about a reply.

Mr Justice Shearman interposed with the remark: He says he decided that unless there was an actual outbreak they would not interfere. If you disarmed publicly these people there must have been some bloodshed, and if you let it blow over it might blow over without any bloodshed at all. I hope I am not wronging you in saying that was the policy pursued.

Witness agreed.

Mr Justice Shearman: The policy chosen was, to leave it alone, in the hope that it would result in nothing.

Witness: Also in the belief that the action against these Volunteers, on the ground that they had been manoeuvring, would have resulted in the alienation of the great bulk of the Irish people, which was not in favour of these people.

Administration

After lunch, the witness, replying to Sir Mackenzie Chalmers, gave details as to the administrative constitution of the Dublin Castle staff and the police—the RIC and the Dublin Metropolitan Police.

What is the strength of the Dublin Police?

The number is 1,121, out of a maximum of 1,160.

Sir Mackenzie Chalmers then asked questions of

Sir Matthew Nathan relative to the cases he had mentioned, the results of which led the authorities to conclude that juries were not to be trusted. The juries in those cases, he said, did not disagree, but definitely acquitted the accused, against whom, in the view of the Crown, the evidence was pretty clear.

Military strength in Dublin

From the 22nd April onwards, how many soldiers had you in Dublin? There must have been about 4,000

Had you any English or Scottish regiments in Dublin? Cavalry. They did not attempt to use them as cavalry. Witness added that there were in Dublin about one thousand unarmed Dublin Police, while at the Depot there were about fifty men of the RIC.

Sir Mackenzie Chalmers: So that your armed force was about 1,050? Yes.

Sir Mackenzie Chalmers: Among the Dublin Police and the Royal Irish Constabulary I imagine you had perfect loyalty? Yes.

Necessarily you are left a good deal in sole charge at Dublin Castle I suppose? If Parliament is sitting, and Mr Birrell is there. The last occasion Mr Birrell was in Ireland was in February, when he was there about ten days or a fortnight.

The Sinn Fein movement.

The witness was then questioned about the Sinn Fein movement, and read a statement to the effect that it was started in 1905, giving as its aims and objects national development on the lines successfully adopted by the Hungarians in their struggle with Austria. By a policy of Sinn Fein, 'ourselves alone', it was to deal with all movements originating within Ireland, not looking outside Ireland for the accomplishment of their aims.

Sir Mackenzie Chalmers: Was there any connection between the Larkinites and the Clan-na-Gael? We knew that Larkin appeared on Clan-na-Gael platforms in America. That was after he left Dublin.

Where is Larkin

Mr Justice Shearman: Is it quite certain, Sir Matthew, that he is in America? We believe so.

Sir Matthew went on to explain the nature of the Gaelic League. It was formed, he said, for the study of Irish literature and language, and included people of all political opinions. Gradually those who were not anti-British dropped out, and afterwards the Executive was practically captured by the leaders of the Irish Volunteers.

The Gaelic Athletic Association was anti-British, and soldiers in uniform were not allowed to attend its gatherings.

Sir Mackenzie Chalmers: Was any notice taken of that? No action was taken.

Mr John MacNeill's notice

Witness was asked about the notice signed by John MacNeill, saying that there would be no movement of the Irish Volunteers on Easter Sunday. 'Was that a blind?' asked Sir Mackenzie Chalmers.

'I should very much like to know,' was the reply. 'I don't think so. He probably wanted to stop it at the last moment.'

Sir Mackenzie Chalmers: I cannot understand why you suggest that if these men were disarmed the loyal Nationalist Volunteers and the Ulster Volunteers should also disarm, when there is no connection between them.

Sir Matthew Nathan: We did not know at the time who were loyal and who were disloyal. A good many of them went over from the loyalist to the disloyal side afterwards. If we had left the National Volunteers we should have left a large number of disloyal people.

STRIKING ADMISSION BY MR BIRRELL.

On Friday, 19th May, Mr Augustine Birrell, late Chief Secretary for Ireland, appeared before the commission at the Royal Commission House, Westminster. He said that he had seen Sir Matthew Nathan's statement, and he had no additions to make in regard to it. Mr Birrell added that he had prepared a statement of a rather general character on Sinn Feinism, and at once proceeded to read it.

The statement was as follows:

The spirit of what to-day is called Sinn Feinism is mainly composed of the old hatred and distrust of the British connection, always noticeable in all classes and in all places, varying in degree, and finding different ways of expression, but always there as the background of Irish politics and character. Dr Newman, on coming over to Dublin as an English Catholic, in the very middle of the last century, discovered it for himself, and was amazed and disgusted at its virility, and was very glad to get away from it. This dislike, hatred, disloyalty (so unintelligible to many Englishmen) is hard to define, but easy to discern, though incapable of exact measurement from year to year. You may assume it is always there, and always dangerous. Reasons are often given for its persistency despite efforts to obliterate it. Had Catholic Emancipation accompanied the Act of Union, had the land tenure reform been ante-dated half a century, had the Protestant Church of Ireland been disestablished a little more to please the Irish people and not so much to gratify the British Nonconformist, had the University question been earlier settled, it is possible, though not obvious, that this spirit of Sinn Feinism might by now have been exorcised. It has, in point of fact, been immensely weakened and restricted, and out of many Irish breasts it may, perhaps, have been removed altogether.

Transformation

The last twenty years have worked transformation. The face of the country is changed. Self-government has been established in the counties on the most democratic plan, and with the most democratic results ever devised or accomplished, even by Tories, and though the experiment was a risky one, it has, on the whole, succeeded. The Irish Local Government Board, though much exposed to criticism, and coming in for a fair share of abuse, is essentially an Irish Board, and wholly outside what is called, often most uninstructedly, 'the Castle' influence. The Congested Districts Board, with enlarged statutory powers and a very considerable income, is also essentially an Irish Board, and within its powers and within its income supreme. The Department, as it is called, of Agriculture and Technical Instruction is Irish in all its ways, quarrels and pursuits. And yet, despite these things, and in the face of prosperity among the farmers, cottages for the labourers, and control over her most important affairs, no close observer of Ireland as a whole during the last two years or so could fail to notice that this Sinn Fein spirit was increasing. For a number of years the Home Rule controversy, which seemed at last to be on its way to a Parliamentary solution, absorbed most of the energies of active politicians, whilst those who were out of real sympathy with a movement which seemed to them limited and unromantic, were content to allow the controversy to be conducted in Parliament by able leaders, and to run its course, whilst they stayed at home and attended, or at least supported, the Gaelic League and other kindred and influential societies.

The Irish Literary Revival

This period was also marked by a genuine literary Irish revival, in prose, poetry and the drama, which has produced remarkable books and plays, and a school of acting, all characterised by originality and independence of thought and expression, quite divorced from any political party, and all tending towards and feeding latent desires for some kind of separate Irish national existence. It was a curious situation to watch, but there was nothing in it suggestive of revolt or rebellion, except in the realm of thought. Indeed, it was quite the other way. The Abbey Theatre made merciless fun of mad political enterprise, and lashed with savage satire some historical aspects of the Irish revolutionary. I was often amazed at the literary detachment and courage of the playwright, the relentless audacity of the actors and actresses, and the patience and comprehension of the audience. This new critical tone and temper, noticeable everywhere, penetrating everything, and influencing many minds in all ranks, whilst having its disintegrating effects upon old fashioned political beliefs and worn-out controversial phrases, was the deadly foe of that wild sentimental passion which has once more led so many brave young fellows to a certain doom, in the belief that in Ireland any revolution is better than none. A little more time, and, but for the outbreak of the war, this new critical temper would, in my belief, have finally prevailed, not indeed to destroy national sentiment (for that is immortal), but to kill by ridicule insensate revolt. But this was not to be.

Some 'causes' of antipathy

There are a number of contributory causes, which lately have created antipathy to constitutional methods and tended to increase in numbers. First—growing doubts about the actual advent of Home Rule. If the Home Rule Bill had not been placed on the Statute Book there must have been in Ireland and the United States a great and dangerous explosion of rage and disappointment, which when the war broke out would have assumed the most alarming proportions in Ireland. All (outside parts of Ulster) would have joined hands, whilst our reports from Washington tell us what the effect in America would have been. Still, even with Home Rule on the Statute Book, the chance of its ever becoming a fact was so uncertain, the outstanding difficulty about Ulster was so obvious, and the details of the measure itself were so unattractive and difficult to transmute into telling platform phrases, that home Rule as an emotional flag fell out of daily use in current Irish life. People left off talking about it, or waving it in the air.

Second—In Ireland, whenever Constitutional and Parliamentary procedure cease to be of absorbing influence, other men, other methods, other thoughts, before somewhat harshly snubbed, come rapidly to the surface, and secure attention, sympathy and support. The sneers of the O'Brienites, the daily naggings in the Dublin *Irish Independent* also contributed to the partial eclipse of Home Rule, and this eclipse foretold danger.

The Ulster Rebellion

Third—The Ulster rebellion, the gun running at Larne, the Covenant, the Provisional Government, and its members, its plan of warfare in Belfast, its armed volunteers and public drillings, and all the rest of the pomp and circumstances of revolution, had the most prodigious effect upon disloyalists elsewhere. There was no anger with the Ulster rebels. Catholic Ireland was very proud of them. 'What they are allowed to do we can do.' This needs no elaboration from me.

Fourth—Then came the war on the 4th August, 1914. This was the moment of the greatest risk. Nobody could foretell what would happen in Ireland, or what her attitude would be. It might easily have demanded 60,000 soldiers to keep her down. Mr Redmond's spontaneous, patriotic, courageous, but British, speech, was a bold stroke, and bravely has it succeeded. One hundred and fifty thousand Irish volunteer soldiers are fighting as Irish soldiers know how to fight, on the side of Great Britain. To me it is marvellous. But there were in Ireland men and women who thought that Mr Redmond had thrown away a great opportunity, and that he should have struck a bargain with the Crown ere he consented to become a recruiting officer for it. These men were in a small minority. Ireland preserved an unbroken front with the rest of the United Kingdom and the Empire, and this she did to the bitter disappointment of Germany. But the minority were still there, and were shortly to be increased in numbers.

Fifth—The Coalition Government, with Sir Edward Carson in it. It is impossible to describe or over-estimate the effect of this in Ireland. The fact that Mr Redmond could, had he chosen to do so, have sat in the same Cabinet with Sir Edward Carson, had no mollifying influence. If Mr Redmond had consented, he would, on the instant, have ceased to be an Irish leader. This step seemed to make an end of Home Rule, and strengthened the Sinn Feiners enormously all over the country.

Sixth—The prolongation of the war, and its dubious end. Irish criticism of the war and its chances were not of the optimistic cast that prevail in Britain. Every event and result was put in the balance, and weighed. The excitement was immense. So long as the war lasted—and it soon became obvious that it might last for years—there were not wholly unreasonable expectations of a German landing in England or a landing in Ireland, and of partial risings in different parts of the country, which if timed so as to synchronise with a German bombardment of the English coasts, and hosts of Zeppelins flying over the north of England and the Midlands, would be quite enough—so it might well be thought by an Irish revolutionist—to secure a fair chance of an immediate Irish success, which, were Germany ultimately victorious, could not but greatly damage British authority and rule in the future. German assistance was at the bottom of the outbreak. The war turned many heads and upset prudent calculations. To this, in Dublin, was added the hoarded passions of the labour disputes and Bachelor's Walk.

The witness examined

The Chairman: I imagine that last year or so you realised that there was a dangerous movement in Ireland? Yes—further back than that. Certainly, during the last two years.

But after consultation with the Irish leaders you came to the conclusion that the policy of non-intervention was the safest? Yes, that is so.

What would you exactly mean by intervention? The misery of the whole thing was this—you had armed bodies of Volunteers all over the place, and to some extent drilled, and if you could have got disarmament all round it would have been a blessing, but to disarm any one section of the population on the evidence that we had appeared to me to be a very dangerous and doubtful proposition.

You need not answer this question unless you like, Who were the Irish leaders who advised you most? Well, in the first place I formed a pretty clear estimate of my own, and I do not think that I was enormously influenced by other people. But Mr Redmond, for example, always took the view that the Sinn Feiners were negligible; and was good enough to say so in the House of Commons. I did not attach too much importance to his opinion in that matter, because I was quite sure that they were dangerous. At the same time, he expressed that opinion strongly. It did affect my mind to this extent, that I gave it great consideration. But I came around to another view. Mr Dillon, for example, was strongly the other way, not in the sense of taking action, but strongly of opinion that the Sinn Fein movement and the insurrectionary movement undoubtedly were a danger. On that point there was a strong difference of opinion between the two, but both were equally in favour of non-intervention.

Warning of impending trouble.

What specific warnings of impending trouble did you have? Do you mean in Dublin?

Anywhere, but especially in Dublin? I think you have to distinguish very clearly between the two. As far as the country generally was concerned, we had reports of the Royal Irish Constabulary, who sent them in daily from every district in Ireland. Ireland lives under the microscope. We had in them expert information which would enable anybody in London or Dublin to form a very correct general estimate of the feeling in the country side. The feeling varied very much in different localities. It varied very much according to the character of the priest. If the curates of the administrators, as they were called, were not Sinn Feiners, then the movement would die out in those localities. If on the other hand, the Sinn Feiners were favoured and fostered by the clergy, they extended. From these reports I had no difficulty in coming to a pretty just view as to the general effect of Sinn Feinism, or of the Irish Volunteers, all over the country.

The Dublin Difficulty

But when you come to Dublin, continued the witness, you are under the Metropolitan Police, not the RIC.

I always felt I was very ignorant of what was actually going on in the minds and cellars, if you like, of the Dublin population. I was always exceedingly nervous about would happen. Therefore I distinguish very much between the state of things going on in Dublin and that in the rest of the country. So far as Dublin is concerned I do not know that Sir Matthew Nathan was not more in a position to know than I was. I am not conscious of any warning until towards the end—the 16th of April. I heard at different times that there were opinions that the Castle was going to be taken, but it never came off. I am not aware of any warning beyond what I saw in the streets., and on that I took very decided views. I had a conference in the war office on March 20th, 1916, and at the Horse Guards on March 23rd, in reference to the supply of more soldiers in Dublin. The view I put before Lord Kitchener and the other military authorities was that we should have more soldiers in the streets of

Dublin. The impression I got, walking around the streets, was that Sinn Feinism was in a certain sense in possession. I put that as forcibly as I could to General Friend. I said:

'Let the soldiers be seen in the streets: march them about, and let the people see the force they will have to contend with.'

I was told by the military authorities that they were busy training the soldiers, and they could not be spared, and that, if there was any trouble, the troops could be transported from Liverpool, perhaps as quickly as in any other way.

The military were considering our proposals.

Mr Justice Shearman: Were many of the priests turbulent? I should not like to say. There are a considerable number. One of the most formidable anti-recruiting pamphlets was written by the Catholic Bishop of Limerick, Bishop O'Dwyer. He is a very clever man, but he has never been a friend of the Nationalist Party.

When there were sittings of the Cabinet in London you had to be in London?

A Jackdaw or Magpie

Mr Birrell said that was so. I have held the office of Chief Secretary for nine years, he proceeded, and from the beginning I held the view that it was my business to be present at Cabinet meetings in order to see whether Ireland was affected. Bills are sometimes instituted in a great hurry, and Ireland is either left out or put in without any consideration whatever of her needs or history. Therefore it was necessary to be at the Cabinet meetings not merely for the general purposes of the Cabinet, but for Irish purposes also. A jackdaw or a magpie would do just as well as the Chief Secretary to cry out at intervals 'Ireland'. We were in constant communication with the Castle, continued Mr Birrell, and connected by wire with the Under Secretary. Parliament has unfortunately been sitting for the past few years all the year round, and therefore my visits to Ireland have been at Christmas, Easter, and Whitsuntide, and sometime or other during the summer. 'I have not lived much at the Lodge, but during all these years I have spent short holidays, three or four times a year, in Ireland, and owing to the use of motors I have been far more in all parts of Ireland than any Chief Secretary who has preceded me.'

The repeal of the Arms Act

The Chairman: What circumstances brought about the repeal of the Arms Act? It was before my time—in Mr Bryce's time. But I was in the Cabinet, and I remember it came up. It was allowed to drop. I have a sort of recollection that it had been a great deal evaded.

If the Act had been in force it would have operated against Ulster? Yes.

Even though the Arms Act had lapsed, had you ample powers to deal with stores of ammunition and explosives under the Explosives Acts, 1875 and 1883—I can't say.

The Chairman: Many months prior to August 4th, 1914, I think you will agree that Ireland was in a state of internal unrest. For obvious reasons, therefore, one would have thought it was desirable to restrict the importation of arms. Why was the restriction removed on August 5th, 1914, the day after the declaration of war?

Mr Birrell: I have a note about it. I will put that in. I have a recollection about it.

Mr Justice Shearman: I take it the resolution to revoke the Arms Act had been arrived at before war was declared? Yes. It was found that the proclamations could not be maintained, and in order to avoid scandal they were revoked.

The Sinn Fein military movement

Sir Mackenzie Chalmers: Can you tell us, Mr Birrell, what turned this Sinn Fein literary movement into a military movement? It was the war and the excitement.

Sir Mackenzie Chalmers: I think you had a certain number of prosecutions for anti-recruiting and seditious meetings, but you could not get any convictions from the juries? That is so.

It was not merely a case of juries disagreeing, but of acquittal? Yes.

Do you put that down to fear or to favour? I put it down to hatred of any case in Ireland in which the Attorney-General appears prosecuting for the Crown. It is nothing treasonable, or quasi-treasonable, or anything of the sort. If the Attorney-General is there or is represented it is enough. If you have a jury you are done.

Sir Mackenzie Chalmers: You had a thousand unarmed men in the Dublin police, and not more than a thousand soldiers. We are told, of course, it is easy to be wise after the event.

The rebellion a failure from the beginning

Mr Birrell: I do not know that so very large a number of soldiers, unless employed beforehand, would have been able to do much when these places had been seized. I do not think it was a question of numbers from a military point of view. The thing was a failure from the beginning, because the soldiers were there before the end of the day in quite a sufficient force from the Curragh and Belfast. Those from Liverpool did not come until next day. But I do not think another odd thousand soldiers on the spot at the time, unless they had been arranged beforehand at the post offices and places of that sort would have affected the position.

If there had been a little more success in Dublin, do you think many would have joined in the country? Was there a large body of men sitting on the fence? I don't think so, apart from the German landing. If the Germans had really landed men and guns, I do not think anybody could say what the effect on the population would have been. But I do not think the mere holding up of Dublin, even for another week, would have affected the result, apart from Germany. They believed that England was surrounded by submarines, and that troops could not come from Liverpool, because there were submarines in the Channel. They thought that England was cut off, and the moment they discovered that soldiers were pouring over—(Here Mr Birrell broke off his reply with a significant gesture).

Mr Justice Shearman: As soon as you had the Defence of the Realm Act you could have forbidden drilling in any part of the United Kingdom, and I cannot understand why it did not occur to anybody to say—'We won't have armed Volunteers drilling while the war is on.' That could have been equally applied to any part of Ireland,

Mr Birrell: Of course, that would have been a challenge to the Volunteers.

Mr Justice Shearman: Everybody knew. These people were known to be disloyal, and known to be having sham fights and training people in the field, including ladies for ambulance work.

Almost ridiculous

Mr Birrell: I quite agree. It seems almost ridiculous. But, on the other hand, the alternative would have been to employ policemen to have done it. You would have attacked these people and disarmed them, and whether it was done North, South, East, or West it would have resulted in bloodshed.

Mr Justice Shearman: Assuming they had been forbidden to march out with arms and knew if they had done it, they would have been attacked by the military, would they have done it? Oh, yes, they would.

At any rate that method of stopping the drilling was considered, I suppose? It was all part and parcel of a policy. It may have been right, or it may have been wrong, that we could not advisedly or properly or safely proceed by soldiers to disarm these forces. It was the same thing that prevented us from acting in Ulster.

The case of Ulster

The Chairman: Was the policy of non-intervention a Cabinet or an Irish Government decision?

Mr Birrell: I won't say with regard to that. Ulster in the earlier days before the war undoubtedly was a Cabinet decision, in which I am bound to say I entirely concurred.

The Chairman: If you had not concurred I suppose you would not have remained Chief Secretary? I would not.

But it was not a Cabinet decision about the Sinn Feiners? No, not a Cabinet decision.

Lord Kitchener corrects Mr Birrell

The third sitting of the Commission took place on Monday, 22nd May, at the Royal Commissions House, Westminster. The Chairman, on the resumption of the inquiry, said—Since we met on Friday I have received the following letter from General Macready, Adiutant-General of the Forces: 'Dear Lord Hardinge,—In view of the statement made by Mr Birrell before your Commission yesterday in regard to the supply of more soldiers for Dublin, inferentially to guard against any outbreak, Lord Kitchener has asked me to write to you and put the facts of the case as they appeared to affect the War Office at the time. Mr Birrell, together with Lord Wimborne and others, came over from Ireland, and had a conference at the War Office on March 20th, purely in relation to the state of recruiting in Ireland. Various proposals were made at the time, among them a proposal that troops should be sent from England to Ireland, to be quartered in various localities other than Dublin, for the sole purpose of encouraging recruiting. It was not considered that the presence of these troops would have an effect on recruiting in Ireland commensurate with the delay that would take place in training the men and the unpopularity of the movement. I attach some correspondence that had taken place on the subject.

'Mr Birrell afterwards saw Lord French, and, so far as we are aware, no question ever arose of sending troops for the purpose of overawing Sinn Feiners. Some time before this General Friend had written to me indicating that there might be trouble in the South of Ireland, and, if so, he might require the assistance of some extra troops, and arrangements were made with Lord French to have a reserve brigade ear-marked to be sent at once, if called for by the Irish authorities. This is what I referred to in my letter to General Friend of the 3rd April. So far as I am aware, Mr Birrell's visit on the 20th to 23rd March had no connection whatever with the sending of troops to Ireland for the purpose of quelling and anticipating any rebellion, although, of course, had troops been sent for recruiting purposes they would have been available in case of emergency. If there is any other information that I can give from the War Office point of view, I shall be most happy to do so.'

Mr Birrell's explanation

Mr Birrell, who was present, at once replied to this letter. He said he would like to say that when he gave evidence he had in his mind three sets of interviews. One was with the War Office, referred to in General Macready's letter, on 20th March, and at the Horse Guards with Lord French, and many other interviews at different times in Ireland with General Friend. My recollection, he went on, is that at all these interviews, notably at those with Lord French and General Friend, I made the point I was always making—that it was a most desirable thing to let the people of Dublin see our troops marching about the streets, and so on. I quite agree that so far as the interview at the War Office on the 20th March is concerned the object was to promote recruiting. It was thought desirable, in order to make recruiting more popular in Ireland, that there should be more soldiers there. Mr Birrell, continuing, said that stress was laid on the fact that there were really fewer soldiers, because there were some whose places in the battalion were taken by wounded soldiers, which was not animating. He thought, therefore, that more troops might be sent for the purpose of obtaining recruits. Inferentially that would have served his other object, because it would have enabled them to have more soldiers in Ireland, and presumably they would have made more show in the streets. The agreed, however, that that was only a by-point at the interview, but he made the other point so frequently that he was 'surprised' if he let the opportunity pass without laying stress on it. In regard to Lord French, he undoubtedly did make the point. While the Commission were in Ireland they would, perhaps, see General Friend, and ask him what he (Mr Birrell) said to him.

Viscount Midleton's warnings

Viscount Midleton, PC, was then called. He said he was acting as the mouthpiece for an influential section of Irishmen in Dublin and the south. He gave evidence as to drawing the attention of the members of the Irish Government to seditious publications in Ireland in November, 1914, and periodically he brought under the notice of Lord Wimborne, Mr Birrell, Sir Matthew Nathan, General Friend, and others what he considered proof of the growth of the Sinn Fein movement, and evidence upon which he urged they should take action. On one occasion after trying to impress Mr Birrell with the seriousness of the position, he was met with this statement of the Chief Secretary—'I laugh at the whole thing.'

Witness said he saw certain leaders of Irish opinion in Great Britain, and agreed with them that a committee should be asked to assemble in Dublin and send a report as quickly as possible as to the state of Ireland.

He subsequently attend a meeting on February 28th, at Queen Anne's Gate, and was asked to bring Lord Barrymore, President of the Irish Unionist Alliance, with him. Matters which had been discussed before were brought up at this meeting, and Sir Matthew Nathan pressed upon him that since their previous interview the movement in Ireland had been developing more seriously. He mentioned to witness the name of the chief conspirators, who were known to the Government, and especially showed him an article which Mr Sheehy Skeffington had written in the January number of *The Century*.

General Friend and the ringleaders

General Friend showed at this time that he was most anxious to deal with some of the ringleaders, but witness gathered that General Friend, although he did not say so in so many words, was unable to move in the matter further, owing to the general attitude of the Government towards Ireland, which it was impossible to alter. Later in the same week, Lord Midleton continued, he had an interview with some Irish gentlemen who had the report made by the Dublin Committee, which had been sitting. He sent this in substance to Mr Birrell.

The Dublin Committee's report

The report of the Dublin Committee was read by the clerk, and set forth details as to the origin of the Sinn Fein movement and its development up to the time of the rising. Advantage was taken of the recruiting campaign of Mr Redmond to develop the anti-British feeling, and this feeling was indicated by the breakdown of certain criminal prosecutions, and the freedom with which seditious journals were published and arms and explosives were accumulated by the rebels through funds supplied from German and Irish-American sources.

The committee recommended:

(1) That Lord Parmoor's clause should be suspended by proclamation, so that charges under the Defence of the Realm Act might be dealt with by the military,

(2) That immediate action be taken against the printers of journals against recruiting, and the suppression of their plant.

(3) The suppression of the Irish Volunteers with the confiscation of their arms and explosives.

Sir Matthew Nathan and the Sinn Fein manifesto

On April 14th he went to Ireland, and had a further interview at Dublin Castle with Sir Matthew Nathan, who spoke strongly of the advice given by Mr Dillon and Mr Redmond, and 'I protested,' said Lord Midleton, 'against the Government in any way putting their responsibility on the shoulders of Mr Dillon and Mr Redmond.'

Witness said that in his interview with Sir Matthew Nathan he put to him this point:

The Irishman is the worst man in the world to run away from, and in all possibility the inaction in dealing with the conspiracy has had the result that even Mr Redmond is in danger of his life. Sir Matthew seemed to think that any activity in that direction would be rather against some of the officials. He was quite alive to the fact that he was dealing with desperate men. Witness added that he did not go to see General Friend on April 14, as he felt that he was powerless to make any move, but he had a private conversation with him before the outbreak.

Lord Wimborne's Revelations
Information withheld from him

Lord Wimborne, Lord Lieutenant of Ireland, gave evidence after luncheon. In the course of a lengthy statement, he made a few preliminary remarks on the position of the Lord Lieutenant and the Irish Government, both in general and in particular. Although the Viceroy was nominally responsible and the prerogative of mercy still devolved upon him, yet, since the Chief Secretary for Ireland had been in the Cabinet these powers had fallen upon the Chief Secretary. The doctrine of the Lord Lieutenant's total irresponsibility was held by the late Chief Secretary. Very soon after assuming office he had reason to complain of this state of affairs, and ask for a clear definition of his position. He pointed out that he had to rely upon the Press for his information of current events, and it was not till March 17, 1916, that he was furnished with daily police reports. These were supplied for his information, and not with the view of obtaining his opinion. At this point Lord Wimborne said that Sir Matthew Nathan was perfectly frank, and, in view of the fact that he differed from him in regard to their relative positions and on matters of policy, he was never in any sense of the word disloyal, and he always had the greatest admiration for his whole-hearted devotion to the public service.

Lord Wimborne next referred to a tour he made through Ireland soon after his appointment, when he received the impression of loyalty everywhere. The Sinn Fein movement was belittled, derided. He fixed the introduction of Compulsion in England as the time at which their numbers began to increase steadily and their confidence developed.

The charge against the Government

The charge which he understood would be brought against the Government would be one of supine blindness and irresolution in dealing with the seditious propaganda. Regarding the military precautions, he stated that he had several conversations with General Friend, and questions him as to his plans in case of trouble, but he was thinking more of raids than internal disturbance. Ever since the departure of the Irish Division to the front last summer he (Lord Wimborne) had been of opinion that the Irish garrison was inadequate. He mentioned a conference he had at the War Office with Lord Kitchener on December 13th, 1915, when he pressed for reinforcements, and strongly opposed the suggestion that artillery should be withdrawn.

The President: Was it all withdrawn? No. At that time artillery was very badly needed at the front, and Lord Kitchener was surprised to hear that we had some 16-pounders in Ireland.

Application for a division of troops

Lord Wimborne continued, that on March 23rd he pressed for a division of troops to be sent to Ireland.

The Chairman: That was not to encourage recruiting?

Witness: That was one object, but so long as troops were obtained I did not care about the plea on which they were obtained. The reply of the War Office was, that if troops were sent it would involve a delay of a whole fortnight in sending troops to the front. He replied that it was most important that troops should be sent to Ireland. He feared internal disorder.

The Chairman: That was on March 23rd; but did you mention then your fear of internal disorder as the reason for the troops being sent? No; but a week later I urged the desirability of troops on that ground. On March 23rd Mr Birrell had a private conversation with Lord French before the conference. Mr Birrell always advocated the presence of more troops in Dublin. Several times in my year of office he expressed his anxiety for a display of power in the capital.

Fear of internal disorder

In connection with the fear of internal disorder, he (witness) wrote to Sir Matthew Nathan on April 4th, informing him that he was going to press for a division of troops on the ground that this division would be a powerful deterrent. Up to the end of 1915 the Sinn Fein movement was practically negligible as a force, but early in the year reports of the Royal Irish Constabulary began to disquiet him. These he had only seen in a monthly summary. They told of movements which gave him serious misgivings. Of the intelligence of the Royal Irish Constabulary he could not speak in too high terms.

Night marches and intimidation

At the close of the year the Sinn Feiners only numbered 1,800 in the provinces and 800 in Dublin: but later he heard rumours of night marches and intimidation, of which he could get no official information. He had no grounds at the beginning of March for apprehending grave developments, but the state of affairs was unsatisfactory, especially in view of the ignorance of the movement and the difficulty in obtaining conviction by juries. These facts convinced him that the proper policy was to intern or deport the leaders who were under suspicion. In March Lord Midleton called on him in Dublin and expressed his uneasiness, but had nothing tangible to report. He undertook to support any amendment of the Defence of the Realm Act which might be found necessary. In March Lord Wimborne said he had had a conversation with the Chief Secretary in London, and expressed his inclination in favour of interning rather than deporting the suspects. The next day there was a conference in the House of Commons, when the Chief Secretary was present. He then again advocated a policy of internment. The reason for this was that two men who had been convicted had refused to comply with the order of deportation, and had been sentenced in consequence to imprisonment.

In answer to a question, witness said that there was an obscurity about the order of deportation. If the suspect left Ireland there appeared to be no control over him when he left the country. When Sir Edward Carson was Attorney-General he advised the Chief Secretary to exclude men from the military area, and that deportation was rather an extreme interpretation of the Act.

Letter to the Under-Secretary

On March 15th he (Lord Wimborne) wrote to the Under-Secretary informing him that he had had a conversation with the Chief Secretary on the previous day, and he thought it was best to wait till after St Patrick's Day before proceeding with any internment. One of the men previously deported had reappeared in the rebellion, showing that it was not very effective. The Sinn Fein parade on March 17th was poorly attended. Sir Matthew Nathan, who reported an attendance of 4,500, said he considered that the situation had slightly improved. This amelioration was short-lived. The seizure of the Press increased the tendency to armed opposition, which was significant, and confirmed his contention as to the requirement of troops. Armed resistance and the discharge of firearms at Portadown were further signs. There was the shooting of police at a meeting on March 30th. On the whole, he thought they had reason to be satisfied at the result of the activity against Sinn Feiners.

The Mansion House meeting was a disgrace to the Lord Mayor. The Beresford place meeting was a climb-down after it was seen what interpretation was placed on the speeches.

Immediate action urged

On April 17 witness said he was informed that a ship, accompanied by two German submarines, was expected to arrive on the 21st, and on the following morning 'the situation was revolutionised' by the arrest of two men (Sir Roger Casement being one) who had landed in a boat, and the blowing up of a ship supposed to be bearing arms, three officers, and 19 crew, all Germans, being taken into custody. Then appeared the notice countermanding the Easter Sunday parades of the Irish Volunteers in Dublin. He thought that dismay had been caused in the ranks of the rebels by the failure of the landing party, but on the Saturday he urged immediate action. He thought it quite likely that the parades having been countermanded the leaders would be sitting in conclave on the Saturday, conspiring against the authorities. On Sunday he heard of the seizure of a large quantity of gelignite, which was said to have been taken to Liberty Hall by the rebels, and he strongly urged that the leaders should be arrested. He wrote his views to the Chief Secretary, and suggested that if he agreed with them he (Mr Birrell) should write and 'ginger up Nathan'. He realised it was no good to stir up a hornet's nest unless they could capture the hornets. He was strongly in favour of an earlier arrest of suspects, but was told that there were legal questions involved. When it was proposed to raid Liberty Hall the Under-Secretary disagreed on the ground of illegality, and it was decided not to go forward that night, though he (Lord Wimborne) pointed out that the arrest of the leaders was the more important matter. He did not want them to leave Dublin and spread the revolt. He eventually signed the warrant for the arrest and other operations, and took full responsibility. He wanted to have at least 100 arrested on Saturday night or Sunday.

'The worst has happened'

On Easter Monday at 10 a.m. the Under Secretary called with a report that Bailey, who had landed with Casement, had been arrested, that a man called Monteith was still at large, that a rising had been planned for that day, and that the Castle was to be attacked. He urged the strengthening of the Castle guard, but the Under Secretary did not agree. He was of opinion, however, that in view of the disorganisation of the Sinn Fein plans the rising would not take place. The Under-Secretary also read him a cipher telegram from Mr Birrell agreeing to the arrests being made.

'I had completed a letter to the Chief Secretary, and was in the act of writing to the Prime Minister,' Lord Wimborne continued, 'when at 12.30 we had a telephone message from the Chief Constable saying that the Castle had been attacked, the Post Office seized, St Stephen's Green occupied, and that the insurgents were marching on the Viceregal Lodge. I wrote to the Chief Secretary saying:

The worst has happened...If only we had acted last night with precision and arrested the leaders as I wanted it might have been over...Nathan still besieged in the Castle. I hope he will be safe. ...Everybody away on holiday...Post Office taken, bridges blown up...If we can get through the night I hope we shall settle it tomorrow...No news from the provinces. I hear there will be trouble there...We must have troops—at least a brigade. I should prefer a division. The situation is very serious, and we need energetic help.'

The Chairman asked what powers the Lord Lieutenant possessed over the military movements. Could he himself give orders which the military must obey?

Lord Wimborne: I don't think so. It is a curious position. The name of the Lord Lieutenant appears on the Army List in the Irish Command, but with no rank of any kind connected with it, and no uniform.

The absurdity of the Lord Lieutenant's position

The Chairman: You have pointed out the effect on your position—the absurdity of the Lord Lieutenant having to rely on the Press and the divergence between yourself and the Under Secretary. Did you ever point this out to Mr Asquith or any influential person in the Government?

Lord Wimborne: The Chief Secretary was aware of the situation.

The Chairman: You never took any steps yourself to have it rectified, were it possible to do so? I am of the opinion that whoever represented the Irish Government in the Cabinet is the head of the Irish Government in practice. In this case I was the youngest of three Ministers in age, and in tenure of office.

The Chairman: You have already stated that in your opinion the troops were insufficient, but they did co-operate with the civil authorities thoroughly on Dublin? Oh, yes.

Although you brought your own anxieties before the Chief Secretary, did you bring them before anyone else in the government? Yes.

'Everyone seems to be away'

Lord Wimborne went on to say that when the trouble began General Friend was not in Ireland. He left for England on short leave on the Thursday.

The Chairman: Who would have given him leave?

Lord Wimborne: Upon the system in Ireland everybody seems to be away. There is no co-ordination. Lord Wimborne added that he was aware that General Friend was on leave. He did not think it was suggested to General Friend that it was undesirable he should go. Witness asked him to write down the name of his subordinates if anything should happen, and if all his plans were ready and in the possession of his subordinates.

The Chairman: Does it not seem extraordinary that General Friend should have gone away, in view of what happened two days afterwards?

Lord Wimborne: I imagine there had been a good many of these false alarms.

An Extraordinary Circumstance

The Chairman: I was much struck by the statement you made just now to the effect that when the Admiralty obtained the information respecting the German ship accompanied by two German submarines due to arrive on the 21st, it was communicated to the Admiral at Queenstown, but not direct to the Irish Government.

Lord Wimborne: It was not; so far as I know.

The Chairman: Is it not a very extraordinary fact that the Admiral at Queenstown should have communicated this information in conversation with General Stafford, and the Irish Government should not have received any information at all?

Why the raid was delayed

The Chairman said he did not understand why, after the conversation witness had on Sunday evening, when it appeared that the Under Secretary was in favour of raiding Liberty Hall and two other Sinn Fein arsenals, this did not come off.

The witness replied that the military did not think that there was time to do this successfully, as it would take three or four hours to get the guns up.

The Chairman: When you urged that the Castle guards should be strengthened, did the Under Secretary give any reason for demurring ? No.

Surely that was the most obvious measure to take? Well I think at that time of day it did not much look like a revolution. My idea is—these things began earlier than half-past twelve, and my belief is the whole thing was an eleventh hour decision, otherwise they would have started sooner.

Sir Mackenzie Chalmers: You think a rebellion ought to begin immediately after breakfast? (Laughter.)

Lord Wimborne added that he thought the fact that recent Lords Lieutenant had not been in the Cabinet led to a loss of their personal power in Ireland. It was a question whether the Lord Lieutenant was the responsible Minister or not. Impetus was given to the Sinn Fein movement by the fact that the people were afraid of compulsion. Many people did not want to fight for England. Of course, they had obtained many Volunteers in Ireland—150,000 altogether. Besides the Sinn Feiners who were opposed to England, many of the farmer class were apathetic. In the towns all over Ireland the Government were very successful in getting recruits.

Sir Mackenzie Chalmers: Had the rebels any old soldiers among them? I do not know.

It seems to have been exceedingly well arranged? Yes, and yet not well enough, fortunately.

Lord Wimborne added that he believed the greater number of the Sinn Feiners thought they were out for a route march, and did not know they were out for a rebellion until they were ordered to seize houses.

Not satisfied with the police reports

Sir Mackenzie Chalmers: Were you satisfied with the police reports? I am not satisfied.

You think with an efficient detective force you ought to have had rather more information than you had? Yes: but the problem was a difficult one. The secret was kept in a very few hands.

There had been firing in Ireland at some places in March, but there were no arrests? No. I was very much annoyed about that. It was difficult, but at the same time I think the police ought to have taken notice of it. It was a Sinn Fein demonstration to protest against our deportation order.

Then how came it be held at the Mansion House?

Lord Wimborne replied that he understood that the Lord Mayor was away at the time, and it was his deputy who was responsible.

Mr Justice Shearman: Up to the end of 1915 you did not think the Sinn Fein movement was dangerous? Yes.

Early in 1915 you thought it was getting dangerous? I thought it was getting unsatisfactory, but I did not apprehend a rebellion.

You saw the military authorities in England about recruiting, and at those interviews you did not say you thought it was dangerous? No.

Mr Justice Shearman: You thought that the danger was so serious that you did not stop the route marches? It would have been extremely foolish to provoke a meeting, and it could not have been done without dealing with all the Volunteers. You would have wanted 100,000 men to enforce it.

The cause of inaction

The President: I suppose this general inaction was largely due to the policy of non-intervention, which was the acknowledged policy of the Government at the time?

Lord Wimborne: No; it was due to the difficulty of doing anything effective without provoking a collision, when, in the first place, we had not the troops to enforce it, and, secondly, because we were anxious to avoid a collision, in view of the major consideration of the war.

Sir David Harrel

Sir David Harrel, who ten years ago retired from the Civil Service in Ireland, where he held various appointments, including that of Permanent Under Secretary to the Lord Lieutenant, made a short statements, in which he said that as a member of the Congested Districts Board he had many opportunities of understanding how feeling ran in Ireland, and he was reluctantly obliged to conclude that the state of affairs for many years had been unsatisfactory. The permission to carry arms was attended with danger, and likely sooner or later to end in catastrophe. The decision some years ago to stop the admission of firearms was an improvement, but it was not sufficiently vigorously enforced. The fact, however, that people carrying arms were obliged to obtain licences was a most useful ordinance, and an advance in the right direction. He contended that the Irish generally were a peaceful, law-abiding people, but they were impressionable, and easily led.

Sir Mackenzie Chalmers: Then you hold that a peaceful majority are led astray by a turbulent minority? I am afraid that I must admit that.

The Commission in Dublin

The Commission appointed by the Government to inquire into the cause of the recent outbreak of rebellion in Ireland, and the conduct and degree of responsibility of the military and the civil authorities in Ireland in connection therewith, which was opened in London, resumed its sitting in the Shelbourne Hotel, Dublin, on Thursday, 25th May.

The Commission was presided over by Lord Hardinge, the other Commissioners being Mr Justice Shearman and Sir Mackenzie Chalmers.

Sir Neville Chamberlain, Inspector-General, RIC

Sir Neville Chamberlain, Inspector-General of the Royal Irish Constabulary, who was the first witness, read from a typewritten document. He explained that the system in force in the Royal Irish Constabulary to obtain information regarding what went on in Ireland has been in existence for many years. Every report containing information was furnished by witness to the Under Secretary for the information of the Government. He said that the Peace Preservation Act, otherwise known as the Arms Act, was repealed in 1906, and at that time he recorded a strong protest against its abandonment, and suggested the extension of the Pistols Act of 1903 to Ireland, as its restrictions, though small, would be a safeguard, some safeguard, against the purchase of revolvers for improper purposes, and he pointed out that the lapse of the Peace Preservation Act would result in the formation of rifle clubs in many places. In May, 1914, he drew the attention of the Government to the undesirable state of things that had arisen, which had, he considered, imperilled the maintenance of law and order in the country by the unrestricted arming of the Ulster and the National Volunteer forces, which had come into existence owing to the acute dispute over the Home Rule question. He held the view that in Ireland the training and drilling to the use of arms of a great part of the male population was a new departure, which was bound in the not distant future to profoundly alter all the existing conditions of life. Obedience to the law had never been a prominent characteristic of the people.

The growth of Sinn Fein

The growth of the Sinn Finn movement arose out of the various disloyal societies which had existed in Ireland prior to 1905, or which came into being under various names since 1905. He had furnished reports on these matters. For some years between 1906 and 1912 the movement fluctuated a good deal, and it seemed to have merely afforded the usual clique of extremists a means of airing their sedition without apparently doing much harm. Dublin had remained the centre of the movement hitherto, but in 1907 it extended to certain districts of the country, and the branches had increased from 30 to 74. In 1908 evidence went to show that the bond between the Sinn Fein and the Irish Republican Brotherhood had become closer, and the object of the two bodies was practically the same. It was also evident that the extreme section of the Gaelic Association had endorsed the Sinn Fein doctrines. The branches of the Sinn Fein Association continued to increase, and in 1910 its activities were directed to the capture of the provinces. This at first resulted in little success, but in a few places their numbers were strong enough to make a show of opposition in connection with the Coronation of King George.

Countess Markievicz

In that year the Countess Markievicz came into prominence by establishing the National Boy Scouts, which was really a training ground for young rebels. In 1911 interest in the movement was kept alive by means of occasional violent speeches. The annual Sinn Fein Convention was held in Dublin in October in that year, and its report went to show that its aims and most important work was the formation of extremist committees. One of the extremists at a meeting in Glasgow in 1912 spoke of a revolution in Ireland in the near future, which would end in total separation from England. Later in that year it was ascertained that money was coming from America to the Sinn Fein party for revolutionary purposes, and revolutionary doctrines were being advocated at meetings. On the question of Home Rule they came into antagonism with the Irish party, the Sinn Feiners declaring they would accept no measure which 'leaves a single vestige of British rule in Ireland.' Towards the end of 1913 the Ulster movement suggested the formation of the National Volunteers. Leading Sinn Feiners seized the opportunity of controlling it, and the Parliamentary party got suspicious of this, and protests were made against the movement being controlled by 'Dublin cranks and extremists'.

The physical force policy was looked upon askance by the majority of Nationalists, who were agitating for Home Rule on constitutional lines. He referred to the formation of the Provisional Committee of twenty-seven members to organise the Volunteer movement. On this Committee were some of the men who had since paid the extreme penalty for their part in the recent rebellion. Prominent figures in the earlier organisation were Sir Roger Casement and Colonel Maurice Moore, of the Connaught Rangers. On the 4th May, 1914, the movement received the full recognition of the Irish Parliamentary Party. At the end of July, 1914, the membership of the Volunteers had increased to 160,000. A good deal was done to place it on a military basis, and its constitution was modelled somewhat on that of the rival volunteers of the North. Mr Redmond's declaration on the outbreak of the war did not find favour with the extremists in Ireland, and Mr Redmond's policy was openly denounced by such men as Bulmer Hobson and Major MacBride. It was evident from such a state of things as then existed that a split would take place, and in 1914, as the war broke out, the Sinn Feiners detached themselves from the main body of the Volunteers. The Sinn Fein movement was then carried on by the Irish Volunteers. In Sir Roger Casement they had an agent for carrying out their schemes in connection with Germany. The National Volunteers in the meantime relaxed their activity in military practice, and a considerable number enlisted in the Army. The disloyal section embodied in the Irish Volunteers continued its activity, and reports were received that they were receiving arms through the country, chiefly from Dublin. A certain amount of rifles and ammunition was received in Dublin in September, 1914, for the disloyal section of the Volunteers.

During 1915 the instructors of the Sinn Fein Volunteers were busy spreading revolutionary doctrines, and the military authorities ordered the deportation of ten of their number under the Defence of the Realm Act Regulations, but some of them came back.

Witness further stated that he realised that this disloyal movement was highly dangerous. It was financed by Irish extremists in America and also by Germany, and its promoters in this country were men who were not usually in good circumstances.

In reply to the Chairman, witness stated that he agreed with the general résumé of facts given by Sir Matthew Nathan in London before the Commission. It appeared to have been based largely on reports sent to the Government from the RIC.

Strength of the RIC

The Chairman: Can you give me the strength of the RIC at present? On 24th April, 1916, there were 165 District Inspectors, 235 Head Constables, and 9,101 men. Ten years ago the total number of men was 9,479.

What is the highest number of the Royal Irish Constabulary in the last twenty years? The highest number was in 1883, which was 14,115. When I assumed command of the force in 1900 its strength was 10,662.

Were you favourable to recruiting from the RIC at the beginning of the war? On my suggestion two hundred men were allowed to join the Irish Guards. No more men were allowed to join, except about twelve officers, until June, 1915, when the Press urged the desirability of more Royal Irish Constabulary joining. Witness discussed the matter with the Under Secretary and with the Chief Secretary, and it was agreed to let seventy-two volunteers join the Army. On 29th September Mr Birrell wrote to witness that Lord Kitchener was very anxious to secure more men of the RIC for the Irish Guards, but he (Mr Birrell) said he was alive to the danger of stripping the Constabulary of their strength, especially having regard to the large numbers of armed men in Ireland.

Lord Kitchener's promise

Lord Kitchener asked how many men he could get, he undertaking that should any grave emergency arise in Ireland he would not leave them (that was, the Irish Government) in the lurch. Mr Birrell told witness he could provide 1,000 men. Witness said he would do everything he could to obtain the 1,000 men, but for various reasons only 350 men were enlisted since that date. Altogether 745 joined, and, in addition, we lent to the Army the services of 41 trained drill instructors. Witness went on to refer to speeches that had been made at public meetings advocating the reduction of the police force, and in particular he quoted a speech made on February 2nd, 1916, in Galway, in which Mr Redmond remarked that the police force was twice too large.

Did you not think an undesirable state of affairs had arisen in 1914 imperilling the maintenance of law and order by the unrestricted arming of the Ulster, and later of the National, Volunteer forces? In May 1914, I drew the attention of the Government officially to the undesirable state of affairs that existed. I suggested that events were moving rapidly, and that every county would soon have an armed body outnumbering the police, that, in fact, the situation was seriously embarrassing the police. This representation was made to the Government in May, 1914. Sir Neville said that the RIC had always had anxiety as regarded explosives.

Photo by] [*Lafayette.*
HIS EXCELLENCY LORD WIMBORNE,
Lord Lieutenant of Ireland.

Photo by] [*Lafayette.*
THE RIGHT HON. AUGUSTINE BIRRELL, M.P.,
Late Chief Secretary of Ireland.

Photo by] [*Lafayette.*
SIR NEVILLE CHAMBERLAIN, late Inspector-General of the Royal Irish Constabulary.

Photo by] [*Lafayette.*
COL. E. JOHNSTONE. Chief Commissioner Dublin Metropolitan Police.

He had suggested that all persons unconnected with the forces of the Crown should be obliged to have a military permit to carry rifles or revolvers. That representation was made to the Government in January, 1916.

Why has the requirement of a licence for a rifle not been enforced? The Government would not enforce it.

Is there no law in Ireland against drilling—could it not be dealt with under the law against illegal assemblies? It could, but really it would be no use here, because where you have magistrates who would give them power you cannot prevent them from drilling.

But in carrying out your duties were you fully supported by the Executive in what you considered were necessary measures? The position is this, sir, that I have made various recommendations to the Government on the advice of very experienced officers who advised me in such matters, especially for the maintenance of law and order in Ireland, and the Government have not seen fit to adopt them in many instances.

Did you consider that this policy of non-intervention in practice tended to discourage activity on the part of the Constabulary, and inclined them to turn a blind eye to what was gong on? I think that unquestionably the policy on non-intervention, not only as regards Sinn Fein, but other things that have arisen, tended to discourage the officers and men of the force, but I am confident that it had no effect on the zeal of the men.

Destroying the railway

Was there any destruction of the railway line on the morning of the 24th or night of the 23rd at Kildare? There was.

You say that in November there was great anxiety to get arms and ammunition into Dublin. What I want to know is, what was the date of the proclamation which prohibited the importation of arms?

Mr Justice Shearman: Your view of Sinn Fein is that it was not dangerous until the men were armed? Not actively dangerous.

What was your view as to permitting any volunteer organisation to be armed or drilled—what was your view of its results? With the growth of large bodies of trained men the police eventually would become powerless.

You represented that view in the ordinary way to the authorities? In a special monthly report. Witness indicated that he would furnish copies of his reports to the Commissioners.

Have you recommended to the Government any prosecution that they have not instituted? Some of our recommendations the Government didn't carry out, probably on the advice of the law officers.

The witness here handed in a file, which he said contained a volume of police private information on the subject.

Sir Mackenzie Chalmers said he only wanted to know if where the police thought there was a reasonable case the Government declined to prosecute.

The witness's answer was not heard.

In answer to further questions by Sir Mackenzie Chalmers, the witness said that he did not know that there was any hostility to the Government on the part of the Gaelic Athletic Association, except that soldiers, police, or naval sailors were not allowed to take part in their sports. No one in uniform would be permitted to join them.

Sir Mackenzie Chalmers: We have heard that the Dublin Metropolitan Police and the Royal Irish Constabulary act loyally together? Yes.

Don't you think that two different forces are less effective than if you had but one force? I should say that is so.

Colonel Moore's position

You mentioned earlier in your evidence the name of Colonel Moore. What happened to him?

Witness was understood to say he was then speaking about the National Volunteers, which came into existence on the growth of the Ulster Volunteers. He wished it to be clearly understood that he did not cast any imputation upon Colonel Moore. That gentleman was associated with the Volunteer movement in its early days, but when the disloyal element got into it he would have nothing more to do with it.

Sir Mackenzie Chalmers: You have had frequent communications with Mr Birrell when he is here?

Witness: Yes, when he is here.

Sir Mackenzie Chalmers: When was he here?

Witness: He was here in February.

The examination of the Inspector-General then concluded. His answers to questions during the latter portion of his examination were in many cases either inaudible or indistinctly heard at the Press table.

DEPUTY INSPECTOR-GENERAL WA O'CONNELL, RIC

Mr WA O'Connell, Deputy Inspector-General, RIC, was next called, and referred to certain recommendations he had made as to amendments in the Defence of the Realm Regulations. There was a conference at the Castle to consider them, at which were present the Under-Secretary, General Friend, and the Solicitor-General. The only suggestion accepted was one dealing with the question of explosives, it being the only one discussed. It was his impression that the other recommendations had been discussed by the higher authorities and ruled out.

COLONEL EDGEWORTH JOHNSTONE, CHIEF COMMISSIONER, DMP

Colonel W Edgeworth Johnstone, Chief Commissioner, Dublin Metropolitan Police, was examined. He described his functions and duties. In the case of ordinary breaches of the law the police under his control acted without instructions, but in any case of a political kind everything had to be referred to the Under Secretary. In such cases, he (witness) was directly under control of the Chief Secretary or in his absence the Under Secretary. Take the particular time they passed through. Anything that would involve the arrest of a Sinn Feiner, or anything of that sort had to be referred to the Under Secretary's Department.

Mr Justice Shearman: I am at a loss to understand the difference? I will give you an instance. Supposing we got some information that there was stolen property in a house, we could get a magistrate's warrant, but supposing that I got information that a Sinn Feiner had arms and explosives in his possession I go to the Chief Secretary.

If you think it is a crime why cannot you act on your own initiative? These are my instructions.

The system is that in political matters you ask for the Castle to help you? I ask for instructions as to what action, if any, is to be taken.

It was stated by Sir Matthew Nathan in his evidence in London that there had been a mimic attack on Dublin Castle. 'No such thing took place,' said the witness; 'it is a fairy tale. On the night of the 16th October a large portion of the Sinn Fein Army marched by Ship street, close to the Castle, but these manoeuvres took place between the Castle and Stephen's Green. There never was a mimic attack of any kind on the Castle, nor did the Castle form any portion of these manoeuvres.'

Mr Justice Shearman read a report of Superintendent Dunne, which contained the following: 'It is a serious state of affairs to have the peace of the city endangered by a gang of roughs with rifles and bayonets, at large at that time of night with a female like the Countess Markievicz in charge.'

Witness said they (the Citizen Army) went in two parties, as they were surrounding somewhere. The other party was manoeuvring in Stephen's Green.

No Attempt to search Liberty Hall

Mr Justice Shearman: As to the subject of explosives, was there any attempt to search Liberty Hall for explosives?

Witness: That was another account that got into the papers that was not correctly stated. There was no attempt to search it. The police seized the printing press of the *Gael*, and they searched a newspaper shop for copies of the publication. They went into a paper shop which apparently belonged to the Transport Workers' Union, and there they discovered that this shop led by a back passage into Liberty Hall, where the police met the members of the Liberty Hall organisation. They asked for the production of the warrant, and the police telephoned to him. He told a superintendent that he had better go down and take the warrant with him, and the police were not interfered with in searching the shop. There was no warrant to search Liberty Hall, nor was there any intention of so doing. The statement in the newspapers that such a search had taken place was not correct.

Volunteer rifles stolen

Asked by the Chairman about the importance of arms, witness said that in 1915 there were a number of rifles: 100 rifles—consigned to the National Volunteers, which came in openly with the permission of the Government, but they were stolen from the railway company, without doubt with the connivance of someone in the employment of the company. The rifles were taken away at about two o'clock in the morning of 14th of August, 1915, and apparently removed in a motor car. These particular rifles were consigned to Mr John Redmond by name at a hall in Rutland square. The seizure of arms in the port of Dublin totalled 500 rifles and guns, 6 revolvers, 207,000 rounds of ammunition, and 765 bayonets. A certain number of these were delivered. The figures did not cover one seizure, but were for the whole time.

Witness said he had always advocated the suppression of seditious newspapers. Asked by the chairman as to the steps taken for dealing with alien enemies, witness explained that he pointed out that these aliens were in possession of a number of sites overlooking Kingstown, Monkstown, and other places. They were interned. They were generally men of good character and there was nothing against them, but they were mostly of military age. He did not connect them with the Sinn Fein movement. 'My other recommendations,' continued the witness, 'were those dealing with the Sinn Fein party and the Citizen Army. I always held one view about them—that they were dangerous organisations. My view was that the only way to stamp them out was to arrest the leaders, and intern them in England during the war, and disarm the rank and file.'

Plan for dealing with the leaders

The Chairman: did you recommend that at the conferences? I was not present at the first conference, but I was present at the Viceregal Lodge on 23rd April, when a conference was called for the purpose of deciding whether the explosives traced to Liberty Hall should be raided at once. That was on Sunday at 10 o'clock. In the absence of Major-General Friend the officer acting in his stead stated that they wanted more time to have proper preparations. I agreed with him, but I stated that by searches we were only nibbling at the thing. He agreed to it, the Under Secretary agreed, and it was the unanimous opinion of the members of the conference that my plan should be put into execution. My plan was that the police, assisted by the military if necessary, should simultaneously arrest all leaders, some 20 to 30, in their homes in Dublin about two o'clock in the morning, send them immediately across Channel, and intern them on the other side. Meanwhile their strongholds in Dublin should be occupied by strong pickets, so that the rank and file, hearing of the arrest of the leaders, would not be able to mobilise and arm. I considered that after that a house to house search should be carried out, and all known Sinn Feiners should be disarmed, and all drilling and marching and arming, except with Government permission, should be stopped.

Mr Justice Shearman: Before anything was done you would have to have the sanction of the Chief Secretary? Yes.

Did the military authority say that he had not enough men? I think so, and I don't think he had. I would not be in favour of doing it myself that night. It would have taken a few days' preparations. Mr Birrell was rather favourably inclined to the plan, and I think it would have been carried out.

Sir Mackenzie Chalmers: What stopped it? I don't know. He left next day, and we never got any further. That was at the interview on February 9th.

Stolen Dynamite

Witness in the course of further evidence explained that the conference at the Viceregal Lodge was called in reference to dynamite stolen at Brittas by rebels on Easter Sunday, which the police located at Liberty Hall. The course which he recommended to be adopted was recommended to the Under Secretary on March 7th, in addition to the recommendation in February. As regards the arrest of the Sinn Fein organisers, witness stated that he was not in favour of it, as it was only stirring them up and they were paid organisers. Four night manoeuvres were held. And there was a series of recruiting meetings arranged like Army meetings. They got a great deal of recruits, probably between 300 and 400.

The witness handed in a report which was made to him by an officer of the 'G' Division, referring to the recruiting meetings held by the Sinn Feiners. In that report it was stated that these meetings were undesirable and that they were causing annoyance and uneasiness to loyal citizens. It was also stated that the meetings were having an adverse effect upon recruiting for the Army, and that the Sinn Fein party were gaining in numbers and equipment. That report was dated 8th April, and it was sent to the Under Secretary, and must have been seen by the Chief Secretary and by the Lord Lieutenant. The Lord Lieutenant had made a note of the document, but it did not come back to witness until he sent for it a day or two ago. The Irish Volunteers in Dublin numbered 2,225, and they had 825 rifles, the Citizen Army 100, and they had 125 rifles; the AOH (American Alliance) 140, and they had 25 rifles. The National Volunteers in Dublin numbered 4,100, and they had 793 rifles.

Information for Mr Birrell

The Chairman: Mr Birrell in his statement said that everybody seemed to have known that the outbreak was about to take place, but that he never had any information as regards what happened in Dublin?

The Witness: I beg to assure you that our 'G' reports, with what I consider full information, and I think fairly accurate, were submitted.

Was there any minute about not seizing arms? No, but I was told directly, before making any search for arms in any house, to get directions from the Under Secretary. When I came here first I had several homes searched without reference to the Under Secretary, but there was a question in Parliament.

You say you got express directions not to search houses. Yes.

And not to stop armed processions? No. I dare not interfere with any of them on my own responsibility.

It was clear, the witness said, in answer to questions by Sir Mackenzie Chalmers, that there was mischief going on for a considerable time in Liberty Hall and in the other strongholds of the rebels throughout the city. He did not think much ammunition was kept in Liberty Hall, as he believed it was pretty well scattered about. There might have been useful documents found if the place had been raided, and perhaps bombs were manufactured there.

Major Price on Leaders and Funds.

Major Ivor H. Price, LLD, a County Inspector of the Royal Irish Constabulary, and at present holding an appointment as Intelligence Officer at the Irish Military Headquarters, stated that he acted as intermediary between the military authorities in Ireland, the Under Secretary, Dublin Castle, the Royal Irish Constabulary, and the Dublin Metropolitan Police. Between August and November, 1914, 900 rifles were sold to the Irish Volunteers by an English firm. In many places in Ireland it was perfectly hopeless to try a man by summary jurisdiction under the Defence of the Realm Regulations. During the past ten years people had been made magistrates who had no local standing, and were practically of no principle. When anything was done by the authorities in the way of suppressing a paper it was at once deprecated by the Nationalist Press. His information was that the Army lost 50,000 men as the result of the Sinn Fein propaganda in Ireland.

A report on Ireland

Witness, continuing, said that a fortnight before the outbreak he had been asked for a report on the state of Ireland, which he supplied, and in which he pointed out that while recruiting was satisfactorily going on, it was not so amongst the farmers and shop-keeping classes. Prejudice and the attitude of the official Nationalist Party up to the outbreak of the war, the lukewarmness of the clergy, and the fact that the farmers and shop-keepers looked down on the Army were reasons why recruiting amongst that class was not satisfactory. As to the Sinn Feiners, the work of organisation was very complete, and they had their members well trained. They practised rifle shooting and drill, and had officers' training schools, etc. No members would join the Army, and they acted as an anti-recruiting league. Considerable amounts of money had come from America, and the Sinn Feiners were able to pay eight organisers £150 per annum; while they kept up their policy through the medium of a series of disloyal papers. They also got control of the Gaelic League. They procured rifles, revolvers, ammunition, and high explosives wherever they could get them. On occasion 500 bayonets were seized by the police, and on another occasion guns and revolvers were seized on being brought from Dublin to Wexford. They were working up for rebellion in Ireland if they got the chance. The Government were aware of this report, and witness had sent five copies to the War Office.

'Only Typical'

Continuing, witness read an account of the parade of the Irish Volunteers in College Green on St Patrick's Day, and said it was a translation of a letter, dated 14th April last, written in Irish from St Mary's College, Rathmines, Dublin. He had described that as an extremely bad letter, pointing to some outbreak during the summer of this year. The letter had been sent to the Chief Secretary, the Under Secretary, and the Lord Lieutenant. The Under Secretary wrote, 'The outbreak in the summer—look upon as vague talk.' Mr Birrell wrote, 'The whole letter is rubbish,' and Lord Wimborne initialled it. (Laughter) 'That is only typical,' added the witness, amidst renewed laughter.

Continuing, witness said that the document read at the Corporation meeting by Alderman T Kelly had been printed at Liberty Hall.

Mr Justice Shearman: Have you any notion who invented that story? I am told it was the Countess Markievicz—at any rate there was a lot of clever people there. The O'Rahilly had an income of about £900 a year of his own, and MacNeill about £600. I think that money was expended in the cause by these men. There was one firm—Messrs Lawler—implicated, and we had to seize the stock.' In reference to members of the Irish Executive, Major Rice stated that on a matter of policy it always struck him that they were guided by the opinion of outsiders, members of the Parliamentary Party, and 'they went against my opinion altogether.'

Mr Justice Shearman: You could see that the outbreak was boiling up? Yes.

On that particular day? No, not until a few days before, until we heard about Casement's landing. About five days before I saw a letter in which it was stated that the ship was coming.

That was for an outbreak generally, not in Dublin specially? Yes. Of course, the heads were in Dublin. Witness further stated that he was present at the conference at the Viceregal Lodge. The Lord Lieutenant did not realise things, and he was rather hasty. His Excellency wanted to rush Liberty hall for the purpose of getting back the 250 lbs of dynamite. The proposal was that 100 soldiers and 100 policemen should rush the hall. Those who knew that the bombs were being made there, at Kimmage, and at Croydon park, knew that the leaders would not be there. Probably 100 lives would have been lost, and then the Press would come down and say, 'Nothing was going to happen; you should not have interfered with them; it is Bachelor's Walk again.'

The Chairman: Is it a good military reason not to do a thing because somebody might say something afterwards? No of course not, but I knew what would have been said. What we meant to do was surround the place in the morning with about 1,000 soldiers, and take all the leaders simultaneously.

Major Price further stated that the order of Mr MacNeill preventing the parade deceived everybody. At that time he knew that the ship had gone down and that Casement was arrested.

In reply to the Chairman, the witness said that he had not been able to trace who the money came from in America. It was brought over by hand. He had seen letters from Denis A Spellesy, who was secretary to an organisation in the United States for arming the Irish Volunteers.

Witness went on to say that the ammunition used by the rebels in the fighting in Dublin was of a terrible character. There were flat nosed bullets, split bullets, and in the Post Office reverse bullets were found.

Sir Mackenzie Chalmers: That is a German trick that has been played in Flanders? Yes. There were buckshot, slugs and bombs made out of workman's cans. He mentioned that there were now at the Ordnance Stores 365,000 rounds of ammunition captured from the rebels.

Captain RC Kelly.

Captain RC Kelly, Munitions Department, Dublin, deposed to his connection with recruiting in Ireland. At a conference at the War Office at which Lord Kitchener, Lord Wimborne, and Mr Birrell were present, he (witness) at the close of the conference asked would the increased Sinn Fein activities be again allowed to interfere with recruiting. He was stopped by His Excellency and Mr Birrell from proceeding. The arrangement was made to send a large number of troops to Ireland in May of this year, to discourage Sinn Fein activities, but not to suppress the organisation.

Mr Norway and the Post Office.

Mr AH Norway, secretary of the Post Office in Ireland, read a long report, in the course of which he referred to a statement that the Post Office in Dublin was a nest of Sinn Feiners. In March 1915, the government decided to issue a warning letter to all members of the Irish Post Office staff, who were active members of the Irish Volunteers. He had been supplied with the names of 48 persons forwarded to him by the Under Secretary, and to his mind in the case of some of these the suspicion was light and indefinite. Punishment was meted out where punishment was deemed necessary.

The Chairman: Do you know what was the attitude of the officials of the Post Office when it was attacked? I understand all the officials of the Post Office were turned out, except one female telegraphist, who remained behind to nurse a wounded sergeant. Upon this question of the loyalty of the Post Office staff—and I do not wish to exclude the possibility that there may have been disloyalty—it is well to remember that the conduct of the staff during this crisis and throughout the war has been quite excellent. In the restoration of the public service after the insurrection they acted with a zeal and public spirit which seem to banish some of the reasons for thinking that there can be many disloyal persons amongst them.

Major-General Friend

Major-General the Right Hon. LB Friend was called at the sitting of the commission on Friday, 26th May.

The Chairman: Would you please tell the Commission how long you have been in your present command? I came to Ireland in January, 1913, as Major-General in Charge of Administration, and I continued in that office until September, 1914 when I was told to take over command of the troops in addition to my other duties. From then up to April 28th I was doing both duties, and on that date Sir John Maxwell came and took over command of the troops, and I reverted to General in Charge of Administration.

General Friend then read from his notes. He stated that during 1913 and the first part of 1914 he saw and watched the progress and arming of various bodies of Volunteers in Ireland. On the outbreak of the war these movements took a new turn, and the existing volunteer organisations all over Ireland came forward and helped the military organisations energetically, and large numbers joined the ranks of the Army. About October, 1914, a new organisation of Volunteers came prominently before his notice. It was opposed to recruiting, and its members were obliged, he understood, to take an obligation that they would not enlist in the Army. That organisation, popularly called Sinn Fein or Irish Volunteers, fluctuated in its character and numbers but its members gradually increased, and arms obtained in various ways had increased until the military authorities that they would be obliged to take action, which consisted chiefly of trial before a magistrate, deportation of organisers, and the suppression of certain newspapers. His anxiety was increased in the beginning of this year, when the Sinn Fein organisation became bolder and more openly anti-military and anti-recruiting, and he thought that possibly a collision might happen at any moment, especially in Dublin, Cork, and Killarney, where there had been demonstrations against recruiting. In addition to this anxiety which he felt, he had also seen various reports from the War Office, and from the Admiralty at Queenstown. The first warnings began in December, 1914, of a possible landing of arms from Germany, America, and other places, accompanied by risings of disaffected persons, as well as of the Irish Volunteers. These alarms were going on for eighteen months, and the south and west of Ireland were mentioned as probable places of these landings, especially the Counties of Cork, Limerick, Kerry, Clare and Galway. On February 9th he attended a meeting at which the Chief Secretary and the Under Secretary were present. In consequence of that meeting he wrote specially to the General Headquarters of the Home Forces, and to the Adjutant-General at the War Office, and a correspondence ensued between himself and those officials, and there were certain interviews.

Greater Power Needed

The Chairman: Did you make any demands? Yes. I told Headquarters of the Home Forces of the interview I had with Mr Birrell and Sir Matthew Nathan, of the importance I attached to this bolder and more open anti-military nature of the Sinn Fein organisation. I thought that under the Defence of the Realm Act I could not do much more than I had done up to date. I thought that greater power should be given me to take stronger action.

Was that approved by the War Office? I will show you the correspondence afterwards in consequence of which Lord French saw Mr Birrell in London.

Witness then handed in a number of letters which the Chairman read, and said that in the public interest their contents should not be disclosed.

Witness, resuming, said that during April of this year the military received further warnings of possible landings of arms and simultaneous risings of disaffected persons. They took some further precautions with the troops they had at their disposal in Ireland.

You consulted Dublin Castle, I suppose? No; not in regard to the movement of the troops.

The Chairman: Did you consider the forces you had at your disposal sufficient to meet the possibility of a rising or internal trouble? I had to balance between the requirements in England, knowing they were pretty much in need of troops, and whether I should call on them in extreme emergency for more troops, or do the best I could with what troops I had. Up to April I took the responsibility of saying myself that I had sufficient to meet any emergency, with the condition that they were ready at short notice to send me additional troops from England.

To whom were you directly responsible? To the War Office.

And now to Lord French? Yes.

Departure for England

On 17th April Lord Wimborne was informed that a ship, accompanied by two German submarines, was expected to arrive on the 21st? I think he got the information through me from the Under Secretary. There was no date, I think. 'Not later than 22nd,' I think that was the way it was stated.

You left on the 23rd for England? On the evening of the 21st, Friday.

Was that not a little risky? I may say I heard about the capture of the boat before I started, and on arrival in London on Saturday morning I went straight to Home Forces Headquarters.

Up to the time you left had you heard of the sinking of the ship? I heard that on Saturday, in London, at the War Office. If I had heard the other news, I think I should have returned to Ireland immediately.

The Chairman: But you heard of Casement's arrest? I did on Friday evening. I think I should have started in any case, and returned the following day.

Mr Justice Shearman: Did it not occur to you that risings and riots might occur on a bank holiday when people were at leisure? Well, we had St Patrick's Day and Christmas. I was within touch with the Irish Headquarters, and I waited, of course, on Saturday to hear of anything likely to occur. I went back to the War Office on Monday, and heard this serious news, and I came back to Ireland at once.

When you prepared to go on leave on the 21st you had leave from the War Office? From the headquarters of the Home Forces.

From Lord French? I mentioned to him that I was going over about several things.

And I suppose in a case like that, you always told the Lord Lieutenant you were going away? I did in this case. I remember His Excellency asking me who would act in my absence, and I told him that General Lowe would act at the Curragh, and Colonel Cowan, Adjutant-General of the Irish Command, would act in Dublin.

On what date did you suggest Liberty Hall should be opened up? I have several dates on which I suggested it—when they were getting bolder.

Consulting the Nationalist Leaders

Mr Justice Shearman said he had a document before him on which was endorsed—'Before acting we should consult the Nationalist leaders.'

General Friend: 'We' means Dublin Castle.

Sir Mackenzie Chalmers: You were not in touch with the Nationalist leaders? No, sir; I saw them and had letters from time to time from many Irish members of Parliament. Witness, proceeding, said that what he wanted was that the Irish Government should agree to a raid on Liberty Hall, and those other places where there was a store of arms. He wanted notice in order to get a force of troops from England. His idea was to make one big blow.

When did you first suggest that? I think it was in October last year.

Sir Mackenzie Chalmers: The negotiations never got to the stage that you applied to the War Office for extra troops? No.

In your various communications did you communicate with Sir Matthew Nathan or Mr Birrell direct? With Sir Matthew Nathan.

He was the neck of the bottle—the communications went through him to Mr Birrell? Yes.

The Chief Danger Spot

Before the Rising, where did you think the chief danger spot was—in the South or in Dublin? In the South as regards this organised attempt to land arms.

And when you heard that Casement's invasion had failed, I suppose you thought that probably would put an end to all risings in Ireland? Yes.

Colonel Cowan.

Colonel HV Cowan, CVO, CB, the next witness, said that he would like to make it clear what occurred at the Conference at the Viceregal Lodge at the interview on Sunday, 23rd April. At 8 o'clock that evening, Sir Matthew Nathan called upon witness, and told him that His Excellency wished to see him. He accompanied Sir Matthew in a motor car to the Viceregal Lodge. On the way he told witness that 250lbs. of gelignite had been stolen that morning from a quarry, and had been brought to Liberty Hall, and that His Excellency wanted a raid on the Hall. His Excellency repeated that to witness, and suggested that a raid should be made in order to recover the gelignite the following morning, Monday, 24th April. He was aware that Liberty Hall was strongly guarded and that Volunteers were constantly coming and going, and that for some months they had been getting supplies of high explosives in small quantities. He felt, therefore, that the raid on Liberty Hall would not be successfully carried out without considerable fighting, and that it was very improbable they would succeed in getting the gelignite. It was manufactured in small sticks, and could be easily removed in pockets or haversacks. One man could carry away 2lbs or 3lbs at a time, and as they were continually coming and going, witness thought there would be very little left when the raid would take place. It would be only stirring up a hornet's nest with the force available.

A Bad Day to Choose

Witness also felt that Easter Monday would be a peculiarly bad day to choose, but before expressing a definite opinion witness told His Excellency he should like to see the Chief Commissioner of Police. An arrangement was made that witness should return to the Viceregal Lodge at 12 o'clock that night. He knew that General Friend's view was that if such a raid was to be made they would have to get reinforcements from the Curragh and Athlone, and the time left between half past eight o'clock, when the witness left the Lodge, and dawn the following morning, which was the best time for the operation, was too short to get up these troops. Witness returned to the Lodge at 10 p.m., accompanied by Major Owen Lewis and Major Price, and found Sir

Matthew Nathan and Colonel Johnstone, already there. The question was discussed, and Colonel Johnstone was very much of the same opinion as witness that Easter Monday was a bad day, as the city would be full of Volunteers and holiday makers, that if they raided Liberty Hall they should also raid the other depots, and that the leaders should be arrested at the same time. Several other suggestions were made, and it was ultimately decided that the thing should be postponed until a later day. That was principally on Sir Matthew Nathan's representation that before the leaders could be arrested authority would have to be obtained from the Government. That is, Mr Birrell.

So, if this outbreak had not taken place, military action would have taken place? Yes, shortly afterwards.

Sir Mackenzie Chalmers: Was there any special reason for making a raid that time? Only for the object of getting the gelignite that was known to have come in on the Sunday morning. That to my mind was a small matter, because we knew they had got other high explosives before.

Were there 1,000 soldiers available in Dublin at the time? We had more than that, but a good many of them were recruits. The total number available in Dublin on the Monday morning was 120 officers and 2,265 men.

Officers on Leave

I see it stated that a great many officers were away on leave? I will refer to that.

'The absence of officers on leave has been commented upon under an entire misapprehension,' said the witness. 'Leave has been most sparingly given since the beginning of the war, except in the case of urgent private business or a medical certificate. On the day of the outbreak all officers of the Headquarters Staff were on duty with the exception of two absent on sick leave and one officer on urgent private affairs.'

It is currently reported in the press that a large number of officers were away at the races some miles away? At Fairyhouse.

Why was that? In Dublin there was a large number of officers on leave from England and only a few officers in Dublin were given leave for the day.

Sir Mackenzie Chalmers: Were the guards strengthened? Not on Monday morning.

There was a suggestion to do so, but Sir Matthew Nathan objected? I knew of no such suggestion. In Ship street there were from twenty or thirty armed men at hand. At the outbreak they were brought into the Castle. The guard of six was overpowered and shut up.

Candidly, you were not expecting this? No, not in the least. We were anxious on Saturday when Casement was being brought up. We thought they would hear of his arrival and there would be trouble in an attempt to release him. He arrived at 5.30 and he was on the boat before 8 o'clock. People apparently did not know of his arrival.

Who held the Bank of Ireland against the rebels? It never was attacked.

Major Owen Lewis

Major Owen Lewis stated that at the request of General Friend he had an interview with Sir Matthew Nathan about three months before the outbreak, on the question of the suppression of certain newspapers, and also about the arrest of the leaders. Sir Matthew Nathan was not in favour of taking action against the newspapers.

The Attorney-General

The Right Hon. James H Campbell, KC, MP, Attorney General for Ireland, was examined after the luncheon adjournment.

The Chairman: Since your reappointment, can you give us any information as to what you have been doing? I am not here for the purpose of making any complaint, but simply answer questions, and let you know the facts. During the nine days I was there before the rebellion broke out I received no official communication of any sort, kind, or description intimating the probability or possibility of any trouble. I was not present at the conference which was stated to have taken place on the part of the Executive at the Viceregal Lodge on the Sunday. I never heard of it until I read of it in the newspaper the other day. I wish to add, further, that I never saw the Under Secretary during that nine days, though we were only separated in the Castle by a partition. I had no interview with the Lord Lieutenant during that time, and the only official act that I was called upon to do during that period was in connection with one file which I have here. It was with reference to the method or propriety of dealing with men who were parading on the public streets, carrying arms which were admittedly service rifles, and had been stolen or abstracted in some way from the military authorities.

Mr Justice Shearman: What date did you get that? On the 22nd April.

Sir Maurice Dockrell.

Sir Maurice Dockrell, DL, explained the operations of the City and County of Dublin recruiting Committee, and mentioned that recruiting activity reached high water mark in April, May, and June last year. It then fell off owing to the efforts made to undermine the Committee's work by anti-recruiting methods. As a result of the special effort of Lord Wimborne recruiting improved, but subsequently fell off.

Sir Maurice also referred to the troubles caused by the labour strike in 1913, and to what merchants and others had suffered by that. He wished to say that, in his opinion, that strike was largely due to feeble government. The then Under Secretary's conception of government was that he was what he called 'the keeper of the ring'—in other words, that the citizens of Dublin and the strikers should fight it our. He met the Under Secretary in the street, and told him that the citizens were suffering a great deal of intimidation, and the answer he made was: 'Don't you think the police could deal with the strikers?' He also said: If you bring any case under my notice I will deal with it.' Dublin was in such a state at that time that any man who acted as his own policemen did so at the risk of his life.

Mr Justice Shearman: Was the Citizen Army in existence then? No; it was formed after that. Witness employed a number of ex-policemen to protect his men, and he fought the strike out to a finish. The point he wished to make was that there was no military protection for the citizens. He believed that protection had been asked for, and that the military authorities did not see their way to grant it.

Mr Justice Shearman: Were your men armed? They were, and the strikers were armed. We took out licences for our men. (Laughter.)

Mr RW Booth

Mr RW Booth, JP, President of the Dublin Chamber of Commerce, was the next witness. He gave an account of a number of industrial strikes that had taken place in Dublin since 1908. Larkin, he said, left the Dockers' Union in 1909, and started, in a small way, the Irish Transport Workers' Union. He was convicted of embezzlement, and sentenced by Mr Justice Boyd to twelve months' imprisonment, but he was released by Lord Aberdeen after three months. (Laughter.) From that time dated the power of Larkin over the Irish Administration.

County Inspector Ruttledge, RIC, Galway, West

At the sitting of the Commission on Saturday, 27th May;

County Inspector George Bedell Ruttledge, Royal Irish Constabulary, stated that he had been 27 years in the police force, and was now stationed in the West Riding of County Galway. Describing the origin of the Irish Volunteer movement, he said that the first branch of the Irish Volunteers was formed in Galway town on December 12, 1913, at a meeting which was addressed by Sir Roger Casement, Mr PH Pearse, Professor John MacNeill, and a man named George Nicholls. At that meeting 248 members were enrolled, and George Nicholls, of Galway, became an active organiser. At the end of May, 1914, there were ten branches, with a membership of 964: on June 24 there were 24 branches with a membership of 1,938; in July 42 branches with 3,704 members; in August 54 branches and 5,179 members. Up to this time drilling was actively carried on by the various branches. After the outbreak of the war and Mr Redmond's declaration in Parliament offering the services of the Volunteers for home defence a marked change took place. No drilling practically took place, as many of the drill instructors, being military reservists, rejoined the Army, and there was also a fear that they might also be called on to serve in the Army. The Volunteer movement then fluctuated, and the branches became less and less. Then in March, 1915, William Mellowes took up his headquarters in Athenry, and became an active organiser in the locality, which had always been disaffected on account of agrarian agitation. He gathered together all the young men who were members of a secret society, and who had pronounced disloyal views. Three branches were formed with a membership of 144 in May, and in the same month a meeting was held in Tuam, which was addressed by William Mellowes and Seán MacDermott. The latter's speech was most seditious, and he was prosecuted and sentenced to four months' imprisonment. In November a large public meeting was held in Athenry, and was attended by all the extremists in the district. Owing to the influence of the leaders the members of three branches of Mr Redmond's Volunteers turned over and joined the Sinn Fein section. These three branches had been in localities which were always disturbed and

Honeycombed with Secret Society Influence

In February an organiser called Alfred Monahan arrived in Galway, and displayed great activity. He was ordered to leave Ireland before the 8th April. He left Galway and evaded arrest. On St Patrick's Day a large Sinn Fein demonstration took place in Galway. It was attended by 562 Sinn Feiners from Galway East and West Riding;: 200 of them had rifles and shot guns, and 20 carried pikes. There were 1,070 Sinn Feiners in the Riding.

The Chairman: Now tell us about the outbreak.

The Witness: The rebellion commenced in the County Galway at 7.20 a.m. on Tuesday, 25th April, by an attack on the police barrack at Gort, 9½ miles from Galway. That attack continued till 10.30. The barrack was fired upon, and the windows were smashed. The rebels numbered 100 at first, but the number increased as time went on. Stone barricades were built across the road at each end of the village. The barrack was defended and held by five policemen, who were first called upon to surrender by a leader of the rebels, who threatened to blow up the barrack.

The Chairman: What is his name?

The witness gave the name privately, and continued: The rebels withdrew to Clarenbridge, where they were reinforced by others. An attack was made on Oranmore Barrack. The attack there commenced between 12 noon and 1 p.m. The railway line and the telegraph poles were cut, and a large hole was made in the bridge. The barrack at Oranmore was defended by four policemen until relief came at 7.30 through the arrival of a party of police and military from Galway. The rebels took to flight towards Athenry in motor cars. Ten Sinn Feiners were arrested, and placed on board ship in Galway Bay. Special constables were sworn in, and three neighbouring police stations were closed, and the police concentrated in Galway. Two hundred troops arrived on Wednesday, and next morning at 4 o'clock the party went out, and were met by a considerable party of rebels at Cahermore crossroads. A sharp encounter took place, in which one constable was shot dead and others were slightly wounded. The rebels were put to flight. On April 26th it was reported that the rebels were marching on Galway. A party of police went out to meet them. The rebels did not come on, but took cover on a hill, which was fired on by sloop of war in the bay. On Friday, April 28th, military went out to Athenry, where it was learned that the rebels were concentrated at Moyvore. The rebels broke up and abandoned five police prisoners and much loot. The rebels surrendered, having been advised by a priest to go home. Since then 211 men had been arrested in the West Riding of Galway, and were conveyed to Dublin.

The Chairman: You mentioned in the course of your statement that a number of seditious speeches were made on a number of occasions at various places—now were all these speeches reported to the Government? They were reported to the Inspector-General.

Was any action so far as you know taken in Galway over those speeches? No action.

The spokesman still at large

The person who acted as the spokesman for the rebels and who threatened to blow up the barracks at Clarenbridge—was any action taken against him? None.

Is he a free man now? Yes.

He is still there? Still there.

At the close of your statement you say that the party broke up on being advised by the priests to go home. Were the priests acting in co-operation with these rebels? Some of the younger ones were.

Did they participate actively? Yes.

Has any notice been taken of it? No notice was taken.

Mr Justice Shearman: There was no action or arrest of any priest? No.

To Sir Mackenzie Chalmers: The priest who appealed to the rebels was acting as a peace maker, and he told them that they were acting very foolishly, that there was a large force of military there, and that their camp could be reached by them and that it would be far better for them to go home.

To the Chairman: Witness did not know the name of the priest, nor whether he was one of the younger or the older clergy.

To Mr Justice Shearman: In Galway some of the younger clergy were disaffected, but a good many of them were very loyal.

Secret society at work

Have you formed any estimate as to the number of people who were engaged in your district in active rebellion? I think about 400 went out.

The Chairman: Have you got any direct proof of the influence of secret societies in Galway? There has been a secret society in Galway since 1882.

Has it always been in touch with the Clan-na-Gael? Always, and it is connected with the Gaelic Association. It has led to all the crime in Galway, and is at the back of this Sinn Fein movement now.

When you say 'crime' do you mean political crime or agrarian crime? Agrarian crime before this last stage.

Do you think the fear of conscription had much effect in increasing the ranks of the Sinn Feiners? I think so, amongst the ordinary village boys.

Shirkers? Shirkers. They won't fight for England.

Do you consider that the prevention of emigration has had some effect? I do. In November, 1915, upwards of 50 left Galway to emigrate, and then that scene occurred at Liverpool when they were jeered at. Those men came back, and ever since then there had been a very hostile feeling.

Were they also Sinn Feiners? Yes.

German money

Have you any information of German money coming over to Galway? Not directly, but we noticed that people who were not well off had a god deal of money to spend, wherever they got it.

Sir Mackenzie Chalmers: The main organiser was a man named Nicholls? Yes, in Galway.

What has happened to him? He is under arrest.

Are the people doing pretty well on their farms in Galway? They are. I did not think the farmers were ever better off. They were afraid of being disturbed. The men who took part in Sinn Fein marches were farmers' sons and labourers. The town of Galway was very loyal, and recruited very well, indeed, for the Army. The town of Galway had no sympathy with the rebellion at all.

Mr Justice Shearman: What is the origin of the agitation in Athenry? It is the headquarters of a secret society.

Has the Clan-na-Gael got any organisation in Ireland? I think that secret society is connected with it.

County Inspector Clayton, Galway, East

County Inspector EM Clayton, RIC, next gave evidence regarding Sinn Fein activities in Galway, East Riding. The Sinn Fein organisation was first established in Craughwell in February, 1907. That branch was really a secret society. Branches were subsequently established at Loughrea, Athenry, and Kilrea, and though their numbers were small it was necessary to watch them closely, as the worst-disposed individuals joined them. Further branches were established in November, 1915, as the result of a meeting held in Athenry. Six hundred and seventy members attended, and 161 were armed with rifles and shot guns. The police were excluded from the meeting. Inflammatory speeches were made. Five branches were immediately formed around Loughrea and Athenry. The total number of branches was eleven at the time of the outbreak, and the membership amounted to 371. There were in addition 350 Sinn Feiners who did not belong to any branch. The black spots of the districts included portions of Athenry and Loughrea, and secret societies existed in these places for years past. Sinn Fein organisers had very little trouble there. The Craughwell members linked themselves up with the Sinn Feiners under the leadership of a famous criminal.

The Chairman: Who is the famous criminal? Thos. Kenny. He took a leading part in the rebellion, and is now on the run. Mellowes came to Athenry in April, 1915, and succeeded in enrolling practically all the young men of the countryside. He was paid a salary of £3 a week.

Sinn Feiners busy at Athenry

The first intimation the police had of the outbreak was on Tuesday, April 25th, when word came in that a constable at Moyvore had been shot and seriously wounded. Nothing occurred until 5.30 on that day, when a message was received that the Sinn Feiners were very busy at Athenry. It was believed that they were going to take the barracks, and it was necessary to reinforce the police there. The attack, however, did not take place. The Sinn Feiners seized the town hall, established their headquarters there, and made bombs during the night. The next morning they moved out about two miles to a farm belonging to the Department of Agriculture, where they were joined by the Sinn Feiners of the West Riding. They remained there for the night. They cut the telegraph wires, tore up the railway line, and commandeered foodstuffs. Next morning they marched to Moyvore Castle. There were about 1,000 of them altogether. The police concentrated at Loughrea and 200 extra men were expected from Belfast. As soon as the latter arrived a message was sent out to the rebels, and efforts were made to induce them to disperse. The priest, whose name witness heard, was not a disloyal man, and there was a contest between him and Mellowes as to who would have the upper hand. Desertions had been going on.

The Chairman: What happened to Mellowes? He is on the run, too. Proceeding, witness stated that 270 arrests were made. Most of them were deported to England. Twelve were convicted and sentenced by courtmartial,. The military and police seized seven rifles, 86 shot guns, and 7 revolvers; 35 rifles were unaccounted for. The majority of the rifles were foreign ones, and of modern pattern.

Influence of seditious newspapers

The Chairman: In your district had the Press much influence? Yes, the seditious papers, which went into the district weekly. The trouble was chiefly confined to the districts of Loughrea and Athenry. The population of the two districts was about 3,000, and they had always been the centre of secret societies.

The Sinn Feiners were pretty well known to you, I suppose? They were.

Were there any people of superior class or education among them? None.

What class did they come from? One of the leaders was a blacksmith, and the Colonel of the Irish Volunteers was a publican. They were all small shopkeepers and farmers' sons.

There were none of them of the literary type? None.

Mr Justice Shearman: Were the priests assisting this movement in your district? Yes, the younger ones.

It has been said by another witness that the priests in considerable numbers assisted? Yes, a considerable number: some of them were more active than others.

Sir Mackenzie Chalmers: As a man gets older he gets more sensible? Yes, he gets more careful.

County Inspector Hill, Kerry

County Inspector HOH Hill, RIC, who said he was 35 years in the force, and 3½ years in County Kerry, gave evidence. He had had general experience as a police officer all over Ireland. The Sinn Fein movement, he said, first came into prominence in Kerry in October, 1914, after Mr John Redmond had announced the decision of the Nationalist Party to support the war. At a meeting in Tralee in that month it was decided that Mr Redmond's policy should be adopted. Others decided to remain loyal to Mr John MacNeill's party in Dublin. The Sinn Fein party produced a Union Jack, which they waved in the face of the Redmondites, and afterwards burned. Then green flags were produced and waved. The decision to remain loyal to MacNeill's party was a snatch decision, because a great many of Mr Redmond's followers were at Listowel Races. He estimated that there were 646 Sinn Feiners in the county after that. On the 30th November there were four distinct branches of Sinn Fein in the county, the estimated strength of which was 1,041 persons. Until Mr Redmond had declared in favour of recruiting the Sinn Fein movement was of no account, but afterwards he found that it would have to be reckoned with, as many of the leaders were pro-Germans and against recruiting. Up to October, 1914, nearly everyone in Kerry was in favour of winning the war, and assisted the police in hunting up spies. But after that all that stopped. Shortly afterwards a number of the Sinn Fein party marched through Tralee, and 118 of them carried rifles. In February, 1915, the number of branches of Sinn Fein had increased to seven, with a membership of 1,039. In March there were eight branches, but they were all mostly inactive. In April the number of Sinn Feiners had increased to 1,044, which was due to the activity of Ernest Blythe, an organiser who came to Kerry during the month. After a meeting on March 18, at which the Irish Guards' band attended, some members of the Sinn Fein party marched through the town, and called upon the people to enrol in the Volunteers. In May the number had increased to 1,060, and Blythe and a man named Cotton were very active in organising work.

The Killarney parade

During that month Mr John MacNeill held a parade in Killarney of 550 armed Volunteers immediately after some Gaelic athletic sports. This parade was to show the strength of the Volunteers in Kerry, and men came from all parts of the county. In June there was a decrease of 38 in the number of Sinn Fein Volunteers in Kerry. This was due to some members resigning because they could not make up their minds as to which section of the Volunteers they should belong to. Blythe and Cotton were very active during the month. In July the numbers had been reduced to 982, a lot of members having seceded from one branch and formed a branch of their own. In August the Sinn Fein party paraded in Killarney in memory of O'Donovan Rossa, whose funeral was taking place in Dublin on that day. In September the numbers increased to 945, and a good deal of skirmishing was carried out throughout the county. They also carried out night manoeuvres, much to the terror of the people of Kerry. In October the number of Sinn Feiners had increased to 1,018, and during that month the Volunteers marched out into the country and practised rifle-shooting. On the 8th October a deputation of Sinn Feiners waited on the Listowel Race Committee, and succeeded in getting them to rescind a resolution they had passed to give 1d. in the 1s. of their receipts to the Royal Munster Fusiliers' Fund. The Sinn Feiners then demanded that 1d. in the 1s. be given by the Race Committee to the Irish Volunteers. This was agreed to, but it was rescinded at a later meeting. (Laughter.)

Playing on the people's fears

In November 1915, the total Sinn Feiners for the County Kerry was 1,143, and the organisers showed great activity, playing on the people's fears of conscription, and on the recruiting letters which were being sent out to persons of military age. Cotton was organising around Kenmare and Killarney, and a man named Michael Moriarty distributed sixteen revolvers at Dingle.

Several meetings were held, and disloyal speeches made by a Dublin organiser who was trying to make the Sinn Fein and the Labour Parties one. In Ballymacelligott district house to house visits were being made for the purpose of purchasing arms. In December the total of the Sinn Feiners was 1,233, an increase of 99. Blythe and Cotton were very active during the month, and a Dublin man delivered a lecture on Wolfe Tone to 200 people in Tralee. Branches of the Transport Workers' Union were established. In the following month the number of Sinn Feiners increased by 59, the increase being due to active organising. During the month a meeting of the County Board of the Sinn Feiners was held at Tralee. In February, 1916, there were 18 branches with a membership of 1,278, and during the month Cotton was giving instruction in the use of the rifle and revolver in Dingle, and special instruction was also given in bayonet exercises and skirmishing.

Mr Justice Shearman: Had Cotton been a soldier? No, he was in the Labour Exchange before he became a Sinn Fein organiser. During the month Mr Partridge, of Dublin, made speeches of a disloyal character, and Mr PH Pearse reviewed 248 Volunteers in Tralee. In March Cotton was organiser, Blythe having been arrested and sent to England. Cotton left Kerry finally on the 27th March after being served with notice when in Belfast not to return to Kerry.

All the leading suspects

Witness went on to detail later events connected with the Sinn Fein movement. On St Patrick's Day they paraded in Tralee in full strength, And on 25th March a woman named Marie Perolze had arranged to deliver a lecture on the Fenian Rising. The Countess Markievicz was to have given the lecture, but she was forbidden to visit Kerry, and she sent this other woman. Nearly all the leading suspects visited Kerry from time to time.

Mr Justice Shearman: Was there any actual rising in Kerry? No, but two constables were shot at.

The Chairman: Were there any leaders of any kind in Kerry at the time of the landing of Sir Roger Casement? No. The principal man there was Austin Stack, and I arrested him the same day as I arrested Casement. I have a note of it.

Witness then read his note of what occurred at the time of the landing of Sir Roger Casement, his capture, the sinking of the arms ship, and a number of arrests he made in Tralee in connection with the landing. He added that 316 Irish Volunteers had mobilised in Tralee evidently to assist in the rebellion and the landing of arms. Owing to the general state of unrest and the rumours that were flying about witness asked the officer commanding the troops in Tralee if he could send him some soldiers to assist the police in case of necessity. The officer replied that he had none to spare. Witness then got into communication with the General Commanding at Queenstown, and he promptly sent on 100 soldiers by train. They arrived at 5 a.m. on 22nd April. On the 21st he had also wired for extra police for Tralee, and they came in from outlying stations. Extra men were placed at Waterville and Valentia to protect the cable stations.

Why there was no rising in Kerry

The Chairman: You said there was no rising in Kerry? No, and I attribute this to the arrest of Casement and the local leaders, the arrival of troops from Cork and of extra police from the country. Austin Stack was in charge of everything, and when he was arrested the Irish Volunteers who were assembled in Tralee became nervous. Those of them who were from the country districts gradually left for home.

Mr Justice Shearman: How many had assembled? 316.

Had the question of conscription a great deal of influence? Yes, a great deal. The number of Sinn Feiners largely increased at that period.

In reply to Mr Justice Shearman, witness said he never expected danger from the Redmondite Volunteers, but he did with regard to the Irish Volunteers. Although he did not expect a rising he knew there would be great danger in the case of a German invasion. The railway lines and the telegraph wires would be cut, and it would be difficult for the military to operate. There were only four young priests connected with the movement. Several parish priests prevented the formation of Sinn Fein branches. Out of a population of 165,000 in the county there were only a little over 1,000 Sinn Feiners.

Sir Mackenzie Chalmers: Were there sympathisers of the Sinn Feiners who would have been with them if they thought they would succeed? Yes. It was hard to know whether some people were Sinn Feiners or Redmondites.

Perhaps they did not know themselves? (Laughter.) That is so. Many Sinn Feiners thought they were insulted when they were called MacNeillites. (Laughter.)

The German ship intended to land at Tralee? Yes, by force.

There was not much preparation to receive it—only two men in a motor car? There was a large number in Tralee. My idea is that the ship came in a day or two too soon. She was unpunctual.

You had not enough men to deal with 370? No. I had only thirty men in Tralee. In the whole county I had 338 before the war; since then 272, not counting officers.

County Inspector Sharpe, Wexford

County Inspector John Robert Sharpe, Royal Irish Constabulary, Wexford, was next examined. He said he had been 29 years in the RIC, five of which he has spent in the County Wexford. Besides the County Inspector there were four District Inspectors, four head constables, and 204 constables in the county.

Asked by the Chairman what he knew of the Sinn Fein movement, he said it was first started in Enniscorthy about 1904, its founders being persons who had been connected with the old Fenian conspiracy. Its aims were the overthrow of English rule in Ireland, the establishment of Irish industries, and the boycotting of English manufactures. It had seven branches, with a membership of 325, in the County Wexford. They had 95 rifles, most of modern pattern, 47 shot-guns, 34 revolvers, a number of bayonets, and some ammunition. He could not state accurately how much. Several branches held weekly and bi-weekly, drills and route-marches, some indoor and some outdoor, and they sometimes went out under arms. They were occasionally visited by PH Pearse, JJ O'Connell, Mellowes, and other organisers. Prior to the outbreak of the rebellion in Dublin the county was peaceful, and none of the political organisations was active, save the Irish Volunteers, which latter had been very active for the past two years.

The Enniscorthy Rising

Beyond the fact that they were in possession of rifles, there was no indication of an intended rising until the 25th April last, when some men marched into Enniscorthy, where they remained that night and dispersed the following morning. The Irish Volunteers took possession of the town at 4 a.m. on April 27.

The Chairman: How many men were there? There were 600 men, and 200 of them had rifles and shot-guns. They established themselves in the Athenaeum as their headquarters, and appointed 'Irish Republican Police'. They appointed sentries, and allowed no one to enter or leave the town without a permit. They commandeered motor cars, food and every description of goods, including arms, and they searched houses for arms. Five constables and the District Inspector held the police barrack, and the sergeant and one man was in the bank. The bank was in view of the barrack. The rebels took possession of the Castle on the hill, and from that they fired on the barrack, and they also fired from the slope of Vinegar Hill. There was an open space around the barrack, and that saved the barrack. On the morning of the 28th the Administrator of the parish, Father McHenry, and a Mr O'Neill wanted the police to surrender. He (witness) was very glad they did not surrender. They held out until relief sent by the military arrived on the 1st May.

Welcome supply of ammunition

The Chairman: What ammunition are the police supplied with? They are supplied only with thirty rounds each man, but they had seized a thousand rounds of Sinn Fein ammunition before that, and it came in very handy, for it fitted the police rifles. (Laughter.) The 600 Sinn Feiners were not all armed. The military told him that a man in a house was equal to eighteen men outside in a fight of this sort.

Sir Mackenzie Chalmers: They did not try to rush the thing at night? No.

Mr Justice Shearman: You say there were about 325 in the county, and that 600 men turned out? Yes, two hundred of them armed.

That is about double the estimated number? Oh, yes; but they terrorised the whole of the inhabitants into joining them.

To Mr Justice Shearman: The population of Enniscorthy was about 5,000. There was no bloodshed in the county with the exception of one head constable wounded. There was a small disloyal element in the county. The only disloyal people were the Sinn Feiners, whom the police were watching. There were four young priests who were Sinn Feiners, but the rest of the priests helped the authorities in every way possible, and were thoroughly loyal. In fact, one of the priests, Father Murphy, of Ballymun, was most abusive of the Sinn Feiners in his sermons, and 99 per cent of the priests were thoroughly against them. Over 200 persons assisted the police to hold the town of Enniscorthy, and witness armed them with shot-guns and other weapons. Then the National Volunteers, Hibernians, Unionists, and, in fact, everyone was most keen in helping the police.

National Volunteers assisting the police

The Chairman: Did the National Volunteers turn out? They turned out everywhere. There were 200 Redmondite Volunteers assisting the police before the military arrived. Wexford was about 14½ miles from Enniscorthy. Witness intended to go to the relief of Enniscorthy, but he received a message from the General Officer Commanding in Cork stating that men were urgently required to guard the railway, and it would be no use to send them to Enniscorthy, and on no account to send them there. Subsequently 1,100 men and 70 cavalry, with a 4.7 gun, were sent to take Enniscorthy.

In reply to the Chairman, witness said that 375 Sinn Feiners were arrested, and of these 319 were sent to Dublin, 52 were discharged, and 2 were taken to hospital. The police seized 46 rifles, 66 shot-guns, 8 pistols, 6 revolvers, 1 bomb, 21½ stone of blasting powder, 667 rounds of sporting ammunition, 4,067 rounds of rifle and revolver ammunition, and a quantity of gelignite and other explosives.

The Chairman: A regular arsenal? Yes. The rifles were mostly of German pattern, and amongst the ammunition was a quantity of soft-nosed bullets. They were not filed, but were made clean cut.

Plan of Campaign in a pass book

Mr Justice Shearman: Did you find amongst the prisoners any copies of the circular read by Alderman Kelly in Dublin? No, but on one of the prisoners we found the whole programme of the rebels in Dublin. It was written out in a pass-book, and contained all details as to the attack on the General Post Office and everything else. That document remains to be produced before the courtmartial. It was an ordinary penny pass-book, with the whole programme written in it. It was written in pencil, and was evidently a copy of the original programme.

County Inspector Power, Kilkenny

County Inspector PC Power, RIC, who has been stationed in County Kilkenny for the past six years, stated that the first appearance of the Sinn Fein movement in the Kilkenny district was about the year 1912. In its initial stages it was intended to encourage Irish industries. On 5th March, 1914, Sir Roger Casement, accompanied by Thomas MacDonagh, held a meeting in Kilkenny City for the purpose of forming a branch of the Irish National Volunteers,. At that meeting about 500 persons attended. Sir Roger Casement advised them to drill and become proficient in the use of firearms, which he stated would be supplied to them. A branch of the INV was formed then, and a number of members were enrolled. Drilling and training were actively carried on from that time, and a large sum of money was collected in the town towards this organisation. Then Mr Redmond and his party about June, 1914, got partial control of the Volunteers. A split occurred, and the local treasurer, without any apparent authority, forwarded about £90 to Mr John MacNeill in Dublin. The next movement of note was when JJ O'Connell, a Sinn Fein organiser, arrived in Kilkenny. That was in April, 1915. From that time forward the movement showed much activity and began to spread over the country districts. The attitude of Mr Redmond towards recruiting for the Army and also the fear of conscription rather gave an impetus to the Irish Volunteers. Witness also noticed at that time that the number of the Irish National Volunteers rather decreased, and that movement more or less became dormant. On the other hand the Irish Volunteers were well organised and stimulated by paid organisers. One of these men, Edward O'Kelly, described himself as a lieutenant. The others were John McDermott and William Mellowes. A good deal of seditious literature was circulated. The first occasion that the Irish Volunteers appeared on the streets under arms was on 23rd November, 1915, at the celebration known as the 'Manchester Martyrs'.

A seditious speech

The Chairman: Where did they get their rifles from? I am unable to say. They were modern magazine rifles, and looked like Enfields. John McDermott attended on this occasion and delivered an address behind closed doors to the Irish Volunteers in the Gaelic League Rooms. In March, 1916, Lieutenant O'Kelly, on the occasion of an Irish Volunteer parade at St John's Well, near Kilkenny, made a very seditious speech. I reported it at the time.

Was any action taken upon it? No. in February and March of this year the Irish Volunteers were under arms on two or three occasions. No actual outbreak occurred in Kilkenny during Easter Week. We noticed a considerable amount of activity and restlessness among the Irish Volunteer men. On Easter Monday they moved about in groups and in a state of excitement. They also attended the railway station, apparently for the purpose of receiving some information which did not arrive. Their cyclists were also very active going out into the country, and one of their number who owned a motor car was pretty well kept on the run.

You never found what they were up to? Not at that time.

Searchlight signalling

Witness went on to say that he took immediate steps to assemble as many armed men as he could, and by Wednesday morning he had about seventy. It was necessary to hurry a force to protect the Barrow bridge. The military subsequently took it over. On the morning of the 27th he observed signalling going on apparently from Mount Leinster, which overlooks Enniscorthy. It looked like searchlight signalling. There were answering signals from a northerly direction. On 5th May the police raided the local Sinn Fein hall and seized a number of bayonets and pikes. In the hall was a scroll with the inscription—'A felon's cap is the noblest crown an Irish head can wear.' There had not been a general surrender of arms, and they believed they were got into Kilkenny, but they were concealed somewhere. Kilkenny did extremely well in recruiting, and he believed that there were not more than 200 or 300 Sinn Feiners in the whole country.

County Inspector Gelston, Clare

County Inspector Gelston, in his evidence, said he had had 26 years' service in the RIC, three years of which he had spent in the Co. Clare. The first branch of the Volunteers was started in the Co. Clare in March, 1914. The number of branches increased to four, and the membership to 400, and that went on until September, 1914, when a split occurred in their ranks and many of them seceded from Mr Redmond's party. At that time about 300 Volunteers became what was subsequently the Sinn Fein party or the MacNeill party.

The Chairman: What brought about the split? I don't quite know. It was, I think, dissatisfaction with Mr Redmond's policy regarding the war and recruiting, and regarding the Home Rule Bill. At that time they had no leaders—the Sinn Fein party—in the county. A Sinn Fein branch, composed of very few people, was organised by Thomas O'Loughlin, and he and his little party became the centre of the Sinn Fein movement, but nothing was done until May, 1915, when a paid organiser named Ernest Blythe came to the county and made himself very active. He went on creating branches until July, 1915, when he came to be looked upon as a danger, and a deportation order was served upon him. Blythe underwent a term of imprisonment for disobedience to the order. When Blythe left the county the movement stood still until a man named O'Hurley, a Gaelic teacher and organiser, became very active, with the result that at the beginning of this year there were ten branches of the Sinn Fein in the county, with a membership of over 400. They drilled, and some of them wore uniform and practised shooting with miniature rifles.

Alarming the Populace

The Chairman: What number of arms had they? In the whole county they had about 35 rifles. They were not well armed, but they had plenty of shot-guns and miniature rifles. These branches became more or less aggressive in some parts of the county, and people got afraid of them. Complaints were made to him of the marching with arms of these men through the county. On one occasion a man named Michael Brennan, a captain of one of the branches, paraded his men after Mass on Sunday on the road, and before proceeding on a route march he distributed ammunition to them. That created a great deal of alarm in the minds of the people. Brennan, addressing his branch of the Volunteers, made the remarks: 'I want to say a few words for your own information about the seizure of arms. My advice to you is, if such an attempt is made, to use them, and not to use the butts of them, but the other ends, and what is in them.'

The Chairman: What is the date of that?

Witness: It was on the 17th March last. It was on the 15th December, 1915, that he handed the ammunition to the men. Brennan further said at that meeting on the 17th March—'Some of you may not like to commit murder, but it is not murder, it will be only self-defence. You know well if your arms are taken that the next thing will be conscription.'

Why Clare did not Rise

He was prosecuted for that speech, and sentenced to three months' imprisonment. The Sinn Feiners in the Co. Clare did not rise, and gave no trouble, but at the time of the rising there was considerable activity. Organisers were moving about, and the Sinn Feiners were evidently anticipating something. On Easter Sunday many of the Sinn Feiners met along the banks of the Shannon, evidently anticipating the landing of arms from the Kerry side of the river. He attributed the fact that there was no rising in Clare to the failure to land arms from Kerry.

The Chairman: What was the state of recruiting in Clare? Recruiting was very good in the County Clare, taking it all round, amongst the labouring classes and in the towns, but there was no response from the farming classes—otherwise the recruiting was surprisingly good.

Was the Sinn Fein movement a small one in Clare? Well, at first it was very small, but it grew rapidly at the end of last year and the beginning of this year. We had a record of over 400 Sinn Feiners in the county, but of course there were a great many sympathisers who did not openly join, but showed themselves in sympathy with the Sinn Fein movement. My own opinion is that if they had had a rising in Clare we would have had a great many more than 400—we would probably have had about three times that number.

Mr Justice Shearman: Did you have any seditious sermons or remarks from priests? We had—there were quite a number. There was one clergyman who addressed a meeting, and told them to arm, and if they could not get long-range rifles to use shot guns—that shot guns were very useful in the hands of Irishmen.

Was this reported to headquarters? No. He also told them if they could not get guns to get revolvers, and if they could not get revolvers to get pikes—that the blacksmith could make them—and if they could not get pikes to get hatchets or slashers in their own houses.

How long ago was that speech made? In January last.

The Chairman: Was that speech made by a young priest? Yes.

As a rule, are the younger priests hostile? Any of the priests in the county who had Sinn Fein tendencies were of the younger variety. The older men, as a rule—the parish priests in a number of cases—have spoken against the Sinn Fein movement.

Have they given assistance to you in the performance of your duties? Well, no, except to the extent of denouncing the rising from the pulpit. In one case a parish priest addressed the Sinn Feiners, and asked them to give up their rifles to us. That was the only case in which rifles were given up to any extent.

Sir Mackenzie Chalmers: There are arms in the county still? Yes; quite a number.

Mr JC Percy

Mr JC Percy, JP, who stated he was an honorary recruiting worker, gave his impressions of the effect of the Sinn Fein movement upon the recruiting for the Army and Navy. Latterly he had confined his efforts to recruiting for the Navy. Killarney was the first place where he found Sinn Fein operating against recruiting. He could not get a chairman to preside over the meeting. He tried the member of Parliament, the Chairman of the Town Commissioners, and the Administrator. The latter had been very kind to them at a previous recruiting meeting over which he presided. He excused himself by saying that he did not think he should be asked to take the chair a second time, and that some other person should do so.

The Chairman: Who is the member of Parliament? I think it is Mr O'Sullivan.

Witness, continuing, said: I then went to Sir Morgan O'Connell, and he gave me an entirely different reason from the others for refusing. He said there had been a review announced to be held of 5,000 people who came from Kerry, that this would be an anti-recruiting meeting, and would put an end to recruiting in Kerry if it was allowed to be held, and that he had wired to Mr Birrell and Lord Wimborne to have it suppressed, but that neither of them had moved in the matter. Under these circumstances, said Sir Morgan, he would not move his little finger to help the British Government. Others, continued the witness, gave me as their reason for refusing to take the chair the reported appointment of Mr James Campbell as Lord Chancellor of Ireland. (Laughter.)

Effect of seditious newspapers

Witness further stated that he had reported to Great Scotland Yard that the seditious newspapers published in Dublin were libelling the speakers at recruiting meetings. The Recruiting Committees in London got interested in the matter and asked for copies of these papers. For two months prior to the outbreak witness sent a weekly file of these papers to the Admiralty and to the Recruiting Committee in London. He also brought the matter up at the Dublin City and County Committee. They made a very serious attack on one of the Dublin priests, Father Doherty. That attack appeared in the *Irish Worker*, and witness sent a marked copy of the paper to Sir Matthew Nathan. Speaking from memory it was to the following effect: 'His Holiness the Pope does not ask us to recruit; Cardinal Logue does not ask us to recruit; the Archbishop does not ask us to recruit; but here is this whipper-snapper of a priest asking us to lay down our lives for this rotten Empire.' The paper also stated that Fr Doherty had a brother in Dublin Castle as a second-class messenger, and that his speech was doubtless made for the purpose of getting his brother promoted. (Laughter.) Witness mentioned that as a sample of what was going on in Dublin for the last twelve months. The Committee was finding it increasingly difficult to get speakers for meetings. All the attacks on speakers at recruiting meetings were marked, and the papers were sent to the recruiting authorities.

Much More Daring

Witness went on to state that he found in his recent travels through Ireland that the Sinn Feiners had become much more daring. He came across their paid organisers on motor bicycles and on horseback all over the country. One of the recruiting committees reported that these organisers were to be found at fairs and markets, and that they were signing on the people not to fight for England. That was done openly, in broad daylight. That, of course, had been reported by witness to the Admiralty.

Mr Justice Shearman: Have you ever run up against Major MacBride? Yes. There are two towns in the West of Ireland only forty miles apart—Ballina and Westport. Ballina did splendidly in recruiting. Then you go to Westport and you cannot get recruits. We were told that Major MacBride dominates the place. At Ballina we were taken to the recruiting meeting by a brass band and torchlight procession. My experience in the West of Ireland is that the towns are fighting for their country.

Too Fat and Prosperous

Sir Mackenzie Chalmers: The country people are doing extremely well with their farms, and are not anxious to lose their money? Yes. They are too fat and prosperous. A great many farmers' sons are joining the Sinn Fein movement, and using it as a kind of umbrella in excuse for not fighting.

If the farmers enlisted would there be difficulty in getting labour; is their labour essential? It is not essential in France. I found a number of women working hard in the fields in Coleraine and district. In County Down, I found fifty men of military age who were doing nothing but driving carts containing seaweed.

The Chairman: How are you getting on now; are you still recruiting? No, I have returned to private life and given up recruiting. (Laughter.) We found as time went on that the Sinn Feiners were getting more daring, and our work was getting more difficult.

Have you done successfully in recruiting for the Navy? Yes. I don't think there is the same prejudice against the Navy as the Army. We had a fine meeting in Westport, although we did not get any recruits. (Laughter.) There were five or six hundred in the hall of military age, and they did not interrupt. I asked them if they wanted to fight for Ireland, and they said 'Yes'. I told them then that they could not fight for Ireland without the Navy, and they agreed. (Laughter.)

Colonel Sir John Ross of Bladensburg, Late of DMP

At the sitting of the Commission on Monday, 29th May;

Colonel Sir John Ross of Bladensburg, until lately the Chief Commissioner of the Dublin Metropolitan Police, was examined. He read a long statement dealing with the events which culminated in the rebellion. The landing of arms at Howth on 26th of July, 1914, he said, was an event which was intimately connected with it, but before he dealt with that event he thought it would be well to allude to a few matters that occurred previously. First—the Government allowed the Arms Act to lapse in 1906, and thereby everyone in Ireland was enabled to arm. This appeared to witness to be an extraordinary step for any Government to take, and, as Ireland was divided into many factions, all having different ideals and aspirations, to give them an invitation to arm themselves seemed like a suggestion to bring a lighted candle into a powder magazine. The repeal of the Act benefited no one, and was of no public utility. Secondly—There had been a great deal of labour unrest in Dublin in recent years, which culminated in a number of serious strikes in 1913, headed by Larkin and Connolly, a very prominent leader in the recent rebellion. The DMP had great difficulty in preserving order. There were numerous riots and considerable unrest: but by firm action disorder was suppressed.

The Sackville Street Riot

On 31st August a meeting was announced to be held in Sackville street, close to the head office of the Tramways Company, many of the employés of that company being involved in the strike. The meeting was proclaimed. Nevertheless, Larkin attempted to hold it, and he was arrested. A riot ensued, which was soon quelled, but in the *mélée*, which was natural, some people were unfortunately hurt. Thereupon the Dublin Corporation demanded that an inquiry should be held into the action of the police. Although it was in the midst of the unrest, the demand was immediately acceded to by the Irish Government, and before they got any report from the police. As a matter of fact, the first official intimation witness had that an inquiry was to be held was about two months later, when Lord Aberdeen wrote to say he thought it might soon take place. Witness had an opportunity of seeing Mr Birrell in October, and complained of this hasty way of condemning the police before anything could be done. It appeared to witness that this throwing over of the police was a weak proceeding, calculated to bring about further disorder, and that it would easily persuade the disorderly that the Government was afraid to resist them. The result of that inquiry was that the action of the police was held to be justified.

The Strikers Drilling

Thirdly—Later it came to his knowledge that the strikers were beginning to drill. He submitted a detailed report on the subject, which he forwarded to the Government with a minute of his own. In that he said that it was the first occasion in his experience that an organisation of a semi-military character had been formed in Ireland. He requested instructions before the movement became stronger. In reply he was told to keep the matter under observation, and to furnish further reports. A few weeks later he had to write again, saying that more men seemed to be enrolling, and that some of them were carrying hurleys. He repeated his first request, and got a similar reply. Connolly had said that they were arming for the purpose of resisting the violence of the police, who were, he declared, in the dock. That took place in November, and the inquiry took place in December. On July 1st, 1914, another report was submitted relative to the so-called Citizen Army, some of whom paraded in uniform with side-arms and a disused type of German bayonet. In reply a somewhat similar instruction was given—to keep the movement under observation, and to get the names and addresses of the men.

The Landing at Howth

Then came the landing of arms at Howth on Sunday, 26th July, 1914, which, as he had already said, was closely connected with the rebellion. He did not think until this landing that arms were in possession of any irregular forces in Dublin police area, which covered not only the city but a large portion of the County of Dublin, about 35 square miles in all. He found, however, a report of drilling by armed Volunteers, made on the 16th July, 1914. That was the first time in which drilling with arms was observed in Dublin. But the arms carried on the 16th July consisted only of four rifles and six dummies. The introduction of arms, after the lapse of the Arms Act, was easily accomplished. The points he wished to make were—First, that the government viewed with alarm the facilities afforded to those organising to arm themselves, and they attempted to prevent the importation of arms into the country under Customs regulations. Arms that were henceforth landed were seized and forfeited. Arms that were not imported illegally could not be touched. The Dublin Metropolitan Police had several times been called upon to assist in carrying out the Customs regulations.

The Larne Gun-Running

Some arms were smuggled into the North of Ireland, and they were secretly and unostentatiously distributed. That proceeding was, of course, very wrong, but the authority of the Government was not defied. But the secrecy with which those arms were landed and distributed testified that those importing them did not wish to come into collision with the police. As soon as the arms disappeared from the port of landing the police were unable to discover their whereabouts. Some arms were illegally landed in Ireland, and hence when persons got arms in that way the Customs regulations had little effect, and the RIC had special instructions as to how to deal with such persons and their arms when caught. Owing to the way in which the landing had been conducted in the North of Ireland, the police had not been able to put their instructions into force, and the arms remained in possession of their owners. The case in Howth differed altogether from the method of the landing in the North. At Howth the arms were ostentatiously landed in daylight, and the Constabulary there, as well as the coastguard officers, were overpowered with violence. The body then marched on to Dublin with their illegally imported arms.

Mr Harrel's Action

Witness said he wished to say that the landing of arms at Howth was in open violation of the law. Mr Harrel, then Assistant Commissioner of the DMP, having heard of the events at Howth, and that the Constabulary were overpowered there, went with a large body of the police, as it was his duty to do, and eventually succeeded in taking some of the rifles illegally landed there from the men engaged in this disorderly conduct. The next day—that is Monday 27th July—Mr Harrel gave me a detailed report on the matter, and I forwarded it to the Irish Government with my own minute. It was as follows: 'Under Secretary, I beg to point out that this gun-running operation of the National Volunteers differed from any other yet attempted in Ireland. Up to now, at all events, those busy in getting arms for themselves have acted surreptitiously, and not, as was done yesterday, in broad daylight, and in face of the police. I further draw attention to the fact (the report continued) that the National Volunteers yesterday were found in possession of arms which had been landed in Howth in defiance of a proclamation, and there was ample evidence to identify the weapons they were carrying with those illegally landed at Howth. It appears, moreover, that a body of more than 1,000 men, marching upon Dublin, which is the seat of the Irish Government, is a menace to the King's Government, and such a body constituted an unlawful assembly of a peculiarly audacious character. The police have been instructed to assist in carrying out a proclamation which prohibits the carrying of rifles in Ireland, and it was held, therefore, to be their duty to take rifles which had just been landed at Howth by force and in defiance of the Government proclamation. Yesterday, however, a minute was sent by you to the Assistant Commissioner, which appears to me to alter the instructions previously given to the police. I beg, therefore, to request His Excellency's directions in the matter in order that it may be made plain how in the future the police were to act in face of a proclamation.'

A Belated Minute

The Under Secretary's minute that this referred to was received by Mr Harrel about 5.15 p.m., when he was returning to Dublin after having taken rifles from some of the men who were carrying them, and after having dispersed an unlawful assembly. It was addressed to him (witness), although the Under Secretary stated at the subsequent inquiry that he knew that witness was in his office. The minute was as follows: 'To the Assistant Commissioner. As regards the steps which you have taken on your own responsibility to deal with the arms landed in Howth this morning, His Excellency has advised that forcible disarmament of the men now marching on Dublin should not, in all the circumstances, be attempted, but the names of the men carrying the arms should, as far as possible, be taken, and a watch kept to ascertain the destination of arms illegally imported. His Excellency cannot authorise any further steps in this matter at present.' That was initialled 'JBD,' the then Under Secretary.

Mr Harrel's Suspension

It was true, remarked witness, that the Under Secretary, having first concurred with Mr Harrel's plan of action, later on changed his mind, but two hours elapsed before that change of mind was notified to Mr Harrel. If it had been communicated at once it would have reached Mr Harrel long before any contact with the gun-runners took place. They delay was one of the mysteries which had never yet been explained. Mr Harrel's account of the Howth landing of arms and witness's covering minute were in the Under Secretary's possession the following day. Witness's minute, at least, was telegraphed to the Chief Secretary—at all events Mr Birrell told him he got it at 6 p.m. that day, but long before that—at 3 p.m.—Mr Harrel had received a communication informing him that he was suspended.

Sir John Ross's Resignation

Under these circumstances he (witness) immediately resigned in the following letter:

'Dear Lord Aberdeen,—It has just been reported to me that Mr Harrel, my Assistant Commissioner, has been suspended from office and duties by order of Your Excellency. This, I beg to say, in the case of an officer in his position amounts to a determination of his office. No explanation has been given to me of the reasons for placing such an indignity upon him and the force. I feel that the course pursued with reference to Mr Harrel so deeply affects myself that under the circumstances I am compelled to ask your Excellency to relieve me from my office and duties.'

Witness went on to say that he found it was quite impossible to remain under the Irish Government after what had been done to Mr Harrel. Not only was Mr Harrel condemned in the manner stated, and before his own version of the story and witness's notes could be considered, but other reasons weighed with witness. On account of the exigencies of the moment and the critical state of public affairs, which in a very few days culminated in the outbreak of the great European war, witness remained at his post until relieved by the Lord Lieutenant. During those few days two applications for the return of rifles seized by Mr Harrel were received, but witness could not say whether that request had been complied with. In July, 1914, there was only one set of Volunteers, known as the Irish National Volunteers, but it was a fact that some of the men who conducted the gun-running at Howth belonged to the extreme section.

An Act of Injustice

The inquiry took place early in August, and a few months later Mr Harrel was removed from the Irish public service, and so his career was broken and his usefulness was lost. Witness begged leave to state that in his opinion an act of injustice had been committed, and this was the more remarkable because he believed this was the first occasion that an Irish public servant had been sacrificed to public clamour. The Irish Civil Service suffered, and its efficiency must have been impaired, for it was impossible that men could do their duty fearlessly and impartially and usefully unless they had confidence in their superiors. He always held the opinion that the armed force which overpowered the Customs officers at Howth and marched on Dublin was obviously an unlawful assembly which a magistrate was bound to disperse, and he would retain that opinion until the contrary was decided by a competent authority. He held that the action of the Executive in removing an official who did his duty prevented all public servants from acting with resolution, and was the essential cause of the recent rebellion.

A Question of Insurrection

Mr Justice Shearman (to Sir John Ross): Before the Howth incident, were instructions issued to police inspectors as to the circumstances under which they could call in military aid? Instructions were given to the Irish Constabulary, but not to us. These instructions were vital to the inquiry that was held, and they were to be embodied in it, but they were not.

They must be in writing somewhere? They were written, but I have never seen them. We all wanted to see them.

It may be that they do not exist.

Mr Harrel: I am aware that they exist.

Mr Justice Shearman: Can you tell me of any occasion on which the military had been called in to assist the police? Yes, during the riots of 1913 we had the military frequently ready, but we only called them out once.

Commander WV Harrel

Mr WV Harrel, late Assistant Commissioner in the Dublin Metropolitan Police, and now a Commander in the Royal Naval Reserve, having detailed the periods of his public service went on to say that he attributed the recent outbreak to, in the first instance, the existence at all times of an extreme party in Ireland, who were always ready, directly or through Irish-American channels, to give trouble on receiving financial and other assistance. Their settled policy had been for years to join, and if possible control, any organisation or movement which might reasonably be expected to strike at constitutional authority. Witness was aware that there were communications between persons in Dublin and others in America, and he considered that these communications were being influenced by Germans in America. Some of the persons who were prominently connected with the recent outbreak were also connected with the societies that were formed during the South African War, notably Major MacBride. He formed the Irish Brigade in South Africa which fought against the British troops. Later there were other suspicious circumstances which came to the notice of witness, and led him to believe that the people in Ireland were being influenced in favour of Germany: but of course a good many of these documents he should not care to refer to. In the second place, he thought the repeal of the Peace Preservation Act had a good deal to do with the outbreak. Save for sentimental reasons, there was no reason for its repeal, against which witness reported at the time to the Under Secretary, then Lord MacDonnell. That Act applied to all Ireland, but it was only put in force by proclamation of the Lord Lieutenant, and it was not of necessity imposed on the country at large, nor even on whole counties, but might be imposed on portions of counties. Witness mentioned to Lord MacDonnell his objections to the repeal of the Act, and he asked witness to put them in writing. He did so, and went fully into the matter. Lord Mac-

Donnell sent witness's report to the law officers and asked them if what witness had stated was the case. They replied that he had accurately stated the law on the subject.

The Larkinite Conspiracy

Witness proceeded to refer to the failure of the Government to enforce the law in the early stages of the Larkinite conspiracy in Dublin from 1908 to 1913, when it was found that it was not a genuine labour movement but one hostile to law and order. Witness said that he thoroughly agreed with the remarks of Sir John Ross in regard to the failure of the Government to support the Dublin Metropolitan Police during the labour troubles. The work of the police during that period was very laborious, but it was well and cheerfully done. It was felt that it was a reflection on them to order an inquiry to be held when they had carried out the orders of the Government. There was a sort of impression that the proceedings taken by the police to prevent the unlawful meeting in Sackville street were taken by the police themselves. That was not so. Everything was done by order of the Government.

Outside advice

The Chairman: By the Under Secretary? Yes. I swore the information on which the magistrates' proclamation was issued. Witness then proceeded to relate how trouble occurred in Sackville street, how Larkin was arrested, and almost immediately released after being convicted by a Dublin jury and sentenced. 'Of late years,' continued witness, 'there was a tendency on the part of the Government to rely on the advice of outside forces rather than that supplied by the police. The Government undoubtedly accepted both, but it was quite clear that in many cases advice was given not in agreement with that given by the police, and he had some reason to believe that it was accepted—on police matters. Towards the end of 1913 the Irish Volunteers were formed. There was a public meeting held on November 25, presided over by John McNeill, and on that occasion a strong contingent of the Transport Workers' Union attended. Following that the proclamation against the introduction of arms was issued.

The Government and gun-running

As regards the actual gun-running at Howth the condition of affairs then existing was that the National Volunteers had been increasing their membership, and that in the spring Mr Redmond had made proposals for assuming, in any case partial control. From what I knew as to some persons controlling the movement I had doubts if they would succeed. But up to the time of the gun-running there was no political difference—there was no actual breach between the two parties. I had interviews with Sir James Dougherty and the Law Officers, and I always understood that the government took a serious view of the gun-running in the North of Ireland. Some weeks before the Howth gun-running witness was one morning sent for by the Under Secretary, and went to discuss with him some information that had been obtained as to the possible landing of arms, which seemed at the time, from the information at the Under Secretary's disposal, to be more or less imminent. He told the Under Secretary that he thought it would be a very good thing if there was a conference of the police, the military authorities, and the coastguards as to what should be done, because, so far as witness could see, no-one understood what his duties and responsibilities were. Witness said: 'Suppose these arms were landed in the early morning, and a large number of men assembled, what could a few unarmed Dublin police do? Now, I think in that case we would have to get military assistance.' He said, somewhat doubtfully: 'I suppose so.' 'Well,' said witness 'would it not be well to address the matter with General Friend, because if such a thing occurs as a sudden landing of arms it would be well to have some orders and understanding about it, and in such case it would be necessary to have a special plan.' At the time witness was only thinking of his own district, and was not thinking of Howth. So far as witness could see, the Under Secretary agreed with him that it was a good idea. At that time there were gun-boats and torpedo boat destroyers up and down the coast, which showed that the matter was a serious one in the view of the Government at that time, and that they wished the proclamation to be enforced.

A Motor Car Searched

There was a gentleman in Dublin at that time who was suspected of being engaged in the importing of arms, and his motor car was stopped and searched by a coastguard officer, and a question was put in Parliament to the First Lord of the Treasury about it—as to the right of the coastguards to do this, and what authority they acted upon. The First Lord said that the vehicle was searched in consequence of a report that some arms had been landed in the locality, and that the duties were imposed on the coastguards by the Customs laws. To a further question suggesting that there was a difference between the treatment of persons in the Co. Dublin and those in the northern counties, and that the importation at Larne was permitted without let or hindrance from the coastguards or anyone else, the First Lord of the Admiralty replied: 'I can only say that it will always be the duty and should be a point of honour with every person serving under the Crown in an official capacity to maintain the law of the Land impartially in all circumstances.'

An incident at Howth

Then followed the Howth gun-running, continued witness, and, as he had said, he never had any doubts that the terms of the proclamation would be enforced. He would like to draw attention to an incident which took place at Howth when the gun runners assembled to the number of 1,000 or 1,200. The coastguards at Howth endeavoured to do their duty and prevent the carrying away of arms, and one coastguard was struck on the head with a rifle, and a Volunteer held his revolver to the breasts of four other coastguards, and threatened to fire if they endeavoured to send a message for assistance. The chief officer found that the wires had been tampered with, and had to send a coastguard in plain clothes with a message to Dublin. The police who attempted to occupy the pier were stopped by a number of men, who had drawn themselves across it, and were armed with heavy clubs hanging from their wrists with leather thongs. These men had assembled to take away the rifles by force, and they certainly were violent in what they did. The police at Howth were powerless to do anything. They followed these Volunteers with the rifles, and ultimately were with them when witness met them at Malahide road. In taking the action that he did on that occasion he never had the slightest doubt that it was his duty to interfere and to intercept these people, as he always understood that if persons were in possession of arms or other offensive weapons it was the duty of the police to disarm them.

Calling out the troops

As regarded the calling out of the troops, he was one of the persons who were specially authorised to do so. The recent Royal Commission in their report state that, 'It appears to be clear he (Mr Harrel) had from the first resolved to invoke the assistance of the military in the operations which he contemplated.' That was not quite correct. He supposed that opinion was based on his instructions which were given, when he heard of this matter, to his superintendent to warn the military. That was done invariably when anything serious was likely to arise, and had nothing whatever to do with the ultimate calling out of the troops. Later on, in a few minutes, he did see the necessity of having armed forces to protect his men, and he then instructed the superintendent to try and get the military on the telephone. He could not do so. He then endeavoured, also without success, to get the RIC Depot in the Park, but he could get numbers of other places, whether by accident or design he did not know. Witness then telephoned to the Kildare Street Club, on the chance of getting into communication with General Capper. It so happened the General was there, but witness had no previous knowledge that he was there.

Mr Justice Shearman intimated that it would not be necessary for witness to detail all the events of that day, as they were already on record, and in any event they were not within the scope of the present inquiry, save in so far as they were reflected on the recent rebellion.

Some of the chief actors

Witness said the only reason he mentioned the fact about the Kildare Street Club was that it was an important factor subsequently, strange as it might seem. He went on to refer to the composition of the body of men carrying rifles from Howth to Dublin. Amongst them were some of the men who had been prominently identified with the rebellion. Thomas J Clarke and John McDermott were going about in motor cars, evidently organising the whole thing. Darrel Figgis, Bulmer Hobson, and Professor MacDonagh were also there.

Mr Justice Shearman: The military were called out because the police were unarmed, and you could not get the RIC? Yes.

Sir Mackenzie Chalmers: Was the action you took successful; was there any trouble? Very little. There were two soldiers wounded and three Volunteers. Twenty-five rifles seized. The soldiers were doing nothing except marching back when they were attacked? Nothing whatever. They had been dismissed by me from duty. In the first instance when I met the Volunteers I was careful not to bring the soldiers into conflict with them, and they were not brought into conflict with them. The police did their work well, but when the two soldiers were wounded there was slight conflict.

Government Servants in secret societies

In reply to further questions witness stated that from time to time during the period in which he was Assistant Commissioner he had occasion to make investigations in reference to secret societies and dangerous political organisations, and it came to his knowledge that persons in the Government service belonged to these organisations.

Answering Sir Mackenzie Chalmers, witness stated that during the labour troubles he had on several occasions, reason to think that the police were in danger, and he ordered them to carry revolvers. There was, however, no occasion to use them.

Sir Mackenzie Chalmers: You are of opinion that there are instructions somewhere about the gun-running? I have no doubt of it.

But they were so secret that they were never issued to the police? They were issued to the Royal Irish Constabulary.

Sir Mackenzie Chalmers: That is, I suppose, because gun-running was likely to take place in their district and not in yours? I do not know: but by law they have some powers as Customs officers that the Dublin police have not. They were told in their instructions that they might use force, and I know that in the country every preparation was made for their doing so.

Sir Morgan O'Connell

Sir Morgan O'Connell was next called and he read a statement in which he said that in August, 1914, on the outbreak of the war, the County of Kerry was absolutely peaceful. A good number of Volunteers were carrying out drills and route marches, mostly on Sundays. At that time there were not many arms in the county, and wherever one met these bodies on the roads they were well conducted, and considerate for other traffic. Although the Sinn Fein existed in Kerry it was until May, 1915, a more or less moribund concern, with no real vitality or following. To remedy that state of affairs the heads of the Sinn Fein party in Dublin determined to hold a demonstration in Killarney on May 23, 1915. The holding of that meeting was advertised throughout the county. Mr John MacNeill was billed to make a speech and to personally enlist recruits for the Army of Ireland. He (witness) realised that the authorities were going to allow that demonstration to take place. The police had warned the Government of the object of the demonstration, and stated that it was plainly anti-recruiting and seditious.

Message to the Lord Lieutenant

Witness went on to say: On May 22nd—the Saturday previous to the Sunday meeting—I telegraphed to the Lord Lieutenant: 'A meeting under auspices of Sinn Fein party is to be held here tomorrow, calling itself a football match, but with the perfectly open and avowed intention of being turned into an anti-recruiting meeting. Will Your Excellency do anything to stop this?' The reply I received was 'The Lord Lieutenant is not advised to prevent meeting referred to taking place, but if any breach of Defence of Realm Regulations occurs it will be dealt with by Competent Military Authority —(Signed), Nathan.' After receiving that I wired to His Excellency: 'If you will have all special trains to Killarney cancelled tomorrow the meeting will be an absolute failure, and we can quite well deal with the local disaffected party.' I received no reply to that telegram until, I think, the following Thursday, when I received the following telegram—'Your telegram has been placed before His Excellency—(Signed) Secretary to Lord Lieutenant.' In addition to that I sent a copy to the Central Recruiting Committee of Ireland in Dublin. The Central Recruiting Committee had been in constant correspondence with me about recruiting in Kerry. I telegraphed to them to see whether they could use any influence to get this thing stopped. The Lord Lieutenant is president of the Central Recruiting Council. I received a letter stating that the Council had been in communication with General Friend, but nothing would be done to stop the meeting. The meeting was held on the 23rd May, and Mr John MacNeill made a seditious anti-recruiting speech. There were five special trains at cheap fares to Killarney, bring thousands of country people to hear this speech, as well as some 500 armed Sinn Feiners, who paraded the streets all day, whilst the whole country for ten mils around flocked into Killarney as well.

From that 23rd May, 1915, Sinn Feinism spread in Kerry like fire on a mountain. Large quantities of arms and ammunition found their way into the county. Recruiting meetings still continued to be held, but the forces against recruiting became more and more hostile. The last recruiting meeting was held on the 26th February, 1916, when a hostile mob of Sinn Feiners, headed by a band, did their best to break it up. This mob was led by a local JP for the County Kerry, and it took the authorities fourteen days to make up their minds whether or not they would deprive him of his JP-ship—he sat in the Killarney Court a week after this anti-recruiting meeting. The authorities were apparently afraid to institute any legal proceedings against this Sinn Fein mob, as no prosecutions followed.

Aliens in Kerry

It is more than probable, continued the witness, that the German connection with Sinn Feinism in the County Kerry was worked through an alien German who acted as manager of the five hotels of the Great Southern and Western Railway Company. This man had his headquarters in Kerry, and there was a hotel in Killarney which was made a dumping ground for alien enemies, who came there as waiters. These understudies were from time to time interned, but the alien manager was left there until April, 1915. It was at this hotel that Lody was arrested—he was afterwards shot as a spy. The manager himself was arrested at that time, but was subsequently released, and returned to Killarney. During the first nine months of the war much German money undoubtedly found its way into Kerry. I have the strongest reason to believe that the police authorities in Kerry did their best to get these men removed. Private effort to get this alien German removed from Killarney was quite fruitless for the first nine months of the war. He appeared to have powerful friends at Court. At the outbreak of the war he was allowed to move freely through Kerry, but subsequently he was restricted to moving about only on a police pass. In witness's opinion, Mr Birrell and his Government were entirely responsible for the present condition of affairs in Ireland by their criminal neglect of all warnings and their refusal to take any steps to stop sedition and disloyalty when both these things could have been easily put an end to in their earlier stages, and by allowing John MacNeill and others in receipt of salaries from public funds to preach open and avowed treason. Mr Birrell had stated that trial by jury in Ireland was a farce. A far greater farce, said witness, in rural Ireland was trial at ordinary petty sessions. The Government had appointed to the Commission of the Peace in the South of Ireland scores and scores of men who were absolutely unfitted for the position, and who attended petty sessions courts solely for the purpose of carrying out the most open and flagrant jobbery. The Roman Catholic Bishop of Kerry had over and over again protested in the strongest possible language against the open corruption at petty sessions. Witness handed in a copy of the Bishop's pastoral letter. The one bright spot in this deplorable chapter of Irish history, said witness, was the unswerving loyalty and devotion to duty of the Royal Irish Constabulary. They knew the country and the people; they were of the people themselves;

COLONEL SIR JOHN ROSS OF BLADENSBURG, formerly Chief Commissioner, Dublin Metropolitan Police.

COMMANDER W. V. HARREL, R.N., formerly Assistant Commissioner, D.M.P.

Photo by] [*Lafayette.*

MAJOR PRICE, Intelligence Officer at the Irish Military Headquarters.

Photo by] [*Lafayette*

Brigadier-General JOHN ALOYSIUS BYRNE, new Inspector-General of Royal Irish Constabulary.

their warnings of the trouble that everyone knew must come were unheeded.

Sir Morgan O'Connell related an incident in which Sinn Feiners returning from a demonstration in Castleisland marched through Tralee discharging shots in the air. He also told how recently his wife and he were standing outside the cathedral in Killarney when some children gathered about them and, to the tune of Tipperary, sang 'it's a wrong, wrong thing to fight for England.' (Laughter.) In Killarney there was a place which was really a Sinn Fein club, and a policeman told him that the person who 'ran' it sent off parcels of seditious literature to the schools in the country.

Sir Mackenzie Chalmers: Who distributes them? I should think the schoolmasters. Witness then handed in a document which he had received connecting people in Dublin with the anti-recruiting campaign in the country.

Magistrates and jobs

In reply to Mr Justice Shearman, witness stated that the Roman Catholic bishop actively used his influence in preserving order. After the outbreak in Dublin he went to his lordship and said that it would be for the peace of the country if he could get the Sinn Feiners to surrender their arms, and he used his influence, which had great weight, with them. In Kerry he did not think that there was a single Sinn Fein parish priest. There were a few of the younger clergy who were a little hot-headed, perhaps. With reference to the licensing cases witness stated that every case was heard before it came into court. A great many magistrates seemed to think that their only duty was to do jobs for their friends.

The witness before leaving the witness chair begged to be allowed to tell a little story in illustration of what the bishop and himself had referred to. A client, he said, came to a solicitor in Killarney to engage him to appear for him in a court at some distance away. They were negotiating about the fee which the client should pay. The solicitor mentioned two guineas. 'Oh,' replied the client, 'I can get two magistrates cheaper than that,' and so the solicitor was not employed (Laughter.)

Colonel Maurice Moore

Colonel Maurice Moore was next called.

The Chairman said the Commissioners had received and read with interest a statement from Colonel Moore, and in due course copies of it would be furnished to all the members. It was not considered necessary, however, that it should be read in public, but he understood that Colonel Moore would like to make an explanation in connection with the mention of his name some days ago, and the Commission would be please to hear him on that point.

Colonel Moore: As my statement is not going to be read in public, and statements were made in public by officials and others, some of which were ludicrously wrong, it would be absurd of me to make any statement at all.

The Chairman afterwards stated, in reply to a question from the Press, that Colonel Moore's name had been mentioned by a previous witness, and that he had been allowed by the Commission to attend to make a personal statement, and nothing else.

Sir James Dougherty

The Commission sat again at Westminster on Wednesday, 7th June, Sir James Dougherty, a former Under-Secretary for Ireland, giving evidence. Sir James said he was Under-Secretary for Ireland from July, 1908, to October, 1914. He went to Dublin Castle in 1895, when he was appointed Assistant Secretary. During his whole term of office the labour world of Dublin was in a state of continual unrest. Throughout these troubles he action of the Irish Executive was directed to two ends. First, to the maintenance of public peace, and, secondly, to the re-establishment of industrial peace by mutual agreement between employers and employés. In the carters strike the police force was adequate to maintain peace, and it was settled as the result of negotiations carried on by the Lord Lieutenant and the Under-Secretary. There were scenes of violence in the tramways strike. Tramcars were wrecked, and from time to time the police had to make baton charges. In the end Larkin completely failed, and left for New York, whence he was not likely to return.

Sir James Dougherty next dealt with the question of the use made of troops during the various strikes, and referred to the activities of the Government in trying to bring employers and strikers together. In some cases, at least, he said, those efforts resulted in satisfactory settlements, although the masters complained constantly, and, I believe with some justice that the engagements entered into by the men were not faithfully kept. For their action the Irish Government was assailed from first to last by a hailstorm of lies. I never saw Larkin alone. When I saw him it was when he was with other members of his union. The political opponents of the Government were not ashamed to put about ridiculous stories as to the relations of members of the Government with Larkin. It was alleged that we were on most intimate terms with him, and that he had been invited to tea.

The Volunteers

The National Volunteers, Sir James declared, were the response of the Nationalists to the Volunteer movement in Unionist Ulster, and the gun-running at Howth was but a natural sequel to the gun-running at Larne. 'I do not care,' he continued, 'to enter into details as to the rise and progress of the Ulster movement. I can only say that those who led and encouraged it shouldered a very heavy burden of responsibility. They were, indeed, the persons who played with matches in a powder magazine. It has been sometimes said that Ireland has been made the playground of English politicians, and some confirmation of this saying in the present case may be found in the fact that the earliest attempt to import into the North of Ireland discarded rifles from Continental armies was promoted and directed in London. Rifles bought in Hamburg were landed here. They were paid for by an English cheque, and persons most intimately connected with the reception and distribution of the imported arms were closely connected with the political organisation in the important London borough where the arms were found.'

Sir James went on to say that the failure to distribute these arms was ignominious and complete. Consignments amounting to 1,166 rifles in all were seized at various Irish ports, including Dublin, Belfast, Coleraine, Londonderry, Greenore, and Drogheda. The balance of the consignment was subsequently seized by the authorities of the Birmingham Proof House under the powers contained in their special Act. The guns which were landed at Howth were brought to Ireland by an English yacht, and steered into Howth by the English wife of the English owner. Events like these threw some light upon the difficulties which beset the path of the unfortunate Government of Ireland.

The Chairman said he wanted to get it specifically, in regard to the Howth gun-running, whether any instructions were given in his time to the Royal Irish Constabulary with regard to the enforcement of the prohibition of the importation of arms. They had been informed that there was a circular, but they had been unable to obtain a copy of it in Dublin.

Sir James said there was a confidential circular addressed to County Inspectors by the Inspector-General but actually signed by the Deputy Inspector-General. He then handed in a copy of this document.

Referring to the bloodshed following the Howth gun-running, Sir James said that his instructions unfortunately did not reach Mr Harrel. They were in writing. That order was, if possible, to take the names and addresses of the leaders.

STATEMENTS FURNISHED TO THE COMMISSIONERS

By Sir Henry Blake, GCMC

In an appendix to the published Minutes of Evidence given before the Royal Commission there were included statements made by Sir Henry Blake, Mr William Martin Murphy and County Inspector Howe, Royal Irish Constabulary, Cork City. The statement by Sir Henry Blake is headed:

Memorandum on the Causes that bear upon the Present Position in Ireland.

And we quote the following from it:

The evidence given before the Royal Commission on Rebellion in Ireland covers so completely all the incidents from the foundation of the National Volunteers that I can add but little to the ascertained facts.

That Germany has been preparing for an Irish adventure may be assumed from the following. Some time in 1914 a foreigner arrived at the railway station of Mogeely, nine miles from Youghal, where he engaged a car, desiring the driver to go to a position between the village of Lady's Bridge and the sea, where, he mentioned, that he wished to see a farm that he intended to purchase. Arrived at the neighbourhood he asked a peasant, at whose house they had stopped to make an inquiry, where the farm was situated, and mentioned it by a name that was only known locally. He spoke to the peasant for some time, and looked carefully over the country, making some notes, or possibly a rough sketch, but made no close examination of the farm mentioned. Having obtained all the information that the peasant could give he handed to him, his wife, and a small child each a sovereign, and on discharging the car on his return to Mogeely station he gave a similar sum to the driver. This visit was, in my opinion, for the purpose of examining the country in the neighbourhood of Ballycotton Bay, with a view of a possible landing.

Dislike of England

The root of this and other adverse movements in Ireland is dislike of England, which, if I can believe statements widely and generally made, is fostered in the national schools, where no emblem of the United Kingdom is shown. In at least one case, publicly reported, the Union Jack was removed as a party emblem. The feeling is fostered by the influence of Irish-Americans, and foreign assistance is kept before the people as a promise in the event of England finding herself in difficulties. This was the immediate impulsion for the Fenian rising in 1867, and for the land agitation begun in 1879.

The speeches of the Irish Nationalist members at home and in the United States before the introduction of the Home Rule Bill showed that the measure was regarded merely as a step towards the ultimate goal of total separation, and an independent Ireland: and if the speeches are examined of the Nationalists who supported the recruiting campaign it will be seen that the name of England was studiously avoided, men being called upon to join 'the Allies' in the fight for freedom. How the adverse action of the Sinn Fein rebels was given free scope, and all official warnings and recommendations ignored has been fully shown in the evidence already published. In effect many of the Sinn Fein branch of the Irish Volunteers thought that they had with them the sympathy of the Government in their demand for total separation.

My experience since my return to Ireland in 1907 is that the Unionist portion of Ireland has been steadily ignored. Even in the arrangements for securing recruits, in which every section of the community, Nationalist and Unionist, joined, no general intimation was given to His Majesty's

Lieutenants of Counties who ought, in my opinion, to have been invited to lend their aid. That it was given without invitation does not affect the fact.

Degradation of the Magistracy

Sir Morgan O'Connell and Major Price have in their evidence mentioned the effect of the degradation of the magistracy by improper appointments made against the protests of the Lieutenant of the County, who, as *custos rotulorum*, usually recommended the names of gentlemen for the position of Justice of the Peace. The change in the practice began when Mr Morley, now Lord Morley, was Chief Secretary, and the result has been a diminution of confidence in the petty sessions courts in certain districts, where the bench is sometimes found to be packed by magistrates who apparently vote by previous arrangement in given cases. In a report in the public Press of a case before an Assize Court in a southern county, about two years ago, it was stated, in answer to the judges' desire to have a Justice of Peace examined in a case of forgery, that the evidence of the gentleman would not assist the court, as, unfortunately, he could neither read nor write!

The dislike of England of which I have written does not necessarily involve active disloyalty, but it is a predisposing influence that makes the younger and more volatile portion of the people liable to be led away by any agitator who promises them relief from a phantom tyranny. The great majority of the people desire peace and security, but have not the moral courage to make any open stand against an anti-English agitation, however wild. The priesthood, it must be remembered, share the feelings of the people, than whom their experience of the world is no wider. The elder clergy desire peace, the younger are as easily led astray as the young hot bloods around them: but, on the whole, their influence makes for good, and its loss would be a misfortune.

People not law-abiding

The people are not law-abiding, but they yield to a real control if it is impartial and just. That those who have been placed in the control of the Executive have been asleep is no proof that the machinery is inefficient. The immediate cause of the present rebellion, prepared as it has been by German influence and money, has been an absence of any attempt at control that would have acted as a warning and saved much bloodshed and destruction of property. A firm and just administration of Ireland that gives assurance of protection of life and property would secure the moral and material support of the great mass of the population and prevent the recurrence of such a danger as that with which we are now dealing.

Mr William Martin Murphy

The statement submitted by Mr Wm Martin Murphy, 39 Dame street, Dublin, Chairman of the Dublin United Tramways Co., at the request of the Dublin Chamber of Commerce, recalled the circumstances of the strikes and disorders in 1911-12-13, and proceeded:

The conception of the Citizen Army appears to have been due to Captain White, who was recently convicted of an offence against the Defence of the Realm Act, in South Wales. He called one day to my office for the purpose, as he said, of settling the strike. I told him there was a great many candidates for the office he was seeking. He then explained to me that his method was to drill the strikers. I pointed out to him that it was difficult enough for the police to keep any kind of order in the city when dealing with an undrilled mob, but if they were all drilled and possessed fire-arms, it would be quite impossible for any force of police to deal with them. He said he had not thought of that, but it would be all right, because when they were drilled they would be disciplined, and it would raise their moral tone, and then they would be no longer guilty of outrages.

One of the most amazing things outside Mexico

That the authorities allowed a body of lawless and riotous men to be drilled and armed and to provide themselves with an arsenal of weapons and explosives was one of the most amazing things that could happen in any civilised country outside Mexico. This body was even allowed to hold meetings with uniforms and arms, and to discharge their rifles at night in the streets of Dublin without any attempt to check them or prosecute them. Fortunately the long strike was coming to an end when the Citizen Army commenced to drill. If they had been in existence in the early days of the strike, when the disorders were at their height we should have had a foretaste of the recent fighting in the city.

It has been said so often, and it is so obvious, that it is hardly necessary for me to repeat it, that the entire cause of this rebellion was permitting any people, no matter what their object, to be armed and drilled, and to possess arsenals, unless they belonged to the regular forces of the Crown. If there were no organised armed men in the country there could have been no attempt at rebellion.

Chief inspector TA Howe, RIC, Cork

County Inspector's Office, Cork,
12 June, 1916

In 1903, a branch of the Celtic Literary Society was started in Cork City. The Society at its formation consisted of about 20 members, all of whom were anti-British. Every member subsequently became an active member of the Sinn Fein movement. At the same time a Society called the 'Daughters of Erin' was established here by Miss Maude Gonne, and its ideals were the same as the Celtic Literary Society. These societies worked hand in hand. As showing the object for which these societies were formed, I give the following resolution adopted by them in June, 1903, a short time previous to the visit of His late Majesty King Edward VII to Cork: 'That we call upon the members of the Cork Corporation, Cork County Council, and other public bodies to reject any addresses to the English King that may be proposed for adoption.' I am glad to say, however, that the resolution had no effect, as the late King received a most enthusiastic reception on his visit to Cork. These Societies may be said to have ceased to exist after January, 1905, when a meeting organised by their members was held for the purpose of forming a branch of the Sinn Fein organisation, but a branch was not formed till the following year, when it absorbed the above-named societies and 'The Young Ireland Society'. On 2nd December, 1906, a meeting was held in the City Hall, under the auspices of the Sinn Fein Society, for the purpose of furthering the movement in the South of Ireland. About 200 persons attended, and a large number of anti-recruiting leaflets were distributed by a man named Wright, subsequently connected with the Dublin rebellion. The Sinn Fein movement did not spread to the country districts till 1907, when four branches were formed. Nothing of note occurred in 1908.

Mitchelstown

On 28th March, 1909, a Sinn Fein meeting was held near Mitchelstown to commemorate the memory of Peter O'Neill Crowley, who was shot there by the police when attempting to effect his arrest for prominent participation in the Fenian rising of 1867. The meeting was addressed by John McDermott, Dublin—lately executed—who was sent to Cork to organise the movement. He spent about two months here. On April 25th, 1909, a Sinn Fein meeting was held in Mitchelstown, addressed by McDermott and Edward Sheehan, a school teacher. The latter, in the course of his remarks, said the Billeting Bill recently passed through Parliament provided free quarters for English soldiers in the coming war between England and Germany, and he advised his hearers to resist the bill and never allow a British soldier to cross their threshold.

The year 1909 was not marked by any incident of importance.

In April, 1911, the Sinn Feiners of Cork City appointed a vigilance committee to canvas the members of the Corporation and other public bodies with the view of preventing the presentation of any loyal addresses to His Majesty the King on the occasion of his visit to Ireland that year. A meeting of the Cork Corporation was held in June 1911, for the purpose of discussing whether or not an address would be presented. A number of Sinn Feiners gained admission to the place of meeting, and when the resolution approving of the presentation of the address was adopted, the Sinn Feiners unfurled a black flag, and on the same night they draped in black the four figures of the monument erected to the 'Manchester Martyrs'. In October, 1911, a branch of the Irish National Boy Scouts was formed in Cork by the Countess Markievicz.

Drilling and Arming

Early in December, 1913, Professor John McNeill and Sir Roger Casement attended a meeting in Cork convened for the purpose of forming a branch of the Irish Volunteers, but the object was not achieved. The first branch of the Irish Volunteers was started in Cork on 23rd December, 1913. From this time forthwith members of this society commenced to purchase arms, chiefly revolvers. Drilling commenced in January, 1914, with an approximate strength of 500. About 200 men attended the drills, which were held openly. So far the movement had not spread outside the city, but in June, 1914, it had spread to the country districts, with a membership of 2,921.

In July, 1913, the Volunteers in city and East Riding numbered 3,460.

On 4th August, 1914, the Volunteers had arranged to travel to Skibbereen by special train, ostensibly for the purpose of taking part in a review, but in reality to get arms that were expected to be landed in Skibbereen, the landing being prevented. The excursion was cancelled at the last moment by Captain Crosbie, RFA, who was in command. I may add that Captain Crosbie re-joined the Army shortly afterwards. In a few days afterwards Mr Redmond's pronouncement in the House of Commons on the outbreak of war caused the split, together with the action of Captain Crosbie in telegraphing to the Secretary of State for War offering to organise the Cork Volunteers for the service of the Government. The original committee of the corps, principally Sinn Feiners, disassociated themselves from the action of Captain Crosbie, and about 30 members seceded and formed what is known as the 'Irish Volunteers'.

Bank account secured by Sinn Feiners

About this time about £800 stood to the account of the Volunteers in the names of two members of the committee, who were advanced Sinn Feiners. This money was appropriated by the newly formed Sinn Fein branch and devoted to the purchase of rifles, ammunition, etc. The organisation of this movement was henceforward carried on by paid organisers and its progress fairly rapid. The membership of the Sinn Feiners in city and riding was at first 200. The membership of the Irish National Volunteers—loyal section—rapidly dwindled away, principally owing to a large number joining the colours, and this body remained loyal throughout, and offered their services to me, to use them in any direction I pleased, after the insurrection in Dublin had broken out.

In March, 1916, the Irish Volunteer membership was 653 in Cork, East Riding, and City, at which it practically stood. It received no support from any influential persons from its inception up to the rebellion. It was principally composed of shop assistants, clerks, artisans, labourers, and, in country districts, of small farmers' sons as well. The country members joined to resist conscription, but the leaders always kept the real object of the movement a secret from the members. Extra activity prevailed for some months previous to the rebellion. Organisers, liberally paid, were employed. These men worked strenuously in the advancement of the movement, and there is no doubt that their exertions, together with the distribution of seditious literature, brought to the ranks a great number of new members. Money was plentifully distributed, but the only definite information as to its source is that a portion came from Dublin—please see receipts attached for salary paid weekly to TJ MacSweeney, a local organiser.

A Magistrate's statement

Two men—Thomas Kent, since shot for murder of Head Constable Rowe—and TJ MacSweeney, were, some months ago, arrested and prosecuted before the Magistrates in Cork Police Court, for delivering seditious speeches at a public meeting—Sinn Fein. The speeches were very violent, disloyal utterances, and merited severe punishment, but the magistrates, of whom seven were present, including the Lord Mayor and Wm Starkie, RM, dismissed the cases against Kent, and fined MacSweeney 1s.—the resident magistrate dissenting. One of the magistrates had publicly stated a few days previously: 'So long as they were bound up with that accursed Empire, so long would they be on the verge of starvation.' On the occasion of this trial the court was packed with sympathisers of the accused, and repeated cheers were raised for Germany and the Kaiser, notwithstanding the protests of the resident magistrate and district inspector.

On 17th March last, 'St Patrick's Day', about 1,600 Sinn Feiners from Cork City and East and West Ridings of the county, assembled in Cork City, most of whom carried rifles and shot guns.

Easter Sunday Orders

Nothing further occurred until Easter week. A general parade of Volunteers was ordered for Easter Sunday, to be held at all places where a branch of the organisation existed. Each man was ordered to be fully equipped, and to take with him two days' rations, and to march to various named destinations—all situated in the direction of Co. Kerry. There is no doubt that this order was given for the purpose of taking over arms from the German ship which was expected to land them. If these arms had been landed and distributed there is no doubt there would have been serious trouble in Munster. When it was ascertained on Easter Sunday, that the German ship was sunk, the Volunteers returned to their respective places of assembly, and were regarded as mobilised until after the surrender of the Dublin insurgents.

Awaiting orders from Dublin

During the week of the rebellion, an armed guard, day and night, was maintained at the Sinn Fein Hall, Cork City. No one was allowed to enter except in possession of the password. The leaders here, who were apparently ready for any contingency, were awaiting orders from Dublin, but those orders never came.

On 24th April, the Lord Mayor, accompanied by the Most Rev. Dr Coholan, Assistant RC Bishop, visited the Sinn Fein Hall, and strongly advised the members present to commit no act that would involve them in trouble and compel the military to take drastic action. The Sinn Feiners promised to act on the advice, and, in fact, carried it out in so far as they committed themselves to no action beyond retaining their arms in the hall and maintaining a guard over them. Negotiations were entered into with the military authorities at Queenstown by the Lord Mayor and Bishop with the view of inducing the Sinn Feiners to surrender their arms to the Lord Mayor. A date was fixed on which all arms were to be handed in on certain conditions. The fulfilment of the contract was not carried out by the Sinn Feiners, who failed to have the arms in at the appointed time. An extension was granted, and eventually, on a given date, they handed in, at night, 76 rifles and shot guns, and two revolvers. They were known to have had in their possession at the time 116 rifles and shot guns, and 150 revolvers. About 500 rounds of ammunition were handed in, but this quantity was only a fraction of what they possess. Since then a large quantity of ammunition and explosive has been found, abandoned, by the police.

Many weapons still missing

In country districts large quantities of ammunition and a number of rifles and guns were surrendered, and large seizures were also made by military and police, but there is still a great number unaccounted for.

As I have already stated, no person of any stake took part in the movement. It was piloted by advanced extremists or failures in the various walks in which they had started.

A great number in the ranks were young men under 21 years, amongst whom the reading of the pernicious literature that was being circulated had such a deleterious effect.

There are no documents in my possession to support the foregoing statements. All matters referred to were duly reported to the Inspector-General for the information of government, as they arose. The information now supplied is taken from extracts recorded in my office.

It is stated in the Report of the Commissioners that four persons submitted signed statements. The writer of the fourth statement requested the Commissioners not to publish his narrative, and the Commissioners decided to treat it as confidential.

THE 'SINN FEIN' ORGANISATION

The following report, which was produced at the Commission by Sir Matthew Nathan, is also included in the appendix:

The above organisation was started in 1905 and gave as its aims, objects, and policy, the following:

'National self development on the lines successfully adopted by the Hungarians in their struggle with Austria by a policy of relying on Sinn Fein (ourselves alone).

'To give the strongest adhesion to the Gaelic and Industrial Revival Movements, and to all movements originating from within Ireland instinct with national tradition, and not looking outside Ireland for the accomplishment of their aims, and to carry this policy into effect by utilising to the utmost the powers of all representative bodies, and by the recognition of an assembly, meeting in Dublin, composed of delegates from such bodies, and other popularly elected representatives as the sole authority entitled to national obedience.'

A National Council was formed to control the organisation, of which Edward Martyn was the first Chairman, and the first Convention was held in the Rotunda on 28th November, 1905, when disloyal speeches were made and resolutions were passed in favour of the policy indicated.

During the proceedings at this Convention the Chairman stated: 'The most important of all matters was the anti-enlisting crusade. By the work of the National Council the recruiting statistics in Ireland had considerably decreased. The Irish Nationalist who entered the English Navy deserved to be flogged.'

This organisation developed for some time and various branches were formed and affiliated, but during the past few years these branches have practically disappeared, and all that now remains in Dublin is the central body which is still controlled by a National Council, and at present their offices and place of meeting are at 6 Harcourt street.

The members of this organisation may, and no doubt do, differ from each other on many points, but no difference of opinion exists regarding their opposition to any form of English Government in Ireland and their support of the anti-enlistment crusade.

If any member announced his opposition to the National Council on these points, he would soon find that he was no longer wanted as a member.

Some members are, of course, more active in their display of disloyalty than others, but all members are disloyal, whether displaying great activity or not.

It can hardly be said that any effort is made to enforce uniformity of view, except as already stated regarding opposition to English Government in Ireland and anti-enlistment, and it is not known that any difference of opinion on these points has ever arisen.

WM DAVIES,
Commissioner.
16th December, 1914.

[Note: Mr Davies, who is now Deputy Inspector-General of the Royal Irish Constabulary, was at the date of this Report acting as Chief Commissioner of the Dublin Metropolitan Police for a period between the resignation of Sir John Ross and the appointment of Colonel Edgeworth Johnstone to that office.}

NIGHT MANOEUVRES OF CITIZEN ARMY AND IRISH VOLUNTEERS

The following report, which was produced by Colonel Edgeworth Johnstone, Chief Commissioner Dublin Metropolitan Police, at the Commission, is also included in the appendix:

6th October, 1915

Citizen Army—At 12.45 a.m. 85 members carrying rifles, in command of James Connolly and Countess Markievicz, left 'Liberty Hall,' Beresford place, and marched through portion of the city to Werburgh street. After manoeuvring in the vicinity of Dublin Castle they returned to their Hall at 1.50 a.m.

24th October, 1915

Citizen Army—At 12.15 a.m. about 120 persons, including 12 women and 20 Sinn Fein Boy Scouts, left 'Liberty Hall,' Beresford place, in command of James Connolly and Countess Markievicz, and marched to Christ Church place. Eighty of the men carried rifles. The party divided up into small sections and manoeuvred in the neighbourhood of Francis street and the Coombe, having been joined at the latter place by 20 other members with rifles under the command of William P Partridge. They remained in the locality until about 3 a.m. and then left for Emmet Hall, Inchicore, where they took part in a dance which was being held there.

At 5.20 a.m. 70 of the party left the Hall and marched back to College Green where they were dismissed about 6 a.m. About 35 returned to 'Liberty Hall' and broke-off there, each man bringing his rifle to his home.

5th December, 1915

Citizen Army—At 12.5 a.m. 76 members (62 with rifles) assembled at 'Liberty Hall,' Beresford place, in command of James Connolly, James Mallin, and Countess Markievicz, and proceeded to Cross Guns Bridge, Phibsborough, where they broke up into sections—some going along Whitworth road and others along the Canal Bank to Newcomen Bridge—and went through manoeuvres as they went along. They returned to their Hall, at Beresford place, at 3 a.m. and broke off there.

5th February, 1916

Irish Volunteers—Between 10.30 and 11 p.m. about 350 members (about 200 with rifles) assembled at Blackhall place and engaged in manoeuvres which extended as far as the Phoenix Park, North Circular road, Kingsbridge, and Thomas street. The party manoeuvring on the

South side returned to Blackhall place at 1.30 a.m., and marched from there to 41 Rutland square, where they disbanded at 2 a.m. on 6th.

The principal persons engaged in these movements were: Edward Daly, EJ Duggan, Frank Fahy, Joseph McGuinness, Pierce Beasley, Edward De Valera, George Irvine, Fenton Lynch, and James Byrne.

REPORT OF THE COMMISSION

Mr Birrell held primarily responsible

Police and Military action approved

The Commissioners issued the following report on Monday, 26th June:

1. We the undersigned now humbly submit to Your Majesty our Report on the matters into which we were directed to inquire.

2. The terms of reference to us were 'to inquire into the causes of the recent outbreak of rebellion in Ireland, and into the conduct and degree of responsibility of the civil and military executive in Ireland in connection therewith.'

3. In pursuance of these instructions we have held nine meetings, of which five were held in London and four in Dublin. At the first sitting the Commission of Your Majesty was read.

4. We have examined twenty-nine witnesses. They were examined in public except in so far as their evidence dealt with German intrigues or police information. Four other persons submitted to us signed statements, and these will be found in the appendix immediately following upon the evidence taken in public.

5. We had interviews with various persons who kindly discussed with us the subjects into which we had to inquire. We also received statements from several persons who offered to give evidence, but, having regard to the scope of our inquiry, we did not think it necessary to call them as witnesses.

6. We purpose to consider the matters referred to in the following order, namely—(a) the constitution of the Irish Executive, in so far as it is concerned with the maintenance of law and order; (b) the legal power vested in that Executive; and (c) the history of events leading up to the outbreak of the 24th April, 1916, together with our observations and conclusions thereon.

The Irish Government

The executive government of Ireland is entrusted to three officers—namely, the Lord Lieutenant, the Chief Secretary to the Lord Lieutenant, and the Under-Secretary; and for the purpose of maintaining order they have at their disposal two police forces—namely, the Royal Irish Constabulary and the Dublin Metropolitan Police Force. 'Theoretically,' says Sir William Anson, 'the executive government of Ireland is conducted by the Lord Lieutenant in Council, subject to instructions which he may receive from the Home Office of the United Kingdom. Practically it is conducted for all important purposes by the Chief Secretary to the Lord Lieutenant.' (Law and Customs of the Constitution, ed. 1892, p. 189.)

The Lord Lieutenant (who is also Governor-General) is resident in Ireland. By the terms of his patent he is responsible for the civil government of the country, and the naval and military forces of the Crown in Ireland are under his orders. But, when the Chief Secretary is in the Cabinet and the Lord Lieutenant is not, all powers and responsibility are in practice vested in the Chief Secretary. His policy is the policy of the British Government as a whole, and it is obviously impossible that there should be any other independent authority or responsibility in Ireland. For many years past the office of Lord Lieutenant has been a ceremonial office; apart from the exercise of the prerogative of mercy he has no executive functions. Proclamations, appointments, and other State documents are issued in his name, but they are put before him for signature, without previous consultation. He is only furnished with information as to the state of the country which he nominally governs, when he asks for it, and then as a matter of courtesy. The military and naval forces in Ireland take their orders from the War Office and Admiralty respectively.

Entire control of Chief Secretary

The office of Chief Secretary is a political office, changing with the Government. The executive government of Ireland is entirely in his hands, subject to the control of the Cabinet. When the Chief Secretary is a member of the Cabinet, as has been the case in recent years, he is, of necessity, to a great extent an absentee from Ireland. He has to attend Cabinet meetings, and he is the only person who can, with authority, answer questions and defend the Government policy in the House of Commons. Although the Chief Secretary is in the position of a Secretary of State, he has no Parliamentary Under-Secretary, and the Irish law officers are frequently not members of the House of Commons. During the last two-and-a-half years of Mr Birrell's nine years' tenure of office, Parliament has been in almost continuous session. He had, therefore, during this critical period but little opportunity of making himself personally acquainted with the state of affairs in Ireland. He was dependent for information on the reports of his Under-Secretary and the advice given by those Irish members of Parliament whom he chose to consult.

The Under-Secretary is a civil servant, residing in Ireland. For practical purposes he can only take action under authority delegated to him by the Chief Secretary. His duty is to report fully and fairly to his Chief all information that he can obtain, to give his advice freely as to what should be done, and then loyally to carry out the instructions of his Chief without regard to any personal opinion of his own.

The police forces

For the ordinary maintenance of law and order the Irish Government have two police forces—viz., the

Royal Irish Constabulary and the Dublin Metropolitan Police Force. Both forces are under the direct control of the Irish Government, though a rate is levied in Dublin as a contribution to the expenses of the Dublin force (see 12 and 13 Vict. c. 91, ss. 29, 30). It appears that since 1905 the Dublin Corporation have refused to pay the proceeds of this rate into the police fund, and that the matter has been adjusted by deducting the amount from the local taxation account. The Royal Irish Constabulary is a quasi-military force. Its members are armed with carbines and taught to shoot. They police the whole of Ireland, except the Dublin police district. When the rebellion broke out the Constabulary was somewhat under strength, as it had furnished a good many recruits to the Army. The military authorities were naturally anxious to get recruits from a body of men with splendid physique and a fine record of honourable service. The Dublin police is also a fine body of men and its numbers were also slightly diminished by reason of enlistments. The force is unarmed, consequently when an armed rebellion broke out in Dublin the police had to be withdrawn from duty. If Dublin, like Cork and Belfast, had been policed by the Royal Irish Constabulary, a thousand armed and disciplined policemen, knowing every nook and cranny of the city, would have been a formidable addition to the thousand soldiers who were available when the rebellion first broke out, and the rebels might have hesitated to face them. As Sir Matthew Nathan expressed it in his letter of the 18th December, 1915, to Mr Birrell, in the event of an outbreak, 'Each policeman would be worth three soldiers.' It is clear from the evidence that the two police forces work cordially together, but it is obvious that two separate forces, under separate commands, cannot be in a time of emergency as efficient as a single force under one command. Each of the forces has a small special Crimes Branch, drawn from uniformed men. For ordinary police purposes this branch does its work well, but it is not specially qualified to deal with political crime, which takes no notice of the boundaries of police districts, and which in the case of Ireland assumes an international complexion.

Irish Government anomalous and unworkable

If the Irish system of government be regarded as a whole it is anomalous in quiet times, and almost unworkable in times of crisis.

The legal powers vested in the Irish Government for the maintenance of law and order, and the suppression of sedition must now be considered.

From 1881 to 1906 the Peace Preservation (Ireland) Act, 44 and 45 Vict. c. 5 (commonly known as the Arms Act), was in force in that country. Under that enactment the Government had complete control over the importation and sale of arms and ammunition, and over the carrying of arms or the possession of ammunition. The Act was a temporary one continued from year to year by the Expiring Laws Continuance Act. In 1906 the Act was allowed to lapse by Sir Henry Campbell-Bannerman's Government. But the Irish Government had other, though less efficient, powers for dealing with unauthorised bodies who sought to arm themselves. If the ordinary excise duty on carrying a gun had been enforced a complete register of firearms would have been obtained, and the poorer members of the community might have found difficulty in paying the licence duty (see the Gun Licence Act, 1870 (33 and 34 Vict. c. 57) It seems that no attempt was made to enforce this law, the only reason alleged being that the people concerned would have refused to take out the licence and pay the duty.

The Explosive Substances Act, 1883, (46 and 47 Vict. c. 83), which applies to the whole of the United Kingdom, gives drastic powers for dealing with explosives, and it may be assumed that the term 'explosive' would include stores of ammunition as well as high explosives. Under that Act if any person has in his possession any explosive substance he is guilty of felony and liable on conviction to 14 years' penal servitude, unless he can show that he was in possession thereof for a lawful object (sec. 4). Accessories are liable to a like punishment. For the purpose of discovering stores of explosives, the Attorney-General, if he has reasonable ground for believing that the Act has been disobeyed, may order an inquiry at which witness may be examined on oath, although no person is charged with any crime under the Act.

Unlawful Drilling

The Unlawful Drilling Act, 1819 (60 Geo. 3, c. 1), is an Act 'to prevent the training of persons to the use of arms, and to the practice of military evolutions and exercise.' It prohibits drilling and military exercises unless authorised by the Crown, the lieutenant, or two county justices, and authorises any justice or peace officer to disperse any meeting un-authorised for drilling, and to arrest the persons attending it. As regards procedure, the Criminal Law and Procedure (Ireland) Act, 1887 (50 and 51 Vict. c. 20), besides providing for special jury trials in proclaimed districts, empowers the Lord Lieutenant by proclamation to prohibit or suppress 'dangerous associations' and defines as dangerous any association which (*inter alia*) interferes with the administration of the law or disturbs the maintenance of law and order.

It may be noted too that the old Acts, known as the Whiteboy Acts, some of which were passed by the Irish Parliament, appear to be still in force. These Acts give the Government extensive powers for dealing with riotous or unlawful assemblies.

The Irish Government have also the ordinary common law powers for proceeding against persons who publish seditious libels or engage in seditious conspiracies. But legal powers are of no avail unless the Government make up their minds to put them into execution, and can rely on juries and magistrates to do their duty when prosecutions are supported by adequate evidence.

Defence of the Realm Act

War broke out on the 4th August, 1914, and on the 8th August the Defence of the Realm Act, 1914 (4 and 5 Geo. V, c. 29), was passed. This Act authorised His Majesty in Council to issue Regulations, during the continuance of the war, 'for securing the public safety and the defence of the realm,' and instituted trial by courtmartial for serious offences against the Regulations. Under these provisions there appeared to be ample powers for dealing with any manifestations of sedition or rebellion. But as regards Ireland, the teeth of this enactment were drawn by the Defence of the Realm Amendment Act, 1915 (5 Geo. V, c. 34), which was passed on the 18th March, 1915. That Act provided that any British subject (not being a person subject to military law) charged with an offence under the Defence of the Realm Acts might claim to be tried by a jury in a civil court, instead of by courtmartial. Power was given to His Majesty to suspend the operation of this provision 'in the event of invasion or other special military emergency'. But it certainly would have been difficult to have justified the exercise of this suspensory power in Ireland before any actual outbreak in arms had occurred. It was impossible, as stated by Mr Birrell and other witnesses, to get a conviction, in any case tried by a jury, for an offence against law and order, however strong the evidence for the Crown might be. The power of internment conferred by the Regulations applied primarily to foreigners, and only extended to British subjects when 'hostile association' could be established. Therefore, however serious an offence might be, the only remedy was a prosecution before a court of summary jurisdiction, where six months' imprisonment was the maximum punishment that could be imposed, and when a case was tried before justices there was no certainty that the decision would be in accordance with the evidence.

Causes of the outbreak

In dealing with the series of events which led up to the outbreak of the 24th April, 1916, and in endeavouring to elucidate the causes of the rebellion in Ireland, the fact should be borne in mind that there is always a section of opinion in that country bitterly opposed to the British connection, and that in times of excitement this section can impose its sentiments on largely increased numbers of the people. As Mr Birrell described it: 'The spirit of what today is called Sinn Feinism is mainly composed of the old hatred and distrust of the British connection, always noticeable in all classes, and in all places, varying in degree, and finding different ways of expression, but always there as the background of Irish politics and character.'

The incidents which preceded the rising in April, 1916, are fully detailed in the evidence of the witnesses, but may be summarised as follows: In the winter of 1913, while industrial strikes were in progress in Dublin, an armed force of working men, officially called the Citizen Army, was first created. As this force was partly armed, and the Dublin Metropolitan Police are an unarmed force, the employers were in some cases compelled to arm their carters to resist intimidation by the strikers. This lawless display of force should have been a warning against the recent policy of permitting the indiscriminate arming of civilians in Ireland in times of turbulence and faction. In periods of peace it may be desirable in an orderly community to disregard some seditious utterances as mere vapouring, but when a country is engaged in a serious struggle sedition alters its aspect and becomes treason, dangerous to the community, and should promptly be suppressed. As stated by Sir David Harrel in his evidence the Irish people 'are easily led, and it is therefore the more incumbent on Government to nip lawlessness and disorder in the bud. Neglect in this respect has invariably led to things getting out of hand, with the result that strong repressive measures become necessary, and much hardship is imposed upon misled, but perhaps comparatively inoffensive people.'

On the 13th December, 1913, in view of information that arms were entering the province of Ulster from foreign countries, including Germany, a Proclamation was issued under the Customs Consolidation Act, 1876, prohibiting the importation of arms into Ireland. In defiance of this, large quantities of arms were surreptitiously imported by night at Larne and other places, in April, 1914. Before this date other similar consignments had been seized and confiscated. It has been stated that as a matter of policy it was decided by the Government not to take proceedings against those responsible for this breach of the law. The validity of the Proclamation was afterwards questioned in an action brought by a gunsmith of Ulster against the Customs authorities, but on the 15th June, 1914, a majority of an Irish Court upheld its validity. Notwithstanding this decision the Irish Government decided to withdraw the Proclamation, and the withdrawal, though decided on before the outbreak of war, was publicly notified on the 5th August, 1914, the day after war broke out.

On Sunday, the 26th July, 1914, a large consignment of arms and ammunition from abroad was landed at Howth, near Dublin, for the use of the Irish National Volunteers, who will be hereafter described. Members of that force overpowered the Customs officers and landed and distributed the arms. An attempt was made by the Dublin Metropolitan Police acting under orders of Mr WV Harrel, the Assistant Commissioner, to enforce the Proclamation by seizure. After trying fruitlessly to obtain the co-operation of a detachment of the Royal Irish Constabulary he called in a military force to assist him, and a few arms were taken, but most of the Volunteers retired with the weapons before the arrival of the military. Whilst the troops were returning to barracks they were attacked by a mob and an unfortunate incident occurred by which some members of the public lost their lives through shots from the soldiers in Bachelor's Walk. Mr Harrel was immediately suspended by the Chief Secretary pending further investigation. A Royal Commission was appointed to enquire into this matter, and sat from the 6th to the 11th August, 1914. In their report which was submitted to Your Majesty, Mr Harrel was censured by the Commission for his conduct in invoking the assistance of the troops, and he resigned his position. The Chief Commissioner—Sir John Ross, of Bladensburg, had previously resigned his position after the order of temporary suspension had been issued against Mr Harrel. The resignation of Mr Harrel was looked upon by the public in Dublin as tantamount to dismissal, and while it appears that it had no effect on the loyalty of the Dublin Metropolitan Police, it tended to discourage the officers of that body from initiative in enforcing the law. Further, there can be no doubt that his dismissal tended to weaken the authority of the police, as it gave rise to the opinion amongst the more ignorant classes that in any case of disorder the Government might not support their action.

In spite of the breach of the Proclamation of December, 1913, in the landing of arms at Howth, the Irish Government decided (as in the case of the arms imported at Larne) to take no action, and to institute no prosecution, and on the 5th August, as has been above stated, the restriction upon the importation of arms into Ireland was removed.

Communication with Germany

From the evidence given before the Royal Commission it is clear that the insurrection was caused by two bodies of men allied together for this purpose, and known as the Irish Volunteers and the Citizen Army. It is now a matter of common notoriety that the Irish Volunteers have been in communication with the authorities in Germany, and were for a long time known to be supplied with money through Irish American societies. This was so stated in public by Mr John McNeill on the 8th November, 1914. It was suspected long before the outbreak that some of the money came from German sources.

The following facts show what was known of the origin and development of these two bodies, and the action taken by the Irish Government in dealing with their activities.

The Irish National Volunteers owed their origin to a meeting at Dublin in November, 1913, of twelve men who came together to discuss the formation of an Irish Volunteer Army. The founders of the force included Bulmer Hobson, PH Pearse, and The O'Rahilly. After the decision to enrol volunteers had been taken, a meeting attended by some thousands of people was held in Dublin, and the movement took shape. ('Secret History of the Irish Volunteers,' by The O'Rahilly.) It was started quite independently of any Irish political party by men strongly opposed to any political connection of Ireland with England. By June, 1914, 65,000 men were reported to have been enrolled, and Mr Redmond in that month succeeded in securing the addition of enough members to the Committee to secure to himself and his party the control of the movements of the body, to the great dissatisfaction of the original founders. On the eve of the Prime Minister's meeting in Dublin on the 25th September, 1914—where Mr Redmond spoke strongly in favour of recruiting—a manifesto was issued attacking Mr Redmond's attitude. This was signed by Mr McNeill and six others (afterwards involved in the rebellion), and concluded by regretting that Sir Roger Casement's absence prevented his being a signatory. On September 30th this party dissociated themselves from the Irish National Volunteers, and formed a new force under the name of the Irish Volunteers. By the end of October the force enrolled numbered over 13,000, including 2,000 in Dublin. Of these, more than 8,000 were known to be actively engaged in drilling at the end of 1914, and to be in possession of over 1,400 rifles.

Forces of disloyalty

It was of paramount importance that, after the outbreak of the present war, no opportunity should have been given for the drilling and arming of any body of men known to be of seditious tendency, and no other consideration should have interfered with the enforcing of this duty. After the war broke out there was a considerable wave of feeling in Ireland in favour of the Allies. Reservists joining the Colours were greeted with enthusiasm, and recruiting was successful. It was owing to the activities of the leaders of the Sinn Fein movement that the forces of disloyalty gradually and steadily increased, and undermined the initial sentiment of patriotism.

The words 'Sinn Fein' (ourselves alone) rather describe a movement than an association, and the principal efforts of those connected with the movement before the outbreak of the war had been active opposition to any recruiting of Irishmen for the British Army and Navy, and a passive opposition to all Irish Parliamentary parties. From the fact that some leaders of the Sinn Fein movement also led the Irish Volunteers, the latter have frequently been called the Sinn Fein Volunteers, and the two expressions from the end of 1914 are synonymous. Between the 5th August, 1914, and the 5th December, 1914, there was no law in force prohibiting the importation of arms into Ireland. Certain warrants had been issued by the Lord Lieutenant, authorising the police to seize arms, but on the 5th December an amendment of the regulations under the Defence of the Realm Act empowered the police to seize arms and explosives which might be landed on the coast, an exception being made in favour of sporting shot guns, which was, however, cancelled on the 5th February, 1915. Nevertheless, arms and explosives continued to be smuggled into Ireland. A flood of seditious literature was disseminated by the leaders of the Irish Volunteer Party early in the war, and certain newspapers were suppressed, but according to the statement of the Under-Secretary for Ireland, action against the seditious Press was not very consistently taken, and prominent members of the Irish Parliamentary Party were strongly against newspaper suppression.

Lack of attention in Parliament

By the end of March, 1915, the Irish Volunteers do not appear to have increased much in numbers, although they had acquired more arms. On Mach, 16th, 1915, the Defence of the Realm Act, No. 2, was passed, by which any British subject could claim the right to trial by jury for an offence against the Defence of the Realm Regulations, and this Act, to a great extent, hampered the Irish Executive in dealing with cases of sedition in Ireland. Insufficient attention appears to have been paid to the state of affairs in Ireland in both Houses of Parliament.

Throughout the whole of the remainder of the year 1915 the Irish Volunteer Party were active in their efforts to encourage sedition. Seditious papers were published, pamphlets of a violent tone issued and circulated, paid organisers were throughout the country to enrol and drill volunteer recruits, and the leaders themselves were active in attending anti-recruiting meetings at which disloyal speeches were openly made. A considerable number of the younger members of the priesthood in certain districts joined in the movement, and schoolmasters who were followers of the Sinn Fein movement disseminated treason amongst the younger people through the medium of the Irish language.

Irish Party's action

Action was taken during this period against seditious newspapers, and against certain paid organisers of the Irish Volunteer Party, but this course was strongly opposed by members of the Irish Parliamentary Party and the Nationalist Press. Major Price, in his evidence says: 'One unfortunate thing which hindered us a good deal was the attitude of the official Nationalist Party and their Press. Whenever General Friend did anything strong in the way of suppressing or deporting these men (the organisers) from Ireland, they at once deprecated it, and said it was a monstrous thing to turn a man out of Ireland.'

Irishmen, no doubt, appreciate the maintenance of order, but they appear to have an inveterate prejudice against the punishment of disorder.

So seditious had the country become during 1915 that juries in Dublin, and magistrates in various parts of the country—through fear or favour—could not be trusted to give decisions in accordance with the evidence. The only tribunals which could be relied upon at this time were those presided over by resident magistrates in Dublin or Belfast, who had no power to impose a greater sentence than six months' hard labour.

Effect of compulsory service

The question of the application of compulsory service gave a great stimulus to the Irish Volunteer movement in the autumn of 1915, and shortly before the recent outbreak the number of Irish Volunteers was estimated by the police authorities to be about 15,000, armed with over 1,800 rifles, and about the same number of shot guns and pistols.

During the greater part of this period the Citizen Army remained distinct from the Irish Volunteers. The movement which led to the formation of the former body, composed chiefly of Dublin workmen, was to a large extent inspired by anarchist sentiment based on Irish discontent. The leader was James Connolly, who is described as a man of great energy and ability. By the month of November, 1915, it was known that the two bodies were acting in combination in Dublin.

In the newspaper, *The Worker's Republic*, edited by James Connolly, the following passage occurs:

'The Irish Citizen Army was the first publicly organised armed citizen force south of the Boyne. Its constitution pledged and still pledges its members to work for a Irish Republic and for the emancipation of labour.'

Throughout the whole of this year Ireland was in a state of great prosperity, so that Irish discontent could hardly be attributed to economic conditions, except that the housing conditions of the working classes in the City of Dublin may have accounted for an underlying sense of dissatisfaction with existing authority.

In the meantime the Volunteers were steadily drilled and practised military manoeuvres by day and by night. Ambulance classes were formed in imitation of a similar organisation in Ulster formed by the Ulster Volunteers. In Dublin the Irish Volunteers held officers' training schools and carried out night attacks, and some manoeuvres took place in the middle of the city and in the neighbourhood of the Castle.

During this period the National or Redmondite Volunteers had sunk into almost complete stagnation, and towards the close of the year 1915 the largest armed and drilled force in the provinces of Leinster, Munster and Connaught—excluding soldiers—were the Irish Volunteers.

An Intercepted Letter

In a letter intercepted by the censor in the post on the 24th March, 1916, and believed to have been written by one of the teaching staff of St Mary's College, Rathmines, to a friend in America, the following extract appears, and is of interest as an indication of the spirit that was abroad in disloyal members of the community:

'On St Patrick's Day there was a lot of people put into prison under the Defence of the Realm Act. There was a rumour that they intended to seize the arms of the Volunteers. The police raided lots of places, but only got one fire-arm in a house, and gave up the job. The Castle is watching them closely, but is afraid to do anything against them. There was a march in the streets of Dublin, right through the city, in front of the foreign College of Trinity and before the Parliament House. The Volunteers were all armed with rifles. Eoin MacNeill was present, and they saluted him as they marched by, and all this under the nose of the Castle. It is a dangerous thing to do but the Volunteers do not care. They are getting stronger every day. Many efforts are being made, for it is known now that they are our only hope, since they put conscription down some time ago. Redmond is done for. Whoever wins the war, this country will be wronged and plundered, but the people of Ireland are not disposed of yet. Their spirit is always improving and growing more Irish. One thing is clear, if not others. An end is being put to the rule and insolence of the 'Peelers.' They are not nearly so arrogant as they used to be. I hope to God that we may see you in Ireland when you have finished your time over there. We want the like of you to strike a blow at John Bull. Easter will soon be over: then there will be summer coming on. May and June will pass by—not very hot as yet—and then—you know as well as I do, and no doubt much better.'

Confidential police reports

Before turning to the events of the present year it is desirable to refer to the confidential reports of the Inspector-General of the Royal Irish Constabulary and the Chief Commissioner of the Dublin Metropolitan Police, to show that even before the outbreak of war, and during the war, full knowledge of the existing state of affairs was supplied to the Under-Secretary, and through him to the Chief Secretary. On the 15th June, 1914, a report was submitted from the office of the Inspector General in which it was stated:

'In Ireland the training and drilling to the use of arms of a great part of the male population is a new departure which is bound in the not far distant future to alter the existing conditions of life. Obedience to the law has never been a prominent characteristic of the people. In times of passion or excitement the law has only been maintained by force, and this has been rendered practicable owing to the want of cohesion among the crowds hostile to the police. If the people became armed and drilled effective police control will vanish. Events are moving. Each county will soon have a trained army far outnumbering the police, and those who control the Volunteers will be in a position to dictate to what extent the law of the land may be carried into effect.'

Warning from Dublin

As early as the 7th September, 1915, the Dublin Metropolitan Police were warning the Government of the danger to be expected within Dublin itself. On that date the following statement was made to the government:

'There is no doubt that so far as Dublin is concerned the majority of the Irish National Volunteers would follow the lead of the extreme section, and hints have been given that they are not without hope of being able to assume and establish control of the Government of Ireland before the present difficulties are over, and that they may attempt some escapade before long.'

On the 26th October 1914, the detective Department of the Dublin Metropolitan Police submitted to the Under-Secretary notes of the speeches made by the Irish Volunteers at their first annual convention. The demonstrators had marched to the meeting nearly 1,000 strong, 230 of their number armed with rifles, and 20 of the National Boy Scouts, similarly equipped. Speeches of the most inflammatory and revolutionary character were delivered. The leaders predicted rebellion and the shedding of blood 'in the great fight of Ireland against the British Empire.'

These documents were seen by the Chief Secretary, but he wrote no comment on their contents and no proceedings were taken.

From the commencement the Dublin Metropolitan Police were in all respects as diligent as the Royal Irish Constabulary in forwarding to the government regular information as to the conduct and progress of the hostile organisations within their jurisdiction.

In the annual report of the Inspector General, delivered at the end of the year 1914, the following words occur: 'In the *personnel* of the Committee, in its declaration of policy, in the utterances of its leading representatives in the Press, and at public meetings, in its opposition to the efforts of Mr Redmond and the Irish Parliamentary Party to bring Ireland into line at the present national crisis, and in its crusade against enlistment in the Army, the Irish Volunteer organisation has shown itself to be disloyal, seditious and revolutionary, if the means and opportunity were at hand.'

On the 12th February, 1915, a further report was submitted, in which it was stated that at certain meetings of the Irish Republican Brotherhood in Tyrone members were reminded of the opportunity afforded by the present crisis to strike a blow for the independence of Ireland, and they were promised arms and ammunition when the time arrived.

At certain places in Wexford, after the promulgation of military orders under the Defence of the Realm Act for the action of the inhabitants in the event of an invasion, counter-notices were placarded calling on people to disobey the orders issued, and welcome the German troops as friends.

Money from America

In a report submitted on the 13th July, 1915, it was stated that information had been received from a reliable source that a sum of 3,000 dollars had been recently sent from America to the Council of the Irish Volunteers.

In a report submitted on the 14th September, 1915, the following passage occurs:

'According to the information confidentially obtained, communications are passing between the leaders of the Clan-na-Gael in America and the Sinn Fein in Ireland, and money has been sent over to the latter to help them in a campaign of disloyalty. As the leaders of the Irish Volunteers apparently aim at national independence, the force bears resemblance to the old Fenian movement, but, unlike the latter, is ready to drill and arm its members, and is not regarded as a secret society. As already reported, according to the confidential information, at a meeting of the council of Irish Volunteers held in Dublin on the 30th May, 1915, Professor McNeill in the chair, a resolution in favour of the Irish Volunteers declaring themselves in favour of immediate insurrection, proposed by Bulmer Hobson, was only defeated by the casting vote of Professor McNeill.'

Disloyal and Bitterly Anti-British

A report dated the 13th November, 1915, contained the following statement:

'This force is disloyal and bitterly anti-British, and is daily improving its organisation. Some drill is practised, but its activities are mainly directed to promoting sedition and hindering recruitment for the Army, and it is now pledged to resist conscription with arms. According to information from a reliable source, the Sinn Feiners have already planned a rising in the event of conscription, and, as this is, perhaps, the one object in which they would find many Redmondites in agreement with them, they might give a serious amount of trouble.'

On the 14th December, 1915, a report was submitted that:

'The Irish Volunteers were very active during the month, and gained 1,300 new members. Lieutenant O'Leary, VC, was hooted and insulted by a party of Volunteers route marching. A party of 800 held military manoeuvres at Artane, Co. Dublin. The liberty of action at present enjoyed by the openly disloyal and hostile Sinn Feiners is having a very undesirable effect.'

Anxiety to the Military

On the 29th November, 1915, a special report was delivered which deserves study. It contains the following statement:

'It is a fact that this body of Irish Volunteers numbers 10,000 strong in the provinces, with control of 1,500 rifles, and possibly more, thoroughly disloyal and hostile to British Government, is apparently now on the increase, and I desire to point out that it might rapidly assume dimensions sufficient to cause anxiety to the military authorities. As it is in the event of an invasion, or of any important reverse to our troops in the field, the Irish Volunteer Force would seriously embarrass arrangements for home defence.'

In addition to the information contained in the above mentioned reports of the Royal Irish Constabulary, Lord Midleton, in November, 1915, had an interview with the Chief Secretary, in which he strongly urged that the Irish Volunteers should be disarmed, and not be permitted to parade, and he pressed for the prosecution of those responsible for seditious speeches. His warnings were entirely neglected.

Serious and menacing situation

On the 18th December, 1915, a letter was sent by the Under-Secretary to the Chief Secretary, of which the following passage is an extract:

'What is Redmond up to, with his comparisons between Ireland and Great Britain in the matters of police and crime? He knows, or should know, after what Dillon wrote to him over a month ago in the enclosed 'confidential' letter, and repeated verbally on the 3rd inst. The present situation in Ireland is most serious and menacing. Redmond himself sent me the other 'private' enclosure on the 9th. He knows, or should know, that the enrolled strength of the Sinn Fein Volunteers has increased by a couple of thousand active members in the last two months to a total of some 13,500, and each group of these is a centre of revolutionary propaganda. He knows, or should know, that efforts are being made to get arms for the support of this propaganda—that the Irish Volunteers have already some 2,500 rifles, and that they have their eyes on the 10,000 in the hands of the supine National Volunteers, and that they are endeavouring to supplement their rifles with shot guns, revolvers and pistols. New measures, possibly requiring additional police at the ports, will be required to counter these attempts, and unless in other matters we keep these revolutionaries under observation, we shall not be in a position to deal with the outbreak, which we hope will not occur, but which undoubtedly will follow any attempt to enforce conscription, or, even if there is no such attempt, might take place as a result of continual unsuccess of the British Arms.'

Lord Midleton's action

On the 8th January, 1915, Lord Midleton called attention in the House of Lords to the condition of Ireland. In the course of his evidence he said: 'I also named four seditious newspapers, and pressed the Government to oppose them, and to say exactly what was the status of the Irish Volunteers. Lord Crewe's reply, which I hand in, minimised the increase of the organisation, expressed sanguine hopes that regulations issued by the military authorities would practically put a stop to this dissemination of seditious newspapers, and undertook, under renewed pressure from me, that the full attention of the Irish Government and the military authorities would be given to the status of the Volunteers.' Lord Midleton further said: 'On the 26th January, 1916, I had an interview with the Prime Minister by appointment, and I brought all these facts before him. The Prime Minister asked me to hand him a memorandum giving the views which had been placed into my hands, into which he undertook to make most careful examination. I sent him subsequently at his wish a memorandum, which I produce.' He added: 'I had an appointment with the Prime Minister for the 14th March on another very important subject, and I proposed then to lay before him the Report of this Committee' (which had met to discuss this subject) 'and to give him a copy of it.

Unfortunately the Prime Minister was taken ill on the 13th, and subsequently had to go to Rome. In the result the interview never took place.'

Besides the warnings above mentioned Lord Midleton gave further warnings at later periods. In his evidence he stated that on February 28th he saw Sir Matthew Nathan, and on March 6th Lord Wimborne, and that:

'All the questions which had been discussed before were brought up at this meeting, and Sir Matthew Nathan especially pressed on me that since our previous interview the movement had been developing much more seriously in Dublin. He mentioned to me the names of those who were known to the Government as the chief conspirators, and urged me to read as a specimen an article by Sheehy Skeffington in the January or February number of the *Century*. I felt so strongly that Sir Matthew had not the necessary powers that I asked the Lord Lieutenant of Ireland whether I could go over and see him, and as he was in London he was good enough to arrange a meeting with me on March 6th in Arlington street. I found Lord Wimborne took rather a more favourable view of the position in Ireland than Sir Matthew Nathan... but the general trend of the conversation showed that he was most anxious to deal with some of the ringleaders, and I gathered, although he did not say so in words, he was unable to move further owing to the general attitude of the Government towards Ireland which it was impossible to disturb.'

Procuring arms and high explosives

Between January, 1916, and the outbreak of the insurrection, the Irish Volunteers steadily increased in numbers and discipline. During this time they were known to be supplying themselves with quantities of arms and high explosives by theft, or otherwise, when opportunity offered. In the early months of the year the state of various parts of the country was known to be lawless. In January the heads of the Royal Irish Constabulary submitted to the Under Secretary suggestions for the amendment of the Defence of the Realm Act and Regulations. They pointed out that trial by jury had proved to be a failure, and that in many parts of Ireland the magistrates could not be relied upon to enforce the existing regulations. A conference was held at the Castle to consider these recommendations early in February. Amendments of the law and prohibition of the carrying of arms by the Irish Volunteers were suggested as remedial measures in a carefully written paper of recommendations submitted to the conference. It was attended by Mr O'Connell, Deputy Inspector-General of the Royal Irish Constabulary, the Under Secretary, General Friend, and the Solicitor-General. The only suggestion discussed was that dealing with explosives—the more serious matters were not even brought forward. Upon this point Mr O'Connell remarked—'it was my impression, rightly or wrongly, that they had been discussed by higher authorities.'

The publication of newspapers containing seditious articles continued during the spring of 1916. A number of seditious books called 'Tracts for the Times' were circulated. Major Price, of the Army Intelligence Department, informed the Commission that he had consultations with regard to this matter, but added: 'I liken myself to John the Baptist preaching in the Wilderness as to taking steps on the subject. The civil authorities did not think it desirable to take steps.'

'A pack of rebels'

On St Patrick's day, the 17th March, there was a parade of the Irish Volunteers, throughout the provinces, under orders from their headquarters. About 4,500 turned out, of whom 1,817 were armed. The report of the Inspector-General of the Royal Irish Constabulary, dealing with this parade, contained the following remarks:

'There can be no doubt that the Irish Volunteer leaders are a pack of rebels who would proclaim their independence in the event of any favourable opportunity, but with their present resources and without substantial reinforcements it is difficult to imagine that they will make even a brief stand against a small body of troops. These observations, however, are made with reference to the provinces, and not to the Dublin Metropolitan area, which is the centre of the movement.'

At the end of last March the Council of the Irish Volunteers assembled in Dublin, and issued a manifesto warning the public that the Volunteers: 'Cannot submit to be disarmed, and that the raiding for arms and the attempted disarming of men, therefore, in the natural course of things can only be met by resistance and bloodshed.'

On the 7th April, 1916, public meetings of the Irish Volunteers were held for the purposes of protesting against the deportation orders and to enlist recruits. The speeches were very violent, threats being used that persons attempting to disarm the Volunteers would be 'shot dead.'

The Chief Commissioner, DMP

The Chief Commissioner made a report to the Under-Secretary, and that document shows clearly the view that Colonel Edgeworth-Johnstone took of the situation:

'These recruiting meetings are very undesirable development, and are, I think, causing both annoyance and uneasiness amongst loyal citizens... The Sinn Fein Party are gaining in numbers, in equipment, in discipline, and in confidence and I think drastic action should be taken to limit their activities. The longer this is postponed the more difficult it will be to carry out.'

This report reached the Under-Secretary on the 10th April, who wrote on it: 'Chief Secretary and the Lord Lieutenant to see the Chief Commissioner's minute'. On the 12th the Chief Secretary wrote upon it: 'Requires careful consideration. Is it thought practicable to undertake a policy of disarmament, and, if so, within what limits, if any, can such a policy be circumscribed?' Upon the same day the Lord Lieutenant wrote upon it: 'This is a difficult point: could the disarmament be satisfactorily effected?'

No answer to the minute was returned to the Royal Irish Constabulary, and the file did not find its way back to the Inspector-General until the 24th May.

For some months before the rising, a newspaper campaign was carried on suggesting that if an attempt were made by the Government to disarm the Irish Volunteers, it could only arise from the deliberate intention of Englishmen to provoke disorder and bloodshed.

There is no doubt that these articles were intended to intimidate the Irish Government, and to prevent their taking active repressive measures.

The arms ship and the bogus circular

On the 18th April news reached Dublin Castle that a ship had left Germany for Ireland on April 12th, accompanied by two German submarines, but the news was accompanied by a caution as to its accuracy. The statement added that the ship was due to arrive on the 21st, and that a rising was timed for Easter Eve. On the 19th April a special meeting of the Dublin Corporation was held at the Mansion House to discuss the police rate. Alderman Thomas Kelly, in the course of a speech attacking Mr Justice Kenny (who had alluded at the opening of his Commission to the state of disorder in Dublin and had urged military action) made a statement to the effect that he had received that morning from the Editor of *New Ireland* a circular which he would read. It was from a man named Little, *New Ireland* Office, 13 Fleet street, Dublin 16th April, 1916:

'Sir, The gravity of the present situation in Ireland compels me to invite your serious attention to the enclosed. It is a copy of portion of a document recently addressed to, and on the files in, Dublin Castle. In view of the deliberate intention here revealed on the part of the Government to cause bloodshed in Ireland by an attack on the Irish Volunteers—a body formed openly in pre-war times—in a manner certain to provoke armed resistance, I appeal to you to use your influence, public and private, in whatever manner you may consider would best benefit this country. The cipher from which this document is copied does not indicate punctuation or capitals.'

Alderman Kelly then read the document which appears on pages 6 and 7. Continuing, he said the document was evidently genuine, and he had done a public service in drawing attention to it, in order to prevent these military operations being carried on in a city which he declared was under God the most peaceable in Europe.

This document was an entire fabrication. Copies of it found since the outbreak are shown by identification of type to have been printed at Liberty Hall, the headquarters of the Citizen Army. It is not known who was the author of this invention, or whether Mr Little was in any way responsible for it. Many copies of this forged document were printed and distributed, and it was widely considered by the people to be genuine, and no doubt led to the belief by the members of the Irish Volunteers and Citizen Army that they would shortly be disarmed. This undoubtedly became one of the proximate causes of the outbreak.

On the 22nd April, 1916, the news of the capture of the German ship, and of the arrest of a man believed to be Sir Roger Casement, was published. The 'Irish Volunteer' newspaper announced in its issue of that day under the title of Headquarters' Bulletin:

'Arrangements are now nearing completion in all the more important brigade areas for the holding of a very interesting series of manoeuvres at Easter. In some instances the arrangements contemplate a one or two day bivouac. As for Easter the Dublin programme may well stand as a model for other areas'.

Reference was also made to a more elaborate series of manoeuvres at Whitsuntide.

It is clear that the leaders of the movement expected the arrival of the ship, since emissaries of the Irish Volunteers were sent to meet it. The vessel, however, and Sir Roger Casement, appear to have arrived a little sooner than was expected.

On the news of the capture of the ship orders were given at the Headquarters of the Irish Volunteers cancelling throughout all Ireland the arrangements for the following day—Sunday. The order was signed 'McNeill, Chief of Staff'. This appeared in the early evening papers of Saturday, the 22nd April.

In the evening of the 22nd it was known to the authorities that the man arrested was Sir Roger Casement. A conference was held at Dublin Castle on the same evening. The abandonment of the parade of the Volunteers for Sunday was then known. No movements of the Volunteers took place on that day. A report was received on Sunday afternoon that there had been a robbery under arms at about 8 o'clock a.m. of 250 lbs. of gelignite from quarries a few miles south-west of Dublin, and that it was believed the stolen material or part of it, had been taken to Liberty Hall. Conferences held during Sunday, the 23rd April, at the Castle are fully detailed in the evidence of Lord Wimborne, Sir Matthew Nathan and other witnesses. It was eventually decided that the proper course was to arrest all the leaders of the movement, there being by this time clear evidence of their 'hostile association', but it was agreed that before this could be safely done military preparations sufficient to overawe armed opposition should be secured.

Early in the morning of the 24th April the Chief Secretary's concurrence with the proposed arrest and internment in England of the hostile leaders was asked for and obtained, but before any further effective steps could be taken the insurrection had broken out, and by noon many portions of the City of Dublin had been simultaneously occupied by rebellious armed forces.

There is no doubt that the outbreak had been carefully planned beforehand. A pocketbook discovered upon one of the rebels who took part in the rising in Wexford contained a list of the places actually seized in Dublin when the outbreak occurred.

Conclusions

The following are the conclusions arrived at by the Commission :

It is outside the scope of Your Majesty's instructions to us to enquire how far the policy of the Irish Executive was adopted by the Cabinet as a whole, or to attach responsibility to any but the civil and military executive in Ireland: but the general conclusion that we draw from the evidence before us is that the main cause of the rebellion appears to be lawlessness that was allowed to grow up unchecked, and that Ireland for several years has been administered on the principle that it was safer and more expedient to leave law in abeyance if collision with any faction of the Irish people could thereby be avoided. Such a policy is the negation of that cardinal rule of government which demands that the enforcement of the law and the preservation of order should always be independent of political expediency.

We consider that the importation of large quantities of arms into Ireland after the lapse of the Arms Act, and the toleration of drilling by large bodies of men first in Ulster, and then in other districts in Ireland, created conditions which rendered possible the recent troubles in Dublin and elsewhere.

It appears to us that reluctance was shown by the Irish Government to repress by prosecution written and spoken seditious utterances, and to suppress the drilling and manoeuvring of armed forces known to be under the control of men who were openly declaring their hostility to Your Majesty's Government and their readiness to welcome and assist Your Majesty's enemies.

Pressure of the Irish Party

This reluctance was largely prompted by the pressure brought to bear by the Parliamentary representatives of the Irish people, and in Ireland itself there developed a widespread belief that no repressive measures would be undertaken by the Government against sedition. This led to a rapid increase in preparations for insurrection, and was the immediate cause of the recent outbreak.

We are of opinion that from the commencement of the present war all seditious utterances and publications should have been firmly suppressed at the outset, and if juries or magistrates were found unwilling to enforce this policy further powers should have been invoked under the existing Acts for the Defence of the Realm.

We are also of opinion that on the outbreak of war all drilling and manoeuvring by unrecognised bodies of men, whether armed or unarmed, should have been strictly prohibited, and that as soon as it became known to the Irish Government that the Irish Volunteers and the Citizen Army were under the control of men prepared to assist Your Majesty's enemies if the opportunity should be offered to them, all drilling and open carrying of arms by these bodies of men should have been forcibly suppressed.

It does not appear to be disputed that the authorities in the spring of 1916, while believing that the seditious bodies would not venture unaided to break into insurrection, were convinced that they were prepared to assist a German landing.

We are further of opinion that at the risk of a collision early steps should have been taken to arrest and prosecute leaders and organisers of sedition.

For the reasons before given, we do not think that any responsibility rests upon the Lord Lieutenant. He was appointed in February, 1915, and was in no way answerable for the policy of the Government.

Mr Birrell Responsible

We are, however, of the opinion that the Chief Secretary, as the administrative head of Your Majesty's Government in Ireland is primarily responsible for the situation that was allowed to arise and the outbreak that occurred.

Sir Matthew Nathan assumed office as Under-Secretary to the Irish Government on September, 1914, only. In our view he carried out with the utmost loyalty the policy of the Government, and of his immediate superior, the Chief Secretary, but we consider that he did not sufficiently impress upon the Chief Secretary during the latter's prolonged absences from Dublin the necessity for more active measures to remedy the situation in Ireland, which on December 18th last, in a letter to the Chief Secretary, he described as 'most serious and menacing.'

We are satisfied that Sir Neville Chamberlain, the Inspector-General of the Royal Irish Constabulary, and Colonel Edgeworth-Johnstone, the Chief Commissioner of the Dublin Metropolitan Police, required their subordinates to furnish, and did receive from their subordinates, full and exact reports as to the nature, progress, and aims of the various armed forces in Ireland. From these sources the Government had abundant material on which they could have acted many months before the leaders themselves contemplated any actual rising.

Police Praised

For the conduct, zeal, and loyalty of the Royal Irish Constabulary and the Dublin Metropolitan Police we have nothing but praise.

We do not attach any responsibility to the military authorities in Ireland for the rebellion or its results.

As long as Ireland was under civil government those authorities had nothing to with the suppression of sedition. Their duties were confined to securing efficiency in their own ranks and to the promotion of recruiting, and they could only aid in the suppression of disorder when duly called on by the civil power. By the middle of 1915 it was obvious to the military authorities that their efforts in favour of recruiting were being frustrated by the hostile activities of the Sinn Fein supporters, and they made representations to the Government to that effect. The general danger of the situation was clearly pointed out to the Irish Government by the military authorities, on their own initiative, in February last, but the warning fell on unheeding ears.

In conclusion, we desire to place on record our high appreciation of the services rendered with ability and energy by our Honorary Secretary. For several months Mr Grimwood Mears gave his services voluntarily to the Government in their investigation into cases of alleged German atrocities, and subsequently served as joint Honorary Secretary to the Committee on alleged German outrages, generally known as Lord Bryce's Committee. The experience thus gained by him has been of great advantage to Your Majesty's Commissioners.

We offer our cordial thanks to the Secretary of the Commission for the assistance he has given us in the performance of our task.

All which we humbly submit and report for Your Majesty's gracious consideration.

(Signed) Hardinge of Penshurst,
(Signed) Montague Shearman,
(Signed) Mackenzie Dalzell Chalmers.

E Grimwood Mears,
Secretary.

June 20th, 1916.

SHOOTING OF THREE MEN IN PORTOBELLO BARRACKS
Royal Commission of Inquiry

A Royal Commission of Inquiry opened in the four courts, Dublin, on Wednesday, 23rd August, and concluded on Thursday, 31st August, 1916, into the circumstances connected with the shooting of Francis Sheehy Skeffington, Thomas Dickson, and Patrick J. MacIntyre, on 25th April, 1916, at Portobello Barracks. The Commissioners who presided were:

Sir John A. Simon, KCVO, KC, MP (Chairman)
Lord Justice Molony
Mr Denis Henry, KC, MP

The Commissioners' Report

On 29th September, 1916, the following report was issued by the Commission:

1. In accordance with Your Majesty's command, signified by your Royal Commission dated the 17th day of August, 1916, we have conducted an inquiry into 'the facts and circumstances connected with the treatment of Mr Francis Sheehy Skeffington, Mr Thomas Dickson, and Mr Patrick J MacIntyre upon and after their arrest on the 25th day of April last.'

2. We held the first sitting for the examination of witnesses on Wednesday morning, the 23rd day of August, 1916, at 11 o'clock, at the Four Courts, Dublin. The inquiry was then opened and Your Majesty's Commission was read in open court.

3. The following counsel appeared:

i The Right Hon. J. H. M. Campbell, KC, Attorney-General, and Mr Cusack, on behalf of His Majesty's Government.

ii Mr TM Healy, KC, and Mr PA O'C White, and Mr RJ Sheehy, on behalf of the family of Mr Sheehy Skeffington and also on behalf of the family of Mr Thomas Dickson.

iii Mr JB Powell, KC, and Mr Swayne on behalf of the Military Authorities.

iv Mr TW Brown on behalf of Major Rosborough and Lieutenant Morgan.

v Mr JA Rearden on behalf of Alderman JJ Kelly.

Mr Brennan, solicitor, appeared on behalf of the family of Mr PJ MacIntyre.

4. Our sittings closed on the 31st day of August, 1916, having occupied six days, during which the evidence of 38 witnesses was taken.

The command of the barracks

5. The Barracks of Portobello were, on the 24th day of April last, occupied by the 3rd Reserve Battalion of the Royal Irish Rifles. The battalion was commanded by Lieutenant-Colonel McCammond, but he was unfortunately on sick leave from the 22nd to the 29th April, and in his absence the command devolved upon Major Rosborough.

6. The insurrection broke out early on the 24th of April, and at noon on that day many buildings and places in the city were occupied by the rebels. When the knowledge of the rising spread through the city officers and soldiers on leave repaired to the nearest barracks and reported for duty, and consequently at Portobello Major Rosborough had under his command many officers and men who were quite unknown to him, but of whose services he was glad to avail himself in the restoration of order.

7. The Portobello Barracks lie outside the city boundary of Dublin on the south side, being bonded on the north by the Grand Canal, on the east by the Rathmines road, and on the south by the suburb of Rathmines. The barracks cover a very large area (about 40 acres) and were built for the accommodation of two infantry battalions, but at the time of the insurrection not more than 600 men were quartered there, and of these quite half would be on duty outside the barracks. On the 24th and 25th April various alarming rumours were current as to an impending attack on the barracks, and as to various alleged successes of the rebel forces, and undoubtedly at the time both officers and men thought that they were in serious peril, which could only be averted by taking strong measures for the safety of the troops and the barracks. In considering the events of the week we think it very necessary that the position of the military at the time should be borne in mind and their conduct should be viewed in the light of the abnormal circumstances then prevailing.

The order of events

We now proceed to describe in order of time the events into which we have been directed to inquire.

8. Mr Sheehy Skeffington was the first of the three individuals to be arrested; his arrest had no connection with the arrest of Mr Dickson and Mr MacIntyre, which occurred some three hours later.

9. Mr Francis Sheehy Skeffington was a well-known figure in Dublin, and shortly before 8 p.m. on April 25th he was walking from the city in the direction of his home, which was situated at 11 Grosvenor place, Rathmines. His way led over Portobello Bridge, and about 350 yards further on he would have passed the turning which leads to the main entrance of Portobello Barracks.

10. It was conceded on all hands before us that Mr Sheehy Skeffington had no connection with the rebellion; his views were opposed to the use of physical force; and it appears that he had been engaged that afternoon in making some public appeal to prevent looting and the like. Mrs Sheehy Skeffington gave evidence of this fact, and her evidence is confirmed by a document which was found on him when he was searched and which contained a form of membership of a proposed civic organisation to check looting. As he approached Portobello Bridge he was followed by a crowd, some of the members of which were shouting out his name.

Arrest of Mr Sheehy Skeffington

11. It was about dusk and the disturbances had now continued for some thirty hours. A young officer named Lieutenant MC Morris, who was attached to the 3rd Battalion of the Royal Irish Rifles at Portobello Barracks, had taken up duty an hour before in command of a picket at Portobello Bridge, occupying premises at the corner known as Davy's publichouse. His orders were to do his utmost to avoid conflict but to keep the roadway as clear as possible. Lieutenant Morris heard people in the street shouting out Mr Sheehy Skeffington's name, and he determined to detain him and send him to the barracks. Lieutenant Morris did not himself leave his post for many hours afterwards. He sent Mr Sheehy Skeffington under an escort of two men to the barracks

12. We consider that there is no good ground for complaint against the action of Lieutenant Morris in causing Mr Sheehy Skeffington to be detained and sent to the barracks. He told us that he had taken the same course with one or two others who seemed likely to cause a crowd to congregate; his picket had been fired at from time to time from houses close by; there was no police force in the streets; and it was obviously better to require pedestrians who appeared to be attracting notice to go to the barracks rather than the risk of altercations in the roadway. No charge was made against Mr Sheehy Skeffington, and he went quite willingly. Many other civilians against whom no charge was made were sent, in the course of the disturbances, to the barracks in similar circumstances, and the fact that they were innocent of all complicity in the rebellion does not necessarily imply that their temporary detention cannot be explained or justified. The really important matter in such cases is not the fact of detention but the subsequent treatment of the individuals detained.

In the Guardroom

13. On arrival at the barracks, Mr Sheehy Skeffington was taken to the main guardroom: three young officers, named Dobbin, Tooley and Alexander Wilson were sharing duty there, Mr Dobbin being the senior of the three. Mr Dobbin was only eighteen years of age, having left school in the previous year, and he had held his commission only a few months; he had at that time seen nothing of fighting. He and the other two second lieutenants had arranged among themselves spells of duty, and it was not clearly established before us which of them was in actual charge when Mr Sheehy Skeffington was brought in. Sergeant Maxwell, who was in the guardroom, was ordered to take Mr Sheehy Skeffington across to the orderly room to be interrogated, and he was there interviewed by the Adjutant of the Battalion, Lieutenant Morgan, who is an officer of experience. Evidence as to this interrogation is not quite precise or consistent, but the witnesses agreed that Mr Sheehy Skeffington stated that he was not a Sinn Feiner, but that he was in favour of passive resistance and opposed to militarism. Since there was no charge of any sort against Mr Sheehy Skeffington Lieutenant Morgan thought it best to communicate by telephone with the Garrison Adjutant for instructions as to whether Mr Sheehy Skeffington should be further detained or not. Orders having been received that he should be detained for further inquiries, he was brought back to the guardroom.

No incriminating documents

14. Mr Sheehy Skeffington was searched by Captain Bowen-Colthurst. This gentleman was an officer of sixteen years' service. He belonged to the Royal Irish Rifles, and had considerable experience of warfare. He had been with his battalion of the regiment at the front when he was seriously wounded and invalided home. At the time of the Dublin disturbances he was attached to the 3rd Battalion at Portobello Barracks. Having searched Mr Sheehy Skeffington, Captain Bowen-Colthurst about 9 o'clock handed over to the Adjutant what he had found upon him. The Adjutant made copies of these documents and produced them before us; they were few in number, and none of them had anything to do with the disturbances save the document already referred to, which was a draft form of membership for a civic guard. There was nothing of an incriminatory nature found on Mr Sheehy Skeffington. When we come to deal with the cases of Mr Dickson and Mr MacIntyre, it will again be seen that nothing of consequence was found upon them, and the absence of compromising documents in all three cases is, in the light of a report subsequently made by Captain Bowen-Colthurst, a fact of considerable importance.

15. Later, on the same evening, Captain Bowen-Colthurst went out of the barracks in command of a party under orders to enter and occupy premises at the corner of Camden street and Harrington street, occupied by Mr James Kelly for the purposes of his tobacco business. Mr Kelly is an Alderman of the City and a Justice of the Peace, and had recently held the office of High Sheriff of the City. There is no question that the suspicion entertained against Mr Kelly's loyalty was due to a misunderstanding, and that Mr Kelly was, in fact, quite innocent of any connection with the outbreak. Mr Kelly's premises are some 300 yards on the city side of Portobello Bridge, and the route for Captain Bowen-Colthurst's party therefore lay from the main gate of the barracks along the lane leading into the Rathmines road, and then along the Rathmines road over Portobello Bridge past Davy's publichouse.

A 'Hostage'

16. Captain Bowen-Colthurst adopted the extraordinary, and indeed, almost meaningless, course of taking Mr Sheehy Skeffington with him as a 'hostage.' He had no right to take Mr Sheehy Skeffington out of the custody of the guard for this or any other purpose, and he asked no one's leave to

do so. Captain Bowen-Colthurst's party consisted of a junior officer (Second Lieutenant Leslie Wilson) and about forty men. Before they left the barracks Mr Sheehy Skeffington's hands were tied behind his back and Captain Bowen-Colthurst called upon him to say his prayers. Upon Mr Sheehy Skeffington refusing to do so Captain Bowen-Colthurst ordered the men of his party to take their hats off and himself uttered a prayer, the words of it, according to Lieutenant Wilson's evidence, being: 'O Lord God, if it shall please Thee to take away the life of this man forgive him for Christ's sake.'

The shooting of Coade

17. The party proceeded from the main gates of the barracks to the turning into the Rathmines road, where a shooting incident occurred which we thought it right to investigate since Mr Sheehy Skeffington was present and since it was suggested (but not proved) that it might have led to some protest on his part, or might have had some bearing on his subsequent treatment. We find it impossible to reconcile all the testimony given on this matter, but it was established that a youth named Coade with a friend named Laurence Byrne were in the Rathmines road when Captain Bowen-Colthurst's party came by. Captain Bowen-Colthurst asked them what business they had to be in the road at that hour, and warned them that martial law had been proclaimed. The evidence as to what happened next is not consistent, but there is no suggestion that either of the two young men showed any violence, and it was clearly established before us that Captain Bowen-Colthurst shot young Coade, who fell mortally wounded, and was subsequently taken by an ambulance to the hospital in the barracks. Lieutenant Wilson testified that Captain Bowen-Colthurst fired with a rifle, but two civilian witnesses—whose good faith there is no reason to doubt—asserted positively that they saw Captain Bowen-Colthurst (whose identity was unmistakable, since he is a man of exceptional stature) brandish and fire a revolver. There was admittedly other firing as Captain Bowen-Colthurst's party marched down the road, which Lieutenant Leslie Wilson told us was for the purpose of securing that the people at the windows should keep indoors. The evidence of the different witnesses can only be reconciled by inferring that more than one case of shooting occurred during the progress of Captain Bowen-Colthurst's party.

A delusion

18. None of the evidence offered to us afforded any justification for the shooting of Coade; it is, of course, a delusion to suppose that a proclamation of martial law confers upon an officer any right to take human life in circumstances where this would have been unjustifiable without such a proclamation, and this delusion in the present case had tragic consequences.

19. On reaching Portobello Bridge Captain Bowen-Colthurst divided his party into two and left half of it in the charge of Lieutenant Leslie Wilson, while going forward with the rest to attack Alderman Kelly's shop; he also left Mr Sheehy Skeffington at the bridge, giving Lieutenant Leslie Wilson orders that, if he (Captain Bowen-Colthurst) and his men were 'knocked out,' Lieutenant Leslie Wilson was to take command, and if they were fired upon Lieutenant Wilson was to shoot Mr Sheehy Skeffington.

Arrest of Dickson and MacIntyre

20. The advance party then went on its way and was absent about twenty minutes; they threw a bomb into Alderman Kelly's shop and met with no resistance there. Alderman Kelly was absent; Mr MacIntyre, who was a friend of Alderman Kelly, had been on the premises some time, and Mr Dickson, who lived close by, took refuge there when he heard the soldiers firing as they approached. Miss Kelly, who is a sister of Alderman Kelly, gave us a detailed account of the raid on her brother's premises; it is evident from her account that Captain Bowen-Colthurst was in a state of great excitement. Dickson and MacIntyre, together with other men who were shortly afterwards released, were taken into custody, and Captain Bowen-Colthurst returned to barracks with them, picking up Mr Sheehy Skeffington and the other section of his party on the way.

21. Meanwhile, the news of Mr Sheehy Skeffington having been taken out of barracks reached the ears of the Adjutant, who fixed the time when he heard this from Sergeant Maxwell at about 10.20 p.m. The Adjutant saw Lieutenant Dobbin and asked him for a written report; this document was produced, and runs as follows:

'April 25th, 11.10 p.m.

'An armed party under Captain J.C. Bowen-Colthurst has just passed through my guard, demanding and taking with him the last captured prisoner, Sheehy Skeffington.'

It is important to observe that the terms of this document, while they show that Lieut. Dobbin realised that the prisoners were in his custody and under his control, record a 'demand' made upon him by an officer of superior rank and vastly greater experience. The report does not state that captain Bowen-Colthurst was taking out Mr Sheehy Skeffington as a 'hostage', and both the Adjutant and Lieutenant Dobbin assured us that they were ignorant of Captain Bowen-Colthurst's object.

Report to the Adjutant

22. When Captain Bowen-Colthurst returned to barracks he made a verbal report in the presence of the Adjutant to Major Rosborough, in the course of which, according to the Adjutant, he mentioned that he had taken Mr Sheehy Skeffington with him and had arrested Dickson and MacIntyre. The Adjutant was unable to give us a fuller account of the interview, and he had no recollection of any

reprimand being administered to Captain Bowen-Colthurst. Major Rosborough himself had no recollection of the interview at all, and explained that he was working at great pressure and under extreme anxiety and whatever Captain Bowen-Colthurst said it never conveyed to his mind that Mr Sheehy Skeffington had been taken out in the way and for the purpose described. Nothing was said as to the shooting of Coade.

23. We are satisfied that the seriousness of the irregularity committed by Captain Bowen-Colthurst in his treatment of Mr Sheehy Skeffington on this Tuesday night was not fully realised by those under whose commands he was supposed to be acting. Whether from the lateness of the hour or from the strain and anxiety caused by events outside the barracks and the apprehension of even graver trouble, this officer was not effectively reprimanded, and the civilians detained under the main guard were not rendered more secure with the result that Captain Bowen-Colthurst was at liberty the next morning again to over-ride or disregard the officer of the guard, and to deal with civilian prisoners as he pleased.

The night in the barracks

24. Mr Dickson and Mr MacIntyre were searched but nothing material was found on them. They spent the night in the detention room along with some other civilians. Mr Sheehy Skeffington, as being of a superior social position, was put into a separate cell and was made as comfortable as possible.

25. Mr Dickson was the editor of a paper called *The Eye Opener*, and Mr MacIntyre was the editor of another paper known as *The Searchlight*. So far as there was any evidence on the point before us, it appears that the only reason for arresting either of these men was the circumstance that they were found on Alderman Kelly's premises, and, as we have already stated, the suspicion entertained against this gentleman was without any foundation. Mr Dickson was a Scotch-man, and deformed. Neither he nor Mr MacIntyre had any connection with the Sinn Fein movement.

26. On Wednesday morning, April 26th, the officers in charge of the main guard were the same as on the previous evening—namely, Lieutenants Dobbin, Tooley, and Alexander Wilson. The sergeant of the guard was Sergeant John W Aldridge, then of the 10th Royal Dublin Fusiliers. Sergeant Aldridge was on leave at the commencement of the rebellion, and on returning to Dublin reported himself (like many other soldiers at this time) at the nearest barracks: he was in consequence new to his surroundings at Portobello, and the officers at the barracks were not known to him by sight. He mounted guard at 9 a.m. on Wednesday morning.

Three men brought out

27. Shortly after 10 a.m. Captain Bowen-Colthurst came to the guardroom. He appears on his first arrival to have entirely ignored Lieutenant Dobbin, who was standing in the barrack square near to the guardroom entrance, and having passed into the guardroom itself to have given his orders direct to the sergeant. These orders were to the effect that he required the three prisoners, Skeffington, Dickson, and MacIntyre in the yard for the purpose of speaking to them. The yard in question is within the guardroom block of buildings, being reached by a short passage from the guard room. It comprises a space less than 40 ft in length and some 15 ft in width, and is surrounded by high brick walls.

28. Sergeant Aldridge had not seen Captain Bowen-Colthurst before and was not aware of what position he occupied in the barracks, save that his uniform showed him to be a captain. Owing to the sergeant having mounted guard only an hour previously he did not know who were the officers of the guard, and there was consequently nothing which appeared to him to be unusual in Captain Bowen-Colthurst entering the guardroom and giving orders. The orders were complied with. Mr Sheehy Skeffington was called from his cell, and Messrs Dickson and MacIntyre from the detention room, and all three were ordered out into the yard, which was but a few paces away.

Urgent message to the Adjutant

29. During the few moments that were occupied by the calling out of the three prisoners Captain Bowen-Colthurst stepped out of the guard room to the spot where Lieutenant Dobbin was still standing, and informed that officer that he was taking the three prisoners out for the purpose of shooting them, as he thought 'it was the best thing to do.' Lieutenant Dobbin's recollection is not clear as to whether the three men were mentioned by name, but there is no doubt that their number and the purpose for which Captain Bowen-Colthurst was taking them out were distinctly conveyed to his mind. Captain Bowen-Colthurst immediately re-entered the guard room, while Lieutenant Dobbin called to Lieutenant Alexander Wilson who was near-by, and dispatched him with an urgent message to the Adjutant. Lieutenant Wilson had his bicycle with him; he mounted it and rode to the orderly room in which the Adjutant was working and which is some 500 yards distant from the guard room.

30. Lieutenant Wilson's recollection of these vital incidents has varied from time to time, but we think there is no reason to question the sincerity of this witness in ultimately arriving at a conclusion as to what took place differing materially from his earlier impressions. Even so, his recollection of the message he delivered does not altogether agree with the Adjutant's memory on the point; the latter's version is corroborated by the evidence of Sergeant Campbell.

No authority to take out men

31. Lieutenant Dobbin's own statement is that he

told Lieutenant Wilson to inform the Adjutant that Captain Bowen-Colthurst was taking the prisoners out of the guard-room. He does not recollect stating in the message for what purpose they were being taken out. We think it probable that Captain Bowen-Colthurst's purpose was present to the mind of Lieutenant Wilson when he conveyed the message, but we are satisfied that the message itself as received by the Adjutant contained no mention of the fact that the prisoners were about to be shot. The impression made on the Adjutant's mind by the receipt of the message was that Captain Bowen-Colthurst was engaged in repeating his irregular proceedings of the evening before, and the message he returned by Lieutenant Wilson was that Major Rosborough was out, that he (the Adjutant) could give no authority for any prisoners to be taken out of the guard-room, and that in taking them out Captain Bowen-Colthurst would be acting on his own responsibility. Lieutenant Wilson returned with this message on his bicycle, and, while he was giving it to Lieutenant Dobbin just outside the guard-room, the shots of the fatal volley rang out from the adjoining yard.

32. When Captain Bowen-Colthurst returned into the guard-room after his brief statement to Lieutenant Dobbin he ordered some of the guard with their rifles out into the yard, where the three prisoners had preceded them. All the men on duty had their magazines already filled, and seven of the guard, who appear to have been merely those that happened at the moment to be nearest the yard passage, accompanied by Sergeant Aldridge, followed Captain Bowen-Colthurst out into the yard. What then occurred took place so rapidly that we have little doubt that none of the victims realised that they were about to meet their death. We are confirmed in this view by the fact that all the witnesses, including civilian prisoners in the detention room, to whom everything that took place in the yard was audible, agree in stating that no sound was uttered by any of the three.

Prisoners walk to the wall

33. While the soldiers were entering the yard Captain Bowen-Colthurst ordered the three prisoners to walk to the wall at the other end, a distance, as we have stated, of only a few yards. As they were doing this the seven soldiers, entering the yard, fell into line along the wall adjoining the entrance, and immediately received from Captain Colthurst the order to fire upon the three prisoners, who had then just turned to face them. All three fell as a result of the volley. Captain Bowen-Colthurst left the yard, and the firing party began to file out.

The second volley

34. Immediately upon hearing the volley, Lieutenant Dobbin (who was engaged in receiving the Adjutant's message outside) hastened through the guard-room and entered the yard. On looking at the bodies he saw a movement in one of Mr Sheehy Skeffington's legs which gave him the impression that life was not yet extinct, and he exclaimed to Sergeant Aldridge, who was still in the yard, 'Sergeant, that man is not dead.' It is Sergeant Aldridge's impression (and we are inclined to accept the evidence of this witness, who was both experienced and candid) that death had, nevertheless, been instantaneous in all three cases, and that what Lieutenant Dobbin saw was a muscular contraction of the unfortunate gentleman's limb. As a result, however, of what he saw, Lieutenant Dobbin dispatched one of the other officers of the guard, Lieutenant Tooley, to the orderly room to report and obtain instructions. At, or in the neighbourhood of, the orderly room Lieutenant Tooley met Captain Bowen-Colthurst, and received from him the order to 'fire again'. Lieutenant Tooley returned with this message, and thereupon four soldiers of the guard (not all members of the firing party) were ordered into the yard by Lieutenant Dobbin, and upon his direction fired a second volley into the body of Mr Sheehy Skeffington.

No separate shooting

35. Certain civilian witnesses who were in the detention room during the course of these events spoke to having heard a shot, or volley, in addition to, and separated by a distinct interval of time from, the two volleys spoken of by the military. If their evidence be correct (and there is no reason to doubt their good faith), this third shot, or volley, was heard at a moment antecedent to Messrs Dickson and MacIntyre reaching the yard, and the question was raised by those appearing for the relatives of Mr Sheehy Skeffington whether the latter had not been shot separately from the other two prisoners. We are quite satisfied on the evidence as a whole that the three prisoners were shot together in the way we have described, and that the earlier report heard by those in the detention room had no connection with any shooting in the yard. It may perhaps be explained by the accidental discharge of a rifle in the neighbourhood of the guard room, which was the impression conveyed to at least one of those in the detention room.

36. It should be clearly understood that the events we have been recording, from the arrival of Captain Bowen-Colthurst at the guard room, occupied but a very few minutes. The guard room, detention room, detention cells, and yard all closely adjoin one another in the same block, and a very few steps suffice to take a person from one into another.

Captain Colthurst's verbal report

37. Not long after the shooting had taken place, and before 10.30 a.m., Captain Bowen-Colthurst reported verbally to the Adjutant at the orderly room that he had shot Mr Sheehy Skeffington and the editors of the *Eye Opener* and the *Searchlight*. Either then, or later, he gave as his reason for so doing the fear that they would escape or might be rescued by armed force. There was no foundation

whatever for any apprehension as to the escape of these prisoners, and no sane person who honestly entertained such a possibility as a rescue would have seen in it any ground for distinction between these three prisoners and the other detained persons. At or about the same time, Captain Bowen-Colthurst verbally reported his action to Major Rosborough, adding that he had shot the three prisoners on his own responsibility and that he possibly might be hanged for it. Major Rosborough told him to make his report in writing, and instructed the Adjutant to report the matter to the Garrison Adjutant at Dublin Castle.

38. Lieutenant Morgan, after going over to the guard-room and seeing the three bodies carried out, telephoned, in accordance with his instructions from Major Rosborough, a report of the circumstances, as far as they were then known to him, to the Garrison Adjutant (Captain Burton). A telephonic report on other matters was about this time being made to Headquarters, Irish Command, and, in view of the seriousness of the occurrence, the Adjutant, under Major Rosborough's directions, did not confine himself to the usual channel, but also made a direct communication by telephone to Headquarters, Irish Command. Major Rosborough had, in the meanwhile, given directions that Captain Bowen-Colthurst should not be detailed for duty outside the barracks. No further action was taken as regards Captain Bowen-Colthurst until May 6th, when orders were received from the superior military authorities to place Captain Bowen-Colthurst under open arrest. Major Rosborough's directions as to his duties do not seem to have placed any effective check upon his movements in the meantime.

Burial and exhumation of the bodies

39. Later in the day, Lieutenant Morgan telephoned again to the Garrison Adjutant in order to ask for directions as to the disposal of the bodies (which were lying in the mortuary) and was ordered to bury them in the barrack yard that evening. Lieutenant Morgan, accordingly, after consultation with the Medical Officer, Major Balch, and also the Engineer Officer, had the bodies wrapped up in sheets and buried in the barrack square. It should be remembered that, in the then state of the city, coffins were difficult, if not impossible, to secure, and the same mode of burial had to be adopted in the case of soldiers whose bodies were brought into the barracks. We are satisfied that Lieutenant Morgan carried out his duties in connection with the burial as decorously and reverently as was possible in the circumstances at the time. He ascertained that all three of the deceased were Roman Catholics and the religious rites were carried out by Father O'Loughlin, the Roman Catholic chaplain of the barracks. At a later date, at the request of the relatives and by permission of Sir John Maxwell (who had arrived in Ireland some days after these shootings), the bodies of all three men were exhumed and re-interred in consecrated ground. Mr Sheehy Skeffington, Senior, was present at the exhumation of his son's body.

Capt. Colthurst's first report

40. From time to time during the course of Wednesday, April 26th, Major Rosborough pressed Captain Bowen-Colthurst for the written report which he had directed him to make; it was ultimately received at a late hour in the afternoon, and, so far as it is material to our inquiry, it reads as follows:

'Sir—I have to report for your information that yesterday evening, about 11 p.m., according to your orders, I proceeded with a party of 25 men to Kelly's tobacco shop in Harcourt road.

'Some shots were fired at them, but whether from this shop or not I cannot say. Two men were seen standing in conversation outside the shop, who at once bolted inside. An entrance was effected and four men were made prisoners; two of these were subsequently released, and two men were detained. The two men detained were McIntyre, editor of the *Searchlight*, and Dickson, editor of the *Eye Opener*.

'Sniping was going on, and I lodged the two men detained in the Portobello guard room. I may add that I was informed that all of the tobacco had previously been removed. This morning at about 9 a.m. I proceeded to the guard room to examine these two men, and I sent for a man called Skeffington, who was also detained.

'I had been busy on the previous evening up to about 3 a.m. examining documents found on these three men, and I recognised from these documents that these three men were all very dangerous characters. I, therefore, sent for an armed guard of six men and ordered them to load their rifles and keep their eyes on the prisoners. The guard room was full of men and was not a suitable place, in my opinion, in which to examine prisoners. I ordered, therefore, the three prisoners to go into the small courtyard of the guard room. I regret now that I did not have these three men handcuffed and surrounded, as the yard was a place from which they might have escaped. When I ordered these three men into the yard I did not, however, know this. The guard was some little distance from the prisoners, and as I considered that there was a reasonable chance of the prisoners making their escape; and knowing the three prisoners (from the correspondence captured on them the previous evening) to be dangerous characters, I called upon the guard to fire upon them, which they did with effect, the three men being killed. The documents found on these three men have been forwarded to the orderly room.'

An untrue account of events

41. It is to be noted that although this report purports to give an account of the raid on Alderman Kelly's tobacco shop, no mention is made of Mr Sheehy Skeffington having been taken out as a

'hostage' on that occasion, or of the shooting of the young man Coade. The account of the events which took place on Wednesday morning is entirely untrue. Captain Bowen-Colthurst's object in going to the guard-room was not to examine the prisoners, but, as he stated to Lieutenant Dobbin at the time, to have them shot. The armed guard was not ordered out for the purpose of preventing the prisoners' escape, but for the purpose of shooting them. There was no possibility of the prisoners making their escape from the yard, a fact which is obvious to anyone who has seen it. No documents or correspondence whatever were found on the prisoners which showed them to be 'dangerous characters'; and any documents found on them could be thoroughly examined in a few minutes.

Captain Colthurst's second report

42. At a later date, and after he had been placed under arrest, viz., on May 9th, 1916, Captain Bowen-Colthurst forwarded a further report, and addressed to the Officer Commanding 3rd Battalion of the Royal Irish Rifles. This report reads as follows:

'Sir,—In accordance with your instructions, I have the honour to forward for your information a more detailed account of the circumstances connected with the shooting of three rebels in Portobello Barracks, Dublin.

'On Tuesday evening, 25th ult., I was officially informed that martial law was declared in Dublin. There were three leaders of the rebels in the guardroom in Portobello Barracks. The guardroom was not safe for these desperate men to be confined in. Their rescue from outside would have been very easy.

'On Tuesday and up to Wednesday morning rumours of massacres of police and soldiers from all parts of Dublin were being constantly sent me from different sources. Amongst others, the rumour reached me that 600 German prisoners at Oldcastle had been released and armed, and were marching on Dublin, I also heard that the rebels in the city had opened up depots for the supply and issue of arms, and that a large force of rebels intended to attack Portobello Barracks, which was held only by a few troops, many of whom were recruits, ignorant of how to use their rifles, and a number of the others were soldiers and sailors who had taken refuge in the barracks. We had also in the barracks a considerable number of officers and men who had been wounded by the rebels, and whose protection was a source of great concern to me. I believe that it was known that these leaders were confined in the barracks, and that possibly the proposed attack on the barracks was with a view to their release. Rumours of the rising all over Ireland and of a large German-American and Irish-American landing in Galway were prevalent. I had no knowledge of any reinforcements arriving from England, and did not believe it possible for troops to arrive in time to prevent a general massacre. I knew of the sedition which had been preached in Ireland for years past, and of the popular sympathy with rebellion. I knew also that men on leave home from the trenches, although unarmed, had been shot down like dogs in the streets of their own city, simply because they were in khaki, and I had also heard that wounded soldiers home for convalescence had been shot down also. On the Wednesday morning, the 26th April, all this was in my mind. I was very much exhausted and unstrung after practically a sleepless night, and I took the gloomiest view of the situation and felt that only desperate measures would save the situation. When I saw the position described in my previous report I felt I must act quickly, and believing I had the power under martial law I felt under the circumstances that it was clearly my duty to have the three ringleaders shot. It was a terrible ordeal for me, but I nerved myself to carry out what was to me at the time a terrible duty.'

No evidence from Captain Colthurst

43. So far as this second report repeats the previous explanation as to the shooting having taken place with the object of preventing escape or rescue, the observations we have already made on this point apply to it. With the reference to martial law and the powers which this officer claimed to exercise under it, we deal in a later paragraph of this report. He is at present, as was proved to our satisfaction, confined in Broadmoor Criminal Lunatic Asylum consequent upon the sentence of a Court Martial (which found him guilty of murder but insane at the time of committing the crime), and we have therefore felt ourselves debarred from taking his evidence,

44. The disturbances continued throughout the week, and on Friday (April 28th) Mrs Sheehy Skeffington, who had last seen her husband in Westmoreland street on the previous Tuesday afternoon, was still without definite information as to what had happened to him. As a result of alarming rumours about him which reached her from various sources her two sisters, Mrs Culhane and Mrs Kettle, on the morning of Friday, went to the police station at Rathmines to make enquiries. The police had no information to give, but suggested that the two ladies might enquire at Portobello Barracks, where they accordingly went.

Mrs Sheehy Skeffington's sisters

45. To appreciate what followed it is necessary to say a word as to Mrs Sheehy Skeffington and her two sisters. They are the daughters of Mr David Sheehy, MP. Their brother, Lieutenant Sheehy, of the Dublin Fusiliers, was engaged in the fighting which was still taking place in Dublin. The husband of Mrs Culhane, then recently deceased, had been a highly-placed and responsible official in the Irish Courts of Justice, while Mrs Kettle's husband, Lieutenant TM Kettle (who since our sittings has gallantly given his life for his country in France) was with his battalion. In such circumstances Mrs Sheehy Skeffington not unreasonably expected that

whatever fate had overtaken her own husband, her two sisters would at least be treated with candour and consideration at the barracks, and would be able to obtain such information as was available about their brother-in-law.

Mrs Kettle and Mrs Culhane's visit to the barracks

46. Mrs Kettle and her sister arrived at the barracks at about one p.m., and after some slight delay were admitted past the first and second gates. A junior officer, Lieutenant Beattie, came up to enquire as to their business. This gentleman was not called before us, but as regards both this and the subsequent events to which Mrs Kettle and Mrs Sheehy Skeffington speak, we were expressly informed by those representing the military authorities, that the accuracy of the evidence given by these ladies was not called in question. Indeed, Lieutenant Beattie was present at the Inquiry, and we were told that his evidence was unnecessary since it would in no way controvert what Mrs Kettle stated. Mrs Kettle and her sister thought it well to commence their enquiries by asking in the first place as to their brother, Lieutenant Sheehy. To this they received a courteous reply. They then asked as to their brother-in-law, Mr Sheehy Skeffington, whereupon the young officer with whom they were conversing betrayed some confusion, asked them to excuse him, and went away to consult with some other officers. On returning he informed the two ladies that he regretted that he would have to place them under arrest, giving as his reason that they were Sinn Feiners and had been speaking to Sinn Feiners. Mrs Kettle and her sister pointed out the absurdity of the allegation, and referred to the position of Lieutenant Kettle and of the late Mr Culhane; they were, however, placed in charge of some soldiers, and marched across the barrack square to the orderly room, outside which they remained standing, surrounded by soldiers, while a consultation of officers appears to have taken place within. After some minutes Captain Bowen-Colthurst emerged from the guard-room and questioned them. They repeated their enquiries as to Lieutenant Sheehy and as to Mr Sheehy Skeffington. Captain Colthurst, in reply to the latter enquiry, said, 'I know nothing whatever about Mr Sheehy Skeffington.' Mrs Culhane referred to some of the rumours which had reached them, and Lieutenant Beattie, who was the only other officer actually present at this interview, made some remark to Captain Bowen-Colthurst in an undertone. Captain Bowen-Colthurst then said, 'I have no information concerning Mr Skeffington that is available, and the sooner you leave the barracks the better.' There was then an order given to have the ladies conducted back, and, by Captain Bowen-Colthurst's direction, they were forbidden to speak to one another. The guard was dismissed at the gate, and the two ladies were conducted to the tramway line by Lieutenant Beattie.

47. It is obvious to us that throughout the incidents recorded in the last paragraph Lieutenant Beattie acted under superior orders, and the evidence satisfied us that the part he was called upon to play was extremely distasteful to him.

Mrs Sheehy Skeffington informed of her husband's death

48. About four o'clock on the afternoon of Friday, after receiving her sisters' report of what had just taken place in the barracks, Mrs Sheehy Skeffington got into touch with the father of the young man Coade to whose death we have referred. Father O'Loughlin, the Chaplain of the barracks whom we have already mentioned, knew young Coade as a member of the religious sodality of which he (Father O'Loughlin) was spiritual director, and at a meeting of which Coade had been present on the night he met his death. The father of Coade was informed of his son's fate by Father O'Loughlin and was permitted to visit the dead body in the mortuary at the barracks. Here the unfortunate man saw the body of Mr Sheehy Skeffington laid out beside that of his son, a fact which on Friday afternoon he communicated to Mrs Sheehy Skeffington. Mrs Sheehy Skeffington, on Mr Coade's suggestion, at once sought out Father O'Loughlin and besought him for particulars as to her husband. She was told that he was dead and already buried.

Raid on Mrs Skeffington's house

49. At 7 p.m. on this same Friday evening Mrs Sheehy Skeffington was putting her little son, aged seven, to bed, when a body of soldiers from Portobello Barracks headed by Captain Bowen-Colthurst and Colonel Allett (an officer of advanced years who had returned to service after the outbreak of the war and who was killed during the later stages of the rebellion) arrived at the house. Mrs Sheehy Skeffington was alone in the house save for her boy and a young maid-servant. Before any attempt was made to obtain an entrance into the house a volley was fired through the windows. A body of soldiers with fixed bayonets, under Captain Bowen-Colthurst then burst in through the front door. No request for the door to be opened was made nor was any time given to those in the house to open it. Mrs Sheehy Skeffington and her boy had bayonets pointed at them and were ordered to hold their hands above their heads. They were then, by orders of Captain Bowen-Colthurst, placed in the front room together with the maid-servant and kept guarded while the house was searched. All the rooms in the house were thoroughly ransacked and a considerable quantity of books and papers were wrapped up in the household linen, placed in a passing motor car, and taken away. Mrs Sheehy Skeffington has been herself a teacher of foreign languages, while Mr Sheehy Skeffington was at the time the editor of a paper known as the *Irish Citizen*, and a large part of the material removed seems to have consisted of text-books both in German and other languages, as well as political papers and pamphlets belonging to Mr Sheehy Skeffington.

The search lasted until a quarter past ten, when the soldiers departed; Mrs Sheehy Skeffington together with her boy and maid-servant remained under arrest up to that hour.

Second visit to the house

50. On Monday, May 1st, Mrs Sheehy Skeffington's house was again visited by soldiers between 11 a.m. and 1 p.m., but Captain Bowen-Colthurst had nothing to do with this second visit. Neither Mrs Skeffington nor her boy were in the house at the time, the only occupant being a temporary maid-servant, Margaret Farrelly by name, a girl aged nineteen or twenty. Mrs Sheehy Skeffington's previous servant had been terrified by her experiences on the Friday and had left, and the maid Farrelly had been obtained from one of Mrs Skeffington's sisters. Sergeant Claxton told us that he received a message, transmitted through the police, that an unknown person had been seen entering the house. Consequently, two soldiers in charge of this sergeant went there and the maid-servant was arrested and taken to Rathmines Police Station. She was detained until the following Saturday when by the efforts of Mrs Skeffington's sisters her release was effected. Nothing else appears to have taken place on the occasion of this visit to the house.

51. Mr Dickson's house at 12 Harrington street was visited by a military search-party during the course of Wednesday, April 26th, and a bag with some documents in it was taken away and left temporarily with the picket which was still in occupation of Alderman Kelly's tobacco shop near by. It was suggested before us that this was done with the object of attaching suspicion to Alderman Kelly, but we are satisfied that this was not the case and that the incident must be judged merely as an ineffectual attempt to obtain evidence which might justify or excuse the shooting which had already taken place at Portobello Barracks.

The forged document

52. Before the outbreak of the rebellion in Dublin, much attention had been attracted to a printed pamphlet entitled 'Secret Orders Issued to the Military'. This pamphlet had been widely circulated with a view to creating the impression that its contents represented the text of confidential directions issued by the military authorities with the object of an attack upon the Sinn Fein organisation and its supporters. The document was a forgery from beginning to end, and the false representations it contained as to the orders actually issued, no doubt, played some part in precipitating the outbreak of the rebellion. A copy of this document was produced before us with the following note attached to it in red ink and in the writing of Captain Bowen-Colthurst: 'I certify that I found this document on the person of F Sheehy Skeffington.—JC Bowen-Colthurst, Captain RIR, Portobello Barracks, 25-4-'16'. Lieutenant Morgan, who took a careful copy of all the documents found on Mr Sheehy Skeffington on the night that he was arrested, satisfied us that this document was not among them, and, moreover, that it was not attached to Captain Bowen-Colthurst's report written on the day of the shooting. It is quite certain that Captain Bowen-Colthurst added this document, together with the above note appended to it, to those documents actually found on Mr Sheehy Skeffington at a later date than that which the note bears, and that the certificate endorsed upon it was untrue. The document itself was probably found by Captain Bowen-Colthurst at Mr Sheehy Skeffington's house at the search after his death, and the false certificate was added later. It was conceded before us that some copy of the printed document could have hardly failed to have come into the hands of any Dublin journalist. We think it right to state explicitly that no other person is in any way implicated in this misrepresentation, and the matter is only of importance as a further instance of the endeavours made by Captain Bowen-Colthurst, after the event, to excuse his action.

Sir Francis Vane had no responsibility

53. As a result of a communication to the military authorities in London made by Major Sir Francis Vane (one of many officers who had reported at Portobello Barracks at the commencement of the outbreak) Captain Bowen-Colthurst was placed under 'open' arrest upon May 6th, and subsequently on May 11th under 'close' arrest. Major Sir Francis Vane was not an officer of the regiment stationed at the barracks and had no responsibility for any of the events we have described. On the 6th and 7th June, Captain Bowen-Colthurst was tried by courtmartial in Dublin for the murder of the three men and was found guilty but insane.

54. We have thought it formed no part of our duty to conduct any inquiry of our own into the state of Captain Bowen-Colthurst's mind at the time he committed the offence of which he has already been found guilty or to hear any evidence upon the point. The courtmartial pronounced on this matter, and its conclusion is on record. Apart from the defence of insanity, there can be no excuse or palliation for his conduct from first to last, a state of things which was frankly recognised by those who appeared before us on behalf of the military authorities.

General observations

55. We have now set out all the relevant facts and circumstances as they appear to us and as we were able to ascertain them. We desire to add the following general observations which those facts and circumstances suggest to us:

Circumstances of the garrison

'(1) In order to form any fair judgement of the conduct of the officers and men at Portobello Barracks during Easter week, the very exceptional character of the circumstances in which they were placed must be carefully borne in mind. The garrison of the barracks, insufficient as it was for the purpose of resisting any serious assault that might have been made, was reinforced by a medley of soldiers from different regiments, together with some sailors who had reported at the commencement of the week. The officers, too, came from different units, and were in many cases unknown to one another. It is not to be wondered at that this state of things produced a considerable laxity of control and cohesion within the barracks. It was in such novel and disturbing conditions that the battalion stationed at the barracks found itself deprived of its commanding officer, Colonel McCammond, through his serious illness. Captain Bowen-Colthurst was the senior captain in the barracks, and although not the equal in rank, was of longer standing and of greater experience in the Army than Major Rosborough. The latter officer, as well as the Adjutant, Lieutenant Morgan, were fully occupied with the many important duties to which the emergency had given rise. Messages of an alarming character were constantly being transmitted to them from outside, and the exercise of effective control over an officer in Captain Bowen-Colthurst's position was rendered doubly difficult. We are satisfied that the state of things, which rendered Captain Bowen-Colthurst's conduct possible was largely caused by the unfortunate, but inevitable absence of Colonel McCammond, the only officer in the barracks who Captain Colthurst would not have considered himself at liberty to ignore. The officers in charge of the guard were young men who had recently left school, and, of necessity, were without military experience: and this fact, combined with Captain Colthurst's masterful character and superior rank, does much to excuse their failure to offer any effective opposition to his treatment of prisoners who were under their charge.

Raid on Mrs Skeffington's house

'(2) No evidence as to the raid on Mrs Sheehy Skeffington's house on Friday evening, April 28th, was tendered to us on behalf of the military, save that Major Rosborough denied that he had given any orders for it—a statement which we accept. A large number of soldiers took part in the raid, and it is impossible to suppose that the facts as to it remained unknown to all not actually engaged in it, though we cannot believe that the methods employed were either authorised or approved. The discreditable character of the proceeding is intensified by the circumstance that a few hours before, when inquiries were made at the barracks on Mrs Sheehy Skeffington's behalf, information was refused by the officer responsible for her husband's death, who himself then headed the raid. We think it right to say that, in our opinion, it is a circumstance highly regrettable and most surprising that, after the events of Wednesday, Captain Bowen-Colthurst should have found himself free to act in company with a body of soldiers, as he did on the following Friday.

Powers under martial law

'(3) The effect, so far as the powers of military authorities are concerned, of a proclamation of martial law within the United Kingdom has often been expounded, but, nevertheless, in the crisis which evokes such a proclamation, is not always remembered. Such a proclamation does not, in itself, confer upon officers or soldiers any new powers. It operates solely as a warning that the Government, acting through the military, is about to take such forcible and exceptional measures as may be necessary for the purpose of putting down insurrection and restoring order. As long as the measures are necessary, they might equally be taken without any proclamation at all. The measures that are taken can only be justified by the circumstances then existing and the practical necessities of that case. Yet, Miss Kelly told us that when Captain Bowen-Colthurst entered her brother's premises he warned those present that 'as martial law had been proclaimed' he could shoot them as he had shot someone in the street. Captain Bowen-Colthurst, in his second report on the shootings, claims to have acted under the belief that he was exercising powers conferred on him by martial law; and we heard from the young officer who was left with Mr Sheehy Skeffington at Portobello Bridge while Captain Bowen-Colthurst went forward, that he saw nothing 'strange' in the order that he was to shoot Mr Sheehy Skeffington in the event of anything happening to Capt. Bowen-Colthurst's party three hundred yards off. The shooting of unarmed and unresisting civilians without trial constitutes the offence of murder, whether martial law has been proclaimed or not. We should have deemed it superfluous to point this out were it not that the failure to realise and apply this elementary principle seems to explain the free hand which Captain Bowen-Colthurst was not restrained from exercising throughout the period of crisis.

56. We desire to state that we have had every assistance from the military authorities in obtaining all the documents and evidence at their disposal which were required for the purposes of our inquiry, and that we are indebted to all who appeared before us for their help in elucidating the course of these lamentable events.

57. Finally, we desire to express our cordial appreciation of the valuable services rendered to us by our Secretary, Mr Harold L Murphy, both during our Sittings and in the preparation of this Report.

All which we humbly submit and report for your Majesty's gracious consideration

(Signed)JOHN SIMON
THOMAS F MOLONY
DENIS S HENRY
HAROLD L.MURPHY
Secretary
September 29th, 1916.

THE EVIDENCE

The sittings of the Commission were held at the Four Courts, Dublin, Wednesday, 23rd August, Thursday, 24th, Friday, 25th, Saturday, 26th, Monday, 27th, and Thursday 31st August, 1916. In all thirty-eight witnesses were examined, and the evidence given was fully reported in the issues of the *Irish Times* following the dates mentioned. All the facts in the case are set out in the foregoing report of the Commission, and we reproduce here, the chief points in the evidence of the principal witnesses:

Sergeant John Maxwell

At the first day's sitting of the Commission, Sergeant John Maxwell, 3rd Royal Irish Rifles, said he was regimental provost-sergeant at Portobello on April 25th. There was a man in the guardroom whose name he was informed was Skeffington. He was interrogated and was ordered to be detained pending further inquiry.

Cross-examined by Mr Healy : When did you first see a man named Edelstein in the barracks? I cannot remember, I know the man very well.

Was he what is called a 'spotter' for the military? I could not answer that.

Did you see a person called Isaacs coming to the barracks? No, I did not.

Second Lieut. Leslie Wilson describes the shooting of Coade

Second Lieutenant Leslie Wilson, 5th Royal Irish Fusiliers, repeated the evidence he gave at the courtmartial, and was afterwards cross-examined by Mr Healy.

Mr Healy: Was Mr Skeffington handcuffed? No, but his hands were tied behind his back. Before we got to the bridge, Captain Colthurst took a rifle from one of the men and fired in the air several times.

Did you hear of the shooting by Captain Colthurst of a boy named Coade? I could not say whether he was a boy or a man, but I was present.

Where was Skeffington? He was in the middle of the party.

Where was the boy killed? This person was mortally wounded at the tramway end of the lane leading to the barracks. So far as I remember two men were slinking or sneaking about the barracks, as if they were spies. Captain Colthurst asked them what their business was, and they gave some impudence, using blasphemous oaths. One of them said something about Captain Colthurst being a 'bloody fool,' and then ran away like a coward. Captain Colthurst raised his rifle evidently with the intention of stopping him or frightening him, and fired in the air. The bullet, said witness, was evidently misplaced, as it went into the man's abdomen. Skeffington at this time was surrounded by the soldiers.

Mr Healy: Are you aware that Coade was not the only man shot in the street by Captain Colthurst? That is the only man as far as I am aware that was shot by Captain Colthurst.

And you never heard that he had previously shot another man? No.

Sergeant Aldridge tells of the shooting of the three men

Sergeant John William Aldridge, 10th Royal Dublin Fusiliers, answering the Attorney-General, said he was on duty at the guardroom on the Wednesday morning, April 26th. He repeated the evidence given by him at the courtmartial on Capt. Bowen-Colthurst, which was that he heard and saw that officer order out the three men—Skeffington, Dickson and MacIntyre—into the yard behind the guardroom, where they were shot.

Cross-examined by Mr Healy: The men were neither pinioned nor blindfolded.

Did they get any time to say their prayers? They did not.

Did they know they were going to their death? I don't think they did.

Were they shot in the back or in the front? Through the front, and the bullets penetrated through the back.

Do you say that when the guns were presented at them neither of them said anything—didn't they ask for a priest? Not in my hearing.

Beside Captain Colthurst, yourself, and the seven men, were any other persons present? I am sure there were not.

Do you say that none of the men protested against being shot? They didn't mention anything at all in my hearing.

Did they utter even a cry? No

Your account is that these three men remained mute as statues during that proceeding? That is right.

Did they make even a gesture? Nothing at all. They obeyed orders and marched to the wall.

Do you suggest that this man Dickson, a Scotchman, who had nothing to do with the rebellion, made no protest against his death? No, sir; it was all too sudden.

The Chairman: Did you know at the time who was in command of the soldiers at the barracks? No; I had come in only the evening before, like other soldiers who were in danger. There were three sailors who took refuge in a similar way.

Were there any sailors in the firing party? No.

You told us that Captain Colthurst said he wanted the three men out to speak to them? Yes.

Did he speak to them? Only to tell them to go to the wall.

Did he ever accuse them of anything? No.

Did he ever explain to them that he was going to shoot them? No.

Did you feel that you had no alternative but to obey his orders? No. I did not understand that he was going to have them shot. It was a surprise to me, and the men themselves did not realise what was going to happen. When he asked for the seven men I thought he wanted them as an escort.

Did anybody make any sort of protest at all? No; there was no one there to do it.

Lieutenant Tooley

Lieutenant Tooley, 6th Royal Irish Rifles, deposed to having conveyed a message to Captain Colthurst after the shooting to the effect that the body of Skeffington was showing signs of life. Captain Colthurst then ordered Skeffington to be killed.

Lieutenant Morgan

Lieutenant Morgan, 3rd Royal Irish Rifles, adjutant on duty at Portobello at the time of the shooting, repeated the evidence he gave before the courtmartial on Captain Bowen-Colthurst.

Cross-examined by Mr Healy: Did you receive any written communication from Headquarters, Irish Command? No, not till about 6th May, when an order was received to place Captain Colthurst under arrest.

Did you communicate to the Garrison Adjutant, Dublin Castle, the fact of the three murders? I did, about 11.15 in the morning of the occurrence.

Who, as far as you know, was the recipient of that report? So far as I know, it was the Garrison Adjutant, Captain Byrne. In accordance with orders, witness made a written report to the Garrison Adjutant on 1st or 2nd May. Witness went on to say that Mr Skeffington was searched by Captain Colthurst when he was brought in. The things found on him were brought by Captain Colthurst to witness, and he had them locked up in his safe until he handed them over to the Chaplain, Father O'Loughlin, about May 5th. Captain Colthurst never got a key from him for Mr Skeffington's house. There was a document produced at the courtmartial which had upon it an endorsement in the name of Captain Colthurst to the effect that it had been found on the person of Mr Skeffington on the night of April 25th.

Mr Powell: That is a printed document purporting to give the alleged disposition of the troops in Dublin.

Mr Healy: Was that document one of those that were handed to you on the Tuesday night by Captain Colthurst? It was not.

Mr Edelstein intervenes

When the Commission resumed its sitting, on Thursday, 24th August, the inquiry was held in the Court of Appeal, Four Courts, the court of the Land Judge, which was occupied the first day, having been found inconvenient for the accommodation of the many people interested in the proceedings.

Mr Edelstein, rising from one of the back benches, said: Sir, I am the person named Edelstein referred to in the cross-examination by Mr Healy of Sergeant Maxwell, and in that he was made terrible insinuations which imperils my own life, I desire to give evidence.

The Chairman said if Mr Edelstein could make it convenient to attend during the day they would have an opportunity to consider whether they should permit him to give evidence.

Lieutenant Morgan, answering Mr Healy, said the bodies were buried uncoffined under the direction of the medical officer (Major Balch) and the engineering officer (Major Guinness). They were wrapped in sheets and laid in unconsecrated ground.

Was a ring stripped from Mr Skeffington's finger and denied to his wife? That I could not say. The medical officer will probably account for that.

Was Mr Skeffington wearing a little badge: 'Votes for Women'? I could not say.

Was that badge and ring kept from the widow for weeks and weeks, until by persistent applications she got them from Dublin Castle? I don't know.

What became of the effects of Mr Dickson? They were handed over to his mother.

The prisoners Dickson and MacIntyre were, as you know, arrested in Alderman Kelly's tobacco shop? They were.

Who instructed Captain Colthurst to go and effect that raid? We consulted the General Officer Commanding; we told him that we had a report that rebels were in occupation of Kelly's house, and he directed us to send a party to the house.

Now, about this man Edelstein, when did you first see him? The first time I saw Edelstein was on the Sunday following Easter Sunday.

Was that the first you heard of him? I had heard of him on the morning of that day.

Was he then supposed to be in custody? He was not in custody.

Was he ever in your custody? He was.

When did he come into it? On that Sunday night.

Arrest of Dickson and MacIntyre

You knew, of course, that he was in Kelly's shop on the night Dickson and MacIntyre were arrested? Alderman Kelly told me about him.

What was he arrested for? An officer reported that Edelstein was in Kelly's shop giving out cigars wholesale to the public, and as a result of that report I inquired of Alderman Kelly, who was then in prison. In consequence of that report, and Alderman Kelly having told me that Edelstein had no right to be in his house—

Was that why he was arrested? He got into the barracks by some manner on Sunday night and he was detained and brought before Colonel McCammond next day. Colonel McCammond was disposed to release him.

He was not released? There were seventeen men that the colonel was disposed to release, but the GOC's instructions were that all the men were to be detained and sent to Richmond Barracks.

The Chairman: Do you say that when you first saw Edelstein in barracks he was not under arrest? He was under arrest.

Mr Healy: Were the arrangements connected with the barracks so loose that in the middle of a rebellion a man like this could get inside your gates without your knowledge? Well, he should not have got in. Perhaps he made some excuse to get in. he told me that he came to see Major Sir Francis Vane.

Did he make a statement—a remarkable

statement—to the prejudice of Alderman Kelly to justify his (Kelly's) arrest? He had so much to say that it is very hard to remember what he did say. (Laughter.) He had too much to say.

Did he make a statement about bombs shattering Kelly's windows?

The Attorney-General said this was going beyond the scope of the inquiry. If these matters were allowed the inquiry would be endless.

The Commission ruled out the question.

Mr Healy: I want to show that my client Dickson was arrested on the information of this man Edelstein.

Mr Edelstein: That is an awful lie. I will be called as a witness, and Mr Healy can make as much as he likes out of me, and, being a Jew, he has his bait.

Mr Chairman: If you do not keep quiet you must go outside.

Mr Healy: I want to show that Dickson was arrested on the information of this man Edelstein, whose contributor he was. I want to bring out the facts connected with that arrest. I want to show that there was no one in Kelly's shop with hostile intent.

The Chairman: Dickson was arrested on Tuesday night. The conversation between the witness and Edelstein took place on the following Sunday? Yes.

Then that conversation could not have led to the arrest of Dickson.

Was it reported to you that Edelstein was on Alderman Kelly's premises when the arrest of Dickson and MacIntyre took place? It was, by Alderman Kelly.

Mr Healy: Do you know that Edelstein was what was called a 'spotter' for the military? I did not. I heard about him being a great linguist.

Captain Colthurst's report

The Chairman referred to the report of the shooting made by Captain Colthurst on 26th April, in which he stated that from the documents he had found on the three men, he believed they were very dangerous characters, and that he attached to the report the documents referred to.

Witness said he believed the only documents attached were some papers found upon Mr Skeffington. He had seen the previous night the other papers taken from Dickson and MacIntyre, and in his opinion there was nothing incriminating in them. Witness had copies made of these documents, and handed them in.

The Chairman said there were two Skeffington documents, which he read. One was a letter which obviously had nothing to do with the disturbance, and the other was a draft for a proposed civic guard to protect shops.

Witness said he had seen them on the Tuesday night, and attached no importance to them. The added that later on, about the 4th or 5th of May, Captain Colthurst came to witness and asked to attach to his report of the shooting some documents which he had obtained in Mr Skeffington's house. He did attach these documents.

Major Rosborough

Major James Rosborough, of the 3rd Batt. Royal Irish Rifles, examined by the Attorney-General, stated that Colonel McCammond went on sick leave on the 23rd April and did not return till 29th. Witness was in the barracks on Easter Monday and also on Tuesday. He first heard of the shooting of these men about 10.35 on Wednesday morning, when Captain Colthurst himself reported he had ordered them to be shot. He had not known of the arrest of a man named Skeffington until after the shooting. The same applied to the other men. He might have heard that so many people had been detained, but he had no particular information about them. He heard the next day that Captain Colthurst had taken out Mr Skeffington, but he had no recollection of having heard that he had been taken out as a hostage.

Replying to the Chairman, witness said he gave orders to Captain Colthurst to make a search of Kelly's shop, but he gave no order of any kind as to taking Mr Skeffington with him either as a hostage or in any other capacity. In fact, he had no recollection of Skeffington's name being mentioned that night, or of the other prisoners' names being mentioned. There might have been a casual remark about them, and it would be in order for Captain Colthurst to have reported what had happened at Kelly's, but it was a time of great pressure, and it had made no impression on his memory.

It would be a very unusual thing for a captain to take a civilian prisoner out of the guardroom when he was going on an expedition of that sort? Most unusual. I want it very clearly understood that the word 'hostage' was never mentioned. If it had been I am quite certain it would have fixed itself on my mind.

Captain Colthurst's verbal report

In reply to further questions witness said the first he heard of the shooting when he was walking across the barrack square. Capt. Colthurst came up to witness and said he had shot three prisoners on his own responsibility, and he possibly would get into trouble about it, and that he would likely be hanged for it, or something like that.

That is to the best of your recollection? I am quite certain of that.

The Chairman: When you learned that Capt. Colthurst had gone out contrary to your orders on the Friday, did you make an inquiry? I do not think I was in command then. He did go out on a different occasion against orders, and I brought him before the colonel.

Lieutenant Colonel McCammond

Lieut.-Col. McCammond, Commanding the 3rd Royal Irish Rifles, examined by Mr Powell, said he had been in hospital from April 23rd to the 29th. When he returned to Portobello Barracks he heard of the shootings, and that Capt. Colthurst was the author of the tragedies.

In reply to Mr Healy the witness said that Major Sir Francis Vane was 'displaced' in Portobello Barracks on May 1st. There was a Court of Inquiry held at Belfast on May 9th as to the shootings.

Lieut.-Colonel McCammond, referring to an earlier question by Mr Healy relating to the repairing of the marks made in the wall by the bullets which killed the three men, said the marked bricks were taken out and replaced by others so that military prisoners exercising in the yard might not see them.

Major Guinness said that he had authorised the thing to be done.

Captain Murphy

Captain Murphy, 1st Royal Irish Fusiliers, gave evidence of having, by order, with a party of men, visited the house of Thomas Dickson in Harrington street where he found a black bag, which he sent by a lame soldier to the nearest picket, which was at Alderman Kelly's shop. It remained there for a short time, and it was afterwards sent to the barracks.

Sergeant Claxton, 4th Royal Irish Fusiliers, who was stationed in charge of Alderman Kelly's shop deposed to having received the bag and sending it along to the barracks. The witness caused laughter in court when in reply to Mr Healy he said that Alderman Kelly had asked him to arrest him. 'He said he wanted to be arrested, and I told him I wouldn't,' added the witness.

MRS SHEEHY SKEFFINGTON'S EVIDENCE

Mrs Skeffington, widow of Mr Sheehy Skeffington, was examined on Friday, 25th August, and deposed to the difficulty she had experienced in obtaining information as to the fate of her husband. She then described the raid made by Captain Colthurst and a body of soldiers on her residence at Grosvenor place, Rathmines, on the Friday evening. They came to the place after seven o'clock in the evening. The first she heard of it was the sound of a volley of firing, and then the smashing of glass. There was no preliminary knocking or demanding of admission. When the soldiers entered Captain Colthurst ordered witness and her little boy to put up their hands. The little boy gave a cry, and witness put her arms around him. She believed she said, 'These are the defenders of women and children.' The man who was in charge—she later learned that he was Captain Colthurst—asked her very insolently who were the occupants of the house. In the meantime parties of soldiers had burst into the house by the rear and went into all the rooms. Captain Colthurst then placed witness and her child and maid in the drawingroom, and put them under arrest. They were kept there for three hours while the soldiers were ransacking the house and taking away papers and books. The latter included text books in German, French, Russian, and other languages. Referring to the German books, one soldier made the remark 'Apparently, sir he was in correspondence with the Kaiser.' (Laughter.) Her husband being a journalist, and editor of the *Irish Citizen*, had a great lot of papers of all kinds in the house. All these and other property were taken away in a motor car. The soldiers occupied the house for three hours, and others guarded it all night. She also described the incidents of a second raid, when her maid was taken away and detained for some days. Many of the articles taken from her house had not been returned, and it was only on the 23rd May, after endless trouble, and by the assistance of Sir Francis Vane, that she got her husband's ring. She had never received formal notice of the death of her husband. Every scrap of information she had received was gathered as the result of endless research. She would like to have some evidence as to whether any medical man saw the body of her husband immediately after his death.

The Chairman said that would be attended to, and the Court adjourned.

Mr Edelstein's denials.

When the Commission resumed its sittings on Saturday, 26th August, Mr Edelstein again intervened.

The Chairman: We may as well dispose of this at once. Let me ask you this first of all—were you present when Mr Dickson was arrested? No, I was not there.

Were you there when Mr MacIntyre was arrested? No.

Did you know anything at all about their intended arrest before it took place? Not at all. I never knew Dickson, and never spoke to him or wrote for him.

You knew nothing about it at all? Nothing about the arrest of Dickson or MacIntyre. I introduced Major Sir Francis Vane to Alderman Kelly, but I did not know he was going to arrest him.

That is all that happened? Yes.

And you know nothing about the arrest of Mr Skeffington? Nothing at all. It is all bosh, Mr Healy's statement, from beginning to end.

It was stated that you were a 'spotter' to the military, and you have already denied you were a 'spotter' to the military? I was no such thing.

I understand it is not true? Not at all.

Mrs Skeffington recalled

Mrs Skeffington was recalled, and in reply to Mr Healy, KC, she said she had no portrait of the Kaiser in her house at the time of the raid.

In fact had you long before the war a little penny school flag which you used in teaching about the Kaiser? Yes, I got it at a bazaar long before the war.

Did you read a statement on the 2nd May published in the London Press that your husband was killed in a green uniform, fighting on the side of the rebels? I did.

That was, of course, untrue? Yes.

Evidence of Mrs Kettle

Mrs Kettle, wife of Lieutenant TM Kettle, who was

killed in action, and sister of Mrs Skeffington, was then examined, and deposed to conversations about the disappearance of Mr Skeffington. From the Wednesday several reports were received, but they seemed simply fairy tales, and they gave no credence to them. On the Friday they heard from a good source that Mr Skeffington had been shot. Witness and Mrs Culhane, another sister, went to the Rathmines Police Station to make inquiries, but they said they knew nothing, and directed them to Portobello Barracks. As witness thought there might be some difficulty in gaining access to the barracks, they decided to ask in the first instance for her brother, Lieutenant Sheehy, who was on duty in Dublin at the time. Having asked as to Lieutenant Sheehy witness and Mrs Culhane were admitted though the first gate. At the second gate there was some difficulty, but finally they got in. They met a junior officer—she thought he belonged to the Munster Fusiliers—and he said he knew their brother, but had no information as to where he was doing duty. Then they mentioned the name of Mr Skeffington. The young officer got very confused and blushed all over. He said, 'Is he your brother-in-law,' and she said 'Yes.' The officer excused himself for a minute and consulted with some other soldiers and officers. He came back and asked some other questions about Mr Skeffington. He would excuse himself every other minute, and that went on for over half an hour. Then he came back and said he must place both of them under arrest. They asked why, and he replied that they had received information that she and her sister were Sinn Feiners. They replied, 'Of course that is absurd,' that they had never in any way been identified with the Sinn Fein party. The officer then said he regretted he must place them under arrest. He then ordered an armed guard of about twelve men to take them to the orderly room. They were interrogated there. After ten minutes an officer came whom they later recognised as Capt. Colthurst. He was, said witness, 'a cool collected type of Englishman (Laughter). His eye struck us as having the cold cruel look which goes with an unimaginative nature.' (Renewed laughter.) having given them a military salute Capt. Colthurst asked what they wanted. They first said they wanted to inquire about their brother, Lieut. Sheehy. They then said they also wished information about Mr Skeffington. This, said witness, was on the Friday after the shooting. Capt. Colthurst said, 'I know nothing whatever about Mr Skeffington.' The young officer who was also present, at this looked uneasy. Mrs Culhane then said that was strange, as they had definite information that Mr Skeffington had been arrested and brought to Portobello and that they had also heard as a matter of fact that he had been shot. The young officer then said something to Capt. Colthurst *sotto voce*, and Capt. Colthurst said—'I have no information concerning Mr Skeffington that is available, and the sooner you leave the barracks the better.'

The Chairman: Are you quite certain in answer to the first question that Capt. Colthurst said he knew nothing about Mr Skeffington? Absolutely clear, because it gave us a glimpse of hope.

Then his second expression struck you as different? It confirmed our suspicions.

Witness then described their exit from the barracks. They were speaking to each other as they were being conducted to the gate. Capt. Colthurst sent soldiers to tell them not to speak. They were then ordered not to look round—to keep their eyes right. The guard left them at the gate, and a second lieutenant conducted them to the end of the military road, where they were told not to reveal anything they had seen or heard on the premises.

Station Sergeant Murphy

Station Sergeant Murphy, Rathmines Barracks, said he was present in court when Sergeant Claxton, RIF, stated he got directions from the police in Rathmines to effect an arrest at Mrs Skeffington's house in Grosvenor place, but witness could find no record of any such instructions. The military sergeant brought to the police station a maid servant named Farrelly who had been employed by Mrs Skeffington. When he brought the girl in the only statement made by the sergeant was that he found her at Mrs Skeffington's. That girl was kept in custody from the Monday until 6th May when she was released by direction of the Provost Marshal.

Witness handed to the Chairman the police file of directions issued from the station to the military, which he examined as to the method of record followed by the police.

Witness volunteered the statement that although he had no record of instructions being sent to the military he would not go so far as to say that no message was sent.

The shooting of Coade

Laurence Byrne was examined as to the shooting of the young man Coade at the corner of Richmond Hill, Rathmines road. He said he and Coade and another young man named Keogh had been at a sodality meeting and were standing at the corner of Richmond Hill, just about to leave for their homes, when the forty or fifty soldiers emerged from the military road, led by a tall officer. Coade was smoking a cigarette when the officer came forward and asked what they were doing out at that hour of the night, and if they did not know martial law had been proclaimed. Witness said they did not know. The officer turned to a soldier and said 'Bash him'. Coade was then struck with the butt-end of a rifle. No impudent or offensive language had been used by any of them before Coade was struck. They then separated, Keogh going off on his bicycle one way, and Coade and witness in the opposite direction. Then witness saw a flash and heard a report, and looking back he saw that Coade had fallen.

A witness named Devine, who was on the opposite side of the road at the time, said he heard part of the conversation between the officer and Coade and the others. The men used no insulting or blasphemous language to the military. Witness saw the officer take a revolver out of his belt and fire a shot. One of the civilians fell.

A city commercial traveller named Hughes, who was also on the Rathmines road at the time, said he was challenged by the tall officer, who presented a revolver at him. Witness was with a friend at the time. As he saw that other civilians were on the road, and thinking that something had happened, he held up his hands and said, 'Not with anybody,' intending to convey to the mind of the officer that he was not with the other party. The officer then pointed the revolver at witness's friend, and witness said, 'He's with me.' The officer then aimed straight at a man who was walking away, fired, and the man dropped. The man who fell was about twelve or fifteen yards away from the officer who fired. Witness wished to make it plain that, so far as he could see, the man was not running away. He was walking.

Miss Kelly

Miss Kelly, sister of Alderman James Kelly, examined by Mr White, spoke of the raid by the military on their shop and residence on the 25th April. She said she remembered Dickson and MacIntyre coming to her house on Tuesday night. MacIntyre had come to see her brother about some Indian students. Dickson ran into the house when he heard the shooting by the military on the street. The military threw a bomb into the shop, and the shop assistant was wounded by it. The door had been closed, and it was forced open by the soldiers with their bayonets. When the soldiers entered they looked for the telephone, and she was going to show it to them when she heard an officer say: 'Now lads, another bomb for upstairs.' The bomb, however, was not thrown, for she saw that officer coming downstairs with the bomb in his hand. The officer shouted to those in the house, 'hands up,' and said: 'Remember, I could shoot you like dogs. Martial law is proclaimed. I am an Irishman myself. We have shot persons on the street before we came in.' The lieutenant confirmed that by saying: 'We have done it.' The names of those in the house were taken, and MacIntyre said he was the editor of *The Searchlight.* The Captain said: 'Another rebel paper,' and someone said, 'No, a loyal paper,' The captain caught MacIntyre by the collar and said: 'Take that man, and if he resists shoot him like a dog.' When Dickson and MacIntyre were arrested an officer told her to stay where she was or she would be shot. She remembered Dickson's trunk being brought to the house by a lame soldier. The military were then in possession. The trunk arrived after her brother had been arrested and taken away. The soldier sat down on the trunk outside the door, and when someone asked him who he was he said he was the Prince of Wales, wounded home from the front. (Laughter.)

Sir Francis Vane

Major Sir Francis Vane, in reply to Mrs Healy, said that when the rebellion broke out he came to Dublin and reported himself at Portobello Barracks. His original regiment was the Scots Greys. He served in the South African War, and was in Dublin on recruiting business. While in Portobello Barracks he was second senior officer to Major Rosborough, and was superior in command to Captain Colthurst.

On Wednesday morning you were not consulted in any way by Captain Colthurst? No, not in the least. He heard of the death of the three men at nine o'clock on the evening of the day on which the occurrence took place. He first heard of it when on Rathmines road an old woman shouted after him, 'Murderer, Skeffington.'

The Chairman: We know you had no responsibility for the shooting.

Witness: It would not have occurred if I had. In reply to further questions, witness stated that he was instructed to arrest Alderman Kelly by Major Rosborough. When he arrested Alderman Kelly he did not see any trunk taken by the soldiers. Major Rosborough gave orders that Captain Colthurst was not to leave barracks. On the following Monday witness was ordered to give up command and hand it over to Captain Colthurst by Colonel McCammond. He reported the shootings, and in consequence of no action having been taken he went to London, reported the matter to Mr Tennant, and saw Lord Kitchener.

Alderman JJ Kelly

Alderman JJ Kelly, in reply to Mr Healy, said that he was a Justice of the Peace, and was High Sheriff of the City of Dublin for the year 1912-1913. On Easter Monday, when the outbreak occurred, his shop was open as usual. He had no knowledge of the outbreak or that it would take place. On Tuesday his shop was also open. MacIntyre was with him that day and dined with him. He was a leading anti-Larkinite journalist in Dublin, and was strongly opposed after Larkin's departure from Dublin to Connolly. A well-known citizen, a prominent Conservative, also shared his hospitality. About eleven o'clock that night he went out to get fruit for MacIntyre, who was a teetotaller. Up to that time Dickson had not come upon the premises. Dickson never stayed in his house.

Was there, before the soldiers came, anything in the nature of arms, ammunition, seditious literature, or anything prejudicial to the State on your premises? No, on the contrary, there were important documents got on me from the Ministry of Munitions, which I gave to Sir Francis Vane on Portobello Bridge. He was in favour of the Allies. No shots were fired from his premises, and no sniping took place there. He did nothing to provide suspicion. He got fourteen young men commissions in the Army and one in the Navy. He was away about seven minutes getting fruit, and on his way back he saw Captain Colthurst, with about twenty or thirty men in single file, making a raid on his premises. As he was prevented from entering his own house, he lay flat on the street for about twenty minutes to avoid the rushes of the military. He appealed to two gentlemen who were in Messrs Crowe's premises to let him in, but they shut the window. A lady who lived across the street called to him to run across. He had to stay in the house that night. His sister was told by Captain Colthurst that night that he had shot a man in the street fifty yards away, and she naturally assumed it was he. On the following morning he returned to his shop and found it wrecked. He was arrested that evening by Sir Francis Vane's party.

In reply to Mr Rearden, witness said that he had absolutely nothing to do with the Sinn Fein movement or the rebellion. At the outbreak of the war he applied for a commission in the Life Guards. He owed his life to Sir Francis Vane, Major Rosborough, and Adjutant Morgan.

The Chairman stated that it was a time of very great confusion and anxiety, and the Commission was absolutely certain from the evidence that the answers of the witness were entirely confirmed by everything shown there. The Commissioners were satisfied that there was nothing to justify any reflection on Alderman Kelly or on his undoubted devotion to the cause of which he had spoken.

Lieut. AS Wilson

Lieutenant AS Wilson related that Lieutenant Dobbin came to him at the gate, and told him to go to the Adjutant (Lieutenant Morgan) and report to him that Captain Colthurst wanted to take out three prisoners from the guardroom to shoot them. He carried the message to the Adjutant, who told him that he could give no authority for such a proceeding, and that if Colthurst did it he would do it on his own responsibility. Using a bicycle, he lost no time in coming back to Lieutenant Dobbin, and just as he had finished giving him the message he heard shots ring out. To the best of his belief, he told the Adjutant that Captain Colthurst was going to take the prisoners out 'to shoot them.'

Adjutant Morgan said he was perfectly sure that the message he received was that Captain Colthurst was taking three prisoners out of the guardroom. Lieutenant Wilson said nothing about shooting. Witness had already heard that Captain Colthurst had taken out Mr Skeffington the night before, and his impression was that he was taking out the three men just as he had taken out Skeffington.

Mr Skeffington's letters

The Chairman, addressing Dr Skeffington, (Father of the late Mr Francis Sheehy Skeffington), said that they could not travel outside the scope of their reference, but if there was anything he could tell the Commission about the facts they would be glad to hear him.

Dr Skeffington said that he was not in Dublin at the time of the occurrence. He was in County Down, and his son and little boy came to see him the week before Easter. His son was very uneasy about the way things were going on in Dublin.

The Chairman said that nobody in the inquiry made the slightest accusation against him in any attempt to justify the rebellion.

Dr Skeffington said he wished they had, as it had been insinuated in Irish and English papers. There was no opportunity of contradicting it. In Ireland the papers were afraid of the Censor.

The Chairman stated that the Commission would take care to deal with the matter in its report in a way in which it would not be interfered with by the Censor.

Dr Skeffington then proceeded to read extracts from personal letters written to him by his son. In a letter dated 26th March Mr Skeffington wrote: 'Anything may happen in the next months. A safety valve militant, but not militarism, is needed, and will be still more needed if, and when, the inevitable disillusionment comes to the physical force people. Such a safety valve will, I hope, be provided by the anti-taxation movement, which, as you see, is going ahead very fast.' Dr Skeffington also quoted from the headings of articles written by his son in his paper, *The Irish Citizen.*

The alleged secrecy arrangement

Rev. EF O'Loughlin, one of the chaplains to the barracks, was recalled when the Commission resumed on Monday, 28th August.

The Chairman, addressing the rev. gentlemen, said their attention had been called to a statement appearing in some of the newspapers, which might possibly seem to cast some reflection upon the witness, and they thought it fair that he should have an opportunity of explaining the matter. It was a statement which might be thought by the public to suggest that Father O'Loughlin had not given information as freely as he might, and that he had taken part in some arrangement to suppress or not to publish the facts that came to his knowledge. Did you, asked the Chairman, put any difficulties in the way of Mrs Skeffington seeing you? None whatsoever.

Were you in any way a party to any arrangement not to let the relatives know? None whatever.

The Chairman: I think it is right that should be clearly understood.

Witness: I considered, being an official in the public service, that I was debarred from making use of any information that I would acquire in my public capacity.

Mr Healy: May I put this question—Did he not inform the Coade family of the death of their boy?

Witness: I did, because that was not a case that happened inside the barracks. He was brought into the barracks, and I was sent for by the medical officer of the barracks, and the medical officer of the barracks asked me to inform the boy's parents.

The Chairman: We want it to be quite clear as to whether you were a party to any arrangement, if there was an arrangement, to conceal the facts? There was no arrangement to conceal the facts whatsoever.

Doctor who examined the bodies

Mr Healy said he felt specially grateful to the Headquarters Staff for their efforts to produce Lieutenant Dobbin. Counsel went on to to say that Dr Balch had been sent to Sierra Leone. Dr Balch had occupied perhaps the most important position that could have been entrusted to an officer here, having regard to the vast garrison in Dublin. He was the head of a particular branch of the medical service, but had been suddenly jerked out of Dublin.

The Chairman: If you have an application to make—

Mr Healy said Dr Balch examined the bodies after death. He would be in a position to tell them how many bullet wounds each body bore, and they would be able to draw some conclusions from that fact, and if, in fact, he declined to certify that Capt. Colthurst was insane. He would ask that Dr Balch should be produced.

The Chairman: Oh, no. We have made it perfectly and absolutely plain that in our view we are not inquiring into the state of mind of anybody. We have an honest desire and the fixed intention to ascertain the material facts and events. We are not going outside our reference, but we will consider what you have said.

Lieut. Dobbin's Evidence

When the Commission resumed its sittings on Thursday, 31st August,

Lieutenant William Leonard Price Dobbin, of the 2nd Royal Irish Rifles, for whose attendance the Court adjourned on Monday, was examined by the Attorney-General. He said he had been on active service in France. He left the trenches on Monday night and arrived in Dublin on Wednesday. He was on duty at Portobello Barracks on Easter Monday and the following day, and was in command of the guard at the main gate. He repeated the evidence he gave at the Courtmartial.

Cross-examined by Mr Healy, witness said that he left for France on 25th June with a number of officers, and when he returned that morning he reported to Colonel Stanton. The only thing he knew about what was going on at the inquiry was what he read in the newspapers in France. He was not able to get the whole of the proceedings. Witness stated that he knew he was in command of the guard. He never mounted guard before. He did not know in accordance with his duty that he had no power to discharge a prisoner from the guardroom. He did not know that only the Commanding Officer had that power, nor did he know that a prisoner should be brought to the orderly room before he was discharged.

What authority was there to tie Mr Skeffington's hands behind his back and send him out as a hostage, he being under your control? I had no authority.

Did you see him taken out and bound with his hands behind his back? I did.

Who gave the orders for that ? I don't remember.

Did you protest? No.

The Chairman: Was Capt. Bowen-Colthurst there? He was.

Witness also stated that he was not acquainted with the regulations as regards hostages. He was not told what Mr Skeffington was being taken out for, nor did he know where he was being taken.

Mr Healy: What did you do on that Tuesday night to protect the safety of your prisoners? Nothing, except I informed the Adjutant of what was happening. Witness said he sent the following report to the Adjutant:

'April 25, 11.10 p.m.

'An armed party under Capt. JC Bowen-Colthurst has just passed through my guard demanding and taking with him the last captured prisoner, Sheehy Skeffington.'

That would seem to show that you were excusing yourself for letting the prisoner out? No.

Now, with eighteen fully armed men and two lieutenants, why did you not defend your prisoners? Captain Colthurst was my senior officer.

But you were responsible for the guard? Yes.

The Chairman: Captain Bowen-Colthurst came and said he would take the prisoners out, and he did.

Mr Healy: And this gentleman let him do it.

The Chairman: I think on this particular point the situation is quite clear. This is a young officer. Capt. Colthurst was an officer of standing and authority; and, right or wrong, be came and took these prisoners out.

Mr Healy (to witness): Is it your view that you had no authority there as compared with Captain Colthurst? This is my view; I had no authority.

Why didn't you say to Captain Colthurst—'Give us a reprieve for 2½ seconds while I am getting the cyclist back?' Again I say that he was my senior officer.

Why didn't you say to Colthurst—'Go and finish your own dirty work.'

The Chairman: This is very painful. I don't see the advantage of this.

In answer to the Chairman, the witness said that he was only nineteen years of age, and that he had entered the army shortly after he left school. He got his commission in June, 1915. Up to April last he had had no experience at all of fighting, or of shots being fired in anger or in self-defence, and the 25th and 26th of April last was the first occasion on which he had served as an officer of the guard.

Mrs Sheehy Skeffington's Statement

Her Husband's Last Hours

The following statement was published by Mrs Sheehy Skeffington respecting the arrest and shooting of her husband.

I last saw my husband on Tuesday evening, April 25th, between 5.15 and 5.30 at Westmoreland Chambers. He had called a meeting there to stop looting (see enclosed poster), and was waiting to see if any people would attend same. On that and the previous day he had been active personally, with help from bystanders, at the same work, and had succeeded in stopping some looting by personal efforts and appeals. All this, there is independent evidence to testify. On Monday afternoon outside Dublin Castle an officer was reported bleeding to death in the street and, the crowd being afraid, owing to the firing, to go to his assistance, my husband himself went, at imminent danger to his life, to drag away the wounded man to a place of safety, to find, however, that by that time the body had been rescued by some soldiers, there being merely left a pool of blood. This incident can also be corroborated.

He stated to me that if none turned up to help on Tuesday at the meeting to prevent looting that he would come home as usual to his house at 11 Grosvenor place. He was afterwards seen by several friends (whose testimony I possess) going home about 6.30. In the neighbourhood of Portobello Bridge he was arrested, unarmed and unresisting. He never carried or possessed any arm of any description, being, as is well known, a pacifist and opposed to the use of physical force.

He was conducted in military custody to Portobello Barracks, where he was shot without trial on that night or early the following morning. No priest was summoned to attend him, no notification was, or has since been, given to me (his wife) or to his family of his death, and no message written before his death has been allowed to reach me.

Repeated inquiries at the barracks and elsewhere have been met with refusal to answer, and when my sisters, Mrs Kettle and Mrs Culhane, called at Portobello Barracks on Thursday, April 27th, to inquire they were put under temporary arrest.

House Surrounded

On Friday night, April 28th, a large military force surrounded my husband's house at 11 Grosvenor place, fired without warning on the windows in front, which they burst through without waiting for the door to be opened. They put myself, my son, aged seven, to whom they shouted 'Hands up!' and my maid (the sole occupants) under arrest, and remained in the house for over three hours. They found no ammunition of any kind, but burst locks, etc., and took away with them a large number of documents, newspapers, letters and books, as well as various personal property, such as linen, tablecloths, trunks, a photograph of Mr Keir Hardie and Mr Davitt, a picture of the Kilmainham prisoners of 1882, a green flag, etc. Most of the books taken were German and Irish books (grammars, school texts, etc.) relating to my work as a teacher of modern languages and my husband's journalistic work. One officer remarked that this was not a 'very exciting search.'

On Monday, May 1, during my absence, the soldiers again entered the house and searched it, and took prisoner Margaret Farrelly (the only occupant), a temporary maid whom I had engaged, my former maid having been too terrified to stay. She was detained in custody until the following Saturday (May 6) in the Rathmines Police Station, and kept there in custody without the knowledge of her friends, without any charge made against her. Finally the authorities allowed her to be released but without any apology or compensation.

I demand the fullest inquiry into all the above circumstances, and desire, as my husband's next-of-kin, to be legally represented at any inquiry that may take place.

(signed) HANNA SHEEHY SKEFFINGTON
May 9, 1916

P.S.—Since the above was written my husband's body was dug up from Portobello Barracks and transferred to Glasnevin Cemetery, again without my knowledge.

The following are details of his last hours that have reached me through various private sources:

He refused to be blindfolded, and met death with a smile on his lips, saying before he died that the authorities would find out after his death what a mistake they made. He put his hand to his eyes, and the bullet passed through his hand to his brain.

The Poster

The poster referred to above and distributed in the city on Tuesday, April 25, when the police were cleared off the streets, is as follows:

'When there are no regular police on the streets it becomes the duty of the citizens to police the streets themselves to prevent such spasmodic looting as has taken place.

'Civilians (both men and women) who are willing to co-operate to this end are asked to attend at Westmoreland Chambers (over Eden Bros.) at 5 o'clock on this (Tuesday) afternoon.

'FRANCIS SHEEHY SKEFFINGTON.

St John Ambulance Brigade

Dr J Lumsden, Deputy Commissioner of the St John Ambulance Brigade (No. 12) Irish District, issued a detailed report of the work done by that body during the rebellion. The members, he said, lost no opportunity of rendering first aid to military, civilians, and rebels alike. The general efficiency of the various detachments was thoroughly tested, and not found wanting. Dr Lumsden submitted reports by his two chief executive officers, Mr WG Smith and Dr Ella Webb.

Mr Smith, in his report, stated that members of the Brigade performed duty in all the zones where fighting took place. These were roughly divided into three areas—From the Custom House to Kingsbridge; from Kingsbridge to Dublin Castle; and from Dublin Castle to Ringsend. From these areas wounded were collected by men and nurses, who went on foot and in ambulance waggons, rendering first aid and taking patients to hospital under circumstances of great danger and difficulty. The first move towards the organisation of first aid work was made by the late Corps Superintendent Holden Stodart, who, on Easter Monday telephoned the military offering help. On Wednesday a room in the Royal City of Dublin Hospital at Baggot street was placed at the disposal of the brigade, and in this area the first casualty was sustained. Corps Superintendent Holden Stodart, one of the most zealous and conscientious officers, was shot whilst proceeding with a stretcher party to the relief of a wounded soldier. His heroic death and noble example must ever be remembered amongst those who serve under that old order whose motto is 'Pro utilitate hominum'. Tribute is paid to the magnificent work performed by the motor ambulance service provided by the Irish Automobile Club, and the splendid courage and bravery shown by the drivers. A number of these ambulances, staffed by St John orderlies, were placed under the RAMC, and others worked with the civil ambulance under the direction of the Deputy Commissioner. Day by day these cars ran the gauntlet of bullet-swept streets, and were frequently struck by shots, and the dangers were accentuated at night when black darkness prevailed, no street lamps, no head lamps, and streets littered with obstacles.

Emergency Hospital at 40 Merrion Square

Dr Ella Webb, Lady District Superintendent, No. 12, Irish District, in a report of work done by the Nursing Divisions, says the chief work undertaken was the transformation of the War Hospital Supply Depot at 40 Merrion square into a temporary hospital. This was done in three hours, the first of the girls arriving at 2 p.m., and at 5 p.m. an amputation was going on in the improvised operating theatre, and half of the thirty beds hurriedly prepared in the wards were full.

The following staff was appointed:

Medical—Dr Edward Taylor, Dr TE Gordon, Sir Robert Woods, Dr McVittie, Dr Burgess.

Commandant—Dr Ella Webb.

Matrons (Day)—Miss Carson Rae. (Night)—Miss MacDonnell.

House Surgeons (Day)—Dr Crichton: (Night)—Dr Euphan Maxwell.

Canteen (Head)—Mrs Hignett (Assistant)—Mrs Newcomen.

Quartermaster—Mrs J Lumsden.

Sisters in Charge (Trained Nurses)—Misses Doherty, Butler, Elliott, Hall, Monan, Strahan, Ledwidge, Hughes, Hunter, O'Donoghue; Mrs Allman.

Stretcher Bearers—Dr W. Carnegie, and Messrs Haffield, WG Smith, GR Webb, Haughton, James H Webb, RH Keatinge, and Shannon.

VAD Helpers—Mrs Day Booth, Mrs Blood, Misses Boyd and W Butler, Mrs Lloyd Blood, Mrs Booth, Misses Ball, R Best, Ball, Bloxham, M Brown, Stanford, Campbell, Cahill, Cooney, Davies, Doherty, Mrs Draper, Misses Freeman, E Farquaharson, Frazer, Foote, Graham, Heany, Hurley, Booth Jones, Jeffares, Keatinge, Knox Gore, ML King, AK Lloyd, Mooney; Mrs McVittie; Misses D Millar, E McComas, S Mackenzie, Nielson, O'Kelly, Poole, Rawson, Robinson, Mrs Robinson; Misses Rothwell, Seeds, Smythe; Mrs Stokes, Misses Smith, Shaw, Smyth, Taylor, Traynor, Mrs Cecil Thompson, Miss Woods, Mrs Upton, Misses Doris Witz, Wrede; Mrs Barrington; Misses Lloyd Blood, FM Bell, Campbell, Clarke, Dovie, Drury, Darley, Fry, Figgis, Finny; Mrs Ford; Misses MH Farrer, Gray, Hall, Hughes; Mrs Jackson, Mrs Booth Jones, Mrs R Keatinge; Misses E Keegan, Leahy, Ledwidge, Meredith, V MacDonnell; Mrs Mercer, Mrs Manders; Misses Martin, O'Carroll, Orr, Pigott, Reilly, Muriel Poë, Rawson; Mrs R Sankey, Mrs Shannon; Misses Shaw, Stevenson, Slyne, Somerville, Simpson, Renny-Tailyour, Thompson, A Walshe, Wakefield, Wilson, M Webb, West.

Some of these members were unable to report early in the week for orders owing to military regulations.

Auxiliary Hospitals

Several auxiliary hospitals were equipped by other divisions. Among these were:

1. The Litton Hall, Leeson park, kindly lent by the Rev. Percy Phair, and staffed by Dr Winter, Miss A Butler, and the Leeson park Division.

2. The High School, Harcourt street, kindly lent by J Thompson, Esq., Headmaster, and staffed by Dr Cope, Dr Wayland, Dr Lane Joynt, Miss M Hamilton Johnstone, MB, BCh.; Mrs Howard Healy, Miss Weldon, and members of the Dundrum and Harcourt street Divisions. This hospital was greatly helped by a band of ladies at Dundrum, who organised an all-day working party for dressings, etc., and a food supply depot. Large quantities of

Doctor JOHN LUMSDEN, Deputy Commissioner St. John Ambulance Brigade, Director-General Joint V.A.D. Committee for Ireland.

Photo by] [*Stanley.*

Dr. ELLA WEBB, Lady District Superintendent St. John Ambulance Brigade, Dublin.

Dr. REGINALD C. PEACOCKE, Assistant County Director, Co. Dublin Red Cross, Dublin.

CORPS SUPERINTENDENT HOLDEN STODART, St. John Ambulance, killed while discharging his duty.

both food and dressings were provided, and at the time of the evacuation of the hospital at the end of the rebellion these supplies were sent to Mercer's Hospital, where they were most welcome.

Other auxiliary hospitals were got ready in private houses, viz. :

3. Miss Fletcher's house, 35 Fitzwilliam square.
4. Mrs Jackson's house, 11 Bushy park road, Rathgar.
5. Miss Meade's house, 32 Fitzwilliam square.

Happily, owing to the termination of the rebellion, these were not needed.

Other duties taken over by the Divisions or isolated members were the housing of refugee women and children, helping at RAMC dressing stations, carrying bales of dressing on stretchers (often through the firing line) to the various general hospitals that wanted them, feeding the poor, and rendering first aid to numerous civilians.

District Divisions

Great credit is due to the various Dublin Divisions of the St John Ambulance for the admirable promptitude with which they equipped immediately on receiving news of the outbreak. The following details have been officially supplied regarding the work done by the various Dublin Divisions of the Brigade:

City of Dublin Nursing Division.—Lady Superintendent, Miss Mowbray, Mrs Middleton Curtis (Lady Corps Treasurer), and many other members of the unit worked indefatigably in Kingstown, where so many soldiers were stationed.

Alexandra College Nursing Division.—Many members were on duty at the Auxiliary Hospital, 40 Merrion square.

Rathgar Nursing Division.—Lady Superintendent, Mrs Jackson, got 12 beds ready at her house, 11 Bushy park road, Rathgar, where Dr JJ Purser, Divisional Surgeon, gave his time and advice unsparingly. Fortunately, as the surrender of the rebel forces came so soon, it was unnecessary to use this hospital. Six members were on duty from the beginning at 40 Merrion square, including Mrs Lloyd Blood and Miss Wrede, who were put in temporary charge of wards until they were relieved by trained nurses.

Kingstown Nursing Division.—Monkstown House Auxiliary Hospital was immediately placed at the disposal of the Military Authorities, and was soon availed of. All the vacant beds were soon filled with wounded, and in addition several cases of men suffering from exposure and bad weather were sent in from the various districts.

Howth Nursing Division.—Two members of this unit gave valuable assistance at 40 Merrion square, and another worked unceasingly in the Adelaide Hospital.

Leeson Park Nursing Division.—By the kind permission of the Rev. Percy Phair, MA, the Litton Hall was equipped as an auxiliary hospital of 25 beds. Fortunately, it was found unnecessary to utilise this hospital to the full, although a couple of patients were treated there. Too much praise cannot be given to the way this detachment mobilised, worked, and disbanded with promptitude and earnestness, which is greatly to the credit of the months of hard work expended on this Division by their indefatigable Lady Superintendent, Miss MH Archer. In addition to this hospital, 12 of their members helped on 'night' and 'day' duty at 40 Merrion square.

St James's Gate Nursing Division.—Early in that fateful week the members offered their services to the city hospitals, and assisted greatly in looking after soldiers and poor refugees.

North Co. Dublin Nursing Division.—Most of these members took part in helping in 40 Merrion square, George V Hospital, and in the dressing station at the north side of the city. Others assisted refugees.

Dundrum Nursing Division.—Lady Superintendent, Miss Bird, was placed in charge of the High School Auxiliary Hospital, where excellent work was done, many patients being admitted during the week. In connection with this hospital a Food Supply Depot was also organised at Dundrum, and all praise is due to the splendid way in which this Division carried out its various duties. Harcourt Nursing Division worked in conjunction with above at the High School.

Fitzwilliam Nursing Division.—Lady Superintendent, Mrs McVittie was out of town, but returned on Tuesday, immediately reporting at the Deputy Commissioner's house. She, and many members of the Fitzwilliam unit were early on the scene when 40 Merrion square opened as a hospital, and worked untiringly all through.

The following Nursing Divisions were represented at 40 Merrion square: The Irish Nurse's Association by Miss Carson Rae, who acted as Matron (day); Maycourt Nursing Division; South Dublin Nursing Division; Orthopaedic Hospital Nursing Division; Dublin University Nursing Division, and Royal College of Science Nursing Division.

The Ambulance Workers

Appended to Dr Lumsden's report is the following list of names of St John Ambulance Brigade and others who were members of the ambulance divisions on duty during the rebellion:

Albany,—
Archibald, W
Armstrong,—
Baker,
Baker, A, MD
Bamford, J
Barrett, W
Bedlow, WJ
Bennett, L (V)
Bennett, W
Bodkin, J (V)
Boland, R
Bolton, RH
Bone, H
Bone, J
Bone, John
Boyd, WH
Boyle, P (driver)
Brown, R (V)
Burke, Granby
Byrne, R
Camp, A (driver)
Cantley, J (BRCS)
Carnegie, WC, MD
Carroll, J
Carte, W
Cassidy,—
Chadwick,—
Chaytor, HS
Christie, P
Cole VC
Convery, J
Cope, GP, MD
Craig, J
Crampton, Geo. (driver)
Crawford, CG
Cross, R
Delaney, M.
Dennison, P
Dick, W
Douglas, WJ (V)
Dowie, W (V)
Duggan, W
Emery, W (V)
Fetherstonhaugh,—(BRCS)
Fitzsimon, O'C (BRCS)
Fullerton,—
Gahan, J (V)
Gibson, J (driver)
Giltrap, Jas (V)
Gleeson, M (driver)
Gourlie, J
Gray, R
Greaves, J
Greville, J
Haffield, WMP
Halliday, GW
Hamilton, JB
Harrison, SJ
Haughton, CC
Haughton, Hugh
Healy, John
Helen, R
Hely, Howard (BRCS)
Hollinshead, AG
Homan, JF
Hughes,—
Hunt, Henry, MD
Hutchinson, E J
Hutson, Capt. (Pembroke Fire Brigade)
Iley, CE
Irwin, TF
Jameson, RW
Jardin, DS
Jarvis,—
Jewell, LW
Johnston, RE
Jones, EH
Jones, H
Kalia, R
Keatinge, Chas
Keatinge, Reg. H
Keely, CW
Kelly,—
Keogh, Myles, MD
Kimberly, A
King, JL
King, K (driver)
Kinnear, JA
Kiverson, G (V)
Know, A (V)
Land, CB
Law,—
Leach, EW
Leask, R
Lee, A
Lee, J (V)
Lightbown,—
Linehan, MF
Lumsden, J, MD
Lynd, JL
MacCormack, CJ, LRCS
Mahoney,—
Mains, WJ
Manson, Jas
Marlowe, JC
Maude, R
May, GH (wounded)
Maynard, WH
Mayne, HP
McCamley, H
McClaren, J (driver)
McClure, R
McCoy, N (driver)
McCreagh, J
McDonnell, W
McGowran, J
McMahon, JB
Monahan, HJ, BL
Monson, W
Moore, ALB
Moore, J
Morgan, F (driver)
Mulligan, A
Murphy, JJ
Murray, I
Newcomen, G
Nolan, S
Norway, NS (V)
O'Brien, E (driver)
O'Brien, JC
O'Callaghan, L
O'Hara,—
Oates, T
Orr, Professor W
Peat, R (BRCS)
Peck, W (driver)
Pender, G
Penny, W
Phillips,—
Pielou, PL
Prenter, CH
Preston,—
Rea,—
Reynolds, WH
Riley,—
Roberts, NL
Robinson, AH
Robinson, DP
Robinson, M (driver)
Robinson, ST (driver)
Roche, C
Roche, W Cheevers (driver)
Rooney, JW
Scott, HJ
Scott, RH (V)
Shannon, H
Smith, WG
Stodart, Holden (killed 26th April)
Stokes, H (driver)
Stronach, WM
Stuart, R W
Stuart, WB
Sullivan, DS
Symes, JM
Teeling, LA
Thompson, KO
Tolputt, LA
Trundle, JF
Tugwell, J (wounded)
Tyrell Smith, C.
Webb, GR, FTCD
Webb, James H
White, J (driver)
Whitton, HM
Wilson,GW
Woods, B
Woods, R
Young, SG
Young, WJ

Members of Nursing Divisions on Duty

Acton, Miss
Archer, Miss WH
Armstrong, Miss I
Baker, Mrs
Ball, Miss
Ball, Miss M
Barrett, Miss
Barrington, Mrs
Bateham, Miss
Battersby, Miss
Bell, Miss FM
Beresford, Mrs Pack-
Best, Miss
Best, Miss R
Bird, Miss C
Bigly, Miss
Blandford, Miss
Blood, Mrs
Blood, Mrs Lloyd
Blood, Miss Lloyd
Bloxham, Miss
Boud, Miss E
Booth, Mrs Day
Booth, Miss
Booth, Miss E
Boyd, Misses
Brown, Miss M
Brunker, Mrs
Butler, Miss W
Blackham, Miss
Cahill, Miss
Campbell, Miss
Campbell, Miss Stanford
Carroll, Miss
Clarke, Miss
Clay, Miss Keating
Collins, Miss
Cooney, Miss
Cope, Miss W
Courtenay, Miss R
Cox, Miss K
Craig, Miss
Crawford, Miss
Curtis, Mrs Middleton
Cutler, Nurse
Darley, Miss
Davidson, Miss
Davies, Miss
Dixon, Mrs F.
Doherty, Miss
Dovie, Miss
Draper, Mrs
Drury, Miss
Dudgeon, Miss
Duffin, Miss P
Duffin, Miss R
Dillon, Hon. G
Farquaharson, Miss E
Farquaharson, Miss M
Farrer, Miss
Figgis, Miss R
Finny, Miss
Ford, Mrs
Forde, Mrs
Foote, Miss
Fraser, Miss
Freeman, Miss
Fry, Miss
Geates, Mrs
Geats, Miss
Goodbody, Mrs R
Goodbody, Miss G
Gore, Miss Knox
Gorman, Miss
Graham, Miss
Graham, Miss R
Gray, Miss
Griffin, Misses
Griffith, Miss
Grubbins, Mrs
Gallagher, Miss L
Hall, Miss
Hamilton, Miss
Handcock, Hon. Mrs
Handcock, Miss V
Harkness, Mrs
Healy, Mrs Howard
Heany, Miss A
Hickey, Miss
Hignett, Mrs AH
Hodson, Misses
Hopking, Miss
Hughes, Miss
Hunter, Miss G
Hunter, Miss W
Hamilton, Miss
Hurley, Misses
Jackson, Mrs
Jameson, Miss
Jeffares, Miss
Jeffares, Miss J
Johnston, Miss L
Johnstone, Miss
Hamilton, MB
Jolly, Miss
Jones, Mrs Booth
Jones, Miss Booth
Keatinge, Miss
Keegan, Miss
Kelly, Miss
Kelly, Miss D.
Kennedy, Miss N
Kerin, Miss D'Arcy
King, Miss ML
Kough, Miss
Laird, Miss
Lamb, Mrs
Lane, Miss
Law, Miss M.
Leahy, Miss
Ledwidge, Miss
Lloyd, Miss A
Lumsden, Mrs J
McComas, Miss E
MacDonnell, Miss V
McLellan, Miss
MacKenzie, Miss S
MacWilliam, Miss
McVittie, Mrs
Maffet, Miss
Mahony, Misses
Manders, Mrs
Mangin, Miss
Martin, Miss
Meade, Miss
Mercer, Mrs
Meredith, Miss K
Meredith, Miss R
Metze, Miss
Millar, Miss D
Monson, Miss
Mooney, Misses
Moore, Miss E
Morrison, Miss
Mowbray, Miss
Murtagh, Mrs
Newbold, Miss
Newbold, Misses
Newcomen, Mrs
Newell, Miss
Newland, Miss
Neill, Miss
Neilson, Miss
Nichols, Miss
Nowlan, Miss Jones
O'Carroll, Miss
O'Kelly, Miss
O'Kelly, Miss E
O'Neill, Miss
Orr, Miss
Pentland, Miss
Perry, Miss
Pigott, Miss
Poë, Muriel
Poole, Miss A
Poole, Miss E
Pringle, Mrs Seton
Purcell, Miss
Purdon, Miss D
Purdon, Miss F
Pringle, Mrs
Rawson, Miss
Rawson, Miss H
Reilly, Miss F
Reilly, Miss
Rice, Mrs
Ritchie, Miss
Ritchie, Miss
Robertson, Miss
Robinson, Mrs
Robinson, Miss
Robinson, Mrs WH
Roff, Miss
Rothwell, Miss
Sankey, Miss R
Scott, Mrs
Sealy, Miss
Seeds, Miss
Selfe, Miss
Shannon, Mrs
Shannon, Miss
Shaw, Misses
Simpson, Miss
Slevin, Miss
Slyne, Misses
Smith, Miss
Smith, Miss H
Smyth, Miss
Smythe, Misses
Somerville, Miss
Stevenson, Miss
Stokes, Mrs
Stubbs, Miss
Skipworth, Miss K
Taylor, Miss
Thompson, Miss
Thompson, Mrs Cecil
Tobin, Miss S
Trayner, Miss
Trayer, Miss
Upton, Mrs
Vanes, Miss
Wade, Miss
Watson, Mrs
Wadsworth, Mrs
Wakefield, Miss A.
Wakefield, Mrs
Wakely, Miss
Walshe, Miss A.
Webb, Miss M.
Webb, Mrs Ella GA, MD
Weldon, Miss
West, Miss
Whitehead, Miss
Wickham, Miss
Wilkinson, Mrs
Williams, Miss
Wilmot, Miss
Wilson, Miss
Wilson, Miss A.
Wrede, Miss
Witz, Miss Doris
Woods, Miss

Awards to Ambulance Workers

The award of Silver Medals for Ambulance Work in Ireland is unique, the occasion of the Rebellion being the first on record for the conferring of such distinctions. The following is the official list of the recipients of the Silver Medals, Bronze Medals and Certificates awarded by the General Chapter of the Order of St John of Jerusalem for meritorious duty performed at the rising. These medals and certificates were presented to the individuals named by Sir Henry Blake at a meeting in the Lecture Theatre of the Royal Dublin Society on Tuesday, 16th January, 1917:

Silver Medals

Mrs Ella GA Webb, MD, Lady District Superintendent, No. 12 (Irish) District.
Mrs Constance Heppell-Marr, Assistant County Director, City of Dublin Branch, British Red Cross Society.
Mrs Edith C Chaytor, unattached.
J Lumsden, MD, Deputy Commissioner, No. 12 (Irish) District.
William G Smith, District Superintendent, No. 12 (Irish) District.

Bronze Medals—Men

Pte. George May, Four Courts St JAB.
Cpl. J Tugwell, Jacob's St JAB.
Corps Supt. Reg. H Keatinge, Dublin Building Trades St JAB.
Corps Supt., James H Webb, City of Dublin St JAB.
District Officer, Arthur LB Moore.
First Officer Charles Keatinge, Dublin Building Trades St JAB.
Supt. J Healy, Four Courts St JAB.
Supt. R Jameson, City of Dublin St JAB.
Herbert S Chaytor, unattached.
Pte. W Reynolds, Brooks, Thomas St JAB.

Bronze Medals—Women

Mrs Dorothy Hignett, Deputy Head Irish War Hospital Supply Depot.
Mrs Caroline F Lumsden, Quartermaster, Irish War Hospital Supply Depot.
Miss Mabel McCartney, Quartermaster, BRCS.
Miss Florence Renny-Tailyour, Dublin University N, St JAB.
Mrs E Fitzpatrick, City of Dublin BRCS.
Miss O'Neill, City of Dublin BRCS.
Sister M. M'Ginley, Sir P Dun's Hospital.
Sister A. Sproule, Sir P Dun's Hospital.
Sister M Scally, Sir P Dun's Hospital.
Miss Molly Woods, unattached.

Certificate of Honour—Men

Supt. PL Pielou, St James's Gate St JAB.
Sergt. J Gourlie, Dublin Building Trades Division St JAB.
Dr Henry Hunt, Rathmines Ambulance Division St JAB.
Pte. Robert Peat, Co. Dublin BRCS VAD 7.
Pte. William Fetherstonhaugh, Co. Dublin BRCS VAD 7.
Dr Myles Keogh, unattached.
Pte. WH Boyd, Four Courts St JAB.
Quartermaster J Bamford, Royal College of Science St JAB.
Supt. D Robinson, Rathmines St JAB.
Sergt. V Cole, City of Dublin St JAB.
Supt. HT Monahan, Land Commission St JAB.
Officer S Iley, City of Dublin St JAB.
Officer J Homan, City of Dublin St JAB.
Pte. GR Webb, Dublin University St JAB.
Div. Surg. Dr Carnegie, Dublin University St JAB.
Sergt. P Haffield, Glenageary St JAB.
Pte. LW Jewell, Four Courts St JAB.
Corps Supt. A Baker, MD, Dublin University St JAB.
Pte. T Oates, St James's Gate St JAB.
Supt. DJ Jardin, Royal College of Science St JAB.
Pte. Granby Burke, Four Courts St JAB.
Cpl. Kelly, Glenageary St JAB.
District Officer GP Cope, MD.
Pte. GW Wilson, Rathmines, St JAB.
Pte. Simon Nolan, Dublin Building Trades St JAB.
Sergt. J Trundle, St James's Gate St JAB.
Pte. J O'Brien, Land Commission, St JAB.
Pte. D Sullivan, Land Commission St JAB.
Pte. GH Bolton, Rathmines St JAB.
Sergt. H Scott, Royal College of Science St JAB.
Quartermaster Howard Healy, Co. Dublin BRCS VAD 7.
Sgt. J Greaves, Royal College St JAB.
Pte. J Greville, Four Courts St JAB.
Pte. George Newcomen, Dublin University St JAB.
Pte. HP Mayne, Four Courts St JAB.
Pte. EJ Hutchinson, City oF Dublin St JAB.
Neville Norway, unattached.
Sgt. LA Tolputt, Galway City St JAB.
Pte. H Whitton, Four Courts St JAB.
Pte. R Helen, St James's Gate St JAB.
Captain Hutson, Pembroke Fire Brigade.
Pte. WJ Bedlow, Dublin Building Trades St JAB.
Sgt. R Leask, Rathmines St JAB.
Cpl. R Maude, Rathmines St JAB.
Cpl. WM Stronach, Rathmines St JAB.
Robert Woods, unattached.
W Chevers Roche, unattached.

Certificate of Honour—Women

Miss Bird, L. Supt. Dundrum N St JAB.
Miss WH Archer, L.Supt. Leeson park N St JAB.
Miss Katherine Conry, City of Dublin BRCS.
Miss EF Blandford, Lady District Secretary, No. 12 (Irish) District.
Miss Frances Mangan, City of Dublin BRCS.
Miss Eileen McCartney, City of Dublin BRCS.
Mrs Crawfurth Smith, Co. Dublin Branch BRCS, VAD 2.
Mrs McVittie, L. Supt. Fitzwilliam Nursing Division St JAB.
Miss Fry, St JAB member.
Miss Freeman, St JAB member.
Miss Pigott, St JAB member.
Mrs Lloyd-Blood, St JAB member.
Miss Wrede, St JAB member.
Mrs Richard Sankey, St JAB member.
Miss Knox Gore, St JAB member.
Miss Booth Jones, St JAB member.
Miss Graham, St JAB member.
Miss Figgis, St JAB member.
Miss W Butler, St JAB member.
Miss A Poole, St JAB member.
Miss E Poole, St JAB member.

Miss F Reilly, Co. Dublin BRCS, VAD 24.
Miss E Mooney, St JAB member.
Miss SF Mooney, St JAB member.
Miss Smythe, Co. Dublin Branch BRCS.

City of Dublin Red Cross

Too much praise cannot be given to the ladies of the Red Cross Branches of the City and County of Dublin for the work which they performed during the rebellion. Mrs Heppell-Marr, Assistant County Director of the City of Dublin Branch, was at her post at 29 Fitzwilliam street each day, and on Tuesday of Easter week Mrs Gordon FitzPatrick, Commandant of VAD No. 12, and Miss Macartney, Acting Commandant of VAD No. 18, reported themselves for duty. They came again on Wednesday morning, and, with several members of their Detachments, entered with zeal on the work of rescue. The ladies who participated in carrying the wounded under fire, in addition to Mrs Heppell-Marr, were Miss Conroy, Commandant No. 8 VAD; Mrs Gordon FitzPatrick, Commandant No. 12 VAD; Miss Macartney, Quartermaster, No 18 VAD; Mrs Byrne, Commandant No 2 VAD; Miss Kerrigan, Miss E Macartney, Miss O'Neill, Miss Mangin, Miss Kinsley, Mrs Little, Nurse Dowd, Mrs Meade, Lower Pembroke street, generously offered her house, No. 32 Merrion square, to Mrs Heppell-Marr, so that fully a hundred beds were available if wanted. As a matter of fact, twenty-five patients were provided with beds at Fitzwilliam street. Miss Thornton, of Sir Patrick Dun's Hospital, expressed her high appreciation of the valuable aid rendered by Mrs Marr's Detachments, and also by the ladies of No. 40 Merrion square, and by Miss Huxley, of Elpis.

The following is a brief epitome of the work performed by the City of Dublin Branch of the Red Cross.

Thursday, VAD's carried in wounded to Sir Patrick Dun's Nursing Home. A great deal of firing was going on at the time. On that day the offices of 29 Lower Fitzwilliam street were converted into a temporary Hospital—the VAD's collecting supplies from the public. Accommodation for 50 patients was prepared. The following trained nurses—Miss Neill, Miss Dowd, Mrs Dwyer, Mrs Burgess, were assisted in the wards by VAD's who had received hospital experience. Surgeon Wheeler, Dr Rowlett, and Dr Rountree gave their services to the Temporary Hospital.

On Friday Miss Meade kindly lent her house, 32 Fitzwilliam square, which was equipped and set in order by the VAD's under the supervision of Miss Gargan. Twenty-five patients were received, and as, thanks to the generosity of the public, a large quantity of provisions were available, the Temporary Hospital was kept going, and some of the City Hospitals supplied with various articles of food.

All stretcher-bearers were women, and from time to time they made a tour of the city to find out if their services were required, and on several occasions were able to render assistance to wounded people. It was then found that difficulty was experienced by the Castle Hospital in getting their laundry done, and the VAD's were able to fill the gap. Lady Woods kindly lending her laundry for the work. The washing was done by some of the city VAD's, assisted by members of St John Ambulance Brigade and members of the Co. Branch BRCS, the linen being dried in Merrion square by permission of the military authorities. The whole of the work of the Temporary Hospital was done by voluntary workers—washing, cooking, kitchen work, etc., and among others the following rendered very valuable assistance:

Miss Macartney, Mrs Little, Miss Spillane, Miss O'Driscoll, Miss McCullagh, Mrs Gordon FitzPatrick, Miss Ferguson, Miss Kinsley, Miss McMahon, Miss E. Macartney, Mrs Byrne, Miss Barnard, Mrs Burne, Miss Kerrin, Miss Mangin, Miss Langan, Miss Donaldson, Miss Scratton, Miss Mitchell, Miss Hume, Miss Dempsey, Miss Lynam, Miss Slyne, Miss Farran, Miss O'Ratigan, Miss Strahan, Miss Butler, Miss Kerrigan, Miss E Harrison, Nurse Neilan, Miss E Slyne, Miss Swan, Miss Merrick, Miss Isaacs, Miss O'Neill, Miss M Harrison, Nurse Dwyer.

Six VAD's and a trained Nurse were sent over to the Dublin Castle Red Cross Hospital at Matron's request, to assist there.

Owing to the restrictions laid upon the City by the Military Authorities, very few of our VAD's were able to report, and those mentioned worked indefatigably during the whole of the disturbance.

It should be recognised that but for the generosity of the public, who supplied a large quantity of provisions, and other necessaries, it would have been impossible to keep the temporary hospital going, and it should be mentioned that Messrs Wilson, Studley, Holmes, Dempsey, and Hutton rendered great assistance.

Two separate centres were established by members of the Branch, Mrs Elkins and Mrs Edie. The former was at her post in Gardiner's place and rendered great assistance to Captain Gaffiken, RAMC, who spoke very highly of her services. Mrs Edie put her house at the disposal of the military authorities during the time they were stationed at Ballsbridge, and she provided sleeping accommodation and meals for Red Cross men on duty, and rendered assistance to some of the wounded men of the Volunteer Training Corps, for which services she was thanked by the military authorities.

Co. Dublin Red Cross

Dr Reginald Peacocke, Assistant County Director of the Co. Dublin Branch of the British Red Cross Society, in a report of the work done by the members of the VAD of that organisation during the rising, deals first with the work done in Kingstown. Dr Dampier Bennett, the medical officer of the Kingstown Men's Detachment,

County Dublin No. 3, had the men mobilised, and on Thursday, April 27th, twelve of the Detachment, under Sec.-Leader Brimage, left Kingstown and marched into Ballsbridge and reported to the MO in command of the RAMC there. The following day, as their services were not required, they returned to Kingstown, and did excellent work at Corrig Castle Hospital. Excellent work was done at Corrig Castle Red Cross Hospital, which, it is said, the Sinn Feiners had determined to take possession of in the event of a successful rising in Kingstown.

On the evening of Monday, 24th April, there arrived at the Hospital two stokers from HMS Tara, who were among those liberated by the Duke of Westminster's armoured car expedition, and who were passing through Kingstown on their way home, but were unable to proceed. Other military and naval refugees also arrived, and late in the evening the Transport Officer sent 24 men, including eight OTC Cadets, who were on their way to Kildare, to be provided with food and beds. The majority of these men remained about 10 days. On Tuesday, 25th, a number of soldiers were brought in, including Captain Denning, RAMC, who had been wounded, and a number of Staffordshires suffering from vaccination fever; shortly afterwards there arrived five Queen Alexandra nurses on their way to King George V Hospital; from this on there was a continuous procession of refugees, both military and civilian. Owing to the great difficulty in procuring food, the kitchen was turned into a bakery, and even the butter was churned on the premises. Some of the ladies were on duty from 12 to 14 hours a day, and the Matron, Miss Harris, Commandant of VAD, No. 28, was on duty for three days and three nights continuously. Altogether there were 76 fed and 69 beds provided, in addition to the usual work of the Hospital.

Dr Dampier Bennett, Medical Officer, VAD No. 3, and Dr Greer, Medical Officer, VAD No. 14, were in constant attendance. In addition to the Matron and the five Queen Alexandra nurses, the following ladies worked indefatigably: Sister Maddock, Miss Roe, Mrs Murray, Miss Sudlow, Miss Doreen Sudlow, Miss Clifford, Miss Connolly, Miss Burke, Mrs West, Miss Morrison, Miss Cook, the Misses Torney, Miss Boyle, Miss Robinson, Miss Booth, Miss Kelly, Miss Manning, Miss Spears, and Miss Roche; these ladies are members of the Voluntary Aid Detachments No. 14 and No. 28. The Red Cross Work Guild, Kingstown, was asked to send shirts and socks for the troops, and at once sent 108 pairs of socks and one dozen shirts. On the 26th April they were asked if they could give or get loans of blankets or rugs, as the troops who arrived had to sleep on the grass slopes near the Pier, and badly needed covering. Mrs Brereton Barry, her secretary, Miss Nolan, her son, Ralph, and Judge Brereton Barry went round most of the houses in the district, and were fortunate enough to get a large quantity of blankets, rugs, coats, etc. The people were most generous in giving, and they were brought in handcarts by Boy Scouts to the Buffet on the sea front, where they were distributed. The members of the Red Cross Work Guild all worked hard to alleviate the hardships of the soldiers during these trying times.

The members of the Ladies' VAD, Balbriggan, No. 30, County Dublin, Commandant Miss Warren, secured the Technical School and established a canteen, which was open from 7 a.m. to 8 p.m., and at which soldiers secured all their meals. Miss Shaw, Commandant of No. 6, Terenure VAD and Quartermaster Miss Mary Shaw, as well as Miss Clarke and Miss Davies, did duty in the Hospital at 40 Merrion square. Mrs Bolton, Commandant of VAD No. 24, reported good work done by members of her detachment in different parts of the city. Mrs Hely, Lady Superintendent, was on night duty at the High School, and the Quartermaster, Miss Reilly, at 40 Merrion square, where also several other members of the Detachment were hard at work. Sec.-Leader Miss Stanuell kept the canteen going at the Munition Works throughout all the trouble: she never went off duty for 11 days and slept in a chair.

A number of the ladies of this Detachment worked untiringly in the neighbourhood of Pembroke road and Ballsbridge. Others who live on the North side of the town worked at King street, Manor street, and Henry street.

From Detachment No. 22 three ladies—namely, Miss Booth Jones (Quartermaster) and the Misses E and L Smyth—did excellent work at 40 Merrion square: two others helped at Ailesbury park Hospital, to the work of which I must now refer.

Ailesbury Park Emergency Hospital

At the beginning of the Insurrection Mrs Crawfurth Smith, Commandant of the No 2 Detachment, 'phoned me her desire to convert her house in Ailesbury park into an Emergency Hospital. I was delighted with the idea and readily consented to take medical charge of it. Mrs Crawfurth Smith and her VAD, with the kind co-operation of many neighbours, set energetically to work. People around lent beds, mattresses, etc., and soon we got 30 beds, which were all occupied by wounded soldiers. The Commandant, Mrs Crawfurth Smith, her son, Mr Malcolm Smith, and all the ladies of the Detachment carried out their work splendidly. The duties of the Quartermaster were discharged by Miss Eileen Wilson. The other ladies of the VAD were the Misses O'Keeffe, Mrs Phipps, Mrs Truelock, Mrs Gick, Mrs Ersksine, Mrs Millar, Miss Dorothy Millar, Miss Mooney, Miss Hicks, Miss Hall, Miss Hayes, Miss Kellard, Miss Sibthorpe, together with Miss McGarvey and Miss Rodgers, members of VAD No. 22. The members of the Blackrock Branch of the War Hospital Supply Depot and Mrs J Snowden, St Andrew's Sewing Club, Blackrock, supplied all needful bandages, dressings, and night shirts.

In addition to the work carried on at Ailesbury park Hospital, two other members of the No 2

Detachment deserve to be specially mentioned; these are the Misses J and R Fitzpatrick. During the whole of the rebellion their labours never ceased in what was perhaps the hottest and most dangerous fighting zone, namely the district around Northumberland road, Haddington road, and Canal street Bridge. These two ladies, after their heroic labours in the fighting line were over, also worked at Richmond Barracks Hospital, dressing the wounds of Sinn Fein prisoners.

The useful and dangerous work that was done by the members of the County of Dublin No. 7 Detachment, Pembroke, is detailed in a special despatch from the Commandant, Mr O'Connell Fitzsimon, who writes:

'On Monday, the 24th ult., I chanced to be passing the Royal City of Dublin Hospital when the first of the wounded GR Volunteers arrived from Northumberland road. I assisted to carry several of them into the hospital, and then, by direction of Dr Parsons, went to Northumberland road and had Mr Browning removed in an ambulance.

I sent a messenger to our Quartermaster asking him to assemble the members of the Detachment, and in a short time Messrs Hely, Cantley, Olliver, R Peat, and Dillon arrived.

Mr Dillon was only partially recovered from influenza so I sent him home, but on subsequent days he did a good deal of work in the vicinity of Grand Canal street.

Messrs Hely and Cantley took up duty at the City of Dublin Hospital, whilst Messrs Olliver, R Peat, and I went on duty at St Vincent's Hospital. We continued in sole charge of the City of Dublin Hospital until Wednesday, when it was taken over by St John's men; and in St Vincent's Hospital until the end of the trouble on the 30th ult.; staying at the hospitals every night in case of emergency.

Our medical officer, Dr Wayland, in conjunction with Dr Cope, Mr Hely and Mr Smith, of St John's established a Red Cross Hospital at the High School in Harcourt street, and were ably assisted by Messrs R Peat, Fetherstonhaugh, Murphy, and O'Carroll, members of our VAD, Messrs Peat and Fetherstonhaugh bringing in a wounded man from Charlemont street on a stretcher under circumstances of great danger. Before going to the High School Mr Murphy had been on duty at Amiens street Station, and attended several cases.

Our Pharmacist, Mr W Kennedy, rallied around him some of our members who live on the North side, and, assisted by Messrs Harte, Douglas, O'Carroll, Ennis, and Whelan, manned the dressing station established by Lieut., King, RAMC, at Dorset street.

Captain Arthur Beveridge, RAMC, pays a warm tribute to the courage and devotion to duty of Mr S Dixon, an official of the Rathmines Township, and a member of our detachment, who did splendid work as orderly on the Rathmines Ambulance, working day and night at the removal of the wounded from Beggar's Bush Barracks to the Military Hospital at Portobello, and bringing medical supplies to Beggar's Bush.

Another member, Mr Giltrap, attached himself as stretcher-bearer to an Automobile Club Ambulance, and did excellent work on several days. He was slightly wounded in the neck, but considers himself lucky to have escaped so well, as his work was in 'the firing line'.

A recent member, Mr Maguire, acting independently, did some useful work as a stretcher-bearer at Northumberland road and Mount street, and another recruit, Mr McCabe, was indefatigable in his efforts to provide for the urgent needs of the hospitals.

I desire in a very special way to bring under your notice the gallant conduct of Mr Henry Olds, a member of our detachment. Olds had been 'doing his bit' from the commencement, and on the 25th was in South Great George's street, when he was informed that a wounded man was lying on O'Connell Bridge. He hastened there, and found a blind man lying wounded. He applied First Aid, and was bandaging the wounded limb, when he was shot in the shoulder, but despite the pain he completed his work, and brought the wounded man to a place of safety before he himself became unconscious. Mr Olds, as a result of his wound, was unable to resume his employment for a considerable time.

It is only right to state that the men of our detachment are unanimous in declaring that the Sinn Feiners respected the Red Cross, Messrs Olds and Giltrap describing their wounds as the result of chance shots, and Mr Dixon stating that on a couple of occasions they ceased fire whilst the ambulance was passing.'

In concluding his report Dr Peacocke names the following as deserving of special recognition:

Mr O'Connell Fitzsimon, Mr W Kennedy, Mr Henry Olds, Mr Cantley, Mr S Dixon, Mr Giltrap, Mr Olliver, Mr R Peat, and Mr Fetherstonhaugh; and among the ladies , Mrs Crawfurth Smith, Miss Harris, the two Misses Fitzpatrick, and Miss Stanuell.

AT THE HOSPITALS

The Royal City of Dublin

With splendid devotion the Nursing Staff of this Hospital, under the direction of the Lady Superintendent, Miss Eddison, performed their trying duty during the entire period of the outbreak. In this Hospital the first cases arrived on Easter Monday, just as the operations of the rebels commenced, and there was no cessation until the King's forces had quelled the movement. Although a very large number of wounded soldiers, civilians, and rebels were brought in for immediate treatment, the working machinery of the Institution was scarcely disturbed. Dr Parsons and the entire Medical and Nursing staff gave themselves up to the work with zeal.

At the monthly meeting of the Board of Directors

of the Royal City of Dublin Hospital, held on Friday, 12th May, the Hon Mr Justice Barton in the chair, the following resolutions were unanimously passed:

'That reviewing the terrible events of the past few weeks, when the resources of the hospital were taxed to the utmost in treating upwards of 200 casualties, the Directors desire to place on record their warm appreciation of the services of those who responded to the extraordinary and unforeseen calls made upon their skill and energy, especially the members of the medical, surgical, and nursing staffs, who proved their efficiency under very trying circumstances, as they were working often under fire, and always at considerable personal risk.'

'The Board do not find it possible to refer by name to all who shared in the work, but they cannot refrain from expressing their most grateful thanks to Miss EA Eddison, Lady Superintendent; Dr Alfred R Parsons, Mr G Jameson Johnston, FRCSI; Mr R Atkinson Stoney, FRCSI: Dr G Pugin Meldon, Dr Adams A McConnell (surgeon of the Richmond Hospital), Dr Walters (Dispensing Medical Officer of Health, Pembroke Urban District), Dr Gibbon FitzGibbon, Mr Frank C Crawley, FRSCI; and to the house surgeon and resident students.'

'Whilst particularly emphasising the exceptional services rendered by the Lady Superintendent, the Board also desire to mention Sisters Hill, Richardson, Lloyd, Kennedy, Hackett, Downing, both the 'day' and the 'night' nurses and the temporary probationers,'

The hospital is under heavy obligations to the many friends who came forward with gifts of food, bedding, dressings, etc., and with offers of help in innumerable directions. The Board particularly wish to thank those who are mentioned in the following list, but regret that some names may have been unavoidably omitted:

The British Red Cross Society, St John Ambulance Association, Alfred Millar, Lady and the Misses Lenox-Conyngham, Mr and Mrs J Hume Dudgeon, Miss Croker, Miss Dudgeon, WF Wells, MPSI,; City of Dublin Nursing Institution, Henry Dudgeon, Miss E Marrable, Christ Church, Leeson park, working party; Mrs Saunders and friends, Mrs Dockray, Miss Michie, Dr Purser, Geo. Hely, Mrs JT Andrews, Lady Shaw, Mrs A Hamilton, Rathmines working party, per Mrs Humfrey; Mr Leared, G Jacob, the St John Ambulance VAD; Mr Coffey, Lady Wright, Mrs Cole Baker, Mr and Mrs Mayne, Miss A J Hogg, Sir John Nutting, Bart., DL; Mrs WH King, the Misses Biddulph, Mrs R Atkinson Stoney, J Wallis, Mrs Collen, Mrs Werner, BH Conyngham, Miss Reilly, the Misses Nolan, Mrs J Andrew, Mrs Ringwood, Fane Vernon, DL; Mrs Gradner, Mrs Purser, Lady Holmes, Mrs Laydig, Mr Hickey, Miss Preston Walsh, Mrs Richards, TA Tombe, the Pembroke Red Cross VAD, Mrs Murphy, Mr and Miss Willington, James Mahoney, DS Jardin, William Brown, Mrs Dixon, Mrs Walker, Mrs Tenison Robbins, Dr McConnell, Mrs McAllister, Mrs Crookshank, Mrs Barrington Jellett, JL King, Mr and Mrs Delap, Mrs Huggard, John Maloney, Miss CH Agnew, the Blackrock Irish War Hospital Supply Depot, per Mrs GH Heenan; Francis W Breedon, the Belfast War Hospital Supply Committee, per Mrs Fane Vernon; Mrs Henry, Mrs Collum, Mrs McDonnell, Miss H Burgess, Mrs Gordon, Miss Bond, Mrs Brindley, Lady Cullinan, the Misses King-Harman, the College of Science, per Miss Reed; the Greystones Women Working Guild, Mrs Huband, Miss Revell, Mrs Jameson, Mrs Hinde, and Miss Cullinan.

Sir Patrick Dun's

It was on Wednesday evening following Easter Monday that the Sherwood Foresters, marched towards Dublin into the death trap that awaited them in the neighbourhood of Northumberland road. Into the inferno the Lady Superintendent and Nurses of Sir Patrick Dun's Nursing Home bravely stepped forth at about four in the afternoon. They were the first on the scene, and they used quilts to serve as stretchers. The Resident Medical Staff of the Hospital were also gallantly engaged in this rescue work, and between them they carried 79 wounded men, including soldiers and rebels, into the Home. Some idea of the strenuous duty may be gathered from the fact that the time occupied was from four in the afternoon to midnight. Three clergymen also helped to carry the wounded under fire, these being the Rev. Father McNevin, Rev. Father McCann, and the Rev. Mr Hall, of Dalkey. Into the fire likewise entered Miss Huxley, the distinguished Lady Superintendent of Elpis, which is situated almost opposite to the Nursing Home, and some of her assistants.

National Maternity

The National Maternity Hospital in Holles street (Miss Keating, Matron) early in Easter week found itself in the centre of hostilities and cut off by military regulations from undisturbed areas. The problem of maintaining supplies for some of the people, including staff and patients, arose early, and was ably dealt with by the Lady Superintendent and the nursing staff, who, at considerable personal risk owing to rifle and machine gun fire, managed to get out and secure supplies. Many civilians in this district lost their lives in the same quest. On Wednesday, after the military secured Mount street Bridge, the firing round the hospital became so heavy that it was necessary to put out the Red Cross flag. At that time Sir Patrick Dun's Hospital was filled to overflowing with wounded from the Mount street fighting, and its approaches being constantly swept with rifle fire it was found necessary to throw open the Maternity Hospital for the treatment of casualties. The Master, Dr White, and the resident staff, assisted by some civilians from about the poorer district, readily responded to the many calls on their help, carrying in the wounded under fire. In all some forty bullet wounds of a shocking nature were treated at the hospital. Twelve proved fatal. After the surrender on Sunday most of the cases were removed to St Vincent's Hospital by IAC ambulances, which were also used to carry bread from Messrs Boland's to the Maternity Hospital. From the dispensary attached flour was distributed to the hundreds of starving poor during four days. During the week none did better work than the priests attached to St Andrew's Church, Westland row, who were constantly in the thick of the danger, ministering to the wounded and dying. Father MacNevin found it necessary to remain at the hospital, and his devotion to duty will be ever remembered by the people of the neighbourhood. Fathers O'Reilly and Fleming also were constantly engaged in errands of mercy in other parts of the district. Father O'Reilly entered Boland's mill, under cross fire, to attend some dying Sinn Feiners. These priests were also conspicuous at the Mount street Bridge battle, Dr O'Brien, of the Skin and Cancer Hospital, co-operated in all efforts at the Maternity Hospital to alleviate the sufferings of the poor, and also put his hospital at the disposal of the wounded. During the critical time the hospital staff managed to reach the urgent maternity cases, as well as many of the sick not normally within the hospital's sphere of activities.

Jervis Street

In the thick of the battle between rebel snipers and the military, Jervis street Hospital was several times hit by bullets. This did not prevent the doctors and nurses of that institution from performing their duties in a heroic manner. They were on duty constantly, it may be said, from the afternoon of Easter Monday, when the first cases which were brought in were four dead soldiers and a woman who had been shot dead near her own door in Capel street, until the following Monday. Altogether between 600 and 700 cases were dealt with. Except for the cases of looting, and a small number of street accident cases, all were bullet wounds. Forty-three persons died in the hospital and about 38 were brought in dead. Dr Louis Byrne, the City Coroner, was always there, and he gave numerous evidences of courage and devotion to duty. On one occasion, assisted by a porter of the hospital, James Dooley, and a civilian whose name has not transpired, he went out at night and rescued a soldier who lay badly wounded some distance from the hospital. He was assisted with unflagging zeal by Doctors Keegan, Stoker, and Hayden, staff surgeons; by Doctors O'Carroll, Hughes and O'Connor, house surgeons, and by resident students Ryan and Murphy. The Matron (Miss Kelly), the Assistant Matron (Miss Gavigan), the Rev. Mother, and the Sisters joined with the staff of nurses in doing all that was possible for the relief and comfort of the wounded.

Mater Misericordiae

The Mater Hospital, under the care of the Sisters of Mercy, being in the centre of an area where some very keen fighting took place, was called upon to deal with a very heavy casualty list. The medical and nursing staffs worked energetically both day and night, and spared no efforts to relieve the sufferings of the wounded.

Dr Steevens'

Over one hundred cases were treated in Dr Steevens' Hospital during the week of disturbance, and the medical staff and the nursing staff (under the superintendence of Miss Phillips) were constantly on duty during that very trying time.

St Vincent's

The first victims of the rebellion received at St Vincent's Hospital were brought in between 12 and 1 o'clock on Easter Monday. They were two civilians and both were dead. About 45 persons were dealt with altogether, nine of which were either brought in dead or died soon after admission. The hospital was struck once or twice by bullets, one of which passed through the window of the Mother Superior's room, but nobody was injured. Several members of the medical staff, at great personal risk, went out with stretchers and brought in cases from the Green and elsewhere. There was no difficulty in getting supplies of food, and on one day Doctor Day, of Cork street hospital, brought a supply of bread to the hospital and succeeded in bringing supplies to several other places as well. Surgeon Kennedy and Surgeon Tobin attended to the operations, and Doctors Shaw, O'Hea, Meenan, Dargan, and Courtney, the nursing staffs and the students were untiring in their efforts.

Mercer's

There were about 130 persons treated for gunshot wounds at Mercer's Hospital during the rebellion. The cases were attended to by Surgeon Maunsell, Surgeon Wheeler, and Dr CF Coyne, who were ably assisted by the nursing staff under Miss Jordan (Matron.)

Richmond

Richmond Hospital is the centre of an area in which considerable fighting took place during the rebellion. Soon after midday on Easter Monday Father Albert, a priest from Church street, brought in the body of a child, shot through the head. Early in the day the insurgents took possession of the telephone at the Old Richmond, and it was only after vigorous protest that they agreed to regard the Richmond Hospital as neutral territory. Throughout the week, however, they came and went freely at the hospital, visiting their wounded or inquiring about them. Sir Thomas Myles, Dr O'Carroll, and Dr Alfred Boyd, anaesthetist, spent the week assisting the resident staff. When it was seen that the trouble had become general, and was likely to continue, the patients were cleared from the male ward into the North Dublin Union and the auxiliary hospitals to make room for casualties, which numbered about three hundred during the week. The majority of the men were civilians, many of them adults injured while trying, under fire, to get food for their families. As the danger increased the beds were placed on the floor to avoid bullets fired from the housetops. In the middle of the week food ran short at the hospital, and Miss Hezlett, the lady superintendent, co-operated in the organisation of an expedition to obtain more. On a white sheet the words 'Richmond Hospital Supplies' were marked with black tape, and Dr Pollock and two students bearing this banner took out a borrowed horse and cart. Passing several times through the firing, the expedition reached the south side of the city, and returned safely with supplies. The number of persons treated during the week for bullet wounds and detained was 37, and about 100 had their wounds dressed and were discharged. The large number of cases treated put a severe strain on the energies of the surgical, medical, and nursing staffs. At a meeting of the Board of Governors on 12th May a letter was read from the three members of the Visiting Staff (Dr O'Carroll, Sir Thomas Myles, and Dr Boyd), who remained on duty in the hospitals during the week of the rebellion, drawing the Board's attention to the courageous way in which the entire resident medical and nursing staffs and servants devoted themselves to the service of the hospitals during that very trying time. A resolution of thanks and gratitude was, therefore, passed in their favour. The following resolution was passed unanimously:

'The Board of Governors, at their first meeting after the recent rebellious outbreak, wish to place on record their high appreciation of the devotion to duty displayed by the members of the senior visiting staff, Doctors O'Carroll, Sir Thomas Myles, and Boyd. During the entire period of disturbance they remained night and day at the hospital doing everything that was possible for the injured, and, by their example and guidance, safe-guarding the hospital, and showing, in the face of extreme danger and difficulty, a loyal attachment to their duty, which the Board feel will ever live as an honour to them personally and to their profession.' The Secretary reported that during the above trouble the Master of the North Dublin Union, Mr D Fagan, had shown great kindness to the hospitals by supplying them with bread, groceries, butter, and eggs, which could not be obtained elsewhere at the time. He was directed to convey to Mr Fagan the Board's most cordial thanks for the invaluable assistance he had given to the hospitals during the period of the disturbance.

Dublin Castle Red Cross

There were only sixty-seven wounded soldiers from France in the Dublin Castle Red Cross Hospital on Easter Monday when the Sinn Fein rebels made their futile attack upon the Castle, but from that night the medical and nursing staff had a very strenuous time. For five days and nights Dr WK Carew, the Medical Superintendent, had not changed his clothes, so great was the demand upon his services, and he was ably assisted by Surgeons Stokes and Tobin, and by Dr PJ O'Farrell. The nursing staff, under Miss Taylor, Matron, and the resident pupils, Messrs Steele, MacDonagh, and Doyle, performed noble duty all the time, and had little or no rest. They were reinforced by members of the Voluntary Aid Detachment. One hundred and eighteen wounded soldiers were brought in, and in addition to these, thirty-four wounded members of the Sinn Fein party, twenty civilians, and two police constables received the attention of the medical and nursing staff. Thirty-six deaths occurred. All these, and about thirty others who were brought from other hospitals, were interred in the garden at the rear of the Castle, but some of them were subsequently transferred elsewhere for reinterment.

Rotunda

The condition of the Rotunda Hospital during Easter week was described to a meeting of the Board of directors at which a report by Miss Ramsden, the Lady Superintendent, was read. This showed that every one had an extremely anxious time. 'Two bullets entered Ward 7, causing great alarm to the patients, who were then moved out to the back of the hospital. The hospital became very full; on one day there were 113 patients in the wards. Owing to the holidays supplies had almost run out, and the situation outside was so very serious that the tradespeople could not deliver the goods, though milk was sent in up to the 27th at very great risk. Then for two days we had none. Extreme economy had to be practised, but owing to the kind assistance of Mr Kennedy, Mr Conway, and Messrs JL Byrne, Ltd., of Great Britain street, who supplied different articles of food, suffering from want was avoided. Our best thanks are due to these tradespeople, and especially to Mr Kennedy, who sent down a vanload of bread: otherwise we should have been entirely without. His vanman on leaving the hospital was fired at and the van searched by the rebels. Fortunately, the man was unharmed. The highest praise is due to our own men, who risked their lives going across the city on two occasions for meat, and in every possible way they gave me most valuable assistance. The gas was cut off on Tuesday morning, and the electricity on Wednesday, and our having to work in semi-darkness added to the difficulties of the situation. The nursing staff, however, maintained a wonderful degree of calmness under the great stress of work to the accompaniment of roaring cannon and firearms of every description. They cheerfully accepted the limited rations, and worked unceasingly for the welfare of the patients. Many wounded were treated in the dispensary, some cases being very serious, and three deaths took place. Dr Simpson and Dr Gilmor, Assistant Masters, with Dr Datta and the students, worked unceasingly both indoors and outside at great personal risk.'

The Board called Miss Ramsden before them, and

thanked her for her very successful efforts in catering for the patients and staff under circumstances of unprecedented difficulty, and also accorded the whole staff of the hospital best thanks for their devotion to duty.

Adelaide

During the rebellion there were admitted to the Adelaide Hospital the following:

Dead, soldiers, 4: civilian, 1: wounded, soldiers and civilians, 70, who received treatment and of whom four died of their wounds. At the meeting of the Managing Committee on Tuesday, 16th May, the following resolution was unanimously adopted:

'At this, the first meeting of the Committee of Management held since the recent outbreak of rebellion in Dublin, the Committee recognise the very great danger in which the hospital was placed. They desire, in the first instance, to record their profound thankfulness to Almighty God for His great mercy, manifested in the preservation of the lives of the inmates of the hospital, and of the premises. The Committee wish to express their sincere gratitude to the members of the staff and household for the courageous and efficient manner in which they attended to the interests and safety of the patients. They desire specially to thank Mr LG Gunn and Dr Geo. Peacock, both of whom remained in the hospital day and night attending to the wants of the patients, and who, by their practical advice, aided Miss Hill (the Matron) in her arduous duties. The Committee sincerely thank the Matron, the sisters, the nurses, and all the staff of the hospital for their single-hearted devotion to duty during a time of great anxiety. They also warmly thank the Rev. R Northridge for his efforts and work, as well as Dr Fishe (House Surgeon), the residents, and the Registrar, for the faithful way in which all did their duty under the most trying and difficult conditions. They cannot adequately express their gratitude for the loyalty and courage shown by all in a time of great danger, and under trying and difficult conditions.'

Royal Victoria Eye and Ear

The following report by Miss Reeves, the Matron, was placed before the Council at its first meeting in May—On Tuesday, April 25th, at 6 a.m., a soldier came in having been shot through the legs in Leeson street. On Thursday, April 27th, there were thirty empty beds here, and hearing the Royal City of Dublin Hospital was over-crowded, I told Dr Stoney that we could take some patients. Forty-two soldiers were immediately sent over, 13 were convalescent patients, and the remainder Sherwood Foresters who had come in the night before, some only suffering from shock, but three or four with fairly serious wounds. Three more soldiers came here direct, making a total of 46 soldiers. The total number of patients in Hospital on this day was 116. On May 5th we were asked to take seven civilians who had been injured during the riots and treated at 40 Merrion square, as that temporary hospital was being closed. Very great difficulty was experienced for several days in getting sufficient food. Milk and meat came regularly, but it was impossible to get sugar or butter, and for two days the bread van failed to come. However, by sending a message to the castle we were able to get enough. The diet was considerably restricted for five or six days, but I do not think that anyone was hungry. Dr TE Gordon very kindly looked after and operated on any cases that required it, and Dr E Watson took X-ray photographs which were needed, as it was impossible to get in touch with Dr Haughton. The neighbours, Rev. Wm Ballie, Mrs Le Peton, Mrs O'Donnell, Mr and Mrs Leggett Byrne, and Mrs Ring kindly lent beds and offered sleeping accommodation for any soldiers who were able to be up and about. Several shots were fired into the sanitary block of the east end of the Hospital, and one into the out-patient department, but no one was injured. Fifteen of the soldiers were discharged on May the 10th fit for duty, sixteen were transferred to King George V Hospital on May 13th, and twelve more we expect to send away this week. There was a great deal of shooting and sniping all round this locality almost all the time, which made it most dangerous for anyone approaching or leaving the hospital.

City Hospital, Holles Street

At the May monthly meeting of the Managing Committee of the City Hospital for Diseases of the Skin and Cancer, Rev. P Hayden presiding, the following resolution, which was proposed by W Ireland, JP, seconded by the Rev. Chairman, was passed unanimously:

'The Managing Committee at this their first meeting after the recent unhappy revolt, hasten to place on record an expression of their deep sense of appreciation of the valour and unflagging devotion to duty displayed by a member of our honorary medical staff, CM O'Brien, Esq., MD, not only during the now historic battle of Mount street Bridge, in which he played a fearless and humane part under fire, worthy of the best traditions of a noble profession, but more especially for his great foresight and administrative capacity in throwing open this specialised hospital for the admission of the wounded, so as to cope with the unprecedented unforeseen demands for hospital accommodation elsewhere.'

In connection with the commissariat, the Committee expressed their obligations to Messrs Boland, Ltd., for their generous supply of bread not only for the intern patients, but also for the sick and hungry poor attending the dispensaries. The Committee placed on record the great assistance which they received from the Royal Irish Automobile Club, Dawson street, through their courteous Secretary, Mr Chaytor, for the supply of ambulance for removal of the wounded to and from this hospital, and also for the supply of ambulance to bring bread from Messrs Boland's bakeries.

The Committee recognised the whole-hearted and valuable assistance which the hospital received from the Rev. Thos McNevin, CC, who kindly volunteered his services, and accompanied Dr O'Brien to Messrs Boland's bakeries, Ringsend, at a time when the scheme was attended with the utmost danger to life. Father McNevin afterwards assisted in the distribution of the bread to many of the city hospitals and the hungry poor outside.

The Committee felt grateful for the kind and generous assistance unstintingly rendered by Dr White, the Master of the National Maternity Hospital, and the Lady Superintendent, who volunteered meat, bread, and butter to tide over the very acute crisis of this hospital. The Matron of the hospital is Miss McGauran.

Meath

At the Meath Hospital 34 persons were admitted, and 46 were treated but not admitted and twelve deaths occurred from bullet wounds. At the annual meeting of the Governors a resolution was passed recording their appreciation of the untiring and invaluable services rendered both by day and night during the critical fortnight of the rebellion, by the medical, surgical, and nursing staffs, the students past and present of the hospital, and the servants of the institution, and thanking all concerned for their self-denying loyalty to duty. The Matron of the hospital is Miss Bradburne.

The Coombe

A word of praise is due to the staff of the Coombe Hospital for the work they did, both in attending the numerous cases and also for having given shelter to many poor women and children for safety. Owing to the demands made on the hospital resources, the staff was kept going day and night, close on thirty cases having being treated for wounds at the hospital and a large number attended outside. Miss O'Carroll, the Matron, and the Rev. Peter Monahan, of Francis street Presbytery, who assisted at the hospital and in the surrounding district, and worked indefatigably to secure food for the poor of this congested area, were specially thanked by the directors for their services, and the Matron was instructed to convey the thanks of the board to the whole staff.

Dublin University VAD

This hospital, at 19 Mountjoy square, was in charge of Sister Gertrude Wood when the disturbance broke out on Easter Monday, the commandant of the detachment being in the country for Easter. Sister Wood opened the hospital, assisted by Miss Hannan and one St John Ambulance dresser (Arthur Bacon). The military authorities sent a surgeon, Captain Friar, RAMC, to take medical charge. With this small staff the hospital did excellent work, no outside help being able to reach them during the week. The hospital premises were attacked by the rebels from adjacent houses, during the earlier part of the disturbance.

National Children's

Very useful and practical work was done by the medical and nursing staff of the National Children's Hospital, Harcourt street. Several serious cases suffering from bullet wounds occurring in the neighbourhood of Harcourt street were admitted. The Matron, Miss Geraldine Mathews went out in Harcourt street to the assistance of a wounded man regardless of a shower of bullets which she encountered on her way, as a rebel at the time was trying to escape down the street on a bicycle, and he was fired at by the soldiers stationed at Harcourt street Railway Station. Assisted by Dr R Lane Joynt Miss Mathews conveyed the patient on a stretcher to the private hospital attached to the Children's Hospital, and afterwards brought in two women who were shot at the same time. Two of her brave nurses, Bookless and Dawson, and Mr Barrett, resident surgeon, rendered valuable assistance in conveying the patients to the hospital, where they were placed under the care of Sir Lambert H Ormsby, FRCS, and Dr RS Wayland, members of the hospital staff.

STAMPS USED BY THE REBELS

Herewith are reproduced fac-similes of several stamps which acquired an exaggerated value for a short time after the rebellion by reason of the belief that they had been specially prepared for postal service under an Irish Republic. The small stamps shown have been in circulation for years, and evidence exists that the one with the harp was on an envelope that passed through the post as long ago as 1908. The other with the cross design also passed through the post more recently. The stamps were sold at half a crown the gross, the idea being to use them as a means of propagating Sinn Fein ideas, and raising money at the same time. 'It is,' said the Sinn Fein newspaper some years ago, 'to make the sign of Irish nationhood to the other nations that the stamp was designed. It is fulfilling that design as the Finnish stamp some years ago fulfilled a like design in calling the attention of the world to the fact that Finland was no province of Russia, but a nation despoiled, but separate and distinct, asserting its individuality, and defending its liberties against foreign despotism.' The larger stamp with the three heads on it was first used on a Manchester Martyrs' anniversary some years ago, and has been current ever since. The heads are those of Allen, Larkin, and O'Brien, who were executed at Manchester in the sixties, and under the shamrock are the words 'God save Ireland.' The cross stamp is printed in black and blue, and the other with the harp is in yellow, green, and white, the colours of the rebels. The martyrs stamp is also in the same colours. Among other bogus stamps of English manufacture is one printed several years ago showing in the centre a harpist with a frame of shamrock and other Irish emblems, and under the words 'Provisional Government—Ireland—Imperial Union.'

At an auction in Messrs Bennett's rooms, Ormond quay, on 26th January, 1917, a pair of the stamps shown on the left was sold for 20s., and a set of twenty-two of the stamps shown on the right was sold for £1 12s. 6d.

Resignation of Executive

A direct result of the rebellion was the resignation of Lord Wimborne, the Lord Lieutenant:

The Right Hon Augustine Birrell, Chief Secretary, and Sir Matthew Nathan, Under Secretary.

The place of the last-mentioned was taken by Sir Robert Chalmers immediately after the rising had been suppressed, but the office of Chief Secretary was not filled until the appointment of Mr HE Duke, KC, on Monday, 31st July, 1916. The position of Lord Lieutenant remained vacant till August 4, 1916, when it was announced that Lord Wimborne had been re-appointed.

On Monday, 23rd October, 1916, it was officially announced that Sir William Patrick Byrne had been appointed Under Secretary.

Photo by] [Elliott and Fry.
MR. H. E. DUKE, K.C., M.P., New Chief Secretary of Ireland.

Mr Birrell and Mr Redmond share the blame

Mr Birrell was in London when the outbreak occurred, but he travelled from Holyhead to Dublin in a destroyer, and remained in the city until Tuesday, 2nd May. The following day his resignation of the office of Chief Secretary was announced, and in the House of Commons the same afternoon Mr Birrell admitted that he had under-estimated the Sinn Fein movement. At the same time Mr John Redmond said he felt that he had incurred some of the blame, as Mr Birrell might have been influenced by what he said.

Mr Dillon's remarkable speech

A remarkable speech was made by Mr John Dillon, MP, in the House of Commons on Thursday, 11th, May, when he demanded that the executions of the rebels be stopped, and declared that the life work of the Nationalist Party was being washed out in a sea of blood.

'I do not come here to raise one word of defence of murder,' said Mr Dillon. 'If there be a case of cold-blooded murder, by all means try the man openly before a courtmartial if you like, but let the public know what the evidence is and prove that he is a murderer, and then do what you like with him. But it is not murderers who are being executed; it is insurgents who have fought a clean fight, a brave fight, however misguided, and,' he continued, in reply to some Unionist interruptions, 'it would be a damned good thing for you if your soldiers were able to put up as good a fight as did these men in Dublin—three thousand men against twenty thousand with machine guns and artillery.'

Mr Asquith's surprise

The Prime Minister sprang a surprise on the House of Commons on Thursday, 11th May, by announcing his intention of proceeding to Ireland. Mr Asquith arrived in Dublin next morning, Friday, 12th, and remained there until Monday, 15th, when he travelled to Belfast, and returned to the capital in the evening. On Thursday, 18th, he left Dublin for Cork, and after a stay of some hours there proceeded to London. The Prime Minister's time in Ireland was spent in conferring with representatives of all classes of the populace, and he devoted an afternoon in Dublin to visiting the Sinn Fein prisoners in Richmond Barracks, many of whom he entered into conversation with. On Wednesday, 17th May, he attended a meeting of the Privy Council in Dublin Castle, and was sworn a member of that body.

Opportunity for settlement

In the House of Commons on Thursday, 25th May, the Prime Minister, referring to his visit to Ireland, said the two dominant impressions left in his mind were that the existing machinery of Irish administration had broken down, and that there was an almost universal belief among representative Irishmen that there was now a unique opportunity for a settlement of outstanding problems by general consent. Proceeding, Mr Asquith said—

The Government is anxious to do everything in its power to facilitate such a settlement. My right hon. friend who sits beside me (Mr Lloyd George) has undertaken to devote his time and energy and powers to the prosecution of that desire, and if as I believe there is among Irishmen, no less than among the people of Great Britain, an honest and a resolute desire to take advantage of this opportunity for the attainment of that which to us, and the nation and Empire, I do not hesitate to say, is the greatest boon we could possibly achieve.

New Home Rule Proposals

Mr Lloyd George had numerous conferences in London with the leaders of the Irish political parties immediately following the Premier's statement, but the right hon. gentleman did not visit Ireland.

A meeting of the Irish Nationalist Party was held in the Mansion House, Dublin, on Saturday, 10th June, when Mr John Redmond, who presided, intimated that the proposals of Mr Lloyd George were, in substance, as follows:

(1) To bring the Home Rule Act into immediate operation.

(2) To introduce at once an Amending Bill, as a strictly War Emergency Act, to cover only the period of the war and a short specified interval after it.

(3) During that period the Irish members to remain at Westminster in their full numbers.

(4) During this war emergency period six Ulster counties to be left as at present under the Imperial Government.

(5) Immediately after the war, an Imperial Conference of the representative from all the Dominions of the Empire to be held to consider the future government of the Empire, including the question of the government of Ireland.

(6) Immediately after this Conference, and during the interval provided for by the War Emergency Act, the permanent settlement of all the great outstanding problems, such as the permanent position of the six exempted counties, the question of finance and other problems which cannot be dealt with during the war, would be proceeded with.

Ulster Unionist Council decision

A full meeting of the Ulster Unionist Council was held on Monday, 12th June, in the Ulster Minor Hall, Belfast. Sir Edward Carson presided. The meeting was held in private, and at the close the following official report was issued:

The adjourned meeting of the Ulster Unionist Council was held today. It was very largely attended, and Sir Edward Carson presided.

The following protest was entered by the delegates of the Counties of Cavan, Monaghan and Donegal:

'That we protest in the strongest possible manner against the proposals of the Government to revive the Home Rule controversy, owing to the continuance of the war, and during the absence of so many Covenanters serving in His Majesty's forces. And further protest, on behalf of those Covenanters from the three counties we represent, against any settlement of the Irish question, which excludes them from Ulster. But if the six counties consider the safety of the Empire depends on the continuance of the negotiations on the basis suggested by the Government, the responsibility must be clearly understood to be theirs, and the delegates of the three counties must abide by their decision.'

After full discussion the following resolution was passed *nem con*:

We, the delegates constituting the Ulster Unionist Council, representative of the Unionist population of the Province of Ulster, having considered the proposals laid before us for an adjustment of the Home Rule question, on the basis of the definite exclusion from the Government of Ireland Act of the six counties of Ulster, in view of the critical situation of the Empire arising out of the European War, declare as follows:

1. That, as Unionists, proud of our citizenship in the United Kingdom, we re-affirm our unabated abhorrence of the policy of Home Rule, which we believe to be dangerous to the security of the Empire, and subversive of the best interests alike of Ireland and of the United Kingdom: and we decline to take any responsibility for setting up such a form of government in any part of Ireland.

2. As, however, the Cabinet, which is responsible for the government of the country, is of opinion that it will tend to strengthen the Empire to win the war in which it is now engaged, if all questions connected with Home Rule are settled now, instead of as originally agreed, at the termination of the war, and as the suggestions from the Government put before us by Sir Edward Carson have been made with that view, we feel, as loyal Citizens, that in this crisis in the Empire's history it is our duty to make sacrifices, and we consequently authorise Sir Edward Carson to continue the negotiations on the basis of the suggestions explained to this meeting, and to complete them if the details are arranged to his satisfaction.

3. And, further, we hereby pledge ourselves as follows: That, in the event of a settlement being arrived at on the basis above mentioned, we shall use all the influence, power, and resources of Ulster (that is to say, of the six counties to be excluded from the purview of the Act) in the future for the protection of Unionists in the Counties of Cavan, Monaghan, and Donegal against injustice or oppression at the hands of the Irish Parliament or Government.

4. We further desire to make it clear that if, from any cause, the negotiations referred to prove abortive, we reserve to ourselves complete freedom of action in the future in opposition to the whole policy of Home Rule for Ireland.

Ulster Irish Nationalists' Decision

A Convention of Nationalists from the six Ulster counties proposed to be excluded from the Government of Ireland Act under Mr Lloyd George's scheme was held on Friday (23rd June) in St Mary's Hall, Belfast.

The following official report of the proceedings was issued at night; A Conference of the representative Nationalists of the six counties principally affected by the proposals of Mr Lloyd George in connection with the government of Ireland was held today in St Mary's Hall, Belfast, at 12 o'clock noon.

The shaded [illegible] of the map shows the area which it was proposed to exclude under the partition scheme.

The following was the basis of representation:

1. One priest in each parish in the six counties.
2. Nationalist members of Parliament in the six counties.
3. The officers of the Divisional Executives of the UIL for each constituency in the six counties.
4. The county officers of the Ancient Order of Hibernians and the district officers of the Irish National Foresters in the six counties.
5. All Nationalist members of elected public boards in the six counties.
6. For the Cities of Belfast and Derry five additional members, elected by the executives of the UIL, INF, and AOH.

The number of delegates entitled to attend was 1,077: the number actually present was 776. Mr John E Redmond, MP, Chairman of the Irish Parliamentary Party, presided. The Chairman having addressed the Conference, Mr Patrick Dempsey, JP, TC, Belfast, proposed the following resolution:

'That this Conference of representatives from the Counties of Antrim, Down, Derry, Armagh, Tyrone, and Fermanagh, and from the Cities of Belfast and Derry, having considered the proposals of Mr Lloyd George for the temporary and provisional settlement of the Irish difficulty, is of opinion that they should be accepted, and that in view of all the circumstances of the present situation in Ireland, they offer the best means of carrying on the fight for a united self-governing Ireland.'

The resolution was seconded by the Very Rev. Canon McCartan, PP, VF, Donaghmore, Co. Tyrone. The resolution was supported by the Very Rev. Canon Quinn, PP, VG, Camlough, Co. Armagh, National Director, UIL; the Very Rev. John Nolan, PP, VF, Moneyglass, Toomebridge, Co. Antrim; Mr John Dillon, MP; and Mr Joseph Devlin, MP. The resolution was opposed by Mr F J O'Connor, solicitor, Omagh; Mr T McLoughlin, UDC, Armagh; the Very Rev. WB MacFeely, PP, BD, Glendermot, Waterside, Derry; the Very Rev. Canon Keown, PP, VG, Enniskillen; Mr John McGlone, National Director UIL, Mid-Armagh; and Alderman James McCarron, Derry City.

No amendment was moved to the resolution, and at the close of the discussion a division was taken by open vote, the name of every delegate being read out from the chair, and the delegate rising in his place and declaring his vote 'Yes' or 'No'. Messrs Daniel McCann, Belfast, and TJS Harbinson, solicitor, Cookstown, were appointed scrutineers, and after the counting of the votes announced the result as follows:

For the resolution, 475: against, 265—majority for the resolution, 210. The proceedings, which were characterised by great earnestness and entire good feeling throughout, then concluded.

A vital difference

Following publication of the reports of the meetings of the Nationalist Party and Ulster Unionist Council a vital difference of opinion was revealed. The Ulster Unionist Council maintained that the exclusion of the six counties was intended to be final and definite, and not subject to any reconsideration at the termination of the war.

The Nationalists on the other hand contended that the exclusion of the six counties was a temporary expedient, and only for the remaining period of the war. The whole position, they maintained, would be open to revision in the conference that would follow the conclusion of peace.

Cabinet Minister Resigns

The differences of opinion caused a keen discussion in the Press regarding the details of the proposed bill. The Earl of Selborne, President of the Board of Agriculture, resigned from the Cabinet, and explained in the House of Lords on Tuesday, 27th June, that he understood nothing was to be brought into operation until the conclusion of the war, and when he found it was intended to operate immediately he resigned.

Order in Ireland

On Tuesday, 11th July, Lord Lansdowne made a statement in the House of Lords regarding the condition of Ireland as revealed by the report of the Hardinge Commission. He said that during the period pending the passing of the Amending Act care would be taken to preserve order in Ireland. The Government had complete confidence in Sir John Maxwell, who would have the assistance of 40,000 soldiers, and the Defence of the Realm Act would be extended, if necessary. There was no intention to grant an amnesty to prisoners, and an order would be issued prohibiting the carrying of arms. The Government also proposed to have recourse to trial before two resident magistrates, as in parts of Ireland it was idle to expect the magistrates or ordinary jury to do their duty.

Mr John Redmond next day, Wednesday, 12th July, issued a statement in which he said he regarded Lord Lansdowne's speech as 'a gross insult to Ireland,' 'a declaration of war on the Irish people,' and 'the announcement of a policy of coercion.' On the 18th July Mr Redmond sent the Prime Minister a note urging the immediate production of the bill for the settlement, as further delay would be fatal.

Collapse of the scheme

In the House of Commons on Monday, 24th July, in reply to questions by Mr John Redmond,

Mr Asquith said that the agreement come to in regard to Ireland by the Secretary for War, subject to the approval of the Government, embodied two main points, which were accepted by both sections of the Government, Unionists and Home Rulers. The Unionists in the Cabinet agreed that the Government of Ireland should be put into immediate operation, and, on the other hand, the Home Rulers in the Cabinet agreed that six Ulster Counties should not be brought in, except by their own consent and on the express authority of a new Act of Parliament. In course of settling the bill to give effect to these objects, two questions arose which required consideration. The first was as to the form in which the exclusion of the Ulster Counties should be provided for. The Government believed that it was common ground to all parties to the agreement that this area should not be subjected to automatic inclusion, and they did not propose to do more than make that sure. The other question was the retention after Home Rule of the Irish members in the Imperial Parliament in undiminished numbers, provided for by one of the heads of the agreement. But on a full examination of the matter, the Government felt that they could not themselves agree to, or have any expectation that the House of Commons could be brought to accept that arrangement as continuing after the next election, except for the purpose of any proposed alteration of the Government of Ireland Act or the Amending Bill. Mr Asquith concluded: With this explanation, the answer to my hon. and learned friend is that the Government do not propose to introduce any bill in regard to which there does not appear, beforehand, a prospect of substantial agreement among all the principal parties concerned.

No coercion of Ulster

Concluding a debate which followed, Mr Asquith said he had laid it down on the floor of the House that there must be no coercion of Ulster, and that the six counties which were being excluded by the arrangement should not be brought back by any automatic process, but only by express Acts of Parliament.

Text of the partition scheme

A White Paper was issued on Thursday, 27th July, with the simple title, 'Headings of a Settlement as to the Government of Ireland,' and inscribed: 'Presented to both Houses of Parliament by command of His Majesty.' There is nothing in the way of explanation or enlargement, but the opening paragraphs make it clear that the Government of Ireland Act, 1914, was not to apply to the excluded are of Ulster. The following is the full contents of the White Paper:

1. The Government of Ireland Act, 1914, to be brought into operation as soon as possible after the passing of the bill, subject to the modifications necessitated by these instructions.

2. The said Act not to apply to the excluded area, which is to consist of the six counties of Antrim, Armagh, Down, Fermanagh, Londonderry, and Tyrone, including the Parliamentary Boroughs of Belfast, Londonderry and Newry.

3. As regards the excluded area, the Executive power of His Majesty to be administered by a Secretary of State, through such officers and departments as may be directed by order of His Majesty in Council, those officers and departments not to be in any way responsible to the new Irish Government.

A Committee to be appointed, on which both of the Irish parties is to be represented, to assist the Government in preparing the necessary Orders in Council.

4. The number of Irish representatives in the United Kingdom House of Commons to remain unaltered (viz., 103).

5. The Irish House of Commons to consist of the members who sit in the United Kingdom House of Commons for constituencies within the area to which the Act applies.

6. A reduction to be made in the number of Irish Senators proportionate to the population of the excluded area. The Senators to be nominated by the Lord Lieutenant, subject to instructions from His Majesty.

7. The Lord Lieutenant to have power to summon conferences between the members for constituencies in the excluded area and the members for constituencies in the rest of Ireland.

8. A deduction to be made from item (a) of the transferred sum—(Cost of Irish services) when ascertained proportionate to the population of the excluded area.

High Court for Belfast

9. Provision to be made for permanent sittings of a High Court judge or judges to Belfast appointed by the Imperial Government, or for the constitution of a new Court in Belfast, with the same jurisdiction as that of the High Court, but locally limited.

All appeals both from the Courts in the excluded area and those in the rest of Ireland to go the Appeal Court in Dublin, which is to be composed of judges appointed by the Imperial Government, and having the like tenure of office as English judges.

The appeals from the Court of Appeal in Dublin, whether as respects cases coming from the excluded are or from the rest of Ireland, to go to the same tribunal of appeal in England. Whether it should be the House of Lords or the Privy Council is for the present immaterial.

10. Section Thirty of the Government of Ireland Act to be extended to any disputes or questions which may arise between the excluded area and the new Irish Government.

11. His Majesty's power of making Orders in Council for the purposes of the Act to be extended so as to include power to make the necessary adjustments and provisions with respect to the government of the excluded area and relations between that area and the rest of Ireland, Great Britain, etc.

12. Amongst the various questions to which attention must be directed in this connection will be the question of fixing fair rents under the Irish Land Acts. It is proposed that there should be two Commissioners specially allocated for fixing rents in the excluded area, and appointed by the British Government.

13. All Orders in Council under the new Act to

be laid before both Houses of Parliament in the same manner as Orders under the Government of Ireland Act. (See S. 48.)

14. The bill to remain in force during the continuance of the war, and a period of twelve months thereafter, but if a Parliament has not by that time made further and permanent provision for the government of Ireland the period for which the bill is to remain in force is to be extended by Order in Council for such time as may be necessary in order to enable Parliament to make such provision.

It is also understood that at the close of the war there should be held an Imperial Conference, with a view to bringing the Dominions into closer co-operation with the Government of the Empire, and that the permanent settlement of Ireland should be considered at that Conference.

Courtsmartial Reports

In the House of Commons on Tuesday, 24th October, 1916,

Mr Hazleton (for Mr Dillon) asked the Prime Minister whether he would not direct that the proceedings of the Irish Courtsmartial shall be published.

Mr Asquith: I will arrange that this shall be done.

In the House of Commons on Monday, 5th March, 1917,

Mr Dillon asked the Prime Minister whether his attention had been drawn to the pledge by the late Prime Minister on 24th October, 1916, that he would arrange to have the proceedings of the Dublin Courtsmartial now published; and whether he would see that this promise was carried into effect without further delay.

Mr Bonar Law: The subject has been carefully considered by the Government, who have come to the conclusion that in present circumstances it would be most detrimental to the public interest to publish these reports.

Funds.

The following funds were organised immediately after the rebellion:

Unemployment Through Fire—Lord Mayor of Dublin's Fund. A fund for this object was first suggested in the columns of the *Irish Times*, and eventuated in co-operation with that of the Right Hon. the Lord Mayor.

Dependants of Soldiers Killed in Dublin. Opened and administered by the *Irish Times*.

Trinity College Officers' Training Corps Commemoration Fund—Mr Lewis HS Beatty, 14 Grafton street, Dublin, Hon. Secretary and Treasurer.

Volunteer Training Corps Fund for Relief of Dependents—Right Hon. TF Molony, Lord Justice of Appeal, Chairman; Mr RA Anderson, Hon. Secretary, 18 South Frederick street, Dublin.

Irish Police and Constabulary Recognition Fund—President—The Earl of Meath, KP, HML; Hon. Treasurer—Mr RW Booth, Chamber of Commerce, Dublin; Hon. Secretaries—Messrs VC Le Fanu, JP Estate Office, Bray; Edward H Andrews, JP, Orton, Monkstown, Dublin.

Irish National Aid Association—Mr Lorcan G. Sherlock, LLD, Chairman; Mr L Gavin Duffy, Mr FJ Allen, Mr M Davitt, MB, and Mr TJ Cullen Hon. Secretaries, 10 Exchequer street, Dublin.

Irish Volunteers' Dependents' Fund—Mrs Tom Clarke, President; Mrs Eamonn Ceannt, Vice-President; S Nic Mhathghamha, Hon. Treasurer; E Mac Raghnaill, Hon. Secretary; Mrs Pearse, Mrs MacDonagh, Miss O'Hanrahan, Miss Madge Daly, Miss Lila Colbert, 1 College street, Dublin.

Subsequently the last two mentioned were amalgamated under the title of the Irish National Aid and Volunteers' Dependents' Fund, and at a conference of the Executive, held on 18th April, 1917, it was intimated that £107,069 had been collected. The subscriptions to February were made up as follows:

	£
Ireland	32,833
England and Wales	1,105
Scotland	59
New York Committee	29,414
Other American Committees	2,632
Australia and New Zealand	19,605
South Africa	332
South America	227
Spain	125
France	11
China	70
India	8

The disbursements were as follows:

	£
By the National Aid Association	9,709
By the Volunteer Dependents' Fund	5,277
By the Amalgamated Executive of the INA and VD fund	30,058

Leaving a balance on hands on 17th February of £41,701, including bank interest, etc.

Legislation that became necessary

Amid the general distraction caused by the rebellion it was not to be expected that the administration of the law could pursue its ordinary course. The fact that the insurgents were in possession of the Four Courts and its precincts during Easter Week, and that during this occupancy the courts, offices, judges' chambers, and Law Library had been entered and the contents rudely thrown about, and in some cases injured, made it impossible that business could begin as usual. The Easter law term should have begun on Thursday, 27th April, 1916, but on that day, as we have mentioned, the Four Courts were in the hands of the rebels. The Recorders' Courts in Dublin and Belfast and the Courts of the County Court Judges could not be opened at the usual times, as in most cases the judges were not able to secure railway facilities.

By a Royal Proclamation given at Windsor Castle on Wednesday, 26th April, 1916, the King proclaimed martial law in Ireland, and thereby suspended the right of subjects charged with offences to be tried by the Civil Courts. On Friday, 5th May, an informal meeting of the judges of the High Court of Justice in Ireland was held to consider the position arising out of the rebellion. The President of the Incorporated Law Society informed the judges that it would be impossible to commence business at the Four Courts before the 19th May. It was then arranged to have a meeting of the Rule Making Authority on Monday, 8th May, and accordingly on that day new rules were made, which were approved of by the Lord Lieutenant, and came into operation immediately. These rules provided: (a) That the Easter Sittings of the Court of Appeal and of the High Court in the year 1916 should commence on 19th May and terminate on the 10th June; (b) that the time between 24th April, 1916 and 8th May, 1916, inclusive, should not be reckoned in the computation of the times appointed or allowed for the doing of any act or taking any proceeding; and (c) In the taxation of the costs of any action or other proceeding pending in the Courts mentioned at the date of the order, the Taxing Master, in addition to the allowances already prescribed, should be at liberty to allow such further fees as he should decide were reasonably incurred by reason of the alteration in the date of the commencement of the Easter Sittings, 1916. It may also be added that the usual break between Easter Term and Trinity Term lasted only for a day or two.

Jury trials resumed

Jury trials were resumed on Wednesday, 24th Amy. The Under Secretary to the Lord Lieutenant on 16th May issued a statement that in connection with the destruction in Dublin and elsewhere of buildings and their contents the State would assume as the maximum of its *ex gratia* grant the same liability as would have fallen on the insurance companies if the risk had been covered by the policies in force at the time of the disturbances, and accordingly the Lord Lieutenant decided to appoint a committee to ascertain the sums assured and to advise on the claims of insured and uninsured persons. Looting might be deemed burning for the purposes of compensation, but no consequential damages were to be taken into account. No grant could be made in respect of property of any persons in complicity with the outbreak. The Committee soon got to work, and as a result very considerable grants have been made by the Government in respect of the contents of buildings and also for the rebuilding of the structures.

Loss of Title Deeds

Among the buildings and premises which were destroyed by the operations of the military or by fire were the offices of a large number of solicitors, and in most cases not only were furniture and fittings destroyed, but also large numbers of original documents, constituting the title deeds to property. The heat was so intense, and so continuous, that fire-proof safes, believed to be immune from fire, afforded little or no protection, and parchments crumpled up and became useless for any purpose whatever. It is worth noticing that original documents written on paper, while made very brittle by the extreme heat, were quite decipherable in many cases. The loss of these title deeds, wills and other documents affected persons in many parts of Ireland, as numerous documents belonging to solicitors in other parts of Ireland were with their agents in Dublin for registration and other purposes. On 23rd August, 1916, the Royal assent was given to an Act 'to amend the Law and Procedure of Civil Courts in Ireland in relation to conditions arising out of the recent disturbances in that country.' This Act is cited as the Law and Procedure (Emergency Provisions) (Ireland) Act: 1916 (6 and 7 Geo. V c. 46). The first section enacted that the period from 24th April, 1916, to 8th May, 1916, both inclusive, shall not be reckoned, and shall be deemed never to have been reckoned, in computing the times for doing any act or taking any proceeding in any Court in Ireland, and that the Court might grant any extension of time which might appear proper by reason of the recent disturbances. It also enacted that where any original document which required to be filed, enrolled, or lodged has been lost or destroyed in the course of the said disturbances the Court may authorise the filing, enrolment, or lodgment of a properly authenticated copy, which shall be deemed to be the original for all purposes. The fourth subsection of this section (1) provided for the making of title in respect of lost documents, and will probably be the foundation of a large number of applications to the Court; it provides: 'Subject to rules made under this Act, the powers and jurisdiction of the High Court with respect to the perpetuation of testimony shall extend to and may be exercised for the perpetuation of the testimony afforded by any muniment of title or other document which has been lost, destroyed or damaged in the course of the recent disturbances in Ireland, whether the right or claim of the person instituting proceedings is a present right or claim or depends upon the happening of some future event.'

No claims against city

The 6th sub-section took away any right which might have existed in respect of any claim against the city for damages under the acts which give compensation for malicious injuries. It enacted that 'No claim for compensation under any of the enactments relative to compensation for criminal or malicious injuries shall lie against a local authority in respect of any injury to person or property sustained in the course of the recent disturbances in Ireland.'

The 7th sub-section relieved solicitors and others from any action for negligence in the case of deeds entrusted to them, and in any such action or proceeding made it a sufficient defence if it is proved that the deed or other document being at the time of the commencement of the recent disturbance in the possession or under the control of a person entitled to have the possession or control, was lost or destroyed in the course and as a result of those disturbances. The Lord Chancellor of Ireland was empowered to make Rules to give full effect to the provisions of this Act, and Rules have been so made dated 3rd November, 1916. These Rules direct that applications under the Act are to be made to the Chancery Division of the High Court of Justice in Ireland. The only reported case under this Act up to the time of writing is Shanahan v. Shanahan (51 Ir. LTR 21). In that case Mr Justice Barton held that under this Act the Court has power to order that evidence as to a document lost or destroyed in the course of the recent disturbances in Ireland be taken and filed in the proper office of the Court. Such evidence may be given of the existence of the document before the disturbances took place, of its due execution, of its loss or destruction, and of its contents. In the course of the case Mr Justice Barton said one of the incidents of the recent disturbances was the destruction of legal documents and of title deeds in the offices of solicitors who had the custody of them. The Legislature thereupon stepped in to aid the parties by applying the old equitable jurisdiction for perpetuating testimony, a wholesome feature of which was that it could only be invoked in cases in which it was necessary to do so in order to safeguard rights, otherwise it might work injury by heaping up costs. This, however, is a *bona fide* application in which some such ought if possible to be given to the applicant.

Stamp duties and copying fees

As the public are aware, stamp duty and copying fees are payable on memorials of deeds and copies thereof in the Registry of Deeds Office, Henrietta street, Dublin, and the fees on Court documents are also paid by a stamp duty. By a concession of the Treasury contained in a Treasury Letter of the 14th day of December, 1916, the stamp duty and copying fees on copies of memorials of deeds destroyed during the rebellion in Dublin in April-May, 1916, were remitted, and also the fee stamp on Court documents destroyed by fire at the same period. On a certificate by the solicitor copies may be issued free of charge for pending legal proceedings or for Registration purposes.

REBUILDING OF DESTROYED AREAS
Special Act of Parliament Passed

The state of the city in the area affected by the rebellion made reconstruction necessary, and as many interests were affected and it was desirable to give additional powers for the purpose of raising money for building purposes, legislation was again required, and on the 22nd December, 1916, the Dublin Reconstruction (Emergency Provisions) Act, 1916, was passed. This Act is defined as 'An Act to amend the law as to the erection of buildings and the making and improvement of streets in connection with the reconstruction of areas, streets, and buildings recently damaged or destroyed in Dublin, and for other purposes incidental thereto.' The chief provisions of this Act, which consists of 12 sections and a schedule, may be shortly stated as follows:

Section 1 empowers the Corporation of Dublin, for the purpose of street improvements, to purchase land compulsorily by means of an order submitted to the Local Government Board. This section also enables the Corporation, in order to widen any street, to substitute one piece of land for another, and to attach to the substituted land all rights and interests affecting the lands taken.

City Architect's powers

Section 2 provides that a person who proposes to erect a new building on the site of a building which has been damaged or destroyed in the course of the recent disturbances, or to reconstruct or alter a building which has been damaged, shall, in addition to delivering plans and sections to the Town Clerk, deliver elevations on the same scale as that of the plans and sections, and shall furnish to the City Architect, if and when so requested by him, any detailed drawings or other particulars which the City Architect may consider reasonably necessary for the further explanation of the documents delivered. If it appears to the City Architect that the character of the proposed new building, restoration or alteration is such as would be injurious to the amenity of the street which the front of the proposed building faces, he may require such reasonable alterations to be made as respects the design, line of frontage, and materials as he thinks proper, and may require the plans, sections, and elevations to be amended accordingly. The front of a building at the corner of two streets shall be deemed to face each street for the purposes of this provision. If any dispute or difference arises as to the reasonableness of any requirement of the City Architect, the matter shall be settled by arbitration between the Corporation and the building owner, and the Corporation shall appoint the City Architect or a person nominated by him to be arbitrator on their behalf, and Section 217 of the Public Health (Ireland) Act shall apply with respect to the arbitration, subject to certain modifications, including one that the reference to the Local Government Board shall be construed as a reference to the Lord Lieutenant, and another that the arbitrators or umpire shall have power to make such modifications of any requirements of the City Architect as seem proper. The section also provides that the Corporation may, on the recommendation of the City Architect, relax or waive any bye-law of the Corporation relating to buildings, where and so far as such relaxation or waive is necessary to enable a joint plan of reconstruction to be carried out in relation to two or more buildings, subject to the consent of the owners of these buildings.

Advance of Money

Section 3 provides that the Corporation may advance money on the security of the ownership of the site of any house or building which has been damaged or destroyed for the purpose of reconstruction. The advance shall not exceed the difference between the amount which the Local Government Board certify to be the total cost of rebuilding or restoration and the amount of the compensation granted from public moneys in respect of the destruction or damage of, or to, the house or building, and in this connection it is to be noted that an *ex gratia* grant by the Government is a condition of the purpose or loan. The advance shall be repayable within such period as may be agreed upon, subject to the sanction of the Local Government Board, but the rate of interest shall not be more than 10s above the rate at which the Corporation can, at the date of advance, borrow money for the purpose from the Commissioners of Public Works, and the term of repayment shall be six months less than the term for which the Corporation can so borrow, unless a shorter term is agreed on. The balance of any such advance outstanding at any time may be repaid by the borrower on giving six months' notice (in writing) to the Corporation. The repayment of the advance and interest shall be secured by a mortgage of the site of the house or building in such form as may be approved by the Local Government Board.

Section 4 provides that where a person desirous of obtaining an advance is not in a position to secure the repayment owing to defective title or insufficiency of his interest in the site, or of the value of that interest, and the other person who concurrence is necessary, in order to remedy or remove the defect or insufficiency, are unable or unwilling to concur in securing the advance, he may apply to the Land Judge (Mr Justice Ross), for an order changing the ownership of the site, and any interest therein, with the repayment of the advance and interest. On any such application, the Land Judge may make an order changing all such interests, and each of them, with the repayment of the advance, interest, and instalments as between the several interests charged in proportion to the benefit accruing from the advance to the owners of those interests respectively. All interested persons will be given an opportunity of being heard. For the purposes of this section, the Land Judge, in addition to his powers and jurisdiction as Land Judge, shall have, and may exercise, all such powers and jurisdiction as are vested in, or exercisable by, the High Court or any division, court, or judge thereof, under any enactments or rules which are applied for the purposes aforesaid by rules made under this section to which we refer below. The Land Judge may review, rescind, or vary any order made under this section, but no such order shall be subject to appeal, and no proceedings before the Land Judge under this section shall be removed or restrained or questioned by any court.

Land Judge's powers

Under this section the Land Judge has power to ascertain the easements and rights attached to the sites, and to hear and determine all questions relating to such easements and rights.

Section 5 provides that at any time after the expiration of two years from the passing of this Act, if it appears to the Local Government Board, on the application of the Corporation, that the rebuilding or restoration of a house or building has not been commenced or, although commenced, has been discontinued, the Board may, unless they are satisfied that the rebuilding or restoration will be completed within a reasonable time, make an Order authorising the Corporation to acquire the site thereof; and the Corporation may sell, let, or otherwise dispose of the site when required in such manner and on such conditions as may be sanctioned by the Local Government Board, including the erection of suitable buildings on the site.

Section 6 provides that no hereditament or tenement upon which was built any building or house destroyed, nor any such building or house when rebuilt, shall be liable to be valued under the Irish Valuation Acts at a sum larger than the valuation in force on the 1st April, 1916, for a period of twelve years from the passing of this Act.

Section 7 provides that no building or house destroyed, nor the land on which the same stood, shall be assessed or liable to any local rate from the 24th April, 1916, until the expiration of one year from the rebuilding of the said house or building.

Section 8 provides that in the case of any publichouse, hotel, or other licensed premises which have been destroyed or damaged, and in which business has in consequence been suspended during the period of rebuilding or restoration, the licence (for the purposes of renewal and any certificates required for renewal, but for no other purpose) shall be deemed to continue in force up to the time of the completion of such rebuilding or restoration, and to be vested in the person legally entitled to the said premises, and it shall be competent for such person to apply for any justices' certificate required for renewal, and for the Court to consider such application, although the same may not be made to the annual licensing petty sessions. Any certificate as to the conduct of the business, required for the purposes of renewal, shall be a certificate as respects the conduct of the business during the period between the date of the last renewal and the destruction of or damage to the premises, and the Licensing (Ireland) Acts, 1833-1902, shall be deemed to be amended accordingly.

Section 9 provides that where a building destroyed or damaged is held under a lease for a term of years, of which the residue unexpired on the 24th April, 1916, was more than five and less than thirty-one years, section 5 of the Town Tenants (Ireland) Act, 1906 (which relates to compensation for unreasonable disturbance), shall apply to the building when rebuilt or restored.

Section 10 provides that the expenses of the Corporation in the execution of this Act shall be defrayed out of the rate or fund applicable to the purposes of the Public Health (Ireland) Acts, 1878 to 1907, but money so borrowed shall not be reckoned as part of the debt of the Corporation within the meaning of the limitation on borrowing imposed by Sub-section (2) of Section 238 of the Public Health (Ireland) Act, 1878.

The 11th Section contains the Interpretation Clause, and enacts that the expression 'site' includes buildings and other structures on, in, or under the surface, and article 32 of the schedule to the Local Government Order, 1898, is applied in reference to local inquiries. The 12th Section contains only the title of the Act.

The schedules contain provisions as to the compulsory acquisition of and by the Corporation.

The Rules

The Rules referred to above have been made by the Land Judge. They are dated 16th February, 1917. They are full and very explanatory of the Act and the procedure thereunder. They are divided into seven parts, with an Appendix of Forms. Part I consists of definitions, the entitling and description of documents, and certain directions as to the Forms in the appendix. Part II contains various preliminary matters, and directs that a person desirous of obtaining an advance under the Act who is not in a position to secure the repayment in accordance with the provisions of section 3 should endeavour to secure the concurrence of other persons whose concurrence is necessary to remove the defect of title. If such concurrence is refused or cannot be given, the person may lodge an originating statement or preliminary application. If such concurrence is unduly delayed, or if the person desiring the advance is not in privity with the other person whose concurrence is necessary, he may lodge a preliminary affidavit, as prescribed in the Rules. Part III provides various rules of procedure. The cases in which personal service is required and the mode thereof are pointed out in the Rules, and attention is directed to these. Costs are to be taxable by the Taxing Masters of the Court, and any agreement as to costs is to be subject to any order of the Court.

How proceedings may be initiated

Proceedings under section 4 may be initiated under any one of three methods provided in the Rules we have mentioned. (1) By originating statement; (2) by preliminary application, or (3) by preliminary affidavit. The proceedings will be initiated by originating statement when the plans, sections and elevation have been passed pursuant to the said section, and the Local Government Board has verified the amount of the advance, and that the same is necessary, pursuant to section 3 (2) of the Act. This method of procedure is set out in Part IV of the Rules ('Initiation of Proceedings by Originating Statement'). In support of the application the applicant is required to lodge a map of the site, certified copies of the plans, sections and elevations passed, pursuant to section 2 of the Act; the documents mentioned in the statement of title; a certificate of the City Architect; a certificate of the Town Clerk, and a certificate of the Local Government Board. Schedule II (Easements and Rights attached to the Site) requires very careful attention, but the Schedule is very explicit on the points—*e.g.* (1) Full and free right to the uninterrupted access, transmission and enjoyment of light to the ancient windows and apertures of the buildings on the 24th April, 1916, and showing that the same light or a substantial part of the same light, which on the 24th April, 1916, passed through the ancient windows and apertures into the destroyed buildings will pass into the proposed new buildings. Similar provisions are made with regard to the access and flow of air and other rights.

REBELLION VICTIMS' COMMITTEE

AWARDS GRANTED TO SUFFERERS

It was officially announced on Tuesday, 10th October, 1916, that the Lord Lieutenant had appointed a Committee, consisting of

Mr Charles St G Orpen (Chairman), President of the Incorporated Law Society of Ireland;

Mr Charles H O'Conor, Inspector Local Government Board; and

Mr JJ Taylor, CB, ISO, Principal Clerk of the Chief Secretary's Office, Dublin Castle,

To inquire and report with regard to applications for payment out of public funds to

(a) Persons who have suffered loss by reason of personal injuries sustained by them without misconduct or default on their part in the recent rebellion; and

(b) Dependents of deceased persons who, without misconduct or default on their part, were killed or injured in the recent rebellion.

The Secretary of the Committee is Mr HC Love, 13 St Stephen's Green, N, Dublin, where all correspondence regarding claims to the Committee had to be directed.

The entire proceedings of the Committee were conducted in private, and it was not until the 9th February, 1917, there was published a number of awards granted by the Rebellion (Victims) Committee in respect of the claims of persons whose breadwinners were killed during the suppression of the rebellion. To each solicitor acting on behalf of dependents the following letter was addressed:

'Chief Secretary's Office, Dublin Castle.

'I am directed by the Lord Lieutenant to transmit to you the accompanying schedule of cases in which the Irish Government, with the approval of the Lords Commissioners of His Majesty's Treasury, will make payment of *ex-gratia* grants of the amounts stated, in full settlement of claims presented to the Rebellion (Victims) Committee. In the cases of awards to adult and minor dependents, it is proposed that the full amount of the grant in each case be lodged in the County Court, and that the apportionment between the adult and minors be made by the Recorder. It is considered to be necessary in these cases to appoint at least two trustees, and if you submit the names of two suitable persons to act as such, with their consents, you will be informed if they are approved of. On their being nominated as trustees, and obtaining privities to lodge the amount of the grant in Court, arrangements will be made for the lodgement of the money. In other cases where the grants are to adults alone, without minors, it is also proposed to pay the money to trustees, to be administered by them for the benefit of the grantees, and in any such cases in which you are interested I shall be glad to have the names of two suitable persons to act as trustees.'

450 applications

On Monday, 12th February, a deputation of solicitors, representing women and children, to whom the Treasury proposed to make grants of money, waited on the Under-Secretary (Sir William P Byrne) at Dublin Castle with reference to the manner in which the money was proposed to be given to the applicants. The deputation put forward the case that the money ought to be paid directly to the adults to whom it had been awarded, without passing through the hands of the trustees, and that where there were children the mother should receive her share without having it lodged in the Recorder's Court. All the members of the deputation agreed that the money to be given to minors should be lodged in the Recorder's Court, and kept there until the intended beneficiaries shall have attained their majority.

Mr Taylor mentioned that he had had 450 applications.

As a result of the consideration of the points brought to notice by the above deputation of solicitors, it was decided to adhere to the procedure previously communicated to them.

COMPENSATION FOR PROPERTY DESTROYED

Settlement of claims

One of the results of the destruction of property in Dublin during the rebellion was a conference of the leading sufferers, which led to the holding of a very large meeting in the Mansion House on Monday, 9th May, 1916, Mr WM Murphy in the chair, when it was decided unanimously that the Dublin Fire and Property Losses Association should be formed to seek compensation for the terrible losses inflicted on them during Easter Week. The following Committee was elected—Messrs George Stapleton, Charles Eason, Sir Thomas Robinson, Dr JA Mitchell, WM Murphy, JC Percy, William Bewley, Marcus Goodbody, EP Robertson, Sir Joseph Downes, Martin Fitzgerald, MJ Minch, JF Potter, Gerald Curtis, Patrick Rooney, Patrick White, MP, and Dr Lorcan Sherlock. Mr Robert J Kidney, FSAA, who placed his offices, Star Buildings, College Green, at the disposal of the Association, was elected Secretary, and the Committee lost no time in getting to work, and invited all the sufferers to send in full particulars of their losses.

A request was made to the Prime Minister asking him to receive a deputation to lay their claims for compensation before the Government at his earliest possible convenience, and in the meantime a deputation from the Committee waited upon the Under Secretary, Sir Robert Chalmers, when they had a long interview with him. On the 11th May a deputation was also received by the Lord Lieutenant, from whom they got a very favourable reception.

Basis of compensation

On the 17th May a letter was received from Sir Robert Chalmers informing the Committee that the Government had decided to meet the claims of the sufferers, and that they would be dealt with upon the basis of the policies of the insurance companies in force at the time of the destruction of the property, and that the claims of uninsured persons would also be dealt with on analogy with the insured claims. These terms of reference were not considered satisfactory, and a considerable amount of negotiation took place between the Government and the Committee, who pointed out that if the losses were to be dealt with upon the basis of the insurance policies in force only, the uninsured would be in a better position than the partly insured, who constituted more than 75 per cent of the total claims. This was pressed so strongly on the Government that the Prime Minister sent Mr Herbert Samuel, Home Secretary, to Dublin, where he received a deputation from the Association, when he admitted that it would be most unfair to give preferential treatment to the uninsured person. The result of the efforts of the Association were the issue of amended terms of reference to a Committee constituted of Sir Wm J Goulding, Bart., DL: Mr John Osborne, of Messrs Sels and Co., and Mr Samuel J Pipkin, General Manager of the Atlas Insurance Company. Mr James J Healy, 51 St Stephen's Green East, acted as Secretary to the Committee.

Mr Walter Hume, 16 College Green, and Mr Wm Montgomery, 1 Foster place, acted as assessors to the Commission. Both gentlemen are well-known and eminent in their profession.

The question of limiting the amount of claims to the insurance value was for a long time in suspension, and it was some months before the Association's efforts to get beyond that point was successful, and although the greater part of claims for buildings and stock have now been settled, the Association is still faced with problems affecting building owners in connection with the rebuilding of the city.

Re-building

The Government at the request of the Dublin Corporation introduced a Bill giving them large and unprecedented powers of dealing with the structure, design, and alignment of the new buildings, which was carefully considered by the association, and they decided to oppose it, and a petition was presented to the House against the second reading of the bill. The opposition was so strong that the Chief Secretary promised that he would not bring forward the bill for the third reading unless an agreement between the Association and the Dublin Corporation was arrived at. Negotiations then took place, with the result that the present Dublin Reconstruction Act of 1916 was passed as an agreed Bill.

The Goulding Commission

The Government decision regarding the question of compensation for property destroyed in Dublin during the rebellion was set out in the following *communiqué* issued by the Under-Secretary to the Lord Lieutenant on Tuesday, 16th May:

In connection with the destruction, both in Dublin and elsewhere, of buildings and their contents, the State will assume, as the maximum of its *ex gratia* grant, the same liability as would have fallen on the insurance companies if the risk had been covered by the policies in force at the time of the recent disturbances.

Accordingly, His Excellency the Lord Lieutenant has decided to appoint a Committee—

(a) (i.) to ascertain what were the sums covered, for ordinary fire risks, by insurance policies in force at the time of the destruction of the property: (ii.) to advise what part of such sums would normally have been paid by the insurance companies if the destruction had been caused by accidental fire: and (b) having regard to the information obtained under the foregoing heads (i.) and (ii.), to advise how, on analogy, the several claims of uninsured persons could fairly be dealt with.

For the foregoing purposes looting may be deemed to be burning, but no consequential damages of any kind are to be taken into account.

In no case will any grant be made in respect of the property of persons in complicity with the outbreak.

Literature of the rebellion

In addition to the illustrated records referred to on page 156, the following Historical Sketches appeared during he year 1916:

The Irish Rebellion of 1916. By John F Boyle. Constable.

Six Days of the Irish Republic. By LG Redmond-Howard. Ponsonby.

A History of the Irish Rebellion of 1916. By Warre B Wells and Marlowe. Maunsell.

Insurrection in Dublin. By James Stephens. Maunsell.

The Irish Rebellion: What Happened and Why. By FA Mackenzie. Pearson.

The Sinn Fein Rebellion as I Saw It. By Mrs H Norway. Smith Elder.

DEFENDERS OF TRINITY COLLEGE HONOURED

On Saturday, 5th August, 1916, in the Provost's gardens of Trinity College, a presentation from the citizens of Dublin to commemorate the gallant conduct of the Officers' Training Corps during the rebellion was made.

To the prompt measures, defensive and offensive, organised by this Corps was due the preservation of valuable life and property in Grafton street, Nassau street, College Green, College street, Dame street, and Westmoreland street, including not only the historic buildings of the College itself, but the Bank of Ireland and many other of our finest buildings.

Appreciation of this amongst that section of the citizens and property-holders who attributed their immunity from loss to the gallant conduct of the Officers' Training Corps materialised by subscription into a fund, exceeding £700, some of which was expended in presenting silver plate to the College to testify and record their gratitude.

Sir Maurice Dockrell was the President of the Committee, and Mr Lewis HS Beatty, Hon. Secretary and Treasurer. The members of the Committee were: Messrs. WD Burke, E Tenison Collins, Henry Dudgeon, Charles Gamble, MB Mathews, Robert Mitchell, F Thompson, and LA West.

Two large presentation silver cups, each valued at £50, and weighing 170 ozs., were presented to the Commandant of the Officers' Training Corps, who, on behalf of the Corps, handed over the Cups to the Provost of Trinity.

A special silver commemorative replica was presented to Provost Mahaffy, and three special silver replicas to Major RW Tate, Commandant; Major GA Harris, Adjutant, and Capt. EH Alton, the Officer Commanding Infantry. Swords were presented to the officers of the OTC, and silver replicas were given to all ranks of the Corps who participated in the work of defence.

The following is the complete list of those who were awarded replicas of the cup:

Staff

Andrews, W, Pipe Major
Basonnet, JE, Co. Sgt-Maj.
Harris, GA, Major
Howell, GA, Con. Sgt.-Maj.
Hoyes, T, QMS
Tate, RW, Major, Comdt.

Officers

Alton, EH, Captain
Baker, AWW, Lieut.
Crawford, JW, Sec.-Lieut.
Luce, AA, Lieut.
Mitchell, JM, Sec. Lieut.
Robinson, CL, Lieut.
Smyth, LB, Sec.-Lieut.
Waterhouse, G, Lieut.
Wood, GH, Captain
Wylie, WE, Sec.-Lieut.

Honorary Members

Canning, H, (Ex-Lieut. DUOTC), FTCD
Pope, JS, Professor
Joly, J, Prof., TCD

Other Ranks

Aidin, AR, Cadet
Allardyce, WS, Cadet
Ashley, M, Cadet Corpl.
Bailey, DH, Cadet Corpl.
Barnes, RV, Cadet
Beckett, DD, Cadet
Bolton, AD, Cadet
Bowesman, GW, Cadet
Boxwell, WS, Cadet
Boyd, RD, Cadet
Bridge, AV, Cadet
Buchanan, WO, Cadet
Butler, R O'N, Cadet Cpl.
Callaghan, JN, Cadet
Chadwick, R St G, Cadet
Chapman,—, Cadet
Cheeke, WA, Cadet
Chute, CJF, Cadet
Collen, W, Cadet
Corbett, RHM, Cadet
Cox, AE, Cadet
Davison, JC, Cadet Sergt.
Despard, ER, Cadet
Dickenson, CH, Cadet Sgt.
Dowling, P, Storeman
Dundon, HC, Cadet
Edwards,—, Cadet
Elford, WP, Cadet
Ferguson, WJ, Cadet
Fitzgerald, GE, Cadet, Cpl.
FitzGibbon, G, Cadet Sergt.
Frazer,—, Cadet
French, JA, Cadet Corpl.
Freeman, CH, Cadet Cpl.
Goodbody, GM, Cadet
Griffin, G, Cadet
Gurney, S, Cadet Corpl.
Harvey,—, Cadet
Hoey, FC, Cadet
Howell, RH, Cadet Sergt.
Jamison, SW, Cadet
Jones-Nowlan, TC, Cadet
Johnston, JK, Cadet
Jordan, GJL, Cadet
Keatinge, GF, Cadet Sergt.
Keegan, W, Cadet Corpl.
Kennedy, HB, Cadet
Killeen, PJ, Cadet Corpl.
Kough, CN, Cadet Sergt.
King,—, Cadet
Kirker, J, Cadet
Lane,—, Cadet
Lawther, JM, Cadet
Leslie, WE, Cadet
Long, E, Cadet
Lubbe, WP, Cadet
Lynn-Grant, CJ, Cadet
Madill, T, Cadet
Maginess, H A, Cadet
Mahony, D McC, Cadet Sgt.
Malone, JJ, Cadet
Mathews, AH, Cadet Cpl.
Mein, CB, Cadet Sergt.
Molyneux, ET, Cadet
Moran, WA, Cadet
Mooney, HL, Cadet
Moore, TCK, Cadet
Murphy, N, Cadet.
Murray, ER, Cadet Cpl.
McBrien, ME, Cadet.
McCaig, MR, Cadet.
McCann, TS, Cadet.
McCullagh, LS, Cadet
McElroy, FW, Cadet, Cpl.
McFeely, WN, Cadet Cpl.
McQuade,—, Cadet.
Neale, J, Cadet.
Orr,—, Cadet.
O'Meara, HJ, Cadet
Peirce, BJ, Cadet Cpl.
Phipps, JP, Cadet Cpl.
Powell, GH, Cadet.
Powell, PL, Cadet
Price, FW, Cadet QMS
Purcell, W, Cadet.
Quinlan, PF, Cadet.
Quinn, JS, Cadet.
Robertson, FW, Cadet
Russell, JHS, Cadet
Russell, WJA, Cadet.
Rutter, W, Cadet, QMS
Salazar, DS, Cadet
Scallan, RT, Cadet Cpl.
Scanlon,—, Cadet
Seddall, WV, Cadet
Shannon, WA, Cadet
Smith,—, Cadet
Spence, WN, Cadet Cpl.
Sutherland, IG, Cadet
Tweedy, RW, Cadet Sergt.
Varian, WO, Cadet Cpl.
Walland,—, Cadet
Webb, G, (Miss) Lady Clk.
Weldon, HB, Cadet
Weir, JH, Cadet Cpl.
Wheeler, RH, Cadet, Cpl.
Wigoder, L, Cadet Sergt.
Wilson, EF, Cadet

COLONIAL SOLDIERS WHO ASSISTED IN DEFENCE OF TCD

454045	Pte. Cassidy, 39th Res. Canadian Infantry.
9343	Pte. Charlton, 3rd Sth African Infantry.
2/1745	Cpl. Don., NZ FA.
3/1315	Corpl. Garland, New Zealand MC.
9405	Pte. Gibson, 3rd S Afr. Infantry.
2521	Pte. Kinnahan, 3rd S Afr. Infantry.
9208	Pte. King, Sth. Afr. Scottish.
1985	Pte. McHugh, 9th Aus. Infantry Force.
9435	Pte. Moffitt, 3rd Sth African Infantry.
4/666	Lance Corpl. McLeod, NZ Ryl. Eng. (2nd).
3/1347	Sgt. Nevin, NZ MC.
7625	Pte. Russell, Sth Afr. Infantry.
12/1253	Pte. Waring, 6th New Zealand R.
447766	Bugler Webb, 56th Can. Infantry.

Chief Steward Mr Joseph Marshall, and about 20 members of the College Staff also received replicas.

Ladies who served

The following ladies rendered valuable services during the rebellion:

Mrs Dorothy Hignett
Miss Elsie Mahaffy
Mrs Molesworth
Miss Renny Tailyour
Miss Rachel Mahaffy
Mrs Annie Elizabeth Payne

Also

L Fenelon, Cadet
JG Moore, Cadet
V Smythe, Cadet
A Malcolmson, Cadet
E Pinion, Cadet

DEFENDERS OF BEGGAR'S BUSH BARRACKS

Nominal Roll of Officers, Non-Commissioned Officers, and Men of the 1st (Dublin) Battalion Associated Volunteer Training Corps who were on duty in Beggar's Bush Barracks during the period Monday, 24th April, 1916, to Tuesday, 2nd May, 1916.

Officers

Allen, GWF, Pl. Comdr.
Anderson, RA, Pl. Comdr.
Dickinson, C, Co. Comdr.
Miller, HJ, Co. Comdr.
McNair, EA, Pl. Comdr.
O'Toole, J, S.-Major
Webb, Ed, Co. Comdr.
White, J, Adjutant
Wilson, J, Pl. Comdr.

Other Ranks

Atkinson, GR, Private
Bagnall, T St., Sec. Comdr.
Barnes, Jos., A, Bugler
Barnes, Joseph, Private
Beckett, GT, Private
Behan, Timothy, Private
Bennie, DJ, L.-Sergt.
Browne, Geo., Private
Burrowes, E, Sergeant
Callear, HH, Private
Campbell, TW, Private
Carey, Thos. H, P.-Sergt.
Clery, Reg. F, L.-Cpl.
Connell, JW., Private
Cosser, Robt., Private
Cox, W, Private
Crawford, WH, Private
Cullerton, JJ, Sec. Comdr.
Davidson, RA, Sec. Comdr.
Day, GA, P.-Sergt.
Doyle, Fred., Private
Dudley, JJ, Private
Edie, Wm, Private
Ford, John B, Bugler
Ford, GH, Private
Foster, S, Private
Gill, John, Private
Green, Harold, Bugler
Guy, Samuel, Private
Harris, GA, Major
Hamilton, JM, L.-Cpl.
Hanlon, Geo., Private
Harte, N, Corporal
Harrison, RJ, Private
Haughton, AE, L. Cpl.
Hawkins, WT, Corporal
Hinch, J de W, Corporal
Hosford, Jos., Private
Hosford, S, Private
Humphreys, L, Private
Hutchinson, AJ, Private
Iley, CE, L.-Cpl.
Johnston, WJ, Private
Lawson, Wm, Corporal
Leopold, CS, Private
Love, HE, Private
Luke, E, L.-Cpl.
Lyster, AE, Private
Lynn, Grant, Cadet
Manning, John, Private
Millard, Jas. G, Private
Montgomery, JA, Private
Moriarty, LE, Sergt.
Mundy, Wm, Cpl.
Murray, Geo., Private
McCarthy, SV, Private
McConnell, RJ, Private
McCormick, CT, Private
McLindon, JE, Private
McRae, WE, P.-Sergt.
Neale, Wm G, Private
Newnham, Geo. A, Private
O'Cleary, P, Mot. Cyclist
O'Donnell, R, Corporal
O'Mahony, C, Cadet
Orpin, John, Private
Pasley, ET, Private
Pearce, CP, Private
Penney, Thos. L, Private
Rae, Thos., Sec. Comdr.
Reilly, CP, Private
Robinson, JH, Private
Robinson, Rev. JL, Sergt.-Instructor Musketry
Rooke, RA, Private
Russell, RH, Private
Russell, JW, Private
Ryan, John, Private
Ryan, John, Bugler
Sanderson, FG, Ar-Sergt.
Shaw, HGF, Co. QMS
Shea, AH, P-Sergt.
Shea, HW, Private
Sibthorpe, AC, L.-Sergt.
Sibthorpe, John, Private
Sloan, John, Private
Stephens, Fred., Private
Stokes, PH, Private
Strachan, Andrew, Sergt.
Stuart, WB, Private
Trueman, JA, Private
Tulloch, GH, L.-Cpl
Walker, HN, Private
Watters, Chas. T, Corporal
West, FG, Private
Wilson, Geo., Private
Zeland, Hy W, Private

DUBLIN NEWSPAPERS IN THE REBELLION
'*Irish Times*' Record
A Publication Table

April 24. *Irish Times, Freeman's Journal, Express* and *Independent*
25. *Irish Times* and *Independent*
26. *Irish Times* only
27. *Irish Times* only
28. No Paper
29. No Paper

May 1. *Irish Times* only
2. *Irish Times* only
3. *Irish Times* and *Express*
4. *Irish Times, Express* and *Independent*
5. *Irish Times, Express, Freeman's Journal,* and *Independent*

The Irish Times' Unique Position

The *Newspaper World* wrote: 'The position of the *Irish Times* was unique all through the insurrection. Equipped with an independent suction gas plant, the *Irish Times* was able to publish its daily issued up to Thursday of the memorable week when the continued rifle and maxim-gun fire in the Westmoreland street area made it impossible for anyone to venture around. Members of the several departments in the office were in attendance on each day, but the paper was not published on Friday or Saturday. The Government Proclamations as to Martial Law, etc., were published through the medium of the *Irish Times,* and its early issued of the week were wholly devoid of any general news matter, the contents comprising special articles of literary interest and some items of local events. As much as a shilling per copy was paid for the *Irish Times* during the height of the insurrection, and none of the newsvendors would sell one under twopence. The issue published on Monday, 1st May, was dated for "Friday, Saturday, Monday, April 28 and 29, and May 1, 1916", "for the convenience of persons and institutions that file the *Irish Times* for reference," as explained in an editorial statement.'

The 'Weekly Irish Times' breaks all records

The *Weekly Irish Times,* after missing two publications, came out with a triple issued dated April 29, May 6 and 13. The number contained a complete record of the rebellion, with full details of the fighting, lists of casualties, and prisoners sentenced and deported, and pictures of the principals. The issue proved immensely poplar, and had a colossal circulation, which far exceeded anything ever previously claimed by any Dublin newspaper —morning, evening, or weekly.

Other publications

The following publications appeared at various times during the twelve months preceding the Rebellion:

Irish Volunteer—Printed for the Proprietors at Mahon's Printing Works, Dublin, and published at the Volunteer Headquarters, 2 Dawson street, Dublin.
Scissors and Paste—Printed for the Proprietor by Patrick Mahon, at the office, 67 Middle Abbey street, Dublin.
Fianna—Printed by the Irish Industrial Printing and Publishing Co., 49 Middle Abbey street, Dublin, for the *Fianna* Publishing Co, 1 College street, Dublin.
The Eye Opener—Published by the Proprietor, and printed for him by The O'Connell Press, 7 College street, Dublin
Sinn Fein—Printed by Devereux, Newth and Co., 49 Middle Abbey street. Published by Sinn Fein Co. at same address.
The Irish Worker—Printed for the proprietors at the City Printing Works, 13 Stafford street, and published by him at 13 Beresford place, in the City of Dublin.
Irish Freedom—Printed by Patrick Mahon, 3 Yarnhall street, Dublin, for the proprietors and publishers, by them, at their office, 5 Findlater place, Dublin.
The Toiler—Printed for the proprietor, PJ MacIntyre, by the *Western News* Company, at Ballinasloe, Co. Galway.
Irish Review—Simpkin, Marshall, Hamilton, Kent and Co., London. Falconer, Dublin.
New Ireland.—Printed for the *New Ireland* Publishing Co., Limited, by the Wood Printing Works, 13 Fleet street, Dublin.

Seditious Papers

In the published minutes of evidence taken before the Royal Commission on the rebellion there is an appendix of documents in which there is given the following list, produced by Sir Matthew Nathan, of seditious weekly papers circulating in Ireland:
The Irish Volunteer—Owner, Bulmer Hobson, 2 Dawson street. Editor, John MacNeill, Woodtown park, Rathfarnham.
The Spark—Owner, Mariana Peroliz, 10 North Great George's street. Editor (supposed), Countess Markievicz, 49B Leinster road, Rathmines.
New Ireland—Owners, The New Ireland Printing and Publishing Co., 13 Fleet street. Editor, Denis Gwynn, B.A., 37 Aylesbury road.
The Workers' Republic—Owner, Helena Moloney, 70 Eccles street. Editor, James Connolly, 49B Leinster road.
The Hibernian—Owners, Parent Body of AOH. Editor, Mr. Stephen Bollard, 28 North Frederick street.
Nationality—Owner, Sean McDermott, 12 D'olier street. Editor, Arthur Griffith, 122 St Lawrence road, Clontarf.
Honesty—Owner and (supposed) editor, Miss Mary Walker, 101 Lower Mount street.
The Irishman—Owner and editor, Herbert M. Pim, Belfast.
The Gael—Owner, Edward Dwyer, Ballagh, Goold's Cross, Tipperary. Editor, Edward Dwyer.

PASSES GRANTED BY THE MILITARY AND POLICE
Some Specimens

On Wednesday, 26th, and Thursday, 27th, April, the granting of permits to those whose occupations required them to pass to and fro in the city and suburbs was considered by the military authorities. Later on, when the railway and shipping services were resumed, permits to travel from and to Dublin, and to England and Scotland were granted by the military and police authorities. These 'passes' or 'permits' were variously worded according to he issuing body, and the requirements of the individual in whose favour they were drawn. To some of these granted by the Royal Irish Constabulary the photograph of the person in whose favour it had been given was attached. The following are some general specimens:

Headquarters, Irish Command,
Parkgate, Dublin, 29th April, 1916.
To Whom It Concerns

Mr ...., residing at .... is an employé of ...., and is entitled to pass to and from .... office and his residence as necessity may require.

(Signed) IH Price.
GSIC

Headquarters, Irish Command,
Parkgate, Dublin. 2nd May, 1916

No. ....

Pass Bearer .... anywhere at any time ....

RC Kelly, IH Price,
Captain Staff. Major,
Intelligence Officer, General Staff.

Stamp.
A. 4. Issued at Kingstown
22-v.-16

The Bearer .... has permission from the Military Authorities to enter and leave the Kingstown Area for Pier on one occasion only, available 22-v.-'16

Holder's Signature. W Hodson,
Acting APM

Assistant Provost Marshal, Dublin
No. ....
Date—22-5-'16
Lower Castle Yard,
Dublin.

Please pass .... between Dublin and England, via Kingstown

Powerscourt, Major
Asst Provost-Marshal, Dublin

Dublin Metropolitan Police
...................May, 1916

Please pass ...., of .... through the streets of the city and DMP Area.

W Edgeworth-Johnstone
Commissioner

This is endorsed by the RI Constabulary for persons leaving Dublin by rail or road. This endorsement reads:

RI Constabulary Office,
Dublin Castle.

—Within pass is valid for the district outside the DMP area.

Neville Chamberlain,
Inspector General
RIC

3-5-'16

Royal Irish Constabulary,
Kilrush, Co. Clare
18-5-'16

Permit.

The bearer of .... of .... in the County of Clare, is known to me to be a loyal person, and may be permitted to embark for England.

(Signed) Patrick Dowling, DI, RIC

Signature of bearer appended ....

District Inspector's Office,
RI Constabulary
Cork—South, May 2nd, '16
City of Cork.

The bearer................... of ...., has my permission to travel from Cork to Liverpool on 22nd day of May, 1916, for the purpose of visiting friends.

CA Walsh, District Inspector

All concerned.
Photo of bearer attached to this pass.

District Inspector's Office,
King street, Cork
20th May, 1916.
Permit.

The Bearer,..................., of................... has authority to proceed to London via Holyhead on 22nd Day of May, 1916. The object of her journey is Private Business. Description...................,
Eyes..................., Nose...................,
Complexion ...., Height...................,
Age ...., Occupation...................,
Married or Single ....
Signature of Bearer

OR Swanzy, DI, RIC

All concerned.
Photo of bearer attached to this is pass.

IRISH POLICE AND CONSTABULARY RECOGNITION FUND

Distribution of Rewards.

On Thursday, 17th May, 1917, at the Royal Irish Constabulary Depot, in the Phoenix park, Dublin, ninety officers and men of the Royal Irish Constabulary and Dublin Metropolitan Police were presented with certificates of honour for their conspicuous service in the suppression of the rebellion of 1916. The presentation was made by Sir Maurice Dockrell, on behalf of the Irish Police and Constabulary Recognition Fund. The certificate was designed by Mr Richard Orpen, RHA, of the Royal Hibernian Academy. It was worded thus:

Presented in recognition of service to the State during the Sinn Fein Rebellion of 1916 by the Executive of the Irish Police and Constabulary Recognition Fund.

Each certificate was neatly framed and signed by the Earl of Meath, President of the Committee.

Along with the certificate of his honour each of the policeman was given £5 in scrip of the War Loan. The officers did not receive this monetary award.

Brigadier-General Byrne, on behalf of Royal Irish Constabulary, and Colonel Edgeworth-Johnstone, on behalf of the Dublin Metropolitan Police, thanked Sir Maurice Dockrell and the other members of the Committee of the fund.

Awards presented to RIC men at the depot

The following is the official list of officers and men of the Royal Irish Constabulary who were presented with Certificates and War Loan Stocks by the Committee of the Irish Police and Constabulary Recognition Fund at the RIC Depot on 17th May, 1917:

	Amount of Stock
RIC Office	
County Inspector JEL Holmes	–
District Inspector GH Mercer	–
District Inspector CCH Moriarty	–
Meath	
County Inspector George B Heard (Navan)	–
RIC Depot	
Sergt. JJ Bowman	£5 0 0
Sergt. JF Gillespie	5 0 0
Sergt. Patrick Hyland	5 0 0
Sergt. Issaac Reid	5 0 0
Act. Sergt. John Coughlan	5 0 0
Constable Thos. O'Connor	5 0 0
Constable Peter Folan	5 0 0
Constable Joseph Regan	5 0 0
Co. Galway ER	
Head Constable Hugh M Crean (Ballinasloe)	5 0 0
Sergt. Peter O'Regan (Athenry)	5 0 0
Constable John Clarke (Moyville)	5 0 0
Constable Owen M'Glade (Ballinasloe)	5 0 0
Constable Joseph Patton (Laurencetown)	5 0 0
Constable Charles Ginty (Gurteen)	5 0 0
Co. Galway WR	
Sergt. James Healy (Oranmore)	5 0 0
Act. Sergt. Samuel M'Carthy (Clonbern)	5 0 0
Constable Anthony Barrett (Oranmore)	5 0 0
Constable James Shea (Cummer)	5 0 0
Constable Hugh Hamilton (Galway)	*10 0 0
Constable James Farrell (Galway)	5 0 0
Co. Kerry	
Sergt. Daniel Crowley (Ballyheigue)	5 0 0
Act. Sergt. Bernard Reilly (Ardfert)	5 0 0
Constable George Carter (Causeway)	5 0 0
Constable Patrick O'Connell (Tralee)	5 0 0
Co. Louth	
Sergt. Michael Wymes (Dundalk)	5 0 0
Constable Richard Kelly (Ardee)	5 0 0
Constable Jas. Doherty (Drogheda)	5 0 0
Co. Meath	
Sergt. Wm O'Connell (Athboy)	5 0 0
Sergt. John Griffin (Bohermeen)	5 0 0
Act. Sergt. Patrick Sullivan (Moynalty)	5 0 0
Constable Wm E Johns (Navan)	*15 0 0
Constable Tim Finan (Bohermeen)	*15 0 0
Constable Patrick Drinan (Nobber)	*15 0 0
Constable Patk. Conneely (Athboy)	*15 0 0
Constable MJ Duggan (Crossakiel)	*15 0 0
Constable Patrick M'Keon (Slane)	*15 0 0
Constable Eugene Bratton (Navan)	5 0 0
Co. Wexford	
Sergt. Michael Collopy (Wexford)	5 0 0
Sergt. Peter Gunnigle (Olygate)	5 0 0
Constable Michael Moore (Wexford)	5 0 0
Constable Michael M'Carthy (Wexford)	5 0 0
Constable Cornelius Sullivan (Wexford)	5 0 0
Constable John Sullivan (Oylgate)	5 0 0

*Wounded

Awards to Dublin Metropolitan Police at the RIC Depot

The following is the official list of awards of Certificates and Stock made to the Dublin Metropolitan Police at the RIC Depot on 17th May, 1917:

Division	*Rank, Name and Divisional Number*		*Amount of War Stock awarded*
A	Const. Ed. J Sheppard	176	£5 0 0
A	Const. Patrick Downing	45	5 0 0
A	Const. John Whelan	37	5 0 0
B	Sgt. John Barton	11	5 0 0
B	Sgt. John R Megahey	17	5 0 0
B	Sgt. Stephen Murphy	186	5 0 0
B	Sgt. Michael Sheehan	76	5 0 0
B	Sgt. William Gore	59	5 0 0
B	Sgt. Cuthbert O'Connell	48	10 0 0
B	Sgt. Denis Cotter	189	5 0 0
B	Sgt. Patrick H Curley	121	5 0 0
B	Sgt. Michael McSharry	89	5 0 0
B	Sgt. Bernard Reilly	99	5 0 0
B	Sgt. John Lyons	72	5 0 0
B	Sgt. James Neill	115	5 0 0
B	Sgt. John Reddy	161	5 0 0
B	Sgt. Arthur Rellis,	113	5 0 0
C	Stn. Sgt. Patrick Barker	7	5 0 0
C	Sgt. John Young	10	5 0 0
C	Const. Robt. R Doyle	69	5 0 0
C	Const. Andrew Buckley	213	5 0 0
D	Stn. Sgt. John Hughes	6	15 0 0
D	Sgt. Martin Tuohey,	19	5 0 0
D	Const. Thomas Donohoe	39	10 0 0
D	Const. John Healy	175	5 0 0
D	Const. Charles Hales	119	5 0 0
D	Const. Hugh Murphy	69	5 0 0
E	Sgt. John Walsh	14	5 0 0
E	Sgt. Patrick J. Haugh,	21	5 0 0
E	Const. Daniel McMullan	51	5 0 0
E	Const. Matthew Byrne	64	5 0 0
E	Const. Michael Devine	129	5 0 0
E	Const. Michael Grace	30	5 0 0
F	Const. William Harmon	35	5 0 0
F	Const. Andrew Kilgallon	53	5 0 0
F	Const. Michael Davies	78	5 0 0
F	Const. Jeremiah Tangney	68	5 0 0
F	Const. Charles Nicholson	31	5 0 0
F	Const. Timothy Moriarty	97	5 0 0
G	Inspr. Neil McFeely		5 0 0
G	DO Michae McKeogh	31	5 0 0
G	DO Thomas Mannion	35	5 0 0
G	DO Michael McGowan	40	5 0 0
G	Const. Patrick J Myles	7	5 0 0
Corpl. James H. Culter, MF Police (formerly DMP)			5 0 0
Ex-Constable John McGrath			190 0 0
Ex-Constable Edward Dunphy			10 0 0
		Total	£440 0 0

Officers

The following is the official list of officers of the Royal Irish Constabulary who were awarded Certificates of Merit by the Committee of the Irish Police and Constabulary Recognition Fund, but were not present at the Depot parade on 17th May, 1917:

County Inspectors

EM Clayton, Galway, ER (Ballinasloe)
GB Ruttledge, Galway, WR (Galway)
H O'H Hill, Kerry (Tralee)
Hubert W Crane, King's Co. (Tullamore)
FCV Ireland, Louth (Dundalk)
JR Sharpe, Wexford (Wexford)

District Inspectors

Charles Collins, Galway, ER (Athenry—now stationed at Granard)
Philip McDonagh, Galway, ER (Loughrea)
Thomas Neylon, Galway, WR (Oughterard)
Patrick Falvey, Galway, WR (Gort—now stationed at Dunfanaghy)
EA Britten, Kerry (Tralee)
John Fitzgerald, King's Co. (Tullamore—now stationed at Navan)
TD Norris, Louth (Dundalk)
JA Carbery, Louth (Drogheda)
PT Roe, Monaghan (Carrickmacross)
PJ O'Hara, Wexford (Wexford)
Anthony McLean, Wexford (New Ross)
RR Heggart, Wexford (Enniscorthy)
Bernard McGovern, Wicklow (Arklow)
Charles McGowan, Galway, WR (Dunmore)
(At the time of the Rebellion he was a Head Constable at Portumna, Co. Galway, ER)
Dennis Barrett, Clare (Kilrush) (At the time of the Rebellion he was a Head Constable at Turloughmore, Co. Galway)
John Kearney, Roscommon (Boyle) (At the time of the Rebellion he was a Head Constable at Tralee)

Discharged RIC Men

The following is the official list of men of the Royal Irish Constabulary discharged on Injury Pensions as permanently incapacitated, who received Certificates and War Stock (£140 each) from the Committee of the Irish Police and Constabulary Recognition Fund:

Sergt. PJ Scully, Meath (Stirrupstown)
Const. Henry Leckey, Meath (Oldcastle)
Const. Patrick Cunningham, Meath (Dillonsbridge)
Const. Patrick Grace, Wexford (Enniscorthy)

Wounded RIC Men

The following is the list of the seventeen men (wounded) not permanently incapacitated, who received Certificates and War Stock from the committee of the Irish Police and Constabulary Recognition Fund:

	Amount of Stock
Co. Meath	
Constable FP Glennon (Trim)	£10 0 0
* Constable WE Johns (Navan)	15 0 0
* Constable MJ Dugan (Crossakiel)	15 0 0
* Constable T Finan (Bohermeen)	15 0 0
* Constable P Drinan (Nobber)	15 0 0
Constable H McGann (Oldcastle)	15 0 0
Constable J Murphy (Robinstown)	15 0 0
Constable F Kenny (Athboy)	15 0 0
* Constable P McKeon (Slane)	15 0 0
Act. Sergt. M Mulvihill (Trim) (now serving in Co. Tyrone)	15 0 0
* Constable P Conneelly (Athboy)	15 0 0
Co. Galway ER	
Constable J Ginty (Moyvilla)	15 0 0
Co. Galway WR	
* Constable H Hamilton (Galway)	10 0 0
Constable D Manning (Loughgeorge)	10 0 0
Constable M Meany (Galway)	15 0 0
Co. Kerry	
Constable M Cleary (Listowel)	15 0 0
Constable T McLoughlin (Killarney	15 0 0

*The seven men marked with an asterisk are included in the list of men who attended the Depot parade on 17th May, 1917.

Awards to RIC men throughout the country

The following is the official list of 175 NCO's and men of the Royal Irish Constabulary who were each awarded Certificates and £5 War Stock by the Committee of the Irish Police and Constabulary Recognition Fund. This list is in addition to the names of men who were present a the R.I.C. Depot on 17th May, 1917:

Co. Galway ER

Head Constables

John O'Sullivan, Craughwell
John B O'Callaghan, Athenry

Sergeants

Michael Carmody, Monivea, Co. Galway
Matthew Dowd, Athenry
TJ Oates, Ballygurrane
Michael Gibbons, Athenry
TJ Hargaden, Newford

Constables

Michael Reynolds, Athenry
John Lynch, Athenry
Thomas McGovern, Newford
Patrick O'Brien, Athenry
Bernard Gannon, Athenry
Thomas Murphy, Athenry
Michael Reynolds, Loughrea
TJ O'Keeffe, Ballygurrane
Patrick Burke, Athenry
Denis Doherty, Gurteen
Nicholas Collins, Riverville
Patrick Coleman, Colmanstown
Owen Rooney, Ballygurrane
MJ Brennan, Ballygurrane
Joseph McCaffrey, Newford
Thomas Grady, Athenry
(now serving in Co. Westmeath)
Jeremiah Hegarty, Castleblakeney
(now service in Co. Kerry)

Go Galway WR

Head Constables

John Golden, Galway
(now serving in Co. Kerry)
PJ Killacky, Galway
Patrick Duffy, Gort

Sergeants

John Clarke, Galway
James Brennan, Galway
William Elliott, Ardrahan
Thomas Redington, Maam Cross
Thomas Reilly, Kinvarra
(now serving in Co. Armagh)

Acting-Sergeants

Thomas Walsh, Carraroe
John Casey, Galway

Constables

Patrick Smyth, Oranmore
Patrick McShane, Loughgeorge
Daniel Foley, Oranmore
John Conlon, Maam
Michael Lavelle, Laraghmore Hut
James Hannon, Oranmore
Peter Heffernan, Oranmore
Martin McEvoy, Galway
Maurice Walsh, Clonboo
Martin Callagy, Galway
Michael Donegan, Galway
Patrick Durkan, Galway
William O'Sullivan, Errismore
Patrick Rourke, Galway
Florence Sullivan, Mace
James Noonan, Salthill
Patrick McGloin, Galway
DF Kelly, Kinvarra
George Barrer, Tuam
WE McGarry, Tuam
(now serving in King's Co.)
Thomas McLoughlin, Turloughmore
John C Palmer, Corofin, Ballyglunin
Martin Crean, Kilcolgan
Bernard McBreen, Galway
Thomas Kirwan, Kilcolgan
Edward Brennan, Kilcolgan
Edward Reilly, Oranmore
(died 19-3-'17)
James Maguire, Kilcolgan
Eugene Igoe, Galway
James Hanley, Kinvarra
Richard H Noonan, Kinvarra
Michael McCarthy, Kinvarra
Florence McCarthy, Gort
(now serving in Co. Westmeath)

Co. Kerry

Sergeants

Thomas J Hearn, Ardfert
R A Crawford, Tralee
Patrick Brennan, Causeway
Thomas O'Rourke, Tralee
Thomas Rahill, Farranfore

Acting-Sergeant

EJ McKenna, Tralee

Constables

George Neazer, Tralee
Michael J Dowd, Brosna
James Donovan, Ballinillane

Co. Louth

Head Constable

EJ Donnelly, Dundalk

Sergeants

Edmund McDonagh, Drogheda
Christopher Sheridan, Dundalk
(now on pension)

Acting-Sergeant

Patrick Kiernan, Dundalk

Constables

Patrick Donovan, Castlebellingham
Patrick Marren, Drogheda

Co. Meath

Head Constable

Denis McHugh, Navan

Sergeants

Terence McDermott, Ballivor
Hugh Brady, Carnaross
Martin Coyle, Killyon
John Colbert, Navan
Patrick Brady, Kilmoon
Thomas Donoghue, Slane

Acting-Sergeant

Daniel Wynne, Kilmainhamwood

Constables

Peter Murtagh, Slane
Oliver Watson, Kells
Thomas Murphy, Navan
Michael Begley, Kells
John McGearty, Balivor
Thomas Foley, Athboy
John Gronell, Enfield
William Breen, Kells
WV Grey, Kells
John Maddock, Drumconra
William Cox, Dunboyne
JJ Curley, Navan
MJ McMahon, Duleek
Martin Gara, Killyon
Patrick Neill, Nobber
Thomas A. McCavish, Navan
Roger B Kelly, Kells
Denis McGillycuddy, Stirrupstown
John Shanahan, Collon
Francis Furey, Dillonsbridge
Richard Mayock, Carnaross
WT McMillen, Oldcastle
Patrick Gunning, Longwood
JJ Higgins, George's Cross
Patrick Geoghegan, Kilmoon
Thomas Keighary, Dunshaughlin
John Tierney, Dunshaughlin
Robert McMullan, Kilmoon
Michael Mulvihill, Ashbourne

Martin Syron, Ashbourne
RM Tully, Ashbourne
Charles Maguire, Robinstown
Samuel Patterson, Moynalty
(now serving in Co. Tyrone)

Co. Wexford
Head Constables
Michael O'Sullivan, New Ross
Timothy Collins, Enniscorthy
WG McDonough, Gorey
Francis McGrath, Wexford

Sergeants
John Oliver, Enniscorthy
Michael Doyle, Enniscorthy
Patrick Tuohy, Gorey
MJ Lyons, Ferns
John Begley, Wexford
Michael O'Hara, Wexford
Cornelius O'Sullivan, New Ross
Patrick E Davey, Ballinaboola
Henry Murphy, Oulart
James Carlos, Camolin

Acting-Sergeant
Maurice Drake, Coolgreney

Constables
Thomas Griffin, Enniscorthy
Thoms Cahill, Enniscorthy
Thomas Scanlan, Ballybrazil
Peter O'Brien, Ferns
Patrick Sloane, Enniscorthy
Edmond Foran, Hollyfort
RP Tighe, Camolin
Patrick Kelly, Oylgate
Daniel Crowley, Wexford
Matthew Normoyle, Wexford
John Codd, Wexford
John Desmond, Wexford
Bryan Donelon, New Ross
(now serving in Co. Cork, ER)

Co. Dublin
Head Constable
John E Hunter, Balbriggan

Constable
Joseph G Thorpe, Donabate

Co. Kilkenny
Head Constable
George Frizelle, Kilkenny
(now on pension)

Co. Tyrone
Head Constable
Hugh O'Neill, Cookstown

Acting-Sergeant
Timothy S Ryan, Stewartstown

Constables
Bernard Conway, Broughderg
Matthew J Molloy, Rock
Michael Dunne, Cookstown

King's County
Head Constable
Joseph H Stuart, Tullamore
(now on pension)

Sergeants
Philip Ahern, Tullamore
(now on pension)

Cork ER
Sergeants
Samuel Caldbeck, Ballincollig
John O'Sullivan, Newmarket

Constables
Owen Dolan, Fermoy
Francis King, Ahern
James Norris, Fermoy
Thomas Walsh, Fermoy

Co. Mayo
Sergeants
Daniel Fitzgerald, Cong

Constable
Martin O'Donnell, Cong

Co. Cavan
Constable
Agustine O'Brien, Ballinagh

Co. Clare
Constable
JJ Loftus, Morris Mills.

Co. Kildare
Constable
William Kyne, Enfield

ADAMS, JOHN F, (38), a member of the Citizen Army, was killed in the fighting in St Stephen's Green. He left a widow and child.

ALDRIDGE, SERGT. JOHN WM, 10th Royal Dublin Fusiliers, was sergeant of the guard at Portobello Barracks on Wednesday, 26th April, when the three men were shot.

ALLATT, COLONEL HTW, Royal Irish Rifles, was killed in action in the vicinity of the South Dublin Union. He was subsequently mentioned in despatches for distinguished services. In the House of Commons on Tuesday, 13th February, 1917, Mr Macpherson, Under Secretary for War, answering a question by Mr Swift MacNeill, said that Colonel Allat was present during the raid on the house of Mrs Sheehy Skeffington. Being a retired officer re-employed as a draft conducting officer only, Colonel Allat exercised no command, and accompanied the party on his own initiative.

ALLEN, THOMAS, was a native of Co. Meath, aged 29, and an active member of the Volunteers, who devoted a large measure of his leisure to drilling his men. He was made a lieutenant on Easter Monday, and while fighting in the Four Courts was severely wounded, and removed to the Richmond Hospital, where he died. He left a widow and three children. The body of Allen was exhumed at Glasnevin Cemetery on 6th January, 1917, and removed to Longwood, Moyvalley, Co. Meath, where the remains were interred.

ALTON, CAPT. EH, was in command of the Dublin University Officers' Training Corps at the outbreak, and took the initial step in the defence of Trinity College. He was mentioned in despatches, and awarded the Military Cross for his services.

BAILEY, DANIEL JULIAN, who travelled from Germany in the submarine with Roger Casement, was born in Dublin. He joined the Royal Irish Rifles in 1904, and had served with his regiment in India. When the war broke out he was employed as a goods porter at Paddington, and was called up as a reservist. He sailed with the original Expeditionary Force to France. He shared the fortunes of the force during the early days of the campaign, and was taken prisoner by the Germans on September, 4, 1914. When Casement went among the Irish prisoners at Limberg to raise an Irish Brigade, Bailey was one of the few who joined it. He did so, as he afterwards explained in order to get out of Germany and be able to return to his regiment, and when placed on his trial after Casement had been sentenced to death the Attorney-General intimated that the charge against Bailey was withdrawn, and he was released.

BALCH, MAJOR, was the medical officer on duty at Portobello Barracks on Easter Week. He examined the bodies of the three men shot there on Wednesday, 26th April. At the Simon Commission Mr TM Healy said that Major Balch had since been sent to Sierra Leone.

BARRETT, CONSTABLE THOS., 67 B, Dublin Metropolitan Police, was awarded the King's Medal for conspicuous gallantry in arresting and disarming a man who was threatening to shoot two soldiers.

BARTON, CONSTABLE JOHN, 37 B, Dublin Metropolitan Police, was awarded the King's Medal for conspicuous gallantry, exceptional ability, and devotion to duty. On the first night of the rebellion he arrested 27 looters in the vicinity of O'Connell Bridge, and two armed men who were carrying a large quantity of ammunition. He was specially promoted to the rank of sergeant.

BATTENBERG, CAPT. HIS HIGHNESS PRINCE ALEXANDER OF, GCVO, who was on Sir John Maxwell's staff, was mentioned in despatches for distinguished services. Prince Alexander is a brother of the Queen of Spain. His brother, the late Prince Maurice Victor Donald, died of wounds received in action in 1914.

BEALEN, PATRICK (30), foreman in a licensed house at 177 North King street. His body was found buried in the cellar there, and the Coroner's jury found that he had died of wounds inflicted by a soldier. (See pages 23 to 25)

BIRRELL, THE RIGHT HON. AUGUSTINE, who as the Hardinge Commission reported, was 'primarily responsible for the situation that was allowed to rise and the outbreak that occurred,' held the Office of Chief Secretary from 1907. He admitted that he had under-estimated the Sinn Fein movement, and on returning to London after the suppression of the rebellion tendered his resignation, which was accepted. Mr Birrell has sat in the House of Commons for North Bristol since 1906. It was only at intervals of a few months that he visited Ireland during his period of Chief Secretaryship, and he defended his action in this respect before the Royal Commission, presided over by Lord Hardinge. Mr Birrell had the experience of holding the office as Chief Secretary for Ireland longer than most of his predecessors for many years.

BLAKE, SIR HENRY, GCMG, of Myrtle Grove, Youghal, Cork, was formerly Governor of Bahamas, Newfoundland, Jamaica, Hong Kong, and Ceylon. He submitted to the Hardinge Commission of Inquiry a statement regarding the condition of Ireland, which was included in an appendix to the report of the minutes of evidence given to the Commissioners.

BOOTH, RICHARD W, JP, President of the Dublin Chamber of Commerce, gave evidence before the Hardinge Commission regarding the industrial troubles of the city in recent years.

Bowen-Colthurst, Capt. JC, Royal Irish Rifles, had sixteen years' service in the Army. He took part in the Battle of Mons, and was afterwards seriously wounded and invalided home. At Easter he was attached to the 3rd Battalion at Portobello Barracks, where he gave the orders which resulted in Francis Sheehy Skeffington, Thos. Dickson, and Patrick J MacIntyre being shot on Wednesday, 26th April. He was tried by courtmartial on 26th June, and found guilty of the murder of the three men mentioned, the court also finding that he was insane at the time he committed the acts. He was ordered to be detained in a criminal lunatic asylum during His Majesty's pleasure, and removed to Broadmoor Asylum.

Bratton, Constable Eugene, Royal Irish Constabulary. Navan, was awarded the King's Medal for conspicuous gallantry during the rebellion as a motor cycle despatch driver.

Brosnan, Sergeant-Major, had been a Head Constable in the Royal Irish Constabulary, and after leaving that service he was musketry instructor at Armagh and Buncrana since the beginning of the European War. He proved himself a highly efficient officer. It was from Buncrana that he came to Dublin on short leave to see his wife and children, who occupied quarters in Dublin Castle. He had obtained an extension of leave, and was due to return to his station at Buncrana on the 25th April, the day on which he met his death. When the rebels attacked Dublin Castle on the 24th April, Brosnan promptly offered his services to the military within the gate. He went outside for a few minutes, and saw a rebel taking aim at a soldier. He disarmed the rebel, and thus saved the soldier's life, but unfortunately he was soon afterwards shot dead by a soldier, who mistook him for one of the attackers, he being in mufti. Sergeant-Major Brosnan was a man of high character.

Browning, FH, died of wounds received on Easter Monday at Haddington road when returning from a route march with the Irish Association Volunteer Training Corps., of which he was second in command. 'Chicken' Browning, as he was known to his intimates, was one of the best cricketers Ireland has produced. Mr Browning was also keenly devoted to Rugby football, and played with no little distinction at half-back for his University and later for Wanderers, with the fortunes of which latter club he was closely identified up to the day of his death. He was paid the high compliment of being elected President of the Irish Rugby Union two years ago, an honour which was as richly deserved as it was prized by the recipient.

Byrne, James (19), an active Volunteer was shot in the Jacob's Factory area.

Byrne, Brigadier-General John Aloysius, who succeeded Sir Neville Chamberlain as Inspector-General of the Royal Irish Constabulary, acted with marked ability and success as Deputy Adjutant-General on Sir John Maxwell's staff in Ireland from April until his appointment to the Command of the RIC. General Byrne was born in 1874, and joined the Inniskilling Fusiliers in 1893. He was promoted to Captain in 1900, Major in 1914, Brevet Lieutenant-Colonel in 1915, and Brigadier-General in April of the present year. For three years General Byrne commanded the Company of Gentlemen Cadets at Sandhurst. He served in the South African war, and was slightly wounded at the defence of Ladysmith. Afterwards he served as Assistant Adjutant-General at the War Office. He wears the Queen's Medal with five clasps and the King's Medal with two clasps. General Byrne is a Roman Catholic, and an Irishman, being the second son of the late Doctor Byrne, DL, of Londonderry. His eldest brother, Colonel Byrne, late Connaught Rangers, is at the War Office, and two younger brothers are at the front, one in Mesopotamia with the Dorset Regiment, and one in France with the Royal Engineers. On 24th January, 1917, it was announced that His Majesty had appointed General Byrne a Commander of the Order of the Bath, and his name was included in the list of officers and men issued from the War Office on 25th January who had been brought to the notice of the Secretary for War for distinguished services rendered in connection with the war.

Byrne, Joseph (32), a native of Wicklow, was killed fighting at Boland's Mills. He left a widow and two children.

Byrne, Sir William Patrick, KCVO, CB, was appointed Under Secretary to the Lord Lieutenant of Ireland, and took up his duties on Friday, 27th October, 1916, in succession to Sir Robert Chalmers. Sir William Byrne, who was born at Withington, Lancashire, is fifty-eight years of age, and a barrister of Gray's Inn. He was educated at St Cuthbert's College, Ushaw, and St Bede's, Manchester, after which he entered the service of the General Post Office. In 1894 he was transferred to the Home Office, where he became Senior Clerk in 1896, and Assistant Under Secretary of State in 1908. In 1910 he was appointed Registrar of the Baronetage, and in 1913 Chairman of the Board of Control in connection with the Home Office. In 1894 he acted as Secretary to the Inter-Departmental Committee on Riots, and later as Chairman of the Home Office Committee on Inebriate Reformatories, and as a member of the Royal Commission on the Feebleminded. In 1910 he was one of the British delegates to the International Conference in Paris on Aerial Navigation.

Campbell, Right Hon. Sir James H, Bart., KC, MP for Dublin University since 1903, Attorney-General for Ireland, gave evidence before the Hardinge Commission that during the nine days he held office before the rebellion he received no official communication of any kind indicating the possibility of trouble. He was not present at the

Viceregal conference, and only learned of it in the Press. He had no interview with the Viceroy during that nine days, and he never saw Sir Matthew Nathan during that period, although they were only separated by a partition in the Castle. Mr Campbell was subsequently appointed Lord Chief Justice of Ireland, and His Majesty conferred upon him the honour of a baronetcy.

CASEMENT, ROGER DAVID, was born at Magherintemple, Ballycastle, Co. Antrim, on 1st September, 1864. In 1892 he was in the service of the Niger Coast Protectorate, and he became HM Consul for Lorenzo Marques in 1895. In 1898 he was appointed Consul to the Portuguese Possessions in West Africa, and during the South African War he was employed on special service in Cape Town, receiving at the conclusion of hostilities a British South African medal. Subsequently he served in the French Congo, and in June, 1905, he was made a CMG, and appointed Consul to the State of San Paulo. He was promoted Consul-General, and transferred to Rio Janeiro in 1908, and in 1911 he was knighted, receiving in the same year the Coronation medal. In 1914 he became actively associated with the leaders of the Sinn Fein movement in Ireland, and took part in the work of organising branches in the country with PH Pearse, Thos. MacDonagh, and others. He appeared in Germany and canvassed the Irish prisoners of war to join an Irish Brigade to fight for Ireland. He travelled in a submarine from Germany, and landed on the Kerry coast, and was arrested a few hours after landing. He was tried for treason, convicted and sentenced to death. Petitions were submitted to the Government with a view to a mitigation of the extreme penalty, but these were unsuccessful, and Casement was executed in Pentonville prison, London, at 9 a.m. on the morning of Thursday, 3rd August, 1916. Before his execution Casement was received into the Roman Catholic Church.

CHALMERS, SECOND LIEUT. AD, 14th Royal Fusiliers, was captured by the rebels and kept a prisoner in the General Post Office during the period of the rebellion. His extraordinary experiences and escapes are related on pages 9, 10, 11 and 49.

CHALMERS, SIR MACKENZIE DALZELL, KCB, one of the three members of the Hardinge Commission which inquired into the causes of the rebellion. He was permanent Under Secretary of State for the Home Department from 1903 to 1908, a member of the Statute Law Committee, the Royal Commission on Vivisection, and the Royal Commission on the affairs of Malta.

CHALMERS, SIR ROBERT, KCB, who succeeded Sir Matthew Nathan as Under-Secretary for Ireland early in May, 1916, was Governor of Ceylon from 1913 till early in 1916. He was Chairman of the Board of Inland Revenue from 1903 to 1907, and Permanent Secretary of HM Treasury from 1911 till he went to Ceylon. He served on the Royal Commission on Indian finance and currency. Sir Robert did not remain long in Ireland, and was succeeded by Sir William Patrick Byrne, whose appointment as Under Secretary was published on 23rd October, 1916.

CHAMBERLAIN, COLONEL SIR NEVILLE FRANCIS FITZGERALD, KCB, resigned his post as Inspector-General of the Royal Irish Constabulary. The first intimation of his retirement was made by Lord Lansdowne in the House of Lords on Tuesday, 11th July, 1916, when he announced that the Inspector-General had some time previously indicated his desire to be relieved of his duties. At the Commission, presided over by Lord Hardinge, Sir Neville gave evidence showing that he had repeatedly warned the Government of perils that were growing in the country. The Commissioners in their report stated that they had nothing bur praise for the conduct, zeal, and loyalty of the Royal Irish Constabulary, and they were satisfied that Sir Neville Chamberlain and his subordinates furnished the Government with full and exact reports on which they could have acted months before the leaders contemplated any actual rising. Sir Neville Chamberlain held the post of Inspector-General from 1900. He is a son of the late Lieut.-Col. C Chamberlain, Indian Army, and joined the Army in 1873; served in the 11th (Devon) Regt., 1873-76, and in the Central India Horse, 1876; was on the staff of Lord Roberts throughout the Afghan War, 1878-80; was in the Burmah campaign 1886-87 (medal and clasp), was Military Secretary to the Kashmir Government and reorganised the Kashmir, 1890-97. He commanded the Khyber Force, 1899; and was private secretary to Lord Roberts in the South African War, 1899-1900 (despatches, medal, and 5 clasps). He is a CB, KCVO, and a Knight of Grace of the Order of St John of Jerusalem. His retirement was received with general regret throughout the force. From his taking charge of the Royal Irish Constabulary on 1st September, 1900, he always evinced a keen desire to make the force as comfortable and happy as an experienced officer in his position could do.

CLARKE, PHILIP (41), a vanman and a member of the Citizen Army, was killed in the fighting in St Stephen's Green. He left a widow and eight children

CLARKE, THOMAS J, was the first of the seven signatories to the declaration of an Irish Republic. He was condemned by court-martial, and executed in Kilmainham on May 3rd, 1916. Clarke represented the old Fenian conspiracy on the 'Provisional Government'. He was a native of Dungannon, and in 1879 emigrated to the United States, where he became Adjutant of the Irish Volunteers of New York. In 1881 he was sentenced to penal servitude for life in England for complicity in dynamite outrages, and released on ticket-of-leave in 1898. A year later he returned to America, and married the niece of his fellow convict, John Daly, of

Limerick. In 1907 he returned to Dublin, opened a tobacco and newspaper shop in Great Britain street, and became prominent once more as a speaker at Fenian anniversaries. Clarke was president of the O'Donovan Rossa Funeral Committee, and was among the leaders at the General Post Office in Sackville street during Easter Week. He was one of the men who directed operations on the day of the gunrunning at Howth, and his shop in Great Britain street was a rendezvous for his comrades in thought. Remarkable evidence of the forethought and preparation given by this veteran to the cause of the rebellion was provided in the intimation made in the first list of subscriptions to the 'Irish Volunteers' Dependants' Fund':

Left by the late Thomas J, Clarke, c.o. Mrs Clarke, for the relief of distress ......£3,100 0 0.

Clarke left a widow and three young sons.

Clayton, County Inspector EM, Royal Irish Constabulary for the East Riding of Galway, gave important evidence before the Hardinge Commission.

Clery, Lance-Corporal Reginald F, IAVTC, was one of the 'GR's,' and was killed by the rebels at the entrance to Beggar's Bush Barracks on Easter Monday.

Coade, JJ (19) was shot by the military in the Rathmines road on the night of Tuesday, 25th April. The Simon Commission reported that 'none of the evidence offered to us afforded any justification for the shooting of Coade.'

Colbert, Cornelius, was executed in Kilmainham on Monday, 8th May, 1916, for taking an active part in the rebellion. He was a native of Athea, Co. Clare, aged about 23, and was employed as a junior clerk in a Dublin bakery. He had been active in Nationalist movements since leaving school, particularly in organising the National Boy Scouts and the Fianna. He was a facile writer, and had some produced poetry.

Connolly, James Thomas, one of the seven men who signed the proclamation of an Irish Republic, was known as the Commandant General of the Dublin Division of the Army of the Irish Republic, and he was one of the three rebel leaders who signed the document of surrender on 29th April. He was wounded in the middle of the week, but continued to direct operations in the GPO from a couch. After the collapse he was removed to Dublin Castle Red Cross Hospital. He was executed in Kilmainham, on Friday, 12th May, 1916, after trial by courtmartial. He was a Monaghan man, the son of an artisan, and was about fifty years of age. When a young man he went to Edinburgh with his parents and soon afterwards became actively associated with the district branch of the Social Democratic Union, a Socialist body. After about ten years' active work as a Socialist he left Edinburgh and came to Dublin, where he founded in the early nineties the Irish Socialist Republican party. Later he went to the States, where he found congenial associates among the ultra-revolutionary Socialists. He wrote a book, 'Labour in Irish History.' Six years ago he returned to his native land in the belief that times were more propitious for his propaganda. He broke new ground at Belfast immediately after the great dock strike there, which had given James Larkin his introduction to Irish industrial agitation. Connolly subsequently transferred his activities to Dublin, where he became the nominal second-in-command but real leader of Larkin's Irish Transport Workers' Union. He took a prominent part in the Dublin strikes in 1913. He originated and commanded the Citizen Army, and blended it with the Sinn Fein Volunteers. Connolly left a wife and three of a family.

Connolly, John, Captain in the Citizen Army, was reported to have led the attack on Dublin Castle on Easter Monday, and subsequently the attack on the City Hall, where he was killed in the fighting. He had proved his skill as an elocutionist, and had frequently appeared on concert platforms with the Abbey Theatre Co. and National Players. He was a member of the Pioneer Total Abstinence Association. He was thirty-two years of age, and left a widow and three young children.

Corcoran, Jas, (33), a native of Gorey, was killed fighting with the Citizen Army in St Stephen's Green. He left a widow and three children.

Corrigan, Chas, (34), killed in the vicinity of the General Post Office, was born in Glasgow of Irish parents, and took an active part in Glasgow for several years in fostering the cause of the Gaelic League. He came to Dublin a few months before the rising.

Cosgrave, Wm T, one of the officers of the Irish Volunteers, and a member of the Dublin Corporation, was sentenced to penal servitude for life. At a meeting of the Dublin Corporation on Monday, 8th January, 1917, he was co-opted a member of that body for Usher's quay Ward, for which he had become disqualified by reason of absence from the Council for the statutory period.

Costello, John, Second Lieut. Irish Volunteers, belonged to Athlone, and had been some time in Dublin. He was killed in the fighting at Boland's Mills.

Coulter, Constable James H, 187 A, Dublin Metropolitan Police, was awarded the King's Medal for conspicuous gallantry in carrying ammunition under fire to Dublin Castle and disarming a rebel who was attacking pedestrians with a rifle and bayonet.

Cowan, Col. HV, CVO, Assistant Adjutant-General, gave evidence before the Hardinge Commission of Inquiry, and was mentioned in despatches for distinguished services.

Coyle, Henry (28), killed in the fighting in the General Post Office area, was a prominent member of the Davis Hurling team for several years. He left a widow and a young son.

Crenigan, John, of Swords, formerly employed in Dublin, was killed at the battle of Ashbourne.

Daly, Edward, who was Commandant of the rebels in the Four Courts, was executed at Kilmainham on 4th May, 1916. Edward Daly's father was a brother of John Daly, an old Fenian, who was afterwards Mayor of Limerick, where he died two months after the Easter rising. Daly was the only son of his widowed mother, and was born in 1891, six months after his father's death. He was educated at Limerick, and came to Dublin a few years ago, residing with his sister, Mrs Thos J Clarke, and her husband Thomas J Clarke, who was also executed. During the rebellion Daly was in charge of the rebels in the north-west area of Dublin, which included the Four Courts, Linenhall Barracks, Church street, and North King street, where some of the fiercest fighting of the week took place.

Daly, PT, a member of the Dublin Corporation, was deported after the rising and subsequently released.

D'Arcy, Chas., a youth, was a member of the Citizen Army, and was killed in the attack on Dublin Castle.

De Valera, Edward, commander of the rebels in the Ringsend area, was sentenced to penal servitude for life. He was born in New York, his father being a Spanish gentleman who had married an Irish lady. He spent his early days with his mother's people in Co. Limerick. He was educated at Blackrock College, and became a professor of Mathematics, which he taught in several colleges. He was also interested in the Irish Summer School at Tawin, Co. Galway, funded by Sir Roger Casement. De Valera has a wife and young family.

Dickson, Thomas, aged 31, who resided at 12 Harrington street, was shot by the military in Portobello Barracks on Wednesday, 26th April, with Francis Sheehy Skeffington and Patrick MacIntyre. The Simon Commission of Inquiry found that he was in no way connected with the rebellion. He was the editor of a small paper, the *Eye Opener*, which had a short but sensational career, terminating with Dickson's death. During Dickson's business career some of his undertakings had involved himself and other persons in very unfortunate consequences.

Dillon, Robert, who for nearly thirty-five years had carried on business in the old-established premises known as 'The Flag,' at 6 and 8 Moore street, met his death while trying to escape with his wife and daughter from their burning premises on the morning of Saturday, 29th April. He was known as a man of high principle and sterling honesty, and his charitable work amongst the poor of the city in connection with the St Vincent de Paul Society had brought solace and relief to many a desolate home.

Dobbin, Sec. Lieut. Wm Price, 3rd Royal Irish Fusiliers, was in command of the main guard at Portobello Barracks when Francis Sheehy Skeffington was taken out as a hostage. He was recalled from France to give evidence before the Simon Commission the sittings of which were postponed for his return.

Dockeray, Cecil E, 4 Warwick terrace, Leeson park, Dublin, a member of the clerical staff at Guinness's Brewery, was shot dead in the brewery by the military with Sec. Lieut. Worswick, of the 2nd King Edward Horse under circumstances that are described in the reports of the courts-martial. (Pages 122 to 127) Mr Dockeray was a trusted employé of Guinness's, and had no connection with the Sinn Fein movement.

Dockrell, Sir Maurice E, DL, JP, gave evidence before the Hardinge Commission, explaining the operations of the City and County of Dublin Recruiting Committee, in the work of which he took a very active part. He reviewed the course of the labour troubles in Dublin in 1913, and recorded his opinion that the strike was largely due to feeble government. Sir Maurice presided at the functions in Trinity College on Saturday, 5th August, 1916, when the members of the Dublin University, OTC were presented with silver cups in recognition of the service of the Corps in defending the College and other portions of the city during the rebellion. Sir Maurice is the head of the firm of Thomas Dockrell, Sons, and Co. Ltd., South Great George's street.

Donelan, Brendan (19), engaged in the drapery trade in Dublin, was one of the rebels killed in the fighting at the South Dublin Union.

Dougherty, Sir James B, was Under Secretary for Ireland from July, 1908, to October, 1914. He gave evidence before the Hardinge Commission regarding the labour strike in Dublin and the gun-running at Howth.

Doyle, Patrick (36), was a musketry instructor in the Volunteers, and was killed in the fighting at Clanwilliam House. He left a widow and five children.

Duke, The Right Hon. HE, KC, MP, was appointed Chief Secretary of Ireland on July 31st, 1916, after that post had been vacant for about three months. Mr Duke has sat as Unionist MP for Exeter since 1910, when he was elected after the other candidate had been unseated on petition. Mr Duke is the first member of the Press Gallery of the House of Commons to attain Cabinet rank.

Dwan, John (25), a member of the Pioneer Temperance Association, and employed at Inchicore Railway Works, was one of the rebels killed in the fighting in North King street.

Edgeworth-Johnstone, Lieut.-Col. Walter, Chief Commissioner, Dublin Metropolitan Police, gave evidence before the Hardinge Commission showing that he had urged the Government to take drastic action before the rebellion. The

Commissioners in their report praised the Dublin Metropolitan Police for their zeal and loyalty, and recorded their satisfaction that Colonel Edgeworth-Johnstone had supplied the Government with full and exact reports on which they could have acted against the leaders many months before a rising was contemplated. Colonel Edgeworth-Johnstone, who served as a Resident Magistrate, and commanded the 4th Battalion of the Royal Irish Regiment before assuming his present duties, saw active service in the Yonnie and Gambia Expeditions, West Coast Africa, in both of which he was mentioned in despatches and awarded a clasp, and also a medal for the first. In 1894 he was appointed Superintendent of Gymnasia in the Southern District, and from 1895 to 1898, held the post of Assistant Inspector of Gymnasia, and for four years afterwards he was Superintendent of Gymnasia at the Curragh. He is a noted sportsman, and holds many records for football, cricket, and boxing.

ENNIS, EDWARD (33), a member of the Pioneer Total Abstinence Association, was one of the rebels killed in the fighting near Boland's Mills.

FANE, MAJOR AND BT. LT.-COL. CECIL, DSO, Sherwood Foresters, was wounded at the battle of Mount street Bridge, but remained in action. He was mentioned in Sir John Maxwell's despatches, and in the New Year Honours' List he was appointed a Companion of the Order of St Michael and St George.

FARRELL, PATRICK (19), a plasterer, was fatally wounded in Church street. He had severed his connection with the Volunteers at the time of the split, but came out and joined the rising.

FIGGIS, DARREL, a well-known Irish writer, was deported from Achill after the rising, and released about Christmas. He was connected with the Irish Volunteers, and came into prominence at the time of the Howth gun-running. He was among those re-arrested on 24th February, 1917, and deported to England.

FLOOD, QUARTERMASTER-SERGEANT ROBERT, 5th Royal Dublin Fusiliers, was tried by courtmartial on a charge of having murdered Wm J Rice, a clerk in Guinness's Brewery, and Lieut. Lucas, King Edward's Horse, and was found not guilty. (See pages 122 to 127)

FRIEND, MAJOR-GENERAL LB, came to Ireland in January, 1913, as Major-General in charge of Administration. In September, 1914, he took command of the troops in Ireland, and up till April 18th, 1916, he discharged both duties. At that date Sir John Maxwell took the chief command, and General Friend reverted to the charge of Administration. When the rebellion broke out he was in England on leave, and returned to Dublin the following morning. He was mentioned in despatches issued by the War Office on 25th January, 1917, giving the names of officers and men who had rendered distinguished services during the war.

GELSTON, COUNTY INSPECTOR JF, Royal Irish Constabulary for County Clare, gave important evidence before the Hardinge Commission.

GEOGHEGAN, GEORGE (35), a bandsman in the Citizen Army, and employed at the Inchicore Railway Works, was killed in the fighting near the City Hall. He left a widow and three children.

GOULDING, SIR W JOSHUA, BART., J, DL, Chairman of the Great Southern and Western Railway, is Chairman of the Commission appointed by the Government as a tribunal to deal with the claims of the sufferers by fire, and assess the damage in each case. Sir Wm Goulding is also Chairman of Messrs W and HM Goulding, Ltd., and is well known in all parts of Ireland, and especially in Dublin, where he occupies a prominent palace in the business community.

HACKETT-PAIN, BRIGADIER-GENERAL GW, commanded the troops in Ulster, and was mentioned in Sir John Maxwell's despatches and in a War Office list of officers who rendered distinguished services.

HARDINGE, OF PENSHURST, BARON, who presided over the Royal Commission which inquired into the causes of the rebellion, was the Viceroy of India from 1910 till early in 1916. He entered the Diplomatic Service in 1880, and became secretary of the Legation at Teheran in 1896, secretary of the Embassy at St Petersburg, 1898-1903, Assistant Under-Secretary for Foreign Affairs, 1903-4, British Ambassador at St Petersburg, 1904-6, Permanent Under-Secretary of State for Foreign Affairs, 1906-10.

HARREL, SIR DAVID, PC, KCB, KCVO, who was for ten years Chief Commissioner of the Dublin Metropolitan Police, and nine years Under Secretary for Ireland, retiring in 1902, gave evidence before the Hardinge Commission of Inquiry that a turbulent minority had led astray a peaceful majority.

HARREL, COMMANDER WILLIAM VESEY, CB, MVO, Royal Navy, served as a District Inspector in the Royal Irish Constabulary from 1886 to 1898, and then as Inspector of Prisons in Ireland till 1902. From that year he held the post of Assistant Commissioner of the Dublin Metropolitan Police until August, 1914, when he was suspended by the Government for calling the military out to assist his men in dealing with the gun-runners from Howth. Subsequently his suspension was confirmed, and his connection with the DMP severed. At present he occupies a post as Commander of the Navy. He appeared before the Hardinge Commission, and gave his version of the Howth gun-running affair, maintaining that in all he did he was acting within the strict letter of the law.

Harris, Major GA, a Commander of the 1st Dublin Batt. Irish Association of Volunteer Training Corps, was in charge of the 'GR's' on Easter Monday when they were fired upon by the rebels. Subsequently he took command in Trinity College, and with a few of the OTC and a number of Colonial soldiers held the place until the military occupied it. In January, 1917, he was made a Companion of the Distinguished Service Order, and mentioned in despatches for distinguished services rendered in connection with the war. He was also mentioned in Sir John Maxwell's despatches.

Haugh, Sergt. Patrick, 21 E (Terenure), Dublin Metropolitan Police, was awarded the King's Medal for conspicuous gallantry in rescuing a wounded policeman from a position of great danger.

Healy, James (44), labourer, employed at Jameson's Distillery, Bow street. His body was found buried in the cellar of a licensed house at 177 North King street, and the Coroner's jury found that he died of wounds inflicted by a soldier. (See pages 23 to 25)

Healy, James J, 51 St Stephen's Green, East, Dublin, is the Secretary to the Goulding Commission, appointed by the Government to assess the damage sustained by Dublin firms by fire and otherwise.

Healy, John (15), a member of the National Boy Scouts, was killed at Phibsboro' while carrying despatches.

Hearn, Sergt. Thomas J, Royal Irish Constabulary, Ardfert, arrested Sir Roger Casement at McKenna's Fort, with the assistance of Constable Reilly.

Henry, Denis Stanislaus, KC, is one of the Royal Commission appointed to investigate the circumstances surrounding the death in Portobello Barracks of Francis Sheehy Skeffington and two others in Easter Week. Mr Henry is a distinguished member of the Irish Bar, to which he was called in 1885. He became a Bencher of King's Inns in 1898, and is senior Crown Counsel for Co. Westmeath.

Heppell-Marr, Mrs Constance, Assistant County Director City of Dublin Branch British Red Cross Society and Joint Red Cross, wife of Captain Heppell-Marr, 6th Royal Irish Fusiliers, and daughter of Mr George Fletcher, MRIA, Assistant Secretary, Department of Agriculture and Technical Instruction for Ireland. During the rebellion she organised a hospital, attended to the wounded under fire in the streets, and brought supplies through the firing line.

Heuston, JJ, was executed in Kilmainham on 8th May, 1916, for taking a very prominent part in the rebellion. He was a comparatively young man, and was occupied as a clerk on the staff of the Great Southern and Western Railway after being educated by the Christian Brothers, and having a brilliant Intermediate course. He was a lieutenant in the National Boy Scouts.

Hewett, Corporal, 2nd King Edward's Horse, was in the list of soldiers mentioned in the War Office despatch of 25th January, 1917, for distinguished service in connection with the war. With his companion Corporal D'Alroy of the same regiment, Hewett performed magnificent services in clearing the neighbourhood of Thomas street, Cork Hill, Dame street, South Gt George's street, Parliament street, and the lines of the quays, during Easter week. He was wounded five times in all, the final wound, which killed him, having been sustained on the Thursday while he and his companion D'Alroy were engaged bombing a rebel barricade in North King street. They had just jumped over the military barricade in their rush when Hewett fell shot through the heart. On the previous Tuesday Corporals Hewett and D'Alroy took a prominent part in the recapture of the *Daily Express* and *Evening Mail* offices.

Hill, County Inspector Hugh OH, Royal Irish Constabulary for the County Kerry, gave important evidence before the Hardinge Commission.

Hosford, Joseph C, one of the Irish Association of Volunteer Training Corps, Glasnevin Company, was shot dead by a sniper while engaged in defending Beggar's Bush Barracks on Wednesday, 26th April, 1916. He had been in the employment of Brooks, Thomas and Co., Ltd., for 36 years, and was in charge of the colour department.

Howard, John Bernard, aged 17, was wounded in the Church street area, and died in Richmond Hospital. He was a member of the Fiana Pipers' Band. After a successful Intermediate career he went to London as a Boy Clerk in 1914, returned to the Land Commission, Dublin, in 1915, and transferred to the Congested Districts Board. Early in 1916 he left there, and entered the Stanley street Works of the Dublin Corporation.

Howe, TA, Chief Inspector Royal Irish Constabulary, Cork, submitted to the Hardinge Commission of Inquiry a statement which was included in an appendix to the minutes of evidence given to the Commission.

Hume, Walter, of the firm of Walter Hume and Co., fire loss assessors, 16 College Green, is one of the assessors to the Goulding Commission appointed by the Government to assess damage sustained by Dublin firms by fire and otherwise.

Hurley, John (29), belonged to Clonakilty, and was active in Gaelic and Irish Volunteer circles in London. Before the rising he was engaged in the drapery trade in Dublin. He was wounded at Church street, and died in the Richmond Hospital.

Hyland, C Hachette, LDS, RCSI, was shot dead while looking out of his back garden door at 3 Percy place, Northumberland road, on the morning of Thursday, 27th April. The deceased gentleman, who was the son of Mr Charles Hyland, manager of the Gaiety Theatre, Dublin, was aged 29 years and two months. He had been engaged in the practice of his profession for eight years, and had established a reputation that secured his recognition as one of the representative leaders of the younger generation of dental surgeons in Ireland. He was a member of the staff of the Incorporated Dental Hospital of Ireland. On the evening of Wednesday, 26th April, when the battle at Mount street Bridge was at its fiercest, and the Sherwood Foresters had sustained heavy loses, Mr Hyland donned his white coat and went into the firing line, where he worked gallantly for several hours, rendered valuable aid to the wounded men, and assisted the unfortunate victims of the battle into a place of safety. From this ordeal he emerged unscathed, and next morning, while looking out of his garden gate, he had the great misfortune to be shot. His loss was deeply deplored by his professional brethren and the host of friends he had gathered around him by his happy disposition.

JOZE, THOMAS MORAN, a well known chemist, having places of business in Dame street and Arran quay, was shot dead by the rebels when he was going to his private residence at Arran quay. Mr Joze was afflicted with deafness, and it is supposed that he did not hear the challenge of the rebel sentry, who fired upon him.

KELLY, ALDERMAN JAMES JP, was arrested in Easter Week and conveyed to Portobello Barracks after his tobacco shop at the corner of Camden street and Harrington street had been raided by the military. The Simon Commission reported that the suspicion against Mr Kelly was due to a misunderstanding, and that he was in fact quite innocent of any connection with the rebellion.

KELLY, JOHN, who assisted Francis Macken in the conduct of the Irish class at Rathfarnham, was educated at the Christian Brothers' Schools, Kingstown. He was shot at the General Post Office, and died in Jervis street Hospital. He left a widow.

KELLY, CAPTAIN RC, Munitions Department, Dublin, gave evidence before the Hardinge Commission of attending a conference at the War Office, where Lord Kitchener, Lord Wimborne, and Mr Birrell were present.

KENNEDY, LIEUTENANT TJ, Royal Inniskilling Fusiliers, who was mentioned in the War Office despatch of 25th January, 1917, for distinguished services in connection with the war, was one of the officers engaged in Dublin during the rebellion. He was in command of the troops in the vicinity of the Pro-Cathedral, and was complimented by the clergy there on the way in which he conducted the operations for safeguarding the building and the innocent inhabitants of the neighbourhood. Lieutenant Kennedy was a son of Mr Samuel Kennedy, of Cookstown, and prior to offering his services was editor of the Monaghan *Northern Standard.* He was subsequently killed at the front in the memorable operations of July 1st, 1916, while serving with his battalion in the Ulster Division.

KENT, DAVID (brother of Thomas Kent, executed) residing at Bawnard, Castlelyons, near Fermoy, was tried by courtmartial at Richmond Barracks, Dublin, on 14th June, on a charge of having murdered Head Constable Rowe while the officer was engaged in arresting him on a charge of treason. He was found guilty and sentenced to death with a strong recommendation to mercy on account of his previous good character, and the Commander-in-Chief commuted his sentence to five years' penal servitude.

KENT, EDMUND, one of the seven signatories (Eamonn Ceannt) to the declaration of an Irish Republic, was executed on Monday, 8th May, 1916, in Kilmainham. He was born in Galway in 1882, and educated in Dublin, and occupied an important position on the clerical staff in the Treasurer's office of the Dublin Corporation. He was a foundation member of the Gaelic League, and a member of the Coisde Gnotha. Kent commanded the rebels who held the South Dublin Union. He left a widow and one young son.

KENT, RICHARD (brother of Thomas Kent, executed) resided at Bawnard, Castlelyons, Coole, near Fermoy, with his mother. On 2nd May, after Head Constable Rowe had been shot, and the military arrived at the house, the family surrendered, Richard attempted to make his escape, and was shot by the military, and died in Fermoy Military Hospital. He had been arrested in the days of the Land League when a boy. He was an athlete, and well-known in Gaelic athletic circles.

KENT, THOMAS, who was tried on 4th May and executed on 9th May, 1916, at Cork, for the murder of Head Constable Rowe, of the Royal Irish Constabulary, was one of four brothers who resided with their mother at Bawnard, Castlelyons, Coole, near Fermoy. On 2nd May the police went to their house to arrest one of the brothers. Resistance was made, and Head Constable Rowe was shot dead. On the arrival of the military the Kents threw out their weapons, and came out of the house with their mother. Thomas Kent was tried in Cork two months before the rebellion under the Defence of the Realm Act, and the Bench, with the exception of the Stipendiary Magistrate, dismissed the case against him. He had previously been imprisoned in connection with land agitations, and had spent some years in the United States and South Africa. From the beginning of the Volunteer movement he was an active member of the Castlelyons Corps, which claimed to be the first teetotal company in Ireland.

KENT, WILLIAM (brother of Thomas Kent, executed) residing at Bawnard, Castlelyons, Coole, near Fermoy, was tried by courtmartial at Cork on 4th May, charged with the murder of Head Constable Rowe, and acquitted.

KEOGH, GERALD (20), a scout in the Volunteers, was shot dead in front of Trinity College.

Keogh, Nurse, one of the staff of the South Dublin Union, was accidentally killed by a stray shot whilst discharging her duty.

Kettle, Mrs, wife of Lieut. TM Kettle, Royal Dublin Fusiliers (who was killed in France) and sister of Mrs Sheehy Skeffington, gave evidence before the Simon Commission regarding a visit paid to Portobello Barracks in company with her sister, Mrs Culhane, to inquire about the late Francis Sheehy Skeffington.

Kidney, Robert J, FSAA, Star Buildings, College Green, was elected Secretary of the Dublin Fire and Property Losses Association.

King, Second Lieut., Royal Irish Fusiliers, was one of the sixteen captives taken by the rebels and held in the GPO during Easter week.

Love, HC, 13 St Stephen's Green, North, Dublin, is the Secretary of the Rebellion Victims' Committee.

Lowe, Brigadier-General WHM, CB, was in command of the forces at the Curragh when the outbreak occurred, and took an active part in the operations in Dublin, and it was to him that PH Pearse surrendered. He was mentioned in Sir John Maxwell's despatches, and in the New Year Honours' List he was promoted to be Honorary Major-General.

Lucas, Sec. Lieut. AL, King Edward Horse, was shot by military while on duty in Guinness's Brewery on Friday, 28th April, under circumstances that are fully narrated in the courtmartial proceedings to be found on pages 122 to 127. Sec. Lieut. Lucas, who was a Graduate of Cambridge University, had been offered the adjutancy of his regiment just before his death. He left a prosperous business in Canada for active service, and was wounded at Festubert. Subsequent to the trial, Lord Cheylesmore, who presided, stated specifically that 'There was no evidence whatever produced at the courtmartial that Lieut. Lucas was in any way connected with the Sinn Feiners, or that he was in sympathy with them; nor,' his Lordship added, 'was there any evidence whatever to justify any suspicion of the loyalty and good character of Mr Lucas.' These statements were rendered necessary because the deceased's friends and brother officers believed that the public had formed the erroneous impression from the reports of the proceedings that Lieut. Lucas and Lieut. Worswick, who had lost their lives under such tragic circumstances, were in sympathy with the Sinn Feiners, or connected with them. There was no public investigation into the circumstances attending the death of Lieut. Worswick his case being governed by the finding in that of Lieut. Lucas.

Lumsden, Doctor John (MD), Knight of Grace of the Order of St John of Jerusalem, Deputy Commissioner St John Ambulance Brigade, Director General, Joint VAD Committee for Ireland, was awarded a silver medal by the General Chapter of the Order of St John of Jerusalem for his services during the rebellion, when he attended wounded soldiers in the streets under heavy fire. The Chapter General of St John expressed its keen sensibility of the good work done by members of the Order in Dublin, and pointed out to the Deputy-Commissioner that such an example is an excellent encouragement to all concerned for making additional efforts in the objects which all members have at heart.

Macken, Francis, was killed in the fighting in the General Post Office. He was an active member of the Volunteers, and aimed at training the men to obey orders given in the Irish language. With this object he conducted an Irish class at Rathfarnham.

Macken, Peadar, who was killed during the fighting at Boland's mill, was active in labour as well as Gaelic circles, and was a prominent figure at Irish-Ireland gatherings. He sat in the Dublin Corporation as Alderman for the North Dock Ward for a number of years, but did not seek re-election at the expiry of his period of service.

Mackenzie, Robert, provision merchant, was shot on Thursday, 27th April, at midday when sitting in his shop at the foot of Rutland square. Mr Mackenzie was one of the survivors of the Lusitania having had the remarkable experience of being rescued from that great disaster dryshod.

Maguire, W, (37), a confectioner, was killed in Talbot street while engaged in ambulance work. He left a widow and seven children.

Mahony, Lieut., IAMS, was one of the prisoners taken by the rebels and kept in the GPO during the rebellion. He attended to the wounded in the building, and dressed among others the wounds of 'Commandant General' James Connolly.

Mallin, Michael, a Commandant of the Citizen Army, was in charge of the rebels at St Stephen's Green, and afterwards in the Royal College of Surgeons with the Countess Markievicz. He was executed in Kilmainham on 8th May, 1916. He was a silk weaver by trade, a musician, and an active member of the Workingman's Temperance Committee, Church street. He left a widow and five young children.

Malone, Michael (28), carpenter, and a member of the Volunteers cyclist section, was killed in the fighting at Northumberland road.

Manning, Peter Paul, was fatally wounded while fighting with the Volunteers in North Brunswick street on Saturday, 29th April. He was twenty-five years of age.

Markievicz, Constance Georgina, commanded the insurgents in the Royal College of Surgeons. She was sentenced to death by courtmartial, but the sentence was commuted to penal servitude for life. She is a daughter of the late Sir Henry Gore-Booth, Bart., a large landowner of Sligo. After being presented at Court to Queen Victoria in the Jubilee year, she became an art student in Paris, and achieved a certain amount of success. Sixteen years ago she married Count Casimir Markievicz, a Polish artist, who at Easter, 1916, was fighting with the Russian Army. In addition to her activities as a Sinn Feiner she took active part in Suffragist demonstrations. She established the National Boy Scouts in 1910, and this body gave many young lads to the ranks of the rebels. She was prominently associated with James Larkin in his activities which paralysed the trade of Dublin in 1913 and led to grave riots in the city.

Maxwell, Major-General Sir John Grenfell, KCB, CMG, CVO, DSO, was sent to Ireland with plenary powers from the Government on Thursday, 27th April. He arrived at the North Wall at 2 a.m. on Friday, 29th, and found the east side of Lower Sackville street in flames and firing going on in all parts of the city. He ordered his forces to press in on the rebels, and by four o'clock the following afternoon, Saturday 29th, the leaders of the insurgents had surrendered. A notable event occurred on Tuesday, 27th June, when Sir John was present throughout the entire proceedings of a meeting of the Cabinet, which lasted from half-past eleven until two o'clock. Sir John Maxwell remained in command in Ireland until he was appointed to the Northern Command at York. He left Ireland by the mail boat from Kingstown on the evening of Monday, 13th November. Sir John is fifty-six years old, and has had a distinguished record of service, mainly in Egypt, where he first served in the war of 1882. He commanded the Second Egyptian Brigade at Omdurman, and the 14th Brigade in the South African War. He was in command in Egypt when the war broke out, and returned to England in April, 1916, having retired from the command owing to the reorganisation of the forces in Egypt under General Sir Arthur Murray.

Mellowes, Herbert, brother of Liam Mellowes, was deported after the rising, and subsequently released. He was re-arrested on 24th February, 1917, and again deported.

Mellowes, (Liam) William, an organiser of the Irish Volunteers, was deported to England early in 1916, but escaped from there, and took an active part in the rising in Co. Galway. He disappeared, and is supposed to have gone to America.

Midleton, Viscount Baron Brodrick, of The Grange, Midleton, Co. Cork, who, as Mr St John Brodrick, was Secretary of State for War, 1900-3, and Secretary for India, 1903, gave evidence before the Hardinge Commission of Inquiry to show that he had frequently urged the Government to take steps to repress sedition before the rising.

Molony, Right Hon. Lord Justice Thomas Francis, PC, Ireland, one of the three Commissioners appointed to inquire into the death of Francis Sheehy Skeffington and two others in Portobello Barracks, was Solicitor-General for Ireland, 1912-13, Attorney-General, 1913, and in the same year became a Judge of the High Court of Justice in Ireland, King's Bench Division. In 1915 he was promoted Lord Justice of Appeal.

Montgomery, William, of the firm of William Montgomery and Son, assessors of fire losses, 1 Foster place, is one of the assessors to the Goulding Commission appointed by the Government to assess the damage sustained by Dublin firms by fire and otherwise.

Moore, Colonel Maurice George, CB, of Ballyglass, Co. Mayo, joined the Connaught Rangers in 1875, and served in the Kaffir and Zulu Wars, and was present at the battles of Colenso and Spion Kop. He commanded the first battalion from December, 1900, till the end of the South African War, serving in Natal, Transvaal, Orange River Colony, and Cape Colony. For his services he was mentioned in despatches and made Brevet-Lieut.-Colonel, CB. He was a prominent figure in the early organisation of the Irish Volunteers, and a member of the Provisional Committee. Sir Neville Chamberlain, in his evidence to the Hardinge Commission, said he wished it understood that he cast no imputation against Colonel Moore, as when the disloyal element got into the Volunteers he would have no more to do with it. Colonel Moore himself submitted a statement to the Hardinge Commission.

Morgan, Lieut. Samuel Valentine, 3rd Royal Irish Rifles, was Adjutant at Portobello Barracks in Easter Week. He gave evidence before the Simon Commission.

Morris, Lieut. MC, 11th East Surrey Regiment, was in charge of a picket on Portobello Bridge on Easter Tuesday, when Francis Sheehy Skeffington crossed on his way home. He gave orders for the arrest of Mr Skeffington, and detailed two men to convey him to barracks.

Murphy, John, who carried on business at the corner of Henry street and Moore street, and who was Chairman of the Rathdown Rural District Council (No 2), was shot dead on Saturday, 29th April, as he was on his way to visit his sister in another part of the city. He was a Justice of the Peace for Co. Wicklow.

Murphy, Wm Martin, Associate of the Institute of Civil Engineers (Ireland), Director of the Great Southern and Western Railway, President of the Dublin Chamber of Commerce, 1912 and 1913, and Chairman of the Dublin United Tramways Co. initiated the Dublin Fire and Property Losses Association, which led to the appointment of the Goulding Commission. He also submitted a statement to the Hardinge Commission of Inquiry which was included in an appendix to the published minutes of evidence given to the Commission.

Murray, Daniel (27), bookbinder, was wounded in the Royal College of Surgeons, and died in St Vincent's Hospital.

McBride, John, Major, was executed in Kilmainham on May 5th, 1916, for taking an active part in the rebellion. He was associated with Thomas MacDonagh in the command of the forces that occupied Jacob's biscuit factory. He was a native of Westport, County Mayo, who threw over the Irish Constitutional Party in 1895, and joined the physical force party. He emigrated to South Africa, became a naturalised citizen of the Transvaal, and when the Boer War broke out he organised and led the Irish Brigade, which fought against the British. He was a commissioned officer in Kruger's Army with the rank of Major. At the end of the war McBride went to Paris as one of the delegates from the Irish Transvaal Committee to Mr Kruger, then in that city, who told him that he 'would never forget how the Irish Brigade stood by the men of the Transvaal in their hour of need.' It was during this visit to France that McBride met Miss Maude Gonne, whom he married two years later, and who afterwards divorced him. At the end of the war he was presented by Mr Reitz with the flag of the Irish Brigade, with the inscription:

> ''Tis better to have fought and lost
> than never to have fought at all.'

Under the general amnesty after the South African War McBride returned to Ireland, and in 1909, at the celebration at Kilkenny of the anniversary of the death of the 'Manchester Martyrs' he appealed to his hearers to 'do all in your power to prevent your countrymen from entering the degraded British Army.' Speaking at the same time of the prospect of a German invasion, he said: 'Should they land in Ireland they will be received with willing hearts and strong hands...and twelve months later this land will be as free as the Lord God meant it should be.' In 1911 the Dublin Corporation elected McBride to the post of water bailiff.

McCammond, Lt. Col. TVP, Royal Irish Rifles, the Commander at Portobello Barracks, was mentioned in a War Office list of officers who rendered distinguished services. He was on sick leave and in hospital on the day the three men were shot in the barracks.

M'Cullagh, Capt. JT, RAMC, was shot through the base of the left lung on Easter Monday while collecting wounded in the front of Jacob's factory. Captain M'Cullagh was educated in St Andrew's College, St Stephen's Green, and Trinity College, taking his medical degree with honours. When the war broke out he was attached to the Army Medical Staff, and served in the Gallipoli campaign with the 7th Battalion Royal Dublin Fusiliers, where he was wounded. When recovering he contracted typhoid fever, and was sent to Alexandria, afterwards coming home on sick leave. After that he had been doing duty as Medical Officer to Portobello Barracks. He is a son of Mr J M'Cullagh, of Arklow, Co. Wicklow.

McDermott, John, one of the seven signatories (Sean MacDiarmada) to the declaration of an Irish Republic, was executed in Kilmainham on 12th May, 1916. He was a native of Kiltyclogher, County Leitrim, and physically was not a strong man. He edited a weekly paper advocating the cause of the Volunteers. After a political mission to America he became active in organising in the West, and for an anti-recruiting speech he was prosecuted under the Defence of the Realm Act, and sentenced to four months in prison. He was much in request as a speaker.

MacDonagh, Thomas, MA one of the seven signatories to the declaration of an Irish Republic, was executed on May 3rd, 1916, in Kilmainham. He was a native of Cloughjordan, and early in life intended to devote himself to the Church, but did not persevere in that purpose. After the publication of John MacNeill's order cancelling the Easter manoeuvres, MacDonagh issued an order from Dublin Brigade Headquarters on Easter Sunday, 23rd, that 'all Volunteers are to stay in Dublin until further orders,' and he issued a final order on Easter Monday directing the four city battalions to 'parade for inspection and route march at 10 a.m.,' and to bring 'full arms and equipment and one day's rations.' He commanded the insurgents in Jacob's biscuit factory, and was one of the signatories to the document of surrender. MacDonagh was an MA of the National University of Ireland, and a tutor of English literature in University College, Dublin, and was associated with PH Pearse in the conduct of St Enda's College, Rathfarnham, after he had spent some time teaching in Fermoy and Kilkenny. He was a poet and dramatist, and published several books of verse. A play of his, 'When the Dawn is Come' was produced at the Abbey Theatre in 1908, and he was director of the Irish Theatre in Hardwicke street. MacDonagh left two children and a widow, who is a sister of Mrs Joseph Plunkett.

McDowell, Wm, (44), one of the rebels killed in the fighting at the South Dublin Union, was a painter by trade. He left a widow and four children.

McGrath, Constable John, 188B, Dublin Metropolitan Police, was shot while on duty in College street Barracks on 26th April. The contents of a shot-gun came through the window, and McGrath received severe wounds in the stomach. He was under treatment in St Vincent's Hospital, and the Convalescent Home at Stillorgan, for seven months, and was discharged on pension as unfit for further services on account of his injuries. On Saturday, 27th January, 1917, at Great Brunswick street Central Police Station, Constable McGrath, who is a native of Waterford, was handed a valuable gold watch, with a suitable inscription, subscribed for by his comrades, on the occasion of his retirement from the force.

McGuinness, Joseph P, was tried by courtmartial, and sentenced to three years' imprisonment, and is still a prisoner in Lewes Jail. On the death of Mr John Phillips, MP for South Longford, Mr McGuinness was run by the Sinn Fein party for the vacancy. At one time there were four candidates in the field, but before nomination day these were reduced to two, and the contest resolved itself into a straight fight between the Official Nationalist Party and the Sinn Feiners. Polling took place on Wednesday, 9th May, 1917, and the result was declared next day as follows:

JP McGuinness (Sinn Fein)	1,498
Patrick McKenna (Nationalist)	1,461
Sinn Fein Majority	37

MacIntyre, Patrick (38), was shot by the military in Portobello Barracks on Wednesday, 26th April, with Thomas Dickson and Francis Sheehy Skeffington. The Simon Commission of Inquiry found that he was in no way connected with the rebellion. He was the editor of a newspaper, *The Toiler*, and an active opponent of the Larkinites.

MacNeill, John, President and Chief of Staff of the Irish Volunteers, was tried by courtmartial, and sentenced to penal servitude for life. He is a native of Co. Antrim, and was educated at St Malachy's College, Belfast. At the age of twenty years he obtained a clerkship in the High Court of Justice, Dublin, and spent more than twenty years in the Accountant-General's office at the Four Courts. He was from an early age an ardent student of Celtic language and history, and was one of the founders of the Gaelic League, in which organisation he held office as vice-president from the time of its establishment. He edited many of the League's publications, and was well known as an authority on early Celtic culture. In 1909, with the establishment of the National University of Ireland, he was appointed to the chair of Early and Mediaeval Irish History. When the Irish Volunteers were established in October, 1913, MacNeill took an active part in their organisation. He addressed meetings in various parts of the country, and when, in 1914, the Sinn Fein section broke away from the general body of Volunteers, he became President of the seceding body. About the same time he took up the editorship of the Irish Volunteer, the official organ of the Irish or Sinn Fein Volunteers. This he conducted up to the time of the outbreak. By the original plan the rising was to have taken place on Easter Sunday, but on that day the *Sunday Independent* published an order signed by MacNeill cancelling all the arrangements ad forbidding any movements of the Volunteers to take place. This was his last public action in the matter, but evidence exists that MacNeill also endeavoured by private letters to Commandants to stop all action.

Nathan, Lieut.-Colonel Sir Matthew, GCMG, succeeded Sir James Dougherty as Under Secretary for Ireland in September, 1914. The Hardinge Commission reported that while Sir Matthew carried out with the utmost loyalty the policy of the Government they considered he did not sufficiently impress upon the Chief Secretary during Mr Birrell's prolonged absences from Dublin the necessity for more active measures to remedy the situation which he had in December, 1915, described as most serious and menacing. Sir Matthew, who served with the Royal Engineers in the Nile and Lushai Expeditions, has since returned to them and gone on active service. Before coming to Ireland he was Chairman of the Board of Inland Revenue, and previously to that he had been successively Governor of Sierra Leon, Gold Coast, Hong Kong, and Natal, and afterwards Secretary to the Post Office.

Neil, James Crawford, one of the junior staff in the National Library of Ireland, died on 10th May at Jervis street Hospital of wounds sustained in the rebellion. On the evening of Easter Tuesday he was returning from a visit at Glasthule, near Kingstown. To avoid firing in Sackville street he passed along the Southern line of quays, and crossed the Metal Bridge, intending to go to the North side of the city, where he lived. A looter alarmed by his coming, fired a pistol at him, the shot taking effect in the spine, causing paralysis from the waist down. On his death bed he wrote a pathetic statement of these facts. Mr Neil was a writer of great promise. He belonged to no political organisation.

Neilan, Lieut. Gerald Aloysius, who met his death on Usher Island on Easter Monday, while attempting to dislodge rebel snipers from the Mendicity Institution, was the second surviving son of the late John Neilan, J.P., of Ballygalda, Roscommon, and of Mrs Neilan, 43 Mount Harold terrace, Leinster road, Dublin. He was educated at Clongowes Wood College, and on the outbreak of the South African War enlisted in the Sherwood Foresters, and served in South Africa, where he was severely wounded. From South Africa he went to China, where he remained with his regiment for six years, and then left the Army. In December, 1914, he was given a commission in the Northumberland Fusiliers, and later acted as musketry instructor. In February, 1916, he transferred to the Royal Dublin Fusiliers, where he got his promotion, and was appointed bombing instructor. He was aged 34, and unmarried. Lieut. Neilan was a brother of Doctors JA and CJ Neilan, of New Seaham, Co. Durham., and of Dr AJ Neilan, of Leinster road, Dublin.

Nolan, Miss Louisa, was awarded the Military Medal by the War Office for her Bravery in tending wounded officers and men at Mount street Bridge during the fighting there on Wednesday of Easter Week. Miss Nolan went calmly through a hail of bullets and carried water and other comforts to the wounded men. She is the daughter of ex-Head Constable Nolan, of the Royal Irish Constabulary, who resides at Ringsend. After the rebellion Miss Nolan went to London, and took part in the 'Three Cheers' revue in the Shaftesbury Theatre. Two of her sisters are nursing in England, one brother is in the

Army, and another in the Navy, and a third was killed in August last on the Western front. On Saturday. 24th February, 1917, Miss Nolan was decorated with the medal by His Majesty at Buckingham Palace.

NORWAY, AH, Secretary of the Post Office in Ireland, gave evidence before the Hardinge Commission in Dublin regarding the conduct of the postal staff.

ORPEN, CHARLES ST G, President of the Incorporated Law Society of Ireland, is the Chairman of the Rebellion Victims' Committee, appointed to inquire and report regarding applications for payment out of public funds by innocent persons who suffered in the rebellion or the dependents of innocent victims.

OSBORNE, JOHN, a member of the firm of Sels and Co., fire assessors, London, is one of the three gentlemen appointed by the Government as a Committee to assess the damages sustained by the sufferers from the fires.

OWEN LEWIS, MAJOR AF, General Staff Officer, Irish Command, gave evidence before the Hardinge Commission of Inquiry, and was mentioned in despatches for distinguished services.

OWENS, JOHN (24), an artificial limb maker, was one of the rebels killed in the fighting at the South Dublin Union.

O'CARROLL, RICHARD, who was shot in Camden street on 26th April, and died nine days later in Portobello Hospital, was a member of the Dublin Corporation, where he represented the Labour party for several years. Councillor O'Carroll was formerly a member of the South Dublin Board of Guardians, and he was an active official of the Incorporated Brick and Stonelayers' Union. At his death he left a widow and seven children, whose ages varied from thirteen years to a few weeks.

O'CONNELL, SIR MORGAN ROSS, Fourth Baronet, Lakeview, Killarney, gave evidence before the Hardinge Commission regarding the presence of aliens in Co. Kerry and the Sinn Fein movement in that county. He said that the Government had appointed to the Commission of the Peace scores of men who were unfitted for the position, and who attended Petty Sessions Courts solely for the purpose of carrying out the most open and flagrant jobbery. The first Baronet was the youngest brother of the 'Liberator'.

O'CONNELL, SERGT. WM, Royal Irish Constabulary, Drumconrath, Co. Meath, was awarded the King's Medal for conspicuous gallantry during an attack by rebels on a body of police at Ashbourne.

O'CONOR, CHARLES H, Local Government Board Inspector, is one of the three members of the Rebellion Victims' Committee.

O'DUFFY, JOHN, LDS, RCSI, of 54 Rutland square, Dublin, aged 81, was killed by a stray bullet. His death caused genuine regret amongst dental practitioners and hosts of other friends throughout Ireland. The rebellion brought about the loss of two well known Dublin dentists. Mr O'Duffy worthily represented the older school of dentists, and Mr Hyland, the younger, and both of them were justly regarded with esteem by the members of the profession and the public generally. Mr O'Duffy was one of the founders of the Dental Hospital in Lincoln place, and in other ways he did much to advance the status of qualified dentists. His son, Mr Kevin O'Duffy, is a Dentist in ordinary to the Lord Lieutenant.

O'FLANAGAN, PATRICK, one of the rebels killed in the fighting in North King street, was a member of the Pioneer Temperance Association, and a Volunteer from the start. He left a widow and three children.

O'HANRAHAN, HENRY, sentenced to penal servitude for life, is a brother of Michael O'Hanrahan, and was also employed on the clerical staff at the headquarters of the Volunteers.

O'HANRAHAN, MICHAEL, executed in Kilmainham on 4th May, 1916, was a man of considerable literary ability. He was employed in a clerical capacity at the headquarters of the Volunteers in Dawson street, and was one of the most trusted men in the Volunteer organisation. He belonged to New Ross, and spent his early years in Carlow. He was the author of a work of military adventure entitled 'A Swordsman of the Brigade'.

O'KELLY, JJ, a well known Irish writer under the nom-de-plume 'Sceilg,' and editor of *The Catholic Bulletin*, published in Dublin, was arrested on 24th February, 1917, and deported to England.

O'KELLY, JOHN T, Secretary of the Gaelic League, was deported after the rising and released at Christmas. At a meeting of the Dublin Corporation on Monday, 8th January, 1917, he was co-opted a member of that body to represent Inns Quay Ward, for which he had become disqualified by reason of absence from the Council during the statutory period. He was again arrested on Thursday, 22nd February, 1917, and deported to England.

O'LOUGHLIN, REV. FE, Roman Catholic Chaplain at Portobello Barracks, was present at the burial and subsequent exhumation of the three men shot there on Wednesday, 26th April, 1916. He gave evidence before the Simon Commission.

O'RAHILLY, MJ (THE) was shot dead while fighting in Henry place opposite the General Post Office, where he was engaged all Easter Week. Military prisoners who were kept in that building were under the direct care of The O'Rahilly, and they agree that he was very considerate to his captives. The O'Rahilly was the head of an old Kerry clan, and had a private income of £900 a year, which, it is believed, he largely devoted to the cause he espoused. For years he was a keen worker in the Irish language movement, and a member of the governing body of the Gaelic League. He travelled extensively on the Continent, and spent several years in the United States. On Easter Sunday he spent the day motoring through the country and countermanding the orders that had been given, but when the fatal step was taken in Dublin he went ahead, and took up a post in the General Post Office. The O'Rahilly left a widow and five children.

O'Reilly, John, was second in command of the Citizen Army, which occupied the City Hall. When John Connolly was shot down O'Reilly succeeded him, only to be shot down five hours later on Easter Monday evening. He was a man of great physique, and 6ft. 6 in. in height.

O'Reilly, Richard, the youngest of a family of five, was one of the rebels killed in the fighting at the South Dublin Union. Two of his brothers were in the British Army, and one of them was killed in action in France.

Partridge, Wm P, a member of the Dublin Corporation, was sentenced to fifteen years' penal servitude, but five years were remitted. He was released in April, 1917, because he was suffering from Bright's disease.

Peacocke, Doctor Reginald C, (MD), Assistant County Director County of Dublin Branch British Red Cross Society and Joint Red Cross, is a son of the late Most Rev. Dr Peacocke, Archbishop of Dublin, and resides at 4 Avoca terrace, Blackrock, Dublin.

Pearse, Patrick H, BA, BL, one of the seven signatories to the declaration of an Irish Republic, was executed on May 3rd, 1916, in Kilmainham. He was described as 'Commandant-General of the Army of the Irish Republic', and 'President of the Provisional Government.' Pearse, who was 36 years of age, was a member of the Irish Bar, and the founder and headmaster of St Enda's School for Boys, at Rathfarnham, County Dublin. He was born in Dublin, but was of English descent. He was educated at the Christian Brothers' School, Westland row, and the Royal University, and at the age of 17 founded and became President of the New Ireland Literary Society. He had been a member of the Executive of the Gaelic League, was a fine Gaelic scholar, and wrote miracle plays in Gaelic for the pupils of his school, some of whom took part in the rising. Pearse was a noted orator, and represented the Gaelic League at Welsh and Scottish festivals, and on the occasion of the funeral of O'Donovan Rossa in Glasnevin Cemetery in August, 1915, he delivered an impassioned oration. Evidence exists that Pearse intended to occupy the post of Provost of Trinity College in the event of the rebellion being a success. Pearse, spent his last hours in prison writing poetry.

Pearse, William J, executed in Kilmainham on 4th May, 1916, for taking a prominent part in the rebellion, was a brother of Patrick H Pearse. He was educated at the Christian Brothers' School in Westland row, and after a period of work as a sculptor became associated with his brother and Thomas MacDonagh in the management of St Enda's College, Rathfarnham. He was a keen Irish Irelander, attending the Oireachtas and other festivals attired in ancient Gaelic costume. He was a stage enthusiast, and appeared on the boards of the Abbey Theatre and Irish Theatre, Hardwicke street.

Percy, JC, JP, gave important evidence before the Hardinge Commission showing how recruiting for the Army was affected by the Sinn Fein propaganda. He is well known in literary and commercial circles, and is the author of several books of anecdote, which are largely read and quoted.

Pipkin, Samuel J, General Manager of the Atlas Insurance Co., is one of the three gentlemen appointed by the Government as a Committee to assess the damages sustained by sufferers from the fires.

Plunkett, Count George Noble, FSA, who was Director of the National Museum of Ireland, and a distinguished scholar, poet, and antiquary, was arrested after the rebellion with Countess Plunkett, his wife, and after a period of detention in Dublin was removed to England. There they had their liberty, but were debarred from returning to Ireland. Their eldest son, Joseph Plunkett, was executed, and two other sons, George and John, were each sent to penal servitude for ten years. Count Plunkett was created a Count of the Holy Roman Empire by Leo XIII. In 1884 he married Miss Josephine Cranny, of Muckross park, and they had four daughters and three sons. After his arrest Count Plunkett was removed from his position as Director of the National Museum, which carried a salary of £700. On Thursday, 18th January, 1917, a special meeting of the Royal Dublin Society by 236 votes against 58 passed a recommendation of the Council to the effect that Count Plunkett be called upon to resign membership of the Society. The restrictions upon his movements having been relaxed Count Plunkett arrived in Dublin on Wednesday, 31st January, to find himself one of three candidates for the Parliamentary representation of North Roscommon, rendered vacant by the death of Mr JJ O'Kelly. The Count reached the constituency on Thursday, 1st February, and the polling took place on Saturday, 3rd. the result was announced on Monday, 5th, as follows:

George Noble Count Plunkett	3,022
TJ Devine (Official Nationalist)	1,708
Jasper Tully (Independent)	687

After the declaration of the poll the Count said he would not take his seat at Westminster, and has not done so. The payment of Count Plunkett's Parliamentary salary having been the subject of questions in the House of Commons, the Speaker ruled that MPs could not be paid until they had taken the oath in the House of Commons.

PLUNKETT, COUNTESS, wife of Count George Noble Plunkett, FSA, was arrested after the rising, detained in prison for a time, and afterwards with her husband obliged to remain away from Ireland until the early part of 1917, when the restriction was withdrawn. It was she who founded the Hardwicke street Theatre, which her late son, Joseph, directed for a period.

PLUNKETT, JOSEPH, one of the seven signatories to the declaration of an Irish Republic, was executed in Kilmainham on 4th May, 1916. Around him centres the romance of the rebellion, as he was married at eight o'clock the night before his execution to Miss Grace Gifford, whose sister was married to Thomas MacDonagh, another of the rebel leaders executed. He was the eldest son of Count and Countess Plunkett, and two of his brothers, George and John, who also took part in the rising, were sentenced to death, but the sentence was commuted in their cases to ten years' penal servitude. Joseph Plunkett was a poet and a dramatist, and for a time edited 'The Irish Review'. He was 24 years of age, and acted as secretary to James Connolly during Easter week in the General Post Office. He had been in Spain early in the year, and was believed to be there for the purpose of negotiating with Germany. Mrs Joseph Plunkett is the daughter of a well known Dublin solicitor.

PORTAL, LT. COL. B, DSO, Commander of the Mobile Column from the Curragh. He was mentioned in Sir John Maxwell's despatches and also in a War Office list of officers who rendered distinguished services.

POWER, COUNTY INSPECTOR PC, Royal Irish Constabulary for County Kilkenny gave important evidence before the Hardinge Commission.

PRICE, MAJOR IVOR H, LLD, is a County Inspector of the Royal Irish Constabulary, but after the outbreak of the war he became Intelligence Officer at the Irish Military Headquarters, and acted as intermediary between the military authorities, the Under Secretary, Dublin Castle, RIC and DMP. He gave important evidence before the Hardinge Commission. He was mentioned in despatches, and made a Companion of the Distinguished Service Order early in 1917.

PURCELL, THOMAS P, Commander of the Dublin Fire Brigade, had a tremendous task imposed upon him during the rebellion. How he grappled with it is clearly told in the striking narrative which he tells on pages 29 to 32. He was awarded the bronze medal of the British Fire Prevention Committee in recognition of the services rendered by himself and the brigade during the rising. Capt. Purcell holds the silver medal for life saving from fire which was presented to him many years ago by the Lord Mayor of London.

PURSER, LIEUT. AND ACTING ADJUTANT PHILIP ADDISON, who was killed in the rebellion, was trained in the OTC, Dublin University, and was attached to the Duke of Cambridge's Hussars on the outbreak of the war. In October, 1914, he obtained a commission in the Army Service Corps, and in February, 1915, was sent to Flanders. He was invalided home in the following May, but, on the expiration of six months, was able to return to duty. Early in April, 1916, he was sent to the Curragh as Acting Adjutant, Army Service Corps, and on the outbreak of the Sinn Fein rebellion was the bearer of despatches from the Curragh to Dublin. He was 'held up' by the Sinn Feiners before he reached Dublin, but managed to get through and delivered his despatches in safety. He was shot on the evening of the 29th April, while returning from Kingstown to Dublin. Lieut. Purser, who was only 20 years of age, was the son of Mr William Purser, Resident Secretary of the Scottish Widows' Fund Society, Westmoreland street, Dublin.

QUIGLEY, JAMES, County Surveyor of County Meath, was tried at Richmond Barracks by courtmartial and acquitted of a charge of having conveyed information to the rebels by signal when the police were ambushed near Ashbourne.

QUINN, JAMES, a painter, was one of the rebels killed in the fighting at the South Dublin Union. He left a widow and young family.

RAFFERTY, THOMAS (22), of Lusk, Co. Dublin, a well-known hurler and member of the Black Raven Pipers, was killed at the battle of Ashbourne.

RAMSAY, LIEUT. ALAN, Royal Irish Regiment, who was killed while leading the attack on the rebels in the South Dublin Union, was the elder son of Mr Daniel L Ramsay, JP, of the Royal Nurseries, Ballsbridge. He was educated at St Andrew's College, and at Trinity College. In College he joined the Officers' Training Corps, and on the outbreak of war he received a commission in the Royal Irish Regiment. He went to Flanders at Christmas, 1914, and a few months later was wounded.

RICE, WILLIAM JOHN, Glenholme, Sandford terrace, Dublin, and member of the clerical staff at Guinness's Brewery, was shot dead by the military in the brewery with Lieut. Lucas, 2nd King Edward Horse. Mr Rice had no connection with the Sinn Fein movement, and was a trusted official in Guinness's. (See pages 122 to 127)

ROSBOROUGH, MAJOR JAMES, Royal Irish Rifles, was temporarily in command of Portobello Barracks during the rebellion. He gave evidence at the courtmartial following the shooting of Francis Sheehy Skeffington, and also before the Simon Commission.

ROSS OF BLADENSBURG, LIEUT. COLONEL SIR JOHN FOSTER GEORGE, KCB, was Chief Commissioner to the Dublin Metropolitan Police from 1901 until August, 1914, when he tendered his resignation because the Government had suspended the Assistant Commissioner without hearing the police report of the Howth gun-running incident. To the Hardinge Commission Sir John related the official police account of that affair, and recorded his emphatic opinion that an injustice had been done to his late assistant, Mr Harrel. Sir John Ross served in the Coldstream Guards, and in 1885 served in the Suakin campaign, and acted as Assistant Commissioner in Turkey in 1878-79. He was Assistant Private Secretary to the Right Hon. WM Forster, Chief Secretary for Ireland in 1881-2, and served on the staff of Earl Spencer and Earl of Carnarvon, when these noblemen held the office of Viceroy of Ireland in the eighties. While he has written a number of military histories, he devotes much time and interest to horticultural matters, being a great collector of trees and shrubs, of which he has a world famous collection at his place at Rostrevor, Co. Down.

RUTTLEDGE, COUNTY INSPECTOR GB, Royal Irish Constabulary in the West Riding of Galway, gave important evidence before the Hardinge Commission. He was awarded the King's Medal for the conspicuous courage and ability he showed during the rebellion when no troops were available.

RYAN, FRED (17), a member of the Citizen Army, was killed in the fighting at St Stephen's Green.

SHARPE, COUNTY INSPECTOR JOHN R, of the Royal Irish Constabulary for County Wexford, gave important evidence before the Hardinge Commission.

SHEARMAN, MR JUSTICE, one of the members of the Hardinge Commission which inquired into the causes of the rebellion, is a noted sportsman. He played Rugby for Oxford, ran a hundred yards and quarter mile, and was the amateur champion in these events. He is the joint author of 'Football: Its History for Five Centuries' (Athletics and Football, Badminton Library.)

SHEEHY SKEFFINGTON, FRANCIS JOSEPH CHRISTOPHER, was shot, with two others (Dickson and MacIntyre) by the military in Portobello Barracks on Wednesday morning, 26th April, 1916. He was the son of Dr Skeffington, MA, LLD, J., and was born at Bailieboro', Co. Cavan. He was for many years a well-known figure in Dublin, and took a prominent part in the votes for women movement—in fact he was wearing a 'votes for women' badge in his coat the day he was arrested. He was principally engaged latterly as a journalist, and acted as correspondent for foreign papers. He was 37 years of age, and left a widow and one son. The circumstances attending his death were enquired into by a Royal Commission, which found that he was in no way connected with the rebellion. Captain JC Bowen-Colthurst, who ordered him to be shot, was tried by courtmartial, found guilty of murder, and was also found to be insane, and was subsequently ordered to be confined in a criminal lunatic asylum during His Majesty's pleasure.

SHEEHY SKEFFINGTON, MRS, widow of Francis Sheehy Skeffington, who was shot in Portobello Barracks, gave evidence before the Simon Commission appointed to inquire into the circumstances surrounding her husband's death. In December, 1916, she arrived in New York with her son, Owen, aged seven.

SHORTIS, PATRICK (23), was a native of Ballybunion, and was educated in Killarney and Dublin, taking his BA Degree at the National University. He qualified as a wireless telegraphy operator, and while in London was active in Volunteer circles there. He was killed in the fighting in the General Post Office, Dublin.

SIMON, RIGHT HON. SIR JOHN ALLSEBROOK, was the Chairman of the Royal Commission appointed to inquire into the facts connected with the shooting of Francis Sheehy Skeffington and to others in Portobello Barracks. Sir John was Solicitor-General of England from 1910 to 1913, and from the latter date until 1915 he was Attorney-General. In that year he became Home Secretary, but differed with his colleagues in the Cabinet when Compulsory Service was introduced, and in the same year he resigned his office.

SKEFFINGTON, DR JB, Warrenpoint, Co. Down, ex-Senior Inspector National Education Board, the father of the late Mr Francis Sheehy Skeffington, was present at the exhumation of his son's remains in Portobello Barracks. Dr Skeffington also attended the Simon Commission of Inquiry, and put a number of questions and made a statement.

SOMERVILLE, MAJOR HF, was in command of the troops at the North Wall and Custom House. He was mentioned in despatches and made a Companion of the Distinguished Service Order.

STODART, HOLDEN, Corps Superintendent for Co. Dublin of St John Ambulance Brigade, was shot on the afternoon of Wednesday, 26th April, 1916, while going with a stretcher to the rear of Pembroke road to bring in a wounded soldier to the Royal City of Dublin Hospital at Baggot street. Mr Stodart, who was aged 33, and the younger surviving son of Dr Thomas A Stodart, an old and valued member of the *Irish Times* staff, resided at 'Winona', Victoria Villas, Blackrock, and has left a widow and child. He was educated at the High School, Dublin, and held a responsible position in the firm of Messrs Arthur Guinness and Co. Mr Stodart was one of the strongest supporters of the St John Ambulance Brigade in Dublin, and from the outbreak of the war had rendered valuable service as a Superintendent of the Brigade, and he had been awarded the Coronation Silver Medal. To this work he devoted himself with a whole hearted enthusiasm that characterised everything he took an interest in. When the rebellion broke out in Dublin he was the senior St John Ambulance officer then in the city, and he immediately got into touch with the military authorities, who were only too glad to avail of the services which Mr Stodart rendered cheerfully for two days and nights. He had an arduous task in organising bodies of ambulance workers to take duty at various hospitals, but despite what would have seemed insurmountable obstacles to many Mr Stodart gathered his forces, and placed them where their services were most needed. Having completed the work of organisation he settled down to the detail work under his superior officer who was now on the spot, with the Royal City of Dublin Hospital, Baggot street, as his station. From there he went out on the afternoon of Wednesday, 26th April, and died in the discharge of his duty. Acting on the suggestion and under the direction of Dr Lumsden, Deputy Commissioner for Ireland, the members of the St John Ambulance Brigade in Ireland founded the Holden Stodart Memorial Ward in the Duke of Connaught's Hospital for Limbless Soldiers and Sailors at Bray. The list of subscriptions, which totalled £724, showed that many thousands of men and women throughout the country participated in paying tribute to the memory of a gallant comrade. The memorial ward, which contains 14 beds, is now open in the Duke of Connaught's Hospital at Bray. The War Office placed officers and men of the Red Cross and St John Ambulance Brigade in the same position with regard to pensions and compassionate allowances as the equivalent ranks in the Army, and in pursuance of this liberal policy the widow and child of Mr H Stodart were granted the pension and allowance of a Lieutenant killed in action.

TAYLOR, JJ, CB, ISO, Principal Clerk of the Chief Secretary's Office, Dublin, is one of the three members of the Rebellion Victims' Committee.

TRAYNOR, JOHN J, (17), one of the rebels killed in the fighting in the South Dublin Union on Easter Monday, was a member of the Geraldine Football Club and the Mount Argus Pioneer Temperance Association.

VANE, MAJOR SIR FRANCIS, Munster Fusiliers, was engaged on recruiting work in Ireland at the outbreak of the rebellion, volunteered for service, and was attached to the Royal Irish Rifles at Portobello Barracks. He had previously seen service with the Scots Greys in the South African War. In Portobello Barracks he was second senior officer, and superior in command to Capt. Colthurst, who did not consult him about the shooting of the three men on Wednesday, 26th April. Major Vane reported the shootings, and in consequence of no action having been taken he went to London, and saw Lord Kitchener. He gave evidence in Dublin before the Simon Commission, which reported that he had no responsibility for the shooting.

WALSH, EDWARD, one of the rebels, died of wounds in the General Post Office. He left a widow and two children.

WALSH, JJ, sentenced to ten years' penal servitude, was a member of the Cork Corporation, and was employed in Cork Post Office until he was obliged by the authorities, because of certain speeches in public, to transfer to Bradford. Eventually he was dismissed from the Civil Service, and opened a tobacco and newsagent's shop at the corner of Berkeley road, Dublin. Walsh is said to have been appointed Postmaster-General of the Irish Republic.

WALSH, PHILIP, aged 28, was a signal sergeant in the Volunteers, and fought with them at the corner of Church street and Brunswick street, where he was fatally wounded. He was a member of Croke Football Club.

WARMINGTON, CAPTAIN ALFRED ERNEST, Royal Irish Regiment, who was killed while leading the attack on the rebels in the South Dublin Union, was the only son of Mr Alfred Warmington, Manager of the Munster and Leinster Bank at Naas, Co. Kildare. The deceased officer, who was educated at Ranelagh College, Athlone, and by private tuition, served through the South African War, and was with the Cape Mounted Rifles and Thornycroft's Mounted Infantry. He took part in the Battle of Spion Kop and the Relief of Ladysmith, and was awarded the King and Queen's Medals, with seven clasps, for his services in that campaign. On the outbreak of war in 1914 he was gazetted Captain to the 6th Batt. Royal Irish Regiment. He went to France with the Tenth (Irish) Division, and was later attached to the 3rd Batt. of the Royal Irish Regt. at Richmond Barracks, Dublin, in March, 1916. The remains of Capt. Warmington were interred in the grounds of King George V Military Hospital, Dublin, where a suitable monument has been erected to his memory.

WATERS, RICHARD, Recess, Monkstown, Co. Dublin, and an official in the Bank of Ireland, College Green, was shot dead while motoring towards the city on Easter Tuesday when approaching Mount street Bridge. Sir John Maxwell in his despatch dealing with the rebellion mentioned that numerous cases of unarmed persons killed by rebels had been reported to him, and among the instances he selected for the information of the Secretary for War was that of the late Mr Waters, who, he said, was being driven into Dublin by Captain Scovell, RAMC. Both Mr Waters and Captain Scovell were unarmed and the car was not challenged or asked to stop.

WATTERS, THE VERY REV. FELIX JOSEPH, SM, DD, LLD, President of the Catholic University School, Lower Leeson street, had been out on a mission of charity in the vicinity of Mount street Bridge, when he was hit by a bullet, from the effects of which he died on Monday, 8th May, 1916. The Rev. Dr Watters was born at Dundalk in 1851. His brother, the Rev. Michael J Watters, ex-Provincial of the Marxist Society in the Anglo-Hibernian province, predeceased him two years ago, and his only sister presides over a community of Poor Clares in Australia. He received his education at St Mary's College, Dundalk, and became a member of the

Society of Mary in 1872. Two years afterwards he was ordained priest, and his first appointment was to the Catholic University School. In 1884 he left Ireland and went to New Zealand, where he founded the College of St Patrick at Wellington. On his return to Europe in 1897 he was attached to the staff of St Anne's, Underwood street, London: and in 1902 he was appointed Superior of the Catholic University School, Dublin, which position he occupied till his death.

Weafer, Thomas, was a captain in the Irish Republican Army, and belonged to Enniscorthy, where he was born twenty-six years ago. He was killed in the Hibernian Bank at the corner of Sackville street and Lower Abbey street, on Wednesday, 26th April.

Webb, Doctor Ella G (MD), Lady of Grace of the Order of St John of Jerusalem: Lady District Superintendent, SJAB, member of Joint VAD Committee for Ireland, is the wife of Mr George R Webb, FTCD, daughter of the Very Rev. Dr Ovenden, Dean of St Patrick's Cathedral. Her residence is at 20 Hatch street, Dublin. During the rebellion Dr Webb organised hospitals, cycled through the firing line continuously, and visited the city hospitals day by day, ascertaining their needs, and giving all assistance possible. She was awarded a silver medal by the General Chapter of the Order of St John of Jerusalem for her gallant services during that week.

Wheeler, Major H de Courcy, son of the late Surgeon Wheeler, Dublin, accepted the surrender of Countess Markievicz at the Royal College of Surgeons. He was mentioned in a War Office list of officers who had rendered distinguished services.

Whelan, Patrick (23), a member of the Ringsend section of the Gaelic League, was killed near Boland's Mills. He was well known as a hurler.

Williams, Miss Florence, was awarded the Military Medal by the War Office for her gallantry and devotion in tending wounded soldiers in the vicinity of Dublin Castle on Easter Monday. She assisted several wounded soldiers to her mother's house, going through a heavy fire repeatedly, and afterwards rendered much valuable assistance in bringing bread and medical supplies and bandages. Miss Williams' father is a sergeant in the Border Regiment, and on active service in the Balkans, and the heroine resides with her mother and sister in 8 Bristol Buildings, Castle street, Dublin.

Wilson, Lieut. Alexander, one of the three officers sharing guard duty at Portobello Barracks on Wednesday, 26th April. When the three men were taken out to be shot Lieut. Wilson was sent by Lieut. Dobbin with an urgent message to the Adjutant. He rushed over on his bicycle, and while delivering the reply to Lieut. Dobbin the fatal volley was fired.

Wilson, Sec. Lieut. Leslie, 5th Royal Irish Fusiliers, was in command of the party of soldiers which held Francis Sheehy Skeffington as a hostage on Portobello Bridge on Tuesday night, April 25, while Capt. Bowen-Colthurst's party was raiding Alderman Kelly's shop.

Wimborne, Lord, who resigned his post as Lord Lieutenant following the rebellion, was appointed in succession to the Earl of Aberdeen on February 17th, 1915. He was sworn in as Viceroy on the following day, and made his State entry into Dublin on April 14th, 1915. His attentions during the brief period in which he held office were mainly directed to the furtherance of recruiting in Ireland, and in his capacity of Controller of Recruiting he addressed numerous meetings in various parts of the country. His sporting temperament assured his popularity, but, unfortunately, the continuance of the war did not enable him to indulge to any great extent in polo, a pastime with which his name has been closely linked. He is the eldest son of the first Baron Wimborne, and was born on January 16th, 1873. He was educated at Eton and Trinity College, Cambridge, and afterwards joined the Imperial Yeomanry, in which he attained the rank of Captain. In the year 1900 he went to South Africa with his corps, and for his services there he was awarded the Queen's Medal with three clasps. In 1900 he was elected as Conservative member for Plymouth, and he represented the constituency until 1906, when he was elected as the Liberal candidate for the Cardiff Division. He held the seat until 1910, when he became Paymaster-General. In the same year he was raised to the Peerage as Baron Ashby St Ledgers, and in 1913 he was appointed a Lord in Waiting to the King. On the death of his father in 1914 he succeeded to the title as second Baron Wimborne. Lord Wimborne was Chairman of the Royal Commission on Coast Erosion and Afforestation, which took evidence in various parts of the United Kingdom some years ago. At the date of his appointment as Lord Lieutenant he was acting as Aide-de-Camp to Lieutenant General Sir Bryan Mahon, Commander of the 10th (Irish) Division of the First New Army. In 1902 he married the Hon. Alice Katherine Sibel Grosvenor, daughter of the second Baron Ebury. The Hardinge Commission recorded their opinion that no responsibility rested upon the Lord Lieutenant, and that he was in no way answerable for the policy of the Government. When announcing the appointment of Mr Duke as Chief Secretary, Mr Asquith said it was not proposed to appoint a Lord Lieutenant, but a few days later, on August 4, 1916, it was announced that Lord Wimborne had been re-appointed to the post of Lord Lieutenant.

Worswick, Sec. Lieut. B, King Edward Horse, was shot by the military in Guinness's Brewery on Friday, 28th April, under circumstances that are fully reported in the courts-martial to be found on pages 122 to 127. Sec. Lieut. Worswick joined the 2nd King Edward's Horse in August, 1914, when it was first formed, and served with it continuously until the day of his death. He left with the regiment for France on May 4th, and served in the trenches till he was offered his commission by the Colonel while he was still in the trenches serving as a trooper. He returned to England to take up his commission at the end of September, 1915, and was gazetted on October 2nd, 1915. When the rebellion broke out he was stationed with the 2nd King Edward's Horse at the Curragh, and the unanimous testimony of his brother officers and friends is that he had no sympathy or association of any kind with the Sinn Feiners. There was no public investigation into the circumstances attending the death of Lieut. Worswick, his case being governed by the finding in that of Lieut. Lucas (See also, Lucas, Sec. Lieut. AL.)

UNCONDITIONAL RELEASE OF ALL PRISONERS

In the House of Commons on June 15, 1917, Mr Bonar Law said—The Government, after giving long and anxious consideration to the position of the Irish political prisoners, feel that the governing consideration in the matter is the approaching session of the Convention, in which Irishmen themselves will meet to settle the difficult problem of the future administration of their country. They have decided, therefore, upon the release, without reservation, of all prisoners now in confinement in connection with the rebellion.

All male prisoners were assembled at Pentonville Prison, London, on Sunday, 17th June, 1917. The same evening they were placed on a special train at Euston Station, and conveyed to Holyhead, from where they crossed by the mail steamer Munster to Kingstown. At Westland row Station, Dublin, the men arrived on Monday morning, 18th June, 1917, and were welcomed by a large crowd of friends.

Countess Markievicz was not released until Monday, 18th June, from Aylesbury Prison. She arrived in Dublin on Thursday, 21st June, and was met by a large crowd, which accompanied her as she drove through the principal streets.

Before the amnesty several of the prisoners were released on account of ill-health, among them being William Partridge, JF Cullen, and Gerald Crofts.

The following is the list of names of those released by the amnesty. The sentences passed upon them will be found on pages 60 to 66, with the exception of R Donoghue (Enniscorthy), who was sentenced to three years' penal servitude, and Michael Slattery sentenced to eight years' penal servitude:

Ashe, Thomas
Beasley, Pierce
Bevan, Charles
Bevan, Thomas
Boland, Henry James
Brady, Michael
Brennan, J
Brennan, Maurice
Brennan, Robert
Brooks, F
Brosnan, Timothy
Burke, James
Burke, Joseph
Byrne, J
Carrick, Christopher
Carrick, John
Clancy, Peter
Clarke, J
Coleman, R
Collins, Cornelius
Corcoran, Eddy
Corcoran, John
Corcoran, William
Cosgrave, Philip B
Cosgrave, William, TC
Corrigan, William P
Davys, Richard
De Lacy, Michael
Dempsey, James
Dorrington, J
De Valera, E
Doherty, John
Donoghue, R
Downey, J
Doyle, Gerald
Doyle, James
Doyle, Peter
Drennan, Frank
Duggan, Edward
Etchingham, John R
Fahy, Francis
Fahy, Patrick
Faulkiner, John
Fitzgerald, Thomas Desmond
Flanagan, Patrick
Fleming, Michael (senior)
Fogarty, Patrick
Fury, Patrick
Fury, Thomas
Fury, Thomas
Galligan, Patrick
Hayes, Dr Richard
Hehir, Michael
Higgins, Michael
Howley, Joseph
Hughes, James T
Hunter, Thomas
Hussey, William
Irvine, George
Joyce, James
Kelly, P
Kelly, R
Kent, David
King, Richard, F
Lawless, Frank
Lawless, James V
Leahy, Denis
Levins, George
Loughlin, James
Lynch, Finian
Lynch, Jeremiah C
Markievicz, Countess
M'Ardle, John
MacEntee, John
MacGarry, John
M'Ginley, Conor
M'Guinness, Joseph, MP
MacMahon, Philip Joseph
MacNeill, Eoin
MacNestry, Patrick
Marks, J
Martin, Francis
Meehan, W
Melinn, James
Mervyn, Michael
Molloy, Bryan
Morrissey, James
Norton, J
O'Brien, John
O'Callaghan, Denis
O'Connor, Fergus
O'Dea, William
O'Donovan, C
O'Geary, Colin
O'Hanrahan, Henry
O'Kelly, T
O'Sullivan, J
Peppard, T
Plunkett, George
Plunkett, John
Poole, Vincent
Quinn, John
Rafter, James
Reid, JJ
Reynolds, Michael
Sally, James
Scully, Michael
Shouldice, John
Slattery, Michael
Stack, Austin
Sweeney, PE
Tobin, William, J
Tomkins, John
Toole, Michael
Walsh, JJ
Walsh, Thomas
Williams, John
Wilson, James
Wilson, P
Wilson, W

ON WANDSWORTH BRIDGE

A NOVEL

HATTIE POND

On Wandsworth Bridge

A novel

All you need in this life is ignorance
and confidence, and then Success is sure.

Mark Twain

For Martin and Adam

Contents

SECTION THREE: MAURITANIA AND LONDON

SECTION FOUR: ENDINGS

AFTERWORD

PROLOGUE

Arrivals

A YOUNG WOMAN, ENVELOPED IN A WATERPROOF cloak, stands alone in the gloom on Wendelsworth Bridge. She carries a red bag and is wearing pink galoshes. It is not raining, has not rained for some weeks and shows no signs of doing so. A passing cabbie does a U-turn and stops to pick her up.

As the taxi sets off through the streets of Lundenwic, the cabbie begins the story of his life. It has a flow to it, this story, and perhaps he has told it before. In the darkness of the rear of the taxi, the young woman pillows her blonde head on the bag and her mouth hangs open in what might be wonderment or incredulity, but after a while it becomes more likely that she is fast asleep.

Something is sailing up from the estuary. Beneath the grey of the evening waters moves a submersible, an ellipsoid. It looks like a whale, or something military that no one knows about except for a journalist or two. As it moves along the river Tempus, it becomes apparent that this is a vessel similar in size, but not shape, to a single-decker bus. It bobs beneath the surface then reappears. It veers across the water seeking shadow as though it does not wish to be seen. For such a craft concealment would present a problem. The estuary has been comfortably deep but, gliding further and further into the city, under Lundenwic Bridge, Dark Religious Mendicant Bridge, Year Twenty-Hundred Bridge, it becomes obvious that the river is too shallow. Few of the city's occupants realise this. It does not look shallow.

The vessel has passed under most of the city's bridges and, if it is not to flounder in the suburbs, must resort to desperate measures. It shunts backwards and forwards, its engines in danger of burning out. Inch by inch it sinks into the mud until it comes to rest, its lower section level with the riverbed, safe in the silt beneath Wendelsworth Bridge.

The bald dome of its roof can still be seen in the half-light. In response to the vessel's arrival, two obscure gizmos embedded in concrete on either side of the water's edge clunk into activity. At last the vessel is entirely hidden.

Over to the east of the city, the girl with the red bag arrives at her destination and awakes.

Time passes. A year, and then another month or so.

SECTION ONE

Lundenwic

CHAPTER 1

The invitation

HUGO DE LAMARTINE, WHO LIKED HIS name to be pronounced 'Oogo' in the French way, clad rather smartly in a white linen shirt and black trousers, opened his front door and stepped out into the streets of Lundenwic to confront the world and, perhaps, to change it.

There was nothing about him to suggest that the world had much to fear. It might be argued that he was in good company in that respect, as most of the damage done to this earth throughout history has been perpetrated by ordinary-looking people. Many of these wore a moustache, however, whereas he was clean-shaven.

Hugo de Lamartine, author of a book on Photographic Art, his name established for three months now on the lists of People Who Get Invited, was off to a drinks do at Cave Paintings, a small gallery on Hassock Street.

The book had been published two years ago. It began:

> I am pressed into combat with a differing paradigm, my incorporeal self confronting the choppy waves of another reality…

The rest flowed seamlessly from that first sentence, taking on a life of its own and surprising its author who, never having picked up a camera, had not appreciated the inner depths of photography. Neither had he realised, until then, that he had an unusual facility with the written word. The book had transformed his life.

The roots of this transformation could be traced to a small update on his curriculum vitae. He wasn't born Hugo de

Lamartine. The name came to him one day as an inspiration and surely, in a world such as this where you can get anything new from kids to kidneys, it is not such a big deal for a young man leading a decent-enough life to have the cosmetic alteration of a new name. The Hugh conferred on him shortly after birth had not proved an advantage during his education. Hugh. Hugh. Hugh. If you say it often enough it suggests something unpleasant, an accretion of mucus in the nasal passages. There's a whine to it. The boys at his school often dropped the aitch. He could never be sure if shouts of 'Ay you! were not Hey Hugh! Should he turn round or just ignore them?

A sudden move to a boarding school, when his father was posted at short notice to the Middle East and his mother went too, brought with it an opportunity to change one letter on a form. Out went the final aitch, and in came an o. Hugo, pronounced Hugh-go. Such a tiny change. But it helped.

'Hi. I'm Hugo, Hugo Fisher.'

He learned a bit of French, enough to do well in an exam and win a merit star, and that was how his connection with France began, and grew, until many years later, on a quiet day at the office, he began his masterwork, typing with one finger on a clean, white, word-processing page:

TRAPPED LIGHT

An Interpretation of the Photographic Art
by Hugo de Lamartine

There was a nicely alliterative echo to the 'l' of *Light* in Lamartine. It seemed cultured, had gloss. He changed everything into the pseudonym (quite legal under current law, there being no intent to defraud) and after a while, joy of joys, a passport was issued in his new name.

What a delight it is to be me! thought Hugo, as he walked along Thrombold Street, where he lived, past terraces of grand mansions all now reduced by years of multiple occupation to blowsy middle-age and letting themselves go. A rhythm to his step carried him along without effort. It was one of those uncertain evenings of autumn. Although the temperature was balmy there was something rotten in the air, summer beginning to decompose. Young women passing him in the street all seemed to be wearing tartan. How strange that they should be so warmly clad when the night was mild. Only a few days ago they had been scarcely covered at all and, to add to the mystery, why tartan? Having spent a month of his childhood in Pazely, Hugo understood Scotland. What right had these girls to be wearing the colours of Finlaggan, Dinwiddie and Spens? The girls, like ants or bees, were dressed identically, followed chemical cues, operated mindlessly. What a gap between them and someone like himself, an individual invited to a celebration where his profound views on Art would be recognised and welcomed.

In anticipation, he had considered bringing a few copies of his book to leave lying around, but decided that this lacked subtlety. Instead, he had slipped some business cards into his trouser pocket. This evening might be a stepping stone to that most gratifying of events, a book reading. Perhaps he would be invited to return to the gallery at some future date. He imagined himself looking stylish and relaxed, reading from his book, people sitting in neat rows before him hanging on his every word.

But hush, listen! He halted for a moment. Since leaving the bright lights of the Silver Falcon Road some moments ago, the back of his neck had begun to prickle and he sensed that someone was following him. There was a sound like claws skittering on flagstones and a snuffle of heavy breathing. He whirled around and held his breath, but there was no one to be seen, a dearth of passers-by or traffic, so he resumed a no-nonsense stride, and, as he turned into Hassock Street, his gaze penetrated the gloom. Halfway down the street he saw the gallery, Cave Paintings. Lit by an orange glow, it was in a row of shops and businesses, all closed for the night but for a restaurant a little further along.

A receptionist spotted him through the glass frontage and greeted him at the door.

'Hi, I'm Tommy. Can I help you?'

Hugo felt her question might be a challenge to his right to be there. There was something odd about what she was wearing; it resembled an all-in-one flight suit with a zip up the front. The tartan was faded.

'I am Hugo de Lamartine.' *Boff!* he thought, *why didn't I bring my cape?* The announcement of his name ought to have been followed by a swish of black cashmere-mix, giving an impetus to propel him over the threshold. In this instance the name alone sufficed.

'Wow. We've got your book on the list at Uni.'

'Ah! You've perused *Trapped Light!*'

'No. Sorry. Don't have to. Photography's not one of my subjects.'

Hugo raised an eyebrow. The girl ushered him into the gallery and pinned a label to the pocket of his white shirt; 'Hugo de Lamartine' it said in a quirky font. She was clumsy, fumbled a little, scraped his hand briefly with a knuckle-duster of a ring causing him to yelp and make a fuss. She lunged with a napkin, intent on dabbing. He parried, nabbed the napkin, soothed his own wound. She made amends by pouring him a glass of white wine followed swiftly by a top-up.

His feathers now smoothed a little, Hugo made his entrance into the room with what he deemed to be an air of interest and discernment. His invitation had come from Rodney and Wilfred Warlock-Williams, their two surnames conjoined, who owned the gallery. Tonight they had invited clients, art world aficionados and press to a showing of some wonderful examples of Conceptual Art: Umberto Piselli's *Time and String* series covered one wall, and a Mungo Murphy rotating sackcloth installation hung from the ceiling. The other artists displayed were less well known, but they had used a similar palette of colours: taupe, dun, camel and smoke, which worked so well with the white walls and limed-wood floors of the gallery. One wall was empty.

It was always a fraught moment, this business of breaking into an established group. Apart from two vaguely-familiar figures who he thought might be his hosts, and the woman in tartan who did not count, there were five people chatting and pecking on Prinkles. Remembering all the names and faces would be tricky with so many people. Two elderly ladies he took to be Patrons of the Arts. They were probably titled and sat as judges for Famous Art Prizes. Two young men wore tie-less suits, which in this world suggested that they had reached the managing echelons of something, an Auction House maybe, or a National Institution. A young woman was draped in some sort of nightgown, demonstrating the kind of eccentricity so typical of the rich and well-connected.

'Hello, hello!' Rodney, his host, head and face agleam, peered up at Hugo's name badge. 'My dear. . .Hugo! What a delight to see you! You must be wondering why we have an empty wall. It's going to be a surprise for everyone, including me. A friend of Wilfred's . . . You've met Wilfred, haven't you?' He indicated an untidy-looking middle-aged man with boyish hair on the far side of the room.

Hugo nodded. 'There was a summer do . . .'

'Oh, good! As I was saying, a friend of Wilfred's is sending round a painting that he says will cause a sensation with the press. Anyway, we've got the journalists,' he gestured towards the two suits who were laughing immoderately beside a drinks table in the corner, 'but there's no painting yet. Tommy's going to put it up when it arrives. You met her at the door, I presume?'

'Well, yes . . .'

'She's a treasure. An absolute treasure. Just look at her!'

Hugo followed his host's gaze in the general direction of the tartan suit.

'She's perfect, isn't she?' said Rodney.

Hugo's mind was lost in a dark wood, as he tried to decide how this conversation might find a better path, along which it might be possible to encounter the paradise of books and book readings and the not-quite mid-life aspirations of Hugo. But the right words were unavailable, and Rodney appeared not to be waiting for a response.

'Classic features! See the Grecian nose? Such a find! And she works like a bee! A little bee!' He laughed. 'Lovely talking to you, Hugo! We must continue this one later!' And he bustled off. Hugo glared with irritation at the cause of this hiatus. Tommy wasn't buzzing about working at that moment. She looked like an attenuated nursery toy and appeared to be having some sort of tryst with a new arrival, an oriental, no doubt a boyfriend, who was clutching a towel. The boyfriend was also dressed in outlandish clothes: tight flared jeans and a t-shirt, both in a pale, purply sort of a colour that reminded Hugo of the trends of his parents' youth.

With a swing of his long hair tied back in a ponytail, the strange young man raised his head and met Hugo's gaze. A hard look. The air seemed to shimmer. Hugo blinked, shook his head and swivelled around one hundred and eighty degrees to gaze at nothing in particular.

A moment or two thudded by. He was wondering if he should have another glass of wine, when he heard a snorting sound. Something pig-like was rumbling beneath the higher cadences of the gossiping guests, accompanied by a scuttle of claws on the wooden floor.

A female voice rose above the hubbub. 'I say, does anybody own this dog?'

Hugo looked down. A dog! Some idiot had brought a bloody dog to a drinks party and the elderly ladies were gushing over it.

'To whom do you think it belongs, Daphne?' continued the voice, which sprang from the throat of a large-boned lady, gussied up in yellow.

'I believe he just wandered in, Marjorie. Isn't that the Boston terrier who belonged to – um, what's his name? – that film star . . .?' Daphne was small, white-haired and wearing brown; even her voice was soft like a mushroom.

'Give me a clue.'

'You must know who I mean, he's quite famous – anyway he was over here in a play. Apparently, the dog used to hang around backstage. Won whatsisname a lot of brownie points, but then he lost them. Went back to the United Confederacy and left the poor creature behind.'

'He didn't! What a bastard. So you're lost, little fellow! What shall we do about him? Anybody got any ideas?' thundered Marjorie.

To Hugo's irritation everyone gawped at the dog. He was a black-and-white dwarf of a dog with a punched-in muzzle, bulging, bloodshot eyes and bandy legs.

'Don't worry,' said Tommy. 'I'll deal with him.'

'Will you, dear?' shrieked Marjorie. 'What a sweetheart! Thank you.' This seemed to provide a reason for everyone in the room, except Hugo, to grin like idiots.

One of the young men in suits was wearing trainers, which Hugo found unsettling. It was plain that the evening was not easily to be lifted to the abstract heights of the Mungo Murphy swinging above everyone's heads, but at least, Hugo noticed, the time-warp thug in the purplish jeans appeared to have done a disappearing trick.

A van drew up outside.

'Tommy! The picture's here. Will you get a craft knife and open the packaging in the street?' Little Rodney's face was flushed. 'Soon as you've finished we'll help you hang it.'

Hugo stood behind Rodney and Wilfred as through the glass frontage they watched two shifty-looking individuals in jeans unload the van and Tommy hack at the packaging with a blade.

'I hope it's our sort of painting,' said Rodney.

'Trust me, it will be,' Wilfred beamed down at his partner. 'Maurizio is a sweet fellow, and he has impeccable taste.'

Tommy's efforts had revealed an enormous oil painting in an ornate gilt frame. Its subject was difficult to see in the streetlight.

'Oh dear,' said Rodney. 'Look at that frame. It's a turkey.'

'Never mind. It's too late now. We don't want to look silly in front of our guests.' said Wilfred. 'Let's get it inside and up on the wall where we can see it.'

The painting was taller than the doorway and Tommy guided it in diagonally. Wilfred and Rodney stood beside a stepladder to help her ease it up on a row of picture hooks. Conversations tailed away, eyes turned, feet followed. The guests all gathered beside their hosts and surveyed the painting.

The execution was faultless. In the foreground a laughing girl in a headscarf and overalls leant over a heavily-textured concrete wall, her fingers holding up a dandelion, yellow against the grey-green of the wall. She seemed to offer the pis-en-lit to some unseen young man or to the guests in the art gallery. Behind her, a woman in similar working dress stood beside a youth with a cap and a red neckerchief. All three, framed by a rough wooden lintel, were smiling a little too joyfully, given all those overalls and concrete, at some shared joke.

To Hugo it was just an oil painting. Maybe one day he would write a book on oil paintings, but until then he could take them or leave them. Feeling peckish, he looked around him in search of nibbles. Marjorie and Daphne moved up to the painting to examine it more closely. Wilfred's lips were drawn back tightly. Little Rodney was the first to speak.

'Oh dear. Happy workers.'

There was a solemn silence, as though there had been the announcement of some death or dire prognosis, followed by the sound of a dish striking a hard floor, spinning around quickly before slowing down. Hugo held his palms up before him as though absolving himself of blame and damning the errant finger food.

'Don't worry! Not a problem.' Tommy fussed around, which suggested that a few flakes on the floor were indeed a problem. 'I'll fetch a dustpan and brush.'

'Are you knowledgeable about art?' It was the young woman in the nightdress. 'It's a Russian painting, or rather Soviet, isn't it?'

'Isn't that rather the same thing?' said Hugo.

Her voice was English but her nightgown had an ethnic look. Noticing her dark hair and olive skin, Hugo took her to be from the Indian subcontinent and was nettled. For the entire week he had been brooding about a certain Indian woman. Indeed, it was the setting aside of this preoccupation that had caused him to feel so exhilarated earlier that evening, as he left his flat and strode out into the street.

He had received an e-mail on Monday from Nigel, a fixer in the art world who was acting as his agent, which read:

> Chaire Hugo,
>
> Grate news. The University of Shandygore – had a letter but cant find it maybe someone hav stole it. Chiz Chiz. Anyway they want text book's for the Department of the Art's.
>
> They hav scent Ravinda Bat to Lundenwic who is a really grate person to translate your book into indian and some other language which is indian too aparently!!!!!
>
> It was me * three cheers hurray etc * who suggested that your book on Phtography would be a good one!
>
> Ravinder Baht will be ringing you soon to arrange a get together.
>
> je te embarrasse
>
> Nigel
>
> www.molesworthmentoring.com

Hugo had been chasing Nigel throughout the week by telephone, all e-mails having bounced back, intending to persuade him that such a venture was not a good idea. Indeed the prospect of someone meddling with his book appalled him. Nigel was not in his office. The woman from India had not called yet. Hugo had tiptoed around the telephone, regarding it with revulsion, for days. He knew his geography. There was the Near East, the Middle East and the Far East. And where did India come in all that? Somewhere there wasn't a word for, between middle and far. And now here was this young woman, moving in Art Circles, who might possibly be Ms Bat or Bhatt or whatever her name was, asking him to comment on a painting on which he was unable to formulate any opinion whatsoever. He strained to read her name tag, then saw to his relief as she turned towards the light that it began with an 'M'. Megan something or other. Good. Not the woman whose threatened intrusion he feared. He did not bother to decipher the rest of her name and, leaving her dangling in mid-participle, went over to where the two young suits, one plump, both tall, were drinking green liquid with a whitish scum on top.

'Come to join us at the absinthe table?' said the slim one to Hugo, who replied, 'Well, no. Not really. I prefer white wine.'

'It's apple and kiwi juice, actually, with a shot of vodka and three caffeine pills. Charlie Archer.' He extended a hand and smiled. 'Don't tell anyone, but I'm not a journalist, I'm a solicitor at Burton and Crump and this is Terence Bunyan from . . . who're you writing for now, Terence?'

'Whoever will have me. *Art Monthly* mostly. I'm sort of free-lancing and trying to break into TV work. That's where the art world's really happening these days. It's mega. Hey, listen to our hosts! Rodney and Wilfred appear to be having a major set-to!'

Hugo followed his gaze to the doorway of an inner office, through which Rodney's voice could be heard quite clearly wailing:

'He's a complete tosser and you're a complete tosser. He must've had a bloody good reason for sending over that painting! Everyone's looking at it! I've had two offers to buy it, and nobody's even bothering to look at anything else. It's all a complete disaster! You slept with him, didn't you?'

'Of course I didn't.' Wilfred's voice, sincere, placatory.

'Of course you did, and then it went sour, and that turkey, that complete dodo of a painting, is his getting back at you with a vengeance. Isn't it?'

'Let's talk about it later. Everybody's listening.'

'What do I care?' Rodney sounded close to tears. 'Oh lord, I'm getting low blood sugar now. I'm feeling all weak and wobbly.'

'You need dinner. Let's close the show and see who wants to come out to dinner.'

There were certain words and phrases in the English language which, when interpreted in a personal way, were capable of giving Hugo a warm feeling: expressions such as *accolade, beneficiary, invitation, honorary degree, unconditional* and *dinner*. A meal was a step up from a drinks do. 'Dinner!' he whispered to the two young men standing beside him and Marjorie, who had at that moment come banging out of a loo next to the office and left the door wide open. Why hadn't the stupid old woman closed it? Oblivious, she strode on past Hugo, with a reek of cosmetic chemicals and floor cleaner rushing to fill the air she displaced. There was a snuffling noise at his feet, followed by the sound of claws on ceramic and a tongue lapping. The door swung slowly to and clicked shut, removing all these troubling aesthetic crimes together.

'Good idea. Time for some fodder,' whooped Marjorie. 'There's a French restaurant just a few doors down.'

'There is indeed. Tommy, would you be a dear and lock up and set the alarm? Here's the key. You can post it through the letterbox.' Wilfred fished in his trouser pocket. 'Oops, I'm out of cash. Is next week OK?'

'Of course,' said Tommy.

Hugo saw the group of prospective diners begin to gather. He wanted to be among them, but on what terms? Would he still be a guest of Rodney and Wilfred, or would it be each man for himself? It could prove to be a free-for-all at one of those restaurants that embarrassed people into paying silly prices. Perhaps it would be better if he were just to go home, but he hadn't had a chance to discuss his book with anyone yet. All that chit-chat. Nothing had happened this evening that could have any bearing, at all, on his advance across that glorious bridge from obscurity to renown. And it was only half past nine! Some sort of bacteriological warfare involving *helicobacter pylori* and jets of acid was skirmishing in his stomach. They were leaving. He would have to make a decision. Little threads of possibility, pulled from the warp and weft of all those suits and shirts and dresses around him, were already spinning out to who knows where. Faint strains of music from down the street drifted through the open door.

Oh bugger, he thought. Dinner, he thought, and followed the others out of the gallery.

CHAPTER 2

Oh where, oh where, can he be?

THE PARTY GUESTS JOSTLED THROUGH the doorway and went out into the night. Tommy washed the wineglasses, ran the Myson cleaner over the limed-wood floor and switched off the spotlights shining equally on the good, the bad and the uncertain. Was there a scratching sound? No, nothing but her imagination. She set the alarm, locked the front door and, posting the key through the letterbox, walked out into the street, overtaking a little old lady who was staggering along, knees agape, her head moving from side to side as though searching for something. Tommy turned back. 'Anything I can do to help?'

'No, dear. Don't fink so, but bless yer. Goo'night.' The voice was warm, homely, a little drunk. Her eyes, strangely bright for an old lady, glittered in the half-light.

No need to worry then. 'Goodnight.' She picked up speed and hurried off towards the Tube station. Behind her in the quiet road she could hear music playing, something emotional and French with rolling guttural 'Rs' that possibly she had heard before; but then again maybe not.

At last there was time to think. What on earth had happened in there tonight? It had been such a strange experience. She had been worrying over the promised arrival of the mystery artwork, and the practical problem of installing it with the guests already present, when something uncanny occurred. The air before her shimmered and the light seemed split into jagged shards. All of a sudden, there he was, appearing like a projection or a mirage, dimly at first and then more clearly. It was him – she'd know that face anywhere, the slanting grey eyes and high cheekbones – Splintered Dick, or rather their lead singer, dressed in faded mauve jeans and a lavender t-shirt and clutching a towel. He was standing in the doorway, looking anxious and a little stoned. Some indefinable emotion made her stomach lurch.

His voice floated over to her like bubbles pushing through water and she heard him say, 'I've something im . . . portant to tell you . . . Go . . . You go . . . Now!'

'Of course,' she replied, not knowing what he meant or to what she was agreeing. There was something so intense about his gaze that she felt immobilised, while his eyes moved from hers, seeming to peer over her shoulder and beyond, before returning to transfix her once more. She was about to question him when he became less substantial. The figure in mauve faded through grey to silver, thinning until it was one with the air and gone. There was no one there any more. An empty doorway led out into the night. Now what was she to make of that?

It had been a difficult day. Uni was always a struggle, the study of art being such a messy business, and there in the background never quite going away was a niggling concern about Hendrix. Her flatmate Hendrix had not returned the night before and had failed to respond to phone calls made throughout the day. There was obviously some perfectly reasonable explanation. She'd find him on her return, back from wherever it was that he'd been. She wouldn't let him know that she'd been anxious. She'd cook a meal. Paintstripper, her other flatmate, would as usual be drinking beer. Life would be on track again. Yet, behind the background, or maybe underneath it, there was something else. Something she hadn't done. What was it? Fingers scratched in a forgotten corner of her mind.

Tommy waited on the Underground platform. There was a smell of ancient dust and a rush of air. Ghosts seemed to cackle along electric cables. Eyes turned to follow her: a businessman, two young guys. Why were they looking at her? Did they spot something askew, some hint that she was different? A woman with a secret. Or maybe they hadn't really noticed her at all. How did you fit in? How did you know if people liked you or were simply being kind and tolerating you? The world was overcomplicated and inexplicable, and the only response to it was to keep moving, keep busy, never let anything get too untidy and make sure all kitchen surfaces were perfectly clean. It was amazing how quickly microbes could multiply on a damp cloth!

Up she climbed from the grubbiness of the Underground, back to her home turf at last. Even at ten o'clock at night the traffic was heavy in this neighbourhood. Shop windows were aglow with impossibly expensive, incomprehensible clothes. Big men with thick necks stood in doorways taking the night air, for their health she assumed; gangs of middle-aged women swayed by. Tommy felt a wave of compassion for the women who, she imagined, were hurtling towards the menopause, poor things, or binge drinking to relieve the sorrow of empty nests. She side-stepped some street dwellers with a wince of empathy and took a turning along the flank of Horridus, the department store. This would have been a much more convenient place for a part-time job than Cave Paintings, but it always made her shiver. There were dark tales about Horridus and Tommy walked briskly past.

She had found Cave Paintings one day, purely by chance, at the end of a long walk through the streets of Lundenwic. It was meant to be a short walk but she'd taken a wrong turning somewhere. Overcoming her shyness, she had entered, asked for a job and been taken on there and then. It was just one strangeness among many.

Although the neighbourhood had its shortcomings – basic provisions were too expensive and had to be purchased elsewhere – her home, a flat in a mansion block in Klaus Place, was familiar and comforting. She was tired now and grateful for the lift, an ancient engineering miracle of polished wood and brass, which took her up to the third floor.

'Is he back?'

Visible through the open door of her room, Paintstripper was slumped at a desk in front of a monitor. She removed her headphones and ruffled her hair so that it stuck up in clumps.

Tommy repeated her question. 'Is he back yet?'

'No. Not yet.'

The vision of a happy evening blurred and vanished. Paintstripper knew more about males than Tommy did. Paintstripper had left her husband and three boys last year, when the youngest was eight. A practical man her husband, she said, a coper; he'd bring her kids up perfectly well. Her room was clean. A pair of jeans and a sweatshirt, both size 22, were hanging up to dry. There wasn't a photograph or an ornament in sight. Tommy felt the urge to confide her unease.

'It's not like Hendrix to be away all night and all day. Perhaps something's happened.'

Paintstripper smiled at her. 'But then we haven't had a knock on the door or somebody ringing with bad news. Hendrix'll turn up.'

'I hope you're right.'

'Trust me, he'll be OK. Come on.' She heaved to her feet. 'Let's have a beer.'

The kitchen was Tommy's favourite room. The flat's high ceilings sneered at all beneath, and had such an embellishment of cornices, coving and architraves that establishing cosiness on a tiny budget had been a challenge. Tall sash windows lined one wall of the kitchen, but she had brought them down to a more human scale with old flannel sheeting dyed yellow and tie-backs made from black socks. The fitted units were mustard melamine. The rest of the room was furnished with a table, oak chairs and a veneered sideboard with spindly gold legs, all of which still had plenty of wear left in them. Posters from the Notional Portraiture Gallery covered three walls. Tommy bustled about, more at ease now that she was home.

Paintstripper was pouring beer into bulbous tumblers when Tommy reached out and touched her.

'Look at your hands! And your arms! They're bleeding!'

'It's nothing.' Paintstripper shrugged, rubbing a hand over one plump arm as though to wipe away the marks.

'They could get infected. Have you put antiseptic on them?'

Van Gogh waggled an ear in empathy from the wall.

'Don't fuss. I'll do it later.'

'What happened?'

'I was down at the University painting. I'm usually careful, but I was working quickly today and got carried away. The bradawl kept slipping.'

This was the sort of thing that worried Tommy. Possibly even small children knew about bradawls. 'What's a bradawl?'

'It looks a bit like a screwdriver.'

'Couldn't you use a paintbrush like everybody else?'

Dali, opposite her, eyebrows lifted and mustachios a-dance, shared her surprise.

Tommy fetched a bottle of Dabisept and some cotton wool from the cupboard beneath the sink. She treated the cuts while Paintstripper explained how she first applied wodges of paint, waited for them to dry and then scraped strips away to give texture.

'Surely you must have wondered why I'm called Paintstripper?'

When every day was filled with things she did not know and did not understand, and yet others that she immediately felt to be familiar, asking questions was a dangerous business. And responding to them, too, might lead to more unanswerable questions. But Paintstripper was a friend, and maybe this one didn't need an answer. Her missing flatmate was a much more pressing concern. 'I think I'll go and check out Hendrix's room. Maybe he left a message or something.'

Hendrix was a bedroom dweller. She remembered Paintstripper commenting one day that he had presumably been conceived in a bedroom, was probably a home birth, had spent his childhood playing alone in his room and had graduated to a study bedroom with a computer when his first spots arrived. Dear little fellow. Yet, in truth, he was nearly as tall as Tommy and could not be far off in age.

There was a musty smell. The room was filled with clutter: clothes were strewn all over the bed, and shoes, papers, dirty plates and carrier bags covered the floor. Two PCs and three printers huddled together on a table, although she knew Hendrix had no interest in hardware. To him, computers were simply the means of storing and copying the photographs that covered every surface. On the walls were pictures of walls and pictures of cisterns, pipework, train engines, birds, sky, bathroom mould, worms, even his own feet (he had big toes that stuck up at an odd angle); there was little in this world that Hendrix was incapable of finding of visual interest.

He was Tommy's special care. A little guy with soft, brown eyes, caffè latte skin and a corona of wispy, frizzy hair, he was such an innocent. He used to complain, *Why does everyone call me Hendrix? My name is Robert!* But the nickname stuck, and he became resigned to it. Recently, it seemed to Tommy, his mind had been elsewhere; he dragged his slippers over the floorboards even more than usual. He sniffed incessantly and ate cereal from the packet for dinner. She suspected that he took sleeping pills at inappropriate times of day. All these things put together were an indication that something was amiss. He hated being out after dark; it was quite unlike him not to come home.

Tommy picked up his mobile phone from underneath a grubby t-shirt on the bed. Fourteen missed calls. She checked. They were all from her. That he had gone out without his phone was not surprising, for he used it principally to tell the time. Not like his camera. Hendrix would never go out without that. She turned her head a few degrees and there it was, sitting on the suitcase that served as a bedside table. His camera. Why had he left it behind? Tommy sat on the bed holding the camera in one hand and stroking the grubby t-shirt with the other.

Where in all of Lundenwic was he? The world was uncertain and shifting. She began to snuffle and fumbled for a tissue. When had she last shed a tear? For whom? For what? How silly, crying solves nothing. If Hendrix was in trouble she must pull herself together and help him. She blew her nose and went back to the kitchen.

'It's more serious than I thought. He's left his camera behind.'

'Just consider,' Paintstripper leant back from the table, hands splayed on spreading thighs. 'Hendrix comes from a long line of survivors. Over millions of years, not one of his direct ancestors did anything stupid and got killed before puberty.'

'How could you possibly know that?'

'Think about it. We're all survivors.'

Tommy walked over to the window and tried to gaze out, but she couldn't see anything except for the reflection of the kitchen lights thrown back by the darkness. 'Oh I get it.' Her voice was flat. She thought of another universe full of might-have-been people whose parents had all died in infancy, disconnected people, a little like herself.

Meanwhile Paintstripper had refilled the tumblers and was busy tracing whorls of bluish froth with a fingertip on the ancient red formica of the tabletop. 'He's twenty years old, Tommy. He doesn't have to tell us where he's going and when he's coming back. He's probably in some pub doing just what we're doing.'

'That's unlikely. He doesn't like to drink. What was he wearing the day before yesterday?'

'What does he always wear? A saffron t-shirt. Airforce-blue jeans. Oh for goodness' sake.' Paintstripper rose from her chair and stood quietly grimacing as she broke wind. 'You're his friend, Tommy, not his mother.'

'He doesn't have a mother. Somebody apart from us ought to know he's gone missing. Should we tell his father? He won't be in New Bronx, he'll be away on business. Where is it that he goes?'

'The Tribal Kingdoms of Mongolia. I think they send messages by yak.'

'We could find somebody to help us do that, but first, I think, we should tell the police, and maybe have a word at the University, talk to the head of the Photography Department perhaps. What's her name? Über Professor Camber!'

'You don't want to go anywhere near Camber.'

'Why not?'

'She's dangerous. That's why not. She waits for people in the dark and sucks out their souls. Come on, stop worrying, Tommy. Hendrix is young for his age. Think back to when you were – how old – say sixteen, surely sometimes you went off for a bit, just to show your independence, and got annoyed when your parents worried about you?'

Tommy carried on staring at the window and didn't reply. Paintstripper had hit a nerve, touched that place that Tommy kept hidden. For, as far as Tommy knew, such a thing had never happened to her at sixteen. It was her horrible secret. She didn't remember having parents. She had no memory; didn't, in fact, remember anything at all before arriving at University over a year ago.

A voice had said, Wake up, Miss, we're here. She was curled up in the back seat of a black cab, outside the hall of residence where she was to live for the first year, and that was the first thing she knew about anything. She had a red handbag with her containing a toothbrush, enough birth control pills to depopulate China, three hundred pounds sterling which included an assortment of obsolete coinage and notes, a red and yellow toy train engine and a letter from a firm of solicitors, Burton and Crump, suggesting that she contact them.

Tommy had been winging it ever since, hoping nobody noticed the gaps, and never getting around to confessing her appallingly careless loss of her past to anybody. Hendrix and Paintstripper were Tommy's world, all that stood between her and emptiness. And emptiness was not bearable. She would go to the police and, in spite of what Paintstripper said, she would speak to Über Professor Camber tomorrow. The resolution gave her strength. She turned her back on the window and faced her friend.

'You're probably right. I worry too much. It's been an oddish sort of day.' What was it that she hadn't done? Something important, she thought. She swallowed a few of her pills – they always made her feel less confused – and began to rummage in the old gas fridge, looking for leftovers to heat up for their supper. She thought about telling Paintstripper of her strange vision of the lead singer of Splintered Dick, but thought better of it. It sounded too weird. Instead she said, 'The gallery party went really well tonight, except that Rodney and Wilfred had a massive quarrel. And guess what, there was a man there who wrote a book that's on the photography course list. Hugo de Lamartine.' Tommy pronounced it 'Hugh-go', in the English way. 'He was a bit oddish. Walked about with his chin tilted up and his nose in the air.'

'Never heard of him. That's an interesting outfit you've got on.'

'Isn't it a find! Everybody's wearing tartan. Even though I've been a bit on the hot side all day, it's such a nice feeling being in fashion at last.'

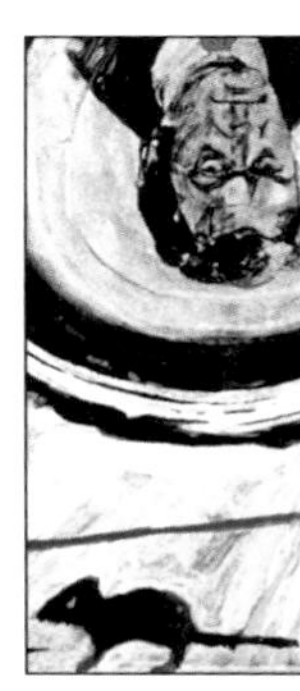

CHAPTER 3

La Pipistrelle

A RECORDING OF A FRENCH SINGER'S passionate *L'hymne à l'amour* played loudly enough to be heard throughout the restaurant, even down to the basement below, which was the territory of the cook – not a Frenchman but a Slav – who had fled the disappointment of communist cuisine many years before. Now he cooked for joy and with love, transmuting basic foodstuffs into flights of fantasy with the application of pressure, heat, cold and friction, the forcing-in of air and the emulsifying of fats. Two kitchen assistants whistled, washed and chopped, and the waiters bore aloft plates of food from a dumbwaiter to the diners. A *plongeur*, whose job was to feed the dishwasher and maintain kitchen hygiene, was impervious to human feeling but had a sympathy for anything that scuttled and scurried; he was able to turn a blind eye to creatures with more than two legs.

Thus it was that rat ^ and rat +, who had recently met and were planning a family, entered through the open back door, ran past the *plongeur* and ascended the stairs to the restaurant. Their favourite haunt was underneath the table in the corner. This was flanked on two sides by church pews, separated by a marble plinth topped by a vase containing a single bare twig. Four oak dining chairs provided seating on the other two sides. On the floor was a cosy rat run in the darkness beneath the pews.

Rat ^ and rat + waited until the diners had decided who was going to sit next to whom, and then dived beneath the tablecloth to greet them. They sniffed Hugo's loafers, Rodney's lizard-skin, size 6 lace-ups, Wilfred's suede smart-casuals and Marjorie's comfortable sandals. They scurried over to Daphne's crocodile peep-toes, Megan's strappy Manuel

Beatniks, Terence's black Psyche trainers and Charlie's brown, all-weather Red Gore boots. Then the two rats sat and waited politely for dinner to be served and crumbs to be scattered.

'We need wine, lots of wine.' Wilfred's arms conducted an unseen orchestra. 'Are you up for a bit more, Hugo?'

'Well yes, actually,' said Hugo.

Things were looking up. The restaurant pleased him. La Pipistrelle was reassuringly clean, with white tablecloths and dark wooden flooring. There were prints on the walls depicting some of the leading lights of the menu in happier times, bucolic scenes of meadow, farmyard and pond. It was understated, yet classy. And the evening was beginning to flow, just as his life had been flowing of late.

The ease with which *Trapped Light* had been written, taken up by Nigel, published by Pangolin, and included on an academic syllabus by Über Professor Camber of the University of Artistry and Design, had restored his faith in humanity. Doors had opened and it was now up to him to ensure that they stayed open. He had hopes of tonight's assembled company. If the conversation could be steered correctly, he might present his card and suggest a trip to the bookshop, Piddlestones, or volunteer a public reading. There was also the prospect of a cuisine beyond his means, a welcome change from his usual Thursday supper of Eminesse sushi. Raw food was risky. He liked it microwaved with a sprinkling of cheese. Au gratin. Thank goodness tonight's dinner would be properly French!

The waiter was approaching. Trained in an old school, a bringer of order and form, he distributed heavy, leather-bound menus. Hugo read his nonchalantly, one elbow draped on the edge of a pew. Daphne, trying to hold hers as far away as possible, struggled with the demands of her focal point. Charlie gripped his menu with both hands and looked grim. It was agreed that as it was late they wouldn't bother with starters but would go straight to the main course.

'Actually, I'm completely lost with this menu,' thundered

Marjorie. 'There's no English translation. What on earth is *Mélange des abats en sauce épatante*?'

'I'm having the same problem, Marjorie.' Wilfred peered over his glasses at her. 'They must have a new chef since we were here last. Rodney and I have a dear little bolt hole in Moncuq that we've been going to for years. Though everyone there speaks far too quickly to understand a word of what they're saying, we've read more menus than most people have had hot dinners. Yet I've never come across half these dishes. Any of you speak French? Oh, of course, how silly of me, we have Monsieur de Lamartine. My dear Hugo, can you help us make head or tail of this menu?'

'Of course I can help in a general sense.' Hugo pulled at his collar and sat a little more upright. '*Oreille de porc* is, in fact, a pig's ear, but if you need me to be more specific than that, then I'm sorry. French is such a brilliant language, but my relationship with it, sometimes, gets complicated.'

'How absolutely fascinating. I smell a mystery!' Marjorie whooped with glee and eyed him skittishly. 'You look French, you have a French name. Where were you born?'

'France.' His fingers rose too late to his lips.

'And what nationality was your father?'

A quiff of hair was in his eyes. He flicked it back. 'French.'

'And what language, pray, did you speak at home?'

His legs seemed in danger of springing out of control. He crossed and uncrossed them under the table. 'English.'

'And what sort of cooking was served at home?'

'... English.' His eyes seemed unable to move away from the yellow of her dress, unforgiving as the sun. 'It's a very long and involved story.'

'Why don't we ask the waiter to give us some recommendations,' said Daphne, 'and then, while we're waiting for the food to be served, we can hear Mr de Lamartine's story. It sounds absolutely fascinating.'

'I would be happy to oblige,' said Hugo. 'And now, if you will kindly excuse me, I need to wash my hands. I'm not too worried about what I eat – not the pig's ear of course – the *Mélange des abats* dish will be fine. Do order for me when the waiter returns.'

He wandered about the restaurant for a while and then, retrieving some sense of direction, headed downstairs. He edged himself into the tiny lavatory and closed the door firmly behind him.

Beyond the wall of the basement bog, in the adjacent kitchen, the Slav chef had just received a new order. He had been wearily resigned to the preparation of five steaks *au poivre* and two *omelettes aux fines herbes*, which weren't on the menu, but the waiters were always telling customers that they might be easily prepared. His heart leaped for joy. A solitary diner had risen to the challenge of one of his special creations. He dived into the walk-in fridge and lovingly removed the ingredients for this dish, each in its own plastic lunch box: coxcombs, gizzards, coiled intestines, assorted genitalia, pancreas, tumours and tripes. As he worked, he overlaid the music from upstairs with a song from the old country, which must surely have penetrated the aforementioned wall.

No one embarking on a meal wants to be faced with the thought of one of their number struggling with appalling intestinal difficulties in some subterranean loo. It had not entered Hugo's head that there might be stirrings of concern at his long absence. Neither was he listening to the singing that wavered and trilled from beyond the wall. Hunched, chin on palm, he was giving careful thought to how best to present to the assembled company the heritage and upbringing of such a one as he. That Hugo de Lamartine was a Frenchman carried with it all the rightness of emotional truth. He had been bored for too long by England and all things English. Nonetheless, that a Frenchman might not be fully in command of his native language was something that needed to be explained with some subtlety.

There was no point beating himself up over what he might or might not have said. These things, once started, tended to flow of their own accord. Perhaps that was the best way, just to let it happen. He rose to his feet. He was ready. They were an audience and must not be disappointed. His story would be heard!

Hugo sloped up the wooden stairs and approached the table.

The conversation had resumed with vigour, everyone seeming to be speaking at once, but it was Rodney's voice that rang out above the rest.

'Come on Megan – you're as English as I am!'

'No, I'm not.' The young woman grinned at him and wrinkled her nose. 'Not quite. I wouldn't be wearing a kaftan if I were as English as you.'

'Ha. Another story!' screeched Marjorie, who had become very red in the face. 'We'd love to hear it!'

'It would only be *another* story if I'd had the opportunity . . .' said Hugo.

'Talking about me is boring.' Megan smiled, revealing perfect teeth.

'Please, Megan, we're all dying to hear it,' said Terence. 'Aren't we, Charlie?'

Charlie nodded his enthusiasm.

'Oh all right then.' Megan clasped her hands together on the table and looked around at each face as she drew breath. 'Well. Before I was born, my father, who was a diplomat, was posted to Morocco. He and my mother, and their three young children, left England and went off to live in a large and crumbling house in Rabat. It must have been a lonely life for my mother, as her husband worked incredibly hard and was often away for weeks at a time . . .'

Hugo was annoyed. His story surely took precedence over this one. He barely heard what Megan was saying, and stared around the room.

'. . . returned to Lundenwic and life from then on was quite ordinary until, when I was sixteen, my father became dangerously ill with . . .'

The food arrived. The waiter placed enormous platters before each of the diners.

'No, don't worry, I can eat and talk at the same time,' said Megan. 'Wow, this omelette is so delicious. Like I was saying, he became very ill with . . .'

Hugo tentatively stuck a fork into the glistening mound of – what? He wasn't sure. It appeared to be mostly of animal origin. There were reddened crinkly twists of . . . whatever, a gleaming smoothness that must be liver. He popped a bit into his mouth. No, it wasn't liver and it wasn't happy in his mouth; so he lifted his napkin as though dabbing grease from his lips and pushed out the animal product with a concealed finger and thumb.

'Well, some weeks after the funeral of the man I *thought* was my father, my mother came into my room and said let's go for a walk. I want to talk to you . . .'

Hugo carried the morsel down below the tablecloth and, with a deft flick of the wrist, lobbed it into the dark recesses of the pew behind his feet. He washed out his mouth with a swig of wine.

'I couldn't believe it at first. My father and I had always got on OK together . . .'

This lump was paler and much softer. It appeared to be fat, but no, there was a protrusion of gristle inside. Up went the napkin. The wrist flicked. He was becoming good at this.

Beneath the table, two dark shadows, largely unsatisfied by the dry flakes of bread carried from fingers to napkin and raining like snow upon the floorboards, quivered with excitement at the tiny, flaccid thud of offal on *terra firma* that only they could hear.

Megan, meanwhile, was saying, 'When I thought about it afterwards, it began to make sense. I looked at myself in the mirror. I had always looked a little different from the rest of the family.'

As manna from heaven it was falling quickly now. The two rats, crouching behind Hugo's black loafers, sat up on their hind legs and held the food in delicate pink fingers, their jaws working furiously on *gésiers, rognons* and *tripes*. Never had they known such abundance!

'I'd been kept in the dark too long.' Megan tossed back her hair, her eyes glistening. 'I needed to know exactly how it happened . . .'

Terence was gazing at her, rapt.

Whiskers, fur, the moist gobbets, all conjoined in a sensual overflow of gorgeousness as they sat together flank to flank.

'He came into her room with a silver pot of tea and two glasses.'

The meal over, the two rats sniffed lovingly at the polyester hems and leather shoes of their benefactor. It was a curious odour, one to be filed away in the rich creases of each tiny cortex and retained forever.

'The simple act of kindness made my mother start to cry.'

Rat ^ pressed his muzzle into the floor behind rat +, where a streak of urine carried a message written in biochemical letters that proclaimed that, now, the moment had arrived!

' . . . and what had begun as a gesture of comfort turned into an expression of such deep love . . .'

Looking coyly at him, and lifting her rump and tail in the air, she wiggled enticingly.

'It was a moment of such danger and madness. My mother was going to have to live with this . . .'

As Megan told her tale, the ten diners, with two animal and one human exception, gave her their full attention. She paused to take a mouthful of omelette and there was a moment of silence, which seemed to be filled with a high-pitched note of exquisite purity, a squeak of passion and ecstasy. The diners felt the noise as a shudder in the spine, and then it was over. Each immediately doubted that such an improbable sound had ever been heard.

'So that's it. That's the story of me,' said Megan.

'Phew!' Daphne exhaled audibly. 'What a wonderful tale. It's better than a novel. Did you ever meet your real father again when you were grown up?'

'I tried to. Three years ago, I travelled to his village. They told me he'd died the year before. They made me so welcome.

Treated me like a member of the family. Showed me a picture of him.'

'So you've lost two fathers! What did the real one look like?'

'He was very, very handsome.'

'My grandfather was very handsome too,' said Hugo, placing knife and fork neatly parallel on an empty plate.

'Thanks, Megan.' Terence smiled warmly at her. 'That was a good one. It would make great television.' He removed the wine bottle from its bucket and refilled Charlie's glass. 'How do you rate Aston City's chances on Saturday?'

'Food's good here, isn't it?' observed Wilfred, patting his belly. 'Yours OK, Hugo?'

'Mine? Um. Unusual. An interesting juxtaposition of contrary flavours. Is there any more bread in that basket? It reminded me of an extraordinary meal which my father told me . . .'

'Cheese anyone? Pud? No? We seem to be the last people here. We'd better get the bill. Rodney! How are we going to do this?'

'I shall pay for Daphne and me,' said Marjorie.

'Megan is my guest.'

'Wilfred, you are very sweet.'

'I'll take care of the two gentlemen of the press.' Rodney bounced up and down in his seat and waved an arm at the waiter. 'A separate bill for three people,' he told him.

That left Hugo unaccounted for. His knuckles whitened on the last solitary bread roll. He tore it into little pieces and masticated each mouthful with bitterness and determination.

It was still a fine night as they filed out of the restaurant into the quiet street.

Megan, turning to the older ladies, said, 'Are you sure you won't come back for a drink?'

'No thank you, my dear. It's very kind of you, but Daphne and I are both larks and we've got a busy day tomorrow. Goodnight everybody. A simply lovely evening!'

'I've got room in my car for five of us. My flat's only a short drive away,' said Megan.

'I'm up for it.' Terence pushed his belly forward and beamed. 'What about you, Charlie?'

'Yeah, great.'

'Rodney and Wilfred?'

'Well, we *could* come. Should we go back and check the gallery first, Wilfred?'

'No. It'll be fine. Tommy locked it up and posted the keys through the door.'

'Did you give her the mortice key as well?'

'No. We don't need it. She knows how to set the alarm. Come on, let's go. What was that vegetable dish you had? Was it tatooine?'

'No. It was ratatouille. It'd only take a second to pop back.'

Hugo contemplated his solitary walk home and felt irritated by their conversation.

'Don't fret, Rodney,' Wilfred was saying. 'We can always rely on Tommy to take her responsibilities seriously.'

Divine Providence? Random Providence? Who knows. The door of La Pipistrelle opened, and whatever else was destined to happen moved down the Agenda of Time. The waiter hurried over to Hugo and handed him his debit card and two slips of paper.

'You 'ave left this behind. I 'ave voided it,' he said.

'I don't understand. Avoided what?'

'I 'ave voided it. The older lady. She pay for three people. We 'ave not need for yours. I am sorry about your order. The chef, 'e is not a Frenchman. Thank you very much. *Bonne nuit. Au revoir.*'

'Would you like to come too, Mr de Lamartine?' asked Megan. 'We haven't heard your story yet. If Terence sits in the front, we could squeeze you four guys into the back.'

'All right,' said Rodney, 'but I'm not sitting on anybody's lap.'

CHAPTER 4

Elsewhen

IN A CITY OF LOST SOULS, DARK WATER lapped against brick and concrete in a realm of the depths beneath Wendelsworth Bridge. It was not a particularly scenic bridge but a solid workaday construction painted dull blues and greys. There was a recycling installation on the fashionable side of the river, a smartish apartment block and a concrete manufacturing plant on the other. No one bothered to walk here at night for this was a city that often turned its back on the river. Few had the sense of history, or place, to comprehend that there was nothing in all this metropolis more interesting than its river. This was where the history of Lundenwic was written. Here the waters of the future rushed in to join swords, coins, arrowheads and the bones of vast swamp creatures.

On this autumn evening it was a place where the imagination might bring forth anything. A little mermaid, confused by abandoned drilling rigs in northern waters and venturing too far south, could have swum here in search of her prince. Diving down to the river bottom, she would have peered through the water and found a vessel, nosing between currents in the rather shallow depths. Through portholes emerging from the mud and glowing with a dim light, she would have seen him, just as in the story.

Sidney Ng was not a prince, but he looked like one. Inside the motionless ship he sat hunched in darkness before a viewscreen. He had the pallor of an olive complexion that has spent too long without sunlight. Shadows lay heavy across almond eyes and the oriental contours of an otherwise caucasoid face with a hawkish nose. His hair was long and caught in a ponytail. He was princely, indeed regal. Dream on, little mermaid, for he was watching, waiting, consumed by the tedium of his task. He was looking at a little blue light on his viewscreen. He had been doing this for fourteen months. A man of action with not enough to do.

Much human unhappiness involves some constraint assumed to be imposed by the laws of physics, usually involving the stubbornness of time in refusing to run back and re-play or alter speed. Sidney also had a time problem. He was a time traveller.

He came from an era, sixty-odd years in the future, that had discovered two forms of time travel. The first was a clever technique, man-made, with a host of tricky technical glitches. The second seemed to have been part of the earth from ancient times and involved slipstreams, which are channels of time that co-exist with now but over to the left a bit. Adjacent. They follow rivers, dive down to the depths of seas, girdle the earth in the upper reaches of the atmosphere and carry with them all manner of strange craft. Such as this one.

The downside of a slipstream is that it is a second-rate form of time travel. All that passes between a slipstream and the world beyond is light. So Sidney could see and be seen, but he could not open the door, swim up through the muddy water and become part of that early 21st-century world. He was like a tourist in a walkway through an aquarium.

This was part of the reason why Sidney's lower lip was clamped over his upper lip, why from time to time he groaned and flailed his arms or legs. The contributing factor was that little blue light on the viewscreen. It represented Tommy Willoughby, who had travelled to Lundenwic from the same era as Sidney but had used the tricky man-made method. She was not a slipstream time traveller but a real one, able to mingle, touch and act. Sidney's plight was particularly cruel as there was no one on whom he could foist responsibility, whom he could edge into a corner and quietly eviscerate. Tommy's journey, his own fossilisation on the riverbed: he had arranged it all himself.

The little blue light on his screen, on which his grey eyes were fixed, followed the pathway of a predictable day. It told Sidney that a few miles from where he was sitting, yet in another world of time beyond the slipstream, Tommy Willoughby was going about her business, which always involved some tedious combination of flat, University and art gallery and never achieved the accomplishment of her mission. He had trained her himself. Her instructions had been clear and specific. She was to establish herself in Lundenwic and then meet up with a man. *Hudelam.* That monstrous cornerstone of culture. *Hudelam.* Sidney's nostrils flared in distaste at the thought of him; arbiter of all things, prophet, writer, man of the arts and destroyer of everything in Britain that made life diverse, interesting and worth living. *Hudelam.* The man Sidney Ng hated.

'What's she doing? Stupid *gwaipo.* She's useless, useless.'

He needed something to relieve his tension. He had already flailed his legs and arms, blown his nose and drunk cups of coffee many times since his afternoon nap. All that was left for him was to brood over the history of this enterprise. Facts were something he could cling to, and he shuffled through them in his mind. The ring. Every story has a ring in it somewhere. The idea of that ring demonstrated Sidney's wizardry. It was a clunky piece of costume jewellery with a blue stone. It enabled Tommy to carry with her, concealed in its paste setting, a DNA probe from another time. It was primed with molecules from the revered corpse of the aforementioned Hudelam that had been stolen, or, more accurately, would on some future day be stolen, from beneath the marble slab of his tomb, built as a National Monument. The probe would activate the moment it came into contact with the living flesh of Hudelam, who was here, in the time of the past Tommy occupied, many years away from his enormous tomb. But in fourteen months of opportunity, Tommy had never met Hudelam. She had paced the streets of Lundenwic and accomplished sod all.

At the beginning it had all been so hopeful, so joyful. Sidney Ng was a flamboyant head of his creation, a remarkable organisation called the Conspiracy. The Conspiracy was formed of young, passionate idealists who looking around them saw a Britain benighted, buggered-up and betrayed. They were committed to action.

One day Sidney was sloshing through the streets of late 21st-century Lundenwic when he came upon an art show. And there it was. The perfect thing. An exhibit in a show of graduate work of the University of Artistry and Design, entitled *Time Ship*. How apt. The outside had been sleek and aerodynamic, the inside whimsical: a shower room inspired by the late 20th century, a rococo fireplace, lamps and furniture from various eras. It had not been a success, and Sidney was able to persuade its student creators to recoup a little of their financial outlay. This was Art, not technology. It had not been designed to work, yet it would do. He cobbled together the working parts and patched them on. Such sweat and pleasure. Yet now, if he faced the truth, nothing really worked properly. Sidney gazed around him. There was an unpleasant side to rococo. The slipstreamer had a certain despairing gloom – yet still, what an achievement.

Time, as ever, needed to be filled. Sidney leant back in his chair, closed his eyes and remembered how positive he had felt planning each detail of Tommy's journey. A few years earlier, the first guinea pigs of time travel, all men, had come to grief. A second generation of women made it feasible. These young pioneers – all of them in rebellion against the regime of the day and committed to the Conspiracy's cause, heedless of risk – performed Sidney Ng's necessary tasks.

One, obsessed with the early 19th century, was delighted to be given the opportunity to travel there to set up a trust fund for Tommy, who would not arrive until two hundred years later. Another, visiting the early twenty-first, had embedded widgets, one on each side of Wendelsworth Bridge. These, set to activate on the day of the slipstreamer's arrival, would provide a Distraction Field, so the vessel would not be seen. On the same trip, a scholarship and a University place had been established to be taken up by Tommy Willoughby. Nothing had been left to chance except, perhaps, Ms Willoughby herself. Sidney recalled the fervour of her application to join the mission. It had certainly not been matched by any demonstration of effectiveness on the job. He sighed.

And then one eyebrow lifted. Sidney leaned forward in his chair. Where there had been one light on the viewscreen there were now two, a red and a blue. There was a red light! After fourteen long months it had happened!

'Yes! Yes! Yes!' shouted Sidney. He was happy. He punched the air.

The two lights separated, just a little. They semicircled, wavered, always a short distance apart. The red light meant that Tommy's hand had touched Hudelam's. The marker had homed in on its target's DNA and activated. The mission had begun. Sidney had waited a long time for this moment. A celebration was in order.

'Bollunk!' he called. 'Bollunk!'

He pressed a button on his keypad, and a sound like an ancient foghorn rose on a crescendo of decibels. A young woman in socks pit-patted into the room.

'What's up, Sidney? Have I missed something? I've been completely stuck in a brilliant book.'

She was short and swarthy with long, black, frizzy hair. Her tunic would have been more elegant had it been longer; her face, although pleasant enough, lacked artifice and was not prepossessing in the gloom. Yet he would share with her this moment of history.

'It has happened. Tommy has put the marker on Hudelam.'

'Hudelam? Really? You can't mean the real Hudelam!'

Sidney blinked. There was no possible rejoinder. This female, a recent recruit who had joined the Conspiracy only a month ago, had been trained in his absence. They had discussed the mission's objectives on many occasions, yet

here she was, failing to grasp its essentials. Why had she been selected? Was the universe suddenly robbed of all women with a grain of common sense?

'I'm sorry.' She pushed back her hair as though to tame it with her hands when an elastic band and a can of UR-30 would have done the job so much more effectively.

'Do you know what this red light is, or this blue one?' Sidney waved a pallid hand towards the screen.

'Well yes, I suppose one must be Tommy, and the other? Oh wow, it's Hudelam, isn't it?'

Sidney was the product of a long, convoluted, Samurai, Shaolin Temple and Cossack history. He should have been on horseback, festooned with *netsuke*, twirling a silver baton through the sacred hills of Guangdong. Instead, here he was, cooped up on a viewing deck barely large enough for one, with a girl who made him long for the strong and clever women who had nurtured and educated him. Still, at least the wait for action was over.

'They don't call him Hudelam in this time. He hasn't got that name yet. Go and get some Maotai,' he said. 'We can celebrate.'

Life's sweetness never lasts. Through the aeroplane-fuel haze of the strong rice spirit, Sidney's stomach suddenly lurched as he became aware that there was only one light on the screen. The red one. A rush of adrenaline overrode the Maotai. He spat out expletives in a variety of languages that might have referred to mothers, or perhaps dogs, depending upon whether the cadence fell as cadences really ought to do, or instead rose in a questioning way. And then in English, 'Oh bother!'

'Where's she gone?' asked Bollunk.

Sidney's hands chopped the air in front of the screen. His arms moved like *tai chi* speeded-up a hundred times, speaking to his viewscreen in a language much faster than any voice. The scale of the map altered, panning out across the city, until once again the blue light came into view. Instead of staying with Hudelam, as intended, he could see that Tommy had wandered back to her flat, leaving her target still in the vicinity of the art gallery.

Sidney put his head in his hands and despaired.

'Oh how wretched,' said Bollunk. 'How unreal. It's like a science fiction story, isn't it?'

'This isn't science fiction.' Sidney rose from his chair. 'This is raw, bleeding comedy.' He picked up the Maotai bottle, filled his glass and knocked back a slug. Still holding the bottle, he lurched towards his sleeping quarters. 'I'm going to drink myself to somewhere catatonics only dream of.'

CHAPTER 5

Knitting Knoll

'OH DEAR,' SAID MEGAN, 'NOW I THINK about it there isn't an awful lot to drink apart from my collection of specialty teas.'

They needed alcohol to provide a reason for being there.

Why were they there? For Megan it appeared to be home. Hugo still had certain objectives to be achieved and was beginning to feel a bit ragged. Rodney and Wilfred were also rather tired and should have thought twice about coming at all. Terence and Charlie were at an age at which going home was a final option, all others having run their course. Perhaps each of the two young men harboured a hope of furthering their acquaintance with Megan, hopes which, if they existed, immediately curled up and died as they entered the house.

It was a beautiful house in Knitting Knoll, one of the most fashionable parts of Lundenwic. On the walls were pen and inks, watercolours, photographs, oils, acrylics, silk tapestries, a papyrus and some very old Kashmiri rugs. It was all far beyond the means certainly of Terence, and even of the solicitor, Charlie. So that left alcohol.

As Megan did not drink, the alcohol was presumably there for the entertainment of guests and, to be frank, it wasn't up to the job. There were three bottles of Konigsbaden beer, and two bottles of the sort of wine that travels from party to party in search of someone stupid enough to open it. There were also some brightly coloured, syrupy liqueurs of a kind usually to be found in bleak duty-free shops in fairy lands forlorn. The solution was for Rodney to bustle into the kitchen, slice some oranges, a mangosteen and six of those little orange things that Wilfred called syphilis, and bung everything together to make a sort of beery, syrupy, light red punch. It didn't have enough kick to it. There was a bottle of cough-mixture on the work top. It improved the colour dramatically, and some synergy of glucose syrup and E-numbers gave a hot rush down the throat that, at this time of night, deceived and sufficed.

Hugo stood in front of three photographs, sipping his gunk, looking knowledgeable and wishing there were some peanuts.

'Do you like them?' asked Megan. 'They're quite old. They show workers in the tanneries in Fez at the beginning of the last century.'

'Like doesn't really come into it. I'm interested in the juxtaposition of the point of penetration within the different areas of light and shade.'

'Wow, that's so cool. Are you some sort of expert?'

Hugo stretched his lips into something that might have been a smile. He was beginning to feel better. 'In a small way,' he replied. 'I believe one of my books on photography is used as a University textbook these days.'

'Brilliant! And you were going to tell us the story of how you came to be so very much a man of England! So rude of me to leave you hanging in the air while I bored the pants off everyone with my story. I do apologise.' She turned to the others and began chivvying them with graceful movements of her hands. 'Come and sit down. Rodney, Wilfred! Wake up! May I interrupt you, Terence and Charlie? Hugo is going to tell us his story. Hang on. I'll turn up the fire a bit. Right. We're ready.'

They were sitting comfortably. All eyes in the room turned towards Hugo, who had settled himself in a leather armchair next to some sort of hi-tech wood-burning stove. It was a moment to be relished. He cleared his throat and began.

'I am partly French. Indeed I was born and spent part of my childhood in France, yet I am not au fait with much of French life, language and food. How this came to be begins with my grandfather, Perrier de Lamartine. Ours was one of those families that kept their heads down and avoided the

Revolution. Our lineage had always inhabited a château in the countryside near Toulouse.'

Hugo was prolix with a pencil but not a raconteur, and yet there's something about a story, especially at that time of night. Where his words were not descriptive, his listeners brought their own talents of imagination to flesh out the narrative. The name *Perrier de Lamartine* could perhaps give rise to an image of a handsome, swashbuckling musketeer of the early 20th century, nimbly descending the stairs of a wondrous building. The very word *château* evoked something from fairy tale, gabled and turreted, encircled by formal gardens, with vistas of low hills draped with grapevines.

Hugo sniffed a bouquet of chemical preservatives from his drink, swallowed a mouthful and continued with his narrative. 'Beautiful as the château was, my grandfather was rarely there, preferring to spend his time in the Capital, deeply involved in the dangerous politics of those responsible for the running of that Museum of Art beyond all museums of art, the magnificent L'Ouvrier. He made enemies. Rich and powerful ones.' Hugo paused and waved one hand in the air in a languid gesture. 'He was forced to flee, to leave France altogether, and to set up home in the one country where his enemies would never follow or find him. *L'Angleterre*.'

Hugo recounted how his grandfather, Perrier, had found a house, Dicker House in Dickers Crossing, a small town on the south coast, and was blissfully happy there, developing a passion for England and all things English. He absorbed language and culture with a speed extraordinary for an adult. The locals adored him. He used to wander around the town in an old plaid dressing gown and bedroom slippers, with a supply of Liquorice Allshapes in his pockets for the local urchins. He married a well-connected woman, Myrtle, and had a son, Hugo's father, Albert. (Hugo pronounced it *Albair*.)

The family employed a local woman, Trish, as a cook. A kindly soul and a heavy smoker, she helped to bring up little Albert. She used to take him down to the beach to collect winkles and bring them home to boil in a large saucepan on the range; then they would eat them, harpooning the soft inner bodies with hairpins.

Alas, in 1939, war with Germany was on the horizon, and Perrier was forced to return to France with his family to take up his role as guardian of the family estates, Hugo's great-grandparents having suddenly expired. Followed by storm clouds, across a grey sea, the journey back seemed to last an age. Perrier was filled with resentment at this disruption to his chosen life. The sight of the château, instead of feeling like a homecoming, sent him half-mad with rage and sorrow. He resolved that he would do what he could to make the place feel like his darling adopted home in Dickers Crossing. Waving an old ceremonial sword above his head, he drove out all the faithful old retainers who lived in the château. He had brought Trish the chain-smoking cook with them, and she sent for her son, Willie, and his wife, Trixie, to come over from England to do what they could in the château and grounds.

Perrier was a strong personality and his word was law. He insisted that English was the only language to be spoken, and that Trish should carry on cooking the food they had eaten in England: toad in the hole, steak and kidney pudding, bubble and squeak, suet pudding and junket. All vegetables were to be boiled for a very long time. The château, for some reason, was reputed locally to be haunted by vampire valkyries and, when France was occupied, the Germans avoided it.

When the war was over, the family still kept themselves to themselves. Myrtle, Perrier's wife and Hugo's grandmother, died and they buried her in the garden. They had little need of contact with the world outside, except for the bargaining that Willie and Trixie would conduct, using signs and gestures, in the local village shops. Essentials not available in France arrived by post from Horridus in Lundenwic. Perrier never again spoke, and none of them ever learned, a word of French. Albert grew up listening to *Grand Hotel* on Sunday evenings, broadcast by the Domestic Service on shortwave wireless, and came to manhood with the Unmarried Irish Singers, Christian Richard and Judy Andrew. There was the King's Speech at Christmas.

Hugo paused, and accepted a refill of punch from Megan. He knocked it back; his audience remained silent, awaiting the rest of the story.

'This is the family I was born into. My mother, Pat, who came from a very old dynasty in the East Midlands, was taking a holiday with an elderly aunt in Toulouse. She wandered into the château one day, separated from her aunt and quite lost. She stayed on, married my father, Albert,' he extended both hands, palms upraised in a gesture of sincerity, 'and gave birth to me. Hugo . . . Rimbaud . . . Mallarmé . . . de Lamartine.'

'On my tenth birthday, I remember waking feeling very excited because there was to be a special party in my honour. I ran downstairs (the château had the most sublime curving staircase) looking forward to the usual plate of porridge, followed by bacon and eggs and a cup of milky tea. I wanted a new *Beagle Annual*, from the stock my father kept locked in the attic, for my present. As my sandalled foot reached the bottom step, there, to my horror, was my grandfather Perrier stretched out on the flagstones in an advanced state of rigor mortis. It transpired that he had bravely borne terrible debt without worrying his family. The château was mortgaged many times over and not a *sou* was left. Our time in France was over.

'I remember vividly how we took the ferry to England – Maman, Papa and I – just as my grandfather had done a generation before. Sadly, Trish, the cook, who was now a very old lady, had to be left behind in France together with Willie and Trixie, because they didn't have enough money for their ferry tickets. As I smelt the salt air and climbed aboard the train for Dickers Crossing, where my late grandmother Myrtle's family still lived, I knew, although my mother was from England and I spoke English like a native, that there was in the very depth of my being a *soupçon* of something

quintessentially French.' He leaned back into the depths of the armchair. '*C'est tout*,' he said with a Gallic shrug.

'Wow. Rambo,' said Terence.

'But that must make you a quarter French, not half-French,' said Rodney.

'No. Half-French,' Wilfred corrected him. 'On the maternal side he has a mother and a grandmother who were from England, and on the paternal side a father and grandfather who were French. That makes him half-English and half-French.'

'That's not the way to look at it. Albert would have been half-English, and he married an Englishwoman,' said Rodney.

'Hang on a minute,' interrupted Charlie. 'Hugo is a male, which means he inherited an X chromosome from his mother and a Y chromosome from his father. Now that Y chromosome, which is passed down on the male side, has to be entirely French.'

'That would mean that, if he had a sister, she would have had the same parents but would be of a different nationality,' gasped Rodney in despair. 'You don't have a sister, do you?'

'No,' said Hugo.

'It's late and this is all too difficult.' Wilfred stretched out his plump legs before him and gave the trousers over his knees a good scratch.

'We have a lot in common, Hugo.' Megan smiled at him. 'We're both the product of two countries.'

'I felt that Megan's story would make great television.' Terence leaned forward on his sofa (all the others were slumping). 'But Lamartine's story, too, is crying out to be dramatised. It just flickered across my eyes. I could even sense the timing of the commercial breaks! It could be a docudrama or a play.'

'Julie Tench would be wonderful as his mother,' said Wilfred.

'Pity Eric Mackisson is dead,' added Rodney. 'He would have been brilliant as Perrier. I can just see him waving that sword.'

'I've got connections,' said Terence in an earnest tone. 'If you like, Hugo, I could have a stab at a script.' He rummaged in his inside pocket and took out a battered wallet from which he drew a card. 'Here's my business card. Give me a ring and let's chat about it. And the same for you, Megan.' He handed her a second card.

'Allow me to present you all with my card,' said Hugo. He handed one to each of the assembled guests. 'I'm always happy to talk about photography and give readings of my book, *Trapped Light: An Interpretation of the Photographic Art*, if anybody…'

'It's two o'clock,' interrupted Rodney. 'How did it get to be two o'clock? I hope we haven't outstayed our welcome, Megan.'

'We can get a cab,' said Wilfred.

'I could call you one, but it would probably be quicker to pick one up on the street,' said Megan.

'Anyone need a lift? We're going to Tempusbury. We're suburbanites,' said Rodney. 'Not even you, Charlie? You're practically our neighbour! Just you, Hugo?'

Leaving the younger people to a longer night, Wilfred, Rodney and Hugo waited outside the house for a while. A few cars came and went, but no taxis.

'This is a fine show,' said Wilfred.

They walked for a while, until they came to a busier road and at last spotted a cab sporting an orange light.

'I'll sit on the little seat by the driver,' said Rodney. 'Would you mind if we stopped at the gallery for a moment? It's on the way. Don't start, Wilfred. I'll only be stopping for two minutes. This isn't going to cause the slightest problem for anybody, I promise. Should've thought about it while we were at Megan's. I'm desperate for a pee!'

CHAPTER 6

Searching for Hendrix

THE IMAGE OF THE LEAD SINGER OF Splintered Dick, contorted by some primal urge, stared down at Tommy from the poster on her bedroom wall as she awoke. It had been a present from Hendrix.

At the beginning of term the three of them, Hendrix, Paintstripper and Tommy, had been sitting in Tommy's bedroom watching what Paintstripper called Friday night dross on television. It was strangely mesmerising to Tommy, as she understood little of it. Chat shows were too fast to follow; music was easier, and some of it familiar. And there he was, making an electric guitar sing, twisting his body this way and that.

'Who is he?' Tommy crouched in front of the television set, waiting for the cameras to pan back to his face. There was a close-up, the almond eyes, the high cheekbones so strangely familiar to her.

'That's Splintered Dick. He's the lead singer, can't remember his name,' said Hendrix.

Tommy knew they thought she fancied the singer. Privately she suspected that this was someone she must have known in her forgotten life. Yet Splintered Dick's music was quite foreign to her. She couldn't name a number and, indeed, found heavy metal disturbing. She preferred the music they played on children's television and loved it when the kids, with piping voices and wrong notes, sang along.

You don't get to see many kids in this part of town, she mused as she lay in her bed. The unhappy thought that Hendrix was still missing returned to her mind. She leapt from her bed and ran to his room, but it remained as before; even the friendly foot photograph seemed a reproach. He had not come home.

She rang the police. After a complicated meander through a series of options on offer by the local police authority, there was a brief conversation. She heard the duty officer echoing her words to a colleague – *young lady here's reporting that her student flatmate hasn't come home for a couple of nights.* His voice had a bantering tone when he told her to call back in a day or so if her friend hadn't returned. So much for help; she had to press on alone. She dressed quickly; there was no time for her usual deliberation. Donning a pair of twill slacks with loops that slipped beneath her feet and a multicoloured sweater with batwing sleeves, she set off for the University.

In the coffee bar, Tommy searched for Hendrix's classmates on his photography course. She managed to find two. One barely remembered who Hendrix was, the other was able to confirm that Hendrix hadn't attended classes for two days, but that was nothing out of the ordinary as he rarely turned up for classes anyway. That left only one course of action. She hurried off to the wing where the lecturers had their offices.

Perhaps she was out. There was a good chance she was lecturing. Tommy hovered near the door of Über Professor Camber's office. Camber's secretary, Mrs Struddlewick, whom Tommy knew as a cheery soul, could be seen within, but the inner office was out of Tommy's line of sight. Camber had a scary reputation in the college. Paintstripper had said that she sucked the souls out of people, yet the description that was most compelling came from Hendrix. He had been summoned by Camber, in her role of Director of Studies, towards the end of the summer term, to account for his failure to observe deadlines.

'She was sitting opposite me', Hendrix confided to Tommy, 'with her arms folded and her legs crossed. She even had her face turned away from me as if she couldn't bear to look at me.'

'She must really hate you, sitting like that. What on earth did you do to make her hate you?'

'It might have been the lectures. She said she couldn't remember seeing my face at her lectures.'

'Were you there?'

'Well no, actually. I told her that. I explained that I hadn't been able to go to her lectures because of all the time pressure I was under with written work.'

'Oh dear, not the way to get on her good side, is it, Hendrix?'

'No, I suppose not.'

Whilst seeing some justification for Camber's attitude, Tommy could not imagine how any woman, faced with Hendrix's fragility, soft eyes and coffee-coloured skin, would not have wanted to give him a big hug and sort out all his problems. Strengthened by the memory of her missing friend, she approached the doorway of the secretary's office.

'Hello! Come on in, my dear, I remember you from somewhere. Where was it?'

'I think it was the "Angles in Flight" visuals display one of my classes put on last summer. My name is Tommy Willoughby.'

'I remember now. What wondrous and bright Angles in Flight they were indeed. Lovely to see you again, Tommy. Sit down, my dear.'

Mrs Struddlewick was seated behind a sliver of a desk. Her hardware was sleek and minimal. She was holding an enormous calendar featuring a picture of a striped beauty and bearing the legend *Olympic Cats in a Leap Year.* The inner office was clearly unoccupied.

'What a lovely calendar,' observed Tommy.

'It is, isn't it. I brought it from home.' She flipped through it. 'Look at August. That's a Maine Coon. My sister had one. He was so heavy she used to get sciatica from having him on her lap. You see, the office calendar was defaced by some of our young lads.'

'Defaced?'

'They had mapped out a rather imaginative alternative agenda for Über Professor Camber for the next two months. Thank goodness I found it before she did, or those lads would be kissing their degrees goodbye. Now where can you find a new calendar when it's most of the way through the year? So I brought this one in from home. The Über Professor was furious and made me take it down again.'

'Doesn't she like cats?'

'I think it's the photographs she objects to. She doesn't approve of photographs of anything heart-warming. She calls it *mass-market art substitution*. You see, photography is an art, not a technology. Über Professor Camber calls it an alchemy, and thinks that people who take wedding photos should be shot. She can be quite extreme sometimes.'

Tommy nodded in sympathy. There was something comforting about Mrs Struddlewick. Even though beyond the door was Camber's grim lair, Tommy felt at ease and was happy to confide in her.

'I have a problem, Mrs Struddlewick. My flatmate, Hendrix, is a student of Über Professor Camber.'

'Oh I know Hendrix. Robert Winston rather. I don't see him often, but when he does come into college he always smiles at me. Does he play the guitar?'

'No, he doesn't like music.'

'Hendrix is an odd nickname. Robert. One would expect him to be called Bob. But he's not really a Bob, is he?'

Tommy, uncertain about the attributes of Bobs, carried on with her tale. 'The problem is, he's been missing for two days.' She recounted the litany of Hendrix's usual daily habits and dislike of being out after dark. How he had seemed not himself of late.

'Perhaps he's gone to a girlfriend's house.'

'I don't think Hendrix has girlfriends yet. He has friends, but he probably doesn't know where they live.'

'Have you told his parents?'

'He only has a father, who lives abroad. He imports cashmere into New Bronx, spends most of his life in the Tribal Kingdoms of Mongolia. I don't want to worry him too early, but obviously if Hendrix was missing for any length of time

I'd have to find a way to contact him. So I guess Hendrix is my responsibility, for the time being.'

'It doesn't seem right that you should be shouldering this on your own, Tommy. I could mention the matter to Über Professor Camber, or do a report, but the University tends to take the line that students are over eighteen and, if they choose to go missing, there's not much the University can do about it. It becomes a police matter.'

The telephone rang. Mrs Struddlewick answered it, motioning to Tommy to stay where she was. Tommy's drifting attention was caught when she overheard a name she recognised.

'Hugo de Lamartine. Indeed I have. Yes, I've met him a few times. Can I be of any assistance, Professor Bhatt? . . . um, um . . . indeed yes. We've got lots of copies . . . No, only English . . . Yes, he speaks English very well, without a trace of an accent. Look, let me take your number and, if Über Professor Camber does have a copy in French, I'll ring you and let you know.'

She jotted a series of digits on a piece of paper and said goodbye. Lifting a tin from a shelf behind her desk, she offered Tommy a biscuit.

'Where was I? Ah yes, your friend. Let's see if I've got anything about him on file.'

She tapped at her keyboard for a while, then frowned. 'Nothing recent here. That doesn't mean that there isn't anything. Über Professor Camber likes to write her own letters, and she keeps records in her private system and transfers them if she gets round to it. It means I'm always a bit out of date, or missing bits of the picture. Sometimes I wonder why I'm here at all. I wish I could be of more help. Believe me, my dear, I do understand how worried you must be.'

Tommy nibbled her biscuit and felt comforted. She had been understood and Mrs Struddlewick had shown no sign of eagerness to be off doing other things. Indeed, she seemed to like her. For a moment Tommy was tempted to confide all the strangeness of her life, but then decided that she must not put her own troubles before finding Hendrix.

'I appreciate your help, Mrs Struddlewick.'

'You're very welcome. Tell me, what's your talent, my dear? Do you paint, draw, do sculptures?'

'I enjoy the fashion course, but I think I'm still looking for something I'm really good at.'

'I hope you find it . . . and about Hendrix, I wouldn't advise you to talk to Über Professor Camber without a very good reason, but, if he still hasn't come home by Monday, call me and I'll see what I can do.'

Tommy thanked her and left. She felt herself to be small and ineffectual as she descended the stairs, dwarfed by the extraordinary building around her. The vast staircase was on the side of the building, with a view that looked out over the city and extended all the way to Larkklingon Tower in the east. The inner walls were composed of square metres of toughened glass, and through them could be seen some of the weirdness of a University given over to the study and practice of the twin gods, Art and Design. There were glimpses of papier maché armchairs, disembodied aluminium heads, flickering screens with repeating video clips. An unpleasant reek suggested that somewhere some animal was getting stuffed.

Tommy stopped on a landing and took in the view. She was assailed by the same sense of not belonging that she had felt for most of her first year at University, when she had worked hard trying to look and behave like any other student.

There is no real sense of identity without memory. Childhood forms a framework, an interpretation of the world that can be added to, detail by detail, over time. Without a past she had felt less than a person, rootless and homeless, and the approach of the end of her first year had threatened to make her homeless in a literal sense. Halls of residence only offered accommodation to first-year students.

The beginnings of a solution had come with a letter from Burton and Crump, the firm of solicitors who supported her financially, to the effect that, with the end of her tenure at the hall of residence approaching, a flat was available and she was welcome to live there for as long as she wished. She picked up the keys, by arrangement with the caretaker, and found the flat to be dusty, spacious and devoid of anything that might be called furniture. There were two empty packing cases in one of the bedrooms. She felt acutely lonely. She placed messages on notice boards: *Tommy Willoughby is looking for two people to share a large flat in Klaus Place behind Horridus. Very cheap.* There were phone calls, meetings in the coffee bar, but always some excuse: too far away, friends who had plans. Nobody wanted to live with her. One applicant was a theology student with a pet python, but even she changed her mind and went away.

Eventually one of her tutors introduced her to Paintstripper, who was the first person prepared to make the journey across town to inspect the flat.

She was typically down to earth. She asked Tommy about the rent.

'Whatever,' said Tommy. 'I'm getting it for free. It needs some furniture.'

'We can get furniture. That's not a problem, but we two need to get on. Where are you from? You're not English I think.'

'Oh I am!' Tommy was surprised. 'What makes you think I'm not?'

'I don't know. Your vowel sounds remind me a little of India. Perhaps it's your clothes. They're unusual. Where did you buy them?'

'Junk shops mostly. And there's a warehouse I found, run by a Ukrainian man.'

'Ah!' Paintstripper appeared satisfied.

'Is there anything else that's wrong with me?'

She looked so forlorn that Paintstripper gave her a friendly pat on the shoulder and said, 'Goodness no. There's nothing wrong with you. It's good to be different.'

'I don't want to be different. I want to blend in.'

'Fine. I'm not very up on fashion myself, but we could alter some of your clothes, and maybe buy some more if there's anything left after buying the furniture. That's if you're happy for me to live here?'

Shortly afterwards, Hendrix became the third potential flatmate. (Tommy had found him in the basement at University looking lost and had asked if she could help.) For the final weeks of the summer term Tommy's isolated life was transformed. The three of them, though two were still living in their respective halls of residence and Paintstripper in a B&B, went to the cinema, cooked curries together, drank coffee and talked: a universal student life.

When the academic year ended and Hendrix went to join his father for the summer, Paintstripper and Tommy toured junk shops, and worse, to buy furniture for the flat. Their best find was a company on webworld called *thediscerningskip.co.uk*. Some of the stuff needed a bit of drying out, but was otherwise perfectly serviceable.

Paintstripper set to work helping Tommy to blend in. She tactfully suggested that some of the ways in which Tommy expressed herself were dated, or odd, as though she had absorbed the slang from movies that spanned the entire 20th century.

'That's a real humdinger! Don't you think it's a bit of a ripsnorter?' said Tommy, gazing in a mirror and holding a dress against her, which, in spite of Paintstripper's efforts to dissuade her, she had bought from a second-hand shop. 'Sorry, that was wrong, wasn't it?'

'Am I bugging you by correcting you all the time?' asked Paintstripper.

'No. I want you to correct me. Please don't stop. What should I have said?'

Paintstripper commented how impressed she was by the younger woman's ability to memorise new expressions and change her vocabulary, being at an age, herself, when the bars of the mind were more widely spaced and things tended to flutter in and out a bit.

Neither of the women talked about anything beyond the here and now. Paintstripper had drawn a line underneath her previous existence and was determined to greet each day as a gift, to which she was probably not entitled yet but which she was bloody well going to enjoy. Tommy clung to these new memories she was making. She accepted the strangeness of her relationship with Burton and Crump, and their provision of a bare minimum of funding. She had never visited their offices. She had thought about it, and once she telephoned, but her contact, some woman in accounts, had a voice so wavering and full of pain that Tommy slid back into her shell. How did you explain to lawyers that you didn't know who you were or where you came from? Lawyers were black and white, had answers; what could they know of the uncertainties of someone like Tommy? And they might realise that paying for her to attend the University, when she really had no aptitude for art whatsoever, was a colossal mistake and cut off her funding! So they exchanged letters when necessary. It was easier not to think too much, to take things one day at a time, and all had been well until Hendrix went missing.

Now, standing on the stairs of the main building of the University, staring out over the bleak city, she feared that her life was beginning to become uncertain again, to unravel. It would be a while before Paintstripper began to share her concern and there was no one she could turn to for help. Where had he gone, and why? The answer might lie somewhere among his possessions. She would have to search his computer files at some point. The thought of such an invasion of his privacy filled her with dread. Hendrix was her friend, he was easygoing and gentle, but she knew that if he were to find out she was going through his private files, he would be angry with her. It felt like a kick in the belly, the very idea of Hendrix, or indeed anybody, being angry with her.

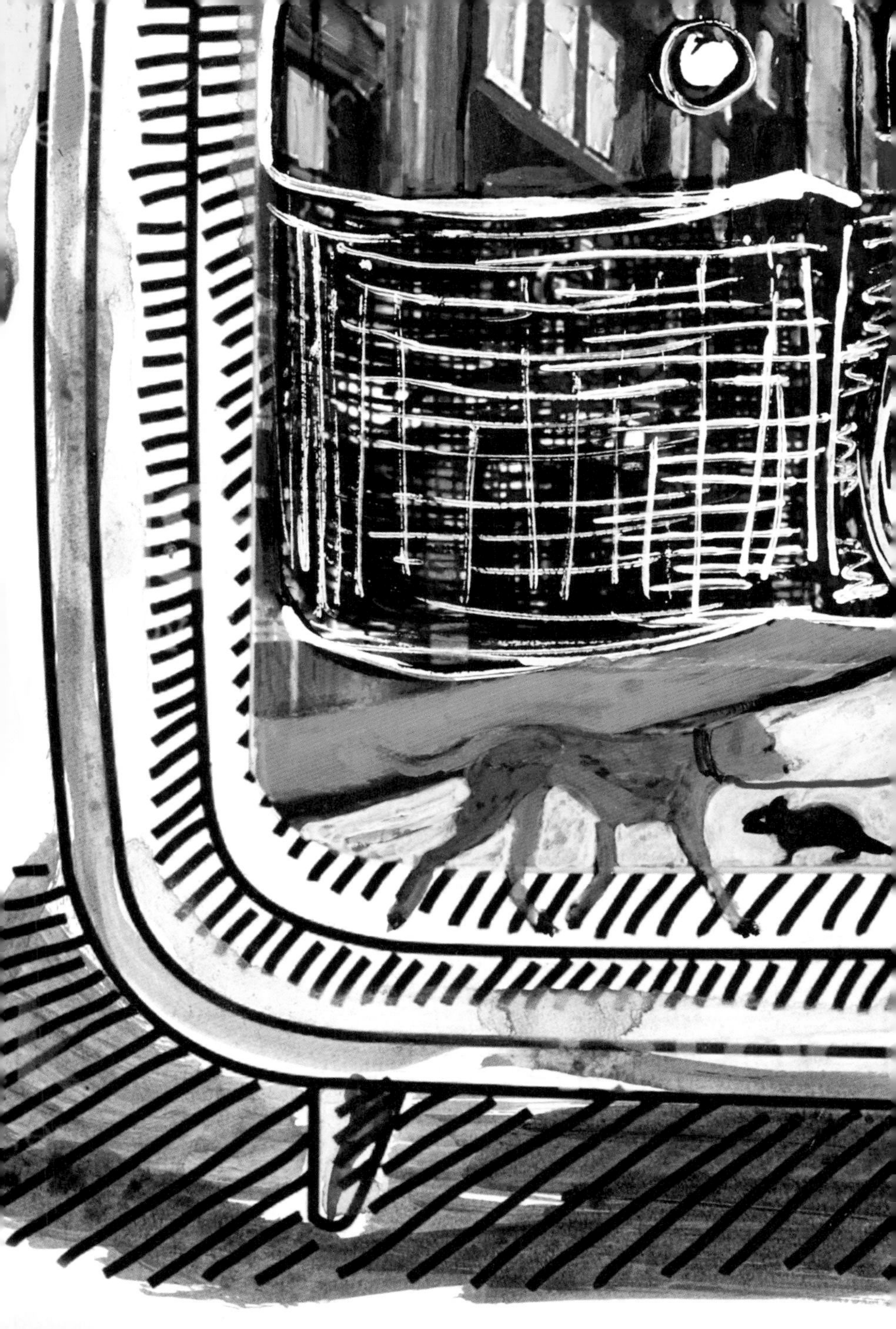

CHAPTER 7

Hugo faces some demons

HUGO WAS ANGRY ENOUGH TO SPLIT OPEN a dozen bouncy castles with a plastic airline knife. No, he was not angry, he was furious, and it was all her fault. Tommy – that fatuous excuse of a woman in tartan! He recalled her, quite clearly, reassuring that bright-yellow Marjorie woman with the loud voice at the gallery, *don't worry, I shall deal with it.* And what had she done? She had locked the wretched animal in the lavatory and swanned off into the night, clubbing no doubt. And why couldn't Rodney have had a pee at Megan's?

Hugo hurled his legs out of bed, straightened up with a groan, threw on a dressing gown and staggered towards the bathroom. Even through the closed door it was louder than a Sunday morning of car alarms: a wailing, yelping howl more appropriate for some demented jungle creature than a dog. Indeed, he thought, as he hesitated outside the door, the creature had left the genus *canis* so far behind that it was nearer to a warthog than a dog. He had locked it in the bathroom rather than have it crap all over the flat, but even the idea of a mess on the tiled floor was enough to make him retch at this hour of the morning.

He opened the door. The dog was sitting on its haunches, in the far corner, by the bath. It regarded him with two bloodshot saucers dripping reproach. Its bowels had held; there was no mess.

'Come on. Downstairs!' ordered Hugo.

The dog followed him down three flights. It was not bred for stairs; it hesitated and descended slowly, its claws scrabbling for purchase on the polished, wooden flooring. Still clad in his dressing gown, Hugo shunted it onto the pavement. All that he needed to do was go back into the building, close the door and have another hour's sleep before work. The dog belonged on the street anyway. But then he remembered Rodney's clear instructions: *You'll have to have him for tonight, Hugo. We can't possibly take him down to Tempusbury because of Akhenaten.* (Akhenaten was apparently some sort of cat-shaped household deity.) *We'll sort something out tomorrow.* He had taken Hugo's home and work telephone numbers. *Goodness gracious. No mobile number?* Rodney had said. Silly prat.

The dog was snuffling at the base of a lamp post. It raised one leg and sprayed a steady stream of urine, then trotted past Hugo through the open doorway and back into the hall. Hugo followed, with heavy tread, as the dog climbed the stairs, its testicles swinging.

Now don't forget to feed him before you go to bed, Wilfred had said. Some chance! It had been nearly three by the time he got home. It probably needed feeding now. But what did dogs eat? Cats ate mice and birds, but Hugo had never heard any mention of dogs being carnivores and so deduced that they had to be vegetarian. He searched under the kitchen sink for an old plastic bowl, filled it with water and put it on the floor. The dog lapped thirstily. Hugo opened the fridge and studied its contents. Nothing seemed appropriate for the sustenance of a small black-and-white dog. He had two passion fruit, but he was buggered if he was going to let the mutt have them. Eventually he opened a can of baked beans, poured the contents into a cereal packet torn in half – better not to let the dog contaminate his plates – and placed it on the kitchen floor. It waddled over, sniffed the food and looked up at Hugo. It had heavy, greying dewlaps framing what appeared to be a small mouth. The lips – if that is what the black shiny stuff around the mouth should be called – had a pursed quality about them. Hugo walked off into his sitting room. Through the doorway he could see the dog eating the beans while following the sliding cereal packet around the kitchen floor.

Hugo checked to make sure Rodney and Wilfred had not telephoned while he was downstairs, then switched on his computer. There was an e-mail from his agent which read:

Hi HI hi Hugo good to see you in the nayberhood!!!

Had a phone call from Ravinda Bat. It is better you deal with her problem.

She sed she was looking evrywhere for an Ariginal coppy of your book.

Woe and alas she tried Piddulston's, Reevers, w.a. jones and nobody have an Ariginal Edishun.

I sed to get one from you or order it from Frans – becos she isunt reddy to see you till shes read it in the Ariginal.

Hi fives

Nigel

www.molesworthmentoring.com

This made no sense to Hugo at all. Not that much about Nigel made any sense, including the fact that he was veering towards elderly yet still had spots. Hugo had not seen Nigel, in the neighbourhood or out of it, since their last communication the previous day. If Nigel had passed him in the street, why had he not greeted him? Nigel held two hundred copies of Hugo's book. There had been two editions with identical content. Who was Fran? Or did he mean Franz? Did high fives mean that Ravinder Bhatt was prepared to pay £5,000 for the privilege of translating his book? Effin-Nigel seemed to cause more problems than he was worth. Who needed an agent anyway? Hugo knew that he would have been much better off just walking into any publishing house in the land with his manuscript of *Trapped Light*. Instead someone had sent him to Nigel and now he was stuck with him. Oh, of course, that was it. The woman wanted to read his original manuscript. But why, when she had a perfectly decent paperback?

He would be late for work if he didn't get a move on. He e-mailed a reply:

> Dear Nigel,
>
> Please tell Ms Bhatt that my original manuscript is very personal and it would be inappropriate for it to leave my possession. She must read a paperback of *Trapped Light* like everyone else. Where was it that you saw me? Why didn't you greet me? What remuneration is Ms Bhatt prepared to offer? Who is Fran/Franz? Is she/he some devotee of my writing who has copied it out by hand?
>
> Regards,
> Hugo de Lamartine

Was everything to be tiresome today? In the kitchen, the dog had left red swirls of tomato sauce on the blue vinyl flooring. Hugo hurriedly ran a dishcloth over the floor with his foot. If you left food lying around it attracted rats, he had heard.

Neither Rodney nor Wilfred had rung by the time he was dressed and had swallowed a cup of coffee, four pieces of toast and a banana. He was unusually hungry this morning.

He had no option but to take the fleabag with him to work. On the journey there it proved a nightmarish companion, exuding clouds of bakedbeanious wind in the overcrowded Tube.

Hugo's place of employment was in Swift Street, on the borders of the financial district, an area once as famous for the publication of newspapers as its neighbouring district was for probity. The papers were long gone, but the area still retained a certain cachet. It is interesting how men of creative genius (for they are usually men) are drawn to certain occupations. Talent needs a job that fills neither brain nor day to overflowing.

As soon as he entered what passed for a reception area, Hugo's ears were assailed by a prolonged high-pitched scream. 'Yeeeeeeeeeeeeeee! Yeeeeeeeeeeeeeeeee! Oh wicked! 'E's a bewiful boy! He's only gotta titchy little tail so he has to waggle his botty instead.' There were no aitches sounded in this statement and the T's in *little* and *botty* were missing too.

The dog put on a revolting display in response, wiggling the aforementioned botty from side to side. What had mistakenly appeared to Hugo as a small mouth was opened to reveal a vast, gaping maw breathing foetid joy in snorting gasps.

'I never would of thought you'd of got a dog, Mister Lamartine.'

Hugo was at a loss to know who repelled him more at this moment, Chertsey Staines bowlegged in pink trousers or the object of her enthusiasm. Chertsey was Hugo's minion in the workplace; she did the tasks he didn't do.

'He's not my dog, I'm just minding him for a few hours. Why don't you take him into your office and look after him.'

'Can I? Oh brilliant. Dogs is great.'

'You can probably have him if you want. I think he's a stray.'

'I'd give the world to have him. But I can't.'

'Why not?'

'He's not up to it. A dog's gotta be able to get respeck where I live. We've got pitbulls and rottweilers an stuff. They'd rip him to shreds.'

The presence of the dog would doubtless mean a long time before a cup of tea arrived. In Hugo's office, the day's work, a heavy pile of folders, awaited him on his desk. This was a midway point for patent applications. It had been set up by the Government in knee-jerk response to a public outcry at the length of time being taken to process patent applications. All applications received by the Patent Office were now dealt with in the first instance by an obscure Government office, Room 5414, situated somewhere in the Ministry of Offence. This office was responsible for sending many patent applications to a certain death; they were returned to their owners stamped with the words *Not In The Interests Of National Security*. This meant that all work on the patent in question must immediately cease, to which their inventors no doubt responded, *Oh well, I'll go and do something else then.* It was

Hugo's job to reduce the pile still further. The patents that remained, by the time Hugo had finished with them, were sent again to the Patent Office. There they were meant to receive final approval or rejection, but Hugo knew that many patents went round in this circle quite a few times.

When interviewed for the job, Hugo had been expected to have a science degree. This seemed to him to be an example of the worst sort of cronyism, and he felt perfectly justified in assuring his interviewers that he was appropriately qualified. Hugo knew that he was degree material, but had always taken the view that most subjects were interesting if you examined them superficially, yet could be deathly boring if you waded in too far. Why anybody should wish to subject themselves to this, especially in science, was beyond him. Besides, doing the job involved only the talents with which he had demonstrated an effortless superiority in primary school.

He picked up the first folder and examined the title:

SUPER REFRACTIVE LENSES
A new type of lens with refractive power
10,000 times more than what we have today

This was a perfect example of what led Hugo to reject a patent application.

Point 1. The use of the word *super*. This was a word more suited to a comic book than a patent application.

Point 2. The clumsy grammar of 'than what we have today'. He also disliked patents that used too many squiggles and diagrams. If something was worth saying, then it should be well expressed, in correct English and properly punctuated, and the failure to do so, quite evidently, was a deliberate attempt to annoy. Thus he had no need of a science degree to know which patents to reject.

His reaction to his agent Nigel's difficulties with the language, which were to dyslexia what Ebola is to the common cold, was more tolerant. Hugo had taken to reading, writing and arithmetic with ease. From the very start of his education, being able to spell was something that happened without effort. At ages five and six, he was top of the class. It was only later on that he failed to see the point of much of what he was being taught. This sense of natural superiority provided a comfortable buffer zone between him and his agent. He was prepared to allow Nigel to manage his literary output because Nigel need not be taken too seriously. The irritation of reading his nonsensical e-mails was balanced by the convenience of not having to undertake the negotiation with tiresome people that Nigel performed on his behalf. Here, in the office, he had the same satisfactory arrangement. He simply signed a form, attached to the patent, with either a green pen, which indicated his approval, or a red one, which relegated the patent to oblivion. The rest of the processing fell to Chertsey.

Hugo's tea had not yet arrived. That noisome dog. He got up and went across the hall to Chertsey's office. As he walked in he noticed that she slid a sheet of paper over whatever she had been reading.

'Oh hi, Mister Lamartine. I expect yer ready for a cuppa tea.'

'Yes, I have been ready for about an hour, but as I see you're busy…'

'I'm sorry. I'll bring it through straightaway. That dog's ever so well-behaved. Look at him. Fast asleep.'

Hugo looked briefly at the dog, who was tightly curled up in a corner of the room on what appeared to be Chertsey's red coat. 'Um,' he said, and returned to his office.

When Chertsey had brought in the tea, very strong with a little milk and two Mussolini biscuits, he removed the next folder on the pile and began to read. It started in a promising way. After the cover, which listed the application's author and personal details, the first page was composed entirely of text which appeared to be written correctly. Hugo read it through:

TIME TRAVEL – PART OF A NEW PARADIGM

by P. Brockworth

The subject of this patent application, time travel, is a natural development of my previous paper on parallel universes which I wrote ten years ago, entitled: SWITCHING BETWEEN UNIVERSES IN THE MULTIVERSE. I am still waiting for this paper to be peer-reviewed and published.

INTRODUCTION

This study intends to show that a paradigm shift is needed to better understand what time is and our position within it. This leads on to practical applications.

It is demonstrated that we have a linear, one-dimensional view of time. It can be shown that a better model would be multiple elliptical lines surrounding a central core (see fig. 1) set within two dimensions of time. The core represents a moment in time. All moments exist in relation to this one moment. It can be argued that, as separate entities, humans, animals, all living things exist within all moments of time.

It can be postulated that our brains have only evolved to perceive time in a one-dimensional, linear fashion that gives rise to a limited experience of cause and effect. Only one section of a time continuum can be perceived. We experience space and time as two different things and cannot conceptualise an effect coming before a cause.

It can be postulated that a change in the way time is conceptualised is necessary to move within time, just as we are conscious of moving within space.

Given the concentric circles of time demonstrated in fig. 1, a move backwards or forwards within time of several hundreds or even thousands of years is more easily accomplished than a move to, for example, the previous day.

The theory also allows for different states of space-time and postulates the existence of temporal anomalies in the form of terrestrial and extraterrestrial highways and skylanes. While it can be postulated that these are physically adjacent they would be temporally extraneous and therefore not of interest for any practical purpose.

The paper will demonstrate the following:

SECTION 1 Justification within existing physics for a new paradigm.

SECTION 2 Changes in cerebral structure in relation to time perception.

SECTION 3 The role of oestrogen and the emotions in time perception.

SECTION 4 Space-time anomalies (skylanes, etc.) – quirks without purpose.

SECTION 5 Practical applications.

SECTION 6 Conclusion.

So far, so good. Hugo liked the word paradigm and used it often himself. He flipped the page. His forehead creased in a frown. Shot to pieces. The second page consisted entirely of diagrams and irritating wodges of numbers and symbols. The first page would have warranted a green signature, even though it contained a worryingly split infinitive and the style was a bit dodgy – there was a lot of postulation going on – but the next – he flipped through more pages – indeed the bulk of the paper was utterly incomprehensible. He turned back to the first page and affixed his signature on the attached docket in red ink. He felt cheered. The elimination of balderdash was always satisfying.

Feeling fatigued, Hugo decided that it was time for lunch and phoned through to Chertsey to ask her to pop out to the White Rose Food Emporium and pick up a prawn and peanut-butter sandwich. When he heard her leave, he entered her office and had a good look on her desk to find

out what she had been hiding, but he could find nothing out of the ordinary.

He returned to his office and read his morning paper, giving particular attention to the Arts pages, with his feet up on his desk. Chertsey popped in with his sandwich and, when he had finished it, he picked up the phone book and decided to find the number of the art gallery. The idea of spending another night with the dog was not a happy one. It was sensible to suggest to Rodney and Wilfred that the animal should be taken to Beatwater Dogs' Home. He looked up Cave Paintings and rang the number. *This call is being diverted* said a fatuous voice, as though Hugo had done something amusing. A further ringing tone was eventually answered by Wilfred, who sounded flustered.

'Oogo? Oogo? Oh, Hugo! How are you?'

'Not too good, actually. I'm not the best person to be looking after a dog.'

'Gosh, yes, the dog. I am sorry. We're having a plumbing nightmare down here in Tempusbury and all the electrics have tripped. Akhenaten doesn't like cold; he needs the boiler on.'

'I see,' said Hugo. 'The problem is, I'm not equipped to look after a dog. I don't have leads or beds or feeding bowls. I don't know what I should be doing with it. Wouldn't it be sensible for me to take it to the Dogs' Home?'

'Hang on a minute.'

Hugo could hear muffled voices as Wilfred, with a hand over the receiver presumably, conferred with Rodney.

'Look,' said Wilfred. 'Leave it with us. We'll get it sorted out. We feel a sort of moral obligation because the dog was locked in our loo for so long. We'll phone the police and say that we've found him, and then we'll find someone to look after him until he's claimed by his owner. It won't be a problem.'

'Good,' said Hugo. 'It was an excellent night last night, by the way. I'll look forward to hearing from you.'

'In the meantime, why don't you find out what the dog's name is?' suggested Wilfred.

'And how, pray, will I do that?'

'Most people give dogs sensible names these days, like Godfrey or Neville. Just keep trying till he answers. Now don't fret. There's bound to be someone who can take him.'

As he put the receiver down, Hugo became aware that Chertsey was standing beside his desk, having placed a fresh mug of tea on a coaster, which said COME TO POLPERRO! She looked pensive and obviously wanted something.

'So the dog got dumped on ya.'

'Yes. That's right.'

'You woulden of chosen to bring him in. I mean, if you could of helped it.'

'No. Obviously not.'

'That's so strange! Like the same fing happened to me! You remember I tole you 'bout my bruvver's girlfriend, the one what was livin' wiv . . .'

'Chertsey, I'm a busy man, what is it that you want? Get to the point.'

'My bruvver's girlfriend wants to drop her kid in, like, for a coupla hours. She won't be no trouble.'

When Hugo entered her office some while later, carrying a pile of patents that he had signed off that day, a fat child in a skimpy top was drawing pictures, and the room had a strong odour of dog combined with the chemical tang of cheap sweets.

'Melony's run out of drawrin' paper. 'Ave you got'ny scrap?'

'No, I haven't.' Hugo felt this morning's anger, which had only been damped down, start to rekindle. 'Oh for goodness' sake.' He turned the patents over, exposing their blank white undersides. 'Let her draw on these. They're heading for the bin anyway. See that I'm not disturbed for the next hour. And try and find out what the dog's name is. Say a few boys' names and see if it responds. And don't come and tell me the result. I've an important report to write.'

Chertsey knew that not being disturbed meant that Hugo had gone back to his office for a nap. That suited her. Melony was producing some wonderful pen sketches of long-haired girls and sleeping dogs. When she had finished, she would give them to Chertsey who would take them home and put them, with all her other gifts of art, in a perspex magazine-holder in the spare bedroom. Chertsey Staines slid a book out from underneath the papers on her desk and, with a sigh of satisfaction at having a perfect hour of afternoon to herself, carried on practising her Mensa tests.

CHAPTER 8

Swallow a pill and go tripping

BOLLUNK WAS LONGING TO GO BACK TO her cubicle and have time to herself to read a book or two, but that was not possible. She always knew how Sidney was feeling and, today, she knew that he was miserable. Indeed, he seemed close to tears as he groaned: 'I've spent a year in this stinking river waiting for this mission to start. Soon as it at-long-bloody-last starts, it stops. He's at work! She's at the University. It's hopeless. Why did I choose her in the first place?'

'There must have been a reason. Why *did* you choose her?'

'She was one of the most boring women I've ever met but, on the upside, she seemed a serious sort who would put on neoprene gloves and do whatever the job required. Men who mess up the world, like Hudelam, often don't have friends or pets. She seemed able to be whatever he needed, bedmate, mother or just someone to cook him a meal and listen to him. How was I to know? She didn't seem the type to get carried away and not do things properly.'

'Can't you just leave the ship and go and speak to her?'

Why had she said it? She could see by the expression on his face that, if he had had a sabre to hand, he would have chopped her up into little bits and splattered them all over the viewing deck. Instead he made a muffled choking noise, leapt to his feet and began to stagger about with his tunic pulled up to his neck.

'What do you think these are?' He indicated his chest.

Bollunk peered at the naked skin of his upper torso and replied, 'I don't know. I don't know what they're called on a man. If you were a girl I'd say they were boobs.'

'Chest buttocks. Baby-chokers. Man boobs. Why do you think I've got 'em?'

'I don't know. Too much trifle? Not enough exercise? They don't look bad on you though . . .'

Of course she knew the right answer. She had just felt embarrassed saying it. And now she was going to get an explanation and she didn't want one. She wanted to go back to her quarters, have a cup of detox tea and get on with reading her book.

'This isn't even proper time travel!' His voice was raised, angry. 'We're only in a slipstream. But for me it's time-travelling enough and that takes more oestrogen than your ovaries churn out in a week. I've got enough female hormone in my body to mess up every neuron in my brain. And you're saying I should talk to Tommy, who is sixty years in the past! Not just in a slipstream but proper time-travelling! Have you any idea just how difficult that is? Have you never heard of Brockworth?'

Why hadn't Bollunk just replied 'yes'? But she hadn't. She'd said that she had read all about Brockworth in her favourite book about famous women . . . And Sidney wouldn't let her finish. He shouted, 'But Brockworth, as anyone with a brain cell knows, was a man!'

Then he crashed off to his sleeping quarters. The sliding door closed automatically, but it felt as though something had been slammed. It was obvious that he couldn't bear to stay in her company. He thought she was educationally underachieving. But her favourite book told the life story of Chertsey Staines, and how she saved Brockworth's theories for humanity, and Chertsey Staines was a famous woman!

There wasn't a development in history that couldn't be traced back to a woman somehow. Usually it was someone's mother or wife. But they all ended up forgotten, rosalindfranklinned into obscurity with a pat on the head and an *I'll take over now, my dear.* Bollunk felt that she herself ought to have accomplished more, but there were always men like Sidney prepared to sit it out and wait for years, happy to calculate every boring detail.

Chertsey Staines had been different, a real achiever. Bollunk remembered seeing her speak at an underground meeting, an elderly woman, rather bowlegged and wearing clashing colours, climbing onto a podium, shaking hands.

Staines had been in her seventies when she presented the work of the long-forgotten physicist, P. Brockworth, to scientists, who were at first incredulous and later rather nervous. No one could predict the consequences of time travel. It might make things messy, perhaps spawn alternate universes – zillions of them, even. *Time Travel – Part of a New Paradigm* looked set to change the world – and then it hadn't. It had all been hushed up. Science was a dirty word in the latter part of the 21st century. The social eruption of time travel had not been considered aesthetically pleasing by leading Senior Artists. Holistic healers persuaded everyone of its inadvisability. Grandparents trembled in their beds and anticipated being murdered, while parents feared winking out of existence. It had all been much too difficult.

Who was it who had first decided that the world could and should be changed? Was it Sidney himself, or some *éminence grise* behind him? Someone with the financial clout to dust down Brockworth's theories and put them into practice?

Sidney had been responsible for training Tommy. At the point where Bollunk had first joined the Conspiracy, Tommy had been a few days from starting her mission. They had exchanged brief words over a cup of coffee. Tommy had seemed anxious, distracted, and then she was gone. It was only a few hours later that Bollunk joined a line of young women, assistants to Sidney, who had been coming and going all morning. That was time travel for you. Over a year of subjective time for Tommy and Sidney was experienced as just a few hours for the organisation supporting them.

Bollunk had been so excited to be playing an active role in all of this. She had been prepared for danger, self-sacrifice, but not for day after weary day with reading her only comfort. To make matters worse, her hair was a mess. The humidity of the slipstreamer made it frizz and she had run out of conditioner. She gazed out of the porthole at the murky water and wished there was something nutritious to eat, but the replicator, set to balance emotional with nutritional need, an example of Sidney's technical wizardry, was refusing to serve up anything but trifle at the moment, extraordinarily dense trifle, topped with glacé cherries, angelica and crystallised violets. The very thought was revolting to her.

She sat in Sidney's flowered-chintz twirly chair, in front of the viewing screen, her ankles dangling a few centimetres from the floor. The chair carried his scent. A mechanical whine intruded on her thoughts. He never seemed to notice the noise of the air refabricator, but it was a constant irritation to her. She wondered, if he hadn't been taking all that oestrogen, whether he might have been attracted to her. Perhaps. He'd been down here for so long with just a quick trip back, now and then, to pick up a new assistant. Had he slept with any of her predecessors? The thought of just sleeping with Sidney, in a bed, without even doing anything, filled her with longing.

Bollunk sighed and picked up her book of haiku based on sagas from the Old North and tried to read. The fusion of northern ideas and oriental form reminded her of Sidney. He and she would make such an interesting couple. Oriental/Prussian combined with Anglo/Arab and black African. Together they spanned the globe. They had world enough and time. She was beginning to nod off when a door opened with a swish. Sidney came out of his quarters carrying three A2 printouts of time charts.

'I've worked it out. It's possible.'

He put the charts down on the table. The top one showed hundreds of ellipses, some nested one after another without touching, others set at odd angles overlaying and here and there connecting. Red swirls on blue paper. She gazed at his face while he spoke, glad to see him animated and positive.

'It's like bungee jumping. The first jump will take me out of the slipstream and back roughly two thousand years.

The calculations are complex, but I think I've got them right. Then forwards for three and half thousand. Stay there for the shortest possible time – no more than five minutes is safe, huddled under a blanket and not looking out, you risk your sanity that way – then back to last night. Those first men who time-jumped didn't have my training and discipline, and they were probably already mentally unstable before they went. I'm going to need a lot of concentration to stay for more than a few minutes, but it is possible. It can be done.'

'But isn't it dangerous?'

'Dangerous?' His handsome mouth twisted in a grimace and he shook his head to and fro in a way that suggested male chutzpah. 'The journey back will be complicated, but it shouldn't be any more life-threatening than that time the Conspiracy broke into Prancing-Gammon House and trashed the pictures the King had painted.'

'Will you have enough time to find out what's happened to Tommy?'

'I've worked it and reworked it, and I'm sure to have a good half an hour with her.'

'How much hormone will you need to take?'

Bollunk was stunned when he told her. Such a dose was inconceivable for a man, its effect on mind and body incalculable. There was a risk, even with the use of an antidote, that its effect might not be reversible and he would end up like those first pitiable pioneers.

'Let me go instead of you, Sidney? It would be so much easier for me. I wouldn't need to take such a megadose of oestrogen, and if you managed to teach the mental time travel techniques to Tommy, I'm sure you could teach them to me.'

Sidney laughed, high-pitched guffaws that seemed painfully loud in the confines of the ship. Bollunk was hurt – it was cruel of him to laugh; he thought her too short and stupid to time-travel – then angry – *let him go, what did she care?*

'Don't forget', he said, 'going was your idea, Bollunk. I've known Tommy for many weeks. I know how she thinks. She needs my authority to snap her out of whatever state of fugue she's in.'

Bollunk stayed curled up in Sidney's chair, electric hair pressed to the antimacassar, while Sidney busied about the slipstreamer. She became aware that he was putting things together for the trip.

'When are you going?'

'Shortly. There's no point brooding about the risks, better to do it now, quickly, and when it's done I'll be that much closer to recovering. I'm sick to death of waiting for this mission to get going.'

He disappeared into his quarters for a while and emerged wearing mauve jeans and a lavender t-shirt and carrying a towel. A tunic would not be appropriate where he was going, yet Bollunk was not sure that he was dressed convincingly for the period.

'Those are very oddish clothes you're wearing.'

'Yes, they're originals. I stole them from the Notional Costume Gallery. I want to look authentic, merge with the crowd. How on earth did they cope with jeans this tight?'

She kept her misgivings to herself, fetched him some water and sat with him while he forced down sixty small, pink pills.

'I'm remaking history,' he said. 'I'm the first man, since those first pioneers, to be making more than one slipstream time jump. I'm boldly going . . .'

He smiled at Bollunk. He'd never smiled at her before.

'I'll be waiting for you,' she reassured him. 'It will be oddish being down here on my own.'

'Hey, don't stress. I'll be back before you know it. Oh God, I feel so sick.' He clutched his stomach. 'I'm going to throw up. Dim the lights.'

Bollunk waved a hand at the viewing screen. She watched Sidney standing in front of a porthole. His brow was creased with the effort of concentration as he stared out on layers of silt topped with dark, dirty water. It was an act of pure faith to envisage the mathematics of time, to trust and love the

numbers of an individual calculation, to shout *Sod it!* to the universe and let go. She saw him cling on to his towel, turn widdershins and begin to fade, return to full-fleshed reality, then fade again. She reached out a hand towards him, but he had gone. She was alone in the half-light with the air refabricator singing its crazy song.

CHAPTER 8½

The slave

THERE'S A MESS ON THE FLOOR. VOMITUS. SOME strange old woman with glittering eyes wandering in from the street. He cleans it up, taking care to remove every trace from the mosaic tiles. Just as he finishes, she reappears clutching an animal to her breast. He drives her away with a broom. All civic order and respect have broken down. He has been up most of the night waiting for first light. He never sleeps much. He's a little man with dirty hair. When he opens his mouth his teeth are small, worn away by gritty bread. There are wads of old rags packed underneath the heavy band of iron which encircles his waist. The skin beneath the band has formed callouses like the soles of his feet, but it is still impossible to sleep sitting up or lie down comfortably at night.

The light is oily grey, and it is presumably morning, though it seems to be getting darker. The powerful ones have been grumbling and rumbling on the mountain. Yesterday they shook the earth briefly; the mountain sent sparks flying high into the air and spewed filth in a huge grey plume. Though the air was foul, this side of the mountain stayed safe. The family fled by boat for the home of friends a day's journey away up the coast, taking jewellery, good clothes, everything of value. He is alone with the lares and penates, the household gods, taking care of the house.

Since yesterday, there has been the clang of carts striking the cobbles with their iron-rimmed wheels. Squealing boys push handcarts laden with household goods. So many people have left or are going.

He wanders down to the harbour and stands beneath the porticos on the seafront. There is a wind and a strong swell rocks the few boats that remain. Mostly they are old worn-out fishing boats but, though a sturdy skiff bobs about within reach, it is already too rough to take safely to the water. He once spent a long time on a boat and learned a little too much about rowing. He respects the Sea God, but trusts him less than the gods of sky and land.

He pays attention to his hunger. The house is full of food and who knows when the family will be back. For once he has a chance of a full belly, unless someone has broken in and stolen everything. He has been charged with the house's safety and is not supposed to leave it, but the seafront has a powerful pull. He hurries back home, glancing only briefly up to the skyline where the outline of the mountain glows a dull red against the sky. Its rank breath envelops him.

The house is safe. The water cistern bubbles in the courtyard. In the coolness of the kitchen, earthenware containers sunk into the ground are filled with wine, flour, oil and garum. Yesterday he fetched loaves from the bakery and they are only a little stale. There is fresh fruit. He is safe here, but he could leave. The thought shocks him. It has not occurred to him before. To go. To walk out. Such a pointless act, it has always seemed, with a band of metal about his waist. Not much future in it. But now, with all manner of people travelling, why not take his chances on the open road? With so much chaos, who will notice one more person travelling? He could steal a robe to cover his metal band – what matter an extra misdeed – and leave the mountain far behind. Yes, he will go.

At the moment of deciding the air shimmers. He had not noticed how dark it has become. He cannot tell what time it is, for the God of Fire has covered the face of the sun these two days past. Just outside the open doorway of the kitchen, lights and colours dance in the air. A pair of leather-clad feet form on the intricate patterns of the courtyard floor. They gain a body, dressed in a colour that mixes asses' milk with dark wine, but he dares not look up at the face and cannot tell which god this is. The air shimmers again and the god quickly fades. The message is quite clear. This house has been visited by a god. It is blessed. It is safe. The gods will not deliver death to the town. He will stay here with the lares and penates, in Hercule Aneum. And maybe he will take another walk down to the harbour to look at the sea.

CHAPTER 8¾

The future

SIDNEY'S EYES ARE CLOSED, BUT HE FEELS HIS FEET make contact with what must be mud, slipping and sucking; he can smell it, the raw smell of earth. He pulls the towel over his head. The distant past was bad enough; he really doesn't want to see the future. Much easier not to know. It is unbearably hot and he struggles to breathe. His lungs fill to capacity yet are not satisfied. He opens his mouth and gulps in heat and too much carbon dioxide. He is dry-drowning. Why is he still here? Why is this taking so long? He is falling . . .

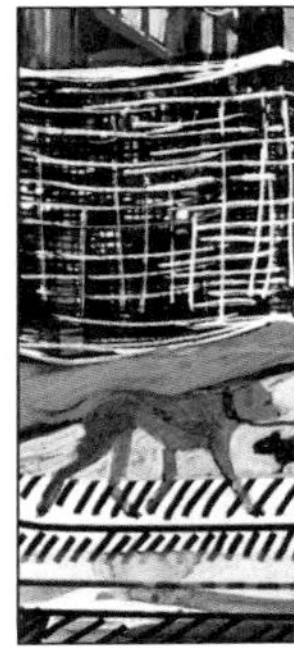

CHAPTER 9

The stuff of nightmares

HUGO JERKED AND NEARLY FELL OFF HIS chair. He had been awoken by the sound of a man talking in the outer office; one of those cheery types who was revelling in the sound of his own voice. That, coupled with Chertsey enthusing over something, and shrill interjections and silly giggles from her repulsive niece, and any peace that Hugo might have been enjoying was blasted out of dreamland as though by the guns of enemy tanks.

Emerging from his office, Hugo had a brief glimpse of someone who looked like a delivery man before the door closed. Chertsey, Melony and the dog were making a visual and olfactory examination of the following items spread out on the floor: one green velour dog bed decorated with a happy puppy motif, a red and white feeding bowl with a drawing of a bone on the inside, an earthenware water bowl with DOG written on it, a fluorescent green lead, a red collar with aggressive studs, three two-kilo packets of dog biscuits, fourteen cans of Bouncing Chow Meatychunks, some worm pills and a plastic chewable effigy of the Pope.

'He doesn't need a collar,' said Chertsey.

'He doesn't need any of this stuff. What's it for?' shouted Hugo.

'The man said it was wiv the compliments of Cave Paintings and you was not to worry 'cause everythink'd be sorted.'

'Why . . .' (Hugo kicked the dog bed. It rose into the air and fell without sound.) '. . . have Rodney and Wilfred sent over this stuff, when they were supposed to be sending someone to take the dog away, not equip him for a bloody lifetime in my office?'

'His name's Botty.'

The dog reacted to its name and stared up at her.

'Botty?' sneered Hugo.

The dog closed its eyes.

'Yeah. Botticelli.' (She pronounced his name with a glottal stop on the T's and a hard anglicised C.)

'Botty Kelly. Ah! So we now know that the people who own the dog are called Kelly, which means it should be possible to give it back to them. But just a minute.' Hugo struggled with the idea of Chertsey, using the suggested system of trial and error, addressing the mutt with one name after another and arriving at both Botty and Kelly. It seemed improbable. 'Are you quite sure that's his name?'

'Oh yeah,' she affirmed. 'Pozzitiff.'

'And how can you be so sure?'

'Is on his collar. I took it off him and found it like stuck on the inside wiv tape. But no phone number. Not very bright really, is it, Mister Lamartine?'

Hugo had not noticed the dog had a collar. He now perceived it to be thin, black, and well camouflaged by the fur at the back of the dog's neck, but quite evident running across his white front. He felt annoyed, but that was the penalty one paid for intelligence. The educated mind so often soars above the mundane, and then is forced to land with a crash back in the irksome mud of reality. 'This place is a mess,' he said. At the tone of his voice, Chertsey, Melony and the dog looked up at him, each with the same sullen expression. Hugo turned on his heel and went back to his office.

He was busy placing his pens and pencils in neat lines, all facing the same way, when the telephone rang. It was Terence. Hugo couldn't remember the name at first, but was soon reminded of his encounter with the journalist the previous evening.

'Absinthe!' said Terence.

'Absinthe?' Hugo replied, totally mystified, having forgotten all about the green drinks.

'I've been chatting about your docudrama with a friend of mine at the EBC. He's as excited by it as I am.'

'Good.' Hugo's heart skipped a beat as he realised what Terence was talking about, and he sent the pencils hurtling into a state of randomness upon the floor.

'Are you available for a chat?'

'Why not.'

'Great, we're in your neighbourhood. We're keen to start building some ideas on a possible film about you. You must have heard of my friend – his name's Gruff Hint. You probably saw his latest documentary series, which transported a certain famous art critic out to the African war zones...'

Hugo had not realised that a chat would involve a meeting, now, and with the illustrious film-maker. He was in no mental state to meet anyone. And then the words *film about you* insinuated themselves into his consciousness. The film-maker's name rang a bell. Indeed, there had been much discussion in the media over the art critic's namby-pamby reaction to the war zone.

'Yes, of course I've heard of him and I'd love to meet him, but at the moment...' Hugo's thoughts turned with anguish to the outer office, to Chertsey, to Melony and her inane scribblings on paper spread all over the desktop, to the dog and his paraphernalia, to the smells of dog, dog food and whatever it was that Melony was incessantly chewing. It was unthinkable that somebody of *Gruff Hint's* eminence and standing should meet with Hugo de Lamartine in such an inappropriate setting. '...at the moment...' Hugo's mind went blank. He thought of sunflowers waving in a green field.

'Are you still there?' asked Terence.

'Well, yes, but...' There were so many things that Hugo might have said. But they escaped him. He could have suggested meeting at a nearby pub as Government Inspectors were in his office. He might have had an important conference scheduled for that very time and set up a mutually convenient date for a meeting in the very near future. But the sunflowers nodded their heads and *No! No! No!* was screaming inside Hugo's head, yet was never articulated, and Terence said they'd be there in five minutes and put the phone down.

When Terence and Gruff Hint arrived, Hugo was sitting at Chertsey's desk. The drawings had been removed, the floor was innocent of canine accoutrements, the door to Hugo's inner office was firmly closed. The window was open, and the afternoon's sudden chill blasted over the three men as they shook hands and sought seats. There were only two. Hugo wheeled his chair next to the other chair for his guests and sat upon the desk, facing them and the window, as though he always did that sort of thing. But a man whose nature it is to sit awkwardly does not suddenly acquire nonchalance and grace when swinging his legs while perched on the side of a rather tall desk. And the wind was blowing his hair over to the wrong side. Still, Hugo was relieved to have the situation under his control. His threats to Chertsey had perhaps been a little severe, but had given him confidence that nothing, short of flood or earthquake, would cause the door of the inner office to be opened while Gruff Hint and Terence were present.

Hugo apologised for the fact that his office was unable to be used. It was in the nature of patent work, he explained, that sometimes the patents' contents were so world-changing that anyone granted admittance to the room where they were kept had to be security-vetted. He also regretted his inability to provide refreshment of any sort.

'That's all right,' said Terence, cheerful despite the cold. 'We were in the pub when I rang you.'

Gruff Hint was a tall man who appeared to be in his late forties, slim in contrast to Terence's bulk and charmingly urbane. He spoke of his upbringing in an impoverished area of Bradford, of atrocities in Africa and of the technical demands of shedding light on Truth through Art via the medium of what he called the *Dramamentary*, and then the phone rang. Hugo waited for Chertsey to answer it until he realised, with some irritation, that she had obviously taken his ban on noise-of-any-sort-whatsoever to include answering the telephone. Excusing himself to his guests, he jumped down, went to the other side of the desk, threw several files to one side looking for the telephone, found it and took the call. It was Chertsey.

'No,' said Hugo, his chin jutting out and the sinews in his neck extending and tightening as he spoke. 'Not at the moment. She'll just have to wait.' He replaced the receiver and nodded to Hint. 'You were saying?'

'I've heard Terence's recording of your story, and I must say I'm riveted. Mind if I shut this?' Gruff Hint rose and closed the window behind him.

'Recording?' Hugo was puzzled.

'Yes, it's all fascinating stuff. I do programmes for the French market as well. Your story seems particularly suitable. There's a lot of examining of the national psyche going on over there at the moment. I understand you've written a book on photography. What's it like?'

'It's a paperback.'

'No, I meant what approach does it take stylistically?'

'It's a philosophical view of the states of mind underlying photography.'

'Ah! Intellectual stuff. The French like that. Have you got a copy with you?'

As this conversation progressed, it had become more and more obvious that a child was sobbing in the adjacent office. Hugo clenched his teeth and made a lot of noise, clumping about the room, searching for the book, even though he knew there were six copies of *Trapped Light* in the bookshelf above Chertsey's desk. He handed over a copy with a 'Ta Da!' and a flourish.

Gruff Hint riffled the pages. His eyes flickered towards the door. The sobs grew louder. 'Ah, this is just what we need! We could use it as a soundtrack behind the visuals. But it would sound so much better in French and subtitled. Would you mind if I translated it?'

'Not at all,' said Hugo. 'How long would that take?'

'My French is a bit African at the moment. Too many months in the Francophone part. But I've got a friend who's

French and a professor of philosophy. He's happy when he's shut up in a room translating stuff. Got Alzheimer's or Asperger's or something. He's incredibly fast. He'd probably do it over the weekend.' He slipped the book into his jacket pocket.

The telephone rang again. Chertsey didn't answer it, so it was probably her again, in which case he would kill her. Hugo mumbled an apology to his guests and lifted the receiver. Wilfred burbled happily, but thankfully was inaudible to Gruff Hint and Terence. Hugo's replies were terse: 'Yes, the packages arrived... But why send the stuff to me?... I thought you would get You-Know-Who round to remove him... I can't really talk now... The police should be told that the owner's name is Kelly... Yes, Kelly... Quite sure... Yes, clever of me that! Ah ha ha ha!... Written where you'd expect it to be written... Round his neck... Goodbye!'

Gruff Hint and Terence straightened a little, looked ghoulishly interested one minute and awfully uncomfortable the next.

Hugo began to apologise, but the howls from the inner office were very loud now and further conversation was not possible. There was also a rhythmic thudding coming from beyond the office entrance. Footfalls could be heard ascending the stairs, echoing in the passageway outside and getting nearer. The door was thrown open.

Some people's appearance seems to be woven of the stuff of nightmares, and such was the case with this visitor who presented a particularly urban bad dream: heavy-booted, thick legs were clad in camouflage trousers, a black sleeveless vest revealed arms strongly muscled and tattooed. The hair was slicked back off a sweating forehead, the face was scowling and the voice deep.

'Want me kid,' she said. 'Where the fuck is she?'

Hugo, his intestines gyrating within him, did not hesitate. He opened the door a fraction and called for Melony to come out, just her, no one else!

He shut the door quickly after the girl as, red-faced and

trailing strings of mucus in her wake, she swept past him and flew into her mother's strong arms.

'What's bin 'appenin'?' said the harsh voice.

'Pleeeeease. Not now, Mum. Wanna sick up! Now!'

'All right,' Mum said, looking each of the men in turn squarely in the eyes. 'I'll 'ear from Melony what 'appened, and if I don't like it I'll be back.' Her departing army boots echoed along the corridor accompanied by the *flop flip* sound of plastic flip-flops.

Hugo, pulling himself together, apologised and explained that it had been rather an unusual day. Yet, even as he spoke, there was a new sound emanating from behind the inner office door. Terence and Gruff Hint exchanged horrified glances. It was a squeaking, an ecclesiastical squeaking; but they were not to know that. There was the sound of a struggle, a growl, then a series of bereft and mournful yelps.

Gruff Hint leapt to his feet. 'I'm sorry. This can't go any further. I really want no part in the abuse of children and animals.'

'Me neither,' said Terence in a high voice. 'We need to leave.'

Wailing that he could explain, Hugo sought some simple explanation for the kerfuffle; failing, and feeling powerless to stop them leaving, he realised that the dream of a docudrama in which he was the star was slipping away. 'Wait!' he cried. He threw open the inner door, revealing everything, bar the revolting child, that he had struggled so manfully to conceal.

Outside distant sirens faded away. A pigeon cooed unseen beyond the window. Never had imagination offered so much and reality delivered so little. Chertsey Staines, in her pink trousers and top, clutching one end of the Pope, and the black-and-white dog with his teeth attached to the other. Both seemed oddly shrunken, irrelevant; midget figurines in a tableau of tacky, pet-shop artefacts. A developmental psychologist would have been fascinated by some of the crayoned drawings spread out over floor and desk, but Gruff Hint and Terence were not really into that sort of thing.

Gruff Hint shook his head in wonder. 'Sometimes I think

life is simpler in Africa. You know where you are in a war zone. Why don't we go back to the pub and continue our meeting there.'

Chertsey stared wordlessly at Hugo and watched as he left. She was not the type to wish ill or want revenge. Sometimes the universe looks after people like her. The squeaking recommenced. Tentatively.

'After my book's been translated, what happens next?' asked Hugo, as they clattered down the stairs.

'We'll need a script from you, Terence, and the legal stuff too, if you can get Charlie Archer to come up with a contract quickly. And I need to be sorting out a film crew... French speakers and wine lovers. Nice time of year for a location shoot.'

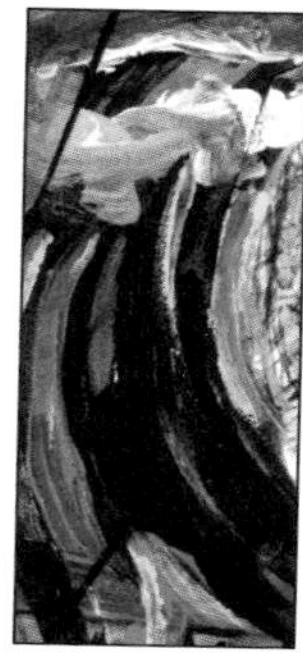

CHAPTER 10

Black light

IT WAS STILL DAYLIGHT. TOMMY WAS locked in some existential hellhole from which the return of her *raison d'être*, Hendrix, would be the only possible release. Paintstripper, who hadn't managed any sympathy yet, had eaten a gargantuan breakfast and gone off for a class on willow-whittling, even though willow-whittling was not the sort of thing one expected Paintstripper to be doing of her own free will. Tommy was frustrated, itching for something practical to do to ease her anxiety. Somewhere there had to be an answer to the mystery of Hendrix's disappearance. Wandering into his empty room, she noticed that it needed a good clean. He'd only been resident such a short time, yet it was extraordinary how grubby it was! She would have to tidy up a bit in order to dust and vacuum.

Underneath the bed she found a plate of rotting food, three trainers and a copy of *Trapped Light* by Hugo de Lamartine. It had a picture on the front of a white lamp, glowing with black light and forming a circle of darkness, like an old-fashioned photo negative. She put it next to the camera on the suitcase beside the bed.

There was a heap of papers on the floorboards that had never been filed. Picking them up, she shuffled through them and saw two letters that bore the crest of the University of Artistry and Design. The first was from Über Professor Camber and was dated 1st July. She read:

> Dear Mr Winston,
>
> It has been decided by The Department that you may be permitted an extension of the deadline on your

Photography Project. You may complete this over the summer vacation, but it must be handed in by the end of the first week of the autumn term. Failing this, we will have no alternative but to reconsider your entitlement to a place at the University.

Yours sincerely,

Amphelisia Camber, D. Phil. MPLO FUTTOC CNT

She knew what the second one was going to say. It was short, to the point, brutal. It was dated the day before Hendrix had left the flat and not returned.

None of this made any sense. How had Hendrix come to be expelled from the University of Artistry and Design for failing to complete a project on a subject about which he was passionate?

She had searched his room, read his personal letters. She was steeped so far now in deeds of a questionable nature that switching on his computer, opening the hard disk and clicking on the first folder, labelled 'Stuff', was not as difficult as she had anticipated. Somewhere there would be his work on the project. Computers irritated her. They were absurdly clunky when they should have known what it was that you wanted, and Hendrix was so disorganised! It took an age to discover what she was looking for, but she found it.

It was in a file labelled with the word *Progect* and dated 18th April. She read:

I have chosen to consider the following two photographs

There were thumbnails of two of Hendrix's photographs. She was familiar with both: a view from a haystack looking down to the ground, and another taken in a Tube train, bodies pressed together; in the bottom right corner, the striking face of a young man emerged from the shadows.

I will consider them in the light of Hugo de Lamartine's book *Trapped Light*

There was nothing more. Not a word. He had ground to a halt back in April and written nothing since. Why?

It was twilight now, and the lamp beside his bed cast a circle of yellow light on *Trapped Light*, echoing the design on its cover. She picked it up and riffled the pages. Hendrix had wandered off into obscurity. Why? Because Über Professor Camber had expelled him from the University. It had been his own fault because he had not written a project, which was to be based on the book which she held in her hand. She felt sure that the book contained the reason for this. Perhaps if she understood this she might have an idea of how to answer the most important question: Where? Hendrix was out there somewhere in the night, lost, alone, perhaps injured, and she would find him. She curled up on the bed and began to read. She read half a page and fell asleep.

Her mobile phone woke her, mewling beneath her like a zombie kitten in a tiny coffin. She held it to her ear. It was Rodney. Where was she? How relieved he was to find her at home. He needed an urgent favour. Would she mind taking a taxi to the gallery? Hugo de Lamartine was on his way there now, and it was simply impossible for Rodney to be there in time to meet him. Hugo was delivering something, would she pick it up?

'I can't.' Tommy swung her legs over the side of the bed and sat up. 'I haven't got the money for the cab fare. You still owe me for the last two times I worked at the gallery, and my last cash went on travelling to and from Uni today.'

There was a silence. 'Oh dear.' Rodney's voice sounded drained of energy. 'Leave it with me and I'll come back to you.'

She was making a cup of tea when he phoned again.

'Sorted. Remember Megan, who was at the party the other night? Attractive, ethnic dress?'

'Yes.'

'If you go via her house in Knitting Knoll, she'll lend you the money for the taxi to the gallery and enough money to take it on back to your house. And she'll give you the back pay we owe you too. When you get to the gallery, Hugo will be there with that dog, you remember, the one that wandered into our do.' Rodney cleared his throat with a cough. 'Tommy, I know this is asking a lot of you, and you'll be well paid, but I'd like you to look after him for a day or so.'

'Look after Hugo?'

'No, of course not. The dog. Name's Botty.'

Since Tommy had woken up in a taxi a year before, she had acquiesced, helped out, agreed and sympathised. She had never put her own needs first. 'No,' she said, surprising herself. She explained that she knew nothing about dogs, couldn't remember ever having encountered one before the party (she had meant to shoo it out of the room with a broom but someone had interrupted her) and certainly wouldn't know where to begin looking after one.

'Oh God!' wailed Rodney. 'Speak to you soon!' And he put the phone down.

Tommy was about to drink her tea when he called back. 'Here's the plan.' He had just been speaking to Megan, he told her, who was prepared to take care of the dog, but who was at home waiting for a guest to arrive. Therefore, would Tommy mind just picking up the dog from the gallery, quickly, for Hugo would be there shortly, and take the dog round to Megan's? He assured her that Botty was a well-behaved dog and didn't bite. He'd pay her £20 for her trouble, and Megan would give her the cab fare and the back pay. Would she do it?

Worn down by the intensity of his need, Tommy agreed. She left the cup of tea half-finished upon the kitchen table and went out into the darkness to hail a cab. It looked as though it was going to rain and her hair felt lank and crumpled. The clothes she was wearing really were very old. Whatever would Mr de Lamartine think of her? There wasn't time to change. She slipped on her raincoat. It had cost her so little yet always cheered her up, reminding her as it did of those ancient stories of Sherlock Holmes.

CHAPTER 11

Voleur de nuit

IT WAS RAINING, ONE OF THOSE AUTUMN evenings that bring back to mind what winter was all about. Hugo had the dog on a lead, the dog bed and biscuits in a heavy-duty dustbin liner, the bowls and six cans of dog food in a canvas shoulder bag, and there wasn't a cab in sight. The underground train was unbearably crowded and a fat middle-aged woman shouted at him, 'Pick the dog up! Pick the dog up!' her face unpleasantly red, her teeth uneven, and her eyes clamped on his like a stage hypnotist's. So he had picked up the dog, and been forced to endure the leathery smell of its body and to remain motionless while it deposited saliva, slowly and lovingly, upon his hand. Emerging from the Underground he felt unclean.

He managed to hail a cab for the remainder of the journey. The driver insisted on dropping him at the end of Hassock Street, having approached the one-way street from the wrong end, and Hugo had been forced to wait on the pavement while the dog, rounding its back and lowering its hindquarters, crapped copiously in the gutter. He imagined the fat woman from the Tube striding up behind him and shouting *Pick it up!* and he shuddered.

He dumped the bags on the pavement. Cave Paintings was in darkness. It would have taken a stronger-willed, more rational man than Hugo not to rattle the handle on the front door. The door, of course, was locked. He looked up and down the street. There wasn't a street in the whole city that did not have someone in it at such an hour, but this one was deserted. His opinion of Tommy was reconfirmed. He had told Rodney on the phone, most emphatically, that he had an important engagement this evening to which it was not possible to bring a dog. At the realisation that, if this were indeed the case, then that stupid woman's failure to appear would now be making him late, and his appearance was not being improved by the rain, he became angrier. Rodney had promised him that Tommy would be there, and she was presumably out clubbing again.

Hugo examined the frontage of the gallery in search of a suitable protuberance. The door handle was too high up for his purposes but, almost at ground level, he found what he was looking for. A metal prong, shaped like a square mushroom, tipped with rubber and attached by a bracket, stuck out from the wall.

Hugo dragged the dog, who was in the middle of investigating an interesting smell, over to the wall, rolled up the wide legs of his trousers to protect them from the wet pavement and, squatting down, knotted the lead firmly to the doorstop.

This was a dog who had been abandoned before. He knew what shirkers of responsibility smelt like. Faced by the rolls of loose cloth on the hip of a squatting Hugo, he sank his teeth in and clung on firmly. Indeed, the strong jaw of his breed might have been given, on a whim, by a benevolent deity, precisely because of the advantage to survival such chomping ability conferred.

Hugo tugged at the dog's collar, swearing, but was not stable enough to gain purchase. So he did a foolish thing. He stood up. For a moment the dog was lifted into the air, and then the cloth of the trousers, and the cotton boxer shorts beneath, gave way, ripping like a loose sail in a wet wind and revealing the elastic waistband of the underpants, a bony hip and an expanse of white, hairy leg.

Hugo shouted out in outrage. 'You wretched little swine!' This dog deserved to be tied up and left.

And then he realised his predicament. One half of his lower body was almost completely naked. His flat in Thrombold

Street was a long, well-lit walk away, and it was pouring with rain. The street was deserted, and his only hope of finding a taxi would be to walk to the Silver Falcon Road, where he would also encounter passers-by. Cab drivers always went off to have coffee with their friends when it was raining and there was no guarantee, if he were to find one, that the driver would be willing to transport the damp and ragged street dweller that Hugo appeared to be.

'Swine, swine, swine!'

He emptied the canvas bag of its contents and, without a backwards glance at the dog, hurried along the road, clutching the flapping cloth of his trousers with one hand and loping lopsidedly through the night. No, he would not seek refuge in La Pipistrelle. He imagined the waiter turning his head away and smirking. Further along the road he came to a garden square, the garden enclosed by railings and surrounded by grand terraced houses. He passed it and came to the well-lit front steps of a police station. It was a large, red-brick, Boadicean building. Forty years ago someone like Hugo might have found assistance in such a place, but nowadays, not a chance. Just past it he came to iron railings, similar to those surrounding the park, and steps leading down to something that he would never have expected to find. It was the entrance to a public lavatory, a convenience hailing from an era that took civic responsibility seriously, and where high-minded public officials would not have dreamed of a world where urgent bodily functions had been expanded to include cottaging and needle-sharing. Presumably it still survived because it was sited right next door to a police station.

Hugo was filled with joy. Now he could get out of the rain and find some privacy to assess, and perhaps mitigate, the damage to his trousers. He trotted down the stairs and entered a large room, where green tiles were topped with a brown dado. Along one wall were cubicles, along another urinals, and a third was lined with a row of stained wash-hand basins. There was a reek of pink liquid soap, and worse. On the quarry-tiled floor, beneath the basins, was curled the sleeping form of a young man. He was obviously asleep, and not dead, because he had some form of dark jacket rolled up beneath his head, and he was snoring. He was wearing a yellowish t-shirt and grey-blue jeans. A halo of wispy hair stuck up around his head.

Hugo washed his hands with the pink soap, dripping from a dispenser, lathering them up and rubbing them together to remove all traces of dog. Then he peed in a urinal. Next he examined his trousers and concluded that they were beyond all hope of repair. It was a shame. They had fitted him in a very stylish way and he had worn them for some years. What was he going to do? He looked down at the recumbent form at his feet and had a bright idea. He would pay the obviously impoverished young man to go and find him a cab. He prodded him with a foot. The kid did not stir. Hugo kicked him. The depth of his sleep must have been extraordinarily profound for he groaned but did not wake. Hugo gazed at himself in a greasy mirror above the basins and felt shock at seeing his own pale face look back at him. What was Hugo de Lamartine doing in this place and in such a predicament? He imagined himself facing humiliation as he made his way home: hoodies mocking his exposed body, women staring. Or worse, he thought of the police station just a few paces away and the Hand of the Law upon his wrist, suggesting that his state of undress was some revolting sexual perversion. Oh, the horror! The horror!

He found himself closing the outer door. He had no means of locking it, but at least it was pulled to. He crouched over the young man and touched, with reluctance, the laces of his dirty trainers. And pulled. With a tug at the heel the trainers slipped off, revealing grubby socks. From the depth of Hugo's being stirred the ghosts of diseases past, present and yet to come, muttering to him, warning him. The legs and feet felt loose and floppy. Ignoring the inner voices, he unbuttoned the grey-blue jeans at the waist and unzipped them. They too were torn. The rips were intended and strategically placed, but all that Hugo registered was that they were in a better state than his own. He slid the jeans from their wearer. The ghosts were shocked into a horrified silence. The youngster appeared not to be as tall as he was; perhaps the jeans would be too short. He took off his own torn trousers and dropped them over the kid's bare legs. The borrowed jeans were revolting and undoubtedly smelled. He put them on with a shiver of disgust. The hems were frayed, and the jeans were probably too long for their former owner because they fitted Hugo quite well. In one of the pockets was half a pork pie wrapped in cling film and a brown plastic bottle of sleeping pills. He dumped both on the floor beside the trainers. Now he was free to escape, but he did not.

Something shifted. For a moment reality seemed lopsided, then it adjusted. In silence.

He stood with his back to the wall, hands pressed against cold tiles. Something had happened, but what? He felt as though he had been lifted by the scruff of his neck and dumped in another universe.

Sound returned. He could hear the throb of a taxi engine idling outside in the London street. London. The word *London* seemed twisted in some way and unrecognisable, yet otherwise all was normal. The dispenser still dripped soap; the kid was snoring. He murmured in his sleep, changed his position and seemed about to wake. If there were a cab outside Hugo could take it and be swiftly home. He opened the door and ran up the stairs just as the cab roared off into the night.

CHAPTER 12

Knick-knacks

DOWN HERE, SUNK IN THE RIVERBED, IT was impossible to know whether it was raining or snowing. It was always gloop and gloom. Still, the replicator had come up trumps and served Bollunk a bacon sandwich. What a treat! Crispy would have been nice, but even a bit slithery was still good.

She had just finished when Sidney reappeared. She was going to say *Well, wonder of wonders – you've only been gone twenty minutes,* but took one peep at him and didn't. He looked terrible: bedraggled, muddy, and his hair not only appeared singed but smelt so. His face was distraught. He really was in need of comfort.

'Would you like a bacon sandwich?' she asked.

Beneath their epicanthic folds, his eyes were wild. He seemed not to have heard her. 'I've done something awful.'

'What? Share it with me.'

'On my jump back I spewed up all over three thousand years in the future! I tried to wipe it off with my towel and bring it back with me . . . but it was too difficult.' He looked down at his hands, palms open, fingers turned inwards, twin dead crabs encrusted with the barnacles of time. Bollunk looked down too and wished she hadn't. The trifle wouldn't have won a prize for presentation the first time round. 'It'll be all right.'

'How do I know that? Much more likely to be a disaster. It could . . . change things.'

'Not in the future, it won't. Just think, there's probably lots of sick from our era three thousand years in the future. Tons and tons of fossilised vomit. A little bit more won't make a difference. Go and have a wash and brush-up. You'll feel much better.'

She gave him a little push. She had never seen him appear so vulnerable. She took him to the tiny cubicle which served as a bathroom. It was always a gamble; would it be working today? Unhooking a nozzle from the wall, she suctioned his hands, and then he must have pulled himself together a bit, for he snatched the nozzle from her and did it himself. 'Go away,' he said.

He returned a while later wearing a black tunic, the towel, lavender trousers and mauve t-shirt no doubt consigned to the replicator. She fetched him some chai in a pretty china cup and saucer, while he sat in his twirly chair and operated his viewscreen, fanning out his now perfectly clean hands like a weather girl showing off.

'Maybe it worked.' He panned from side to side on the viewscreen.

Bollunk noticed that the blue light and the red light were some distance apart, but both were moving swiftly in the same direction. There was a chance that they might eventually meet up at the same spot.

'Maybe it did. What happened?'

'Saw Tommy at the gallery party, and she could see me. Spoke to her, told her to go to Hudelam, or rather Hugo. She'll call him Hugo here. And she said of course.' He gulped the chai down in a mouthful. 'She was acting normally but wearing a very strange outfit, a bit like a tartan sleeping bag but with legs and arms. She looked at me and it was obvious that she knew who I was, so she can't have completely lost it. And over on the other side of the room, I saw Hudelam! It was like peering through soup, but I saw him, dressed as anybody else in that time and place would dress, in some sort of a white shirt and dark trousers.'

'No robes?' said Bollunk.

'No robes,' Sidney confirmed.

Some instinct made him turn back towards the viewscreen.

He yelped in Cantonese, *'Ayee-yaaah!'*

Bollunk's gaze followed his. Tommy's blue light and Hudelam's red light were very close together a short distance from the art gallery.

Sidney focused in. 'How far apart are they? Two, three metres?'

As they watched, Tommy's blue light suddenly sped off, leaving Hudelam far behind. Sidney let out a strangled sob, and Bollunk held his shoulders. She could feel that he was shaking and his voice, when he spoke again, was cracked.

'That was practically the most difficult thing I ever did, that time jump!'

'I know.'

'She's forgotten. Forgotten who she is and what she's supposed to be doing. She's gone native. She's positively feral!'

'It's the oestrogen,' said Bollunk. 'It rots the brain.' *But it makes people nicer too, she thought.*

It had always seemed to Bollunk that, whenever she was with Sidney, she would get nervous and say something stupid. Or perhaps he was so gripped by cabin fever from the long period of enforced idleness that any minor irritation caused him to fly into a rage. Tonight he was different. They chatted together as equals for the first time.

'Could you have warned them about the finance thingy?' asked Bollunk.

'What? The crash?'

'Yes.'

'What good would that do? No point. You couldn't pin that on one man alone. With Hudelam it was possible to do something, but there's no point in anything now.'

It seemed that their mission was over. They would go back to their era and their lives. The world would stay as it was, buggered up. The thought of going home, away from this cramped bubble of air lodged in the mud, filled them both with a sense of failure, yet with a certain calm. Bollunk lit some candles in the hearth of the rococo fireplace and switched on a standard lamp. The light emerging from the fringed velvet lampshade gave the room a warm glow. They shared a bottle of wine and Sidney ate a bacon sandwich.

'What brought you to England and made you care about it so much? It must seem such a dull little place compared with where you grew up!' Bollunk topped up his wine glass.

'Dull? Gracious no. Certainly it is a little cramped compared with the vastness of China and Mother Russia, although Honshu, too, is compact, but I came here when I was six on a school exchange programme and fell in love with the country and the language.' His eyes gazed into the distant depths of the crewelwork on the antimacassar of his twirly chair and his voice softened. 'This little blob, this small grey drift of urban paradise set in the very confluence of worldwide aviation routes! How could I bear to stand aside and see it slowly submerge in a sea of misbegotten ideas? I dreamed of helping it develop into a better place, and when time travel arrived it seemed to offer the means. That dream led to us, sitting here tonight. But I had other ideas too, like setting up a company using slipstreams for ecotourism.'

'How clever! The ultimate hands-off tourist experience! But what would you dream of having for yourself? Where would you live?'

'I've always wanted to have a house in the *Gemütlichkeit* of suburbia, with a garden.'

'And what would you have in that house to make you happy? Children perhaps?'

Sidney rubbed a bruise on his cheek and gave the matter some thought.

'My personal happiness doesn't matter so much, and no, I don't think I'm cut out to have children, but there is something I've always wanted. I've read about people being allowed to own dogs, not just look at them in zoos. Apparently you could throw a stick in a pond, and the dog would jump in and bring it back to you. I'd like to have a dog of my own. And also, from an intellectual point of view, the old game of football seems of interest. And my own rifle range would be nice too. And you? What would you wish for?'

Bollunk found herself rubbing her own cheek in the very same place. She could see he was tired: it made him seem more human somehow. She thought for a moment. What she wanted was a proper relationship with a man. Sex, love, everything. People always assumed that because she had a daughter, she'd had a past. Yet she hadn't. Not really. But she wasn't going to say all that to Sidney, so she replied, 'I'd like to have a place of my own back home. Not live with my mother. I'd have comfortable things in it and, what did they used to call them? Knick-knacks. It would be nice to have some knick-knacks. And more of a life of my own. Not be weighed down all the time by my daughter's problems.'

'What's her name?'

'Dorcas.'

'You must miss her.'

'Yeah. Sometimes.'

'Tommy must . . .' He stopped. The wild look came back into his eyes. 'Stupid! Stupid! Stupid! We can't pack up and go home. What am I going to do about Tommy?'

She must have suffered horribly from homesickness and loneliness, thought Bollunk. She had never got to grips with her mission. Perhaps it was true that her brain had been scrambled. It was possible that, without intervention, she would carry on living out her life in the right place at the wrong time. 'Yes, Tommy's a problem.'

'We need to get her back,' said Sidney.

'What'd happen if she were to stay back there for a lifetime? Would it change the world in some way we hadn't intended?'

'It's unlikely. My vomiting over the future is potentially more important.'

'Why? How do you know that?'

'We worked it out. I say we – but of course it wasn't me. We found two physicists, bright guys, yet approachable. You've probably heard of them: Banks and Bridgewater.'

'The men who built the distraction field?'

'Indeed. They invented that and much more besides. Weird stuff.'

Sidney told her how the two young scientists had spent months, cooped up in a wine cellar, extrapolating data from P. Brockworth. They had sent probes to the past, carried out experiments, like sending stable manure back through time to see if it became unstable. They concluded that there were forces operating in the past which counteracted changes that were too radical. Too big a change induced a form of negative feedback, which bounced backwards and forwards in time and then cancelled the act that had caused problems. Sidney gave the example of a time traveller to the past trying to stab someone. Nobody knew for certain, but the knife would probably shatter before the act could be completed. But if you tried to stab someone who was going to die anyway, you'd probably be successful.

'We can change small stuff in the past that isn't going to happen anyway?'

'Indeed, we can tweak the tweakable. We can bolster relationships, alter the climate of opinions. We can't prevent wars; they have roots that go back too deeply in time. But in the future it's different. There we have the power to change everything.' He explained that Banks and Bridgewater discovered something that frightened them. They theorised that time travel to the future was dangerous. It could break down symmetry. A physical entity that originated in the future, went to the past and then returned to the future, caused no problems; but one brought straight from the past which remained in the future for more than ten minutes or so could send vibrations back into the past that were not controllable. A wave of change might seep back in time, from the future through to the present, perhaps causing bizarre changes. Maybe even change on a vast scale.

'There are changes – quantum leaps, perhaps, so infinitesimally tiny that they cannot be sensed – that mushroom briefly into awareness, then pass away into realms too vast for humankind to perceive. Like a tiny child put in front of an elephant and being quite unable to see it. We only see stuff in such a narrow range.' He glanced towards the porthole. 'Nothing's changed, has it?'

'No. Still the same shades of grey.'

'How many bacteria are there in vomit, do you think?'

'Well, it's only food and stomach acid. I'm sure there isn't anything alive in vomit at all.' Bollunk pointed at the viewscreen. 'It's still the same old world out there.'

They watched. Panning out to a larger scale, they saw that Tommy was back in her flat and Hudelam in his. It did, indeed, seem to be the same old world. 'There's one last thing we could try,' said Bollunk.

'And what would that be?'

'Me. I could go. Maybe I could help Tommy out with her mission, and then I could bring her back.'

Sidney began to laugh. 'Bollunk saves the world.'

'My name's Posy.'

'Hah! Posy! Posy Bollunk neutralises Hudelam and saves the world.'

'And why not?'

'Because you have to do backwards and forwards jumps to coincide with Tommy, and Posy Bollunk's body, spread for eternity over all the future, would probably create enough nasties to wipe the planet clean. Thanks for the offer, my girl, but it's a tough time continuum out there, not a playground for practising bunny hops.'

He belittled her. It hurt.

'I've better things to do with my time than waste it talking to you!' She spun on her heel and marched off to her tiny sleeping place. Suddenly there was no better thought than being as far away as possible from Sidney Ng. Aargh! But why let him get to her? She lay on her bed, breathing out and holding her lungs empty for a minute or two to calm herself. For all his air of superiority, there was something that they never talked about: Sidney had entrusted the mission to Tommy, while he could only sit and watch. Tommy had lived in the past for over a year, yet Sidney had barely managed a few minutes. There really was something dangerous and physical that a woman could do better than a man, apart from having babies, extreme ironing and sailing round the world single-handedly. A woman could time-travel! And Sidney knew that.

By the morning he would have some of his confidence back and would realise that they had an alternative to scuttling back home, defeated, and that she, Posy Bollunk, was their last hope. He would have to train her to time jump, fill her in on the details of Tommy's mission, brief her on Hudelam. A huge dose of the same hormone that enabled her to multitask at home, and had brought her to this river bottom, would send her twanging back and forth in a bungee-jump through the ages. How she longed for freedom, dry air and sleek hair, room to walk and space to dance, away from the confines of this watery prison that reminded her so much of her schooldays.

How exciting. She was going to London.

SECTION TWO

London

CHAPTER 13

Is she on something?

THERE IT WAS! TOMMY DID NOT KNOW why the taxi driver had had so much difficulty finding the right street. Outside the gallery she could see a bin bag, some bowls and tin cans piled higgledy-piggledy on the pavement; but where, oh where, had that odd little animal gone? A lead tied to a doorstop trailed on the wet pavement. Attached to the lead was a collar with its buckle undone. She looked up and down the street but could see no sign of the dog. She untied the lead and picked up the bowls and cans. She piled the soaking bin liner with everything in it, the feeding bowls and the cans, into the back of the taxi.

'Would you mind driving down the road a bit. I'm looking for a lost animal. A dog.'

She walked down the road with the cab slowly following her. 'Botty! Botty!' she called, even though she doubted the ability of a mere dog to recognise its name. It was raining heavily and she was glad of her raincoat. She came to a police station. (She remembered how they'd jeered at her on the phone. No help there, for sure.) Past the police station there were some steps leading down to a men's lavatory. GENTLEMEN said an optimistic sign above the door. Something about those steps, the worn stone, the way they curved and led downwards, encircling gloom, seemed to lure her. Perhaps the dog had gone down them. There was presumably no need of a law to stop women going into Gents' loos, as they have a powerful instinct to keep well away from such places. Tommy was going to have to overcome that instinct to force herself to descend the steps. What if someone else, apart from the dog, was down there? She swallowed and placed one foot on the first step.

'I'm off if you go down there.' The cabbie had emerged from his vehicle and was waving a fist at her.

'Why?'

'Cos there's monsters down there, and I'm not gonna spend the rest of the evening next door in that station giving a statement. You'd be better off ringing the dogs' home than wandering round the streets in the rain!'

She could pay him off, but then he would go and she would be alone in this empty street. She looked once again at the steps. The door of the lavatory was pulled to. It was painted sage green, and the top half was windowed with obscured glass. A light was shining within. It beckoned like the maw of hell. But Tommy felt that going down to that Gents was necessary.

Then something happened, as though the world were a television and someone had changed channels. A shift. A smell in the air like chlorine. She almost lost her balance.

Tommy had never had a migraine before but there was always a first time. The taxi seemed a safe haven. She staggered back to it and climbed in.

'Where d'you wanna go?' asked the cabbie.

'I don't know. Anywhere. Um . . . Knitting Knoll,' she said.

'And I'm a big blue elf,' he said. 'Do you wanna stop at 221B Baker Street on the way?'

When she gave him the address, Blindhome Half Moon Street, he began to lose his bantering tone and his voice had an edge to it. He thought she was unhinged. Feeling that he might be right – there was something worse amiss than a migraine – she called Megan on her mobile and checked the address. The street name was completely different. That settled it. This was some severe psychosis. 'Blenheim Crescent,' she told him.

'Oh, I get it, very funny. Notting Hill it is then.'

She leaned back in the big leather seat and began to feel more herself again. The rain was easing off now, and the street lamps and shop lights reflected off the wet streets. It was Friday night, some people had gone off to the countryside, others had poured into London, from the suburbs, from abroad on city breaks. Workers had gone from offices to pubs, restaurants and cinemas, and youth was out and about seeking affray. The city was always a wonder to Tommy. She was familiar with the bones of it, knew her way around, yet it had always seemed strange to her, too bright, too loud, too in your face. And now, all of a sudden, the air smelt different and she felt as though the street names were unreal. Notting Hill sounded right though. What was it that she thought it was called?

She fingered the dog lead and the sad little collar. No dog could have undone the buckle of the collar, yet surely a thief would not have taken the dog and left his collar behind. She hadn't said anything to Megan on the phone about his being missing; she would prefer to be around when Rodney and Wilfred were informed.

'No dog!' said Megan, leading her into the house. 'Just as well, really, I would only have got emotionally involved. Hope he's found his way back home. But what a bastard, eh? That de Lamartine, not bothering to wait till you got there. Why didn't he call you on his mobile?'

'He doesn't have one.'

Tommy had an inner certainty that she had never before seen such a beautiful house. Megan explained that she was looking after it for a friend of a relative. Megan was looking gorgeous in an orange shift dress; she was going out for the evening with Terence; a first date, she said. Megan phoned Rodney and Wilfred, and Tommy told them her tale. There was much hoo-ing, haa-ing and conjecture. There didn't seem to be anything that anybody could or ought to do. Tommy drank a cup of coffee and hesitated to accept the proffered back pay and the taxi money, which was really too much, she could take the Tube home, but Megan insisted. Rodney and Wilfred could afford it.

Back on the street Tommy did not go to the Tube station or take a taxi. She feared a plethora of confusing names, and where would she tell the taxi driver to go on this strange, upside-down evening? She could ring Paintstripper and ask where it was exactly that they lived. That didn't seem to be a good idea, so she walked.

The streets were full of self-assured people, who appeared to know who they were and where they lived, where they had been and where they were going. She was assailed by the smells of foods she could not name, together with a tang of autumn like burning leaves. She wove in and out of the Friday evening crowds, crossed roads, dodged cars and, by the time she had reached Harrods, her confusion seemed a mental aberration that had now gone away, leaving her relieved to be back in familiar Hans Place. She would kick off her shoes, sink into a sofa and watch Paintstripper's Friday night dross. As Tommy's key turned in the lock, Paintstripper opened the door.

'Shush,' she said. 'I've put her in Hendrix's bed. She's been asleep for an hour and a half,' and as an afterthought, 'It's your old friend Posy. She was in a dreadful state, white as a ghost, shaking. I gave her a beer, but she couldn't keep it down, so I put her to bed.'

Tommy followed her into the kitchen. Not being aware that she had any old friends, she thought it best to seek more information. 'How did she get here?'

'The woman upstairs brought her down. Found her in her sitting room. Seems she had gone up there by mistake. I don't like to ask, but is she on something? I mean, is she the type to be on something?'

'No, I'm sure she isn't,' said Tommy, on the assumption that this was likely to be the right answer. 'I'll go and check on her.'

The woman was curled up in the grubbiness (Tommy feared) of Hendrix's bed. She had long, dark, frizzy hair and a face that seemed rather exotic. Her skin was blotchy. Tommy could not recall ever having seen her before. She was taking quiet breaths of deep sleep. Tommy sat down at Hendrix's desk and thought. Perhaps the woman was a burglar who had been caught in the act of doing over the upstairs flat; yet she had known Tommy's name (presumably) and where she lived. So, maybe she was indeed an old friend, in which case she would know a lot more about Tommy than Tommy knew about herself, which was both exciting and disquieting. Still, she could not help but feel resentment that the wrong person was sleeping in Hendrix's bed and wished the woman would wake up. There was nothing to be done but wait.

She went into the kitchen, cleaned up a bit and made a cheese sandwich. Tommy could hear that Paintstripper was in Tommy's bedroom and, from the sound of it, well into the dross. She took the sandwich and the copy of *Trapped Light* with her, sat at Hendrix's desk, ignored the snores and began to eat and read.

The sandwich was hard, dry and indigestible. The book was wordy, chasing impossibly difficult concepts, but the feel of the words seemed familiar, lulling her into a state of pliancy in which the ideas of meaning or development of thought no longer had any relevance. Life was like that. Some people were academic and had strings of letters after their names, while someone like her struggled to find something she was good at. Hugo de Lamartine inhabited a very different world from Tommy. She presumed that Hendrix, with his instinctive grasp of photography, would find the book easier. There were some illustrations, plates of black-and-white photographs. One appeared to be of the back of a garage; there were pictures of unsmiling people who looked like they had been dead a long time. They were wearing old-fashioned clothes, or their faces were all swollen, or their bodies had bits of bones sticking out. Not surprising they weren't smiling, really.

The woman in the bed made a sound like 'Aaaaragh ermph ermph', and turned over. Tommy was very tired, but she wished she could clean something. She looked at Hendrix's photographs covering the walls and decided they were much nicer than the ones in the book.

The woman turned over again, sat up and said, 'Hello, Tommy.' Seeing that Tommy was in some difficulty, she added, 'I'm Posy Bollunk. We had a cup of coffee together once.'

Tommy hesitated, then asked, 'Where was that? Remind me. Was it at the University?'

Posy looked weak. Tommy picked up a glass of water from the suitcase beside the bed and handed it to her. Posy drank it all, then looked directly at her and said, 'No, it was a long long time after you came to the University. Does that give you a clue?'

Tommy had spent the entire day grappling with the inexplicable. She had had enough. Her expression must have conveyed this to Posy, who added, 'I've come to help you.'

Tommy could hear the sincerity behind the words. 'I'm grateful. I need help badly. Will you help me look for Hendrix? He's gone missing, and I'm desperately worried about him. Oh, I'm sorry. You're not in any state to be helping anyone. You're not well.'

Posy pushed back the covers and swung her feet onto the floor. She was wearing a green tunic and looked like a surgeon about to perform an operation after a night of serious partying. She assured Tommy that she was feeling much better. A change of clothes would help.

'Let me see,' said Tommy, as Posy stood up. 'I'm bound to have something I could shorten for you.'

In Tommy's bedroom, Paintstripper was sprawled on the sofa. She heaved her bulk upright and turned off the television. 'Load of dross,' she said. 'I'll go and make some tea.' Tommy looked through her wardrobe for something suitable. Posy was staring at the poster on the wall.

'Where did you find this?' The tone of her voice suggested that she was looking at something much more interesting than a poster.

Tommy explained that the poster was a gift from her friend and that she didn't know the guy's name, but he was the lead singer of Splintered Dick.

'Really? Are you sure?'

'Of course. That picture was taken at Glastonbury a couple of years ago. It says so at the bottom.'

'So it does. Wow! What a weird coincidence,' said Posy. 'I know this guy's double – well, almost, the eyes should be grey, not brown – his name's Sidney Ng and he's a bit of a genius.'

Tommy realised that there must be a connection with her strange vision of the singer at the gallery, but the name meant nothing to her. She felt that she was being studied very carefully. She picked out a dress from the wardrobe and asked if Posy wore pink.

The three women sat at the kitchen table. Posy was wearing a white t-shirt and some jeans with the legs rolled up, and was feeling much better. She looked better too; indeed, now that she was no longer wearing a shapeless tunic it could be seen that she had a waist. Paintstripper had made mugs of tea and had given Posy a cheese sandwich. Posy concentrated on the sandwich – she had not realised how hungry she was – then leaned back in her chair and looked at Tommy and Paintstripper. Tommy looked at Posy and Paintstripper. Nobody said a word. Explanations hung unspoken in the air. Finally Posy said, 'I understand that Tommy has experienced a loss.'

'Yes,' said Tommy, 'I lost a dog tonight. I was supposed to collect it at an art gallery, but it had been left by the man who was supposed to be delivering it and either someone stole it or it ran away.'

'Oh, how unusual! A dog! I didn't realise Hendrix was a dog!' said Posy.

'No, Hendrix is my friend, our flatmate, I . . . we've lost him too. Those are his jeans and t-shirt you're wearing.'

'Tommy's lost everything, including her memory,' commented Paintstripper in a matter-of-fact voice.

'You knew!' Tommy turned to face Paintstripper. 'That's amazing. How long have you known?'

'Since pretty early on, actually. I've never met anyone of your age who didn't rabbit on about her life. It was quite restful. So presumably you two will have a lot to talk about. I'm tired. You can tell me what you want me to know in the morning. Nice to meet you, Posy. G'night.' She lumbered off to bed carrying a bottle of beer and the bottle opener, leaving Tommy to confront the sibyl in jeans before her.

Here was the person who had the keys to all the locked boxes. Someone who could tell Tommy who she was, where she came from, why she was here in London studying for an Art degree, and someone who could solve the mystery about the lead singer of Splintered Dick. So much to be revealed. Part of her was desperate to know, but another part of her was too tired and didn't care. Posy must have realised this for she said, 'It's late, it's a long story, and I think at the moment I'm too tired to get it right. What day is this?'

It seemed to Tommy an odd question. 'Friday.'

'Good. So tomorrow's Saturday. You won't have to go to University. I want to take you for a trip across London. I'll tell you everything and, when I have, I think you'll be much happier. But if you really want me to tell you now, we can sit up all night talking.'

'No, I don't want you to tell me tonight. I'm going to get you some fresh sheets from the airing cupboard and make up Hendrix's bed for you. Those sheets have probably been on his bed since the beginning of term.'

'I don't give a half-groat from the Gathered Isles about the sheets,' said Posy. 'I'm incredibly stiff and sore for some reason.' She moved her legs about as though shifting knicker elastic. 'How very oddish.' She frowned and then shrugged. 'All I care about is having a good night's sleep and waking up to daylight. I'm really looking forward to seeing proper daylight.'

CHAPTER 14

The blue that doesn't have a name

HUGO WAS RELIEVED THAT THE SUN HAD set on a pretty horrendous day. He always found night-time comforting and it was a joy to be home. He anticipated a quiet supper and an evening spent doing a crossword or two. He took the jeans off as soon as he got through the front door, tied them very tightly in a rubbish bag and put them in the bin in the kitchen. Then he had a bath. He was certain that there was still a whiff of dog in the bathroom. He downloaded his e-mails while rubbing his hair with a towel. As usual there was a message from Nigel. Translating from the proto-Indo-European as he went along, Hugo read it aloud:

> Deer Hugo,
>
> You have a grate sens of humer. When we get together you must explane what you ment in your emale as i dident get all of it.
>
> Ravindar Bart is offring to pay in cash. Wow. Yippee. So i think youd be wize to keep her happy and give her wot she wants which is of coarse your book writen in french.
>
> I am tole their is a lot of french in english so it shuddent be difficult.
>
> May be Proff Camber will help if you are stuck.
>
> c u latur alley gate ur
> Nigel
> www.molesworthmentoring.com

Hugo replied quickly, informing Nigel that the book was being translated even at this very moment as his words were bouncing through the ether. He instructed Nigel to make sure to inform Ravinder Bhatt that the book would be with her *tout de suite*, on the double, not later than the beginning of the coming week.

As he was clicking on *send* another e-mail pinged into his inbox. It was from Professor Amphelisia Camber and read simply, *I was wondering if you were at home tonight? I seem to have mislaid your telephone number. Perhaps you would care to ring me on my mobile.* The number followed.

The effect on Hugo was like a blast of caffeine to the bloodstream. Her voice, when she answered his call, was inch-deep in soft coffee grounds, its richness a product of middle age and years of nicotine.

'Such a *long time* since we've enjoyed a chat! And how is your book selling?'

'Indeed, yes. Quite well.' His bare feet wanted to bounce on the carpet.

'What would you say to a walk in the park tomorrow morning?'

'Tomorrow morning? In the park? A walk? Well, yes. Of course. What a good idea!'

Camber suggested a suitable meeting place.

It is not usual for a youngish man to be set afire by a not particularly attractive woman more than twenty years his senior, but Camber had changed his life.

It was a year ago that he had been summoned to her office at the University of Artistry and Design. Although Mrs Struddlewick, the secretary, had been a friendly enough nonentity, Hugo was aware upon entering Camber's office, two windows of which extended from floor to ceiling and looked down on a bleak winter campus, that he was in the inner sanctum of a daunting presence. The room was vast, yet there was nothing in it beyond two curving chairs and a glass coffee table. Professor Camber, a tall figure, clad in a garment that Hugo's eyes registered as flowing, avant-garde and curiously lopsided, was sitting on one of the chairs smoking a cigarette. She beckoned Hugo to the adjacent chair. On the coffee table was a glass ashtray with a revolving circular top that whisked butt ends away to oblivion, and a copy of *Trapped Light*.

'This,' said Camber in her thrilling voice, picking it up, 'is a most extraordinary book.'

'It's very kind of you to say so.'

She flipped over the pages with fingers that seemed stubby for such a long-limbed person. Her nails, too, were short and painted dark red. She peered from beneath Gothic brows at Hugo and maintained a silence which would have sent lesser souls quite mad in an attempt to end it.

Eventually she spoke again. 'I can use this book.'

And that was all! The details had been arranged between Mrs Struddlewick and Nigel. There had been a new print run. A contract. Every student from then on taking the photography course had a fresh new copy, the cost of which was deducted from their academic fees, and for a paperback it was horribly expensive. From that moment there had also been a steady demand for copies from Universities in the United States, and it became one of the few international academic texts permitted entrance to the Democratic People's Republic of Korea.

The income from the book was not enough for Hugo to give up his day job, but it removed the need to budget carefully. The intangible benefits were much more attractive. Being a writer for one – and there were all sorts of writers, all the way from those who dissect the individual cells of a philosophy through to those hackers and bodgers of the writing world, the novelists. Hugo had read a few novels and found them to belong to one of two camps: they were either tediously simplistic or wearyingly overcomplicated. Hugo knew that the book he had written was more valuable than a novel and worth much, much more than an academic textbook. It was a Guardian of a Portal. Nobody could be thought to know anything about photography without having read it. It offered a key to the kingdom of the cognoscenti. Placed on a bookshelf it denoted Culture, and in passing reference it indicated Learning. As the man behind the book, Hugo embodied the conspiracy of academics and the zenith of intellectual achievement. With all this in mind, Hugo had been out to the shops that week and bought a jacket.

He padded over to his cupboard, slid open a veneered door, and revealed the jacket hanging unjostled by other garments and protected by its own cocoon of navy blue plastic. He unzipped the carrier (which was emblazoned with the words Ettore Stuzzicadenti) and there was the jacket! It was cashmere, with a thread of something silken running through it. It was the sort of blue for which Hugo did not have a name. He put it on, went into the bathroom, came back, fetched a chair, went back to the bathroom, stood on the chair and found that, if he moved up and down whilst bending his knees, over time he could see all of the jacket and it was truly wonderful. But more important was what it felt like: soft to the touch, mimicking every movement like a shadow.

He had bought it intending it to be the jacket he would wear at some celebration of the Arts, when for the first time he was reading out in public a longish excerpt from *Trapped Light*. However, in the brightness of a spotlight in the centre of his bathroom ceiling, Hugo could see that it was the ideal jacket to be worn for a brisk walk in the autumn air. It would reflect light from the sunshine. Young ladies out riding would turn to admire it. Older men walking gun dogs would notice and approve. And Professor Camber? Why, she would expect nothing less of him.

CHAPTER 15

Tommy and Posy don't commit suicide

'HOLD ON TO THE SIDES WITH BOTH HANDS,' shouted Posy.

'I feel a complete idiot!' said Tommy.

It was early morning, and the traffic was up and about but not moving very quickly. The drivers were backed up as though it were a weekday, and they had nothing better to do than stare at the two young women, who were indeed looking very conspicuous standing in the middle of the bridge. Ha! Would-be suicides! At least the drivers really, really hoped that they were. Anyone that stupid deserved to die. Couldn't they find a better place to do it than Wandsworth Bridge, the most prosaic bridge in the whole of London?

'OK, look down at the river!'

Tommy looked down over the painted-metal sides of the bridge at the Thames, and noticed that dark clouds were definitely gathering and this rain wasn't going to stop any time soon.

'And again!'

On the other hand, the seagulls were quite happy wheeling about in the sky looking for someone to dive-bomb.

'You couldn't do it, could you?' Posy sounded smug. 'It's quite impossible, isn't it?'

Tommy had a third try at keeping her gaze fixed downwards, wiped a raindrop from her eye and was forced to agree with her. 'It makes my neck hurt looking downwards.'

'You remember your poster of Spikey Dick?'

Perhaps Posy was unbalanced, in which case Tommy needed to extricate herself from the relationship with some skill; in the meantime it would be wise to humour her. 'Splintered Dick.'

'Oh yes. Well, as I mentioned last night, the guy who looks so like that singer is Sidney Ng. I know him quite well.'

This was something Tommy had been thinking about overnight and her interest was piqued. She nodded for Posy to continue.

'At this very moment, he's sitting in something a bit like a submarine called a slipstreamer. It's just down there, at the bottom of the river. He'll be jumping up and down with excitement, because he can see two lights on his viewscreen that mean that you're here and that I'm with you. He'll be so happy! So . . .'

'It's raining. Can we go now?' The woman was mad and Tommy needed to be searching for Hendrix, not wasting time here.

'Just be patient with me a moment longer. Where's that mirror I asked you to bring? Now, turn your back to the river. Hold the mirror up. Look at the river. Nothing? Let me do it. Like this. You'll have to hold it a bit higher 'cos you're taller. Aim it at the river. Up a bit.'

Tommy screamed. 'It's a whale!' She couldn't see clearly as the looking glass was small. The river was grey and rather choppy, but underneath, its outlines moving and zigzagging when reflected by the water, was a black lozenge shape. She whirled around to look at it without the mirror and wiped more raindrops from her eyes. 'What is it? What's it got to do with me?'

'It's nothing to be frightened about.' Posy took her arm. 'Why don't we find somewhere to sit down and have a cup of tea?'

They walked back the way they had come, to the huge disappointment of the passing drivers.

They trudged awhile in the rain, before finding a café that didn't look threatening and was largely empty. It was a small place called Omega 3 Spoon, offering cooked vegetarian breakfasts. They ordered two cups of jasmine and ginger green tea. Tommy took off her Sherlock Holmes raincoat, revealing what could only have been a school uniform, once, in a less self-conscious age than this.

'Just take the submarine thing on trust,' said Posy. 'I'll give you a full explanation in a minute. Let me tell you the whole story, and then you can ask as many questions as you like.'

Posy explained that Sidney was Tommy's boss. He had trained her for an important mission and somehow the strain of her journey to London had taken away her memory. At some point, hearing about who she was and why she was here, everything might click back into place and Tommy's memory would return. Tommy nodded and held her tongue.

'There's a man living in this city who is about to write a book, a very dangerous book. Your mission is to get to know him, become his friend and stop him writing it.'

Tommy decided that now would be a good time to point out a major inconsistency that appeared not to have occurred to Posy. 'How do you know that it is going to be a dangerous book if he hasn't written it yet?'

'That's a very good question. Take a deep breath. We're not from this time, you and I. We're from the future.' She took hold of Tommy's reluctant hands and gripped them firmly. 'We come from London, but it's a different London, sixty years in the future. You and I met only once, and I don't know you very well. We had a cup of coffee. I told you about my life and my daughter, Dorcas, and you told me about you.' Tommy tried to pull away but Posy held on tightly. 'Like me, you don't have a relationship with a man at the moment. You live in a large house in Putney with lots of other women. You have a little boy. I've forgotten his name. You showed me a picture. He has cute wispy hair sticking up around his head. His name is . . . Harvey? Harry?' She was obviously hoping for a reaction and wasn't getting one. And then she spoke with more confidence: 'Henry!'

'Henry!' Tommy lifted both hands to her face, as though imitating a figure standing on a bridge in a painting. 'Henry! Henry! Henry!' She let out a sob, then a wail of anguish. 'My baby! My son!' Her body shook. She made as if to stand up but sat down again when Posy patted her arm, restraining her. 'I need to get back to my little boy. I told him I'd be back for supper time. I promised him!'

The world seemed to be spinning, as her sense of who she was hurtled forwards and backwards in time. Images appeared in procession, a wrinkled newborn, a toddler plodding across a room, a little boy asleep in sunlight. His voice. *Mummy, where are you?* 'Oh God. He's not even born yet. He's how many years away?'

'How old is he?'

'Five.'

'Fifty-five till he's born.'

'Fifty-five years away!' She buried her face in her arms on the table and cried as though she were a small child herself.

Posy held on to one of Tommy's shoulders to anchor her to some sort of reality. She reassured her that she would be back in time for supper. She could be down here for years, yet still be home again in time. Her little boy would never know that she had been so far away.

'That's why we do this job. Remember, childcare is forbidden where we come from and mums have to stay with their kids if they can't afford boarding school. We can only work when they're at school. That's why we time-travel, Tommy. It's one of those rare jobs. It's well paid and fits in with a short day and school holidays.'

Tommy thought about Henry. How could she have forgotten? Memories of her child flooded back. The last time she had seen him, she had kept hugging him and saying *be a good boy,* until he became annoyed with her. She had wanted to remember every last detail of how he looked; and he had said, *Why do you keep on looking at me? I'm going to school now, OK?* She thought of his hair. Henry. So like Hendrix. That was it! Losing Hendrix had been losing her child all over again. She wanted Henry back. She wanted Hendrix too. She wanted them both.

She unzipped her red bag, searched in a side pocket and withdrew a tiny red and yellow toy train engine. She showed it

to Posy, caressed it with her fingers for some minutes and then put it away again.

The two women needed a trip to the loo. There was only one and it was cramped. They took turns. Afterwards Tommy washed her face and dried it with the hem of her skirt. Posy too ignored the hot air blower, as women always do, and dried her hands with loo paper which broke into little bits and stuck all over her fingers. They held on to each other and hugged. It felt good to both of them to be in the same boat, to be understood. They were both mothers adrift in time. They returned to their table and ordered more tea.

'My grandparents must be alive not too far away.' Tommy sipped her tea. 'Two of them never went outside their front door, and the others were a mean pair. Hope I don't bump into them.'

'My mother's parents would be in Africa still. Pity. I'm told they were amazing. But my father's parents are in Cambridge. They were kind when my dad left home. Is there any reason why I shouldn't get in touch?'

'I've a vague memory that Sidney made me sign a piece of paper. I think that's one of the things we're not allowed to do.'

'Huh. So even he makes mistakes. He forgot to tell me that. It's probably wise.' Posy sighed.

'So we need to get this writer guy sorted out, so we can get back home.'

'That's right.'

'I was supposed to have met him and latched onto him. I've been down here for over a year and didn't remember what I was supposed to be doing. That's why you're here?'

Posy nodded.

'I'm so sorry! I've let everyone down. How twattily twerpish I've been. I can say twerpish now. You say it too, don't you? The memories are still hazy. I can't remember why his book is dangerous.'

Posy explained that, in itself, the book would not have been dangerous. It was a sort of bible of art and design and how life should be lived. Nobody had paid much attention when it was first published. Then it became one of those books that seemed to pop up on search engines when you were looking for something else. People quoted it. It was memorable and full of sonorous phrases. They laughed at some of its more bizarre strictures. But over the years, somehow, it had caught on and, insidiously, it had/would have a huge effect on the way everyone, in the latter half of the 21st century, would be forced to live their lives.

Tommy slipped a packet of pink pills out of her bag and took three. Posy did the same, swallowing them down with the dregs of her tea.

'They help, don't they? I get a tight feeling in my head and begin to feel insubstantial, then I take one of these and suddenly everything's better. What's this writer's name?'

'His name is Hugo de Lamartine and he'll become Hudelam.'

'Of course! He's the one who left the dog in the rain. I met him at a party at an art gallery on Thursday, and he isn't about to write a book, he's already written it!'

'What?' Posy's dark eyebrows lifted. 'He's written it? Already?'

'Yes. There's a copy back in the flat. It's called *Trapped Light*. It's a University textbook. I read some of it yesterday while I was waiting for you to wake up.'

'The name must have changed. We know it as the *Book of Hudelam*.' Posy leaped to her feet, walked from table to table, running her fingers over tables and chairs as she went as though seeking to touch something real, then stood motionless, staring out of the glass front of the café deep in thought. She turned around, walked back to the table, sat down heavily and sighed. 'The mission's over. We've failed. It's too late.'

'And it's all my fault. I remember now. Of course, the *Book of Hudelam*. He's Hudelam! Goodness gracious. How very oddish!' She remembered her mother taking her, a small unwilling child, to see the vast marble tomb of Hudelam.

Posy pointed out that it would have taken longer than a year for the book to be written, published and adopted as a textbook. It had undoubtedly already been too late when Tommy first arrived. Somebody had messed up with the time charts. Sidney had been sitting waiting at the bottom of the river in a slipstreamer for over a year, and it had all been a waste of time. Poor Sidney. He'd even taken pink pills and made himself ill time-jumping further back in a pointless attempt to meet with Tommy.

'He tried to meet me?'

'Yes.'

'Wearing mauve trousers and a t-shirt and carrying a towel?'

'That's right.'

'Yeah, I saw him at the gallery. Just for an instant. I thought I was dreaming. He looks exactly like the lead singer of Splintered Dick.'

'Except for the colour of the eyes,' said Posy. 'They probably wouldn't be so alike if we saw them, side by side, in the flesh. But still it's strange. It's the sort of meaningless coincidence you'd never find in a novel, only in life.'

'And the singer's clothes were different too. Certainly not mauve. And Sidney never wore clothes like that when I knew him. He was always in full combat gear when he was training me.'

Tommy remembered Sidney teaching her to time-jump. It had involved something called *supercoherence*. Atoms deep in the mind latched onto the ellipses of a time chart, and connected with the ghosts of atoms that existed *somewhen*, years before, and followed the path of those atoms throughout the times, past and future, when humans were and will be. It was awfully complicated. She didn't understand it, but something in her, pumped with hormone, had. Her mind still shied away from remembering the horror of that jump. She looked at Posy, who seemed calm and composed.

'How come you time-jumped yet haven't suffered like I did? And you seem to have made yourself at home here so quickly.'

'The jump was horrible, I think. Perhaps my memory is blocked a little too; but no, it didn't scare me too much.

Maybe it's because I've spent most of my life reading and daydreaming. I read anything, even strange stuff. It does prepare you for things.'

'Where do we go from here?'

'We'll go home.' Posy did not appear happy at the idea. 'We'll send a message to the Conspiracy that we're ready to leave and need instructions for the jump. All we have to do is put an ad in *New Woman Scientist* magazine.'

'Of course. I'm remembering bits now. And we get a reply through . . .'

'Your solicitors, Burton and Crump.'

Tommy remembered. It was all coming back. There was a traveller who regularly called in to the 19th century on her way to the Hundred Years' War. She would leave the Conspiracy's reply to their *New Woman Scientist* ad with Burton and Crump.

Posy added, 'Presumably you didn't get all the other letters we sent you?'

'No,' said Tommy. 'Bloody lawyers.'

On the journey home neither of them said much. Tommy kept a lookout for Hendrix. Posy was fascinated by the strange world around her, the city streets and the people on the Underground.

'Wow! The clothes! And they have dogs here too! Aren't they afraid of them? And so many cars. Why do they need so many cars? And the river was practically empty. But what a stink! The air's polluted! It's all so *wild and individual!* And the streets aren't flooded!'

Tommy was busy gathering and re-examining the memories of her lifetime. The need to get away from the pointlessness of her art course, and back to being a mother to her son, was an urgent and intense compulsion. But there was still the problem of Hendrix. He was missing and in need of her help. She couldn't waltz back to the future and forget all about him. It would not affect Henry and Dorcas if they were to stay on a little bit longer.

Posy did not need much persuading to give the proposal

that they delay their jump and continue searching for Hendrix her serious consideration. They discussed the pros and cons in whispers, nervous of being overheard by passers-by. There was a problem. Sidney. He would be sitting watching his viewscreen, expecting them to be linking up with Hugo de Lamartine. Communicating with Sidney was a lot more complicated than putting an ad in *New Woman Scientist*. A slipstream was not properly in their time frame. Sidney had always picked up messages when he popped back to change assistants, which, of course, he was unlikely to do as he would expect Posy to return to the slipstreamer.

'He'll have one of his tantrums,' said Posy. 'He'll see that you and I aren't bothering to link up with Hugo de Lamartine, and he'll geek-freak. But even so, there's no way I'm time-travelling to explain the situation to him. I'm only going to make one more time jump – ever – and that's to go back home for good.'

'There must be a solution.'

'We'll have to think about it. You know, Tommy, I've been thinking. Why does Sidney need so many assistants when he hasn't really got anything to do in that slipstreamer? Do you think he sleeps with them?'

'Sidney? Sleep with his assistants? Goodness no. He's too professional. I've never seen him look at a woman in that way.'

Posy furrowed her brow. 'It's probably the observer effect.'

'Which is?'

'He cannot be measured unless he is observed. He needs to be watched. Needs someone to pass a screwdriver, hold a torch. Some men are like that. And as for a romantic attachment, he'd want someone like himself. You know the type – a woman of noble blood who can do backward somersaults and run up walls.'

'Why's he there anyway?' asked Tommy.

'What do you mean why's he there?'

'Instead of being where he could send and receive messages, he's sitting at the bottom of the Thames and we can't communicate with him. According to you, all he can see are lights wandering about on a viewscreen.'

'It's a man thing, too. He's close to the action.'

Tommy agreed that she was right. Of course, Sidney would rather be there than hunting through copies of sixty-year-old magazines. Also, they were not supposed to use the ads too often in case it looked strange and somebody noticed. She thought of him hunched in his sardine can at the bottom of that cold impersonal river. Part of her resented him as the man responsible for her present predicament; the other saw him as just another human being in need. There had to be some way of getting a message to him. They'd find a way.

CHAPTER 16

Of curtains and carpets

HUGO NEVER BOTHERED TO OPEN THE curtains in the morning at this time of year. There was no point. It saved him the trouble of closing them again when he returned from work in the evening. He washed, dressed, breakfasted at speed, and then he put on the jacket. There is a body sense that has no name that Hugo knew. It is not kinetic, owes nothing to touch. It is a sense of being that can only be felt when the body is perfectly still, which says, yes, this is right, this is just so. Hugo stood with his eyes shut and thought to himself, *I am the essence of pure light.*

When he was ready to leave he lifted the side of the curtain and peeped out at the day. It was raining. This presented a problem. The jacket must not, ever, be worn in the rain. Hugo's raincoat had been commuting to work for many years. It was a long, baggy affair which buttoned up tightly to the neck. It was soiled. It was not just so, or even vaguely right. An umbrella was awkward and, if Professor Camber had not brought one, he would be obliged to be gentlemanly and extend its use to two people, thereby depriving the jacket of its full protection. There was no alternative; he would have to wear his black cape over the jacket. When he walked into the street he noticed that the weather, although wet, was unseasonably mild again.

As he neared the underground, he stopped at a news vendor's stall. A car drew up beside him and a voice said, 'Hugo! Hi! Fucking good job I found you. I've just been to your flat! End of the earth, Gunnersbury!'

It was Terence. His car was on a double yellow line. He hopped as gracefully as his bulk allowed out of the car and, waving a sheaf of papers, strode towards Hugo. 'I need you to sign these.'

'What are they?'

'Bumph. Legal bumph. My mate Charlie got them done in the middle of the night. We can't set up all the people for a TV feature without a contract, insurance, etc. Do you know this man?' he asked the news vendor, indicating Hugo.

'Yeah. See him every day.'

'What's your name?'

'Jaskaran.'

'Great, Jas. Would you witness his signature for a fiver?'

So Hugo signed the forms, Jas witnessed them, Terence was happy as he jumped back into his car and Hugo was left feeling hot and bothered. Why did men like Terence have to be so rushed all the time? And a bit of a cheek going to his home. On a Saturday too!

Hugo hated going anywhere on this day of the week. Saturday pedestrians did not flow as people going to work did. There were too many women, old people and children about, dithering and causing blockages. Reaching the entrance to the park where they had arranged to meet, Hugo realised that he was early. Professor Camber had not arrived yet. In spite of the continuing rain, the park was busy. There appeared to be some sort of convention of youths parading barrel-shaped, muscle-bound bull terriers. There were two groups of girls loitering in tightly-packed conspiracies, ogling the men and eyeing Hugo, who was standing there with nothing much to do. He held his umbrella aloft and strolled away from them; he could always return if he spotted Camber from a distance. He felt unbearably hot. Along the pathway, inline skaters, wet hair slicked back, swerved to avoid him and passed dangerously close. The sky seemed overlarge, the grass was strewn with the first untidy autumnal leaves and infested by grasping little squirrels.

He found a vantage point beneath a tree, from where he could see the park's vast wrought-iron gates. He waited, breathing in the pungent smell of sodden greenery. Ten minutes passed. He must have missed Camber's arrival for, all of a sudden, he became aware that for some minutes he had been observing a figure pacing backwards and forwards by the entrance. Hugo hurried back towards the gates. By the time he reached Camber, the youths and girls, for some reason of their own, were looking uneasy and shuffling away.

'Why on earth didn't you call my mobile? This is no weather for hanging about in the park. Come on. We'll find somewhere to go.' She looked striking in black boots and trousers, underneath a light mac in a pale cream colour which was opened at the neck to reveal a white shirt. Hugo held his umbrella over both of them and they crossed Kensington Gore, with some difficulty, as the traffic hurtled by. They hurried down Exhibition Road with Hugo mumbling platitudes about the weather.

'I always do at least ten miles every weekend,' said Camber. 'I spend too much of the week at my desk. Ah! Here's the solution.' She nodded in the direction of the Science Museum. 'We can walk about in there and still be in the dry. Much better for our purposes than the V&A. Far too many distractions in there.'

The Science Museum was packed with children, accompanied mainly by fathers who either lacked the skills to keep them under control or could not see how annoying they were. Hugo removed a leather purse from his pocket to pay for their tickets, but Camber told him not to be so silly, entrance was free. Hugo removed his cape, but then had the problem of carrying it together with a wet umbrella. He asked an attendant if there was a cloakroom.

'There's always a greater risk of terrorists on a Saturday, and we can't be too careful with children around, can we?' said the man.

'Does that mean there isn't a cloakroom?' Hugo had the feeling that, had he been someone else, there might indeed have been such a facility.

'Not at the moment, mate,' said the attendant with conviction.

They walked into an enormous hall lined with vast engines from the 19th century.

'Look at all this!' Her husky voice, raised to its highest volume, was interrupted for a moment by a burst of chesty coughing, brought on perhaps by the intensity of her disapproval. 'It's all so *ugly!* Tell me, how is your book selling?'

'I really can't complain,' he replied. It was still muggy indoors and Hugo would have been more comfortable without his jacket; but there was only so much one could carry. 'I would like to say how very grateful I am to you for all the support you've given me.'

'Don't mention it. When first your book came to my attention, I thought, this little seed needs sunshine and watering and it will grow.' She turned and studied him. 'You're not married, are you?'

'Oh no. Absolutely not.'

'Do you have any family?'

'Some cousins, but we're not really in contact,' said Hugo.

'Friends?'

'I have many connections in the Art World, a few in Television and of course I meet people in my Work.'

'Remind me, what is it that you do?'

'I'm a Director of Patent Processing for Her Majesty's Government.'

'Ah, yes. But tell me, who do you confide in? To whom do you tell your dreams?'

Hugo made a noise, more a voiced breath than a laugh. 'I keep my own counsel.'

'I do the same. Jolly good. Come on, let's have a cup of coffee.'

It was too early for children to have reached the café. The room was light and airy. They found a secluded alcove in which to sit. Professor Camber removed her mac. Hugo took off his jacket and hung it carefully over the back of his chair. They had coffee, cream cakes and two tarts made of sun-dried tomato and goat's cheese. Hugo had whipped out his little purse and settled the matter before her hand had time to draw a credit card. He felt wildly profligate.

Camber chatted as they ate, telling him about how she had recently overseen a financial restructuring of the University of Artistry and Design. She was having difficulty finding students worthy of the University, education and the development of talent being what they were these days. Hugo nodded, agreed, expressed interest, wiped cream off his upper lip with a paper napkin.

'It is deeply satisfying', she said, 'to have seen my plans for the University come to fruition over the past twenty years. But that's not all. I have other satisfactions. I'm going to tell you a secret.' (Hugo caught his breath.) 'Something that I have told no one before.' Camber leaned out of the alcove, observed that the staff at the food counter were busy chatting to each other, then lit a cigarette, inhaled deeply and began her tale.

'Let's go back some years, quite a few in fact. Obviously I'm a lot younger, but not essentially different in appearance. I am making my way up the ladder in the world of Art. Yes, we all have to start somewhere! I am living in a flat that's small but pleasant and I am counting my blessings. There are dark-brown fitted carpets throughout. They're easy to keep clean, only need a quick once-over with the vacuum cleaner now and then. My sofa is comfortable and covered in a patterned glazed cotton that doesn't show the dirt. My bedroom and sitting room are filled with light and, thanks to flowing voiles, quite private from the flats opposite. Do you see where I'm heading?'

'I think so, but do carry on.'

'I wear shoes with low heels, easy on the feet and one can walk for miles in them. My skirts have elasticated waistbands, which are comfortable, too, and always fit properly. I wear a dab of lipstick and my hair is pushed back in a velvet band. The food I eat is simple, quickly bought and prepared. None of the furniture, the structure of my life, requires time, difficulty or expense. I am free to concentrate on my aspirations for Art! How much do you think this differs from Ms Average living in London today?'

'I wouldn't really know, Professor Camber,' said Hugo.

'No, of course you wouldn't!' She laughed. 'Call me by my first name. It's Amphelisia. Bear with me. What I am saying may not be of interest to you, yet. But it will be.

'These days, Ms Average has a terrible time! And Mr Average too! They're much more conscious of style and it's a constant battle to keep up. You'll find most women, like me, find it's best to be tall and slim with straight hair. They are on view all the time, even through the windows of their homes. Furnishings are pale, floorboards get dusty in a moment. It's hard work keeping knick-knacks out of sight, there's never enough storage space. Clothes absolutely have to be in fashion, and there's such a fast turnaround in manufacturing in the third world that fashions can change overnight. Bodies have to be perfect, because everything's on show! All the bulgy bits have to be exposed to view. No hiding fat arms and bellies under baggy jumpers any more. Heels are high. My dear Hugo, it might surprise you to try on a pair of high heels and try walking all day. You wouldn't manage it! No normal man would be brave enough to stand the pain!

'What we eat, read, listen to, is no longer an easy choice. Hair is a full-time occupation.' She doused her cigarette butt with the coffee slops in her saucer. 'For every aspect of life there are a thousand rules. And, oh, the insecurity of those who are not sure if they know what all those rules are!' Camber gave a low chuckle, lit another cigarette, leaned back in her chair and smiled. 'There are many other things I could mention. It's as bad for men as it is for women, but in different ways. What I've said will give you a rough idea. I have described for you a world that has changed in a way that no one would have predicted at the time when I was a young woman sitting in my flat counting my blessings. And do you know what caused all these changes?'

Hugo's mind raced. They were discussing concepts that had never entered his head before. This was something that was important to Camber. He was hugely intelligent. He ought to have an answer. Would she look down on him if he couldn't answer? God, it was hot in here even without his jacket! Perhaps it was a trick question.

'Give up?' said Camber. 'I'll tell you. Me! I caused all these changes.'

A laugh could express so many things. Hugo laughed. They both laughed.

'Gosh, how did you do that... Amphelisia?' he said.

'I am a visual person. I can go into a room and remove everything except one object, and anyone with a jot of aesthetic appreciation will agree that it is the right object. I also have a gift with language. I write poetry sometimes. But words are not my principal area of interest. Words are such clumsy things. You turn them the wrong way round or back to front and they change completely. They are so flat and two-dimensional. That is why I need you, my dear boy. You juggle them like a...' She searched for the right word.

Hugo couldn't think of the right word either. 'Octopus?' he ventured.

'No matter,' said Camber. 'One evening, sitting in my flat, I said to myself, what if? What if all these things that I value were changed? Not for me, but for other people. For everyone else except me. I sat down and I wrote what I called my Chronicles. Amphelisia Camber's Chronicles! They listed the things that would change. They were all things that no sensible person would dream of changing.

'I had a plan, and I put it into action. I infiltrated snippets of the Chronicles into all sorts of places: the Art press, in conversation, at parties. As I became more and more important at the University of Artistry and Design, there were interviews for TV and radio. I would always preface them with remarks like, *Of course, everyone agrees that... and it is a crime against good taste if... Nobody, but nobody, wears, whatever, any more...* they were such sneaky little snippets. And they were repeated and came back to me!

'Now I can walk down any street in the land, look at the

passers-by, look in the shops, and know I did this. I did all this! They all think they live in a democracy, don't have to obey religion or have good manners. They think they are free. And they are not. They are tied up in more rules than at my boarding school forty-odd years ago!'

Hugo had got it. It was massive. It was a social revolution. He looked at Camber sitting laughing across the table, at her big teeth, the wealth demonstrated by the clunky gold bangles at her wrist, the cool comfort of her white blouse. She was magnificent.

'My God,' he said. 'You could change anything, everything.'

'Exactly,' she said. 'I can, have and will, and that's why I need you.'

'I went to boarding school too,' said Hugo.

A bell chimed in some far-off church. The café filled with people. Families jostled for tables, chairs and food. Children wanted this and not that. Knives clattered, noxious chemicals were slurped through straws. All the airy space was taken up with brollies, pushchairs and rucksacks decorated with tacky cartoon figures. A little girl with dark hair and golden skin tentatively touched Camber's sleeve. She was dressed in up-to-the-minute designer chartreuse. 'I've lost my daddy,' she said.

Camber drew back her arm as though scalded and said quietly and firmly, 'Go away!'

The little girl hesitated, blinked back tears, then went away.

'My father was a complete shit,' said Camber to Hugo. 'One day, she'll realise that losing her daddy was probably a very sensible thing to do.'

They stood up and picked up their belongings. 'Let's go and have a good long walk!' said Camber.

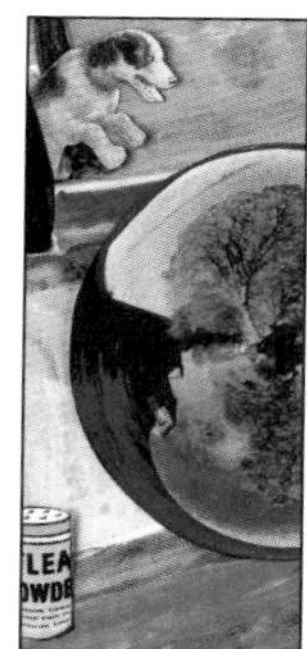

CHAPTER 17

A place of parakeets

TOMMY WAS LOOKING FORWARD TO GETTING back to her flat, but Posy, having been cooped up in a slipstreamer for so long, was living life to the full. They decided to get off the Tube at South Kensington and walk. On the way they encountered the full glory of the Natural History Museum. Even in the rain its patterned bricks exuded a warm glow.

'I remember this building,' said Tommy. 'I came here as a child and I always used to bring Henry here. But it wasn't called the Natural History Museum. It was called the Notional Costume Gallery. They used to let children dress up as dinosaurs.'

'I went there too. Shall we go in?'

'No. Remembering Henry here makes me feel so sad. Although I'd love to be somewhere there are children.'

'Why don't we go to that other museum, around the corner. The Design Museum.'

They were both surprised to find that the museum was called the Science Museum. It was evident that many things were due to change in the forty or so years before their childhood selves would visit this part of London.

The museum was full of children accompanied by fathers and it felt good to be surrounded by them again. Children were so straightforward, said what they meant, showed what they were feeling. Living in a purely adult world, Tommy now realised, had been something of a strain. She studied the crowd; no sign of Hendrix.

'Shall we have an early lunch? I'm starving.' Posy consulted a floor plan, hung on the wall, which indicated the café.

'I'll have to work out if we can afford it.' Tommy had the back pay from Rodney and Wilfred plus the unused taxi fare, but she was concerned now that her meagre finances were going to have to support Posy's meals and travel as well as her own.

'How come? Don't Burton and Crump keep you supplied?'

'Yes, but it's a pittance. It wasn't supposed to be a pittance, was it?'

'No, it certainly wasn't. Sidney gave me a complete rundown of your set-up here, and you were meant to be getting plenty to live on. Another mess-up. We'll sort it out on Monday. Will what you have keep both of us fed over the weekend?'

'Oh yes. If we're careful.'

The café was filled with children and alive with noise and bustle. They ordered some tea, two glasses of tap water and a large green banana to share.

'No, not that table. Follow me.' Tommy chose a table by the window. 'I don't believe it! That's him!' she said. 'Over there! In the alcove.'

Posy looked to where she indicated. A slim man with a full head of dark, wavy hair was eating a cream cake. He was accompanied by an angular woman in her fifties.

'It's de Lamartine. Hudelam!' said Tommy.

'He looks so different from his holograms. He's so young! How amazing! Of all the places in London where we might have come.' Posy gave a whoop. 'This is great! Sidney will be so happy! He'll think we're on track with the mission.'

'The woman with him is Professor Camber. She's a big cheese at the University. She heads up the photography department, but she's in control of a lot more than that. She's supposed to suck out people's souls.'

As they watched, a small dark-haired child approached Camber and touched her arm. They saw the woman turn and speak to her. The child retreated a few feet, looking miserable. Hugo donned a periwinkle blue jacket, picked up his coat and umbrella, and trotted like a dog at the heels of Professor Camber as she swept from the room.

Their duty had been to follow him but their mission was pointless now, yet some close-range surveillance would, at least, give them something to report on their return to their own time, and keep Sidney content as he watched his viewscreen on the riverbed. Duty called where Hugo had gone, yet both women leapt to their feet and rushed over to where the mournful little girl stood alone. She told them that her name was Iphigenia and that she was lost. It took effort and tact to find an appropriate official and have the little girl reunited with her daddy at the information desk in the entrance hall. He picked her up in his arms and hugged her. It was evident that in spite of a somewhat fearsome appearance this was a loving daddy. By this time Tommy and Posy realised that finding Hugo and Camber was going to be difficult.

'We've even left our banana behind,' said Tommy.

'No we haven't. I put it in my bag. Sidney will be getting cross though.'

They ate the banana on the hoof, as they wandered from room to room. Camber would have been distinctive in her cream mac, and Hugo too, in his periwinkle blue, but there was no trace of them. Posy drew to a halt and declared it to be hopeless. The Science Museum was a labyrinth. Perhaps they would be better off planning their search for Hendrix. Tommy had recounted the tale of his disappearance, in some detail, on the way to the bridge that morning, and Posy was mulling over various avenues of possibility. The stumbling block was cash. It would take forever if they had to keep consulting Tommy's purse to see what they could, or could not, do.

'Phone Burton and Crump.'

'They'll be closed. It's Saturday.'

'It's worth a try. You never know.'

There were symbols on every wall, mobile phones in a circle with a cross through them. Tommy did not like breaking rules. She dialled a number and a tired voice answered:

'Charlie speaking.'

'Oh, I'm sorry. Is that Burton and Crump?'

'Yes it is, but we're closed.'

'But you're there.'

'Yes, but I'm not really. The office will be open again on Monday morning.'

Tommy switched off her phone. 'It's no good, they're closed.'

'Who answered then?' asked Posy.

'He said his name was Charlie but that he wasn't really there.'

'Come on, we're going to visit Charlie.' Posy was already striding towards the exit.

'They're closed. It's too far away. They're miles away out in the suburbs.'

'What else are we going to do with the day?'

On the way they stopped at a chemist's and Posy insisted that they buy some make-up: mascara, eyeshadow, kohl, blotch concealer, some proper glycerin-based shampoo with no sulphate foaming agents, three bottles of silicone-free conditioner and some hair gel. Tommy was concerned at the expense.

'Don't worry. We'll have access to funds when we get to Burton and Crump. We can spend what you've got. It would be wonderful to have something to wear apart from your mate's jeans. And you need some clothes too.'

'Me? Need clothes? Why? I agree this outfit is a bit warm for the weather, but it's wonderful quality. Feel it. Pure wool.'

Against Tommy's better judgement they took the Tube to Richmond and then took a taxi the rest of the way. Whenever the cab slowed or stopped at traffic lights Tommy scanned the faces of the passers-by for Hendrix, and Posy did another bit of her eye make-up. By the time they arrived at Thamesbury, she was transformed. Tommy had turned down every offer of sharing the make-up.

'You'd look great with a bit of colour,' said Posy.

'No I wouldn't. I'd look as though I was pretending to be someone else and people would stare at me.'

Burton and Crump's offices were an imposing Georgian house in a smart residential area, but, as such houses

commonly are, it was on a main road. Posy rang the doorbell. The rain had stopped and the air was fresh. The garden at the front was aglow with flowers that had not yet succumbed to autumn. Nobody was answering, so Posy rang the doorbell again. After a long while they heard the shuffling of footsteps. Somebody rattled security chains and inner locks. The door swung open.

'Hello, I'm afraid we're closed.' The young man looked as though he hadn't slept in a week.

'We're clients, here on urgent business,' said Posy. 'This is Tommy Willoughby. One of your oldest clients, I believe.'

'We've met, Ms Willoughby. I'm Charlie Archer.' He shook Tommy's hand. 'Cave Paintings? Thursday? You were working there or something.'

'Indeed we did. Call me Tommy.'

'Have you just come from school?'

'Oh no. I'm at University, but we don't have lectures on Saturday.'

He smiled. Posy thought it rather a sweet smile.

Charlie led them into a tiled hallway. He apologised for asking them to be very quiet but, he explained, the Senior Partner was taking a quick nap. They followed him up three flights of stairs to an attic room in which there was a daybed, a picnic table with a kettle and mugs and a desk with a computer. Charlie explained that they had run out of milk and coffee, but there was some green tea. They had been drinking tea all day. Their bodies were supersaturated with tea.

'Oh how lovely,' said Tommy. 'I'll make it.'

'Just let me find you on the computer and then I'll be in a position to help.'

Posy sat on the day bed and Tommy made the tea. It was very hot, and they had to wait for it to cool.

The women finished their tea and Charlie was still entering folders and sweeping through hierarchies.

'I'm sorry,' he said. 'I'm having to look manually. The search thingy couldn't find you.'

'I'll make some more tea,' said Tommy.

'Gotcha! It's in accounts! I've got a weekly payment of forty-five pounds payable to Miss T. Willoughby. There's no other info here though.'

'Where will that be?' asked Posy, lowering sweeping lashes, touching her hair lightly with her fingertips and giving him an oblique half-smile.

Charlie leaned back in his twirly chair and stretched. 'There has to be a file, but if it's not on the computer it'll be in storage. How long has your family been clients, Tommy?'

She looked at Posy, who frowned, thought about it, then said, 'Since the beginning of the 19th century.'

'Bloody hell,' said Charlie.

The oldest storage facility in the building was in a cellar, which, according to Charlie, extended under much of the garden. 'The whole road used it as a bomb shelter during the war. They had everything they needed down here.'

'That would be the Falklands War, I suppose,' commented Posy. She had read a few history books in her life, bought from faceless people in shadowy side streets. Charlie gulped and said nothing. He climbed a ladder and choked as clouds of dust from the Industrial Revolution swirled about his head. He removed a box and, holding it carefully, came down the ladder and placed it on the only available surface, which was what looked like an ancient iron kitchen range covered with layers of leather-bound volumes. He dusted the box with a handkerchief and revealed embossed golden lettering which read:

Matters and Sundries pertaining to the Affairs of
Miss T. Willoughby

'What the hell?'

'It's a family name,' explained Posy. 'The eldest daughter has always been called Tommy Willoughby since . . .?' She turned to Tommy.

'Oh forever,' said Tommy. 'Since forever.'

They waited while Charlie leafed through yellowing correspondence as thin as the skin on an old lady's hands.

'Where's Klaus Place?'

'Must be a mistake. It's Hans Place,' said Tommy.

'It's mostly arguing over money. It refers to an instruction from 1802, which I haven't found yet, which sets out a system of ... *weekly payments of the sum of forty-five pounds and ten shillings sterling to cover board, sustenance, vestments, travel, entertaining and other manifold sundries of the aforementioned Miss Willoughby, for the pursuance of a standard of living commensurate with the expectations of a young lady of social standing, and for the furtherance*... I can't read any more of this. I've got asthma.' Charlie slid a puffer from his pocket and inhaled up one nostril.

'What's ten shillings?' asked Tommy. 'I haven't had ten shillings.'

'Tommy's been getting forty-five pounds a week,' said Posy tartly.

'That seems to have been the problem.' Charlie flipped through more papers. 'It was a lot of money in 1810, which must have been the time of your great, great...? Whatever. Some of the Partners were of the view that *such a huge sum given over to the management of a young lady of tender years, without a father or the guiding hand of a husband*... You're not married, are you?'

'No,' said Tommy.

'... *might encourage a degree of wanton profligacy and a descent into a World of Vice, to which the fair sex, notwithstanding a feebleness of imagination, may nonetheless*...'

'I think we've got the gist,' interrupted Posy. 'How much is left in the account?'

Charlie riffled through more correspondence, looked startled, consulted a long statement of accounts which seemed to have been written in ginger ink using a quill pen. 'Bloody hell. It seems, from what I've got here, that £1000 was invested in property in 1810, with rental payments accruing at a fixed rate of 2% yearly compound interest. I'd have to work it out, but in financial terms, this undoubtedly makes you the firm's largest client. In fact you probably own the firm. What was it that you wanted?'

'What do you earn in a year?' asked Posy.

'Well I'm up for partnership again this year, and it looks promising, which will involve a substantial increase.'

'Oh, never mind. Let's say someone of about your age, but a bit less talented, in an average firm.'

'Sixty thousand quid,' said Charlie.

'Great. We'll take that.' Posy flicked her hair back. It was always difficult on rainy days, but the gel had helped.

'We don't need anything like that amount,' said Tommy.

Posy shut her up with a sharp elbow. 'Tommy has a hard life. She gets her furniture off skips, buys clothes off mad Ukrainians, she'd boil sheep's heads if they sold them in Asda. She needs some money.'

'Oh, what a load of fuckwits we've been! I really am sorry. What a balls-up.' Charlie took out his puffer and had another snort. 'I'd do anything to give you the money, but it's difficult. I'm not authorised to sign a cheque.'

'What about the Senior Partner?' asked Posy.

'He doesn't sign cheques either. And he's asleep. He hasn't had any sleep for seventy-six hours. He'll kill me if I wake him.'

'Who else is here?'

'Come on,' said Charlie. 'We'll have a look. Mustn't forget these! There are some letters here which probably should have been given to your great-great-grandmother.'

Tommy put them in her red bag.

Charlie led them up from the bowels of the house to the basement. There, in a vast room with little natural light, were three women sitting at computers.

'Weekend typing pool,' explained Charlie. 'Hello, ladies. Everything all right?'

'Hi, Charlie!'

Tommy smiled at the women; they nodded weakly back at

her. One of them was in a wheelchair, one had a bandaged arm, and the arms of the third – who was typing nonetheless – were fully encased in plaster.

'RSI,' explained Charlie.

'Is that one of those sexually communicated thingies?' Posy had read about such diseases being rife in the early 21st century.

'Repetitive strain injury. It's psychosomatic. Women tend to get it.'

Posy was fascinated. Her reading matter had been eclectic, allowing her to cherry-pick from centuries of odd thought. 'In every era there seem to have been ailments invented by men that only women suffered from. Wandering womb in Aristotle's time, hysteria in Freud's, PMS in the 21st century.'

'What's PMS?' asked Tommy.

'Post-menopausal syndrome. It's similar to pre-menstrual syndrome. Has exactly the same symptoms.'

Every room of the building seemed to have some occupant beavering away. As they approached, doors were banged shut. Far away someone was wailing.

'I thought you said you were closed,' said Tommy.

'We are,' replied Charlie. 'You should see this place during the week. Forgive me for being so inefficient. I was on my way out yesterday night and then a client, or rather a friend, called needing an urgent contract for a docudrama. That's the problem. Most of our clients hate us because we earn too much money, so we work harder and harder to justify what we charge them; and then some of our clients are friends, and it's so wonderful to work for someone friendly. It makes it very difficult to say no to anyone. Nobody gets any sleep, and it all spirals downwards. I made the mistake of going out for the evening on Thursday, and now I'm making up for it.'

'But you get paid a lot,' said Posy.

'Yes, but it costs us a fortune to live. I have to pay someone to put my dustbin and recycling out every week because I'm never there. An out-of-work actor phones my relatives. I've

got a writers' group from an adult education college handling personal e-mails for a fee. The list goes on and on. If I could find a double I'd have someone to go out and drink with my mates. Of course, you can earn more in the City but then you have to work harder.'

He knocked on the door of a first-floor room. 'Come in!' trilled a voice. The room was filled with light and plants and elegant antique furniture. In the corner, sitting beside a laptop as gleaming and enticing as Eve's gift to Adam, was a good-looking black woman wearing 80s disco pants, a tiny top and jungle jewellery. She welcomed them in. Charlie presented Domenica O'Reilly, their Financial Controller, and introduced Tommy and Posy. She listened to Charlie's account of their difficulties while pouring each of them a fruit punch with a slice of lime on the glass and a good dollop of rum. There were coconut cakes and two kinds of cocktail biscuits topped with what Domenica explained was either saltfish and ackee or curry goat.

'Do you like parakeets?' asked Domenica. She led Tommy and Posy to a large bay window looking out onto a garden. The noise explained the wailing that the women had heard earlier. Bright green birds with blue tails and red beaks swooped through palm trees and swathes of bamboo, screeching and squabbling over a suspended bird-feeder. Grey squirrels were busy digging holes in the lawn, and patting it down again so that the damage was quite repaired. They retrieved nuts, from time to time, by lifting the wooden lid of a feeding box nailed to a gazebo. Two elderly oriental tabbies dozed on a rug spread out on the lawn.

'But this is London!' exclaimed Tommy.

'This is Thamesbury,' said Domenica. 'I was born here. Many gardens in Thamesbury are like this.'

Returning to her laptop, she typed quickly on the keyboard. 'Now, you need some money. No problem,' she said. 'Just give me your bank account details, and I'll do a transfer. You've got a credit card for the weekend, I presume.'

'Actually, no, I haven't,' said Tommy. 'I'll have to wait till Monday.'

Domenica said something that sounded like *Killiday – oh!* and then, 'No worry, no worry, I'll get you some petty cash.' She took a key from the mantelpiece and opened a drawer of the escritoire. 'How much do you need? Will nine be enough?'

'It's better than nothing,' said Tommy.

'Nine? *Nine?*' exclaimed Posy.

Domenica handed Tommy nine hundred pounds in fifty-pound notes. It seemed that Tommy was about to hand them back, so Posy swiped the notes into the red bag and closed the zip.

When Charlie saw them to the front door, Posy asked him if he had a pen and paper.

'Sure,' he said, taking out a small pad of yellow stickies and a high-pressure, scuba-diving ballpoint.

'What's your mobile number?' she asked Tommy. Posy wrote it down on the sticky pad and handed it to Charlie. 'If you ever get off work, give me a ring.'

He shook the hands of both women in a friendly farewell, but his rather sweet and sad smile was for Posy.

They skipped and whooped along the road, stopping only to enquire the way to Thamesbury railway station of a passer-by, who told them to continue on up the road. There wasn't a taxi in sight.

'Now we've got all the money we need to find Hendrix.' Tommy was happy.

'And I can buy some clothes!' shouted Posy. 'And some shoes. And a bag!'

Then her face fell.

'What's the matter?'

'I suddenly thought about Sidney, down there at the bottom of the river watching us. He'll be absolutely – what was the expression I heard your mate Paintstripper use yesterday? Gutted. He'll be gutted. I like the way people speak here. It's cool.'

CHAPTER 18

A memorial and a memory

'IT IS SO IRRITATING', SAID AMPHELISIA Camber, 'trying to walk with children in the way. They get underfoot and they're a nightmare to overtake because they never keep to a straight course. They run in all directions at once! Is it still raining outside?'

They were in a windowless room. Hugo was at a loss as to how to answer her question.

'Of course, I forgot, you don't have a phone.' Camber took her own from a stylish leather handbag, pressed a few buttons and announced that the weather had cleared and they could resume their walk *al fresco*. They hurried from the building.

'My God, but that place was oppressive,' she said. 'There is no sense of balance or harmony in the world of science. It is like some vast dark garage filled with grubby-fingered mechanics!'

Hugo murmured his agreement. It was remarkable how their world views concurred.

It was, indeed, no longer raining, and the oblique rays of an autumn sun were drying the pavement. They headed back to the park. Hugo marvelled at how well he was managing to keep up with Camber's long strides. He rarely took exercise, yet something was flowing in his veins which denied pain and kept all sense of effort at bay. The pathways were taken up by strollers, amblers and shufflers, so they took to the damp grass. Hugo listened to Amphelisia's arabica voice telling him how she had made a killing on the Art Markets by sending artists into cultural oblivion, buying as others sold and then restoring reputations when she wanted to sell. 'So easy!' Her laugh was almost girlish to see, but not, of course, to hear.

She chattered on, giving her opinion of a New York exhibition of some artist whose name he didn't recognise, whose work was plainly derived from someone else of whom he'd never heard either. It didn't matter. She appreciated his ability as an equal to follow her drift, and then said, 'Ah, here's the Diana Fountain. I want to know what you think about it.'

Hugo looked around him and was relieved that she had named the place. The Diana Fountain was obviously something to do with Diana the Huntress. What was her other name. Artemis? And what did the fountain signify to Amphelisia Camber? It was large. It was modern. The granite waterway extended in a circle. It was a place where children might come in fair weather to paddle and break limbs, though fortunately there was none present now. Water slipped over grey granite. There was a tang of chlorine in the air. Camber was looking at him intently. He cleared his throat, took out a handkerchief and blew his nose. There was no other choice possible. He would have to dive straight in.

'I think', he said, 'that, on the whole, all things being considered, that the Diana Fountain is, to many people . . .' he swallowed, 'a good idea.'

'I am surprised', she took out a cigarette and lit it, 'to hear somebody else saying exactly what I think. This memorial is indeed a triumph of the world of Art over popular sentiment.'

She extended five fingers with dark enamelled tips towards the fountain and made a sweeping gesture. 'There were some who would have made of this place just a sandpit, some swings and benches where teenage gangs gather.'

Hugo followed her gaze and saw, on the far side, that there was indeed such a bench, and on it a figure who could not clearly be discerned, yet who Hugo knew at once to be a dishevelled youngster with torn trousers. His face was in shadow, but the sunlight caught his unruly hair rising, like a burning bush, from his head.

'Let us walk around the fountain,' said Camber.

Hugo looked about him, desperate for some landmark of interest to which he might redirect her, but the orbit, from which the inevitable conjunction with the figure on the bench might be extrapolated, had already begun.

'I have a business proposition to make to you. An idea that will benefit us both.'

Hugo felt that Camber was at last broaching the subject to which the whole day had been a preamble. He wished he could block the figure on the bench from his mind.

'I am offering to extend our arrangement to three books. The third book would be a book similar to your first. There is a need for a slim volume to clarify an area of interest – no matter what, I shall give you the subject at a later date – which, taken together with your first book, would make you – how shall I put it? – a *presence* in the academic world of Art.'

They were approaching the bench. Hugo did not want to appear to notice the seated figure but, by looking away and using his peripheral vision to take a peek, he was convinced that the fellow was looking at them intently. He could not possibly recognise Hugo – he had been unconscious when the unfortunate but necessary trouser swap had taken place – so why was he looking at them?

'How fascinating,' he said to Camber. 'Please tell me more.'

'The second book would be a special book. You see, Hugo, I am a victim of my own success. Everything I have aimed for I have achieved. I need a dream for the rest of my life. I have some ideas for a book, which you, with your gift for expressing things in a way that makes your readers work a little, are the ideal person to write.'

Yes, he was definitely looking at them. His face was expressionless and he was staring straight at Hugo – or was it Amphelisia? It was difficult to tell.

Camber explained that she would provide the financial wherewithal to enable the two further books to be written and published but, before Hugo made a decision on her proposition, she would like him to be aware that there was a downside. The second book would need to be published with some discretion.

Hugo felt excitement welling up. Three books! Three books! Hugo de Lamartine, author of three books. Yes! Yes Yes! And, oh dear, for there could be no doubt, that with the help of some form of attachment (safety pins? string? glue?) those were Hugo de Lamartine's discarded trousers that the kid was wearing, glimpsed on Hugo's right-hand side as they passed the bench – and now he had swivelled round and it was quite obvious that he was staring at them both!

'You must keep a low profile on the second book,' she said firmly. 'There must be no critical reviews in the press. You must not draw attention to yourself beyond the confines of the inner world of Art.' (She appeared not to have noticed the occupant of the bench.) 'The writer must not overshadow the book! Perhaps it could be written under another name. As with my own ideas – which I have jotted down from time to time – the contents of this book will enter society, drip by drip. The internet will make everything much easier. We can use chat rooms and blogs. The book will *infiltrate* and eventually its power will be enormous!'

Thank heavens, the bench was behind them now. The future glittered ahead of Hugo as he traversed the green sward dotted with trees that had seen the reigns of kings and queens come and go. People moved like streams of ants to-ing and fro-ing beneath the branches, their lives enriched by a few significant names of the celebrated, the famous, be they movie stars, singers, footballers or writers like himself. *But,* thought Hugo, *to write a powerful book and not then be acknowledged as its author. Now that was a bit hard!*

Yet, there would be a reward, Camber assured him. For this would be the sort of book whose day would eventually come. Hugo might be an old man by then, or even dead, but his name would be right up there with the most powerful thinkers of all time! Socrates, Plato, the Buddha. This was no time for humility! His reputation would endure!

Hugo halted and stood breathing heavily. His heart was palpitating and his limbs felt like lead.

'Yes, I know I'm asking a lot of you!' said Camber, in a voice which was, for her, curiously gentle. 'I'll tell you my dream. I am a very old lady and I am in my room in a nursing home. This room and the place I know already, for, as I am single with no family to speak of, I have already planned my retirement in some detail. The residence in question caters to an elite, all of whom are already paying monthly for the pleasure of one day coming to live there.

'Anyway, watching the television, or whatever it is that people will watch in that era, I am witnessing everything that you and I will put into the second book coming to pass, bearing fruit, happening on every programme on the box that says something about what the world will then be like! Can you imagine it, Hugo? It'll be so bloody satisfying. Old and full of power! What do you say? Will you do it? In spite of the downside will you do it?'

Hugo felt as though ghostly hands had encircled his throat and were slowly throttling him. He opened his mouth to speak and nothing came out. Then his voice emerged as a thin excited squeak. 'Yes. I'll do it. Of course I will!' But his mind was thinking, *Oh no, oh no, I can't bear it, but I am practically, almost, one hundred per cent certain that I left one of my business cards in the pocket of those trousers!*

CHAPTER 19

Shedding light

THE FLAT WAS QUIET, EXCEPT FOR THE sound of machine gun fire and the shrieks of dying aliens behind the closed door of Paintstripper's room. Posy and Tommy dumped their heavy carrier bags in Tommy's bedroom. Posy had insisted on travelling back via Kingston and stocking up on jeans, skirts, tops, shoes, boots, a mac, a jacket, a glitzy dress and, in Tommy's view, some oddish and totally pointless underwear.

'Who sees it? We aren't going to be in this era long enough for you to need all this stuff, and you can't take it with you when we go home.'

'Course I'll take it with me. I'm going to wear all of it for the return journey.'

Then Posy remembered Sidney's vomit. Oh cruel fate! None of her purchases could go with her, and even in her own time she had admired vintage clothes. She would be travelling back in the green tunic in which she'd arrived, back to a world where everyone had to wear clothes in a similar colour and style each season or risk being slapped down or ostracised. She relented. 'You're right of course, but wow! Wasn't today fun?'

Tommy was set for an evening at home. Posy longed to put on her new skirt and top and go out and hit the clubs. She'd read a story once about life in the early millennium clubbing scene. Her whole body felt full of energy, and she wanted to hear music and dance. When Tommy put her mobile phone on the kitchen table, Posy checked to make sure it was on and still charged.

'We could eat out!'

But Tommy was tired and there was stuff in the fridge that needed finishing. Posy went into Hendrix's room to hang up her new clothes. She looked at his photographs. Each one held the interest in some way. Each was a world, weird yet ordinary. She flipped through the letters from the University of Artistry and Design. She longed for a book, but books appeared not to be a priority for the residents of Hans Place. Then she noticed the copy of *Trapped Light* beside the bed. She picked it up, sat cross-legged on the floor and began to read. In her era books were mostly academic. The few novels considered acceptable were simple tales about love, set in the world of art, their language plain and undemanding; they were ephemera, manufactured to fade in a few days. It was those other forbidden novels and science magazines, obscured in plastic covers, that had taught her to read, comprehend and assess. Her store of books in the timeship was a very special collection.

In the adjacent room, time travellers arrived disguised as religious extremists. They merged with the landscape, then popped out from their hiding places and killed Paintstripper's avatar in devious and inscrutable ways. Tommy gave the kitchen a good clean, chopped some limp and unresisting vegetables, fried leftover cold chicken and mixed it all up with a jar of sauce. If Hendrix were to return after they had eaten, there would still be some bacon to provide a meal. Posy was frowning. From time to time she exhaled audibly and turned a page.

The game ended. Paintstripper announced in a loud voice that she had scored 97,161. Tommy called to all that food was on the table. They made small talk as they ate. Tommy cleared the plates away and washed up. Paintstripper went to watch television, and Posy carried on reading at the kitchen table till she snapped the book shut and said to Tommy, 'We won't be going home any time soon. This isn't the book our mission was all about. This is not the *Book of Hudelam*. Hugo isn't Hudelam yet, and presumably he hasn't yet written or published the book that has caused our era so much trouble. We'll have to find out his precise address. I only remember from Sidney's viewscreen that it was somewhere quite a way to the left of where we are now. That's west, isn't it? We need to get close to him somehow and see what he's up to.'

Posy could tell from Tommy's expression that, with Hendrix still missing, motivating her to carry out their mission was going to be difficult. She would have to keep both projects running in parallel. She tapped the book with a fingernail. 'I've read enough of *Trapped Light* to guess why Hendrix may have had a problem.'

At first glance, the words of *Trapped Light* had revealed themselves to Posy as Artspeak. It was a language she knew well from her education; a wilderness of abstract nouns. Obscure words were used where an ordinary one might have served and some everyday words were given capital letters, or a bold font, till you couldn't be certain if they still meant what they always used to mean. Such language had dogged her as a child. Meaning was something she had discovered for herself, in secret, reading those ancient, crumbling paperbacks. Hendrix, she reasoned, had grown up in a world where every household probably boasted a dictionary and the erosion of logic had not yet spread to all walks of life.

'Was Hendrix much of a reader?'

Tommy thought about it and shook her head.

'Well, he wouldn't be, would he?' mused Posy. 'A twenty-year-old guy who studies photography, even in our own time, is not likely to be the sort of person who would choose to read a book like *Trapped Light*.'

'But you don't need to understand something to write an essay. You only have to quote bits. That's what my teachers told me to do when I was studying.'

'Maybe Hendrix didn't realise that. Perhaps he was trying to understand the world and believed it understandable.'

'It fits. He was always straightforward and honest. If only he had said something to me instead of getting expelled and running away, I could have helped him.' Tommy described how she imagined Hendrix struggling throughout the summer, knowing that his place at the University was dependent on writing this essay, and feeling it was an impossible endeavour. The fact that he had returned at the beginning of the year and said nothing to her suggested that he was not admitting, even to himself, the trouble he was in.

'Denial,' said Posy. 'The big question is, why were they so hard on him?'

There didn't seem to be any obvious answer to that one.

Although they now had an understanding of Hendrix's problem, and Tommy's suspicion that *Trapped Light* was somehow implicated had been confirmed, they were still no nearer to finding Hendrix.

'Tell me everything about him,' suggested Posy. 'All the small details of what he likes and dislikes that might give me a picture of who he is.'

Tommy thought carefully of all she had picked up in six months of knowing Hendrix. She described how he was crazy about photography. A visual person. He wandered around taking pictures of things. That was his joy and reason for living. He struggled to wake up in the morning. Washing and getting dressed were a trial but, once he had managed them, he was OK. He shuffled his feet when he was unhappy. He had no interest in clothes, the news, politics, the economy, history, science or medicine. He wore slippers. Drank hot chocolate. Would have eaten bread and cheese quite happily for every meal, except when he was unhappy and ate cereal for dinner. Ate vegetables occasionally because Tommy insisted. Did not drink alcohol or smoke or do drugs. He had met a girl once at a party whom he had really liked, but she had gone off to University in the North. Not having a girlfriend did not seem to bother him. He loved his father but never spoke about him. New York was OK. He liked taking photos of New York. He had absolutely no interest in sport. He liked animals, especially the way they moved, but did not want to own a pet. He was interested in people but preferred to stay at a distance and view them through a lens. No interest in music. He really loved Audrey Hepburn, Princess Diana and President Putin of Russia. He didn't know why he liked President Putin but it was possibly because nobody else did. Tommy thought hard but couldn't find anything further to add. Except one thing. He'd told her that he'd been passionate about trains as a kid and had trainspotted a bit as a teenager. Her son, Henry, was crazy about trains too.

'And what did other people think of him?' asked Posy.

'Well, Paintstripper said she had never met a chap, young or old, who was easier to live with. He had people he knew, but they were never close. Even with me, the closeness was more on my side than his. Nobody disliked him. Except Professor Camber. She didn't like him.' She told Posy the story of Hendrix's interview with Camber, her folded arms, her body turned away from him.

'And why do you care for him so much?'

'Because he's like Henry, I suppose. But also because he's passionate about photography and, though he's really good at it, never brags or shows off. He's quite humble in his way. Never pretends to be anything other than himself. And because he accepted me, gaps and all.'

Posy was quiet for a while, thinking. Finally she said, 'Camber's the reason why he's gone away but, unless she really does suck out people's souls, I don't think she's the key to where he's gone. The words I've picked up from what you've told me that could be important are: Audrey Hepburn, maybe, and Princess Diana, who are both dead, unfortunately, and trains.'

Tommy said she thought that they should look on Hendrix's computer to see if they could find some missing persons organisation.

'I was wondering', Posy stood up and stretched, 'if you think that Charlie, the solicitor, might be someone who could help with the search?'

'I wouldn't have thought so. He's at work all the time, isn't he?'

'We'll need someone to help, so we've got time for the mission.'

The lights of Saturday night London sparkled. All the music of the planet played from thousands of venues. People went binge drinking, fell in love, and/or had sex, and/or picked up horrible diseases. Posy and Tommy stayed home and the phone never rang.

Sunday morning dawned. Posy leapt from Hendrix's bed, opened the curtains and saw that it was raining again, crashing down from grey skies to grey pavements in a twilight world. She retreated back into bed. *What do people do here on a Sunday when it's raining?* she thought. *Shopping!* But it was doubtful that the guardian of the purse could be persuaded to release any more of the funds which she had considered from the outset to be dwindling. Tommy, she guessed, was likely to see the weather as a good excuse for a bout of radical housecleaning. Which left Hugo or the Hendrix get-out clause.

Now where was Hendrix on this miserable Sunday morning, having perhaps spent since Wednesday roaming the streets? Tommy had told her that she was convinced that he hadn't holed up with a friend sharing spliffs. So, let's trust her, thought Posy. He would need somewhere dry where he could stay without being moved on. A rational guy would have found himself a nice warm police cell, but somehow Hendrix didn't seem the type, and anyway why would he do that when all he had to do was come home to Knightsbridge? Where he would have had a warm bed if someone else hadn't been sleeping in it.

Where are you, Hendrix? Where are you having breakfast? You're eating a sandwich that some shop's let you have because it's gone stale, and you're not in a police station. You're at the *railway station!* You like trains. You won't get moved on there.

Posy threw on yesterday's knickers and a t-shirt, sat in front of Hendrix's computer and waved her arms. Nothing happened. She ordered the computer to wake up, but still nothing

happened. Posy was a bright girl, but it took a while before she managed to plug it in, connect to the internet and find a very small box on the screen where she typed with one finger, *How many train stations are there in London?* She received the following answer:

> People don't like to ask the question, 'How many train stations are there in London?' Causes trouble. Two deaths so far and some breakdowns. What's a station? Underground? Main line? What's a train? Does it have to have a driver? There used to be 274 underground stations. But should it be 273? And where does London end? Birmingham? Counting other systems it could be 1,300. Only Tokyo bears comparison. There's a lot of stations. Let's just leave it at that. A lot.

So much for her bright idea. She typed in Hugo de Lamartine's name and came up with one website which referred to *Trapped Light*. It belonged to Pangolin Press, the publishers. It was plain that the book was going unnoticed by the world and certainly not changing it. There was no trace of his home address, but she had not expected to find it. Posy came from a world where addresses and telephone numbers were kept confidential. In the latter half of the 21st century, letters no longer existed, parcels were sent to Post Office boxes and telephones had become obsolete. She would have been amazed to know that there was a telephone book in a cupboard in the hall, where H. de Lamartine's home address and phone number were freely available.

She heard Tommy's phone ring. She found her in the kitchen leaning against the sink, wearing rubber gloves and an apron, and saying: 'Well, I suppose I could. How many hours would you need? If I come by Tube, I could be there by eleven thirty.'

'That was Rodney. He's in a flap. They've got guests coming, and they want me to go down there and help.'

'But you don't need the money any more.'

'At the rate you're spending it we'll be poor again by next week. I can't let them down. They're friends.'

After much discussion it was decided that Posy would go and explore this new version, or rather old version, of London while Tommy was working. Posy asked for a photograph of Hendrix. Tommy remembered seeing a couple of passport photos in a drawer. The image was slightly blurred but nonetheless recognisable as Hendrix. They took one each.

'Right,' said Tommy. 'I'll change my clothes quickly and then I'm off to Thamesbury.'

'Thamesbury! Where we went yesterday?'

'That's where they live.'

'Why on earth didn't you say so! I'm coming too. They'll be glad of the extra help. I'll be ten minutes getting ready! Hey, Tommy, why don't you wear a pair of Hendrix's jeans? I think in this era people wear jeans for work.' Tommy did not appear convinced. 'They're practical. Good strong material. They might even bring you luck and help you find him.'

CHAPTER 20

Teaia

AMPHELISIA CAMBER TELEPHONED HUGO at nine-thirty on Sunday morning. 'I have thrilling news,' she said. 'Teaia is over from Barcelona for the first time in twenty years! Isn't that amazing? She phoned some friends of mine this morning to say she was coming, so they're having an impromptu gathering.'

Camber outlined the arrangements. There was no point in driving, it was bound to be a boozy day. They could meet at Waterloo and take the train down. It would be smartish, so the Stuzzicadenti jacket would be appropriate wear. They should take flowers. Would Hugo bring some to Waterloo? A big bunch? It was always fun to give a big bunch, people never knew what to do with them when they were entertaining. She would meet him at a quarter to eleven at the coffee shop, the one with the tables outside, on the station concourse.

Hugo never had the chance to say much during this conversation. The importance of the arrival of Teaia presumably overrode any competing arrangements for his day. Camber had pronounced Teaia with a lot of syllables. Tay-aye-ee-ya. She must be very well known, so it would be satisfying to tell people that he had met her. It was gratifying, too, that Amphelisia had realised that his jacket was an Ettore Stuzzicadenti. There was enough time for Hugo to get dressed, go to the supermarket for the flowers and get to Waterloo on time. Just. As all his shirts were in the wash on a Sunday, he would have to wear an orange t-shirt under his jacket, but hey, this was the Art World after all.

He had stayed up well into the night going over in his head all the things that had happened to him in the past few days.

He had arrived! Television, books, inner circles, it was exciting and exhausting in equal measure. And yet, an uncomfortable undercurrent of thought reminded him of the business card in the back pocket of his discarded trousers and the strange figure watching him from the park bench. What if that person were to ring him or turn up on his doorstep? He needed time to decide how to deal with such an event. He had planned a quiet day, but no matter.

The supermarket was busy. There were no bouquets that looked particularly big, so Hugo bought an enormous pink flower with a candelabra of green fronds in a purple pot. *Keep inside in a dark place,* said the label on the pot. *Claustrophilia* was written on a little signpost on a plastic stick. The young man who served him said that, because of the amount he had spent, he was entitled to a free yellow golf umbrella. Hugo had already brought his small collapsible umbrella, but he had owned it for some time now and the frame was wonky, so he threw it away in a litter bin outside the supermarket. The plant and the new umbrella were unwieldy, but at least he was protected from the rain on this miserable morning.

'Hurry up. The Thamesbury train is just leaving!' Her voice was brisk, instant, with no milk or sugar.

'What is that plant?' she asked.

The train was half empty, but Hugo did not like to put the plant on the seat beside him in case the stem broke.

'It had a little signpost but it's disappeared.'

Camber was concerned. 'We can't possibly give them a plant without knowing what it's called.'

'Ah yes,' Hugo studied the pink flower carefully as though seeing it for the first time. 'C something. It's a clostrofidia, I believe.'

'What an odd name. Have you started the book yet?'

'It's mostly in the head stage at the moment. I need more information from you as to the actual content before I can come up with ideas for its structure.'

'It's going to be a bible of Art and Design. Give it the same format as the Bible: short paragraphs divided up into sections which will be grouped into volumes. I'll send you the ideas by e-mail as they come to me day by day. Use the same sort of philosophical language that you used for your first book but make it much, much more authoritative. Got it?'

'Oh, yes. Thank you. That's very clear.'

'It'll be quite large, with leather binding and gold bits. Now the low profile. It's a good idea to begin giving some thought to whom you should or shouldn't be talking to. Most of the people at today's do should be fine. Wilfred and Rodney Warlock-Williams own a gallery and are dear friends of mine.'

'I know them!' piped Hugo. 'I had dinner with them last Thursday!'

'Really? You know them well?' Camber was frowning.

'Not exactly. I gave them my card at the University summer garden party and they sent me an invitation to a do at the gallery. The dinner sort of followed on. Is that a problem?'

'No, of course not. Rodney and Wilfred are part of the inner circle. The low profile really applies to the general public. With Teaia being so famous, there's bound to be a journalist or two who have sniffed out the gathering. Steer clear. We don't want people like that knowing anything about you or the book. Understood?'

'Perfectly,' said Hugo, feeling something uncomfortable lodged in the back of his throat.

The train left Clapham Junction and headed for the suburbs. Camber stared out of the window. There was the faint puckering of a smile on her lips. 'She was his muse for over forty years, you know?'

'Remarkable,' said Hugo.

At Thamesbury the clouds had moved away and the sun was peeking through. The winged residents of autumn were making an uproar; parakeets, magpies and seagulls vied for ascendancy with a multiplicity of decibels. They were joined by the churring of squirrels and the occasional scream of a daydreaming suburban fox. Camber exchanged her high heels for a pair of pumps from her bag and lit up a cigarette. 'It's such a pleasant walk from the station. We won't need a taxi.'

Hugo had been expecting a gracious mansion. It was instead a fairly ordinary 30s semi, but it did back on to the river. Wilfred ushered them in with an effusive greeting for Camber and a quick look of surprise followed by a curt nod for Hugo. Inside there was an eclectic mixture of antique and modern furniture, and even some modern pieces that probably qualified as antique but still looked modern. Art was thick upon the walls. Indeed it was barely possible to discern the colour of the paint between the frames. Someone could be heard clattering about in a kitchen. There was a smell of garlic. A young woman with flowing dark hair wearing a long skirt and a tarty top was busy arranging wine glasses on a side table. She turned and stared at Hugo.

'You're the first to arrive,' said Wilfred, and then, glancing at Camber, he added, 'The others are, of course, late. Teaia is upstairs taking a nap after her journey. She'll be flying to Mauritania tomorrow. Posy here will get you a drink. Rodney has just popped out to get some tequila. We've run out and Teaia drinks Tequila Slammers these days.'

Camber was taking a tour around the paintings like a thoroughbred doing dressage.

Hugo was still holding the plant but had not thought to give it to Wilfred.

'Wow, what an enormous plant!' Posy solved the problem by taking it and the yellow golf umbrella and putting them just outside the French windows opening on to the terrace.

'He says it's a *clostridium*,' commented Camber.

Posy's eyes widened. 'Hi. I'm Posy Bollunk. May I offer you both something to drink?'

Camber said she would have a slug of Polish vodka.

Hugo hummed and ha-ed and then opted for a glass of white wine.

'Why on earth is Teaia going to Mauritania?' asked Camber.

'I have absolutely no idea,' replied Wilfred.

The doorbell rang and everyone seemed to come at once. First was Maurizio, who was presumably the subject of last Thursday's argument. He said '*Ciao bello*!' and patted Wilfred on both cheeks, introduced himself to the assembled guests, thanked Posy for a kir royale and announced how excited he was about meeting Teaia. 'She was 'is inspiration fora nearly fifty yearsa!' he said, beaming at Hugo with a contortion of one side of his face that suggested he was taking in the jacket. His age was uncertain and his clothes too close-fitting, but he exuded energy and charm.

Next came Megan in jeans and a flimsy tunic top, clutching a dustbin bag and a carrier bag of dog food and feeding bowls. Rodney arrived at the same time with six bottles of tequila.

Wilfred fussed over Megan's two bags and appeared not to know where to put them. 'It's all so sad! Poor little doggy!'

'We can take them back to the pet shop tomorrow.' Rodney dumped the tequila on the floor and took charge of the bags. 'I'll put them up in our bedroom for the time being.' He caught sight of Hugo. 'Ah, Mr de Lamartine, tell me, what did happen to little Botty?'

Hugo, looking flustered, suggested that they should ask Tommy. On learning that Tommy had arrived at the gallery and found the dog missing, he assured them that he had tied the lead very securely to the thingy outside the front door.

'You did indeed.' Megan opened her handbag and drew out a collar and lead, which she handed to Wilfred. Wilfred fingered the collar and seemed upset. He took his glasses from his shirt pocket and studied the inside of the collar, and then he laughed. 'Hugo told us the name of the dog was Botty, and we've had the police on the lookout for owners called Kelly, when the name on this collar is Botticelli! Surely you've heard of Botticelli, Hugo? It has a "ch" as in cheese.'

Maurizio clapped Hugo on the back. 'Ita means leetle barrel. Isa nicked name. Someone stole it! Botticelli! Leetle barrel!'

'I was told that the name was Kelly by my secretary.'

'Ah, but you told me the discovery was yours, Hugo.' Wilfred, too, clapped Hugo hard on the back. 'I'm not saying that misplacing a stray dog is the end of the world, but either things matter or they don't. We can draw a line under it now. Let me help you up to the bedroom with those bags, Rodney.' The two hurried upstairs and could be overheard arguing over who had invited Maurizio.

Charlie and Terence arrived together, followed by Loud and Mature Marjorie wearing a vast yellow trouser suit accompanied by her friend, Daphne. More people came, but Hugo did not hear the introductions; he was still seething over the incident with the dog collar. He regretted bitterly that it had been witnessed by Camber. It was his own fault for employing a secretary on the strength of eleven GCSEs and five A-levels. Chertsey's family must have used bribes to get her those A grades. Or perhaps that sister-in-law had threatened somebody. He should have employed a girl with breeding and a knowledge of the world.

The room grew hot and Wilfred opened the French windows. A heron sat looking stuffed on a post on the bank, and cormorants were having flying competitions along a hundred-yard stretch of river. Hugo's plant was attracting flies. It was just like summer. A large stripey cat strolled across the garden and entered through the open windows. 'This is Akhenaten!' Wilfred announced. Nobody seemed to hear.

The cat appeared pleased to see so many people assembled and wandered from person to person wailing a polite greeting. Several guests looked down and saw him but carried on chatting. He showed them the dust of his heels in disgust and strode off to the kitchen. Four thousand years ago his ancestors had hobnobbed with royalty, yet nobody here had the courtesy to acknowledge a greeting!

Tommy, however, liked cats. She knew nothing about dogs, but her family had owned an illegal cat when she was growing up. It was called Blisters and spent most of its life asleep in an airing cupboard. Even though she was rushed off her feet, she gave Akhenaten a quick stroke and filled a bowl with chopped turkey from the fridge. He ate every scrap, licked the bowl to maintain standards of hygiene and then hurried upstairs to find somewhere cosy to sleep. Akhenaten pushed his body into the warm half-circle made by the buttocks and legs of a form, curled up in bed, in the guest room. The body grunted at this outrage and awoke.

Was this Teaia woman ever going to make an appearance, Hugo wondered. He watched tarty-top handing around plates of cocktail sausages mated with cubes of feta cheese. She always seemed to be presenting them to Terence and his lawyer friend Charlie. Hugo was trying to keep to the opposite side of the room from them. He did not want Camber to overhear any discussion of shooting docudramas in France, which would be a certain violation of her low profile injunction. Why did life have to be so difficult? It was a small room for so many people, and both Terence and Charlie were tall. It was hard to avoid them.

Tommy had been let out of the kitchen and instructed by Rodney to move among the guests holding open what looked like some sort of Art Book. She was wearing jeans and a white top with straps that looked like a straitjacket. Hugo drew closer and, glancing over her shoulder, saw two reproductions of paintings of a voluptuous nude. Teaia. Her breasts were twin cantaloupes and her arms and legs unusually thick. Hugo wasn't an expert on the female form, but it did seem an odd shape for a woman who had held a man in thrall for forty or fifty years.

'Hi, Hugo, just the bloke I need to speak to!' Terence was shouting above the hubbub and Hugo had nowhere to run. 'Can I have some photos of your folks?'

Had Camber overheard him? Hugo could imagine the Gothic arch of one eyebrow lifting. However, he had no opportunity to reply for there was a diminuendo of conversations winding down, a gasp from the assembled company and then silence.

A slow, ominous, thudding sound filled the room. Everyone had turned towards where the hallway and staircase could be glimpsed through the open door. A dress was descending the stairs. It was a pinkish floral dress, banded around neck and hemline with ancient black satin and offset by a trailing rose madder scarf. It had been a glorious dress in its day and of quite large proportions. Now it was mostly empty. It hung lifelessly around a stick-thin figure wearing heavy platform shoes that clumped along the hall carpet and entered the room. Camber was dramatic, Camber's presence could fill a room, but Teaia, for it was she, was in another league altogether. She was weird. Really weird. Her hair was like the circular thatch on a Caribbean beach hut. It was dark brown and, from beneath the flying flick-ups of her fringe, a tiny wizened face peered out.

'Hola!' she said.

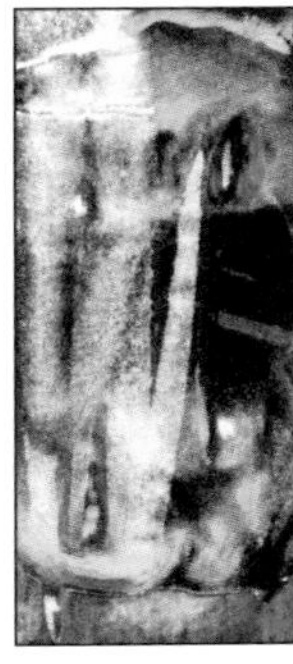

CHAPTER 21

The painful upbringing of Posy Bollunk

The framework of our society is set out in the *Book of Hudelam.*

People look back on what they have lost, a safe, secure, beautiful world squandered through our own foolishness and arrogance. We thought we could control nature. We were wrong. We have learned better. Science has learned its place now.

None of this might have happened if we had followed our own instincts. That is why aesthetics are so important to our age. We know at a glance what is wrong or right. Everything is permitted in our world – science, religion, trade, medicine, sport, technology – but all are subject to the Institute of Aesthetics.

Commentaries on Hudelam, Volume 1, Section 1

OVER A PERIOD OF FOUR WEEKS, AT THE BOTTOM OF THE RIVER, Posy did not have sex with Sidney Ng. But she was, nonetheless, convinced from a number of intimate clues, the nature of which it would be fascinating but perhaps gratuitous to examine, that, at some point since leaving him and before arriving in Hendrix's bed in Hans Place, she had been the recipient, or perhaps the instigator, of a bonk with somebody.

Travelling on the train down to Thamesbury, she had glanced at Tommy, who was sitting on the edge of her seat, gazing out of the window with the disregard of comfort typical of those who are happier when active. The jeans looked good, pity about the jacket. Posy closed her eyes and tried to remember. She recalled swirls of nausea and the wrenching dislocation of the time jump. There was a hand, definitely a hand, touching her. She sank further back in her seat, closed her eyes and concentrated. What was the use of a bonk if you couldn't remember it?

Bonfires. Smoke everywhere. Shrieks. A rumbling. She is lying on sackcloth on a stone floor. A man's voice. *Hic! Hic!* Is he drunk? *Dea! Dea mea!* What he says must mean something. Every time they come together she feels a hard metal band pressing against her skin. It is impossibly painful. *No this way, try it this way!* Whose voice? Her own? The air is thick, and she can scarcely breathe. *Ouch! No! How about like this?* There is the sound of waves crashing against stone. There's a smell of sea and sulphur. At last! On hands and knees on the agony of a stone floor. *Ita vero!* he shouts. There's an almighty bang and the entire earth moves. A man's voice growing fainter, *Atque vale!* Was that goodbye?

She opened her eyes. Birch trees along the route flashed white limbs at her. The first orange leaves leapt gleefully through the air towards the track. Suburban houses nodded and were gone. She shifted in her seat. She was decidedly still sore down there and there had been bruises on her body this morning. Oh well, at least she was full of hormones and couldn't get pregnant.

Pregnancy had been a particular problem in Posy's life. Her education, which was to begin at a primary school in Cambridge forty years in the future, had contained little of the sort of information likely to make a girl realise that there were options available other than a life of aesthetic appreciation. From the moment that she picked up her first paintbrush she was taught to recognise, evaluate and emulate all forms of Art. She was naturally academic and quick to learn. She loved History of Art and could see from her home life that there was scope in her education for an individual point of view. Posy's mother, Virginie, who had exotic blood and had been born in France and understood such things, favoured one artist; her father, Trevor, for whom the word Cambridge indicated a birthplace rather than an attainment, did not agree and preferred another. Once Posy had mastered how Art had developed over the centuries, and the changes brought by each new movement of painting or design or architecture, she would be entitled to have an opinion too.

Sometimes, sitting in the school cloakroom with a few friends, swapping secrets, she was tempted to rebel, and did. 'I hate Braque,' she whispered once. The other girls stared at her and said nothing. It was the start of puberty. She had reached it a long way before them.

Among the memories of her childhood that stood out was late one Saturday afternoon, when she was still at an age when she could only bear witness to what happened and had no power yet to comment or try to change anything. It was a period of wild rain, with the sea and rivers eating up the land. Travel was difficult locally, and impossible beyond the network of living units, workplaces and schools, connected by walkways to the Academy, the Galleries and the Craft Halls, which had been created with high-density, biodegradable plastic and stainless steel and anchored to the foundations of the ancient Colleges demolished to make way for new ideas.

There was a busy timetable of events. People needed to be organised, for too much time spent indoors in cramped units, watching the endless sheets of grey rain falling, could quickly lead to despair. There was ill-feeling between Posy's parents. She could sense it. Trevor Bollunk paced about the flat bristling with repressed energy. He tidied the kitchen, scrubbed down the tiny work surface. Virginie Bollunk slumped on their only sofa. Her eyes were blank, her skin pinkish grey. She was wearing a soiled dressing gown in a shade of pale rust. It had been stylish once. They were due to go out to some function. Posy had been ready, clothes tidy, face washed, hair tied back tightly, for hours and hours, but her mother was not dressed yet. The doors to the clothes cupboards stood open. There was a pile of garments on the bed that she had tried on in a frenzy and discarded. Trevor finished punishing the kitchen and put his jacket on. He stood beside Posy and addressed his wife.

'We need to be going. We're very late.'

'Look at you. Just look at you,' she said to him, rolling her eyes. 'We're not going anywhere. We're staying home.' She groaned, then said in a low voice, 'We've simply nothing to wear.'

Trevor made no reply. He took off his good jacket and cropped trousers and put them on a clothes hanger. He threw on underjeans and a sports vest. He struggled into his rain suit. Posy remembered the rasp of the zip ripping loudly over the sound of drumming rain. He went out. He never came back.

Posy had spent her life wondering if anything said that day might have made a difference. She felt at fault. She knew that she had somehow disappointed her parents. Her skin was too dark and her hair too wild. Her mother had inherited her grandmother's pale skin and Moorish eyes. Both women were great beauties. Posy's genes had sprung instead from an African grandfather whom she had never met. His reputation was impressive, yet Posy felt obscurely that she had let the side down in some aesthetic way. Her mother had tried so hard to do things properly. Their food was always nicely presented. She had a collection of twelve early Poddy Buckthorn abstracts, pale canvases streaked with creams and blues and greys. They were valuable, even then, and gave their small apartment an air of tastefulness. All of Posy's clothes had good labels. Her mother had done her best.

Years later, her mother had confided that it was the uncertainty that she hadn't been able to cope with. There were solid rules for every aspect of life, but that final, awful decision – what to wear – that one had to make and then defend to the world's critical eye, sooner or later had the power to bring the strongest soul, and the closest love match, to breaking point.

'And your father never had taste. No colour sense. No style.'

When Posy got pregnant at the age of eleven it made choosing suitable clothes for her extremely difficult. She had seemed a tall child, a trait seemingly bequeathed by her African grandfather; but of course an early puberty brings a lot of things, growing taller among them, to an end. She was thus tall for her age but short for a grown woman, and it is the beanpoles who have an advantage when it comes to being pregnant. They have somewhere to put a baby. When the centimetres between chest and groin are limited, and not counterbalanced by a slim leg, then the result can be dumpy, indeed squat. Posy's legs were not long. The fashion of that year was inspired by the world of classical dance: long flowing lines, tights, crossover sweaters and hair scraped back off the face and twisted into a bun. Posy loved ballet, but this was not a good look for a pregnant pre-teen. Posy's mother kept her indoors and made her stick her legs and arms out of the window to get vitamin D.

Posy's pregnancy came at a particularly difficult time. The African grandfather and both grandmothers had long since passed away, but her paternal grandfather, an amiable fellow called Digby, who helped them now and then, had also died some months earlier. He had been close to Posy and had left her a little money in his will. Posy's situation, following hard on the heels of bereavement, was not timely. The why and wherefore of her being catapulted into adulthood were never discussed. The subject of underage sex was revolting to Virginie Bollunk. Her mouth settled into a hard line, and she took to dyeing her hair a strictly conformist aquamarine.

Under the rigid childcare laws of the day, Posy had to delay her schooling. When Dorcas was born, Posy was responsible for her care full-time, while her own mother carried on working to support them all in the New Affront Small Concepts Gallery, where she assisted in the gift shop. Posy was slow to get her figure back. Dorcas didn't resemble any of her maternal forebears and showed not the slightest indication of future good looks, but at least her hair was straight. It was a difficult time, and her mother could not be condemned for making the decision to place both girls together in a boarding school when Dorcas, at last, reached the age of four.

Boarding schools were housed in retired cruise liners which made their way around the coastlines of the Gathered Isles, an area which consisted largely of the same nations that had once comprised the United Kingdom, but which now included all the Celtic lands and, of course, excluded those parts which had sunk beneath the waves without trace. Such schools were popular, partly because of a reaction to the childcare laws – most laws achieve the opposite of what they set out to do – but also because they solved the problem of what to wear, as they were the only schools permitted by the Institute of Aesthetics to have a school uniform. With the Gulf Stream a memory, icy currents came down from the north. The academic year was divided into two terms: Winter Term I, which ran from August to December, and Winter Term II, running from January to June.

In her final years at school Posy studied the following subjects:

> Art Appreciation – turning Art into language
> The Visual Arts in Science from Mandelbrot
> to Fibonacci
> Materials Science: paint, clay and metalworking
> Ethnic Art – craftsmanship around the world
> Photographing synchronised swimming
> The Psychology of Creativity: psycho-ceramics
> and poor personal hygiene
> The Universe, from initial concept to final design

In the holidays she bought black-market history books from dodgy traders outside shopping malls. She smuggled novels back to school.

Posy was twenty-five when she finished her education. She was ready for life, love, clothes and terra firma. Dorcas was still safely at boarding school for most of the year. 'I feel I'm a pot of acrylic', Posy told her mother, 'waiting to be hurled onto a canvas.'

And then Dorcas was sent home from school, visibly pregnant. There was no possible way for it to have happened, as she was in a single-sex boarding school, but, in a country where rain falls as bitter sleet or snow for most of the winter and then everything sits in the sun and steams for a month, the unlikely often occurs. Except for Posy, who, to her increasing despair, never seemed to meet anyone attractive and attracted.

Posy contemplated butchering Dorcas. This would present a reality far too brutal for her own mother to cope with, so she would have to be dispatched with too. Losing them both, she felt, would free up a lot of hanging space in the closets. Life could not have been grimmer. That was when she started to go underground.

Every society has its subversive element. In a world where the only sanctioned activities had to involve some branch of a vast, spreading, controlling network called Culture, most of the practical side of existence had been sent underground. Literally. Plastic pipes carried sewage. Other pipes brought treated water from plants beneath rivers and fens, or cables for electricity. Vast tunnels housed a subterranean road network bringing food and supplies. Even larger tunnels, colossal constructions these, housed industrial plants, hydroponic farms, laboratories, the sort of hospitals where arnica and aromatherapy did not have a place and serious and repulsive surgery was performed. Where the grey rain never fell worked doctors, technicians, scientists, researchers, farmers, industrialists and subversives.

Often, at dusk, Posy Bollunk crept down spirals of rusting metal staircases that led deep underground. She drank coffee and savoured ideas that ran contrary to everything she had been brought up to believe. She met intellectuals and humorists. She discovered polemics, politics and, most exciting of all, Science! Ancient copies of *New Woman Scientist* magazine had a clandestine circulation. There was fundraising for research. Scientists were hero-worshipped.

'That was wonderful!' said Posy.

The audience, which had watched Chertsey Staines – oh the quiet dignity, the presence of her – climb up onto the podium and address the gathered scientists, was cheering and clapping. Posy, her face shining with enthusiasm, turned to a woman standing next to her and was immediately seen as a potential initiate to a shadowy group of activists called the Conspiracy, led by the charismatic Sidney Ng.

Which, in the fullness of time, had led to her finding herself sitting in a train opposite Tommy and wondering if she was wearing the right clothes (an avocado skirt and a sexy primrose yellow top) for a gathering of arty types, who must surely be among the movers and shakers of this society. As the party was in Thamesbury and Charlie, she understood from Tommy, had been at a previous party of Rodney and Wilfred's, there was a possibility that he might be there. Perhaps Hugo de Lamartine would also be present, and she would have an opportunity to make a start on some of the objectives of Tommy's original mission.

In which case both men had better watch out. Posy Bollunk was on the prowl.

CHAPTER 22

Four witches and a cat and Terence

IT WAS THE TURN OF HUGO AND CAMBER to attend Teaia's Chesterfield throne. There was sitting room for one supplicant only, so Hugo had to stand. He tried to look as though he was part of this conversation by bending over, with his hands clasped behind his back, and maintaining a fixed smile.

'Ah, *tesoro,*' croaked Teaia.

'I remember. A treasure!' enthused Camber.

'So many years!'

'Too many!'

Teaia and Camber seemed quite relaxed in each other's company. Posy had recently refilled the glasses on the coffee table in front of them with Tequila Slammers. Teaia was propped up by cushions. The satin border of her dress formed a parabola between the fixed points of her widely spaced knees.

Camber exhaled smoke to one side and leaned forward in the direction of the older woman's right ear. 'When are you going to Mauritania?'

'I *have* aeroplane tomorrow!'

'And may I ask, why Mauritania?'

Teaia's tiny eyes lit up beneath the thatch of hair. 'I *have* dreamèd of Mauritania for twenty year! Is most *beeyootifull* place in world. Everywhere is grow sugar plant. Native only *hah-ppy* if make you *hah-ppy!* Is *hot* there but no thing is danger, no snakes – I *hate* snakes – but *hundred* and *hundred* of leetle bird. I dream about lagoon there. Is *big* lagoon. I talk to leetle bird, when up come beyootiful bird with big feet and big yellow – what you say it? – *he* go pick, pick, pick with big yellow thing and eat up peanut! Is dodo. Is just one! Is just one in world! I go with *automobile* and *chofer* and everywhere talk to *leetle* bird. Take picture! Give peanut! All is *hah-ppy!*'

Camber looked confused. Teaia patted her on the cheek and Camber's perfectly painted red lips began to stretch into a smile. Then Teaia leaned back and extended her arm and made a little gesture with her hand as though flicking dust away. It was unmistakable. It was a dismissal. Hugo watched in horror. Teaia flared her nostrils. Camber's smile was frozen in time.

'A call of nature,' said Camber, rising to her feet. 'Excuse me.' The cluster of guests thronging the room shifted to make way as she swept towards the stairs.

'*Ven aquí*.' Teaia indicated the space beside her, and Hugo sat down. She attached a desiccated claw to the sleeve of his periwinkle jacket and yanked him closer with surprising strength. '*Have* you tasted passion?'

Hugo swallowed hard and searched for an answer, but she did not wait for one and continued, 'I have *drownèd* in passion. The young! What they know of *heat* of body? If you weesh, you is Teaia *chofer* in Mauritania!'

Hugo, finding her touch irksome, was wondering how to extricate himself from the claw, when suddenly it occurred to him that now, with Camber upstairs, was an ideal opportunity to talk to Terence. If he could answer his query about family photographs, somehow, he would be spared the embarrassment of dealing with it with Camber in earshot. With some reluctance he pressed his hand to the claw. It relaxed. He leapt to his feet, leaned over and, in the presumed direction of the old lady's ear nestling somewhere beneath the thatch of hair, searched desperately for something, anything to say. The usual sunflowers tried to appear, and he blocked them, and then the words came. 'I am in the service of my Muse!'

Rising, he picked the easiest escape route which took him furthest away from Teaia. From a vantage point near the door he looked back in search of Terence. Only Charlie's head was clearly visible above the huddled mass of more diminutive folk. Where was he? Behind Hugo, across the hallway, was a doorway that led into the kitchen. Perhaps Terence was there.

Hugo put his head round the door. The kitchen was empty except for Tommy who was obviously busying herself between a sea of plates and glasses and the readying of dishes of party food for the guests. It was too late to back off unnoticed. He had been seen.

'Stop,' said Tommy. 'I need to speak to you. It's important.'

'I can explain about the dog. I tied him very securely . . .'

'So I hear. It's not about the dog.' She reached for a red handbag resting on top of a washing machine and searched inside. She handed Hugo a passport photo. 'It's about him. His name is Hendrix.'

Hugo took a quick glance and was about to return the photo, but something struck him and he took a closer look. The hair was unmistakable. What on earth? Hugo felt sick and giddy. What did she know? There wasn't time to think! He didn't know how to respond. Did it show? Could he trust himself to speak? What would be a natural response? He steeled himself to look up. Tommy was staring at him, her brows furrowed. Hugo cleared his throat loudly. 'Yes,' he said in a high voice, handing back the photograph. 'And?' he asked in a low one.

'Have you seen him?'

'Should I have done?'

'Well, he's a photography student at the University.'

This was new information. How did it connect with the slumped figure in the lavatory or the daylight ghost on the park bench?

'He's gone missing. And you're responsible.' She gave him a hard look.

The first sentence was puzzling; the second terrified him. Hugo was sweating now; he hoped it was not visible. 'I'm afraid I don't understand. How could you suppose I have any connection with this young man? I've never seen him before in

FLEA
POWDE

my life. He's a complete stranger. Why should he be anything to do with me?'

Tommy put the photograph back in her handbag, turned her back on Hugo and started to empty the dishwasher. He stood for a moment watching her lift long-stemmed glasses, two at a time, and place them on a tray on the work surface. The conversation appeared to have ended. He retreated and stood in the hallway. He was alone. She had said, *You are responsible.* What could she possibly know? Why on earth was a small incident, one tiny lapse of judgement in a public lavatory that should never have been thought of again, pushing its shadowy legs into all strands of the web of his life? Would people get to know? Would they misinterpret what had happened? Was he facing disgrace?

There were stained-glass windows on the upper half of the front door, and one to the right-hand side of the door. A milky light illuminated the mushroom clusters of watercolours and framed family photographs on the walls. Rodney and Wilfred had what were presumably progenitors and wider family on open display. Hugo thought of two photographs tucked away in a cardboard box in a cupboard in his own hallway: his parents, Pat and Al Fisher. In one photograph they were together, holding hands, looking unhappy. They were young and adrift. Both had long straggly brown hair, both wore t-shirts and jeans with flapping legs and sandals on bare feet. One had boobs and the other one didn't. In the other photograph, thirty years on, they were brimming with happiness. It had been taken in the Middle East ten years after their departure from England. They were both plump now. His father was bald with a bushy beard and no moustache. He was dressed in a jacket over a long tunic. His mother wore the hijab. Her boobs didn't stick out now but were lost in an all-enveloping roundness. His parents were no longer adrift. They had rules and certainty. They didn't phone often, but when they did his mother always said that Hugo must make a trip out to see them one day. Yes, said his father, Hugo really must come out and see them sometime.

Why had Hugo thought of them standing here in the narrow hallway? He envied their certainty. Was it only yesterday that he had said *I am the essence of pure light?* Now he could feel areas of potential difficulty. He had a chance of becoming a television personality. His career as a writer was about to set off in a new direction which required tact and discretion. Could he pull off both ventures without their colliding? Obviously not. So somehow he had to back off from the brinkmanship of the television project. He ached with the pity of it, but it couldn't be helped.

A door upstairs slammed. Someone was approaching the stairs. Perhaps it was Camber. He didn't want to speak to Camber. The front door opened.

'What're you doing there, Hugo?' asked Terence.

'Um, er . . . fresh air. I've come over a bit snuffly.'

There was a footfall on the stairs and Hugo dived out of the half-open front door. 'Let's have a chat outside, shall we?'

'I've just been out for a quick line in the car. Fancy one?'

Hugo wasn't sure what quicklime was, although he was sure it had been mentioned somewhere in a Shakespeare play he studied at school. Or was it birdlime? No matter. 'No thank you,' he replied.

The house opened on to a small front garden. Beyond was a busy road which followed the course of the river. Cars and cyclists whizzed by. It was noisy and the air was tainted with traffic fumes.

'Let's have a stroll up the road,' Hugo suggested.

Terence shrugged and followed him. 'Gruff and I were thinking that it would be good to use your family photos. There will be actors taking the part of the principal characters, but it'll add authenticity to show what they really looked like.'

'There aren't any photographs. They were all destroyed. In a house fire.'

'Pity. But a fire's good. Make a great background shot. Now let me see . . .' Terence ambled along, stopping and looking at Hugo from time to time as he spoke. Hugo wished that they could walk quickly, shoulder to shoulder, with no opportunity for eye contact.

Terence was saying, 'We need the precise location of the château. Also, the names and addresses of any family members or servants still alive, in England or France. How many would that be?' He stopped, turned towards Hugo. He'd even taken a BlackBerry from his pocket and had thumbs poised to take notes.

'This is very awkward.' Hugo stared down as if seeing his own shoes for the very first time. 'I've had second thoughts about going ahead with this project. I've had . . .' A gang of teenagers on bicycles, all riding on the pavement, pushed between them. Hugo waited with his back to a wall until they had passed, then continued, 'I've been invited to participate in a literary project involving a couple of books. This will make huge inroads on my time . . .'

'Just a minute, my friend. It's too late to back out now. Gruff and I have got this project up and running.'

'How can it possibly be too late? We talked about it on Friday and now it's the weekend!'

'Weekends don't count when you've got a BlackBerry. Everything's ready to go.'

'What's everything?'

'Well, we had the financial set-up prepared before we spoke to you on Friday. That was confirmed yesterday. I did the first draft of a script. Gruff's lined up key grips, gaffers, continuity people, make-up, casting, special effects, sound recordists, caterers, etc., etc. Once Charlie had prepared a contract and you signed it, everyone got the green light. So it's all systems go and you can't possibly back out now.'

'Oh my God. This is terrible. You'll have to do it without me.'

'That's not an option.'

'What would happen if I broke a leg or something?'

'We would help you to do it on crutches. We'd film around your hospital bed if we had to. We'd take paramedics with us to France.'

'And if I said no, I won't do it?'

'Oh bloody hell, Hugo. Don't say that! We'd have to sue you for several hundred thousand pounds.'

'I haven't got several hundred thousand pounds.'

'Course you have.'

'No I haven't!'

'That jacket you're wearing. It's what shows above the water when you've got all the stuff underneath. If you wear a jacket like that it says that you don't have a mortgage, that you've already got the car, the computers, the sound system, the holiday flat, the memorabilia collection and you probably spend a lot of time eating out. Oh come on now, Hugo. I'm a nice guy. I don't push people around. I'm saying this because this whole thing's become a lot bigger than just you and me. Believe me, you'll have a ball in France.'

Terence put an arm around Hugo's shoulders. 'Let's turn back now. We both need a drink and Megan will be wondering where I've got to. We'll have lunch tomorrow and sort it all out. Listen to me and I'll tell you some of the things that've happened to me on film shoots . . .'

As soon as they arrived back at the house, Hugo raced upstairs to the bathroom to retch unproductively, surrounded by the wracked, sickened flesh depicted in several framed posters of pictures by Lucian Freud. When he came out, tarty-top was waiting on the landing.

'Hi. I'm Posy. I need to have a word with you.'

'I really can't stop now.'

'I'll be quick. You've written a book and you've got plans for another. Right?'

'What on earth has that got to do with you?'

'Books have consequences.' She reached into her pocket and took out a photo and handed it to him. 'This is Hendrix. At least, that's his nickname. His real name is Robert Winston, and he's a student of photography at the University of Artistry and Design. But I can see that you're aware of all that already. You know him!'

'I don't know him. That woman downstairs in the kitchen showed me this picture earlier. She said he was missing or something. Now, if you'll excuse me, Professor Camber is downstairs waiting for me.'

'This involves Professor Camber too. Why don't we go and have a word with her together?'

Hugo weighed his options. He could just walk away, go downstairs, have a stiff drink and start building an escape plan to get away from all these weird mind readers who were robbing him of his sanity. Or he could talk to this woman and find out how she knew what had happened with this Hendrix fellow. He was terrified that someone – perhaps even Camber, perish the thought – would come upstairs, find them together and overhear their conversation. The door beside them was open. 'Let's go in there and talk.'

The room contained only a bed and bedside table, two large suitcases and a cabin trunk, all packed and ready to go. A soft lamp was lit. The bedclothes had been slept in and were rumpled. Sprawled on the bed, with his legs extended and belly exposed, was Akhenaten. He opened one eye, gave them a dirty look and closed it again. There wasn't much room. Posy sat herself at the top of the bed by the pillow.

'I think we should get rid of the cat,' said Hugo.

'Why? He's not doing any harm. Oh, of course, I'd forgotten you don't like animals.'

Hugo closed the door behind him and leaned on it. 'But you don't know me.'

She bit her lip and looked annoyed with herself. 'I've read your books.'

'I've only written one.'

'Of course, I meant your book, *Trapped Light*.'

'There aren't any animals in *Trapped Light*.'

As though in disgust at such an omission, but more probably because all cats have a profound dislike of closed doors, Akhenaten roused himself and jumped down from the bed. He made a low wuffling sound. Hugo was blocking his way.

'Let him out!' snapped Posy.

Hugo opened the door. With all the cool of one who has been adored by too many humans to fear one, Akhenaten sauntered elegantly past. Hugo hated the cat at that moment with a fierce rush of emotion. He hated its lack of fear, its confidence, its ability to walk out of the door without having to give a monkey's about what anybody else knew or said. If he ruled the world, he'd lock up every cat where it belonged. In a zoo. And dogs too.

Posy was leaning back against the headboard and studying him. Her top was too low, and her bra showed. The expanse of bosom exposed above it was unnerving. Why was he shut in a small bedroom with this woman? 'What do you want from me?' he asked.

'I'd like to think that nobody else was going to be damaged like young Hendrix has been damaged. I'd like you to find something else to do with your time apart from writing. I think it would be better for you, for me, for everyone, if you decided never to write another book.'

'Are you threatening me?'

'Yes, I rather think I am.'

'And why should I worry about someone like you?'

'Well, for one thing, I know an awful lot about you. More than you'll ever realise. And for another, I'm capable of anything.'

'I'm so scared!' Hugo meant it to sound sarcastic, but his voice cracked and his heart was pounding. To his horror, he watched while the woman removed her top, reached behind her and unclasped the bra, and then lay back with her arms behind her head like someone posing for an artist or on the game. And, to make it worse, she had not shaved.

'I've got wonderful lungs,' said Posy. 'When I was at school I could scream more loudly than anyone! And if you so much as touch that door handle, I will scream. Now sit down on the bed.'

What if they were disturbed? There was a key in the door.

'I'm not touching the handle,' he yelped, locking the door. He sat down on the end of the bed, as far away from all that flesh as possible.

'Good, that's better,' she said. 'Now you know, and I know, that *Trapped Light* is a load of landfill. It's a lot of fancy words strung together with no meaning. How it ever came to be published is a mystery. It has nothing to say about photography at all. If you write another book, believe me, I shall know and I will contact everyone I know, in television and newspapers, and tell them about you. I shall tell them the story of Hendrix and what happened to him.' (*Oh God! Oh God, the trousers,* thought Hugo. *She knew!*) 'Do I have your undertaking never to write another book?'

Hugo hesitated and then saw that Posy was inhaling deeply. 'I agree.'

'Say it!'

'I won't write another book.' Curiously, there was something in the words, a presentiment, that made them feel like more than lip service.

'Ever?'

'Ever.' He felt his hopes, dreams and ambitions falling into a bottomless pit, tumbling forever without sound.

'Then you and I have no quarrel any more. Just one last thing. I need you to have a word with Professor Camber. She's expelled Hendrix and it's all your fault. He tried to write an essay on your book and failed, because he couldn't write about something that no one could be expected to understand. That's going to cost him his degree. I don't care how you do it, but get her to send him a letter saying that he's been given another chance. Better still, get her to reinstate him and give him a coursework exemption.'

'I couldn't possibly do that! I don't tell Professor Camber what to do!'

Posy undid a button and slithered out of her skirt. Hugo's unwilling eyes were drawn as though by a gorgon. She was wearing the most ridiculous knickers that Hugo had ever seen:

a horrid mess of shiny lace and green frills with the face of a cat, just like the one he had just let out the door, staring back at him from the crotch. Written above it in green was the word 'Pussy'. It was the most tacky, nauseating and unnerving vision of his life. She began to inhale again. 'I'll do it,' yelped Hugo. He unlocked the door, hurled himself out of it and thundered down the stairs.

Camber was standing in the hallway examining the progenitors. She turned and looked him up and down with some puzzlement. 'Where on earth have you been? I've been looking for you for ages! What's the matter?'

Hugo explained about feeling wobbly and the walk in the fresh air. He was getting on to the episode of retching when she put up a hand and silenced him. At the same moment, it occurred to him that Posy was probably standing at the top of the stairs listening to his every word.

What did anything matter any more? So many men in public life must have felt exactly as he was feeling now. The last moments before being dragged from a pedestal and hurled to the mob. There were some words that he needed to say. He would say them. After that, where would he go? Somewhere grey and anonymous. Bognor Regis. Gateshead. He had never been to either town, but what did that matter? He was too exhausted to find a way of broaching the subject with any skill, so he blurted out what Posy had told him about Hendrix.

'There's a lad called Hendrix or Winston or something. He's one of your pupils and needs your help.'

'My help? Oh I don't think so.'

'It would be very kind of you to give him a coursework exemption.'

'Kind? Kind? A coursework exemption? And how would that benefit *me?* I don't give a shit. I am totally uninterested in appearing in any way disinterested!'

'Quite so, but let me explain.' Hugo felt thrown back to the turmoil of his schooldays. 'He's been expelled, I understand. He couldn't write an essay because he couldn't understand my book. But that wasn't his fault. Apparently it was mine. Please will you write a letter telling him he's not expelled any more.'

Camber was baring her teeth, and Hugo didn't know whether she was smiling or about to bite him.

'Why on earth do you think I wanted your book, you silly boy! I needed it precisely because it was unreadable. Not one student has ever been able to write a satisfactory essay on the subject of your book.'

None of this made any sense. Hugo's world had been turned inside out and he was fighting to construct a new reality. 'Why? Why? Why?'

Camber took a cigarette from her bag, lit it and dragged the smoke deep into her lungs. 'I'd have thought you would have guessed, after all I've told you about me! It gave me an excellent way of getting rid of any student I didn't want on the course! Isn't that clever? Terribly clever?' Her voice softened a little. 'But the next book will be much better. It will make sense. My ideas dressed up in your words! We'll conquer the world together, Hugo!'

Trapped Light was the most important thing in Hugo's life. He cared about it more than about any person he had ever known. It was his beautiful rainbow bubble, and now it had burst.

'There isn't going to be a next book.'

'Of course there's going to be a book. I have it all planned.'

At first she cajoled him. Then she became irritated, stubbing out her cigarette butt on the parquet floor with the sole of one green shoe. He saw a glint in her eye. She was angry.

Finally she said, 'You've become a bore and this party's a drag. Fetch me my coat!'

Hugo went upstairs, pushing past the still figure of Posy on the landing, and retrieved the black coat and green scarf from Rodney and Wilfred's bedroom. He walked slowly down the stairs again and handed the coat to Camber. He didn't help her put it on.

'Don't bother to come with me. I really couldn't bear your company!' She sashayed to the door and went out into the night, slamming it behind her.

Posy hurried downstairs. 'It's a start. Don't ever, for one moment, think about forgetting!' She went into the kitchen, closing the door behind her.

Hugo was alone. He wished to stay alone. He wanted to leave this world, this universe, and escape to another one, fresh and new. But an inner gloominess assured him that any alternate reality was unlikely to be much different from this one. At least now was a moment of quiet and he had time to think.

A voice behind him said, 'Ah! *Mi precioso,* my *beyootiful* young man! You and me, we go to Mauritania?'

Hugo wondered if there were sunflowers among the fields of sugar cane in Mauritania, fields of sunflowers full of little birds overlooking the lagoon. What a thought! Perhaps Mauritania was preferable to the wreckage of his life.

'What time does your flight leave tomorrow?' He enunciated the words carefully to make sure she would hear.

'I take aeroplane to Paris at eleven *hundred* o'clock and then to Nouakchott at fifteen *hundred* o'clock.'

'What airport?'

'London airport.' She looked surprised.

'There are lots of airports.'

'Oh!'

'And which airport in Paris?'

'Paris airport.'

'Right,' said Hugo. 'Maybe I'll meet you on the plane, either the first one or the second one. But don't tell anybody. Let it be our secret.' He went off in search of his yellow golf umbrella.

CHAPTER 23

A message from the future

IT WAS ALREADY DARK BY THE TIME Charlie, the last guest, had left.

Maybe we could have dinner together, he had whispered to Posy. *Here's my mobile number. Ring me any time, day or night.*

He'd been so surprised at finding Tommy once again assuming the role of hired help, and Posy too, that he had had to use his inhaler on more than one occasion.

'We need to get Teaia upstairs to bed. She won't be heavy, but we don't want to break any bones,' said Rodney.

Teaia was slumped unconscious on the Chesterfield, felled by a final Tequila Slammer. Wilfred took her top half and Tommy her legs, and they carried her so gently upstairs to the spare bedroom that she never woke.

'She's got a flight from Heathrow tomorrow morning.' Wilfred looked worried, perhaps imagining Teaia as a permanent house guest. 'I hope she's all right by then.'

They went downstairs, leaving Posy to undress the old lady and remove her teeth. It was the sort of job that Posy would have expected Tommy to perform, but downstairs a mess of dirty crockery and Camber's butt ends was crying out for Tommy's talents.

Posy unwound the scarf encircling Teaia's neck and revealed, hanging on a platinum chain, a pendant curved by the meanders of twin rivers of diamonds, ending in a single pearl drop. She gasped. She had its twin at home, handed down from her maternal grandmother. She turned the sleeping woman on her side and unzipped her dress.

Ha! thought Posy, I'm not the only one who likes sexy

underwear! This stuff must be antique silk. Bet you were the real thing when you were young. Bet you could be a firewire with a man who really wanted you.

She was was straightening the bedclothes when Teaia stirred and awoke.

'Hola.'

'Hello,' said Posy. 'Do you know that at home I've got a necklace exactly the same as yours?'

'There ees no necklace same as this. 'E *had* it made. Ees *only* one!' She held on to Posy's arm with a frail hand 'That *beeyootifooll* young man. What *his* name?' Her voice was scarcely more than a croak.

Posy smiled. 'Charlie. Charlie Archer.'

'What *he* do?'

'He's a solicitor.'

'Really? That why *he* with Amphelisia Camber?'

'Oh no. You must mean Hugo de Lamartine. The one with the nose and dark hair?'

'That *him. He* coming to Mauritania with me. *Hey!* Is exciting no?' Her little eyes wrinkled up so much that they were no longer visible.

'It's astonishing!'

The voice was barely audible by now. '*He* meet me on plane! Maybe in Paris!' She shifted in the bed, snuggled her face into the pillow and was once again unconscious.

'Maybe you'll meet my grandparents,' said Posy softly to the sleeping form, 'although probably you won't.'

When Tommy and Posy reached Waterloo station, Posy insisted on making a circuit of the inside of the station and then walking around outside from the top end, round by the taxi rank and up the stone staircase at the front entrance. 'We're going to find Hendrix.'

'Right. That's great. I'll go wherever you say!' said Tommy.

They took the Tube up to King's Cross. He wasn't there. Then on to Euston, down to Charing Cross, and by then they were feeling weary and took a taxi to Victoria. They had seen a multitude drawn from the four corners of the globe, but no Hendrix.

'What about Paddington?' suggested Tommy.

'Never liked bears. I'm tired. Let's cab it home.'

The stations of London, on a Sunday evening in autumn, are the territory of the relentlessly sociable and the dispossessed. Everyone else wants to be home spinning out the time until Monday. Posy realised that there was a side to this London that was much grimmer and sadder than the world she had left behind in the future. But it was also more honest. People don't always want to be cleaned up and tidied away.

'What about Liverpool Street and St Pancras? They're on the Monopoly board, aren't they?' asked Tommy.

'We'll go there tomorrow morning.'

'Why do you think he's in a station, Posy?'

'Gut feeling. Someone who loves trains is at home in a station.'

As the cab swung round Hyde Park Corner, Posy for once felt, as she knew Tommy always did, that she would be glad to be back at the flat. But it had been a wonderful day. She'd completed the mission. Amazing. What puzzled her was that it had been almost too easy. Some weird instinct had led her to remove a few bits of clothing and threaten him and, to her astonishment, he'd caved in without a fight. She could see by the look in his eyes that she'd beaten him. She'd never imagined it could be achieved so quickly. And the idea of Hugo going to Mauritania with Teaia was hilarious. Pity there was no chance of it being true.

She thought of poor Sidney, another sad and dispossessed person adrift in London on this Sunday evening. Well, not really adrift, but more, in some coexisting way, wedged in mud. He wouldn't know that she'd been successful. But he would have seen the three lights in the same place this afternoon, and then her light and Hudelam's, Hugo's rather, coming together at close quarters. He never would be called Hudelam now. Sidney, had he only known what had happened, might have risked a glass of Maotai at the bottom of the river tonight.

Her reward would be a dinner out with Charlie in the days ahead and maybe more. Who knows. Not much time left here. She'd be home soon. Dorcas would be giving birth and then endlessly wanting her to babysit. She'd be back to the whole child-rearing thing again. Except maybe she wouldn't. The world would be different without the effect of Hudelam's paralysing pronouncements. It could be freer, brighter. People might be able to question Art and learn about Science, wear clothes for fun, go out and party. Even Sidney might lighten up a bit if ever he made it back to the right era.

Tommy paid the cab. They were about to climb the steps to the front door when a voice said, 'Hey!' There was a figure sitting on the pavement. The streetlight illuminated his uplifted face. It was Hendrix.

Tommy squawked and threw herself at him. 'Oh Hendrix! I've been so worried! Where have you been? You smell terrible!'

'Get off me! I can't breathe.' He struggled to his feet and shook himself. His trousers appeared to be in rags. His face was dirty.

'Hi. I'm Posy. An old friend of Tommy's. We've been looking for you. Where've you been?'

He shuffled his feet. Shrugged. 'Here'n there. I was at Paddington all afternoon but the police moved me on.' His voice rose as though this were a question.

'Why are you sitting out here?' Tommy took his arm.

'Lost my key.' Hendrix shook her arm off, yet looked into her face and smiled. 'Rang the doorbell for an hour, but Paintstripper's either out or she's got her earphones on.'

They led him upstairs. Paintstripper emerged from her room with her earphones around her neck. 'Oh hello. You're back. Knew you'd turn up.'

In the bright light of the hallway, Hendrix's mucky disarray horrified Tommy. 'Come on, into the bath. You're filthy! Where did those trousers come from?'

'It's a very strange thing, but I don't know. I fell asleep, and when I woke up somebody had nicked my jeans and left these.'

'They look as though they've been glued together.'

'Yeah, they were a bit torn and I spent the last of my money on a tube of Megashtuck. Dunno why anyone would want my jeans. Even those jeans you're wearing look like an old pair of mine.'

Tommy hurried off to the kitchen and emerged carrying a plastic bucket. 'Put all your clothes in here and I'll deal with them.' She shooed him into the bathroom.

Posy looked at her. Tommy had changed. Her voice was stronger. Her skin glowed. There was a sparkle in her eyes.

'Paintstripper!' Tommy ushered the others into the kitchen. 'We need a beer!'

Paintstripper had eaten earlier, so she went back to her room to attend to her game. There was only a packet of bacon in the fridge. Tommy grilled it, cut it into small pieces and sprinkled it over spaghetti and pesto. She piled it all onto one plate. Hendrix was starving.

'Eat slowly,' she said, 'or you'll be sick.'

He was wearing a checked shirt and green shorts. His hair was damp and curling around his golden brown face. He looked far younger than his years. No wonder, Posy thought, that Tommy, unconsciously in agony from the separation with her son, had become so emotionally attached to him.

'Why did you run away?' Tommy asked him.

'I didn't run away. I just needed some space – to be by myself and think.'

Tommy appeared distressed. 'But why did you have to live on the streets to do that? You might have been attacked. Knifed. You know what happens on the streets of London.'

'Perhaps that's what I needed. The risk. You were always looking after me and making me eat vegetables.'

'Oh God!' said Tommy. 'It's time I went home.'

'Please don't take it personally. I just needed space to get my life sorted. I've made up my mind that I'm going to go and live in New York.'

'You don't have to do that.' Tommy collected up the plates

and stacked them. 'We know that Camber's been a problem. Posy spoke to someone who has dealt with her. You've been treated unfairly.'

Hendrix shook his head. 'I've had time to do a lot of thinking, and the world looks a bit different. The University can't teach me about photography. I just want to take my pictures.'

'We could go over Camber's head, smooth things out for you,' suggested Posy.

'I don't need a degree. I'll never want to teach or work in a company. I just want to take photos. And I want to see more of my father. He'll be in New York between business trips. It'll be better for both of us.'

Tommy nodded. 'Yes. I can see it makes sense.'

'I saw Camber yesterday, in the park. With some man. She really is a scary lady. He was quite odd too. Kept staring at me. Oh well, thanks for the meal, Tommy. It was really nice. Good to meet you, Posy. Sorry if I've caused you all trouble.' He stood up. 'OK if I go into your bedroom and watch some TV, Tommy?'

'Sure. Go ahead.'

Neither of the women spoke. Tommy began to remove Hendrix's clothes from the bucket. His denim jacket and t-shirt might be wearable after a wash. She put them in the washing machine. The underwear was definitely fit only for the bin; the strange trousers were ready to walk there on their own. From force of habit she emptied each pocket and found two business cards. They were damp, dirty but still legible. One introduced Terence Bunyan, of *Art Monthly* magazine and Skirmish Productions, with a London address. The other caused her some surprise. 'Oh wow, Posy! You're never going to believe this! Look at this business card.'

'CEO of Patent Processing, Swift Street. It has to be him! How many Hugo de Lamartines can there be!'

'De Lamartine – Hudelam – was at the party on Thursday and so was Terence. I'll go and ask Hendrix if he met either of them,' said Tommy.

A few minutes later, Tommy returned with the information that Hendrix didn't have a clue where the cards came from and hadn't spoken to anyone on his travels across London.

'Somebody stole his trousers. So, whoever left these trousers must have met both men,' mused Posy. 'We'll probably never know the answer to this one. But, wherever Hendrix was asleep, there must have been a CCTV camera. Isn't there some chap in the Conspiracy who's doing a research project on all the CCTV film of the late 20th and early 21st centuries?'

'Yes, there is,' Tommy agreed, 'but he hears voices all the time and Sidney thinks he's unstable. No, you're right. We'll probably never know. That must have been de Lamartine that Hendrix saw with Camber.'

'Has to be. We saw him ourselves with her yesterday. This is a really strange era. Perhaps it won't be so bad to get back home.'

There was nothing more to be done. No more excuses not to leave. Hendrix was back and didn't need Tommy. Paintstripper would always go her own way. Hugo de Lamartine would not be writing any more books and would never become Hudelam. There was nothing to pack, for there was nothing they could take with them. There was only one problem remaining. Sidney. Somehow they had to get a message to him that it was time for him to leave. Then they could place an ad in *New Woman Scientist* and collect their jumping orders from Charlie's firm.

'What happened to those letters that Charlie gave you on Saturday? The dusty old ones from the box?'

'I'd forgotten all about them!' Tommy unzipped a side pocket of her red bag and pulled out five frail and ancient envelopes. She opened the first one, then the second and third. 'Oh dear, people were so cross with me for not getting on with the mission.'

She opened the fourth letter and read aloud.

Hi Tommy,

I've been speaking on the holo to your housemates. Looks a fun place. How unusual to have so many women

in the same house. They are planning a party tonight and expect you to be there.

Wish we could get in touch with Sidney and Posy, but you know how it is, getting messages to a slipstreamer. Sooner or later they'll have a big row and Sidney will come back looking for a new assistant. Anyway, you can come back any time you feel like it. Go to Wandsworth Bridge. Here are the coordinates for the jump.

See ya!

The Conspiracy (and me, Sandy)

There was a sheet of paper with diagrams of numbered ellipses attached.

Tommy's face was animated as she read, and she was smiling as she put the letter down on the table. 'A party! We really did it. We changed our world!'

Posy felt sniffy at Tommy's use of the word 'we'. But the idea of going back to their own time and finding it not too dissimilar to this age was indeed a joy. Tommy picked up the fifth envelope. Inside was a page from a newspaper. It was the weekly 'Books' section from *The Times*. She glanced at it, shrugged and handed it over to Posy.

Posy scanned it, frowning, and then said, 'Oh my goodness. Listen to this.'

Pictures in the Sand (Pangolin) by Hugh Delam

What brings a man to spend such a long time in Mauritania, one of the harshest places on the globe? Delam gives us no answer to this, but he does open a window on to Africa and gives us some insight into the people who live there. His prose is somewhat florid. Fortunately it's restricted to a few lines of text to explain his photographs, which are startling.

'He went to Mauritania! It has to be him. Hugh Delam is so close. It is him, isn't it, Tommy? What's the date? January. Five years from now. That would fit.' She remembered, earlier that evening, two wrinkled eyes squeezed shut in excitement. 'I wonder what happened to Teaia? My grandparents came from Mauritania and, from what my mother told me, I suspect that it wouldn't be an easy place for an old lady. I wonder why she wanted to go there?'

Posy put the newspaper on the table but, as she did so, a word leapt out at her. *Camber.* Further down the page was another entry. She read it aloud, struggling for breath as she did so.

> *The Book of Camber* (Pangolin) by Professor Amphelisia Camber, University of Artistry and Design
>
> This is the greatest mystery of the year. It has a leather cover embossed with gold. It costs £150. Why did Pangolin publish it? The writing is dire. The content abysmal. Will anybody ever buy it? Will anybody ever read it? Who is Professor Camber? Does anybody care?

The two women hugged each other. There was much that united them – time, the Conspiracy, the mission – yet it had taken shared mirth to bring them together at last.

'So Camber wrote a book too, and not a very good one,' said Tommy. 'It doesn't make sense. The book that Hugo might have written changes the world. He didn't strike me as a particularly dangerous man. Now Camber, you can just imagine her coming up with something truly evil.'

'I suppose it's not what you say but how you say it. What a coincidence about that Camber item. If it hadn't been listed on the same page of reviews, we'd never have known.'

'We've done a good job, haven't we, Posy? But you're still looking thoughtful?'

'I was wondering how it works, this time thing. Do we change anything? Imagine. If we had opened those last two envelopes on Saturday, before I spoke to Hugo, what would have been in them? The letter and newspaper cutting we've just read, or something completely different?'

Later, Posy said, 'I've been good, done good. I deserve a reward. May I borrow your phone?' She went out of the front door to have her phone call on the landing.

Charlie sounded pleased to hear from her. He had gone back to the office, he told her, but was thinking of going home.

'I need a bed for the night,' she murmured, inwardly terrified that he might say no. 'I've got nowhere to sleep except a really lumpy sofa. Can you help?'

Returning to the kitchen, she found Tommy as usual washing up.

'Can I have some money? Hendrix has his bed back, so I'll take a cab down to Thamesbury to see Charlie. I'll be back in the morning and we can go home if you like.'

CHAPTER 24

Packing

HUGO WAS ASLEEP ON THE SOFA. HE turned, woke up, his body stiff and numb. And the memory of yesterday hit him like a blow from a fist.

There had been so much to do last night that he had never made it to bed. A grey, autumnal morning was competing with all the electric lights still burning in the flat, and losing. He'd opened the curtains the previous evening and never bothered to close them. When would they be drawn again?

The first thing he had done on getting back home yesterday was to phone Chertsey at her home.

'Oh hello, Mister Lamartine. How's little Botty gettin' on with yer friends? Is he all right?'

'You mean the dog?' He hesitated. He remembered the ignominy of Wilfred saying earlier, *Surely you've heard of Botticelli, Hugo?* Sod them all! 'No. I don't know. He went missing. The girl Tommy didn't collect him in time from the art gallery.'

'Oh no. That's so sad! Wasn't you supposed to hand him over, Mister Lamartine?'

'His lead was attached quite securely to the door. Somebody unbuckled his collar and stole him. He's probably gone to a good home. He was only a stray after all, for God's sake.'

'He was the very nicest little dog I ever met! I'd of looked after him if I'd of knowed you'd lose him.'

'Well, you did have your chance! He'll probably turn up. Now Chertsey, I've got something very important to talk to you about. I'm going away for a while, and I'm not quite certain when I'll be back. I don't want it to be known officially that I'm not there. Do you think you would be able to field calls for me, answer the odd letter?'

'Oh yeah. Easy peasy. No prob.'

'Good. The only difficulty is that I need to find someone who could deal with the patent applications on a temporary basis.'

'I could do that.'

'Chertsey, patent applications use very long technical words.'

'Yeah. I'm like, *Hey, those words are really hard* all the time now I'm doin' evenin' classes for a chemistry degree. But you can always look 'em up on a computer!'

Hugo lowered the telephone receiver to his chest, held it there and took a deep breath. There was too much in this life that he'd never begin to understand. He returned the receiver to his ear.

'Oh all right then. One other thing. I'll arrange with my bank to pay my bills. If I were to send you a key, could you pop round to my flat every so often and deal with post and stuff? You can let my bank know if there's a problem. Obviously I'll send you a cheque to cover any expenses and something extra to make it worth your while.'

'Yeah, that would be OK, Mister Lamartine.'

'Good. That's all settled then. Your niece, Melony. Is she all right?'

'Not really. She's got mumps and scabies.'

It was too easy. A phone call, a few letters instructing utility companies and the bank, and it was beginning to seem possible that he could step out of his life. Next he used his computer to find the flight. There it was! The 15.00 flight from Charles de Gaulle to Nouakchott, Mauritania. The flights from London City Airport seemed to go to Orly, but there was a choice of flights from Heathrow to Paris, so he picked one at midday. He printed out his e-ticket.

Next was packing. He took his largest suitcase down from on top of the wardrobe. What did one take to Mauritania? In the company of someone like Teaia, there were obviously going to be evening dos. He'd need his DJ, dress shirt and patent leather shoes. There might well be the odd chilly evening and he'd be glad of his Ettore Stuzzicadenti jacket. It was going to be hot in Africa, so no jumpers then. He really needed a new linen jacket. Perhaps he could buy one there. He packed his old one. Next were the usual items of male attire, plus a swimming costume and some shorts that he hadn't worn for fifteen years. Would it rain? He packed his long, grubby raincoat. He even had an old tennis racquet. What the hell, why not? It would be an excellent opportunity to learn to serve. There were some sunglasses that he'd never got round to wearing. There really was no good reason to take the blue and yellow wind-up torch Chertsey had bought him for Christmas; it was typical of her to buy him something so perfectly useless. He had meant to throw it away, but perhaps it would serve as a bribe for a happy native. He packed it.

A few books would be a good idea. Two compilations of crossword puzzles and six months' worth of vintage *Reader's Digests* went into the case. He packed two translated volumes, *Swann's Way*, purchased at the same time as the shorts, with clean pages and a grubby cover, that had been his companions on every trip away since. He removed a copy of *Trapped Light* from his bookshelf and looked at it with sad affection. Poor little book. He couldn't leave it behind. From the kitchen he took a jar of Marmite, some Branston pickle, a tin of Earl Grey tea bags and two packets of Garibaldi biscuits.

It was after two when he thought about picking up his e-mails. He couldn't face the thought of reading something annoying from Nigel M. or, worse, some swingeing attack from Professor Camber. To his surprise there was only a message from Gruff Hint.

> Hugo
>
> As promised here is the French translation of your book. It reads rather well, I'm sure you'll agree. My friend did a good job, I think, but it unhinged him a bit. He's not

communicating much and I haven't been able to pay him.

We could recite bits of it with some music in the background. Adamo singing *Le Ruisseau de mon enfance* or something. Look forward to getting together and sorting out the detailed stuff – places, names, dates, etc.

Cheers

Gruff

He clicked on the attachment and out flowed a bubbling brook indeed of French words: page after page of intelligent-looking French. It was entitled *La Lumière emprisonnée*. It felt as though his book, which had been sullied by the harsh words of Posy and Camber, was now reborn, pure and limpid. Or to confuse the metaphor still further, the light which was trapped had now been set free! How much paper did he have? He hoped to hell he had enough. He shuffled through a cupboard filled with old newspapers, household bumph and copies of irate letters to newspapers till he found a partly-used packet of A4 inkjet paper. He prayed it would be enough.

He waited anxiously as his printer coughed, spluttered and spewed forth page after page of manuscript. There were interruptions. Again and again the paper stuck. Three hours later it was complete, with only two sheets to spare in the printer. He put the sheaf of papers in an envelope and packed it in his suitcase. He hadn't had time to look up tourist web pages for Mauritania. What was the point? He'd find out what it was like soon enough. But he had a feeling they might speak French there, and the manuscript could be useful. Only a few more bits and pieces to do and he would be ready!

Hugo shuffled to the bathroom. Monday morning. At least he didn't have to go to work. It was early. There was still time before he had to leave for the airport. Somebody was knocking on his front door. This meant it had to be a neighbour; not that he knew any of his neighbours, but anyone else would be ringing on the intercom from the front door.

He opened the door. Standing on the mat, dressed in a

smart grey suit was an Asian woman whom he guessed to be in her forties.

'Good morning. I am extremely sorry to disturb you so very early but, not having your telephone number and being rather presumptuous, I dared to call upon your residence. My name is Ravinder Bhatt.'

Even though he was still in his dressing gown, which he excused on the grounds that he had barely slept last night, and informed her he had a flight in a few hours, she wanted to talk. She spoke English better than an enclave of public school headmistresses and it was a steady flow that would not be stemmed. She came into the flat. He ended up making her tea. He had to take the Earl Grey out of his suitcase, for God's sake. She was so bloody polite that it was impossible to do what he really wanted to do, which was to shout at her and kick her out of his flat. What did he care about the improvement of education in the arts in a number of totally unpronounceable Indian regions? Why should he give a toss about *the funding difficulties of Indian Universities, and her absolutely unforgivable, but sadly unavoidable, inability to recompense him adequately for what after all was an extremely important contribution to the academic study of the photographic arts?*

The upshot of it all was that she took his manuscript of *La Lumière Emprisonnée* and paid him fifty quid.

Glancing at it briefly, before putting it in her leather satchel, she said, 'Whoever was responsible for translating this very excellent book into English should be held to account. It was so very evidently a poor translation! I am very delighted indeed to have the original!' And she was gone.

There was no time left to do anything! Barely time to shave, dress and swallow a banana.

He struggled with his suitcase down three flights of stairs and ended up walking for ten minutes before he found an empty cab. He sank back into his seat, feeling totally exhausted.

'Wake me when we get to Paddington, please,' he instructed the driver.

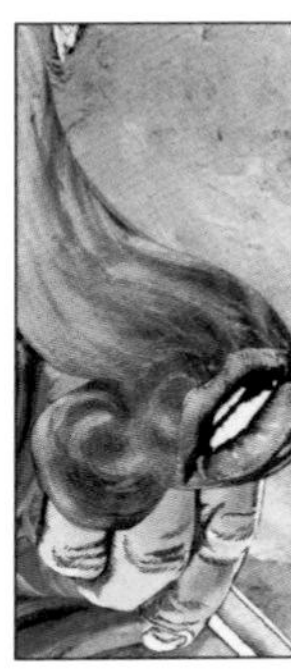

CHAPTER 25

V for Victory

POSY AWOKE, FOR THE SECOND TIME THAT morning, to the sound of magpies cawing. Charlie was asleep beside her in the bed. The first time, she had opened her eyes to find his face a few inches from her face, smiling at her. It wasn't supposed to be like this. She had come down here for the first bonk of her life in a proper bed. Now she was lying in what, it had to be admitted, was a humdrum bedroom and feeling strangely moved.

The flat-roofed house wasn't much larger than a flat. It had a garden which was presumably full of Thamesbury's turbulent wildlife. There was one room downstairs, a bedroom upstairs and a study where Charlie worked when he came back from the office. All was devoid of colour and bachelor-bare, except for a couple of good paintings of country landscapes (*Were they Boddingtons?* she wondered). There was a sculpture of what looked like a workman's apron dipped in plaster of Paris hanging from the bedroom wall. (*Where had he found it? Was art like this as valuable in this era as it would be one day in hers?*) And there were books! A whole wall of battered paperbacks!

Everywhere there were piles of magazines and papers. The kitchen looked unloved. If ever a house had needed the touch of a woman, or indeed a gay man, it was this one. But Posy had not the slightest desire to meddle, even if it were possible for her to stay for more than this one night. And there was the rub. It was so sad. At long last she had met a halfway decent bloke and she was going to have to push off without telling him why.

He looked so peaceful lying there. His hair was sticking up, his skin still slightly tanned from summer past, with shadows of chest hair and new beard. The smell of him was so good. But what future could there be? What would he think of her when he woke and found her gone forever?

She was nearly ready to slip out of the door when he said, 'Why are you dressed? Are you leaving? And why are you crying?'

Everything she said by way of explanation raised more questions. She had to go away today.

'Where to? Why? Is there someone else?'

She tried the truth. 'I'm going to be a grandmother.'

'Wow,' he said, 'you don't look more than twenty-five.'

'I'm nearly twenty-six.'

He did the arithmetic. 'My God, that's young! You're married then.'

So tempting to lie, but being with someone who hasn't got any clothes on, and is looking upset, is not a situation conducive to responding with a convincing fib. 'No.'

'So what's the problem?'

The problem was that, grandmother or not, he was too old for her. Before they had a chance to build a relationship, he'd be in his early nineties. Or maybe – this was a wild idea, totally crazy – what if she didn't go back with Tommy? What if she were to stay? And imagine in thirty-four years' time, knowing that she was sharing space-time with her infant self? Or perhaps she could stay for only a year or so, like Tommy had? But a man who had become so bogged down in his job was bound to want to tie himself down even more securely, in marriage, with children. No, there was no escape. She had to lie.

'I'm dying. I've only got a few weeks to live.'

'Then be with me to the end.'

Oh goddammit, goddammit! He meant it. She was crying uncontrollably now.

So the truth came out.

'I'm from the future. I came in a timeship. Tommy's from the future too. We have to go back.'

He wasn't stupid. He wasn't gullible. His mind had been honed by the law, fenced in by logic, used to functioning within a rule-based system. She could see the struggle that was going on inside him. He went to the bathroom, leaving the door open; she could hear him pissing, cleaning his teeth, throwing water on his face, using his inhaler. He came back wearing a revolting green and orange checked dressing gown and looking utterly miserable.

'Tell me again where you're from.'

'I'm from England. From Cambridge. I'll be born in thirty-four years' time. I've travelled back from sixty years in the future. I came to make our world a little better. I have to take pills that damage my health to be here.'

'Prove it.'

'You've seen the proof. That box in your office. There's only one Tommy Willoughby. The one you met again yesterday.'

'But that's from the past. You said you came from the future.'

'A woman who travels to the past researching history put it there so that Tommy would have the means to live here. Tommy arrived over a year ago.'

'When did *you* get here?'

'Friday night.'

'When are you leaving.'

'Sometime today.'

'Who'll win the World Cup two years from now?'

'What's the World Cup?'

That had an effect. She could see he was beginning to believe her now. 'Come here,' she said. She kissed him, putting everything she had into the kiss. 'This is breaking my heart.'

'Mine too. It's just so hard to believe something illogical.'

'Didn't Einstein say that he couldn't find any forward arrow in space-time? The theory has already been written, now, in this time. It is possible. I could tell you things about what's going to happen, but you've got your life to live. I want you to be able to live a normal life.'

'Normal life? I wouldn't know where to begin. Can I stay with you today, be with you when you go?'

'Yes. OK. If it helps.'

'It'll help. How much time have we got?'

'I'll phone Tommy and find out.'

When Posy spoke to her on the phone, it sounded as though Tommy was anxious and emotional.

'What am I going to say to Hendrix and Paintstripper? I can't leave without saying goodbye.'

'I've told Charlie. I had to. There wasn't any other way.'

'Sidney will kill you.'

'Only if you tell him.'

'Aaargh, this is dreadful. We need to leave from Wandsworth Bridge while it's still daylight. I don't want to take off in darkness. We need to leave before five really. Which means you need to be here at three-thirty.'

'OK. Three-thirty it is then. See you then.'

Charlie said, 'I'll drive you up there. Let's have some breakfast and then go back to bed.'

'What about the office?'

It was good to see him smile again.

Halfway through breakfast, with his mouth full of toast, he asked, 'What about the father of your child?'

'Never knew his name.'

'What! But you were so young. How old were you?'

'Eleven.'

'And you never knew his name? You were raped then?'

'God no. My grandfather on my father's side died and left me some money. In cash, in an envelope. I splurged it all on a course of IVF.'

'Bloody hell! Why on earth did you do that?'

'Haven't the foggiest. Low self-esteem probably.'

Later he asked, 'Could I come with you to the future?'

Posy explained to him about Banks and Bridgewater and that something or someone who came from the past, travelled to the future and stayed there for more than ten minutes would mess up the world. Although it didn't seem as if the world could ever be messed up as much as it was, for them, at that very moment.

Several miles away from the star-crossed lovers, Paintstripper, in the manner of pots and kettles, was saying, 'Look, it's very interesting hearing all about your son, Henry, in such detail, but tell me, you've been here over a year, what on earth are you doing spending all that time away from a six-year-old? He must have been five when you left! And why aren't you rushing to get back to him?'

Tommy had folded all her clothes neatly and put them in dustbin bags together with her few possessions. Perhaps someone would take them to a charity shop. She had left the poster of the lead singer of Splintered Dick where it was. Hendrix had emerged briefly from his room, eaten a bowl of cereal and said that he was going to go back to sleep again, but when he woke up he would book a flight to New York.

Tommy hugged him and said, 'I wish you a wonderful life in New York. I shall look out for your photographs. I won't ever forget you.'

So, without telling him she was leaving, she had said her goodbye. She didn't have to worry about him. He would find his way. The logistics of taking her leave from Paintstripper were proving much trickier.

'Henry's OK. He won't have missed me.'

'A whole year and he hasn't missed you? Oh of course, I didn't realise. And they've managed to find a place for him. In a school! How wonderful, but does he cope?'

Tommy was becoming ever more flustered. 'He's quite normal. He's very bright in fact. Oh dear!'

'Look, don't tell me all the difficult stuff. Why don't you just tell me what I need to know. You're leaving, aren't you?'

'Yes.'

'When?'

Tommy looked up at the kitchen clock. It was three o'clock. 'Soon. In half an hour. When Posy gets here.'

'Can I come and see you off?'

'Yes. I'd like you to be there.'

'Where? Gatwick, Heathrow, Victoria Coach Station?'

'No. Wandsworth Bridge.'

'Funny place to choose. In a car, in a boat?'

'Not exactly.'

'In a TARDIS?'

'If that's a helicopter, then no. We'll be there one minute and gone the next. Do you want me to tell you everything?'

'Oh absolutely not. I wouldn't be able to handle it, I'm sure. Just tell me one thing.'

'What?'

'Why did you come here?'

'To earn money. I'm a single mum. I'm being paid back home for being here.'

'Wouldn't it've been easier to work from home?'

'I did work from home. I was a Sex Nurse. Believe me, it isn't an easy option.'

'Does that mean you dress up as a nurse or something?'

'Goodness, no. I was part of a medical outreach, care in the community, disability facilitation team funded by the Arts Council. It is amazing how medical artists can help keep some bits working when most other bits have closed down, been removed or fallen off completely.'

Paintstripper's eyes opened wide to convey surprise, with a brief nystagmus of some other emotion. 'So you left because you couldn't stomach it any more?'

'Oh no, I loved my work,' replied Tommy. 'It was just that the pay wasn't very good, and they wanted me to work weekends and evenings.'

For once Paintstripper was not drinking beer. She sat with her workmanly hands gripping a coffee mug. Unspoken words hung in the air. What did Van Gogh or Dali, peering down on them, know of the agonies of children left and mothers leaving them? Was there any moral difference between Tommy's deserting a five-year-old and Paintstripper leaving her late-born youngest who was only eight?

'The question is,' mused Paintstripper, 'is the art worth it?'

'Your paintings?'

'No, not the paintings. I'll show you my real art.'

She led Tommy out of the kitchen and into her too-tidy bedroom. How different this room must be, thought Tommy, to the family home filled with the banter and bustle of three boys which Paintstripper had left behind. Tommy drew up a crate, used as a laundry box, and joined her friend at the computer screen.

'This is a computer game which I have created. It starts with a three-minute film sequence.'

The graphics had a man-made quality that Tommy was not used to in her era, where the created could not be distinguished from the real. But there was some sort of strange, jerky, abrasive beauty revealed to Tommy as the film sequence flickered on the screen. The music was surely classical, but she didn't recognise it. She had no natural aptitude for the subject, but she had been trained in art all her life. She could not have said why she knew this was good, but there was a prickling on her skin that insisted it was. There were strange people and animals creeping through a dark landscape towards a château set upon a hill. Faces appeared at the windows. Staircases led up and up and up. A body hurtled down a flight of stairs and a small boy, with dark hair, a sharp nose and a pale face, stood transfixed. Play was set to begin. The images froze. Paintstripper quit the game and returned to her screensaver, a thin white line moving across the screen.

'I have had my vision.' She leant back in her chair. 'That's probably enough to give you an idea.' She looked at Tommy as though she were expecting a judgement.

'It's more than beautiful. How wonderful for your sons to see something like this and know that their mother created it.'

The sun of early morning had long passed behind clouds. This was a day that would end without an obvious sunset. The light would leach away and the darkness encroach. A stream of traffic was making its way over Wandsworth Bridge. There was no procession of the dead, or indeed pedestrians of any kind, except for four people walking onto the bridge two by two. Paintstripper, her hands in the pockets of a donkey jacket, strode a pace ahead of Tommy. Tommy was wearing a grey tunic and a strange cloak fashioned from some waterproof material with long lapels and a scalloped hem. Her galoshes were pinkish and slightly translucent and she carried a red handbag. Behind them were Posy and Charlie, pressed together with arms around each other's waists. Posy was enveloped in a bulky man's coat over her green tunic and bedroom slippers. Charlie's clothes were the sort that men choose when they spend most of their lives dressed in suits and have not got their heads around the concept of smart casual.

'Don't come any further, you two,' said Posy. 'We'll come back when we're ready.'

Posy and Tommy walked together to the middle of the bridge. They stood at the white-painted steel walls, at the edge of the bridge, and stared at the sky above them. They linked hands and began a sort of dance. They moved diagonally backwards, slowly, keeping in step, then shifted forty degrees to the left and moved forward, again diagonally and in step. They repeated this manoeuvre several times, and it was apparent to Charlie and Paintstripper, watching close by, that the women were making the shape of a letter 'V'. Then they stood still and waited. Five minutes passed. It was surely growing chillier. Five minutes more. Once again they performed their creation of an imaginary 'V'. Once more they stood still and waited. It happened. Charlie and Paintstripper, looking down at the water, saw only the grey sky above. Tommy and Posy sensed a pressure of air mounting and being sucked into a vacuum the size of a supermarket. Their bodies curved as though being forced backwards. There was a tiny pop and something that had been present was there no longer. Three lorries and a van drove over the bridge. Somewhere in a neighbouring street a car alarm went off. The city hummed and throbbed and further downriver the London Eye turned, measuring out time.

Posy and Tommy went to the edge of the bridge, standing side by side, and looked down into the water.

'I hope he's been looking after my books,' said Posy.

They walked back over the bridge and rejoined the other two on the riverbank. Below the bridge, it was high tide at the water's edge. Grey water slapped green slime on old brick. There was a smell of age, chemical irresponsibility, inefficient water treatment and mildew.

'What happens next?' asked Charlie.

'Not much. The rest is pretty easy.' Posy encircled his hips with her arms and pressed her face into his stomach. Time, with which she had been so cavalier, had now been frittered all away. 'That money that belongs to Tommy Willoughby, is there any way of giving it to you and Paintstripper and Hendrix?'

'Not really.' Charlie bent over and rested his chin on the top of her head. 'If money suddenly appears and disappears, and there's no trace of the person who was supposed to have owned it, there'd be questions asked. But I'll remove the old box file from the storage room for a keepsake. There's no reason why you shouldn't stay on in the Knightsbridge flat,' he said to Paintstripper.

'I won't be needing it. I'm going home. Back to my boys.'

Charlie shook hands with Paintstripper and kissed Tommy on the cheek.

Tommy hugged Paintstripper. 'Thank you for everything. I'll never forget you.'

Posy and Charlie kissed. What was there left to say? *Thanks for the love, shame we didn't marry and have kids and grow old together. What a sad pity we ever met, but we can't regret, won't ever regret, that we did.*

She took off the coat and gave it back to him. 'Sixty years from now, in Cambridge, on the 22nd October, I shall be twenty-six.' Posy stroked the side of his face with her hand. 'I'll be having a birthday. The party will be held . . . where? Let me think. Let's just say at the best hotel in town. I don't care how old and decrepit you are. I'd love to see you there.'

'What about your grandmother? Is she living in Cambridge now?'

'Forget it. She didn't marry you.'

Posy and Tommy walked side by side to the water's edge, picking up speed as they reached the point where water touched land, and then they carried on walking. It seemed to Charlie and Paintstripper that they saw them hovering above the water, for a moment, and then they were gone.

SECTION THREE

Mauritania and London

CHAPTER 26

In the heat of the day

IT WAS ONE OF THOSE DAYS WHEN LIFE'S hold on the planet seemed particularly marginal. At midday there was no shade. The sky was a single hue of dark blue. It was a world of dust. A hot wind had picked up this dust from the Sahara and lifted each gritty particle to be seared by a relentless sun and sent on its way.

The man was dressed for the demands of his environment. He wore bulky blue robes to reflect the glare. A swathe of cloth was wound as a loose turban around his head and pulled across his face, leaving a crack through which the glitter of his eyes could be seen. He walked slowly, his leather-clad feet emerging briefly with each step from beneath the hem of his robe.

He seemed uncertain of his route. Perhaps it was a way he had walked before, yet memory was not serving him well. He stopped, turning his head from side to side to see the world around him. Where there was soil, it was cracked. Scrubby trees sent roots far down into the ground, searching for any trace of moisture that might have escaped the long months of drought. The white sand, which had travelled so far to get here, was shrouding cars parked along his route. He crossed the road and entered a street, his step a little faster.

There was a row of shops. Each seemed to have been in place for aeons, but he studied them as though searching for somewhere that was no longer there. He walked a little further and stopped beside a restaurant. Its signpost, a grinning bat, could be discerned beneath a layer of white. He stood as though lost in thought. Perhaps he was wondering whether to enter to seek a glass of cool water. The wind tried to play with his heavy robe and gave up. A small shadow crept from beside a door, moved towards the man and sniffed his sandal and bare foot. It was a brown rat, recently widowed and well advanced in years. It limped back through a grating on the pavement and re-emerged with several family members, all of whom scurried in a way which suggested youth and energy.

The man walked on without looking down. He could not know that he was no longer alone. Behind him, the aged patriarch and his sprightly offspring followed, keeping close to the lee of the wall. The man reached a garden square. Here there was no protection for his entourage from the bright glare of day. They dived through the garden railings and trailed him from the shade within. The central area, once laid to lawn, was now bare earth patched with withered blades of yellow and buff. At the end of the square they came to a red-brick Victorian police station. The rats were out in the open again. The man's steps appeared to falter. The rodents stopped, wary of their exposed position, but not wishing to retrace their steps. Tiny peach-coloured feet baked on the paving stones. The caravan took up its forward momentum again, past steps winding down to a public lavatory, across a road and back to the safety of a low wall. There was a journey of several miles ahead of them.

Marjorie and Daphne were lucky to have front row seats. The hall was crowded. Black blinds had been drawn down the long Gothic windows – it had once been a church – to keep out the heat. A crack exposed at the base of each blind let in enough light to see by. The vaulted ceiling was high, and the walls thick. It ought to have been cool.

'Are you perspiring too?' Marjorie's loud voice was softened by the humid air.

'I'm drenched!' whispered Daphne.

'I forgot. I brought two fans! Hold my glass a sec while I try to find them,' said Marjorie, rootling about in her bag.

Life was so overcrowded with ad hoc gatherings – they were both 'Friends' of most of the temples of culture within the Greater London area – that it was a rare thing to have a moment to spare for acting on impulse. Marjorie had been tempted in by a poster at the door which offered a talk and a glass of cold white wine. The promise of a long sit-down in the cool of a former church was irresistible. Daphne, with a little sigh, had followed.

The seats were occupied by the kind of people who were free to attend such an event at lunchtime on a Tuesday: refugees from nearby offices; the unemployed who were, in this well-to-do neighbourhood, a better class of unemployed; parents who worked from home and were glad to escape their stifling flats. The retired were represented in abundance. The event had been organised by a group of middle-aged worthies who, with the collapse of Adult Education, had taken it upon themselves to keep the light of culture burning in the Capital.

'This wine's punching above its weight a bit, isn't it?' Marjorie smacked her lips together.

'Very sweet and sticky. What's that peculiar odour?'

'Smell's like a 60s party. Joss sticks. Horrible stink.'

'I feel a little weird.' Daphne dabbed her forehead with a tissue.

There was an outbreak of coughing, and the two women noticed that a middle-aged dancing queen in a tiered skirt and filmy top had taken her place on the dais.

'Good afternoon, everybody. It really is a *pleasure* to see *so many* of you here today. We are very honoured to have with us Mr Hugh Delam. Now, many of you will remember Mr Delam from his *extraordinary* exhibition of photographs, first in Paris and then at the Serpentine Gallery here in London. For those of you who have not been so fortunate, I shall explain that Mr Delam's photographs were all taken during his stay in Mauritania in Africa a few years ago. The photographs have now been gathered together in a *wonderful* book published by Pangolin Press, called *Pictures in the Sand*. We have a table with the book on display, and we shall be selling copies after the talk and, if we are very lucky, Mr Delam may sign a few. Now, without further ado, allow me to hand you over to Mr *Hugh Delam*.'

Marjorie and Daphne became aware of activity behind them. They turned to see a strange figure emerging from semi-darkness and proceeding up through the the centre aisle towards the lighted dais. It appeared to be a tall male, immensely bulky in a long blue robe and swathes of headgear. His movements were slow and dignified. Reaching the dais, he positioned himself behind the lectern and nodded to a fellow with a laptop to the side of the stage. To the rear of the dais was a white screen where images from the book were presumably going to be displayed.

Hugh Delam lifted the section of headgear obscuring his face and revealed that below dark and glittering eyes was a longish nose and a neatly trimmed black beard. His skin was roughened and blistered. The hand that had performed the operation, although weathered, was thin, with elegant fingers oddly at variance with the immensity of his costume.

He stood very still, saying nothing. People shifted a little in their seats, waiting for the silence to break. The wait did not appear to worry him.

He held himself erect and gazed out over the audience as though he had been waiting all his life to savour this very moment.

At last he spoke.

'Peace be upon you all and upon your houses.' The voice was fairly ordinary, slightly nasal. He had a native's command of the English language. 'I am going to tell you the story of my trip to Mauritania. I was invited there by a very famous woman. Many of you who are familiar with the Art World will recognise the name Teaia.'

There was a murmured hubbub from the audience.

'I was invited to accompany Teaia, at very short notice, to be her companion and protector during her time in Mauritania.

It was her life's wish to visit Mauritania and film its birds. On the flight out from Paris she handed me a very fine old Leica camera together with many rolls of film. *You are to take the photographs,* she told me. My knowledge of photography at that time was extensive but largely theoretical. I was totally unprepared for what happened next . . .'

The details of the memory were personal, not for sharing.

'Now I know it look *muio complicada,* but I have . . .' Teaia scrabbled with one beringed claw in her squat crocodile handbag and produced a notebook. 'This make camera all simple!' She handed the notebook to Hugo with a coy smile. 'Then is money. I is no good with money.' She took out a slim wallet. 'And this.' She gave him a velvet bag secured with gardening twine. 'All gif to me for love. Safer with you. Now why you not get us more cognac from young lady?'

Beneath the velvet Hugo could feel hard edges. Jewellery of some sort? He stood up and placed the camera, the wallet and the velvet bag in his canvas holdall in the overhead locker. The stewardess was nowhere to be seen. The curtain to the galley beside them was closed, and the cabin lights were dimmed for a film. They had eaten and consumed too much wine already. The plane was full, but their two seats were off to one side in the first row of their section and faced a partition. Hugo resumed his seat, glad not to be wedged close to some stranger. His proximity to Teaia was unsettling enough. She was leaning away from the porthole next to her and attempting to snuggle up to him, her head veering dangerously close to his upper arm. He shut his eyes. He felt the weight of the old lady's head against him. He opened his eyes and stiffened. If he turned towards her, the thatch of brown hair would brush his chin. She pressed closer. What could he do? He would fake a sneeze! He inhaled, held the air deep in his lungs for a moment, then exhaled with all his might, reaching for his handkerchief and simultaneously pushing against the intrusive body with some force. She flipped with the lightness of an empty glove and,

above the drone of four powerful engines, Hugo thought he heard the clunk of bone on glass.

Hugo could see that Teaia was now snuggled up to the window but her head was much lower than it ought to have been.

Hugo watched the film, without sound, from a space just by the lavatories. When it was halfway through he returned to his seat and, finding Teaia hadn't moved, thought that he ought to do something, tell somebody.

The steward and the stewardess ignored Hugo and fussed over Teaia. They whispered furiously to each other in French. Hugo could not understand a word. He went off to the lavatory and sat there for a while. When he returned, he saw the cabin staff had erected what appeared to be a small square tent around Teaia's seat. A man's cream chinos could be seen protruding from beneath the tent. Presumably some doctor was in attendance.

Hugo wandered up and down the aisle.

Later the doctor had departed and all had returned to normal except for the tent around Teaia's seat.

'*Asseyez-vous!*' said the stewardess, indicating Hugo's seat beside the tent.

Hugo was insistent. 'I'm not sitting there!'

'Ze plane ees full! Seet down!'

'Why can't you put her in the galley?'

'*Interdit!* Forbidden. We 'ave sanitary rule!'

'But we've had dinner and I want to sit down and I'm not sitting there!' cried Hugo.

The stewardess pouted, shrugged, turned on her heel and disappeared into the galley, swishing the curtain shut behind her. Hugo contemplated taking the matter further. He could insist that the captain was consulted. But there had been a glint in the eye of that stewardess that seemed to suggest that she had power and Hugo did not. He recalled that cabin staff, especially French ones, were more than capable of gripping you with a half-nelson and handcuffing you to the seat struts. He stood in the aisle for ten minutes more, then edged awkwardly into his seat. He sat there for the rest of the flight, imagining waves of cold, dead, contaminated air emanating from the seat beside him.

The large hall was silent. Before him was a sea of expectant faces.

Hugo cleared his throat and said, 'During the flight out, Teaia, as you probably read in the newspapers, succumbed to a stroke or heart attack or something. She died suddenly and with no pain yet was deprived of her dream. She never saw the birds of Mauritania. But she was buried there. At least I think she was.'

He nodded to the man with the laptop. The white screen sprang to life. There was a photograph of Teaia in her youth. She was wearing a dress with a short skirt and an oyster shell of a hat with a light veil. Her eyes were obscured and appeared as dark smudges, but below the veil her lips were bright red, and her smile revealed white teeth. Her breasts were like cantaloupes and distracted the eye from her arms and legs, which were a little on the thick side. She was gleaming, lubricious, suggestive and tantalising.

Hugo coughed drily and continued, 'The airline was very helpful. Indeed it was their assistance, and the disruption that accompanies a death, which enabled me to avoid the formalities which I would normally have encountered on arrival. I emerged into the night air with no visa, no return ticket, not an awful lot of money and a huge conglomeration of Teaia's luggage, which included cabin trunks that had been in transit from Barcelona. But I had her camera. And before me were the lights of Nouakchott!'

CHAPTER 27

Nouakchott

IN FACT IT WAS TO BE MORE THAN TWO days before Hugo ventured out on foot into the streets of Nouakchott.

Hugo's presentation of Mauritania did not include a photograph of his hotel in the Capital. Even if he had taken a snap, he would have rejected it on aesthetic grounds. The hotel room was a suitable candidate for inclusion in a guide entitled *Hotels of the World which we strongly advise you to avoid if you possibly can*. The floor was tiled, the walls bare and of an ageing putty colour at variance with the square modernity of the hotel exterior. The room size had been barely adequate when Hugo first arrived, but by the time the bed had been moved, disturbing an enormous cockroach which had scuttled off towards the bathroom, and Teaia's cabin trunks, valises and hatboxes had been piled against one wall, there was scarcely room for the bed and Hugo's single suitcase. The advent of dawn was already visible through the metal grille of the window. Someone outside with a megaphone could be heard treating the city to a bit of a singsong. It had been a long confusing night. Hugo was exhausted and needed time away from the sound of Arabic to gather his thoughts.

Over the course of the long night at the airport, Hugo had sat on a very hard chair, in the two-dimensional glare of strip lighting in a small office, and tried to work out what was happening to him. A couple of people were involved. One tall man, perhaps, was representing the airline. A small darker-skinned man whom he took to be an immigration official went to and fro bearing forms, onto which information from Hugo's passport had to be transferred. Questionnaires necessitated by Teaia's recent decease needed to be completed and signed by everyone present. Some sort of power play was involved, and someone had blundered. Perhaps the airline was embarrassed by the death and anxious to avoid liability. The body had been carried off somewhere, much to Hugo's relief. Teaia's passport contained a visa, Hugo's did not. Having passed through passport control without let or hindrance, thanks to the accompaniment of a corpse, Hugo now found himself in some technically grey area from which it was not possible to backtrack. The small official was sweating, the tall man blustered, both were smoking heavily and the local variant of Arabic flew fast and guttural. From time to time a very dark-skinned man, in a long robe, with infinite weariness proffered a copper tray with glasses of minty tea. Hugo, who was not fond of sugar, asked if he could possibly have his without any form of sweetener, natural or artificial, and with the addition of a little milk. But nobody appeared to understand what he was saying.

An agreement, written in Arabic and incomprehensible to Hugo, was drawn up by the tallish man and Hugo was urged to sign it. Hugo nodded vigorously afterwards and smiled; everyone seemed tired and relieved. He was taken outside and handed over to an enormously fat man, with a cloth wrapped round his head, sitting in a battered car. A decrepit, roofless truck was commandeered for the luggage. Too weary to care where he was being taken, or to take note of his surroundings, Hugo leaned back against a sheet of plastic covering the back seat and, longing for London, was borne through the night streets of Nouakchott.

Someone had placed a carafe of water in his room while he slept. The water was an unusual colour. He eyed it warily. He was horribly thirsty. He went into the bathroom and peed. The tiling was a bit of a botch job, and the loo was a hole in the ground. A tap with a little hose attached to it dripped beside it and there was no loo paper. He returned to the room. It was imperative that he make arrangements to move to a more suitable, tourist-friendly resort hotel. His thirst assailed him and he drank a glass of the water. Which turned out, an hour later, to have been a mistake.

While he was in the bathroom for the umpteenth time, somebody stole his wallet and passport. Coming back into the room he encountered a wild-eyed Caucasian with Cyrillic tattoos, a ginger moustache and a bullet head. He yelled, and the man fled. Not having a key, Hugo carefully drew the latch down on the door and pushed one of Teaia's heavy suitcases against it.

He did not discover the wallet and passport were missing until the following day, by which time he was feeling a little better physically. The fact that he now had no money of his own, or credit cards or identification of any sort, was only one cause of depression among many. He opened his canvas bag. Teaia's wallet contained an unused chequebook and some very grubby notes, which were presumably Mauritanian money. What were they worth, he wondered.

Hugo discovered that if he placed the empty water carafe outside the door, within a few hours it was refilled. He sat on the bed and ate both packets of Garibaldi biscuits. Later that night he consumed half the Branston pickle. He slept fitfully, and the following morning dipped one finger into the Marmite and licked it. The Earl Grey tea bags obviously did not count as food. He pressed one to his nose and sniffed it. It was the beginning of the third day, and the very maw of hell seemed preferable to staying in this room any longer.

He washed. From the window the weather appeared to be hot and sunny, so he donned a pair of shorts and a short-sleeved cotton shirt. He had forgotten to bring any white socks, so he put on dark ones and white trainers. He placed the Leica and Teaia's jewellery bag and wallet into the canvas bag and slung it over his shoulder. He went out into the corridor. It was a bugger not having a key. But there was a key! It hung on a hook just beside the door. He took it down, turned it in the lock and popped it into his bag. This small act cheered him somewhat.

After a few feet the corridor turned to the right; he followed it, descended two stone steps and emerged into a hallway. There was a man sitting at a desk, fast asleep. Hugo went past him and out the front door into the street. A sign above the doorway read: HOTEL MERHABA GUELB ER RICHAT NOUAKCHOTT in red letters on a black background.

Nouakchott was not a place where he wished to be. It was decidedly short on flowers. Plaster peeled from the discoloured walls of flat-roofed buildings, yet their design appeared to owe nothing to a more gracious age. It looked as though the city had been built less than forty years ago – indeed the passing cars and trucks often seemed older than the buildings. Scrawny animals were penned on wasteland. What were they? Sheep? Goats? It was certainly not the paradise that Teaia's words had led him to imagine. Everywhere there was a coat of powdery sand which blotted out the landscape and made the air hotter and drier.

Hugo walked to a crossroads and stood at the corner of the street with his back to a wall. It was busy here. Humanity flowed past him, men in robes with heads swathed with cloth, other men in cotton trousers and long shirts, women in metres of pink and gold and turquoise. All turned to look at him. Their eyes widened. They looked away. A boy rushed past with a tray piled with a pyramid of loaves. There was no point of contact between Hugo and these people. How he had come to be here seemed to him, at that point, a mystery. Life is simple; it is the explaining of it that gets complicated. He put on his sunglasses to feel a little privacy. The energy he had summoned by washing and dressing was expended. His eyes could not make sense of so much strangeness. He pressed his back against the wall. Not enough money, no food, no language, he would stand here and wait to die.

After a while his legs began to ache. The road before him, milling with people, stretched further than the eye could see and he spotted something, or rather someone. A dark figure, head and shoulders taller than anyone around him, could be seen far off in the distance. Strange that the figure should stand out like that. Every time he looked up it seemed to be a little closer, as though striding through everyone and everything it passed. Closer, he was enormously tall and fearsomely dark. And ragged! People drew aside to let him pass. He was now only a few feet away. Too late Hugo realised that the man was coming towards him and there was nowhere to retreat.

He stopped a few feet from where Hugo stood and squatted with his back to the same wall. Presumably begging, he was motionless for what seemed like an age, yet still exuded power. This had to be a begging spot. Hugo standing stiffly beside him might be taken for a mendicant as well. The author of *Trapped Light* was giving the impression that he was seeking alms from people who probably earned less in a year than he was paid back in London in a week. It was said that people turned their backs to the wall and died. Or was it their heads? Anyway they died. Why on earth was the process taking so long for him?

Hugo became aware that the man was resting his head on one hand and had swivelled to look up at him. Hugo's peripheral vision picked up the glitter of the beggar's eyes and the callouses and grime of his feet. The beggar shifted a little closer. Hugo considered moving away. But where would he go? Would anywhere else be any better? The thought of returning to his hotel room was unbearable. Deep in thought, he was taken unawares by the beggar suddenly standing in one movement, leaning over to him and removing his sunglasses. Hugo yelped in shock, fear and oversensitivity to the searing light. This was theft and an outrage! The man fixed him with a scrutiny that impaled. He was so close that Hugo could smell his acrid breath. Staring deep into another's eyes is an intimate thing. And when nothing is said and there is only the looking, it becomes an assault upon the soul. The fierce eyes searched, and what did they find? Books? Abandoned dogs? Trouserless boys? Old ladies nestled against glass? Did they

see everything? They certainly saw something, for their owner backed off a little, as though satisfied, and said in a harsh and staccato French, *'Affreux!'* The word was full of anger.

The man was caped, bejacketed, festooned with cloths about the hips. His trousers appeared to flutter with assorted strips above calves which gleamed, and his feet were bare and dusty. Why was he so angry?

Once more the beggar drew near. He offered the return of the sunglasses. Hugo took them and put them back on. The man's hand remained where it was, palm upwards. It was an ancient gesture. Give, it said. Hugo wanted to be rid of him. Having resolved to die anyway, he really had nothing further to lose.

He took Teaia's wallet from his canvas bag and handed the dirty notes to the beggar, who counted them out carefully and then shrugged, evidently unimpressed. *'À bientôt!'* Turning his back on Hugo, he continued on his way. His gaunt frame was as powerful in retreat as it had seemed when advancing.

Hugo's back slid down the wall until he was squatting. His protruding knees, pale and unlovely, looked like the domed heads of twin aliens. He couldn't remember having squatted before two days ago, when he had been so ill in the hotel room. Presumably he had squatted when he was a kid. When he was building the sandcastle maybe? There had only been one. He had been thirteen at the time. No, he was probably kneeling in the sand at that point in his life. So all this squatting was a new thing, and it marked a very low point in his existence. Even lower than a few minutes earlier, when he had resolved to die. Hugo greeted his nadir.

'Allô?'

Hugo looked up. Towering above him, the beggar was back and he was bearing what looked like a grey blanket. He gestured for Hugo to get up. Hugo struggled to his feet, and the man offered him the blanket. He made a low noise suggestive of the death of something and whisked the cloth over Hugo's head. It was a robe. Rough fibres prickled exposed skin. There was a smell of ancient sheep. He pulled it across Hugo's body as though protecting him, in spite of the heat, from an imagined cold wind. He wrapped a length of blue material in a turban around Hugo's head. The beggar then stood before Hugo and intoned words in a strange language.

'Asalaamaleikum.' A pause, then, *'jaam nga'm?'* Another pause. *'Nanga def?'*

It was evidently some form of greeting. Satisfied that the formalities had been observed, the man hunkered down beside him and, having twisted off its top, handed a plastic bottle of water to him. Hugo, squatting again, took the bottle tentatively and then, overcome by thirst, drank half. He handed it back to his benefactor. The beggar rubbed a grubby palm over the top and drank the rest. From the recesses of his rags he drew a paper package. Placing it upon his lap, he opened it to reveal a couple of small bread rolls and two boiled cloven trotters. He turned and met Hugo's gaze. He seemed surprised. He proffered a roll. Hugo extended his left hand. The beggar, filled anew with rage, batted the hand away with a sharp blow to the wrist and pushed the roll into Hugo's right hand. The bread was a bit on the dry side, but Hugo ate it in a mouthful. The beggar appeared to regard him with satisfaction. There was going to be no getting past the trotter. Hugo, remembering just in time not to use his left hand – the madman must above all be humoured – picked it up gingerly. He thought of a restaurant in another age. Was it really only a week ago? He nibbled a tiny corner. It was a bit goaty but not as bad as it looked. Indeed, when you were hungry, it was really quite tasty.

The beggar ex machina stood up and extended his right hand to Hugo. Hugo hesitated. Who knew where the hand had been? Then he took it and stood up.

CHAPTER 28

The Ambassador

THE PHOTOGRAPH WAS IN COLOUR, BUT appeared monochromic. There was a figure of a man, the sun turning the blackness of his skin pure white in reflection. His shoulders were broad. He wore a simple robe or *boubou,* Hugo informed his audience. His head was wrapped in a turban, a *howli.*

'A noble savage!' Marjorie informed Daphne with a stage whisper. 'What amazing teeth!'

'He looks terribly fierce. I'd have been petrified.'

'This is the Wolof Abdoulie,' Hugh announced to the crowd. 'My friend. That's how he always introduced himself, although *Wolof* was his tribe and *Abdoulie* the only name he ever used. He put the two words together and they sounded as though they belonged that way. He was used to living where he found himself and had great dignity. Among other languages, he spoke French. If I have any French today, I owe it to him. He told me that once his forefathers had been Kings and Princes, but his family were Kings and Princes no more.'

He paused, gazed around the hall at the faces of his audience in the gloom. They watched, waited, eager to share his story. Hugh knew that he could have written a book about his travels, but what had happened to him was all too raw and real to fit comfortably into a book. The photographs were simpler and yet equally satisfying. So he gave the audience the crumbs from his table. He talked about the play of light on shadow and tacked on a little of his story at the end. Sensing there was much, much more that might yet be revealed, the good people of Kensington felt their appetites whetted, licked their lips in the shadows, and listened.

The meat of the matter was that when Hugo awoke in the morning it seemed unbelievable that, the previous day, he had stood on a street corner, next to a terrifying tatterdemalion, until dusk had fallen abruptly and he had made his way back to his hotel. But there were the robe and turban, rolled up on the floor beside the door.

Reason had returned. He would go to the British Embassy, explain his lack of passport and credit card, and they would help him to fly home. He washed and while he was shaving, peering into the mirror embedded in the inner lid of Teaia's vanity case, he thought with a fierce longing about his flat, his washing machine, a fridge usually stocked with ready-chilled meals, his bathroom, his office. Would Terence and Gruff Hint have forgotten about his dereliction of duty by now? Or would someone be watching for a light in his windows and be there to leap on him when he emerged from his front door to . . . what was it they did? They served writs – whatever a writ was. Would they do that to him? Serve one? And what would happen then? A court case? A fine? And would his book have been quietly dropped from the syllabus of the University of Artistry and Design? And were there still witches around, baring their breasts and sniffing out the details of his private life? He shuddered.

The advantage of being in such a place as Mauritania was that he was safe. Nobody knew where he was. He was beyond the bureaucracy that slavered at the heels of anyone foolish enough to own a mobile phone or a travel card and, through credit cards and bank accounts, knew the comings and goings of everyone. He might as well have stepped off the planet. Still, living here would not do. It was not civilised enough for Hugo. Maybe he could stop off in Paris and lie low among the artists in Montmartre for a few months. An excellent idea! He dressed carefully. He would wear a tie with his shirt and a linen jacket. The Ambassador would shake his hand with a friendly grin, one Englishman to another.

He became aware that someone was whistling outside his window, had indeed been whistling for some time. He peered through the metal grille and saw a tall, dark scarecrow walking up and down in the dusty alleyway within a few yards of his window, exuding impatience and irritation. This was awkward. Yesterday had been all very well, but today was today. He sat down on the bed. *Go away. Go away, please!* The whistling stopped. He went back to the window and looked out again. Bugger, oh bugger, he had been spotted. A few moments later a voice could be heard rumbling in French in the corridor outside his room. 'My friend! Where are you hiding yourself, *mon cher ami?*'

The Wolof Abdoulie had brought another plastic water bottle and a cardboard container with a dollop of cold stew. There was a smell of wet sheep and the beggar was grinning, as though presenting Hugo with something rare and wonderful. It was too early to eat and although Hugo's belly was empty again, he was feeling queasy. He shook his head. The man also brought with him a more personal odour. Not sweat, for moisture does not linger long in a dry land, but a mustiness like train wheels and burnt engine oil.

The Wolof Abdoulie peered wide-eyed into the room. No doubt he had never seen so much luggage. He pushed Hugo aside. *'Mais vous êtes riches!'* It was an accusation.

'No, no no! *Je n'ai pas l'argent.*' Hugo delved into the open vanity case and pulled out a bunch of small keys. He offered them to the Wolof and gestured that he should open whichever piece of luggage he wished. The man put the carton of stew and the water bottle carefully down on Hugo's bed. His head was almost touching the low ceiling and there was scarcely room for Hugo. It took a while, but eventually he succeeded in opening one of the cabin trunks, and lost his French. If he was speaking Wolof, it was a language that lent itself well to what were clearly expletives of angry horror. Why he should be quite so appalled, Hugo was at a loss to understand. The Wolof Abdoulie pulled out a dress, and attempted to communicate with gestures that someone, at some point in the not too distant future, would be placing the end of a gun right up close against Hugo's left temple or slitting his throat with something presumably a bit sharper than a finger.

Surely he could not be imagining that the dresses belonged to Hugo? And if they did, what could this matter in a country where long robes seemed to be worn by both sexes? It was too early in the morning to attempt any French with confidence, but Hugo managed to find words that he hoped meant 'old lady' and 'dead'. He picked up a dress and pulled a face to express his revulsion, then he opened his own suitcase and lifted out trousers, some shirts. '*À moi!*' Hugo asserted. 'All mine!'

The Wolof Abdoulie sat cross-legged on the tiny section of floor not occupied by Hugo and was clearly thinking deeply. He questioned Hugo about the old lady, and somehow, with a few words and a bit of playacting, bits of the story were conveyed. The Wolof Abdoulie nodded his head and again appeared deep in thought. Then, like a snake uncoiling, he leapt to his feet. He had an idea. He began to examine the contents of the luggage without anger and with what appeared to be rising excitement.

Hugo's thoughts had returned to his intended rendezvous with his Excellency, the illustrious Ambassador to Mauritania, and it occurred to him that he would need some assistance in locating the Embassy. Somewhere in this urban conglomerate would be an imposing building framed by trees, smaller than its U.S. counterpart, no doubt, but much more elegant. This fellow would be a useful guide to help him find the way there.

'Stop! Listen!' shouted Hugo in English. '*L'Embassie*' – what was the word? – '*de l'Angleterre!*'

The Wolof Abdoulie stared at him.

'*L'Ambassadeur*' – of course, it wouldn't be England, it would be Great Britain – '*de Grande Bretagne! Nous allons!*'

He understood. The Wolof placed both hands on his chest and looked down towards his feet. His eyes flickered to the robe rolled up on the floor. His head turned towards the bathroom behind him and back to Hugo.

'L'Ambassadeur!'

There was resolve in the angle at which he held his beard that spoke of an iron jaw beneath.

An hour later, Hugo had a sore throat, a headache and was exhausted by the effort involved in restraining himself from running out of the hotel room and never, ever, coming back. The tiny bathroom was awash, and the walls streaked with pink trails of a heavily perfumed shampoo found in Teaia's vanity case. On the tiled floor were mounds of rags and clumps of hair. The sun had risen much higher in the sky outside, and the heat made the room steam like a Turkish bath.

The Wolof Abdoulie was transformed. Clad in rags, he had presence; in the robe, or *boubou*, with a *howli* wrapped around his head, he was regal. Now was the time to consume the mutton stew. Hugo once again shook his head. The Wolof ate delicately with the fingers of the appropriate hand, then licked each one clean. He gestured to the clothes. His new idea had returned to mind. The words that followed were a gabble, but Hugo picked up *possibilité* and *vendre*. There was an interrogative silence and then something about *argent* and *chaussures*. The Wolof stared down at his calloused feet, three sizes or more larger than Hugo's.

Hugo shook his head. '*Plus tard!* First the Embassy!'

Nouakchott was larger and even less appealing than Hugo had imagined. Today was hotter than yesterday. They trailed through streets littered with plastic bags and water bottles squashed flat by generations of Mauritanian feet. The last of their money bought a large one, as yet untrampled and filled with warm water. From everyone they approached with a request as to the whereabouts of the British Embassy, they received only directions to the French Embassy. It seemed that the passers-by could only respond in some sort of affirmative.

Yes, there is the French Embassy. Nobody would say as the English would: sorry mate, can't help you, I don't know where the British Embassy is, but maybe so-and-so can help you. They passed the French Embassy several times on a road that had a name, the Rue Ahmed Ould Hamed, a yellowy-cream, two-storey building, without architectural adornment of any sort and topped with a satellite dish. Hugo was amazed. He had seen County Halls in England that looked more French.

They entered a hotel more worthy of the name than the Hotel Merhaba Guelb er Richat Nouakchott. There were two men at reception and both were awake. At last the word *no*, or rather, *Non!* They were both confident that such a thing as a British Embassy did not exist, had not existed, ever, and was not to be found anywhere.

Hugo, by now, was convinced that he was the victim of a conspiracy. He stormed from the hotel in fury. That a nation whose empire had once spanned the globe and, even now, waged war where it fancied, did not have an embassy in the capital of Mauritania was laughable. Hugo was covered in dust and his feet were aching. They returned to the French Embassy. The guard at the gate had a gun and did not want to let them in. Hugo, by this time, had lost all fear of death. He pushed past him, opened the door and encountered a young Mauritanian woman at the reception desk.

'Bonjour,' said Hugo. *'Je suis Hugo de Lamartine.'*

The Wolof Abdoulie shook his head and backed into a convenient shadow.

'What you weesh, sir?' the receptionist replied, in English.

Hugo was taken aback. He changed to English. 'I am looking for the British Ambassador.'

'*Mais oui, son Excellence, l'Ambassadeur de Grande Bretagne* – I write 'is address.' She wrote slowly and carefully on a very small piece of paper. *'Voilà!'*

And there it was!

'Where is Rabat?' asked Hugo.

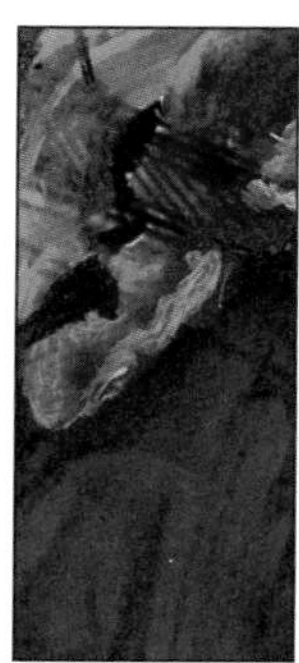

CHAPTER 29

The rag trade

TEAIA'S GOODS FELL INTO THE FOLLOWING major categories:

COATS. Short, long, heavy and light. Two were of fur, very long and incredibly thick.

DRESSES AND SKIRTS. Short ones were not wearable, but could be cut into squares to make blankets or strips for headgear.

UNDERWEAR. Teaia had possessed some very strange items of underwear, some of which undoubtedly had value as antiques. Neither of the men could be sure if they were marketable.

SHOES. Teaia had been a mite stunted and all of her shoes had high heels. There were also boots, the relevance of which, to Mauritanian society, was not immediately obvious; yet they were objects of wonderful craftsmanship and expensive materials. Perhaps they could be used as umbrella stands or vases for dried flowers. There would need to be market trials.

JEWELLERY. Teaia had owned a quantity of rings, necklaces, brooches, earrings and bracelets which were obviously of considerable value. It was very lucky that Hugo had not opened the bag containing them before he was in the Wolof Abdoulie's company. Had he found them at an earlier time, he would have attempted to exchange them at the airport for a return ticket to London. This, he was informed, might have had dangerous consequences. The police were alert to such transactions. In the Wolof

Abdoulie's considered opinion (his mouth turned down, he made a slicing movement with his right hand, the meaning was quite clear) attempting to dispose of this jewellery was a bit of a no-no. Especially by someone who did not have papers of identity.

The costume jewellery, on the other hand, or finger, or ear, was a different matter. Fortunately, Teaia had possessed an enormous collection of obviously fake jewellery. All this was saleable. But it must not be sold too quickly. They did not want to attract the attention of the authorities. Everything must be done very slowly – the Wolof's hands painted the words soundlessly in the air as he spoke them in French – and with great care!

This was all very well, but Hugo had not eaten the previous day, and nothing uses up calories faster than rage. Rabat! There was still fury at the thought. It was, he knew, as a matter of general knowledge, never having read the book, a classic catch-22 situation. He needed to go to Morocco to get a new passport, but he couldn't go to Morocco because he didn't have a passport. It was preposterous! An outrage! What the bloody hell was the British Ambassador to Mauritania doing living in Morocco? Shirking his duty for the comfort of sitting in some palace smoking a hookah pipe and eating tagines all day long!

Oh tagines, the very thought! Hugo had never eaten a tagine, but they stocked them in red, yellow and blue at a kitchen centre off the Fulham Road, and he imagined them filled with little sausages and mashed potato.

The Wolof Abdoulie was adamant. If they were going to eat today, they had to get busy. They bundled some clothes into Hugo's suitcase and into another, larger one of Teaia's that the Wolof confidently asserted he was capable of carrying with one hand.

Mama Oudab sold her goods wherever seemed to be a particularly good place for the day. She would set up her rolls of brightly coloured cloth on a tarpaulin on the ground. She was enormously fat and had a big smile. She did not take much persuading to sell some frocks on their behalf. The clothes were of a very different style to the tangerine robe, draped loosely over head and body, that Mama Oudab was wearing, but their colours were equally bright. And indeed it was not long before the strange dresses attracted the attention of some passing women. Hugo did not know much about women's fashion. The name on the label of one ancient garment indicated that it had been designed by Vivienne Westwood, and, on another, Zandra Rhodes. Neither was of any significance to him, and surely must mean even less to the gaggle of women now fingering the cloth and bargaining with raised voices. But they must have meant something, for the end result was a pile of *ouguiyas* from which Mama Oudab took her cut with a gappy grin.

Time is different in Nouakchott. The moments of each day pass at a dignified and leisurely pace. The days themselves, and the weeks, sink into a morass of timelessness. The Wolof Abdoulie rented a shack with a corrugated iron roof. From the outside it appeared to be a garage or cowshed, of the sort to be found in some rural outpost of the British Isles. The inside, too, was entirely consistent with a garage or a cowshed. But the Wolof Abdoulie was visibly less angry. Hugo continued to live in the hotel where they still jabbered at him in Hassaniya, the local variant of Arabic, but at least he now knew enough to say *Salamaleikum* and *shokran.*

Hugo had taught himself to use Teaia's Leica. He kept it in a plastic bag to protect it from the ubiquitous sand. He took some pictures and had them developed. They weren't very good. The shopkeeper showed him how to make better use of the Leica and gave him a few tips about keeping the sun behind him, not chopping off heads and suchlike. The shopkeeper was a remarkably modest man, probably uneducated. Not the sort to write a book or become well known. He shared his knowledge of photography with ease and grace, simplifying everything so that his foreign visitor could understand. Hugo shook hands with him, promised to return and left feeling surprisingly cheerful.

Later that day, he took pictures of the fishermen at the seashore, which was not far from Nouakchott. The sea was all Atlantic as far as Hugo could squint. Conveying the idea of a lagoon to the Wolof Abdoulie was a little difficult. There did not appear to be one, although there were a few birds.

Dressed in a blue robe with a matching turban wrapped around his head, Hugo did not attract too much attention. Neither did the Wolof Abdoulie. Although all traces of his itinerant past were gone, and sometimes he wore shoes, he still looked a little strange. Something about his height, the intensity and force contained within his form, and his long stride, marked him out as a person on his way to becoming someone a little apart from ordinary men, a branch of *homo* adapted to a very different lifestyle. However, just what that different way of living might be was not apparent to Hugo in the simple flow of daily activity that he was experiencing.

Although the sand-laden wind was a bit of a trial, the climate was quite pleasant, it being winter; but the Wolof was becoming increasingly restless. He was a man who was used to walking. He liked to walk in Nouakchott. Thus it was surprising to Hugo when the Wolof continually talked about the price of camels, who had good strong healthy ones, and who had the damnable effrontery to be selling dromedaries, with floppy humps, that had been force-marched for weeks and were on their last legs. But it took a good eye to spot this!

Hugo was becoming quite proficient in French by now. 'Why on earth do we need camels?' he asked the Wolof.

'It is necessary to give the market in Nouakchott a rest. If we are no longer here with our goods, people will become hungry for them again. We will go to new places where they have not seen old lady dresses and shoes that stop women running away.'

Mama Oudab's cut was a large one, yet they had amassed some money by now. If they had enough to buy camels, there should be funds sufficient for an air ticket home. The thief who had stolen Hugo's passport was known about town. He was a Russian. He was a drug addict. Everybody said so. He had gone to Néma. He was visiting evil foreigners in Chinguetti. He would be back here any day. He would not find the drugs he needed in Néma or Chinguetti.

Hugo had acquired an ability to wait it out that he had never experienced in his former life. The world he had left behind seemed somehow alien to him now. He was surviving in Nouakchott, and what an achievement that was! There were even places here where one could buy a hamburger and chips and coke, but no beer. Ah what a joy. Eating a hamburger made him feel back in civilisation. He longed for a glass of cold white wine. But he had unfinished business. He had not yet seen the wonders of which Teaia had spoken. Perhaps it was his destiny to travel a little bit further.

Hugo had observed groups of travellers setting out from Nouakchott. 'What we need is a four-wheel drive. Something quite large so we can put the trunks and suitcases in the back.'

The Wolof Abdoulie was not happy. He would ride on a camel, and Hugo could drive behind him in a truck if he wished.

'How fast does a camel go?' Hugh wanted to know, and anyway, he insisted, the Wolof Abdoulie would have to do the driving. Driving was one of those things that Hugo had never got around to learning how to do. That appeared to settle the matter; the Wolof Abdoulie had never learned to drive either. He assured Hugo that camels were much safer. They didn't break down or run out of petrol.

Hugo gave way without further argument, relinquishing an impossible dream of riding aloft in a four-wheel drive, and they either rented or bought two camels; he was never precisely sure of the details of the Wolof Abdoulie's negotiations. They arranged with the Hotel Merhaba Guelb er Richat Nouakchott to take Hugo's remaining possessions into storage. He was rather tired of Nouakchott, and an unvarying diet of fish without enough fruit and vegetables. The thought of perhaps finding the lagoon, and a place where there would be fields of sugar cane and exotic birdlife to photograph, lifted his spirits.

CHAPTER 30

Apocalypse in a moment or two

THE DANCING QUEEN LEAPT UP ONTO THE dais, her make-up streaked from the heat and her nose poking redly through.

'It seems *such* a crime to interrupt Mr Delam's lecture and photographs of Mauritania which have us all so *gripped!* But we've got some jugs of iced water and there's still lots of wine left. The water's in paper cups, and we're handing those out now. My husband's coming round with the wine, so anyone who would like some, please pass your glass to the end of the row when he reaches you.'

Marjorie gulped her fourth glass of wine down in one and followed it with a water chaser, then eyed Daphne's newly refilled glass. 'I thought you said the wine was making you feel a bit strange.'

'It grows on you, I think. I can imagine everything. It feels as though I'm there, in Mauritania! There's something about his voice. I'm sure I've heard it before.' Daphne stared into her glass as though divining some truth in its depths.

'I was thinking exactly the same thing!'

'Were you really?'

'Yes, and I was going to say so just before you did!' squawked Marjorie, spreading her stout legs and fanning herself with some violence.

'Extraordinary! He must have been on Radio 4.' Daphne smiled, rather coyly, and held out her glass for a top-up. 'Oh fuck it, if you're going to get sloshed I might as well join you.'

People were popping in and out of the vestry for a quick pee. Hugh Delam remained standing, his hands resting on either side of the lectern. The dancing queen skipped up to him with a jug, offering to refill the glass of water standing on a table beside him. It was still full, so she retreated. He waited until the last bottom had resumed its seat and every throat had been cleared, then he nodded to Laptop Man and the screen revealed another photograph. Two dromedaries. The sun, low on the horizon, visible through their legs. They are seemingly impossibly burdened. The Wolof Abdoulie stands beside one that carries the food and water (a camel can carry a thousand pounds in weight); the other is laden with examples from five decades' output of western fashion houses. The audience said *ah!* at the subsequent photograph, which zoomed in on the camels' faces. People like camels in pictures much more than they do when they meet one in the flesh.

Hugo remembered how the Wolof Abdoulie, who most of the time refused to speak Hassaniya to anyone in Nouakchott, had murmured to the dromedaries in the language they knew. *Shwaia, shwaia, o ishma, ishma,* or something that sounded like that. They were called Ramsi and Mo. Males. Hugo was horrified, that first day, when he realised how close his contact with the two beasts was going to be. They were bad-tempered and sought to bite. They spat or dribbled saliva, groaned as they sank to their knees. Their legs bent in impossible directions. He could smell them. Relieved of their burdens, they would lie on their backs and kick their legs in the air, stupid as puppies. The whole trip revolved around camels. Either they rode them till their groins rose up in agony and rebelled, or they walked behind them blasted by farts; their speed of progress remained the same. Their diet was camel meat, camel meat, or sometimes camel meat, served with couscous or rice on a good day and cooked on dried wood from scrubland when they could find it. The four-wheel drives drove warily by, whenever they shared a road. Driving into camel legs would leave a fearsome tonnage suspended in mid-air; not such a good idea, really, for people wedged in a vehicle underneath.

A map appeared on the screen. Hugh Delam traced their route: Boutilimit, Aleg, Kaédi, Mbout, Sélibaby, Kankossa, Kif,

'Ayoûn el 'Atroûs; Néma. He indicated the separate journeys made to Tichit and Ouadane.

What did the names signify to his audience? What did such a journey mean to these comfortable, cosseted people who hopped into their four-wheel drives in the middle of London? And grumbled when the traffic delayed access to motorways that could take them hundreds of miles in a day. What could they know of the slow reality of mile upon mile upon mile? Look at them sweating in their seats, hot because they could measure the ambient temperature and fuss about it. How would they react if they had to guess whether it was fifty degrees or fifty-five? But he knew how to speak to them and make them feel what it is like to trudge in the sand behind an overburdened camel, fantasising about fruit and vegetables, and with eyeballs so dry they won't move in their sockets. Or what happens in winter when the sun goes down and the temperature drops and drops till it is below freezing.

The weather during the day was pleasant, but the nights with no cloud cover were breathtakingly cold. They would sit, eating the one meal of the day by a small fire, dressed for the evening in Teaia's fur coats. Voluminous for her, they were wearable for Hugo although the sleeves ended at his elbows, and they provided a sort of shoulder cape for the Wolof Abdoulie. The first few days of their journey there was a full moon, but when it had waned the darkness was terrifying. More stars than Hugo had ever seen blazed across the firmament; but at ground level the blackness was total, and once in a while something chitinous could be heard scuttling over the sand dunes. If it got within reach of him, he thwacked it with his tennis racquet.

The dunes themselves shifted and hummed. Then it was that Hugo was grateful for Chertsey's Christmas present, which the Wolof Abdoulie had leapt on with a whoop of delight back in the Hotel Merhaba Guelb er Richat Nouakchott. With his companion asleep, Hugo would sit in the darkness winding and rewinding the torch and forming with it a small circle of safety about his person.

'Switch off the light. When you wind it, it makes a noise.'

'OK. *Excuse-moi.*' Hugo hid it beneath the flayed beavers of his coat.

It was a huge relief to reach a name that was at least marked on a map. An oasis was glorious. You could smell water in the air, and to see the green of palm trees was a joy. But sometimes there was very little: a beautiful old mosque in what was almost a ghost town, crumbling volumes in a dusty library, a few humble dwellings in the middle of nowhere, some tents in the sand. And they were welcomed. Although there were other travellers at this time of year, a visitor was always an event. Tea served in small glasses or watery milk called *zrig* were the currency of social exchange. It was a courtesy, a sharing and a bond. The Wolof Abdoulie would erect an awning and Hugo would lay out his wares on a sheet on the sand. It was Hugo's job to smile and be nice to people. There were muscles in his face that had never been used before, but were not yet atrophied and sprang slowly to life. Sometimes goods were exchanged for water and supplies; usually the travellers departed richer than they had arrived.

Hugo was mystified that towns that seemed so poor had money to throw away on fripperies.

'Here they make money from foreign travellers in the winter months,' explained the Wolof Abdoulie. 'They have few opportunities to buy things from outside.'

'But their lives are hard. Am I doing the right thing selling them this stuff?'

The Wolof Abdoulie looked up from the piece of wood he was whittling with a knife and studied Hugo's face. He grunted as though satisfied about something.

'*Ah, les femmes!* They buy these things. If they have been foolish, they will learn from that. But perhaps they have reasons that we don't know anything about. Anyway, buying old lady dresses makes them happy.'

'Do you have a wife somewhere?'

'No.'

'Where are your people? Where did you grow up?'

He threw away the piece of wood and stood up. 'My people lived down near the Senegal River.'

'Will we go there?'

'No point. My people are gone and the crocodiles have hidden their bones.'

Hugo enjoyed taking photographs, even though the Mauritanians disliked having their photographs taken. He snapped rocky outcrops and smooth undulating dunes of alien orange sand. Women in brightly coloured clothing bared their teeth. Children, shy and cautious, looked up towards the camera lens. The cameraman sees all and remains apart. But, in fact, Hugo was making more friends than he had ever had in his life. Nobody seemed to mind that he could not speak French well, or any Hassaniya beyond a dozen words, and was socially gauche. He had much to learn.

Often, they would encounter local officials keen to join with them in the ritual of checking papers. This was a ceremony designed to increase the status and self-importance of its perpetrators and to give reassurance that the law ruled over the land. A foreigner should not expect to travel far without a visa and a passport. On such occasions the Wolof Abdoulie was happy to speak a little Hassaniya.

'Don't forget,' he said to Hugo, 'you are a deaf mute. Smile and make small religious movements with your hands!'

Two ordinary men, dressed in the traditional way and leading a couple of camels, were of interest to no one. Especially when they gave a cheery greeting and went calmly on their way.

Hugo learned to be respectful and not to give offence. At the beginning of their trip, Hugo had reacted to the lack of washing facilities in a way typical of someone who had always been scrupulously clean. It was an all-or-nothing thing. He became grubbier with each passing day, until one morning the Wolof Abdoulie took him to task and showed him, in quite horrendous detail, how a man attends to his personal hygiene in the desert. Most of it Hugo was delighted to take on board. He was happy

to dig little holes in the ground and bury anything he might choose to leave. He could well see that the abrasive quality of sand would serve to remove grease and dirt. But there was one thing he was not, under any circumstances, going to do.

'*Pourquoi pas? Incroyable!*' The Wolof Abdoulie demonstrated how to scrub, with all the fervour of a weekend washer-upper tackling greasy pans with a brillo pad.

Hugo refused point-blank.

His companion let loose what could only be a tirade of Wolof expletives.

They did not speak for two days.

Then Hugo tried to explain, and the Wolof Abdoulie refused to believe him.

All his life Hugo had been modest to the point of obsession. But he did it. He showed the Wolof Abdoulie why certain measures of hygiene were not appropriate for him.

The Wolof Abdoulie was incredulous, curious, astounded. Never had he seen such a thing on a grown man!

After that Hugo was permitted a tiny quantity of water with which to wash his dick.

Weeks passed and then months. They would be given somewhere to sleep by the villagers, space on a shared floor of a house, barn or tent. Until the Wolof Abdoulie became restless and once again they were off on the road, or complete lack of road, or absence of any sort of track whatsoever.

In films there is always one sandstorm that the heroes survive. Here there were sandstorms, greater sandstorms and sandstorms that were even worse. They were a horrible fact of life. The Wolof Abdoulie would erect a tent, and they would sit out the storm with their noses buried in their *howlis*. They could not converse; it was agonisingly boring.

One evening, towards dusk, Hugo and the Wolof were looking anxiously for a spot to settle for the night, where there was grazing for the camels. The camels weren't fussy eaters. Anything that appeared to contain a soupçon of chlorophyll, or gave the impression that it might have committed an act of photosynthesis some years ago, was fair game for chomping. But vegetation had been getting sparser and sparser as the days heated up. A red Toyota four-wheel drive, which had been approaching them for a half hour, stopped, presumably to ask for directions. There were two young men inside and a Maure driver.

The driver questioned them in Hassaniya, and the Wolof Abdoulie shrugged and assumed a blank expression. One of the young men leaned out of the window. He had long scruffy hair, a broad tanned face and perfect teeth. He pointed at the road ahead and said something in what might have been French. Hugo wasn't sure, but found it vaguely alarming and moved closer to Ramsi's hind legs.

'Drop it, Cody. Those two motherfuckers are dumber'n camels.' The accent was American.

'How dare you!' exclaimed Hugo. 'What appalling rudeness!'

'Well, why didn't y'all give us an answer in the first place?' asked Cody.

'We would if you had asked politely in English.'

Cody stared at him dumbfounded.

It wasn't an ideal place to make camp, but dusk would be falling soon. There wasn't any scrub around – they would have to feed the camels from their stores – but maybe Mo and Ramsi would find something. Hugo unloaded their possessions and hobbled the camels watched by Brandon, the one who had been so rude. His apologies had been grudgingly accepted. More importantly, the Americans had food. The next village was still many hours' journey away, so it made sense to spend the night here.

The meal was a feast. The Wolof Abdoulie cooked, assisted by the Arab driver. They had rice with chicken stew and dried mixed vegetables. And hot coffee and, best of all, cold beer from a plug-in cooler in the Toyota. And cake! The sweet, life-giving cake that Cody asserted was beloved of Homer; and Hugo, who had not studied classics beyond Latin GCSE, was not going to disagree. But he was surprised. Cody did not seem the cultured type.

When the Americans' paper plates had been carefully

collected up by the Wolof, Hugo told them a version of the story of how he came to be travelling across the desert. How he had no identity papers and no means of getting home.

'That's crazy, man,' said Cody. 'The Brits must have some sort of office in Nouakchott. Did you check any websites?'

'No, I was too busy playing shoot-'em-ups to bother looking,' said Hugo wearily.

'Why were you doing that?' asked Brandon.

'How on earth was I supposed to find internet access in Nouakchott? Be sensible!'

'Well, don't see why that's a problem when we've got it here.'

'You have internet access here?'

'Sure thing. We've got a laptop with a satellite link, and the satellite's in range about now.'

Brandon opened the rear of the Toyota and pulled out a plastic case.

It was dark. Brandon, Cody and the Wolof Abdoulie had been sitting on fold-up chairs which the Americans had provided, while the driver sat on coats on the ground and Hugo paced about. But now, Hugo stood peering over Brandon's shoulder as the young man searched for advice for Britons in Mauritania.

'That's it!' cried Hugo 'Foreign Office advice. Try that one.'

There it was indeed, the name of the British Honorary Consul, clearly a Mauritanian name, and his telephone number.

'You ain't supposed to be here!' said Brandon. 'Sez it's dangerous and you shoulda registered with the Honorary Consul before leaving Nouakchott!'

Hugo glanced through the Foreign Office recommendations. Certain words and phrases sprang out at him: *banditry, armed smugglers and extremist groups, avoid large gatherings of people and demonstrations, which can turn hostile, landmines, international terrorism.* It didn't seem to bear much relation to his life over the past months.

'If it's so dangerous why are *you* here?' Hugo asked, scribbling down the name and address of the Honorary Consul with a pencil.

Brandon and Cody exchanged sidelong glances. 'It's different fer us. We're Americans,' said Cody.

'What difference does that make?'

'People are skeered. Any trouble and they know our President'll send in the troops.'

Hugo changed the subject and asked what the two were doing in Mauritania. Once again the reply was not quickly forthcoming. They were looking for a business colleague. What business? Import export. And their colleague, was he American too? No, he was a Russian. There was a discussion. Cody let slip the name Vassily. Hugo was immediately curious at this. He described the tattooed, bullet-headed thug with the ginger moustache who had stolen his passport.

'That don't sound nothing like Vassily,' Cody assured him, a little too firmly.

Before they settled down for the night, Hugo whispered to the Wolof Abdoulie that it would be a good idea for one of them to remain awake. Hugo took the first watch. There was no moon, and the night was very dark. Hugo was conscious of the velvet bag containing Teaia's jewellery nestled inside his robe in a pocket that he had sewn there for that purpose. The Americans had bedded down quickly, and the Wolof Abdoulie, as usual, fell immediately asleep. Hugo could barely make out their huddled forms; only the driver's cigarette end burned redly in the darkness.

The sky was plastered with pinpricks of light. Hugo had never been interested in astronomy in his former life. The study of the stars had seemed a pointless activity. What difference could it make to one's daily life? They were all so impossibly far away. There was a sound nearby. Hugo wound up his torch and flashed it briefly around him. Nothing. All clear. It took his eyes a few minutes to readjust to the darkness and for all the distant suns to reappear. Maybe some of them were galaxies. Perhaps it would have been interesting to know a few names and where they were. Andromeda or Sirius perhaps. And then he saw it. A flash of light. A shooting star? But no, it grew larger, rushing across the sky. How high up was it? Impossible to know. It appeared like a huge spinning soundless disk, whirling, coming nearer, rotating more slowly, until Hugo could discern circular holes ringing the circumference – of what? A flying saucer? A bloody flying saucer! He wanted to shout out, alert the Wolof Abdoulie and the sleeping Yanks, but his mouth was open yet no breath would come out. And it was enormous, and really, really near.

Hugo's shocked mind, for some crazy, inexplicable reason, was hurled back some years to a guided tour of southern France. There had been some mix-up over timing. Lunch had been tardily served, and they needed to be elsewhere in time for tea. The place they had come to visit – what was it? A château? Some edifice redolent with history's bloodshed and oily politicking? There had not been time to go there. Hugo and his fellow travellers had stayed aboard their coach, peering out of the windows, while their guide did a quick run-through of who had been who and done what. Then off they sped for a *tisane* and a madeleine.

The contraption hung motionless in the air. Were there eyes peering from the portholes? What was there here to see apart from huddled sleeping forms and Hugo standing with his mouth open? Were they all about to be killed? Nothing happened. Absolutely nothing happened except for a gentle whooshing noise followed by a cataclysmic acceleration, and the craft was gone.

Hugo waited for his breath to return. There wasn't a sound. Could the others still be sleeping after such an event? He was no longer able to see the red end of the driver's cigarette. He felt around him in the darkness and found the torch. He wound it up. The others were curled up asleep, but the driver was head down, rump raised, praying. Hugo rushed over to him and began shouting, and all hell broke loose.

It need not have happened like that. It would not have come to blows, with the two Americans involved, if only the driver had said something intelligible. Hugo was not attacking him. He was only trying to get the man to admit that he must have seen it too. But the driver wasn't saying anything, or didn't speak French, and the Americans had made the entirely unwarranted assumption that Hugo was beating up their driver. And afterwards Brandon kept saying, 'Yeah sure, flying saucers, yeah sure.' So that Hugo had to be forcibly restrained from attacking him too. Then there was peace, at last, with only the red tail lights of the Toyota fading away in the far distance.

Hugo's cheekbone felt as though it were on fire, and he was sure that two ribs, one on each side, were broken. The Wolof Abdoulie had refused to listen to him and had gone straight back to sleep. Even the camels were nowhere to be seen. There was nobody to tell what he had witnessed. The same stars were up there jeering at him. Hugo shivered. The temperature was probably in the low twenties Celsius at night at this time of the year, but the days were so hot that Hugo felt cold. He rolled himself up in one of Teaia's light spring coats and eventually fell into a fitful sleep. He dreamed that the world was about to be destroyed. The US Marines led by Ivan the Terrible had joined forces to attack him. He was on the ground, and they were borne aloft in an enormous black helicopter whose rotors were kicking up a hell of a racket and, in the background, someone was playing the 'Ride of the Valkyries' on a mouth organ.

Suddenly, over a sand dune, came a wonderful figure riding a grey steed. He was dressed in a gleaming white uniform with golden epaulettes.

'Watch him!' yelled one of the marines, dangling from the helicopter by his heels. 'He's ornery!'

Hugo leapt up on the horse behind the strange figure.

'Come,' said the man. 'I shall take you to a meeting of the Borough Council!'

Down in the dust, Br'er Rabbit hopped behind them as they rode.

After that the dream became silly, and Hugo sank into a deeper, dreamless sleep.

CHAPTER 31

Violence and sex

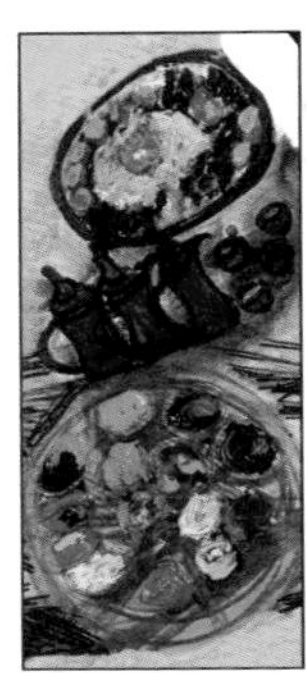

THEY AWOKE JUST BEFORE DAYBREAK. IT was best to try to put some miles behind them before the hottest part of the day. Hugo was an unwilling traveller. Their journey was taking them further away from Nouakchott, and he was eager to return there and track down the Honorary Consul. But the Wolof Abdoulie insisted that they should press on to the next village, where they could rest the camels and stock up on food and water.

'What if those Americans are there?' asked Hugo.

'Then we decide.'

'Why can't we decide now?'

'Do you see a red Toyota?' asked the Wolof Abdoulie.

'Well obviously not. Why do you ask?'

'If we see a red Toyota, then we decide.'

Soon the sun was high in the sky, and it was unbearably hot. The wind was blowing sand like a hair dryer on full power, and it was difficult to see more than a few feet ahead. The camels swished their tails and endured. The Wolof Abdoulie maintained his customary pace, never seeming to need to stop for water, never complaining. Hugo had had enough. His cheekbone was sore, his ribs painful, his feet aching, sweat dripped down his neck, his back and his legs. He had a headache, his eyes hurt, his ears throbbed, his knees felt strained, his shoulders were stiff, one of his back teeth was crying out for a dentist, there was a queasy feeling in his stomach and a rumbling in his bowels that boded ill. He was very conscious of the ever-present threat of parasitical infestation, or worse, kidney stones, brain haemorrhage, atrial fibrillation, cirrhosis of the liver, COPD and Ménières disease.

A swelling in his groin suggested Burkitt's lymphoma. Above his head was the terrible, terrible sun. In addition, he was fed up. It felt almost like the lowest descent of a bipolar slump. If the Wolof Abdoulie walked ahead of him Hugo felt that he was being left behind, if he walked beside him he felt crowded, and if he walked behind him the paranoia was unbearable. They reached a promontory of rock, providing some shelter from the wind, where the Wolof Abdoulie stopped, turned around and hit him. Hard.

The sand was much too hot to lie there on his back for very long. Hugo got up with difficulty, shuffled over to the rock and slumped beside it, while the Wolof Abdoulie removed poles and a length of canvas from the camels and erected the tent. Hugo took out his water bottle and drank deeply. The Wolof Abdoulie looked on disapprovingly, pulled out his own water bottle, took a small sip and put it away again.

'For God's sake,' shouted Hugo. 'Why don't you have a proper drink? You're not human.'

The Wolof Abdoulie thumped him again, with some force, on the shoulder.

Hugo yelped.

'Don't ever tell me that I'm not human again,' said the Wolof. 'I am a human. You are a human. We are all human beings.'

Hugo could see that his companion was very angry, so he turned his back on him and tried to sleep. He could not decide why his life had turned suddenly so violent. The Americans had beaten him up, now the Wolof Abdoulie was hitting him. Why? Even at school people had done little more than flick used chewing gum at him. What had changed?

He thought about the strange aircraft he had seen the previous night. The world was less straightforward than he had always assumed. If flying saucers were real, then other distasteful flights of the imagination might be too. And what could he, one lone man, do against a universe of flakey ideas become orthodox? Yet was it a sign? Some celestial portent? Certainly he was no ordinary fellow. The extraordinary experiences he was living through attested to that. Maybe his role in life was to be even greater than that of a writer of influential books. One thing was certain, he could either follow or lead. It was time to take charge of his destiny. Time to find his way back to England. And on the next occasion somebody presumed to lift a fist . . . well, there wouldn't be such an occasion. There were some people who had too much gravitas to be subject to intimidation. And he would be one!

He formed in his head a list of men that you just wouldn't think about hitting: Gruff Hint, the Dalai Lama, Prince Charles, David Attenborough, Pope John Paul II (but not any other recent ones), Nelson Mandela, the Wolof Abdoulie . . . He jumped to his feet. 'Come on!' he said to the Wolof Abdoulie. 'We can't be hanging around here all day.' Or words to that effect.

As they trudged along behind the camels, it occurred to Hugo that there were some men whom nobody wanted to hit because they weren't sufficiently robust, mentally or physically. Rodney, for example, or Stephen Hawking or Prince Edward. So maybe, until yesterday, he had been in a sort of *noli me tangere* situation, had progressed to being hittable and now was on his way to attaining untouchable eminence. He needed to get the walk right. He had heard once about American presidents doing the power walk. He extended his arms from his sides and tried it. It didn't feel right on him somehow. Perhaps more of an archbishop's glide, with the upper body held firm and erect. It wasn't easy on sand, but yes, there was a certain rightness to it. The folds of his robe scarcely moved as he walked, which he felt to be excitingly dignified. He became aware that the Wolof Abdoulie was looking at him as though something were amiss. Tough. Let him wonder. He was going to have to get used to the new Hugo.

They left their camels hobbled and headed off to the village ahead, which was little more than a hamlet: a series of single-storey huts not large enough for more than a dozen people. The occupants were Maures, who welcomed them in a friendly enough way, but the Wolof Abdoulie was always slightly withdrawn with such people. Hugo's new walk and poise also involved a certain restraint. He was eager to see how this would affect his position in this newly realised pecking order. His host did seem to be demonstrating a degree of deference, and nobody looked in the least inclined to attempt any form of physical aggression upon his person.

Their host, a tall thin man with a long beard, spoke Hassaniya to them. The Wolof Abdoulie replied in French, which worked perfectly well, but he used Wolof to Hugo, perhaps as some form of put-down, and Hugo, irritated, responded in English, neither of which languages worked at all. Nonetheless, Hugo understood most of what was going on. Such a household was a novelty to him. The Wolof had only ever before taken him inside homes where the people were much darker-skinned. He was introduced to their host's brother, his sister's son, his aunt's second husband, his cousin's neighbour's son, three goats and a chicken. They were served glasses of tea, and then the rest of the family arrived. It was all very jolly. The host was delighted to receive his new guests as there was going to be a festival in a few days' time, and his daughter, Maymouna, would be thrilled to have a new dress.

'A few days' time!' said Hugo in English, scowling, to the Wolof Abdoulie. 'There's no way we're staying here that long!'

Their host noticed the scowl and gave a little bow. 'My daughter, Maymouna,' he reiterated loudly, fixing a beady eye upon two female family members, who both slipped out of a back door without a word.

The rest of the women came in and out with plates of food. Hugo was delighted to be out of the sun, sitting down, and eating and drinking. He couldn't understand most of the conversation, so he assumed a severe expression and every so often nodded wisely.

There was a commotion. All heads turned towards the door, where a young woman, who looked about thirty years old, was squeezing herself through the narrow doorway. She

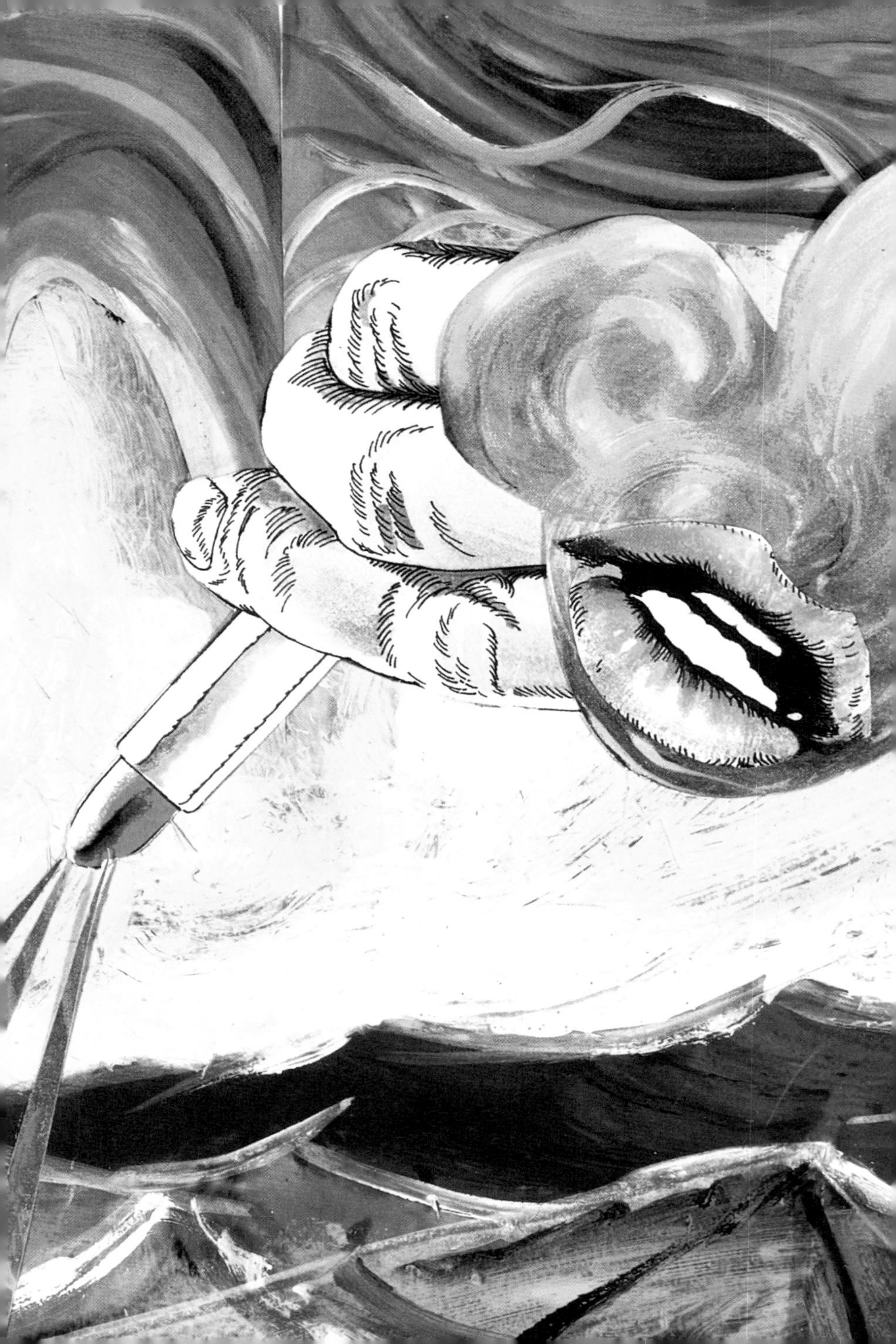

turned around breathlessly, her mouth hanging open, took a quick glance at Hugo and cast her gaze upon the floor. She was enormous.

'My daughter, Maymouna!' announced the host.

'Not a word!' whispered the Wolof Abdoulie. 'Leave this to me.'

The conversation was not of interest to Hugo. He could understand the Wolof Abdoulie's observations and questions – what a beautiful girl! How old is she? – but the host's answers went far beyond Hugo's few words in Hassaniya, and there was a French word, *gavage*, that he did not understand. He was used to Mauritanian women being large. It was often a problem with Teaia's dresses. She had been well endowed in her youth, and many were a good size 16, but sometimes it was a mystery to Hugo how some of the women here were ever going to get into the dresses they had purchased. In Nouakchott many found them a good fit and some of the youngest women would need to take in the seams, but in the countryside things were different and the women were big. Maymouna, however, was vast.

'Our host wishes you to know that his daughter is twelve years old,' said the Wolof Abdoulie.

Hugo nodded and frowned.

There was a further exchange of conversation, then the Wolof Abdoulie said, 'Our host observes that his daughter, of course, has had a surgical intervention to ensure that her appetites will never outstrip those of her husband and she will always be faithful.'

Hugo nodded again. He was feeling sleepy now, having eaten so much, and was anxious for the evening to conclude so that he and the Wolof Abdoulie could find a comfortable place to go to sleep, outside, under the stars.

'Her aunts – her mother being dead, according to His will, praise Him – must take the credit for making sure that you find Maymouna as beautiful as she is today. She is young and will grow larger and even more beautiful.'

The Wolof Abdoulie turned to their host and said that their conversation was a joy and they looked forward to continuing it in the morning, and to Hugo's huge relief they left and went off to find just the sort of clean, soft sand that Hugo had been anticipating. They could hear the murmur of conversation where the evening's gathering continued and the gentle snickering of goats in the night.

'Well?' said the Wolof Abdoulie.

'What's *gavage?*' asked Hugo.

The Wolof explained that it meant making sure that someone ate a huge amount even if they didn't want to. Sometimes a tube would be used and milk and couscous poured down it.

'Bloody hell, force-feeding!' muttered Hugo. 'Why do they do that?'

'To make her beautiful.'

'But she's not beautiful. She's fat. She's more than fat. She can barely walk.'

'Don't be so cruel,' said the Wolof. 'She is beautiful and she's a young girl having a difficult life.'

'And what was that about an operation?'

The Wolof described it in a few words, then, 'Presumably where you come from the women do it too?'

'No, I don't think so. I'm pretty sure that they don't. What exactly is it that happens?'

The Wolof explained in greater detail.

'Yuck,' said Hugo. 'Does that hurt?'

'Yes, and I have heard it goes on hurting if you get married. But it's the way here. Everybody does it, or is supposed to. We the Wolofs do not do things like this. But none of this matters. Are you going to marry her or not?'

'Marry her? Yes sure, now let's go to sleep.'

'Our host has made you a serious offer. Do you wish to marry his daughter, Maymouna?'

Hugo sat up straight and looked the Wolof Abdoulie in a moonlit eye to find out if he was being serious. 'No, of course I don't want to marry her.'

'You're not likely to do better.'

'I don't want to marry anyone, and if I were going to marry someone that girl would be the last person on earth. In fact I'd rather marry one of those goats.'

'That can be arranged,' said the Wolof Abdoulie.

They set off very early the following day, before anyone in the hamlet was awake. It took an age to find the camels, and the going was likely to be hard. They had taken water from a well the previous evening, but they hadn't sold any dresses or stocked up on food.

The Wolof Abdoulie was very silent along the way, as though sulking about something. At first, Hugo was glad to think his own thoughts, but after an hour or so he summoned up the energy to winkle out what was bothering his companion. Finally it emerged.

'Nobody has ever wanted to offer me their daughter in marriage,' said the Wolof. 'And there you are, treating it as some sort of a joke. You should be honoured! Do you realise how much that family didn't eat so that there was enough food to force-feed their daughter?'

The morality of this was beyond Hugo. He had always found the whole business of what you were supposed to feel, do and say in human society a complete mystery, and it bored him so. But he felt disposed to be kind to the Wolof Abdoulie. He explained that marriage was not for him and that, although Mauritania was hugely interesting, he was looking forward to returning to his own country. And he was not in any position to support a wife.

The matter seemed settled but, as the journey went on, the Wolof still seemed dejected.

'It's not so bad,' said Hugo. 'They were friendly people. We had a good dinner last night. Did you enjoy yourself?'

'No. Not at all.'

'Why not?'

'I used to be a slave in a household like that.'

Hugo stopped in his tracks. He didn't know what to say.

The Wolof Abdoulie was trudging on ahead of him, with the two dromedaries; up in the sky buzzards were wheeling, and perhaps there wasn't another soul within miles. Hugo hurried to catch up. 'Do you mean really a slave? Were you chained, or something?'

'No. I wasn't chained, but I worked hard and I wasn't paid and I thought I had nowhere else to go.'

'So what changed things?'

'One day I just walked out.'

'And then?'

'I walked and I walked and one morning . . . ' he turned and looked solemnly at Hugo, 'I came to a crossroads and I found *you*.'

CHAPTER 32

I am monarch of all I survey

HUGO WAS CHEERED TO BE HEADING BACK in the direction of Nouakchott, and was in the mood for a chat.

'What did it feel like being a slave?' he asked.

The Wolof Abdoulie quickened his pace and ignored him.

'Does it feel very different now being a free man?'

'I mentioned it once,' the Wolof replied. 'That doesn't mean I want to talk about it.'

'What shall we talk about then?'

'How about you? What are you searching for? What do you hope to find at the end of your journey?' asked the Wolof.

'Let me have a think and I'll tell you.'

It was a good question. On one level Hugo would be delighted to find his passport and his credit card, and the thought of a plane ticket to Heathrow or the City Airport was a joy, and even one to Stansted would be good. But he sensed that his companion was being rather more philosophical. He probably meant some sort of a life goal. Hugo had never been motivated by the sort of things that seemed to interest other men: football, cars, motorbikes, drugs, girlfriends, wives, kids, garages. What did he really want? Some sort of recognition perhaps. To be a someone. But for what? Being a writer had been good, and he liked the world of Art. It was made up of the right sort of people. You could say something quite fine-sounding or nebulous and they didn't say *What do you mean by that?* or *Give me an example.* They said, *Oh how fascinating, and what do you think of so and so?* They believed you. So, yes, he wanted to be involved with the Visual Arts in some way. He wanted people to listen to him and believe what he said.

'I wish to devote my life to the Visual Arts,' Hugo said very loudly in the direction of Mo's bottom and the Wolof Abdoulie.

A lively discussion ensued. The Wolof did not appear to have any idea of what constituted Visual Arts. He had no concept of paintings or sculpture. Indeed, he seemed to find the notion of the depiction of the human form offensive. He drew the line at pictures of animals, although street scenes without people were OK too. Trying to explain Abstract or Conceptual Art to the Wolof was an exhausting and pointless exercise. Hugo had not come across any obvious signs of art since he had arrived in Mauritania. Was there any art in Mauritania? After a lengthy debate it was agreed that calligraphy and designs on walls were acceptable art forms, but the Wolof Abdoulie did not think that such things could really fill up a life. Once you had seen one page of writing, or a pattern on the wall of a house, you had seen them all really. What a man needed was a full belly, a roof over his head, some sort of smallholding where he could grow vegetables, tend goats and chickens and, most importantly, have a wife. The right woman was really the key to everything. And, by the by, did Hugo realise that they were being followed?

Hugo looked behind him and, a few miles in the distance, made out the shape of a heavily laden camel. He expressed the opinion that just because they could make out a lone camel, which, although heavily burdened, did not appear to have a human being accompanying it, did not mean they were being followed. The Wolof disagreed, but they needed a rest anyway as the sun was overhead, so he got out the awning and they settled back in the shade to watch the camel's approach.

The Wolof had keen eyes and Hugo did not, and thus it was a goodly time between the first traces of a smile appearing on the former's lips and the first wrinkling of a frown on the brow of the latter.

'Come on! We need to get out of here fast!' said Hugo. 'You're right, we're being followed, and it's that she-elephant from last night!'

Maymouna looked very hot and uncomfortable perched

aloft on the camel. She was too stout to slide her legs onto its neck and rest them there as Hugo did. She was all dangling and awobble.

'Don't let her come under the tent! You have to make it absolutely clear that I have no intention of marrying her!' said Hugo.

The Wolof held her camel firmly while it knelt and she lumbered to the ground.

Without touching her, he ushered Maymouna under the awning and fetched her some water while she lurched about stretching her legs.

'Don't give her water. You'll encourage her to stay.' Hugo hopped about on the sand with the sun beating down on him. 'We need to get her back on her camel and off in the direction of her home, before her family arrive and think we've kidnapped her.'

'*Shokran*,' said the girl in a voice that did indeed sound about twelve, and then, in perfect French, 'Thank you very much from me and from my camel who is called Habibi. You've been most kind.' She turned to face Hugo. 'Please understand that I have no wish to get married either. That is why I've run away. I can't face any more being kept indoors and force-fed. I want to go to Nouakchott and find a job.'

'How old are you?' asked the Wolof Abdoulie.

'Sixteen.'

'Is that the truth?'

'Yes. I swear.'

'Right. Let's get her home,' said Hugo.

'Do you understand what a hard journey it is to go to Nouakchott at this time of the year?' asked the Wolof Abdoulie.

'Of course. I understand many things and I think it is the second hardest thing in the world,' Maymouna replied.

'What's the first hardest?' asked Hugo.

The Wolof Abdoulie gave him a withering look and began to take down the awning. 'We'll see how you manage for the next two days. You need to get a little weight off, just enough so that you can walk. If after two days I feel that you aren't going to make it, then we'll take you home. Agreed?'

'Agreed,' said Maymouna.

'You cannot possibly be serious!' said Hugo. 'How is she going to get weight off in two days without amputation or something?'

'I won't eat till I get to Nouakchott.'

'Don't be silly,' said the Wolof. 'You are going to need to keep your strength up. Now we need to be off quickly. We don't want anyone to catch up with us. If you aren't in agreement, Hugo, then you are going to have to make your own way to Nouakchott.'

When Maymouna was back in the saddle, Hugo took the Wolof to one side and asked him, 'Why on earth are you doing this? She belongs with her family.'

'Well not according to her family she doesn't. They were trying to give her to you. Maybe she's not property. I'm not going to take her back without giving her a chance, and that's final.'

Every hour the Wolof insisted that Maymouna should dismount and walk a little way.

Throughout the journey, he made sure that she drank small amounts of water and gave her some salt to lick. When they could see the next hamlet some way in the distance, he led them off into the scrub and then suggested that they make camp. He went alone to meet the inhabitants and returned some while later with water and supplies. To Hugo's disgust, Maymouna showed no inclination to busy about and cook them a meal. She flopped semi-comatose onto a blanket. When Hugo had finished cooking, the Wolof gave her some food and told her that it was important for her to eat, as she needed to retrain her appetite.

'What is appetite?' she asked. 'At home they fed me even when I slept. I used to wake up feeling full.'

Still she ate a little, and then settled down for the night and slept fitfully, moaning from time to time.

Hugo sat looking up at the sky. His stomach battled to digest its daily ordeal of camel meat. No flying saucers appeared to cheer him on. He realised that the company of the taciturn Wolof had been a source of pleasure. Now something had gone. It wasn't just the two of them any more. He looked forward to the time when they would take Maymouna back. It was very hot weather. There was no way she would make it for a second day. He begrudged the effect the detour would have on their schedule. Or would have done, if they'd had one.

The next day Maymouna struggled. And she made everything difficult for Hugo. Washing, urinating, defecating could not be accomplished in the presence of someone of the opposite sex. Riding along, he could hear her whimpering from time to time and it got on his nerves. And the Wolof Abdoulie seemed to be going back to his slave roots attending to her needs. Her little girly voice was so pathetically grateful. He discovered that when she was practising her walking, like some overgrown toddler, she did not like having her photograph taken! Too bad. As someone *in loco parentis*, Hugo was there to put all progress, or lack of it, on record.

She appeared to have developed a fever when they set up camp. They left her to sleep, and Hugo and the Wolof went into the village and sold some dresses and trinkets. The following morning, she heaved her bulk up from the ground and seemed prepared to continue their journey.

'Surely you're taking her home now?' said Hugo.

'No,' replied the Wolof Abdoulie.

A day or so later and even Hugo had to admit that her walking had extended in duration, and that she was quite useful in helping to sell Teaia's dresses. There was some knack involved in matching up a dress with a person that the two men had not mastered. And she understood underwear. These virtues, however, were outweighed by two major blots, which must have flown once like huge, black harpies from Pandora's box, to wit: singing and religion. Maymouna sang. Her speaking voice was small and sugary, but her singing voice was penetratingly high-pitched and loud, a soprano stiletto that pierced through the layers of cloth wound around Hugo's ears and scythed the delicate hairs lining his cochlea.

The second, religion, was not something that had inconvenienced Hugo too much up until now. The Wolof had encouraged him to prostrate himself or stand with villagers when they prayed, and he had not given the matter too much thought. When they were alone, the Wolof never bothered. But now Maymouna expected them to pray. Her bullying was subtle and insidious. She chivvied, gave them space, smiled a lot, and instead of standing up to her the Wolof Abdoulie got down on his hands and knees and made Hugo do it too. In the middle of the desert! Miles from anywhere!

Hugo began to think about this, how an ineffectual blob like Maymouna could have two grown men down on their knees. He thought about priests and clergymen, and curates, and mullahs, and popes, and archbishops, and archimandrites and suchlike. What power they wielded! When they addressed a throng, the throng listened, and it really did seem as though many of them believed. These authority figures often wore robes and had resonant voices. Such a voice might be cultivated. It would take some practice. It was a lot to think about all at the same time, the walk and the voice, but, not having brought any chewing gum with him, and trudging along in the desert day after day in the burning heat, a man had to do something or he would go mad. Thus, when Maymouna began to trill, using a voice that made the dunes vibrate, Hugo would recite the only poem that he knew, apart from nursery rhymes and limericks.

He couldn't remember if it was written by Cowper, about the solitude of Selkirk, or by Selkirk, about the loneliness of Cowper, yet he remembered every word of the poem. It had been consigned to memory as one of those group punishments in which teachers at his school used to delight, and which to Hugo had always seemed so maddeningly illogical. The very idea of punishing people for something they had not done, simply because they were part of an arbitrary group, called the whole system of education into question. The teacher had been . . . what? Hugo struggled to remember. A thin, joyless fellow. An English teacher? No. A geography teacher. Lately, the poem had been ringing in his brain as he watched Maymouna edging close to the Wolof Abdoulie, for whose benefit, it appeared, she was sliding up and down those weird Arab octaves.

'Verses supposed to be written by someone about someone!'

It was a joy to hear his own voice ring out in manly English tones across the alien sands.

I am monarch of all I survey,
My right there is none to dispute;
From the centre all round to the sea,
I am lord of the fowl and the brute.
O solitude! where are the charms
That sages have seen in thy face?
Better dwell in the midst of alarms,
Than reign in this horrible place.

Maymouna's trill had faltered and then stopped. Hugo's voice was just getting into its stride, relishing its command of his native language.

I am out of humanity's reach,
I must finish my journey alone,
Never hear the sweet music of speech;
I start at the sound of my own.
The beasts that roam over the plain,
My form with indifference see;
They are so unacquainted with man,
Their tameness is shocking to me.

The camels flicked their tails. They only paid attention to Hassaniya and had forged a new allegiance to Maymouna, which had mercifully removed most of the responsibility for their care from Hugo. So he was free to spread his arms wide and declaim:

Society, friendship, and love,
Divinely bestowed upon man,
Oh had I the wings of a dove,
How soon would I taste you again!
My sorrows I then might assuage
In the ways of religion and truth,
Might learn from the wisdom of age,
And be cheer'd by the sallies of youth.

Hugo had known a girl called Sally in primary school and hadn't liked her.

Religion! what treasure untold
Resides in that heavenly word!
More precious than silver and gold,
Or all that this earth can afford.
But the sound of the church-going bell
These valleys and rocks never heard,
Ne'er sigh'd at the sound of a knell,
Or smil'd when a sabbath appear'd.

None of which was strictly applicable, as there seemed to be an awful lot more religion here than Hugo had ever experienced back in England, but the verse did resonate with his earlier thoughts on the matter. A katabatic wind swept aptly through the valley they were traversing, cooling him a little and giving him strength to continue.

Ye winds, that have made me your sport,
Convey to this desolate shore
Some cordial endearing report
Of a land I shall visit no more.

My friends, do they now and then send
A wish or a thought after me?
O tell me I yet have a friend,
Though a friend I am never to see.

He stopped to drink water. His voice was becoming a little cracked. Was there anybody he missed? The names faded and the faces had always been a little blurred. But he must finish the poem! What a long one it was.

How fleet is a glance of the mind!
Compar'd with the speed of its flight,
The tempest itself lags behind,
And the swift-wing'd arrows of light.
When I think of my own native land,
In a moment I seem to be there;
But alas! recollection at hand
Soon hurries me back to despair.

But the sea-fowl is gone to her nest,
The beast is laid down in his lair,
Even here is a season of rest,
And I to my cabin repair.
There is mercy in ev'ry place,
And mercy, encouraging thought!
Gives even affliction a grace,
And reconciles man to his lot.

It took a pretty good brain to remember all that! Hugo noted to his surprise that the Wolof Abdoulie and Maymouna had lagged a long way behind him.

CHAPTER 33

Where men dither and dogs howl

HUGH DELAM RECITED HIS POEM AS THE slide show flicked through a phantasmagoria of solitude and distance. The heads of his audience appeared to sway ever so slightly from side to side, in unison. And when he stopped speaking there was a silence, followed by a self-conscious stirring, then somebody clapped, and someone else did too. For several minutes everyone applauded rhythmically. The dancing queen's husband, moving surprisingly quickly for someone his age, resumed his row-by-row distribution of the wine.

'The *horrible place* was hardly appropriate,' said Hugh, 'but I am sure that those of you who are or have been expatriates will be familiar with some of the emotions described. Ah! How I longed to be here in London, but now, strangely, I dream of that vast sky and orange sands. Maybe it is in the nature of man to be always on a journey in search of somewhere else.'

There was a clock on the wall. He had been talking for exactly one hour. He glanced at the faces of the organisers in the front row. It looked as though everyone was happy for him to carry on. So, he would take them with him on his continuing journey. He signalled to Laptop Man and the audience was treated to a photograph of two figures, a man and a woman, leading camels.

Maymouna was indeed moving with greater ease, yet her garments were so voluminous that it was difficult to tell if she had lost any weight.

'I think she is definitely a lot thinner,' observed Hugo.

'Do you think so?' The Wolof Abdoulie looked worried. 'I wouldn't want her to get too thin and lose her beauty.

Apparently her mother was a great beauty too. She died when Maymouna was twelve.'

'What will happen when we reach Nouakchott?'

'What will happen will happen.'

Their conversation was interrupted by Maymouna crashing out of the scrub bushes, giving them both a cheery wave, and climbing back onto her kneeling camel. She could do it without any difficulty now.

They were forced these days, by the increasing temperature, to confine most of their travel to the mornings and late afternoons, sheltering under the awning from the heat of the major part of day. Maymouna would chatter on merrily, the Wolof Abdoulie listened, made a comment or posed a question from time to time, and Hugo fantasised about beating his own brains out on a nearby rock. The air was suffused with the stink of the rancid goat fat, mixed with couscous, that the Wolof insisted Maymouna use to protect her complexion from the sun. Hugo wondered what he had done in his life to deserve all this. The desert is close to the bones of the Earth; the fripperies of nature and culture are stripped away, and man is alone with such thoughts. The only possible conclusion was that it was all monstrously fucking unfair. Life owed him. When he was through with all this shit, he would extract some recompense. He sank into gloom for a long period, which was only relieved when darkness fell one evening and there was a glow upon the horizon: the lights of Nouakchott!

Two days later, they waited until dawn to make their entrance into the city. Maymouna walked all the way there with a spring in her step. The Wolof Abdoulie strode like a general into a conquered city. His shoulders held back, his chin uplifted, he seemed somehow even taller than when the journey had begun. Yet reality lurked. There were practical problems; a young Maure woman in the company of a Wolof and an Englishman turned native, neither of whom were bound to her by blood or matrimony, was inappropriate in this society.

They left Ramsi, Mo and Habibi at the cattle market pending their sale. The Wolof ensured they would be well fed and gave each one a pat. Maymouna stroked Ramsi and Mo and embraced Habibi with passion. Hugo was eager to be off. Mama Oudab was easily found in the central market. She was delighted to see her old suppliers again. Yes, she could help. There was an old woman, Madame Aishitu mint Abba, a widow with no children, whose husband had been a rich man who had fathered children elsewhere but had not cut her off entirely. She had a house. She was lonely. So Maymouna found herself with a roof over her head and the company of someone not unsympathetic to her situation. The Wolof Abdoulie went joyously to his abandoned cowshed, yet felt terribly alone when he got there, and Hugo resumed his occupation of the Hotel Merhaba Guelb er Richat Nouakchott.

The luxury of the place was a joy to his soul: roof, walls, a bed with sheets, running water and a loo of sorts. Not even a scorpion, quickly crunched with a shoe, could mar his joy. And his belongings! His suitcases had been brought from storage: clean underwear, his copy of *Trapped Light,* shaving foam and shampoo! His old green flannel and Martin, his belovèd loofah. How had he survived without Martin loofah?

He had just completed his ablutions, his chin festooned with fresh cuts and oddly white against the mahogany of the rest of his face, when the Wolof Abdoulie banged on his door demanding the use of the bathroom.

Hugo found it impossible to dress quickly. He had become accustomed to completing tasks slowly and methodically. His shirt and trousers clung uncomfortably to his body and hindered his movements. He left the Wolof whistling in the bathroom and went off to find a telephone. The phone at the Hotel Merhaba Guelb er Richat Nouakchott wasn't working, so he went to the big hotel on the Rue Ahmed Ould Hamed, where he had called in briefly so long ago on the day he had visited the French Embassy. They were happy for him to make a local call, so Hugo called the number given to him by Cody and Brandon's laptop.

'Good afternoon,' said a heavily accented voice. 'Welcome to the office of the British Honorary Consul.'

'Good day to you too,' replied Hugo. 'My name's Hugo de Lamartine. I'm a British subject in a spot of bother. My passport's been stolen and all my money, and I have to get back to England. I need to see the Honorary Consul quite urgently.'

'Oh, I so sorry. So very sorry.'

There was a pause.

'Hello?' said Hugo.

'Hello,' said the voice. 'Can I help you?'

'Well yes. As I explained, I need to see the Honorary Consul. Would you give me your address so that I can come over.'

'I so very, very sorry.'

'Yes, I know you are, but would you answer my questions. I want to see the Honorary Consul.'

'Honorary Consul not here at moment. I very very sorry. But he very pleased and meet with you when he get back.'

'And what time will that be?'

'Oh very very soon.'

'But when, precisely?' The telephone receiver dripped sweat from Hugo's hands.

'Oh, very surely he back in more than one month or two.'

'But I've lost my passport! Where is the Honorary Consul?'

'He with Ambassador in Rabat at moment. Cooler there. Nouakchott very, very hot now.'

'But what's the point in having an Honorary Consul if he's not in the country? Or an Ambassador too for that matter. There must be somebody there in authority.'

'I here. I authority in everything!'

'Fine. Perhaps you would be kind enough to give me your address, so that I can come over and get this matter sorted out.' There was another pause. 'Hello?'

'I seeking date.'

'Good.' Hugo waited. The hotel lobby appeared to have some rudimentary form of air conditioning. Hugo was used to heat. He felt cold, yet his hands were sweating. He wanted to bring down the receiver hard against the wood of the hotel reception and batter the bakelite to pieces. The silence at the other end of the line continued.

'HELLO?' said Hugo.

'Hello.'

'Well?'

'Very well indeed, thank you.'

'DO YOU HAVE A DATE? A DAY? A TIME?'

'Yes.'

'WHEN IS IT?'

'Wednesday. Not this one. How say you? After this one another Wednesday.'

'But that's ridiculous! Why can't I come over to your office now, this afternoon, and do whatever it is that needs to be done to have a replacement passport issued?'

'Sir, I advise much patience. There nothing do with passport until Honorary Consul he return. You phone when Nouakchott cooler.' Hugo heard the click of the receiver being replaced at the other end of the line.

The Wolof Abdoulie and Hugo were invited to dinner at the home of Madame Aishitu mint Abba who was, for politeness' sake, called a widow. They had bought new *boubous* and shining white *howlis* from Mama Oudab for the occasion. They sat on the floor and ate a wondrous tagine from a central bowl. They drank *bissap* juice. The widow was quite old and a little batty. She spoke a mixture of French and Hassaniya and cackled merrily without any provocation. Maymouna was wearing some sort of sparkling dress under her *muluffa,* and she was sporting a pair of Teaia's red stiletto heels. The shoes appeared to be a perfect fit. She looked somehow altered to Hugo. A different face was emerging as the fat receded. It was a face that Hugo felt he had seen before, but could not place. She now seemed much younger than thirty, but older than sixteen, and there was a hint of something tarty about her. The Wolof Abdoulie seemed to glow from within and said very little.

Outside the sky was low. There would be rain, and the humidity would get even worse. They could hear dogs howling nearby. The dogs here all seemed to be wild, snarling curs and the locals gave them a wide berth.

'I like the way dogs are kept outside here,' commented Hugo. 'I think it is very sensible.'

'Where else would they be?' asked Maymouna.

'Well, where I come from in England, the dogs live inside people's homes. Even when their houses or apartments are very small, say a couple of rooms, they can share them with enormous dogs.'

'But dogs are unclean!' Maymouna was horrified.

'Exactly. But they do wash them I believe.'

Maymouna shook her head in wonderment. 'They must be very brave, your people, to live so close to dogs. They must surely fear that their throats will be ripped out!'

'Well yes, we English are a brave race. In fact, I had a dog in my home overnight shortly before I left England last year. I owed a duty to a friend.'

'And did it attack you?'

'It's all a question of letting them know who's in control. I wasn't going to stand for any nonsense and the dog knew that.'

Maymouna was intrigued by the concept of another country where people did things differently from Mauritania. She wanted to know what people ate, what the weather was like, what clothes people wore. But most of all she wanted to know about marriage. What were the rules about marriage? The subject was not particularly to Hugo's taste.

'I imagine that marriage in England is about the same as here. People have a ceremony, religious or otherwise, and then both families and all the friends have a reception where they gather together and eat a lot and drink a lot.'

'What, they all eat together?'

'Of course.'

'Even the in-laws?'

'Absolutely.'

'Amazing!' said Maymouna. 'Here a man would never eat with his wife's parents.'

'Whyever not?'

'It wouldn't be respectful. A woman wouldn't want her parents to think of her as married.'

'Good lord,' said Hugo. 'The parents aren't important at all. Marriage is between the two people concerned, I believe.'

'But the parents decide that they are going to get married?'

'Not at all. People tell their parents that they have decided to get married and then the families arrange the wedding.'

'But what if the man was . . . say, white, and spoke a different language, and the woman was black? What would happen then?'

'A few families might not like it very much. There could be a bit of a row, but the married couple could always go off and live somewhere far away from their families.'

'Could they really? Together?'

'Yes. No problem.'

'And does everyone speak French and Hassaniya in England?'

'Good gracious, no. They struggle to speak English.'

'What do they speak then?'

'Well, they sort of mumble and swear a lot.'

The old lady staggered in with a big bowl of camel milk. It was passed from person to person. Hugo had never got the hang of drinking milk on its own. He didn't like the smell of it. In the desert you had to make do with whatever you could get, and there was an allure to anything that wasn't camel meat. Here it was different, and he didn't care what people thought, he wasn't going to drink it.

The Wolof Abdoulie, cross-legged on the carpet, eventually grew bored with scowling at Hugo and picked up the thread of the conversation again. 'If I had a lot of money I would go and live in France where everybody speaks French, I think. Is France a long way from England?'

'No. It's quite close,' said Hugo.

'What's marriage like in France?' asked Maymouna.

'Well, it starts out the same as in England, but I think it ends up a bit more complicated,' mused Hugo. 'But goodness, who cares? Can't we talk about something interesting?'

'Like what?' asked the Wolof Abdoulie.

'Like Art or photography or me,' said Hugo.

'May I ask you, Monsieur Hugo, why did you come to Mauritania?' asked Maymouna.

Hugo thought for a moment and then replied that it had something to do with birds.

'Birds!' exclaimed Madame Aishitu mint Abba, showing interest for the first time in a while.

'I wanted to photograph birds. I've taken snaps of the odd one or two, but it's all been a bit disappointing really.'

The old lady became animated. Hugo must go to the Banc d'Arguin National Park! It was a direct journey straight up the road towards Nouadhibou. There he would find birds!

She had nodded off by the time Hugo and the Wolof left, so they didn't thank her. They bade goodnight to Maymouna and stepped outside, just as the heavens opened. The sand and dust sucked up the rain, the water drowned the feeble glow from street lamps, and all was a quagmire of mud and darkness. They both hurried to Hugo's hotel. His room was more spacious now. The Wolof had mended his shack's corrugated iron roof, and all Teaia's remaining clothes had been moved there. They could only hope that the roof would stand up to the rain.

Hugo quickly changed into his pyjamas and hung his soaking robe in the bathroom.

The Wolof sat on the floor and steamed. 'Can you grow crops in France?' he asked.

'Of course. Farming is very popular there. They all take it very seriously and all the neighbouring countries pay them a lot of money to do it.'

'Do they really?' asked the Wolof. 'That is kind.'

'Why are you and Maymouna so interested in Europe tonight?'

'Well, it's difficult. I have no family and she will never go back to hers. This is a place where family and friends make life. Being married is impossible if you haven't got any family to tell you that you are.'

'Who wants to get married?'

Hugo had been fiddling with his pyjama buttons, straightening his sheet, squashing a cockroach here and there with the first volume of *Swann's Way*. Now he stopped and turned to look at his companion.

'Maymouna and I would like to. I hope that you will slaughter a goat and join in our happiness.'

'Join in your happiness? I think it's a horrible idea. She's still fat, but her face has a sharp look to it, and she sings. How can you possibly think about marrying her?'

'To me she is an oasis in the desert. She is the warmth of a camel's breath on a cold night. She is the grass that grows after rain. She is the sweetness of *zrig* and honey . . . '

'But hasn't she had a nasty operation?'

'Her mother spared her. Swore her to secrecy. She is ripe as a *bissap* upon the tree.'

'Oh for God's sake,' said Hugo. 'I'm going to bed. Do you want to sleep on the floor?'

'No,' said the Wolof, 'I'm going home.'

He banged the door behind him, but Hugo hardly heard for the noise the rain was making outside.

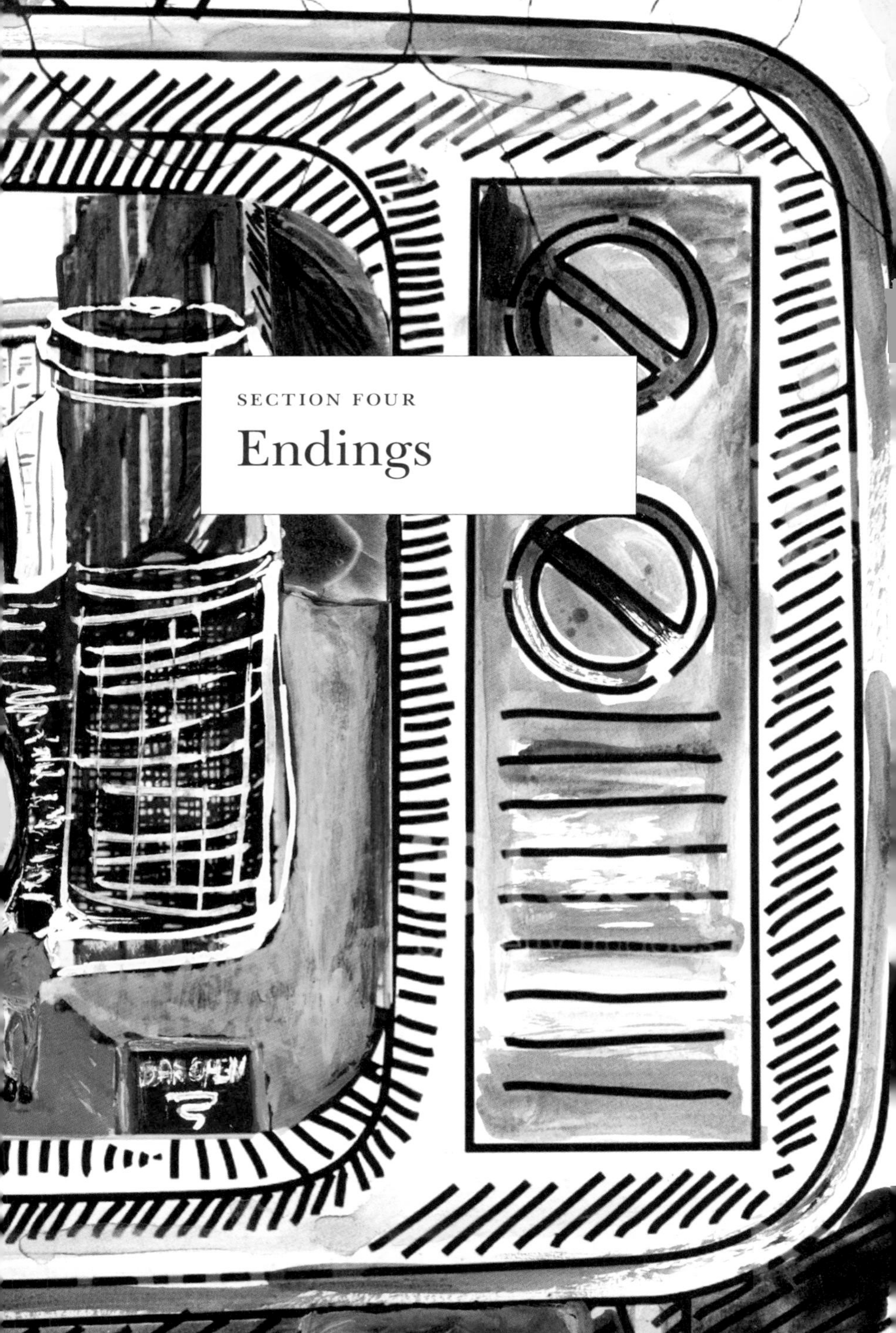

SECTION FOUR

Endings

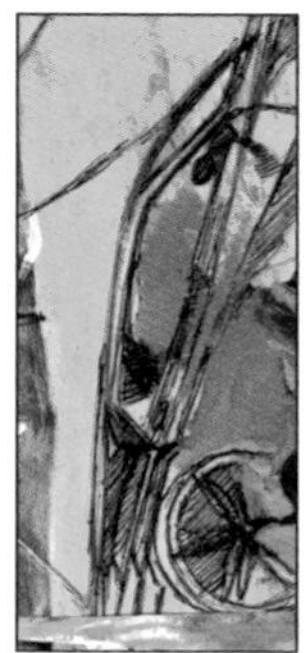

CHAPTER 34

On the road to Nouadhibou

ABDOULIE MISSED HUGO'S FUNERAL. IT was over by the time he came to England from France, but he stopped off in London on his way to Cambridge, where a job on a farm awaited him, and attended the laying of the stone. Even that was a very great affair. It was difficult finding the place. Rural France had not prepared him for London and the complexities of bus and Underground, and May had insisted on bringing the buggy. She was so proud of that buggy. In the end he had to carry it while May held Virginie. For all his strength, May was better at carrying their little girl; she had a nice padded seat between rib and hip just right for the purpose. And even for this lesser ceremony, the crowds were fearsome. Nobody made way for them or seemed to care that they had a child to look after. So May didn't see much, mostly the backs of heads, but Abdoulie being immensely tall saw all the way across the crowds to the vast marble tomb.

All this fuss was about Hugo. Hugo! Not Hudelam, as everyone was calling him now. Abdoulie had seen a picture in France. Hudelam holding a scroll, carefully posed. Those long fingers, the nose, the uplifted chin! Who could it be but Hugo? And if someone like Hugo was seen as touched by a divine hand, what, God be praised, were the rest of them like? He looked around him at the faces in the crowd: grey skin, grey clothes, glum as camels in a sandstorm. And oh, it was cold here, even colder than France. Not that Abdoulie couldn't cope. He could block out all thought of discomfort, but he worried about his wife and child. Virginie was well wrapped, and May seemed warm enough. May kept spluttering and exclaiming that the English were mad and that they must have mixed up Hugo with someone else. But Abdoulie had fond recollections. There had been a spark to Hugo and, looking back on their friendship, there were so many wonderful images, but the one that was clearest and best in his memory was always Hugo at the Banc d'Arguin National Park.

From the moment Hugo first heard of the place, he was determined to go there. But it was too difficult, they had neither the time nor the money to make the journey. Abdoulie was desperate to make enough to begin to think seriously about marriage, and there were four of them now to be provided for, with Madame Aishitu and of course Maymouna. Not that Maymouna wasn't an active partner in their enterprise, but satellite television was bringing a more modern world to Nouakchott, and their women customers now had ideas about fashion. They knew what the girls were wearing in Egypt and Lebanon, so it was not easy to make money with clothes that smelled of mothballs and were years out of date. Hugo even gave English lessons. The pupils never seemed to last very long before there was a falling-out, but there was an unceasing supply.

Abdoulie knew that Hugo still hankered for home. Autumn came. He made written applications to see the Honorary Consul. Winter came. He had a reply! A summoning. The Honorary Consul would see him. It was a warm day, but Hugo wore a smart blue jacket that Abdoulie had never seen before and considered shaving off his beard, but then didn't. He returned angrier than Abdoulie had ever seen him. He had argued with the Honorary Consul!

It was Hugo's fault. That was quite clear from his ranting account of the meeting. He was asked why he had a French name, and why it had taken him well over a year between losing his passport and credit cards and applying to the Consulate, and how had he been earning his living in the meantime, which were reasonable enough questions, and Hugo should have answered them properly. The Honorary

Consul said that he would write a letter and find out what had been on Hugo's original visa application, and Hugo, very rudely, had stormed out of the place. But that was Hugo for you, the sort of man who would always end up killing a bleating goat rather than a calm one.

Something snapped. Hugo changed. He didn't seem to fuss so much about small things any more. He wanted to be off, travelling away from Nouakchott. Perhaps he thought that if they went away together, Abdoulie would stop wanting to marry Maymouna. Abdoulie refused to hire camels and go with him on a long trip, so Hugo found a driver to take them to the Banc d'Arguin.

Now the driver, a fellow called Nagid, didn't have a four-wheel drive, and indeed his wheels were very old. Some sort of eastern European car of a type that someone had been importing into Nouakchott; there were a few of them about. Nagid insisted that the road to Nouadhibou was a good straight one, and his car had the soul of a camel. There was room in the boot for Hugo's suitcase. Abdoulie told him they wouldn't need much in the way of clothes, but Hugo took all his *boubous* and *howlis* and rolls and rolls of film, used and unused. People didn't want film any more in the rest of the world, so somebody enterprising was importing it into Mauritania.

The car had broken down a few times, and the journey had taken much longer than it should. Darkness was falling as they drew near to their destination, so they left the road and set up camp for the night. It was just like old times: the light of a small fire, the stars in a huge sky; but instead of camel meat they ate fish they had bought from a vendor by the roadside.

As dawn broke, Abdoulie realised that he was in the most beautiful place he had ever seen. They came down from perfect sand hills, scored with parallel tracks from winds that had blown all the way over the Sahara, crossing thousands of miles to hurl themselves against the winds from the sea and rise upwards to the sky. And out, across, the glittering bay spread before them.

The images of that scene would stay always with Abdoulie, although much that he saw, having not yet been educated by teaching a child, he lacked the concepts to name. The emotions were there and the ideas came later. Far back in history, when the Sahara had not been all desert, but rich green lands, huge rivers had flowed to this estuary. The rivers were gone, but somehow their highways remained. Spread out on mudflats the seals lolled as they had always done. Mangroves joined the land to the ocean and as far as the eye could see were birds, thousands upon millions of birds: flamingos, herons, plovers, good terns and bad terns, redshanks, pelicans, spoonbills and godwits, feasting upon fish and seagrass and all the living protein fashioned by helical twists that sea and land could provide. Hidden by acacia, heliotrope and euphorbia, eyes watched. A gazelle stood close to its mother, a fennec fox bared its teeth at a jackal, a sand cat dozed and waited for night. Far out in the bay, between white-sailed boats, sported dolphins. Turtles ploughed the waves with leathery arms, and fin whales sailed the sea highways and moved forwards and backwards from one age to another.

It was all glorious. Abdoulie watched Hugo pick up his skirts and run. He capered down to the sea, stopping, every so often, for a click of the shutter here and there, and yelling at the top of his voice, in English, *Birds! Birds! Birds!* And the birds flew up in the sky ahead of him and swooped down to the ground as he passed.

How long did they stay there? Hugo sat for hours looking out to sea and smiling. Abdoulie had never seen Hugo smile for so long. It wasn't something he was good at.

'Teaia was right,' he said. 'I was meant to come here. It has all been for a reason. This must be what she meant by a lagoon, the sea between the land and those islands out there. What a wonderful place it must have been in centuries past when there were dodos!' That was what he said, Abdoulie was sure, dodos. It was something he was to ponder upon in later years, when Virginie brought home school books and ideas, and he came to realise that once there had been hippopotamuses and lions here, and further back there might have been pterosaurs and plesiosaurs, so perhaps Hugo had some special knowledge about dodos.

It was late afternoon when they made their way back to the road. Nagid had erected a tent in the sand and was dozing beneath it.

They bought fish again that night from Imraguen tribesmen who lived in the park and fished the waters, as their ancestors had done for thousands of years. Hugo was not usually so perspicacious, yet he latched onto the idea that this was an ancient, numinous place.

The road to Nouadhibou is dangerous at night. Some vehicles drive slowly, others too quickly and many don't have lights. Besides, they were in no hurry to leave this place. They slept serenaded by the calls of animals, the yelping grunts of seals and the tumultuous hubbub of the birds.

In the morning, Hugo was his usual touchy self. They drove a mile or two, then the car broke down. Nagid was very passive about this. It was as God willed. There was nothing to be done. They waved at two lorries, but nobody wanted to stop. Then a red Toyota passed them at speed and was disappearing off into the distance, when it did a u-turn and came back.

'Hi, you guys! How ya doin'?'

Teeth gleamed in the sunshine. It was Brandon and Cody. The contretemps of their former encounter appeared forgotten. They had a new driver who looked terrified. He stared from side to side, and the whites of his eyes flashed a warning. They climbed out onto the road, lit a couple of spliffs, spat in the dust and explained that they were off home. Vassily had gone back to Russia. There was no business here. They planned to cross the border into Western Sahara and then drive to Rabat, where they had stuff to pick up, then they'd take a flight from Casablanca. Sure they could take Hugo and Abdoulie. There was room for both of them. Hugo translated the conversation for Abdoulie's benefit, and Abdoulie said a couple of words in Hassaniya and gestured to the north to Nagid.

Nagid drew Hugo and Abdoulie to one side. A conference between the three established the following: Nagid felt that the Americans were not to be trusted. The journey was too dangerous. All along the border to the north were landmines. There were bandits and police checkpoints. There was trouble between Western Sahara and Morocco. His cousin had told him all this only last week. He knew it to be true. Besides, his car would soon be working again. He was sure of it.

Hugo chatted to Brandon and Cody. Abdoulie couldn't understand what they were saying, but he guessed Hugo was asking them how he was going to manage a border crossing without papers. Then Hugo turned away from the men and stood for a while, with his back to them, inspecting something he had taken from inside his robe. He returned with a pair of diamond earrings and showed them to the men. Brandon and Cody looked at their nervous driver and then muttered again with Hugo. Abdoulie guessed that, when the four-wheel drive crossed over the border, the driver's papers would be making the journey and their owner left behind with five litres of water and a long walk ahead of him.

Hugo's manner had changed again. He had speeded up. He spoke more quickly, and even in his French there was the structure of another language.

'This is your chance,' he said to Abdoulie. 'Come with me. I'll find you work in England.'

'I'll come, but not without Maymouna.'

Hugo spoke to the men, who had climbed back into their vehicle and seemed eager to be off.

'There's no time to go back to Nouakchott. You have to decide now.'

Abdoulie said that he was sorry, that his soul would always follow Hugo and one day he would come to England, but now he was going home to Maymouna.

Hugo wrinkled up his mouth, then nodded, and then he winced as though remembering something. 'My stuff,' he said. 'It's yours now.' He felt inside his robe and took out Teaia's jewellery pouch. 'There's the key to my hotel room at the Merhaba Guelb er Richat Nouakchott in here. You can have what I own: my torch, my tennis racquet, my clothes . . .' Then he thought of something else and writhed in a sort of agony. He stood up straighter as though drawing himself together. 'And you can have my jacket. My special one. *Sacré bleu!* It's too small for you, but it should be worth a lot in the market. And these.' He proffered the pouch of jewellery. 'This doesn't really belong to me. There must be some way to sell it without causing trouble. Use it to pay for your ticket out of here. All I'll need are this and this.' He took out a couple of golden bangles and some rings and secreted them about his person.

Abdoulie shook his head and pushed the pouch away.

'Oh bloody hell,' said Hugo. 'Let Maymouna wear them for your wedding.'

Abdoulie took the pouch. The two men embraced in a way that was commonplace for men in Mauritania, but never had been for Hugo and never would be again. Hugo climbed into the front of the vehicle, beside the driver, and it sped off towards the north.

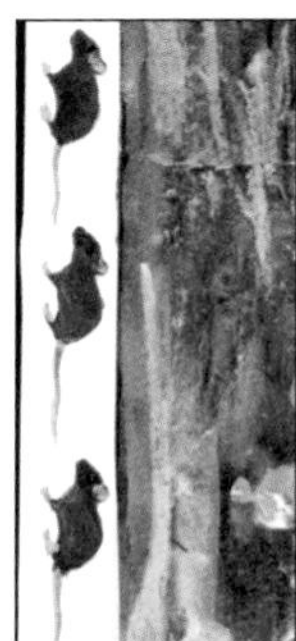

CHAPTER 35

Of rats and men, homo habilis and otherwise

IT WAS KIND OF RODNEY AND WILFRED, Daphne thought, to suggest accompanying her to the laying of the stone. She did not get out these days half as much as she should. Marjorie had been a good influence. She missed her. Cirrhosis of the liver had not been a pleasant way to go; yellow never had been Marjorie's colour.

Being sure of a good seat was a challenge, but she was determined. A night could as easily be spent sitting in a fold-up chair here as at home, and although it was winter the weather, as usual, was far too warm for the season. Some people thought that next door to the Diana monument in Hyde Park was not an appropriate place for Hudelam, but it was a wonderful spot (the grass, the trees), Daphne thought, and she was sure that if Hudelam were looking down on them now he would be in full agreement.

Rodney and Wilfred had volunteered to take turns to sit with her but, when it came to it, Rodney preferred to stay with her the whole night. He couldn't sleep anyway, he said. Rodney, too, was bereaved and his was the grief that couldn't be mentioned for fear that no one would take it seriously. Their cat, Akhenaten, age fifteen and a half, had died. The hole in their lives unfillable, Wilfred soldiered on in denial, his face drawn, his hair whiter. He was better off asleep back in Thamesbury, said Rodney, pulling his coat around him more for comfort than warmth.

Already a line snaked behind them. People talked in hushed voices, a civilised gathering of dedicated souls.

'Look at that tomb. Isn't it astonishing!' Daphne took Rodney's arm.

'I've never seen anything like it. It makes the Albert Memorial look like brutalism. I'm amazed they ever got planning permission.'

'I just had to come! Marjorie and I were there right at the beginning, at the very moment when Hugh Delam turned into Hudelam!'

'I didn't know he was called Hugh Delam. You make it sound as though someone waved a magic wand!' he said, pouring hot chocolate from a thermos and handing her a cup.

'It was like that. Extraordinary.'

'Go on. Tell me about it.'

She remembered every detail perfectly. What a sweltering day it had been, gathered together in that little church in North Kensington. Or was it South Kensington? No matter. Hugh Delam had shown them his photographs of Mauritania and it had been as though they were there with him. At the end, when he showed photographs of sea birds, something had happened. They had all been transported. Sort of.

'It doesn't sound like very much,' said Rodney.

'No, it doesn't, but it was. You have to see it in context: that awful government, nothing working properly, the church busy hounding people like you… Nobody believed in anything. We lacked all conviction, you know, and Hudelam, well, he was full of what d'you call it? Intensity. That was it. Passionate intensity!'

The incense. The wine. The birds. The very air had wings and flew. Laptop Man had switched off and sat staring ahead in some sort of trance. The audience sweated through cotton, linen, silk and a few unpleasant acrylic mixes. A hundred nostrils drew in incense and breathed out hot fumes of Wangaratta Frottage Hill red. Yet Hugh Delam, elevated upon his dais, was as cool in his blue robe as a Pope in winter. The glass of water stood untouched. He didn't even need to wipe his brow. There was the sound in the audience of someone humming one of Leonard Cohen's songs. Another person took it up. Somebody opened a door at the front of the church and a shaft of light, presumably travelling at the speed of light, traversed the ancient tiles, ascended the dais and illuminated the hem of the robe of Hugh Delam. Something ran along the path of light. A small dark shadow. In pursuit, many more. They ran up to the base of Hugh Delam and, forming a crescent, waited. There were rats in the hall, yet no one screamed. They seemed as unthreatening as rats on a television screen or behind glass in a zoo. The robed figure was invested with the power of a Pied Piper or a David Attenborough. Nobody was afraid. Hugh Delam was in charge. Hugh Delam was so full of confidence, he appeared not even to notice the rats. He lifted a hand. A sigh rose up from the audience. 'Hudelam!' shrieked the voice of a woman, in received pronunciation. Was it a drunken slurring of first name with surname, or the inspired birth of a new appellation? Who knows, who will ever know? But the woman's cry was swiftly joined by a burbling bass calling 'Hudelam!' And everyone joined in, chanting *Hudelam! Hudelam! Hudelam! Hudelam!*

Time passed. Hudelam descended from the dais and walked slowly down the central aisle. The rats followed. Somebody on bended knee reached out and touched the hem of his garment, but Hudelam did not notice her and walked on.

Hudelam! Hudelam! Hudelam!

'When will we see you again?' cried a voice.

Hudelam turned, smiled. 'I shall be here in two days, in the evening. I welcome you all.'

And then he was gone from the building in a flash of blue robes and little scurrying feet. Some said that he climbed into a black cab, others that it was a bus. But it could equally well have been a stretch limo or a chariot.

Back in the hall, a woman who had a packet of the Prince's organic biscuits fed them to some rats left behind, who sat up on their haunches and dined politely, then filed out neatly like

the quasi-mystical embodiments of transcendent attributes that they were. Men and women, and women and women, and men and men and some who were even harder to classify, put aside their reserve and held hands and wept.

It really was all quite extraordinary.

'Kaplaa!' mused Rodney. 'He won your souls. What an incredible experience. Would you like a crayfish and rocket sandwich?'

'Oh how lovely! I brought some sandwiches but nothing as nice as these. This is spelt bread, isn't it?'

Rodney nodded. 'We make it ourselves. So how did all that stuff about art and animals happen?'

Daphne swallowed a mouthful of sandwich, dabbed her lips with a paper napkin and said, 'Two days later, it was much more informal. Somebody had cleared the chairs away and we were all on cushions on the floor. Hudelam sat on the floor with us and talked to us, about Art, about animals, about everything. I remember poor Marjorie was rather uncomfortable. She was much too large and stiff to be sitting on cushions.'

The heatwave had continued; the day had been unbearably hot and muggy and then, just as Hudelam swept into the hall, the first crash of thunder came. There were far more people present than had been there previously. He put everyone at their ease and told them to make themselves comfortable on the cushions on the floor. He unrolled a small north African carpet and sat on it cross-legged. People had brought wine with them and plates of tapas, dim sum and little canapés. Everyone shared. There was a flash of lightning visible through the darkened windows, followed quickly by the rolling borborygmi of giants. Then the rains came, crashing down like designer chef pans on quarry tiles.

'*Shantih, shantih, shantih*,' murmured a woman to a tall grey-haired man beside her.

'No, but there's lager,' he replied, reaching into a cold bag and handing her a can.

Hudelam began to address them, and sometimes his words were muffled by the drumming of the rain.

Each person who was there came away with a slightly different version of what had been said. It was always Hudelam's way to talk to people, never to write anything down. He left that to others, indeed he encouraged note takers. *Who knows,* he would say, *someone might write a book of Hudelam one day!* Sometimes there would be quite strange versions of things he was supposed to have said. Yet here there was a broad consensus. Hudelam told them on that evening, with the rain falling and the air clearing even as he spoke, that right at the dawn of time there were two sorts of men. He didn't say anything about women. The first men made tools from flint and hunted wild beasts, the second took the gift of fire deep into caves and made paintings on rocks. From the first had arisen science and technology and consumerism and from the second, the greater good of Art. It was Art that expressed our better nature, Hudelam assured them.

Not everyone, fortunately, had it in them to be a scientist or a technologist, but all had the potential for Art. You didn't need to learn anything to pick up a paintbrush, or see something from a different viewpoint or reinterpret, or put two things together, or just look at something and see the Art in it. Art was everywhere. Art was everything. Art didn't damage the world. Economies could be powered by Art. But Art was subtle. It took training and dedication and vision to spot real Art and know the difference between a dribble and a trace of the mystical.

Alas, this gift of Art was not possessed by animals. That is how we could be sure of their position in the hierarchy of being. Animals were lowly things, but birds were not. Some birds, and even insects, had achieved craftsmanship, to wit: the building of a nest, hive or termite mound. And in its attempts to woo, one bird alone, the bowerbird, with its arrangements of what lay to hand, pebbles and twigs and flowers, had achieved that glorious gestalt that we call Art.

Our homes were Art. Dogs were not Art and should not be living in homes. Dogs were unclean.

Motherhood was an Art and women were to be responsible for the full-time care of their children.

Cooking was a form of Art. Food should never be eaten raw. Preparation was everything.

Clothing was Art. People should tread carefully and seek guidance.

Photography was the highest Art, trapping light in its purest form.

As they departed that evening, filing out into the summer air, which once again could be breathed deeply, all of London seemed sparkling and new. Each man or woman carried a fragment of knowledge, a seed to be planted in conversation, e-mail, blog, newspaper article, television discussion, book or even film. The word and world of Hudelam were on their way.

'Did he say anything about cats?' asked Rodney.

Daphne thought hard. 'No. I don't think so. Camels were OK, but I'm not sure why. Dogs were out, of course, but cats? He probably did, but I can't remember.'

'People seem not to be having them as they used to,' he said, blinking hard.

'No,' Daphne agreed, 'and, dare I say it, but it's been a pity about dogs. So difficult for the blind.'

'Yes, every day more of them die crossing roads. But the rats were presumably OK though?'

'Oh I think they were there just to demonstrate that he was right. They sort of showed the animal kingdom bending its knee in front of Hudelam. They probably went off and killed themselves afterwards, like lemmings.'

It was as dark as it ever got in London, so Rodney and Daphne could see the gathering around them quite clearly. The timbre of the hubbub, the candles wavering far away, suggested an ever-increasing throng. Television people had set up their equipment hours earlier and appeared to be working through the night. Deference was shown to a scruffy young man with coffee-coloured skin and a bald head, who was taking photographs from peculiar angles. A circle of young students – presumably of Art, for they were dressed cheaply yet stylishly – surrounded the tomb itself. They knelt, heads bent, keeping a vigil.

'What did he sound like? Did he speak English well?' asked Rodney.

'A bit nasal and yes, his English was perfect.'

'Yet he came from Mauritania?'

'Oh no. I don't think so. I think he came from France originally. Of course, he's enormous over there, and I've heard him on television preaching in French.' Daphne smiled at the memory.

'That was where Teaia was going when we saw her last.'

'France?'

'No, Mauritania. She died on the plane on her way there.'

'Of course she did. When was that?'

'Oh, ages ago. Must have been ten years ago, I think.'

'I've got a vague memory about some sort of connection between Teaia and Hudelam. I think he said he knew her.'

'Really?' Rodney packed away the remains of the sandwiches and produced two small ramekins of elderflower and berry fool. He handed one to Daphne. 'Of course, now Hudelam is dead, all this will probably fade away.'

'Do you think so?'

'Well, it's been very good for Cave Paintings, everyone feels that not buying art is a bit socially irresponsible, but I should think the bubble will burst.' He looked out at the assembled masses. 'Or then again, maybe not.'

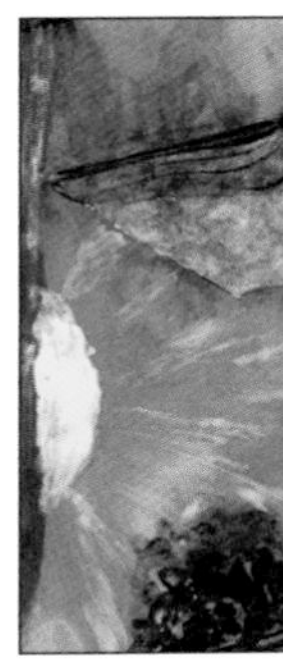

CHAPTER 36

Betty has a vision

CS Funny thing, space-time. Bit like a cauliflower. Every thousand years a flower thingy.

NWS Floret. The flower thingy. I think it's caled a floret.

CS Floret? Doesn't that mean the same thing? Anyway, maybe every million years a stalk. Stalk-et. Wouldn't it be great to travel right back down to the roots? Maybe you could jump to another cauliflower and come up somewhere else.

Chertsey Staines, Interview
New Woman Scientist Magazine

CHERTSEY'S BLADDER WAS READY TO BURST. BLOODY lucky she was in a bathroom.

Phew, that was better! She sat looking around her. Not a very nice bathroom. The tub was bright blue and biodegradable; it was already beginning to crumble away around the edges. Where was she, and *when?* She picked up a bottle of shampoo. Full of sulphates! And the liquid soap, same horrible stuff. So, whoever used this bathroom would have a flaking scalp, dry skin and a problem with their wee; she eyed two large boxes of extra-large, heavy-duty granny nappies with stay-dry, mop-up gusset. But hang on a minute, they didn't have biodegradable baths in the time she had been hoping to reach. They didn't come in till – when? Oh ever so much later. What a pisser! Wrong time, and obviously wrong place too. All this time-jumping was much more complicated than P. Brockworth had worked out, whoever he was. Nobody had ever succeeded in finding out. Perhaps he had done it himself, gone off to somewhere really lovely in the past and never found out what had happened to his extraordinary paper on time travel.

She tried to flush the toilet but it appeared to be blocked and the flush button or sensor taped over. From the room beyond, she could hear what sounded like a television. She opened the door, just a crack, and peered through. There was a leather armchair with its back to her, but she couldn't see its occupant. The television was an ancient LED with a two-dimensional picture. The room looked as though someone had made an attempt at early 21st-century minimalism, then messed it up with an oil painting in a massive gilt frame, which nearly covered one entire wall. The smell of the room, and the nature of the blinds, flooring and an adjacent bedspread, were the same in any age. This had to be a nursing home.

How long was she likely to be here? She wasn't that far away in time from where she had hoped to end up, so the next jump would have to be a long way into the future, then back to a distant past, to enable her to stand a chance of coming back to the right time on the next bounce-back.

'I can see you in the mirror you know!' said a loud voice. 'Why don't you stop skulking in there? You must have finished cleaning it ages ago!'

Typical, thought Chertsey. She had spent her working life single-handedly running British patent processing, had been slightly famous for a few minutes through her discovery of P. Brockworth's time travel theories, had lived for more than eighty years, and yet she was still being mistaken for either a personal assistant or a cleaning lady! Oh well, let's face the music and dance, as they used to say in her Nan's time. 'Ello!' She moved out into the room.

The occupant of the chair eyed her with a sour expression. Although she was seated, it was obvious that she was tall and gaunt. She wore a black dress and green strappy shoes. Her enormous toenails were painted red and most were chipped. Her hair was dyed a uniform black, ageing the face it framed, yet this was not an old lady. Chertsey put her at about seventy.

'Go away!' The woman's voice was husky, yet still loud and assertive.

'I know this sounds silly, but please could you tell me what day and what year this is?'

The woman looked at her as though she were mad. 'I haven't the foggiest. They keep bringing me appalling calendars – cats, dogs, revolting stuff – which I rip into tiny pieces and use to block up the loo.'

Chertsey tried again. 'Maybe you could tell me who's Prime Minister?'

At that moment, the door opened and a middle-aged woman in a maroon uniform bustled in.

'How lovely!' she said. 'You have a visitor. It's not often Betty has visitors, you know, except the ones she sees and nobody else does.' The last sentence was directed at Chertsey. 'And forget about asking who's Prime Minister. I don't think there's anyone in the entire place who could answer that one! We've all lost interest.'

'My name isn't Betty,' said the occupant of the chair.

'I know, I know, but your real name's such a mouthful and I never get it right! Betty is a friendly name.'

'You may call me Professor Camber.'

'Come now, Betty, let's not be stuffy. How about a nice cup of tea for you both?'

'My given name is Amphelisia. It is no more complicated than any other name. I would like a glass of red wine and a cigarette. I do not want tea. If you won't bring me what I want, then go away and take this old hag with you.'

'And what about tea for your visitor? No? Call me if you need anything. I'll be just at the end of the corridor.' She closed the door quietly behind her.

'Pleased to meet you, Professor Camber. I'm Chertsey. Chertsey Staines.' She held out her hand, but Camber merely rolled her eyes and turned back to her television programme.

Chertsey sighed. She had been here too long already. That bungee rope of time travel was surely ready to whisk her off again. She was much too old for this sort of thing. Oestrogen, when you were way past the change, was risky. It could make tumours grow, and her head felt all wrong. Still, at her time of life you could take a chance and she'd earned this one.

The Camber woman was having some sort of a fit. One arm was stretched out before her, and her breath came in gasping pants. 'Isssssss! Issssss Isssssss!' she hissed.

Chertsey wondered if she should stick a spoon in her mouth to stop her swallowing her tongue, but she didn't have a spoon (maybe she should have accepted that cup of tea) and it really wasn't her business to get involved.

'Issssim! Issssim!' gasped Camber, and then more clearly, 'It's bloody well him!'

Chertsey turned to the television, just in time to see a tall, blue-robed figure in front of some public building before the picture switched to an aerial shot of sand dunes. The glimpse was enough to inform her. She had already seen this docudrama, filmed shortly before his death. Some well-known producer had made it. ''Udelam,' she said. ''Ugo de Lamartine.'

'That's right,' said Camber, sitting up and looking much more with-it. 'I keep telling everyone that he's Hugo de Lamartine, and nobody'll listen to me. How do you know who he is?'

'I used to work fer 'im. Did all the work 'e was supposed to do and didn't.'

The camera panned back to Hudelam. He was saying something about the pre-eminence of the Visual Arts.

'And do people believe you when you tell them that?' asked Camber.

'Don't usually say nuffink. Don't wanna be classed as somebody who noo 'im well. People'd make a fuss, and I wouldn't be able to come and go like I wanted.'

'You're probably right. When I spoke up about who he was

and told people that I taught him everything, how he got all of his ideas about Art from me, they shut me up in this place! This place! Look at it! Isn't it awful? I didn't pay into a fund for thirty years for this!'

Chertsey nodded, then added, 'That's a lovely picture though, innit?'

'That thing?' She glanced at the oil painting on the wall, the happy Russian workers, the smiling girl with a dandelion. 'That's state intervention that is! As if there weren't better ways of spending our money than trying to foist such crap on the sick and the dying! And I'm not even sick! I asked for a Damien Hirst and they gave me that Communist thing! I begged them to take it away, but they wouldn't; so I made the decision to become incontinent, as an expression of rage, and I'll go on refusing to use the loo for anything except calendars until they remove it!'

'Remove the toilet?'

'No, the painting, the fucking painting, damn it! Have you got a cigarette? I'd kill for a cigarette.'

Chertsey shook her head.

'He's altered things I wouldn't have touched!' Camber's face was twisted into a gargoyle of disgust. 'And making himself into some sort of Pope figure, instead of staying in the background as I told him to!'

'But 'e did some good things as well.'

'The power of Art?'

'He started a wave of tourists. Got everyone talking about mutilatin' and force-feedin' women and trappin' sea birds in fishin' nets. Now Mauritania's reeelly, reeelly popular.'

'I don't give a toss about such things,' said Camber. 'Also, the way they said he died was a complete nonsense. Didn't believe a word of it. Are you going to help me to get out of here?' She stood up and, opening her wardrobe, took out a huge green bag with straps and padlocks on it. She began stuffing make-up from a drawer into its depths. 'I need to leave, now!'

'I'd help you if I could, but I'm only going to be here one minute and gone the next...'

Chertsey felt the room begin to fade. Camber was looking at her with her mouth hanging open; then there was darkness, but she could still hear Camber's voice shrieking.

'And I don't imagine things!'

CHAPTER 37

The wonder and heartbreak of Wendelsworth Bridge

CHERTSEY SWALLOWED. THAT LAST JUMP had left a horrible taste in her mouth and a stench like black smoke in her nostrils. She'd been sick on a mosaic floor somewhere, or somewhen. She breathed out, emptying her lungs, and held it, with eyes closed, until she felt better. She opened them. Hole in one! She'd come to the right place. It was a beautiful evening and Hassock Street was deserted; nobody to see her arrive. But what day was it? And where was he?

Lundenwic. What a thrill to be back, solid and living in what had become just a memory. Even the word *Lundenwic* rolled about in her mind, like something that hadn't been thunk for sixty years, which was strange as she had lived here all her life. Even the air smelt different. Chertsey trod her way cautiously along the road and stared in at the glass frontage of Cave Paintings. There was a girl in a let's-frighten-the-natives sort of tartan romper suit. Chertsey admired her nerve. She was setting out glasses. A party. Yippee! This should mean she had landed on the right day, but there was no sign of him yet. It was still early. She wandered further down the road until she came to a restaurant, La Pipistrelle. How long had it been since she'd had a good French nosh? At least forty years! Why not? There was time and she needed to cheer herself up after meeting that mad, elderly crone.

Inside, the restaurant was quite posh, but she liked the pictures of animals on the walls. A waiter approached her.

'Hello,' said Chertsey. 'Table for one, please.'

He showed her to a small table at the top of a flight of

stairs, which appeared to lead down to the toilets and kitchen.

'Do you have a copy of today's paper?'

'I'm sure I could find one somewhere, Madame.'

The waiter departed, and returned with a leather-bound menu and a Twilight Herald.

Chertsey checked the date at the top of the paper. Bingo!

'Would Madame care for something to drink?'

'Do you have any Steel-Brew Headbashers?'

'No, I don't think I've heard of that one, Madame, but if you tell me what's in it, I'm sure I could make one for you.'

'Silly me! I use to drink stuff like that when I was a gel. Doesn't matter. A slosh of Glenfluddoch 12 Year Old, just by itself, would be ever so nice. Thank you.'

Chertsey examined the menu. At the next table two men were dining. One of them had his handphone beside his plate. She thought it would be very strange if she was to ask him if she could use it, and then phone up Melony and ask her *How are you, darlin'*? But it was so many years ago, and even a mind like hers, which collected all sorts of strange things, couldn't remember the phone number. And she would see Melony when she got back home again. Who'd have thought, when she was a kiddie, that Melony would become so famous and have an exhibition in the Loyal Academy? Perhaps there was a telephone book here. Who could she phone? Hugo de Lamartine! That would be funny. What would she say? What a laugh it would be if she played a practical joke, told him that there was a burst water main and the road was closed and he shouldn't come to the party. Would he recognise her voice? She must surely sound a lot different now from sixty years ago. Or she could phone herself. Now there was a strange thought!

The food on the menu seemed a little weird. She didn't know what to choose.

'Might I suggest an *omelette aux fines herbes*,' said the waiter, 'or a steak *au poivre?*'

'Brilliant. I'll have the steak. Bloody. Wiv chips. And peas. An' a bottle of red. What's that one like? Château Rieussec?'

'Can't be sure. Came as part of a job lot. Very old, so it's a bit of a gamble. It's the last bottle; you can have it half-price if you like.'

'Done.'

The service was slow, but she was in no hurry and the food, when it arrived, was good, although the wine needed to breathe a bit. She savoured each mouthful. Where she had come from, she thought, they were more concerned with presentation than taste and everything was cooked to buggery. She liked the music that was playing. Piaf. *L'hymne à l'amour.* She'd learned all the words once. In French, too. Though saying them was a bit difficult. *Dieu réunit ceux qui s'aiment,* they promised, which cheered her up even though she didn't go along with the God bit.

She was just finishing a final cup of coffee when a group of people entered the restaurant and took a table in the corner, beside a plinth with a vase containing a single twig. As they sat down, she noticed two rats run under one of the pews. How amazing! Two huge rats! The party was too far away for her to hear what the people were saying. She didn't recognise most of them, except for Hugo de Lamartine and one of the young men. Wasn't that the fellow who had visited Hugo with the film director all those years ago? And there was something familiar about the face of that other young man; he had ever such a nice smile. Their clothes are sort of quaint and they're still young, she thought, and I've got old!

Hugo stood up, trotted here and there as though he was pissed, then made his way across the restaurant, passing right by her without even a glance, and descended the stairs. Well, what else could she expect after all these years?

She called for the bill and paid it with some very ancient, grubby notes that she had retrieved from a money belt tucked in her knickers. The waiter took the cash with good grace, so she left him a hefty tip. *Bye bye, Hugo, I'm off!*

The music began to fade as she walked out into the night. She gazed about her. Where was he? The young woman with the tartan suit was coming out of the gallery and locking up

as Chertsey passed by. Tartan suit overtook her, then turned back and asked, 'Do you need any assistance?'

What a sweetheart! Chertsey said thank you, but no, and wished her a good night.

No sign of him anywhere. He must have been in the street a while later. She'd just have to hang around a bit. She'd had too much to eat and drink and was tired and longed to put her feet up. She waited.

It was still hard to come to terms with what Hugo had or would become. Maybe she had misjudged him. Perhaps there was more to him than met the eye. And why had he suddenly gone to Mauritania of all places, all those years ago, leaving her to do his job for a third of the pay? There was so much that was really, really mysterious. His death, too, had been the strangest thing; it was still hard to accept that it had really happened. It had been on the news.

She remembered. It was an ordinary summer's evening. She was watching a film, sitting on the sofa wearing her comfy clothes, and sucking cherryade from a bottle with a straw. There was a newsflash. She stood up, unaware of the falling bottle. When television is suddenly real, you have to do something different. She couldn't just sit back and watch; that was for entertainment. She stood up and bent down with her face close to the screen. Hugo, or rather Hudelam, as he was called by then, had been at Wandle, Wendle, whatever Bridge doing his favourite thing, talking at people. Thousands of people. There wasn't room for them, no space for cars to go past, and the crowd was blocking the bridge and lining the banks of the river on either side.

There was a long shot showing the sun setting beyond Wendelsworth Bridge. It was just an ordinary bridge then, painted blue and grey, and not impressive-looking at all. Hudelam, just visible in his blue robes, was raised above the crowds on a platform. All they showed on the TV was that short clip and an announcer talking in the studio. She remembered standing there, her mouth open and body shaking, and only afterwards seeing a pattern of cherryade swirled on the blue carpet. Time had stopped still, all moments somehow part of this one.

A few hours later, video clips of the event began to appear on webworld. Chertsey had to know what had happened, forced herself to watch. There was a disturbance, a lot of shouting, and there he was! Of all the people you didn't expect to see, there, then. Somebody had filmed him quite clearly, the lead singer of that band, Splintered Dick, what was his name? You'd have thought, with all the fuss there had been at the time, that she would have remembered his name – she'd loved Splintered Dick in her teens, downloaded all their music – and there he was, dressed in an odd-looking tunic, riding a horse and twirling a baton in his hands.

There was a silence as he rode over to Hudelam, dismounted and, as though performing something between a ballet and a martial art, poleaxed him. Slow, graceful madness. Speared him with a metal-tipped baton. Hudelam too surprised even to defend himself. Loads of people had caught it on their handphones, but nobody did anything to help. Poor old Hugo, beaten to death with a stick in front of all those people. It didn't make any sort of sense at all. The lead singer of Splintered Dick, for crying out loud!

There was a confused shot of victim and assailant stretched out on the ground, swirls of red blood on a blue robe; one was dead and the other God knows what – nobody had touched him – he had slaughtered Hugo, then collapsed. The camera jerked up and down. People shouting, women screaming. The whinny of a horse.

All those cameras must have used up their memory at the same time. Nobody knew what happened next. When the ambulances and police arrived, the singer was nowhere to be found. Even the horse had disappeared into thin air.

Later they'd tracked the singer down and given him thirty years. Minimum. But he'd produced an alibi – how do you figure that one? An alibi! – and he'd been released on appeal.

Celebrities always get off somehow. And afterwards. That had been strange too. The man who performed the post-mortem, it was reported in the papers, whipped out all Hudelam's innards and stuck them in jars. Big ones like the Egyptians used to have. Canopic jars. Some people said that Hudelam wasn't dead at all, but had done a deal with the Government and had slipped off to spend his retirement in the South of France, in a château. But she didn't believe that. He'd been murdered on Wendelsworth Bridge that evening. Slain like a warrior in his moment of glory. They'd put up a plaque. Very simple. Hudelam died here, and the date.

Of course, Wendelsworth Bridge had become a very different place, but that was much later and had nothing to do with Hudelam. That lawyer – what was his name? Old guy, very tall, with a nice smile? Sir Charlie Archer! He'd said it was his Taj Mahal, that bridge. Reminded him of a woman he loved once. He'd spent all that money! They said his kids and his ex-wife were really pissed off. But it did look wonderful. All those rainbow colours shading from reddish through yellowy to purple. A proper bridge. And when they took away the lights from all the other Lundenwic bridges, they still kept them shining on Wendelsworth Bridge.

Oh lord, her feet were killing her. Where was he? Ah, at last something was happening. She saw Hugo – looking a bit hot and bothered, but wonderfully alive – coming out of the restaurant with his friends. Two elderly ladies went off; the waiter came out and spoke briefly to Hugo, then he and the rest of the men climbed into a car with a young woman. They drove off. Still no sign of him. Oh Botty! Where are you?

Two cops in a patrol car stopped beside her and asked her if she was all right. Perhaps they thought she was looking for business, hanging about in the street like that. At her age! She'd find a hotel. Get some sleep. After all, there'd be another opportunity the following day. She'd have to take loads more pills!

The next evening it was raining and cold. Just down from Cave Paintings was a chemist's shop with an awning. She stood underneath it and waited. A taxi arrived. Hugo alighted dragging a dustbin bag, and with him was Botty! She watched him dump the bag on the pavement, then tie Botty to something at ground level. She heard Hugo shout, 'You wretched little swine!'

There was the sound of tin cans landing on the pavement; Hugo yelling 'Swine, swine, swine!' He loped along the road, passing her, a canvas bag clasped to his hip, a trouser leg flapping in the rain and one white leg exposed. He was whimpering like someone who had been wounded. For God's sake, it was only a bloody trouser leg missing, not a limb amputated! If he'd seen her and stopped, she might have offered him a safety pin, the one in her knickers that fixed her money belt in place. Though he'd probably have needed a few more than just one. His figure carried on down the road, growing smaller and smaller, and then disappeared as though swallowed up by the earth.

Little Botty was sitting in the rain, a wet stray abandoned yet again. You had to judge people by their actions. It wouldn't have hurt Hugo to find some better way of passing Botty on to someone who cared.

She patted him on the head. 'Hello, Botty!'

He sniffed her fingers, remembered her, and wiggled his bottom, half-mad with delight. Just goes to show that a dog's nose-memory works better than a human eye.

'Now, we've got a bit of a journey, little fellow, and leads and things aren't part of the bargain.'

She unloosed his collar and removed it, still attached to the lead, which was tied to a doorstop. She gave his wet neck a good scratch. Then she took a napkin with a lump of steak inside from her pocket, and a bottle of pills. The dog watched her, ears pricked, sensing some sort of reward. She stuffed a few pills into the gobbet of meat. A small dog surely wouldn't need much. She tossed it into his open mouth. He swallowed it whole and looked up, expectantly, wanting more.

'You can have some more when we get home, little fella.'

She hoped he liked cats. She had four big gingers, three tabbies and a black and white back home. They were ferals when she found them and now were busy repopulating England, and they wouldn't take any attitude from Botty. She should have come and fetched him earlier. Old age wasn't much fun. Bollocks to what the law said; you needed cats to talk to and sleep with and a dog to cheer you up and keep you taking exercise.

There was no one around to see her. She looked left and right, then up to the one-eyed gawp of a security camera. It seemed to wink at her. No hoodlums here, she thought, just Chertsey and her dog. She took a cloth baby carrier from her pocket, put it around the dog's body and, picking him up, strapped him firmly to her chest. He didn't object. There he was, his little legs flapping and his spine pressed up against her belly. He snorted, and she gave him a quick peck with her lips on the top of his head, inhaling his leathery smell. The juddering engine of a black cab was approaching. She didn't want its occupant to see her.

'We'd better hurry up. We're goin' to the past an' then the future,' she told him. 'Wiv a bit a luck, a coupla jumps and we'll be there. Jus' like the song said.' She tried to sing, *J'irai voler la fortune!* But her voice wasn't much used to singing, or French, and cracked.

A quick stroke on his neck. It would be all right. He was a stray, after all, so what harm could taking him do?

Some Vast Entity – set apart, elsewhere or elsewhen, who had generated the first seeds of this multiverse on a random whim, as a geography project perhaps, and could be imagined gazing down upon it – would have so many questions about time (was it this, or that, and what will be?) that would bounce like light trapped among perfect mirrors. Endlessly and wondrously complicated.

But Chertsey only saw joy ahead, and she jumped.

Afterword

HATTIE POND was a born storyteller. Given any topic, she was able to devise a storyline within minutes, almost always with a beginning, a middle, an ending and a twist. As a child she made up ghost stories for her classmates. As an adult she wrote many short stories, mainly for her own amusement. She always wanted to write a full-length novel and, like many would-be writers, made part-completed attempts in her teens and 20s. But it was not until she was in her 50s that she felt she had sufficient time, space and knowledge to commit herself wholeheartedly to *On Wandsworth Bridge*.

Writing *On Wandsworth Bridge* was possibly the happiest, and certainly the most intellectually satisfying and fulfilling, time of Hattie's life. After a day's writing she would come downstairs from her study glowing with joy and enthusiasm. 'You can't imagine what Hugo has done now,' she would say. Or sometimes, 'The story has just spun off somewhere weird – I've no idea where it's going, but it's great.' She was always amazed at where the story took her. She said it seemed almost to write itself. Storyline twists near the end of the book tied in miraculously with things she had written many months before. She did not plan out the story in advance – it just flowed out of her – but somehow the loose ends all disappeared as the pieces fitted together. It was as if it was all there, fully plotted in her subconscious, even before she began to write.

Hattie was a woman who thought and cared deeply about many things. She was always totally honest and gave her full commitment to whatever she did. She was in love with the English language and the sound and beauty of words. She valued clear and articulate communication, correct grammar, words being used properly, accurate spelling and consistent punctuation. Having studied English at Manchester University, she became fascinated by the wonders and constant new discoveries in the sciences. She read *New Scientist* cover-to-cover every week for 25 years. She despaired at the general public's ignorance of science and inability to evaluate scientific questions rationally. She was very concerned at the continuing prevalence of C. P. Snow's 'two cultures' – the split between the sciences and the humanities. *On Wandsworth Bridge* is, in part, about this.

The novel's structure is a sardonic and satirical spin on multiverse theory. I recommend anyone unfamiliar with the concept to look up 'multiverse' on Wikipedia, although those sufficiently intrigued to work their way through the whole entry are likely to require both dictionary and analgesics. While there are many different multiverse hypotheses, in essence the theory states that everything that exists is contained within a (possibly infinite) series of parallel or alternative universes, and that it may be possible for these different universes to interact to some extent. Like so much of modern physics (or metaphysics, if you prefer) the theory is mind-stretching, counter-intuitive and probably unprovable, but no less serious for that – eminent supporters of the theory include Erwin Schrödinger, Stephen Hawking, Michio Kaku and Leonard Susskind. Hattie loved having her mind stretched by ideas such as this, and she was keen to share this joy with her readers. She told me that all the structural elements of *On Wandsworth Bridge* were based on either proven science or respectable scientific theories, and (other than oestrogen being a prerequisite to time travel) I have no reason to disbelieve her.

Hattie was also a very funny person, told good jokes and adored puns, strange-sounding words and unexpected juxtapositions. While she loved many novels – *Mary Swann* by Carol Shields was perhaps her all-time favourite – she was always drawn in particular to writers who combined serious purpose and insight with humour. Terry Pratchett, for example – 'our greatest social satirist since Jonathan Swift', as she called him. She was very annoyed by the refusal of much of the literary establishment to take humour seriously. This side of Hattie is also very obvious throughout *On Wandsworth Bridge*.

Hattie died in 2013. It is immensely sad that *On Wandsworth Bridge* could not be published in her lifetime. I am therefore both delighted and grateful that Sylph Editions, renowned for its eclectic range of high-quality illustrated publications, has chosen *On Wandsworth Bridge* to be one of its first full-length novels. My unqualified thanks are due to Ornan Rotem as book designer and typographer, to Num Stibbe for her fantastic illustrations, and to them both for their unfailingly sage advice and unwavering support. Thank you also to Mona Gainer-Salim for her insightful and sensitive 'lightest-touch' editing – I cannot imagine how she could have done a better job – and to Debra Naylor for her assistance in the early stages of this project. And, on Hattie's behalf, my sincere thanks also to the novelist and journalist Elspeth Barker, who reviewed the near-final manuscript and, together with many helpful specific comments, provided Hattie with enormous encouragement and reassurance with remarks such as 'I would like to say that none, or little, of the above matters, because everything else is so exceptionally brilliant' and 'I can only admire your astonishing tightrope feats' – it warms my heart to read these again now.

Hattie would have been so proud and happy to hold this book in her hands. She was my wife and best friend for 33 years. I miss her terribly.

Martin Bridgewater
February 2018

COLOPHON

Hattie Pond

On Wandsworth Bridge

TEXT: ©Martin Bridgewater, 2018
IMAGES: ©Num Stibbe, 2018

DESIGN: Ornan Rotem

The original layout was developed by Debra Naylor of Naylor Design, Inc.

Set in ITC New Baskerville

PRINTED AND BOUND BY Syl, Barcelona on Munken Lynx 100gsm

ISBN: 978-1-909631-25-0
SYLPH EDITIONS · LONDON | 2018
www.sylpheditions.com